HANDBOOK
of
INTERNATIONAL RELATIONS

HANDBOOK
of
INTERNATIONAL RELATIONS

Edited by
WALTER CARLSNAES, THOMAS RISSE
and BETH A. SIMMONS

Los Angeles • London • New Delhi • Singapore • Washington DC

First published 2002
Reprinted 2003, 2005, 2006 (twice), 2007, 2008

SAGE Publications Ltd
1 Oliver's Yard
55 City Road
London EC1Y 1SP

SAGE Publications Inc
2455 Teller Road
Thousand Oaks
California 91320

SAGE Publications India Pvt Ltd
B 1/I 1 Mohan Cooperative Industrial Area
Mathura Road, New Delhi 110 044
India

SAGE Publications Asia-Pacific Pte Ltd
33 Pekin Street #02-01
Far East Square
Singapore 048763

British Library Cataloguing in Publication data
A catalogue record for this book is available from the British Library
Library of Congress Control Number: 2001135896

ISBN 978-0-7619-6304-2
ISBN 978-0-7619-6305-9 (pbk)

Typeset by SIVA Math Setters, Chennai, India
Printed and bound in Great Britain by
Cromwell Press Limited, Trowbridge, Wiltshire

Contents

Notes on Contributors   ix

Preface   xv

Acknowledgements   xix

Part One   HISTORICAL, PHILOSOPHICAL AND THEORETICAL ISSUES IN INTERNATIONAL RELATIONS   1

1   On the History and Historiography of International Relations   3
Brian C. Schmidt

2   Philosophy of Social Science and International Relations   23
Colin Wight

3   Rationalism *v.* Constructivism: A Skeptical View   52
James Fearon and Alexander Wendt

4   Rational Choice and International Relations   73
Duncan Snidal

5   Constructivism and International Relations   95
Emanuel Adler

6   Linking Theory to Evidence in International Relations   119
Richard K. Herrmann

7   Norms and Ethics in International Relations   137
Andrew Hurrell

Part Two   CONCEPTS AND CONTEXT IN INTERNATIONAL RELATIONS   155

8   State, Sovereignty and Territory   157
Thomas J. Biersteker

9   Power and International Relations   177
David A. Baldwin

10   International Organizations and Institutions   192
Beth A. Simmons and Lisa L. Martin

11   Diplomacy, Bargaining and Negotiation   212
     Christer Jönsson

12   From Interdependence to Globalization   235
     Michael Zürn

13   Transnational Actors and World Politics   255
     Thomas Risse

14   Feminist Perspectives on International Relations   275
     J. Ann Tickner

15   Psychological Explanations of International Conflict   292
     Janice Gross Stein

16   Domestic Politics and International Relations   309
     Peter Gourevitch

           **Part Three   SUBSTANTIVE ISSUES IN
              INTERNATIONAL RELATIONS**   **329**

17   Foreign Policy   331
     Walter Carlsnaes

18   War and Peace   350
     Jack S. Levy

19   Security Cooperation   369
     Harald Müller

20   Peace-making and Conflict Resolution   392
     Lilach Gilady and Bruce Russett

21   Nationalism and Ethnicity   409
     Lars-Erik Cederman

22   International Finance   429
     Benjamin J. Cohen

23   International Trade   448
     Helen V. Milner

24   International Development   462
     Sylvia Maxfield

25   Comparative Regional Integration   480
     Young Jong Choi and James A. Caporaso

26   International Environment   500
     Ronald B. Mitchell

27   International Human Rights   517
     Hans Peter Schmitz and Kathryn Sikkink

28   International Law, International Relations and Compliance   538
     Kal Raustiala and Anne-Marie Slaughter

Index   559

Notes on Contributors

Emanuel Adler is the Andrea and Charles Bronfman Chair in Israeli Studies at the University of Toronto and a Professor at the Hebrew University of Jerusalem. Publications include *The Power of Ideology* (1987), *Progress in Postwar International Relations* (with Beverly Crawford, ed. 1991), *Security Communities* (with Michael Barnett, ed., 1998) and articles in *International Organization, European Journal of International Relations* and the *Review of International Studies*. Current projects include Mediterranean pluralistic integration, global governance, and a constructivist theory of institutionalization in international relations.

David A. Baldwin is Ira D. Wallach Professor of World Order Studies and a member of the Institute of War and Peace Studies at Columbia University in New York. His writings on power have appeared in *World Politics*, *Journal of Politics*, *Journal of Conflict Resolution*, *International Organization*, *American Political Science Review*, *International Security* and *Security Studies*.

Thomas J. Biersteker is Director of the Thomas J. Watson Jr Institute for International Studies and Henry R. Luce Professor of Transnational Organizations at Brown University. His research focuses primarily on International Relations theory and international political economy of development. His most recent books include *State Sovereignty as Social Construct* (edited with Cynthia Weber, 1996), *Argument without End: In Search of Answers to the Vietnam Tragedy* (co-authored with James G. Blight, Robert K. Brigham, Robert S. McNamara and Herbert Y. Schandler (1999) and *The Emergence of Private Authority in Global Governance* (edited with Rodney B. Hall, forthcoming).

James A. Caporaso is Professor of Political Science in the Department of Political Science of the University of Washington. He is a past president of the International Studies Association as well as a former Chair of the Executive Committee of the European Community Studies Association. He most recently published *The European Union: Dilemmas and Regional Integration* (2000) and co-edited with Maria Green Cowles and Thomas Risse *Transforming Europe: Europeanization and Domestic Change* (2001).

Walter Carlsnaes is a Professor of Government at Uppsala University, as well as Adjunct Professor at the Norwegian Institute of International Affairs. He has published five books, including two co-edited volumes, and was founding editor of the *European Journal of International Relations*. His main research interests are in foreign policy analysis, IR theory and the philosophy of social science, EU external relations and Swedish foreign and security policy.

Lars-Erik Cederman is Frederick S. Danziger Associate Professor of Government at Harvard University. He is the author of *Emergent Actors in World Politics: How States and Nations Develop and Dissolve* (1997), has edited *Constructing Europe's Identity: The External Dimension* (2001) and published several articles. His research interests include nationalism, state-formation, general IR theory and computational modelling.

Young Jong Choi is Research Professor at the Asiatic Center at Korea University. He is interested in the institutionalization of regional economic relations in Asia and the Pacific, Japan's foreign economic policy and US–Japan economic relations. He has published 'An Exploration into the Institutional Underdevelopment in Asia and the Pacific' and 'Japan's Preference for Japan–US Dispute Settlement Institutions' appeared in *Pacific Focus*. He has also published several articles on Asia-Pacific regional cooperation and Japan's foreign policy in *Korean Political Science Review* and *Korean Journal of International Studies*.

Benjamin J. Cohen is Louis G. Lancaster Professor of International Political Economy at the University of California, Santa Barbara. He has previously taught at Princeton University and the Fletcher School of Law and Diplomacy, Tufts University. He is the author of nine books, specializing mainly in the political economy of international monetary and financial relations. His most recent book, *The Geography of Money*, was published in 1998.

James D. Fearon is Professor of Political Science at Stanford University. His research has focused on democracy and international disputes, explanations for interstate wars and, most recently, the causes of civil and especially ethnic violence. Representative publications include 'Domestic Political Audiences and the Escalation of International Disputes' (*American Political Science Review*, September 1994), 'Rationalist Explanations for War' (*International Organization*, Summer 1995) and 'Violence and the Social Construction of Ethnic Identity' (with David Laitin, *International Organization*, Autumn 2000).

Lilach Gilady, a graduate of the Hebrew University of Jerusalem, and a former fellow at the Stockholm Peace Research Institute, is a PhD candidate in the Department of Political Science, Yale University.

Peter Gourevitch is Professor of Political Science at the University of California at San Diego and founding Dean's of UCSD's Graduate School of International Relations and Pacific Studies. He was co-editor with David Lake of *International Organization*, and author of articles and books on international relations and comparative politics, including *Politics in Hard Times: Comparative Responses to International Economic Crises*. He was elected to the American Academy of Arts and Sciences, and chairs the International Area Fellows Selection Commitee at the Council on Foreign Relations.

Richard K. Herrmann is Professor of Political Science and Associate Director of the Mershon Center at the Ohio State University. He is interested in International Relations theory and political psychology and has written on US and Russian foreign policies and political conflicts in the Middle East. His research has concentrated on the role perceptions play in world affairs and particularly on a theory of images. His current research focuses on identity and emotion and their relationship to perception as well as the relationships between multiple social identities and political institutions.

Andrew Hurrell is University Lecturer in International Relations at Oxford University and Fellow of Nuffield College, Oxford. His major interests include International Relations theory with particular reference to international law and institutions, and the international relations of Latin America with particular reference to the foreign policy of Brazil and US–Latin American relations. Recent publications include *Regionalism in World Politics* (co-editor with Louise Fawcett, 1995), *Inequality, Globalization and World Politics* (co-editor with Ngaire Woods, 1999) and *Hedley Bull on International Society* (2000).

Christer Jönsson is Professor of Political Science at Lund University, Sweden, and served as President of the Nordic International Studies Association (NISA) 1996–99. In addition to international negotiation, his research interests include international organization and transnational networks. He is the author of *Soviet Bargaining Behavior* (1979), *International Aviation and the Politics of Regime Change* (1987), *Communication in International Bargaining* (1990), co-author of *International Cooperation in Response to AIDS* (1995) and *Organizing European Space* (2000). He has also contributed numerous articles to edited volumes and scholarly journals.

Jack S. Levy is Board of Governors' Professor of Political Science at Rutgers University. He is the author of *War in the Modern Great Power System, 1495–1975* and numerous articles and book chapters. His research interests focus on the causes of war and on foreign policy decision-making.

Lisa L. Martin is Professor of Government at Harvard University. Her publications include *Coercive Cooperation: Explaining Multilateral Economic Sanctions* (1992) and *Democratic Commitments: Legislatures and International Cooperation* (2000).

Sylvia Maxfield holds a Professorship at the Simmons Graduate School of Management, a Boston-based business school 'training women for positions of power and leadership'. She is also an associate of Harvard's David Rockerfeller Center for Latin American Studies. Sylvia Maxfield has published over twenty-five articles on the political economy of developing countries in *International Organization, World Politics, World Development, Journal of Democracy* and elsewhere. Her most recent books are on central bank independence and government-business relations in developing countries.

Helen V. Milner is James T. Shotwell Professor of International Relations at Columbia University. She is the author of *Resisting Protectionism* (1988) and *Interests, Institutions and Information* 1997).

Ronald B. Mitchell is an Associate Professor in Political Science at the University of Oregon. His *Intentional Oil Pollution at Sea: Environmental Policy and Treaty Compliance* (1994) received the 1995 Harold and Margaret Sprout Award from the International Studies Association. He has published articles in *International Organization, Journal of Theoretical Politics, International Studies Quarterly* and *Journal of Environment Development*. From 1999–2001 he was a Visiting Professor at Stanford University's Center for Environmental Science and Policy.

Harald Müller has directed the Nuclear Nonproliferation Program of the Peace Research Institute Frankfurt (PRIF) since 1986, working with colleagues from thirteen European countries. He became Director of PRIF in 1996. He is Associate Professor of International Relations at the Technical University Darmstadt, a Visiting Professor at the Johns Hopkins University Center of International Relations in Bologna and a Visiting Lecturer at the NATO Defense College in Rome. Since 1999 he is Professor of International Relations at the Goethe University, Frankfurt. He is a member of the Advisory Board on Disarmament Matters of the Secretary General of the United Nations.

Kal Raustiala is Acting Professor at UCLA Law School and the UCLA Institute of the Environment. In addition to compliance, his current research interests include the role of law in international agreements, the democracy and sovereignty concerns raised by cooperative regimes, and the design of effective international institutions. He is editor, with David Victor and Eugene Skolnikoff, of *Implementation and Effectiveness of International Environmental Committments: Theory and Practice* (1998).

Thomas Risse holds a PhD from the University of Frankfurt and is Professor of International Politics at the Free University of Berlin. He has previously taught at the European University Institue, Florence, Italy, the University of Konstanz, Germany, and at various US universities including Cornell, Yale, and Stanford. He is the author of *Cooperation among Democracies: The European Influence on US Foreign Policy* (1995) and co-editor of (with Stephen C. Ropp and Kathryn Sikkink) *The Power of Human Rights: International Norms and Domestic Change* (1999), and of (with Maria Green Cowles and James Caporaso) *Transforming Europe: Europeanization and Domestic Change* (2001). He has contributed articles to *World Politics, International Organization, International Security*, the *European Journal of International Relations*, and others. He is associate editor of *International Organization*. His research interests include international relations theory, comparative foreign policy, norms and identity in international politics and European integration, and transnational governance.

Bruce Russett is Dean Acheson Professor of International Relations and Director of United Nations Studies at Yale University. He has edited the *Journal of Conflict Resolution* since 1972. He has held visiting appointments at the Richardson Institute in London, the Netherlands Institute for Advanced Study and various universities (Columbia, Michigan, Brussels, North Carolina, Tel Aviv, Harvard and Tokyo). The most recent of his twenty-two books are *The Once and Future Security Council* and *Triangulating Peace: Democracy, Interdependence and International Organizations* (with John R. Oneal).

Brian C. Schmidt is Assistant Professor of Political Science and International Relations at the State University of New York, New Paltz. The final draft of his chapter was completed while on leave at the University of Wales, Aberystwyth. He is the author of *The Political Discourse of Anarchy: A Disciplinary History of International Relations* (1998) and has published several journal articles on the history of the field. His research interests are in the areas of International Relations theory and disciplinary history.

Hans Peter Schmitz is Assistant Professor of Political Science at the Maxwell School of Citizenship and Public Affairs, Syracuse University. Previously he was a Post-Doctoral Fellow in the Human Rights Program at the University of Chicago. His research interests include the role of non-state actors in international politics, their transnational promotion of norms and the conditions for regime change and democratization in East-African nations.

Kathryn Sikkink is the Arleen Carlson Professor of Political Science at the University of Minnesota. Her publications include *Ideas and Institutions: Developmentalism in Brazil and Argentina; Activists Beyond Borders: Advocacy Networks in International Politics* (co-authored with Margaret Keck) and *The Power of Human Rights: International Norms and Domestic Change* (co-edited with Thomas Risse and Stephen Ropp). She is a member of the editorial board of *International Organization* and of the Council of the American Political Science Association.

Beth A. Simmons is Professor of Government at Harvard University. Her book *Who Adjusts? Domestic Sources of Foreign Economic Policy during Interwar Years* (1994) won the 1995 American Political Science Association's Woodrow Wilson Award. She was also awarded the International Studies Association's Karl Deutsch Award for research contributions in International Relations in 2000. Her research interests are in international political economy, international institutions and international law.

Anne-Marie Slaughter is the J. Sinclair Armstrong Professor of International, Foreign and Comparative Law and Director of Graduate and International Studies at Harvard Law School. In August 2000 she delivered a short course at the Hague Academy of International Law on International Law and International Relations Theory, to be published in the Recueil de Cours in 2001. She is currently finishing a book on vertical and horizontal networks among different government institutions operating beyond national borders.

Duncan Snidal is Associate Professor of Political Science and Public Policy at the University of Chicago and Director of the Program on International Politics, Economics and Security (PIPES). His past research has focused on theoretical issues of international cooperation. He is currently working on issues of international legalization and international institutional design. His research on these topics has appeared in the *American Political Science Review, Journal of Conflict Resolution, Journal of European Public Policy, Journal of Theoretical Politics, International Organization, International Studies Quarterly, and World Politics.*

Janice Gross Stein is the Director of the Munk Centre for International Studies at the Univesity of Toronto, the Harrowston Professor of Conflict management, and a Fellow of the Royal Society of Canada. Her most recent publications are *Networks of Knowledge: Collaborative Innovation in International Learning* (2001), *The Cult of Efficiency* (2001), and *Street Protests and Fantasy Parks: Globalization, Culture, and Society* (2002). She is currently working on the social understanding of accountability at the global and local levels.

J. Ann Tickner is a Professor in the School of International Relations at the University of Southern California and the Director of USC's Center for International Studies. She is the author of *Self-Reliance Versus Power Politics: The American and Indian Experiences in Building Nation States* (1989); *Gender in International Relations: Feminist Perspectives on Achieving Global Security* (1992) and *Gendering World Politics: Issues and Approaches in the Post-Cold War Era* (2001). She has written numerous articles and book chapters on feminist International Relations theory.

Alexander Wendt is Associate Professor of Political Science at the University of Chicago. He is the author of *Social Theory of International Politics* (1999), and a number of articles in *International Organization, Review of International Studies, International Security*, and *American Political Science Review*.

Colin Wight is Senior Lecturer at the Department of Politics, University of Sheffield. His research interests are in the interface between the philosophy of social science, social theory and IR theory. He is currently researching the role played by the 'idea of science' in the formation of IR as an academic discipline. He has published in the *Philosophy of the Social Sciences, International Studies Quarterly, European Journal of International Relations* and *Millennium*.

Michael Zürn is Professor for Transnational and International Relations at the Institute of Political Science and Co-Director of the Institute for Intercultural and International Studies (InIIS), both at the University of Bremen. He is editor of *Zeitschrift für International Beziehungen* and author of *Regieren jenseits des Nationalstaates* (1998), *Gerechte internationale Regime* (1987) and *Interessen und Institutionen* (1992). He has contributed articles to *World Politics, International Studies Quarterly, European Journal of International Relations, Politische Vierteljahresschrift, Zeitschrift für Internationale Beziehungen* and numerous book chapters on such themes as international institutions, globalization and denationalization, and theories of international relations.

Preface

The beginning of a new millennium is a particularly fitting occasion for taking stock of the past achievements and present condition of International Relations (IR). However, there is an additional reason as well, and one with considerable more intellectual clout: the surprising dearth of such attempts at stocktaking within this discipline during most of its short history. Those that have been published in the past few decades have either been brief guides to the subject matter (Groom and Light, 1994; Light and Groom, 1985), or have had the encyclopaedic ambition of covering not only the major analytical approaches within the discipline of IR but also all the significant political developments, events and personages which have characterized modern international relations *qua* empirical domain (Krieger, 1993). These (and similar) repositories of disciplinary knowledge and accumulated wisdom certainly deserve the space which they occupy on the shelves of our scholarly libraries. However, given the specific goals which their editors have set for themselves, they do not provide for the needs of those advanced students, both undergraduate and graduate, as well as more established scholars within or outside the field, who are in need of in-depth introductions to, and critical discussions of, the major theoretical and analytical concerns of contemporary IR research. In other words, this *Handbook* is intended to fill what we submit is currently a significant lacuna within the discipline: providing a single volume of extensive, systematic and authoritative overviews of the state of the art within the various sub-fields of the discipline.

In pursuing this ambition Fred Greenstein and Nelson Polsby's magisterial *Handbook of Political Science* (Greenstein and Polsby, 1975a) has served as an awe-inspiring exemplar. At the same time, their landmark effort – consisting of eight volumes altogether – is obviously a feat that is virtually impossible to repeat today, as is frankly acknowledged by the editors of its successor, the one-volume *New Handbook of Political Science* (Goodin and Klingemann, 1996). However, what can be replicated even when operating on a considerably more modest scale is the seriousness of the intellectual tone which suffuses their achievement; and we hope that we have succeeded at least to some degree in the delicate task of transferring this timbre to the present *Handbook*. In one major respect we do contend to have succeeded rather better than either of the above works of reference: covering the entire spectrum of IR as a field of scholarly endeavor. Thus, whereas the Greenstein and Polsby volume on *International Politics* (Greenstein and Polsby, 1975b) consists of only six chapters (one of which, it must be acknowledged, subsequently turned into Kenneth Waltz's epochal *Theory of International*

Politics), and the *New Handbook* has allotted only four chapters to IR, we have made space for twenty-eight chapter-long presentations, covering what we perceive to be the major areas of study and controversy characterizing the contemporary IR research community.

Choosing and agreeing on which topics to include – and hence which to exclude – has been a major task facing the three co-editors, but one which turned out to be far less divisive than we had first anticipated. The underlying structure which we have opted for is to make a distinction between three analytically different intellectual domains within the field, defining what in our view constitute three types of research discourses. The first pertains to the intellectual history of the discipline, as well as to the meta-theoretical, theoretical and normative concerns that characterize current thinking *about* IR as a distinctive field of research. Here we have, to a large extent, opted for a focus based on the current debate between 'rationalism' and 'constructivism', although we are fully aware of the controversial nature of this distinction itself. The second group of chapters has an essentially conceptual thrust, incorporating within its ambit the various *analytical* concerns, perspectives and contextualizations which have come to characterize current IR scholarship, cutting across the various issue-areas and substantive questions lying at the core of contemporary research. Instead of reinforcing thinking along the traditional lines of various substantive theories of IR – such as realism, liberalism, institutionalism and so forth – we have deliberately organized the *Handbook* in a way that would entice our authors to probe approaches such as these primarily in terms of their analytic utility in issue-based empirical research. The third, final and largest group of chapters focuses on the various *substantive* processes, actions and interactions which can be said to define the core empirical domain of international relations. Obviously, it is not always easy to maintain a clear distinction between these substantive issues areas and the analytic and cross-cutting conceptualizations highlighted in Part Two. However, from the point of view of the presumptive readers of this *Handbook* we have found it important to be able to offer separate and chapter-long discussions on conceptual topics such as 'sovereignty', 'power' and 'globalization', on the one hand, and substantive issues such as the pursuit of 'foreign policy', 'war' and 'peace', on the other. Although intimately linked, they at the same time belong to distinguishable discourses within IR.

Our choice of authors has been guided by two simple principles: to entice the best possible expertise to participate, and to make this a truly international (or at least trans-Atlantic) enterprise, despite the putative nature of IR as an essentially 'American social science' (Hoffmann, 1977; Waever, 1998). Hence, we are grateful that such a distinguished and international group of scholars has agreed to participate in this project. And although not primarily intended as such, it is nevertheless our hope that this *Handbook* will itself contribute further to the ongoing denationalization of IR as a scholarly profession. Whatever else its publication may achieve, enhancing this process during the coming years of the new millennium would indeed be a fitting side-effect of what has been a truly intensive and mutually rewarding trans-Atlantic collaboration between the editors and the authors of this *Handbook*.

References

Goodin, Robert E. and Klingemann, Hans-Dieter (eds) (1996) *The New Handbook of Political Science*. Oxford: Oxford University Press.

Greenstein, Fred I. and Polsby, Nelson W. (eds) (1975a) *Handbook of Political Science*, vols 1–8. Reading, MA: Addison–Wesley.

Greenstein, Fred I. and Polsby, Nelson W. (eds) (1975b) *Handbook of International Relations, Volume 8: International Politics*. Reading, MA: Addison–Wesley.

Groom, A.J.R. and Light, Margot (eds) (1994) *Contemporary International Relations: A Guide to Theory*. London: Pinter Publishers.

Hoffmann, Stanley (1977) 'An American Social Science: International Relations', *Daedelus*, 106: 41–60.

Krieger, Joel (ed.) (1993) *The Oxford Companion to Politics of the World*. Oxford: Oxford University Press.

Light, Margot and Groom, A.J.R. (eds) (1985) *International Relations: A Handbook of Current Theory*. London: Frances Pinter.

Waever, Ole (1998) 'The Sociology of a Not So International Discipline: American and European Developments in International Relations', *International Organization*, 52: 687–727.

Acknowledgements

An editorial and publishing venture of the size of this *Handbook of International Relations* is impossible without incurring a number of debts. These require public acknowledgement, but unfortunately all cannot be named here, not only because the list is so long, but also because some of the most valued advice we have received has been provided under a veil of anonymity. However, except for those whom the publishers enlisted as external reviewers of our initial proposal, we know who they are, and will always remain grateful for their help even if we cannot identify them openly here. The same goes for those who continue to remain unknown to us, but whose written advice has been an equally valuable part of the editorial process.

The only reason why the names of the members of the International Advisory Board will not be mentioned here is that this list of distinguished colleagues is published elsewhere in this volume. Apart from this, we have a number of very good reasons to acknowledge openly and fully their invaluable contributions since the very beginning of this project. Always forthcoming when we sought their help in various ways, they provided us with the solid intellectual and disciplinary foundations which are a *sine qua non* for a venture of this kind. Some of them contributed considerably more by accepting to author or co-author individual chapters as well.

The idea to publish this *Handbook* was first broached by the publishers, who thus deserve more than the usual passing tribute, particularly since Simon Ross and Lucy Robinson never faltered in providing constant encouragement, friendly advice and cheerful admonitions throughout the long process between the initial conception and final delivery of what has become this heavy tome. In this connection we would also like to mention Vanessa Harwood, who came late into the process as senior production editor but who not only quickly caught on to the informality of our working style, but who was also highly instrumental in saving us from completely missing our publication date. Although all three undoubtedly knew much better than the editors how treacherous and difficult the production of a volume of this kind and size can be, they kept their nerve and never gave any indications that they did not believe fully in our capacity to deliver. For this trust, and for challenging us to pursue this venture in the first place, we owe them considerable gratitude.

This also goes for our individual working places, not least for underwriting the costs – in terms of both time, money and in other ways – which are incurred in a project of this kind. In this regard we are particularly grateful to the Department of Government at Uppsala University which has functioned as the administrative center of the project since its inception, freely providing copying, mailing and other facilities, as well as an inspiring environment in general. The European University Institute in Florence must also be mentioned here, especially for hosting – in what must be one of the most breathtakingly beautiful academic milieus in existence today – the initial brainstorming session which launched the *Handbook* as a dynamic (and demanding) part of our professional lives for over three years.

Finally, it would be totally remiss of us not to acknowledge our profound debt to the individual authors themselves. Without their hard and conscientious work, performed with enthusiasm but without remuneration, this *Handbook of International Relations* would obviously never have seen the light of day in the first place.

Walter Carlsnaes
Thomas Risse
Beth A. Simmons

Uppsala, Berlin and Berkeley

Part One

HISTORICAL, PHILOSOPHICAL AND THEORETICAL ISSUES IN INTERNATIONAL RELATIONS

1

On the History and Historiography of International Relations

BRIAN C. SCHMIDT

Thus, today, after a quarter-century of activity, the study of international relations is still in a condition of considerable confusion. The scope of the field, the methods of analysis and synthesis to be followed, the proper administrative arrangements to be made in college curricula, the organization of research – all these are matters of continuing controversy. (Kirk, 1947: 7)

In brief, as a field of inquiry, international relations today resembles a poorly marked-out arena in which a multiplicity of research programs and strategies compete, coexist, overlap, or retain splendid isolation. (Plating, 1969: 11)

The field of international studies has become a little like the Tower of Babel, filled with a cacophony of different voices – or, as some have implied, a set of tribes that are very territorial, sniping at those who come too close and preferring to be with those like them. As a result, the field of international relations has become an administrative holding company rather than an intellectually coherent area of inquiry or a community of scholars. (Hermann, 1998: 606)

These quotations indicate a preliminary reply to those who question the value of engaging in research on the disciplinary history of the field of international relations (IR).[1] While a common

diagnosis of the contemporary state of the field is that it lacks a coherent identity, the statements above indicate that the identity of the field has never been as secure as many might imagine. A cursory review of recent books and articles found in the ever-expanding number of specialized journals, and the programs of the annual meetings of the International Studies Association (ISA) and British International Studies Association (BISA), reveals a complex field of extraordinary scope, yet an element of suspicion continues to be cast on the task of examining its history. One possible explanation for the reluctance to grant legitimacy to this research task is the common notion that we already know the history. Another possibility is that those in the mainstream are satisfied with the dominant story that is told about the development of the field. In any event, there is no shortage of brief synoptic accounts of this history in introductory textbooks, state-of-the-field articles and ISA Presidential Addresses.

These renditions frequently retell a conventional story of how the field has progressed through a series of phases: idealist, realist, behavioralist, post-behavioralist, pluralist, neorealist, rationalist, post-positivist and constructivist. The image of the first three phases has been so deeply ingrained in the minds of students and scholars that there almost seems to be no alternative way of understanding the early history of the field. Hedley Bull, for example, claimed that it is 'possible to recognize three successive waves of theoretical activity': the 'idealist' or 'progressivist' doctrines that were dominant in the 1920s and early 1930s, the 'realist' or conservative theories that developed in the late 1930s and

1940s, and lastly the 'social scientific' theories that arose in the late 1950s and 1960s 'whose origin lay in dissatisfaction with the methodologies on which both earlier kinds of theory were based' (Bull, 1972: 33). This story of the field's evolution is, in turn, often buttressed by the closely related account of the field evolving through a series of 'great debates', beginning with the disciplinary defining 'great debate' between 'idealists' and 'realists' and extending perhaps to the latest debate today between 'rationalists' and 'reflectivists' (Banks, 1986; Katzenstein et al., 1999; Keohane, 1988; Lijphart, 1974a; Maghroori, 1982; Mitchell, 1980). This particular construction of the field's history tends to have the effect of making the present debate a matter that all serious students of IR must focus on while relegating previous debates to obscurity.

Finally, the field's history is commonly chronicled by reference to the external events that have taken place in the realm that has been conventionally designated as international politics. There is a strong conviction that significant developments in international politics such as wars or abrupt changes in American foreign policy have, more fundamentally than any other set of factors, shaped the development of IR. The birth of the field, for example, often associated with the founding of the world's first Chair for the study of international politics, in 1919 at the Department of International Politics at the University College of Wales, Aberystwyth, is characteristically viewed as a reaction to the horror of the First World War (Porter, 1972).

My main intention in this chapter is to problematize these prevalent interpretations of how the field has developed and to indicate that the history of the field is both more complicated and less well known than typically portrayed in the mainstream literature. While it is quite evident that we do not possess an adequate understanding of how the field has developed, there are a number of reasons why it is crucially important for contemporary practitioners and students of IR to possess an adequate familiarity with this history.

First, numerous theoretical insights, of largely forgotten scholars, have been simply erased from memory. Yet, once recalled, these insights can have critical purchase in the present. Second, the field has created its own powerful myths regarding the evolution of the field that have obscured the actual history (Booth, 1996; Kahler, 1997; Osiander, 1998; Schmidt 1998a, 1998b; Waever, 1998; Wilson, 1998). Third, an adequate understanding of the history of the field is essential for explaining the character of many of our present assumptions and ideas about the study of international politics. While current intellectual practices and theoretical positions are often evoked as novel answers to the latest dilemmas confronting international politics, a more discriminating historical sense reminds us that

contemporary approaches are often reincarnations of past discourses. Without a sufficient understanding of how the field has evolved, there is the constant danger of continually reinventing the wheel. There is, in fact, much evidence to support the proposition that much of what is taken to be new is actually deeply embedded in the discursive past of the field. Finally, a perspicacious history of the field offers a fruitful basis for critical reflection on the present. Knowledge of the actual, as opposed to the mythical, history may force us to reassess some of our dominant images of the field and result in opening up some much needed space in which to think about international politics in the new millennium.

My purpose in this chapter is not to provide a comprehensive history of the broadly defined field or discipline of IR. Not only would such an endeavor be impossible in this context, but, as I will indicate below, there is sufficient ambiguity concerning the proper identity of the field, with respect to its origins, institutional home, and geographical boundaries, that simply writing a generic history of IR without addressing these sorts of issues in detail has reached the point of being counter-productive. Moreover, while much of the previous work on the history of the field has not exhibited sufficient theoretical and methodological sophistication in approaching the task of providing an adequate historical account, some recent work in this area is forcing scholars to confront a number of historiographical issues. This latest wave of scholarship clearly recognizes the necessary link that exists between establishing the identity of the discipline and presenting an image of its history. Furthermore, the manner in which the history of IR is reconstructed has become almost as significant as the substantive account itself, and therefore it becomes crucially important to address the basic research question of how one should approach the task of writing a history of the field.

I will begin by briefly discussing a number of lingering and contentious issues concerning the extent to which there is a well-defined field of IR that has a distinct identity, as well as the equally controversial question of whether the history of the field should be written from a cosmopolitan frame of reference – that does not pay significant attention to distinct national and institutional differences – or whether it is necessary to approach this task from within clearly demarcated national contexts. Although it should be evident that IR is a discrete academic field after more than fifty to a hundred years of evolution, depending on how one dates the genesis of the field, ambiguities have continually arisen regarding both the character of the subject matter and the institutional boundaries of the field. Adding to the confusion surrounding the identity of the field is the fact of the overwhelming and continuing dominance of the American IR scholarly community that sometimes leads to the erroneous conclusion that the history of IR is synonymous with its development in the United States. While there is much merit in Stanley Hoffmann's (1977) assertion that IR is an American social science, despite the influence of a great many European-born scholars, it is also the case that notwithstanding the global impact of the American model, there are many indigenous scholarly communities that have their own unique disciplinary history. This is, for example, clearly the case with the English School, whose contributions have only recently begun to be properly documented and assessed (Dunne, 1998; Little, 2000). Certainly these communities have been deeply impacted by theoretical and methodological developments in the United States, but there are nevertheless differences in how the subject is studied in different parts of the world (Jorgensen, 2000). The interdisciplinary character of the field and differences in national settings sometimes lead to the conclusion that a distinct discipline or field of IR does not really exist, but despite ambiguities about disciplinary boundaries and an institutional home, IR, as an academic field of study, has a distinct professional identity and discourse.

I next focus on the historiography of IR, that is, both the scholarship on the history of the field and the methodological principles involved in that research and writing. My attention will focus on two fundamental problems: first, presentism, which involves the practice of writing a history of the field for the purpose of making a point about its present character; and second, contextualism, which assumes that exogenous events in the realm of international politics have fundamentally structured the development of IR as an academic field of study. I will attempt to illustrate these issues by reviewing the existing literature. Recently, there has been a notable increase in both the quantity and quality of literature on the history of the field, and it can be argued that, in general, the history of the social sciences is becoming a distinct research specialty. This new literature has cast increasing doubt on the conventional images of the development of IR. My critical purpose in this chapter is to challenge the dominant understanding of how the field has progressed and to encourage more sophisticated work on the disciplinary history of IR.

Throughout the chapter, I will occasionally make reference to a conceptual framework developed by John Gunnell (1998). The framework, which Gunnell terms the 'orders of discourse', is applicable to analyzing various issues in the field of IR, since it shares many of the characteristics associated with the other social sciences. In Gunnell's terminology, the social sciences are second-order metapractices that 'are identified, in terms of logic, function, and self-understanding, by the fact that in various ways they speak about and sometimes to first-order activities' (Gunnell, 1998: 22). First-order practices, which include natural science, religion, music, art and politics, are defined by Gunnell as 'modes of activity that are primordial and "given" in that their various forms and historical manifestations represent functionally necessary elements of human activity' (1998: 19). With respect to the relationship between the orders of discourse, the crux of the issue concerns that between second-order and first-order practices. The former have sought in various ways to acquire epistemic and practical authority over the latter. Gunnell writes that 'the history of the social sciences has largely been driven by the issue of how to vindicate its cognitive claims and translate them into a basis of practical authority' (1998: 3). In applying this framework to the intellectual history of IR, we can see how the various theoretical, methodological and epistemological positions that have arisen since the field first came into existence have often been involved with seeking to achieve authority over the practice of international politics. And histories of IR, like many of those offered in the other social sciences, have often served to vouchsafe a particular rendition of the field in order to legitimate a contemporary image of a scientific approach. This search for validation explains in part the attraction in social science of turning to the history and philosophy of natural science, another second-order practice, in accounting for the growth of the field. It will be through the medium of disciplinary history which, in Gunnell's terms, qualifies as a 'third-order discourse' (i.e., those that have another metapractice as their object) that I will explore the manner in which the field of IR has sought to acquire the authority of knowledge that would provide theoretical and practical purchase in its relationship to international politics.

INTERNATIONAL RELATIONS AS AN ACADEMIC FIELD OF STUDY

The task of demarcating the disciplinary boundaries of the field is an important prerequisite to establishing authority over its object of inquiry. Yet the question of whether a distinct field or discipline of IR exists has been a matter of consistent controversy (Gurian, 1946; Kaplan, 1961; Neal and Hamlett, 1969; Olson, 1972; Olson and Groom, 1991; Olson and Onuf, 1985; Palmer, 1980; Thompson, 1952; Wright, 1955). While the controversy is, in some ways, related to the contentious issue of the origins and geographical boundaries of the field, it more fundamentally involves the question of the identity of IR as a second-order discourse and the status of its subject matter. Although it is apparent that this question has never been answered satisfactorily, disciplinary history does provide an insightful vantage point for viewing the manner in which the field has attempted to establish its own identity.

The period that precedes the point at which we can discern the identity of the field as a distinct academic practice can be termed its 'prehistory'. Here there was a gradual change 'from discourse to discipline' (Farr, 1990). This period is important for identifying many of the themes and issues that would later constitute the field as it took form during the early decades of the twentieth century (Schmidt, 1998b). The field's antecedents included international law, diplomatic history, the peace movement, moral philosophy, geography and anthropology (Olson and Groom, 1991). In *The Study of International Relations* (1955), Quincy Wright identified eight 'root disciplines' and six disciplines with a 'world point of view' that had contributed to the development of IR.[2] Wright, along with a number of others, argued that the task of synthesizing these largely autonomous fields of inquiry hampered the effort to create a unified coherent discipline of IR (Bailey, 1932; Gurian, 1946; Kirk, 1947; Wright, 1955). Moreover, Kenneth Thompson observed that 'there was nothing peculiar to the subject matter of international relations which did not fall under other separate fields' (Thompson, 1952: 433). The interdisciplinary character of the field and the fact that other disciplines studied various dimensions of its subject matter has sometimes led to the question of whether 'international relations is a distinctive discipline' (Kaplan, 1961). This is an interesting and important question that has often been answered by pointing to the field's unique subject matter, typically defined in terms of politics in the absence of central authority as well as by adducing various epistemological grounds. Yet while the question of whether IR is a distinct discipline is intriguing, it is important not to let this become an obstacle to reconstructing the history of the study of international politics.

These issues do, however, highlight the importance of clearly identifying and focusing on the institutional context of the field. The variability in institutional context is, in part, responsible for the wide range of dates that have been used to mark the birth of the field. It makes a large difference, for example, whether IR was institutionalized as a separate discipline, as was largely the case after the First World War in the United Kingdom, where a number of independent Chairs were created, or as a sub-field of political science, as was the case in the United States, Germany and France.[3] Yet orthodox histories have been more inclined to emphasize the impact of significant political events on the development of the field than the character of the institutional setting of the field. In the case of the United States, for example, it is impossible to write the history of IR without locating it within the disciplinary matrix of American political science. This is different from the historical experience of IR in the United Kingdom, where it was not a part of political science, but rather a new field of inquiry with a separate departmental home (Hill, 1987; Waever, 1998). In addition to these institutional variations, there are numerous differences with respect to intellectual climate, access to information, research support, links between government and academia, and the general structure and character of the university system (Simpson, 1998; Smith, 1985).

The significance of institutional context is closely related to the issue of the national context of the field. Variations in institutional structure are intimately related to the national setting in which IR is situated. The issue of whether the boundaries of IR should be demarcated in terms of one particular country or whether it should be viewed as a more cosmopolitan endeavor without regard to national differences complicates the task of writing a history of the field. Yet while the creation of a truly global discipline may, perhaps, be an aspiration, studies continue to indicate that the academic study of international politics is marked by British, and especially American, parochialism. Ever since Stanley Hoffmann published his famous article 'An American Social Science: International Relations', discussion has ensued about the extent to which the American academic community dominates the 'global discipline' of IR, and about the profound consequences that this dominance has for the discipline as a whole (Alker and Biersteker, 1984; Crawford and Jarvis, 2001; Goldmann, 1996; Hoffmann, 1977; Holsti, 1985; Kahler, 1993; Krippendorf, 1987; Smith, 1987, 2000; Waever, 1998). Yet despite the alleged American hegemony, it is a fundamental mistake to associate the American study of international politics with the 'global discipline of IR'. For although it is often the case that many national IR communities seem to be susceptible to embracing American theories, trends and debates, IR, as Waever notes, 'is quite different in different places' (1998: 723). I argue that disciplinary histories of IR should be committed to reconstructing the discursive history of the field in both its global and indigenous dimensions. Although limitations of space prevent me from commenting on the history of IR in every country in the world, and much of what follows focuses on developments in the United States and the United Kingdom, it is important that more country-specific studies of the development of IR be undertaken.[4]

THE HISTORIOGRAPHY OF INTERNATIONAL RELATIONS

One of the most significant problems in work on the history of IR is that these histories have failed to address adequately the question of how one should write a history of the field. The tendency has been to describe the history of IR as if a complete consensus existed on the essential dimensions of the field's evolution. In the absence of any significant controversy concerning how the field has developed, there has been little or no attention devoted to historiographical issues. Yet as a number of related academic disciplines such as political science have begun to examine more closely their disciplinary history, several theoretical and methodological controversies have arisen over what in general constitutes proper historical analysis and, particularly, what is involved in disciplinary history (Bender and Schorske, 1998; Collini et al., 1983; Dryzek and Leonard, 1988; Farr et al., 1990; Gunnell, 1991; Ross, 1991; Tully, 1988). The historiographical concerns that this literature has raised have, however, made little if any impact on those who reflect on the history of IR. A major exception to this generalization is found in Ole Waever's article 'The Sociology of a Not So International Discipline' (1998), which is a significant contribution to the literature. With respect to the existing state of the available literature on the history of the field, Waever disapprovingly notes that it is 'usually not based on systemic research or clear methods' and that it amounts to little more than 'elegant restatements of "common knowledge" of our past, implicitly assuming that any good practitioner can tell the history of the discipline' (Waever, 1998: 692). But while the lack of theoretical sophistication is definitely rooted in the assumption that practitioners already know the history of the field, additional factors are at work in reinforcing the tendency to simplify, and thus distort, that history.

Traditions: Analytical and Historical

There is a general assumption that the history of the field can be explained by reference to a continuous tradition that reaches back to classical Athens and extends forward to the present. The IR literature contains numerous references to the idea that there are epic traditions of international thought that have given rise to coherent schools or paradigms such as realism and liberalism (Clark, 1989; Donnelly, 1995; Holsti, 1985; Kugler, 1993; Zacher and Matthew, 1995). Furthermore, and more importantly for the discussion at hand, there is a widespread conviction that these ancient traditions represent an integral part of the field's past and, therefore, are relevant for understanding the contemporary identity of the field. One example of this belief can be found in Jacek Kugler's survey of the literature on conflict and war in which he claims that the 'classic account of international war comes from the realist tradition in world politics', and that the realist 'approach to the study of war has a very long tradition that can be traced from Thucydides

(400 BC), to Machiavelli (1513), to Hobbes (1651), to Hume (1741), to von Clausewitz (1832), to Morgenthau (1948), to Organski (1958), to Waltz (1979) and to Gilpin (1981)' (Kugler, 1993: 483–4). While it is certainly the case that the study of the theorists associated with the classic canon of Western political thought constitutes an element of the practice of IR, as evidenced, for example, by Kenneth Waltz's *Man, the State and War* (1959), it is, nevertheless, a fundamental misconception to presume that the work of classic political theorists such as Thucydides or Kant can be construed as constitutive antecedents of the literature of contemporary IR.

There is a certain irony in the widespread tendency of contemporary scholars to make reference to the writings of classic political theorists in that one of the dominant assumptions for many years was that the canon of classic texts from Plato to Marx did not have very much to say about international politics. This was the view popularized in Martin Wight's polemical essay 'Why is There No International Theory?' (1966), which was presented at the inaugural meeting of the British Committee on the Theory of International Politics in 1959. Wight's argument contributed to the widespread view that there was a rich and well-defined tradition of political thought but an impoverished and essentially contested tradition of international thought. This view, along with the scientific ambitions of the behavioralists who directly challenged the relevance of the canon, led the fields of political theory and IR to drift apart, producing a profound sense of estrangement that only recently has begun to change (Boucher, 1998; Brown, 1992; Knutsen, 1997; Schmidt, 2000; Walker, 1993; Williams, 1992). David Boucher has argued that one of the reasons why IR does not have an established canon of classic texts stems from the mistake that IR theorists made when they 'cut themselves adrift from the mainstream of political theory in order to develop their own theories and concepts' (1998: 10).

The strained and troubled relationship between political theory and international relations theory has not, however, prevented scholars from constructing numerous typologies and traditions for classifying the ideas of classic political theorists and linking them to the work of contemporary students of international relations (Boucher, 1998; Donelan, 1990; Doyle, 1997; Holsti, 1985; Kauppi and Viotti, 1999; Wight, 1992). While, symbolically or metaphorically, contemporary practitioners may wish to describe themselves as descendants of Thucydides or Kant, a serious conceptual mistake is made when the history of the field is written in terms of the development of an epic tradition beginning with classical Greece or the Enlightenment and culminating in the work of contemporary scholars. This common practice, which can be found in a multitude of synoptic accounts of the history of the field, commits the error of confusing an analytical and a historical tradition, resulting in significant obstacles to tracing the actual historical development of IR (Schmidt, 1994). Although discussions of a tradition of IR are widespread and, as Rob Walker (1993) has noted, far from monolithic, they tend to refer less to actual historical traditions, that is, self-constituted patterns of conventional practice through which ideas are conveyed within a recognizably established discursive framework, than to an analytical retrospective construction that largely is defined by present criteria and concerns. In the case of the disciplinary history of IR, such retrospectively constructed traditions as realism are presented as if they represented an actual or self-constituted tradition in the field, and serious problems in understanding and writing the history of IR result when the former is mistaken for, or presented as, the latter.

Perhaps the greatest difficulty is that such epic renditions of the past divert attention from the actual academic practices and individuals who have contributed to the development and current identity of the field. Instead of a history that traces the genealogy of academic scholars who self-consciously and institutionally participated in the professional discourse of IR, we are presented with an idealized version of the past in the form of a continuous tradition stretching from ancient times to the present. These epic accounts, which are the norm in many of the leading undergraduate texts, serve to reinforce the idea that we already know the history of the field. Attention usually is devoted to 'founding fathers' such as Thucydides, Machiavelli and Kant, while a host of individuals who contributed to the institutionalized academic study of international politics are routinely neglected. While academic scholars such as James Bryce, Frederick S. Dunn, Pitman Potter and Paul S. Reinsch may not be as historically fascinating, they are much more relevant for tracing the actual development of the field.

Presentism

The widespread tendency to write the history of the field in terms of its participation in an ancient or classic tradition of thought often serves to confer legitimacy on a contemporary research program. One of the primary purposes of the various histories of IR is to say something authoritative about the field's present character, and this often contributes to the tendency to distort the history of the field. In order either to advocate a new direction for the field and to criticize its current structure, or, conversely, to defend the status quo, scholars often feel compelled to justify their position by referring to and characterizing the general evolution of the field. For example, histories that seek to account for the rise and subsequent dominance of realist theory frequently feel obliged to demonstrate the timeless insights of the realist tradition, beginning with Thucydides or Machiavelli. And those who periodically criticize the pluralistic character of the field quite often make reference to an earlier period when there was supposedly a dominant paradigm or approach that united it. The crux of the matter is that many of the attempts to reflect on the history of IR are undertaken largely for 'presentist' purposes rather than with the intention of carefully and accurately reconstructing the past.

'Whig' history, which Herbert Butterfield (1959: v) described as the tendency 'to emphasize certain principles of progress in the past and to produce a story which is the ratification if not the glorification of the present', and the problem of presentism in general, has become a controversial issue among those who are engaged in writing the history of the social sciences (Collini et al., 1983; Dryzek and Leonard, 1988; Farr et al., 1990; Gunnell, 1991; Ross, 1991). The problem with presentism is not that historical analysis is utilized to make a point about the present, but that history is distorted as it is reconstructed to legitimate or criticize a position that the writer has set out in advance to support or to undermine. Whig history 'consists in writing history backwards', whereby the 'present theoretical consensus of the discipline … is in effect taken as definitive, and the past is then reconstituted as a teleology leading up to and fully manifested in it' (Collini et al., 1983: 4).

Given the elusive but persistent goal of mainstream IR in the United States to achieve the status of a 'true' science, it is understandable why so many of the existing accounts of the history of the field continue to be Whiggish in character. Histories of the field, and images of that history, are frequently advanced for the purpose of either illustrating theoretical progress and scientific advance or diagnosing an obstacle that is preventing the field from making scientific progress (Brecher, 1999). George Stocking provided an early and persuasive explanation for why the professional social scientist was likely to be Whiggish. According to Stocking, there is 'a sort of implicit whiggish presentism virtually built into the history of science and by extension, into the history of the behavioral sciences' (Stocking, 1965: 213). The reigning logical positivist account of science that was offered by philosophers of science during the 1950s and 1960s, which is the medium through which most social scientists acquired their understanding of science, was one of incremental and cumulative progress whereby a greater understanding of the natural world was made possible by an increasing correspondence between theory and fact. Since logical positivists claimed that there was an essential unity and hierarchy of scientific method, the history of social science was bound sooner or later to replicate the same forward advance of knowledge.

Thomas Kuhn's *The Structure of Scientific Revolutions* (1970) challenged the logical positivist account of science and provided a basic impetus for post-positivist philosophers and historians of science. Not only did Kuhn attack logical positivism's central premise of the separation of theory and fact, as well as the correspondence theory of truth, but he sought to replace the orthodox textbook account of the history of science with the idea of a discontinuous history marked by scientific revolutions, that is, 'those non-cumulative developmental episodes in which an older paradigm is replaced in whole or part by an incompatible new one' (Kuhn, 1970: 92). Kuhn's theory of paradigms and scientific revolutions represented a significant challenge to the orthodox account of scientific development. The crucial point of Kuhn's revisionist account of the history of science was his argument that there was no transcendental vantage point from which to claim that the replacement of one paradigm by another constituted 'progress', because the criteria for progress was paradigm-specific. While Kuhn made a significant impact on philosophers and historians of science, many of whom were displeased by the relativistic implications of the argument that resulted in the inability to vindicate scientific progress, his book had an equally dramatic impact on the field of IR, especially with respect to how many scholars have come to understand the history of the field. The fact that IR scholars increasingly have turned to Kuhn and other philosophers of science, particularly Imre Lakatos (1970), who, for many, appeared to re-establish evaluative criteria of progress, serves to illustrate the point that the task of writing the history of the field often has been subordinate to the more fundamental task of demonstrating progress in the field.

Paradigms and the Historiography of IR

There are two principal ways in which the work of Kuhn in particular, and the literature emanating from the philosophy and history of science in general, has had an impact on the historiography of IR. First, IR scholars quickly set out to establish their own paradigms. The situation was very much the same in political science where political scientists began to use the word paradigm to denote specific schools of thought such as behavioralism (Almond, 1966). In IR, realism has been assumed by many to be the leading candidate for a paradigm, and scholars have repeatedly undertaken the task of defining and operationalizing the core assumptions of the realist paradigm (Guzzini, 1998; Keohane, 1983; Lijphart, 1974b; Vasquez, 1983). In a historical sociology of realism, Stefano Guzzini argues that the realist paradigm that was most eloquently articulated by Hans J. Morgenthau served the

disciplinary function of defining an independent field of study. Realism, according to Guzzini, 'set the paradigmatic boundaries of the discipline' (1998: 27). While Morgenthau argued that international politics, like politics in general, was characterized by a continuous struggle for power, he maintained that the struggle was qualitatively different in the international field where an over-arching central authority was missing (Morgenthau, 1948). The notion, which later would become the cardinal claim of neorealists, that the international system was characterized by a condition of anarchy, helped to differentiate domestic politics from international politics (Waltz, 1979). The exclusive focus that neorealists placed on the anarchical structure of the international system subsequently came to provide the predominant framework for analyzing a wide variety of issues in the areas of international security, international organization, foreign policy and political economy.

The prevalence by which references are made to the realist paradigm have led some to term it the 'traditional paradigm' which, according to Arend Lijphart, 'revolves around the notions of state sovereignty and its logical corollary, international anarchy' (1974b: 43). Quite frequently references to the realist paradigm are used interchangeably with references to the 'realist tradition' or the 'realist school of thought'. Recently, a number of scholars have problematized the notion that realism represents a singular, coherent theoretical position, and instead have argued that there are actually a variety of realisms (Ashley, 1981; Doyle, 1997; Dunne, 1997; Frankel, 1996; Goldmann, 1988; Guzzini, 1998). Nevertheless, almost everyone in the field is able to identify the central tenets that are associated with realism, which typically include the following claims: that the sovereign state is the most important actor in international politics; that state behavior can be explained rationally; that states are unitary actors; that there is a sharp distinction between domestic and international politics; that states pursue power in an anarchical self-help setting; and that the issues of war and peace are paramount. The dominance of realism has led Jack Donnelly to suggest that 'tracing the fate of realism provides a partial yet still useful survey of the development of the field of international relations' (1995: 175).

Yet while realism is considered by many to be the leading paradigm in the field, it has certainly not been the only candidate for paradigmatic status. Scholars have made reference to a host of alternative paradigms, which are almost always defined in opposition to the propositions of realism and whose origins are typically linked to developments in international politics. A classical example of this, even though it allegedly predates the realist paradigm, is the so-called idealist paradigm of the inter-war period. John Vasquez claims 'that the first stage of international relations inquiry was dominated by the idealist paradigm', which was 'important in terms of institutionalizing the field and creating the emphasis on peace and war' (1998: 33–4). The central features of the so-called idealist paradigm, which largely have been defined retrospectively by post-Second World War realist critics, are the exact antithesis of the tenets attributed to realism (Bull, 1972; Carr, [1939] 1964; Guzzini, 1998; Hollis and Smith, 1991; Kegley and Wittkopf, 1989; M.J. Smith, 1986; Vasquez, 1998). Some of the other rival paradigms to realism have included the 'behavioralist paradigm' (Lijphart, 1974a), 'world politics paradigm' (Keohane and Nye, 1972), global society and neo-Marxist paradigms (Holsti, 1985), a 'new paradigm for global politics' (Mansbach and Vasquez, 1981), and pluralism (Little, 1996; Viotti and Kauppi, 1999).

The Great Debates

Kuhn's concept of a paradigm as well as other concepts borrowed from the philosophy and history of science, such as Lakatos's (1970) conception of a 'scientific research programme', have not only been used to provide grounds for defining distinct 'schools of thought', but also to evaluate the overall evolution of the field as well as specific approaches in the field (Ferguson and Mansbach, 1993; Guzzini, 1998; Keohane, 1983; Kugler, 1993; Lijphart, 1974b; Smith, 1987; Tellis, 1996; Vasquez, 1998; Walt, 1997). Arend Lijphart, for example, has argued that 'the development of international relations since the Second World War fit's Kuhn's description of scientific revolutions' (1974a: 12). The underlying purpose of utilizing analytical frameworks borrowed from the philosophy and history of science largely has been to demonstrate that scientific advances are being made and that the field as a whole is progressing. In the quest for cognitive authority over the subject matter of international politics, IR has been drawn to philosophers of science in the belief that they can provide the grounds for empirical judgment and evaluation. Ferguson and Mansbach, for example, note that the attraction of the Kuhnian framework for describing the history of IR is that it allowed 'international relations scholars to see progress in their field while surrounded by theoretical incoherence' (Ferguson and Mansbach, 1993: 22). Yet this is simply a misuse of Kuhn, since he argued that his account of the development of science was not applicable to the history of the social sciences, since they were 'pre-paradigmatic'. Moreover, analytical constructs such as idealism and realism do not meet the criteria of a paradigm as Kuhn described it. And while Kuhn's framework has been employed to demonstrate progress, his basic argument was that it was not possible to speak of progress from a second-order perspective.

Within the orthodox historiography of IR, it has been through the organizing device of the image of a series of 'great debates' that the story of the field's development has been framed. This has served to demonstrate either coherence or incoherence but, most commonly, scientific progress. The widespread belief that the field's history has been characterized by three successive great debates is so pervasive and dominant that, as Waever notes, 'there is no other established means of telling the history of the discipline' (1998: 715). The story of the field's three great debates is, as Steve Smith (1995) and Kjell Goldmann (1996) have argued, one of the most dominant self-images of the field. While all academic disciplines experience their share of disciplinary controversy, IR may be unique in that most practitioners believe that the history of the field has been singularly marked by these defining debates. This view has been reinforced by explaining the debates in terms of exogenous influences such as the outbreak of the Second World War, the rise of OPEC, the Vietnam debacle and the end of the Cold War. For many in the field, it seems self-evident that changes in the practice of international politics necessarily and directly bring about a transformation in how the subject is studied and taught. This is, for example, the standard explanation of the alleged paradigm shift from 'idealism' to 'realism' that occurred after the Second World War. Perhaps more than any other claim about the general history of the field, that which postulates three great debates must be critically examined (Kahler, 1997; Schmidt, 1998a, 1998b; Smith, 1995; Waever, 1998; Wilson, 1998). It is not entirely clear that all of the debates actually have taken place, and an examination of the discursive artifacts of the field leads one to ask if the field's history has been seriously distorted by viewing it within this framework. I do not deny that the field has experienced numerous controversies, but I question the appropriateness of understanding them in terms of the conventional story of the field's three great debates.

According to the conventional wisdom, the first great debate, which Miles Kahler (1997) has termed the 'foundational myth of the field', was between the interwar 'idealists' and the post-war 'realists'.[5] Almost every historical account concedes that the realists won the first debate and, as a result, reoriented the field in a more practical and scientific direction (Dunn, 1948; Fox, 1949; Guzzini, 1998; Kirk, 1947; M.J. Smith, 1986; Thompson, 1960). The alleged superiority of the realist view has made it appear unnecessary to consider carefully the nature of the claims made by those writing in the field prior to the Second World War or even the writings of many of those who are considered as early realists. The interwar 'idealists', who are greatly disparaged, are typically depicted as a group of utopian pacifists and legalists who focused their attention on reforming international politics rather than on analyzing the realities of politics among nations. The 'debate', which allegedly took place as the League of Nations system broke down, is often described in Kuhnian terms. While the idealists supposedly envisioned ever-lasting peace, the Second World War is depicted as a glaring anomaly representing a severe crisis in the idealist paradigm, which eventually resulted in its replacement by the realist paradigm, which was superior in its ability to rationally explain the persistent and ubiquitous struggle for power among nations (Guzzini, 1998; Hollis and Smith, 1991; Vasquez, 1998). Sometimes the idealists are represented as alchemists who were concerned with 'what ought to be' while the realists are portrayed as scientists focusing on 'what is', which was a prerequisite for creating a science of politics (Carr, [1939] 1964). This story of the 'debate' between 'idealists' and 'realists' continues to exert a strong influence on how the field understands its own history, and this accounts in part for the perpetual need to retell the tale of how IR was once rooted in idealism but was fortunate, after the Second World War, to have embraced realism.

The second great debate, as characteristically described in the literature, took place within the context of the behavioral revolution that was already deeply impacting the social sciences, especially political science, and which pitted 'traditionalists' against 'behavioralists' or 'scientists'. The debate is symbolized by the intellectual exchange between Hedley Bull (1966), who sought to defend what he termed the 'classical approach', and Morton Kaplan (1966), who was one of the early advocates of what came to be known as the 'scientific approach'. A growing sentiment among American scholars was that the field was losing ground in its quest to acquire the mantle of science. While realism, it was argued, served a number of paradigmatic functions, some scholars claimed that its tenets, such as the a priori foundational claim that the struggle for power stemmed from basic biological drives rooted in human nature, as well as its methodology, which relied heavily on historical examples, were preventing the field from achieving scientific status.

As in the case of political science, the debate became polarized between those who believed that the methods of the natural sciences, or at least those described by logical-positivist philosophers of science as the hypothetico-deductive model, could be emulated and adopted in the study of international politics, versus those who argued that the study of the social world was not amenable to the strict empirical methods of natural science (Knorr and Rosenau, 1969; Morgenthau, 1946; Nicholson, 1996; Reynolds, 1973; Rogowski, 1968; Vital, 1967). George Liska described the period in which the debate between traditionalists and behavioralists

took place as the 'heroic decade' and suggested that the key division was 'between those who are primarily interested in international relations and those who are primarily committed to the elaboration of social science' (1966: 7). The debate over the merits and adequacy of a positivistic approach surely has not diminished, but there is, nevertheless, a common view that the debate helped to foster the scientific identity of the field through the widespread acceptance and utilization of scientific methods which aided in the task of developing a cumulative theory of international politics. Morton Kaplan's (1957) systems theory, Karl Deutsch's (1953, 1964) communications and cybernetics theory, Thomas Schelling's (1960) early game theory, Richard Snyder, H.W. Bruck and Burton Sapin's (1954, 1962) development of decision-making theory, and J. David Singer and Melvin Small's (1972) data collection in their correlates of war project at the University of Michigan, are generally viewed as contributing to the scientific identity of the field.

Historical accounts of the third debate tend to be more ambiguous than that of the other two debates, but it is commonly described as an inter-paradigm debate that took place in the early 1980s among realists, pluralists and structuralists (Banks, 1985; Maghroori, 1982; Olson and Groom, 1991; Waever, 1996). The typical explanation of the origins of the third debate holds that, during the 1970s, realism fell on some difficult times when events in the realm of international politics, particularly in the economic sphere but also regarding matters of peace and security, appeared to contradict some of the key realist assumptions about the nature of inter-state politics (S. Smith, 1987). As a result of this apparent incongruity, it is generally believed that alternative 'approaches' such as Robert Keohane and Joseph Nye's ([1977] 1989) theory of 'complex interdependence', Immanuel Wallerstein's (1974, 1980) 'world systems theory', John Burton's 'cob-web theory' (1972), and 'dependency theory' (Cardoso and Faletto, 1979; Evans, 1979) were developed and directly challenged many of the central tenets of realism. Most fundamentally, critics of realism attacked the core claims of state-centrism, the notion that independence rather than interdependence characterized the condition of international politics, and that a clear distinction could be made between 'high politics' (i.e., military and security issues) and 'low politics' (i.e., economic, environmental and human rights issues). It has been suggested that it was within this context of a growing focus on interdependence (Cooper, 1968; Rosecrance and Stein, 1973) that the distinct subfield of International Political Economy emerged (Katzenstein et al., 1999).

While it was argued that the publication of Waltz's *Theory of International Politics* (1979) gave a new lease on life to realism in the form of neorealism, which rapidly became the new orthodoxy, most accounts of the third debate do not conclude that realism was the victor. Unlike the previous two 'great debates', the 'third debate' is, according to Waever, 'seen as a debate not to be won, but a pluralism to live with' (Waever, 1996: 155). In other words, claims about the ascendancy of neorealism did not mean that adherents of a liberal (pluralist) or Marxist (globalist) approach stopped contributing to the discourse of IR, and some have even questioned whether the three 'paradigms' were ever in competition with one another. Adding to the confusion of understanding this period of disciplinary history in terms of a 'third debate' was the emergence, during the 1980s, of a number of postpositivist approaches that were sharply critical of all the mainstream approaches in the field (Der Derian and Shapiro, 1989; George and Campbell, 1990; Peterson, 1992). According to Yosef Lapid, the attack by feminists, Frankfurt School critical theorists, and post-structuralists on what they perceived to be the positivist epistemological foundations of the field signaled the dawn of a 'third debate', which he claimed consisted of a 'disciplinary effort to reassess theoretical options in a "post-positivist" era' (1989: 237). That the literature can simultaneously make reference to two fundamentally different controversies under the same label of the 'third debate' should be enough to indicate that there is something seriously wrong with this understanding of the history of the field.

What's Wrong With the Image of the Great Debates?

The newest cohort of disciplinary historians have both noted the peculiarity of the field's self-image being derived from the idea of a set of recurrent debates and pointed to some of the problems that are involved in viewing the history of the field in this manner (Goldmann, 1996; Kahler, 1997; Schmidt, 1998a, 1998b; Smith, 1995; Waever, 1998; Wilson, 1998). There are so many problems and difficulties involved in understanding the history of the field within the framework of the three great debates that we might be better off simply to reject discussing this account of how the field has developed. In the first place, when attention is directed to the details of the field's history, it is not evident that all of the three debates actually took place. This is especially the case with respect to the first 'great debate' (Wilson, 1998). Second, the stylized versions of the debates do not do justice to the nature of the controversies that were in fact taking place. Third, by focusing only on the three great debates, a number of additional and, extremely important, disciplinary controversies continue to be overlooked. Finally, the use of the analytical

framework of a series of great debates to account for the field's history is a conservative move that gives the field a greater sense of coherence than the actual history of the field warrants (Waever, 1998).

One of the surprising findings to emerge from the recent scholarship on the history of the field is that, contrary to popular belief, the field was never dominated by a group of utopian scholars who adhered to something akin to what has been described as the idealist paradigm (Baldwin, 1995; Kahler, 1997; Little, 1996; Long, 1991; Long and Wilson, 1995; Osiander, 1998; Schmidt, 1998a, 1998b; Wilson, 1998). In most cases, it is difficult to find a scholar who was self-consciously and institutionally a member of the field of IR who adhered to the tenets that are frequently associated with a construct termed 'idealism' or 'utopianism'. While it is the case that the interwar scholars had a practical mission to reform the practice of international politics, this objective, which is endemic to the very nature of second-order metapractices, has continued to animate the history of the field. This objective, I argue, does not in and of itself qualify the enterprise as utopian. Many of those who have been dubbed 'idealists' turn out, upon closer inspection, to subscribe to a position that is quite different from the manner in which they have been characterized in the secondary literature. The conventional label of idealism that has been attached to the interwar period of IR scholarship seriously misrepresents the actual character of the conversation that was being directed toward understanding international politics (Osiander, 1998; Schmidt, 1998a; Wilson, 1998). Apart from seriously distorting the formative years of the field's history, the idealist tag has inhibited understanding some of the deep discursive continuities that exist between the present and the past.

Perhaps the most important continuity is the concept of anarchy that has given the field of IR a distinct discursive identity. Although it might appear to those who are not familiar with the institutional history of IR that anarchy is some newly discovered research puzzle that lends itself to the latest tools of social scientific inquiry, anarchy – and the closely related concept of sovereignty – has served as the core constituent principle throughout the evolution of the field (Schmidt, 1998b). The interwar scholars were keenly aware of the fact that their subject matter, which included an analysis of the causes of war and peace, directly dealt with issues arising from the existence of sovereign states in a condition of anarchy (Dickinson, 1916, 1926). Many of those writing during the interwar period understood that sovereignty and anarchy were inextricably associated with, and mutually constitutive of, each other, and this explains why much of the interwar discourse focused on the concept of state sovereignty. In their study of the state, political scientists established a theoretical link between the internal and external aspects of state sovereignty as well as between domestic and international politics. The juristic theory of the state, which, during the early 1900s, was the most influential paradigm for the study of political science, depicted the international milieu as one where states led an independent and isolated existence (Willoughby, 1918). Proponents of juristic theory evoked the pre-contractual image of individuals living in a state of nature to describe the external condition of states and drew many of the same pessimistic conclusions that realists have made about politics conducted in the absence of a central authority.

Beginning in the 1920s, juristic theory was challenged by a new group of thinkers who collectively put forth the theory of pluralism that fundamentally transformed the discourse of both political science and IR (Gunnell, 1993; Little, 1996; Schmidt, 1998b). Pluralists such as Harold Laski (1921, 1927) and Mary Parker Follett ([1918] 1934) argued that juristic theory was entirely inconsistent with the modern condition of interdependence, and this clearly indicated that the state was no longer omnipotent and immune from all other sources of authority. The interdependent quality of international politics, which pluralists took to be axiomatic, along with the existence of many international public unions (Reinsch, 1911), raised serious doubts about the validity of the claim that each nation-state was entirely sovereign in relation to all other actors. There are many similarities between the pluralist critique of juristic theory and the debate over interdependence that took place during the 1970s, and yet there is almost no recognition of this earlier discourse (de Wilde, 1991). Richard Little argues that one of the main reasons why the intellectual heritage of pluralism has been obscured stems from the 'willingness of the discipline to accept the attachment of the idealist tag to this seminal literature' (1996: 69). The 'idealist tag' has also obscured the manner in which the interwar scholars approached the study of international security (Baldwin, 1995) and international organization. While the interwar scholarship is most often associated with the ill-fortunes of the League of Nations, not everyone writing during this period assumed that the introduction of this new international organization would by itself alter fundamentally the logic of international politics (Duggan, 1919; Hicks, 1920). The most pressing theoretical issue for those involved in the study of international organization concerned the manner by which various conceptions of state sovereignty could be reconciled with the operation of the League of Nations. This was certainly the case for Pitman Benjamin Potter, who was the person responsible for giving specific form to the study of international organization in the United States (Potter, 1923, 1925).

Refuting the notion that the interwar period was distinguished by idealism does not, however, rest on denying that the field experienced a change of emphasis after the Second World War. By the early 1940s, it was apparent that the field was undergoing a transition, which was best exemplified by the argument that the study of international politics should replace international organization as the central focus of the field (Dunn, 1948; Fox, 1949; Kirk, 1947; Schuman, 1933; Schwarzenberger, 1941). Those who began to enter the profession under the self-proclaimed 'realist' identity were responsible for changing the emphasis in the field, but it is important not to exaggerate the discontinuities between the pre- and post-war discourse of IR. Like those writing before the Second World War, the aim of many of the 'realists' was to speak truth to power. This was especially the case with the émigré scholars who deeply impacted the discourse of both political science and IR. A careful reading of the texts by E.H. Carr ([1939] 1964), Hans J. Morgenthau (1948) and Frederick L. Schuman (1933) reveals a number of continuities with the earlier discourse which have been entirely overlooked as a consequence of viewing their work in terms of the dubious dichotomy between idealism and realism. While it is the case that Morgenthau and the other 'realists' helped to make 'international politics' the nucleus of the field, it was not the case that those writing before the outbreak of the Second World War were unfamiliar with many of the core claims of the 'new' power politics model (Bryce, 1922; Reinsch, 1900). The discursive artifacts of the field's history do not lend much support to the claim that a debate, in the sense of an intellectual exchange between opposing theoretical positions or paradigms, ever took place between the interwar and the post-Second World War scholars.

Compared with the recent research on the interwar period of the field's history, the details generally associated with the 'second great debate' or the 'traditionalism versus scientism debate' have not been carefully and systematically investigated. Consequently, this later period is not very well understood, and additional research is required. Within the existing literature on the second debate, which typically construes it as a debate about the scientific status of the field, two different accounts of the nature of the controversy have been put forth. Many of the early accounts of the controversy heralded it as a 'great debate' that contributed to a major transformation in the field (Bull, 1972; Kaplan, 1966; Lijphart, 1974a, 1974b). Lijphart, for example, claimed that the 'traditionalism-science debate of the 1960s' was more substantive and fundamental than the earlier debate between idealism and realism (1974a: 11). He argued that the behavioral revolution in IR resulted in a new paradigm – 'the behavioral paradigm' – that was at great odds with the substantive claims of the traditional realist paradigm. According to this view, the traditionalists – those who approached the study of international politics from a legal, philosophical, historical, or inductive point of view – lost out to what was perceived to be a scientific approach that sought to emulate the methods of the natural sciences. The result was that IR became more scientific, realism lost its dominant position, and the field was brought more in line with the other social sciences.

Beginning with John Vasquez's influential book *The Power of Power Politics* (1983), an alternative view of the 'second debate' began to emerge that argued that the controversy was really only a pseudo debate which was largely confined to methodological issues and did not involve substantive aspects of the subject matter of international politics (Guzzini, 1998; Hollis and Smith, 1991; Holsti, 1985, 1998; Vasquez, 1998). Vasquez (1983) sought to demonstrate that the behavioralists largely worked within the realist paradigm and merely sought to advance the methodological credentials of the field. In this manner, the debate has been construed as a 'methodological debate' which took place 'within a single [realist] theoretical orientation', and that it was 'about how to conduct inquiry within that approach' (Hollis and Smith, 1991: 31). Holsti endorses this view and argues that the 'behavioural revolution did not inaugurate a new way of looking at the world, a new paradigm, or a new set of normative problems' (1998: 33). One of the more significant implications of this revisionist interpretation is the view that the 'field has been far more coherent, systematic, and even cumulative than all the talk about contending approaches and theories implies' (Vasquez, 1998: 42).

While I concede that there is some merit in each of these accounts, neither sufficiently captures the nature of the disputes that occurred during the 1950s and 1960s. One way of coming to grips with this period is to view the events in terms of Gunnell's framework of the orders of discourse. A crucial issue that informed the behavioral debate was the problem of IR's cognitive authority as a second-order discourse. It increasingly became the case, especially within the American context, that science provided the model for achieving the authority of knowledge, and the quest during the 1950s and 1960s, as well as before and after this period, was to emulate what were believed to be the canons of inquiry in natural science. The commitment to achieving a body of knowledge about international politics that was scientifically credible and that could command practical authority has always been a defining goal of the field. What has changed over the course of time is the content of the idea of science.

One of the consequences of neglecting a careful study of the history of the field has been a failure to recognize adequately the work of the members of the Chicago School of political science. In the 1920s and 1930s, Harold Lasswell, Charles Merriam and Quincy Wright believed that they were at the forefront of developing a universal science of politics (Fox, 1975; Kahler, 1997). As William T.R. Fox has noted, when *World Politics* began publication in 1948, there were two very different schools of thought reshaping the academic study of IR: the realist school and the school led by Merriam, which 'had its roots in homegrown American political science, in pluralist pragmatism, and in an abiding faith in the power of the human intellect gradually to create a better world' (1975: 597). The Chicago School's idea of a science of international politics was one that viewed international relations as merely a single subdivision of a more inclusive approach that focused on the role of power across a broad range of associations from the local to the global level.

There are a number of explanations of why the idea of science that the bahavioralists brought to the field during the 1950s and 1960s largely centered on the concept of an international system (Kaplan, 1957; Rosenau, 1969). The idea of a system was central to the behavioral movement, but its application to IR took on a number of distinctive and problematic properties. Within political science, the systems approach (Easton, 1953) was meant to replace the study of the state, which the behavioralists deemed to be archaic and contributing to the backwardness of the discipline. Yet within IR, where the influence of the behavioral persuasion arrived late and where the theory of realism was dominant, the adoption of the concept of a system did not supersede the focus on the interaction of states, since it would have risked the very identity of the field (Little, 1978, 1985). The properties accorded to the 'international system' were largely derived from a detailed, and increasingly quantitative, analysis of the units (states) (Buzan and Little, 2000). The systems approach gave rise to what has been termed the 'level of analysis problem', which involves the question of the relative weight that should be attributed to the units as opposed to the system as a whole (Buzan, 1995; Hollis and Smith, 1991; Singer, 1969). Waltz's (1979) later attempt to construct a systems theory was based on the model of microeconomics, which sought to overcome the problem of reductionism that he attributed to the earlier generation of systems thinkers. It would appear that Buzan and Little (2000) are correct to argue that the concept of an international system is deeply contested, and I would suggest that carefully examining the period that has been construed in terms of the second debate might add a sense of clarity to the present conversation.

Whether or not we accept the idea that a 'great debate' took place, it is important that we do not de-emphasize the consequences that the increasing attachment to scientism had for the development of the field. First, it has resulted in IR surrendering its intellectual autonomy to a number of cognate fields that appeared, for whatever reason, to be more scientific. This is plainly, and I would argue unfortunately, the case today with the field's fascination with, and incessant borrowing from, microeconomic models of analysis. Second, the commitment to science contributed to a growing rift between the American scholarly community, which sought to emulate the positivist approach to knowledge, and much of the rest of the world that remained deeply suspicious of studying international politics in this manner. The members of the English School, Hedley Bull, Herbert Butterfield, John Vincent, Martin Wight and others, were, for example, 'skeptical of the possibility of a scientific study of International Relations' (Dunne, 1998: 7). They chose to focus on what they termed an 'international society' that involved the study of history, culture, religion and philosophy (Dunne, 1998; Epp, 1998; Grader, 1988; Little, 2000). Yet their work, as well as most of the scholarship from Britain, was, until recently, almost completely ignored by American scholars. A third consequence was a divorce between political theory and international relations theory (Boucher, 1998). Just as the history of political thought became a focal point of attack by behavioralists in political science, the idea that the study of international political theory could advance the scientific credentials of the field was rejected. Fourth, the bifurcation of political theory and international theory had the effect of marginalizing normative concerns and contributed to what Steve Smith has termed the 'forty-years detour' whereby it became 'simply old-fashioned, and very unacademic, to introduce normative concerns into analysis unless they were themselves to be the objects of analysis' (1992: 489). The field has only recently begun to recover from this detour and has rediscovered normative international political theory.

The limitations of utilizing the 'great debates' framework for understanding the history of the field is plainly apparent when we come to the 1980s and the so-called 'third great debate'. As the field has become increasingly pluralistic, perhaps owing, in part, to its institutional growth, there seems to be a plethora of debates. In addition to the two versions of the 'third debate' mentioned earlier, the interparadigm and post-positivism debates, there is the debate between neorealism and neoliberalism (Baldwin, 1993; Kegley, 1995); between rationalists and reflectivists (Keohane, 1988; Walker, 1989); between rationalists and constructivists (Katzenstein et al., 1999; Ruggie, 1998; Wendt, 1999; see also Fearon and Wendt, Chapter 3 in this volume); between 'offensive' and 'defensive' realists (Mearsheimer, 1994/1995; Schweller, 1996); and between communitarians and cosmopolitans (Brown, 1987, 1992; Hoffman, 1988). Yet this

listing only begins to scratch the surface, since there are also numerous debates within specific approaches such as constructivism, feminism, realism and post-structuralism.

Although it is difficult to provide an adequate historical perspective on these more recent developments, it is simply impossible to lump all of these controversies under one grand master debate. No matter what general characteristics we assign to the debate, it would not help us to understand the most recent history of the field. Waever has suggested that one way to get beyond the confusion of viewing recent developments in terms of a singular third debate is by acknowledging that we have entered a 'fourth debate' (1996). Here Waever, like several others in the field (Lapid, 1989; Smith, 2000; Vasquez, 1995), suggests that we make a sharp differentiation between, on the one hand, approaches, such as critical theory, post-structuralism, postmodernism and specific versions of constructivism and feminism, that fall under the post-positivism label and, on the other hand, the mainstream, which he argues is wedded to a rationalist orthodoxy. The latter is seen as resulting from what Waever (1996) terms a 'neo-neo synthesis' in which, during the 1980s, neoliberalism and neorealism essentially became indistinguishable on the basis of their shared commitment to a rationalist research program. This view of a 'neo-neo-synthesis' is more popular outside the United States than within, where neoliberalism and neorealism continue to represent the basic divisions within the field despite the new emphasis on constructivism.

Post-positivism has sparked a considerable amount of meta-theoretical reflection on the current identity and composition of the field. The activity of reflecting on the nature of theory has come to comprise a significant component of the discourse in IR. As in other fields where the challenge to positivism has been mounted, post-positivists in IR view the traditional epistemological foundations of the field, often assumed to emanate from the Enlightenment, as no longer a philosophically defensible basis for making authoritative judgments about validity in political inquiry. In this manner, 'post-positivism has placed the scientific study of world politics in a serious crisis' (Vasquez, 1995: 234). Many of these 'alternative' or 'dissident' approaches seek to deconstruct the traditional positivist foundations of the field and to embrace a radical anti-foundationalism that can enable multiple voices or perspectives to be heard. This is seen by some as leading to a major restructuring of IR, allowing for additional space in which to think about the issues that currently comprise the subject matter of the field (George, 1994; George and Campbell, 1990; Neufeld, 1995). For others, post-positivism, and postmodernism in particular, has raised fears about relativism, as the loss of an epistemological foundation is believed to undermine the authority of scholars to provide transcontextual grounds for truth (Rosenau, 1990; Vasquez, 1995).

While there is little doubt that various post-positivist approaches have contributed to the field's pluralistic character, generated an expansive body of interesting literature, and forced the field to confront a host of new meta-theoretical questions, how large an impact they have made on the mainstream core of the field is still not clear. Like previous 'alternative' approaches, the main object of the post-positivist critique has been realism, yet realism, in one form or another, survives and continues to provide what many would argue to be the initial essential assumptions for explaining international politics as it has been traditionally defined by the field of IR (Grieco, 1997; Jervis, 1998; Mearsheimer, 1994/5). This can partly account for why, of all the alternative approaches that have entered the field since the early 1980s, Wendt's particular conception of constructivism, which accepts many of the assumptions of realism, is the approach being taken most seriously by the mainstream today. To the dismay of some of the critical scholars in the field, Wendt (1999) claims that his version of constructivism is able to entertain the role of ideas, norms and the process of identity-formation while at the same time subscribing to a realist world-view and a positivist epistemology. In this manner, some of the most recent literature on the state of the field is heralding constructivism as the field's newest approach or paradigm to the study of international politics (Katzenstein et al., 1999; Walt, 1998).

CONCLUSION

Although there is a general sense that we already know the field's history, I have attempted to demonstrate that there are many problems with the conventional story about how the field has developed. Some of the more recent work on the history of IR suggests that many of our dominant understandings of the field are nothing more than myths (Booth, 1996; Kahler, 1997; Wilson, 1998), and one of the problems with such myths is that they often not only misrepresent the past but continue to misinform the present. Research on the history of the field is not simply an exercise in antiquarianism but an attempt to increase our capacity to examine critically the contemporary nature of the field by an understanding of the intellectual roots from which it has evolved. There is an intimate link between disciplinary identity and the manner in which we understand the history of the field. For a field that appears to be perpetually consumed by identity crises, careful attention to some of the previous

identities by which we were possessed would represent a fruitful research agenda. There is ample opportunity for the diverse approaches in the field to explore their own intellectual roots and, thereby, to recognize some of the continuities between the past and the present. Such an exercise might even help to prevent the tendency for the field to proclaim something quite old as new.

In order for the investigation of the history of the field to receive the same intellectual respect as other areas of research, more attention should be placed on the theoretical and methodological assumptions involved. The absence of such attention in much of the existing literature on the history of the field has served to reinforce the view that the history of IR is self-evident or trivial. One example is the explicit as well as implicit contextualism that has informed so many of the orthodox accounts of the field's development. Although it is often suggested that the external context provided by 'real world' political events can be conceived as an independent variable that explains the character of the field at a specific historical juncture, the actual link between the two is seldom as straightforward and self-evident as it might appear. The relationship between external events and the internal disciplinary response manifested in conceptual or theoretical change must be empirically demonstrated and not merely assumed. Although IR is conceived as an academic enterprise devoted to the study of international politics, this does not automatically imply that the exogenous events that comprise the subject matter at any given point in time can explain what happens inside the field. From the point of view of disciplinary history, the crux of the issue should be how the field has, or has not, responded intellectually to external factors rather than how these factors can account for the dynamics inside the field. And more attention should be placed on the internal context of the field such as its setting in the university system, sources of funding and professional norms. An internal as compared to an external focus may well help to account for the distinct national differences in how the field has developed.

While I have suggested that it might, for various reasons, be beneficial for the various approaches or schools of thought in the field to chronicle their own discursive development, this does not mean that disciplinary history should merely serve as a vehicle for legitimation and critique. As Gunnell has stated, truth is very often more convincing than fiction and carries as much critical force (1991). Although there might be a tendency for histories of the field to be presentist, it has become obvious that this often results in serious distortions. Rather than seeking to say something authoritative about the field's present character, it might be more useful to attempt to say something definitive about the field's past.

It is quite evident that a number of different approaches and methodologies can be used to recover the disciplinary history of IR. While I have elsewhere advocated a historiographical approach that can be described as a critical internal discursive history (Schmidt, 1998a, 1998b), Guzzini (1998) advocates a historical sociological approach, Waever (1998) embraces a sociology of science view, and Smith (1995) advocates a genealogical method informed by the work of Foucault. There is room for all these approaches and more, but the important point is that disciplinary history can be a vehicle in fostering critical insights and opening additional space in which to think about the central dilemmas that continue to confront the study of international politics. These insights, however, depend on dispelling the misconceptions that have plagued past work on the history of IR.

Notes

I wish to thank John G. Gunnell, Steve Smith and the editors for their helpful comments and suggestions on earlier versions of this chapter.

1 The abbreviation IR refers to the institutionalized academic field of international relations.

2 The eight root disciplines included international law, diplomatic history, military science, international politics, international organization, international trade, colonial government and the conduct of foreign relations. The disciplines with a world point of view included world geography, world history, psychology, sociology, language and biology.

3 Waever, 1998 provides a very useful discussion of the evolution in IR in Germany, France, the United Kingdom and the United States.

4 Although few in number, there is a growing body of literature that examines the development of IR from within a specific country setting. For example, the edited volume by Hugh C. Dyer and Leon Mangasarian (1989) includes chapters on the study of IR in the former Soviet Union, China, Brazil, the Federal Republic of Germany, South Africa, France, Japan, Italy and the United Kingdom among others. Other examples of this undertaking include Chan, 1994; Groom, 1994; and Jorgensen, 2000.

5 The first generation of self-ascribed academic realists and their most influential work included: E.H. Carr 1939; George F. Kennan, 1951; Hans J. Morgenthau, 1948; Reinhold Niebuhr, 1940; Frederick L. Schuman, 1933; Georg Schwarzenberger, 1941; and Nicholas J. Spykman, 1942.

Bibliography

Alker, Hayard R. and Biersteker, Thomas J. (1984) 'The Dialectics of World Order: Notes for a Future Archeologist of International Savoir Faire', *International Studies Quarterly,* 28 (2): 121–42.

Almond, Gabriel A. (1966) 'Political Theory and Political Science', *American Political Science Review*, 60 (4): 869–79.

Ashley, Richard K. (1981) 'Political Realism and Human Interests', *International Studies Quarterly*, 25 (2): 204–36.

Bailey, Stanley H. (1932) *The Framework of International Society*. New York: Longmans, Green, and Co.

Baldwin, David (ed.) (1993) *Neorealism and Neoliberalism: The Contemporary Debate*. New York: Columbia University Press.

Baldwin, David (1995) 'Security Studies and the End of the Cold War', *World Politics,* 48 (1): 117–41.

Banks, Michael (1985) 'The Inter-Paradigm Debate', in Margot Light and A.J.R. Groom (eds), *International Relations a Handbook of Current Theory.* London: Francis Pinter Publishers. pp. 7–26.

Banks, Michael (1986) 'The International Relations Discipline: Asset or Liability for Conflict Resolution?', in E. Azar and J. Burton (eds), *International Conflict Resolution: Theory and Practice.* Boulder: Lynne Rienner. pp. 5–27.

Bender, Thomas and Schorske, Carl E. (1998) *American Academic Culture in Transformation: Fifty Years, Four Disciplines*. Princeton: Princeton University Press.

Booth, Ken (1996) '75 Years On: Rewriting the Subject's Past – Reinventing its Future', in S. Smith, K. Booth and M. Zalewski (eds), *International Theory: Positivism and Beyond.* Cambridge: Cambridge University Press. pp. 328–39.

Boucher, David (1998) *Political Theories of International Relations: From Thucydides to the Present*. Oxford: Oxford University Press.

Brecher, Michael (1999) 'International Studies in the Twentieth Century and Beyond: Flawed Dichotomies, Synthesis, Cumulation', *International Studies Quarterly*, 43 (2): 213–64.

Brown, Chris (1987) 'Not My Department? Normative Theory and International Relations', *Paradigms*, 1 (2): 104–30.

Brown, Chris (1992) *International Relations Theory: New Normative Approaches*. New York: Columbia University Press.

Bryce, James (1922) *International Relations*. Port Washington: Kennikat Press.

Bull, Hedley (1966) 'International Theory: The Case for a Classical Approach', *World Politics*, 18 (3): 361–77.

Bull, Hedley (1972) 'The Theory of International Politics, 1919–1969', in Brian Porter (ed.), *The Aberystwyth Papers: International Politics 1919–1969.* London: Oxford University Press. pp. 30–55.

Burton, John W. (1972) *World Society*. London: Cambridge University Press.

Butterfield, Herbert (1959) *The Whig Interpretation of History*. London: G. Bell and Sons.

Buzan, Barry (1995) 'The Level of Analysis Problem in International Relations Reconsidered', in Ken Booth and Steve Smith (eds), *International Relations Theory Today*. University Park: Pennsylvania State University Press. pp. 198–216.

Buzan, Barry and Little, Richard (2000) *International Systems in World History: Remaking the Study of International Relations*. Oxford: Oxford University Press.

Cardoso, Fernando Henrique and Faletto, Enzo (1979) *Dependency and Development in Latin America*. Berkeley: University of California Press.

Carr, E.H. ([1939] 1964) *The Twenty Years' Crisis, 1919–1939: An Introduction to the Study of International Relations*. New York: Harper & Row.

Chan, Stephen (1994) 'Beyond the North-West: Africa and the Rest', in A.J.R. Groom and Margot Light (eds), *Contemporary International Relations: A Guide to Theory*. London: Pinter Publishers. pp. 237–54.

Clark, Ian (1989) *The Hierarchy of States: Reform and Resistance in the International Order*. Cambridge: Cambridge University Press.

Collini, Stefan, Winch, Donald, and Burrow, John (1983) *That Noble Science of Politics: A Study of Nineteenth Century Intellectual History*. Cambridge: Cambridge University Press.

Cooper, Richard N. (1968) *The Economics of Interdependence: Economic Policy in the Atlantic Community*. New York: McGraw-Hill.

Crawford, M.A. and Jarvis, Darryl S.L. (2001) *International Relations: Still an American Social Science? Toward Diversity in International Thought*. Albany, NY: State University of New York Press.

Der Derian, James and Shapiro, Michael J. (eds) (1989) *International/Intertextual Relations: Postmodern Readings of World Politics*. Lexington: Lexington Books.

Deutsch, Karl W. (1953) *Nationalism and Social Communication*. Cambridge, MA: MIT Press.

Deutsch, Karl W. (1964) *The Nerves of Government*. New York: The Free Press.

Dickinson, G. Lowes (1916) *The European Anarchy*. New York: Macmillan.

Dickinson, G. Lowes (1926) *International Anarchy, 1904–1914*. New York: Century.

Donelan, Michael (1990) *Elements of International Political Theory*. Oxford: Clarendon Press.

Donnelly, Jack (1995) 'Realism and the Academic Study of International Relations', in James Farr, John S. Dryzek and Stephen T. Leonard (eds), *Political Science in History: Research Programs and Political Traditions*. Cambridge: Cambridge University Press. pp. 175–97.

Doyle, Michael W. (1997) *Ways of War and Peace: Realism, Liberalism, and Socialism*. New York: W.W. Norton.

Dryzek, John S. and Leonard, Stephen T. (1988) 'History and Discipline in Political Science', *American Political Science Review*, 82 (4): 1245–60.

Duggan, Stephen Pierce (ed.) (1919) *The League of Nations: The Principle and the Practice*. Boston: The Atlantic Monthly Press.

Dunn, Frederick S. (1948) 'The Scope of International Relations', *World Politics*, 1: 142–6.

Dunne, Tim (1997) 'Realism', in John Baylis and Steve Smith (eds), *The Globalization of World Politics: An Introduction to International Relations*. Oxford: Oxford University Press. pp. 109–24.

Dunne, Tim (1998) *Inventing International Society: A History of the English School*. London: Macmillan.

Dyer, Hugh C. and Mangasarian, Leon (eds) (1989) *The Study of International Relations: The State of the Art*. London: Macmillan.

Easton, David (1953) *The Political System: An Inquiry into the State of Political Science*. New York: Alfred A. Knopf.

Epp, Roger (1998) 'The English School on the Frontiers of International Relations', *Review of International Studies*, 24 (special issue): 47–63.

Evans, Peter (1979) *Dependent Development: The Alliance of Multinational, State, and Local Capital in Brazil*. Cambridge, MA: Harvard University Press.

Farr, James (1990) 'Francis Lieber and the Interpretation of American Political Science', *Journal of Politics*, 52 (4): 1027–49.

Farr, James, Seidelman, Raymond, Gunnell, John G., Leonard, Stephen T. and Dryzek, John S. (1990) 'Can Political Science History Be Neutral?', *American Political Science Review*, 84 (2): 587–607.

Ferguson, Yale and Mansbach, Richard (1993) *The Elusive Quest: Theory and International Politics*. Columbia: University of South Carolina Press.

Follett, Mary Parker ([1918] 1934) *The New State: Group Organization the Solution of Popular Sovereignty*. London: Longmans, Green and Co.

Fox, William T.R. (1949) 'Interwar International Relations Research: The American Experience', *World Politics*, 2: 67–80.

Fox, William T.R. (1975) 'Pluralism, the Science of Politics, and the World System', *World Politics*, 27 (4): 597–611.

Frankel, Benjamin (ed.) (1996) *Roots of Realism*. London: Frank Cass.

George, Jim (1994) *Discourses of Global Politics: A Critical (Re)Introduction to International Relations*. Boulder: Lynne Rienner.

George, Jim and Campbell, David (1990) 'Patterns of Dissent and the Celebration of Difference: Critical Social Theory and International Relations', *International Studies Quarterly*, 34 (3): 269–94.

Goldmann, Kjell (1988) 'The Concept of "Realism" as a Source of Confusion', *Cooperation and Conflict*, 23: 1–14.

Goldmann, Kjell (1996) 'International Relations: An Overview', in Robert E. Goodin and Hans-Dieter Klingemann (eds), *A New Handbook of Political Science*. Oxford: Oxford University Press. pp. 401–27.

Grader, Sheila (1988) 'The English School of International Relations: Evidence and Evaluation', *Review of International Studies*, 14 (1): 329–51.

Grieco, Joseph M. (1997) 'Realist International Theory and the Study of World Politics', in Michael W. Doyle and G. John Ikenberry (eds), *New Thinking in International Relations Theory*. Boulder: Westview. pp. 163–201.

Groom, A.J.R. (1994) 'Introduction: The Past as Prelude', in A.J.R. Groom and Margot Light (eds), *Contemporary International Relations: A Guide to Theory.* London: Pinter Publishers. pp. 1–6.

Gunnell, John G. (1991) 'Disciplinary History: The Case of Political Science', *Strategies: A Journal of Theory, Culture and Politics*, 4/5: 182–227.

Gunnell, John G. (1993) *The Descent of Political Theory: A Genealogy of an American Vocation.* Chicago: University of Chicago Press.

Gunnell, John G. (1998) *The Orders of Discourse: Philosophy, Social Science, and Politics.* Lanham: Rowman and Littlefield.

Gurian, Waldemar (1946) 'On the Study of International Relations', *The Review of Politics*, 8 (3): 275–82.

Guzzini, Stefano (1998) *Realism in International Relations and International Political Economy: The Continuing Story of a Death Foretold.* London: Routledge.

Hermann, Margaret G. (1998) 'One Field, Many Perspectives: Building the Foundations for Dialogue', *International Studies Quarterly*, 42 (4): 605–24.

Hicks, Frederick Charles (1920) *The New World Order: International Organization, International Law, International Cooperation.* New York: Doubleday, Page.

Hill, Christopher (1987) 'The Study of International Relations in the United Kingdom', *Millennium: Journal of International Studies*, 16 (2): 301–8.

Hoffman, Mark (1988) 'States, Cosmopolitanism, and Normative International Theory', *Paradigms*, 2 (1): 60–75.

Hoffmann, Stanley (1977) 'An American Social Science: International Relations', *Daedalus*, 106: 41–59.

Hollis, Martin and Smith, Steve (1991) *Explaining and Understanding International Relations.* Oxford: Clarendon Press.

Holsti, Kal J. (1985) *The Dividing Discipline: Hegemony and Diversity in International Theory.* Boston: Allen & Unwin.

Holsti, Kal J. (1998) 'Scholarship in an Era of Anxiety: The Study of International Relations During the Cold War', *Review of International Studies*, 24 (special issue): 17–46.

Jervis, Robert (1998) 'Realism in the Study of World Politics', *International Organization*, 52 (4): 971–91.

Jorgensen, Knud Erik (2000) 'Continental IR Theory: The Best Kept Secret', *European Journal of International Relations*, 6 (1): 9–42.

Kahler, Miles (1993) 'International Relations: Still an American Social Science?', in Linda B. Miller and Michael Joseph Smith (eds), *Ideas and Ideals: Essays on Politics in Honor of Stanley Hoffmann.* Boulder: Westview. pp. 395–414.

Kahler, Miles (1997) 'Inventing International Relations: International Relations Theory After 1945', in Michael Doyle and G. John Ikenberry (eds), *New Thinking in International Relations Theory.* Boulder: Westview. pp. 20–53.

Kaplan, Morton (1957) *System and Process in International Politics.* New York: John Wiley.

Kaplan, Morton (1961) 'Is International Relations a Discipline?', *Journal of Politics*, 23: 462–76.

Kaplan, Morton (1966) 'The New Great Debate: Traditionalism vs. Science in International Relations', *World Politics*, 19 (1): 1–20.

Katzenstein, Peter J., Keohane, Robert O. and Krasner, Stephen D. (eds) (1999) *Exploration and Contestation in the Study of World Politics.* Cambridge, MA: MIT Press.

Kauppi, Mark V. and Viotti, Paul R. (1999) *International Relations Theory: Realism, Pluralism, Globalism, and Beyond*, 3rd edn. Boston: Allyn and Bacon.

Kegley, Charles W. (ed.) (1995) *Controversies in International Relations Theory: Realism and the Neoliberal Challenge.* New York: St Martin's Press.

Kegley, Charles W. and Wittkopf, Eugene (1989) *World Politics: Trend and Transformation.* New York: St Martin's Press.

Kennan, George F. (1951) *American Diplomacy 1900–1950.* Chicago: University of Chicago Press.

Keohane, Robert O. (1983) 'Theory of World Politics: Structural Realism and Beyond', in Ada W. Finifter (ed.), *Political Science: The State of the Discipline.* Washington, DC: American Political Science Association. pp. 503–40.

Keohane, Robert O. (1988) 'International Institutions: Two Approaches', *International Studies Quarterly*, 32 (4): 379–96.

Keohane, Robert O. and Nye, Joseph S. (eds) (1972) *Transnational Relations and World Politics.* Cambridge, MA: Harvard University Press.

Keohane, Robert O. and Nye, Joseph S. ([1977] 1989) *Power and Interdependence*, 2nd edn. Boston: Scott, Foresman.

Kirk, Grayson (1947) *The Study of International Relations in American Colleges and Universities.* New York: Council on Foreign Relations.

Knorr, Klaus and Rosenau, James N. (eds) (1969) *Contending Approaches to International Politics.* Princeton: Princeton University Press.

Knutsen, Torbjorn L. (1997) *A History of International Relations Theory*, 2nd edn. Manchester: Manchester University Press.

Krippendorf, Ekkehart (1987) 'The Dominance of American Approaches in International Relations', *Millennium: Journal of International Studies*, 16 (2): 207–14.

Kugler, Jacek (1993) 'Political Conflict, War and Peace', in Ada W. Finifter (ed.), *Political Science: The State of the Discipline II.* Washington, DC: American Political Science Association. pp. 483–509.

Kuhn, Thomas S. (1970) *The Structure of Scientific Revolutions*, 2nd edn. Chicago: University of Chicago Press.

Lakatos, Imre (1970) 'Falsification and the Methodology of Scientific Research Programmes', in Imre Lakatos and Alan Musgrave (eds), *Criticism and the Growth of Knowledge.* Cambridge: Cambridge University Press. pp. 91–195.

Lapid, Yosef (1989) 'The Third Debate: On the Prospects of International Theory in a Post-Positivist Era', *International Studies Quarterly*, 33 (3): 235–54.

Laski, H.J. (1921) *The Foundations of Sovereignty and Other Essays*. New York: Harcourt, Brace and Co.

Laski, H.J. (1927) 'International Government and National Sovereignty', in *The Problems of Peace: Lectures Delivered at the Geneva Institute of International Relations*. London: Oxford University Press. pp. 288–312.

Lijphart, Arend (1974a) 'International Relations Theory: Great Debates and Lesser Debates', *International Social Science Journal*, 26 (1): 11–21.

Lijphart, Arend (1974b) 'The Structure of the Theoretical Revolution in International Relations', *International Studies Quarterly*, 18 (1): 41–74.

Liska, George (1966) 'The Heroic Decade and After: International Relations as Events, Discipline, and Profession', *SAIS Review*, 10: 5–11.

Little, Richard (1978) 'A Systems Approach', in Trevor Taylor (ed.), *Approaches and Theory in International Relations*. New York: Longman. pp. 182–204.

Little, Richard (1985) 'The Systems Approach', in Steve Smith (ed.), *International Relations: British and American Perspectives*. New York: Blackwell. pp. 71–91.

Little, Richard (1996) 'The Growing Relevance of Pluralism?', in Steve Smith, Ken Booth, and Marysia Zalewski (eds), *International Theory: Positivism and Beyond*. Cambridge: Cambridge University Press. pp. 66–86.

Little, Richard (2000) 'The English School's Contribution to the Study of International Relations', *European Journal of International Relations*, 6 (3): 395–422.

Long, David (1991) 'J.A. Hobson and Idealism in International Relations', *Review of International Studies*, 17 (3): 285–304.

Long, David and Wilson, Peter (ed.) (1995) *Thinkers of the Twenty Years' Crisis: Inter-War Idealism Reassessed*. Oxford: Clarendon Press.

Maghroori, Ray (1982) 'Introduction: Major Debates in International Relations', in Ray Maghroori and Bennet, Ramberg (eds), *Globalism Versus Realism: International Relations' Third Debate*. Boulder: Westview. pp. 9–22.

Mansbach, Richard, W. and Vasquez, John, A. (1981) *In Search of Theory: A New Paradigm for Global Politics*. New York: Columbia University Press.

Mearsheimer, John (1994/1995) 'The False Promise of International Institutions', *International Security*, 19: 5–49.

Mitchell, C.R. (1980) 'Analysing the "Great Debates": Teaching Methodology in a Decade of Change', in R.C. Kent and G.P. Nielsson (eds), *The Study and Teaching of International Relations*. London: Pinter Publishers. pp. 28–46.

Morgenthau, Hans, J. (1946) *Scientific Man versus Power Politics*. Chicago: University of Chicago Press.

Morgenthau, Hans, J. (1948) *Politics Among Nations: The Struggle for Power and Peace*. New York: Alfred A. Knopf.

Neal, Fred and Hamlett, Bruce D. (1969) 'The Never-Never Land of International Relations', *International Studies Quarterly*, 13 (2): 281–305.

Neufeld, Mark A. (1995) *The Restructuring of International Relations Theory*. Cambridge: Cambridge University Press.

Nicholson, Michael (1996) *Causes and Consequences in International Relations: A Conceptual Study*. London: Pinter.

Niebuhr, Reinhold (1940) *Christianity and Power Politics*. New York: Charles Scribner's Sons.

Olson, William (1972) 'The Growth of a Discipline', in Brian Porter (ed.), *The Aberystwyth Papers: International Politics 1919–1969*. London: Oxford University Press. pp. 3–29.

Olson, William and Groom, A.J.R. (1991) *International Relations Then and Now: Origins and Trends in Interpretation*. London: HarperCollins.

Olson, William C. and Onuf, Nicholas (1985) 'The Growth of a Discipline Reviewed', in Steve Smith (ed.), *International Relations: British and American Perspectives*. New York: Blackwell. pp 1–28.

Osiander, Andreas (1998) 'Rereading Early Twentieth-Century IR Theory: Idealism Revisited', *International Studies Quarterly*, 42 (3): 409–32.

Palmer, Norman D. (1980) 'The Study of International Relations in the United States', *International Studies Quarterly*, 24 (3): 343–64.

Peterson, V. Spike (1992) 'Transgressing Boundaries: Theories of Knowledge, Gender and International Relations', *Millennium: Journal of International Studies*, 21 (2): 183–206.

Plating, E. Raymond (1969) 'International Relations as a Field of Inquiry', in James N. Rosenau (ed.), *International Politics and Foreign Policy: A Reader in Research and Theory*. New York: The Free Press. pp. 6–19.

Porter, Brian (ed.) (1972) *The Aberystwyth Papers: International Politics 1919–1969*. London: Oxford University Press.

Potter, Pitman B. (1923) 'Political Science in the International Field', *American Political Science Review*, 27 (3): 381–91.

Potter, Pitman B. (1925) *An Introduction to the Study of International Organization*. New York: Century.

Reinsch, Paul S. (1900) *World Politics at the End of the Nineteenth Century, As Influenced by the Oriental Situation*. New York: Macmillan.

Reinsch, Paul S. (1911) *Public International Unions Their Work and Organization*. Boston: Ginn and Co.

Reynolds, Charles (1973) *Theory and Explanation in International Relations*. Oxford: Martin Robertson.

Rogowski, Ronald (1968) 'International Politics: The Past as Science', *International Studies Quarterly*, 12 (4): 394–418.

Rosecrance, Richard and Stein, Arthur A. (1973) 'Interdependence: Myth or Reality?', *World Politics*, 26 (1): 1–27.

Rosenau, James N. (ed.) (1969) *International Politics and Foreign Policy: A Reader in Research and Theory*. New York: The Free Press.

Rosenau, Pauline (1990) 'Once Again Into the Fray: International Relations Confronts the Humanities',

Millennium: Journal of International Studies, 19 (1): 83–110.

Ross, Dorothy (1991) *The Origins of American Social Science*. Cambridge: Cambridge University Press.

Ruggie, John G. (1998) *Constructing the World Polity: Essays on International Organization*. London: Routledge.

Schelling, Thomas C. (1960) *The Strategy of Conflict*. New York: Oxford University Press.

Schmidt, Brian C. (1994) 'The Historiography of Academic International Relations', *Review of International Studies*, 20 (4): 349–67.

Schmidt, Brian C. (1998a) 'Lessons from the Past: Reassessing the Interwar Disciplinary History of International Relations', *International Studies Quarterly*, 42 (3): 433–59.

Schmidt, Brian C. (1998b) *The Political Discourse of Anarchy: A Disciplinary History of International Relations*. Albany: State University of New York Press.

Schmidt, Brian C. (2000) 'Resurrecting International Political Theory', *Millennium: Journal of International Studies*, 29 (1): 153–63.

Schuman, Frederick L. (1933) *International Politics: An Introduction to the Western State System*. New York: McGraw-Hill.

Schwarzenberger, Georg (1941) *Power Politics: An Introduction to the Study of International Relations and Post-War Planning*. London: Jonathan Cape.

Schweller, Randall L. (1996) 'Neorealism's Status-Quo Bias: What Security Dilemma?', *Security Studies*, 5 (3): 90–121.

Simpson, Christopher (ed.) (1998) *Universities and Empire: Money and Politics in the Social Sciences During the Cold War*. New York: New Press.

Singer, J. David (1969) 'The Level-of-Analysis Problem in International Relations', in James N. Rosenau (ed.), *International Politics and Foreign Policy: A Reader in Research and Theory*. New York: The Free Press. pp. 20–9.

Singer, J. David and Small, Melvin (1972) *The Wages of War, 1816–1965: A Statistical Handbook*. New York: John Wiley.

Smith, Michael Joseph (1986) *Realist Thought from Weber to Kissinger*. Baton Rouge: Louisiana State University Press.

Smith, Steve (1985) *International Relations: British and American Perspectives*. Oxford: Blackwell.

Smith, Steve (1987) 'Paradigm Dominance in International Relations: The Development of International Relations as a Social Science', *Millennium: Journal of International Studies*, 16 (2): 189–206.

Smith, Steve (1992) 'The Forty Years' Detour: The Resurgence of Normative Theory in International Relations', *Millennium: Journal of International Studies*, 21 (3): 489–506.

Smith, Steve (1995) 'The Self-Images of a Discipline: A Genealogy of International Relations Theory', in Ken Booth and Steve Smith (eds), *International Relations Theory Today*. University Park: Pennsylvania State University Press. pp. 1–37.

Smith, Steve (2000) 'The Discipline of International Relations: Still An American Social Science', *British Journal of Politics and International Relations*, 2 (3): 374–402.

Snyder, Richard C., Bruck, H.W. and Sapin, Burton (1954) *Decision-Making as an Approach to the Study of International Politics*. Princeton: Princeton University Press.

Snyder, Richard C., Bruck, H.W. and Sapin, Burton (eds) (1962) *Foreign Policy Decision-Making*. New York: The Free Press.

Spykman, Nicholas J. (1942) *America's Strategy in World Politics: The United States and the Balance of Power*. New York: Harcourt, Brace and Co.

Stocking, George W. (1965) 'On the Limits of "Presentism" and "Historicism" in the Historiography of the Behavioral Sciences', *Journal of the History of the Behavioral Sciences*, 1: 211–17.

Tellis, Ashley J. (1996) 'Reconstructing Political Realism: The Long March to Scientific Theory', in Benjamin Frankel (ed.), *Roots of Realism*. London: Frank Cass. pp. 3–100.

Thompson, Kenneth (1952) 'The Study of International Politics: A Survey of Trends and Developments', *Review of Politics*, 14 (4): 433–67.

Thompson, Kenneth (1960) *Political Realism and the Crisis of World Politics*. Princeton: Princeton University Press.

Tully, James (ed.) (1988) *Meaning and Context: Quentin Skinner and His Critics*. Princeton: Princeton University Press.

Vasquez, John A. (1983) *The Power of Power Politics: A Critique*. New Brunswick: Rutgers University Press.

Vasquez, John A. (1995) 'The Post-Positivist Debate: Reconstructing Scientific Enquiry and International Relations Theory After Enlightenment's Fall', in Ken Booth and Steve Smith (eds), *International Relations Theory Today*. University Park: Pennsylvania State University Press. pp. 217–40.

Vasquez, John A. (1998) *The Power of Power Politics: From Classical Realism to Neotraditionalism*. Cambridge: Cambridge University Press.

Viotti, Paul R. and Kauppi, Mark V. (1999) *International Relations Theory: Realism, Pluralism, Globalism, and Beyond*, 3rd edn. Boston: Allyn and Bacon.

Vital, David (1967) 'On Approaches to the Study of International Relations Or, Back to Machiavelli', *World Politics*, 19 (4): 551–62.

Waever, Ole (1996) 'The Rise and Fall of the Inter-Paradigm Debate', in Steve Smith, Ken Booth, and Marysia Zalewski (eds), *International Theory: Positivism and Beyond*. Cambridge: Cambridge University Press. pp. 149–85.

Waever, Ole (1998) 'The Sociology of a Not So International Discipline: American and European Developments in International Relations', *International Organization*, 52 (4): 687–727.

Walker, R.B.J. (1989) 'History and Structure in the Theory of International Relations', *Millennium: Journal of International Studies*, 18 (2): 163–83.

Walker, R.B.J. (1993) *Inside/Outside: International Relations as Political Theory*. Cambridge: Cambridge University Press.

Wallerstein, Immanuel (1974) *The Modern World System*. New York: Academic Press.

Wallerstein, Immanuel (1980) *The Modern World System II*. New York: Academic Press.

Walt, Stephen M. (1997) 'The Progressive Power of Realism', *American Political Science Review*, 91 (4): 931–5.

Walt, Stephen M. (1998) 'International Relations: One World, Many Theories', *Foreign Policy*, 110: 29–46.

Waltz, Kenneth N. (1959) *Man, the State and War: A Theoretical Analysis*. Columbia: Columbia University Press.

Waltz, Kenneth N. (1979) *Theory of International Politics*. Reading, MA: Addison-Wesley.

Wendt, Alexander (1999) *Social Theory of International Politics*. Cambridge: Cambridge University Press.

Wight, Martin (1966) 'Why is There No International Theory', in Herbert Butterfield and Martin Wight (eds), *Diplomatic Investigations: Essays in the Theory of International Politics*. London: George Allen and Unwin. pp. 17–34.

Wight, Martin (1992) *International Theory: The Three Traditions* (eds Gabriel Wight and Brian Porter). New York: Holmes & Meir.

Wilde, Jaap H. de (1991) *Saved from Oblivion: Interdependence Theory in the First Half of the 20th Century*. Aldershot: Dartmouth Publishing Co.

Williams, Howard (1992) *International Relations in Political Theory*. Buckingham: Open University Press.

Willoughby, Westel Woodbury (1918) 'The Juristic Conception of the State', *American Political Science Review*, 12: 192–208.

Wilson, Peter (1998) 'The Myth of the "First Great Debate"', *Review of International Studies*, 24 (Special Issue): 1–16.

Wright, Quincy (1955) *The Study of International Relations*. New York: Appleton–Century–Crofts.

Zacher, M. and Matthew, R. (1995) 'Liberal International Theory: Common Threads, Divergent Strands', in Charles Kegley (ed.), *Controversies in International Relations Theory: Realism and the Neoliberal Challenge*. New York: St Martin's. pp. 107–50.

2

Philosophy of Social Science and International Relations

COLIN WIGHT

When a discipline begins to reflect on its own practices there are various resources on which it can draw and a range of foci upon which the gaze can be turned. In Chapter 1 of this volume Brian Schmidt has addressed the history and historiography of the discipline. Inevitably, many of the issues deemed important in any historical account of disciplinary development will necessarily touch upon issues of relevance to the philosophy of social science (Gordon, 1991; Manicas, 1987). The philosophy of social science is inseparable from the history of social science, and many of the debates that have shaped international relations (IR)[1] have been concerned with issues integral to the philosophy of social science. Where Schmidt deals with the manner in which these issues have historically (mis)shaped the discipline, this chapter will focus on their content and attempt a critical analysis of them in relation to their deployment in terms of disciplinary development, disciplinary politics and wider sociopolitical concerns.

A key issue for any social science discipline is the extent to which it might be considered a science,[2] and Schmidt identifies this question as a 'defining goal of the field' (See Chapter 1). However, where Schmidt sees the development of IR in terms of a continuing attempt to provide scientific credentials for its knowledge claims, I see a discipline that is structured around a set of deep contestations over the very idea of science itself and the extent to which IR can, and should, be a science. The development of IR cannot be understood as the inexorable march towards science since many within the discipline are opposed to a science of IR, irrespective of any benefits that might derive from the label. What science is and whether IR can or should be a science is a subject of impassioned debate within the discipline (Bull, 1969; Ferguson and Mansbach, 1988; Hollis, 1996; Hollis and Smith, 1990; Kaplan 1969; Nicholson 1996a, 1996b; Ogley 1981; Reynolds, 1973; Wendt, 1999). For many working within the philosophy of social science this issue effectively defines the content of its subject matter (Bhaskar, 1979: 1; Brown, 1979: vii; Fay, 1996: 1). Following conventional usage within the philosophy of social science I shall call this the problem of 'naturalism' (Bhaskar 1979; Hollis, 1996).[3] Within the context of this overarching question a range of subsidiary issues are typically subsumed: the nature of explanation, the nature of causation, the nature of laws and so on (Bunge, 1996; Nicholson, 1996a; Reynolds, 1973; Suganami. 1996).

Inevitably, answers to this question have been legitimated by recourse to the philosophy of social science. The philosophy of social science, however, is itself parasitic upon the philosophy of science, and to a large extent much of the literature that addresses the science question in IR bypasses the philosophy of social science completely (Vasquez, 1995, 1998; Waltz, 1979).[4] This is a regrettable, although understandable, development, and the unreflective importation of the frameworks of philosophers of science to either legitimate a scientific IR (Kuhn, Lakatos, Popper), or to defend IR from science (Kuhn, Feyerabend) has done perhaps serious damage to the discipline (Ferguson and Mansbach, 1988). This damage pales in comparison, however, to that inflicted by the assumption that what science is, is self-evident.

None of this, of course, is to argue that the philosophy of social science, and hence by extension the philosophy of social science in IR, is only concerned with the question of science. Another fundamental question has revolved around what is known in IR as the agent–structure problem (Carlsnaes, 1992; Dessler, 1989; Wendt, 1987; Wight, 1999a). This issue defies easy definition, and within IR the confusion over what exactly is at stake in the agent–structure problem has led one pair of commentators to suggest that it is not at all clear if the contributors to the debate in IR are referring to the same problem (Friedman and Starr, 1997). Whatever this problem does involve, however, all parties agree that a substantive element of it concerns a conundrum best elaborated by Marx: 'Men make their own history, but they do not make it just as they please; they do not make it under conditions chosen by themselves' (Marx, 1962). The agent–structure problem then, is concerned with the relationship between active and self-reflecting agents and the structural context in which their activity takes place.[5] There are many aspects to this problem and it has surfaced under various guises within the philosophy of social science[6] (Singer, 1961). When combined with the issue of naturalism, it is tempting, as indeed many have done, to picture these problems in terms of a matrix such as Figure 2.1 (Hollis and Smith, 1990; Wendt, 1999; see also Carlsnaes, Chapter 17 in this volume).[7]

The problems with such pictorial representations go well beyond the self-evident point that they have their limitations in terms of how much detail they can represent (Bourdieu, 1977; Hollis and Smith, 1992: 216; see also Carlsnaes, Chapter 17 in this volume). The real difficulty with such diagrammatic devices is that their inability to deal with the complexity of the issues introduces a high level of distortion as to what the actual fault lines are. That is, the matrix provides an image of rigid boundaries that do not hold when the issue is considered in other discursive and less dichotomous ways. Moreover, taking seriously the fact that its practitioners largely construct IR, we can see how the fault lines of contemporary IR might themselves be an artefact of the pictorial representation of them in two-by-two matrix form. In short, the use of such devices to explain disciplinary divisions contributes to their construction. Such devices may be valuable aids in teaching and understanding complex issues, but we should always be aware of what Mario Bunge calls the 'Myth of Simplicity' (Bunge, 1963; see also Carlsnaes, Chapter 17 in this volume).

The aim of the chapter is not simply to outline the various uses of the philosophy of social science within IR. Nor is it simply to reiterate the well-worn, and overused, claim that things are more complicated than the literature portrays them. The primary aim of the chapter is to provide an account of the philosophy of social science within IR in

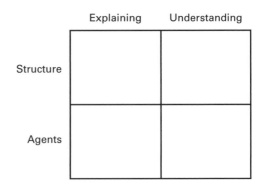

Figure 2.1   *A landscape of philosophical positions in relation to social study*

order to demonstrate that the contemporary theoretical cleavages that structure the discipline are unable to contain the weight they are being asked to bear. In short, the contemporary meta-theoretical framework the discipline employs is: a bar to constructive dialogue; a hindrance to much-needed research into issues of vital concern; a confused misrepresentation of the issues; and most importantly, a construct of those working in the field, hence they have it within their power to change it.

I begin by providing legitimations for taking the philosophy of social science seriously and give a brief sketch of the development of the philosophy of social science. In the following section I briefly discuss the early development of the discipline in the context of claims to be a science of social affairs. The philosophy of social science is largely missing from this period of the discipline's development, as, of course, it must be given that the philosophy of science had not yet emerged as a sub-discipline of philosophy. The third section deals with the first genuine attempt to constitute IR as a science on the basis of literature drawn from the philosophy of science and the philosophy of social science. A key component here will be understanding the role of positivism and its use within the discipline.[8] In the fourth section I will concentrate on contemporary debates and will, in particular, attempt to throw some light onto what is increasingly becoming what one commentator has called 'a philosophical swamp' (Walker, 2000). Here I demonstrate how the current ways of framing disciplinary debates are rapidly deconstructing themselves.[9]

LEGITIMATION: DOES IR NEED THE PHILOSOPHY OF SOCIAL SCIENCE?

The utility of examining the philosophy of social science within IR is not self-evident. Critical voices have often doubted whether the discipline has either the intellectual resources, or the need, to engage in such an exercise (Griffiths and O'Callaghan, 2001: 199; Skocpol, 1987). Many would prefer to leave such esoteric speculation to those more able – philosophers perhaps (Wallace, 1996). Others doubt whether philosophy as a different 'order of discourse' can provide the kind of legitimation claimed on its behalf (Gunnell, 1975: 54; 1998: 6). Often this skepticism towards disciplinary self-reflection derives from a belief that such inquiries lead to the neglect of more substantive forms of knowledge generation (Gunnell 1998: xii; Halliday, 1996: 320; Mann, 1996; Skocpol, 1987). There are also legitimate concerns about naïve appropriations of 'Gurus' from cognate disciplines (Hollis and Smith, 1991).

There is, of course, something deeply ironic in the fact that the social sciences feel the need to legitimate their activities in relation to the philosophy of social science. After all, apart from some notable exceptions, scientists rarely legitimate their practices in terms of the philosophy of science (Gordon, 1991; Gunnell, 1998; Nicholson, 1996a). Indeed, modern science only emerged as a science once its autonomy from philosophy was firmly established (Easton, 1965; Gordon, 1991; Gunnell, 1975; Little, 1980). Given the success of the natural sciences, allied to the desire to emulate them, some have argued that it was inevitable that social inquiry and philosophy would likewise divorce if such forms of inquiry were to constitute themselves as sciences (Little, 1980: 3; Nicholson, 1996a: 8–10).

To view this process as inevitable, however, is probably too strong a characterization. Whilst most natural scientists were happy to leave speculative philosophy behind, many concerned with social inquiry were not (Gadamer 1977; Winch, 1958; in IR see Bull, 1969; Garnett, 1984; Hollis and Smith 1990; Little, 1980). This is an intellectual split that still structures the contemporary social sciences, but it is important to note that it emerges not only out of a desire to maintain a philosophical presence within social inquiry, but also from a desire to keep a certain form of science out (Bull, 1969; Reynolds, 1973). In general, those who reject a scientific IR are not against systematic inquiry *per se* (Garnett, 1984; Reynolds, 1973). Indeed Vico, often cited as an authoritative source by those against a social science, entitled his major work *New Science*[10] (Vico, [1744] 1984). When hermeneutics first emerged as a distinctive approach to inquiry, its early proponents still conceived of themselves as being engaged in the development of a science of meaning (Bauman, 1978; Dilthey, 1976; Husserl, 1982; Outhwaite, 1975). Often the rejection of a science of the social world is derived from deep-seated fears in relation to some claimed dehumanizing aspects at the heart of science itself (Aliotta, 1914; Ashley, 1987, 1989; Morgenthau, 1946; Thompson, 1981).

The philosophy of science only really emerged as a recognizable field of study in the 1930s (Dingle, 1952; Gordon, 1991; Gunnell, 1998; Oldroyd, 1986). Early understandings of science were rudimentary and were generally based upon accounts developed by Thomas Hobbes, John Stuart Mill, David Hume and Rene Descartes (Gordon, 1991). However, conscious reflection on the nature of human inquiry can be said to have played a role in the human sciences ever since reflection on the human condition became a recognizable activity (Gordon 1991; Manicas, 1987). Thucydides, for example, is said to have been the first scientific historian (Abbott, 1970; Gilpin, 1986: 306; Tellis, 1996), or perhaps even a positivist (Bluhm, 1967).

It is doubtful if this characterization of Thucydides as a positivist can be sustained (Bagby, 1994; Garst, 1989), particularly if one places the development of positivism in a historical perspective (Kolakowski, 1969; Oldroyd, 1986). Yet, it does highlight the manner in which positivism and science became interchangeable terms in the twentieth century (Bhaskar, 1986). Equally, it points to an important reason for considered reflection on the nature of the knowledge claims of all social sciences. For despite doubts concerning the ability of the philosophy of science to provide a justificatory framework for natural science, the results of science, particularly in the form of technological innovation, can hardly be doubted (Gunnell, 1998; Nicholson, 1996a, 1996b). This success has given science enormous prestige in modern societies – a prestige, which despite some dissenting voices, it still largely holds (Appleyard, 1992; Dunbar, 1995).

If social inquiry is to emulate the natural sciences it needs to examine its methods, procedures and underlying rationale. It needs a yardstick against which claims to be science can be measured. Where better to look than the philosophy of science? Hence, whereas the natural sciences became sciences through an enforced divorce from philosophy, social science turned to philosophy for legitimation. Since knowledge claims in social science are almost always couched in terms of some philosophical justificatory framework, the various disciplines have felt the need to examine the status of them (Reynolds, 1973: 14). Not least because claiming that one's research is science is exactly to claim legitimacy not accorded to other forms of knowledge (Ashley and Walker, 1990; Smith, 1987).

Gunnell (1975: 54) sees this as an impossible enterprise and argues that political 'science must chart its own methodological route, and that the defence of that route cannot be achieved by invoking the authority of science'. There are two problems with this claim. First, the influence of the philosophy of science on social inquiry is not simply methodological, and second, his argument relies on the assumption that the philosophy of science can tell us nothing about the practices of science; and, of course, if this were the case then he would be correct. But the philosophy of science *does* claim to reflect on the practice of science and to pronounce on some of its essential elements. No doubt it will get much wrong, but there is no a priori reason to assume it will get it all wrong. Since the philosophy of science does claim some legitimacy in terms of its understanding of science, then it is perfectly appropriate for social inquiry to look to it for resources. If Gunnell's argument were to be followed to its logical conclusion, political science and IR would be excluded from drawing on any resources other than those developed within the discipline (see Reynolds, 1973 for arguments counter to Gunnell's). Moreover, academic disciplines are not as hermetically sealed as Gunnell seems to suggest and include philosophical concepts as essential elements within their frameworks.

Many of the concepts developed in the philosophy of science have been thoroughly integrated into the fabric of the discipline (Gunnell, 1975: xiii) and, perhaps more than any other factor, have shaped the discipline's self-image and continue to do so (Nicholson, 1996a, 1996b; Smith, 1995). In this respect, IR has little alternative but to engage with the philosophy of social science. This accounts for the fact that introductory sections and chapters on this issue feature in almost all textbooks. Another reason is that conceptual inquiry is a prerequisite to empirical research (Walker, 1993: 82). Before empirical research can proceed, researchers need to have some idea of what it is they are attempting to explain and how best to explain it. All inquiry begins from certain premises, and understanding the basis of these is an essential part of inquiry.

The final reason why such abstract conceptual inquiries are important is that whereas natural scientists may disagree on the actual content of specific explanations, they at least agree on what an explanation of a given phenomenon would look like (Nicholson, 1996a: 2; Reynolds, 1973). Social scientists, on the other hand, do not (Hollis and Smith, 1990; Reynolds, 1973). For a discipline supposedly born out of a desire to uncover the causes of war, not knowing the conditions under which such a discovery might be made seems a damning indictment (Nicholson, 1996a: 3). Knowing the causes of war is one thing; knowing that we know them is an altogether different matter.

Yet engagement alone does not guarantee success, and it has to be admitted that many of the complaints against the use and abuse of the philosophy of social science within IR have some substance (Halliday, 1994: 23; Kratochwil, 2000; Wallace, 1996). In general, these problems occur due to a lack of conceptual clarity, the misuse of key terms and the naïve appropriation of key concepts developed in cognate disciplines with little awareness of the specifics of their use or the context of their

development. The most glaring examples of these concern the use of terms such as ontology, epistemology and methodology, although the widespread and uncritical adoption of Kuhn's notion of paradigms comes a close second (Banks, 1985; Vasquez, 1998). Within the philosophy of social science and the philosophy of science these terms have very specific uses and function to maintain analytical clarity and as ways of delineating very specific aspects of the field. In IR, on the other hand, these terms are often thrown around like philosophical hand grenades, with little consideration given to how they are deployed, or to what end.

Michael Nicholson, for example, in a series of otherwise exemplary works, has variously referred to positivism as an 'epistemology' (Nicholson, 1996a, 1996b), a 'methodology' (despite the chapter title being 'The Epistemology of International Relations') (Nicholson, 1996a; Nicholson and Bennett, 1994), 'behavioralism'[11] (Nicholson, 1996a; 129) and any 'sort of scientific approach to social behaviour' (Nicholson, 1996a: 190) – although admittedly this latter is with a sense of regret. Likewise, Steve Smith refers to positivism as: an epistemology (Smith, 1996: 24); as *having* an 'empiricist epistemology' (Smith, 1996: 22); and as being the 'methodology' that underpins realism (Smith, 1997: 166). I highlight these two eminent scholars not as the worst examples of this tendency, but merely representative ones. But clearly, there is some confusion here.[12]

EARLY IR: A SCIENCE WITH NO PHILOSOPHY

There was a time in the discipline's pre-history when science was not a problematic term (Bluhm, 1967; Boucher, 1998; Dougherty and Pfaltzgraff, 1996; Tellis, 1996). Early practitioners were perhaps not clear on how the term was deployed, but there was a general acceptance that IR could and should be a science. Ashley J. Tellis argues that the development of realism from Thucydides to the present day can be understood as a 'Long March to Scientific Theory' (Tellis, 1996). And despite a number of critiques questioning the extent to which Thucydides can be considered a realist, few have doubted that his discussion of the Peloponnesian War is 'severe in its detachment, written from a purely intellectual point of view, unencumbered with platitudes and moral judgments, cold and critical' (Bury, 1975: 252).

Hobbes, of course, had provocative views about which subjects could be deemed to be scientific, but there is little doubt that he considered his own work a science and he perhaps even thought of himself as the inventor of political science (Ryan, 1996; Sorell, 1996). Within Hobbes's notion of political science there were already the seeds of a very clearly demarcated difference between what he called 'political science' and 'political prudence' (Ryan, 1996). According to Hobbes, Thucydides's analysis was based at the level of political prudence; in general it equated to practical wisdom and was achieved through the best advice we could draw from a range of historical examples. Political prudence was a genuine form of knowledge, yet it is inevitably knowledge of particulars. Charles Reynolds seems to suggest that all historical explanations are of this form (Reynolds, 1973). It is a form of knowledge based upon experience of the past and of what has happened. It is not, however, knowledge of how things *must* work and what *must* happen. Science, for Hobbes, must be hypothetical, general and infallible. But none the less, politics could, and indeed should, be a science.

Even interwar idealism can be interpreted as committed to the role of science in human progress (Carr, 1946; Long, 1995: 306). And insofar as this period of IR was driven by Enlightenment ideals of progress based on knowledge, this point seems hardly in doubt (George, 1994: 74–7). Richard Little, however, argues that early IR differed from other social sciences that emerged at the time in that it did not attempt to model itself on the natural sciences and was not 'concerned with uncovering laws which would assist in the comprehension of an infinitely complex reality' (Little, 1980: 7; see also Smith, 1987). Little's position, however (see also Smith, 1987), suffers from two problems.

The first demonstrates the validity of Schmidt's claim that bad histories of the discipline can distort current understandings (See Chapter 1 in this volume). For Little's sharp demarcation between IR and other social science disciplines only makes sense if one accepts that when the first academic department was set up in 1919 in Aberystwyth this constituted a unique moment with no disciplinary prehistory. What Schmidt very clearly shows, is that although 1919 does mark the emergence of a specific academic department of IR, knowledge production of the subject had a much longer prehistory. In this respect the disciplines that Little claims did attempt to model themselves as sciences were the sources upon which the new discipline of IR was to draw (Schmidt, 1998; see also Butterfield, 1951).

The second problem with Little's analysis is that he is projecting a very particular account of science back onto the work of the interwar idealists. He seems to assume that a normative dimension to inquiry precludes it from being a science; that science is concerned with factual analysis and value-driven inquiry is something different (Little, 1980: 7). This is a very particular, and contentious, account of the fact/value relationship within science, and there is no evidence that it is one held

by the early members of the discipline. Moreover, there are many defenders of a scientific IR who are committed to providing scientific explanations precisely in order to bring about social change (Nicholson, 1996a: 3; 2000: 197; Wright, 1962).

The charge that the early origins of the discipline were 'unscientific' is located within the damning critique launched by E.H. Carr. In what can only be considered a strategic polemic, Carr argued that the 'science of international politics is in its infancy' (Carr, 1946: 14). According to Carr, realism could provide such a science through its emphasis on 'the acceptance of facts and on the analysis of their causes and consequences' (1946: 14). The alternative to this science, according to Carr, was idealism, which he characterized as 'alchemy' (1946: 14).

Interestingly, despite Carr's avowed commitment to science, some have argued that he is best considered part of the interpretive tradition within the discipline (Dunne, 1998: 7), whereas others see him as operating with both a scientific and interpretive outlook (George, 1994: 77). But whichever tradition (if indeed there are clear borders) Carr should be considered to be within, his critique of the idealists does indicate something important about the disciplinary politics of such labels. Carr's claim that realism was based upon acceptance of the facts and analysis of their causes and consequences is mirrored by Norman Angell's plea for the development of education about international political affairs. The lack of such education, claimed Angell, was a barrier to the 'impartial search for truth, the true interpretation of all the facts' (Angell, 1947: 17); without this belief we render 'inoperative the only method by which we can hope to make steady progress: the correction of social theory and doctrine in the light of fact and experience; the scientific method applied to society' (Angell, 1947: 23). Given the similarities between Angell's idealist approach to IR and Carr's more realistically inclined tendencies, Carr's science/alchemy dichotomy can only be seen as a conscious attempt to seize some 'scientific' high ground – a ground to which Angell also staked a claim.

Hans Morgenthau is an interesting figure in terms of this development because he was one of the first major figures in the discipline to openly argue against IR as a science. His anti-scientific turn, however, had very specific origins. His early work was conceived as an attempt to provide a 'scientifically unassailable classification of international disputes' (Honig, 1996: 289). And this commitment to science was still evident in his 1940 essay 'Positivism, Functionalism and International Law' (Honig, 1996; Morgenthau, 1940). In this piece he bemoaned the attempt to construct international law at a technical level devoid of scientific principles (Morgenthau, 1940: 284). This position was completely reversed in *Scientific Man and Power*

Politics, where he rejects all hope of a scientific IR (Morgenthau, 1946, 1972). Still, Morgenthau's clear renunciation of science and positivism, which he claimed was fictional, metaphysical and dogma (Griffiths, 1992), has not stopped scholars from aligning him with a science of IR (Hollis and Smith, 1990: 23), with some even going as far as to label him a positivist (George, 1994; Hollis and Smith, 1990: 28; see Bain, 2000 for an alternative view, Garnett, 1984; Nicholson, 1996a).

The assertion that Morgenthau should be viewed as committed to a science of IR is generally made on the basis of his claim that politics was governed by 'objective laws that have their roots in human nature' (George, 1994: 93; Hollis and Smith, 1990: 23–4; Morgenthau, 1948: 4). But to construe this claim as supporting a commitment to scientific IR is to miss the point. In conceding that politics is governed by objective laws of human nature Morgenthau is actually saying that there is no need for a science of IR, because IR is governed by laws that are explained by biology, not social science (Griffiths, 1992: 39). There is nothing for a science of IR to discover. Morgenthau's theory is best viewed as a manual for state leaders. It is a technical guide to policy based on an understanding of the laws that govern human behavior. More important is the fact that Morgenthau does not ground his arguments about human nature in any scientific content, but in metaphysical ones (Griffiths, 1992: 38, 43; Honig, 1996: 305).

What is interesting about these developments is the absence of any sustained discussion on the nature of the science that was either being advanced or rejected. There was little attempt to legitimate claims about science by recourse to bodies of literature developed in other disciplines, and no real attempt to spell out the actual content of the science being proposed. Indeed, for someone like Herbert Butterfield, science simply *was* traditional forms of inquiry (Butterfield, 1951; Dunne, 1998: 123). This lack of legitimation in terms of the philosophy of science is understandable given the underdeveloped state of the philosophy of science at the time. However, developments were moving on rapidly and a consensus was emerging which was, for better or worse, to stamp its mark on IR in ways that could not have been envisaged. The science of IR was about to rediscover some philosophy.

ADOLESCENT IR: THE LEGITIMATION
OF SCIENCE

The systematic use of the philosophy of science within IR begins with what John Vasquez terms the 'behavioral revolt' (Vasquez, 1998: 39). Although this 'revolt' had been taking place within political science and other social sciences since the early 1950s, it did not begin to emerge into IR in a substantive way until the l960s (Knorr and Rosenau, 1969a). There had been calls for its introduction into IR prior to this (Guetzkow, 1950), and some argue that works such as Quincy Wright's 1942 book on war are behavioralist (Knorr and Rosenau, 1969b: 5; Schmidt, Chapter 1 in this volume). Vasquez, however, sees these developments, whilst validly described as behavioral in intent, as not substantively contributing to the coming 'revolt' (Vasquez, 1998: 40). Given this periodization of the 'revolt', the sources of the 'behavioral revolt' are generally located in Deutsch (1953, 1964), Kaplan (1957), Schelling (1960) and Snyder, Bruck and Sapin (1954, 1962); (Hollis and Smith, 1990; Vasquez, 1998; Schmidt, Chapter 1 in this volume). Schmidt, however, claims in Chapter 1 that the role of the Chicago School of political science generally goes unrecognized in the dominant accounts of the development of behavioralism. And from the perspective of the philosophy of science Schmidt's point seems broadly correct.

In 1950, Harold Lasswell and Abraham Kaplan explicitly argued that their attempt to provide a framework for political science was informed by developments in logical positivist philosophy of science (Gunnell, 1975; Lasswell and Kaplan, 1950).[13] This turn to the philosophy of science was validated by David Easton (1953, 1965), who very clearly did influence the 'behavioral revolt' in IR, and Robert Lane, who argued that 'the widespread acceptance of the philosophy of science as a basis for social inquiry represents a "take off" phenomenon in social science, promising sustained growth in social interpretation' (Lane, 1966).[14]

A key component of logical positivism that served to legitimate the turn to the philosophy of science was its 'unity of science thesis' (Nagel, 1961). This, of course, is self-validating; logical positivism declares that the sciences can be unified and logical positivism defines the content of science. So any social science deserving of the label science needs logical positivism just as logical positivism provides the legitimation for the turn to the philosophy of science (Bhaskar, 1986). This usurping of the label science was to be an important move in the 'great debate' (Dunne, 1998) between traditionalists and scientists, because essentially the label *science* was conceded to logical positivism.

This is an important point and highlights something often missed in disciplinary discussions relating to the study of IR, for the model of science that underpins the 'behavioral revolt' in IR is based upon a very specific philosophy of science and not the practices of scientists (Gunnell, 1975: 19). Despite claims to be following the scientific method, behavioralism was actually an attempt to implement a particular philosophy of science that was dominant at that time. The relationship between the actual practices of scientists and logical positivism was not yet a question that would be subject to challenge (Chalmers, 1992). Once IR had turned to the philosophy of science to legitimate its practices it was inevitable that when the philosophy of science began to question the account given by logical positivism then IR would follow. This has led to various modifications to logical positivism and eventually the term 'logical' would be dropped in favor of a less austere version under the label of positivism (S. Smith, 1996: 14–18).

This also helps explain many of the contemporary confusions surrounding science in IR, since it is never clear whether it is science *per se* that is being rejected, the logical positivist version, or other less extreme positivist versions. This problem is compounded by the fact that there is no longer a consensus on what positivism is, with one commentator identifying twelve versions of it (Halfpenny, 1982). Moreover, the philosophy of science itself was soon to reject positivism and to claim that the practices of scientists did not conform to the positivist model. This held out the rather paradoxical prospect that all approaches that had attempted to emulate the positivist model were not actually following scientific procedures. Yet, whatever problems emerged in terms of philosophy's own quarrel with logical positivism, when the behavioralists turned to philosophy a consensus had emerged within the philosophy of science around the validity of positivism, hence it was perfectly correct for the discipline to adopt that model. In fact, given the level of consensus that existed within the philosophy of science around logical positivism/positivism it would have been perverse not to adopt it (Chalmers, 1992).

Before proceeding to examine its reception within IR it is important to consider something of the claims being made on its behalf that had a significant impact on IR. Two in particular stand out: operationalism and instrumentalism were at the heart of the 'behavioral revolt', and both are firmly embedded within logical positivism/positivism (Gunnell, 1975). The commitment to operationalism is generally well understood: since, the validity of a theory ultimately rests on the 'facts', all concepts that are considered to be scientific or empirical must be defined operationally. Within behavioralism this has generally being taken to mean the language of observation (Gunnell, 1975; Nicholson, 1996a). Less well understood is the closely related instrumentalism that pervaded logical positivism/positivism.

Instrumentalism was the device employed by positivists to get around some tricky questions concerning the status of non-observable terms in theories. From the instrumentalist perspective, theoretical concepts are judged not by their truth or falsity, but by their theoretical utility (Singer, 1969: 76; Waltz, 1979: 8; Wasby, 1970: 66). For the instrumentalist, theories cannot be taken as assertions about the way the world is. Theoretical terms that could not be translated into observational ones were to be treated 'as if' they existed. Facts are what matter and theory is simply a better way of collecting them (Gunnell, 1975: 26–7). This incipient instrumentalism helps explain why a philosophy so firmly embedded within the requirements of validity through observation became so adept, and so insistent, on the need to build models and, in particular, models of the system.

From this instrumentalist perspective, 'truth' was not part of the lexicon of positivism, nor was any search for underlying causes (see Griffiths, 1992: 96–8, for an account of why Kenneth Waltz is not concerned with truth). Indeed, positivism since Comte had long given up according ontological status to anything beyond the phenomena or the search for truth (Comte, [1854] 2000: 28). According to Comte:

> In the final, the positive state, the mind has given over the vain search after Absolute notions, the origin and destination of the universe, and the causes of phenomena, and applies itself to the study of their laws – that is, their invariable relations of succession and resemblance … I merely desire to keep in view that all our positive knowledge is relative, and, in my dread of our resting in notions of anything absolute … (Comte, [1854] 2000: 68, 190)

This also helps illuminate how some contemporary confusions emerge in relation to positivism. For example, Hollis and Smith's claim that Morgenthau's version of realism is 'an essentially positivistic way of analysing events, since it relied on a notion of underlying forces producing behaviour' (Hollis and Smith, 1990: 23) is problematic given positivism's rejection of the search for underlying causes.

Underpinned by logical positivism, a more overt scientific approach took a firm hold in the discipline (Alker, 1965; Dunne, 1998; Hollis and Smith, 1990; Hoole and Zinnes, 1976; Rosenau, 1971). When viewed from the perspective of the philosophy of social science, four aspects stand out. First, whatever the merits of logical positivism, behavioralism in IR was at least consistent with its fundamental principles and attempted to validate its 'scientific' credentials as opposed to simply taking them as given. Abraham Kaplan's *The Conduct of Inquiry* (1964) is perhaps the most important work in this respect, but others had preceded it (Brecht, 1959; Van Dyke, 1960; see also Meehan, 1968). The behavioralists seemed to understand the philosophy and applied it consistently; something which could not be said of many of its detractors, both then and now.

Second, its critique of realism, which it claimed was not scientific enough, injects a real tension in any subsequent account that attempts to claim that realism is positivist (George, 1994; Smith, 1996). The behavioralists were scathing about the lack of rigour within classical realism (Hollis and Smith, 1990: 28). Consistent application of their logical positivism entailed that assumptions about human nature were metaphysical, non-observable and hence unscientific. Given the variations in realism and the variations in positivism, it is highly unlikely that a blanket claim that realism is positivist can be sustained.

Third, the importation of this approach to IR was not without sustained resistance. At the forefront of this resistance was Hedley Bull's polemical attack on what he called the scientific approach (Bull, 1969: 361). Against this scientific approach, which he clearly sees embedded within logical positivism (Bull, 1969: 362), Bull argues for the 'classical' approach embodied within the works of Zimmern, Carr and Morgenthau (for a detailed and sophisticated treatment of the debate see Dunne, 1998). Because of the polemical nature of Bull's attack and Morton Kaplan's (1969) rejoinder, there is a tendency within the discipline to see this 'debate' in terms of a growing rift between American social science and academic communities in the rest of the world (Hoffman, 1977; Smith, 1987; see also Schmidt, Chapter 1 in this volume).

Donald J. Puchala, however, argues that within American IR the new version of science peddled by behavioralists was rejected by major American figures in the field (Ferguson and Mansbach, 1988; Puchala, 1991). Stanley Hoffmann, in an early critique characterized as a 'wrecking operation', was scathing about Kaplan's proposed science of IR (Hoffman, 1961). But also Leo Strauss (1953) attacked the onwards march of 'scientism in political science' and Michael Haas (1969) identifies many American critics. As already noted, an important aspect of this debate was the manner in which all of the critics allowed the behavioralists to take control of the label science. From this point on, science became inextricably linked to positivism and any reference to science was taken to imply positivism.

Fourth, whilst the introduction of behavioralism was initially hailed as a dramatic stride forward in terms of the development of a 'scientific' IR (Lijphart, 1974a, 1974b), later accounts now argue that this debate did not fundamentally change underlying assumptions and was essentially only a very limited debate about methodology (Guzzini, 1998; Hollis and Smith, 1990; Holsti, 1985, 1998; Vasquez, 1998). This is a problematic claim (Dunne, 1998: 124; see also Schmidt, Chapter 1 in this volume); debates about science can never simply be 'methodological'. Positivism is a philosophy of, and for, science and its adoption requires the taking of a series of implicit ontological and epistemological

assumptions as well as methodological ones. It is for partly this reason that contemporary claims that positivism is an epistemology are wide of the mark (Nicholson, 1996a).

Positivism embodies certain epistemological commitments, but it is not itself an epistemology; unless, that is, one is stretching the use of the term epistemology to such lengths as to make it meaningless[15] (Smith, 1996: 17). But one only has to examine the substance of Bull's arguments to see that they were primarily ontological not methodological. His critique of the scientific approach was precisely that the following of its methodological strictures left a large, and important, area of international politics unexamined. So even though his target might be considered to be the proposed new procedures of science, these were based on ontological assumptions. Moreover, as a philosophy of science with well-formulated accounts of cause, explanation, law and the nature of the world, it is also incorrect to consider positivism as simply a methodology.

Another neglected aspect of the behavioral revolution within IR is the extent to which its adherents conceived of themselves as going beyond social science and instituting a 'behavioral science' (Easton, 1965: 18). The 'behavioral revolt' was not only about placing IR on a more scientific basis, but about taking part in an ambitious attempt to unify all of the human sciences into a seamless whole. David Easton accepted that prior to the 'behavioral revolt' the social sciences were deserving of the label science (Easton, 1965: 22). He also accepted that the 'behavioral revolt' could not only be about the introduction of more scientific rigor. Indeed, he argued that more rigour would mean 'rigor mortis, as its critics from the traditional points of view ... have been so quick and correct to point out' (Easton, 1965: 22). In a very Comteian manner, Easton saw the behavioral movement as the next stage in the development of human knowledge, where the human sciences would be united into one research programme, centered on the notion of behavior. This was a very strong version of the unity of science thesis.

Whatever the overall impact of the 'behavioral revolt' on the discipline, it legitimated the turn to the philosophy of social science and the philosophy of science. References to Hempel, Nagel, Popper, Kuhn, Feyerabend and Lakatos became commonplace. Waltz devoted a chapter of his *Theory of International Politics* (1979) to the philosophy of science, and strongly defended an instrumentalist treatment of theoretical terms (Griffiths, 1992: 93). And, of course, Thomas Kuhn has shaped the discipline in fundamental ways. Moreover, Kuhn's framework implicitly continues to shape the discipline today, even if the language used is no longer that of paradigms. That Kuhn's framework was adopted so universally across the discipline is puzzling when one considers that Kuhn himself thought that the social sciences were in a pre-paradigmatic state and doubted whether they could ever be 'mature sciences' (Kuhn, 1962: 164–5; see also Kuhn, 1970: 245; see Ferguson and Mansbach, 1988 for a critique of the attempt to apply Kuhn to IR).

Yet, reasons for Kuhn's success in the social sciences are not hard to find. Political scientists, sociologists and anthropologists recognized in their own practices and disciplinary conflicts Kuhn's picture of paradigms. They were delighted to hear that what had previously been thought an embarrassment was the way it was done in respectable sciences. Traditionalists could now portray themselves as working in a different paradigm, thus making themselves immune to critiques from the scientists. The scientists could continue unabashed, safe in the knowledge that they were actually contributing to knowledge growth under the guise of normal science. And dissidents could now portray themselves as revolutionary heroes of a new paradigm. Here was a philosophy of science that not only seemed to put science in its place, but legitimated what social scientists already did and required little in the way of change. Kuhn's ambiguous terminology was also a key factor. His master concept, that of paradigm, was particularly subject to various interpretations; Margaret Masterman (Masterman, 1970) identified twenty-one different ways Kuhn used the term – a criticism Kuhn accepted (Kuhn, 1970). This ambiguity allowed the framework a large measure of flexibility and ensured its welcome into disciplines that made definitional debate a key component of their research practices.

Kuhn's framework was almost universally adapted. Arend Lijphart saw the 'great debates' of the discipline in terms of paradigms (Lijphart, 1974a, 1974b). From the 1980s onwards, IR caught the paradigm bug so comprehensively that paradigms and Kuhn became part of the unreflective subconscious of the discipline. Textbooks were organized according to paradigms, and Kuhn was perhaps cited more than home-grown disciplinary figures (Banks, 1984; Hollis and Smith, 1990; Little and Smith, 1991; Viotti and Kauppi, 1987). But Kuhn's framework came with two related and major problems.

The first was an incipient conservativism (Guzzini, 1993: 446; Smith, 1992: 494; Wight, 1996). Science progressed, argued Kuhn, in periods of normal science (Kuhn, 1962; see Toulmin, 1970 for a critique). This claim had normative force. It meant that if progress in terms of knowledge production were to be achieved, then IR scholars needed to find themselves a dominant paradigm. Realism seemed an obvious candidate, but it would have come as no surprise to Kuhn to see competitors quickly

emerging. The inter-paradigm debate that developed in IR vindicated Kuhn's assertion that the social sciences were pre-paradigmatic (Kuhn, 1962: 164–5). But if IR scholars were to achieve progress and move into normal science then the discipline needed a dominant paradigm. This meant that pluralism could be seen as a threat to progress. But Kuhn had already built into his framework a mechanism where paradigms could flourish, even if progress could not.

This was the issue of incommensurability (in IR see Guzzini, 1993; Neufeld, 1995; Nicholson, 1996a; Rengger, 1989; Waever, 1996; Wight, 1996; see also Sankey, 1994, 1997). Kuhn had seemed to suggest that the move from one paradigm to another was a revolutionary process and that there was no way to compare paradigms (Kuhn, 1962, 1970). Paradigm choice, Kuhn seemed to suggest, was a matter of faith; or what Imre Lakatos would call 'mob psychology' (Lakatos, 1970: 178). This made any notion of an inter-paradigm 'debate' oxymoronic (Nicholson, 1996a: 82). Which, of course, did not deter people from continuing as if there was a debate. However, incommensurability became another Kuhnian buzzword that seemed to offer non-mainstream approaches some shelter. After all, did not incommensurability leave the world safe for critical theory?

Dissenting voices, however, were soon to see the perils in the incommensurability thesis (Guzzini, 1993; Waever, 1996; Wight, 1996). Incommensurability not only provided a safe haven for critical theory, but also for the mainstream (Guzzini, 1993). If incommensurability meant that cross-paradigmatic conversation was in principle impossible, how could the critics critique the mainstream (however defined)? Steve Smith, invoking ontological grounds for incommensurability, argued that it meant that proponents of different paradigms literally lived in different worlds (Smith, 1992, 1996). If so, there is little point in trying to critique the world of the mainstream from another world. However, it is very doubtful if Smith's reading of incommensurability was Kuhn's interpretation of it. Kuhn went to great lengths to dispel the idea that incommensurability meant that theories were non-translatable (Kuhn, 1970, 1982, 1990). Also, some in the discipline began to challenge the philosophical grounds of the incommensurability thesis itself (Wight, 1996).

There is little doubt that Kuhn's work has fundamentally – for better or worse – shaped the discipline. However, the discipline has typically seen this as a resource to be mined as opposed to displaying any awareness of either the complexities of his ideas, or the many trenchant critiques of his position. Even in those instances where the difficulties are acknowledged these are brushed aside in the attempt to apply the framework (Vasquez, 1998; see Katzenstein et al., 1998 for similar treatment of

Lakatos). Often, Kuhn's notion of paradigms was grafted onto a Lakatosian framework for theory choice with little in the way of justification (Christensen and Snyder, 1997; Elman and Elman, 1997; Vasquez, 1997; for a critique see Waltz, 1997). Philosophy of science was now in IR and the discipline needs to consider it much more carefully if it is to play such a fundamental role. Unfortunately, before the discipline could reflect on its turn to the philosophy of science there was to be an explosion of alternative philosophical sources of inspiration.

CONTEMPORARY IR: PHILOSOPHY, BEGINNING AND END?

If the Kuhnian experience within the discipline once again vindicated the turn to the philosophy of science then the philosophy of social science was surely everywhere. Unfortunately this was not the case. Despite a vast body of literature on the philosophy of social science the number dealing with these issues specifically in relation to IR is small (George, 1994; Hollis and Smith, 1990; Neufeld 1995; Mackenzie, 1967, 1971; Nicholson, 1983, 1996a; Reynolds, 1973; Sylvester, 1993). There are, of course, many references to the philosophy of social science, but these are scattered around the discipline in fragments (Alker, 1996; Campbell, 1988; Carlsnaes, 1992; Dessler, 1989; George and Campbell, 1990; Wendt, 1987). Hollis and Smith, in the first sustained presentation of this argument within IR, argue that the discipline could do better than turning to the philosophy of science and that there were models of social science not based on the natural sciences that might be more appropriate (Hollis and Smith, 1990: 68–91). The philosophical inspiration for their argument is Peter Winch, although they also draw on a range of hermeneutic thinkers as well, particularly Weber (Weber, 1949; Winch, 1958).

In fact, Hollis and Smith's argument had already played a fundamental role in structuring the discipline, even if those arguing against a science of IR have never specifically located their argument in a sustained engagement with the philosophy of social science. Reynolds (1973) perhaps stands out as a notable exception, but his work is concerned with the distinction between science and history, as opposed to that between science and hermeneutics. Moreover, Reynolds still draws heavily on the philosophy of science and includes no specific references to Winch, although Winch's book does appear in his bibliography (Reynolds, 1973). More importantly, and contrary to Hollis and Smith, Reynolds argues that the traditionalists and the scientists have 'more in common than their advocates have perhaps realized' (Reynolds, 1973: 15).

Likewise, W.J.M. Mackenzie (1967, 1971) might also be considered an early contributor but he sees no fundamental conflict in the attempt to integrate a scientific IR with more traditional forms of inquiry. Even Bull's attack on a 'scientific' IR is notable for its lack of references to a philosophical rejection of the natural science model, though his arguments seem to imply an awareness of the issues (Bull, 1969).

Hollis and Smith's book emerged in the context of what has come to be called the post-positivist turn (Biersteker, 1989; George, 1989, 1994; Holsti, 1989; Lapid, 1989), and has given the anti-science wing of the discipline a series of formidable philosophical arguments on which to draw. Hollis and Smith argue that one can have either an explanatory account (based on scientific principles), or an understanding account (based on hermeneutic principles); what one cannot have is some combination of the two (Hollis and Smith, 1990, 1994). In reality, Hollis and Smith's 'two stories' thesis is not wholly consistent with that of either Winch or Weber (Hollis and Smith, 1990, 1991, 1992, 1994, 1996). Winch (1958) had rejected all attempts to construct a science of the social, and Weber (1949) had insisted on the necessity of both forms of analysis.

Weber rejected both the positivist contention that the cognitive aims of the natural and the social sciences were basically the same and the opposing historicist doctrine that it is impossible to make legitimate generalizations about human bevavior because human actions are not subject to the regularities that govern the world of nature. Against the historicists Weber argued that the method of science, whether its subject matter be things or men, always proceeds by abstraction and generalization. Against the positivists, he took the view that the explanation of human behavior could not rest only on its external manifestations, but required also knowledge of the underlying motivations. Hence Weber's definition of sociology as that science which aims at the *interpretative understanding (Verstehen)* of social behavior in order to gain an explanation of its causes its course and it effects. According to Weber, what distinguishes the natural and social sciences is not an inherent difference in methods of investigation, but rather the differing interests and aims of the scientist. Both types of science involve abstraction. Hence there is no insurmountable chasm between the procedures of the natural and the social scientist; they differ only in their cognitive intentions and explanatory projects (Weber, 1949).

Weber saw the notion of interpretative understanding as only a preliminary step in the establishment of causal relationships. The grasping of subjective meaning of an activity, he argued, is facilitated through empathy *(Einfuehlung)* and a reliving *(Nacherbleben)* of the experience to be analyzed. But any interpretative explanation *(verstehende Erklaerung)* must become a causal explanation if it is to reach the dignity of a scientific proposition. *Verstehen* and causal explanation are correlative rather than opposed principles of method in the social sciences (Weber, 1949).

Given the philosophical justification of the arguments of Hollis and Smith, however, the only alternative is a philosophical refutation, not simply a rejection of the position, or a creative redescription (Suganami, 2000; see Patomäki, 1996 for a philosophical engagement). This task is complicated by the fact that many of the labels currently being deployed in the discipline are not clearly delineated, or the content of them sufficiently explained (see Smith, 1995 for an account of the discipline's self images; see also Waever, 1996). In this respect, despite the appearance of philosophical sophistication, the discipline has moved from throwing philosophical hand grenades to a largely untargeted artillery barrage against an ill-defined series of enemies.

Often this phase of disciplinary development is called the 'third debate', (Dougherty and Pfaltzgraff, 1996; George, 1989; Lapid, 1989; Neufeld, 1994, 1995; Sylvester, 1993) but there are problems with such a designation. In particular, it is not clear what the content of the 'third debate' is, or who the debaters are (Smith, 1995: 14; Vasquez, 1995: 217–18; Waever 1996). Mark Neufeld, for example, claims both that the 'third debate' is the 'inter-paradigm debate' between realism, pluralism and structuralism (Neufeld, 1994: 19; see also Banks 1984, 1985), and that it represents the discipline's attempt to move beyond the positivist orthodoxy (Neufeld, 1994: 19). Christine Sylvester treats it as simply the move beyond positivism (Slyvester, 1993: 140–68). Ole Waever provides a solid critique of the confusion surrounding the 'third debate' (Waever, 1996).

The dominant way the discipline views this period is in terms of a vehement set of reactions to a scientific IR; or what has been called a post-positivist phase (Biersteker, 1989; Holsti, 1989; Lapid, 1989). Many of the current meta-theoretical debates are primarily concerned with the extent to which the positivist model of science can, or should, be applied to IR (Hollis and Smith, 1990; King, et al., 1994; Kratochwil, 2000; Nicholson, 1996a; Smith, 2000; Wendt, 2000). And all of the contributors to the current meta-theoretical debates have addressed the nature of inquiry itself, as opposed to the nature of the international system, or some other chosen object of inquiry (Ashley, 1987; Biersteker, 1989; Hollis and Smith, 1990; Holsti, 1989; Lapid, 1989; Nicholson, 1996a, 1996b). However, as Yosef Lapid suggests, this period is not simply a continuation of debates about the relevance of the philosophy of science to IR, but is also the 'confluence of diverse antipositivistic philosophical

and sociological trends' (Biersteker, 1989; Holsti, 1989; Lapid, 1989: 237). For the purposes of this last section I will label this the 'post-positivist turn' and attempt to indicate the contemporary landscape of IR, highlight some of the problems, and indicate some potential avenues of future research.

The post-positivist turn began in the mid-1980s. Just as Kuhn was becoming well embedded within the literature a number of other developments were being imported into IR. Often these interventions would include references to Kuhn and Feyerabend as ways of delegitimating claims to science (George, 1989: 271; Neufeld, 1994: 14); with defenders of science tending to draw on Kuhn, Popper or Lakatos (Dougherty and Pfaltzgraff, 1996: 5; Herman and Peacock, 1987; Keohane, 1989; King et al., 1994; Nicholson, 1996a; Vasquez, 1998). But the philosophy of science no longer provided the only fertile ground for sources of legitimation. Moreover, the overturning of the positivist orthodoxy within the philosophy of science now meant that there was no 'secure' account of a scientific methodology on which to draw (Chalmers, 1992; Hollis and Smith, 1990; Oldroyd, 1986; Stockman, 1983; Trigg, 1993; Tudor, 1982). This meant that a range of disparate positions was now being imported into the discipline, with the relationships between them being unclear and unspecified.

Critical theorists criticized mainstream commitments to science (Cox, 1981; Hoffman, 1987; Linklater, 1990; see also Habermas, 1988; Horkheimer, 1982, 1993; Morrow and Brown, 1994). The extent of this critique, however, is not clear. For some, critical theory is seen as a replacement for a positivist form of social science (Brown, 1994; S. Smith, 1996: 24). Yet, as Mark Hoffman points out, critical theory did not denigrate positivism, but rather aimed to show how scientific knowledge aimed at mere technical control was not the only legitimate type of knowledge (Hoffman, 1987: 236; see also Adorno et al., 1976). Certainly, Habermas viewed positivist, hermeneutic and critical research as legitimate components of all social inquiry (Habermas, 1988). Likewise, Andrew Linklater seems to accept the validity of positivist informed research, whilst rejecting the idea that it exhausts the possibilities (Linklater, 1990). Positivism as a valid philosophy of science is accepted and only the boundaries of its legitimate use within social science are disputed. As such, a critical theory approach to social science will incorporate elements of positivism as well as hermeneutics, but attempt to go beyond them in terms of emancipatory potential (Morrow and Brown, 1994).

Feminist approaches in IR, as in other social science disciplines, critiqued science on the basis of its male-centered assumptions and lack of attention to gendered forms of knowledge construction

(Elshtain, 1997; Enloe, 1990, 1993; Sylvester, 1993; Tickner, 1992; Zalewski, 1993). However, while many seem happy to view feminism as a project dedicated to the critique of something called the 'positivist mainstream', there is within feminist approaches very little in the way of agreement about appropriate standards of inquiry within feminism (Zalewski, 1993; see also Tickner, Chapter 14 in this volume). Some feminists view their work in terms of science, even if they would not accept the label positivist (Enloe, 1990; Harding, 1991; Hartsock, 1983). In general, the discipline, following Sandra Harding's framework, tends to divide feminists into empiricist, standpoint and postmodern positions (Zalewski, 1993), although it is doubtful whether this characterization comes close to engaging with the nuances of this important body of work (Harding, 1991).

Often described as the most radical attack on the assumptions of social science, postmodernism and post-structuralism are difficult bodies of thought to characterize (Ashley, 1987, 1989; Ashley and Walker, 1990; Campbell, 1998a; Der Derian and Shapiro, 1989; Devetak, 1996; George, 1994; Jarvis, 2000; Rosenau, 1990, 1992; Smith, 1995; Walker, 1993). Also, the discipline seems unable, or unwilling, to attempt to make any differentiation between postmodernism and post-structuralism, and tends to treat the two terms as synonymous (Rosenau, 1990: 84–5; Vasquez, 1995). This is problematic in terms of the philosophy of social science.

Post-structuralism emerges out of a general critique of structuralism (Harland, 1987). It is critical of structuralism's attempt to develop an objective science of social structures, but equally important is that post-structuralism expresses no desire to return to a form of inquiry based upon the subjectivity of agents (Harland, 1987, 1993; Rabinow, 1982; Rosenau,1990). Structural forms of inquiry had come to dominate many forms of social science (Althusser and Balibar, 1970; [1938] Durkheim, 1964; Harland, 1987, 1993). Structuralism proposes that understanding social practices requires the decentering of individual subjectivities and a focusing of attention on the structural modalities and organizing principles within which social practices are framed (Harland, 1987, 1993; Kurzweil, 1980). Structuralism was an attempt to scientifically describe the structural principles under which activity could be explained (Harland, 1993; Jackson, 1991). Waltz's structural realism, although not specifically embedded with a structuralist meta-theory, can be understood as a structuralist theory of IR (Waltz, 1979; see Ashley, 1984 for a critique of Waltz that makes this explicit).

Post-structuralism departs from two central tenets of structuralism (Harland, 1987, 1993). First, the logic of structures, which structuralism had thought was clear and determinate, is challenged

(Derrida, 1988). For post-structuralism, structures do not operate according to one organizing principle or logic (Harland, 1987). Indeed, for post-structuralism there is no underlying logic to structures and hence there is structural indeterminancy (Doty, 1997; Harland, 1987; see Wight, 1999b for a critique). Social outcomes, which are products of social structures, are also indeterminate (Doty, 1997). Attempts to ascribe a logic to social activity must necessarily either fail or impose a logic on the situation through claims to some form of legitimacy – generally science (Derrida, 1988).

But science, as a social practice dependent upon structures, also falls to the same logic, and its outputs are either indeterminate, or such determinacy that does emerge can only be the outcome of practices that attempt to tame the indeterminacy of structures (Ashley, 1987, 1989; Ashley and Walker 1990). This means that all claims to scientific objectivity are actually social practices imposing order through practices of power (Ashley, 1987, 1989; George, 1994; Walker, 1993). Postmodernism expands on this post-structuralist position and grafts onto it various other wholesale critiques of reason, reality, truth and so forth (Brodribb, 1992; Callinicos, 1990; Dews, 1987; Eagleton, 1996; Farrell, 1996; Nicholson, 1993; Owen, 1997; in IR see, Brown, 1994; Devetak, 1996; Jarvis, 2000; Rengger and Hoffman, 1990; Vasquez, 1995).

The fourth source of influences and ideas that began to be imported is that of social theory. This position has been labelled constructivism within the discipline (Adler, 1997; Guzzini, 2000; Hopf, 1998; Kratochwil, 1989; Onuf, 1989, 1998; Ruggie, 1998; Vasquez, 1997a; Wendt, 1987). This is a very problematic term because there are some very conflicting positions being imported under this label (Adler, 1997; Hopf, 1998; see also Chapter 5 in this volume; Ruggie, 1998). The confusion is evident when one considers that John Ruggie, in his typology of constructivism, includes post-structuralism (Ruggie, 1998: 35; see also Adler, Chapter 5 in this volume), whereas Smith sees a clear demarcation between them (Smith, 1995, 1996, 1997). David Campbell likewise sees certain forms of constructivism as inimical to his version of post-structuralism (Campbell, 1998a, 2001).

The philosophy of social science can help throw some light on this situation. In relation to the science question, Ruggie's neoclassical constructivism and Alexander Wendt's scientific realist version are united; both are committed to the idea of social science (Ruggie, 1998: 35–6).[16] Friedrich Kratochwil, on the other hand, is much closer to Winch's anti-science perspective (Kratochwil, 1989, 2000). Why Ruggie draws such a firm distinction between his neoclassical constructivism and Wendt's more naturalistic form is not immediately clear. Ruggie sees the work of philosopher

John Searle as playing a fundamental role in his neoclassical constructivism (Ruggie, 1998: 35). Yet, there is very little in Searle's *The Construction of Social Reality* (1995) that Wendt and other scientific realists would find objectionable (compare Bhaskar, 1979; Outhwaite, 1987).

Indeed, Searle begins with a statement that could function as a *leitmotif* for scientific realism: 'We live in exactly one world, not two or three or seventeen. As far as we currently know, the most fundamental features of that world are as described by physics, chemistry, and the other natural sciences' (Searle, 1995: xi). Moreover, Searle openly declares his hand with both philosophical realism and science (Searle, 1995: xiii). Equally, Weber's attempt to combine *eklaren* and *verstehen* into one seamless account is exactly the project that scientific realists, such as Roy Bhaskar, are engaged in (Bhaskar, 1979; Weber, 1949). Indeed, Ruggie actually accepts 'relational social realism' as an accurate description of his account, of international structure (Ruggie, 1998: 34; for a scientific realist account, see Porpora, 1987).

This raises the question of just why Ruggie feels it so necessary to distinguish his neoclassical constructivism from that of Wendt. The answer, of course, is the label 'scientific', in scientific realism. Kratochwil also objects to Wendt's constructivism on similar grounds (Kratochwil, 2000). Ruggie's depth of engagement with scientific realism, however, does not seem to extend any further than an almost verbatim restatement of Hollis and Smith's rejection of it (Hollis and Smith, 1991; Ruggie, 1998: 36). And Hollis and Smith can hardly be said to have provided a sustained assessment of it (Hollis and Smith, 1991; S. Smith, 1996). As a philosophy of science that is non-positivist, scientific realism is very poorly understood within the discipline and this is certainly one area where much research is still required.

Wendt (1987, 1999) and David Dessler (1989, 1991, 1999) provide good introductions to scientific realism (see also Shapiro and Wendt, 1992). Ashley J. Tellis (1996) writes of something called 'scientific realism' and aligns it with Karl Popper's 'critical rationalism'. It seems unlikely, however, that by 'scientific realism' Tellis means the philosophy of science version of it, and his scientific realism can only be political realism that attempts to be scientific. None the less, precisely because the labels are deployed with little clarification, confusion abounds. Kratochwil provides a recent attempt to address scientific realism, but ultimately his treatment lacks, an understandable, depth of analysis (Kratochwil, 2000; see also Doty, 1997, and the critique by Wight, 1999a, and the subsequent exchange: Doty, 1999; Wight, 2000). Heikki Patomäki and Colin Wight have begun what might be a closer examination of scientific realism, although the tenacity of the view

that science equals positivism is a serious obstacle to any serious evaluation of alternative views of science (Patomäki and Wight, 2000; see also Patomäki, 1996, 2001; Lane, 1996; Wendt, 1999).

Smith calls scientific realism an epistemology, which is a strange reading given that scientific realism is a philosophy of science that does not privilege any particular epistemological stance (S. Smith, 1996). The problem here is the use of the term epistemology within the discipline. Smith, for example, talks of something called a 'postmodern epistemology', and of postmodern work on epistemology being diverse (Smith, 1996). But this can only be to misuse the word epistemology, since epistemology is the branch of philosophy concerned with the theory of knowledge and not a philosophy of science; or an account of the reality (Haack, 1993; Taylor, 1987). In fact, very few books on epistemology include references to positivism (Haack, 1993; Taylor, 1987).

The main problems with which epistemology is concerned include: the definition of knowledge and related concepts; the sources and criteria of knowledge; the kinds of knowledge possible and the degree to which each is certain and the exact relation between the one who knows and the object known (Haack, 1993; Taylor, 1987). Epistemological questions are typically concerned with the grounds we have for accepting or rejecting beliefs. Insofar as many postmodern positions reject these as valid questions they also reject epistemology; which is evident in Smith's own table, since he indicates 'no' in every category pertaining to postmodern positions on criteria of assessment (S. Smith, 1996).

In short, postmodernism as yet has no epistemology, and is unwilling to advance one (see the debate between Campbell, 1998b, 1999 and Wight, 1999b; and between Doty, 1999 and Wight 2000; also Osterud, 1996, 1997; Patomäki, 1997; Smith, 1997). It is for this reason that Peter Katzenstein, Robert Keohane and Stephen Krasner argue that it falls outside the social science enterprise (Katzenstein et al., 1998: 678; Sørenson, 1998: 88). Equally, however, Smith locates Michel Foucault as representative of postmodernism, which would seem to imply he had no criteria of assessment, whereas Foucault declared himself an empiricist (Foucault, 1990: 106). No doubt he was being 'ironic'! Unfortunately the discipline tends to use epistemology to mean any generalized approach to study. But this only serves to hide a range of hidden ontological assumptions.

A key factor that the discipline has yet to take seriously is that the demise of the positivist orthodoxy within the philosophy of science now means that there is 'no definitive or agreed cannon of scientific explanation' (Hollis and Smith, 1990: 67). This means that science is not synonymous with positivism. This should have been the lesson drawn

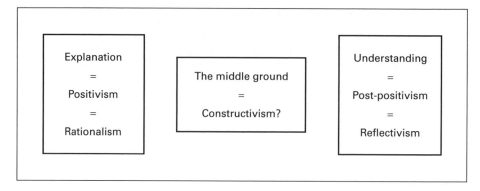

Figure 2.2   *Contemporary IR*

from developments within the philosophy of science (Vasquez, 1995). Yet the discipline seems tenaciously wedded to the idea that science is positivism (Nicholson, 1996a, 1996b, 2000; S. Smith, 1996). Even Hollis and Smith, despite a highly sophisticated discussion of this issue, draw the line between explaining and understanding on positivist principles (Hollis and Smith, 1990). This demonstrates the problem with simplistic diagrammatic representations of complex theoretical landscapes (see Figures 2.1 and 2.2). Explaining, for Hollis and Smith, seems to suggest a unitary scientific approach, whereas recent work within the philosophy of science shows just how untenable this is (Chalmers, 1992), with many, including Paul Feyerabend and Roy Bhaskar, maintaining that there is no generalized account of the 'scientific method' that could facilitate the drawing of such a line (Bhaskar, 1978; Feyerabend, 1975).

For Bhaskar, and other scientific realists, there cannot be one scientific method, or one appropriate epistemology, because each of the sciences is concerned with differing object domains, and no one method, or epistemology, could be expected to fit all cases (Bhaskar, 1978; Mackinnon, 1972; Psillos, 1999). For scientific realists, the correct epistemological stance is one of epistemological opportunism. As Einstein put it, '[c]ompare a scientist with an epistemologist; a scientist faces a complicated situation. So in order to get some value in this situation he cannot use a simple rule, he has to be an opportunist' (see Feyerabend, 1995). Equally, given that there is no agreed cannon of scientific explanation, post-positivism should not be interpreted as anti-science.

The term 'post-positivist' is ambiguous as to whether it constitutes an outright rejection of positivism, an outright rejection of science, or a reformulation of the idea of science on the basis of new developments within the philosophy of science (Laudan, 1996). Indeed, many of the developments

within the philosophy of science that deserve the label 'post-positivist' are certainly not anti-science, although they may well be anti-positivist (Bhaskar, 1978, 1986; Kuhn, 1962, 1970, 1982, 1990; Laudan, 1996). This opens up the possibility of a non-positivist, yet still scientific IR; a science of IR, that is, that does not follow positivist principles.

There is little doubt, however, that for many within the discipline a commitment to science still remains a commitment to positivism (Nicholson, 1996a, 1996b, 2000). Even Wendt, whilst advocating a scientific realist philosophy of science, can declare, 'I am a strong believer in science … I am a "positivist"' (Wendt, 1999: 39). This is an impossible position to hold. One cannot be both a scientific realist and a positivist; the two accounts of science are diametrically opposed on some very fundamental issues (Bhaskar, 1978; Feyerabend, 1981; Hollis, 1996; Mackinnon, 1972; S. Smith, 1996).[17] Positivism, in this sense, has lost all meaning. Indeed, the discipline's understanding of positivism seems a caricature of what is a very sophisticated, although in my opinion highly flawed, philosophy of science.

This confusion surrounding the meaning of positivism threatens to destabilize any attempt to employ it (Nicholson, 1996a, 2000; S. Smith, 1996). And if positivism cannot be given coherent content, then post-positivism is equally meaningless. Many seem to equate positivism with realist (in the philosophical sense) accounts of science (Campbell, 2001; George, 1994); or treat it as meaning any approach that relies on a belief in a 'world out there' – a form of philosophical realism (Campbell, 2001; George, 1994). However, Hollis argues that positivism, insofar as it is committed to an empiricist epistemology, is actually an anti-realist (in the philosophical sense) philosophy (Hollis, 1996: 303; George also admits this, 1994: 53).

There have been some serious attempts to clarify the content of positivism in the discipline (compare

George, 1994; Hollis, 1996; Nicholson 1996a, 1996b, 2000; S. Smith 1996), but it is doubtful, given the disciplinary baggage surrounding the label, if there is anything to be gained from its continued deployment (Nicholson, 1996a, 1996b, 2000). Smith provides a good account but one that omits many of the most fundamental issues – particularly positivism's commitment to a Humean account of cause; its anti-realism and associated phenomenalism and instrumentalism; and the covering law model of explanation (S. Smith, 1996; see Kowlakowski, 1969, for a more in-depth account of positivism).

More problematic is that Smith's (1996) own positivistic (on his own terms) attempt to spell out four essential characteristics of positivism simply begs the question of how many of the chosen principles a given theorist need commit to before being deserving of the label?[18] Is it a case of 'three strikes and you're out', or are you a positivist if you just accept one of them? Nicholson (1996a, 1996b) also produces a good account, but it suffers from the conflation of positivism with empiricism (see Smith, 1996, for a critique of this conflation). Hollis makes an often-missed point in his claim that all positivists are naturalists, but not all naturalists are positivists (Hollis, 1996: 303).

All of this adds up to a very confused picture in terms of the philosophy of social science. IR has struggled to incorporate an increasingly diverse set of positions into its theoretical landscape. In general, the discipline has attempted to maintain an unsophisticated and outdated two-category framework based on the science/anti-science issue. The terminology of this framework may have changed, but ultimately contemporary disciplinary categories seem to be mirror images of a Carr's distinction between science and 'alchemy'. Currently there are three continuums that the discipline seems to consider line up in opposition to each other. The first of these is the explaining/understanding divide (Hollis and Smith, 1990). The second is the positivism/post-positivism divide (Lapid, 1989; Sylvester, 1993). The third is Keohane's distinction between rationalism and reflectivism (Keohane, 1989). The newly emerging constructivism claims the 'middle ground' in between (Adler, 1997; Price and Reus-Smit, 1998; Wendt, 1999). This constitutes a field configured as in Figure 2.2.

The problems with such a framework should be evident from the above discussion, but it is particularly worth noting the irony of aligning something called 'rationalism' with positivism. Particularly if the claims that positivism embodies an empiricist epistemology are correct (Nicholson, 1996a, 1996b; S. Smith, 1996); rationalism and empiricism are normally considered epistemological opposites[19] (Haack, 1993). Moreover, if the 'science = positivism' equation is accepted this would mean that post-positivism is necessarily anti-science. But, this cannot be the case since many post-positivist positions are pro-science. Moreover, Marxist approaches to IR sit uneasily in this framework as they are also committed to science, but not positivism (Maclean, 1981; H. Smith, 1996). There is a move within some sections of the discipline to substitute the rationalist/reflectivist axis for a rationalist/constructivist one, and this is certainly evident in many of the chapters in this volume. However, this can only make sense if the category of constructivism is further disaggregated into competing, and sometimes incompatible positions (see Chapter 5 by Adler in this volume for an attempt to construct just such an account). It is difficult to see what is gained by such a move since to use one label to cover a range of positions can only be of benefit if they share substantial elements in common.

Another complicating factor is that of causation (Harré and Madden, 1975; Lerner, 1965; Suganami, 1996; Wright, 1974). Hollis and Smith ultimately reduce the distinction between explaining and understanding, and by implication positivism and post-positivism, to the issue of causation: 'To understand is to reproduce order in the minds of actors; to explain is to find causes in the scientific manner' (Hollis and Smith, 1990: 87). This would suggest that all causal accounts are necessarily positivist. Indeed, David Campbell, in accepting the logic of this framework, argues: 'I embrace the logic of interpretation that acknowledges the improbability of cataloguing, calculating and specifying the "real causes"' (Campbell, 1992: 4). This seems to suggest that interpretative (understanding) accounts eschew causation. But what kind of causation is being rejected here? Hollis and Smith view cause in Humean positivist terms, whereas Campbell offers no explanation of what he means by 'real causes' (Hollis and Smith, 1991: 407; 1994: 248–50).

Ruggie, presumably still on the post-positivist/reflectivist side, is committed to causation, but discusses it in the context of the covering law model of explanation and contrasts this with a narrative form of explanation (Ruggie, 1998: 34). Hidemi Suganami has also addressed the issue of cause in a very similar manner, but the ontology of his account is unclear and he seems to imply that the narration itself is the cause (Suganami, 2000). This is a very idealistic account of cause, and would seem to suggest that Thucydides's narrative of the Peloponnesian War was actually its cause (Patomäki and Wight, 2000; Suganami, 2000). Missing from Suganami's discussion is the difference between 'narration-of-causes' and 'narration-as-cause'. Both are equally valid in terms of social science, but the distinction is important in temporal terms. A narration of the causes of the First World War cannot literally be the cause of the First World War, whereas a narrative that portrayed certain groups as inferior could be part of the cause of their being treated as inferior. Dessler (1991) has a good discussion of cause from a non-Humean position and contrasts this to correlation.[20]

The distinction between constitutive and explanatory theory is another issue that has emerged within the discipline as a result of the contemporary way of framing the issues (Burchill and Linklater, 1996; Smith, 1995; Wendt, 1999). Steve Smith sees this as the main meta-theoretical issue facing the discipline today (Smith, 1995: 26). Smith clearly sees explanatory theory as being essentially positivist in orientation and constitutive theory as post-positivist (Smith, 1995: 26–7). According to Smith, explanatory theory seeks to offer explanations of international relations, whereas constitutive theory sees 'theory as constitutive of that reality' (Smith, 1995: 26–7). It is difficult to know how to interpret this distinction. Smith formulates it as a basic ontological difference embedded within competing visions of the social world (Smith, 1995: 27). But underlying Smith's formulation is still the science/anti-science schema; is the social world to be 'seen as scientists think of the "natural" world, that is to say as something outside of our theories, or is the social world what we make it' (Smith, 1995: 27)?

But just whom does the 'we' refer to here? Setting this distinction in opposition to explanatory theory that attempts to explain international relations, we can presume that Smith means 'we' IR theorists, not 'we' members of society. But this seems implausible. It seems to suggest that 'we' IR theorists make the world of international relations. On the other hand, if the point is simply that the world is socially constructed then it would be difficult to find many social scientists, whether on the science wing or not, who think otherwise (Holsti, 1998: 29; Searle, 1995). Even such a mainstream scholar as Kenneth Waltz accepts that the social world is socially constructed (Waltz, 1979: 48).[21]

It may well be that academic theories eventually filter down into society and fundamentally change it, but as yet, there is little to suggest that 'we' are in a privileged enough position to say 'we' IR theorists make the world we study. Wendt's reply to Smith on this issue seems basically sound, and even though social objects do not exist independently of the concepts agents have of them, they do exist 'independent of the minds and bodies of the individuals who want to explain them' (Wendt, 1999: 75). Wendt rejects Smith's science/anti-science framing of this issue, and argues that both explanatory theory and constitutive theory transcend the natural–social science divide (Wendt, 1999: 78; see Smith, 2000 for a reply). According to Wendt, constitutive theory is concerned with 'how' social

objects are constituted, and what is 'X' (Wendt, 1999: 78). State theory would be a good example here. It asks 'what is a state?' and does not attempt to link causes in time (Bosanquet, 1899; Jessop, 1990; Laski, 1935). Wendt also argues that some of the most important theories in the natural sciences are constitutive – the double helix model of DNA for example (Wendt, 2000: 107).

The issue of constitutive theory and explanatory theory is often linked to that of whether reasons can be causes (Hollis, 1994; Smith, 2000). This used to be a major issue of concern for the philosophy of social science (Winch, 1958, although compare Winch, 1990; Davidson, 1963; MacIntyre, 1973). Today the construal of reasons as causes is generally accepted as a necessary component for interpretative accounts; although Smith suggests that it is still hotly disputed, but does not indicate by whom (Smith, 2000: 158). In general, understanding reasons as causes has come to be seen as necessary in order to preserve the difference between action and behavior (Bhaskar, 1979; Carlsnaes, 1986; Collin, 1985; Davidson, 1963; Porpora, 1987).

For if the reason for an act is not part of the causal complex responsible for the act, then the contrast drawn between an act and a bodily movement, upon which hermeneutic accounts insist, is negated; such as that between signalling to a friend or scratching one's head, for example (Bhaskar, 1979: 169–95). The difference between a waving arm and signalling to a friend depends upon the possession, by an agent, of a *reason* to wave one's arm in that manner, namely, the desire to signal to a friend. In this respect, the desire to wave to one's friend can rightly be considered as part of the causal complex responsible for the waving of the arm in the appropriate manner (Carlsnaes, 1986; Patomäki, 1996). If reasons are stripped of their causal function, behavioralism beckons.

This issue again demonstrates the tenacity of the positivist vision of science, for Smith's rejection of reasons as causes is derived from his acceptance of a positivist account of cause. Winch accepted that his rejection of causal accounts in social explanations was based on a Humean/positivist account of cause, and that devoid of such an account causal talk was not only appropriate, but necessary for social explanation (Winch, 1990). Because of this Wendt has suggested that Hollis and Smith's 'two stories' thesis is 'a legacy of positivist conceptions of explanation' (Wendt, 1991: 391).

The explanatory/constitutive divide is linked to the rationalist/reflectivist dichotomy by a number of authors (Adler, 1997; Laffey and Weldes, 1997; S. Smith, 1996; Wendt, 1999). The division of the discipline into rationalist and reflectivist camps is generally attributed to Robert Keohane (Keohane, 1989), although in recent years it has played less of a role, with many within the discipline preferring to talk of a rationalist/constructivist divide. The original distinction was specifically formulated by Keohane to capture the difference between two approaches to international institutions, but the terms have rapidly come to signify two radically opposed approaches to the study of IR itself (Keohane, 1989; S. Smith, 1996; Wendt 1992). According to Keohane, rationalists are theorists who accept what he calls a 'substantive' conception of rationality. By this he means that behavior can be considered rational insofar as it can be adjudged objectively to be optimally adapted to the situation (Keohane, 1989: 160). Reflectivists, on the other hand, take a 'sociological approach to the study of institutions' and stress the 'role of impersonal social forces as well as the impact of cultural practices, norms, and values that are not derived from a calculation of interests' (Keohane, 1989: 160). Reflectivists emphasize 'the importance of "intersubjective meanings" of international institutional activity' (Keohane, 1989: 161).

As formulated, this is an ontological difference, not an epistemological or methodological one. Keohane claims that the study of international politics will require both approaches if empirical research is not to suffer (Keohane, 1989: 161). Keohane's rationalist/reflectivist distinction can be understood as one in which rationalists focus their attention on how institutions function; whereas reflectivists are more interested in how institutions come into existence, how they are maintained and how they vary across cultural and historical contexts (Keohane, 1989: 170). According to the reflectivist critique, rationalist theories are said to be one-dimensional, static, universalistic, ahistorical and decontextualized (Keohane, 1989: 170–3). Keohane acknowledges all of these limitations, yet argues against a wholesale rejection of rationalist approaches in favour of a broadening of the research agenda to incorporate the reflectivist perspective (Keohane, 1989: 171). The problem is that, although these reflectivist critiques of the rationalist perspective seem telling, the reflectivists have yet to develop what Keohane calls a 'research program' able to demonstrate the veracity of their claims (Keohane, 1989: 173). Without such a 'research program' reflectivist criticisms of the rationalist mainstream will remain marginal to the discipline (Keohane, 1989: 173).

In essence, Keohane's Lakatosian call for a 'research programme or perish' intervention can be understood as a plea, or perhaps challenge, to reflectivist scholars to move beyond incessant critique and to demonstrate empirically the validity of their claims (Katzenstein et al., 1998). The reflectivist response has, predictably enough, been to ask on whose terms (S. Smith, 1996)? After all, isn't the demand to develop a 'research programme' based upon empirical validation an appeal to exactly those same positivist principles that the reflectivists are challenging (George, 1994)? To many reflectivists still wedded to an outmoded view of science this is to accept positivism. It is in this manner that positivism comes to be aligned with rationalism.

There is something to this alignment at the level of ontology. Positivism, in all its varied manifestations, has always been ontologically coy, preferring to either remain agnostic about the ontological status of theoretical terms, or denying outright that they have any ontological status. This, of course, is its instrumental treatment of theoretical terms. Keohane's rationalists do not believe that any actual agents meet the rational man model; any more than economists think that any firms are perfectly rational utility maximizers (Katzenstein et al., 1998; Keohane, 1989). Rationality is an assumption deemed necessary in order to get research under way. Reflectivist critics can be interpreted as either rejecting the validity of the 'as if' (assumptive) mode of theorizing, or merely rejecting the particular assumptions being made; or perhaps both.

Whereas Keohane originally based the distinction on ontological grounds and accepted the need to broaden the ontological horizon of investigation, the reflectivist reaction to it is based upon the epistemological criteria that Keohane sees as non-negotiable (Keohane, 1989: 174; Katzenstein et al., 1998). That the reflectivist reaction to Keohane's position has been primarily based upon epistemological issues demonstrates the depth of the science/anti-science split within the discipline. Moreover, the fact that the vast majority (if not all) of so-called reflectivists within the discipline do indeed supply empirical support for their claims throws yet more doubt on the validity of this particular cleavage (Campbell, 2001; Wendt, 1999: 67; 2000: 173). If the distinction between a rationalist and a reflectivist is made on these epistemological grounds alone then there are simply no practicing reflectivists in IR today. Even the severest critics of Keohane's epistemological concerns enlist empirical support for their arguments (Ashley, 1987, 1989; Ashley and Walker, 1990; Campbell, 1998b, 2001; George, 1994; Smith, 1997; Walker, 1993).

There is one final dichotomy that demonstrates the inability of this crude framework to contain the weight it is being asked to bear. This is the material/ideational split. There is little constructive to be said about the way the discipline currently frames this issue. From a philosophy of social science perspective it makes little sense. Rationalists, explainers and positivists are said to concentrate on material factors; reflectivists, understanders, constructivists and post-positivists are said to focus on ideational ones (Laffey and Weldes, 1997; Ruggie, 1998; S. Smith, 1996, 2000; Wendt, 1995, 1999, 2000).

This issue again is derivate of the science/anti-science split. But there is simply no philosophy of science position that can legitimate this split. Positivists of all sorts of persuasion can legitimate analysis of ideational factors; it is how they treat them that matters (Haas, 1991: 190; Laffey and Weldes, 1997). Likewise, non-positivist philosophies of science and social science can privilege material factors (Marx, 1966). Of course, different theorists can focus their attention of these factors to varying degrees, but even in these instances this would be an ontological choice related to the object of inquiry, not one derived from an a priori commitment to some mythical epistemological position. If the difference between rationalists and reflectivists, or positivists and post-positivists, or even constructivists and rationalists, is based on the material versus ideational issue, then Keohane, given his claim that 'institutions can be defined in terms of their rules', is not a rationalist or a positivist (Keohane, 1989: 163).

Many on the so-called non-rationalist/post-positivist side of the current landscape seem to assume that Wendt's argument for maintaining a social science embedded within nature suggests that *only* material factors matter (Campbell, 2001: 445). But Wendt is not suggesting this (1999). What he is suggesting is that IR should leave open the possibility that material factors play a role; why this should be interpreted as saying that *only* material factors matter is not clear, although understanding the logic of the contemporary framework partially explains it since the framework sets up an either/or distinction. Ultimately, however, this issue is not helped by the lack of conceptual clarity that is deployed when discussing it. David Campbell, for example, can both claim that 'nothing exists outside of discourse' (Campbell, 2001: 444), and that the 'undeniable existence of that world external to thought is not the issue' (Campbell, 2001: 444).

There may, of course, be coherent ways in which these two claims can be reconciled, but this would require much greater conceptual clarity. Moreover, despite the commitment to objects external to thought, Campbell is still essentially advocating a form of philosophical idealism in tying the existence or those objects to discourses; without humans no discourses; without discourses no objects; in a sense a version of positivism. To say more on the material/ideational issue within IR would confer on it a legitimacy that it clearly does not deserve. It does, however, demonstrate how the current way of framing the issues throws up such absurdities.

CONCLUSION

Mervyn Frost once declared IR the 'backward discipline' (Frost, 1986). It was 'backward', he argued,

due to a lack of self-conscious reflection concerning its analytical and research endeavors (Frost, 1986: 39). On these grounds IR can hardly be considered 'backward' today. However, it would be a mistake to consider that self-reflection necessarily constitutes progress. It may be that Holsti's characterization of the discipline as dividing is a more accurate description (Holsti, 1985). And even then there is the difficult question of where the dividing lines are and whether division is something the discipline desires? When positivism dominated the philosophy of science the choice for the discipline was simple, but stark. Either science, or not science; which effectively translated into 'positivism or perish'. When the positivist orthodoxy began to crumble hopes were high for a more pluralistic IR: one less grounded in austere visions of a deterministic science and one much more amenable to the introduction of alternative patterns of thought. Is this where we are today?

Unfortunately not. Unable to shake the positivist orthodoxy because it never really understood it, the discipline simply poured the newly emerging patterns of thought into the old framework. But, as any mathematician could testify, a 'thousand theoretical flowers' into two will not go, and hence the current framework bursts at the seams. Simply adding a new 'middle ground' category does not help and nor does subsuming a range of differing categories under one label. And so the current framework 'disciplines' and demands that one declares one's allegiance. Once declared, one's analytical frame of reference is specified and one's identity firmly fixed. As a rationalist you *will* privilege material factors, causation and science; as a post-positivist/reflectivist you *will* privilege ideational factors, deny causation and are anti-science. Any attempt to challenge this categorization is tamed and forced into one or other extreme. This is exactly the reaction from both sides of the divide to Wendt's attempt to occupy the middle ground. The idea that one has to declare which tribe one belongs to and that this determines one's ontological frame of reference, epistemology and appropriate methods seems a bizarre way for a discipline to proceed. However, some within the discipline have begun to question the validity of the framework itself (Ashley, 1996; Patomäki and Wight, 2000; Sørenson, 1998; Waever, 1996).

These objections notwithstanding, and given the long history of the discipline's attachment to this framework, its rejection looks unlikely. Part of the explanation for this deeply embedded attachment is surely a form of disciplinary identity politics that stakes out borders over which only the foolhardy might tread (Campbell, 1998a, 2001). After all, without borders what would the border police do? If this is the result of the philosophy of social science in IR, then perhaps the discipline can do without it. But such an assessment would miss the point. The philosophy of social science is not something the discipline can use or discard in that manner. The subject we study is not wholly empirical, hence philosophy constitutes part of what we study, part of what we are and helps inform what we do. In this case, perhaps the best we can hope is that we can do it better. In the final analysis, it is worth keeping in mind that meta-theoretical debate on the issues I have covered in this chapter tend to be much more tribalistic in language than in practice. When it comes to concrete empirical research it is doubtful if anyone could consistently occupy any one of the positions and still maintain coherence. Hopefully the following chapters in this volume will demonstrate the veracity of this claim.

Notes

1 Throughout this chapter the abbreviation IR refers to the institutionalized academic discipline of international relations.

2 It would be normal to indicate the contested nature of this label by enclosing it in 'inverted commas'. Given that this chapter is centrally concerned with the meaning of the term such a form of enclosure seems unnecessary.

3 The problem of 'naturalism' is concerned with the extent to which society can be studied in the same way as nature (Bhaskar, 1979: 1).

4 The success of modern science led to the emergence of the philosophy of science. The philosophy of science reflects on the practice of science and attempts to examine what is distinctive about scientific explanations and theoretical constructions; what marks science off from guesswork, speculation and pseudo-science; what makes the predictions of science worthy of confidence; and, to question whether science reveals a hidden truth about an objective reality. In short, the philosophy of science attempts to grasp the nature of science. The philosophy of social science attempts to grasp the nature of social science. Both attempt to give a generalized account of what might constitute the practice subsumed under the label. It should be noted, of course, that given the success of science, philosophies of science are not simply explanatory schemes, but represent normative claims. A philosophy of science that claims to grasp the nature of scientific practice implies that if you want to practice science you 'ought' to follow the principles explicated in the philosophy. Equally, it should be clear that any philosophy of science will include ontological claims (claims about existence); epistemological considerations (claims about what would constitute a valid knowledge claim, and the grounds for such claims); and methodological implications (if you believe in X (ontology) and wish to ground the claim re X in Y (epistemology) then you should follow method Y). It is for this reason that a philosophy of science is much more than an epistemology or methodology. There are no ontologically neutral philosophies of science.

5 Again, subsumed under this question are a range of issues relating to the nature of the entities; for example, what is a 'person'; the collective action problem; the nature of social structures and so on.

6 Although this debate was labelled the agent–structure debate, it has been argued that this was simply a different terminology for what used to be called the individual/society problem, or the macro/micro problem. However, although these problems are related there are good grounds for considering them as distinct problems (see Layder, 1994).

7 Figure 2.1 is said to represent four possible positions that can be taken when the problem of naturalism is combined with the agent–structure problem. The top left box, where explanation meets structure, can be understood as a scientific approach to social study that concentrates its attention on structural forces. The bottom left box (explanation and agents), a scientific approach focussing on agents. The boxes on the right-hand side of the diagram represent a non-scientific approach to social study (hermeneutics perhaps), which, of course, can either focus on structural factors (top right) or agential ones (bottom right).

8 I view positivism as a philosophy of science. As such, it is only one account of what constitutes science. There are many other accounts of science that reject many of the central tenets of positivism. As should be clear, one of the main aims of this chapter is to problematize the idea that positions such as positivism can be given a clear and unequivocal meaning. There are many versions of positivism and much that divides those who claim to be positivists. However, these caveats aside, positivism can be characterized in the following manner. (i) Phenomenalism: the doctrine that holds that we cannot get beyond the way things appear to us and thereby obtain reliable knowledge of reality – in other words, appearances, not realities, are the only objects of knowledge. (ii) Nominalism: the doctrine that there is no objective meaning to the words we use – words and concepts do not pick out any actual objects or universal aspects of reality, they are simply conventional symbols or names that we happen to use for our own convenience. (iii) Cognitivism: the doctrine that holds that no cognitive value can be ascribed to value judgements and normative statements. (iv) Naturalism: the belief that there is an essential unity of scientific method such that the social sciences can be studied in the same manner as natural science (see Kolakowski, 1969). From these philosophical assumptions most positivists adhere to the following beliefs about the practice of science. (1) The acceptance of the 'covering-law' model of explanation (often referred to as the D–N model). An explanation is only valid if it invokes a law which covers, in the sense of entailing, all cases of the phenomena to be explained. (2) An instrumentalist treatment of theoretical terms. Theoretical terms do not refer to real entities, but such entities are to be understood 'as if' they existed in order to explain the phenomena. There is, however, no epistemological warrant (grounds for belief) that such entities really exist. The proper way to evaluate theoretical concepts and propositions is not through the categories of truth and falsity but through judging their

effectiveness. (3) A commitment to the Humean account of cause. To say that event *a* necessitated event *b* need be to say no more than when *a* occurred, so did *b*. This leads to causal laws being interpreted as 'constant conjunctions'. (4) A commitment to operationalism, which entails that the concepts of science be operationalized – that they be defined by, and their meaning limited to, the concrete operations used in their measurement. For example, the meaning of a mental term is *exhausted* by the observable operations that determine its use. So '*P* is thirsty' means *P* says she is thirsty if asked, drinks water if given the chance, and so on.

9 My analysis is an Anglo-American perspective on the issues, and it might be argued that Continental European IR would address the issues in a different manner. However, many of the anti-science positions that I address in this chapter take their inspiration from German idealism, and in this respect, one could argue that the underlying issues are the same even if the terms of debate might differ (see Jørgenson, 2000).

10 The original title of the text was *Principles of a New Science Concerning the Common Nature of Nations*.

11 Adopted from political science, behavioralism in IR is a strictly behavioral approach in which explanations are based on agents' overt, expressed and observable behavior; on 'what is really going on' rather than on non-measurable values and motives. Behavioralists emphasize that theories should be 'operational'; that is, capable of being empirically tested.

12 It is important to maintain the distinctions between ontology, epistemology and methodology. *Ontology*, in philosophical terms, was originally understood as a branch of metaphysics; it is the science of being in general, embracing such issues as the nature of existence and the categorial structure of reality. In the philosophy of science and the philosophy of social science, it is used to refer to the set of things whose existence is claimed, or acknowledged, by a particular theory or system of thought: it is in this sense that one speaks of 'the' ontology of a theory, or of a theory having such-and-such an ontology (for example, an ontology of anarchical structures, or of material substances). The term *epistemology* comes from the Greek word *epistêmê*, meaning knowledge. In simple terms, epistemology is the philosophy of knowledge or of how we come to know. *Methodology* is also concerned with how we come to know, but is much more practical in nature. Methodology is focused on the specific ways – the methods – that we can try to understand our world better. Epistemology and methodology are intimately related: the former involves the *philosophy* of how we come to know the world and the latter involves the *practice*. It is common in IR for these aspects to be conflated and confused. Adler (in Chapter 5 of this volume), for example, claims that '*Materialism* is the view that material reality exists, regardless of perception or interpretation, and that what we know is a faithful representation of reality out there.' It should be clear that two claims are being advanced here; two claims that do not *necessarily* follow from one another. First, there is the *ontological* claim that

'material reality exists'; second, is the *epistemological* claim that what we 'know is a faithful representation of reality'. But it is important to see that a materialist might accept the first ontological claim, without necessarily accepting the second epistemological claim. Materialism is a theory of existence (an ontological claim) and the epistemological claim is either superfluous, or will require further support. However, I doubt that anyone within IR would argue that what we 'know is a faithful representation of reality'.

13 Logical positivism, sometimes also known as logical empiricism scientific empiricism and consistent empiricism, was a school of philosophy founded in Vienna during the 1920s by a group of scientists, mathematicians and philosophers known as the Vienna Circle. Among its most prominent members were Moritz Schlick, Rudolf Carnap and Kurt Godel. They derived much of their inspiration from the writings of Ernst Mach, Gottlob Frege, Bertrand Russell, Ludwig Wittgenstein and George Edward Moore. The logical positivists made a concerted effort to clarify the language of science by showing that the content of scientific theories could be reduced to truths of logic and mathematics coupled with propositions referring to sense experience. Members of the group shared a distaste for metaphysical speculation and considered metaphysical claims about reality to be meaningless. For the logical positivists only two forms of knowledge were valid; that based on reason and that based on experience. The main theses of Logical Positivism may be briefly stated as follows. (1) A proposition, or a statement, is factually meaningful only if it is verifiable. This is understood in the sense that the proposition can be judged probable from experience, not in the sense that its truth can be conclusively established by experience. (2) A proposition is verifiable only if it is either an experiential proposition or one from which some experiential proposition can be deduced in conjunction with other premises. (3) That which cannot be experienced cannot be said to exist. Theoretical entities are treated instrumentally, 'as if' they existed. (4) A proposition is formally meaningful only if it is true by virtue of the definitions of its terms – that is, tautological. (5) The laws of logic and mathematics are all tautological. (6) A proposition is literally meaningful only if it is either verifiable or tautological. (7) Since metaphysical statements are neither verifiable nor tautological, they are literally meaningless. (8) Since ethical, aesthetical and theological statements also fail to meet the same conditions, they too are cognitively meaningless – although they may possess 'emotive' meaning. (9) Since metaphysics, ethics, philosophy of religion and aesthetics are all eliminated, the only tasks of philosophy are clarification and analysis. Thus, the propositions of philosophy are linguistic, not factual, and philosophy is a department of logic; hence the label logical positivism.

14 Easton, in a claim that is a mirror image of contemporary calls for a 'return to normative theory' (Frost, 1986, 1996; Smith, 1992), argued that 'the dominance of historical and ethical theory' had excluded empirical theory from the discipline (Easton, 1953, 1965: ix).

15 Understanding why positivism came to be referred to as an epistemology is a simple task once one understands the manner in which logical positivism claimed only scientific knowledge could be considered real knowledge (a position few positivists would hold today; Nicholson, 1996a). There are two important reasons why this conflation of epistemology and positivism should be rejected. First, those working on issues related to the philosophy of social science within IR should be able to take a much more sophisticated approach, and second positivism should no more be allowed to appropriate the label knowledge (epistemology) than that of science.

16 Again, as with positivism and other such positions, there is no easy definition of scientific realism. However, within the philosophy of science scientific realism has been the dominant alternative to positivism. Hence, one way to understand scientific realism is as a non-positivist philosophy of science. As such it rejects the tenets of positivism outlined in notes 5 and 12. Scientific realism is the belief that the objects posited in scientific theories should be considered to be real and their ontological status subject to test. Scientific theories and hypotheses, even about unobservable entities, are attempts to grasp the nature of real entities and processes that are independent of our theories about them – even non-observable ones. Scientific realism does not deny that theories are dependent on minds (or languages or judgements) if only because such theories have to be expressed by minds and in languages. It accepts that we construct theoretical accounts of the world, but it denies that these theoretical accounts exhaust the world. As should be clear, scientific realism is not committed to the view that all the objects posited in theories exist. Whether or not an entity posited in a theory exists is what science tries to discover. Some theories simply get the world wrong. Its point is that, and contrary to a positivist philosophy of science, scientists, in their practices, do treat theoretical entities as real. It has a fallibilist view of knowledge, since knowledge claims constructed in scientific theories are of a realm independent of specific claims. This means that scientific realism accepts epistemological relativism; all knowledge claims are socially constructed. Moreover, given that the world is populated by a diverse range of objects that science tries to grasp, no one epistemological and/or methodological position can be privileged. This is essentially what Feyerabend meant by 'anything goes' (Feyerabend, 1975). However, since competing knowledge claims are claims about a realm of independent objects, then some claims may be better than others. This means that despite the acceptance of epistemological relativism, judgmental rationalism (the possibility of rational judgement) may well be possible. Social realism refers to the assumption that social reality – social structures and related social phenomena – has an existence over and above the existence of individual members of society, and independent of our conception or perception of them. Contrary to positivists, social realists consider that the purpose of science is to provide explanatory knowledge. For the realist, there is an important distinction between explanation and prediction, a distinction which positivism conflates. Social realists believe that explanation should be the primary objective. They claim that explanation in both the natural and social sciences should entail going beyond simply demonstrating that phenomena are instances of some observed regularity, and uncovering the underlying and often-invisible mechanisms that causally connect them. Frequently, this means postulating the existence of unobservable phenomena and processes that are unfamiliar to us. Realists believe that only by doing this will it be possible to get beyond the mere 'appearance' of things to deeper forms of explanation.

17 The most important of which are: (i) the treatment of theoretical terms; (ii) the account of causation – scientific realists reject Hume's account and focus their attention on causal mechanisms rather than constant conjunctions; (iii) no epistemological position is privileged in scientific realism. In fact, the only thing scientific realism shares with positivism is a commitment to science. Where they differ, however, is what they think science entails (Psillos, 1999).

18 Adler (Chapter 5 in this volume) accepts Smith's account. However, Smith's own account is essentially positivist in his own terms; (i) Smith must believe that there are people who regularly hold such views (his own regularity principle); (ii) Smith can only be understood as asserting that his account of positivism accurately reflects something of the 'facts' of the position and these four principles are not simply a reflection of his values (the fact/value distinction); (iii) Smith supplies empirical evidence in support of his factual claims (the commitment to empirical validation); (iv) Smith applies all of these principles to a social object (positivism) (the commitment to the unity of science). Hence, Smith's account of positivism is a positivist account if his definition is correct. The point of this is not to demonstrate that positivists would reject Smith's four criteria. In fact, most positivists would accept them. But then again so would many others who would not wish to be considered positivists (including Smith himself).

19 Empiricism is the philosophical belief that all knowledge is ultimately based on experience, that is, information received through the senses. It is opposed to rationalism and denies that we have any a priori knowledge or innate ideas: we owe all our concepts to experience of the world. Rationalism is the opposite epistemological position that claims that reason rather than sense-experience is the foundation of certainty in knowledge (Aune, 1970).

20 See King et al., 1994, Nicholson, 1996a, and Patomäki, 1996 for alternative discussions of cause; see also Deutsch, 1996.

21 Waltz's acceptance that the social world is socially constructed problematizes the use of the label 'constructivist' to indicate that those falling under the label share at least one thing in common – the idea that the social world is socially constructed; if this is the key factor, then Waltz is also a constructivist – a conclusion few constructivists would be willing to accept.

Bibliography

Abbott, G.F. (1970) *Thucydides: A Study in Historical Reality*. New York: Russell and Russell.

Adler, Emanuel (1997) 'Seizing the Middle Ground: Constructivism in World Politics', *European Journal of International Relations*, 3 (3): 319–63.

Adorno, Theodor, Abert, Hans, Dahrendorf, Ralf et al. (eds) (1976) *The Positivist Dispute in German Sociology*. London: Heinemann.

Alker, Hayward (1965) *Mathematics and Politics*. New York: Macmillan.

Alker, Hayward (1996) *Rediscoveries and Reformulations: Humanistic Methodolgies for International Relations*. Cambridge: Cambridge University Press.

Aliotta, Antonio (1914) *The Idealistic Reaction Against Science* (trans. Agnes McCaskill). London: Macmillan.

Althusser, Louis and Balibar, Etienne (1970) *Reading Capital*. London: New Left Books.

Angell, Norman (1947) *The Steep Places*. London: Hamish Hamilton.

Appleyard, Brian (1992) *Understanding the Present: Science and the Soul of Modern Man*. London: Pan Books.

Ashley, Richard (1984) 'The Poverty of Neorealism', *International Organization*, 38 (2): 225–86.

Ashley, Richard K. (1987) 'The Geopolitics of Geopolitical Space', *Alternatives*, XII: 403–34.

Ashley, Richard K. (1989) 'Living on Border Lines: Man, Poststructuralism, and War', in James Der Derian and Michael J. Shapiro (eds), *International/Intertextual Relations: Postmodern Readings of World Politics*. Lexington: Lexington Books. pp. 259–321.

Ashley, Richard K. (1996) 'The Achievements of Poststructuralism', in Steve Smith, Ken Booth and Marysia Zalewski (eds), *International Theory: Positivism and Beyond*. Cambridge: Cambridge University Press. pp. 240–53.

Ashley, R.K. and Walker, R.B.J. (1990) 'Reading Dissidence/Writing the Discipline: Crisis and the Question of Sovereignty in International Studies', *International Studies Quarterly*, 32 (4): 367–416.

Aune, Bruce (1970) *Rationalism, Empricism and Prgamatism: An Introduction*. New York: Random House.

Bagby, Laurie M. Johnson (1994) 'The Use and Abuse of Thucydides in International Relations', *International Organization*, 48 (1): 131–53.

Bain, William (2000) 'Deconfusing Morgenthau: Moral Inquiry and Classical Realism Reconsidered', *Review of International Studies*, 26 (3): 445–64.

Banks, Michael (1984) 'The Evolution of International Relations Theory', in Michael Banks (ed.), *Conflict in World Society*. Brighton: Wheatsheaf Books. pp. 3–21.

Banks, Michael (1985) 'The Inter-Paradigm Debate', in Margot Light and A.J.R. Groom (eds), *International Relations: A Handbook of Current Theory*. London: Francis Pinter. pp. 7–26.

Bauman, Zygmunt (1978) *Hermeneutics and Social Science*. London: Hutchinson.

Bhaskar, Roy (1978) *A Realist Theory of Science*, 2nd edn. Brighton: Harvester.

Bhaskar, Roy (1979) *The Possibility of Naturalism: A Philosophical Critique of the Contemporary Human Sciences*, 2nd edn. Brighton: Harvester.

Bhaskar, Roy (1986) *Scientific Realism and Human Emancipation*. London: Verso.

Biersteker, Thomas J. (1989) 'Critical Reflections on Post-Positivism in International Relations', *International Studies Quarterly*, 33: 263–7.

Bluhm, William T. (1967) 'Thucydides', in Paul Edwards (ed.), *The Encyclopedia of Philosophy*: New York: Macmillan. p. 123.

Bohman, James (1991) *New Philosophy of Social Science*. Cambridge: Polity.

Bosanquet, Bernard (1899) *The Philosophical Theory of the State*. London: Macmillan.

Boucher, David (1998) *Political Theories of International Relations: From Thucydides to the Present*. Oxford: Oxford University Press.

Bourdieu, Pierre (1977) *Outline of a Theory of Practice*. Cambridge: Cambridge University Press.

Brecht, Arnold (1959) *Political Theory*. Princeton: Princeton University Press.

Brodribb, Somer (1992) *Nothing Mat(t)ers: A Feminist Critique of Postmodernism*. Melbourne: Spinifex Press.

Brown, Chris (1994) 'Critical Theory and Postmodernism in International Relations', in A.J.R. Groom and Margot Light (eds), *Contemporary International Relations: A Guide To Theory*. London: Pinter Publishers. pp. 56–68.

Brown, S.C. (ed.) (1979) *Philosophical Disputes in the Social Sciences*. Brighton: Harvester Press.

Bull, Hedley (1969) 'International Theory: The Case for a Classical Approach', in James Rosenau (ed.), *Contending Approaches to International Politics*. Princeton: Princeton University Press. pp. 20–38.

Bunge, Mario (1963) *The Myth of Simplicity: Problems of Scientific Philosophy*. Englewood Cliffs: Prentice Hall.

Bunge, Mario (1996) *Finding Philosophy in Social Science*. London: Yale University Press.

Burchill, Scott and Linklater, Andrew (1996) 'Introduction', in Scott Burchill and Andrew Linklater (eds), *Theories of International Relations*. London: Macmillan. pp. 1–27.

Bury, J.B. (1975) *History of Greece*, 4th edn. New York: Macmillan.

Butterfield, Herbert (1951) 'The Scientific versus the Moralistic Approach to International Affairs', *International Affairs*, 27: 411–22.

Callinicos, Alex (1990) *Against Postmodernism: A Marxist Critique*. New York: St Martins Press.

Campbell, David (1988) 'Recent Changes in Social Theory: Questions for International Relations', in R. Higgott (ed.), *New Directions in International Relations: Australian Perspectives*. Canberra: Australian National University. pp. 11–65.

Campbell, David (1992) *Writing Security: United States Foreign Policy and the Politics of Identity.* Manchester: Manchester University Press.

Campbell, David (1998a) *Writing Security: United States Foreign Policy and the Politics of Identity*, rev. edn. Manchester: Manchester University Press.

Campbell, David (1998b) 'MetaBosnia: Narratives of the Bosnian War', *Review of International Studies*, 24 (2): 261–81.

Campbell, David, (1999) 'Contra Wight: The Errors of a Premature Writing', *Review of International Studies*, 25 (2): 317–21.

Campbell, David, (2001) 'International Engagements – The Politics of North American International Relations Theory', *Political Theory*, 29 (3): 432–48.

Carlsnaes, Walter (1986) *Ideology and Foreign Policy.* Oxford: Blackwell.

Carlsnaes, Walter (1992) 'The Agent–Structure Problem in Foreign Policy Analysis', *International Studies Quarterly*, 36 (3): 245–70.

Carr, E.H. (1946) *The Twenty Years Crisis, 1919–39*, 2nd edn. London: Macmillan.

Chalmers, Alan F. (1992) *What is This Thing called Science?*, 2nd edn. Buckingham: Open University Press.

Christensen, Thomas J. and Snyder, Jack (1997) 'Evaluating Theories', *American Political Science Review*, 91 (4): 919–22.

Collin, Finn (1985) *Theory and Understanding: A Critique of Interpretive Social Science.* Oxford: Blackwell.

Comte, Auguste ([1854] 2000) *The Positive Philosophy of Auguste Comte.* Kitchner: Batoche Books.

Cox, R. (1981) 'Social Forces, States and World Orders: Beyond International Relations Theory', *Millennium: Journal of International Studies*, 10 (2): 125–55.

Davidson, Donal (1963) 'Actions, Reasons and Causes', *Journal of Philosophy*, 60: 685–700.

Der Derian, James and Shapiro, Michael J. (eds) (1989) *International/Intertextual Relations: Postmodern Readings of World Politics.* Lexington: Lexington Books.

Derrida, Jacques (1988) 'Structure, Sign and Play in the Discourse of the Human Sciences', in David Lodge (ed.), *Modern Criticism and Theory.* Harlow: Longman. pp. 108–24.

Dessler, David (1989) 'What's at Stake in the Agent–Structure Debate?', *International Organization*, 43 (3): 441–73.

Dessler, David (1991) 'Beyond Correlations: Towards a Causal Theory of War', *International Studies Quarterly*, 35: 337–55.

Dessler, David (1999) 'Constructivism within a Positivist Social Science', *Review of International Studies*, 25 (1): 123–37.

Deutsch, Karl W. (1953) *Nationalism and Social Communication.* Cambridge, MA: MIT Press.

Deutsch, Karl W. (1964) *The Nerves of Government.* New York: The Free Press.

Deutsch, Karl W. (1966) 'Recent Trends in Research Methods in Political Science', in C. Charlesworth James (ed.), *A Design for Political Science: Scope, Objectives, and Methods.* Philadelphia: American Academy of Political and Social Science, monograph 10.

Devetak, Richard (1996) 'Postmodernism', in Scott Burchill and Andrew Linklater (eds), *Theories of International Relations*, London: Macmillan. pp. 179–209.

Dews, Peter (1987) *The Logics of Disintegration: Post-Structuralist Thought and the Claims of Critical Theory.* London: Verso.

Dilthey, Wilhelm (ed.) (1976) *Selected Writings.* Cambridge: Cambridge University Press.

Dingle, Herbert (1952) *The Scientific Adventure: Essays in the History and Philosophy of Science.* London: Pitman.

Doty, Roxanne Lynn (1997) 'Aporia: A Critical Exploration of the Agent–Structure Problematique in International Relations Theory', *European Journal of International Relations*, 3 (3): 365–92.

Doty, Roxanne Lynn (1999) 'A Reply to Colin Wight', *European Journal of International Relations*, 5 (3): 387–90.

Dougherty, James E. and Pfaltzgraff, Robert L. (1996) *Contending Theories of International Relations: A Comprehensive Survey*, 4th edn. New York and Harlow, UK: Longman.

Dunbar, Robin (1995) *The Trouble with Science.* London: Faber and Faber.

Dunne, Timothy (1998) *Inventing International Society: A History of the English School.* Basingstoke: Macmillan.

Durkheim, Emile ([1938] 1964) *The Rules of Sociological Method.* London: The Free Press.

Dyke, Vernon Van (1960) *Political Science: A Philosophical Analysis.* Stanford: Stanford University Press.

Eagleton, Terry (1996) *The Illusions of Postmodernism.* Cambridge, MA: Blackwell.

Easton, David (1953) *The Political System: An Inquiry into the State of Political Science.* New York: Alfred A. Knopf.

Easton, David (1965) *A Framework for Political Analysis.* Englewood Cliffs: Prentice Hall.

Elman, Colin and Elman, Miriam Fendius (1997) 'Evaluating Theories', *American Political Science Review*, 91 (4): 923–6.

Elshtain, Jean Bethke (1997) 'Feminist Inquiry and International Relations', in M. Doyle and J.G. Ikenberry (eds), *New Thinking in International Relations Theory.* Boulder: Westview. pp. 77–90.

Enloe, Cynthia H. (1990) *Bananas, Beaches and Bases: Making Feminist Sense of International Politics.* London: Pandora

Enloe, Cynthia H. (1993) *The Morning After: Sexual Politics At the End of the Cold War.* Berkeley: University of California Press.

Farrell, Frank B. (1996) *Subjectivity, Realism and Postmodernism.* Cambridge: Cambridge University Press.

Fay, Brian (1996) *Contemporary Philosophy of Social Science.* Oxford: Blackwell.

Ferguson, Yale H. and Mansbach, Richard W. (1988) *The Elusive Quest: Theory and International Politics.* Columbia: University of South Carolina Press.

Ferguson, Yale H. and Mansbach, Richard W. (1991) 'Between Celebration and Despair – Constructive Suggestions for Future International Theory', *International Studies Quarterly*, 35 (4): 363–86.

Feyerabend, Paul K. (1975) *Against Method: Outline of an Anarchistic Theory of Knowledge.* London: New Left Books.

Feyerabend, Paul K. (1981) *Realism, Rationalism and Scientific Method.* Cambridge: Cambridge University Press.

Feyerabend, Paul K. (1995) 'Three Interviews with Paul K. Feyerabend', *Telos*, 102: 115–48.

Foucault, Michel (1990) 'On Power', in Lawrence D. Kritzman (ed.), *Michel Foucault: Politics, Philosophy and Culture*, London: Routledge. pp. 96–119.

Friedman, Gil and Starr, Harvey (1997) *Agency, Structure and International Politics. From Ontology to Empirical Inquiry.* London: Routledge.

Frost, Mervyn (1986) *Towards a Normative Theory of International Relations.* Cambridge: Cambridge University Press.

Frost, Mervyn (1996) *Constitutive Theory: Towards an Ethics of International Relations.* New York: Cambridge.

Gadamer, H.G. (1977) *Philosophical Hermeneutics.* Berkeley: University of California Press.

Garnett, John C. (1984) *Commonsense and the Theory of International Politics.* London: Macmillan.

Garst, Daniel (1989) 'Thucydides and NeoRealism', *International Studies Quarterly*, 33 (1): 3–27.

George, Jim (1989) 'International Relations and the Search for Thinking Space: Another View of the Third Debate', *International Studies Quarterly*, 33: 269–79.

George, Jim (1994) *Discourses of Global Politics: A Critical (Re)Introduction to International Relations.* Boulder: Lynne Rienner.

George, Jim and Campbell, David (1990) 'Patterns of Dissent and the Celebration of Difference – Critical Social-Theory and International Relations', *International Studies Quarterly*, 34 (3): 269–93.

Gilpin, Robert (1986) 'The Richness of the Tradition of Political Realism', in Robert Keohane (ed.), *Neorealism and its Critics.* New York: Columbia University Press. pp. 301–21.

Gordon, Scott (1991) *The History and Philosophy of Social Science.* London: Routledge.

Griffiths, Martin (1992) *Realism, Idealism and International Politics: A Reinterpretation.* London: Routledge.

Griffiths, Martin and O'Callaghan, Terry (2001) 'The End of International Relations?', in Robert M.A. Crawford and Darryl S.L. Jarvis (eds), *International Relations – Still an American Social Science: Towards Diversity in International Thought,* Albany: State University of New York. pp. 187–201.

Guetzkow, Harold (1950) 'Long Range Research in International Relations', *American Perspective*, 4 (Fall): 485–507.

Gunnell, John G. (1975) *Philosophy, Science, and Political Inquiry.* Morristowns, NJ: General Learning Press.

Gunnell, John G. (1998) *The Orders of Discourse: Philosophy, Social Science and Politics.* Oxford: Rowman and Littlefield.

Guzzini, Stefano (1993) 'Structural Power: The Limits of Neorealist Power Analysis', *International Organization*, 47 (3): 445–78.

Guzzini, Stefano (1998) *Realism in International Relations and International Political Economy: The Continuing Story of a Death Foretold*. London: Routledge.

Guzzini, Stefano (2000) 'A Reconstruction of Constructivism in International Relations', *European Journal of International Relations*, 6 (2): 147–82.

Haack, Susan (1993) *Evidence and Inquiry: Towards Reconstruction in Epistemology.* Oxford: Blackwell.

Haas, Ernst B. (1991) 'Reason and Change in International Life', in Robert L. Rothstein (ed.), *The Evolution of Theory in International Relations.* Columbia: University of South Carolina Press. pp. 189–220.

Haas, Michael (1969) 'A Plea for Bridge Building in International Relations', in Klaus Knorr and James N. Rosenau (eds), *Contending Approaches to International Politics.* Princeton: Princeton University Press. pp. 158–76.

Habermas, Jurgen (1988) *On the Logic of the Social Sciences.* Cambridge: Polity.

Halfpenny, Peter (1982) *Positivism and Sociology.* London: George Allen & Unwin.

Halliday, Fred (1994) *Rethinking International Relations.* Basingstoke: Macmillan.

Halliday, Fred (1996) 'The Future of International Relations: Fears and Hopes', in Steve Smith, Ken Booth and Marysia Zalewski (eds), *International Theory: Positivism and Beyond.* Cambridge: Cambridge University Press. pp. 318–27.

Harding, Sandra (1991) *Whose Science Whose Knowledge?* Milton Keynes: Open University Press.

Harland, Richard (1987) *Superstructuralism: The Philosophy of Structuralism and Poststructuralism.* London: Routledge.

Harland, Richard (1993) *Beyond Superstructuralism.* London: Routledge.

Harré, Rom and Madden, Edward H. (1975) *Causal Powers: A Theory of Natural Necessity.* Oxford: Blackwell.

Hartsock, Nancy (1983) 'The Feminist Standpoint: Developing the Ground for Specifically Feminist Historical Materialism', in Sandra Harding and Merrill Hintikka (eds), *Discovering Reality: Feminist Perspectives on Epistemology, Metaphysics and the Philosophy of Science.* Dordecht: D. Reidel. pp. 283–310.

Herman, C.F. and Peacock, G. (1987) 'The Evolution and Future of Theoretical Research in Comparative Study of Foreign Policy', in C.F. Herman (ed.), *New Directions in the Study of Foreign Policy.* Boston: Allen & Unwin. pp. 13–32.

Hoffman, M. (1987) 'Critical Theory and the Inter-Paradigm Debate', *Millennium: Journal of International Studies*, 16 (2): 231–49.

Hoffman, Stanley (1961) 'International Relations, the Long Road to Theory', in James N. Rosenau (ed.), *International Politics and Foreign Policy.* Glencoe: The Free Press. pp. 421–37.

Hoffman, Stanley, (1977) 'An American Social Science: International Relations', *Daedalus*, 106 (3): 41–60.

Hollis, Martin (1994) *The Philosophy of Social Science: An Introduction.* Cambridge: Cambridge University Press.

Hollis, Martin (1996) 'The Last Post?', in Steve Smith, Ken Booth and Marysia Zalewski (eds), *International Theory: Positivism and Beyond.* Cambridge: Cambridge University Press. pp. 301–8.

Hollis, Martin and Smith, Steve (1990) *Explaining and Understanding International Relations.* Oxford: Clarendon Press.

Hollis, Martin and Smith, Steve (1991) 'Beware of Gurus: Structure and Action in International Relations', *Review of International Studies*, 17 (3): 393–410.

Hollis, Martin and Smith, Steve (1992) 'Structure and Action: Further Comment', *Review of International Studies*, 18 (2): 187–8.

Hollis, Martin and Smith, Steve (1994) 'Two Stories About Structure and Agency', *Review of International Studies*, 20 (3): 241–51.

Hollis, Martin and Smith, Steve (1996) 'A Response: Why Epistemology Matters in International Theory', *Review of International Studies*, 22 (1): 111–6.

Holsti, K.J. (1985) *The Dividing Discipline: Hegemony and Diversity in International Theory.* Boston: Allen & Unwin.

Holsti, Kal (1989) 'Mirror, Mirror on the Wall, Which Are the Fairest Theories of All', *International Studies Quarterly*, 33 (2): 255–61.

Holsti, Kal J. (1998) 'Scholarship in an Era of Anxiety: The Study of International Relations During the Cold War', *Review of International Studies*, 24 (Special Issue): 17–46.

Honig, Jan Wilhelm (1996) 'Totalitarianism and Realism: Morgenthau's German Years', in Benjamin Frankel (ed.), *Roots of Realism.* London: Frank Cass. pp. 283–313.

Hoole, Francis W. and Zinnes, Dina A. (eds) (1976) *Quantitative International Politics: An Appraisal.* London: Praeger.

Hopf, Ted (1998) 'The Promise of Constructivism in International Relations Theory', *International Security*, 23 (1): 171–201.

Horkheimer, Max (1982) *Critical Theory: Selected Essays.* New York: Continuum.

Horkheimer, Max (1993) *Between Philosophy and Social Science: Selected Early Writings.* Cambridge, MA: MIT Press.

Husserl, Edmund (1982) *Ideas Pertaining to a Pure Phenomenology and to a Phenomenological Philosophy* (trans. F. Kersten). The Hague: M. Nijhoff.

Jackson, Leonard (1991) *The Poverty of Structuralism.* Harlow: Longman.

Jarvis, D.S.L. (2000) *International Relations and the Challenge of Postmodernism.* Columbia: University of Southern Carolina.

Jessop, Bob (1990) *State Theory: Putting Capitalist States in their Place.* Cambridge: Polity.

Jørgenson, Knud Erik, (2000) 'Continental IR Theory: The Best Kept Secret', *European Journal of International Relations*, 6 (1): 9–42.

Kaplan, Abraham David Hannath (1964) *The Conduct of Inquiry: Methodology for Behavioral Science.* San Francisco: Chandler.

Kaplan, Morton (1957) *System and Process in International Politics.* New York: John Wiley.

Kaplan, Morton (1969) 'The New Great Debate: Traditionalism vs. Science in International Relations', in James Rosenau (ed.), *Contending Approaches to International Politics.* Princeton: Princeton University Press. pp. 39–61.

Katzenstein, Peter J., Keohane, Robert O. and Krasner, Stephen D. (1998) 'International Organization and the Study of World Politics', *International Organization*, 52 (4): 645–85.

Keohane, Robert O. (1989) 'International Institutions: Two Approaches', in Robert O. Keohane (ed.), *International Institutions and State Power.* Boulder: Westview Press. pp. 158–79.

King, Gary, Keohane, Robert O. and Verba, Sidney (1994) *Designing Social Inquiry: Scientific Inference in Qualitative Research.* Princeton: Princeton University Press.

Knorr, Klaus and Rosenau, James N. (1969a) *Contending Approaches to International Politics.* Princeton: Princeton University Press.

Knorr, Klaus and Rosenau, James N. (1969b) 'Tradition and Science in the Study of International Politics', in Klaus Knorr and James N. Rosenau (eds), *Contending Approaches to International Politics.* Princeton: Princeton University Press. pp. 3–19.

Kolakowski, Leszek (1969) *The Alienation of Reason: A History of Positivist Thought* (trans. Norbert Guterman). New York: Anchor Books.

Kratochwil, Friedrich V. (1989) *Rules, Norms and Decisions: On the Conditions of Practical and Legal Reasoning in International Relations and Domestic Affairs.* Cambridge: Cambridge University Press.

Kratochwil, Friedrich V. (2000) 'Constructing a New Orthodoxy? Wendt's "Social Theory of International Politics" and the Constructivist Challenge', *Millennium: Journal of International Studies*, 29 (1): 73–104.

Kuhn, Thomas (1962) *The Structure of Scientific Revolutions.* Chicago: University of Chicago Press.

Kuhn, Thomas S. (1970) 'Reflections on my Critics', in Imre Lakatos and Alan Musgrave (eds), *Criticism and the Growth of Knowledge*. Cambridge: Cambridge University Press. pp. 231–78.

Kuhn, Thomas S. (1982) 'Commensurability, Comparability, Communicability', paper presented at the PSA, East Lansing, Michigan.

Kuhn, Thomas S. (1990) 'Dubbing and Redubbing: The Vulnerability of Rigid Designation', in C. Wade Savage (ed.), *Minnesota Studies in the Philosophy of Science*. Minneapolis: University of Minnesota Press. pp. 298–318.

Kurzweil, Edith (1980) *The Age of Structuralism: Lévi-Strauss to Foucault*. New York: Columbia University Press.

Laffey, Mark and Weldes, Jutta (1997) 'Beyond Belief: Ideas and Symbolic Technologies in the study of International Relations', *European Journal of International Relations*, 3 (2): 193–237.

Lakatos, Imre (1970) 'Falsification and the Methodology of Scientific Research', in Imre Lakatos and Alan Musgrave (eds), *Criticism and the Growth of Knowledge*. Cambridge: Cambridge University Press. pp. 91–195.

Lane, Robert E. (1966) 'The Decline of Politics and Ideology in a Knowledgable Society', *American Sociological Review*, 31 (October): 656–7.

Lane, Ruth (1996) 'Positivism, Scientific Realism and Political Science', *Journal of Theoretical Politics*, 8 (3): 361–82.

Lapid, Yosef (1989) 'The Third Debate: On the Prospects of International Theory in a Post-Positivist Era', *International Studies Quarterly*, 33 (22): 235–54.

Laski, Harold J. (1935) *The State in Theory and Practice*. London: George Allen & Unwin.

Lasswell, Harold Dwight and Kaplan, Abraham (1950) *Power and Society: A Framework for Political Inquiry*. Oxford: Oxford University Press.

Laudan, Larry (1996) *Beyond Positivism and Relativism: Theory, Method and Evidence*. Boulder: Westview.

Layder, Derek (1994) *Understanding Social Theory*. London: Sage.

Lerner, Daniel (1965) *Cause and Effect*. London: The Free Press.

Linklater, Andrew (1990) *Beyond Realism and Marxism: Critical Theory and International Relations*. Basingstoke: Macmillan.

Lijphart, Arend (1974a) 'International Relations Theory: Great Debates and Lesser Debates', *International Social Science Journal*, 26 (1): 11–21.

Lijphart, Arend (1974b) 'The Structure of the Theoretical Revolution in International Relations', *International Studies Quarterly* 18 (1): 41–74.

Little, Richard (1980) 'The Evolution of International Relations as a Social Science', in R.C. Kent and G.P. Nielsson (eds), *The Study and Teaching of International Relations: A Perspective on Mid-Career Education*. London: Frances Pinter. pp. 1–27.

Little, Richard and Smith, Michael (eds) (1991) *Perspectives on World Politics*. London: Routledge.

Long, David (1995) 'Conclusion: Inter-war Idealism, Liberal Internationalism and Contemporary International Theory', in David Long and Peter Wilson (eds),

Thinkers of the Twenty Years Crisis. Oxford: Clarendon Press. pp. 302–28.

Long, David and Wilson, Peter (eds) (1995) *Thinkers of the Twenty Years Crisis*. Oxford: Clarendon Press.

MacIntyre, Alasdair (1973) 'The Idea of Social Science', in Alan Ryan (ed.), *The Philosophy of Social Explanation*. Oxford: Oxford University Press. pp. 15–32.

Mackenzie, W.J.M. (1967) *Politics and Social Science*. Harmondsworth: Penguin.

Mackenzie, W.J.M. (1971) *The Study of Political Science Today*. London: Macmillan.

Mackinnon, Edward A. (ed.) (1972) *The Problem of Scientific Realism*. New York: Appleton–Century–Crofts.

Maclean, John (1981) 'Marxist Epistemology, Explanations of Change and the Study of International Relations', in Barry Buzan and R.J. Barry Jones (eds), *Change in the Study of International Relations: The Evaded Dimension*. London: Frances Pinter. pp. 46–67.

Manicas, Peter T. (1987) *A History and Philosophy of the Social Sciences*. London: Blackwell.

Mann, Michael (1996) 'Authoritarian and Liberal Militarism: A Contribution from Comparative and Historical Sociology', in Steve Smith, Ken Booth and Marysia Zalewski (eds), *International Theory: Positivism and Beyond*. Cambridge: Cambridge University Press. pp. 221–39.

Marx, Karl (1962) 'The Eighteenth Brumaire of Louis Napoleon', in *Karl Marx and Fredrick Engels: Selected Works*. Moscow: Foreign Languages Publishing House.

Marx, Karl (1966) *Capital*, vol. III. London: Lawrence & Wishart.

Masterman, Margaret (1970) 'The Nature of a Paradigm', in Imre Lakatos and Alan Musgrave (eds), *Criticism and the Growth of Knowledge*. Cambridge: Cambridge University Press. pp. 59–89.

Meehan, Eugene J. (1968) *Explanation in Social Science: A System Paradigm*. Homewood: Dorsey Press.

Morgenthau, Hans J. (1940) 'Positivism, Functionalism and International Law', *American Journal of International Law*, 34 (April): 260–84.

Morgenthau, Hans J. (1946) *Scientific Man vs. Power Politics*. Chicago: University of Chicago Press.

Morgenthau, Hans J. (1948) *Politics Among Nations: The Struggle for Power and Peace*. 5th edn. New York: Alfred A. Knopf.

Morgenthau, Hans J. (1972) *Science: Servant or Master?* New York: W.W. Norton.

Morrow, Raymond A. and Brown, David D. (1994) *Critical Theory and Methodology*. London: Sage.

Nagel, Ernest (1961) *The Structure of Science*. New York: Harcourt, Brace and World.

Neufeld, Mark (1994) 'Reflexivity and International Relations Theory', in Claire Turenne Sjolander and Wayne S. Cox (eds), *Beyond Positivism: Critical Reflections on International Relations*. London: Lynne Rienner. pp. 11–35.

Neufeld, Mark (1995) *The Restructuring of International Relations Theory*. Cambridge: Cambridge University Press.

Nicholson, Linda J. (ed.) (1993) *Feminism/ Postmodernism*. New York: Routledge.

Nicholson, Michael (1983) *The Scientific Analysis of Social Behaviour: A Defence of Empiricism in Social Science*. London: Pinter.

Nicholson, Michael (1996a) *Causes and Consequences in International Relations: A Conceptual Study*. London: Pinter.

Nicholson, Michael (1996b) 'The Continued Significance of Positivism?', in Steve Smith, Ken Booth and Marysia Zalewski (eds), *International Theory: Positivism and Beyond*. Cambridge: Cambridge University Press. pp. 128–45.

Nicholson, Michael (2000) 'What's the Use of International Relations?', *Review of International Studies*, 26 (2): 183–98.

Nicholson, Michael and Bennett, Peter (1994) 'The Epistemology of International Relations', in A.J.R. Groom and Margot Light (eds), *Contemporary International Relations: A Guide to Theory*. London: Pinter; New York: St Martin's Press. pp. 197–205.

Ogley, Roderick C. (1981) 'International Relations: Poetry, Prescription or Science', *Millennium: Journal of International Studies*, 10 (2): 170–86.

Oldroyd, David (1986) *The Arch of Knowledge*. London: Methuen.

Onuf, Nicholas Greenwood (1989) *World of Our Making: Rules and Rule in Social Theory and International Relations*. Columbia: University of South Carolina Press.

Onuf, Nicholas Greenwood (1998) *The Republican Legacy in International Thought*. Cambridge: Cambridge University Press.

Osterud, Oyvind (1996) 'Antinomies of Postmodernism in International Studies', *Journal of Peace Research*, 33 (4): 385–90.

Osterud, Oyvind, (1997) 'Focus on Postmodernism', *Journal of Peace Research*, 34 (3): 337–8.

Outhwaite, William (1975) *Understanding Social Life: The Method Called 'Verstehen'*. London: Allen & Unwin.

Outhwaite, William (1987) *New Philosophies of Social Science: Realism Hermeneutics and Critical Theory*. London: Macmillan.

Owen, David (ed.) (1997) *Sociology after Postmodernism*. London: Sage.

Patomäki, Heikki, (1996) 'How to Tell Better Stories About World Politics', *European Journal of International Relations*, 2 (1): 101–33.

Patomäki, Heikki (1997) 'The Rhetorical Strategies and the Misleading Nature of Attacks on "Postmodernism": Reply', *Journal of Peace Research*, 34 (3): 325–9.

Patomäki, Heikki (2001) *After International Relations. Critical Realism and the (Re)Construction of World Politics*. London: Routledge.

Patomäki, Heikki and Wight, Colin (2000) 'After PostPositivism: The Promise of Critical Realism', *International Studies Quarterly*, 44 (2): 213–37.

Porpora, Douglas V. (1987) *The Concept of Social Structure*. Westport: Greenwood.

Price, Richard and Reus-Smit, Christian (1998) 'Dangerous Liaisons? Critical International Theory and Constructivism', *European Journal of International Relations*, 4 (3): 259–94.

Psillos, Stathis (1999) *Scientific Realism*. London: Routledge.

Puchala, Donald J. (1991) 'Woe to the Orphans of the Scientific Revolution', in Robert L. Rothstein (ed.), *The Evolution of Theory in International Relations*. Columbia: University of South Carolina Press. pp. 39–60.

Rabinow, Dreyfus (1982) *Michel Foucault: Beyond Structuralism and Hermeneutics*. Chicago: University of Chicago Press.

Rengger, Nicholas J. (1989) 'Incommensurability, International Theory and the Fragmentation of Western Culture', in J. Gibbins (ed.), *Contemporary Political Culture: Politics in a Postmodern Age*. London: Sage. pp. 237–50.

Rengger, N. and Hoffman, M. (1990) 'Modernism, Post-Modernism and International Relations', in J. Doherty (ed.), *Postmodernism in the Social Sciences*. London: Macmillan. pp. 127–47.

Reynolds, Charles (1973) *Theory and Explanation in International Politics*. London: Robertson.

Rosenau, James N. (1971) *The Scientific Study of Foreign Policy*. New York: The Free Press.

Rosenau, Pauline (1990) 'Once Again into the Fray: International Relations Confronts the Humanities', *Millennium: Journal of International Studies*, 19 (1): 83–110.

Rosenau, Pauline (1992) *Post-modernisn and the Social Sciences: Insights, Inroads and Intrusions*. Princeton: Princeton University Press.

Ruggie, John Gerard (1998) *Constructing the World Polity: Essays On International Institutionalization*. London: Routledge.

Ryan, Alan (1996) 'Hobbes's Political Philosophy', in Tom Sorell (ed.), *The Cambridge Companion to Hobbes*. Cambridge: Cambridge University Press. pp. 208–45.

Sankey, Howard (1994) *The Incommensurability Thesis*. Aldershot: Ashgate.

Sankey, Howard (1997) *Rationality, Relativism and Incommensurability*. Aldershot: Ashgate.

Schelling, Thomas C. (1960) *The Strategy of Conflict*. New York: Oxford University Press.

Schmidt, Brian (1998) *The Political Discourse of Anarchy: A Disciplinary History of International Relations*. Albany: State University of New York Press.

Searle, John R. (1995) *The Construction of Social Reality*. London: Penguin.

Shapiro, Ian and Wendt, Alexander (1992) 'The Difference that Realism Makes: Social Science and the Politics of Consent', *Politics and Society*, 20 (2): 197–223.

Singer, J. David (1961) 'The Level-of-Analysis Problem in International Relations', in Klaus Knorr and Sidney Verba (eds), *The International System: Theoretical Essays*. Princeton: Princeton University Press. pp. 77–92.

Singer, J. David (1969) 'The Incompleat Theorist: Insight Without Evidence', in Klaus Knorr and James N. Rosenau (eds), *Contending Approaches to International Politics*. Princeton: Princeton University Press. pp. 62–86.

Skocpol, T. (1987) 'The Dead End of Metatheory', *Contemporary Sociology*, 16 (1): 10–12.

Smith, Hazel (1996) 'The Silence of Academics: International Social Theory, Historical Materialism and Political Values', *Review of International Studies*, 22 (2): 191–212.

Smith, Steve (1987) 'Paradigm Dominance in International Relations: The Development of International Relations as a Social Science', *Millennium*, 16 (2): 186–206.

Smith, Steve (1992) 'The Forty Years Detour: The Resurgence of Normative Theory in International Relations', *Millennium*, 21 (3): 489–506.

Smith, Steve (1995) 'The Self Images of a Discipline: A Genealogy of International Relations Theory', in *International Relations Theory Today*, Cambridge: Polity. pp. 1–37.

Smith, Steve (1996) 'Positivism and Beyond', in Steve Smith, Ken Booth and Marysia Zalewski (eds), *International Theory: Positivism and Beyond*. Cambridge: Cambridge University Press. pp. 11–44.

Smith, Steve (1997) 'Epistemology, Postmodernism and International Relations Theory', *Journal of Peace Research*, 34 (3): 330–6.

Smith, Steve (2000) 'Wendt's World', *Review of International Studies*, 26 (1): 151–63.

Snyder, Richard C., Bruck, H.W. and Sapin, Burton (1954) *Decision-Making as an Approach to the Study of International Politics*. Princeton: Princeton University Press.

Snyder, Richard C., Bruck, H.W. and Sapin, Burton (eds) (1962) *Foreign Policy Decision-Making*. New York: The Free Press.

Sorell, Tom (ed.) (1996) 'Hobbes Scheme of the Sciences', in Tom Sorrell (ed.), *The Cambridge Companion to Hobbes*. Cambridge: Cambridge University Press. pp. 45–61.

Sørenson, G. (1998) 'IR after the Cold War', *Review of International Studies*, 24 (Special Issue): 83–100.

Stockman, Norman (1983) *Antipositivist Theories of the Sciences*. Dordrecht: Reidel.

Strauss, Leo (1953) *Natural Right and History*. Chicago: Chicago University Press.

Suganami, Hidemi (1996) *On the Causes of War*. Oxford: Oxford University Press.

Suganami, Hidemi (2000) 'Agents, Structures and Narratives', *European Journal of International Relations*, 5 (3): 365–86.

Sylvester, Christine (1993) *Feminist Theory and International Relations Theory in a Postmodern Era*. Cambridge: Cambridge University Press.

Taylor, Charles (1987) 'Overcoming Epistemology', in K. Baynes, J. Bohman and P.A. McCarthy (eds), *After Philosophy: End or Transformation?* Cambridge, MA: MIT Press. pp. 464–88.

Tellis, Ashley J. (1996) 'Political Realism: The Long March to Scientific Theory', in Benjamin Frankel (ed.), *Roots of Realism*. London: Frank Cass. pp. 3–94.

Thompson, John B. (ed.) (1981) *Hermeneutics and the Human Sciences*. Cambridge: Cambridge University Press.

Tickner, J. Ann (1992) *Gender in International Relations: Feminist Perspectives On Achieving Global Security*. New York: Columbia University Press.

Toulmin, Stephen (1970) 'Does the Distinction Between Normal and Revolutionary Science Hold Water?', in Imre Lakatos and Alan Musgrave (eds), *Criticism and the Growth of Knowledge*. Cambridge: Cambridge University Press. pp. 39–47.

Trigg, Roger (1993) *Rationality and Science: Can Science Explain Everything?* Oxford: Blackwell.

Tudor, Andrew (1982) *Beyond Empiricism: Philosophy of Science in Sociology*. London: Routledge & Kegan Paul.

Vasquez, John A. (1995) 'The Post-Positivist debate', in Ken Booth and Steve Smith (eds), *International Relations Theory Today*. Cambridge. Polity Press. pp. 217–40.

Vasquez, J.A. (1997a) 'War Endings: What Science and Constructivism Can Tell Us', *Millennium*, 26 (3): 651–78.

Vasquez, John A. (1997b) 'The Realist Paradigm and Degenerative versus Progressive Research Programs: An Appraisal of Neotraditional Research on Waltz's Balancing Proposition', *American Political Science Review*, 91 (4): 899–912.

Vasquez, John A. (1998) *The Power of Power Politics: From Classical Realism to Neotraditionalism*. Cambridge: Cambridge University Press.

Vico, Giambattista ([1744] 1984) *The New Science of Giambattista Vico: unabridged translation of the third edition*. London: Cornell University Press.

Viotti, Paul R. and Kauppi, Mark V. (1987) *International Relations Theory: Realism, Pluralism, Globalism*. New York: Macmillan.

Waever, Ole (1996) 'The Rise and Fall of the Interparadigm Debate', in Steve Smith, Ken Booth, and Marysia Zalewski (eds), *International Theory: Positivism and Beyond*. Cambridge: Cambridge University Press. pp. 149–85.

Walker, R.B.J. (1993) *Inside/Outside: International Relations as Political Theory*. Boulder: Lynne Rienner.

Wallace, William (1996) 'Truth and Power, Monks Technocrats: Theory and Practice in International Relations', *Review of International Studies*, 22 (3): 301–21.

Walt, Stephen M. (1997) 'Evaluating Theories', *American Political Science Review*, 91 (4): 931–4.

Waltz, Kenneth (1979) *Theory of International Politics*. Reading, MA: Addison–Wesley.

Waltz, Kenneth N. (1997) 'Evaluating Theories', *American Political Science Review*, 91 (4): 913–7.

Wasby, Stephen L. (1970) *Political Science – The Discipline and Its Dimensions*. New York: Scribner's.

Weber, Max (1949) *The Methodology of the Social Sciences* (trans. Edward A. Shils and Henry A. Finch). New York: The Free Press.

Wendt, Alexander E. (1987) 'The Agent–Structure Problem in International Relations Theory', *International Organization*, 41 (3): 335–70.

Wendt, Alexander, E. (1991) 'Bridging the Theory/Meta-Theory Gap in International Relations', *Review of International Studies*, 17 (4): 383–92.

Wendt, Alexander (1992) 'Anarchy is What States Make of it: The Social Construction of Power Politics', *International Organization*, 46 (2): 391–425.

Wendt, Alexander (1995) 'Constructing International Politics', *International Security*, 20 (1): 71–8.

Wendt, Alexander (1999) *Social Theory of International Relations*. Cambridge: Cambridge University Press.

Wendt, Alexander (2000) 'On Constitution and Causation in IR', *Review of International Studies*, 24 (Special Issue): 101–17.

Wight, Colin (1996) 'Incommensurability and Cross Paradigm Communication in International Relations Theory: What's the Frequency Kenneth?', *Millennium*, 25 (2): 291–319.

Wight, Colin (1999a) 'They Shoot Dead Horses Don't They? Locating Agency in the Agent–Structure Problematique', *European Journal of International Relations*, 5 (1): 109–42.

Wight, Colin (1999b) 'MetaCampbell: The Epistemological Problematics of Perspectivism', *Review of International Studies*, 25 (2): 311–6.

Wight, Colin (2000) 'Interpretation All the Way Down? A Reply to Roxanne Lynn Doty', *European Journal of International Relations*, 6 (3): 423–30.

Winch, Peter (1958) *The Idea of a Social Science*. London: Routledge and Kegan Paul.

Winch, Peter (1990) *The Idea of a Social Science*, 2nd edn. London: Routledge.

Wright, George Edward (1974) *Causality and Determinism: Woodbridge Lectures: 10*. London: Columbia University Press.

Wright, Quincy (1942) *A Study of War*. Chicago: University of Chicago Press.

Wright, Quincy (1962) *Preventing World War III: Some Proposals*. New York: Simon and Schuster.

Zalewski, Marysia (1993) 'Feminist Theory and International Relations', in Mike Bowker and Robin Brown (eds), *From Cold War to Collapse: Theory and World Politics in the 1980s*. Cambridge: Cambridge University Press. pp. 115–43.

- similarities between both of them are what make me more receptive to post-structuralism.

3

Rationalism v. Constructivism:
A Skeptical View

JAMES FEARON AND ALEXANDER WENDT

- are they that different?

could I go against this?

In the introduction to the fiftieth anniversary issue of *International Organization*, Peter Katzenstein, Robert Keohane and Stephen Krasner (1998) suggest that the main axis of debate in the field of international relations (IR) in the coming years is likely to be rationalism versus constructivism.[1] In at least one important respect, this would be a remarkable development. For whatever they are, rationalism and constructivism are not in the first instances theories of international politics. Rather, rationalism seems to refer to a methodological approach that may imply a philosophical position on what social explanation is and how it ought to work, the nature of which is debated. And constructivism seems to refer to a set of arguments about social explanation that may imply preferences over specific questions and methods of social inquiry, the nature of which are debated. If the field does focus on rationalism versus constructivism, then the central debate in IR will not be about international relations but rather about how to study international relations.

To be sure, the concern in IR with questions of method and philosophy of social science has precedents, in recent arguments over positivism and post-positivism and in the earlier debate over behavioralism versus historical traditionalism.[2] The terms of the emerging debate between rationalism and constructivism are different than these, but the concern with second- rather than first-order issues is similar.

One may reasonably ask whether progress in understanding international relations and improving human (and planetary) welfare is best served by structuring the field of IR in this way, as a battle of analytical paradigms. At the very least it can encourage scholars to be method-driven rather than problem-driven in their research, which may result

in important questions or answers being ignored if they are not amenable to the preferred paradigmatic fashion. For this chapter, however, we leave this important question aside. Supposing that 'rationalism v. constructivism' does orient some debate in IR in the coming years, we ask what the contrast amounts to. What are the 'isms' referred to? And do the differences between them provide grounds for a war of paradigms?

We answer the last question mainly in the negative. Although there are some important differences between the two approaches, we argue that there are also substantial areas of agreement, and where genuine differences exist they are as often complementarities as contradictions. Our objective is not to suggest that there is no need for discussion, or that rationalism and constructivism should or could be synthesized into one perspective. It is to suggest, rather, that the most interesting research is likely to be work that ignores zero-sum interpretations of their relationship and instead directly engages questions that cut cross the rationalist/constructivist boundary as it is commonly understood.[3]

A key argument towards this conclusion is that, in our view, rationalism and constructivism are most fruitfully viewed *pragmatically* as analytical tools, rather than as metaphysical positions or empirical descriptions of the world.[4] Since the ontological and empirical interpretations of the debate seem more common in the literature and lead to more zero-sum pictures, it may be useful to explain briefly why we resist them.

The ontological reading treats rationalism and constructivism as sets of assumptions about what social life is made of and what kinds of relationships exist among these elements. For example, *const-ructivism?.*

→ *these different ontologies guide the debate*

strongly argued - should I criticise Wendt's

from this perspective rationalism is usually seen as assuming an individualist ontology, in which wholes are reducible to interacting parts, and constructivism as assuming a holist ontology, in which parts exist only in relation to wholes. In each case, certain empirical arguments and analytical tools are prescribed or proscribed a priori as legitimate or illegitimate, scientific or unscientific, and thus the stage is set for a genuine war of paradigms.

It is important to understand these ontological issues, since failure to do so can lead to analytical tools or frameworks becoming *tacit* ontologies (Ruggie, 1983: 285), foreclosing potentially interesting lines of argument without justification. However, we do not believe this framing of the rationalist–constructivist debate is the most useful, for three reasons. First, the issues are by definition philosophical, and as such not likely to be settled soon, if ever, and almost certainly not by IR scholars. Second, although some rationalists and constructivists may in fact have strong ontological commitments, others may not, since there is no inherent *need* to commit to an ontology to work in these traditions. Just as quantum physicists can do their work without any idea how to interpret its ontological implications, social scientists too can proceed pragmatically, remaining agnostic about what society is 'really' made of. Finally, it seems doubtful that as a discipline we know so much about international life that we should rule out certain arguments a priori on purely philosophical grounds. Thus, while recognizing the role that ontological issues play in structuring the rationalist–constructivist debate, in this chapter we will largely avoid them, adopting a stance of ontological pluralism instead.[5]

A second way to frame the debate is in empirical terms, as a disagreement about substantive issues in the world like how often actors follow a logic of consequences or logic of appropriateness, or whether preferences really are exogenous or endogenous to a given social interaction. We explore some of these questions below, and find some genuine differences, but this too is not our preferred way to proceed. First, in their purest, most stripped-down forms, neither approach makes many interesting empirical predictions about the world. To a large extent it is only with the addition of auxiliary assumptions – a particular theory of preferences, for example – that such predictions emerge. Moreover, although one *can* interpret an assumption of, say, exogenous preferences, as a factual claim about a certain social system, there is no *need* to do so. It is perfectly legitimate to view it instead as merely a methodological convenience necessitated by the fact that one cannot study everything at once. As in the ontology case, there is always a danger here that analytical assumptions will become tacit empirical ones, but given sufficient methodological self-consciousness this problem can be avoided.

This brings us to the pragmatic interpretation of rationalism and constructivism, as analytical tools or lenses with which to theorize about world politics. Analytical lenses do not in themselves force the researcher to make ontological or empirical commitments. What makes a comparison of them interesting none the less is that they view society from opposing vantage points – roughly speaking, rationalism from the 'bottom-up' and constructivism from the 'top-down'. As a result they tend in practice to ask somewhat different questions and so bring different aspects of social life into focus. It would be surprising if this did not lead to different pictures of world politics, and thus to 'paradigmatic' debate about what world politics is really like. Emphasizing these differences would have been one way to write this chapter. Yet, in IR today there is ample perception already of conflict between rationalism and constructivism, in our view much of it unnecessary or ill-founded, based either on treating them in ontological or empirical terms or on misunderstandings about what they entail. Moreover, we are also struck by two areas of potential convergence that are insufficiently appreciated. First, the two approaches often yield *similar*, or at least complementary, accounts of international life. This redundancy may arise because in the end they are studying the same underlying reality. Second, even though their respective vantage points tend in practice to highlight some questions and not others, in many cases there may be much to be gained by using the tools of one to try to answer questions that tend to be asked primarily by the other. Such a cross-paradigmatic exchange of characteristic questions and answers is in our view the most fruitful way to advance not only these two research agendas, but more importantly, our understanding of world politics. With these considerations in mind, we shall write this chapter with a view toward deconstructing some of the supposed contradictions between the two approaches, and highlighting the convergences. Again, this is not to suggest that there are no differences, many of which we discuss below. But once viewed in an analytical, tool-kit fashion, we believe many putative disputes lose much of their force.

From this pragmatic stance, we seek to clarify what each approach brings to the table and how they relate. In standard representations of the debate, two issues seem most at stake: (1) whether and how ideas matter in world politics, and (2) the relationship between international actors and the structures in which they are embedded. These are large issues and we do not attempt a full discussion of both here. We will argue, however, that on the first issue there is considerably less difference than is often thought. Rationalism is sometimes portrayed as emphasizing material as opposed to ideational factors, but this misunderstands what is entailed by the approach.

This allows us to focus most of our attention on the second issue. Here it seems useful to begin by dividing the debate into two issues, conceptions of structure and conceptions of agency. In the literature it has become increasingly common to assume that one approach is agent-centric and one structure-centric,[6] but this can be misleading insofar as it suggests that one is only about agents and the other only about structures. In fact, both have an agentic and a structural aspect.

Although we believe that there is much useful work to be done thinking through the structural side of the debate, given space constraints we shall set this issue aside in favor of an approach to the problem through the agency side.[7] We do so in part because there seems to be more interest in contemporary IR in agency than in structure. But this focus also makes sense given that constructivism entered the field in part by criticizing the rationalist view of agency as being exogenous to structure, and constructivism is now in turn being criticized for lacking a theory of agency.[8] As such, even though what follows neglects some important issues in the rationalist/constructivist debate, we do hope it will speak to one of its major concerns so far.

The next section provides brief overviews of the positions typically denoted by 'rationalism' and 'constructivism'. The rest of the chapter examines five common ways of characterizing the debate with respect to the agent side of the agent–structure problem: material versus ideational; logics of consequences versus logics of appropriateness; norms as useful versus norms as right; exogenous versus endogenous actors, when this is understood in causal terms; and exogenous versus endogenous actors, when understood in constitutive terms.

This list by no means exhausts the possibilities for discussion. A particularly interesting one that we take up only in passing is the role of 'performativity' in the constitution of actors. Although associated with postmodernism and thus constructivist in a broad sense, a divide has emerged between postmodernism and constructivism as this term has come to be defined in IR, and as such performativity has not figured in the rationalist/constructivist debate *per se*.[9] We hope the implications of performativity for this debate will be addressed soon.

OVERVIEW OF RATIONALISM AND CONSTRUCTIVISM

Rationalism

As used in IR contexts, 'rationalism' seems to refer variously to formal and informal applications of rational choice theory to IR questions, to any work drawing on the tradition of microeconomic theory from Alfred Marshall to recent developments in evolutionary game theory, or most broadly to any 'positivist' exercise in explaining foreign policy by reference to goal-seeking behavior. In the first two senses, rationalism can be characterized as a method, that is, as a cookbook or recipe for how to explain actions (and especially actions taken in a strategic or multi-actor context). The recipe may be summarized as follows.

1   One starts with an action or pattern of actions to be explained.[10] Some international relations examples would include decisions to send troops into battle, the formation of a balance of power, an arms race, currency devaluations, the imposition of a tariff, or protests at the meetings of an international organization.

2   One posits a set of actors with the capacity to take the actions in question, and probably others who can take actions that may bear on their considerations. Especially in IR, this step typically involves simplification and abstraction (for example, states or international organizations as actors instead of individuals).

3   One proposes a structure of interaction, a sequence of choices for the actors identified in (2), that embeds the pattern of actions to be explained in a larger universe of possibilities. For instance, to explain an arms race one needs a structure of interaction that allows, in principle, for actions that would not produce an arms race. In any structure of interaction some elements will be taken as exogenous for the purpose of the analysis. Exogenous elements of a rationalist model or argument are features not explained within the argument, such as (mostly) preferences over outcomes, the beliefs that actors hold at the start of the posited interaction, or technological capabilities (such as the time it takes to move X troops Y miles given Z terrain). Endogenous features are things explained within the model/argument, such as actor preferences over actions, and beliefs about other actors in light of their actions. The variation of exogenous elements – for instance the relative size of two armies or a state's current account balance in a specific model – allows statements about when the (endogenous) outcome to be explained is more or less likely.

4   Either (a) one makes arguments about the actors' preferences over the universe of possible outcomes identified in (3). Or (b), in evolutionary game-theoretic models/arguments, one may posit rules for how different outcomes associate with the differential reproduction of actors and their 'programs' or decision rules in subsequent rounds. In addition, in some models/arguments, one may posit a structure of initial beliefs held by the actors in question.

5   One shows how or under what conditions the outcome or pattern of actions in question would

emerge if the actors were choosing rationally in light of their beliefs and the other actors' choices, or as the result of the longer-term selection of decision rules or habits in more evolutionary models.[11] In game-theoretic models, beliefs are themselves subject to criteria of rational revision, both through Bayesian and more boundedly rational forms of learning.

Steps 2, 3 and 4 (which need not occur in any particular order) are all both empirical and theoretical. They are empirical in that each is open to criticism on the grounds of being consequentially unrealistic. For instance, a critic might reasonably say 'it is empirically implausible that in your argument state A has no opportunity to concede the territory at stake rather than fight, and this restriction drives your conclusions'.[12] They are theoretical in that each involves the creative simplification and re-presentation of a complex reality in schematic form, which may or may not yield valuable insights and clarity. In other words, this is art as much or more than science. Following the recipe does not guarantee tasty or filling results.

Two Common Misunderstandings about Rationalism

Scientism and the status of formal models The recipe for explanation described above may be pursued informally, in ordinary language, or formally, in the language of game or decision theory. In the latter case, many scholars infer from the appearance of mathematics and symbols that the 'rationalist' must believe that there are no fundamental differences between social and natural science, and that social science can and should aspire to be the same as, say, theoretical physics. While there may be scholars who believe this, the position is definitely not entailed by the use of formal models in the microeconomic tradition. Quite the contrary, the rationalist recipe described above embraces intentionality and the explanation of actions in terms of beliefs, desires, reasons and meanings.[13] Models in physics purport to describe invariant laws governing a world of inanimate objects to which we have no immediate, intuitive access. Microeconomic models purport to show how initially puzzling patterns of action may emerge from individual choices that make sense (are comprehensible) to us in light of the beliefs, desires and constraints they face. They are a form of ethnography more than an effort to find equations that govern putative laws of behavior.

Here is another way to make this point: a formal model is just an argument. Models in the rationalist tradition are arguments that formalize and explore the collective consequences of a fundamental principle of folk psychology – that actions are explained by showing how they make sense in light of particular beliefs and desires.[14] Some users of game models present them instead as if they were magic boxes. Assumptions go in at one end and (presto!) out come hypotheses and results at the other end, with little or no attention paid to explaining what is happening in between to make the connection. In our view, this is bad practice. It should always be possible to translate the action within a model of intentional decision-making into readily comprehensible, ordinary language terms, and it is incumbent on users of such models to do so.

'Rationalism' is a moving target Rationalist analyses in IR have drawn and continue to draw heavily on the results of the evolving program of microeconomic theory.[15] It is worth pointing out that the makers of this program, mainly economic theorists, have spent little time reflecting on the defining features or philosophical foundations of their approach and its results. Instead, efforts to delimit 'rationalism' (or under other names) almost invariably come from without, from philosophers, sociologists, psychologists and political scientists. One consequence is that these efforts sometimes become dated as microeconomic theorists progress from one set of problems to another. It is difficult and hazardous to try to define rationalism by picking out a set of core assumptions said to characterize all past and all future 'rationalist' work.

Two examples are useful to develop the point. First, in the late 1950s Herbert Simon persuasively delimited rationalism by the assumption of perfectly rational agents, whom he characterized as possessing (1) perfect information and (2) a perfect ability to perform calculations. Beginning (more or less) with Akerlof's work on the 'lemon's problem' in 1970 and continuing through the development of incomplete information game theory in the 1980s, microeconomic theory developed a powerful set of tools for explaining action in contexts where people lack knowledge about some important aspect of the situation they face. These developments helped clarify that imperfect information did not entail 'bounded rationality', as Simon had assumed, but rather that bounded rationality should be identified with an imperfect ability to perform calculations, to remember or envision states of affairs.

Second, it is striking that for roughly a decade the cutting edge of microeconomic theory has been devoted *almost entirely* to models in which the actors are less than fully rational in this second, more narrow sense.[16] The 1980s had seen an explosion of work exploring the meaning and consequences of the rationality assumption in models with imperfectly informed agents. By the early 1990s this research had either answered its questions, pushed them as far as they could reasonably go, or had made older questions (such as the problem of equilibrium selection) more pressing.

This effective completion of a research program in non-cooperative game theory with rational agents led directly into work on evolutionary models with agents who use fixed decision rules or adjust their actions in some myopic, boundedly rational way.[17]

Notably, no economic theorist has decried this shift away from models about fully rational agents as a betrayal of the premises of 'rationalism' (so far as we know). Rather, the spirit of the research has been, as before, 'what happens in a model of this problem if one makes such-and-such assumptions?' In addition, many of the main results from evolutionary and bounded rationality models show how less-than-full rationality assumptions often yield similar or identical aggregate implications as did the earlier models with full rationality. If the shift reveals anything about the philosophical commitments of the current microeconomic program, it makes clear that the core commitment is to the formalization of arguments to explore the consequences of different assumptions rather than to any particular assumption of actor rationality.

This second example raises the question of what exactly rationality has to do with 'rationalism'. Certainly it would be odd to define rationalism as whatever it is that the users of microeconomic theory do, and certainly the program's point of departure has long been the explanation of action by reference to optimality in light of beliefs and desires.[18] But perhaps a more plausible candidate for a constitutive feature of rationalism is a commitment to explaining macro-social phenomena in terms of more micro-level phenomena – as Thomas Schelling (1978) suggested, going from 'micromotives' to 'macrobehavior'[19]. Note that in the rationalist recipe posed above, one might employ all sorts of rationality assumptions, or perhaps none at all, as in a model that explained an aggregate outcome such as a balance of power by reference to the differential selection of culturally or otherwise given state 'programs'. By contrast, the recipe is more fundamentally characterized by an effort to explain a whole – an outcome, or pattern of actions – in terms of component parts.

This does *not* imply that 'rationalism' lacks any account of how macro-level phenomena, such as social structures, impinge on and even 'socially construct' individual actors. Indeed, the point of equilibrium analysis is to elaborate how certain 'macro' structures select for or create incentives for individual actions that in turn constitute the structure. We briefly take up such accounts and their relationship to constructivism in the penultimate section of the chapter. But it is still fair to say that as a provisional starting point, rationalist analyses begin from the micro level and try to work to the macro level.

It is not clear whether 'from micro to macro' is or needs to be an expression of an ontological commitment to some form of methodological individualism, or just a pragmatic proposal about a potentially productive way to pursue social explanation. Some rationalists seem inclined toward the former position,[20] in which case the rationalist/constructivist debate is pushed into the domain of metaphysics and the game becomes more winner-take-all. Such 'ontologizing' of rationalism, whether tacit or explicit, worries many constructivists (like Wendt), and this concern underlies some of their critical reaction to the rationalist research program. However, many users of rationalist methods (like Fearon) see no need to make broad metaphysical claims about this approach, and want simply to explore its implications for social explanation. This pragmatic stance does not rule out constructivist approaches to social explanation a priori and as such does much to deflate any notion of a new 'Great Debate'.

Constructivism

Like rationalism, constructivism can be seen in either ontological, empirical, or analytical terms. In either case, however, it is not a substantive theory of world politics. This is important to note because constructivism has sometimes been identified with the latter, and then compared to bona fide theories of world politics like realism or liberalism.[21] This is problematic. As in rationalist IR scholarship, in its constructivist counterpart one can find state-centric and non-state-centric theories, second-image and third-image theories, pessimistic and optimistic theories, and so on. As such, there is a great deal of variation on substantive issues within constructivist IR, and indeed, given the often self-consciously political character of constructivist scholarship, these issues are if anything even more intense sources of disagreement than they are among rationalists. Fortunately, we do not need to address these substantive variations here, but let there be no mistake up front that when it comes to the content and nature of international politics, constructivism is not a 'theory' at all, any more than is rationalism.

Even narrowing the focus in this way, however, there seems to be considerably less agreement among constructivists than among rationalists. Thus whatever the risks of stipulating a single 'recipe' for rationalist research above, it is even more difficult to do so here. This is an important part because whereas rationalists generally agree on questions of epistemology, the debate over the nature of knowledge and truth claims is very much alive within constructivist IR. Indeed, since rationalists have tended not to have deep epistemological qualms about social science and thus not to see the point of debating epistemology in the first place, it seems fair to say that it is primarily within constructivism that these questions are being argued.[22]

In particular, constructivist IR scholarship is currently divided on at least two epistemological questions: (1) whether knowledge claims about social life can be given any warrant other than the discursive power of the putative knower (call this the relativism issue); and (2) whether causal explanations are appropriate in social inquiry (the naturalism issue). These questions are partially independent, which has allowed three distinct epistemological positions to emerge within constructivism: a 'positivist' position that answers yes to both questions; an 'interpretivist' position that answers yes and no respectively; and a 'postmodern' position that (seems to?) answer no to both. These epistemological differences are deep and sufficiently contentious as to raise the question of whether one can speak of 'constructivism' in the singular at all. Moreover, in the eyes of many constructivists epistemological positions have implications for the ontological and analytical questions they believe are at stake in arguments over rationalism and constructivism, making it impossible or illegitimate to separate them. So on the constructivist side at least, the basic parameters of the 'rationalism *v.* constructivism' issue are essentially contested.

This leaves the authors two options in handling constructivism: we can either show how epistemological and ontological issues are or are not intertwined, or we can bracket that nexus and focus just on the latter. Ultimately we believe that the first option needs to be pursued. Some of the issues in the rationalist/constructivist contrast do involve questions of what it means to know something and how this is possible. However, in our view this does not mean that the epistemological differences are the whole of the matter – the rationalist/constructivist contrast does not reduce to positivism versus post-positivism. Given its less developed state, therefore, as well as the limitations of time and space, we adopt the second option above, although some differences among constructivists with respect to rationalism arising from epistemological disputes emerge below. In bracketing epistemological questions in this chapter, however, we emphasize that the result is only a partial and debatable interpretation of 'constructivism'.

So, what generalizations can be made about constructivism? To start with the obvious, constructivists are interested in how the objects and practices of social life are 'constructed', and especially those that societies or researchers take for granted as given or natural. Naturalization is problematic because it obscures the ways in which social objects and practices depend for their existence on ongoing choices, and as such it can be oppressive and a barrier to social change. However, while the general purpose of de-naturalizing a previously unquestioned object or practice – for example, power politics, ethnic identity, or sovereignty – is therefore to open up possibilities for progressive transformation, it need not have that effect. In some cases actors may decide that a practice should not

be changed, but if so at least its acceptance would then be more self-conscious and democratically accountable.

One can identify at least four characteristic and inter-related features of constructivist thinking about the construction of social objects and practices. First, constructivism is centrally concerned with the role of ideas in constructing social life. These ideas will often be shared by many people, and in order to have social relevance they need to be instantiated in practices, which on both counts means they may have considerable objectivity, facticity, or 'materiality'. Constructivism is not subjectivism or pure idealism. Instead, the emphasis on ideas is meant to oppose arguments about social life which emphasize the role of brute material conditions like biology, geography and technology. This is not to say that these have no role whatsoever, but rather that their impact is always mediated by the ideas that give them meaning.

Second, constructivism is concerned with showing the socially constructed nature of agents or subjects. Rather than taking agents as givens or primitives in social explanation, as rationalists tend to do (though see below), constructivists are interested in problematizing them, in making them a 'dependent variable'. This concern operates on two levels. On the more superficial level the focus is on the causal processes of socialization by which particular agents acquire their identities and interests. On a deeper level, constructivists are concerned with the constitutive conditions of possibility for certain modes of subjectivity in the first place. Some of these conditions are historical, in the sense that understandings of what it means to be an agent may change over time, and thus are culturally relative rather than reducible to universal features of human beings' biological constitution. In modern liberal society, for example, we often take it for granted that agents are 'individuals' with powers of reason, autonomy and responsibility. But as John Meyer and Ron Jepperson, among others, have shown, this is very much a culturally specific way of thinking about subjectivity.[23] Other conditions of possibility for subjectivity are synchronic, in the sense that the ideas that actors have in their heads about what they want to do depend for their content or meaning on discursive structures shared with other actors, so that one cannot be a certain kind of subject – say, a witch-doctor – unless others in the society make that possible. At stake in all this is partly an explanatory question of whether social forms can be adequately understood by starting with given agents, but also ultimately a political question of whether society can be normatively grounded on the liberal conception of the individual as some kind of natural baseline.

Third, constructivism is based on a research strategy of methodological holism rather than methodological individualism. In a strict form,

[margin handwritten notes: are they mutually constitutive? — conflict understood in terms of prot v catholic - loyalist v nationalist]

methodological individualism requires that explanations in social science be reducible in the last analysis to 'micro-foundations', which is to say statements about ontologically primitive individuals and/or their interactions. For various reasons holists argue that this effort must ultimately fail, and so we need to make social wholes and internal relations rather than individuals the primitives in social scientific explanation.[24] The commitment to holism, while related to the second point above about endogenizing the given individual, is not the same thing. As will become clear below, it is possible to explain certain aspects of agents' subjectivity in ways that do not violate the individualist requirement of reducibility. (Note that this is not to suggest that rationalism is necessarily individualistic. Whether rationalism is committed to a reducibility requirement depends on how it is interpreted: if as an ontology then probably yes, if only as a pragmatically useful strategy of social explanation, then no.)

Finally, what ties the three foregoing points together is a concern with constitutive as opposed to just causal explanations.[25] Causal theorizing seeks to establish the necessary and sufficient conditions relating a pre-existing cause to a subsequent effect in a more or less mechanistic way. An assumption of such theorizing, therefore, is that cause and effect are independently existing phenomena. Constitutive theorizing, in contrast, seeks to establish conditions of possibility for objects or events by showing what they are made of and how they are organized. As such, the object or event in question is an 'effect' of the conditions that make it possible, but it does not exist independent of them. A common example illustrating this point is the master–slave relationship. The nature and meaning of 'master' and 'slave' as modes of subjectivity are constituted by their relationship in the sense they cannot *be* 'masters' and 'slaves' except in relation to the other. This highlights the way in which social relations can be a primitive in analysis, or irreducible to propositions strictly about pre-existing individuals. This is not to say that constructivists, particularly on the 'positivist' wing, are uninterested in causal explanations. After all, masters and slaves are also effects of shared ideas in the causal sense that their identities and interests are generated and sustained by the interaction between them. But the constitutive aspect of constructivist scholarship is more distinctive.[26]

BONES OF CONTENTION?

We turn now to the substance of the rationalist–constructivist debate. The discussion takes place on many fronts simultaneously and continually evolves, and as such it is difficult to know what all

the issues are, much less cover them all in any detail. However, as we indicated at the outset, one way of organizing the terrain and slicing off a manageable piece for this chapter is to distinguish questions about agents from questions about structure. In this chapter we address only the former. Here there seem to be at least five ways of characterizing what 'rationalism v. constructivism' is about. Although judging from the literature it may seem that they are equally divisive, we argue that this is not the case. Some involve genuine rival hypotheses about what is going on in social contexts; others involve differences in emphasis or research question, and as such more complementarity than contradiction; and still others seem to involve hardly any difference at all.

Material versus Ideational

It is not uncommon in the literature to see the rationalist–constructivist divide characterized in terms of the former being about material factors and the latter being about ideas. Put into the frame of this chapter's concern with conceptualizations of agency, this often translates into the proposition that rationalists believe that people are always acting on material self-interest, and constructivists believe that people are always acting on the basis of norms or values. Whatever the relative merits of self-interest versus non-self-interest descriptions of actor motivation, we think that seeing this as an issue of material conditions versus ideas is not very useful. The problem here lies more in the perception of rationalism than of constructivism.

Constructivism is correctly seen as defined in part by opposition to materialism. The character of this opposition depends on how materialism is understood, which we shall not get into here, and it should not be over-stated. Constructivism does not imply a radical, 'ideas *all* the way down' idealism which denies any role whatsoever to material considerations. As John Searle points out, brute (material) facts are logically prior to institutional facts (Searle, 1995: 34–5). And neither does constructivism imply that the ideational structures of social life are not objective or real. 'Material' is not the same thing as 'objective'. But given those qualifications, John Ruggie is correct to say that constructivism emphasizes the role of consciousness in social life, Emanuel Adler to stress its focus on Popper's World 3 of shared understandings, and so on (Adler, 1997; Ruggie, 1998: 856). Material factors matter at the limit, but *how* they matter depends on ideas.[27]

The picture is more complicated on the rationalist side. On the one hand, proponents and critics alike have sometimes associated rationalism either tacitly or explicitly with materialism. In their influential treatment of the role of ideas in foreign

[Handwritten margin notes: "one historically situated", "D the very arguments for why materialism is emphasis-ed", "how can desires be material?", "materialism the issue"]

policy, for example, Judith Goldstein and Robert Keohane argue that explanations emphasizing ideas are 'rivals' to the 'rationalist' concern with explanations emphasizing preferences (Goldstein and Keohane, 1993: 4). This putative rivalry suggests that preferences or interests[28] are not themselves ideas and thus, presumably, material.[29] Similarly, Ruggie's point about constructivism's focus on ideas is meant as a contrast with rationalism, which he argues does not encompass 'normative factors' and treats ideas either not at all or only 'secondarily' (Ruggie, 1998: 864, *passim*).

These associations of rationalism with materialism may stem from the sociology of knowledge of how rational choice theory entered IR. Early in the 1960s, it was seen as a useful way of exploring the logic of nuclear deterrence and military strategy more generally.[30] Since these intellectual enterprises were influenced by political realism, and realism gives pride of place to material power in international politics, it was perhaps natural for 'rationalism' to acquire a materialist connotation. This may have been reinforced by the publication in 1979 of Kenneth Waltz's *Theory of International Politics*, whose neorealism combined an implicitly materialist definition of system structure with microeconomic analogies for thinking about the logic of anarchy (Waltz, 1979). (We say 'implicitly' because Waltz does not actually defend materialism or argue that ideas do not matter. Rather, he suggests that due to evolutionary pressures in a self-help system, perceptions will tend to reflect the reality of who has the material power to hurt whom, which leads to his equating international structure with the distribution of material capabilities.) Finally, facing what they saw as a disciplinary hegemony of rationalist realists, postmodern and constructivist critics in the 1980s and early 1990s failed to disentangle the two strands, reinforcing the perceived materialist bent of rational choice theory.[31]

It is true that in the hands of rationalists who were influenced by materialist conceptions of politics the explanatory role of ideas has tended to be ignored or minimized. But this should be seen as a function of materialist commitments, not rationalism. At least three considerations bear on this conclusion.

First, rationalist explanations are a species of intentional explanation, the basic structure of which is the formula, 'Desire + Belief = Action'.[32] This means that at their core – the level of individual choice – ideas are an essential, not just secondary, element of rationalist explanation. Second, at the level of social interaction, game theory typically explains aggregate outcomes by reference to 'equilibria', which are *made up of* patterns or structures of beliefs that satisfy various stability properties.[33]

Finally, it is not clear in what sense even desires are necessarily material. Some desires may be material in the sense of having a biological basis, like the desire for food or sleep. But in what sense is, say, a desire to get tenure material? It is in the sense that getting tenure will result in pecuniary rewards. On the other hand, the fact that one sees oneself (and is seen by others) as a professor, such that one could plausibly have a preference for tenure in the first place, seems more a fact about ideas than biology. At some level there is always a material base to desire because human beings are physical creatures, but in most cases this base is 'directionless' in the absence of ideas that give it content (Howe, 1994). This does not violate the 'Desire + Belief' model, since there is nothing in the model which requires that 'Desire' be material. It *may* be material, but then again it may not; rational choice theory, as a theory of choice given desires and beliefs, is strictly speaking agnostic on this question.

Two lessons can be drawn from this discussion. One is that there is little difference between rationalism and constructivism on the issue of *whether* ideas 'matter'. Constructivists might criticize rationalists for the way in which they study ideas, for example by imputing the content of actors' consciousness on the basis of some deductive theory rather than proceeding inductively from what kind of ideas actors really do have, and rationalists might criticize constructivists for failing to explicate whether and how a given pattern of actions and a system of beliefs are mutually reinforcing.[34] But that is a different point. The logic of both approaches depends crucially on actors making choices on the basis of their beliefs. That there should be no fundamental difference here makes sense if we pause to consider that rationalism and constructivism can both trace roots to Weber. The differences between 'intentional' and 'interpretive' explanations notwithstanding, they also have a lot in common.[35]

The other lesson follows from the first, which is that when rationalist models *do* seem to downplay ideas (and sometimes they do) this is a function of materialism rather than rationalism. John Ferejohn's distinction between 'thin' and 'thick' rationalist models is useful here (Ferejohn, 1991). The thin model is simply the logic of intentional explanation referred to above, which says nothing about the content of desires or beliefs. The thick model adds assumptions about the content of desires and beliefs (for example, 'self-interest' and 'complete information about preferences') in a given case. Where those assumptions come from, however, is a question about which rationalism in the thin sense is agnostic. There are materialist rationalisms and idealist rationalisms, and as such if we want to debate the relative importance of ideas in social life it makes more sense to focus on thick theories of interest than it does on rationalism and constructivism.

All of this is not to suggest that there are no significant differences between rationalism and constructivism with respect to *how* they think ideas matter. In particular, as we noted above, rationalists tend to draw a clear distinction between ideas/ beliefs and desires or preferences. This may be related to a more basic feature of rationalist thinking about ideas, which one of the authors here thinks is to treat their explanatory role in more causal than constitutive terms. Ideas are a causal mechanism like any other, existing independently of other causal mechanisms and explaining some portion of the variance in actors' behavior. Constructivists, on the other hand, tend to emphasize the constitutive role of ideas, the ways in which ideas give other factors the explanatory role that they have by investing them with meaning and content. From this perspective ideas permeate social life rather than form a distinct variable whose explanatory force can be isolated. This may be an important difference, to which we return below. But it is a difference *within* a largely shared agreement that ideas 'matter'.

The Logic of Consequences versus the Logic of Appropriateness

Another typical way of interpreting 'rationalism *v.* constructivism' in IR is in terms of the contrast between *homo economicus* and *homo sociologicus*. The former is a calculating machine who carefully assesses different courses of actions, choosing whichever provides the most efficient means to her ends. The latter is a rule-follower who acts out of habit or decides what to do by posing the question 'how is a person in my role (or with my identity) supposed to act in this circumstance?' In March's terms, *homo economicus* is said to follow a 'logic of consequences' in her mode of decision-making, while her sociological counterpart follows a 'logic of appropriateness'.[36]

Partisans face powerful temptations to reduce one logic to an instance of the other. Economists are apt to see the logic of appropriateness as consequentialist – it is simply that the consequence of concern is conformity of one's actions with a set of norms or an identity. Economists stress that nothing in their approach prevents taking desires (or 'interests' or 'preferences') as being informed by or based on norms. On the other side, sociologists are apt to see the logic of consequences as simply rule-following in settings where it is regarded as socially appropriate to be calculating about the choice of efficient means to given ends.

As blanket statements – ontological claims about the nature of decision-making – we agree with March and Olsen's skepticism about either reduction being a good idea (March and Olsen, 1998: 953–4). Surely the distinction between the two logics points to an empirically interesting phenomenon. Sometimes actors do decide by attempting

to calculate consequences. On the other side, some choices seem so tightly constrained by webs of norms and roles that they scarcely seem like 'choices'. And even if not tightly constrained, in some settings the problem of figuring out what to do seems to entail primarily the interpretation and application of conflicting normative claims, rather than estimating the likelihood that such-and-such action will lead to such-and-such result. Even if it were possible to subsume one logic theoretically as an instance of the other, if we are not to obscure these empirical differences we would then simply need to introduce a new linguistic or conceptual distinction to capture them.

There are also good reasons to think that both rationalist and constructivist analyses as commonly practiced may have a comparative advantage in analyzing settings where one or the other mode of decision-making is predominantly at issue. Arguably, decisions with great importance for international politics have often proceeded from a person's or group's interpretation of the internal logic of a complicated ideological or religious system (for example, Marxist-Leninism, Islam, or liberalism). Rationalist methods in their present form are ill-suited to provide insightful analyses of the ideational logics embedded in such systems, or their consequences for debates and actions. Constructivists, by contrast, are in their element here. On the other hand, rationalists have developed a powerful set of tools for thinking about the choice of means to diverse ends in multi-actor settings. Even a constructivist committed to 'reduction' in favor of the logic of appropriateness might concede some value to such analyses in domains where norms permit consequentialism.

But this division-of-labor framing should not be pushed too hard. There is no reason to rule out, a priori, the possibility that a rationalist (constructivist) analysis might yield valuable insights applied to a domain where the logic of appropriateness (consequences) predominates. For example, suppose that for some recurrent pattern of behavior the truth is that people or states are purely acting out norms, or out of habit, or both. An analysis that assumes the agents are acting as calculators-scheming-consequences might none the less be valuable for revealing how the observed pattern can be stable and self-reproducing over time. To be stable, a social pattern of habitual or norm-based actions still needs to be robust against 'entry' by agents espousing alternative norms and against agents who experiment with new (non-habitual) actions. Game-theoretic models are well-suited for analyzing this sort of robustness in social settings. On the other side, IR research that problematizes logic-of-consequences thinking by challenging its empirical universality or theoretical necessity may yield valuable insights as well.[37]

are both theories too deterministic?

↳ where is capacity for agency?

Norms as Useful versus Norms as Right

A closely related framing of 'rationalism *v.* constructivism' sees the two approaches as differing in their understanding of social norms and the reasons thought to explain norm compliance. Here the issue is not so much '*Do* people follow a logic of consequences or appropriateness in their behavior?' as '*Why* do people follow norms? What motivates them to do so?' Some see rationalists as arguing that people follow norms only because (and when) it is useful to do so, whereas constructivists allow that people can be motivated to follow norms simply because they think it the right or legitimate thing to do.[38]

Of course, the idea that actors may desire to follow norms for their own sake rather than just because it is useful is perfectly compatible with the 'thin theory' of rational choice (Ferejohn, 1991). The latter, after all, is agnostic between different 'thick theories' about the content of preferences, and as such does not rule out actors having a preference to follow a norm for its own sake. Indeed, interpreting norms as preferences probably represents the first way that rationalists tried to conceptualize norms.[39] Constructivists might point out that the idea of a 'preference for a norm' could refer simply to a 'taste', like for chocolate, and as such does not capture their interest in the perceived normative or obligatory force of norms.[40] But the logical ability of rationalism to accommodate a preference for rule-following nevertheless does seem to take much of the wind out of the sails of at least this one framing of 'rationalism *v.* constructivism'.

In order to generate a real debate on this issue, therefore, it is necessary to arbitrarily restrict the rationalist position to a particular thick theory of actor preferences, namely one in which actors do *not* have an intrinsic preference to follow norms. This amounts to saying that actors' attitudes toward norms is a 'realist' one of 'self-interest', since the norms would not be seen as having intrinsic worth or being ends in themselves.[41] This move in effect limits the role of norms to the Belief side of the intentional action equation, rather than allowing them to appear as arguments in actors' utility functions (Desire).

The constructivist position then becomes equivalent to a different, 'non-Realist', thick theory of preferences, namely one in which actors *do* have an intrinsic desire to follow norms, perhaps rooted in a belief that this is the right or obligatory thing to do given a certain identity. This seems to imply that actors possess non-selfish or collective interests toward norms, which is to say that they identify with or make them part of their conception of self, and as such make the group's interest in upholding norms their own individual interest as well (Wendt, 1999: 337).[42] Norms here figure as arguments in

actors' utility functions, rather than being limited to beliefs about the environment.

Having imposed such a constraint on the 'rationalist' view, rationalists and constructivists would now have a genuine empirical disagreement. On one level, the issue at stake is about actor motivations. But it may also be seen as about the degree to which norms are internalized. Saying that norms have become desires with perceived obligatory force implies deeper internalization than saying that norms are only beliefs about the environment to which actors relate instrumentally. As such, there may be something to the common characterization – given the arbitrary domain restriction we have imposed – that in rationalism the main explanatory role of norms is 'regulative' of the behavior of exogenously given agents, whereas in constructivism norms are 'constitutive' of actors' identities and interests in the first place.[43]

These differences might have observable implications for both discourse and behavior. On the discursive side, actors might justify their actions differently under the two logics, the one by appeal to instrumental considerations, the other by appeal to normative ones. For example, is a norm of reciprocity in trade or other international negotiations defended on the grounds of intrinsic fairness or as a useful means to an end? Such evidence is not decisive, since actors may talk publicly in normative terms even if they are motivated primarily by instrumental and selfish concerns.[44] But unless we are prepared to dismiss all talk as cheap then the kinds of discourse that actors use should count for something. On the behavioral side, in turn, we might expect to see observable differences at both the individual and aggregate levels in rates of norm compliance. If actors are motivated to follow norms for their own sake then they should be more inclined to observe them (other things being equal).

So in the end there does seem to be something at stake, both theoretically and empirically, in the distinction between the two motivations for norm compliance. Yet, beyond the difficulty already noted that rationalists need not exile norms from preferences, there are at least three further reasons not to treat the rivalry between these two views of motivation in zero-sum, let alone paradigmatic, terms.

First, there is little reason to think that human behavior toward norms is either *always* self-interested or *always* a function of perceived legitimacy. Different people may vary in the extent to which they have internalized a given norm, and the same person may vary in the extent to which she has internalized different norms. The theoretical challenge is therefore one of identifying the conditions under which each hypothesis holds, rather than showing that one is always right or wrong. In the larger scheme of things, both hypotheses are probably true.

A second problem is that empirically it may be impossible to discriminate between the views, especially when both predict – as they may often do – the same outcome. This will be particularly problematic if we have access only to behavioral evidence, whether because of data unavailability or because no conscious or explicit 'choice' was made to follow a norm in the first place. Why did Germany not annex Denmark last year? Both hypotheses offer plausible explanations: because the consequences would have been too grave, and because the German leadership believed that this would have been wrong. Which is the 'real' reason, and how would we know, given that Germany probably never made a conscious decision not to invade last year in any case? Moreover, what is to stop someone from saying that he obeyed a norm for *both* reasons, perhaps with one in the foreground and the other in the back? Clearly, the two hypotheses need not be mutually exclusive for a given case. These empirical problems will be less debilitating in situations where the two hypotheses generate different behavioral predictions (like compliance versus violation), since we can then substitute observable behavior for assessments of subjective intention. But it is unclear what percentage of cases this will be (or even how we could find this percentage out), nor what to do with the remaining cases where predictions are the same, nor what kind of metric one could develop to assess the relative importance of normative versus non-normative motivations in a useful way.

Finally, there is the problem that the two motivations for norm compliance – fear of bad consequences and desire to do right – may interact with each other over time, in either direction. On the one hand, if in a given situation 'second-' or 'third-party enforcement' (punishment by society or state) is consistent enough that actors repeatedly comply with a norm, then over time they may internalize it to the point of acquiring a preference to comply for the sake of doing right or acting appropriately. Indeed, that seems a fair description of the socialization process we all go through as children. First we get punished for doing bad things, later we learn to see doing bad things as morally wrong.

But on the other hand, desires to do right may also decay over time if there is not enough enforcement against norm violators. Consider someone who stops at a red light at 3a.m. on an empty road, which is plausibly taken as evidence of internalization. If it happens that police enforcement suddenly plummets and traffic violations increase, then this person is more likely to ask 'Why should I follow the rules when no one else does?'[45] Thus, third-party enforcement of norms may sometimes undergird 'first-party enforcement', the desire to comply because one believes it the right thing to do. These potential interactions suggest a developmental division of labor between first- and third-party enforcement. When norms are new, we might expect the fear of bad consequences for violation to dominate. Over time, with internalization, the logic of appropriateness may take over, but may still depend in part on social or legal institutions that use the threat of punishments to prevent the entry and proliferation of 'exploiters'.[46]

In sum, although under at least one important formulation there are some differences between the 'rationalist' and constructivist explanations for why people follow norms, there are also good reasons not to make too much of them. In the aggregate the two explanations are complementary rather than mutually exclusive, may be hard to distinguish empirically, and in some cases there might not even be any fact of the matter to distinguish at all. At the extremes or 'tails' of the case distribution the rivalry between the two claims is clear, but in the middle there may be no deciding between them. This muddy empirical situation may encourage partisans to privilege their favored hypothesis on purely theoretical grounds, trying to subsume the other as a special case, but that seems unlikely to advance our understanding of the world.

Problematizing Actors I: Preference Formation

Perhaps the most widely cited issue thought to divide rationalist and constructivist scholarship concerns what the dependent variable or explanandum should be, in particular whether to take actors as 'exogenously given' and focus on explaining their actions, or to 'problematize' or 'endogenize' actors themselves. Rationalism is usually seen as doing the former and constructivism the latter, although we shall argue that this difference is difficult to sustain in a hard and fast form. Since the issue is many-sided and thus fraught with potential confusion, however, we should say a few words about how we see the analytical terrain going into the discussion. In particular, it is useful to make two distinctions, one between different ways in which actors might be problematized or explained, the other between different kinds of actor properties which could be at stake in such a process.

There are two broad senses in which one might try to 'endogenize' actors, causal and constitutive.[47] The causal approach asks where actors came from, or came to have the qualities that they have today. Hendrik Spruyt's explanation of how over the centuries states became the dominant actors in world politics by driving out competitors like city-states and city-leagues, or Rodney Hall's account of how changes in the domestic organization of states from dynastic to national foundations transformed inter-state relations, are good examples of what can be learned when we problematize state actors rather than take them as given (Hall, 1999; Spruyt, 1994; see also Reus-Smit, 1999). More generally, a number of constructivists in IR have advanced variations on the causal argument that state identities and interests have evolved over time through interaction with other states and NGOs.[48]

In contrast, the constitutive approach asks not where actors or their properties come from, in an historical or process-tracing sense, but about their social conditions of possibility at a given moment. What is it about Costa Rica that enables it to participate as an equal in the UN? The recognition by other states of its sovereignty as a right. What is it that, for a time in the early 1990s, made Iraq a 'rogue' state with which most other states refused to have contact, when in the past its aggressiveness might have been evaluated differently? Shared understandings that determine the boundaries of acceptable foreign policy practice. Constitutive explanations of actors 'explain' in the sense of telling us what actors are made of, or how their properties are made meaningful or possible by the society in which they are embedded. As we argue below, the causal approach to endogenizing actors is not that much at odds with rationalism, whereas the constitutive approach may be more difficult to reconcile with it.

Because these two ways of thinking about problematizing actors are different, and have different implications for the debate between rationalism and constructivism, we address them in different sections. In this section we take up the causal issue, in the next the constitutive one.

Turn, then, to the second analytical distinction, between the kinds of actor properties that might be at stake. Whether approaching actors from a causal or constitutive standpoint, we can take three different things about them as given or not: their bodies, beliefs, or desires. These should be kept distinct in discussions about exogenous versus endogenous actors, since they vary in the extent to which they are a source of disagreement between rationalists and constructivists.

A *body* is the platform on which actorhood is constructed. The social position and meaning of bodies will vary, but before this variation can occur bodies must be constituted by an internal organizational structure and process that enables them to move, act and acquire meaning in the first place. In the case of individuals this internal organizational structure is given by biology. In the case of corporate actors like states it is constituted by biologically given people engaging in ongoing collective action enabled by the structure of the organization.[49] Interestingly, on the question of whether to take bodies as given the main theoretical cleavage is not between rationalists and constructivists, but between rationalist and constructivist 'moderns'

who both see themselves as part of the Enlightenment, liberal project in which the individual or agent is granted a privileged status, and 'postmoderns' who reject that project and want to deconstruct the individual or agent all the way down (this is one place where the performativity argument referred to in the introduction comes into play). Thus, like rationalists, modern constructivists have been largely content to take as 'exogenously given' that they were dealing with *some* kind of actor, be it a state, transnational social movement, international organization or whatever. As such, the constructivist concern with identity-formation has typically focused on the construction of variation within a given actor class (type or role identities), rather than on explaining how organizational actors come into being in the first place (corporate identities).[50]

Actors also have *beliefs*. Here too there is little disagreement between rationalists and constructivists (of any stripe), this time because rationalists have been perfectly willing to try to explain beliefs and changes in beliefs. All non-cooperative game-theoretic solution concepts (such as Nash equilibrium) amount to proposals about what sort of patterns of beliefs one would expect to arise in different social settings. Further, dynamic games with incomplete information can explicitly model the evolution of actor beliefs about others' preferences and beliefs (including, for instance, beliefs about others' beliefs about oneself, which figure prominently in discussions of 'identity'). And it is perfectly possible within such an analysis for a person's beliefs even about their *own* preferences to change and evolve as a result of acquiring new information.

To be sure, there is debate about how *deeply* rationalism can explain beliefs – for example, whether it can handle the 'complex' learning involved in preference formation, or the ways in which individuals' beliefs may be constituted by social collectives. But it is clear that at least with respect to 'simple' learning about an external environment rationalism is itself very much in the business, with constructivism, of problematizing actors.[51] Since we address preference formation as a separate point in a moment, and there is otherwise relatively little to disagree about, we shall not address this aspect of the exogenous actor problem in this chapter.

That leaves *preferences*, desires, or in constructivist parlance, 'identities and interests'. This is where most of the debate has occurred, with rationalists tending to treat preferences as given, and constructivists trying to endogenize them. Our view is that while there are characteristic differences here, they are not as fundamental as is sometimes supposed.

Before turning to that argument, however, we emphasize up front that the choice of whether to treat preferences as given is an important one in social inquiry, for both theoretical and political reasons. It matters theoretically because to assume exogeneity is implicitly to make an empirical claim about the world, namely that what actors want is constant within the context of the study in question. If this claim is not accurate, then we are led to question the subsequent causal story being told about behavior. And an exogeneity assumption can matter politically because if what actors want is not stable, or could be made not stable, then policies based on an assumption of stability may not have the desired effect or may understate the potential for social change. The latter is of course the main reason why constructivists are concerned to endogenize identities and interests. If it can be shown that these are produced and reproduced by social interaction then the possibilities for change may be greater than if, say, a 'prisoners' dilemma' is treated as an unchangeable fact about some aspect of world politics.

Yet there are also at least three reasons for caution about making it the basis for a deep, paradigmatic divide. One is that the choice of exogenous versus endogenous preferences can be treated as purely analytical, rather than as a substantive claim about the nature of the world.[52] By this we mean that, on one level, the choice can be about nothing more serious than what question, or dependent variable, researchers are personally interested in. After all, there *are* two questions here – 'what are the causes of X behavior?' (an action in the world) and 'what are the causes of X preference?' (a state of mind) – and it is not obvious that we have to answer one in order to answer the other. It is perfectly legitimate to answer the former while holding preferences constant, and to answer the latter while bracketing the causes of behavior. Jeffrey Legro has summarized this overall situation with a dance metaphor, the 'two-step': first we explain preferences, then we explain behavior (Legro, 1996).

This is not to say that there is no risk in separating the two questions. As we noted above, the assumption that preferences are given brings baggage with it, an implicit assumption of stability. Probably few rationalists are committed to this assumption as a matter of principle, that is, to the proposition that preferences *really are* stable, for all time.[53] For most it is merely a 'methodological bet', an analytical convenience that allows them to answer the question that interests them, which is the effect of context on choice behavior. But there is nevertheless a danger that, through a process of forgetting what we are doing, what starts out as merely an analytical convenience can become something more than that, a tacit assumption about what the world is really like which limits our theoretical and/or political horizons. The assumption that states are self-interested, for example, is harmless when made as an analytical convenience, but if turned into a tacit universal claim it can lead us to conclude, mistakenly, that anarchic systems are necessarily

self-help worlds rather than contingently so in particular historical circumstances. This transformation of harmless analytical assumptions into tacit ontologies seems particularly likely to happen in a 'division-of-labor' approach to the two-step, where constructivists and rationalists address their respective questions in isolation from each other. The best way to keep the two-step honest is to make sure that the partners are coordinated, rather than go their separate ways.

A second reason for not putting too much weight on whether preferences are taken as given is that the boundary between preferences and action, on which the debate over this issue inherently turns, is relative and unstable. One researcher's preference over outcomes is another researcher's preference over actions. Consider the Cuban Missile Crisis. A 'rationalist' might ask, why did US decision-makers, given their preference that the Soviets remove their missiles from Cuba but an even stronger preference to avoid nuclear war, choose a strategy of naval blockade? And why did this convince the Soviets, given their preferences and available actions, to retreat? On the other hand, one could also ask the 'constructivist' question, as Jutta Weldes has done, of how US policy-makers constructed the removal of Soviet missiles as their interest in the first place, since such an interpretation was not absolutely necessary (Weldes, 1999). Weldes answers by reference to a national security discourse and its associated Cold War identity, that constituted US interests in a certain way. Yet, the collective agreement within the Kennedy administration on this assessment of 'US interests' can also be seen as the outcome of strategic behavior in an intra-administration game of talk and access, conducted in the shadow of expectations about likely public and élite reactions to different courses of action and outcomes. Insofar as the determination of collective interests is itself the result of a set of choices, we could then ask a new 'rationalist' question in which *that* was the 'action' to be explained, and the problem was to show how that choice emerged in light of higher or 'meta'-preferences (for example, 'security of the United States as a capitalist, democratic state'), and 'lower' preferences concerning re-election and relative power within the administration.

We have, in other words, a potentially endless means–ends chain in which any given end can be seen as a means to some other ends depending on what question is being asked. As such, the decision to call something an outcome over which preferences are assumed, or an action (or set of actions) to be explained is not a statement about the world but rather an analytical move by the investigator. This absence of a fixed boundary between action and interests may help explain their occasional conflation in constructivist critiques of rationalist models, in which the claim to explain interests sometimes turns out to be difficult to separate from an explanation of action.[54] And in any case, if 'rationalists' can be turned into 'constructivists', or *vice versa*, simply by pushing the research question one step up (or down), whether or not preferences are taken as given seems like a slippery foundation for a paradigm war.

A final issue is that it is not even clear that the 'two-step' accurately describes the division of labor between rationalists and constructivists, on either side. Thus, on the one hand, some 'rationalists' do not take preferences as exogenously given. In IR, for example, Andrew Moravcsik accepts the logic of the two-step but nevertheless seeks to explain foreign policy-makers' preferences by reference to domestic politics (Moravcsik, 1997). That rationalists could do this is not surprising in light of the dependence of what counts as a preference on what question is being asked: a preference (end) on one level of theory can be a choice (means) on another. In evolutionary game theory some rationalists have gone even farther, building models in which actors acquire preferences either as a result of differential reproduction or a process of imitation or adaptation; thus actor preferences are explained endogenously by some kind of selection or evolutionary stability (equilibrium) argument.[55] As such, Ruggie goes too far in suggesting that rationalism cannot accommodate complex learning, unless we restrict the label 'rationalist' arbitrarily to models that do not address it (Ruggie, 1998: 868).

If 'rationalists' can justifiably claim to offer some insight into the formation of preferences, then 'constructivists' in turn can justifiably claim to offer some insight into the second half of the two-step, the choice of action. As we discussed above, constructivism has become associated with the hypothesis that much of human behavior is driven by a normative logic of appropriateness rather than an instrumentalist logic of consequences, and as such invades the turf of the 'rationalist' step of the supposed division of labor.

In sum, the decision about whether to causally explain preferences does not seem like an occasion for a profound or divisive debate. The boundaries between preferences and choice of action are in important part question-relative and thus unstable, and even less do they have to constitute significant epistemological or ontological cleavages. This is not to say that in every case it will be useful to explain preferences over outcomes by translating them into means to higher ends. And certainly it remains reasonable to criticize an argument or model that draws policy conclusions without exploring the possibility of preference endogeneity, just as it may be warranted to criticize an analysis that does not treat identity and interest-formation as the consequences of choices that are potentially amenable to rationalist explanation. But these are relatively concrete issues that can be handled without implicating 'paradigmatic' sensibilities.

Problematizing Actors II: On the Constitution of Subjectivity

One of the most persistent and at least superficially plausible ways of characterizing 'rationalism *v.* constructivism' in IR is by reference to the divide between methodological individualism and holism in the philosophy of social science. We already gave credence to this view by picturing rationalism as an approach that tries to explain macro-level phenomena (such as a 'balance of power system') by reference to more micro-level phenomena (such as state motivations and capacities). Holists in a range of fields have expressed serious doubts about whether many central features of social life, in international politics and elsewhere, can be adequately or at all understood by somehow resolving them to component parts. In practical terms, constructivists in IR argue for understanding parts, such as states, in terms of wholes like international systems or reigning ideas, rather than exclusively the other way around.

Another way of expressing this opposition is by contrasting causal and constitutive forms of explanation. Causal explanations, which refer to the action of pre-existing, temporally prior causes that produce the effects to be explained, would seem to have an affinity with the micro-to-macro program of rationalism. Constitutive explanations, which characterize systems of beliefs and practices that in effect create or define social objects and actors – such as master and slave, or states, for instance – would seem to illustrate holism in action.

Even here, though, we encounter difficult issues that caution against drawing too sharp a line. Perhaps the main question concerns whether rationalism has the conceptual resources for a defensible and useful account of how structures constitute agents. We lack the space here to provide anything like a full investigation of rationalist/constructivist differences on questions about social structure (as opposed to agency). But we do want to suggest how some standard formulations in the literature may be 'too quick'.

In a broad sense, rationalist studies do typically involve efforts to explain wholes in terms of the actions and interactions of parts. Contrary to a common misconception in IR theory, however, this does *not* imply that rationalists have no account of how macro-level phenomena, such as 'social structures', impinge on individual actors. An example is useful to illustrate how this account works.

Consider the following application of the rationalist recipe to explaining why, in the United States, people drive their cars almost exclusively on the right side of two-lane roads. Imagine a model/argument in which the actors are a large number of individuals who must choose simultaneously whether to drive on roads or not, and if on a road on the left, in the middle, or on the right side. Individuals are assumed to desire to arrive at their destination quickly but without damage to body or car. This is a coordination problem – a problem in which one's optimal choice depends on how others choose and in which some patterns of choice are better for all than some others. The observed pattern in which more or less everyone drives on the right side of the road is explained as an equilibrium pattern of optimal choices. That is, given that everyone else is expected to drive on the right, driving on the right is an efficient means to reach one's destination quickly but without harm.[56]

Notice that there are *two* sorts of 'structure' implicit in this story, exogenous and endogenous. Individuals in the argument face exogenous structure in the sense of physical constraints. If you drive off the road, your car is likely to be damaged and it may be impossible to get where you want to go.[57] But in an equilibrium, they also face a social structural constraint that derives from the fact that everyone expects everyone else to drive on the right. This is endogenous structure in that it is *mutually constituted* by the beliefs and attendant actions of all individuals in the model, and it is explained within the model rather than postulated. From the vantage point of any one actor, this endogenous structure of beliefs and attendant actions is just as objective and real as the trees on the side of the road, even though the actor's own actions contribute to making the reality and it could be made otherwise. Note also that this social structure is not determined by material conditions; the convention could just as well be to drive on the left.

If this is a *causal* explanation, it is not causal in the most straightforward sense of pre-existing causes that reliably produce subsequent effects. Actions are explained in part by reference to beliefs in this account, but at the same time beliefs are explained as correct perceptions of actions (in an equilibrium). Explanation by reference to an equilibrium pattern of beliefs and behaviors answers a 'how is this possible?' question more than it does a 'what caused this to come about?' question.[58] In this respect it appears closely akin to the constitutive form of explanation associated with holism.

The convention of driving on the right is regulative rather than constitutive; what it means to drive is not constituted by this convention.[59] But a convention account can also be offered for the constitutive rules that define the meanings of words and actions or, say, actor identities. The mappings from behaviors such as speech sounds and gestures to meanings (which mappings constitute 'actions') are obviously also matters of coordination within a culture. In the United States a wave with a smile generally means 'Hi!' and not 'I want to kill you', though it could be otherwise.[60]

Now consider a question of social identity, such as the master–slave dichotomy. In contrast to a property such as being six feet tall, the social identity 'master' or 'slave' cannot be defined solely by reference to facts about an individual. There are no masters without slaves and vice versa. Instead, to be a master (for example) is to be accorded certain powers with respect to certain other individuals, *by social convention*. Just as in the case of driving conventions, the coordinated actions and beliefs that constitute a system of slavery could be otherwise, but none the less have for any one individual an objective reality posed by the beliefs and expected actions of others in various contingencies. In this approach, an actor's identity, a complex of beliefs about self, others and relations between them, would be endogenously explained as an equilibrium in a coordination game rather than posited as an exogenously given fact about an individual.[61]

It is true that, in practice, emphasizing the ways in which actor identities are constituted by social conventions is not how rationalist arguments usually proceed. Rather, the rationalist strategy is usually to build in or presuppose some social structures and the identities they constitute, and then to explain from the 'bottom-up' a pattern of choices and the structures they imply. Constructivists have objected to this building in of structurally constituted identities, since they are interested in how these are constituted in the first place.[62] So in showing how identities can be seen as constituted by an equilibrium in a coordination game we are going beyond the typical rationalist story, in effect using a rationalist approach to answer a question normally asked only by constructivists.[63] The value of such a move is both rhetorical and substantive. By highlighting the flexibility of rationalism to accommodate 'constructivist' insights it suggests there may be less opposition here than is often thought.[64] And by emphasizing the mutual determination of social structure and individual choice in equilibrium, it highlights an aspect of the micro-foundations of actor constitution that constructivists have sometimes neglected.

Even so, constructivists may wonder if a rationalist approach to conventions is really up to the task of comprehending the constitution of social identities and structures of meaning more broadly. One question is whether such an account can explain the constitution of one identity without presupposing some other (or others). If not, then the convention account may be missing an important aspect of the constructivist position.[65] In practical terms, this might imply that the rationalist approach to conventions would sometimes be useful for 'cutting into' a network of social identities to understand how one particular identity is sustained given others, but less useful for gaining insight into the bigger picture.

A second issue is whether a rationalist approach necessarily implies that conventions are aggregates of, and thus ontologically reducible to, pre-existing beliefs and meanings. If so, this would conflict with the holist argument that the contents of the actor beliefs that sustain social conventions do not exist apart from those conventions. But in themselves, the equilibrium explanations just given of the driving and master–slave conventions carry no such implication of reducibility. The meanings that constitute and sustain these conventions may be pre-existing in actors' heads or they may not. If rationalism is viewed in analytical rather than ontological terms it can be agnostic on this question, and thus be compatible with holism. And well that is, since it would be unfortunate if constructivists could not avail themselves of the insights provided by equilibrium arguments in their own work just because they are associated with 'rationalism'.

We are not suggesting that the ontological debate between holism and individualism is thereby settled or unimportant. Philosophers have been arguing about their relative merits for decades.[66] The eventual 'solution', if there is one, may matter in a broad sense for IR insofar as it speaks to the question of whether or not rationalism and constructivism reduce to the same vantage point on international life, and thus to what the search for 'micro–foundations' in IR can mean. We are in no position to settle this dispute. However, if the rationalist–constructivist debate in IR is understood in methodological rather than ontological terms, as we recommended in the introduction, then it is not clear that IR scholars *need* to settle it to do their work. A lesson to take away from this discussion is that there seem to be at least two ways of telling stories about the constitution of actor subjectivity, which may or may not on close examination turn out to be the same. Although constructivists have tried to make this issue exclusively their own – an effort abetted by relative neglect from rationalists – the rationalist approach appears to have the conceptual resources for an endogenous account of actor identities, both constitutive and, as we saw in the previous section, causal. This account may or may not ultimately capture the essence of the constructivist argument, and it may or may not yield insightful analyses of the phenomenon in question. This remains to be seen. But in the meantime, there is a strong pragmatic case for treating the two stories as complementary at the least. This will encourage IR scholars to pursue questions about the constitution of actors in whatever way seems to yield insights, and to think creatively about how they might be combined.

CONCLUSION

The idea of a battle royal or 'Great Debate' between rationalism and constructivism is appealingly dramatic, but properly understood many of the issues dissolve upon close inspection. Although often framed as an argument about ontology or empirical descriptions, we have argued for a pragmatic interpretation in which these are two approaches to answering questions about international politics, rather than two competing *Weltanschauungen.*

If the debate is defined as a matter of ontology, then it approaches zero-sum and a great deal rides on who wins. Yet it is not clear how much this would tell us about world politics. Knowing that international reality consists 'ultimately' of wholes or parts, for example, tells us little about how states, non-governmental organizations or multinational corporations affect international politics; about the conditions under which world politics is more conflictual or cooperative; about whether and how anarchy can be transcended – in short, about most of the political questions of concern to IR scholars. To answer such questions we need to make further assumptions that go beyond those supplied by rationalism and constructivism.

Again, this is not to say that ontological (and for that matter epistemological) issues should not be engaged by IR scholars, or that doing so will have no benefits. Indeed, some benefits are already apparent. Of the empirically oriented sub-fields of political science, IR is probably the most philosophically self-conscious and informed, the most interested in the continuous examination of fundamental questions about what social inquiry is supposed to be and do. On the whole, this engagement makes it harder for scholars to lapse into an unthinking 'normal science' or 'normal postmodernism' that cannot defend or think through its standard practices. But we should also be conscious of the limits of philosophical debates for making sense of international politics. If 'rationalism *v.* constructivism' is to be another 'Great Debate' in IR, then let it not be constructed as an argument about ontology.

If the debate is viewed in more empirical terms then the relationship between the two approaches is more complex. In some cases they offer rival hypotheses, in others they seem complementary, in others they are redundant. Discussion about issues like these is likely to provide more insight into world politics than will ontology, but here too it is problematic to see the question as 'rationalism *v.* constructivism'. Neither perspective necessarily commits the researcher to a claim about the world like 'preferences *really are* exogenous (endogenous) to interaction'. It is equally valid to treat rationalism and constructivism as merely analytical statements about what the researcher is interested in, which can never be everything at once. Moreover, even if we do choose to test the claim that, for example, in context *X* preferences 'really are' exogenous (endogenous), this may tell us little about *Y* or *Z*, where the opposite claim might be true. Even when defined as an empirical dispute, in other words, the eventual result of a 'Great Debate' would probably be that both approaches are true some of the time. This does not mean we should never try to adjudicate between 'rationalist' and 'constructivist' hypotheses in those cases where they can be made to generate rival empirical predictions. But we should be clear about what those cases are, and about what does and does not follow 'paradigmatically' from one hypothesis prevailing over the other.

In short, we believe the most fruitful framing of 'rationalism v. constructivism' is a pragmatic one, treating them as analytical lenses for looking at social reality. It is common in articles of this sort to try to delimit (or legislate) the types of problems for which each lens works best. Although we have offered some suggestions of this kind, on the whole we have argued that the standard ways of drawing lines between the two 'isms' and their presumed competences are on shaky grounds. Thus, even the question of what lens to use for a particular research question should be left open and not fixed by a priori, methodological or theoretical considerations.

Our discussion has focused on the 'agency' side of the problem. We did not explore the structural side of the equation except indirectly in our discussion of the constitution of agents. Some additional 'bones of contention' between rationalism and constructivism might be found in their approaches to structure, involving issues such as micro versus macro structure, common versus collective knowledge, external versus internal relations, and the reality of 'deep' structures. An exploration of these issues would be worthwhile, but we suspect the result would parallel our conclusion here, that the relationship of the two approaches, when understood pragmatically, is largely either complementary or overlapping.

It should be stressed that in advocating a pragmatic view we are not endorsing method-driven social science. Too much research in international relations chooses problems or things to be explained with a view to whether the analysis will provide support for one or another methodological 'ism'. But the point of IR scholarship should be to answer questions about international politics that are of great normative concern, not to validate methods. Methods are means, not ends in themselves. As a matter of personal scholarly choice it may be reasonable to stick with one method and see how far it takes us. But since we do not know how far that is, if the goal of the discipline is insight into world politics then it makes little sense to rule out one or the other approach on a priori grounds. In that case a method indeed becomes a tacit ontology, which may lead to neglect of whatever problems it is poorly suited to address. Being conscious about these choices is why it is important to distinguish between the ontological, empirical, and pragmatic levels of the rationalist–constructivist debate. We favor the pragmatic approach on heuristic grounds, but we certainly believe a conversation should continue on all three levels.

This prompts a concluding suggestion: that the rationalism–constructivism issue be seen not as a debate but as a conversation. The connotation of 'debate' is of a zero-sum conflict between two sides with firm substantive commitments about what the world is like. This might have been appropriate in the first 'Great Debate' between realists and idealists, who disagreed about the essential nature of world politics. But all of the subsequent 'debates', including this one, have been more about method than substance, and on that level considerably less is at stake. Rationalists and constructivists approach international life from different analytical standpoints, which has led them to ask characteristically different questions and develop characteristically different answers. Rather than a dialogue of the deaf in which each side tries to marginalize or subsume the other in the name of methodological fundamentalism, the challenge now should be to combine insights, cross boundaries and, if possible, synthesize specific arguments in hope of gaining more compelling answers and a better picture of reality.

We have tried to contribute to such a conversation by working through a number of commonly perceived points of conflict and disagreement. Our own experience going back and forth on ten (!) drafts of this chapter might suggest that a conversation across these 'isms' is too difficult to pursue or sustain. But interestingly, most of our difficulties arose not from clear substantive disagreements but rather from matters of presentation and efforts to gain clarity about just how 'the other side's' argument works on specific points. In any event, we believe that the blind men's best hope of progress in understanding international politics lies in a conversation of truth-seekers rather than lawyerly debate.

Notes

The authors gratefully acknowledge comments on earlier drafts by Walter Carlsnaes, Thomas Risse, Joel Westra, the participants at a PIPES workshop and the Stanford Reading Group on International Relations, and one anonymous reviewer.

1 As if confirming this suggestion, the editors of the present volume have organized the theory section in these terms as well.

2 Which have since become known as, respectively, the third and second 'Great Debates' (see Lapid, 1989). By this reckoning, rationalism v. constructivism would be the 'fourth debate'.

3 For other recent discussions in this spirit see Fierke and Nicholson, 2001 and Katzenstein, Keohane and Kraser, 1998.

4 See Wendt, 1999: 33–8 for further discussion of these three ways of interpreting the debate.

5 For an exploration of ontological aspects of the debate see Wendt, 1999.

6 For example, Clark, 1998; Finnemore, 1996.

7 For a complementary discussion emphasizing the structure side, see Wendt, 1999: ch. 4.

8 On the latter criticism see Checkel, 1998.

9 For entries into the literature on performativity in IR see Campbell, 1998; Laffey, 2000; Weber, 1998.

10 'Outcomes', such as a balance of power, are understood in this approach as labels for patterns of actions or the result of sets of actions.

11 'Rationally' in this sentence refers to instrumental rationality.

12 Specific features of specific rationalist models/ arguments are often taken to task for being unrealistic *per se*, which is probably never a valid criticism.

13 Omitting the case of pure evolutionary models in which 'actions' might be explained as the result of a genetic or totally unreflective cultural 'programming'. This qualification applies at several places in the discussion that follows.

14 Where 'makes sense' is understood in terms of instrumental rationality.

15 Much of this program has been textbookified; see, for a good recent example, Mas-Collel, Green and Whinston 1995. For examples of work closer to the frontier, see Fudenberg and Levine, 1998; Rabin, 1993; Rabin and O'Donoghue, 2001.

16 A major exception being work on the epistemic foundations of decision theory; for an overview see Dekel and Gul, 1997.

17 See, for overviews and main results, Fudenberg and Levine, 1998, Weibull, 1995, or Young, 1998. The political scientist Robert Axelrod has been a pioneer in evolutionary models, and there is now a small community of IR scholars working on evolutionary game-theoretic and related computational models (Cederman, 1997). This intriguing line of work remains curiously disconnected from the much larger set of theoretical results developed by economists and theoretical biologists.

18 On the other hand, one might also ask what is the point of delimiting 'rationalism' in the first place, except to fit out one side for an interparadigmatic battle.

19 In the 1970s, Schelling explored models with agents that were far less than rational by the meanings that evolved in subsequent game-theoretic work. Indeed, his analysis of tipping models illustrates that evolutionary thinking is not a new thing in 'rationalism'.

20 See, for example, Elster in some of his earlier work (e.g., Elster, 1985).

21 For example, Walt, 1998; Wendt, 1992, 1994.

22 See, for example, Kratochwil, 2000; Searle, 1995; Smith, 2000; Wendt, 1999.

23 Meyer and Jepperson, 2000.

24 For discussion and illustration see Emirbayer, 1997; Jackson and Nexon, 1999; Wendt, 1999: ch. 4.

25 There are various ways to render this distinction other than 'causal-constitutive'; this particular language is developed at greater length in Wendt, 1998, 1999.

26 The causal-constitutive distinction is in turn often thought to have implications for the epistemological debate between positivist 'Explanation' and interpretivist 'Understanding' (see Hollis and Smith, 1990); we are not convinced that explanation and understanding require fundamentally different epistemologies, but have chosen to set the issue aside in this chapter.

27 For further discussion see Wendt, 1999: ch. 3.

28 We shall use these terms interchangeably to denote the subjectively perceived wants that actors do have rather than normative or objective wants that they arguably should have, which is how Fearon thinks the concept of interests should be understood (in contrast to non-normative 'preferences'). For an overview of this distinction, with further references, see Wendt, 1999: 231–3.

29 Though Keohane has since made clear that he does not see rationalism as a 'materialist' theory; see Keohane, 2000.

30 See especially Schelling, 1960.

31 See Ashley, 1984; Dessler, 1989; Walker, 1987; Wendt, 1992.

32 For an overview see Wendt, 1999: 113–19.

33 For example, in a Nash equilibrium, players' beliefs about others' actions are such that every player prefers to take the action that confirms the others' beliefs as correct.

34 See Ferejohn, 1991.

35 On the affinities between rationalism and interpretive sociology, see Esser, 1993; Ferejohn, 1991; Norkus, 2000.

36 See March and Olsen, 1998.

37 See Wendt, 2001, for example, for some suggestions along these lines.

38 For a good discussion of this contrast highlighting the role of legitimacy see Hurd, 1999.

39 See, for example, Gary Becker's (1957) explaination of the practice of racial discrimination in terms of 'tastes', or Ellickson (1991) on 'first party enforcement' of social norms (referring to the internalization of a norm as a preference).

40 See Finnemore and Toope, 2001. Note that this is not to say that constructivists have yet generated an adequate theory of obligation; though see Kratochwil, 1989 for a start.

41 For further discussion see Wendt, 1999: 238–43.

42 For a more rationalist discussion of this idea see Sugden (1993) on 'thinking as a team'.

43 But see also the discussion below about whether the constitution of actor identities and preferences can be comprehended in terms of a coordination (or convention) account.

44 Indeed, this is often to be expected. Since the argument that you should do *X* because it is in my self-interest is not likely to persuade unless you happen to care independently about my welfare, there are strong incentives to cast arguments in public-spirited terms even when the underlying motives are selfish. See Elster, 1995 and Fearon, 1998.

45 On this point see Philip Pettit's (1995) interesting discussion of the 'virtual reality' of *homo economicus*, where he argues that instrumental thinking will tend to kick in when it becomes highly advantageous for actors to use it, but otherwise most actors most of the time will do what is socially appropriate.

46 This example raises a deeper question, however, about the idea of following a norm because one believes that it is right to do so. Has one internalized a norm if one's desire to abide by it is in fact conditional on whether others do so?

47 See Wendt, 1998, 1999.

48 For example, Barnett, 1998; Checkel, 1997; Cronin, 1999; Finnemore, 1996; Lynch, 1999; Wendt, 1999.

49 On corporate actorhood see Wendt, 1999: ch. 5.

50 For typologies of identity concepts see Wendt, 1999: 224–30 and Fearon, 2000. Note that for rationalists, at least, the decision about where to locate 'the body' can be a methodological rather than an ontological question. See, for example, Lake and Powell, 1999; Elster, 1986.

51 The terms complex and simple learning are Nye's (1987).

52 Lake and Powell (1999) call it a 'methodological bet'.

53 Though see Stigler and Becker, 1977.

54 On this point see Clark, 1998 and Lake and Powell, 1999.

55 See, for example, Bowles, 1998; Cohen and Axelrod, 1984; Gerber and Jackson, 1993; Raub, 1990.

56 Of course, the account does not explain why the convention is to drive on the right rather than on the left, since driving on the left is equally a social equilibrium. This is an example of the type of 'equilibrium selection problem' that motivated the turn to exploring more evolutionary models in 1990s microeconomic theory; see, for example, Young, 1998.

57 Of course, these physical constraints are constraints only if one has a desire to get from one place to another without injury. Constraints on action are always relative to desires.

58 Indeed, the main criticism of equilibrium explanations in game theory is that they give no causal account of how an equilibrium state of affairs would or does come about. This is the main reason for the great attention to evolutionary models by 'rationalist' economic theorists in the 1990s.

59 Though we could say that the convention does constitute part of the role identity 'good driver'.

60 See Lewis, 1969 for the most philosophically developed effort to understand meaning in terms of coordination in games, and Weingast, 1995 for a rationalist analysis of the institution of sovereignty that highlights a number of constitutive effects on the meaning of state action.

61 Schelling (1960: 92) had hinted that 'roles' in the sociologist's sense might be productively analyzed and understood in terms of a coordination account. For a more developed empirical analysis along these lines see especially Laitin, 1998.

62 For a useful exchange on this and related issues see Fierke and Nicholson, 2001.

63 Although this 'rationalist' approach to the social construction of meanings and identities is hardly unprecedented. Lewis (1969) had suggested it with regard to meanings in language (and he says it is just a development of arguments about convention by David Hume); Sugden (1989) gives an evolutionary account of social norms and normativity in terms of social conventions; and Fearon and Laitin (1996, 2000), Kalyvas (1996) and Laitin (1998) have all pursued arguments along these lines in political science.

64 The potential convergence is also evident in Kratochwil's (1989: 69–94) discussion of the emergence of norms, which draws favorably on 'rationalist' scholars like Schelling and Lewis.

65 This is the central message of Mandelbaum (1955), one of the earliest statements of the holist position in the modern philosophical debate.

66 See Bhargava, 1992; Collin, 1997; Gilbert, 1989; and Lewis, 1969; among others; Wendt (1999: ch. 4) offers an interpretative review of this literature.

Bibliography

Adler, Emanuel (1997) 'Seizing the Middle Ground: Constructivism in World Politics', *European Journal of International Relations*, 3: 319–63.

Akerlof, George (1970) 'The Market for "Lemons": Quality Uncertainty and the Market Mechanism', *Quarterly Journal of Economics*, 84: 488–500.

Ashley, Richard (1984) 'The Poverty of Neorealism', *International Organization*, 38: 225–86.

Barnett, Michael (1998) *Dialogues in Arab Politics*. New York: Columbia University Press.

Becker, Gary (1957) *The Economics of Discrimination*. Chicago: University of Chicago Press.

Bhargava, Rajeev (1992) *Individualism in Social Science*. Oxford: Clarendon Press.

Bowles, Samuel (1998) 'Endogenous Preferences: The Cultural Consequences of Markets and Other Economic Institutions', *Journal of Economic Literature*, 36: 75–111.

Campbell, David (1998) *Writing Security*, 2nd edn. Minneapolis: University of Minnesota Press.

Cederman, Lars-Erik (1997) *Emergent Actors in World Politics*. Princeton: Princeton University Press.

Checkel, Jeffrey (1997) 'International Norms and Domestic Politics: Bridging the Rationalist–Constructivist Divide', *European Journal of International Relations*, 3: 473–95.

Checkel, Jeffrey (1998) 'The Constructivist Turn in International Relations Theory', *World Politics*, 50: 324–48.

Clark, William (1998) 'Agents and Structures: Two Views of Preferences, Two Views of Institutions', *International Studies Quarterly*, 42: 245–70.

Cohen, Michael and Axelrod, Robert (1984) 'Coping with Complexity: The Adaptive Value of Changing Utility', *American Economic Review*, 74: 30–42.

Collin, Finn (1997) *Social Reality*. London: Routledge.

Cronin, Bruce (1999) *Community Under Anarchy: Transnational Identity and the Evolution of Cooperation.* New York: Columbia University Press.

Dekel, Eddie and Gul, Faruk (1997) 'Rationality and Knowledge in Game Theory', in David M. Kreps and Kenneth F. Wallis (eds), *Advances in Economics and Econometrics: Seventh World Congress*, Volume 1. Cambridge: Cambridge University Press, pp. 87–172.

Dessler, David (1989) 'What's at Stake in the Agent–Structure Debate?', *International Organization*, 43: 441–73.

Ellickson, Robert (1991) *Order Without Law: How Neighbors Settle Disputes.* Cambridge, MA: Harvard University Press.

Elster, Jon (1985) *Making Sense of Marx.* Cambridge: Cambridge University Press.

Elster, Jon (1986) *The Multiple Self.* Cambridge: Cambridge University Press.

Elster, Jon (ed.) (1995) 'The Strategic Uses of Argument', in Kenneth Arrow et al. (eds), *Barriers to Conflict Resolution.* New York: W.W. Norton. pp. 236–57.

Emirbayer, Mustafa (1997) 'Manifesto for a Relational Sociology', *American Journal of Sociology*, 103: 281–317.

Esser, Hartmut (1993) 'The Rationality of Everyday Behavior', *Rationality and Society*, 5: 7–31.

Fearon, James (1998) 'Deliberation as Discussion', in Jon Elster (ed.), *Deliberative Democracy.* Cambridge: Cambridge University Press. pp. 44–68.

Fearon, James (2000) 'What is Identity (As We Now Use the Word)?', mimeo, Stanford University.

Fearon, James D. and Laitin, David D. (1996) 'Explaining Interethnic Cooperation', *American Political Science Review*, 90: 715–35.

Fearon, James D. and Laitin, David D. (2000) 'Violence and the Social Construction of Ethnic Identity', *International Organization*, 54: 845–77.

Ferejohn, John (1991) 'Rationality and Interpretation', in K. Monroe (ed.), *The Economic Approach to Politics.* New York: HarperCollins. pp. 279–305.

Fierke, K.M. and Nicholson, Michael (2001) 'Divided by a Common Language: Formal and Constructivist Approaches to Games', *Global Society*, 15: 7–25.

Finnemore, Martha (1996) *National Interests in International Society.* Ithaca: Cornell University Press.

Finnemore, Martha and Toope, Stephen (2001) 'Alternatives to Legalization: Richer Views of Law and Politics', *International Organization*, 55: 743–58.

Fudenberg, Drew and Levine, David K. (1998) *The Theory of Learning in Games.* Cambridge, MA: MIT Press.

Gerber, Elisabeth and Jackson, John (1993) 'Endogenous Preferences and the Study of Institutions', *American Political Science Review*, 87: 639–56.

Gilbert, Margaret (1989) *On Social Facts.* Princeton: Princeton University Press.

Goldstein, Judith and Keohane, Robert (eds) (1993) *Ideas and Foreign Policy.* Ithaca: Cornell University Press.

Hall, Rodney (1999) *National Collective Identity: Social Constructs and International Systems.* New York: Columbia University Press.

Hollis, Martin and Smith, Steve (1990) *Explaining and Understanding International Relations.* Oxford: Clarendon Press.

Howe, R. (1994) 'A Social-Cognitive Theory of Desire', *Journal for the Theory of Social Behaviour*, 24: 1–23.

Hurd, Ian (1999) 'Legitimacy and Authority in International Politics', *International Organization*, 53: 379–408.

Jackson, Patrick and Nexon, Daniel (1999) 'Relations before States', *European Journal of International Relations*, 5: 291–332.

Kalyvas, Stathis (1996) *The Rise of Christian Democracy in Europe.* Ithaca: Cornell University Press.

Katzenstein, Peter, Keohane, Robert and Krasner, Stephen (1998) '*International Organization* and the Study of World Politics', *International Organization*, 52: 645–85.

Keohane, Robert (2000) 'Ideas Part-way Down', *Review of International Studies*, 26: 125–30.

Kratochwil, Friedrich (1989) *Rules, Norms, and Decisions.* Cambridge: Cambridge University Press.

Kratochwil, Friedrich (2000) 'Constructing a New Orthodoxy? Wendt's "Social Theory of International Politics" and the Constructivist Challenge', *Millennium*, 29: 73–101.

Laffey, Mark (2000) 'Locating Identity: Performativity, Foreign Policy and State Action', *Review of International Studies*, 26: 429–44.

Laitin, David (1998) *Identity in Formation: The Russian-Speaking Populations in the Near Abroad.* Ithaca: Cornell University Press.

Lake, David and Powell, Robert (1999) 'International Relations: A Strategic Choice Approach', in D. Lake and R. Powell (eds), *Strategic Choice and International Relations.* Princeton: Princeton University Press. pp. 3–38.

Lapid, Yosef (1989) 'The Third Debate: On the Prospects of International Theory in a Post-Positivist Era', *International Studies Quarterly*, 33: 235–54.

Legro, Jeffrey (1996) 'Culture and Preferences in the International Cooperation Two-Step', *American Political Science Review*, 90: 118–37.

Lewis, David (1969) *Convention: A Philosophical Study.* Cambridge, MA: Harvard University Press.

Lynch, Marc (1999) *State Interests and Public Spheres: The International Politics of Jordan's Identity.* New York: Columbia University Press.

Mandelbaum, Maurice (1955) 'Societal Facts', *British Journal of Sociology*, 6: 305–17.

March, James and Olsen, Johan (1998) 'The Institutional Dynamics of International Political Orders', *International Organization*, 52: 943–69.

Mas-Collel, Andreu, Green, Jerry R. and Whinston, Michael D. (1995) *Microeconomic Theory.* New York: Oxford University Press.

Meyer, John and Jepperson, Ronald (2000) 'The "Actors" of Modern Society: The Cultural Construction of Social Agency', *Sociological Theory*, 18: 100–20.

Moravcsik, Andrew (1997) 'Taking Preferences Seriously: A Liberal Theory of International Politics', *Intenational Organization*, 51: 513–53.

Norkus, Zenonas (2000) 'Max Weber's Interpretive Sociology and Rational Choice Approach', *Rationality and Society*, 12: 259–82.

Nye, Joseph (1987) 'Nuclear Learning and US–Soviet Security Regimes', *International Organization*, 41: 371–402.

Pettit, Philip (1995)'The Virtual Reality of *homo economicus*', *The Monist*, 78: 308–29.

Rabin, Matthew (1993) 'Incorporating Fairness into Game Theory and Economics', *American Economic Review*, 83 (5): 1281–302.

Rabin, Matthew, and O'Donoghue, Ted (2001) 'Choice and Procrastination', *Quarterly Journal of Economics*, 116 (1): 121–60.

Raub, Werner (1990) 'A General Game-theoretic Model of Preference Adaptations in Problematic Social Situations', *Rationality and Society*, 2: 67–93.

Reus-Smit, Christian (1999) *The Moral Purpose of the State*. Princeton: Princeton University Press.

Ruggie, John (1983) 'Continuity and Transformation in the World Polity', *World Politics*, 35: 261–85.

Ruggie, John (1998) 'What Makes the World Hang Together? Neo-utilitarianism and the Social Constructivist Challenge', *International Organization*, 52: 855–85.

Schelling, Thomas (1960) *The Strategy of Conflict*. Cambridge, MA: Harvard University Press.

Schelling, Thomas (1978) *Micromotives and Macrobehavior*. New York: W.W. Norton & Co

Searle, John (1995) *The Construction of Social Reality*. New York: Free Press.

Smith, Steve (2000) 'Wendt's World', *Review of International Studies*, 26: 151–64.

Spruyt, Hendrik (1994) *The Sovereign State and its Competitors*. Princeton: Princeton University Press.

Stigler, George and Becker, Gary (1977) 'De Gustibus Non Est Disputandum', *American Economic Review*, 67: 76–90.

Sugden, Robert (1989) 'Spontaneous Order', *Journal of Economic Perspectives*, 3 (4): 85–97.

Sugden, Robert (1993) 'Thinking as a Team: Toward an Explanation for Nonselfish Behavior', *Social Philosophy and Policy*, 10: 69–89.

Walker, R.B.J. (1987) 'Realism, Change, and International Political Theory', *International Studies Quarterly*, 31: 65–86.

Walt, Stephen (1998) 'International Relations: One World, Many Theories', *Foreign Policy*, 110: 29–46.

Waltz, Kenneth (1979) *Theory of International Politics*. Boston, MA: Addison–Wesley.

Weber, Cynthia (1998) 'Performative States', *Millennium*, 27: 77–95.

Weibull, Jorgen (1995) *Evolutionary Game Theory*. Cambridge, MA: MIT Press.

Weingast, Barry R. (1995) 'A Rational Choice Perspective on the Role of Ideas: Shared Belief Systems and State Sovereignty in International Cooperation', *Politics and Society*, 23 (4): 449–64.

Weldes, Jutta (1999) *Constructing National Interests: The US and Missiles in Cuba*. Minneapolis: University of Minnesota Press.

Wendt, Alexander (1992) 'Anarchy is What States Make of It: The Social Construction of Power Politics', *International Organization*, 46: 391–425.

Wendt, Alexander (1994) 'Collective Identity Formation and the International State', *American Political Science Review*, 88: 384–96.

Wendt, Alexander (1998) 'On Constitution and Causation in International Relations', *Review of International Studies*, 24, Special Issue: 101–17.

Wendt, Alexander (1999) *Social Theory of International Politics*. Cambridge: Cambridge University Press.

Wendt, Alexander (2001) 'Driving with the Rearview Mirror: On the Rational Science of Institutional Design', *International Organization*, 55 (4): 1021–51.

Young, H. Peyton (1998) *Individual Strategy and Social Structure: An Evolutionary Theory of Institutions*. Princeton: Princeton University Press.

4

Rational Choice and International Relations

DUNCAN SNIDAL

CHALLENGES TO RATIONAL CHOICE

Rational choice is one of the major approaches to the post-war study of international relations (IR). It has helped define contemporary theoretical debates about international politics and has advanced our understanding of such topics as the implications of anarchy and the possibility of cooperation. In some eyes, rational choice has been on a mission to establish its hegemony over the field and has failed to appreciate both its own limitations and the value of alternative approaches. Several vigorous critiques of this approach – both internal and external – are now well-established and rational choice might appear to be in retreat in the face of those.[1]

This chapter evaluates the challenges raised by those criticisms with an eye toward how rational choice can deal with them.[2] I begin with a discussion of the critiques and argue that each contains some significant element of truth. But they are more usefully thought of as stimulants to improving rational choice than reasons for rejecting it. I then briefly investigate this claim in terms of a set of the substantive and theoretical puzzles that rational choice and the IR field more generally are currently trying to deal with. Rational choice offers no simple solutions to these problems and it is not the only way to address them. But it is a powerful and flexible approach that, if it takes the criticism seriously, will rise to these new challenges.

Internal critiques about the way rational choice conducts its analysis can be divided into two primary categories. The first is that rational choice has developed a fetishism over mathematical technique

that leads it to substitute abstract and complicated models for common-sensical theoretical development. At its best, this line of argument continues, rational choice simply reproduces what we 'already know' in a more obscure language; at its worst, it uses obfuscation to hide its emptiness. Worse yet, explanations not cast in the language of rational choice, and even arguments highly compatible with rational choice but not couched in its technical garb, have not been appreciated. Technique has falsely triumphed over substance.

While it contains an element of truth, this critique fails to appreciate the value of technical approaches used properly. More importantly, it conflates a discussion of particular ways to do rational choice with the approach taken as a whole, which need not be technically complicated or mathematically obscure. Proponents should realize that formalization is not the *sine qua non* of rational choice but only a tool. Applications of, and even deductions within, rational choice can be entirely 'verbal'. That is often the best way to proceed. But skeptics should appreciate that the power of approach derives in no small part from established results that might not have been obtained except through formalization.

The second internal critique is that rational choice has no strong empirical legs. According to this view, proponents have not tested it adequately and, when they have, have found little support. Instead of remedying this deficiency, they argue, rational choice has retreated to theoretical speculations that are increasingly irrelevant.

Again, there is an element of truth here, since some rational choice has been more heavily oriented toward developing theoretical arguments about international politics than toward evaluating them. Moreover, the versatility and flexibility of rational choice create special difficulties for testing. But this critique is mistaken in two important respects. First, it confuses the (im)possibility of testing rational choice as a general approach with the more reasonable project of testing specific hypotheses or substantive theories based on a rational choice perspective. Second, it seriously under-appreciates the extent to which rational choice is driven by empirical considerations and plays a central role in a wide range of empirical work. Nevertheless, the greatest challenge to rational choice is to strengthen its range and depth of empirical application. This is an ongoing project, however, and I document substantial work that addresses this challenge. In the end, the most interesting debates should be over how best to evaluate rational models empirically, since there is no disagreement over the need to do so.

More recently, an important set of external critiques, grouped loosely under the constructivist label, have pointed out that rational choice emphasizes certain problems and sets aside other issues by assumption. This leads some to doubt the value of rational choice contributions altogether, whereas others are sympathetic to the contributions of rational choice but see it as having run its course or being unable to answer big questions. Rational choice is found deficient in explaining who the key actors are, in explaining their interests, explaining the origin of institutions, or in explaining how these change. These deficiencies present challenges that need to be understood and, where possible, addressed. But the deficiencies are also overstated and (in their weaker form) justifiable as savvy methodological moves by which rational choice analysis gains its power.

My goal here is not to engage the constructivist–rationalist debate but to draw on constructivist criticisms as posing important challenges that rational choice can and should address.[3] I argue that IR rational choice analysis cannot resolve all of these challenges but it can improve itself by taking them seriously and selectively modifying itself in response.

I address these different critiques first from a methodological direction and then, building on that, from a substantive direction. The next section begins by asking 'What is rational choice?' I propose that rational choice is a methodology incorporating general theoretical assumptions but that it is wide open in terms of specific substantive content. Indeed, its association with particular substantive positions – especially ones deriving from its tradition in realism, neorealism and, more recently, neoliberalism in IR – makes it too easy to confuse the limits of these substantive approaches as inherent limits of rational choice. In fact, rational choice is extraordinarily flexible and is compatible with a wide range of substantive approaches. Other reputed

limitations are not inherent to rational choice but represent tactical methodological choices to facilitate analysis. That does not eliminate them as limitations but closer examination suggests how they are potentially surmountable or, alternatively, why it may be unwise to surmount them.

Building on this, I consider the two internal critiques of rational choice methodology. I argue that formalization is not a necessary feature of rational choice but has played an indispensable role in its development. But softer, non-mathematical approaches have been equally central in the development of the theory and in its application to specific problems. Most importantly, formal and soft approaches are highly complementary, not competitive. On the empirical side, rational choice faces some special limitations and so its empirical development lags behind its theoretical development. But it also is much stronger empirically than its critics claim; a significant body of empirical research illustrates the wide range of approaches that are being used to strengthen it further in this regard.

The final section of this chapter considers how rational choice can handle three important challenges facing its broader application to IR. The first is the general problem of change. I argue that while some substantive theories employing the rational choice approach may reject the study of change, that is not true of rational choice in general. Although rational choice imposes some methodological limits on incorporating change, it can address important issues of change in the international setting. The second challenge is the problem of explaining preferences and actor identities within rational choice. This continues the discussion of change and I argue that rational choice can relax its assumption of fixed preferences provided it does so in a systematic manner. The third substantive challenge is incorporating normative concerns. Although I do not engage a full normative discussion, I show that rational choice is capable of engaging normative considerations in a number of different ways and that addressing these, in turn, will feed back on the positive theory in useful ways.

WHAT IS RATIONAL CHOICE?

Rational choice is a broad enterprise with permeable boundaries. It is not a substantive theory except at the most general level.[4] Therefore it is usually viewed as a methodological approach that explains both individual and collective (social) outcomes in terms of *individual goal-seeking under constraints*. This broad conception needs to be filled in considerably before it can have much specific content, either theoretically or empirically. There is a myriad of possible ways to do so – some of which respond to important critiques of the approach.

Yet any theoretical methodology such as rational choice entails some very general substantive commitments.[5] The focus on goal-seeking presumes that explanation should proceed in terms of relevant actors, the goals they seek and their ability to do so. The approach also requires some specification of constraints – which may be technological, institutional, or arise from interdependencies among actors' choices. Within and beyond this, rational choice is remarkably open to alternative specifications. Notably, the goals are *not* restricted to self-regarding or material interests but could include other-regarding and normative or ideational 'goals'. Moreover, while the baseline theory is often developed in terms of hyper-rational actors with powerful calculating abilities, the theory is open to incorporating limits to their capacities or constraints on their decision-making. Finally, the theory is most often used as a positive theory of how actors behave in practice, but it can also be used as a normative theory to evaluate how actors behave or to indicate how they should behave.

Any application of rational choice that aspires to be a theory 'of something' requires more detailed substantive commitments. In IR, the 'neo-' tradition has assumed that states are the key actors, that they seek goals such as power or wealth, and that they are relatively effective at pursuing their interests. The warrant for these assumptions comes not from rational choice, however, but from substantive knowledge of international politics. For example, the social choice literature raises thorny questions about treating aggregates as actors (Arrow, 1951) so that use of the state-as-actor assumption depends on implicit substantive claims. Alternative assumptions that propose other actors (for example, transnational activists or subnational interests), or actors pursuing different goals (for example, moral values or profits) or actors with differential abilities to do so (for example, in terms of more limited calculating ability or lack of information), are equally compatible with rational choice. Thus rational choice is not at all limited to conceptions of self-interested, materialistic 'economic' actors, or to anomic, power-seeking state actors in international affairs. Different substantive specifications can lead to different theories within the broader umbrella of rational choice.

Goal-seeking obviously does not cover all aspects of human (or state) behavior in any straightforward way. There are other rich traditions of research in IR based on (for example) psychological or cognitive limits of decision-makers (Jervis, 1976; Steinbruner, 1974) or, more recently, explanations that depend on identity or culture (Katzenstein, 1996), or on the role of 'appropriateness' as an alternative basis for behavior (Finnemore, 1996; March and Olsen, 1989).[6]

The elasticity of the rationality concept makes it tempting (and a little too easy) to reduce these alternative conceptions to a form of goal-seeking.

Treating 'appropriateness' as an element of utility function, or bounded rationality as information costs, simply misses the difference between the approaches which need to be taken more seriously (Sen, 1977). Nevertheless, rational choice is often a central part of the explanation even where different motivations are also at play. Many behavioral findings about the limits of decision-making – hysteresis and framing effects, for example – are implicitly defined in terms of deviations from a rational choice baseline. Similarly, while human rights activists or other actors may be driven by different considerations and use different techniques than are typically captured by rational choice, the analysis of their behavior in international politics requires careful attention to their strategically rational behavior (Johnston, 2002; Keck and Sikkink, 1998). Conversely, rational choice analysis can advance by taking the alternatives seriously and seeing what elements it can incorporate. An example is the effort to understand communication (Morrow, 1994a) and rhetoric (Goldsmith and Posner, 1999; 2002b) among states. But rational choice does not have to be a closed system in this process and the resulting explanations may blend elements of rational choice with alternative approaches.[7]

One criticism of rational choice is that it takes the identity and interests of actors as outside the analysis – and thereby brackets one of the most interesting aspects of international politics and change. Leaving that issue to later, it is not true on the constraint side, which is determined by both exogenous and endogenous factors. Some constraints derive from available 'technology' but the more interesting ones are political and social. In many equilibria, for example, each individual is 'constrained' by others' choices in the sense that its best choice, and what it can achieve, depends on the choices of others. Institutions themselves are equilibria – sometimes emerging endogenously within a game and sometimes the legacy of interaction in a prior game – that serve as constraints for actors in a game (Calvert, 1995; Snidal, 1996). These institutional constraints also provide the means by which rational choice can move beyond its focus on actors (that is, its 'ontological commitment') to investigate how institutions impose structural constraints on the actors. This is especially important with regard to beliefs which straddle individual goal-seeking and collective institutional constraints. Beliefs are properties of individuals but their impact often comes because they originate in and depend on intersubjective 'common knowledge' among the collective (Morrow, 2002; Wendt, 1999).

Operating as a causal theory, rational choice is often criticized for assuming what is of greatest interest – including the identities of the actors, their interests and the institutional structures or rules of the game. To be sure, a causal rational choice account needs to be clear about what is exogenous and what is endogenous in order to proceed. It may specify these things according to substantive knowledge of which elements are (relatively) fixed compared to other elements more subject to change. It therefore defines the scope of what is being analyzed, and identifies various factors as endogenous (to be explained) or exogenous (taken as given). The latter category includes 'deep' assumptions that the researcher uses implicitly without highlighting or perhaps even realizing (for example, market institutions in traditional neoclassical economics; sovereignty in neorealist arguments). In other cases, a 'partial' equilibrium analysis reflects an explicit understanding that certain factors are being held constant which might otherwise affect the analysis. The justification for this bracketing is that the excluded effects are small – or change slowly – compared to the effects of the included variables.

Moreover, rational choice analysis is not inherently causal, as is reflected in the centrality of equilibrium analysis in the theory (Marshall, 1910). An equilibrium is a statement of consistency among specified elements, that there is no pressure on any of the elements to change given the values of the other elements. It is thus an evaluation of a whole state of affairs and claims only that the elements can co-exist with one another while stipulating nothing about their sequence or causal relation. In this respect, equilibrium analysis is constitutive rather than causal (cf. Lake and Powell 1999b: 32; Wendt 1999). Causal analysis is induced when substantive assumptions of exogeneity and endogeneity are introduced for tactical methodological reasons to trace the implications of change in one element on another while holding other elements fixed or constant. Comparative statics does this by assuming an exogenous change in one element will result in an endogenous change in one or more other elements. But the choice of what is fixed and what fluctuates is not inherent to rational choice but to the interpretation put on the model.

Rational choice is also associated with some further methodological commitments that are neither logically entailed by it nor necessarily distinguish it from other research approaches. One commitment is to simplification, the notion that good explanations are lean and minimize the assumptions made. This simplicity – and the structure of some of the problems that are analyzed – lends itself to formalization, discussed below. Another reason rational choice stresses simplicity is to constrain its own versatility so that its explanations do not become tautologies. But the price of making simplifying assumptions such as fixed interests and fixed environments is that rational choice sets aside potentially important questions (for example, what determines interests) by assumption. Even if this self-imposition of theoretical blinders is for good reason, it nevertheless raises the question whether rational choice can

relax those assumptions (possibly by tightening others) to broaden its analysis.

A second commitment of rational choice is to generalization. One virtue of abstract concepts and models (for example, prisoners' dilemma, agency problems, asset specificity) is that they transcend substantive problems. Thus similar rational choice analyses have been offered of such disparate phenomena as the family, the market and war. This greatly facilitates the transference of insights and intuitions across fields, for example from the study of American politics to IR (Martin, 2000; Milner, 1998). It has also been an important factor in the spread of international relations theory into other areas such as international law (Abbott, 1989; Burley, 1993; Setear, 1999). But this commitment to generalization is not simplistic in the sense of requiring that human action can be reduced to fully generalizable 'laws', as is often implied by critiques. Instead, it is in the spirit of showing how a very broad framework can encompass compatible analyses that explain many different situations. Indeed, the development of rational choice in its game-theoretic mode has involved a proliferation of increasingly specific and therefore different structures or contexts (that is, game specifications), each of which may exhibit substantial further variation as its parameters vary. Generality obtains at the level of transferable insights rather than mechanical rules or scientific laws.

An immediate implication is that rational choice is not a singular approach but rather a large family of approaches. These are highly complementary at the level of basic methodology, but they can be completely inconsistent in terms of their substantive arguments. Thus many of the debates within rational choice – and certainly most of those within IR – are actually debates driven by substantive assumptions that originate outside the methodological framework.[8] Rational choice can play a useful role in clarifying and even adjudicating these debates because it provides a common conceptual framework for specifying the problem and a machinery for checking consistency and implications of arguments. Gaining the full advantage of these capabilities explains the importance both of formalization of arguments and of developing empirical connections.

METHODOLOGICAL DEBATES AND CHALLENGES FOR RATIONAL CHOICE

This section examines 'internal critiques', which are largely methodological in terms of debating 'how to do rational choice' rather than the advantages or disadvantages of the approach taken as a whole. I focus on the relation of rational choice to formal mathematical models and to empirical testing. My argument is that formalization is highly complementary to 'softer' (that is, non-technical) rational choice and that neither can be successful without close attention to the other. The complaint that rational choice has paid insufficient attention to empirical testing holds some merit but nevertheless greatly undervalues the substantial empirical work of various types that is based on rational choice approaches. More importantly, attention to empirical issues has grown considerably among rational choice researchers and a new concern for evaluating theoretical arguments is apparent.

Rational Choice and Formalization

Rational choice has an elective affinity for formalization, by which I mean the use of mathematical models to represent theoretical arguments and simplified versions of the real world. Formalization is by no means a necessary feature of rational choice. Many important applications of rational choice can be properly described as 'soft', meaning that they are not closely tied to formal models or arguments. Indeed, one indicator of the success of formal rational choice is the extent to which key analytic arguments and conclusions such as those emerging from theories of collective action, cooperation theory, principal-agent models, and signaling models, have become part of our verbal vocabulary and common understanding of international politics. This is not to say that mathematics is not central to rational choice – far from it – since many important developments have been generated or significantly improved by formalization. Moreover, the persuasiveness of soft rational choice often rests on the 'hard' formalization that stands behind it.[9]

Theoretical rational choice need not rest on mathematical models. Early rational choice political economists, including Adam Smith and David Hume, did not invoke mathematics. Much of the contemporary economics that has been most influential on IR – notable examples include the work of Ronald Coase (1960) Douglass North (1990) and Oliver Williamson (1975, 1985) – is not mathematical to any significant extent. Moreover, traditional IR contained significant though informal elements of rational choice thinking long before any move towards formalization (Morgenthau, [1948]1978: 4–10). Contemporary rational choice theorizing in IR often draws on formal results but is not formal itself (e.g., Keohane, 1984; Koremenos et al., 2001a; Lake, 1999; Oye, 1986).

Conversely, mathematical models need not involve rational choice. Recall Lewis Frye Richardson's (1960) arms race model using coupled differential equations to represent a dynamic action-reaction process where each nation-state acquires weapons in response to the others' level of armaments. Richardson describes it as a model of 'what men would do if they did not stop to think'. Even game-theoretic models have no necessary connection to rationality. Evolutionary game models are of this sort and their relation to rational models is an area of on-going research (Kahler, 1999). Barry O'Neill (1999) uses game theory to underpin an explicitly non-rational choice framework – indeed he allies his work closely with constructivism – and to explain a wide range of international phenomena through symbolism.

There is also no singular way to model rational choice. Non-cooperative game-theoretic models are the predominant approach and they largely subsume traditional microeconomic and decision-making approaches.[10] But choice within this broad family of models entails increasingly detailed substantive commitments. In deciding on a specific model – for example, between a strategic game model versus a non-strategic decision-making model, or between an extensive (tree) form game versus a simultaneous (matrix) form game, or between complete versus incomplete information games – we are making substantive judgments as to what are the most important features of the problem. The tendency to assume that one class of models (often more complex ones or newer ones) is inherently superior is generally misguided. Proper model choice, including the level of formalization, depends on the substantive problem being analyzed.

Simple representations have been as important as technically complex ones in promoting rational choice analysis. The obvious example is the prisoners' dilemma game (PD), which is now so much part of our common theoretical vocabulary that Stephen Walt (1999: 9) seeks to exclude it as an example of formalization in his critique of such approaches even though it fits his definition of a formal theory. Like other simple games, including 'assurance', 'coordination' and 'chicken', PD carries an impressive analytical load that has considerably clarified and advanced our thinking about international politics. The fact that it has become a standard metaphor for international anarchy is an indicator of its power as soft theory; the fact that its clarity has made its limitations apparent and stimulated a large family of extensions and refinements shows the power of its formal representation.

Many soft rational choice arguments that have become standard in the literature are ultimately based in mathematical derivations. Although Walt treats Olson's (1965) analysis of collective action as not placing 'much emphasis on mathematical rigor', that claim seriously misunderstands Olson's enormous debt to Paul Samuelson's (1954) very rigorous and quite technical analysis of public goods. The economics field was befuddled by public goods until Samuelson's formalization provided a clear conceptual basis to move forward.

Olson's great contribution was to connect the formal analytics to wide-ranging political examples and to extend the analysis through soft theory (for example, selective incentives). It provides an excellent example of how soft rational choice can build off formalized work to overturn well-entrenched conventional wisdom and create a common framework for substantial advances.

Similarly, the result that cooperation can be supported by strategies of reciprocity is referred to as the 'folk theorem' because a simple version had been widely known (at least among game theorists) for a long time.[11] The understanding of the effectiveness of reciprocity also pre-dates its mathematization, while explicit 'tit-for-tat' policies pre-date game theory by four hundred years and informal 'eye-for-an-eye' behavior goes back much further. Yet the folk theorem result that seems so obvious in the light of game theory was a novel claim for IR theory when expressed in terms of the possibility of 'cooperation under anarchy' (Oye, 1986), just as tit-for-tat's victory surprised most game theorists who participated in Axelrod's (1984) tournament. Formalization of the cooperation argument was essential for establishing the conditions under which cooperation was possible and for overcoming substantial intellectual resistance on that point. By identifying the precise preconditions for cooperation, formalization also opened up avenues of analysis regarding the limitations of those arguments (for example, poor information, large numbers, distributive issues) as well as ways to overcome those limitations (for example, different strategies, issue-linkage, institutional roles).

While proponents make much of how rational choice formalization has produced results that are 'counter-intuitive', critics respond that most of these results are 'obvious'. The debate is pointless for two reasons. First, most good results cease being counter-intuitive once they are properly understood. Collective action and PD are good examples where what was once surprising is now conventional wisdom (Barry and Hardin, 1982). Second, and more important, counter-intuitiveness is vastly over-rated as a criterion. In a field that has no shortage of unsubstantiated 'surprising' claims, formalization performs a more important service by helping us work out the underlying logic and clarifying the grounds for the different claims. A prime example has been the improved understanding of the role of information in the deterrence (Powell, 1990) and assurance problems (Kydd, 2000).

A related contribution is that formalization provides a systematic framework for exploring detailed implications and extensions of arguments. While this happens within any one model, it also occurs across analyses. A good example is the set of interconnected advances that follow from the initial formalization of how cooperation is possible among states. For example, Downs and Rocke (1995) show how domestic uncertainty will impede cooperation and the impact this may have on preferred institutional arrangements. James Fearon (1998) shows that when bargaining differences among alternative cooperative outcomes are introduced, the 'shadow of the future' that enforces decentralized cooperation among states also creates incentives that may impede the attainment of cooperation. Barbara Koremenos (2001) demonstrates that introducing flexibility to cooperative agreements provides an institutional means to overcome such problems in many circumstances. Although the specific models vary, their close relationship and clarity allow their conclusions to be readily compared and integrated.

A different complaint against formalization is that with a little cleverness one can derive virtually any conclusion (Stein, 1999). Unfortunately, the complaint is not generally valid as demonstrated, for example, by the difficulty of finding a realistic mechanism for optimal public goods provision and by the difficulty of providing a satisfactory rationalist account of war (Fearon, 1995; Garzske, 1999). Even if a model can be trumped up, however, the whole point of formalization is to insist that its assumptions and logic be explicit so that any 'tricks' can be discovered. It is true that tricks can be buried in the mathematics, but they can also be unearthed and more readily revealed as tricks than can tricks in comparably complicated verbal arguments. The explicitness, precision and clarity of formal analysis lend themselves to this goal.

Usually, of course, it is not a matter of tricks but of different assumptions. Here formal analysis provides an excellent way to clarify the terms of a substantive debate. An example is the 'relative gains' debate. Grieco (1988) argues that liberal theories misspecify the cooperation problem as an absolute gains problem (that is, how much each received) whereas states also care about relative gains (that is, who gets more). He shows that cooperation is much more difficult under relative gains, although Snidal (1991) demonstrates that even under Grieco's assumption, the inhibiting effect on cooperation is significantly limited in multilateral settings. Powell (1991) challenges the need to use the relative gains assumption by showing that the relative gains concerns can be induced as a by-product of strictly absolute gains concerns for survival.

This raises an interesting question about the aesthetics of models and theories. Should we prefer Powell's more parsimonious explanation because it assumes only absolute gains and derives relative gains concerns within the model? This does not by itself invalidate Grieco's assertion that states seek relative gains for primordial reasons. Indeed, one might equally be able to derive absolute gains preferences as a by-product of relative gains concerns (that is, I want more in order that I have more than you). This difference can be resolved only by finding a way to investigate the assumption itself or by generating divergent predictions from the two approaches. Either way, the formalization of the argument and the logical derivations sharpen the issues at stake (Grieco et al., 1993).[12]

In addition to the complaint that rational choice can predict anything, another complaint is that rational choice predicts everything and therefore predicts nothing. It is not true of all models, of course, since some give quite precise predictions. Therefore it is usually expressed in terms of the multiple equilibria produced by the folk theorem result that (under certain conditions) any point of cooperation that makes everyone better off can be attained. But should game theory be blamed for creating this multiplicity, or credited for revealing it and raising new questions about how the resulting indeterminacy is resolved? Regardless, there is a need to narrow the prediction, a problem on which the formal theory has had only partial success.[13] Any solution almost certainly requires bringing additional substantive considerations into the theory – perhaps through psychological theories of decision-making, or social norms, or historical analyses of path dependence.

Thus we can endorse and extend to IR more generally Walt's approving quotation of Schelling's warning that we should not 'treat the subject of strategy as though it were, or should be, solely a branch of mathematics'. But this caveat must be understood in the context of Schelling's general concern that 'the promise of game theory is so far unfulfilled' with respect to his goal of improving 'the retarded science of international strategy'. Schelling's point is *both* that mathematics isn't sufficient for developing good theory *and* that the verbal theory of military strategy that developed without formalization is moribund. His work shows how formal analysis can provide an invaluable basis upon which to build a largely verbal theory. Schelling's brilliance, of course, is that he is able to keep the mathematics in the background and in the appendices, while connecting it to a rich set of anecdotal examples and broad theorizing.

The challenge for rational choice is to find an appropriate combination of hard and soft approaches. Because the formal theory is now so much more developed, the contemporary mixture does and should include some highly technical pieces. At the same time, the real success of these models depends on several things. One is that the model itself not be so complex that it ceases to be a reasonable representation of what actors are actually capable of doing.[14] Another is that the underlying logic be expressed in softer terms, even if that means less precisely, in order to exploit the complementarities between hard and soft approaches. Formal results can provide a new impetus for informal speculation, now informed by a clearer baseline and better able to proceed on problems that defy hard formalization.

Finally, an important criterion for gauging the success of a model is whether it can be connected to empirical evidence, to which we turn next.

Empirical Evaluations of Rational Choice Arguments

Rational choice has also been criticized as insufficiently attuned to empirical matters, especially testing. This is an important and partly valid complaint. Enthusiasm for the theory's deductive power sometimes displaces attention to empirical realism and testing. This problem is aggravated by the difficulty or impossibility of observing some key variables such as preferences and beliefs, and by the flexibility of the theory, such that it can be adapted to fit the data in an *ad hoc* manner. However, the partial validity of the complaint should not be misconstrued as indicating an inherent fault of the approach as much as a failure of application. Below, I discuss some of the significant and growing body of empirical rational choice IR research, both quantitative and qualitative, that illustrates the empirical usefulness of the perspective.

Rational choice as a whole cannot be tested; only specific hypotheses and substantive theories within rational choice can be tested. Rational choice operates at such a general level, and covers such a range of models, that it makes no sense to think of testing it than it would to test 'statistics'. Furthermore, at the most abstract level, the conclusions of rational choice are 'true' by logical derivation. They are made empirically relevant – and falsifiable – only by mixing them with substantive assumptions (for example, goals of actors, 'rules of the game'). Thus what can be tested are applications of particular rational choice models to specific substantive problems. If the finding is negative, we reject the application of that model and the associated substantive assumptions and theory to that issue – not the model itself, and certainly not rational choice as a whole. This is the same as (say) when a Poisson model of war initiation fails and we reject the attached substantive theory of war initiation, not the Poisson model or its potential application to other areas of international politics. Of course, if a Poisson, signaling, or whatever type of model fails across a wide variety of circumstances and succeeds on few, we should conclude that it isn't much help for understanding IR. Only in this very limited sense can we 'test' rational choice as a whole.

For this reason, much of the antagonism between rational choice and its critics is again misplaced. Rational choice should not claim to explain everything and should not be held to that standard. The appropriate question is whether it can explain a fairly wide range of phenomena. Although the standard IR approach is to line up one theory against another so that the success of one is tied to the failure of another, that is not a necessary condition for understanding international politics. It is perfectly plausible, bordering on the obvious, that actors are motivated by both the 'logic of consequences' and 'the logic of appropriateness', for example, and our empirical task is to sort out under what conditions each logic operates – including the recognition that they operate together in some circumstances (March and Olsen, 1989). It is equally apparent that actors sometimes deviate significantly from the strict assumptions of rational choice so that conclusions need to be tempered by consideration of whether the simplification is adequate for the problem.[15] Conversely, many of these deviations can only be understood in terms of a baseline of rationality. For example, James Fearon (1995: 409) points out that a better rational explanation of war may increase our estimate of the importance of 'irrational' factors. So the complementarities of explanations may be more important than their differences – especially if the goal is understanding substantive problems rather than scoring debating points. In brief, rational choice should claim to explain, and be expected to explain, only some important aspects of international life, not all.

A generic difficulty in empirical testing is that when an argument or model fails, proponents will re-specify it before abandoning it. This is simultaneously a virtue and a defect, which though not unique to rational choice is magnified by its versatility. It is a virtue because the 'thinness' of any general theory means that its conjectures are unlikely to perfectly match any case or set of cases. Reformulation allows us to capture nuances and details of the case that we did not theoretically anticipate, or to relax simplifying but unrealistic assumptions (for example, replacing the unitary state assumption with a specification of domestic interests). It allows us to revise rather than reject the model. In this sense it is not unlike the use of different models in statistical work, or different specifications within any particular model. The corresponding defect is that revision undercuts testing, and heavy-handed revision merges into curve-fitting. This even erodes the logic of discovery if patching up a model to fit a case displaces the effort to identify a very small number of unexpected revisions that improve our understanding. In the extreme case, we end up 'rationalizing' the model rather than testing it.[16]

But while 'rationalization' is certainly a concern, rational choice offers safeguards that limit the danger posed. First, formalization restricts curve-fitting. As noted, it is difficult to generate a reasonable model that produces a particular result, especially since formalization makes assumptions and arguments explicit and subject to scrutiny. Verbal theory ('soft rational choice') provides more latitude in this respect, but even here the theory imposes significant limitations on acceptable explanations. Arguments drummed up to rescue the empirical failings of a model are more likely to appear *ad hoc* when compared to the systematic theory. Second, the emphasis on parsimony works against curve-fitting in both formal and verbal theory. (To expand the analogy, it is more difficult to 'curve-fit' with a straight line than with a higher order polynomial, or with one or two independent variables rather than with many variables.) Third, rational choice's aspirations to generalization limit its ability to modify models to fit particular cases. Finally, and most important, rational choice has adopted methodological strategies to limit the possibility of rationalization. The much-maligned assumption of fixed preferences, for example, arises not from a metaphysical belief that preferences are fixed but from methodological considerations of enabling empirical disconfirmation through limiting the possibilities of 'curve-fitting' via imputed preferences.[17]

Thus rational choice is caught between the 'rock' of empirical criticisms and the 'hard place' of theoretical (constructivist) criticisms of its conception of international politics. Fixed preferences increase the potential for falsifying a rational model but make it difficult to accommodate change in the character of actors and of the system. However, this difficult tradeoff is not unique to rational choice. It emerges from the more general problem of reconciling expansive theory with empirical testability. In other words, the 'revealed preference' problem, whereby rational choice explanations tend to tautology if preferences are induced from behavior, is no more or less severe than the *revealed norm* problem of constructivism when social 'norms' are induced from observation of social practice.

Although the empirical application of rational choice has lagged behind its theoretical development, a significant and growing amount of attention has been devoted to testing rational choice-based theories using both quantitative and qualitative methods. On the quantitative side, an excellent example is the emphasis on empirical analysis in the 'expected utility' theory of war pioneered by Bruce Bueno de Mesquita (1981). In addition to strengthening the attention to theoretical issues over earlier correlational investigations, this line of analysis has paid careful attention to the difficult measurement problems inherent in expected utility arguments and, especially as it has developed into a fully strategic model, to the difficult problems of estimation associated with equilibrium predictions (Signorino, 1999; Smith, 1999). The implications of the theory are testable and it has received considerable empirical support (Bennett and Stam, 2000; Bueno de Mesquita and Lalman, 1992), but also much criticism. The point here is not whether the theory is right or wrong but that it demonstrates that quantitative testing is an achievable goal for rational choice arguments.[18]

A second cumulative empirical agenda guided by rational choice has been the analysis of sanctions. The basic model is of one actor (the 'sender') imposing a demand on another actor (the 'target') and threatening to impose a sanction unless the demand is met. In addition to a progression of theoretical efforts to develop improved models of sanctioning (Drezner, 1999; Kirschner, 1997; Martin, 1992; Smith, 1995; Tsebelis, 1990), there has been extensive empirical work in both the qualitative and quantitative traditions to evaluate the theoretical claims (Dashti-Gibson et al., 1997; Drezner, 1999, 2000; Drury, 1998; Pape, 1997; Shambaugh, 1999). Debate continues on the efficacy of sanctions, on the selection of evidence, and on exact theoretical specifications, but there is no debate that this is a serious effort to join theory and data.

On the more qualitative side, rational choice has implicitly underpinned many important arguments which have been evaluated through historical and comparative case studies. One of the difficulties here, as noted earlier, is that rational choice arguments are so pervasive that it is sometimes easier to distinguish analyses that are predominantly not rational choice (for example, organization theory, normative, psychological) rather than ones based on rational choice. Nevertheless, a list of empirical analyses that are closely tied to rational choice theory would include such important books as those by Vinod Aggarwal (1996) on international debt, Jeffry Frieden (1991) on debt and development, Robert Gilpin (1981) on war and change, Hein Goemans (2000) on war termination, Joanne Gowa (1994) on alliances and trade, Joseph Grieco (1990) on the Tokyo Round, Lloyd Gruber (2000) on NAFTA, David Lake (1999) on US foreign policy, Lisa Martin (2000) on making credible commitments, Walter Mattli (1999) on regional integration, Helen Milner Ronald Mitchell (1994) on environmental compliance, (1997) on domestic politics and IR, Andrew Moravscik (1998) on European integration, Kenneth Oye (1992) on economic discrimination, Beth Simmons (1994) on inter-war monetary politics, Jack Snyder (1991) on imperial over-extension and Daniel Verdier (1994) on trade policy, and even Stephen Walt (1987) on alliance formation.[19] This is necessarily a partial list of books, and it ignores the much greater number of relevant articles. [20] But it certainly illustrates an impressive quantity and range of empirical applications significantly guided by rational choice. It also illustrates a wide variety of styles in the empirical application of rational choice. Some use explicit models to guide their analysis, others use verbal models as heuristics to guide their verbal argument, and still others simply focus on goal-seeking behavior as their fundamental explanatory factor.

Qualitative testing of models based in whole or part on rational choice has the same possibilities and drawbacks as similar tests of other theories. However, there are two routes (neither exclusive to rational choice) by which this capacity can be enhanced. First, the generality and systematic character of rational choice makes it particularly well suited for evaluation through connected case studies. The potential for development in this regard is seen in comparing the early Cooperation Under Anarchy project (Oye, 1986) to the recent Rational Design project (Koremenos et al., 2001a). The Oye volume shows the value of using very general rational choice insights (for example, 'Iteration promotes cooperation in PD') to guide understanding across a wide range of empirical cases. The RD project builds on this by increasing the specificity of independent and dependent variables and developing a series of precise conjectures based directly on formal rational choice results (for example, 'Institutional flexibility will increase with uncertainty'). These institutional design conjectures can be clearly evaluated in specific cases and are sometimes found wanting. However, the overall success of the conjectures demonstrates the value of rational choice for understanding international institutional design.

Second, Robert Bates et al. (1998) have coined the term 'analytic narratives' to describe a more systematic use of rational choice as a qualitative empirical research tool for individual case studies.[21] Their method uses a rational choice framework to guide the description of the case in terms of actors, preferences, choices, environmental constraints, strategic interdependencies, etc. and then invokes stronger theoretical results to assess the underlying mechanisms that lead to equilibrium outcomes. Its distinctiveness rests on a self-conscious effort to connect explicit and detailed rational choice models to historical events. In doing so, analytic narratives engage the tension between the formal logic and parsimony of the rational choice framework on the one hand, and an effort to capture specific contexts and analysis of developments over time characteristic of the narrative on the other hand. This combination has attractive advantages, including opening up the rational choice framework by pushing for a deeper and tighter analysis of the underlying mechanisms of change. The analytic side encourages generalization while the narrative side encourages closer contextual specification. While the approach can be seen as a form of rational choice imperialism, the authors argue it can more fruitfully be understood as an effort to find a 'middle ground'.

The rhetoric of 'analytic narratives' is exaggerated in a number of respects. First, the approach is not as novel as the name which, as Bates et al. (2000) point out, effectively describes what a number of rational choice and other case specialists have already been doing without the label. In particular, the well-established approach of 'process tracing' (George and McKeown, 1985) is similar in spirit and can be applied using a variety of theoretical perspectives (for example, analytical Marxism, prospect theory). Nevertheless, Jon Elster

(2000: 694), in an otherwise unyielding critique of analytical narratives, argues that rational choice has a special advantage because it 'is the only theory in the social sciences capable of yielding sharp deductions and predictions'. Of course, this requires that the predictions are sharp – a potential problem if multiple equilibria are pervasive – and that *ex post* choice among *ex ante* predictions doesn't dull the sharpness of the latter.

This richness of predictions poses a challenge for the use of analytic narratives. Proponents present it as a method not only of interpretation and theoretical discovery but of 'testing' – although these are rarely so neatly separated in practice – whereas critics may see it as little more than a more formalized approach to curve-fitting (Dessler, 2000; Green and Shapiro, 1994). As with any case-oriented approach, this limitation is attenuated (but not eliminated) to the extent that the narrative explains a rich variety of facts within the case and to the extent the same theory fits across cases (King et al., 1994; Van Evera, 1997). Analytical narratives are stronger tools than process-tracing or other qualitative approaches to the extent that rationalist theory restricts the range of predictions and enable skepticism, if not strict falsification, of the application. By this reasonable standard of comparison, analytic narratives hold substantial potential.

Elster's severe critique of analytic narratives implicitly applies to any systematic explanation that would meet (say) the standards of Green and Shapiro (1994). It nevertheless contains a series of points that should promote modesty in the development of analytic narratives in IR. First, actors should not be endowed with extraordinary powers of computation (for example, able to anticipate complicated strategic contingencies over long periods, or to deal rationally with any type of uncertainty). Overly sophisticated models that require equally sophisticated actors are not plausible representations of the international life and these complications make testing that much harder. Second, Elster is suspicious of aggregate actors such as the states, international organizations or non-governmental organizations (NGOs) that populate many IR arguments. While his preferred solution of disaggregating down to individuals is generally impractical – as well as denying the importance of collective properties that cannot be captured in the individual units – his alternative solution that the 'aggregate as actor' assumption be justified is wholly appropriate. This also provides insight into state 'preferences', a point I expand on below. Finally, Elster makes the important point that rational choice models not only must recognize that rational motives need not be material but, equally importantly, that they co-exist with other motivations whose impact may not be understood through rational models. Thus strategic actors can be moral, and moral actors can be strategic. This

delimits the scope of rational approaches but it doesn't necessarily undermine their power. Proper scope delimitation should make rational choice more effective in the range it applies (Abbott and Snidal, 2002).

Whether in response to its critics or simply as a natural continuation of its research program, rational choice is responding to its weaknesses as an empirically applied theory. The resulting growth in empirical work will have several salutary effects. Closer attention to empirical issues promotes explanations that are 'thicker' in specifying key features and context of issues and in identifying underlying mechanisms. While empirical successes in explanation and systematic testing will strengthen the grounds for accepting these explanations, empirical failures will identify aspects of international politics that rational choice does not explain well. Proponents will treat failures as anomalies that need to be accommodated. This will occur first through retrofitting and reformulating the theory – a form of curve-fitting which is inherently unsatisfactory from a testing perspective but may be illuminating both of the individual case and of more general mechanisms. The ultimate empirical test, of course, is whether these reformulated models have a more general applicability to other empirical cases.

SUBSTANTIVE CHALLENGES FOR RATIONAL CHOICE

The ultimate challenge for rational choice is not whether is has been too formal or has focused insufficiently on empirical matters in the past, but how well it can handle emerging issues in the future. While many of these issues will be driven by changing substantive problems – increasing globalization, shifting economic and military power, emerging issues, and so forth – rational choice will be judged by how it addresses the theoretical and empirical questions that they raise. To explore these prospects, I consider three important questions that face international relations in theory and practice.

Incorporating Dynamics and Change

Rational choice might seem ineffective for studying change. The concept of equilibrium is inherently static since it is defined as the absence of any tendency to change. And the standard way to model 'dynamic' choice is by redefining it as a static choice of an optimal strategy for all time, typically under an assumption of stable preferences (Kreps, 1990). Thus, even game models that represent sequences of choices through time, whether in the extensive form or as repeated play of a normal form game, typically take the fundamental structure of the situation as fixed and then focus on determining the equilibrium outcome.

Change is usually introduced through comparative static analysis of how the equilibrium shifts in response to exogenous change. The actual dynamic process and time path are not described, but bracketed under the assumption that actors adjust to a new equilibrium as it emerges. This failure to engage the process and mechanisms of change becomes even more glaring when there are multiple equilibria so that choice among equilibria also needs to be explained. This is a particular shortcoming of the cooperation literature where the central question of when or how there will be a transition between equilibria – from anarchy to cooperation, or from one cooperative arrangement to another – is thereby ignored. Similarly, for historical analysis, it leaves open the question of when the prevailing equilibrium path will persist for reasons of path dependency or when there will be a shift to a superior time path.

There are some examples of more properly dynamic IR rational choice analysis. Power-transition theory (Gilpin, 1981; Organski and Kugler, 1980) argues that rapid shifts in power caused, for example, by differential economic growth will make war more likely. Powell (1999b) proposes a formal model that emphasizes the informational problems. By decomposing the concept of power shift, he shows that the size of a shift affects the probability of war but that its speed does not. James Fearon (1997) deepens this analysis by making shifts in power endogenous as concessions between states affect their future power balance. His finding that such changes do not lead to war (except in specifiable and unlikely circumstances) is an excellent example of a non-obvious result that could only be found through formalization.[22]

This sort of change, while important, is only partial. The reason is that the underlying substantive interpretation is deeply rooted in realism. Realism is fundamentally a theory of stasis that is premised on an enduring international anarchy with states as the primary actors.[23] Rational choice offers a number of analyses of change within this overarching 'anarchy' equilibrium. Change is typically driven by shifts in the distribution of power; adjustment mechanisms include war, changing coalition patterns (Niou et al., 1989; Wagner, 1986), or decisions to acquire arms (Intriligator and Brito, 1984). Similarly, realist analysis of political economy incorporates change driven by a changing distribution of power – as in hegemonic stability theory (Gilpin, 1981). Although all of these analyses focus on change at one level, their underlying presumption is one of stability in the overall nature of system. However, this restriction on the scope of change inheres in substantive assumptions drawn from realist theory rather than in the rational choice approach.[24]

Rational choice analyses of cooperation and institutions introduce the possibility of broader change in international politics.[25] The cooperation literature establishes the possibility of attaining a different equilibrium than envisioned by realists. Institutions are seen as facilitating the attainment of cooperative equilibria and reinforcing and stabilizing those equilibria over time. Important mechanisms include improving information about potential joint gains from cooperation, reassuring actors that others also intend to join in the cooperative equilibrium, and providing timely information about behavior to diminish incentives to cheat. The impact cumulates within actors as they learn about the world and about each other, and changes their individual expectations regarding each other's preferences and behavior. It also takes place at the collective level through the creation of norms of behavior and shared beliefs about the new equilibrium outcome. Here, rational choice moves beyond its individualism since equilibria and common knowledge are properties of the collective. Through this, institutional analysis is developing an analysis of institutions as independent factors in international politics and, possibly in some cases, as autonomous actors.

The foregoing is only a sketch of the past and evolving trajectory of rational choice institutionalism. My purpose is to show that rational choice potentially encompasses a wide range of change in international politics, although it has not fulfilled this broad agenda by any means. How successfully it can meet the constructivist challenge of explaining fundamental change in actor preferences (and identity), as well as change in the international political settings, remains an active research question. My claim is only that it has the potential to do much in this regard.

Before turning to some (slightly) more detailed considerations of actor and preference change, let me distinguish two reasons why IR rational choice analysis has been reluctant to take on such issues. The first is because of substantive assumptions that are used in specific arguments but are not intrinsic to rational choice. Most realist analyses and some institutionalist analyses reject the assumption of fundamental change by maintaining a substantive emphasis on states as the central actors with constant goals and facing problems analytically similar to those of the past. Other analyses accept the notion of change both through institutions and within actors but tend to see it operating more incrementally. This goes to a second methodological reason for reluctance to incorporate change, which essentially goes back to the revealed preference problem. Because considerations of change introduce even more flexibility into rational models, and preferences cannot be directly observed, the concern is that explanation will reduce to tautology. To avoid this, rational choice imposes limits on itself, such as fixed preferences. But in doing so it also limits its ability to examine possibly important phenomena. The next section considers some possible strategies for improving its analysis of changes in actors and in preferences.

Endogenous Actors and Preferences

Rational choice has traditionally assumed that the actors and interests are fixed in any analysis and has explained change in terms of changing constraints. The reason is that preferences are impossible to observe directly whereas constraints are usually more observable. Under these conditions, fixed preferences allow for a tight analysis of many issues in an empirically falsifiable way, whereas assumptions of changing preferences lead to slippery and untestable arguments. However, the fixed preference assumption is not always valid and cannot handle all problems. In an article that is widely cited to justify the fixed preferences assumption, Stigler and Becker (1977) assert 'not that we are clever enough to make illuminating applications of utility-maximizing theory to all important phenomena ... [but that] no other approach of remotely comparable power and generality is available'. Their central argument is that fixed preferences *sometimes* provide a powerful analytic premise whereas 'assumptions of unstable tastes ... really have only been *ad hoc* arguments that disguise analytical failures'.[26]

Even this position – or at least the conventional interpretation of it – is overstated. Becker (1992, 1996) has moved well beyond it to consider 'the evolution of preferences out of past experiences [which] seems far more intuitive, even when extended to institutions and culture, than the opposite assumption so dominant in economics that preferences are independent of the path'. These two positions – which Becker reconciles through the notion of stable meta-preferences – reflect the tension between sound methodological strategies and addressing certain, substantively important problems. IR rational choice analysis faces the same tension between maintaining the power of the approach while expanding its scope of coverage. Here I briefly sketch several different ways in which it can do so.[27]

While treating states as aggregate actors with well-defined preferences is often a troublesome assumption for rational choice analysis, enriching the assumption provides a useful window for analyzing preference change. In IR, this has occurred as part of an effort to create a richer understanding of 'state' motivations by unpacking them into their domestic components, both theoretically and empirically (Milner, 1998; Walsh, 2001).[28] A wide range of examples includes analyses of political and economic coalitions (Frieden, 1991; Milner, 1988;

Moravscik, 1997; Rogowski, 1989), the analysis of two-level games (Evans et al., 1993; Putnam, 1988), principal–agent models (Downs and Rocke, 1995), audience costs (Fearon, 1994), domestic commitment problems (Drezner, 2001), and macro-historical explanations of the evolution and changes in state preferences (Rosecrance, 1986; Spruyt, 1994). The logic is that aggregate preference change can be explained in terms of the changing relative influence of underlying constituencies, and their coalitional behavior, even where the preferences of the underlying constituencies are stable. Preference change can also result from variations in the regime type that determine how groups are aggregated (Goemans, 2000) or, within regime type, by variations in the specific aggregation rules (Rogowski, 1999). Such derivations of aggregate preferences impose strong theoretical and empirical requirements, but they offer a way to specify state preferences that is prior to state behavior.

A different type of preference change occurs when new actors with different goals enter an issue. Globalization, for example, may empower new actors ranging from activists to experts to firms. Insofar as they can be treated as goal-seeking actors, rational choice can explore the implications of their addition to international setting. Of course, the heterogeneity of these new actors dramatically increases the complexity of the problem being analyzed and makes modeling more difficult. For that reason, analysis will lean towards soft rational choice informed by formal results. Examples of introducing non-state actors include bankers (Lipson, 1986), ship owners (Mitchell, 1994), environmental NGOs (Raustiala, 1997), soldiers (Morrow, 2001), airlines (Richards, 2001) and international business firms (Mattli, 2001). Indeed, even Keck and Sikkink's (1998) constructivist analysis of transnational activists treats them as strategically rational agents at the international level. While this illustrates the complementarity of constructivist and rational approaches in examining the impact of new actors, there is no reason in principle why rational choice explanations may not be valuable in explaining the emergence of these non-state international actors through the same logic used to explain the rise of domestic interest groups (Hansen, 1991; Schattschneider, 1935).

A third case is that of deliberate decisions to change actors and their preferences. This occurs when the members of an international arrangement, and therefore the preferences of the relevant actors, are objects of choice. Rational choice has had some preliminary empirical success in addressing membership within international institutions as a solution to an institutional design problem (Downs, et al., 2000; Koremenos, et al., 2001c). The new members can be states, but they also can be firms or NGOs admitted to participate on some international problem (Raustiala, 1997) or IOs that are either created or empowered on some issue (Abbott and Snidal, 1998; Thompson, 2001). In other cases, the membership is fixed but some actors seek to change the nature of other actors. Examples include human rights activists who seek internal reform in repressive states, international financial institutions that require program beneficiaries to adopt market reforms, or organizations such as the EU and NATO that impose 'democracy' requirements on prospective members.

Finally, actors sometimes deliberately seek change in their own national 'preferences'. This is what free trade coalitions hope will be the case as non-competitive industries decline and what political leaders seek when they bind themselves to international arrangements to solve commitment problems (Drezner, 2001). States also engage in processes ranging from joint scientific research to cultural and political exchanges in order to learn more about the world, about each other and about their joint expectations. By changing not only their own information but also their shared beliefs with respect to equilibrium behavior, they change their preferences over courses of action even if their underlying preferences are stable. Again, if the processes strengthen the relative position of some domestic actors, that may also change aggregate state preferences. More dramatically, states make rational plans to join international institutions like the EU, WTO or international legal agreements with the understanding – often reflected in resistance from some quarters – that those institutions will significantly shape their own future course. Rational choice has a largely unfulfilled role to play in analyzing this sort of deliberate preference change.

The examples illustrate different strategies for introducing preference change through aggregation processes, the introduction of additional actors, through the choice of actors, or through changing information and the external institutional environment. They are speculative, although in each case some progress has been made. But these approaches also raise tensions between the advantages of parsimony and the value of empirical richness, and between formal and softer analyses. Finally, despite these possibilities, rational choice (and for that matter other approaches) should remain modest about the extent to which it can offer systematic analyses of the complicated problem of actor and preference change.

Normative and Policy Analysis

Because the research impetus of rational choice has been heavily 'scientific' such that it is even labeled 'positive' theory, both proponents and critics often see it as far removed from normative analysis. This is ironic since rational choice began as a normative enterprise (Stein, 1999) and lends itself readily to normative analysis, at least along the utilitarian lines from which it developed. So it is fair to say that rational choice in IR has not fulfilled its normative potential, but not fair to say that it cannot do so (Wendt, 2001).

Rational choice already contains important normative elements. At an individual actor level, it is implicitly a theory of how people should behave – What is the best choice? – in a given situation. At a collective level, it examines how groups can do better through cooperation to attain a superior equilibrium. But while these efficiency considerations have important normative content – and, to reiterate, efficiency need not be defined in terms of material interests – rational choice can and should engage other normative considerations.

Distributional questions are slowly emerging as an important area of inquiry in IR rational choice and bring both a positive and normative dimension. Theoretical work has moved beyond the use of coordination problems to exemplify 'the' distributional problem to a realization (especially via the folk theorem) that distributional issues are pervasive. An important literature has emerged exploring how distributional differences inhibit cooperative efficiency gains (Fearon, 1998; Krasner, 1991; Morrow, 1994a). Empirical work has begun to examine the impact of cooperative arrangements on distributive outcomes at both the international and domestic levels (Goldstein, 1996; Gruber, 2000; Oatley and Nabors, 1998). By emphasizing that there may be losers as well as winners from 'cooperative' schemes, analysis of this sort invites a normative evaluation of the achieved equilibrium in comparison to alternative possibilities.

Institutional design questions bring rational choice yet closer to normative analysis. Analyses of institutional arrangements have addressed how issue linkage (Mitchell, 2001; Sebenius, 1983), membership (Koremenos et al., 2001c; Pahre, 2001), and incorporation of escape clauses and other forms of flexibility (Koremenos, 2001) can remedy distributional impediments to cooperation. Since institutional analysis is premised on the analysis of alternative equilibria, it is a short step from asking what institutions states *will* design to asking what institutions they *should* design. For example, bargaining models typically predict the outcome among individuals in particular circumstances but can equally be used to ask what protocols and institutions will lead to preferred outcomes. Brams and Taylor (1996) illustrate the possibilities in their investigation of how to devise fair allocation devices among rational agents. International relations has only begun to engage this type of analysis, but rational choice is eminently suited for it and already offers a large number of insights (Young, 1994).

It is less clear how fully rational choice can incorporate other normative issues – such as justice, appropriateness, or autonomy – but it can certainly contribute to an analysis of their impact in IR. Of course, insofar as other values can be treated as objectives of actors, rational choice can readily incorporate them. Despite the danger of trivializing other values by simply re-labeling them as interests, this can be valuable for understanding their impact (and perhaps the impact of the actors who carry them), as well as the possibilities of and strategies for attaining them. Finally, by showing that good institutional design must be consistent with interests to be effective, rational choice can help normative analysis avoid foundering on naïve idealism.

Rational choice can further benefit by addressing the 'positive' impact of normative conceptions by way of their influence on actors' behavior. This is one of the central insights raised by constructivist critiques of interest-based approaches. Rational choice often has nodded implicitly to it through reference to the role of normative considerations in creating 'focal points' to guide choice among multiple equilibria. But no adequate theory of focal points – normative or otherwise – has been deveoped.

Another area where normative considerations appear important is in international legalization. Rational choice has now begun to explain the form and content of legalization (Goldstein et al., 2000). While significant insights have been generated in seeking to explain legalization from a strictly ratio-nalist perspective (Goldsmith and Posner, 1999, 2002a,b), a purist approach may overlook the norma-tive force of law reflected in such key concepts as legitimacy, obligation or compliance pull (Abbott and Snidal, 2000, 2002; Hurrell, 1993; Finnemore and Toope, 2002). Because these concepts are notoriously vague, however, rational choice can play an important role in tightening the theoretical discussion and sort-ing out the logic of the claims. An important example is the debate on compliance initiated by the Downs et al. (1996) critique of 'managerial approaches' (Chayes and Chayes, 1995) and its extension into a more general critique of the legal 'transformational-ist' school (Downs et al., 2000). However, the goal should not be to show how rational choice can make the normative perspective redundant, but to explain how rational incentives and normative understand-ings interact through legalization.

A turn to normative questions also suggests a need to shift the emphasis of tools within the rational choice toolkit. Primary concern for problems of enforcement and associated problems of commit-ment and information led to an emphasis on non-cooperative game theory as the appropriate method of analysis. While enforcement remains an important issue, it is not the only one. Other models that de-emphasize enforcement problems may be more valuable for these new problems. Cooperative game theory with its focus on how the gains from cooper-ation are divided may provide better insights to dis-tributional issues.[29] Similarly, attention to questions

of mechanism design – that is, how to design institu-tional arrangements so as to achieve the desired ends – may be more relevant as the field shifts to address normative issues.[30] Now, instead of using rational choice to ask the positive question 'Given actors' interests and (institutional and other) con-straints, what will be the outcome?', we turn the analysis around to ask 'Given actors' interests, how should we rearrange institutional constraints to achieve our normatively desired outcome?' Rational choice analysis in IR is barely on the threshold of asking such questions, but they are the means through which its normative and policy potential can be unleashed.

CONCLUSION

While the analysis of international relations in terms of goal-seeking agents has long been a central part of IR theory, rational choice analysis has become more explicitly theoretical by drawing upon both formal and informal analytic results. Its considerable successes have led to optimism and even arrogance regarding its future prospects, but there have also been failures and shortcomings which critics appropriately have been quick to point out. Rational choice cannot resolve all of these chal-lenges, but by addressing them seriously it can increase its own power to enhance our understand-ing of international affairs.

The view of rational choice adopted here is expansive. In particular, I did not draw a line between formal and soft rational choice because their relation is highly symbiotic. Formal results often provide the hard kernel behind softer analysis, while softer analysis encourages a wider range of interpretation and application of the model. For this reason, soft rational choice approaches lie behind many of the empirical tests of the theory because they facilitate the adaptation of the abstract theory to different issues, cases and historical periods.

While rational choice has numerous short-comings, some of its seeming failings are best understood either as important features of the world or as a result of appropriately cautious strategies for analyzing it. The existence of multiple equilibria, for example, may indicate not a failure of a model but an important indeterminacy in the world, and in our ability to predict outcomes. Of course, it remains a reasonable goal for rational choice – in concert or in competition with other approaches – to explain how and why a specific equilibrium is attained. Similarly, rational choice models that leave out important considerations such as change in preferences thereby restrict their ability to handle some important international issues. But this limita-tion may have a benefit in allowing other questions to be studied more carefully. Of course, rational choice should seek to expand its range of coverage with regard to excluded issues but, in doing so, it should remember that the power of its analysis rests partly on the limits it imposes. Without such limits, rational choice (like other approaches) explains nothing by pretending to explain everything.

Thus rational choice in IR should be neither defensive nor arrogant. It does not have to be defensive because it has led to significant advances in our understanding of international politics. Many of its limitations are self-imposed for good reasons and others provide challenges that it can be expected to address. But rational choice should not be arrogant because its critics have identified significant shortcomings in its theoretical and empirical work. Rational choice cannot answer all these challenges and the answers it can give are often 'soft' compared to its aspirations.

Notes

I thank an anonymous referee, Susan Pratt, Alexander Thompson and the editors of this volume for helpful comments on an earlier draft of this chapter.

1 For a representative range of critiques, not all specifically addressed to international relations, see: Elster, 1989; Friedman, 1995; Green and Shapiro, 1994; Katzenstein, 1996; Monroe, 2001; Ruggie, 1998; Walt, 1999; Wendt, 1999; Yee, 1997.

2 For other recent efforts to look at this question from different perspectives, see Lake and Powell, 1999a, a number of the articles in Katzenstein, et al., 1998 and Hasenclever et al., 1997.

3 Fearon and Wendt discuss the relation between constructivism and rationalism in their contribution to this volume.

4 As always, the word 'theory' is a bit elusive here. Rational choice is essentially a normative theory of how actors should choose in different (abstract) circumstances that becomes a positive theory when actors are assumed rational and the empirical circumstances (e.g., of IR) are specified. Formalization introduces a parallel mathematical 'theory' which provides an abstract representation with minimal substantive content. A particular empirical interpretation of this abstract theory turns it into a substantive theory.

5 I thank Thomas Risse for pressing me on this point.

6 Here and elsewhere I use specific references as iconic representations of work in the field. There are too many relevant contributions to provide an exhaustive bibliogrphy.

7 Axelrod's work on the evolution of cooperation (1984) and agent-based models (1997; see also Cederman, 1997) are illustrative. See also Rubinstein's (1998) effort to model bounded rationality and the chapter by James Fearon and Alexander Wendt in this volume.

8 Even differences within rational choice methodology – for example, over the use of one solution concept rather than another – are ultimately debates over how the actors would (or should) handle a particular problem.

9 Powell (1999b) and Lake and Powell (1999b) provide a good overview of important issues pertaining to the use of models in international relations. See Walt, 1999 for a critique and the subsequent responses by Bueno de Mesquita and Morrow (1999), Martin (1999), Niou and Ordeshook (1999), Powell (1999a) and Zagare (1999).

10 Allan and Dupont (1999) provide an excellent overview of the diversity of alternative models. They develop a typology of sixteen different types of social model, of which they categorize eight as rational. They also pay special attention to the relation between model choice and empirical applicability.

11 The 'folk theorem' says that any feasible payoff combination can be an equilibrium in an on-going interaction provided that the players are sufficiently patient (i.e., don't discount the future too heavily) and that every player receives at least as much as they can guarantee themselves even if everyone else gangs up on them. An important consequence is that most such interactions will have 'multiple equilibria'.

12 See Hasenclever et al., 1997 for an excellent overview of this debate.

13 A clear success is the introduction of 'subgame perfection' to eliminate incredible threats, while concepts like sequential or Perfect Bayesian equilibria have also been widely used to good effect. But the value and empirical applicability of more complicated equilibrium 'refinements' has been increasingly challenged (Allan and Dupont, 1999).

14 This does not mean that the actor must be able to 'solve' the model or understand it in its entirety, but it must be able to reasonably perform the tasks assigned to it. For example, an international negotiator need not understand the Arrow (1951) theorem in order to recognize opportunities for strategic agenda-setting or linkage.

15 Well-known deviations include the bureaucratic and psychological schools of decision-making, especially the literature which builds on work such as that by Kahneman and Tversky (1979) in challenging rational choice directly (Levy, 1997). Some of the internal rational choice critiques of key concepts like discounting (Laibson, 1997) and risk (Rabin and Thaler, 2001) also suggest limits inherent in the logical theory as a representation of rational decision-making.

16 Without diverting my argument that rational choice can meet the challenge of testing head-on, the value of curve-fitting in IR should not be dismissed. Establishing systematic empirical relations is a real contribution to a field that remains fairly short of clear and correct systematic facts. The 'democracies don't go to war' correlation, for example, has stimulated important work on both the theoretical and empirical fronts. Even identifying a situation as fitting a particular model (e.g., as prisoners' dilemma) may enhance our understanding of it.

17 See not only the standard cite to Stigler and Becker (1977) but Marshall's (1910) early discussion of preferences and time periods.

18 For a critique of the empirical contributions of rational choice, including the expected utility theory of war, see Walt, 1999 and replies by Bueno de Mesquita and

Morrow (1999), Martin (1999), Niou and Ordeshook (1999), Powell (1999) and Zagare (1999).

19 The most controversial inclusion here is (deliberately) the work of Walt, who has been highly critical of rational choice and especially formal models. See Frieden, 1999: 50–1 for a cogent analysis of Walt's work as fitting in the rational choice tradition – or at least of how it could be improved by a more self-conscious attention to the (soft, not formal) rational choice approach.

20 Consider also examples like Goldstein, 1993 and Goldstein and Keohane, 1993 which are critical of rational choice as too limited (by leaving out ideas) but proceed in a largely complementary manner; works like Spruyt, 1994 that engage important elements of rational choice arguments but move significantly beyond them; or works like Pape, 1996 that use a rational choice framework to sort out different verbal arguments.

21 Analytic narratives can be seen partly as an elaboration of earlier discussions of the use of rational choice approaches in 'interpretive' accounts (Ferejohn, 1991; Johnson, 1991). Indeed, the possibility of its strictly interpretive usage reminds us that rational choice has no necessary connection to positivism and 'testing'.

22 Another example of more dynamic analysis that has been applied to IR is Axelrod's (1984, 1997) analysis of the evolution of cooperation, which can be interpreted from a rational choice as well as other perspectives. It shows how dynamic processes of selection, imitation or learning may lead to changed outcomes.

23 Thus Robert Gilpin's (1981: 211) study of change maintains 'that the nature of international relations has not changed fundamentally over the millennia'. See also Waltz, 1979: 65–6 and Krasner, 1999 with respect to sovereignty.

24 Of course, the realist substantive position may be right. See Grieco, 1997 for a persuasive case for the value of studying the constant factors in international life across time and systems.

25 For a full treatment of international institutions see Simmons and Martin's contribution to this volume. Here I offer more of a speculative sketch of the trajectory of rational choice approaches.

26 Choice over time also raises deep problems of inconsistency even when preferences are constant (Strotz, 1955–6) which are further aggravated by changing preferences (Hammond, 1976). One could interpret such results as indicating the inability of rational choice to deal with changing preferences over time. In my view, a superior interpretation is that the models reveal deep problems relevant to any analysis of changing preferences. See Schelling, 1978 and Elster, 1979 for extensions of these problems that bridge beyond rational choice, and Becker, 1996 for an effort to incorporate them within rational choice.

27 See Milner, 1998 for a general overview of the IR unitary actor assumption and Frieden, 1999 for an overview of general issues and strategies for determining preferences.

28 Empirical work, often but not always closely guided by rational analysis, has taken the lead, but Milner, 1998 discusses how theoretical rational choice can catch up to it.

29 The standard distinction between cooperative and non-cooperative games is that agreements are binding in the former and not in the latter. Moulin (1995) argues that this misunderstands the self-enforcing nature of the core and other stability concepts in cooperative game theory. More important, for some IR problems – such as agreements within the EU or many agreements among the OECD countries – there is no more doubt that parties will abide by their agreements than in domestic contexts. In such cases, cooperative game models can allow for a tighter focus on the bargaining–distribution problem by de-emphasizing the enforcement problem. For a different view see Morrow, 1994: 76.

30 I thank an anonymous reviewer for suggesting that I mention this literature. For an overview of mechanism design see Myerson, 1991, Mas-Colell et al., 1995 and, for a less technical introduction, see Dutta, 1999.

Bibliography

Abbott, Kenneth (1989) 'Modern International Relations Theory: A Prospectus for International Lawyers', *Yale Journal of International Law*, 14 (2): 335–411.

Abbott, Kenneth and Snidal, Duncan (1998) 'Why States Act through Formal International Organizations', *Journal of Conflict Resolution*, 42 (1): 3–32.

Abbott, Kenneth and Snidal, Duncan (2000) 'Toward a Theory of International Legalization', *International Organization*, 53 (3): 421–56.

Abbott, Kenneth and Snidal, Duncan (2001) 'Transformation: Alternative Pathways to International Legalization'. paper presented at a conference on 'The Impact of Norms and Institutions on Cooperation in International Environment and Trade: Theoretical Perspectives', Hebrew University, Jerusalem, 3–5 June.

Abbott, Kenneth and Snidal, Duncan (2002) 'Values and Interests: International Legalization in the Fight against Corruption', in Jack Goldsmith and Eric Posner (eds), *Rational Choice in International Law* (Special issue of *The Journal of Legal Studies*).

Abbott, Kenneth, Keohane, Robert, Slaughter, Anne-Marie, Moravscik, Andrew and Snidal, Duncan (2000) 'The Concept of Legalization', *International Organization*, 54 (3): 401–19.

Achen, Christopher H. and Snidal, Duncan (1989) 'Rational Deterrence Theory and Comparative Case Studies', *World Politics*, XLI (2): 143–69.

Aggarwal, Vinod K. (1996) *Debt Games: Strategic Interaction in International Debt Rescheduling*. Cambridge: Cambridge University Press.

Allan, Pierre and Dupont, Cédric (1999) 'International Relations Theory and Game Theory: Baroque Modeling Choice and Empirical Robustness', *International Political Science Review*, 20 (1): 23–47.

Allan, Pierre and Schmidt, Christian (1994) *Game Theory and International Relations*. Brookfield, VT: Edward Elgar.

Arrow, Kenneth (1951) *Social Choice and Individual Values*. New Haven: Yale University Press.

Axelrod, Robert (1984) *The Evolution of Cooperation*. New York: Basic Books.

Axelrod, Robert (1997) *The Complexity of Cooperation: Agent-Based Models of Competition and Collaboration*. Princeton: Princeton University Press.

Barry, Brian M. and Hardin, Russell (1982) *Rational Man and Irrational Society: An Introduction and Sourcebook*. Beverly Hills: Sage.

Bates, Robert H., Greif, Avner, Levi, Margaret, Rosenthal, Jean-Laurent and Weingast, Barry R. (1998) *Analytic Narratives*. Princeton: Princeton University Press.

Bates, Robert H., Greif, Avner, Levi, Margaret, Rosenthal, Jean-Laurent and Weingast, Barry R. (2000) 'Analytic Narratives Revisited', *Social Science History*, 24 (4): 9522–34.

Becker, Gary S. (1992) 'Habits, Addictions, and Traditions', *Kyklos*, 45 (3): 327–45.

Becker, Gary S. (1996) *Accounting for Tastes*. Harvard: Harvard University Press.

Bennett, D. Scott and Stam, Allan C. III (2000) 'A Universal Test of an Expected Utility Theory of War', *International Studies Quarterly*, 44 (3): 451–80.

Bhandari, Jagdeep and Sykes, Alan (eds) (1997) *Economic Dimensions in International Law*. Cambridge: Cambridge University Press.

Brams, Steven J. and Taylor, Alan D. (1996) *Fair Division: From Cake-Cutting to Dispute Resolution*. Cambridge: Cambridge University Press.

Bueno de Mesquita, Bruce (1981) 'Risk, Power Distributions, and the Likelihood of War', *International Studies Quarterly*, 25 (4): 541–68.

Bueno de Mesquita, Bruce and Lalman, David (1992) *War and Reason: Domestic and International Imperatives*. New Haven: Yale University Press.

Bueno de Mesquita, Bruce and Morrow, James D. (1999) 'Formal Methods, Formal Complaints: Debating the Role of Rational Choice in Security Studies – Sorting Through the Wealth of Notions', *International Security*, 24 (2): 56–73.

Burley, Anne-Marie (1993) 'International Law and International Relations Theory: A Dual Agenda', *American Journal of International Law*, 87: 205.

Calvert, Randall L. (1995) 'Rational Actors, Equilibrium and Social Institutions', in Jack Knight and Itai Sened (eds), *Explaining Social Institutions*. Ann Arbor: University of Michigan Press.

Cederman, Lars-Erik (1997) *Emergent Actors in World Politics: How States and Nations Develop and Dissolve*. Princeton: Princeton University Press.

Chan, Steve and Cooper, A. (eds) (2001) *Economic Statecraft: Theory and Practice*. New York: Macmillan/St. Martin's Press.

Chayes, Abram and Chayes, Antonia (1995) *The New Sovereignty: Compliance with International Regulatory Agreements*. Cambridge, MA: Harvard University Press.

Coase, Ronald (1960) 'The Problem of Social Cost', *Journal of Law and Economics*, 31: 1–44.

Dashti-Gibson, Jaleh, Davis, Patricia and Radcliff, Benjamin (1997) 'On the Determinants of the Success of Economic Sanctions: An Empirical Analysis', *American Journal of Political Science*, 41: 608–18.

Dessler, David (2000) 'Analytic Narrative: A Methodological Innovation in Social Science?', *International Studies Review*, 2 (3): 176–9.

Downs, George W. and Rocke, David M. (1995) *Optimal Imperfection: Domestic Uncertainty and Institutions in International Relations*. Princeton: Princeton University Press.

Downs, George, Danish and Barsoom, Peter (2000) 'The Transformational Model of International Regime Design: Triumph of Hope or Experience?', *Columbia Journal of Transnational Law*, 38 (3): 465–514.

Downs, George W., Rocke, David M. and Barsoom, Peter M. (1996) 'Is the Good News about Compliance Good News about Cooperation?', *International Organization*, 50 (3): 379–406.

Drezner, Daniel W. (1999) *The Sanctions Paradox: Economic Statecraft and International Relations*. Cambridge: Cambridge University Press.

Drezner, Daniel W. (2000) 'The Complex Causation of Sanctions Outcomes', in Steve Chan and A. Cooper (eds), *Economic Statecraft: Theory and Practice*. New York: Macmillan/St. Martin's Press.

Drezner, D.W. (2001) 'Outside the Box: Explaining Sanctions in Pursuit of Foreign Economic Goals', *International Interactions*, 26 (4): 379–410.

Drezner, Daniel (ed.) (2002) *The Interaction of Domestic and International Institutions*. Ann Arbor: University of Michigan Press.

Drury, A. Cooper (1998) 'Revisiting Economic Sanctions Reconsidered', *Journal of Peace Research*, 35: 497–509.

Dutta, Prajit K. (1999) *Strategies and Games: Theory and Practice*. Cambridge, MA: MIT Press.

Elster, Jon (1979) *Ulysses and the Sirens: Studies in Rationality and Irrationality*. Cambridge: Cambridge University Press.

Elster, Jon (1989) *The Cement of Society*. Cambridge: Cambridge University Press.

Elster, Jon (2000) 'Book Reviews – Rational Choice History: A Case of Excessive Ambition', *American Political Science Review*, 94 (3): 696–702.

Evans, Peter, Jacobson, Harold and Putnam, Robert (eds) (1993) *Double Edged Diplomacy: International Bargaining and Domestic Politics*. Berkeley: University of California Press.

Fearon, James (1994) 'Domestic Political Audiences and the Escalation of International Disputes', *American Political Science Review*, 88 (3): 577–92.

Fearon, James D. (1995) 'Rationalist Explanations for War', *International Organization*, 49 (3): 379–414.

Fearon, James (1997) 'Bargaining Over Objects that Influence Future Bargaining Power'. Paper presented at 93rd Annual Meeting of the American Political Science Association, 28–31 August, Washington, DC.

Fearon, James D. (1998) 'Bargaining, Enforcement, and International Cooperation', *International Organization*, 52 (2): 269–305.

Ferejohn, John (1991) 'Rationality and Interpretation: Parliamentry Elections in Early Stuart England', in Kristen R. Monroe (ed.), *The Economic Approach to Politics*. New York: HarperCollins.

Finnemore, Martha (1996) *National Interests in International Society*. Ithaca: Cornell University Press.

Finnemore, Martha and Toope, Stephen (2002) 'Alternatives to "legalization": Richer Views of Law and Politics', *International Organization*.

Frieden, Jeffry A. (1991) *Debt, Development and Democracy*. Princeton: Princeton University Press.

Frieden, Jeffry (1999) 'Actors and Preferences in International Relations' in David Lake and Robert Powell (eds), *Strategic Choice and International Relations*. Princeton: Princeton University Press. pp. 39–76.

Friedman, Jeffrey (ed.) (1995) *Rational Choice Theory and Politics. Critical Review* (Special Issue), 9 (1–2).

Garrett, Geoffrey and Tsebilis, George (1996) 'An Institutional Critique of Intergovernmentalism', *International Organization*, 50 (2): 269–99.

Gartzke, Erik (1999) 'War is in the Error Term', *International Organization*, 53 (3): 567–88.

George, C., Alexander, L. and McKeown, Timothy J. (1985) 'Case Studies and Theories of Organizational Decision-Making', in R.F. Coulam and R.A. Smith (eds), *Advances in Information Processing in Organizations*, vol. 2. Greenwich, CT: JAI Press. pp. 21–58.

Gilpin, Robert (1981) *War and Change in World Politics*. Cambridge: Cambridge University Press.

Glaser, Charles (1997) 'The Security Dilemma Revisited', *World Politics*, 50: 171–210.

Goemans, H.E. (2000) *War and Punishment: The Causes of War Termination and the First World War.* Princeton: Princeton University Press.

Goldsmith, Jack and Posner, Eric (1999) 'A Theory of Customary International Law', *University of Chicago Law Review*, 66 (4): 1113–77.

Goldsmith, Jack and Posner, Eric (eds) (2002a) *Rational Choice in International Law*. Special Issue of *The Journal of Legal Studies*.

Goldsmith, Jack and Posner, Eric (2002b) 'Moral and Legal Rhetoric in International Relations: A Rational Choice Approach', in Jack Goldsmith and Eric Posner (eds), *Rational Choice in International Law*. Special Issue of *The Journal of Legal Studies*.

Goldstein, Judith (1993) *Ideas, Interests and American Trade Policy*. Ithaca: Cornell University Press.

Goldstein, Judith (1996) 'International Law and Domestic Institutions: Reconciling North American "Unfair" Trade Laws', *International Organization*, 50 (4): 541–64.

Goldstein, Judith and Keohane, Robert (1993) *Ideas and Foreign Policy: Beliefs, Institutions and Political Change*. Ithaca: Cornell University Press.

Goldstein, Judith, Kahler, Miles, Keohane, Robert O. and Anne-Marie Slaughter (2000) *Legalization and World Politics*. Special Issue of *International Organization*. 54 (3).

Gowa, Joanne (1994) *Allies, Adversaries, and International Trade*. Princeton: Princeton University Press.

Green, Donald P. and Shapiro, Ian (1994) *Pathologies of Rational Choice Theory: A Critique of Applications in Political Science*. New Haven: Yale University Press.

Grieco, Joseph M. (1988) 'Anarchy and the Limits of Cooperation: A Realist Critique of the Newest Liberal Institutionalism', *International Organization*, 42 (3): 485–507.

Grieco, Joseph M. (1990) *Cooperation Among Nations: Europe, America, and Non-Tariff Barriers to Trade*. Ithaca: Cornell University Press.

Grieco, Joseph M. (1997) 'Realist International Theory and the Study of World Politics', in Michael W. Doyle and G. John Ikenberry (eds), *New Thinking in International Relations Theory*. Boulder: Westview. pp. 163–201.

Grieco, Joseph, Powell, Robert and Snidal, Duncan (1993) 'The Relative Gains Problem for International Cooperation', *American Political Science Review*, 87 (3): 729–43.

Gruber, Lloyd (2000) *Ruling the World: Power Politics and the Rise of Supranational Institutions*. Princeton: Princeton University Press.

Hammond, Peter L. (1976) 'Changing Tastes and Coherent Dynamic Choice', *Review of Economic Studies*, 43 (1): 159–73.

Hansen, John Mark (1991) *Gaining Access: Congress and the Farm Lobby, 1919–1981*. Chicago: University of Chicago Press.

Hasenclever, Andreas, Mayer, Peter and Rittberger, Volker (1997) *Theories of International Regimes*. Cambridge: Cambridge University Press.

Hurrell, Andrew (1993) 'International Society and the Study of Regimes', in Volker Rittberger with Peter Mayer (ed.), *Regime Theory and International Relations*. Oxford: Clarendon Press. pp. 49–72.

Intriligator, M.D. and Brito, D.L. (1984) 'Can Arms Races Lead to the Outbreak of Conflict?', *Journal of Conflict Resolution*, 28 (1): 63–84.

Jervis, Robert (1976) *Perception and Misperception in International Politics*. Princeton: Princeton University Press.

Johnson, James D. (1991) 'Rational Choice as a Reconstructive Theory' in Kristen R. Monroe (ed.), *The Economic Approach to Politics*. New York: HarperCollins.

Johnston, Alastair Iain (2002) 'The Social Effects of International Institutions on Domestic (Foreign Policy) Actors', in Daniel Drezner (ed.), *The Interaction of Domestic and International Institutions*. Ann Arbor: University of Michigan Press.

Kahler, Miles (1998) 'Rationality in International Relations', *International Organization*, 52 (4): 919–42.

Kahler, Miles (1999) 'Evolution, Choice, and International Change', in David Lake and Robert Powell (eds), *Strategic Choice and International Relations*. Princeton: Princeton University Press. pp. 165–96.

Kahneman, Daniel and Tversky, Amos (1979) 'Prospect Theory: An Analysis of Decision Under Risk', *Econometrica*, 47: 263–91.

Katzenstein, Peter (ed.) (1996) *The Culture of National Security: Norms and Identity in World Politics.* Columbia: Columbia University Press.

Katzenstein, Peter, Keohane, Robert and Krasner, Stephen (eds) (1998) *International Organization at Fifty: Explorations and Contestation in the Study of World Politics. International Organization* (Special Issue), 52 (4).

Keck, Margaret E. and Sikkink, Kathryn (1998) *Activists Beyond Borders: Advocacy Networks in International Politics.* Ithaca: Cornell University Press.

Keohane, Robert (1984) *After Hegemony: Cooperation and Discord in the World Political Economy.* Princeton: Princeton University Press.

King, Gary, Keohane, Robert O. and Verba, Sydney (1994) *Designing Social Inquiry: Scientific Inference in Qualitative Research.* Princeton: Princeton University Press.

Kirschner, Jonathon (1997) 'The Microfoundations of Economic Sanctions', *Security Studies*, 6: 32–64.

Koremenos, Barbara (2001) 'Loosening the Ties that Bind: A Learning Model of Agreement Flexibility', *International Organization*, 55 (2): 289–326.

Koremenos, Barbara, Lipson, Charles and Snidal, Duncan (eds) (2001a) *Rational Design: Explaining the Form of International Institutions: International Organization.* Special Issue of *International Organization*, 55 (4).

Koremenos, Barbara, Lipson, Charles and Snidal, Duncan (2001b) 'The Rational Design of International Institutions', in B. Koremenos, C. Lipson and D. Snidal (eds), *Rational Design: Explaining the Form of International Institutions.* Special issue of *International Organization*.

Koremenos, Barbara, Lipson, Charles and Snidal, Duncan (2001c) 'Moving Forward with the RD Project', in B. Koremenos, C. Lipson and D. Snidal (eds), *Rational Design: Looking Back to Move Forward.* Special issue of *International Organization*.

Krasner, Stephen D. (1991) 'Global Communications and National Power: Life on the Pareto Frontier', *World Politics,* 43: 336–66.

Krasner, Stephen D. (1999) *Sovereignty: Organized Hypocrisy.* Princeton: Princeton University Press.

Kratochwil, Friedrich V. (1993) 'The Embarrassment of Changes: Neo-Realism as the Science of Realpolitik without Politics', *Review of International Studies*, 19: 63–80.

Kreps, David M. (1990) *A Course in Microeconomic Theory.* Princeton: Princeton University Press.

Kydd, Andrew (1997) 'Game Theory and the Spiral Model', *World Politics*, 49 (3): 371–400.

Kydd, Andrew (2000) 'Trust, Reassurance, and Cooperation', *International Organization*, 54 (2): 325–58.

Kydd, Andrew (2001) 'Trust Building, Trust Breaking: The Dilemmas of NATO Enlargement', in B. Koremenos, C. Lipson and D. Snidal (eds), *Rational Design: Explaining the Form of International Institutions.* Special Issue of *International Organization*.

Laibson, David (1997) 'Golden Eggs and Hyperbolic Discounting', *Quarterly Journal of Economics*, 112 (2): 443–78.

Lake, David (1999) *Entangling Relations: American Foreign Policy in its Century.* Princeton: Princeton University Press.

Lake, David and Powell, Robert (eds) (1999a) *Strategic Choice and International Relations.* Princeton: Princeton University Press.

Lake, David and Powell, Robert (1999b) 'International Relations: A Strategic-Choice Approach', in David Lake and Robert Powell (eds), *Strategic Choice and International Relations.* Princeton: Princeton University Press. pp. 3–38.

Levy, Jack (1997) 'Prospect Theory, Rational Choice, and International Relations', *International Studies Quarterly*, 41: 87.

Lipson, Charles (1986) 'Bankers' Dilemmas: Private Cooperation in Rescheduling Sovereign Debts', in Kenneth A. Oye (ed.), *Cooperation Under Anarchy.* Princeton: Princeton University Press. pp. 200–25.

March, James G. and Olsen, Johan P. (1989) *Rediscovering Institutions: The Organizational Basis of Politics.* New York: The Free Press.

Marshall, Alfred (1910) *Principles of Economics, an Introductory Volume*, 6th edn. London: Macmillan.

Martin, Lisa L. (1992) *Coercive Cooperation: Explaining Multilateral Economic Sanctions.* Princeton: Princeton University Press.

Martin, Lisa (1999) 'Formal Methods, Formal Complaints: Debating the Role of Rational Choice in Security Studies – The Contributions of Rational Choice: A Defense of Pluralism', *International Security*, 24 (2): 74–83.

Martin, Lisa L. (2000) *Democratic Commitments: Legislatures and International Cooperation.* Princeton: Princeton University Press.

Martin, Lisa L. and Simmons, Beth (1998) 'Theories and Empirical Studies of International Institutions', *International Organization*, 52 (4): 729–58.

Mas-Colell, Andreu, Whinston, Michael and Green, Jerry (1995) *Microeconomic Theory.* New York: Oxford University Press.

Mattli, Walter (1999) *The Logic of Regional Integration: Europe and Beyond.* Cambridge: Cambridge University Press.

Mattli, Walter (2001) 'Fora of International Commercial Dispute Resolution for Private Parties', in B. Koremenos, C. Lipson and D. Snidal (eds), *Rational Design: Explaining the International Institutions.* Special Issue of *International Organization*.

Milner, Helen (1988) *Resisting Protection: Global Industries and the Politics of Free Trade.* Princeton: Princeton University Press.

Milner, Helen V. (1997) *Interests, Institutions, and Information: Domestic Politics and International Relations.* Princeton: Princeton University Press.

Milner, Helen (1998) 'Rationalizing Politics: The Emerging Synthesis of International, American, and

Comparative Politics', *International Organization*, 52 (4): 759–86.

Milner, Helen and Rosendorff, Peter (2001) 'The Optimal Design of International Trade Institutions: Uncertainty and Escape', in B. Koremenos, C. Lipson and D. Snidal (eds), *Rational Design: Explaining the International Institutions*. Special Issue of *International Organization*.

Mitchell, Ronald B. (1994) 'Regime Design Matters: Intentional Oil Pollution and Treaty Compliance', *International Organization,* 48 (3): 425–58.

Mitchell, Ronald B. (2001) 'Reciprocity, Coercion or Exchange: Symmetric and Asymmetric Externalities in Institutional Design', in B. Koremenos, C. Lipson and D. Snidal (eds), *Rational Design: Explaining the International Institutions*. Special Issue of *International Organization*.

Monroe, Kristen (2001) 'Paradigm Shift: From Rational Choice Theory to Perspective', *International Political Science Review*, 22 (2): 151–72.

Moravscik, Andrew (1997) 'Taking Preferences Seriously: A Liberal Theory of International Politics', *International Organization*, 51 (4): 513–53.

Moravscik, Andrew (1998) *The Choice for Europe*. Ithaca: Cornell University Press.

Morgenthau, Hans J. ([1948] 1978) *Politics Among Nations: The Struggle for Power and Peace,* 5th edn. New York: Alfred A. Knopf.

Morrow, James D. (1994a) 'Modeling the Forms of International Cooperation', *International Organization*, 48 (3): 387–423.

Morrow, James D. (1994b) *Game Theory for Political Scientists*. Princeton: Princeton University Press.

Morrow, James D. (2001) 'The Institutional Features of the Prisoners of War Treaties', in B. Koremenos, C. Lipson and D. Snidal (eds), *Rational Design: Explaining the International Institutions*. Special Issue of *International Organization*.

Morrow, James (2002) 'The Laws of War, Common Conjectures, and Legal Systems in International Politics', in Jack Goldsmith and Eric Posner (eds), *Rational Design: Explaining the International Institutions*. Special Issue of *The Journal of Legal, Studies.*

Moulin, Hervé (1995) *Cooperative Microeconomics*. Princeton: Princeton University Press.

Myerson, Roger B. (1991) *Game Theory: Analysis of Conflict.* Cambridge, MA: Harvard University Press.

Niou, Emerson and Ordeshook, Peter C. (1999) 'Formal Methods, Formal Complaints: Debating the Role of Rational Choice in Security Studies – "Return of the Luddites"', *International Security*, 24 (2): 84–96.

Niou, Emerson, Ordeshook, Peter and Rose, Gregory (1989) *The Balance of Power and Stability in International Systems*. Cambridge: Cambridge University Press.

North, Douglass C. (1990) *Institutions, Institutional Change and Economic Performance*. Cambridge: Cambridge University Press.

Oatley, Thomas and Nabors, Robert (1998) 'Redistributive Cooperation: Market Failure, Wealth Transfers and the Basle Accord', *International Organization*, 52 (1): 35–54.

Olson, Mancur Jr (1965) *The Logic of Collective Action*. Cambridge, MA: Harvard University Press.

O'Neill, Barry (1999) *Honor, Symbols and War.* Ann Arbor: University of Michigan Press.

Organski, A.F.K. and Kugler, Jacek (1980) *The War Ledger.* Chicago: University of Chicago Press.

Oye, Kenneth A. (ed.) (1986) *Cooperation Under Anarchy*. Princeton: Princeton University Press.

Oye, Kenneth A. (1992) *Economic Discrimination and Political Exchange: World Political Economy in the 1930s and 1980s*. Princeton: Princeton University Press.

Pahre, Robert (2001) 'Most-Favored-Nation Clause and Clustered Negotiation', in B. Koremenos, C. Lipson and D. Snidal (eds), *Rational Design: Explaining the International Institutions*. Special Issue of *International Organization*.

Pape, Robert A. (1996) *Bombing to Win: Air Power and Coercion in War*. Ithaca: Cornell University Press.

Pape, Robert (1997) 'Why Economic Sanctions Do Not Work', *International Security*, 22: 90–136.

Powell, Robert (1991) 'Absolute and Relative Gains in International Relations Theory', *American Political Science Review*, 86 (4): 1303–20.

Powell, Robert (1999a) 'Formal Methods, Formal Complaints: Debating the Role of Rational Choice in Security Studies – The Modeling Enterprise and Security Studies', *International Security*, 24 (2): 97–106.

Powell, Robert (1999b) *In the Shadow of Power: States and Strategies in International Politics.* Princeton: Princeton University Press.

Putnam, Robert D. (1988) 'Diplomacy and Domestic Politics: The Logic of Two-Level Games', *International Organization*, 42: 427–60.

Rabin, Matthew and Thaler, Richard H. (2001) 'Anomalies: Risk Aversion', *Journal of Economic Perspectives: A Journal of the American Economic Association*, 15 (1): 219–232.

Raustiala, Kal (1997) 'States, NGOs, and International Environmental Institutions', *International Studies Quarterly*, 41: 719–40.

Richards, John (2001) 'Institutions for Flying: How States Built a Market in International Aviation Services', in B. Koremenos, C. Lipson and D. Snidal (eds), *Rational Design: Explaining the International Institutions*. Special Issue of *International Organization*.

Richardson, Lewis F. (1960) *Arms and Insecurity: A Mathematical Study of the Causes and Origins of War*. Pittsburgh and Chicago: Boxwood Press/Quadrangle Books.

Rittberger, Volker, with Mayer, Peter (eds) (1993) *Regime Theory and International Relations*. Oxford: Clarendon Press.

Rogowski, Ronald (1989) *Commerce and Coalitions*. Princeton: Princeton University Press.

Rogowski, Ronald (1999) 'Institutions as Constraints on Strategic Choice', in D. Lake and R. Powell (eds), *Strategic Choice and International Relations*. pp. 115–36.

Rosecrance, Richard (1986) *The Rise of the Trading State: Commerce and Conquest in the Modern World*. New York: Basic Books.

Rubinstein, Ariel (1998) *Modeling Bounded Rationality*. Cambridge; MIT Press.

Ruggie, John G. (1998) 'What Makes the World Hang Together: Neo-Utilitarianism and the Social Constuctivist Challenge', *International Organization,* 52 (4): 55–86.

Samuelson, Paul Anthony (1954) 'The Pure Theory of Public Expenditure', *Review of Economics and Statistics*, 36: 386–9.

Schattschneider, E.E. (1935) *Politics, Pressures and the Tariff: A Study of Free Private Enterprise in Pressure Politics, as Shown in the 1929–30 Revision of the Tariff*. Hamden, CT: Prentice Hall.

Schelling, Thomas C. (1978) 'Egonomics, or the Art of Self-Management', *American Economic Review*, 68: 290–4.

Schultz, Kenneth (1998) 'Domestic Opposition and Signaling in International Crises', *American Political Science Review*, 92 (4): 829–44.

Sebenius, James K. (1983) 'Negotiation Arithmetic: Adding and Subtracting Issues and Parties', *International Organization,* 37 (2): 281–316.

Sen, Amartya (1977) 'Rational Fools', *Philosophy and Public Affairs*, 6: 317.

Sen, Armatya (1979) 'Utilitarianism and Welfarism', *Journal of Philosophy*, 76: 463–89.

Setear, John (1999) 'An Iterative Perspective on Treaties: A Synthesis of International Relations Theory and International Law', *Harvard International Law Journal*, 37: 139.

Shambaugh, George (1999) *States, Firms and Power*. Albany: State University of New York Press.

Signorino, Curtis S. (1999) 'Strategic Interaction and then Statistical Analysis of International Conflict', *American Political Science Review,* 93 (2): 297–316.

Simmons, Beth (1994) *Who Adjusts?* Princeton: Princeton University Press.

Smith, Alastair (1995) 'The Success and Use of Economic Sanctions', *International Interactions,* 21: 229–45.

Smith, Alastair (1999) 'Testing Theories of Strategic Choice: The Example of Crisis Escalation', *American Journal of Political Science*, 43 (4): 1254–83.

Snidal, Duncan (1985) 'The Game Theory of International Politics', *World Politics*, 38 (1): 25–57.

Snidal, Duncan (1991) 'Relative Gains and the Pattern of International Cooperation', *American Political Science Review*, 85 (3): 701–26.

Snidal, Duncan (1996) 'International Political Economy Approaches to Institutions', *International Review of Law and Economics*, 16: 121–37.

Snyder, Jack (1991) *Myths of Empire: Domestic Politics and International Ambition*. Ithaca: Cornell University Press.

Spruyt, Hendrik (1994) *The Sovereign State and Its Competitors*. Princeton: Princeton University Press.

Stein, Arthur (1999) 'The Limits of Strategic Choice: Constrained Rationality and Incomplete Explanation', in David Lake and Robert Powell (eds), *Strategic Choice and International Relations*. Princeton: Princeton University Press. pp. 197–228.

Steinbruner, John P. (1974) *The Cybernetic Theory of Decision: New Dimensions of Political Analysis*. Princeton: Princeton University Press.

Stigler, George J. and Becker, Gary S. (1977) 'De Gustibus Non Est Disputandum', *American Economic Review,* 67 (2): 76–90.

Strotz, R.H. (1955–56) 'Myopia and Inconsistency in Dynamic Utility Maximization', *Review of Economic Studies,* 25 (3): 165–80.

Thompson, Alexander (1999) 'Coercion through International Organizations: The US and the UN in the Gulf War', presentation to the Annual Meeting of the American Political Science Association, Atlanta, GA, 2–5 September.

Thompson, Alexander (2001) 'Channeling Power: International Organizations and the Politics of Coercion'. PhD dissertation, University of Chicago.

Tsebelis, George (1990) 'Are Sanctions Effective? A Game-Theoretic Analysis', *Journal of Conflict Resolution*, 34: 3–28.

Van Evera, Stephen (1997) *Guide to Methods for Students in Political Science*. Ithaca: Cornell University Press.

Verdier, Daniel (1994) *Democracy and International Trade: Britain, France and the United States, 1860–90*. Princeton: Princeton University Press.

Wagner, R. Harrison (1986) 'The Theory of Games and the Balance of Power', *World Politics*, 38 (4): 546–76.

Walsh, James I. (2001) 'National Preferences and International Institutions: Evidence from European Monetary Integration', *International Studies Quarterly*, 45: 59–80.

Walt, Stephen (1987) *The Origins of Alliances*. Ithaca: Cornell University Press.

Walt, Stephen (1999) 'Rigor or Rigor Mortis? Rational Choice and Security Studies', *International Security*, 23 (4): 5–48.

Waltz, Kenneth (1979) *Theory of International Politics*. New York: Random House.

Wendt, Alexander (1999) *Social Theory of International Politics*. Cambridge: Cambridge University Press.

Wendt, Alexander (2001) 'Driving With the Rearview Mirror: On the Rational Science of Institutional Design', in B. Koremenos, C. Lipson and D. Snidal (eds), *Rational Design: Explaining the International Institutions*. Special Issue of *International Organization*.

Williamson, Oliver (1975) *Markets and Hierarchies: Analysis and Antitrust Implications*. New York: Free Press.

Williamson, Oliver (1985) *The Economic Institutions of Capitalism*. New York: Free Press.

Yarbrough, Beth V. and Yarbrough, Robert M. (1992) *Cooperation and Governance in International Trade: The Strategic Organizational Approach*. Princeton: Princeton University Press.

Yee, Albert S. (1997) 'Thick Rationality and the Missing "Brute Fact": The Limits of Rationalist Incorporation of Norms and Ideas', *Journal of Politics*, 59 (4): 1001–39.

Young, H. Peyton (1994) *Equity in Theory and Practice*. Princeton: Princeton University Press.

Zagare, Frank C. (1999) 'Formal Methods, Formal Complaints: Debating the Role of Rational Choice in Security Studies – All Mortis, No Rigor', *International Security*, 24 (2): 107–14.

Zürn, Michael (1993) 'Bringing the Second Image (Back) In: About the Domestic Sources of Regime Formation', in Volker Rittberger with Peter Mayer (eds), *Regime Theory in International Relations*. Oxford: Clarendon Press.

5

Constructivism and International Relations

EMANUEL ADLER

In this chapter I will explore where constructivism came from, what brings constructivists together – and thus sets them apart from adherents of other international relations (IR) approaches – what divides constructivists, and where constructivism is and should be going. In particular, I will show that constructivists deal extensively with metaphysics and social theories less for their own sake than because constructivism provides a firm basis for building better IR theories.

In addition, I will argue that despite the divisions among constructivists concerning serious issues, all constructivists (modernist, modernist linguistic and critical) – with the exception, perhaps, of the extreme postmodernist wing of radical constructivism – share two understandings: what Stefano Guzzini (2000: 149) summarized as *the social construction of knowledge* and *the construction of social reality*. In combination, these understandings are construc-tivism's *common ground*, the view that the material world does not come classified, and that, therefore, the objects of our knowledge are not independent of our interpretations and our language. This means that different collective meanings are attached to the material world twice, as social reality and as scientific knowledge. In other words, knowledge is both a resource that people use in their day-to-day life for the construction of social reality, and the theories, concepts, meanings and symbols that scientists use to interpret social reality.

This dichotomous description is offered for ana-lytical purposes only. For reflexive knowledge or interpretation *of* the world, when imposed on mate-rial reality, becomes knowledge *for* the world – the

power to change the world in accordance with collective understandings and, concurrently, with human motives and intentional acts. The above analysis means not only that there is no perfect correlation between objects 'out there' in nature and our classifications of nature, but also that social facts, which are the objects of our study, emerge from the interaction between knowledge and the material world, neither of which is invariant.

Unlike positivism[1] and materialism,[2] which take the world as it is, constructivism sees the world as a project under construction, as becoming rather than being. Unlike idealism[3] and post-structuralism and postmodernism,[4] which take the world *only* as it can be imagined or talked about, constructivism accepts that not all statements have the same epistemic value and that there is consequently some foundation for knowledge.

I start by tracing four constructivist IR approaches to their philosophical and sociological roots and suggest a synthesis between pragmatism and realism. The next section provides a brief historical account of the evolution of IR construc-tivism. In my third section I describe three aspects of IR constructivism: (1) the common ground (in ontology, epistemology and methods), (2) con-ceptual contributions to IR theory (what I call its 'added value') and (3) substantive empirical contri-butions. The fourth section then introduces the major debates within constructivism. Finally, I pro-pose an agenda for helping constructivism become more firmly established in IR. In particular, I emphasize the need to focus constructivist debates on methodological issues.

The Philosophical and Sociological Foundations of Constructivism

Constructivism, which reached the shores of IR in the 1980s, describes the dynamic, contingent and culturally based condition of the social world. It has major implications for an understanding of knowledge, including scientific knowledge, and how to achieve it. Constructivism thus has the potential to transform the understanding of social reality in the social sciences. It stresses the reciprocal relationship between nature and human knowledge and suggests a view of the social sciences that is contingent, partly indeterminate, nominalist,[5] and to some extent externally validated (Kuhn, 1970). With the exception of its radical postmodern wing, however, constructivism does not challenge science, rationalism and modernity; it merely makes science more compatible with the constructivist understanding of social reality.

Let us begin by putting to rest the widely held assumption that constructivism is yet another IR 'ism', paradigm, or fashion, which, highlighting the role of norms in IR and offering a more optimistic approach to IR, has recently joined the ranks of 'realism' (neorealism) and 'liberalism' (neoliberalism). Constructivism is in fact a three-layered understanding – involving metaphysics,[6] social theory and IR theory and research strategies – of social reality and social science and of their dynamic mutually constitutive effects.

First, constructivism is a *metaphysical stance* about the reality that scholars seek to know and about the knowledge with which they seek to interpret reality. This position has been applied not only to IR but also to the social sciences in general (for example, sociology, psychology and education), to mathematics and, via the philosophy of science and the sociology of knowledge, to the natural sciences.[7] Thus from an IR perspective in which paradigms are associated with broad world-views of international political life (such as realism, liberalism and Marxism), constructivism is more like a paradigm of paradigms.

Second, building on the metaphysical position, constructivism is a *social theory* about the role of knowledge and knowledgeable agents in the constitution of social reality. It is as social theory that, for example, we should understand the role of intersubjectivity and social context, the co-constitution of agent and structure, and the rule-governed nature of society.

Finally, constructivism is an IR *theoretical and empirical perspective* that, building on the other two layers, maintains that IR theory and research should be based on sound *social* ontological and epistemological foundations. IR constructivism has led to new and important questions, for example,

about the role of identities, norms and causal understandings in the constitution of national interests, about institutionalization and international governance, and about the social construction of new territorial and non-territorial transnational regions.

Debates within IR constructivism take place on all three levels – metaphysics, social theory and IR theory. IR constructivists have often inadvertently 'jumped around' the three levels, without specifying whether the points they are making are about metaphysics, social theory, or IR. This may be one of the reasons for the misunderstanding and confusion that exist outside the constructivist camp and for the charges that constructivists do only 'metatheory'. Constructivists, however, are the first group of political scientists to have grounded IR theory on an explicit metaphysics and social theory. Not only does this grounding promote more realistic social assumptions; in the wake of the flood of recent empirical constructivist work, it also disposes of the charge that IR constructivists are metatheorists. Constructivists could not have reached level three (IR constructivist theory and research) without levels two and one (social theory and metaphysics). Indeed, constructivists could not have approached non-constructivists without letting the latter know that the constructivist picture of the social world (and the way to attain knowledge of the world) is not at all similar to theirs. In fact, the argument of non-constructivists – that IR does not need to be grounded on metaphysics and social theory, or that metaphysical and social theory assumptions should remain unspoken – is a social-construction move *par excellence*.

Because constructivism in the social sciences builds on centuries of intellectual developments in philosophy, sociology and social theory, it is not easy to speculate about its origins. This is not the place for an intellectual history of constructivism. To illustrate the roots of the debates within IR constructivism, however, I will present four currents of thought that have affected IR constructivism: neo-Kantian 'objective hermeneutics', linguistic 'subjective hermeneutics', critical theory and pragmatist philosophy of science. I will then describe four IR constructivist approaches – modernist, modernist linguistic, radical and critical – which rely, directly or indirectly, on one or more of the above currents of thought – and a strategy for bridging between them.

Constructivism can be traced back to Immanuel Kant – whom Ian Hacking describes as 'the great pioneer of constructivism' (1999: 41) – and to nineteenth- and early twentieth-century 'neo-Kantians'. Kant believed that although knowledge can tell us something about objective reality, it must nevertheless be 'restricted to the realm of phenomena, or that which appears to consciousness' (Delanty, 1997: 45). Neo-Kantians took Kant's insight – that to know means imposing the a priori forms of our minds on the structures of nature – and carried it from nature to culture. For example, in the late nineteenth and early twentieth centuries, Wilhelm Dilthey (1989) and Edmund Husserl (1962) set the human sciences apart from the natural sciences. Max Weber (1978) called for an autonomous social science, based on the understanding of meaning ('*verstehen*') and the explanation of motivations that lead to actions. More recently (building on Alfred Schutz (1962)), Peter Berger and Thomas Luckmann (1966) – who like Georg Simmel (1955) stressed the intersubjective nature of everyday knowledge, and the interpreted nature of social reality – coined and developed the concept of 'the social construction of reality'. Neo-Kantianism, in sum, is an *objective approach to hermeneutics.*[8] Working within the realm of reason, it stresses the need to understand consciousness. Because it believes in the possibility of attaining empirical knowledge without the mediation of language, it aims at explaining society. Neo-Kantianism generally follows a 'particularizing positivist strategy[9] that reconstructs historical processes and narratives, rather than Carl Hempel's (1965) covering-law type positivism,[10] which aims at prediction. Neo-Kantianism, which I will hereafter call the 'weak programme' of constructivism in the social sciences, looms large in modernist versions of IR constructivism.[11]

Constructivism's 'strong programme' in the social sciences is based on a turn from consciousness to language and from objective to *subjective hermeneutics*. Led by Martin Heidegger (1962) and Ludwig Wittgenstein (1953), this current of thought directly challenged positivism and argued that social facts are constituted by the structures of language and that, accordingly, consciousness can be studied only as mediated by language. To be sure, as with John Austin's (1962) student, John Searle (1995) – who adopted the notion of the construction of social reality while rejecting the social construction of nature – not every turn to linguistics was a relativist turn. In general, however, the turn to linguistics radicalized the anti-positivist movement by taking science as being at best 'forever constrained by its social context' (Delanty, 1997: 53) and at worst as a discourse that cannot attain objective knowledge or criticize society. Peter Winch (1958), who argued that social action is '"rule following" within a concrete form of life' (Delanty, 1997: 55), brought the radical linguistic logic to the social sciences. Arguing that the objects of science are socially constructed in laboratories, Bruno Latour and Steve Woolgar (1986) carried this linguistic logic from society to nature itself. Poststructuralists like Jacques Derrida (1978) and postmodernists like Michel Foucault (1980), however, challenged reason, science and modernity, thereby bringing radical linguistics to its ultimate relativist destination. We can trace two IR constructivist approaches – a 'modernist linguistic' approach and a 'radical' approach – to constructivism's strong programme in the social sciences.

Critical theory, which resulted from an attempt by the so-called Frankfurt School to turn a Marxist critique of political economy into a critique of ideology (Adorno, 1976; Horkheimer, 1972), falls between the weak and the strong programmes of constructivism in the social sciences. Jürgen Habermas (1978, 1984, 1987, 1996) combined objective hermeneutics and language philosophy in order to extend critical theory into (a) a powerful critique of instrumental rationality and (b) a social theory of 'communicative action' and 'deliberative democracy'. Habermas's critique of instrumental rationality showed that the social sciences should abandon the cognitive interest in control, which is characteristic of instrumental rationality, in favour of a cognitive interest in emancipation. In turn, his social theory explained how emancipatory interests become reconstructed in both theory and practice and especially how deliberative democratic processes help people free themselves from distorted communication. 'Critical' IR constructivism builds on Habermas's blend of insights from the philosophy of language with beliefs in the distinction between the natural and social sciences, the possibility of explanation in the social sciences and human progress.

Another current of thought that bridges the weak and strong programmes of constructivism in the social sciences is *pragmatism*. Dismissing the Cartesian notion that we must choose between objectivism and relativism, pragmatism (Dewey, 1977; James, 1975; Peirce, 1966) suggests that we need to adjust our ideas about truth as experience unfolds (Smith, 1996: 23). More specifically, it underscores the role of choice, deliberation, judgement and interpretation by communities of scientists, who immerse themselves in a type of rational persuasion that must aspire, but cannot always be assimilated, to models of deductive proof or inductive generalization (R. Bernstein, 1985). For example, Thomas Kuhn's (1970) pragmatist philosophy of science played a large role in the development of the four IR constructivist approaches mentioned above. Although not a pragmatist, Karl Popper (1982), who stressed the role of background expectations in the development of scientific theories, also contributed to the development of IR constructivism.

The above philosophical and sociological approaches imprinted the various strands of IR constructivism, which I will describe in brief. A *modernist* type of constructivism in IR (John Ruggie (1998a: 35) called it 'neo-classical') results from the combination of objective hermeneutics with a 'conservative' cognitive interest in understanding social reality. Thus, for example, IR structivists, such as Emanuel Adler arnett (1998), Jeffrey Checkel (2001), more (1996), Peter Katzenstein s Risse-Kappen (1995), John Ruggie (1998a), and Alexander Wendt (1999), uncover the causal social mechanisms and constitutive social relations that make IR more intelligible.

Modernist linguistic (or 'rules') constructivism results from the combination of subjective hermeneutics with a 'conservative' cognitive interest in explaining and understanding social reality. Modernist linguistic or rule-oriented constructivists, such as Friedrich Kratochwil (1989) and Nicholas Onuf (1989), believe that, because of the primacy of epistemology, understanding social reality means uncovering the processes by which social facts are constituted by language and rules. They are interested in explaining how social rules (including legal rules) and what Austin and Searle have called 'speech acts'[12] 'make the process by which people and society constitute each other continuous and reciprocal' (Onuf, 1998a: 59). Other proponents of modernist linguistic constructivism, such as Karen Litfin (1994), Neta Crawford (1999) and Jutta Weldes (1999), though emphasizing discourse and its power to construct social reality, nevertheless conduct empirical historical and interpretive research with the aim of understanding the emergence of social reality.

Radical constructivism in IR, which often embraces postmodern and post-structuralist perspectives, results from a combination of a radical turn to language (and thus to subjective hermeneutics) with a dissident emancipatory or deconstructionist attitude toward knowledge in general. As such it lies at the extreme edge of the strong programme of constructivism in the social sciences. In general, radical constructivists do not question the existence of material reality; sometimes they even conduct empirical research (Der Derian, 1987; Doty, 1996; Gill, 1988; Weber, 1995). Because, however, they believe that material reality cannot be truly represented, they are agnostic about material reality and prefer to concentrate on discourse, narratives and texts (Ashley, 1987; Campbell, 1992; Der Derian, 1990; Peterson, 1992; Walker, 1993). What drives many radical constructivists outside the constructivist 'common ground' is neither their emancipatory or deconstructionist cognitive interest, nor their insistence on uncovering power structures disguised as truth and their pessimistic view about the social world. Rather, it is their view that no statements can be more valid than others, that nothing can be done to assess the validity of normative and epistemic claims, and that science is accordingly just one more hegemonic discourse.

Critical constructivism in IR results from the combination of objective hermeneutics (mainly the approach of Habermas and his followers) with a dissident interest in the emancipatory effects of knowledge. Critical constructivists, such as Andrew Linklater (1998) and Robert Cox (1986) (who follows Antonio Gramsci (1971)), share the view that striving for a better understanding of the mechanisms on which social and political orders are based is also a reflexive move aimed at the emancipation of society. In general, critical constructivists follow a pragmatist approach, to which I now return.

Pragmatic realism, a term I borrow from Hilary Putnam (1990, 1998) to designate a combination of modernist pragmatism[13] and scientific realist philosophy (especially a 'critical realist' view of the construction of social reality[14]), may provide a way to consolidate the common ground within IR constructivism. Pragmatic realism says that although representations of the natural and social world are always made from a point of view and are thus interpretations, there none the less exists a material reality outside human interpretations; social facts emerge from the attachment of collective meaning to a previously existing material reality. It follows that rules that evoke *reasons* for action, individuals' reasoning processes, and collective understandings within dialogical communities – all of which are part of a pragmatist interpretation of social reality – may also be interpreted as being part of the social mechanisms that scientific realists believe help explain social reality. These mechanisms, and the structures on which they are based, involve the intersubjective 'stuff' that makes material reality meaningful; they do not exist outside human practices. Hence pragmatic realism does not postulate the sameness of the natural world and the social world.

THE EVOLUTION OF CONSTRUCTIVISM IN INTERNATIONAL RELATIONS

One often reads (e.g., Price and Reus-Smit, 1997) that IR constructivism was a result of IR theory's 'third debate' (Lapid, 1989) and that the end of the Cold War made it popular (Checkel, 1998; Hopf, 1998). This is true if one looks at the immediate conditions of its acceptance and growing influence, including the partial disenchantment with materialist and positivist views of social science and, in the wake of the end of the Cold War, by the dismal record of prediction in IR. More generally, the IR discipline has also responded to some earthshaking changes, such as the decline of sovereignty, the growing social and economic importance of knowledge, globalization, the Internet, and changes in the natural environment. These and other changes have been bringing home the post-positivist message that 'science is not independent of its object but constructs it' (Delanty, 1997: 8). Despite all this, it was in fact a century or more of interpretative sociological scholarship that penetrated IR at least a decade before the end of the Cold War that made IR constructivism possible.

Another common narrative, which, though it gives due credit to some pioneers of constructivism, is narrow and suffers from a short memory, is that in the beginning there was Onuf (1989), who coined the concept of constructivism in IR; then there was Wendt (1992b) – and the rest is history. To refine this narrative, we should add some synergetic links between people, trends and research programmes that made IR constructivism possible. Because I have done no research on the matter and have only a few pages in which to tell the story, however, I will not pretend to write a full history of IR constructivism here.

Some of the credit for the development of IR constructivism should go to the radical constructivists who, in the late 1970s, shocked the IR community by building their arguments around Foucault (1980) and Derrida (1978). Dialectically, they opened a space for the development of less radical strands of constructivism, which I have identified as the 'middle ground' (Adler 1997). Particularly influential were works by Ashley (1987) on power, practice and international community, by James Der Derian (1987) on diplomacy, by David Campbell (1992) on US foreign policy, by Andrew Linklater (1990) on moral community, and by R.B.J. Walker (1993) on sovereignty. Also influential were the neo-Gramscian critical theory of Robert Cox (1986) and Ann Tickner's (1992) feminist theory. It was mainly their work that Yosef Lapid (1989) had in mind when he wrote his powerful article on the 'third debate' in IR theory.

IR constructivism, however, has older and deeper roots. Karl Deutsch et al. (1957) and Ernst Haas (1958) anticipated modernist constructivism. In the 1950s Deutsch promoted a research programme on security communities, which dealt with peaceful transnational collective identities. Deutsch himself was not a constructivist – constructivism had yet to make its way from sociology to political science – and favoured a positivist epistemology. His sociological approach, however, which emphasized social transactions and social communication, had an indelible influence on later developments in constructivism. For example, Hayward Alker (1996), who studied with Deutsch, became a leading methodologist working within the constructivist tradition. And Peter Katzenstein (1996), who also was a student of Deutsch's, edited a trailblazing book on culture and national security. Many of its chapters were written by Katzenstein's students, who also became leading and widely published constructivists, including Audie Klotz (1995), Richard Price (1995), Christian Reus-Smit (1999), and Nina Tannenwald (1999). Also in this book,

Iain Johnston (1995, 1996) and Elizabeth Kier (1996, 1997) introduced a distinctive perspective on strategic culture. More recently, Adler and Barnett (1998) put a constructivist spin on Deutsch's security community concept.

Although Raymond Duvall did not study with Deutsch, he collaborated with Bruce Russett, who did (Russett and Duvall, 1976). Duvall became the mentor of, among others, Wendt (1999), Michael Barnett (1998), Roxanne Doty (1996), and Jutta Weldes (1999). In a seminal 1987 article, Wendt brought Giddens's (1979, 1984) structuration theory[15] and scientific realism to the attention of IR scholars; David Dessler (1989) followed suit shortly thereafter. Wendt then wrote a series of very important articles (1992b, 1994) and a book (1999); these established him as one of the leading constructivist scholars. I am not saying that Duvall and Wendt owe their constructivist perspective to Deutsch. It is noteworthy, however, that the substantive part of Wendt's theory deals with security community-like collective identity formation. It is also noteworthy that in the early 1960s Onuf, one of the most influential early constructivists, studied with Deutsch at Yale. According to Onuf, Deutsch 'got him thinking' about constitutive and regulative legal action (personal communication). Onuf's 1989 book, where he first referred to the interpretive turn in IR as 'constructivism', along with Kratochwil's 1989 book on rules, norms and decisions, became a beacon for modernist linguistic and rule-oriented constructivist research. It was no coincidence that both books promoted a legal theoretical approach; Kratochwil briefly studied with Onuf at Georgetown and they afterwards maintained a dialogue that lasted fifteen years.

In the early 1980s Ernst Haas (1983) suggested a powerful sociological of international co-operation based on learning, that is, on the introduction to politics of scientific consensual understandings. Borrowing the concept of 'episteme' from Foucault, Ruggie (1975), who studied with Haas, further developed this programme, which P. Haas (1992) and Adler and P. Haas (1992) turned into an agent-oriented constructivist research programme on 'epistemic communities'.[16] Adler (1991) also used E. Haas's ideas to develop the concept of 'cognitive evolution', a constructivist interpretation of collective social learning, which involves the innovation, selection and international diffusion and institutionalization of collective understandings. In 1986, Ruggie joined forces with Kratochwil, who came to constructivism via insights from international law and language-based 'speech-act theory'; together they wrote a seminal article on international regimes from a constructivist perspective (Kratochwil and Ruggie, 1986). Robert Keohane (1988) picked up the gauntlet thrown down by these two scholars, whom he called 'reflectivists', and challenged them and other 'reflectivists' to develop empirical research along positivist lines. This call stimulated a second generation of constructivists to engage in empirical research, although generally not along positivist lines. Ruggie and Kratochwil later wrote a series of important articles that helped establish the modernist type (Ruggie, 1993b, 1998a) and linguistic type (Kratochwil, 1993, 1996) of IR constructivism.

In addition to Kratochwil, other German scholars were prominent in the development of constructivism, mainly by initiating an important debate between instrumental rationalists (e.g., Keck, 1997) and Habermas-inspired communicative rationalists (Müller, 1994). For example, Risse (2000) not only did important work on communicative rationality,[17] but also became a 'conveyer belt' of ideas between German and American constructivist scholarship.

The English School, which interprets IR as being social and historical, and which stresses the existence of an international society that is driven by norms and identity (Buzan, 1993; Hurrell, 1993), played a role in promoting constructivist ideas (see Jepperson, Wendt and Katzenstein, 1996). In fact, some theorists of the English School (e.g., Dunne, 1999) argue that the differences between 'middle ground' constructivism and the English School are small (but see Finnemore, 1996; Waever, 1999). Moreover, the work of English School scholars (e.g., Jackson, 1990; Linklater, 1998), especially those of the latest generation (Dunne, 1995; Epp, 1998; Rengger, 1999) has sometimes gone further than modernist constructivism in stressing discourse and the critical aspects of knowledge.

We cannot talk about the English School's influence on IR constructivism, however, without also referring to the collaboration between Buzan and Waever (1997). In addition to Buzan and Waever's 'Copenhagen School',[18] many other Scandinavians have had a strong impact on the evolution of constructivism in IR. Walter Carlsnaes (1992), for example, was one of the first scholars to build on critical realism; he was followed by Heikki Patomäki (1996). Iver Neumann (1999), in turn, conducted important studies of collective identity formation. Scandinavians (e.g., Carlsnaes, 1992, 1994) also played an important role in early agent–structure debates and helped establish important IR journals, such as the *European Journal of International Relations*, that became a forum for the publication of constructivist ideas. Lately, Scandinavian scholars, such as K. Erik Jørgensen, have also played a role in bringing constructivism to studies of European integration (Christiansen et al., 1999).

Back in the United States, Martha Finnemore (1996) brought John Meyer's (1980) 'sociological institutionalism' to IR; her stress on the diffusion of Western norms to the Third World reinforced constructivist arguments about the constitutive effect of cultures. Constructivists (Barnett and Finnemore, 1999; Finnemore and Sikkink, 1998) also used other forms of sociological institutionalism (March and Olsen, 1998; Powell and DiMaggio, 1991) to explain the generation, diffusion and institutionalization of culture. In addition, a sociological turn toward social movements and networks also made inroads into IR constructivism, especially the idea of 'transnational advocacy networks' (Keck and Sikkink, 1998).

IR CONSTRUCTIVISM'S COMMON GROUND, 'ADDED VALUE' AND SUBSTANTIVE EMPIRICAL CONTRIBUTIONS

IR Constructivism's Common Ground: Ontology, Epistemology and Methods

All strands of constructivism converge on an *ontology* that depicts the social world as intersubjectively and collectively meaningful structures and processes. In this world, 'material resources only acquire meaning for human action through the structure of shared knowledge in which they are embedded' (Wendt, 1995: 73). Several crucial implications follow from this. First, the social world is made of intersubjective understandings, subjective knowledge and material objects (Popper, 1982; Searle, 1995). The world that constructivists see, therefore, is neither better nor worse than the world seen by neorealists and neoliberals. But it is a world that is broader, more contingent, more unexpected, more surprising and endowed with more possibilities. Second, social facts, which are facts only by human agreement and which account for the majority of the facts studied in IR, differ from rocks and flowers, because, unlike the latter, their existence depends on human consciousness and language. In other words, social facts depend, by way of collective understanding and discourse, on the attachment of collective knowledge to physical reality (Searle, 1995). For example, when we classify and refer to some people as 'self' and to other people as 'the other', a notion of what is in 'our' interest, as opposed to the 'other's' interest, emerges. Third, although individuals carry knowledge, ideas and meanings in their heads – where else would they be? – they also know, think and feel only in the context of and with reference to collective or intersubjective understandings, including rules and language. In other words, it is from this context or background that people borrow the epistemic, normative and ideological understandings, rules and discourses that 'make individuals into agents by enabling them to act upon the world in which they find themselves' (Gould, 1998: 81). Fourth, constructivists (except for radical constructivists) all consider the mutual constitution of agents and structures to be part of constructivism's ontology.

Again with the exception of the radicals, constructivists share, albeit only partially, an *epistemology* that makes interpretation an intrinsic part of *social* science and that stresses contingent generalizations. Contingent generalizations do not freeze understanding or bring it to closure; rather, they open up our understanding of the social world. Moreover, constructivists of all types are not interested in how things *are* but in how they *became* what they are. In addition, most constructivists agree with the premise that the validation for knowledge is only partly internal. In other words, constructivists argue that even were it possible to grasp social reality's minimalist foundations and thereby inch toward truth, in practice theories are far from being true pictures of the world.

This consensus notwithstanding, there are also wide epistemological disagreements among constructivists. For example, some modernist constructivists follow scientific realism (Carlsnaes, 1992; Wendt, 1999) and look in the workings of social mechanisms for causal and/or constitutive explanations of social phenomena. Other modernist constructivists (Barnett, 1998; Reus-Smit, 1999; Ruggie, 1998a) establish causality by means of abduction or 'a process of successive interrogative reasoning between explanans and explanandum' (Ruggie, 1998b: 880), thereby teasing out tentative explanations from thickly described narratives. Still other modernist constructivists embrace a 'particularizing positivist strategy' (Katzenstein, 1996; Sikkink, 1993), or, like Checkel (2001), take constructivism to be consistent with positivism's generalizing or covering-law strategy.

Modernist linguistic constructivists (Kratochwil, 1989; Onuf, 1989) and critical constructivists (Cox, 1986; Williams and Krause, 1997) reject the natural-science concept of causation and argue that 'to ask for a reason for action is to try and find the rule that led to the action' (Smith, 2000: 159). Consequently, their approach to the social world is based on consensus within a community of research practitioners; to arrive at 'truth' they use argumentative procedures, abduction, narrative analysis and practical reasoning. Finally, a majority of radical constructivists embrace postmodernist pragmatism and study how the world is 'talked into existence' by means of signs, discourse and narratives.

Constructivists use a large variety of *methods*: positivist, post-positivist, quantitative, qualitative, and combinations thereof. The conventional qualitative methods most used by constructivists include case studies (Klotz, 1995); process tracing, including process tracing of ideas and their institutionalization in practice (Sikkink, 1993); counterfactuals (Checkel, 2001); and the comparative method (Reus-Smit, 1999). A combination of quantitative

and qualitative empirical methods – what Alker (1996) calls 'emancipatory empiricism' – has also been used to promote a critical approach. Some constructivists have followed the conventional path of grounding research on one concept, such as 'epistemic communities' (Adler and Haas, 1992; P. Haas, 1992); others have used formal methods, such as agent-based models (Cederman, 1997); while some have used statistics (e.g. Adler, 1987). Interpretive methods applied with great success have included genealogy[19] (Bartelson, 1995; Price, 1995), ethnography [20] (Zabusky, 1995), semiotics[21] (Bially, 1998), discourse analysis (Milliken, 1999), narrative analysis[22] (Barnett, 1998) and a combination of cognitive mapping[23] and symbolic analysis[24] (Johnston, 1995). All of these methods have proven useful in identifying background intersubjective meanings and social structures and the agents involved in social processes. They also have helped identify the reason why some discourses and practices become established, but not others, and the minimal foundations that validate some statements rather than others.

Several things stand out in this diversity, uniting many constructivists and setting them on a collision course with positivism, however. First, there is the notion that the quest for explaining causal processes requires the interpretive practice of uncovering intersubjective meanings. Second, constructivists generally draw descriptive inferences by means of traditional quantitative and qualitative methods and draw causal or constitutive inferences by means of historical narratives. Wendt (1999: 86), for example, argues that constitutive theories are explanatory and not merely descriptive (but see King et al., 1994). Constructivists generally believe that the barriers to true knowledge are posed not only by poor or defective methods, but also by the nature of social reality, which is at least partly indeterminate and contingent. Constructivist explanations, therefore, usually include reconstructed narratives that – because the manner in which social facts become established in the social world is relevant to the way in which they exert their influence (Adler, 1997: 339) – are as much about partly indeterminate processes as they are about partly determinate outcomes. The use of narratives and other interpretive methods, however, does not mean that all statements or all variables have the same weight; rather, such methods are used to uncover the validity of statements (Morrow, 1994) and to reveal social structures, social mechanisms and empirical regularities.

Constructivism's 'Added Value' and Substantive Empirical Contributions

By *added value*, I mean substantial improvements in the understanding of some of the conceptual building blocks of IR theory, especially knowledge, change, social communication, rationality, language and power.

(1) Constructivism considers intersubjective *knowledge* and ideas to have constitutive effects on social reality and its evolution. When drawn upon by individuals, the rules, norms and cause–effect understandings that make material objects meaningful become the source of people's reasons, interests and intentional acts; when institutionalized, they become the source of international practices. Constructivism's added value, therefore, is that it helps explain why people converge around specific norms, identities and cause–effect understandings, and thus where interests come from (Adler, 1987, 1991; Finnemore, 1996). Moreover, it puts to rest the naïve notion that *either* material objects *or* 'ideas' – but not both – constitute interests. Instead, constructivism advances the notion that interests *are* ideas; that is, they are ontologically intersubjective but epistemologically objective interpretations about, and for, the material world (Weldes, 1996). This means that interests cannot be mechanically deduced from international anarchy and the distribution of material resources. As Wendt (1999) has shown, international anarchy may be consistent with a state of permanent war, a state of calculated partial cooperation, and a state of more or less permanent peace.

(2) Contrary to the argument that constructivism is agnostic about *change* in world politics (Hopf, 1998: 180), it may be only a slight exaggeration to say that if constructivism is about anything, it is about change. For rather than using history as a descriptive method, constructivism has history 'built in' as part of theories. Historicity, therefore, shows up as part of the contexts that make possible social reality, the path-dependent processes involving structural and agent change, and the mechanisms involved in the explanation of change.

Constructivism's added value, therefore, is to take change less as the alteration in the positions of material things than as the emergence of new constitutive rules (Ruggie, 1998b), the evolution and transformation of new social structures (Dessler, 1989; Koslowski and Kratochwil, 1995), and the agent-related origins of social processes. In reference to agency, constructivism has generated theoretical and empirical studies about, for example, policy entrepreneurs (Checkel, 1998), epistemic communities (Adler and Haas, 1992), and transnational advocacy networks (Keck and Sikkink, 1998). Regarding the mechanisms of change, some constructivists emphasize collective learning, cognitive evolution, epistemic change and the 'life cycles of norms', all of which involve the institutionalization of people's novel knowledge, practices and discourses (Adler, 1991; Finnemore and Sikkink, 1998; Haas, 1990; Ruggie, 1993b). Critical constructivists (Cox, 1986; Linklater, 1998),

instead, take change not as something to be passively observed and explained, but as something that may occur as a result of reflexive analysis. Thus critical constructivism points to potential alternatives to prevailing structures (Hopf, 1998: 180).

(3) *Social communication* is another important added value of contemporary constructivism. Not only do collective understandings diffuse across time and place by means of it; it also enables agents to *fix the meanings* of material reality (Luhmann, 1989: 17). When fixing meanings, agents select from 'a "horizon" of possibilities' (Mingers, 1995: 157). In so doing they contribute to the institutionalization of practices and consequently to the unintentional survival of social structures. We also may find added value in constructivist theories that build on Habermas's (1984, 1987) theory of 'communicative action'. The main idea behind this theory is that social actors do not bargain to achieve the utilities they expect – as rational choice theory maintains. Rather, they engage in a discourse that helps demonstrate the validity of their arguments; this discourse in turn promotes collective understandings (Risse, 2000). So, rather than studying instrumental bargaining and choice, constructivism focuses on the effects of social communication on social relations; for example, how debate and persuasion help promote shared understandings. Recently, some rationalists have started to address social communication issues such as socialization, pointing to the rhetorical and thus instrumental nature of agents' actions (e.g., Schimmelfennig, 2000). By contributing to a better understanding of the micro-foundations of social construction, they are adding to the pool of knowledge from which some constructivists also draw.

(4) The relationship among acting, communication and *rationality* is critical for constructivists. Contrary to common belief, constructivists consider rationality and reason to be of critical importance for their explanations. Constructivists, however, cannot accept the notion that rationality means only instrumental rationality.[25] Thus they advance the notion of *practical* or *communicative rationality*, which, though sometimes calculating and choice-related, is also based on practical reason, is sensitive and contingent to historical, social and normative contexts, and emphasizes the communicative and persuasion logic in social theory. Practical rationality is one of constructivism's most important recent contributions to IR theory and research. When scholars emphasize the role of norms, the logic that stands in contradistinction to rational choice is that of 'appropriateness' (Finnemore, 1996; March and Olsen, 1998). Accordingly, agents do not choose between the most efficient alternative, but 'follow rules that associate particular identities to particular situations, approaching individual opportunities for action by assessing similarities between current

identities and choice dilemmas and more general concepts of self and situations' (March and Olsen, 1998: 951). When scholars stress social communication, Habermas's notion of 'communicative rationality' suggests itself.

Regardless of the route we follow to characterize practical rationality, however, what stands out is the significance of intersubjective understandings; the capacity for rational thought and behaviour is above all a background capacity (Bourdieu, 1977; Searle, 1998). Rationality lies less in choosing instrumentally on the basis of true theories than in behaving in ways that stand to reason, given people's background expectations and dispositions. It follows, then, that, because instrumental action is prompted by expectations and intentions, which are drawn from previously constituted social structures, constructivism subsumes rational choice under its more general principles. In other words, rational actors live and act in a socially constructed world and instrumental action takes place as a backdrop, not only to the knowledge that individuals share qua individuals, but also to all institutionalized knowledge (such as norms). Although very few rationalists accept this argument, some of them (Bates et al., 1998a; Fearon and Laitin, 2000, Zürn, 1998) have become more sensitive to the effect of discourses, narratives, identities and norms on rational choice. This demonstrates not only that constructivism has already left its mark on the discipline, but also that rationalists and constructivists are now in a position to cooperate on IR theoretical work.

(5) Social communication and practical rationality depend on *language*, which is the vehicle for the diffusion and institutionalization of ideas, a necessary condition for the persistence in time of institutionalized practices, and a mechanism for the construction of social reality. Constructivism's added value, therefore, consists in spelling out the role of language in social life. To begin with, language is the medium for the construction of intersubjective meanings. The sense of right, obligation and duty that political actors borrow from social structures depends on language that is oriented toward collective purposes. Second, 'speech acts' (e.g., 'this meeting is adjourned') have an 'illocutionary' dimension ('doing something by saying something'); hence, not only do they describe a reality, they also construct it (Kratochwil, 1989: 8). Third, and moving toward constructivism's 'strong programme', discourse – in Foucault's (1980) celebrated interpretation – is power, in the sense that 'it makes us understand certain problems in certain ways, and pose questions accordingly. It thereby limits the range of alternative policy options, and it enables us to take on others' (Diez, 1999: 603). Finally, if we start from the premise that language expressions represent a potential for new constitutions of reality (Derrida, 1978; Diez, 1999: 607), then discourse is also a source of change.

(6) Stressing material capabilities and overlooking the intersubjective dimension of *power*, traditional IR theoretical perspectives lost touch with some of the main forms of power, such as speech acts (Onuf, 1998a), hegemonic discourses (Cox, 1986), dominant normative interpretations and identities (Checkel, 2001), and moral authority (Hall, 1999). When, for example, someone uses guns and tanks, or makes a threat, it usually means that the ability to impose meanings, status, or functions on physical objects by collective agreement has already failed. As the case of the disintegration of the Soviet Union shows, guns and tanks were of no use when the regime's legitimacy and the system of collective understandings about identity, status and functions collapsed (Searle, 1995: 92). The imposition of meanings on the material world is one of the ultimate forms of power, and thus is where constructivism's added value with regard to power lies. The added value that results from interpreting power from a constructivist perspective also includes what Hacking (1999) has called 'making people'; in other words, labelling people in such a way that they change their identity, status and functions in reaction to the labelling. It also includes the power branded by social groups 'to provide the authoritative vision of the world' (Guzzini, 2000: 172), as well as Gramscian hegemonic power, which brings the interests of powerful groups into harmony with weaker groups and incorporates these interests into 'an ideology expressed in universal terms' (Cox, 1983: 168). Finally, it lies in the discursive ability to force one meaning of the world onto others (Bially, 1998).

Substantive empirical contributions Contrary to the still-common belief that constructivists avoid empirical research, there is a growing empirical constructivist literature about, for example, norms, identity, sovereignty, institutionalization and international governance, which has already made a substantive mark on the field.

(1) *Norms* constitute social identities and give national interests their content and meaning. Constructivist research grounds the notion that how people apply norms to classify the world is not irrelevant to the manner in which world politics unfolds. For example, Katzenstein and his associates (Katzenstein, 1996) have persuasively shown that states face security choices, and act upon them, not only in the context of their physical capabilities but also on the basis of normative understandings. Klotz (1995), in turn, has shown that the end of the apartheid regime in South Africa became possible because of the emergence and institutionalization of a global norm of racial equality. Moreover, according to Finnemore (1996), international organizations 'teach' or help diffuse norms and thereby help constitute the national interests of states that adopt these norms.

(2) *Identity* lies at the core of national and transnational interests. Consequently it is crucial

for an understanding of international behaviour, practices, institutions and change. It is just as important for an understanding of international conflict and war as for an understanding of international cooperation. Constructivism's critics argue that though it may be true that identity lies at the core of people's interests, identities do not change as often as constructivists say they do; hence there is no reason not to assume that interests are fixed (Mearsheimer, 1994). Adler and Barnett (1998), however, have shown that the 'we feeling' or identities of national groups may expand across national borders and lead to the development of security communities. Moreover, if identities are fixed, it would be difficult to explain the case of post-war Germany, which came to include Europe as part of its identity (Banchoff, 1999). And while the Middle East seems to be the area where realist thinking would take us the farthest, Barnett (1998: 15) has shown that 'Arab politics can be understood as a series of dialogues concerning the relationship between identities, norms, [and] regional order'. Lynch (1999), in turn, has elucidated the notion that changes in Jordan's foreign policy are foremost changes in Jordan's identity.

(3) Constructivism has made important contributions to the understanding of *sovereignty* (e.g., Bartelson, 1995; Biersteker and Weber, 1996; Walker, 1993). For example, constructivists have shown that the components of state sovereignty, such as territory, authority and national identity, are not fixed, but evolve with changing practices (Biersteker and Weber, 1996: 15). Building on Ruggie's insight (1983, 1993b)[26] about the transient nature of the Westphalian international system, constructivists have also been drawing attention to alternative constitutive norms – for example, human rights (Risse et al., 1999) – around which future systems might develop. Hall (1999) traced the social construction of national sovereignty in recent centuries and demonstrated its differential impact on interests (and thus behaviours), and, more generally, on international order and international systems. Moreover, constructivist analysis of sovereignty has shown how people collectively draw the boundaries between 'inside' and 'outside' (Walker, 1993) and how these boundaries are 'produced, reproduced, legitimated, contested, changed and naturalized' (Thompson, 1994: 13).

(4) Constructivists understand *institutions* as reified sets of intersubjective constitutive and regulative rules that, in addition to helping coordinate and pattern behaviour and channel it in one direction rather than another (Ruggie, 1998a: 54), also help establish new collective identities and shared interests and practices. For example, based on case studies of ancient Greece, Renaissance Italy, absolutist Europe and the present international system, Reus-Smit (1999) has shown that societies are constituted by 'deep institutions' that result from

beliefs about the moral purpose of the state, sovereignty, and the norm of procedural justice. Adler and Barnett (1998), Finnemore (1996) and Keck and Sikkink (1998) have shown that socialization, learning and emulation may enable international institutions to establish, articulate and transmit norms across nations, to define what constitutes legitimate behaviour, and to shape the identities of their members. Constructivism, however, has yet to provide more convincing answers to two questions: first, why certain ideas are institutionalized and others are not (Kowert and Legro, 1996; Legro, 2000); second, what keeps international institutions stable.

(5) Empirical constructivist work about new actors on the global scene – such as epistemic communities (Adler, 1992; P. Haas, 1990), NGOs and transnational advocacy networks (Keck and Sikkink, 1998), and moral communities (Linklater, 1998) – is enriching our understanding of *international governance*. Uncovering previously unrecognized 'chunks' of international and transnational social reality that occupy previously unidentified transnational spaces, it suggests diverse ways of organizing the study of international political reality, which transcend IR's 'domestic analogy'.

DEBATES WITHIN CONSTRUCTIVISM

The most salient and sustained constructivist debate in IR, which blends ontological, epistemological, and theoretical issues, has revolved around the 'agent–structure' problem. Three other epistemological debates have dealt with: (1) constitutive vs. causal theory, (2) explanatory vs. emancipatory cognitive interests, and (3) modernism vs. postmodernism. In addition, three debates about IR theory deal with: (1) the nature of agency in IR, (2) the role of rationality in the construction of social reality; and (3) liberal constructivism and its discontents. A methodological debate, which is imperative, has yet to begin.

The Agent–Structure Debate

The agent–structure debate focuses on the nature of international reality; more precisely, whether what exists in IR, and the explanation for it, should revolve around actors, structures, or both. Kenneth Waltz's structural theory of IR (1979) became the debate's point of entry for early constructivists, especially Wendt (1987). Wendt argued that Waltz's international structure and system, being creations of states, can only constrain state agency, but cannot generate state agents themselves; this argument meant that Waltz was 'not at all the structuralist he claimed, but, to the contrary, an ontological individualist' (Gould, 1998: 84). By contrast, claimed Wendt, Immanuel Wallerstein's (1974) 'world systems' are all structure and no agency, productive of states, which have no productive powers themselves. In order to avoid having to choose between agency and structure and to make it possible to deal with the nature of their relationship, Wendt imported Giddens's (1984) social structuration theory and Bhaskar's (1979) critical realist theory to IR.[27] He argued that just 'as social structures are ontologically dependent upon and therefore constituted by the practices and self-understandings of agents, the causal powers and interests of those agents, in their own turn, are constituted and therefore explained by structures' (1979: 359).[28] Similarly, Dessler (1989: 452) challenged Waltz's 'positional' model with a 'transformational' model of international structure, in which 'all social action presupposes social structure, and vice versa'. Wendt's and Dessler's work on the agent–structure problem was a crucial moment for constructivism, but also the basis of a new agent–structure debate within constructivism itself.

Reacting to Wendt's claims, Hollis and Smith (1990: 1) used an epistemologically driven approach to the agent–structure problem, along with a 'level of analysis' argument, to suggest that, as far as the social world is concerned, there are always two stories to be told. One story is about 'explaining' from the perspective of an outsider or observer, as in the naturalist approach to science. The other story is about 'understanding' – a hermeneutic inside view that involves getting to 'the point' or the meaning of things. This notion led to several interconnected sub-debates, which were framed by a series of articles by Wendt (1991, 1992a, 1998) and Hollis and Smith (1991, 1992, 1994, 1996), and which I distinguish for analytical purposes only.

First, there is the question whether, as Hollis and Smith argue, we can *explain* social phenomena from the 'outside' and *understand* people's meanings from the 'inside', or whether, as Wendt (1991: 391), Carlsnaes (1994) and Dessler (1999) maintain, we may be able to explain social phenomena, even when studying people's meanings from the 'inside'. What divides these scholars is the question of whether one should start from ontology or from epistemology. Scientific realists, such as Carlsnaes, Dessler and Wendt, first seek to identify social essences and only then to explain and/or understand the social world. They thus argue that it is possible to explain and understand from the inside or from the outside. Hollis and Smith (1996: 111, 113), however, hold that one can make ontological judgements only after deciding 'what kinds of criteria allows us to judge what kinds of things exist in the social world. ... Ontological statements without an epistemological warrant are mere dogma.'

Second, the above controversy directly impinged on Hollis and Smith's (1990) 'level of analysis'

argument, according to which, at every level of analysis, one can explain or understand IR by proceeding either from system to unit or from unit to system. In their view, at one level of analysis the international system is the 'whole' or structure and the state is the unit or agent. At a lower level of analysis, however, the state is structure and the bureaucracy is the agent. The same is true with the bureaucracy vs. the individual. Wendt (1991) retorted that the level of analysis argument, as originally formulated by David Singer (1961), is best suited for 'assessing the relative importance of causal factors at different levels of aggregation in explaining the behaviour of a given unit of analysis' (Wendt, 1991: 387). But in Hollis and Smith's account, 'the phenomenon to be explained *changes*; first it is the behaviour of state actors, then behaviour of the international system. This is a problem of ontology: of whether the properties or behaviour of units at one level of analysis can be reduced to those of another' (Wendt, 1991: 388). To avoid confusion, Wendt (1992a: 185) suggested reserving the level-of-analysis discourse 'for questions about what drives the behaviour of exogenously given actors, and agent-structure talk for questions about what constitutes the properties of those actors in the first place'. For Hollis and Smith (1992: 188), however, the question of ontology emerges at any level of analysis. Thus a distinction between explaining unit behaviour and identifying its properties is empty (Patomäki, 1996: 107).

The third question that Wendt (1991, 1992a) and Hollis and Smith (1991, 1994, 1996) debated directly followed from the previous question. Arguing that there can be only one kind of international system, that is, Waltz's, Hollis and Smith strongly objected to Wendt's portrait of Waltz as an individualist. Wendt, for whom a systemic theory must account for how states are constituted in the course of their interactions, and thus also for how identities and interests are socially constructed, retorted that the fact that Waltz's system can only constrain behaviour is indicative of an individualist approach. According to Wendt (1992a: 183), therefore, it was Waltz's *de facto* individualism that allowed Hollis and Smith 'to reduce the question of systemic causation to the question of whether the international system conditions the foreign policy behaviour of states' – in other words, 'to reduce the agent–structure problem to one of levels of analysis'.

If Wendt thought that Hollis and Smith (1990) conflated the agent–structure problem and the levels of analysis problem, Carlsnaes thought that Wendt conflated agent and structure in ways that made it difficult to do empirical research. Carlsnaes's important contribution was to invoke Margaret Archer's (1989) early morphogenesis theory[29] in order to introduce the time dimension to the agent–structure debate. He argued, with special reference to foreign policy, that what is needed to explain an action is 'indicating the reciprocal *interplay over time* – in terms of developmental patterns or cycles – that exists between structure and action' (Carlsnaes, 1992: 264). Hollis and Smith (1994: 244) were not persuaded; they retorted that the addition of the time dimension does little to solve the agent–structure ontological problem. On the contrary, it may actually make things worse, because morphogenesis means 'treating agents and structures as if they take turns affecting the social world' (Gould, 1998: 92); furthermore, it is not clear how adding the time dimension helps judge rival accounts of agents and structures. Replying to Hollis and Smith, Carlsnaes (1994: 280–4) suggested that a single integrative conceptual framework, which involves 'intentional', 'dispositional' and 'structural' levels of explanation, may go a long way towards resolving the agent–structure debate. Structures, '*cognitively* mediated by the actors in question rather than affecting policy actions directly', may thus be part of causal interpretive explanations.

In recent years, Patomäki (1996), Wight (1999), and Patomäki and Wight (2000) entered the agent–structure debate with a critical realist argument based on the work of Archer (1995) and Bhaskar (1979). For example, Patomäki (1996: 108) took explanation as a mode of interpretation, reasons as causes, and actors and regulative and constitutive rules as involved in the production of reality. Wight (1999), criticizing Wendt's (1992b) identification of states as agents, argued that only individuals can be agents and suggested a multilayered definition of agency, involving individual attributes, sociocultural systems and roles. This realist position, however, did not sit well with Doty (1997; cf. Suganami, 1999); making a rare contribution to the agent–structure debate from radical constructivism, she advanced the post-structuralist argument that what matters is neither structures nor agents, but the role of discursive practices.

I doubt whether the agent–structure debate will ever be fully resolved. Because of the debate, however, we now have a much better understanding of the metaphysical and social-theory foundations of the relationship between agents and structures. While constructivists have disagreed markedly about agent–structure, there is much more in common in their work than they are aware of or care to acknowledge. The agent–structure debate can thus profit from some 'consolidation', by which I mean concentrating on the consensus already achieved and that still can be achieved, and then turning our efforts to translate the agent–structure metaphysical and social theory positions into theoretical and empirical propositions.

In particular, theoretical and empirical discussions of how social structures act on the subjective level and how ideas held by individuals become institutionalized and taken for granted seem to be a good place to restart the debate. Constructivists have

started to pay attention to the *micro-foundations of intersubjective phenomena* and to the *macro-foundations of reasoned acts* and are beginning to search for mechanisms that link them. These mechanisms include ideational diffusion and learning (e.g., Adler, 1992; Checkel, 2001; Finnemore and Sikkink, 1998; Wendt, 1999), socialization (e.g., Checkel, 1999; Johnston, 2001; Schimmelfennig, 2000; Wendt, 1999), social communication and persuasion (e.g., Checkel, 1998; Lynch, 1999; Risse, 2000), and institutionalization (Adler and Haas, 1992; Legro, 2000; Ruggie, 1993a).

Searching for the mechanisms that can make social action more intelligible and make the agent–structure problem more manageable, however, will require learning more about the development of communities of shared meaning, discourse and practice, and focusing on the dynamic aspects of agent–structure. Learning processes, for example, occur in people's heads, but their outcomes exist in the intersubjective world. Thus, only when practices change as a result of a re-conceptualization of reality, can multiple interacting actors and future actors draw upon these understandings and, thus, learn the same or similar lessons over time. And when people's collective knowledge is institutionalized, it becomes a building block of their reasons and the spring of subsequent social action.

The Epistemological Debates

A debate about causal vs. constitutive explanations, which deals primarily with the kind of knowledge that constitution entails, has been brewing mainly between Wendt (1998, 1999, 2000) and his critics. In Wendt's view, causal theories 'answer questions of the form "why?" and, in some cases, "how?"'; whereas constitutive theories 'account for the properties of things by reference to the structures in virtue of which they exist'. Thus, for example, the factors that constituted the Cold War – which 'do not exist apart from a Cold War, nor do they precede it in time' (Wendt, 1998: 104–6) – are not the same as its causes. Echoing linguistic and critical constructivist approaches, Smith (2000: 157) claims that Wendt's view of constitution looks very much like a causal theory, 'or at least … a form of theorizing that leads to, or is prior to, causal explanation'. It thus differs from the 'understanding' hermeneutic-like view that is dominant in the interpretive social sciences. For Smith (2000: 157–8), the problem with Wendt's rendition of causal theory and constitutive theory is his Cartesian separation between ideational and material forces, according to which 'at some level material forces are constituted independently of society, and affect society in a *causal* way' (Wendt, 1999: 111). This is far from what Smith considers to be a hermeneutic strategy of rule- and language-constituting action.

Some of the differences between Wendt and his critics may be reconciled by pragmatic realism. *Contra* Smith, we need a realist ontology 'about what it is that brings about changes in the world outside of the texts we are writing ourselves' (Patomäki and Wight, 2000: 229). *Contra* Wendt (1999), however, we need a pragmatic epistemology that, without neglecting human agents, does not separate between the material (causation) and social structure (constitution). Pragmatic realism consolidates the two arguments by taking social constitution as the dynamic collective attachment of meaning, function and value to material reality (Searle, 1995), and causal explanation as the identification of the mechanisms that are involved in the social constitution of institutions and practices. Expectations, for example, are intentional, and are thus part of the causal relation between mind and the world (Searle, 1998: 100–7). On the other hand, expectations are simultaneously drawn upon the background of intersubjective dispositions that constitute but do not determine human reasons.

The *cognitive interest* debate within constructivism has pitted modernist constructivists, who believe that explaining social reality is the main goal of social knowledge, and critical theory scholars, who believe that the main goal of social knowledge is emancipation from oppressive structures. Critical theorists say that there can be no explanations of the world as it is, if only because there is no world until we explain it. Thus constructivists should take a normative and ethical stand (Inayatullah and Blaney, 1996) and use theory as a tool for improving the world; for example, advancing democratic transnational community (Linklater, 1998), empowering women (Enloe, 1990; Peterson, 1992; Tickner, 1992), and redefining security (Williams and Krause, 1997: xiv).

Modernist constructivists do not disagree with their critical counterparts about the occasional need to take a critical position against the social world and pursue normative agendas, or about the capacity of knowledge 'carriers' to help bring about changes in the social world. But they also believe that the best way to advance normative goals is not to take theory as an instrument for the emancipation of ideologically chosen underclasses but instead to produce systematic knowledge, including about how knowledge and political power interact. Critical constructivists retort that, in their zeal to provide contingent explanations of social reality, modernist constructivists legitimize the existing situation. Thus they really are not constructivists at all, but liberals and positivists in disguise, who stick close to the precepts of rationalist theories (Ashley, 1996; Campbell, 1996; George, 1994).

Price and Reus-Smit (1997), two modernist constructivists with critical leanings, have recently attempted to narrow the rift between the two types of constructivism; they maintain that modernist constructivists share some of the normative concerns held by critical theorists and that, in fundamental ways, modernist constructivists have been advancing a critical agenda. Price and Reus-Smit suggest, therefore, that only through a dialogue between normative arguments and empirically informed accounts can we arrive at better and more ethical practices. Their point is that improving the world requires bringing the two cognitive interests together; without explanation there can be no emancipation.

This is certainly the case with regard to the relationship between social knowledge and political practice. We need theories about the emergence and consolidation of practices that enhance human interests across national borders, including about the manner in which theoretical knowledge intervenes in struggles over meaning and affects these processes (Adler, 1997). Constructivist theory, therefore, can be both 'critical' *and* 'problem-solving', in Robert Cox's (1986: 208–9) sense.

Finally, an attitude of mutual disengagement and benign neglect (rather than a debate) characterizes the relations between constructivists and post modernists. They differ about (a) the status of material reality, (b) the ontological status of unobservable mechanisms, (c) agency and especially reason, and (d) the notion that a *social* science, separate from the other sciences, is possible. As a consequence, constructivists have taken postmodernism to lie outside constructivism's 'middle ground' (Adler, 1997). Postmodernists, in turn, tend to regard constructivists as positivists in disguise, aiming to take interpretive action out of postmodernism. Do these differences mean that postmodernists are 'inside' constructivism or 'outside' it? The question, of course, indicates that we are dealing with a social construct. Until recently, postmodernists have explicitly chosen to remain on the outside. Calling themselves 'dissidents' (Ashley and Walker, 1990; George, 1994), they carried over to IR their deep suspicions about anything that looks like discipline and foundation and thus divorced themselves from other streams of constructivism. The 'middle ground' thesis, therefore, rather than aiming to exclude postmodernists (Milliken, 1999: 227), echoed the fact that postmodernists explicitly and self-consciously placed themselves beyond what Waever (1996: 169) called 'the boundary of negativity'. There is no 'essential' reason, however, why constructivists and postmodernists cannot hold a fruitful and constructive debate, aiming to achieve not supremacy of one approach over the other, but mutual learning.

Theoretical Debates

The constructivist debate over the *nature of agency* in IR is about whether constructivists, following Wendt (1999), should theorize about agency as the attribute of states, or whether, as other constructivists say, they should open constructivism to domestic politics, non-state actors, and the possibility of state transcendence. Wendt (1999, 2000) defends his decision to focus on the state, because his theory is about the inter-state system and states possess a monopoly on the use of force, which they can use on behalf of individuals, domestic organizations and governments. Although, he admits, non-state actors increasingly play critical roles in world politics, these roles are important only through state action. He also believes in the progressive nature of the state. Finally, Wendt holds that states are structures that exhibit macro-level regularities and these, although dependent on individuals' beliefs, are not explained by them.

Wendt's state-orientation has been sharply criticized within the constructivist camp. To begin with, his critics have argued that although constructivism is supposed to open structures to different constructions and to different understandings of world politics, Wendt's theory, like Waltz's, is conservative and consecrates the existing inter-state system (Inayatullah and Blaney, 1996). Moreover, they say, Wendt's theory should have assigned equal status to agents and structures, thus permitting the study of the domestic societal manifestations of collective identities (Hall, 1999: 27). Because Wendt brackets the domestic sources of state identity, however, he cannot explain the rise and decline of international societies (Reus-Smit, 1999: 166). Wendt may be able to explain change within systems, but not change between them.

Wendt's reification of the state has also been faulted as being unhelpful for studying, for example, transnational communities (Koslowski, 1999) and security communities (Cederman, 1997). His critics add that it can be shown empirically that subjects who act in the name of the state are aware that it is not a unitary state (Doty, 2000: 139) and that ontologically, as Bhaskar (1979) has shown, only individuals can express agency (Wight, 1999: 127). Thus, they say, although Wendt may have articulated a 'via media' with regard to epistemology, mainly because of his reification of the state and his almost exclusive reliance on social structures for explanation, that middle path eluded him when it came to ontology.

Wendt's (2000: 175) reply to his critics is simple. 'It all depends on the question one is asking. Against a book on the states system, therefore, calls to "stop reifying the state!" should be seen really as calls to "change the subject!" I am all for that, but it complements the systemic question, rather than replaces it.' Wendt is right, as far as *his* theory is concerned. But, one should ask, why did Wendt settle for such a limiting constructivist theory? As a constructivist, Wendt should have been aware that constructivist theories ought to leave room for new and unexpected structural possibilities. Instead, he

offers a theory and a portrait of agency and the state that locks in politics as the study of inter-state relations and ultimately gives up on bringing into the theory *the ultimate constructor of worlds* – by which I mean the thinking, often reasonable, sometimes surprising, and even at times creative human individual.

Within constructivism, a dialogue that may soon turn into a full debate has been taking place about how to approach *rationality*. In the background is the increasing realization that constructivism and rationalism are complementary rather than contradictory. Three factors catalyzed the dialogue. First was a debate that took place in the 1990s between rationalists and constructivists in the pages of the *Zeitschrift für Internationale Bezienhungen* (ZIB, Journal of International Relations). A second factor was the lead article by Peter Katzenstein, Robert Keohane and Stephen Krasner (1998: 680) in the fiftieth anniversary issue of *International Organization*, with its thesis that 'rationalism and constructivism are generic theoretical orientations that are complementary on some crucial points'. For example, constructivism may contribute to a better understanding of what rationalists call 'common knowledge'[30] and of the role of norms in situations of multiple equilibria. The article also envisions a division of labour whereas constructivists explain where alternatives come from and rationalists explain instrumental choice (Katzenstein et al., 1998: 680–2). The third factor has been the growing trend in the rationalist camp to develop theories of institutional behaviour (Young, 1998) and rational choice-based narratives (Bates, et al., 1998b).

The emerging debate within constructivism is thus whether and how to reconcile rationalism and constructivism, and on whose terms. I can identify four (preliminary and still vague) constructivist responses to the challenge to integrate rationalist and constructivist approaches. The first 'response' is no response at all, but an unwillingness to contemplate or even talk about the possibility that rationalism and constructivism may be compatible. This response is common mainly among radical constructivists. Risse (2000) and a small but growing group of constructivists provide a second response, namely, that constructivists should confront the 'logic of consequentialism' not only with the normative 'logic of appropriateness' but also by adopting Habermas's (1996) concept of 'communicative rationality' and the 'logic of arguing'.

Checkel (2001) suggests a third response, which is really about scope: in some circumstances, a rational approach is called for; in other circumstances, a constructivist approach is more suitable. Following in the footsteps of Katzenstein, Keohane and Krasner (1998), who take constructivism as a supplement to rational choice, Finnemore and Sikkink (1998: 911) offered a fourth response; namely, a 'staged analysis' that 'could run either way: one could model rational choice as producing social knowledge as easily as one could model social context as a background for rational choice, depending on the empirical question being researched'. The second, third and fourth responses are consistent with the view that a synthesis between rationalism and constructivism may be possible. A real synthesis, in my view, would integrate rationalism and constructivism into a theory that ultimately transcends both.

Another dialogue, which pits liberal vs. non-liberal constructivist approaches, is just getting under way. In general, constructivist scholars have been critical regarding liberal approaches. This includes postmodernists (Ashley, 1987; Latham, 1995), critical constructivists (e.g., Cox, 1986), and feminist constructivists (Runyan and Peterson, 1991). Some modernist constructivists, however, while distancing themselves from liberal explanations (Moravcsik, 1999) and neoliberal explanations (Keohane, 1984), have nevertheless explicitly followed liberal research agendas, for example, about the democratic peace (e.g., Risse-Kappen, 1995). A possible constructivist debate of the future may thus be about making liberalism more compatible with constructivism without undercutting the latter's meta-theoretical basis. Another possible debate would follow Onuf's (1998b) book *The Republican Legacy in International Thought*, and address constructivism's Kantian and Weberian roots. Still a third possibility is a debate about the liberal agendas that most modernist constructivists follow. In this generally West-oriented discipline such a debate may engender an increased attention to the Third World, its culture, problems and agendas, which are frequently not liberal and may even be anti-liberal.

A BLUEPRINT FOR ACTION

In this concluding section I offer a blueprint for action within the constructivist camp. I am less interested in chartering an agenda for specific IR theory and empirical research than in emphasizing those issues that, if constructivism is to become firmly established in IR, need to be taken into account and dealt with.

(1) *Methodology* is the major missing link in constructivist theory and research (but see Alker, 1996; Dessler, 1999; Friedman and Starr, 1997). It would be only a slight exaggeration to say that whether constructivism ultimately has a profound effect on the IR discipline will depend on the development of a coherent constructivist methodological base that suggests a practical alternative to imitating the physical sciences. The explanatory endeavour, I believe, should revolve around the historical reconstruction of social facts (Dessler, 1999), on the basis of interpretive narratives, practices and discourses. A coherent constructivist methodological approach also means approaching research less as a predictive enterprise than as an effort to explain how past and present events, practices and interests became possible and why they occurred in time and space the way they did.

This does not mean, however, that constructivism should not be 'forward reasoning'. As eloquently proposed by Bernstein et al. (2000), an alternative to deductive-nomological methodology may be offered by an evolutionary approach, in which we read into narratives the 'so-called lessons of the past' (p. 50) and, by building scenarios, learn about the likely but not certain path that reality may take. This is appealing for constructivists, because it makes it possible to deal both practically and empirically with what Hacking calls 'looping effects' (Hacking, 1999)[31] and with the reflexivity of human knowledge, including how world events affect our knowledge, which then affects us and the world.

(2) It is time for constructivists to tone down epistemological and ontological debates and concentrate more directly on *building constructivist IR theory*. This does not means neglecting meta-theory and social theory, but concentrating on them only when they are necessary for building substantive IR constructivist theories. In spite of the differences and debates within constructivism, there exists enough common ground among most types to permit dealing with meta-theoretical issues on the basis of IR theoretical and empirical questions.

(3) We should redouble our efforts to develop *the micro-foundations of constructivist theory*. In recent years, perhaps because most constructivists have relied on structural/functional sociological theories (Sterling-Folker, 2000), there has been a call to 'go micro' (Checkel, 1998). For example, Wendt (1999) suggests relying on cognitive theory; Schimmelfennig (2000), on rational choice; Checkel (2001), on rational choice and social psychology, mainly social learning; and Johnston (2001), on social psychology, mainly status theory. I believe that all these paths should be explored further and assessed on their merits. At the same time, the micro-foundations of constructivism and thus constructivist theories of action should not be disconnected from the social structures that *individual* agents draw upon for their intentional acts. To put this another way, we do not need a structural theory over here and a micro theory over there. Rather, we need a mechanism or, if possible, a theory whose micro-foundations are clearly understood by us.[32] The point is that we first need to know what type of overall social mechanism or theory of institutionalized international behaviour this micro theory is part of.

(4) Alex Wendt's (1994) 'corporate identity' black box should be opened up. In fact, this has started

to happen, as constructivist scholars increasingly pay attention to the *domestic determinants of change* (Reus-Smit, 1999; Risse et al., 1999) and to the domestic impact of international norms (Checkel, 1997; Cortell and Davis, 2000; Risse et al. 1999). This agenda should be broadened and deepened, however. First, the domestic arena, which to liberals (Moravcsik, 1998) is the mechanical bureaucratic backdrop of a rational choice theory of inter-state bargaining, to constructivists is the place where national preferences are born, and international practices are produced, reproduced and transformed. To constructivists, therefore, the socio-cognitive domestic 'sources of state preferences' (Moravcsik, 1998) are part of the mechanisms that connect agents and structures in dynamic ways. These mechanisms may help explain individuals' socially constructed reasons in domestic political settings, which come to constitute social structures at later times and in different places. They also may help explain the domestic selection processes that partly determine what and whose collective understandings, including norms and causal beliefs, become the 'national interest'.

Second, Robert Putnam's concept of 'two-level-games' – according to which national leaders play strategic material power games, albeit domestically and internationally constrained (R. Putnam, 1988) – lends itself to a constructivist reading of *conceptual games*. In conceptual games, not only leaders of states, but also other state and non-state actors bargain about who gets to impose meanings on material reality and thus to socially construct the situation in their own image. A research programme on conceptual games will help constructivists explain how power affects the domestic sources of corporate identity. Third, constructivists should pay more attention to the role of domestic practices in the constitution of regional, international and even global social structures (Lumsdaine, 1993; Nadelmann, 1990). Finally, constructivists must bring the individual back in – for example, studying how individuals purposefully use social capital and carefully chosen words to legitimize or delegitimize opponents and sometimes entire populations. In fact, this kind of social construction, especially in the information age, is a large part of what politics is all about.

(5) Constructivists will need to face the problem of *blending normative theory with explanatory theory*. Here, I believe, we have much to learn from the English School, whose 'international society approach' is simultaneously historical, normative and systematic/analytical. One of the English School's key points is that normative and critical goals are part of the frame of systematic problems that scholars set themselves to explain.

(6) Constructivists should stress the *practical and political consequences* of their approach. First, constructivism can help sensitize practitioners to the sometimes crucial role that learning plays in international politics. For example, constructivism can contribute to a better understanding of the role of intersubjective meanings and identities in conflict prevention and resolution. Second, constructivism can make practitioners more sensitive to the functions, practices and discourses of transnational epistemic communities and transnational advocacy networks. Third, constructivism holds the potential to change how practitioners think about security, for example, the idea that people's identities lie at the root of conflict and peace. Fourth, constructivism can be conducive to a better understanding of the design of international organizations, stressing that design may be a function not only of efficiency (Koremenos et al., 2001) but also of the way the designers intersubjectively interpret the organizations' purposes and functions. Fifth, constructivism may help produce a new understanding of strategy and strategic relations. For example, insights about 'communicative rationality' may be used to reformulate our understanding of conventional and non-conventional strategy. Finally, a critical understanding of the role of socially constructed knowledge in the practical day-to-day construction of social reality – for example, via epistemic communities – may help advance practical and politically oriented understandings of sustainable development, globalization, arms control and human rights.

(7) There are several directions of *interdisciplinary research* that, if pursued, may help constructivists better to understand how social construction processes work. I am referring mainly to a cross-fertilization between constructivism, on the one hand, and international law (Dezalay and Garth, 1996), social psychology (Johnston, 1995), evolutionary theory (Adler, 1991; Bernstein et al., 2000), cognitive psychology (Wendt, 1999) and complexity theory[33] (Alker, 1999; Hoffmann, 1999), on the other. Because I do not have enough space to refer in detail to these and other areas of collaboration, I will say a few words about the last two areas only.

Cognitive science can help develop constructivism's micro-foundations. This does not mean reducing constructivism's micro-foundations to information processing and AI (artificial intelligence), let alone neurons (Lycan, 1999). Cognitive psychology and its connections to analytical philosophy, however, may lead to a better understanding of reasoning processes, human dispositions, expectations, intentional acts, and the relationship between mind and language (Searle, 1995, 1998).

Complexity theory raises more difficult issues, if only because it is a relatively new field that still lacks a scientific consensus. Again, I do not suggest reducing *social* issues to the new kid on the physical and natural sciences' block. Complexity theory, however, has developed some insights that can be particularly useful to constructivists, for example, about interactions that are interconnected in unanticipated and non-linear ways. Non-linearity is consistent with self-fulfilling and self-defeating prophecies and 'looping effects'. The idea that small and basically unpredictable changes can become large social transformations may help shed light on how to study amplification processes, such as the social diffusion of norms. Complexity theory may also illuminate the agent–structure problem. For example, the critique that structuration theory is circular is based on a linear approach to change. From a non-linear perspective, however, the possibility that one variable is 'involved in causing change in another, while the other variable is similarly involved in causing change in the first' (Brown, 1995: 7) makes perfect sense.

Constructivism has come a long way. It has become an alternative way of doing IR theory and research and has made a substantial contribution to the IR discipline. Constructivism's common ground, however – the social construction of knowledge and the construction of social reality – which is often concealed by theoretical differences and debates, can and should be articulated more explicitly, not only through dialogue, but also by convergence around shared academic practices. Moreover, IR constructivism is at a preliminary stage only; much work still remains before it becomes a normal and taken-for-granted way of doing IR theory and research. For this to happen, however, constructivism must manage to bridge, first, metaphysics and social theory on the one hand, and IR theory research and methodology on the other, and then bridge IR theory and practice.

Notes

I would like to thank my students Yael Bala, Sharon Bouchnik, Tal Dingott, Leah Gedalia, Gadi Heimann, Piki Ish-Shalom, Tommy Steiner and Elias Vilderman for helping me think through some of the issues I have dealt with in this chapter. I also would like to thank Michael Brecher, Raymond Duvall, Harry Gould, Stefano Guzzini, Peter Haas, Robert Keohane, Nicholas Onuf and Richard Price for helpful comments. Finally, I would like to thank an anonymous reviewer, Walter Carlsnaes, Thomas Risse, and Beth Simmons for their thoughtful comments and suggestions.

1 Positivism is a metaphysical theory that holds (a) 'a belief in the unity of science' (it applies to the social as well as to the natural sciences); (b) 'the view that there is a distinction between facts and values'; (c) 'a powerful belief in the existence of regularities in the social as well as the natural world'; and (d) 'a tremendous reliance on the belief that it is empirical validation or falsification that is the hallmark of "real" enquiry' (Smith, 1996: 16).

2 Materialism is the view that material reality exists, regardless of perception or interpretation, and that what we know is a faithful representation of reality out there. Materialism informs functionalist and rational choice social theories, which are the basis, respectively, of neorealism and neoliberalism in IR.

3 Idealism holds that the physical is just a collection of ideas and that, therefore, the foundation for all knowledge is in the mind.

4 As a radicalized version of idealist philosophy, *poststructuralism* aims to deconstruct the dominant readings of reality; *postmodernism* aims to uncover the discourse and power structures that control practice. Both approaches are in agreement that subjects are ontologically unimportant, reason is a chimera, no foundational point whatsoever exists, and that science is just power disguised as knowledge. Unless a distinction is necessary, I will refer to both approaches as postmodernism.

5 Nominalism is the philosophical view that the world does not come already classified and that it is human beings who classify it (Hacking, 1999).

6 Metaphysics studies the fundamental nature of reality and being, which is outside objective experience.

7 On mathematics, see Bishop, 1967; Troelstra and van Dalen, 1988. On education and mathematics, see Davis et al., 1990. On psychology and education, see Piaget, 1932, 1973 ('cognitive constructivism'); Vygotsky, 1962, 1978 ('social constructivism'); Glaserfeld, 1995. On sociology, the seminal work is Berger and Luckmann 1966. On natural science, see Barnes, 1977; Bloor, 1976; Golinski, 1998; Pickering, 1984.

8 Hermeneutics subordinates explanation and description to interpretation and understanding of meaning. 'Objective hermeneutics' refers to the perspective that 'the study of human meaning can aspire to objectivity' (Delanty, 1997: 41).

9 By means of historical reconstruction, the 'event is explained as the end-point of a concrete historical sequence, not as an instance of a particular type' (Dessler, 1999: 129).

10 It treats 'the event to be explained as an instance of a certain *type* of event, which is then shown to accompany or follow regularly from conditions of a specified kind' (Dessler, 1999: 129).

11 I borrow the language of strong and weak programmes in the social sciences from the sociology of knowledge, in particular the Edinburgh School's 'Strong Programme in the Sociology of Knowledge'. See Barnes, 1977; Bloor, 1976.

12 'The act of speaking in a form that gets someone else to act' (Onuf, 1998a: 66).

13 Modernist pragmatism follows in the footsteps of early American pragmatists, such as Peirce, in using a 'modernist discourse of democratic deliberation in which communities of inquiry [test] hypotheses in order to solve problems; such contemporary pragmatists as Richard J. Bernstein and Hilary Putnam sustain that tradition' (Kloppenberg, 1998: 84). Postmodern pragmatists like Richard Rorty 'present pragmatism as a postmodern discourse of critical commentary that denies that we can escape the conventions and contingencies of language in order to connect with a world of experience outside texts, let alone solve problems in that world' (Kloppenberg, 1998: 84).

14 Scientific realism subsumes events under causal laws and mechanisms. According to scientific realists, therefore,

causal investigations of natural and social orders presuppose a natural and social reality that exists prior to our descriptions of it. 'Critical realism' shares with constructivism the view that the social world is endowed with meaning and that, therefore, 'observations are theory-dependent and ... we cannot have pure access of the independent world' (Mingers, 1995: 88). Unlike idealists, however, critical realists believe that the natural world is not constructed by perception. Instead, reality describes the causal mechanisms and entities that compose them (Archer et al., 1998; Baert, 1998: 191; Smith, 1999: 25).

15 Giddens's (1979: 5) structuration theory incorporates the mutually constitutive relationship between irreducible and potentially unobservable social structures and intentional human agents into a dialectical synthesis that overcomes the subordination of one to the other (Wendt, 1987: 356). According to structuration theory, 'structure enters simultaneously into the constitution of the agent and social practices, and "exists" in the generating moments of this constitution'. This means that, as rules and resources, structures, 'are both the precondition and the unintended outcome of people's agency' (Baert, 1998: 104).

16 'An epistemic community is a network of professionals with recognized expertise and competence in a particular domain and an authoritative claim to policy-relevant knowledge within that domain or issue area'. Epistemic communities have a shared set of principled and causal beliefs, shared notions of validity, and a common policy enterprise (P. Haas, 1992: 3).

17 Accordingly, rational members of a community deliberate to reach intersubjective understandings, or a 'reasoned consensus', and this can be attained only when members of this community share a 'common life world', i.e., 'a supply of collective interpretations of the world and of themselves' (Risse, 2000: 11).

18 The 'Copenhagen School' is associated with the Centre for Peace and Conflict Research in Copenhagen.

19 Genealogy is a non-chronological history of present institutions with reference to past bodies of knowledge that embodies discursive and practical social power.

20 Ethnography is a descriptive and interpretive method aimed at understanding culture.

21 Semiotics is the study of linguistic, cultural and behavioural signs.

22 A 'narrative concerns a story that is joined by a plot' (Barnett, 1998: 15).

23 Cognitive mapping is a technique for measuring mental representations, in particular those that capture subjects' causal axioms (see Johnston, 1995: 50).

24 Symbolic analysis refers to the study of symbols as a means of identifying the relationship between culture and behaviour (Johnston, 1995: 51).

25 Instrumental rationality is 'the efficient pursuit of exogenously determined interests within the constraints of available information, the interests and strategies of other actors, and the distribution of power' (Reus-Smit, 1999: 159–60).

26 Ruggie (1983) studied the historical transition from a medieval 'heteronomous' to a sovereign system of rule.

27 Although conceptually similar to Giddens's structuration theory (1984), Bhaskar's critical realism (1979) has a different conception of structure (sets of internal and external social relations, instead of Giddens's rules and resources) and a different epistemological outlook (it endorses realism, rather than Giddens's hermeneutics).

28 Wendt's empirical 'bracketing strategy', according to which one looks first at agents and then at structures, did not provide an easy solution to the agent–structure problem.

29 Archer's morphogenesis theory introduces the time dimension to solve structuration's 'two realities' problem and circularity. Archer's (1995: 76) main insight is that 'structure necessarily pre-dates the action(s) which transform it; and that structural elaboration necessarily post-dates those actions'. Thus morphogenesis breaks with the flow of the recursiveness of social life into intervals and accords 'full significance to the time scale through which structure and agency themselves *emerge*, *intertwine* and *redefine* one another'.

30 Rationalists use the concept of 'common knowledge' to describe what players must know in order to be part of the same game.

31 A 'looping effect' is the reflective process by which the way people are collectively classified affects who they are, what they do and, in turn, how they affect the very classifications that made them 'this kind' of people (Hacking, 1999: 34).

32 Evolutionary theory, which first relied only on Darwin's macro theory about the differential survival rates of organisms, now has also a good account of the micro-level genetic processes of evolutionary change and of their relation to Darwin's macro theory (Bohman, 1991: 147).

33 Complexity theory, 'the emerging science at the edge of order and chaos', deals with adaptive self-organizing systems. See Waldrop, 1992.

Bibliography

Adler, Emanuel (1987) *The Power of Ideology: The Quest for Technological Autonomy in Argentina and Brazil.* Berkeley: University of California Press.

Adler, Emanuel (1991) 'Cognitive Evolution: A Dynamic Approach for the Study of International Relations and their Progress', in Emanuel Adler and Beverly Crawford (eds), *Progress in Postwar International Relations*. New York: Columbia University Press. pp. 43–88.

Adler, Emanuel (1992) 'The Emergence of Cooperation: National Epistemic Communities and the International Evolution of the Idea of Nuclear Arms Control', *International Organization*, 46 (1): 101–45.

Adler, Emanuel (1997) 'Seizing the Middle Ground: Constructivism in World Politics', *European Journal of International Relations*, 3 (3): 319–63.

Adler, Emanuel and Barnett, Michael (eds) (1998) *Security Communities.* Cambridge: Cambridge University Press.

Adler, Emanuel and Haas, Peter (1992) 'Conclusion: Epistemic Communities, World Order, and the Creation of a Reflective Research Program', *International Organization*, 46 (1): 367–90.

Adorno, T.W. (ed.) (1976) *The Positivist Dispute in German Sociology*. London: Heinemann.

Alker, Hayward R. (1996) *Rediscoveries and Reformulations: Humanistic Methodologies for International Studies*. Cambridge: Cambridge University Press.

Alker, Hayward R. (1999) 'Ontological Reflections on Peace and War', *Santa Fé Institute Working Paper Series* 99-02-011. New Mexico: Santa Fé.

Archer, Margaret S. (1989) *Culture and Agency*. Cambridge: Cambridge University Press.

Archer, Margaret S. (1995) *Realist Social Theory: The Morphogenetic Approach*. Cambridge: Cambridge University Press.

Archer, Margaret S., Bhaskar, Roy, Collier, Andrew, Lawson, Toni and Norrie, Alan (1998) *Critical Realism: Essential Readings*. London: Routledge.

Ashley, Richard (1987) 'The Geopolitics of Geopolitical Space: Toward a Critical Social Theory of International Politics', *Alternatives*, 12 (4): 403–34.

Ashley, Richard (1996) 'The Achievements of Post-Structuralism', in Steve Smith, Ken Booth and Marysia Zalewski (eds), *International Theory: Positivism and Beyond*. Cambridge: Cambridge University Press. pp. 240–53.

Ashley, Richard and Walker, R.B.J. (eds) (1990) 'Reading Dissidence/Writing the Discipline: Crisis and the Question of Sovereignty in International Studies', *International Studies Quarterly*, 34 (3): 367–416.

Austin, John L. (1962) *Sense and Sensibilia*. Oxford: Clarendon Press.

Baert, Patrick (1998) *Social Theory in the Twentieth Century*. New York: New York University Press.

Banchoff, Thomas (1999) 'German Identity and European Integration', *European Journal of International Relations*, 5 (3): 259–89.

Barnes, Barry (1977) *Interests and the Growth of Knowledge*. London: Routledge and Kegan Paul.

Barnett, Michael (1998) *Dialogues in Arab Politics*. New York: Columbia University Press.

Barnett, Michael and Finnemore, Martha (1999) 'The Politics, Power, and Pathologies of International Organizations', *International Organization*, 53 (4): 699–732.

Bartelson, Jens (1995) *A Genealogy of Sovereignty*. Cambridge: Cambridge University Press.

Bates, Robert H., de Figueiredo, Rui J.P., Jr and Weingast, Barry R. (1998a) 'The Politics of Interpretation: Rationality, Culture, and Transition', *Politics and Society*, 26 (4): 603–42.

Bates, Robert H., Greif, Avner, Levi, Margaret; Rosenthal, Jean-Laurent and Weingast, Barry R. (1998b) *Analytical Narratives*. Princeton: Princeton University Press.

Berger, Peter L. and Luckmann, Thomas (1966) *The Social Construction of Reality*. New York: Anchor.

Bernstein, Richard J. (1985) *Beyond Objectivism and Relativism: Science, Hermeneutics, and Praxis*. Philadelphia: University of Pennsylvania Press.

Bernstein, Steven, Lebow, Richard Ned, Stein, Janice Gross and Weber, Steven (2000) 'God Gave Physics the Easy Problems: Adapting Social Science to an Unpredictable World', *European Journal of International Relations*, 6 (1): 43–76.

Bhaskar, Roy (1979) *The Possibility of Naturalism: A Philosophical Critique of the Contemporary Human Sciences*. Brighton: Harvester.

Bially, Janice (1998) 'The Power Politics of Identity'. PhD dissertation, Yale University.

Biersteker, Thomas J. and Weber, Cynthia (eds) (1996) *State Sovereignty as Social Construct*. Cambridge: Cambridge University Press.

Bishop, E. (1967) *Constructive Analysis*. New York: McGraw-Hill.

Bloor, David (1976) *Knowledge and Social Imagery*. London: Routledge.

Bohman, James (1991) *The New Philosophy of Social Science*. Cambridge, MA: MIT Press.

Bourdieu, Pierre (1977) *Outline of a Theory of Practice*. Cambridge: Cambridge University Press.

Brown, Courtney (1995) *Serpents in the Sand: Essays on the Nonlinear Nature of Politics and Human Destiny*. Ann Arbor: University of Michigan Press.

Buzan, Barry (1993) 'From International System to International Society: Structural Realism and Regime Theory Meet the English School', *International Organization*, 47 (3): 377–52.

Buzan, Barry and Waever, Ole (1997) 'Slippery? Contradictory? Sociologically Untenable? The Copenhagen School Replies', *Review of International Studies*, 23 (2): 241–50.

Campbell, David (1992) *Writing Security: United States Foreign Policy and the Politics of Identity*. Minneapolis: University of Minnesota Press.

Campbell, David (1996) 'Political Prosaics, Transversal Politics, and the Anarchical World', in Michael J. Shapiro and Hayward R. Alker (eds), *Challenging Boundaries: Global Flows, Territorial Identities*. Minneapolis: University of Minnesota Press. pp. 7–32.

Carlsnaes, Walter (1992) 'The Agency-Structure Problem in Foreign Policy Analysis', *International Studies Quarterly*, 36 (3): 245–70.

Carlsnaes, Walter (1994) 'In Lieu of a Conclusion: Comatibility and the Agency-Structure Issue in Foreign Policy Analysis', in Walter Carlsnaes and Steve Smith (eds), *European Foreign Policy: The EC and Changing Perspectives in Europe*. London: Sage. pp. 274–87.

Cederman, Lars-Erik (1997) *Emergent Actors in World Politics*. Princeton: Princeton University Press.

Checkel, Jeffrey (1997) 'International Norms and Domestic Politics: Bridging the Rationalist-Constructivist Divide', *European Journal of International Relations*, 3 (4): 473–95.

Checkel, Jeffrey (1998) 'The Constructivist Turn in International Relations Theory', *World Politics*, 50 (1): 324–48.

Checkel, Jeffrey (1999) 'International Institutions and Socialization', paper presented at the Annual Meeting of the International Studies Association, Washington, DC.

Checkel, Jeffrey (2000) 'Social Learning and European Identity Change', *International Organization*, 55 (3): 553–88.

Christiansen, Thomas, Jørgensen, K. Erik and Wiener, Antje (1999) 'The Social Construction of Europe', *Journal of European Public Policy*, 6 (4): 528–44.

Cortell, Andrew P. and Davis, James W. (2000) 'Understanding the Domestic Impact of International Norms: A Research Agenda', *International Studies Review*, 2 (1): 65–87.

Cox, Robert W. (1983) 'Gramsci, Hegemony and International Relations: An Essay in Method', *Millennium*, 12 (2), 162–75.

Cox, Robert W. (1986) 'Social Forces, States and World Orders: Beyond International Relations Theory', in Robert O. Keohane (ed.), *Neorealism and Its Critics*. New York: Columbia University Press. pp. 204–54.

Crawford, Neta (1999) 'The Passion of World Politics: Propositions on Emotion and Emotional Relationships', *International Security*, 24 (4): 116–56.

Davis, R.B., Maher, Carolyn A. and Noddings, Nel (eds) (1990) *Constructivist Views of the Teaching and Learning of Mathematics*. Reston: NCTM.

Delanty, Gerard (1997) *Social Science: Beyond Constructivism and Realism*. Minneapolis: University of Minnesota Press.

Der Derian, James (1987) *On Diplomacy*. Oxford: Blackwell.

Der Derian, James (1990) 'The (S)pace of International Relations: Simulation, Surveillance and Speed', *International Studies Quarterly*, 34 (3): 295–310.

Derrida, Jacques (1978) *Writing and Difference* (trans. Alan Bass). Chicago: University of Chicago Press.

Dessler, David (1989) 'What's at Stake with the Agent–Structure Debate', *International Organization*, 43 (3): 441–73.

Dessler, David (1999) 'Constructivism Within a Positivist Social Science', *Review of International Studies*, 25: 123–37.

Deutsch, Karl W., Burrell, Sidney A., Kann, Robert A., Lee, Maurice Jr, Lichterman, Martin, Lindgren, Raymond E., Loewenheim, Francis, L. and Van Wagenen, Richard, W. (1957) *Political Community and the North Atlantic Area*. Princeton: Princeton University Press.

Dewey, John (1977) *The Essential Writings*, ed. David Sidorsky. New York: Harper & Row.

Dezalay, Yves and Garth, Bryant G. (1996) *Dealing with Virtue: International Commercial Arbitration and the Construction of a Transnational Legal Order*. Chicago: University of Chicago Press.

Diez, Thomas (1999) 'Speaking "Europe": The Politics of Integration Discourse', *Journal of European Public Policy*, 6 (4): 598–613.

Dilthey, Wilhelm (1989) *Selected Works: Introduction to the Human Sciences*, vol. 1. Princeton: Princeton University Press.

Doty, Roxanne L. (1996) *Imperial Encounters*. Minneapolis: University of Minnesota Press.

Doty, Roxanne L. (1997) 'Aporia: A Critical Exploration of the Agent–Structure Problematique in International Relations Theory', *European Journal of International Relations*, 3 (3): 365–92.

Doty, Roxanne L. (2000) 'Desire All the Way Down', *Review of International Studies*, 26 (1): 137–9.

Dunne, Tim (1995) 'The Social Construction of International Society', *European Journal of International Relations*, 1 (3): 367–89.

Dunne, Tim (1999) 'Constructivism in the Altered Landscape of IR Theory', paper presented at the Annual Meeting of the International Studies Association, Washington, DC.

Enloe, Cynthia (1990) *Bananas, Beaches and Bases: Making Feminist Sense of International Politics*. Berkeley: University of California Press.

Epp, Roger (1998) 'The English School on the Frontiers of International Relations', *Review of International Studies*, 24 (5): 47–63.

Fearon, James D. and Laitin, David D. (2000) 'Violence and the Social Construction of Ethnic Identity', *International Organization*, 54 (4): 845–77.

Finnemore, Martha (1996) *National Interests in International Society*. Ithaca: Cornell University Press.

Finnemore, Martha and Sikkink, Kathryn (1998) 'International Norm Dynamics and Political Change', *International Organization*, 52 (4): 887–917.

Foucault, Michel (1980) *Power/Knowledge: Selected Interviews and Other Writings, 1972–1977*, ed. Colin Gordon. New York: Pantheon.

Friedman, Gil and Starr, Harvey (1997) *Agency, Structure, and International Politics: From Ontology to Empirical Inquiry*. London: Routledge.

George, Jim (1994) *Discourses of Global Politics: A Critical (Re)Introduction to International Relations*. Boulder: Lynne Rienner.

Giddens, Anthony (1979) *Central Problems in Social Theory*. Berkeley: University of California Press.

Giddens, Anthony (1984) *The Constitution of Society*. Berkeley: University of California Press.

Gill, Stephen (1988) *The Global Economy: Perspectives, Problems, and Policies*. New York: Harvester.

Glaserfeld, Ernst von (1995) *Radical Constructivism: A Way of Knowing and Learning*. London: Falmer Press.

Golinski, Jan (1998) *Making Natural Knowledge: Constructivism and the History of Science*. Cambridge: Cambridge University Press.

Gould, Harry D. (1998) 'What *Is* at Stake in the Agent–Structure Debate', in Vendulka Kubalkova, Nicholas Onuf and Paul Kowert (eds), *International Relations in a Constructed World*. London: M.A. Sharpe. pp. 79–98.

Gramsci, Antonio (1971) *Selection From the Prison Notebooks* (ed. and trans. by Quinton Hoare and Geoffrey N. Smith). New York: International.

Guzzini, Stefano (2000) 'A Reconstruction of Constructivism in International Relations', *European Journal of International Relations*, 6 (2): 147–82.

Haas, Ernst B. (1958) *The Uniting of Europe: Political, Social, and Economic Forces, 1950–1957*. Stanford: Stanford University Press.

Haas, Ernst B. (1983) 'Words Can Hurt You; or, Who Said What to Whom About Regimes', in Stephen Krasner (ed.), *International Regimes*. Ithaca: Cornell University Press. pp. 23–59.

Haas, Ernst B. (1990) *When Knowledge is Power*. Berkeley: University of California Press.

Haas, Peter M. (1990) *Saving the Mediterranean: The Politics of International Environmental Cooperation*. New York: Columbia University Press.

Haas, Peter M. (1992) 'Introduction: Epistemic Communities and International Policy Coordination', *International Organization*, 46 (1): 1–35.

Habermas, Jürgen (1978) *Knowledge and Human Interests*, 2nd edn. London: Heinemann.

Habermas, Jürgen (1984) *The Theory of Communicative Action*, vol. 1. (trans. Thomas McCarthy). Boston: Beacon Press.

Habermas, Jürgen (1987) *The Theory of Communicative Action*, vol. 2. Boston: Beacon Press.

Habermas, Jürgen (1996) *Between Facts and Norms: Contributions to a Discourse Theory of Law and Democracy*. Cambridge, MA: The MIT Press.

Hacking, Ian (1999) *The Social Construction of What?* Cambridge, MA: Harvard University Press.

Hall, Rodney B. (1999) *National Collective Identity: Social Constructs and International Systems*. New York: Columbia University Press.

Heidegger, Martin (1962) *Being and Time* (trans. John Macquarrie and Edward Robinson). London: SCM Press.

Hempel, Carl (1965) *Aspects of Scientific Explanation*. New York: The Free Press.

Hoffmann, Matthew J. (1999) 'The Complexity of Mutual Constitution: Co-evolving Agents and Structures in Environmental Politics', paper presented at the Annual Meeting of the American Political Science Association, Atlanta, GA.

Hollis, Martin, and Smith, Steve (1990) *Explaining and Understanding International Relations*. Oxford: Clarendon Press.

Hollis, Martin and Smith, Steve (1991) 'Beware of Gurus: Structure and Action in International Relations', *Review of International Studies*, 17 (4): 393–410.

Hollis, Martin and Smith, Steve (1992) 'Structure and Action: Further Comment', *Review of International Studies*, 18 (2): 187–8.

Hollis, Martin and Smith, Steve (1994) 'Two Stories About Structure and Agency', *Review of International Studies*, 20 (3): 241–51.

Hollis, Martin and Smith, Steve (1996) 'A Response: Why Epistemology Matters in International Theory', *Review of International Studies*, 22 (1): 111–16.

Hopf, Ted (1998) 'The Promise of Constructivism in International Relations Theory', *International Security*, 23 (1): 171–200.

Horkheimer, Max (1972) *Selected Essays*. New York: Herder and Herder.

Hurrell, Andrew (1993) 'International Society and the Study of Regimes: A Reflective Approach', in Volker Rittberger (ed.), *Regime Theory and International Relations*. Oxford: Clarendon Press. pp. 49–72.

Husserl, Edmund (1962) *General Introduction to Pure Phenomenology*, trans. W.R. Boyce Gibson. New York: Collier.

Inayatullah, Naeem and Blaney, David L. (1996) 'Beyond Parochialism in International Relations Theory', in Yosef Lapid and Friedrich Kratochwil (eds), *The Return of Culture and Identity in IR Theory*. Boulder: Lynne Rienner. pp. 65–84.

Jackson, Robert (1990) *Quasi-States: Sovereignty, International Relations and the Third World*. Cambridge: Cambridge University Press.

James, William (1975) *Pragmatism: A New Name for Some Old Ways of Thinking*. Cambridge, MA: Harvard University Press.

Jepperson, Ronald L., Wendt, Alexander and Katzenstein, Peter J. (1996) 'Norms, Identity, and Culture in National Security', in Peter J. Katzenstein (ed.), *The Culture of National Security: Norms and Identity in World Politics*. New York: Columbia University Press. pp. 33–75.

Johnston, Alastair I. (1995) *Cultural Realism: Strategic Culture and Grand Strategy in Chinese History*. Princeton: Princeton University Press.

Johnston, Alastair I. (1996) 'Cultural Realism and Strategy in Maoist China', in Peter Katzenstein (ed.), *The Culture of National Security: Norms and Identity in World Politics*. New York: Columbia University Press. pp. 216–68.

Johnston, Alastair I. (2001) 'Treating Institutions as Social Environments', *International Studies Quarterly*, 45 (3).

Katzenstein, Peter (ed.) (1996) *The Culture of National Security: Norms and Identity in World Politics*. New York: Columbia University Press.

Katzenstein, Peter, Keohane, Robert and Krasner, Stephen (1998) 'International Organization and the Study of World Politics', *International Organization*, 52 (4): 645–86.

Keck, Margaret and Sikkink, Kathryn (1998) *Activists Beyond Borders: Advocacy Networks in International Politics*. Ithaca: Cornell University Press.

Keck, Otto (1997) 'The Information Dilemma: Private Information as a Cause of Transaction Failure in Markets, Regulation, Hierarchy, and Politics', *Journal of Conflict Resolution*, 31 (1): 139–63.

Keohane, Robert (1984) *After Hegemony: Cooperation and Discord in the World Political Economy*. Princeton: Princeton University Press.

Keohane, Robert (1988) 'International Institutions: Two Approaches', *International Studies Quarterly*, 32 (4): 379–96.

Kier, Elizabeth (1996) 'Culture and French Military Doctrine Before World War II', in Peter Katzenstein (ed.), *The Culture of National Security: Norms and Identity in World Politics*. New York: Columbia University Press. pp. 186–215.

Kier, Elizabeth (1997) *Imagining War: French and British Military Doctrine Between the Wars*. Princeton: Princeton University Press.

King, Garry, Keohane, Robert and Verba, Sidney (1994) *Designing Social Inquiry*. Princeton: Princeton University Press.

Kloppenberg, James T. (1998) 'Pragmatism: An Old Name for Some New Ways of Thinking?', in Morris Dickstein (ed.), *The Revival of Pragmatism: New Essays on Social Thought, Law, and Culture*. Durham, NC: Duke University Press. pp. 83–127.

Klotz, Audie (1995) *Norms in International Relations: The Struggle against Apartheid*. Ithaca: Cornell University Press.

Koremenos, Barbara, Lipson, Charles and Snidal, Duncan (eds) (2001) 'The Rational Design of International Organizations', *International Organization*, 55 (4).

Koslowski, Rey (1999) 'A Constructivist Approach to Understanding the European Union as a Federal Polity', *Journal of European Public Policy*, 6 (4): 561–78.

Koslowski, Rey and Kratochwil, Friedrich (1995) 'Understanding Change in International Politics: The Soviet Empire's Demise and the International System', in Richard N. Lebow and Thomas Risse-Kappen (eds), *International Relations Theory and the End of the Cold War*. New York: Columbia University Press. pp. 127–66.

Kowert, Paul and Legro, Jeffrey (1996) 'Norms, Identity, and Their Limits: A Theoretical Reprise', in Peter J. Katzenstein (ed.), *The Culture of National Security: Norms and Identity in World Politics*. New York: Columbia University Press. pp. 451–97.

Kratochwil, Friedrich (1989) *Rules, Norms, and Decisions*. Cambridge: Cambridge University Press.

Kratochwil, Friedrich (1993) 'The Embarrassment of Change: Neo-Realism and the Science of *Realpolitik* without Politics', *Review of International Studies*, 19 (1): 63–80.

Kratochwil, Friedrich (1996) 'Is the Ship of Culture at Sea or Returning?', in Yosef Lapid and Friedrich Kratochwil (eds), *The Return of Culture and Identity in IR Theory*. Boulder: Lynne Rienner. pp. 201–22.

Kratochwil, Friedrich and Ruggie, John G. (1986) 'International Organization: A State of the Art on an Art of the State', *International Organization*, 40 (4): 753–75.

Kuhn, Thomas (1970) *The Structure of Scientific Revolutions*. Chicago: University of Chicago Press.

Lapid, Yosef (1989) 'The Third Debate: On the Prospects of International Theory in a Post-Positivist Era', *International Studies Quarterly*, 33 (3): 235–54.

Latham, Robert (1995) 'Liberalism's Order/Liberalism's Other: A Genealogy of Threat', *Alternatives*, 20 (1): 111–46.

Latour, Bruno and Woolgar, Steve (1986) *Laboratory Life: The Construction of Scientific Facts*. Princeton: Princeton University Press.

Legro, Jeffrey W. (2000) 'Whence American Internationalism', *International Organization*, 54 (2): 253–90.

Linklater, Andrew (1990) 'The Problem of Community in International Relations', *Alternatives*, 15 (2): 135–54.

Linklater, Andrew (1998) *The Transformation of Political Community: Ethical Foundations of the Post-Westphalian Era*. Columbia: University of South Carolina Press.

Litfin, Karen (1994) *Ozone Discourses: Science and Politics in Global Environmental Cooperation*. New York: Columbia University Press.

Luhmann, Niklas (1989) *Ecological Communication*. Cambridge: Polity Press.

Lumsdaine, David (1993) *Moral Vision in International Politics: The Foreign Aid Regime, 1949–1986*. Princeton: Princeton University Press.

Lycan, William (1999) *Mind and Cognition: An Anthology*. Oxford: Blackwell.

Lynch, Marc (1999) *State Interests and Public Interests: The International Politics of Jordan's Identity*. New York: Columbia University Press.

March, James G. and Olsen, Johan P. (1998) 'The Institutional Dynamics of International Political Orders', *International Organization*, 52 (4): 943–69.

Mearsheimer, John J. (1994) 'The False Promise of International Institutions', *International Security*, 19 (3): 5–49.

Meyer, John W. (1980) 'The World Polity and the Authority of the Nation-State', in Albert Bergesen (ed.), *Studies of the Modern World System*. New York: Academic Press. pp. 109–37.

Milliken, Jennifer (1999) 'The Study of Discourse in International Relations: A Critique of Research and Methods', *European Journal of International Relations*, 5 (2): 225–54.

Mingers, John (1995) *Self-Producing Systems: Implications and Applications of Autopoiesis*. New York: Plenum.

Moravcsik, Andrew (1999) *The Choice for Europe: Social Purpose and State Power From Messina to Maastricht*. Ithaca: Cornell University Press.

Morrow, Raymond A. (1994) *Critical Theory and Methodology*, vol. 3, *Contemporary Social Theory*. Thousand Oaks: Sage.

Müller, Harald (1994) 'Internationale Beziehungen als komunicatives Handeln zur Kritik der utilitaristischen Handlungstheorien', *Zeitschrift für Internationale Bezienhungen*, 1 (1): 15–44.

Nadelmann, Ethan (1990) 'Global Prohibition Regimes: The Evolution of Norms in International Society', *International Organization*, 44 (4): 479–526.

Neumann, Iver (1999) *Uses of the Other: 'The East' in European Identity Formation*. Minneapolis: University of Minnesota Press.

Onuf, Nicholas (1989) *World of Our Making: Rules and Rule in Social Theory and International Relations*. Columbia: University of South Carolina Press.

Onuf, Nicholas (1998a) 'Constructivism: A User's Manual', in Vendulka Kubalkova, Nicholas Onuf and

Paul Kowert (eds), *International Relations in a Constructed World*. London: M.E. Sharpe. pp. 58–78.

Onuf, Nicholas (1998b) *The Republican Legacy in International Thought*. Cambridge: Cambridge University Press.

Patomäki, Heikki (1996) 'How to Tell Better Stories about World Politics', *European Journal of International Relations*, 2 (1): 105–33.

Patomäki, Heikki and Wight, Colin (2000) 'After Postpositivism? The Promises of Critical Realism', *International Studies Quarterly*, 44 (2): 213–38.

Peirce, Charles S. (1966) *Selected Writings* (ed. Philip Wiener). New York: Dover.

Peterson, Spike V. (1992) *Gendered States: Feminist (Re)visions of International Relations Theory*. Boulder: Lynne Rienner.

Piaget, Jean, (1932) *The Moral Judgement of the Child*. London: Routledge and Kegan Paul.

Piaget, Jean (1973) *To Understand is to Invent*. New York: Grossman.

Pickering, Andrew (1984) *Constructing Quarks: A Sociological History of Particle Physics*. Edinburgh: Edinburgh University Press.

Popper, Karl R. (1982) *The Open Universe: An Argument for Indeterminism*, ed. by W.W. Bartley III. Totowa: Rowman and Littlefield.

Powell, Walter W. and DiMaggio, Paul J. (eds) (1991) *The New Institutionalism in Organizational Analysis*. Chicago: University of Chicago Press.

Price, Richard M. (1995) *The Chemical Weapons Taboo*. Ithaca: Cornell University Press.

Price, Richard and Reus-Smit, Christian (1997) 'Dangerous Liaisons? Critical International Theory and Constructivism', *European Journal of International Relations*, 4 (3): 259–94.

Putnam, Hilary (1990) *Realism with a Human Face*. Cambridge, MA: Harvard University Press.

Putnam, Hilary (1998) 'Pragmatism and Realism', in Morris Dickstein (ed.), *The Revival of Pragmatism: New Essays on Social Thought, Law, and Culture*. Durham, NC: Duke University Press. pp. 37–53.

Putnam, Robert D. (1988) 'Diplomacy and Domestic Politics: The Logic of Two-Level Games', *International Organization*, 42 (3): 427–60.

Rengger, Nicholas (1999) *International Relations, Political Theory, and the Problem of Order*. London: Routledge.

Reus-Smit, Christian (1999) *The Moral Purpose of the State: Culture, Social Identity, and Institutional Rationality in International Relations*. Princeton: Princeton University Press.

Risse, Thomas (2000) '"Let's Argue!": Communicative Action in World Politics', *International Organization*, 54 (1): 1–40.

Risse, Thomas, Ropp, Stephen and Sikkink, Kathryn (eds) (1999) *The Power of Human Rights: International Norms and Domestic Change*. Cambridge: Cambridge University Press.

Risse-Kappen, Thomas (1995) *Cooperation among Democracies: The European Influence on US Foreign Policy*. Princeton: Princeton University Press.

Ruggie, John G. (1975) 'International Responses to Technology: Concepts and Trends', *International Organization*, 29 (3): 557–83.

Ruggie, John G. (1983) 'Continuity and Transformation in the World Polity: Toward a Neorealist Synthesis', *World Politics*, 35 (2): 261–85.

Ruggie, John G. (ed.) (1993a) *Multilateralism Matters: The Theory and Praxis of an Institutional Form*. New York: Columbia University Press.

Ruggie, John G. (1993b) 'Territoriality and Beyond: Problematizing Modernity in International Relations', *International Organization*, 46 (1): 139–74.

Ruggie, John G. (1998a) *Constructing the World Polity: Essays on International Institutionalization*. London: Routledge.

Ruggie, John G. (1998b) 'What Makes the World Hang Together? Neo-Utilitarianism and the Social Constructivist Challenge', *International Organization*, 52 (4): 855–86.

Runyan, Ann S. and Peterson, Spike V. (1991) 'The Radical Future of Realism: Feminist Subversion of IR Theory', *Alternatives*, 16 (1): 67–106.

Russett, Bruce and Duvall, Raymond (1976) 'Some Proposals to Guide Research on Contemporary Imperialism', *Jerusalem Journal of International Relations*, 2 (1): 1–27.

Schimmelfennig, Frank (2000) 'International Socialization in the New Europe: Rational Action in an Institutional Environment', *European Journal of International Relations*, 6 (1): 109–39.

Schuz, Alfred (1962) *Collected Papers*, vol. 1 (ed. by Maurice Natanson). The Hague: Martinus Nijhoff.

Searle, John R. (1995) *The Construction of Social Reality*. New York: The Free Press.

Searle, John R. (1998) *Mind, Language, and Society: Philosophy in the Real World*. New York: Basic Books.

Sikkink, Kathryn (1993) 'The Power of Principled Ideas: Human Rights Policies in the United States and Western Europe', in Judith Goldstein and Robert O. Keohane (eds), *Ideas and Foreign Policy: Beliefs, Institutions, and Political Change*. Ithaca: Cornell University Press. pp. 139–70.

Simmel, Georg (1955) *Conflict and the Web of Group Affiliations*. New York: The Free Press.

Singer, David (1961) 'The Level of Analysis Problem in International Relations', in Klaus Knorr and Sidney Verba (eds), *The International System*. Princeton: Princeton University Press. pp. 77–92.

Smith, Steve (1996) 'Positivism and Beyond', in Steve Smith, Ken Booth and Marysia Zalewski (eds), *International Theory: Positivism and Beyond*. Cambridge: Cambridge University Press. pp. 11–46.

Smith, Steve (1999) 'Social Constructivisms and European Studies: A Reflectivist Critique', *Journal of European Public Policy*, 6 (4): 682–91.

Smith, Steve (2000) 'Wendt's World', *Review of International Studies*, 26 (1): 151–63.

Sterling-Folker, Jennifer (2000) 'Competing Paradigms or Birds of a Feather? Constructivism and Neoliberal

Institutionalism Compared', *International Studies Quarterly*, 44 (1): 97–120.

Suganami, Hidemi (1999) 'Agents, Structures, Narratives', *European Journal of International Relations*, 5 (3): 365–86.

Tannenwald, Nina (1999) 'The Nuclear Taboo: The United States and the Normative Basis of Nuclear Non-Use', *International Organization*, 53 (3): 433–68.

Thompson, Janice (1994) *Mercenaries, Pirates, and Sovereigns*. Princeton: Princeton University Press.

Tickner, J. Ann (1992) *Gender in International Relations*. New York: Columbia University Press.

Troelstra, A.S. and van Dalen, D. (1988) *Constructivism in Mathematics: An Introduction*, vols 1 and 2. Amsterdam: North-Holland.

Vygotsky, L.S. (1962) *Thought and Language*. Cambridge, MA: MIT Press.

Vygotsky, L.S. (1978) *Mind in Society*. Cambridge, MA: Harvard University Press.

Waever, Ole (1996) 'The Rise and Fall of the Inter-Paradigm Debate', in Steve Smith, Ken Booth and Marysia Zalewski (eds), *International Theory: Positivism and Beyond*. Princeton: Princeton University Press. pp. 149–85.

Waever, Ole (1999) 'Does the English School's Via Media Equal the Contemporary Constructivist Middle Ground?', paper presented at the Annual Meeting of the British International Studies Association, Manchester. http://www.uck.ac.uk/politics/english school/ waever99.htm

Waldrop, M. Mitchell (1992) *Complexity: The Emerging Science at the Edge of Order and Chaos*. New York: Touchstone.

Walker, R.B.K. (1993) *Inside/Outside: International Relations as Political Theory*. Cambridge: Cambridge University Press.

Wallerstein, Immanuel (1974) *The Modern World System: Capitalist Agriculture and the Origins of the European World-Economy in the Sixteenth Century*. New York: Academic Press.

Waltz, Kenneth (1979) *Theory of International Politics*. Reading, MA: Addison–Wesley.

Weber, Cynthia (1995) *Simulating Sovereignty: Intervention, the State and Symbolic Exchange*. Cambridge: Cambridge University Press.

Weber, Max (1978) *Economy and Society* (ed. by G. Roth and C. Wittich). Berkeley: University of California Press.

Weldes, Jutta (1996) 'Constructing National Interests', *European Journal of International Relations*, 2 (3): 275–318.

Weldes, Jutta (1999) *Constructing National Interests: The United States and the Cuban Missile Crisis*. Minneapolis: University of Minnesota Press.

Wendt, Alexander (1987) 'The Agent–Structure Problem in International Relations Theory', *International Organization*, 41 (3): 335–70.

Wendt, Alexander (1991) 'Bridging the Theory/Meta-Theory Gap in International Relations', *Review of International Studies*, 17 (4): 383–92.

Wendt, Alexander (1992a) 'Levels of Analysis vs. Agents and Structures: Part III', *Review of International Studies*, 18 (2): 181–5.

Wendt, Alexander (1992b) 'Anarchy is What States Make of It: The Social Construction of Power Politics', *International Organization*, 46 (2): 391–425.

Wendt, Alexander (1994) 'Collective Identity Formation and the International State', *American Political Science Review*, 88 (2): 384–96.

Wendt, Alexander (1995) 'Constructing International Politics', *International Security*, 20 (1): 71–81.

Wendt, Alexander (1998) 'On Constitution and Causation in International Relations', *Review of International Studies*, 24 (5): 101–17.

Wendt, Alexander (1999) *Social Theory of International Politics*. Cambridge: Cambridge University Press.

Wendt, Alexander (2000) 'On the Via Media: A Response to the Critics', *Review of International Studies*, 26 (1): 165–80.

Wight, Colin (1999) 'They Shoot Dead Horses Don't They? Locating Agency in the Agent–Structure Problematique', *European Journal of International Relations*, 5 (1): 109–42.

Williams, Michael C. and Krause, Keith (1997) 'Preface: Toward Critical Security Studies', in Keith Krause and Michael C. Williams (eds), *Critical Security Studies*. Minneapolis: University of Minnesota Press. pp. vii–xxiv.

Winch, Peter (1958) *The Idea of a Social Science*. London: Routledge and Kegan Paul.

Wittgenstein, Ludwig (1953) *Philosophical Investigations*. Oxford: Blackwell.

Young, H. Peyton (1998) *Individual Strategy and Social Structure: An Evolutionary Theory of Institutions*. Princeton: Princeton University Press.

Zabusky, Stacia E. (1995) *Launching Europe: An Ethnography of European Cooperation in Space Science*. Princeton: Princeton University Press.

Zürn, Michael (1998) 'The Rise of International Environmental Politics: A Review of Current Research', *World Politics*, 50 (4): 617–50.

6

Linking Theory to Evidence in International Relations

RICHARD K. HERRMANN

As is clear in this handbook, the study of international relations includes diverse theories purporting to explain substantive patterns in world politics. The field is also characterized by different perspectives on how to defend these claims. One strategy, of course, is to connect the concepts that constitute a theory to observable indicators, spell out what expectations follow from the theory, and then demonstrate whether these expectations materialize or not. Although this positivist strategy sounds straightforward, its implementation is anything but simple. Demonstrating that the chosen indicators validly connect to the abstract concept is difficult, as is determining the specific expectations that should follow. The subsidiary theories, data generating methods and analytic techniques associated with these tasks also provoke controversy. Of course, some scholars conclude that trying to link theory and evidence in a positivist fashion is misguided. It confuses constructed concepts and categories with natural categories, treats created data as if they were facts, and employs the label of science in an effort to empower particular political preferences.

Despite the disagreements over how theory and evidence should be related there are benefits to attempting the endeavor. The process compels the production of specific definitions and concrete expectations. By taking the empirical step, it is easier to identify at what stage of the enterprise disagreement is most clear and what the substance of this disagreement is. One criticism of both rational choice and constructivist theorizing is that too little of it has made the connection to evidence. The confusion that can be generated when theories are not clearly linked to evidence is easy to spot. Fearon and Wendt (see Chapter 3 in this volume), for instance, make a

convincing case that the main differences between rationalist and constructivist theories are often misunderstood or misidentified as related to assumptions about the causal role of ideas or substantive assumptions about the motives of actors.

Connecting theory to evidence not only sharpens the understanding of theory, it also creates a common ground across the boundaries established by disciplines, sub-disciplines and intellectual communities. Most substantive questions such as why wars happen and what causes collective identities to form provoke research in many fields. Although scholars have reasons to claim their work is different and to align with people using similar languages and methods, focusing on the substantive question and the empirical evidence connected to theoretical answers can promote common ground. One purpose of this chapter is to explore this common-ground and to review the progress and problems in connecting theory to evidence. This will entail crossing sub-community boundaries. For instance, it will include bridging rationalist interest in subjective expectation with social psychological research on perception which, heretofore, have typically been seen as antithetical rational and irrational explanations. It will also include connecting the constructivist focus on collective identity formation with the literature on the emergence of nationalism.

Although rationalist and constructivist labels are relatively recent and often associated with a rather thin empirical record, the substantive research linking theories and evidence in international relations is large. Far too large to summarize in a single chapter. That is the task of the entire handbook. Instead, this chapter concentrates on the major efforts and problems encountered as rationalists and constructivists have attempted to link theory and evidence. I start with the rationalist tradition in its objectivist version. This has generated a huge body of work. I concentrate primarily on that portion of this research that focuses on war and security. Most of it takes as a starting assumption that there are rational actors sensitive to distributions of power. Following this, I turn to theories that abide by the most general form of rationalist models offered by Fearon and Wendt (that is Desire + Belief = Action). These are theories of purposeful action. Most of them relax both the assumptions of substantive and procedural rationality. They also emphasize the agent's subjective understanding of the environment as distinct from the scholar's objective description of the environment.

Following the discussion of how ideas have been studied at the level of agents, I turn to the study of ideas as constituting an element in the structure of the international system. I use the study of ideas and phenomenological perspectives as a bridge to cross from rationalist to constructivist endeavors. I pay special attention throughout to the tension within the constructivist umbrella between objectivist and phenomenological perspectives. I do this in some detail in the context of research on norms. Finally, I take up the question of where collective identities come from. This involves linking the constructivist approach to this question to the long-standing efforts to explain identity in comparative politics, sociology and history.

RATIONALIST THEORIES

Many theories of international relations assume that actors have a set of desires or motives and pursue these according to beliefs about the environment. Various forms of realism, for instance, accept the formula Desire + Beliefs = Action. Of course, determining an actor's desires or motives is a difficult task. Hans Morgenthau (1973) argued that it was an impossible task. He explained that single motives, like national security or the desire for wealth, did not associate with single behaviors but could lead to many different behaviors. Specific behaviors, like defense spending or military intervention, also did not associate with only a single motive. The same behavior could be attributed to diverse motives. With no empirical way to infer an actor's motives, Morgenthau suggested that motives be held constant and variation in action be explained by variation in the other variable, that is beliefs, especially beliefs about power. Assuming that whatever an actor's desires were they would need power to achieve them, Morgenthau defined interests in terms of power.

The central realist simplification, treating means as a common aim, led to a focus upon beliefs about

what was possible. Of course, determining an actor's beliefs is also difficult. This information is central to strategic bargaining and actors have many incentives to disguise their real beliefs and to manipulate what other actors think their beliefs are (Jervis, 1972). Two approaches to the problem developed: I will label them objectivist and phenomenological.

The objectivist strategy assumes the external environment can be described by the scholar in terms that are objectively accurate. It then assumes that actors correctly see objective power distributions and incentives in the environment. This strategy leads to the study of the environment, especially the distribution of power. It also leads to the prediction of outcomes more than actions. Realists accept that states may misread the situation and make mistakes. The objective distribution of power, however, is assumed to determine the outcome of these actions. In addition, some realists add a social Darwinian notion, suggesting that actors that misread the situation are over time eliminated from the system, leaving actors that can be assumed mostly to understand objective reality.

The phenomenological strategy doubts that the scholar's view of the situation and the actor's view of the situation are likely to be the same. It also assumes that an actor's action will follow from the actor's perceptions not the scholar's perception, no matter how objective scholars claim their view to be. The phenomenological strategy, therefore, puts primary emphasis upon the empirical identification of the perceptions and world-views held by actors. It seeks to explain action by referring to the cognitive understandings and ideas actors have, rather than searching for primary explanatory leverage in the objective structure of the environment. The phenomenological strategy focuses on action but also doubts the objectivist claim that environment determines outcomes. The main constraints in the system are typically seen to be the actions of the great powers. If these actions are determined by the perceptions held by the great powers, then predicting outcomes of interaction also requires knowing the perceptions of the key actors.

In both phenomenological and objectivist strategies, it is necessary to introduce auxiliary assumptions about what percentage of the opportunity (or perceived opportunity) that is available actors will seize. Often a maximizing assumption serves this purpose.

Although objectivist and phenomenological strategies are ideal-types and practical research often combines elements of both strategies, the differentiation captures an important distinction in efforts to link theory and evidence. I will look first at research in the more objectivist tradition and then turn to the phenomenological efforts. This sequencing should not be interpreted as suggesting one perspective supersedes another. Contemporary empirical research in both veins has proceeded simultaneously for many years.

Objectivist Strategies

Hans Morgenthau doubted that international relations could be dealt with appropriately by adopting the logic of science employed in the physical sciences. Despite the insight in his work, his theoretical formulations were inconsistent with positivist methods. Concepts were defined loosely, often without empirical referents, and causal claims were sometimes contradictory. For instance, power was defined in multiple dimensions with no strategy for aggregating a net power score, and while Morgenthau (1973: 4–16) argued that states defined their interests in terms of power and behaved accordingly, he also argued that balance of power systems were impossible in an era of mass politics (1973: 241–56, 327–37). Mass politics, Morgenthau argued, led states not to pursue their power interests but instead to pursue normative crusades, what he called nationalistic universalism.

Power determinism Scholars like William Riker (1962) recognized scientific shortcomings in traditional realist formulations and proposed more precise renditions that clarified the concepts and teased out individual causal claims. This led, at first, to stark power determinist models with explicit maximizing assumptions. The ideal-typical formulation paralleled B.F. Skinner's (1960) model of personal behavior. That is, it assumed that actors had similar motives, mostly to survive and satisfy material needs, and that actions responded to objective incentives in the environment. The environment was characterized as anarchic, leading to a concentration on the distribution of power among actors assumed to follow self-help strategies. The empirical task then was to operationally define the variation in power and see if this corresponded to predicted variation in behavior.

Measuring power was not easy but indicators were devised (Cline, 1975, 1994; Knorr, 1975). The best known of these are associated with the Correlates of War (COW) project headed by J. David Singer. COW identified a set of indicators and treated them as objective measures of power (Singer and Diehl, 1991). Data sets were also created that measured the conflict and cooperation between states, which was taken to be the dependent variable in these models. The Correlates of War project focused on states involved in war. Subsequently, in the 1980s, this data was expanded to include states involved in militarized disputes (Gochman and Maoz, 1984). A number of events data projects sought to study a wider set of countries and a wider range of behaviors. They typically arrayed behaviors on a scale ranging from very cooperative behaviors (like unifying two states into a single state) to very conflictual behavior (like military attack). Events data sets like COPDAB (Azar, 1980), WEIS (McClelland, 1976, 1983) and KEDs (Gerner et al., 1994) drew information from news reporting services, papers and the wire, and expanded their coverage of sources as funds and technology permitted.

The expansion of sources reduced concerns that the editorial selection of news biased badly the events and behaviors reported. It did not, however, solve the problem of translating categories of behaviors into a scale that associated numbers with each category. To translate this categorical information into a scale across which interval distances would be substantively meaningful (that is a conflictual behavior coded as 4 points from the neutral point would be substantively twice as conflictual as a conflictual behavior coded as 2 points from the neutral point), scholars endeavored to create a weighted conflict-to-cooperation scale reflecting their agreed upon judgments about the relative cooperativeness and conflictualness of behaviors (Azar, 1980).

The COW power measure and the events data sets refined increasingly reliable methods so that measures were reproducible and consistent across cases. This did not, however, eliminate concerns about the validity of the measures. In terms of power, the indicators originally employed by COW emphasized material resources and industrial capacity, leaving aside aspects of power associated with the government's ability to mobilize people, lead wisely and take advantage of geo-strategic bargaining leverage (Baldwin, 1979). The weighted COPDAB scores also raised concerns about validity. Moreover, events data sets concentrated only on bilateral directed behaviors and resisted reading three-way significance into behavioral moves. Consequently, positive moves toward one country would not be coded as negative moves toward a third country, making it difficult to capture political moves like Washington's playing of the China Card against the Soviet Union (Goldstein and Freeman, 1990). Reading in meaning of this sort required substantial area expertise coders may not have had, and more importantly, it injected still more subjective interpretation into the collection of what was seen as objective data.

Empirical tests of power determinist models did not affirm the accuracy of these models (Ferris, 1973; James, 1995; Sullivan, 1990). Behavior was not predictable from power distributions alone. To refine the basic theory, attention turned to the concentration of power in the system (Mansfield, 1994: 71–116) and to the changing distribution of power. Theoretically, the basic model was adjusted to expect conflict as more likely when relative power between states was in transition and uncertainty about the likely outcome of conflict was high

(Gilpin, 1981; Organski, 1968). These theoretical modifications were also coupled with attempts to improve the measure of power, for instance by including indicators of the government's ability to tax and mobilize the polity (Kugler, 1996; Organski and Kugler, 1980). These models did better empirically but still fell short of aspirations.

Power activation   Power was found to limit a state's options but typically not determine its behavior. Within the parameters of the options available, there evidently was still substantial choice. Also, leaders of states may have understood the power circumstances differently than the objective measures indicated. Theoretically, power theory could take this into account by concentrating on perceived power, that is the power situation as understood by the actor (Christensen, 1997; Wolhforth, 1993). When models highlighted perceptions of shifting relative power, they seemed to produce more empirically accurate predictions about behavior (Ferris, 1973). Although some realists made this adjustment as if it were consistent with the basic objectivist paradigm, others saw the contradiction and resisted the reformulation on essentially phenomenological terms (Powell, 1991). Of course, shifting from a conception of objective power to a conception of perceived power raises difficult empirical problems. The perception of power must be determined in operational terms independent of the observed behavior, otherwise the explanation is tautological. It is not clear how to establish these perceptions for many states across the last two centuries and produce a measure commensurate with the scope of the existing COW data.

Rather than shift to perceived power and phenomenological premises, some power-based theories revised basic assumptions about the motivation of actors. In ideal-typical power determinism, the motives of actors are held constant as power maximization. This allows the model to make a prediction about behavior from the empirical analysis of relative power and objective opportunities in the environment. If the state does not behave as expected, or the expected outcome does not occur, for instance the much more powerful state concedes to the much weaker state, this can be attributed in a post-hoc way to a lack of desire, will or insufficient motivation stemming from a substantive understanding of interests. States, after all, may not exert 100 per cent of their capability in all situations and instead activate different amounts of their power depending on the interests at stake.

By moving toward power activation theories, as James March (1966) called them, we can capture this possibility in our models, but as Robert Keohane (1984: 35) points out, only at a substantial cost. When motivation level varies, as well as beliefs about power, we cannot solve the equation, that is predict action from the empirical estimate of relative power. Instead, we can explain any action

post hoc by referring to various degrees of power activation. To avoid this problem an actor's motivation needs to be set by assumption or identified empirically. Neorealist theorizing has pursued both avenues, devoting most attention to the former.

Kenneth Waltz (1979) revised power theory by substituting the power maximizing motivational assumption with a security maximizing assumption. Determining the objectively best way to maximize security is, of course, no easier than establishing objectively the best way to maximize power, but as long as the maximizing assumption is in place empirical attention is focused on relative power. Waltz's formulation, however, also acknowledged the power activation issue and argued that states did not always seek maximum security. For instance, states did not always pursue relative gains when this meant forgoing absolute gains. Waltz (1979: 102–28) spelled out some of the conditions that lead states to pursue relative gains. Joseph Grieco (1990) and Ducan Snidal (1991) have refined the theory further, paying special attention to the delineation of these conditions. If these conditions were defined primarily in objective terms, then the basic scientific perspective could be sustained. Powell (1991) has tried to remain within these parameters, associating the activation of relative gains behavior with situations in which the use of force is involved. Whether these situations, especially in a nuclear age when force is often symbolically engaged, can be determined in any agreed upon way remains to be seen.

Joseph Grieco (1990: 40–50) associated the activation of relative gains behavior to perceptions of future power, common enemies and past relationships. In this regard, his reformulation of neorealist theory is similar to Stephen Walt's. Walt (1987: 22–6, 263–6) built a model of alliance formation that attributed behavior to aggregate power, proximity of actors, offensive capability and the perceived intentions of other actors. This balance of threat theory allowed the activation of power to vary, but like Grieco's formulation rested the operational identification of the factors predicting this variation on phenomenological factors. There is nothing wrong with this theoretically, but it has serious implications for empirical testing. To make the model produce predictions, we must operationally and empirically identify these actor perceptions. On this front, neorealists offered little instruction. Rather, they frequently illustrated the basic function of their theory, treating phenomenological variables as mostly non-controversial facts. In other words, rather than inventing a method for determining what an actor's perceptions of threat might be, they assumed these perceptions were known to area experts and/or historians.

Another way to introduce variation in power activation is to assume states are of different types. Some are offensively motivated and others are defensively motivated. Morgenthau made this distinction, although he quickly pointed out that differentiating one from the other in practice is nearly impossible. Subsequently, neorealists have returned to differentiating between offensive and defensive states but have not addressed the central empirical dilemma of how to tell one from the other (Glaser 1997; Rose, 1998; Schweller, 1996; Snyder, 1992: 11–12).

If offensive and defensive distinctions are to be central parts of international relations models, then we need to have methods for empirically distinguishing one type from the other. James Fearon (1995) has shown in formal terms why this endeavor will not be a simple one. Although propagandists may assert with great confidence what the motives of other states are, Fearon shows that careful observers will always entertain doubts. This is because actors have incentives to mislead other actors with regard to what motivational type they are and because actors face serious limits in the credible commitments they can make and thus face inherent limits in their ability to signal what type they are.

The most successful effort to explain variation in conflict and cooperative behavior that abides by the core premises of the scientific paradigm is democratic peace theory. In this paradigm, relative power is controlled for statistically and the conflict and cooperation among a pair of states is attributed theoretically to the types of governments in the interacting states. The distinction is between democratic and non-democratic governments. The indicators of each are specified and fairly large data sets have been collected, categorizing states accordingly. The Polity data is best known in this regard (Jaggers and Gurr, 1995).

Democratic peace theory predicts war will not occur between two democracies or at minimum will not occur as often, and if it does occur will remain at a lower level of violence, than between other pairs of states (Russett, 1993). The empirical test of the theory involves associating the type of government in states and the wars between states. Questions have been raised about the validity and reliability of measures of democracy (Gleditsch and Ward, 1997) and scholars have debated whether democracy should be measured in terms of elections or civil liberties (Owen, 1997), and scholars have discussed whether differentiations should be made between consolidated democracies and democratizing states (Mansfield and Snyder, 1995). Questions have also been raised about the association between regime type and war, focusing attention on the sample of pairs of states that have been studied and the statistical implications of different sampling choices in this regard (Russett, 1995; Spiro, 1994). Although these debates have been important, they have taken place within the basic parameters of the normal positivist paradigm. If we agree for sake of argument that the statistical

relationship exists, we are still left with substantial uncertainty about how the mechanisms inside this relationship operate.

The most common form of the democratic peace theory argues that it is as if democratic states share norms of compromise and expect peaceful and fair outcomes when dealing with other democracies (Russett, 1993). It could also be that trust develops because of strategic associations that vary with regime type in the period after the Second World War (Gowa, 1999). Moreover, it could be that leaders of certain personality types prevail more often in democracies (Hermann and Kegley, 1995). As might be expected in positivist science, models of sub-mechanisms consistent with the overall theory have led to additional empirical investigation. They have also, however, evoked concepts like trust, shared norms and expectations, which to verify at the micro-level require investigation into the black box of actor decision-making. Unlike neorealists, the democratic peace theorists have not imported into their objectivist theory phenomenological concepts or concepts that are not operationally defined, but their research agenda has demonstrated the need for a bridge between objectivist and phenomenological perspectives.

Phenomenological Strategies

In the 1950s and early 1960s, while scientific realists operating in the objectivist perspective sought to refine power theory other scholars developed an essentially phenomenological perspective. These phenomenological scholars conceived of the relations between states as the product of the actions of individual states and they believed the values, mindsets and beliefs of actors guided these actions (Kelman, 1965; Sprout and Sprout, 1965). Scholars therefore turned to the study of foreign policy decision-making (Hudson, 1995) and in particular to the identification of the cognitive lenses through which actors understood the world. Richard Snyder, H.W. Bruck and Burton Sapin (1962) offered a framework identifying key concepts that could be used to describe such a mediated decision-making process, including the values, mindsets and domestic players that comprise them. Kenneth Boulding (1956, 1959), meantime, argued that the cognitive images leaders have of other countries guide choices about action and that the two most important components of this image are perceptions of the threat or opportunity the other country poses and the perception of the other country's capability. He argued that by identifying the factors empirically, foreign policy action could be explained.

In the 1970s, Michael Brecher (1972) offered an elaborate conceptual framework with which to study Israeli decision-making, illustrating how the basic phenomenological argument could be connected to empirical evidence in a specific case. Robert Jervis (1976) illustrated how a phenomenological perspective modified international relations theory and drew attention to the advances made in social psychology. He identified substantive common misperceptions and a host of common perceptual tendencies that could guide the empirical study of world-views and beliefs. Robert Axelrod (1976) proposed a strategy for mapping an actor's cognition, including the actor's central concepts, objectives and causal beliefs.

The focus on cognitive and decision-making variables in international relations ran parallel to the cognitive revolution in social psychology and the social sciences more generally (Gardner, 1985). This revolution advanced the proposition that human cognition was not predictable from environmental factors alone. It did not contend that actor cognition is unaffected by environmental forces, personality characteristics and personal experience. What it argued was that the processes and factors affecting the formation of an actor's images and understandings of the world are so complicated, with so many possible causes, that it is not adequate in scientific terms to assume the scholar can know what the actor thinks without direct empirical investigation of this matter. In psychology, this meant including manipulation checks in experiments to tap directly what participants were thinking rather than just assuming they were apprehending the experimenter's manipulation as planned. In international relations and other natural settings, it meant devising strategies for identifying the mindset of leaders and other actors rather than assuming scholars could predict what these must be from the scholar's construction of the environmental situation.

Phenomenological models connect cognitive and decisional concepts to predicted international actions. Alexander George made an initial effort to spell out the causal nexus between operational codes and action (George, 1979). Stephen Walker (1977) and Harvey Starr (1984) went further in this vein. A cognitive model that has been developed extensively is the inherent bad faith model (Holsti, 1967; Stuart and Starr, 1982). In this model, an enemy image with relatively few sub-concepts is predicted to produce aggressive action toward the country seen in enemy terms. The enemy image is also predicted to be invulnerable, or at least highly resistant, to disconfirming information. The internal validity of the model has been shown to be quite strong empirically and it has been applied in a number of concrete analytic settings (Herrmann et al., 1997; Silverstein, 1989).

The most influential framework in a basically phenomenological perspective is the subjective expected utility (SEU) paradigm. In this framework, the most important concepts are the actor's values and the actor's perceptions of the situation which give rise to the actor's expectations about the utility of action. As Herbert Simon (1985, 1995) has argued, if this framework is to say more than that people have reasons for what they do, then it is necessary to identify empirically both an actor's values (motives from which utility is established) and an actor's perceptions (subjective constructions of situations and beliefs about causes). It is also necessary to introduce a subsidiary theory specifying how calculations are made, such as (1) a statistically rational maximizing theory, (2) a satisficing theory that assumes actors will not search indefinitely for the optimal choice but take the first one that is satisfactory (Simon, 1979, 1982), and (3) a prospect theory that argues that the framing of probabilities in terms of gains and losses affects choice (Kahneman et al., 1982; Levy, 1992a, 1992b, 1997).

It is important not to confuse subjective expected utility theory with an objectivist version of scientific realist theory. In the latter, objective incentive structures are presumed to exist in the environment and the behavior of actors is predicted from a theory that says they will behave 'as if' they understood these incentive structures and calculated in a statistically rational power maximizing fashion (Lake and Powell, 1999). SEU theory emphasizes the subjective character of utility calculations, allowing actors to define different utility hierarchies and to operate with different cognitive constructions of the environment. This distinction in international relations research has been blurred.

The language of a phenomenological subjective expected utility framework has been adopted but often coupled with an empirical strategy that remains essentially objectivist and non-phenomenological. For instance, in Bruce Bueno de Mesquita's (1981) influential book *The War Trap*, and later in his book with David Lalman (1986), *War and Reason: Domestic and International Imperatives*, the central variables of the expected utility model, that is utilities and expectations, are measured with objectivist indicators. Utilities are estimated by comparing the objective configuration of alliance portfolios and expectations are measured by assuming they equal the objective measure of power as indicated in the COW data with an objective discount factor built in to account for logistic complications that increase as the proximity of the combatants decreases. The conceptual discussion organizes the traditional power determinist data into a decision-making language, but the empirical test still relies on associations of COW measures of power complemented by the contribution made by an ally which is now treated as utility rather than as a modifier of power (for treatment of alliances in COW, see Singer, 1990).

Other studies, like Dan Reiter's *Crucible of Beliefs: Learning, Alliances, and World Wars*, have also clearly adopted the language and labels of phenomenological perspectives but in operational terms treat these concepts as if they were determined objectively by the environment as the scholar understands it. Reiter (1996: 85), for instance, assumes an actor's perception of a great power's intentions, that is revisionist or status quo, are equal to whether the great power initiated a militarized crisis with another great power or regional ally of the great power in the previous year, with this objective picture of the previous period constructed by the scholar. Similarly, Reiter (1996: 86) determines an actor's perception of the probability that war will break out by examining the relative share of great power capabilities held by the potential revisionist, using COW data to determine capabilities.

Another method for linking cognitive concepts to empirical evidence is to study an actor's statements and choices. The study of statements has been done with systematic content analysis, linguistic discourse analysis, closed-ended survey instruments, structured interviews, free-wheeling interviews, as well as through focus groups and interactive dialogues. Although some of these methods have produced reliable measures for an actor's values and perceptions, they have not been employed to generate large cross-national data sets that are commensurate to the Correlates of War coverage of states over time. Most of these methods remain labor-intensive and often require highly skilled labor at that, meaning people who have language and area expertise sufficient to carry out the interviews and who can construct instruments embedded in the context and vernacular of the actor.

The construction of valid observable indicators, for phenomenological variables, cannot be accomplished by improving the reproducibility of measures alone. It is naive both for philosophical and political reasons to believe that a scholar can simply listen to what an actor says or watch what they do and know how to describe the actor's values and world-views. The very idea of values and world-view are concepts that belong to the scholar not the observed actor. Unless we believe in pure induction unmediated by language and concepts, it is impossible to approach this task except in a deductive manner. That is, the scholar needs to develop concepts, perhaps in an interactive fashion with the actor, and then devise propositions about what concepts might accurately describe the mindset of the actor, and finally employ questions designed to probe these possibilities or watch for choices deemed by the scholar to reveal these mental dispositions. The investigation can be carried out with different techniques as noted above but typically follows this basically positivist logic. Perhaps several illustrations will make the point more clearly.

For example, if Gorbachev is the actor under study, then competing models of his values and world-views could be constructed. In the case of each model of Gorbachev, the scholar could reason that if this model is an accurate representation, then we ought to see Gorbachev saying and doing a set of predicted things. William Riker (1995) suggested we would be wise to systematize in formal language the logic of these deductions and then examine the empirical record to see which model made the best predictions. In this way, international relations research could parallel economic research using a modified version of searching for revealed preferences. Of course, as in economics, if these preferences are then used to explain the action from which they are inferred, the enterprise becomes tautological. Consequently, the inferred values and perceptions need to be derived from statements and actions different from those they are being used to explain. This can be done by focusing on statements in a different domain than international relations, or by using the values and perceptions inferred in one time period to predict action in another time period, the way economists use revealed preferences to predict future market trends.

Another approach to the Gorbachev task would be to conduct in-depth interviews and analyze text. Rather than spelling out models, scholars might prefer to reproduce the narrative Gorbachev offers. There will be by necessity selection of text in this process. Only part of the narrative will be reproduced. Inevitably, this will include the part of the text the scholar believes is most reflective of Gorbachev's values and world-view. Typically, scholars will spell out the inferential logic they have employed, but, at times, they may simply assert expertise and their feel for the region and subject. This, of course, does not make their representation invalid, but it does make it impossible to reproduce. Because pure induction is impossible, and, unless we accept illogical reification claiming that the mental concepts used by the scholar are actually in the head of Gorbachev, there is no way to avoid the deductive leap whether it is spelled out or not.

Many phenomenological approaches rely on concepts and theories drawn from psychology, not because they believe actors are irrational as much as they believe that to understand action we need to appreciate the actor's point of view not only the scholar's. Instead of comparing the actor's construction of reality to the scholar's and declaring deviations irrational, scholars operating in a phenomenological perspective forgo this comparison and use psychology and the cognitive sciences to refine the conceptual apparatus they use to represent actor values and world-views (Cottam, 1977; Herrmann, 1985). By anticipating that actors will organize their thinking in schematic and script-like fashion, use existing information to bias incoming information, allow emotion to affect memory and cognitive processing, and combine information in ways that do not follow statistical rules, scholars in this tradition hope to devise conceptual models that are more accurate and useful representations of the observed world (Herrmann et al., 1997; Kahneman and Tversky, 2000; Vertzberger, 1990). The phenomenological tradition in international relations does not abandon the positivist approach to science. It applies it to identify actor values and beliefs instead of the nature of the international environment and builds a picture of the environment by combining the pictures drawn of individual actors.

Treating international actors as anthropomorphic agents with psychological properties requires a simplification that presents formidable obstacles in the path of empirical research. First, these approaches need to define operationally whose values and mindsets matter, equally whose voice and choices should be studied. Does the top leader matter or are the beliefs and world-views of other people in the polity relevant? Second, if multiple people matter, then how should we aggregate and construct a picture of them as a collective actor? How can we decide what portion of whose point of view to include in the overall representation? Likewise, how can we guard against picking and choosing from among many different people's statements and choices and constructing a representation of the group that is driven by our pre-existing biases and impressions? Moreover, how should we generalize to the group from the individual data we have? The problems with the stereotyping of out-groups, attributing to them essential and immutable features, are well-known.

Although rationalist perspectives conceive of agents taking purposeful action, they recognize that any single actor is part of a social system which entails multiple actors interacting. There are several ways that rationalist theories have studied the properties of systems and interaction.

Rationalist Theories and Interaction

Both objectivist and phenomenological perspectives have developed theories that explain the interaction between multiple actors and, at the same time, describe the system as a whole. Modeling behavior such as arms races provided an early application of game theory to international relations (Richardson, 1960). These models posited decision rules for two actors and then predicted the pattern of interaction in the system. By constructing multiple models that made distinct predictions about the pattern in the interactive acquisition of weapons, these models could then be compared to the historical record to see which models were most accurate.

For example, the interactive process could be modeled as one of reciprocity in which one actor's acquisition of weapons was met by an equivalent counter-move by the other actor. Alternatively, a model of inverse reciprocity would predict that one actor's acquisition or demonstration of strength would lead to appeasement and compromise on the part of the other actor. Russell Leng (1984, 1993) used such models to study the Soviet–American Cold War and other bilateral crises. He concluded that the Cold War evidenced more tit-for-tat spiral escalation than peace-through-strength inverse reciprocity. William Gamson and Andre Modigliani (1971) employed a similar strategy to test alternative theories of the Cold War that were explicitly phenomenological in form.

Game theorists have explored the logical dynamics of various bargaining relationships. The identification in formal mathematical terms of how different relationships work, for example, how a prisoners' dilemma game differs from a chicken or stag hunt game. A number of game theorists have tried to gauge the resemblance between the observed world and their formal models of various systems of interaction (for example, Bueno de Mesquita and Lalman, 1986; Mansfield et al., 2000; Niou, et al., 1989). Of course, judgments about this empirical resemblance can produce as much controversy as the explication of the logic of the model (Walt, 1999).

Employing simulations is another strategy for studying whole systems as patterns of interaction. Simulations allow scholars to re-run their experiments many times to see if their models consistently produce similar outcomes and to identify the consequences of manipulating different possible causal factors. This experimental strategy is not available to history-based research in any fashion other than counterfactual arguments. Simulations provide a systematic method for running such counterfactual thought experiments. For example, Robert Axelrod (1984) used simulations to explore the logical outcomes expected of tit-for-tat strategies given different types of actors. Lars Eric Cederman (1997) built a computer model to represent the formation and interaction of nations. In Cederman's simulations, distributions of national strength emerge over time as the actors interact. These emergent structures describe the history of the particular simulation. Cederman uses this method to test whether structural distributions occur and associate with war in the fashion realists expect. Just as with game-theoretic models, scholars could compare the predicted patterns Cederman's models produce to a historical record of the observed world, and, in this fashion, judge the accuracy of competing models.

Game theory and simulations include sub-models of actors, but they typically focus on evidence related to interaction. In other words, they do not establish operational indicators for each actor's motives and perceptions, but instead posit these in a model and deduce from the model what the interaction would look like if these assumptions about motives and perceptions were accurate. Scholars proceeding this way, then compare the type and amount of conflict and cooperation expected in the model of the systemic relationship to empirical evidence regarding these matters. It is also possible to identify empirically the values and world-views of two or more actors and then predict interaction from these estimates. Herrmann and Fischerkeller (1995), for instance, have argued for a cognitive approach of this type. They identify empirically the world-views in Iran, Iraq, the United States and the Soviet Union, use these to predict action and use the simultaneous and lagged prediction of strategic action to predict the pattern of interaction. To avoid some of the problems of trying to associate a motive and world-view with a single act, they employ a concept of a strategic script grouping events into sets that have strategic meaning.

Although interaction and the whole system of relations can be built by aggregating up from models that start with agents, it is also possible to concentrate on the character of the whole and consider the effect of the system on individual units. Given how complex the system of interaction can be in international relations, just describing the constitutive parts of the system can be a demanding theoretical task. Constructivists have emphasized at least two tasks that are part of examining the whole: (1) identifying the most important ideas that actors share and which thus define relationships, and (2) critically examining the power relationships that are embedded in the language scholars use to describe the whole and the political stage the scholar is acting upon.

Constructivist Theories

Critical Theory

Both objectivist and phenomenological theories of purposeful choice operate as if the scholar is not part of the political process being examined. Phenomenological approaches, for example, although not assuming that an objective reality leads to common perceptions among actors, treat the description of actors with distinct world-views interacting with one another as an objective description of the relationship. Conceiving of the scientific enterprise as comprising two distinct worlds, one that is conceptual and theoretical and the other which is empirical and observed, is at the core of positivist perspectives but it is not immune from criticism. A very common criticism is that the pictures scholars draw become part of the political process they are describing and thus affect the process being explained, either reinforcing it or changing it.

Phenomenologists argue that the social sciences are not similar to the physical sciences because subjects can be creative and proactive in ways objects cannot be. Critical theorists go further and suggest that the social sciences are also different than the

physical sciences because the subjects of study are affected by the knowledge about them that is created by the scholars. Typically, patterns found in the physical movement of objects are not changed by the scholarly theories that explain these patterns. Human subjects, on the other hand, can learn from social science and this learning can produce change in subsequent behavior.

Because the production and dissemination of social science theory can affect the future behavior of those who come to believe it is true, the scholarly enterprise becomes part of the political interaction between actors. This leads to a concern that the construction of concepts, models and empirical testing is part of a strategic agenda serving material self-interests not simply academic ends. For instance, the conceptualization of the environment as anarchic, governed only by rules of self-help, may appeal more to powerful states than to weaker ones and make realist conceptions more popular in superpowers like the United States. Conceptions that argue that societal bonds and norms govern behavior in the environment, on the other hand, may be more popular in less powerful states, for instance, the contemporary United Kingdom (Bull, 1977; Buzan, 1993).

The effects of theory as it becomes part of the mental world of contemporary actors can be diverse. When leaders reify models, they turn them into self-fulfilling prophecies. When they decide to undo the previously observed pattern, now that they understand what it is, they create a new reality. For example, if the Cold War was a spiral model of mutual suspicion, then once this neorealist insight became part of the mindset of leaders they could see the dynamic of the security dilemma and act to change it (Osgood, 1962; Wendt, 1992). This philosophical point, perhaps most associated with Hegel (1952) and the early work of Marx (Marx, 1975: 57–198) has concrete implications for international relations theories. For instance, it leads to the expectation that ideas that become institutionalized change actors. They can, therefore, persist beyond the confines of the original agent-based calculations that led to their initial creation.

Institutions and Ideas

Ernst Haas (1990) has shown how this process can work. He argues that international organizations can promote certain ideas and establish a way of thinking about issues that then affects the way states come to understand the issues and identify their own interests. Haas begins with organizations coordinating affairs in technical domains where scientific expertise is often respected and shows how the adoption of the technical language and mindset common in the international organization can affect processes in the state. The evidence used to support this theoretical claim often includes a set of case studies of international organizations and states.

The empirical strategy typically involves showing that ideas popular in the organization come to be accepted in later periods by key leaders in the participating states. Often the causal claim rests primarily on the presentation of a sequential time-line emphasizing that the idea was evident in the international organization before it was evident in the top leadership circles of the state (Finnemore, 1996). This method can include an effort to trace the process by which the idea moved from the international organization to state-level discussions about interests. One way to strengthen the causal logic that is not always a part of these efforts would be to include a correlational logic. This would explore whether states that belong to an organization adopt different ideas than states that do not belong to the organization.

A somewhat different neoliberal theory of institutional effects has been developed by Robert Keohane (1989, 1993). In this theory, institutions promote cooperation by managing both communication inefficiencies and risks that are inherent in international relationships. By providing verification of compliance with agreements, early-warning of defections and sanctions of some sort for violation as well as mechanisms for adjudication, some institutions help actors overcome security dilemmas (Keohane and Martin, 1995). Neoliberal institutional theories have been tested empirically quite often in the economic realm. Some efforts have also been undertaken in the security realm (Wallander, 2000). The evidence in these studies typically involves a measure of institutionalization and a measure of cooperation. Both are typically treated in objectivist terms and a correlation is sought between higher and deeper levels of institutionalization and higher levels of cooperation.

Of course, a relationship between institutionalization and cooperation does not necessarily sustain the causal claim that institutions cause cooperation. The causal arrow could point in the opposite direction. The argument stressing the causal significance of institutionalization and membership in shared ideational communities often rests on a claim regarding the effect institutions have on agents, particularly on the ideas, identity and understanding of self-interest that drives agent behavior. How much institutions can change agents is a question that sits at the crux of contemporary debates between realists and neoliberal institutionalists (Jervis, 1999).

Norms

Theoretical development The broad constructivist argument that the ideas instantiated in institutions affect the identity of members has been investigated empirically in the domain of norms.

The theoretical argument is that, unlike coercive material power that can change behavior by compulsion, norms affect behavior by changing an actor's motives and beliefs, that is their understanding of their interests. Norms produce, therefore, not only a logic that spells out the consequences of what will happen if they are violated but also a logic of what behavior is appropriate. That is, what someone ought to do. The instantiation of norms in institutions is expected to socialize actors, both those in the institution and those who want to join, and produce in these actors a sense of what they ought to do, and, in turn, affect how they behave. The strongest test for this constructivist theory is to show that in the consciousness of actors the logic of appropriateness is operative more than a utilitarian logic calculating material consequences.

Martha Finnemore (1996) examines UNESCO and the creation of state science bureaucracies, the Red Cross and the operation of the Geneva Conventions, and the norms established in the World Bank and strategies for dealing with poverty. She argues across these cases that the norms instantiated in the international institution led states to re-evaluate what their national interests were and to adopt the behavior identified by the institution as appropriate even when there was no compelling material reason for this choice. Finnemore's empirical strategy is to trace the evolution in thinking about these matters inside the states and to demonstrate both that the ideas for change came from the international institutions and that the sort of reasoning they led to was not simply utilitarian but deontic, meaning states came to believe that certain behaviors were appropriate. The evidential base includes statements made by officials taken to represent the state, funding decisions taken by the state, and changes in state-level bureaucratic organization and rules taken as instantiated norms.

Richard Price (1997) with regard to chemical weapons and Nina Tannenwald (1999) with regard to nuclear weapons investigate the effect of the norms that proscribe the use of weapons of mass destruction. In these cases, theory is connected to evidence by demonstrating that states do not even consider using weapons of mass destruction. The case is strongest when there is a practical battlefield value that could be achieved by the employment of such weapons and states still do not even consider their use. In these case studies of decision-making, Price and Tannenwald trace the process by which war-fighting decisions were taken and try to demonstrate taboo weapons were not used because they were seen as inappropriate on normative grounds. The evidence includes interviews with policy-makers asked to provide retrospective pictures of the decision process, archival documents when available, and memoir literature. Of course, the non-use of these weapons is behavioral evidence consistent with the argument but indeterminate with regard to why these choices were eschewed. The central interpretative claim that system-wide normative ideas coupled with conceptions of state identity led to this behavioral outcome raises methodological problems not unique to constructivists endeavors. It is quite parallel to the motivational attribution problem that has been prominent in rationalist theories as discussed above.

Empirical obstacles   Efforts to link constructivist theories regarding the role of norms and empirical evidence face a number of obstacles just as rationalist efforts to link theory and evidence do. One obstacle relates to the definition of a norm and the relationship between norms and interests. On one hand, the resurgence of research on norms has been fueled by arguments about how much norms matter compared to other motives. Martha Finnemore and Stephen Krasner, for example, have argued at length about the relative importance of logics of appropriateness and logics of consequences, with Finnemore (1996: 31, 87–9) contending norms are a potent motive and Krasner (1999: 6, 40–2, 66, 72, 238) arguing interests are trump. On the other hand, constructivists deny that norms and interests should be opposed to each other as distinct motives, arguing that norms shape interests.

The argument that norms shape interests, of course, can be taken as either a truism that refers to the definition of these concepts or as an empirical claim. If a scholar defines interests and norms as indistinguishable, for example, by defining normative desires as interests, then the two cannot be opposed as alternatives. This need not be the case, however. It is possible, to define norms and interests as distinct notions at the level of foreign policy motivation and then to recognize that interests are based on different norms. If the norms underpinning interests (for example, a norm that wealth is good) are different norms from those directly relevant to foreign policy (for example, a norm that sovereignty should be respected), then the norms and interests at the foreign policy level could be treated as independent factors. Assuming we are dealing with distinct concepts that have operational meaning at the same level of analysis, the relationship between norms and interests becomes an empirical question. Do norms shape interests? If so, how much and when? And do they also affect behavior?

There is not much controversy that norms affect verbal and rhetorical behavior. For realists, like Hans Morgenthau, however, the effect of norms was to generate the need for ideological disguises. Norms established desired practices, not the practices that actually prevailed. They give rise to justification, excuses and denials; 'organized hypocrisy', to use Krasner's label. Constructivists do not disagree that norms have discursive importance, but they go farther. They argue that the study of discourse provides insight into the meaning of norms and action. Moreover, they argue that norms constrain states from doing what otherwise would make utilitarian sense. To link this theoretical debate to evidence is complicated. It requires identifying what a state would do if it were motivated by material concerns that is different from what it would do if it were motivated by normative ideas.

Although it is possible to identify violations of normative principles, it is more difficult to demonstrate compliance. The empirical problem is quite similar in this domain to the problem plaguing the identification of successful deterrence. When a state complies with the normative principle, it might be doing this for several reasons. One of these reasons may be that they saw no material payoff for violating the norm. Politicians have many incentives to mislead observers on this score. For bargaining purposes, for example, leaders may want to claim they gave up an easy gain in the name of justice and now want reciprocation. As Morgenthau argued, leaders also have plenty of reasons to mislead themselves and to believe in normatively self-serving stories. How to establish what sort of mindset was active in decision-making and which beliefs were decisive is an empirical challenge quite similar to that faced by rationalists when attempting to determine motives and beliefs.

Empirical strategies and evidence   There are several methods for determining what norms are shared in a community. One way is to look for evidence of the norm in codified laws. Another strategy is to examine patterns in behavior and to argue these patterns reveal certain norms. This process of attaching meaning to observed behavior, of course, can be controversial, as is evident in efforts to determine proclivities to racism. A third strategy is to examine the discourse in a community by some form of content analysis, discourse analysis, survey, or in-depth interviews.

Regardless of which method constructivists employ to identify empirically the norms that are shared in a community, they need to guard against over-generalizing and evoking essentialist stereotypes. Because they often aim to describe the ideas that are common in a community, the task of generalization is central to the constructivist enterprise. Of course, sub-communities can be identified, but the problem still remains. When constructivists draw a picture of shared norms and beliefs at the national and even world-wide level the magnitude of this empirical challenge is clearly large. For instance, Alastair Iain Johnston (1995), in his study of Chinese culture and its affect on Chinese strategic ideas, uses texts that are many centuries old to draw a picture of an essential Chinese culture. Price (1997) draws on legal texts, the discourse of leaders and state behavior to draw inferences about the norm *vis-à-vis* chemical weapons that is shared world-wide. It is possible to identify different zones of the world in which certain norms are shared, but this distinction drawn from limited evidence in each zone has political implications. This is especially true when zones of war and zones of peace are identified, or more pointedly when this identification of zones really means the identification of those people who share peaceful and good norms like us and those who do not.

The risks of essentialist and self-serving biases are certainly not unique to constructivist research. However, given this tradition's emphasis on generalization to the level of shared ideas and many of its practitioners' preference for ethnographic in-depth interviews and broad-ranging discourse analysis, the risks are worth considering in some depth. They are also raised by the constructivist interest in constitutive theory (Wendt, 1999). That is, theory that describes the component parts of a system and the essential elements that make up the political phenomenon and entities under investigation. The empirical challenge inherent in trying to describe the elemental ideational parts of a social system may be illustrated by considering the case of US hegemony. Because prominent constructivists operate from an objectivist perspective *vis-à-vis* the ideas that define the ideational structure of an international system (Jepperson et al., 1996), they examine the nature of US hegemony and the shared norms and ideas that it represents (Cronin, 2001; Ruggie, 1996, 1997). The shared ideas in this system might be identified as norms of free trade, liberal civil rights and democratic governance.

In defining the ideational character of a system defined by US hegemony, the ideas that are shared among those who oppose US hegemony are also described. This often includes characterizing this opposition as opposed to the ideas the United States promotes, including free trade, civil rights and democracy. Islamic fundamentalists are sometimes identified as concrete examples of this ideational opposition. The problem, of course, is in defending empirically the picture drawn of the United States and the ideas it is presumed to represent. The contrast between the picture of a democratic human-rights promoting United States and the authoritarian human-rights denying other is of course very reminiscent of the imperial and colonial stereotypes examined in some detail in the debate over Orientalist essentialism (Halliday, 1995; Said, 1978). Although this picture of a benign and worthy hegemon opposed by an unreasonable and unworthy opposition may be popular in the United States, it is a description of the United States that many people in the Third World and Europe find unpersuasive. They do not believe that the United States promotes human rights, democracy, or non-proliferation for that matter. In their picture, the United States has not promoted norms of free trade, liberalism, democracy or non-proliferation, but has instead instantiated a system of norms that give priority to the pursuit of self-interest, wealth as the arbiter of truth and justice, and dictatorship where expedient.

The key point here is not to debate the substantive reality of US hegemony. Rather, it is to emphasize the challenge facing the effort to describe empirically the norms extant in a system. Whether there is US hegemony, and, if there is, what norms it empowers may be seen as especially controversial. Other claims about the ideas that prevail in a system, however, raise similar issues and the general problem cannot be avoided. For example, Jepperson, Wendt and Katzenstein (1996) point to the idea that Moscow and Washington were locked in a competitive relationship as a system-wide belief that was extant during the Cold War. This may be true, but voices in Beijing and throughout the Third World often doubted it. How to establish the prevalence of ideas or norms in a system without engaging in ethnocentric and essentialist stereotyping is a question both constructivists and rationalists need to pursue.

Norms may be conceived of as part of a 'suprapersonal objective order' (Heider, 1958: 219), but they are enacted at the level of individual agents. Constructivists explain variation in enactment mostly as a result of whether an actor shares the norm or not. This interpretation, however, may underestimate the importance of variation across situations. Most norms take the form: moral people do X, in situations A, B or C unless Q and/or R prevail. In other words, situations are part of the definition of the norm and so are the exceptional conditions that define exemptions from the moral obligation. This is obvious in the literature on just wars (Walzer, 1977). Situations, however, are not necessarily objective givens. If perceptions of situations are integral to the process of norm enactment, then so are the cognitive and political processes that affect actor-level perception. In this regard, a number of constructivists have indicated the need for a complementary theory of agency (Adler, 1991; Checkel, 1998; DiMaggio, 1997).

Identity

Constructivists, of course, have not confined their research to the system level exclusively, or at least they have not always defined the international system as the system they are investigating. A number of constructivist efforts have explored the processes of identity formation. Collective identity can be thought of in at least three different ways. First, it can refer to the boundaries of the group and explore who is considered a part of the group. Second, it can refer to the attributes of a prototypical group member or to the features and values shared by the modal member. Third, identity can refer to the relationship a collective actor assumes *vis-à-vis* other collective actors. This third usage of the word treats identity as quite analogous to role or to the combination of self-image and image of other. In this regard, it generates empirical research parallel to that done in role theory (Walker, 1987) and image theory (Herrmann and Fischerkeller, 1995). Identity has also been used to refer to both the attributes of the collectivity and its role. Robert Herman (1996) uses this method to interpret change in Soviet foreign policy.

Using identity to mean the construction of group boundaries or providing answers to the question who is us, opens the long-standing question of why collective identities form. In other words, why do people come to understand themselves as part of a nation or other political entity? And why does this become an important part of their conception of themselves? Social identity theorists (Tajfel, 1981; Tajfel and Turner, 1986) have provided psychological reasons for why people attach a part of their understanding of self to groups, but they do not explain why nations and certain other groups take on such political importance. Political scientists and historians often explain this by the rise of mass politics and the emergence of nationalism. From the French and American revolutions onwards, the idea of popular sovereignty and mass-based legitimation of political authority has played an important role in world politics. The study of why nationalism forms has produced a very large literature.

Although the literature on nationalism cannot be reviewed here, four causal factors have received a great deal of attention. They are (1) the importance of nationalism to leaders; (2) the character of the mass public, particularly its attentiveness to politics; (3) the viability and functional advantage of a nation-state, concentrating especially on the economic base, the communication base and the attitudes of neighboring states and (4) the commonality of features shared by members of the in-group and the uniqueness of these features vis-à-vis out-groups. Shared language that is unique to the in-group and common memories of group history are often pointed to in this regard.

The empirical literature investigating the relationship between these four factors and the development of nationalism is large and covers a diverse set of communities. Rupert Emerson's (1960) classic study entitled *From Empire to Nation*, outlines part of the story for each factor. Benedict Anderson (1991) and John Breuilly (1982) have developed the empirical case for the importance of leaders. Richard Cottam (1964) made a case for the importance of mass politics and attentiveness, while Karl Deutsch (1953) built a theory based on the importance of language and the viability of communication. Ernst Gellner (1983) developed an elaborate economies of scale argument and empirical test. Constructivist scholars like Geoff Eley and Ronald Suny (1996) have traced the emergence of common memory. All four factors have been found to relate

to the emergence of common identity but no overarching all inclusive integrative theory has been successfully proposed and empirically defended.

Very few scholars treat collective identity as a primordial given. Most accept the conventional wisdom that these categories are social constructions (Hall, 1999; Spruyt, 1994). There is debate, however, over how malleable and flexible these identities are (Connor, 1994). Once constructed and institutionalized, they might be very difficult to change. This is likely to be especially true when states derive their legitimacy from these mass-beliefs, and, consequently, work hard at preserving (or establishing) these socially shared beliefs. Many of the early studies of nationalism also explored internationalism. Given that nation-states were relatively recent historical constructions, these students of nationalism who investigated the combination of previous units into nations wondered if still larger units were likely to form.

This question becomes more energized when it is connected to the observation that conceptions of nationalism and in-group versus out-group discrimination play a role in war. David Mitrany (1966) and Ernst Haas (1964) argued that moving beyond the nation-state was not simply an academic question, but a vital objective in conflict resolution. By promoting identification with a superordinate collective, cross-group hostility and conflict between two nations might be reduced. This was the hope in neofunctionalist strategies. The idea was to promote functional cooperation in technical areas in the anticipation that over time this narrow common ground would spill over to involve a broader array of people and functions. By combining this functional notion with Deutsch's emphasis upon communication, it might also be possible to promote larger security communities over time.

Theories of regional integration generated empirical research, especially in the context of Western Europe. More recently, predictions of an emerging European identity have led to substantial empirical research (Inglehart and Reif, 1991; Niedermayer and Sinnott, 1995). Studying mass identities through survey instruments, scholars have found that national identities remain even if European identities increase. In fact, it appears that in many European countries the people who say Europe is an important part of their identity also say that their nation is an important part of their identity (Martinotti and Stefanizzi, 1995). The two identities do not seem to be mutually exclusive nor is it clear that a stronger identity with Europe is associated with a less negative view of other nations in Europe. Substantially more investigation is needed on these questions.

Emanuel Adler and Michael Barnett have revitalized the study of security communities from a constructivist perspective, looking at more than half-a-dozen inter-state cases. It is not possible to summarize the evidential argument they mount but it is possible to note a continuing dilemma in linking theory and evidence. Barnett and Gause (1998), for example, examine the relative lack of success in building community in part of the Arab world. They identify a number of factors that explain this lack of success, poor Arab leadership playing a significant role for instance. Ian Lustick (1997), in contrast, explains the failure of an Arab great state to emerge largely in terms of the intervention of outside powers. He contends that, unlike in Europe where nation-states were built with substantial coercion and force, in the Arab world the European powers have intervened to prevent any Bismarck-like regional hegemon from establishing the great Arab state. Obviously, we cannot settle this interpretative debate here, but it does remind us that the interpretative task is inevitably tied to contemporary politics. If we want to persuade other scholars that our picture is warranted by empirical investigation and not simply national bias, then we will need to defend quite explicitly how the key concepts are linked to indicators and how we established the relative importance of various factors.

THE ROAD AHEAD

This chapter has reviewed progress and problems faced in linking theory and evidence. Four broad lessons will serve to bring this chapter to a close.

First, the form in which theory is presented is less important than the substance of the theory. It also is important not to confuse the language in which a theory is presented with the substance of the theory. For example, formal theory is not synonymous with rational choice theory. Both the rational choice calculating engine associated with micro-economics and other calculating engines can be represented in formal terms. Computational models use formal theory and advanced computing technologies to construct formal models of rational choice and other types of choice and variations on these themes. Barry O'Neill (1999) has used formal language to present a phenomenological theory of symbols and honor in international relations that is very different from the rational choice theory associated with Bueno de Mesquita (1981), even though both use formal language to organize their theoretical ideas.

A second overarching lesson is that attention needs to be devoted to the validity of the indicators used to operationalize concepts. Although a good bit of debate has focused on the methods of data creation, this has often concentrated on techniques for improving reliability. Often this means systematizing the data generation and quantifying the evaluations. Clearly, reproducibility is a valuable feature of evidence, but it is not the most essential feature. The most essential feature is the relevance of the evidence and its appropriateness to the argument.

For example, the crux of the debate about attitudinal evidence is not whether structured survey instruments tap attitudes more reliably than do open-ended extensive dialogues, but whether either strategy of interviewing has a persuasive and valid theory for interpreting what the responses and verbal input from the participants mean. What strategy of interpretation underpins the logic of the data generation? Are verbal statements, however lengthy, taken at face value or is an inferential theory employed to translate the statements into meaningful data that is taken to be the operational measure of a concept?

Third, although rationalist theories have adopted the language of phenomenological subjective expectations and constructivist theories emphasize the importance of shared ideas and consciousness, the empirical challenge posed by this phenomenological shift has not been addressed adequately. Operational measures for these concepts still often rely on objective factors and the assumption that the subjects under study must see the world the way the scholar does. What other strategies might be used to create operational estimates for phenomenological concepts is a question that has not received the attention it deserves. Too often theorists assume that area specialists can simply provide these variables as if they were facts.

Finally, international relations scholars have made substantial strides in connecting theory to past history but have made rather little use of theory to predict the future. On the one hand, there is a widespread recognition that the future cannot be predicted from international relations theory, yet, on the other hand, there is apparent confidence that empirical patterns found statistically are sound and inform our understanding of causation. Because we cannot re-run history and create a true control condition, however, the validity of the causal claim remains suspect. Looking forward, scholars recognize the importance of contingency, path sequencing and stochastic events. When looking backward, these complications play a less prominent role in the evaluation of causal tests. Logically, they should play the same role as when thinking about the future (Dawes, 1993).

Predictive accuracy is surely not the only way to judge theory, but making future-oriented predictions and evaluating the outcome over time may be a very effective way to improve theorizing and improve the linkage of theory to evidence. The exercise will surely humble any theorists who exaggerate the success international relations theorists have had in linking theory and evidence, but this is not an altogether negative outcome. Overconfidence in what we already take to be demonstrated can be a serious impediment to improving theory and empirical knowledge (Tetlock, 1999). The predictive task has had a positive effect on other fields such as meteorology, where experts are now quite well calibrated, that is, aware of how confident they ought to be in their theory and empirical tests. A similar improvement in the calibration of international relations theorists could be a positive outcome from a broader practice of making predictions, as might the increasing sophistication of theories purporting to explain international relations and improvement in their linkage to empirical evidence.

Bibliography

Adler, Emanuel (1991) 'Cognitive Evolution: A Dynamic Approach for the Study of International Relations and their Progress', in Emanuel Adler and Beverly Crawford (eds), *Progress in Postwar International Relations*. New York: Columbia University Press. pp. 43–88.

Adler, Emanuel and Barnett, Michael (1998) *Security Communities*. Cambridge: Cambridge University Press.

Anderson, Benedict (1991) *Imagined Communities: Reflections on the Origins and Spread of Nationalism*. London: Verso.

Axelrod, Robert (ed.) (1976) *The Structure of Decision: The Cognitive Maps of Political Elites*. Princeton: Princeton University Press.

Axelrod, Robert (1984) *The Evolution of Cooperation*. New York: Basic Books.

Azar, E.E. (1980) 'The Conflict and Peace Data Bank (COPDAB) Project', *Journal of Conflict Resolution*, 24: 143–52.

Baldwin, David (1979) 'Power Analysis and World Politics: New Trends versus Old Tendencies', *World Politics*, 31 (2): 161–94.

Barnett, Michael and Gause, Gregory F. III (1998) 'Caravans in Opposite Directions: Society, State and the Development of a Community in the Gulf Cooperation Council', in Emanuel Adler and Michael Barnett (eds), *Security Communities*. Cambridge: Cambridge University Press. pp.161–97.

Boulding, Kenneth (1956) *The Image*. Ann Arbor: University of Michigan Press.

Boulding, Kenneth (1959) 'National Images and International Systems', *Journal of Conflict Resolution*, 3: 120–31.

Brecher, Michael (1972) *The Foreign Policy of Israel: Setting, Images, Process*. London: Oxford University Press.

Breuilly, John (1982) *Nationalism and the State*. Chicago: University of Chicago Press.

Bueno de Mesquita, Bruce (1981) *The War Trap*. New Haven: Yale University Press.

Bueno de Mesquita, Bruce and Lalman, D. (1986) *War and Reason: Domestic and International Imperatives*. New Haven: Yale University Press.

Bull, Hedley (1977) *The Anarchical Society*. New York: Columbia University Press.

Buzan, Barry (1993) 'From International System to International Society: Structural Realism and Regime Theory Meet the English School', *International Organization*, 47 (3): 327–52.

Cederman, Lars-Erik (1997) *Emergent Actors in World Politics: How States and Nations Develop and Dissolve*. Princeton: Princeton University Press.

Checkel, Jeffrey (1998) 'The Constructivist Turn in International Relations Theory', *World Politics*, 50 (2): 324–48.

Christensen, Thomas (1997) 'Perceptions and Alliances in Europe', *International Organization*, 51 (1): 65–97.

Cline, Ray S. (1975) *World Power Assessment: A Calculus of Strategic Drift*. Boulder: Westview.

Cline, Ray S. (1994) *The Power of Nations in the 1990s: A Strategic Assessment*. Lanham Rowman and Littlefield.

Connor, Walker (1994) *Ethnonationalism: The Quest for Understanding*. Princeton: Princeton University Press.

Cottam, Richard (1964) *Nationalism in Iran*. Pittsburgh: University of Pittsburgh Press.

Cottam, Richard (1977) *Foreign Policy Motivation: A General Theory and a Case Study*. Pittsburgh: University of Pittsburgh Press.

Cronin, Bruce (2001) *Community Under Anarchy: Transnational Identity and the Evolution of Cooperation*. New York: Columbia University Press.

Dawes, Robin (1993) 'Prediction of the Future versus an Understanding of the Past: A Basic Asymmetry', *American Journal of Psychology*, 106 (1): 1–24.

Deutsch, Karl (1953) *Nationalism and Social Communication: An Inquiry into the Foundations of Nationality*. Cambridge, MA: MIT Press.

DiMaggio, Paul (1997) 'Culture and Cognition', *Annual Review of Sociology*, 23: 263–87.

Eley, Geoff and Suny, Ronald (eds) (1996) *Becoming National: A Reader*. New York: Oxford University Press.

Emerson, Rupert (1960) *From Empire to Nation: The Rise to Self-Assertion of Asian and African Peoples*. Boston: Beacon Press.

Fearon, James (1995) 'Rationalist Explanations for War', *International Organization*, 49 (3): 379–414.

Ferris, Wayne (1973) *The Power Capabilities of Nation-States: International Conflict and War*. Lexington, MA: Lexington Books.

Finnemore, Martha (1996) *National Interests in International Society*. Ithaca: Cornell University Press.

Gamson, William and Modigliani, Andre (1971) *Untangling the Cold War: A Strategy for Testing Rival Theories*. Boston: Little, Brown.

Gardner, Howard (1985) *The Mind's New Science: A History of the Cognitive Revolution*. New York: Basic Books.

Gellner, Ernest (1983) *Nations and Nationalism*. Ithaca: Cornell University Press.

George, Alexander (1979) 'The Causal Nexus between Cognitive beliefs and Decision-Making Behavior: The "Operational Code"', in L.S. Falkowski (ed.), *Psychological Models in International Politics*. Boulder: Westview.

Gerner, Deborah, Schrodt, Philip, Francisco, Ronald and Weddle, Judith (1994) 'Machine Coding of Event Data Using Regional and International Sources', *International Studies Quarterly*, 38 (1): 91–119.

Gilpin, Robert (1981) *War and Change in World Politics.* New York: Cambridge University Press.

Glaser, Charles (1997) 'The Security Dilemma Revisited', *World Politics*, 50 (1): 171–201.

Gleditsch, Kristian and Ward, Michael (1997) 'Double Take: A Reexamination of Democracy and Autocracy in Modern Polities', *Journal of Conflict Resolution*, 41 (3): 361–83.

Gochman, Charles and Maoz, Zeev (1984) 'Militarized Interstate Disputes, 1816–1975', *Journal of Conflict Resolution*, 29 (4): 585–615.

Goldstein, Joshua and Freeman, John (1990) *Three-Way Street: Strategic Reciprocity in World Politics.* Chicago: University of Chicago Press.

Gowa, Joanne (1999) *Ballots and Bullets: The Elusive Democratic Peace.* Princeton: Princeton University Press.

Grieco, Joseph (1990) *Cooperation Among Nations.* Ithaca: Cornell University Press.

Haas, Ernst (1964) *Beyond the Nation-State: Functionalism and International Organization.* Stanford: Stanford University Press.

Haas, Ernst (1990) *When Knowledge is Power: Three Models of Change in International Organizations.* Berkeley: University of California Press.

Hall, Rodney (1999) *National Collective Identity: Social Constructs and International Systems.* New York: Columbia University Press.

Halliday, Fred (1995) *Islam and the Myth of Confrontation: Religion and Politics in the Middle East.* London: I.B. Tauris.

Hegel, Georg W.F. (1952) *Philosophy of Right* (trans. T.M. Knox). London: Oxford University Press.

Herman, Robert (1996) 'Identity, Norms, and National Security: The Soviet Foreign Policy Revolution and the End of the Cold War', in P. Katzenstein (ed.), *The Culture of National Security: Norms and Identity in World Politics.* New York: Columbia University Press. pp. 271–316.

Hermann, Margaret and Kegley, Charles, Jr (1995) 'Rethinking Democracy and International Peace: Perspectives from Political Psychology', *International Studies Quarterly*, 39 (4): 511–33.

Herrmann, Richard (1985) *Perceptions and Behavior in Soviet Foreign Policy.* Pittsburgh: University of Pittsburgh Press.

Herrmann, Richard and Fischerkeller, Michael (1995) 'Beyond the Enemy Image and Spiral Model: Cognitive-Strategic Research after the Cold War', *International Organization*, 49 (3): 415–50.

Herrmann, Richard and Voss, James, Schooler, Tonya and Ciarrochi, Joseph (1997) 'Images in International Relations: An Experimental Test of Cognitive Schemata', *International Studies Quarterly*, 41 (3): 403–33.

Holsti, Ole (1967) 'Cognitive Dynamics and Images of the Enemy', in D. Finley, O. Holsti and R. Fagen (eds), *Enemies in Politics.* Chicago: Rand McNally. pp. 25–96.

Hudson, Valerie (1995) 'Foreign Policy Analysis Yesterday, Today, and Tomorrow', *Mershon International Studies Review*, 39 (Suppl. 2): 209–38.

Inglehart, Ronald and Reif, Karlheinz (1991) *Eurobarometer: The Dynamics of European Public Opinion.* London: Macmillan.

Jaggers, Keith and Gurr, Ted Robert (1995) 'Tracking Democracy's Third Wave with the Polity III Data', *Journal of Peace Research,* 32: 469-82.

James, Patrick (1995) 'Structural Realism and the Causes of War', *Mershon International Studies Review*, 39 (Suppl. 2): 181–208.

Jepperson, Ronald, Wendt, Alexander and Katzenstein, Peter (1996) 'Norms, Identity, and Culture in National Security', in Peter Katzenstein (ed.), *The Culture of National Security: Norms and Identity in World Politics.* New York: Columbia University Press. pp. 33–75.

Jervis, Robert (1972) *The Logic of Images in International Relations.* New York: Columbia University Press.

Jervis, Robert (1976) *Perception and Misperception in International Politics.* Princeton: Princeton University Press.

Jervis, Robert (1999) 'Realism, Neoliberalism, and Cooperation: Understanding the Debate', *International Security*, 24 (1): 42–63.

Johnston, Alastair Iain (1995) *Cultural Realism: Strategic Culture and Grand Strategy in Chinese History.* Princeton: Princeton University Press.

Kahneman, Daniel and Tversky, Amos (eds) (2000) *Choices, Values, and Frames.* Cambridge: Cambridge University Press.

Kahneman, Daniel, Slovic, Paul and Tversky, Amos (1982) *Judgment under Uncertainty: Heuristics and Biases.* Cambridge: Cambridge University Press.

Kelman, Herbert (ed.) (1965) *International Behavior: A Social-Psychological Analysis.* New York: Holt, Rinehart and Winston.

Keohane, Robert (1984) *After Hegemony: Cooperation and Discord in the World Political Economy.* Princeton: Princeton University Press.

Keohane, Robert (1989) 'Neoliberal Institutionalism: A Perspective on World Politics', in Robert Keohane (ed.), *International Institutions and State Power: Essays in International Relations Theory.* Boulder: Westview.

Keohane, Robert (1993) 'Institutional Theory and the Realist Challenge After the Cold War', in David Baldwin (ed.), *Neorealism and Neoliberalism: The Contemporary Debate.* New York: Columbia University Press.

Keohane, Robert and Martin, Lisa (1995) 'The Promise of Institutionalist Theory', *International Security*, 20 (1): 39–51.

Knorr, Klaus (1975) *The Power of Nations: The Political Economy of International Relations.* New York: Basic Books.

Krasner, Stephen (1999) *Sovereignty: Organized Hypocrisy*. Princeton: Princeton University Press.

Kugler, Jacek (1996) *Parity and War: Evaluations and Extensions of the War Ledger*. Ann Arbor: University of Michigan Press.

Lake, David and Powell, Robert (1999) 'International Relations: A Strategic Choice Approach', in David Lake and Robert Powell (eds), *Strategic Choice and International Relations*. Princeton: Princeton University Press. pp. 3– 38.

Leng, Russell (1984) 'Reagan and the Russians: Crisis Bargaining Beliefs and the Historical Record', *American Political Science Review*, 78: 338–55.

Leng, Russell (1993) *Interstate Crisis Behavior, 1816–1980: Realism versus Reciprocity*. Cambridge: Cambridge University Press.

Levy, Jack (1992a) 'An Introduction to Prospect Theory', *Political Psychology*, 13: 171–86.

Levy, Jack (1992b) 'Prospect Theory and International Relations: Theoretical Applications and Analytical Problems', *Political Psychology*, 13: 283–310.

Levy, Jack (1997) 'Prospect Theory, Rational Choice, and International Relations', *International Studies Quarterly*, 41 (1): 87–112.

Lustick, Ian S. (1997) 'The Absence of Middle Eastern Great Powers: Political "Backwardness" in Historical Perspective', *International Organization*, 51 (4): 653–83.

Mansfield, Edward (1994) *Power, Trade, and War*. Princeton: Princeton University Press.

Mansfield, Edward and Snyder, Jack (1995) 'Democratization and the Danger of War', *International Security*, 20 (1): 5–38.

Mansfield, Edward D., Milner, Helen and Rosendorff, B. Peter (2000) 'Free to Trade: Democracies, Autocracies, and International Trade', *American Political Science Review*, 94 (2): 305-46.

March, James (1966) 'The Power of Power', in David Easton (ed.), *Varieties of Political Theory*. Englewood Cliffs: Prentice Hall.

Martinotti, Guido and Stefanizzi, Sonia (1995) 'Europeans and the Nation State', in O. Niedermayer and R. Sinnott (eds), *Public Opinion and Internationalized Governance*. Oxford: Oxford University Press. pp. 163–89.

Marx, Karl (1975) *Karl Marx Early Writings* (Introduction by Lucio Colletti, trans. by Rodney Livingstone and Gregor Benton). New York: Vintage Books.

McClelland, Charles (1976) *World Event/Interaction Survey Codebook*. (ICPSR 5211). Ann Arbor: ICPSR.

McClelland, Charles (1983) 'Let the User Beware', *International Studies Quarterly*, 27 (2): 169–77.

Mitrany, David (1966) *A Working Peace System*. Chicago: Quadrangle Books.

Morgenthau, Hans J. (1973) *Politics Among Nations: The Struggle for Power and Peace*, 5th edn. New York: Alfred A. Knopf.

Niedermayer, Oscar and Sinnott, Richard (eds) (1995) *Public Opinion and Internationalized Governance*. Oxford: Oxford University Press.

Niou, Emerson M.S., Ordeshook, Peter and Rose, Gregory (1989) *The Balance of Power: Stability in International Systems*. Cambridge: Cambridge University Press.

O'Neill, Barry (1999) *Honor, Symbols, and War*. Ann Arbor: University of Michigan Press.

Organski, A.K.F. (1968) *World Politics*, 2nd edn. New York: Alfred A. Knopf.

Organski, A.K.F. and Kugler, Jacek (1980) *The War Ledger*. Chicago: University of Chicago Press.

Osgood, Charles (1962) *An Alternative to War or Surrender*. Urbana: University of Illinois Press.

Owen, John (1997) *Liberal Peace, Liberal War: American Politics and International Security*. Ithaca: Cornell University Press.

Powell, Robert (1991) 'Absolute and Relative Gains in International Relations Theory', *American Political Science Review*, 85 (4): 1303–37.

Price, Richard (1997) *The Chemical Weapons Taboo*. Ithaca: Cornell University Press.

Reiter, Dan (1996) *Crucible of Beliefs: Learning, Alliances, and World Wars*. Ithaca: Cornell University Press.

Richardson, Lewis (1960) *Arms and Insecurity*. Pittsburgh: The Boxwood Press.

Riker, William (1962) *The Theory of Political Coalitions*. New Haven: Yale University Press.

Riker, William (1995) 'The Political Psychology of Rational Choice Theory', *Political Psychology*, 16 (1): 23–44.

Rose, Gideon (1998) 'Neoclassical Realism and Theories of Foreign Policy', *World Politics*, 51 (1): 144–72.

Ruggie, John Gerard (1996) *Winning the Peace: America and the World Order in the New Era*. New York: Columbia University Press.

Ruggie, John Gerard (1997) 'The Past as Prologue? Interests, Identity, and American Foeign Policy', *International Security*, 21 (4): 89–125.

Russett, Bruce (1993) *Grasping the Democratic Peace: Principles for a Post-Cold War World*. Princeton: Princeton University Press.

Russett, Bruce (1995) 'Correspondence: And Yet it Moves', *International Security*, 19 (4): 164–75.

Said, Edward (1978) *Orientalism*. New York: Random House.

Schweller, Randall (1996) 'Neorealism's Status Quo Bias: What Security Dilemma?', *Security Studies*, 5: 90–121.

Silverstein, Brett (1989) 'Enemy Images: The Psychology of US Attitudes and Cognitions Regarding the Soviet Union', *American Psychologist*, 44: 903–13.

Simon, Herbert (1979) *Models of Thought*. New Haven: Yale University Press.

Simon, Herbert (1982) *Models of Bounded Rationality*. Cambridge, MA: MIT Press.

Simon, Herbert (1985) 'Human Nature in Politics: The Dialogue of Psychology with Political Science', *American Political Science Review*, 79 (2): 293–304.

Simon, Herbert (1995) 'Rationality in Political Behavior', *Political Psychology*, 16 (1): 45–62.

Singer, J. David. (1990) *Models, Methods, and Progress in World Politics: A Peace Research Odyssey*. Boulder: Westview.

Singer, J. David and Diehl, Paul (eds) (1991) *Measuring the Correlates of War*. Ann Arbor: University of Michigan Press.

Skinner, B.F. (1960) *Behavior Theory and Conditioning*. New Haven: Yale University Press.

Snidal, Duncan (1991) 'Relative Gains and the Pattern of International Cooperation', *American Political Science Review*, 83 (3): 701–26.

Snyder, Jack (1992) *Myths of Empire: Domestic Politics and International Ambitions*. Ithaca: Cornell University Press.

Snyder, R., Bruck, H. and Sapin, B. (1962) *Foreign Policy Decision-Making: An Approach to the Study of International Politics*. New York: Free Press.

Spiro, David (1994) 'The Insignificance of the Liberal Peace', *International Security*, 19 (2): 50–86.

Sprout, Harold and Sprout, Margaret (1965) *The Ecological Perspective on Human Affairs with Special Reference to International Relations*. Princeton: Princeton University Press.

Spruyt, Hendrik (1994) *The Sovereign State and its Competitors*. Princeton: Princeton University Press.

Starr, Harvey (1984) *Henry Kissinger: Perceptions of International Politics*. Lexington: University of Kentucky Press.

Stuart, D. and Starr, H. (1982) 'Inherent Bad Faith Reconsidered: Dulles, Kennedy, and Kissinger', *Political Psychology*, 3: 1–33.

Sullivan, Michael (1990) *Power in Contemporary International Relations*. Columbia: University of South Carolina Press.

Tajfel, Henri (1981) *Human Groups and Social Categories*. Cambridge: Cambridge University Press.

Tajfel, Henri and Turner, John (1986) 'The Social Identity Theory of Intergroup Behavior', in S. Worchel and W. Austin (eds), *Psychology of Intergroup Relations*. Chicago: Nelson-Hall. pp. 7–24.

Tannenwald, Nina (1999) 'The Nuclear Taboo: The United States and the Normative Basis of Nuclear Non-Use', *International Organization*, 53 (3): 433–68.

Tetlock, Philip (1999) 'Theory-Driven Reasoning about Plausible Pasts and Probable Futures in World Politics: Are We Prisoners of Our Preconceptions?', *American Journal of Political Science*, 43 (2): 335–66.

Vertzberger, Yaacov (1990) *The World in Their Minds: Information Processing, Cognition, and Perception in Foreign Policy Decisionmaking*. Stanford: Stanford University Press.

Walker, Stephen (1977) 'The Interface between Beliefs and Behavior: Henry Kissinger's Operational Code and the Vietnam War', *Journal of Conflict Resolution*, 21: 126–68.

Walker, Stephen (ed.) (1987) *Role Theory and Foreign Policy Aanalysis*, Durham, NC: Duke University Press.

Wallander, Celeste (2000) 'NATO After the Cold War', *International Organization*, 54 (4): 705–35.

Walt, Stephen (1987) *The Origins of Alliances*. Ithaca: Cornell University Press.

Walt, Stephen (1999) 'Rigor or Rigor Mortis? Rational Choice and Security Studies', *International Security*, 23 (4): 5–48.

Waltz, Kenneth (1979) *Theory of International Politics*. Reading, MA: Addison–Wesley.

Walzer, Michael (1977) *Just and Unjust Wars: A Moral Argument with Historical Illustrations*. New York: Basic Books.

Wendt, Alexander (1992) 'Anarchy Is What States Make of It', *International Organization*, 46 (2): 391–425.

Wendt, Alexander (1999) *Social Theory of International Politics*. Cambridge: Cambridge University Press.

Wolhforth, William (1993) *The Elusive Balance: Power and Perceptions during the Cold War*. Ithaca: Cornell University Press.

7

Norms and Ethics in International Relations

ANDREW HURRELL

This chapter examines the study of norms and ethics in the field of international relations (IR). In particular, it explores the links between normative theory (What would a just world order look like? How should it constructed?) on the one hand, and the historically created normative practices embedded within the institutions of international and global society on the other. For all the 'norm-talk' inspired by constructivist scholarship, the status of normative political theory remains somewhat elusive. The first section therefore seeks to give a general overview of how the sub-field of international ethics or international normative theory has developed; the main approaches adopted; the reasons for its continued importance; and the different ways in which normative theorists have engaged with the empirical study of norms and institutions in world politics.

Building on this last point, the second section of the chapter explores the work of those writers (political theorists, historical constructivists, international lawyers and those working within the tradition of the English School) who have sought to understand how the normative structure of international and global society has changed and evolved through the period of the classical European state system and into the age of globalization. It also seeks to underline the importance of focusing on normative structures in order to understand better the nature and meaning of specific rules, how they affect behaviour, and how they change through time. The final section examines the difficult and contested subject of cultural difference and diversity. Cultural diversity and value pluralism have been central themes in both historical and contemporary normative analysis of what a just world

order might look like. And they are equally central to all attempts at evaluating the breadth, depth and degree of consensus that exists in international society at the present time.

NORMATIVE POLITICAL THEORY

One can approach the subject of norms and ethics in IR from three distinct perspectives: the first considers the role that normative ideas play in the practice of politics ('How have ideas about what should be done influenced political behaviour?'); the second seeks to engage in rational moral debate as to the nature of ethical conduct ('What ought we to do?'); and the third examines the extent to which moral behaviour is heavily constrained by the dynamics of political life ('Given the realities of political life, what can be done?'). Mervyn Frost argues that the academic study of international relations remains resistant to normative theory, especially in this second sense:

The post-positivists have given us rich accounts of the complex social structures within which we are constituted and within which we act. They have shown how these structures are not static but are in constant flux. They stress the important role which normative considerations play in the practices which we study and in our practices of scholarship themselves. But, once again, following a long tradition of IR scholarship, they stop short of engaging in detailed normative theorizing about what ought to be done. In particular they fail to take on that most important normative question of all: in what would a just world order consist? (Frost, 1998: 129; see also Smith, 1992)

Nevertheless, one of the most striking developments of the past fifteen years has been the re-emergence of normative political theory. This has involved the forging of closer links between IR and mainstream political theory, a more sophisticated reworking of classical traditions of thought on international relations, and the development of a rich and impressive literature on topics ranging from nationalism and national self-determination, to intervention and just war, to global distributive justice.

In part this resurgence has followed from attempts to rethink the way in which we mark off international politics from domestic politics. As the academic study of international relations developed, it became common to stress the uniqueness of the international – either as a realm of anarchy and conflict or as a society but one structured around institutions that were distinct from those that existed within the state (Bull, [1977] 1985; Schmidt, 1998). For Wight this meant that 'international theory' differed fundamentally from 'political theory' and looked to its own history and to its own traditions (Wight, 1966).

And yet as Boucher (1997, 1998), Brown (1992), Linklater (1998), Rengger (2000), Walker (1993), and others have argued, this approach involved a strangely limited view of politics and of political theory. If we shift the focus of the question and if we alter the way in which we conceive of the divide between the domestic and the international, then we get a rather different set of theoretical questions and a rather different set of historical debates and traditions that might help enlighten them (Mapel and Nardin, 1992, 1998). A concern with the nature and extent of community, for example, places the moral basis of the state in question and opens up a fundamental division between cosmopolitan and communitarian answers to normative issues (Brown, 1992; Frost, 1996). For others it is that very division that is problematic and normative theory is intrinsically bound up with the principles and practices of state sovereignty and with the recognition that 'Sovereignty is a claim to particularity that can be meaningful *only in relation* to something more general' (Walker, 1999: 154–5, 1993). Or, to quote Boucher:

> political theory and international relations theory become genuinely united in focusing upon the issue of identity, that is, answers to the question 'Who am I?' The consequent politics of recognition, inclusion and exclusion bring into focus not only the politics of the nation, state and cosmopolitanism, but also of gender, race, religion and ethnicity. (Boucher, 1997: 193)

The revived interest in normative inquiry also followed from broader doubts as to the purposes of social theory. In part, this reflected the power of Robert Cox's simple but powerful statement that 'Theory is always *for* someone and *for* some purpose' (Cox, 1986: 207), and his influential development of the distinction between critical theory and problem-solving theory. In part, it followed from the attacks by a wide range of critical and postmodern theorists on positivism – the idea that the observable regularities in the social world can be analysed with the same methods that have proven successful in analysing the natural world and that social interaction is governed by objective forces the causal workings of which can be formulated in terms of general laws which hold independent of human subjectivity. On this view, then, the return of the normative reflects the failure of social science to provide definitive answers as to how the political world operates and the continued role of moral choice even in those cases where we think we know how the political world operates. Post-positivist routes into the normative have been especially important for critical theorists such as Linklater, concerned with the possibility of expanding the character and range of political community (Linklater, 1998); and for anti-foundationalist postmodern approaches to both political theory (for example Rorty, 1993) and IR (Campbell and Shapiro, 1999; Der Derian, 1987; George, 1994; Walker, 1993).

However, the expansion of normative writing on international relations also reflected changes within the mainstream of Western political theory. In part this had to do with broader 'resurgence of political theory', as David Miller characterized it in 1990 (Miller, 1990: esp. 427–34; see also on this topic, Parekh, 1996) and, in particular, with the torrent of work that followed from the publication of John Rawls's *A Theory of Justice* in 1971. The intense debates between individualist and communitarian liberals inevitably involved competing understandings of global politics. On the one hand, communitarians were concerned to provide moral justification for a world of separate units and for the problems that followed from the different character of these units (peoples, nations, states, nation-states). On the other, cosmopolitans were inevitably drawn to question that very division and to delineate more carefully the range of our 'duties beyond borders' (Hoffmann, 1985). Thus, for example, Beitz and Pogge took up Rawls's arguments in favour of egalitarianism within the state and argued that the changing conditions of justice now required distributive justice to be applied on a global scale (Beitz, [1979] 1999b; Pogge, 1989).

But engagement was also forced upon political theorists by the intensity and complexity of the moral dilemmas of world politics. This had of course been true of the Cold War period which saw major work on just war (Walzer, 1977), on the ethics of nuclear deterrence, and, for a rather brief moment in the 1970s, on distributive justice (for example Singer, 1972). But the inevitability of engagement grew stronger in the post-Cold War world – as a result, for example, of the frequency of ethnic and nationalist conflict; the so-called 'new interventionism', the increased activism of the UN and the revival of debates around the concept of humanitarian intervention; the degree to which increasingly intrusive international rules (for example on human rights) combined with renewed US hegemony and Western dominance sharpened the issue of cultural diversity; or the continued growth of global inequality and the manifest failure of the global system to provide even the most minimal conditions of human welfare and well-being for a very large proportion of humankind (for details see UNDP, 1998). It would be an odd kind of political theory that was not led to ponder on the manifest injustices of contemporary world politics.

Yet lurking behind these specific examples has been a more general and potentially important shift. For many theorists (and for much political and public opinion), increased economic interdependence, an increasingly dense and activist transnational civil society and an expansion in the number and scope of international institutions have shifted understandings of global justice. In the first place, they have necessarily altered the scope of justice. It is, for example, no longer possible to accept Martin Wight's classic distinction between domestic society as the arena within which understandings of the good life might be debated, developed and, potentially, realized, whilst international relations are condemned to remain the arena of 'mere survival'. To take only the most obvious example, 'mere survival' in relation to the protection of the global environment depends fundamentally on how societies are organized domestically and on how their various conceptions of what the good life entails can be brought together and reconciled. Material and moral circumstances have therefore pushed international society inevitably beyond Nardin's practical association – 'an association of independent and diverse political communities, each devoted to its own ends and its own conception of the good'(Nardin, 1983: 9).

Second, integration and globalization have undermined the boundedness of political communities whose particular cultures, traditions and ways of living are given so much weight by communitarians. For many they have given a new reality to the sense of sharing a single world and to the nature of plurality, connection and finitude (O'Neill, 1996: ch. 4). In an integrated world, after all, what possible sense can one make of Rawls's taking as his starting point the idea of a basic social structure built around the 'self-sufficient schemes of cooperation *for all the essential purposes of human life*' (Rawls, 1993: 301; emphasis added)?

This is not to suggest that the tide is flowing in a clearly cosmopolitan direction. Indeed, it is striking to note that a more or less traditional vision of international society is defended by some of the most important contemporary political theorists, including most notably John Rawls (Rawls, 1999). Other examples include Robert Jackson's powerful reworking and extension of the case for normative pluralism and of the rules and institutions of the state system as providing the framework for that pluralism (Jackson, 2000). But it is to note how even more pluralist and communitarian theorists such as Miller or Walzer have been forced to defend their view of the limits to global justice more carefully (David Miller, 1995b, 1999), or to accept the thin obligations that have already been established in the practices and principles of contemporary international society (Walzer, 1994).

The range of issues and problems addressed by normative political theorists is therefore extremely wide. So too is the range of approaches – consequentalist (Singer); Kantian constructivist (O'Neill); Rawlsian (Rawls, Pogge, Beitz, Teson); pluralist or communitarian (David Miller, Walzer); Habermasian (Habermas, Linklater); constitutive (Frost, Brown); pragmatic (Cochran). It is impossible in a short chapter of this kind to enter into a substantive discussion of or even to survey the main schools of thought (for such a survey see Brown, 1992; Thomson, 1992; also see Cochran, 1999; Frost, 1996). Instead I will develop one particular theme: the relationship between normative theory and the role of norms in the practices of world politics. The conventional position is, of course, to insist on the fact/value distinction and to see normative and empirical theory as separate enterprises. As Charles Beitz puts it: 'The analytical and the normative, although related, are different domains, and it is a virtue, not a shortcoming to observe the distinction' (Beitz, 1999a: 270). Yet, even leaving aside the foundational doubts of critical and postmodern theorists, this distinction is far from clear-cut and involves a number of difficult issues.

One dimension concerns feasibility. At one extreme are those who stress the constraints of international politics. Thus classical realists (who were of course themselves passionately committed to a moral project and to uncovering and exposing the dangers of utopianism) believed that moral politics were closely tied to rational statecraft and to the ethics of responsibility that would inevitably dominate the choices of political leaders. This was itself both a moral project and, together with the idea of the national interest, provided the moral basis for realism. In a related vein, English School theorists argued that normative theory should concentrate on the ways in which the law of the jungle might be at least marginally deflected; on the kinds of international society that it might be just possible to establish; and on the principles of prudence and moral obligation and the consensus of shared values that actually existed within international society and that might form a part of achieving this goal. The difficulty with these positions is that they risk becoming an apologia for state practice and that they forswear any clear argument as to what principles ought to guide the practice of international politics and on what sorts of foundations they rest. Prudential ethics are all very well, but, although they speak to the difficulties of going anywhere, they do not give a very clear sense of where we ought to be trying to go. (For a critique of the alleged greater 'realism' of an ethics of responsibility, see McCormick, 1999: ch. 1.)

For those at the other extreme, political theory is in the business of stating clearly what justice requires, and of pushing out the normative boat at least to the margins of what conventional opinion takes to be plausible. For some, there is no great concern with the relationship between what is normatively desired and the chances of it coming about. As Brian Barry puts it: 'most truths are pointless in that sense [i.e. efficacious] and none the worse for that. It rebounds to the honor of the human race that there should be people going about saying that slavery is an absolute evil, even if this cuts no ice with the beneficiaries' (Barry, 1990: 368). For others, the aim should be to delineate a grounded utopia or a realistic utopia. As Rawls puts it: 'Political philosophy is realistically utopian when it extends what are ordinarily thought of as the limits of practical political possibility' (Rawls, 1999: 6; see also 11–16). What might constitute the realism of this realistic utopia depends partly on the time-frame and partly on judgements and assessments that derive from the empirical study of politics.

Here the more empirically minded political scientist is likely to enter two caveats. The first concerns the important distinction drawn by O'Neill between abstraction and idealization and between ideal and idealized theory. 'For example, if human beings are assumed to have capacities and capabilities for rational choice or self-sufficiency or independence from others that are evidently not achieved by many or even by any actual human beings, the result is not mere abstraction; it is idealization' (O'Neill, 1996: 41; see also discussion in Hoffmann, 1998: 40–1). The second concerns the way in which empirical evidence is incorporated into normative argument. In some cases the problem might lie with the weight placed on a particular finding (as, for example, when Rawls uses Sen's work on famines to conclude that it is domestic political culture rather than, say, external vulnerability, that determines the conditions for minimal economic justice). In other cases the problem lies in the uncritical elevation of a contingent and contested argument – as, for example, when Rawls talks in *The Law of Peoples* of the 'Fact of Liberal Democratic Peace' (Rawls, 1999: 125; capitals in original).

The other dimension is more fundamental and relates to the foundations of the normative arguments being presented. Again, let us take two extreme positions whilst acknowledging the reality of many intermediary possibilities. At one extreme, it is precisely human reason that provides both the foundation of moral argument and the hope that it can be acted upon. The normative theorist begins with his/her best considered judgement based on reasons that are suitably coherent and generalizable. Whatever people may actually believe, he or she seeks to find good reasons why they should alter their beliefs and their patterns of behaviour. Showing that certain values are widely accepted in social practices is not the same as providing valid arguments as to why they are justified. But even many of those who wish to start with their own 'best considered judgements' as to what justice requires and who seek to build theories of justice around principles that would be chosen by any rational individual do not end the story there. Thus, for example, Rawls insists that the theorist's considered judgement be related to the values that are available within the political or moral culture of a given society (the idea of a so-called reflective equilibrium) and that valid principles of justice must be publicly justifiable. (See the discussion in Miller, 1999: ch. 3.)

For other theorists, normative theory should begin with the norms and values that exist within particular communities. The critical side of this position is to stress that both the concerns and the methods of political theory are themselves the product of particular historical traditions and are rooted within a particular cultural tradition. Thus, Freeden, for example, seeks to contextualize contemporary American philosophical liberalism and to uncover the way in which its inherently ideological character is disguised by the methods and style that it adopts. 'Liberal principles are consequently stated in such a way as to blur the distinctions between the theory and the ideology; in particular – again, as with Marxism – to disengage the theory from a diachronic tradition of thought against which its identity has been subject to continuous appraisal' (Freeden, 1996: 227, but see especially ch. 6). Or Rogers Smith analyses the ways in which Rawls's work fits within and grows out of broader patterns of American liberal political thought (Smith, 1997: 481–5). From this perspective, abstract theoretical analysis, whether normative or empirical, can never be wholly divorced from the historical circumstances against which it arose. It can never be treated as though it had neither a past nor a future – nor, of course, that it is connected to particular structures of political power.

The more positive aspect is to seek to ground normative theory in the existing normative practices of particular communities. As Michael Walzer puts it, 'principles of justice are … the inevitable product of historical and cultural particularism' (Walzer, 1983: 5–6, quoted in Barry, 1990: 365). Theory should uncover, interpret and critically develop understandings of morality that exist within specific international historical and cultural contexts. The theorist or social critic 'gives expression to his people's deepest sense of how they ought to live'. On this view, as David Miller puts it: 'There are no universal principles of justice. Instead, we must see justice as the creation of a particular political community at a particular time, and the account we give must be given from within such a community' (Miller in Miller and Walzer, 1995: 2).

This is an approach to grounding normative debate that ties in closely with English School perspectives on IR: the need to nurture (but not uncritically accept) the normative consensus that has come to develop within international society; to build arguments and proposals for greater justice out of the values and modes of reasoning that have already begun to take root; and to pay very close attention to the balance between substantive principles of global justice on the one hand and the principles of fair institutional process that underpin the reality of some kind of international community on the other. This conventionalist or internalist position has been central to communitarian theorists. But there is no reason in principle why such accounts of justice cannot provide a fuller account of the pluralist case for the state system (as with Jackson, 2000), or indeed push beyond pluralism. Thus, for example, changes in the practices of international institutions or of transnational civil society may well move different states and societies towards 'shared understandings of the meaning of social goods', to use Walzer's phrase (Hurrell, 2001).

In a different idiom, critical theorists also seek to push towards emancipatory reform but on the basis of tendencies and that are already potentially immanent in current practices. To quote Andrew Linklater:

> No critical theorist influenced by Marx would deny that normative theory must engage with actual social structures and real social conflicts. ... critical theory in the broadly Marxian tradition avoids the extremes of resignation to international political fate and retreat into utopian fancy. Normative theory in this tradition focuses on what is immanent within existing social structures, and intimated by the decisive social struggle in any epoch – not on the requirements of disembodied reason. (Linklater, 1999: 165)

It is well beyond the scope of this chapter to try to defend a single resolution of these intrinsically difficult and contested issues. Although it remains important to try to separate out questions of normative rightness or plausibility from questions relating to the sociology of norms (How did such an idea arise? What function does it serve?), finding stable criteria for adjudicating these distinctions is fraught with difficulty. And yet we might still wish to deny the claim, made by both realists and Marxists, that *all* moral discussion can be reduced to simple-minded

notions of self-interest or viewed as simply reflective of material forces. Nor is it correct, as so much postmodern ethical argument suggests, that *all* moral debate can be reduced to a clash of incommensurable contending discourses.

No doubt in a politically and culturally fragmented world there are examples of true conflict. But there will always be scope for rationally grounded moral debate and discussion. Much moral argument involves issues of facts and the application of shared moral principles to particular empirical circumstances. Equally, a good deal of moral debate is concerned with the definition of rules and their logical relationship to one another. When we move beyond these shared premises and into the realm of true incommensurability, then there is no alternative but to strive to nurture the political institutions through which normative consensus might be developed and extended; and, in particular, through which respect for pluralism and coexistence might be reconciled with the need for more active cooperation and for an overlapping moral consensus. This is, after all, part of the specificity of politics: that arena in which the practical results of different moral visions are to be negotiated and rationally constructed if they are not to be imposed by coercion and unequal power.

NORMATIVE STRUCTURES

As is evident from the previous section, normative theory has for a long time (and necessarily) interacted closely with ideas and arguments about the changing character of international society and capacity of that society to provide a satisfactory basis for international or global order. What kinds of ordered cooperative relations have states and their governments sought to establish amongst themselves? What kinds of shared purposes and values (if any) can be discerned in the norms, rules and institutions that structure and regulate their interaction? How far have these been successfully achieved and what explains the gap between normative ambition and political realization? Such questions have been explored most directly in the classic studies of international order (Aron, 1966; Bull, [1977] 1985; Falk, 1972, 1975, 1999; Hoffmann, 1987, 1998; Mayall, 2000; Lynn Miller, 1990; Vincent, 1974). It also connects with more recent discussion of global governance (Diehl, 1997; Keohane, 2001; Nye and Donahue, 2000; O'Brien et al., 2000; Reinecke, 1998; Woods, 1999; Young, 1999). There is an obvious overlap with the literature on institutionalism surveyed elsewhere in this volume. But the focus here is less on theoretical understanding how particular institutions or regimes emerge and develop, and more on assessing the overall character of institutionalization in world politics, the normative commitments of different varieties of institutionalism, and the adequacy of existing institutions for meeting practical and normative challenges.

There are many aspects of change that are of potential importance for normative theory. Equally, the range of writing on the broad subject of change and transformation in world politics has been enormous. We have seen major works of synthesis (for example Buzan and Little, 2000; Ruggie, 1998), as well as a flood of work examining the links between globalization and transformation (see in particular Held et al., 1999; Held and McGrew, 2000; Scholte, 2000). But the concern here is with a particular sub-set of the analysis of change, namely change in what may be called the normative or constitutional structure of international society, as this is manifest in international legal rules and practices, in international political norms and in the dominant ideologies and practices that animate them.

Many of the proponents of deep change offer a stark and highly implausible choice: between a grossly simplified image of a Westphalian past and an invariably complex, but usually underspecified, post-Westphalian present and future. Even the most suggestive and sophisticated of those arguing for change tend to skirt rather quickly around juridical and normative structures, to conflate claims about power and control with claims about law and authority, and to rely on a range of plausible but elusive concepts. Ideas about 'post-sovereign states' or 'multilayered geo-governance' do indeed point to potentially very important changes but they are embedded in a discourse of normative transformation that is in most cases extremely difficult to pin down. On the other side, those who stress continuity rely on such a one-dimensional view of the role of norms and such a very thin notion of the legal order that it becomes impossible to make sense of the tremendous changes that have indeed taken place, above all in the period since 1945 (for example, Krasner, 1999).

One question, then, involves seeking to delineate and trace models of the international normative order, both in terms of the different goals to be promoted and the different means of achieving them. Thus Falk distinguished between Westphalian and Charter conceptions of the international legal order (Black and Falk, 1969), a theme developed by Cassese (1986). Bull distinguished between 'pluralist' and 'solidarist' models of international society (Bull, [1977] 1985; Alderson and Hurrell, 2000), a way of thinking developed more recently by Wheeler (2000). Nardin (1983) distinguished between purposive and practical associations. Reus-Smit (1999) sought to analyse different international societies by distinguishing between issue-specific regimes, fundamental institutions and constitutional structures. Philpott (2000) has traced the development of 'revolutions in sovereignty'.

Others have engaged with the immensely difficult task of trying to think through the possible nature of a post-sovereign normative order.

Thus political theorists such as Held have sought to chart the contours of cosmopolitan democracy (Archibuggi and Held, 1995; Archibugi, Held and Köhler, 1998; Held, 1995), whilst others such as Linklater have delineated the possible character of the post-sovereign state (Linklater, 1998). Within international law, Chayes and Chayes (1995) and Koh (1996) have developed transnational process and managerial models of the emerging legal order; whilst Slaughter has provided an important depiction of how a liberal international legal order would differ from traditional understandings (Slaughter, 1995, 1997 and 2000; for two very useful collections on the changing roles of International Law see Byers, 2000 and Goldstein et al., 2001).

This branch of international relations has brought together political theorists, analytically minded international lawyers, historical constructivists, and those working within the tradition of the English School. There are many differences and shades of opinion, but also a series of general commitments. From this perspective, the international system cannot be viewed solely in material terms as a decentralized, anarchic structure in which functionally undifferentiated units vary only according to the distribution of power. Central to the 'system' is a historically created, and evolving, structure of common understandings, rules, norms and mutual expectations. The concepts of state sovereignty, international law or war are not given by the game of power politics. Rather shared and historically grounded understandings of war or sovereignty define what the nature of the game is and how it is to be played and, very critically, how it might change or evolve. IR cannot therefore be taught or analysed as part of an abstract 'game' independent of its human or historical origins. It grows out of its past, although never fully outgrows it. The system is the result of historical processes of change and development and therefore cannot be understood in terms of timeless, immutable laws.

Material structures matter, but these material structures cannot be understood outside of the shared knowledge and shared understandings held by the actors themselves. Amongst these shared understandings and intersubjective knowledge, norms and institutions play a number of fundamental roles. They may well serve as regulatory rules designed to constrain choices and/or as parameters within which individual agents pursue their own preferences. But the critical point is that they do far more than this. In the first place, they help explain how actors are constituted. As Wendt puts it, this is 'one of the most important things a structure can explain' (Wendt, 1999: 16). Second, they help us make sense of the identity of actors and hence of the sources of their preferences. Norms can be understood as expressions of what states are, where they belong and of the kinds of roles they play. And third, norms do not simply constrain but also enable and empower action. In Martin Hollis's words: 'They enable not only by making collective action easier but also by creating forms of activity' (Hollis, 1991: 13).

A great deal of recent work has involved more detailed historical understanding of how the institutional structure of the classic European state system emerged and developed. Although bland (and often inaccurate) references to 'Westphalia' still blight many textbooks, the past two decades have seen a sustained attempt to get beyond the textbook stereotypes. Thus the study of classical theories of international relations has grown significantly (for general studies see Boucher, 1998; Clark and Neumann, 1996; Doyle, 1998; and Knutsen, 1992) and there have been important reassessments of the major traditions of thought in international relations (Dunne, 1998; Nabulsi, 1999; Walker, 1993). Westphalia has been demythologized by Osiander (1994 and 2001), Philpott (1999) and Krasner (1999). Biersteker and Weber (1996) and Bartelson (1995) have emphasized the importance of seeing state sovereignty as a social construct. Work on the history of international law remains underdeveloped but important works for the study of international relations include Koskenniemi (1989) and Grewe (2000). And finally there has been a very important move into the area of 'international relations' on the part of those working within the history of political thought – a move which has expanded immensely the degree of historical sophistication in the study of the subject (see in particular Hont, 1994; Pagden, 1995; Rothschild, 1995; Tuck, 1999).

Understanding the historical evolution of the normative structure matters for the obvious reason that it is only by understanding the past that we can gauge and assess claims for change and transformation. But understanding normative structures matters for other reasons and shapes our understanding of the role of norms in international life: how we interpret and understand specific rules, how they affect outcomes, and how they change through time.

What Norms Are

All normative analysis revolves around the two classic meanings of the term 'norm'. On the one hand, norms are identified by regularities of behaviour among actors. Norms reflect actual patterns of behaviour and give rise to expectations as to what will in fact be done in a particular situation. On the other, norms reflect patterned behaviour of a particular kind: a prescribed pattern of behaviour which gives rise to normative expectations as to what ought to be done. Thus regularity is combined with an internal attitude involving criticism of oneself or

others on the ground that a particular norm is being violated. Norms can therefore be defined (and will be so used in this chapter) as 'a broad class of prescriptive statements – rules, standards, principles, and so forth – both procedural and substantive' that are 'prescriptions for action in situations of choice, carrying a sense of obligation, a sense that they *ought* to be followed' (Chayes and Chayes, 1994: 65).

Deciding which norms matter and in which circumstances will be difficult, if not impossible, without being able to systematically distinguish levels of authority or normativity among the different principles or rules within a particular regime (Brunneé and Toope, 2000). Equally, compliance cannot be reduced to following a static set of clear sharped-edged rules (see Chayes and Chayes, 1995; Kingsbury, 1988; Koh, 1997). But for the sceptic, it is the very ubiquitousness of norms in international life, their frequent ambiguity, and the variety of interpretations to which they may give rise that is the problem. Powerful actors can always find a norm to support their consequentially based choice. Norms are often in conflict. As Krasner puts it: 'International rules can be contradictory ... and there is no authority structure to adjudicate such controversies.' Or again: 'The international environment has been characterized by competing and often logically contradictory norms, not some single coherent set of rules' (Krasner, 1999: 6, 54). The strong can always pick and choose amongst existing rules or set new ones, through formal agreement or through custom – a source of international law which places disproportionate weight on the actions and arguments of powerful states (Byers, 1999).

It is important to recognize the seriousness of the problem and to avoid a stylized or idealized view of the legal order. But it is one thing to accept that indeterminacy and instability are problems but quite another to argue that anything goes, that anything can be claimed and said, and that powerful states can simply pick and choose the rules that suit their purposes.

In the first place, it is in the very nature of norms that there will always be questions as to which norms are relevant and how they should be interpreted. The critical issue is the degree to which interpretation reflects shared practices. The theoretical point is well made by Kratochwil: 'As a practice, a rule not only tells me how to proceed in a situation that I have never faced before, it is also governed by certain conventions of the community of which I am part. To this extent, my interpretations of a rule as well as my uses of words are monitored and reinforced by a group of competent speakers' (Kratochwil, 2000: 52). The institutional point is that international law is built around an interpretative community of lawyers (and others who argue in and through law) who inhabit a more or less unified conceptual universe and who share a common set of discursive practices. It is by dint of this that questions relating to the determinacy of rules or the meaning of contested concepts can be rationally debated, if never fully resolved. Second, international law has to be understood as an integrated institution and as an interconnected normative system in which historical development and the evolution of specific legal doctrines or concepts over time play a crucial role. Thus the content of a particular norm and the degree of obligation that attaches to it is related to its place within this broader normative order. Doubtless there are many cases where competing principles animate controversy. Similarly, many rules are capable of widely differing interpretations. But the integrity of law sets limits to the range and influence of eligible principles, and to the range of legitimate interpretations. If indeed 'organized hypocrisy' is a useful term, we still need to reflect on the crucial fact that it is just that: *organized* hypocrisy.

Something similar is true of moral and normative argument. All human societies rely on historical stories about themselves to legitimize notions of where they are and where they might be going. Over time, understandings of normative problems and categories of normative arguments become organized into intelligible patterns, traditions, or ideologies. Thus to take the case of war: the continual involvement of individuals and societies in war and conflict, the moral and political necessity of trying to make sense of what war involves, and the limited range of plausible arguments have led over time to the creation of intelligible patterns, traditions and ideologies. As Michael Walzer puts it: 'Reiterated over time, our arguments and judgements shape what I want to call *the moral reality of war* – that is, all those experiences of which moral language is descriptive or within which it is necessarily employed' (Walzer, 1977: 15).

How Norms Affect Outcomes

For neorealists norms do not matter in themselves but only to the extent that they reflect, or are backed by, the power of powerful actors. For rationalists, norms and institutions matter to the degree that they affect actor strategies (but not their underlying preferences) by reducing transaction costs, by identifying focal points for coordinated behaviour, and by providing frameworks for productive issue-linkage (see Chapter 10, this volume). Moving beyond rationalism, cognitive approaches highlight the role of knowledge, and especially of scientific or technical knowledge, in shifting state understandings of interest in ways that foster cooperation.

Attempts to go beyond these kinds of approaches (for a survey see Hasenclever et al., 1997) rely on two well-established steps. The first is to challenge the rationalist account of human choice and human

agency. Rationalists like to claim that they adopt an 'actor-centred' theory and that, if this is rejected, then one is necessarily committed to a view of human agents blindly following internalized norms. Much recent writing within both political science and social theory has relied on this stark and, to many, implausible dichotomy (March and Olson, 1998). Thus Elster contrasts instrumentally rational action that is hypersentive to consequences with norms understood as internalized Kantian imperatives ('blind, compulsive, mechanical or even unconscious'; Elster, 1989). Krasner distinguishes between consequential action on the one hand and 'taken for granted' 'deeply embedded' 'internalized' norms on the other (Krasner, 1999). And Keohane has written on the differences between instrumental and normative 'optics' (Keohane, 1997).

As against this, the critics of rationalism highlight the complexity of human choice and the inevitability of deliberation, of moral conflict and of moral purpose (O'Neill, 2000). As Jackson puts it: 'People are not automated or mechanical things. People are human beings who make choices, and whose policies and actions must be justified to other people' (Jackson, 2000: 8). It was, after all, for this reason that Carr believed that political realism had to accept the importance of utopian ideas (Carr, 1939). Or, as Robert Musil (1995) puts it: 'If there is a sense of reality, then there must also be a sense of possibility.' The critics also point to the difficulties of any clear-cut distinction between a rational logic of consequences and a norm-following logic of appropriateness. How we calculate consequences is often far from obvious and not easily separable from our understanding of legal or moral norms. Think, for example, of how states sought to calculate the consequences of alternative courses of action in the Kosovo bombing campaign and how these calculations were deeply shaped by the existing legal and moral normative framework. Moreover, time and process are especially important in understanding how logics of consequences and of appropriateness interrelate. At any point in time it may indeed to be helpful to think of actors making choices between consequentialist calculations and normative appropriateness. But over time the obviousness of certain sorts of norms (for example against slavery or military conquest) becomes such an accepted part of the international political landscape that it becomes part of how actors routinely calculate consequences.

The second well-established challenge to rationalism is to question the rationalist account of how norms are related to causality. The issues are complex and murky but the basic point is a simple one – that there are many routes to explaining social action.

Thus, contrary to Popper and the predominant epistemology, 'explaining' does not seem to involve simply the procedure of the 'subsuming' of a single case under a general law, but comprises a rather heterogeneous set of procedures by which we try to understand actions and events. Explaining often means providing a context, such as when we make a series of actions and events part of a wider narrative. However, explaining an action might also involve us in elaborations and justifications of the choices made, or of our reasons for choosing certain beginnings and endings. (Kratochwil, 2000: 64)

Or, in the earlier classic statement with John Ruggie:

Norms may 'guide' behaviour, they may 'inspire' behaviour, they may 'rationalize' or 'justify' behaviour, they may express 'mutual expectations' about behaviour, or they may be ignored. But they do not effect cause in the sense that a bullet through the heart causes death or an uncontrolled surge in the money supply causes price inflation. (Kratochwil and Ruggie, 1986)

If these two points have been frequently made, there are two further areas on which much work remains to be done. Both concern the way in which normative structures (as opposed to individual norms) may affect political outcomes. The first relates to constitutive norms. 'Constitutive rules define the set of practices that make up any particular consciously organized social activity – that is to say, they specify *what counts* as that activity' (Ruggie, 1998: 22). The distinction between regulatory norms and constitutive norms has a long history within philosophy and jurisprudence (Rawls, 1955; Searle, 1995) – although it is by no means universally accepted (for example by Raz, [1975] 1999: 108–11). Constructivist writing has laid great emphasis on the importance of constitutive rules and the theoretical and general debate has been intense and often illuminating (see especially, Kratochwil, 1989; Onuf, 1989) .

Yet many puzzles remain. What actually are the most important constitutive rules in international relations and what are the criteria for assessing their importance? How are we to understand the normative force of constitutive rules? How do believers in the importance of constitutive rules answer the sceptical response that powerful actors can find new constitutive norms to suit their interests (as in the case of revising sovereignty in the post-Cold War world)? Answers to these questions may well involve sharper distinctions between different sorts of rules that can loosely be placed under the 'constitutive' banner: transactional or facilitative norms as, for example, in the law of treaties or diplomatic law; 'power-conferring norms' (to use Raz's term) which determine the capacity to participate in political or legal processes; membership norms that govern the participation of actors in individual institutions or in international society more generally; and finally those international norms which

both reflect and seek to shape the domestic constitution of major actors – their corporate as opposed to social identities to use Wendt's rather problematic distinction (Wendt, 1999: ch. 5). This last category is especially important. Constitutive norms are powerful not only (or indeed primarily) because they formally create or enable certain kinds of activity; but rather because they foster group identification and therefore allow for the coordination of great social power. It is for this reason that national self-determination is the most important constitutive norm of the modern era.

The second set of on-going puzzles concerns the many different mechanisms by which norms are diffused across the international system and internalized by actors. It is easy to suggest in broad terms that past institutional choices affect the present choice of norms and the framework within which strategic interaction takes place. But, as Krasner argues with his usual clarity of purpose, it is much harder to establish how institutions become embedded: 'that is, dictate actual behaviour and endure over time or across different environmental conditions' (Krasner, 1999: 226). Within the rationalist agenda, the systemic dimension is incorporated through hard notions of path dependence (and maybe also of sunk costs) that 'lock' actors into patterns of behaviour. Patterns are followed because the costs of divergence are high. Within a sociological account the explanatory work will have to be done by some version of individual socialization.

Whether individual-level socialization is important is an empirical question and not one that can be settled by theoretical fiat. But, very importantly, it is by no means the only mechanism by which actors may come to 'internalize' norms that originate elsewhere in the system. Three other mechanisms deserve brief mention. The first can be labelled *discursive enmeshment* and highlights the importance of argumentation, deliberation and persuasion. Words are not always cheap. The reasons for making normative claims or framing interests in normative language may well be purely instrumental. Such a course of action legitimizes and makes universal claims that would otherwise seem partial and particular. It may also reflect straightforward calculations of interest (talking the language of human rights in order to secure aid or investment or, as with China, its acceptance as a legitimate Great Power; Foot, 2000). But entering into a particular debate and accepting particular principles, ideas and arguments shapes and constrains the sorts of arguments that can be made in the future and provides institutional and normative platforms for different forms of political mobilization. On the importance of legitimacy see Brunneé and Toope, 2000; Franck, 1990; Hurd, 1999.

A second mechanism concerns *bureaucratic enmeshment*. Individual leaders may well remain completely unsocialized into international norms. And yet they may find that external norms have been incorporated into bureaucratic structures in ways that preclude or raise the costs of certain sorts of policies. There may, for example, be very powerful situational pressures to deviate from the laws of war. Yet politicians and generals may find themselves effectively constrained by the incorporation of these rules into bureaucratic operating procedures and national military codes. Similarly, national and international bureaucratic procedures in the field of human rights (to compile reports or to attend review meetings) help explain the continuity of human rights policies despite the changing attitudes and commitment of individual leaders. Third, there is *legal internalization*. As should by now be well known, international legal rules cannot be understood in any straightforward sense as simply 'international'. At one level, rule-governed behaviour does reflect the dynamics of inter-state politics and of inter-state institutions. But that inter-state dynamic is very often heavily influenced by the degree to which international rules have been incorporated into national legal systems and also by transnational groups and pressures that act across the domestic/international divide (Goldstein et al., 2001).

How Norms Change

Change matters. As Hollis put it: 'Norms are no less effective for being fluid and no less real for being negotiable. Both ideally and actually the stuff which binds societies is more like mastic than cement' (Hollis, 1991: 13). But how are we to understand normative change? Realists and neorealists argue, often correctly, that changes in the normative structure are closely bound up with power and the distribution of power – within the state system but also within the global economy and transnational civil society. Rationalist institutionalists are inclined to see institutions as responses to the increasingly serious collective action problems generated by growing societal, ecological and economic interdependence. Such interdependence creates huge scope for joint gains and hence a powerful 'demand' for institutions (although their supply is an altogether more difficult matter).

More recently, liberal pluralists have emphasized the role of transnational civil society. Transnational civil society refers to those self-organized intermediary groups that are relatively independent of both public authorities and private economic actors; that are capable of taking collective action in pursuit of their interests or values; and that act across state borders (Scholte, 2000; see also Chapter 13 in this volume). Their role in norm formation and norm development is important (although by no means obviously greater than, say, in the late nineteenth

and early twentieth centuries): first, in the formal process of norm creation, standard-setting and norm development; second, in the detailed functioning of many international institutions and in the processes of implementation and compliance; and third in direct participation in many governance activities (disbursing an increasing proportion of official aid, engaging in large-scale humanitarian relief; leading efforts at promoting democracy or post-conflict social and political reconstruction). In all of these areas the analytical focus has been on transnational networks – for example, knowledge-based networks of economists, lawyers, or scientists; or transnational advocacy networks which act as channels for flows of money and material resources but, more critically, of information, ideas and values (Finnemore and Sikkink, 1998; Keck and Sikkink, 1998).

Four points deserve to be highlighted. First, as the density and complexity of the international legal system increases and as globalization opens up new channels of transnational political action, so the process of norm creation becomes harder for even powerful states to control. Thus transnational NGO networks have carved out important roles and relatively weak states have been able to promote new and often far-reaching legal rules and institutions (as with the International Criminal Court). In part this success has depended on material or ideational resources. But it also reflects the ability of non-state groups to exploit institutional platforms. State action may be shaped by NGO lobbying but it is often state action that is crucial in fostering the emergence of civil society in the first place and in providing the institutional and normative framework that enables it to flourish. In addition, success will often depend on the capacity to build on already established patterns of legal argument and to import and adapt already accepted principles from other areas – in other words, to exploit internal logics of norm development.

All of this points to a broader change. In the traditional legal order, dominant norms were created by states and depended directly on the consent of states. Over recent decades, the process of norm creation has been opened to a wider range of actors, both states and non-state groups, and there is an easing of the degree to which states can only be bound by those rules to which they have given their explicit consent. Lest this appear too cosy and liberal, two important caveats are in order. First, civil society is an arena of politics like any other in which the good and thoroughly awful coexist and in which outcomes may be just as subject to direct manipulation by powerful actors as the world of inter-state politics. And second, the degree of effective pluralism varies greatly across issue areas. It is most apparent in fields such as human rights and environment but far less so in the hierarchically structured institutions and institutionalized practices that shape the global economy.

Second, there is the inherent tendency for all normative systems (especially reasonably well-institutionalized judicial systems) to expand from within and to enmesh actors within certain patterns of discourse, reasoning and argumentation. As Stone Sweet put it: 'norms ... develop in path-dependent, self-reinforcing ways, one mechanism of which is the ubiquity, and naturalness, of normative reasoning itself. Normative systems are inherently expansionary to the extent to which they enable people to reason from one situation to another, by way of analogy' (Stone Sweet, 1999: 157). In complex legal institutions, such as the ECJ or the WTO dispute settlement procedures, norm development does not simply reflect periodic bargains amongst states. It often takes place internally through the practices of the institutions themselves: filling in gaps in treaties, developing answers to new problems, establishing precedents (even where precedent is not formally admissible).

Third, institutions act as platforms for normative debate, for the mobilization of concern, and for debating and revising ideas about how international society should be organized. However much social scientists insist on analysing international institutions solely in terms of the provision of international public goods, normative issues cannot be kept out of the actual practices of those institutions. It is, for example, politically and theoretically significant that this should be true even of economic institutions that define their own purposes in instrumental terms. Thus arguments about the effectiveness and efficiency of the World Bank or the IMF are increasingly having to be made in the language of legitimacy or even of moral purpose.

Finally, normative change reflects changes in the organization of domestic society and in the powerful transnational ideological forces that have shaped those changes. Thus the legitimacy of governments (democratic and authoritarian) has come to depend on their capacity to meet a vastly increased range of needs, claims and demands. In part this has involved increased expectations of the role of the state in economic management (something that remains substantially true even in an era of deregulation, privatization and globalization). In part it reflects changed notions of political legitimacy and broadened understandings of self-determination, of human rights and of citizenship rights. In addition, although it may be true, as realists tell us, that the international system tames and socializes revolutionary regimes, it is also true that each of the great social revolutions of the modern era has left an indelible mark on the dominant norms of international society (Armstrong, 1993; Halliday, 1999). In one sense this may be obvious. But it is obscured by the very common tendency in IR to distinguish too sharply between 'thick' domestic norms and 'thin' international norms. Many international norms (national self-determination, economic liberalism,

sustainable development) are powerful precisely because of the way in which they relate to the transnational structures within which all states are embedded and to the broad social forces that have transformed the character of states and altered the dynamics of the state system.

Much work has been done on non-state groups (both firms and NGOs) either as lobbyists within individual states or as participants directly within international regimes and institutions. But much more needs to be done, for example, on the emergence of convergent state norms and forms of 'world law' that develop not through explicit or formalized inter-state bargaining but rather through regulatory competition, pressure from international bodies or mimesis (Meyer et al., 1997); or the emergence of private authority structures that exist largely autonomous from the framework of both municipal and international law: private systems of arbitration and dispute settlement, privatized rule-production resulting from technical standardization, internal regulations within transnational firms; and private regimes governing particular sectors of the global economy (Cutler et al., 1999; Ronit and Schneider, 1999; Teubner, 1997).

NORMS AND CULTURAL DIVERSITY

What Sen calls 'the empirical fact of pervasive human diversity' (Sen, 1992: xi) has long been seen as a major issue confronting normative theorists: What value should be accorded to the traditions and practices of particular human communities? How might obligations owed to such communities be balanced with obligations owed to humankind in general? Cultural diversity has also long been a central problem for those who ask: How broad and how deep is international society? How strong is the consensus on the nature of a desirable world order and the means by which it might be achieved?

A deep-rooted tradition of Western thought has associated social order and political institutions (both domestic and international) with the existence of common values and with the shared culture within which those values are embedded. It was, for example, axiomatic to the classical European writers on international society that the society of states was in some way related to shared values (Bull, [1977] 1985). Some stressed the shared international political or diplomatic culture of élites; others emphasized shared societal values whether those of Christianity, of Europe or of civilization (Watson, 1992; Wight, 1977). On this view, the interests and identities of actors are shaped by particular histories and cultures, as well as by historically constituted relationships and ongoing processes of interaction with other states. It is perhaps for this reason that English School approaches resonate so strongly outside the world of Western political science. But certainly for Bull (if less so for Wight), the role of values is an empirical question to be investigated, not an analytic assumption. Although shared values may have been important at particular times, Bull did not believe that international society *necessarily* rested on the existence of a common value system as, for example, suggested by Krasner (Krasner, 1999: 47; see discussion in Alderson and Hurrell, 2000: 6–7 and 69–70).

This way of thinking about the role of culture in international relations has attracted significant criticism. There are many problems with the view (often associated with Parsonian sociology) that simply equates order with the existence of a common value system and with normative consensus, and which sees norms in terms of the social functions that they serve. Value systems, after all, do not just happen. They are created by social agents for particular purposes and they are maintained because it will often pay people in some way to ensure that they are (Barry, 1970: 75–98; and Coleman, 1990: chs 10 and 11). Functionalist accounts of social norms run the risk of circularity, of *post hoc* reasoning, and of reducing human agents to automata blindly following internalized norms. In addition, if cooperation does not necessarily follow from shared values, conflict need not necessarily be the result of their absence (see Cederman in this volume and Hardin, 1995). More generally in political science, after a brief flourishing in the 1950s, concern with culture as an analytical concept faded away. (The emphasis on strategic culture formed one partial exception, see Booth, 1979 and Snyder, 1977).

The 1990s, however, witnessed a renewed interest in culture. Three aspects can be highlighted. In the first place, changes in the international system seemed to underline the renewed importance of cultural factors. Thus trends towards globalization appeared to many to make cultural differences more salient and indeed to act as a spur to the reassertion of cultural traditionalism and particularism. The resurgence of nationalism and ethnic conflict seemed to push questions of identity and culture centre-stage and to focus attention on the construction of boundaries and the production of meaning (Lapid and Kratochwil, 1996). And the increasing emphasis placed by Western states on human rights and democracy gave new life to old arguments about cultural relativism and 'Asian values' (Bauer and Bell, 1999; Dunne and Wheeler, 1999).

Second, the concern with culture formed part of a more general interest in the role of ideas and non-material forces in explaining social phenomena (Goldstein and Keohane, 1993). Theorists argued, for example, that the models that dominated mainstream IR were incapable of dealing with the complex dynamics of integration and disintegration that were producing many different political forms and political affiliations, both above and below the state. Moreover, those models were themselves socially and culturally constructed so that, for example, even realism could be traced to culturally specific roots (Johnston, 1995). It was also argued that rationality is not static and that experience and shifting identity can change or modify behaviour even where the strategic environment remains constant (as in the cases of Germany and Japan; see Berger, 1996; Katzenstein, 1996a). Equally, actors may be culturally unaware of the range of potential options open to them or may be culturally inhibited from adopting particular paths (Katzenstein, 1996b). Although the range of arguments has been very wide, culture was seen to matter in terms of its effects on the definition of interests; the way that it shapes links between interests and identity; and its impact on normative structures such as identity (Kowert and Legro, 1996).

It is not possible to provide here a full analysis of these claims and the interested reader is referred to other chapters in this volume. But a couple of points need to be made. First, within this literature it is not always easy to pin down what is meant by culture. The terms 'culture' and 'identity' have often been used interchangeably and with a significant degree of imprecision. And second, the links between culture and language remain underdeveloped. It is certainly true that linguistic constructivists have added a very great deal to our understandings of how social meanings and intersubjective structures are produced and reproduced (Fierke, 1998; Kratochwil, 1989; Onuf, 1989). But it is not just language in general that matters; it is also the specificities of particular languages and linguistic systems. Here it is not necessary to accept determinist claims about the way in which different languages map the world differently or predetermine certain modes of observation and interpretation. The point is rather to stress the complex ways in which language affects the way people think and act; the role of particular languages in both symbolizing culture and producing culture; the difficulties of translating ideas across linguistic boundaries (Steiner, 1992; Wierbicka, 1997); and the very different value connotations of apparently similiar words (for examples of how this matters politically see Cohen, 2000; Inoue, 1991; Komatsu, 1999).

The third dimension of the return of culture has to do with broad characterizations of the post-Cold War international order. In the influential view of Samuel Huntingdon the world is fundamentally divided along cultural or civilizational lines and it is these divisions that will determine the shape of global politics in the coming century (Harrison and Huntingdon, 2000; Huntingdon, 1997). Minimizing conflict for Huntingdon involves accepting the reality of civilizational difference, forsaking vain attempts to promote Western liberal values globally, and, implicitly at least, returning to a pluralist order of coexistence, based, in the post-Cold War world, not on balanced power but on hegemonic self-restraint.

The problems with this image of clashing civilizations are well known. It is difficult to identify clear territorial boundaries to civilizations, and harder still to imbue them with the capacity to act as a coherent unit. It places far too much in the undifferentiated category of 'civilization', reifying and essentializing cultures and downplaying the multiplicity of trends, conflicts and contradictions within any particular cultural tradition. Cultures are not closed systems of essentialist values and it is difficult to see the world as consisting of a limited number of cultures each with its own indestructible and immutable core, particularly given the expansion of channels, of pressures and of agents through which norms are diffused across the world. Of course there are cultures and communities that militantly refuse to be globalized. But there are also many examples of powerful normative diffusion; and still more cases in which deep-rooted, inherited local traditions come up against powerful globalizing pressures. The result is neither fusion nor fragmentation but rather continued eclectic and syncretic diversity.

And yet despite these difficulties, human diversity and value conflict remain important. All communities and polities have to find ways of dealing with diversity and value conflict. Conflict is, after all, intrinsic to all morality and even within a single value system conflicts arise: how different principles are to be related to one another; how shared principles are to be applied to the facts of a particular case. For international society the problem has always run much deeper. The creation of any kind of universal society of states or any other kind of world society has to face up to the existence of fundamental differences in religion, social organization, culture and moral outlook. Diversity is a basic and common feature of humanity. The clash of moral, national and religious loyalties is not the result of ignorance or irrationality but rather reflects the plurality of values by which all political arrangements and notions of the good life are to be judged.

It is certainly true that great care needs to be taken as to what should be placed under the heading of 'culture': how far the problems of cultural diversity reflect differences in national histories, in social and economic circumstances and conditions, and in political contexts, rather than in culture *per se*. And yet the question of how to mediate amongst opposing moral and political worlds remains one of the greatest and most difficult challenges to normative discussion of what might constitute a feasible and desirable international order.

One aspect of this problem concerned the transition from a European to a global international society and the incorporation on at least slightly more equal terms of a much wider range of cultural, religious and social traditions (Bull and Watson, 1984). Here the optimists can point to the alacrity with which those Third World leaders who had so vehemently denounced imperialist international law came to appreciate its benefits (as had French, Soviet and Chinese revolutionary leaders before them). Being mostly weak it made great sense to buy into the political advantages that sovereign statehood provided and such protection as international legal rules might afford. Moreover, as Robert Jackson and Christopher Clapham have shown, external support and access to the instruments of juridical statehood played major roles in the battle for domestic survival (Clapham, 1996; Jackson and Rosberg, 1982a, 1982b).

And yet, as the international legal order moves in more solidarist and transnational directions and as the 'waterline of sovereignty' is lowered, so the political salience of societal difference rises. International rules relating to human rights, to the rights of peoples and minorities, to an expanding range of economic and environmental issues impinge very deeply on the domestic organization of society. Divergent values also become more salient as the legal order moves down from high-minded sloganizing towards detailed and extremely intrusive operational rules in each of these areas and towards stronger means of implementation. And divergent values come into sharper focus as inequalities of power grow more extreme and as the debate on 'Western values' meshes with debates on US hegemony.

Finally, the stakes have risen substantially. The capacity to opt out of what was previously a largely consent-based legal system has declined. Refusal to accept either non-derogable core legal norms or those norms that are particularly prized by powerful states run the risk of being branded a 'rogue' or 'pariah' state. And the post-Cold War period witnessed a revival of formal or informal criteria by which full membership of international society is to be judged. All of these developments have magnified a fundamental tension in the character of the international legal order: between sets of rules that seek to mediate amongst different values and those that seek to promote and enforce a single set of universal values. The political problems are, of course, still more acute when the purportedly universal values are those of the most powerful states.

Values also enter the picture because of the role that they play in explaining cooperation. One aspect has to do with the degree to which successful cooperation may depend on some prior sense of community. Rationalist models of cooperation may indeed explain how cooperation is possible once the parties have come to believe that they form part of a shared project or community in which there is a common interest that can be furthered by cooperative behaviour. They assume the accepted legitimacy of the players; a common language for bargaining; a shared perception of potential gains;

and some mechanism for at least potentially securing contracting. Once there is a common identification of, and commitment to, some kind of moral community (however minimalist in character) within which perceptions of potential common interest can emerge, then there may indeed be prudential reasons for the players collectively to cooperate. But rational prudence alone cannot explain the initiation of the game and why each player individually might choose to begin to cooperate. Rationalist approaches neglect the factors that explain how and why contracting is possible in the first place and the potential barriers that can block the emergence of any such a shared project.

The role of values in rational action is complex and difficult. As Michael Hechter argues, values are *ex ante* reasons for taking action, or relatively general and durable internal criteria for taking and evaluating action (Hechter, 1994). Whereas rationality is conditional and future oriented, values are the product of history. They are what differentiates one society from another and one international system from another. They might indeed be incommensurable, or, more often, they may shape the meanings of rational action in ways that can either help or hinder cooperative endeavours. Offer has, for example, demonstrated how values and rational action can be combined in his analysis of how codes and notions of honour pervaded the cultural script of pre-1914 Europe and how this script in turn shaped understandings of how the game of power politics should be played and what constituted 'rational action' (Offer, 1995: 213–41).

In some areas, such as human rights, the potential importance of differing societal and cultural values has been extensively debated and analysed (see Chapter 27 in this volume). But the relevance and frequent intractability of these problems extends well beyond human rights. Thus the politics of security is not only driven by problems of trust and credible contracting but also by deep disputes as to which values are to be incorporated into understandings of security and as to whose security is to be promoted (states? nations? regimes? individuals?). Equally, liberal governance approaches to global environmental negotiations can easily overlook the absence of a shared cultural or cognitive script that allows the largely rhetorical consensus value of 'sustainability' to be translated into stable and effective operational rules. Or again, arguments about international trade in GMOs are not about how scientific standards of risk assessment might be applied but rather about the intrinsic validity of those standards and the criteria by which international institutions might decide upon the permissible sphere of legitimate societal difference. Culture does not necessarily matter but difference and diversity do. Understandings of world order vary enormously from one part of the world to another, reflecting differences in national and regional histories, in social and economic circumstances and conditions, and in political contexts and trajectories. Why is international order so difficult to achieve and why are common interests so hard to capture? First, because of the intractability of the problem of power in international relations. But second, because of the persistent difficulty of accommodating human diversity and the continuity of pervasive value conflict.

CONCLUSION

What is distinctive about IR is its concern with what makes the world hang together, as Ruggie puts it so nicely (Ruggie, 1998). It is a zone of academic endeavour united not by particular methods or by the insights of a single academic discipline, but rather by a concern with certain central questions. The appropriate methods and disciplinary approaches follow from these central questions and from the particular puzzles and research questions to which they give rise, and not the other way around. This chapter has focused on a series of questions related to the role of ethics and norms in international relations: How have ideas on international ethics and on the nature of a just world order evolved? How has the normative structure of international society developed and how do normative structures influence what norms are, how they operate and how they change? And how has the issue of culture and the role of cultural diversity affected the possibility of international order and conceptions of what a just world order should be like? This chapter has identified some of the major lines of enquiry that have emerged in answer to these complex issues. In all of these areas we can look back to a range of rich traditions of thought in which links between political science and other disciplines (especially international law, history and political theory) have always been apparent; and where those links are likely to gain ever greater importance in the future.

Acknowledgements

I would like to thank Carol McQueen for her research assistance with this chapter and Chris Jones for his help with the section on norms and cultural diversity.

Bibliography

Alderson, Kai and Hurrell, Andrew (eds) (2000) *Hedley Bull on International Society*. Basingstoke: Macmillan.
Archibugi, Daniele and Held, David (eds) (1995) *Cosmopolitan Democracy: An Agenda for a New World Order*. Cambridge: Polity.

Archibugi, Daniele, Held, David and Köhler, Martin (eds) (1998) *Re-Imagining Political Community: Studies in Cosmopolitan Democracy*. Cambridge: Polity.

Armstrong, David (1993) *Revolution and World Order: The Revolutionary State in International Society*. Oxford: Clarendon Press.

Aron, Raymond (1966) *Peace and War: A Theory of International Relations* (trans. Richard Howard and Annette Baker Fox). London: Weidenfeld & Nicolson.

Barry, Brian (1970) *Sociologists, Economists and Democracy*. London: Collier Macmillan.

Barry, Brian (1990) 'Social Criticism and Political Philosophy', *Philosophy & Public Affairs*, 19 (4): 360–73.

Bartelson, Jens (1995) *A Genealogy of Sovereignty*. Cambridge: Cambridge University Press.

Bauer, Joanne R. and Bell, Daniel A. (eds) (1999) *The East Asian Challenge for Human Rights*. Cambridge: Cambridge University Press.

Beitz, Charles R. (1999a) 'International Liberalism and Distributive Justice: A Survey of Recent Thought', *World Politics*, 51: 269–96.

Beitz, Charles R. ([1979] 1999b) *Political Theory and International Relations* (new edition with afterword). Princeton: Princeton University Press.

Berger, Thomas U. (1996) 'Norms, Identity, and National Security in Germany and Japan', in Peter J. Katzenstein (ed.), *The Culture of National Security: Norms and Identity in World Politics*. New York: Columbia University Press. pp. 317–56.

Biersteker, Thomas J. and Weber, Cynthia (eds) (1996) *State Sovereignty as a Social Construct*. Cambridge: Cambridge University Press.

Black, Cyril Edwin and Falk, Richard A. (eds) (1969) *The Future of the International Legal Order*. Princeton: Princeton University Press.

Booth, Ken (1979) *Strategy and Ethnocentrism*. London: Croom Helm.

Boucher, David (1997) 'Political Theory, International Theory, and the Political Theory of International Relations', in Andrew Vincent (ed.), *Political Theory: Tradition and Diversity*. Cambridge: Cambridge University Press. pp. 193–213.

Boucher, David (1998) *Political Theories of International Relations: From Thucydides to the Present*. Oxford: Oxford University Press.

Brown, Chris (1992) *International Relations Theory: New Normative Approaches*. London: Harvester Wheatsheaf.

Brunneé, Jutta and Toope, Stephen J. (2000) 'International Law and Constructivism: Elements of an Interactional Theory of International Law', *Columbia Journal of Transnational Law*, 39: 19–74.

Bull, Hedley ([1977] 1985) *The Anarchical Society: A Study of Order in World Politics*. London: Macmillan.

Bull, Hedley and Watson, Adam (eds) (1984) *The Expansion of International Society*. Oxford: Clarendon Press.

Buzan, Barry and Little, Richard (2000) *International Systems in World History: Remaking the Study of International Relations*. Oxford: Oxford University Press.

Byers, Michael (1999) *Custom, Power and the Power of Rules*. Cambridge: Cambridge University Press.

Byers, Michael (ed.) (2000) *The Role of Law in International Politics: Essays in International Relations and International Law*. Oxford: Oxford University Press.

Campbell, David and Shapiro, Michael (eds) (1999) *Moral Spaces: Rethinking Ethics and World Politics*. Minneapolis: University of Minnesota Press.

Carr, E.H. (1939) *The Twenty Years' Crisis, 1919–1939: An Introduction to the Study of International Relations*. London: Macmillan.

Cassese, Antonio (1986) *International Law in a Divided World*. Oxford: Clarendon Press.

Chayes, Abram and Chayes, Antonia Handler (1994) 'Regime Architecture: Elements and Principles', in Janne E. Nolan (ed.), *Global Engagement. Cooperation and Security in the 21st Century*. Washington, DC: Brookings Institution.

Chayes, Abram and Chayes, Antonia Handler (1995) *The New Sovereignty: Compliance with International Regulatory Agreements*. Cambridge, MA: Harvard University Press.

Clapham, Christopher S. (1996) *Africa and the International System: The Politics of State Survival*. Cambridge: Cambridge University Press.

Clark, Ian and Neumann, Iver B. (eds) (1996) *Classical Theories of International Relations*. New York: St Martin's Press.

Cochran, Molly (1999) *Normative Theory in International Relations: A Pragmatic Approach*. Cambridge: Cambridge University Press.

Cohen, Raymond (2000) 'Meaning, Interpretation and International Negotiation', *Global Society*, 14 (3): 317–35.

Coleman, James S. (1990) *Foundations of Social Theory*. Cambridge, MA: Belknap Press of Harvard University Press.

Cox, Robert W. (1986) 'Social Forces, States and World Orders: Beyond International Relations Theory', in Robert O. Keohane (ed.), *Neorealism and its Critics*. New York: Columbia University Press. pp. 204–54.

Cutler, Claire A., Haufler, Virginia and Porter, Tony (eds) (1999) *Private Authority and International Affairs*. Albany: State University of New York Press.

Der Derian, James (1987) *On Diplomacy. A Genealogy of Western Estrangement*. Oxford: Blackwell.

Diehl, Paul F. (1997) *The Politics of Global Governance: International Organizations in an Interdependent World*. Boulder: Lynne Rienner.

Doyle, Michael W. (1998) *Ways of War and Peace: Realism, Liberalism, and Socialism*. New York: W.W. Norton.

Dunne, Tim (1998) *Inventing International Society: A History of the English School*. Basingstoke: Macmillan.

Dunne, Tim and Wheeler, Nicholas J. (eds) (1999) *Human Rights in Global Politics*. Cambridge: Cambridge University Press.

Elster, Jon (1989) *The Cement of Society. A Study of Social Order*. Cambridge: Cambridge University Press.

Falk, Richard A. (1972) *This Endangered Planet: Prospects and Proposals for Human Survival*. New York: Vintage Books.

Falk, Richard A. (1975) *A Study of Future Worlds*. New York: The Free Press.

Falk, Richard A. (1999) *Predatory Globalization: A Critique*. Cambridge: Polity.

Fierke, Karin M. (1998) *Changing Games, Changing Strategies: Critical Investigations in Security*. Manchester: Manchester University Press.

Finnemore, Martha and Sikkink, Kathryn (1998) 'International Norm Dynamics and Political Change', *International Organization*, 52 (4): 887–918.

Foot, Rosemary (2000) *Rights Beyond Borders. The Global Community and the Struggle over Human Rights in China*. Oxford: Oxford University Press.

Franck, Thomas M. (1990) *The Power of Legitimacy Among Nations*. New York: Oxford University Press.

Freeden, Michael (1996) *Ideologies and Political Theory. A Conceptual Approach*. Oxford: Oxford University Press.

Frost, Mervyn (1996) *Ethics in International Relations*. Cambridge: Cambridge University Press.

Frost, Mervyn (1998) 'A Turn Not Taken: Ethics in IR at the Millennium', *Review of International Studies*, 24 (Special Issue): 119–32.

George, Jim (1994) *Discourse of Global Politics: A Critical (Re)Introduction to International Relations*. Boulder: Lynne Rienner.

Goldstein, Judith and Keohane, Robert O. (1993) *Ideas and Foreign Policy: Beliefs, Institutions, and Political Change*. Ithaca: Cornell University Press.

Goldstein, Judith L., Kahler, Miles, Keohane, Robert O. and Slaughter, Anne-Marie (eds) (2001) *Legalization and World Politics*. Cambridge, MA: MIT Press.

Grewe, Wilhelm Georg (2000) *The Epochs of International Law* (trans. Michael Byers). Berlin: Walter de Gruyter.

Halliday, Fred (1999) *Revolution and World Politics: The Rise and Fall of the Sixth Great Power*. Basingstoke: Macmillan.

Hardin, Russell (1995) *One For All: The Logic of Group Conflict*. Princeton: Princeton University Press.

Harrison, Lawrence E. and Huntingdon, Samuel P. (2000) *Culture Matters: How Values Shape Human Progress*. New York: Basic Books.

Hasenclever, Andreas, Mayer, Peter and Rittberger, Volker (1997) *Theories of International Regimes*. Cambridge: Cambridge University Press.

Hechter, Michael (1994), 'The Role of Values in Rational Choice Theory', *Rationality and Society*, 6 (3): 318–33.

Held, David (1995) *Democracy and the Global Order: From the Modern State to Cosmopolitan Governance*. Cambridge: Polity.

Held, David and McGrew, Anthony (eds) (2000) *The Global Transformations Reader: An Introduction to the Globalization Debate*. Cambridge: Polity.

Held, David, McGrew, Anthony, Goldblatt, David and Perraton, Jonathan (1999) *Global Transformations: Politics, Economics and Culture*. Cambridge: Polity.

Hoffmann, Stanley (1985) *Duties Beyond Borders: On the Limits and Possibilities of Ethical International Politics*. Syracuse: Syracuse University Press.

Hoffman, Stanley (1987) *Janus and Minerva: Essays in the Theory and Practice of International Politics*. Boulder: Westview.

Hoffmann, Stanley (1998) *World Disorders: Troubled Peace in the Post-Cold War Era*. Lanham: Rowman and Littlefield.

Hollis, Martin (1991) 'Why Elster is Stuck and Needs to Recover his Faith', *London Review of Books*, 24 January: 13.

Hont, Istvan (1994) 'The Permanent Crisis of a Divided Mankind: "Contemporary Crisis of the Nation State" in Historical Perspective', *Political Studies*, 42: 166–231.

Huntingdon, Samuel (1997) *The Clash of Civilizations and the Remaking of World Order*. New York: Simon & Schuster.

Hurd, Ian (1999) 'Legitimacy and Authority in International Politics', *International Organization*, 53 (2): 379–408.

Hurrell, Andrew (2001) 'Global Inequality and International Institutions', *Metaphilosophy*, 32 (1/2): 34–57.

Inoue, Kyoko (1991) *MacArthur's Japanese Constitution: A Linguistic and Cultural Study of its Making*. Chicago: Chicago University Press.

Jackson, Robert H. (2000) *The Global Covenant: Human Conduct in a World of States*. Oxford: Oxford University Press.

Jackson, Robert H. and Rosberg, Carl G. (1982a) *Personal Rule in Black Africa: Prince, Autocrat, Prophet, Tyrant*. Berkeley: University of California Press.

Jackson, Robert H. and Rosberg, Carl G. (1982b) 'Why Africa's Weak States Persist: The Empirical and the Juridical in Statehood', *World Politics*, 35: 1–24.

Johnston, Alastair Iain (1995) *Cultural Realism, Strategic Culture and Grand Strategy in Chinese History*. Princeton: Princeton University Press.

Johnston, Alastair Iain (1996) 'Cultural Realism and Strategy in Maoist China', in Peter J. Katzenstein (ed.), *The Culture of National Security: Norms and Identity in World Politics*. New York: Columbia University Press. pp. 216–70.

Katzenstein, Peter J. (1996a) *Cultural Norms and National Security: Police and Military in Postwar Japan*. Ithaca: Cornell University Press.

Katzenstein, Peter J. (ed.) (1996b) *The Culture of National Security: Norms and Identity in World Politics*. New York: Columbia University Press.

Keck, Margaret and Sikkink, Kathryn (1998) *Activists Beyond Borders: Advocacy Networks in International Politics*. Ithaca: Cornell University Press.

Keohane, Robert O. (1997) 'International Relations and International Law: Two Optics', *Harvard International Law Review*, 38 (2): 487–502.

Keohane, Robert O. (2001) 'Governance in a Partially Globalized World', *American Political Science Review*, 95 (2): 1–13.

Kingsbury, Benedict (1988) 'The Concept of Compliance as a Function of Competing Conceptions of International

Law', *Michigan Journal of International Law*, 19: 345–75.

Knutsen, Torbjorn L. (1992) *A History of International Relations Theory: An Introduction.* Manchester: Manchester University Press.

Koh, Harold H. (1996) 'Transnational Legal Process', *Nebraska Law Review*, 75: 181–207.

Koh, Harold H. (1997) 'Why do Nations Obey International Law?', *Yale Law Journal*, 106 (8): 2598–659.

Komatsu, Keiichiro (1999) *Origins of the Pacific War and the Importance of 'Magic'.* Richmond: Japan Library.

Koskenniemi, Martti. (1989) *From Apology to Utopia: The Structures of International Legal Argument.* Helsinki: Lakimiesliiton Kustannus.

Kowert, Paul and Legro, Jeffrey (1996) 'Norms, Identity, and Their Limits: A Theoretical Response', in Peter J. Katzenstein (ed.), *The Culture of National Security: Norms and Identity in World Politics.* New York: Columbia University Press. pp. 451–97.

Krasner, Stephen D. (1999) *Sovereignty: Organized Hypocrisy.* Princeton: Princeton University Press.

Kratochwil, Friedrich V. (1989) *Rules, Norms and Decisions: On the Conditions of Practical and Legal Reasoning in International Relations and Domestic Affairs.* Cambridge: Cambridge University Press.

Kratochwil, Friedrich V. (2000) 'How Do Norms Matter?', in Michael Byers (ed.), *The Role of Law in International Politics: Essays in International Relations and in International Law.* Oxford: Oxford University Press. pp. 35–68.

Kratochwil, Friedrich V. and Ruggie, John Gerard (1986) 'International Organization: A State of the Art on an Art of the State', *International Organization*, 40 (4): 753–76.

Lapid, Yosef and Kratochwil, Friedrich (eds) (1996) *The Return of Culture and Identity in International Relations Theory.* Boulder: Lynne Rienner.

Linklater, Andrew (1998) *The Transformation of Political Community: Ethical Foundations of the Post-Westphalian Era.* Cambridge: Polity.

Linklater, Andrew (1999) 'Transforming Political Community: A Response to the Critics', *Review of International Studies*, 25 (1): 165–75.

Mapel, David and Nardin, Terry (eds) (1992) *Traditions of International Ethics.* Cambridge: Cambridge University Press.

Mapel, David and Nardin, Terry (1998) *International Society: Diverse Ethical Perspectives.* Princeton: Princeton University Press.

March, James G. and Olsen, Johan P. (1998) 'The Institutionalist Dynamics of International Political Orders', *International Organization*, 52 (4): 943–70.

Mayall, James (2000) *World Politics: Progress and Its Limits.* Cambridge: Polity.

McCormick, John P. (1999) *Carl Schmitt's Critique of Liberalism.* Cambridge: Cambridge University Press.

Meyer, John W., Boli, John, Thomas, George M. and Ramirez, Francisco O. (eds) (1997) 'World Society and the Nation State', *American Journal of Sociology*, 103 (1): 144–81.

Miller, David (1990) 'The Resurgence of Political Theory', *Political Studies*, 38: 421–37.

Miller, David (1995a) *On Nationality.* Oxford: Clarendon Press.

Miller, David (1995b) 'Introduction', in David Miller and Michael Walzer (eds), *Pluralism, Justice, and Equality.* Oxford: Oxford University Press.

Miller, David (1999) *Principles of Social Justice.* Cambridge, MA: Harvard University Press.

Miller, David and Walzer, Michael (eds) (1995) *Pluralism, Justice and Equality.* Oxford: Oxford University Press.

Miller, Lynn H. (1990) *Global Order: Values and Power in International Politics*, 2nd edn. Boulder: Westview.

Musil, Robert (1995) *The Man Without Qualities* (trans. Sophie Wilkins and Burton Pike). London: Picador.

Nabulsi, Karma (1999) *Traditions of War: Occupation, Resistance and the Law.* Oxford: Oxford University Press.

Nardin, Terry (1983) *Law, Morality, and the Relations of States.* Princeton: Princeton University Press.

Nye, Joseph S. and Donahue, John D. (eds) (2000) *Governance in a Globalizing World.* Washington, DC: Brookings.

O'Brien, Richard, Goetz, Anne Marie, Scholte, Jan Aart and Williams, Marc (2000) *Contesting Global Governance.* Cambridge: Cambridge University Press.

Offer, Avner (1995) 'Going to War in 1914: A Matter of Honour?', *Politics and Society*, 23 (2): 213–41.

O'Neill, Onora (1996) *Towards Justice and Virtue: A Constructive Account of Practical Reasoning.* Cambridge: Cambridge University Press.

O'Neill, Onora (2000) 'Four Models of Practical Reasoning', in Onora O'Neill *Bounds of Justice.* Cambridge: Cambridge University Press.

Onuf, Nicholas Greenwood (1989*) World of Our Making: Rules and Rule in Social Theory and International Relations.* Columbia, SC: University of South Carolina Press.

Osiander, Andreas (1994) *The States System of Europe, 1640–1990.* Oxford: Clarendon Press.

Osiander, Andreas (2001) 'The Westphalian Myth', *International Organization*, 55 (2): 251–87.

Pagden, Anthony (1995) *Lords of All the World: Ideologies of Empire in Spain, Britain, and France c. 1500–c. 1800.* New Haven: Yale University Press.

Parekh, Bhikhu (1996) 'Political Theory: Traditions in Political Philosophy', in Robert E. Goodin and Hans-Dieter Klingemann (eds), *A New Handbook of Political Science.* Oxford: Oxford University Press. pp. 503–18.

Philpott, Daniel (1999) 'Westphalia Authority and International Society', *Political Studies*, 47: 566–89.

Philpott, Daniel (2000) *Revolutions in Sovereignty.* Princeton: Princeton University Press.

Pogge, Thomas W. (1989) *Realizing Rawls.* Ithaca: Cornell University Press.

Rawls, John (1955) 'Two Concepts of Rules', *The Philosophical Review*, 44: 3–32.

Rawls, John (1971) *A Theory of Justice.* Oxford: Oxford University Press.

Rawls, John (1993) *Political Liberalism*. New York: Columbia University Press.

Rawls, John (1999) *The Law of Peoples*. Cambridge, MA: Harvard University Press.

Raz, Joseph ([1975]1999) *Practical Reason and Norms*. Oxford: Oxford University Press.

Reinecke, Wolfgang H. (1998) *Global Public Policy: Government without Government?* Washington, DC: Brookings.

Rengger, Nicholas (2000) *International Relations, Political Theory and the Problem of Order*. London: Routledge.

Reus-Smit, Christian (1999) *The Moral Purpose of the State: Culture, Social Identity, and Institutional Rationality in International Relations*. Princeton: Princeton University Press.

Ronit, Karsten and Schneider, Volker (1999) 'Global Governance through Private Organizations', *Goverance*, 12 (3): 243–66.

Rorty, Richard (1993) 'Human Rights, Rationality, and Sentimentality', in Stephen Shute and Susan Hurley (eds), *On Human Rights*. New York: HarperCollins. pp. 111–34.

Rothschild, E. (1995) 'What is Security?', *Daedalus*, 124 (3): 53–98.

Ruggie, John Gerard (1998) *Constructing the World Polity: Essays on International Institutionalization*. London: Routledge.

Schmidt, Brian (1998) *The Political Discourse of Anarchy: A Disciplinary History of International Relations*. Albany: State University of New York Press.

Scholte, Jan Aart (2000) *Globalization: A Critical Introduction*. New York: St Martin's Press.

Searle, John R., (1995) *The Construction of Social Reality*. London: Penguin Books.

Sen, Amartya (1992) *Inequality Reexamined*. Oxford: Clarendon Press.

Singer, Peter (1972) 'Famine, Affluence, and Morality', *Philosophy and Public Affairs*, 1: 229–43.

Slaughter, Anne-Marie (1995) 'International Law in a World of Liberal States', *European Journal of International Law*, 6: 503–38.

Slaughter, Anne-Marie (1997) 'The Real New World Order', *Foreign Affairs*, 76 (5): 183–97.

Slaughter, Anne-Marie (2000) 'Governing the Global Economy Through Government Nerworks', in Michael Byers (ed.), *The Role of Law in International Politics*. Oxford: Oxford University Press.

Smith, Rogers M. (1997) *Civic Ideals. Conflicting Visions of Citizenship in US History*. New Haven: Yale University Press.

Smith, Steve (1992) 'The Self-Images of a Discipline: A Genealogy of International Relations Theory', in Ken Booth and Steve Smith (eds), *International Relations Theory Today*. Cambridge: Polity. pp. 1–37.

Snyder, Jack (1977) *The Soviet Strategic Culture* (Rand Report R-2154-AF).

Steiner, George (1992) *After Babel: Aspects of Language and Translation*, 2nd edn. Oxford: Oxford University Press.

Stone Sweet, Alec (1999) 'Judicialization and the Construction of Governance', *Comparative Political Studies*, 32 (2): 147–84.

Teson, Fernando R. (1994) *Humanitarian Intervention: An Inquiry into Law and Morality*, 2nd edn. Dobbs Ferry: Transnational Publishers.

Teson, Fernando R. (1998) *A Philosophy of International Law*. Boulder: Westview.

Teubner, Gunther (ed.) (1997) *Global Law Without a State*. Aldershot: Dartmouth Publishing.

Thomson, Janna (1992) *Justice and World Order. A Philosophical Inquiry*. London: Routledge.

Tuck, Richard (1999) *The Rights of War and Peace: Political Thought and the International Order from Grotius to Kant*. Oxford: Oxford University Press.

UNDP (1998) *Human Development Report 1998*. Oxford: Oxford University Press.

Vincent, R.J. (1974) *Nonintervention and International Order*. Princeton: Princeton University Press.

Walker, Robert B.J. (1993) *Inside/Outside: International Relations as Political Theory*. Cambridge: Cambridge University Press.

Walker, Robert B.J. (1999) 'The Hierarchicalization of Political Community', *Review of International Studies*, 25: 151–6.

Walzer, Michael (1977) *Just and Unjust Wars: A Moral Argument with Historical Illustrations*. New York: Basic Books.

Walzer, Michael (1994) *Thick and Thin: A Moral Argument at Home and Abroad*. Notre Dame: University of Notre Dame Press.

Watson, Adam (1992) *The Evolution of International Society: A Comparative Historical Analysis*. London: Routledge.

Wendt, Alexander (1999) *Social Theory of International Politics*. Cambridge: Cambridge University Press.

Wheeler, Nicholas J. (2000) *Saving Strangers: Humanitarian Intervention in International Society*. Oxford: Oxford University Press.

Wierbicka, A. (ed.) (1997) *Understanding Cultures Through Their Key Words: English, Russian, Polish, German, Japanese*. Oxford: Oxford University Press.

Wight, Martin (1966) 'Why Is There No International Theory?' in Martin Wight and Herbert Butterfield (eds), *Diplomatic Investigations*. London: Allen & Unwin. pp. 17–34.

Wight, Martin (1977) *System of States*. Leicester: Leicester University Press.

Woods, Ngaire (1999) 'Order, Globalization, and Inequality in World Politics', in Andrew Hurrell and Ngaire Woods (eds), *Inequality, Globalization, and World Politics*. Oxford: Oxford University Press. pp. 8–35.

Young, Oran (1999) *Governance in World Affairs*. New York: Cornell University Press.

Part Two

CONCEPTS AND CONTEXT IN INTERNATIONAL RELATIONS

8

State, Sovereignty and Territory

THOMAS J. BIERSTEKER

The concepts of state, sovereignty and territory are central to the study and practice of international relations. For generations of scholars, the concept of the state has been the principal subject and unit of analysis in international politics (Morgenthau, 1948; Waltz, 1979). The principle of sovereignty has provided one of the central bases for order in international relations, particularly in its codified form since the end of the Thirty Years War (Hinsley, 1986). Disputes over territory or struggles over territorial control have figured in virtually every major inter-state war of the past hundred years (Agnew, 1998; Mackinder, 1904).

However, forms of state, meanings of sovereignty and conceptions of territoriality are neither fixed nor constant across time and place. The absolutist states of the seventeenth century are profoundly different from the liberal states of the nineteenth and twentieth centuries. The meaning of the sovereignty of states that prevailed prior to the French Revolution bears only a limited resemblance to the application and assertions of sovereignty today. The formidably armed territorial boundaries that separated and defined the major states of Europe throughout most of the twentieth century were fundamentally redefined within the European Union by the beginning of the twenty-first.

One of the most important analytical challenges for scholars of international relations is to identify different meanings of state, sovereignty and territory, and to understand their origins, comprehend their changes of meaning, analyze their interrelationships, and characterize their transformations. The purpose of this chapter is to illustrate important changes of meaning of these central concepts over the course of the twentieth century and to suggest some ways of thinking about them.

The concepts of state, sovereignty and territory are each socially constructed. They are defined, and redefined, by the rules, actions and practices of different agents, including in the case of states, by themselves. An examination of the contestation of different practices, resistances, rules, norms, legal challenges and public justifications provides important insights into the changing composition and definition of state, sovereignty and territoriality. It is for this reason that I will take a decidedly constructivist approach to this review.

State and sovereignty are mutually constitutive concepts. As F.H. Hinsley reminds us, 'In a word, the origin and history of the concept of sovereignty are closely linked with the nature, the origin and the history of the state' (Hinsley, 1986: 2). States define the meaning of sovereignty through their engagement in practices of mutual recognition, practices that define both themselves and each other. At the same time, the mutual recognition of claims of sovereignty is an important element in the definition of the state itself (although there is a school of thought within international law that maintains that states can exist without formal recognition by other states) (Shaw, 1997: 146–7). Both the concepts of state and sovereignty also have territorial conceptions associated with them. The idealized, Westphalian state has distinct boundaries, and the Westphalian ideal of sovereignty stresses the principle of the inviolability of those borders.

The modern state and sovereignty have been co-determinitive since their common origins as concepts and associated practices in the sixteenth and seventeenth centuries. But while they have always been closely associated, they have not remained constant or been mutually constitutive in the same ways over time (Bartelson, 1995). That is, different forms of state have constituted different meanings of sovereignty and been associated with different conceptions of territoriality over time and across place.

Broad generalizations and timeless categorizations of forms of state, types of sovereignty and concepts of territory are highly problematic. Thus, I will attempt to ground – to historicize and to contextualize – this discussion with consideration of different twentieth-century forms of state, changing meanings of sovereignty and conceptions of territory. The preceding introductory comments suggest how easy it is to demonstrate changes of meaning over a broad range of time (contrasting the sixteenth-century absolutist state with the nineteenth-century liberal state, for example). However, I want to illustrate changes of meaning over a more limited time span. This should be considered a harder test of the principal thesis about the changing meaning of our core concepts. That is, if we can see significant changes of meaning over the course of a single century, it should sensitize us further to the importance of historicizing and contextualizing the concepts over longer time periods.

This characterization of changes in meaning over the course of the twentieth century is being made for illustrative purposes. I do not intend to imply a unitary directionality to the changes described in the next section or to deny the possibility of dramatic reversals, change and/or transformation. Indeed, as I will illustrate, there was evidence at the end of the twentieth century of states attempting to strike back at (or reverse) the redefinition of their sovereignty . Rather, I want to illustrate qualitative changes in meaning across time and place and to suggest how we should try to comprehend the changing meaning of some of the core concepts of our discipline.

HISTORICIZING AND CONTEXTUALIZING STATE, SOVEREIGNTY AND TERRITORIALITY

Forms of State

It is common for scholars and practitioners of international relations to employ concepts of state (or to invoke lessons from the history of state practices) as if the term described a fixed and unchanging institutional phenomenon. This tendency was especially evident during the latter half of the twentieth century, when scholars first began to articulate the need for 'a scientific approach' to the subject in the 1940s (Carr, 1939; Morgenthau, 1948), a movement that was developed further by the behavioral scientific 'revolution' that emerged in the 1950s and 1960s (Kaplan, 1962; Singer, 1961). Neorealists

writing in the 1970s and 1980s are commonly associated with broadly positivistic assertions about states and about state behavior across time and place (Gilpin, 1981; Waltz, 1979). For Kenneth Waltz, the enduring anarchic character of international politics accounts for the 'striking sameness' in the quality of international life over the millennia (Waltz, 1979: 53). While for Robert Gilpin, states 'throughout history' have had as a principal objective 'the conquest of territory in order to advance economic, security, and other interests' (Gilpin, 1981: 23).

However, the tendency to treat states as fundamentally similar units across time and place is by no means restricted to neorealist analyses. It is also commonly found among neoliberals (Keohane, 1984), contemporary behavioralists (Russett and Starr, 1985), and even among some constructivists (Wendt, 1999: 8–9).[1] Not every scholar consistently employs the word 'state' to describe the core units of international relations. Although he is commonly associated with state centrism, Hans Morgenthau wrote more extensively about 'nations' than about 'states' in his classic text *Politics among Nations*. Nevertheless, the Weberian roots of his core unit of analysis – the state – are both clearly recognizable and firmly grounded in Morgenthau's classic work (Smith, 1986: 15–16).

While scholars of international relations commonly recognize and acknowledge the presence of a great variety of state forms over time, an explicit analysis of the variation and its implications rarely figures prominently in their theories. The lure of positivist generalization either proves too seductive, or the complexity of differentiation turns out to be too difficult to accommodate.

The literature on the nature of the state typically distinguishes between its origins and absolutist forms in the sixteenth century (Bodin, [1576] 1962; Hobbes, [1651] 1958; Machiavelli, 1965) and the variation in its modern forms. This includes variations from the era of popular sovereignty to the nineteenth-century liberal state, the twentieth-century totalitarian state, and what some have described as the late twentieth-century 'post modern' state (Held, 1983). Perry Anderson (1974) has chronicled the origins and functions of the absolutist state, while Charles Tilly (1975), Anthony Giddens (1985) and Michael Mann (1988) have each described the role of war in the making of the modern state. Douglass North (1981) has emphasized the early state's critical role in establishment and enforcement of property rights, central to the development of capitalism. The relationship between the absolutist state and the origins and functioning of the classical European balance of power system has also been examined extensively in the scholarly literature (Claude, 1989; Little, 1989; Schroeder, 1989). The absolutist nature of the state in the sixteenth and seventeenth century was highly correlated with the diplomatic practices of the period, especially the ease with which diplomats and heads of state were able to settle disputes with the division, re-division and allocation of territory. This absolutist residue is a characteristic of the balance of power system that has troubled democratic leaders of the liberal state throughout the twentieth century. Woodrow Wilson abhorred the political immorality of the balance of power system prevalent at the beginning of the twentieth century and preferred open diplomacy to secrecy, and self-determination over the 'unconscionable bartering of helpless and innocent peoples'. The tension between the frequently illiberal practices of balance of power diplomacy and the proclivities of democratic liberal states has persisted throughout the twentieth century (Craig and George, 1995).

The very conceptualization of the meaning of the modern state has generated extensive scholarly and political debate. Max Weber's conception of the state as an institution that possesses a monopoly over the legitimate means of coercion and the ability to extract tax revenues has been widely utilized throughout the scholarship of international relations, either explicitly or implicitly (Weber, 1949). The Weberian conception of the state has been particularly influential on the scholarly tradition identified with political realism (Smith, 1986). Indeed, Weber's construct of the state is central to all of the works of the classical, postwar realists, from E.H. Carr and Hans Morgenthau, to John Herz, Reinhold Niebuhr and Henry Kissinger.[2]

Alternatives to Weberian conceptions of the state have been provided by scholars working within the Marxist tradition. Karl Marx and Friedrich Engels anticipated the eventual withering away of the state, and in some of their early work the state is characterized as little more than the executive committee of the ruling class (Marx and Engels, [1848] 1978). As such, the state could have no autonomous role, independent of the interests of the ruling bourgeoisie.

There is enough ambiguity in the broader corpus of Marx's early work (as well as in the collected works of more than a few so-called 'revisionists') to ensure the emergence of other interpretations of the state within the broader Marxist tradition. Nicos Poulantzas argued that the state could theoretically work against the ruling class, if it served the broader purpose of preserving capitalism as a system (Poulantzas, 1975). Peter Evans and many Latin American dependentistas argued that the state could, in some instances, act relatively independently of dominant social forces and serve its own material interests (Evans, 1979) – a point shared by statist scholarship from outside the Marxist tradition (Evans et al., 1985; Wade, 1987). Suffice it to say, that there have been significantly different conceptions of the state over time, and that there have been significant disagreements about the conceptualization of the state construct. There is enough

variation at least to render problematic the tendency within much of international relations to assume the constancy of the state as a unit across time and space.

Discussions of the modern state sometimes conflate the concepts of state, nation and nation-state. The three are analytically separable, and the chapter by Lars-Erik Cederman in this volume explores them at some length. While there is no unanimity on the definition of the state, both the Weberian and Marxist conceptions of the state regard it as a set of institutions and relationships of governance closely connected to, but analytically distinct from (and partially independent of) society. Nations consist of peoples, often with a shared language, history and identity, who might find themselves contained within states, divided between them, or granted self-determination over their own affairs in the form of the nation-state. The coincidence of nation and state in the form of the nation-state has more often than not proven to be an ephemeral phenomenon, however.

It is one thing to establish changes in the form, meaning and conceptualization of the state over time, but yet another to establish its implications for our analysis and understanding of international relations. The basic affinities between the absolutist state and the operation of the classical European balance of power system have already been suggested. Martin Wight identified relationships between the emergence of other forms of state – revolutionary, democratic state forms – and the international systems that developed in later periods (Wight, 1977). More recently, Mlada Bukovansky has illustrated how the French and American revolutions produced new forms of state that challenged the dynastic principles that governed the international system during the eighteenth and the early nineteenth centuries (Bukovansky, 1997, 1999). These were principles that had been derived from, and were in many ways a continuation of, principles associated historically with the absolutist state. However, enlightenment ideas played an important role in the transformation of the state and of the international political culture that was shaped and formed by state interactions.

It would be possible to trace changes in the meaning of the modern state and their implications for our understanding of the states system from their origins in the sixteenth and seventeenth centuries (both the origins of the modern state and the origins of the modern states system) (Hall, 1999). However, we can also illustrate the importance of changes in the meaning of states with more contemporary illustrations drawn exclusively from the twentieth century. The great powers (and their imitators) were more than mere states or nation-states at the beginning of the century: they were empires. It was not until the middle of the twentieth century that the nation-state form was truly globalized, following the break-up of formal empires and the transformative process of decolonization. By the century's end, we had evidence of both 'failed' states in Africa and the emergence of a distinctly different polity (or a potential 'superstate') in Europe. Thus, while states remained central to international politics throughout the course of the twentieth century, the meaning of 'state' has not remained fixed in time or place.

At the beginning of the twentieth century, empires were the 'natural' state form for the great powers. The British, French, Austro-Hungarian, Ottoman and Russian empires governed most of the world, while Germany, Japan and the United States aspired to empires of their own. According to J.A. Hobson, it was an era 'of competitive forms of imperialism' (Hobson, 1902). World maps reflected empires as the principal units in territorial terms, and the language of geopolitics and imperialism tended to take the imperial state for granted. Sir Halford Mackinder worried in 1904 that if Russia, the pre-eminent land power, were to ally with Germany, 'the empire of the world would then be in sight' (Mackinder, 1904: 436). Advocates of imperial expansion, from Jules Ferry in France to Cecil Rhodes in England, asserted the economic, political and strategic benefits of imperialism, along with the moral imperative of assuming 'the selfless burden of empire' (Kipling, 1903). Imperial expansion was natural and unproblematic, while primacy was given to the physical occupation and possession of territory (a point to which I will return later). The 'hierarchy of civilizations' ensured that the world was very much a European world (with Europe on top), and there was widespread belief in the benefits to be derived from the historically progressive aggregation of political units, from nations to states to empires. Adam Watson has described this in terms of 'the worldwide expansion of European international society' (Watson, 1992).

The beginning of the twentieth century also saw the emergence of mass politics, and increasingly, at least in some parts of the world, the emergence of mass, democratic politics (Barraclough, 1967). As urbanization and industrialization both advanced, labor became increasingly mobilized and eventually became a political force that generated reform movements within liberal democratic states, and revolutionary upheavals in more autocratic places like Russia and China. Similar forms of mass mobilization and proto-nationalist movements began to emerge throughout the colonial possessions of the empires by the 1920s, from Africa and South Asia, to the Middle East and East Asia. It was the presence of these movements for reform and self-determination, in combination with the great world wars of the twentieth century, that would lead eventually to the demise of the imperial form of the twentieth-century state.

The primacy of the nation-state form is most strikingly apparent during the middle years of the twentieth century, from the 1930s through the 1970s. The 'welfare state', the 'territorial state', the 'national security state', and the 'developmental state' are all prominent constructs of the middle part of the twentieth century. The decolonization process following the Second World War distributed the nation-state form throughout the territories of the former colonial empires. At the beginning of the twentieth century, Sir Halford Mackinder commented on the significance of the end of the age of exploration (that had begun with Columbus) and the emergence of a period where 'there is scarcely a region left for pegging out a claim of ownership' (Mackinder, 1904: 421). Most of this remaining territory was claimed by empires, a fact that prompted V.I. Lenin to observe that this would inevitably prompt conflict over the division and re-division of territory, since wars between rising and declining capitalist imperial powers would recur (Lenin, 1939). By the middle of the twentieth century, virtually all the empires were gone, and the world was increasingly divided into nation-states. Where new states contained more than one nation, new 'nation-building' efforts predominated.

One of the best ways to illustrate the change in the meaning of the state in the twentieth century is to examine changing norms about the legitimate role of the state, both in the economy and in the provision of security. Between the First and the Second World Wars there was a genuine contestation between radically different alternative political forms of the state, from the welfare-nationalist state to the alternatives of the fascist state and the socialist state (Cox, 1987). Each of these three different state forms entailed substantial increases in the degree of the state's intervention in the economy (Gerschenkron, 1962; Polanyi, 1957). It was not until the end of the twentieth century that there were significant initiatives to reverse the degree of state economic intervention in the economy (Biersteker, 1992).

The struggle between different state forms, resulting in the defeat of fascism during the Second World War, and subsequently the defeat of socialism at the end of the Cold War, led to substantial increases in the security apparatus of the twentieth-century nation-state (Lasswell, 1941). These are increases that have often proven more resilient than the increases in state economic intervention, particularly in much of the developing world. The imitative behavior of the United States and the Soviet Union during the Cold War led to replications of each other's tactics, behavior and strategies, although in the US case it was tempered by its anti-statist tradition (Friedberg, 2000). At the end of the Cold War, both the United States and the Soviet Union were spending significant amounts on the maintenance of the national security apparatus of the state.

Another indication of the predominance of the nation-state form at the middle of the twentieth century is contained in the Charter of the United Nations. The UN Charter is founded on the defense of the inviolable norm of non-intervention into the affairs of member nation-states, inscribed in Article II, Chapter 7 of the Charter. The United Nations as an institution has, since its founding in 1945, been strongly associated with asserting the rights and defending the concerns of its member states. It is a profoundly statist institution.

Although the nation-state form was universalized during the middle part of the twentieth century, not every observer viewed this development as benign. The intense nationalism associated with the origins of the Second World War also contributed to a global search for institutions that would transcend the nation-state construct, from an interest in regional integration (Deutsch et al., 1957; Haas, 1958) to the expansion of global institutions more generally (Ruggie, 1993a).

By the end of the twentieth century, the intense statism associated with its middle decades began to show evidence of waning. There were substantial reductions in the degree and nature of state intervention in the economy, beginning in the late 1970s. By the early 1990s this transformation was virtually universalized, as the global expansion of capitalism was achieved under the banner of 'economic reform' and the neoliberal state. The national security state was increasingly challenged by the transparency of the Internet, but it was doing its best to defend itself by enhancing its surveillance capacity. Governance had become increasingly complex (Held, 1995).

At the same time, the failure of the explicit state-building project of the post-colonial era was becoming increasingly apparent in many parts of Africa. The considerable promise of post-colonial development and nation-building was replaced by recurring crises of development and the specter of state failure and incapacity. Also at the same time, Europe, the birthplace of the nation-state, was moving away from the separate nation-state form, in the direction of a polity whose definition remains ambiguously situated between a collection of nation-states and a single, superstate (Wallace, 1983). While there is no consensus on a label for the modal state form at the beginning of the twenty-first century, candidates range from the self-restrained, neoliberal or postmodern state to the defective, retreating or failed state.

Up to this point, most of the discussion about different forms of state has focused on its change of meaning over time. The form of the state has changed across the centuries, and it has also shown significant changes within them. However, not only does the form of the state change over time, but it also changes across location, place and space. That is, the salience, importance and meaning of state economic intervention and the nature of the relationship between state and society are profoundly different in different places on the globe at the same point in time. The differences are most apparent when we compare the salience of the nation-state in contemporary Western Europe with its contemporary salience throughout most of the developing world. The contrasts between Europe and North America on the one hand, and Asia on the other, are equally striking, regardless of level of development. These contextual differences have implications both for the ways we need to understand the nature of state economic intervention, as well as for the nature of the relationship between state and society (Katzenstein, 1978).

In the final analysis, why should differences between twentieth-century forms of state – between the imperial state and the nation-state, for example – concern us? Why should this be of interest to students of international relations in particular? State forms matter, because they provide essential forms of political identity, around which people mobilize, kill others and commit their lives. The defense of empire is far more abstract and qualitatively different from the defense of the nation-state. State forms also play a critical role in the construction of the culture of international relations. The culture of international relations during the era of empires, balance of power geopolitics and competitive imperialisms was significantly different from the culture of international relations during the high point of the nation-state, with its imperfect norms of non-intervention and multilateralism. Different state forms can also define the likelihood of international conflict. This is especially the case, if advocates of the democratic peace hypothesis are correct about their assessment of the probability of conflict among democratic states.

It may often appear to be convenient to ignore differences in state form over time and place, in an effort to increase the number of historical cases from which to generalize about international relations. However, the gains in terms of increased sample size may not justify the losses in terms of the misunderstanding of important international phenomena, a point to which we will return in the conclusion of this chapter.

States of Sovereignty

Stephen Krasner has characterized sovereignty as 'organized hypocrisy' (Krasner, 1999: 42). Krasner argues that although the institution of sovereignty affirms the principle of non-intervention in the affairs of other states, intervention has always been a normal feature of international affairs. Organized hypocrisy refers to a stable game-theoretic solution to the contradictory practice of asserting the inviolability of territorial boundaries on the one hand and the practice of constant interference on the other. The informal understanding that states are sovereign, yet subject to constant intervention, is best characterized as organized hypocrisy.

Krasner is basically correct, as far as he goes. In constructivist terms, the practices of states serve to define the operational meaning of sovereignty, and these practices are by no means consistent. States are hypocritical and have always intervened in each other's affairs. The Westphalian ideal of sovereign non-intervention has always been just that: an ideal. As Daniel Deudney has suggested, 'although the Westphalian system of authority and power has been hegemonic in modern world politics, it has not been universal' (Deudney, 1996: 191).

The principal limitation with Krasner's conceptualization of sovereignty is that it is essentially a static one. It does not help us comprehend the possibility of change in the operational meaning of sovereignty, and it does not suggest (or allow for) any typology for the different forms and meanings of sovereignty over time and across place. Like the tendency to treat states as fundamentally like units, Krasner's conceptualization of sovereignty is essentially fixed and unchanging. It does not help us understand the significance of challenges to sovereignty or the possibility of its transformation.

In this sense, Krasner's work does not take us very far beyond the insights about state sovereignty contained in the pioneering work of Carl Schmitt or in the work of F.H. Hinsley and Alan James. For Schmitt, '[S]overeign is he who decides the exception' (Schmitt, 1985: 5). For Hinsley, sovereignty is 'the idea that there is a final and absolute political authority in the political community' and that 'no final and absolute authority exists elsewhere' (Hinsley, 1986: 26). For James, sovereignty is defined in terms of constitutional independence, an authority derived from a state's constitution, 'which exists in its own right' (James, 1986: 40). While each of these works defines the essence of the concept of sovereignty, like Krasner, they concentrate on its transcendent characteristics rather than its variation in form, its change in operational meaning across time and space, or the possibility of its transformation. We need a framework and an approach to help us understand this phenomenon, something I will propose later.

Like the previous discussion of changing forms of state, I will also illustrate changing states or forms of sovereignty across time and place. While it would be easier to demonstrate the magnitude of changes by contrasting the sovereignty of the absolutist state with that of the contemporary state, as in the preceding discussion, I will illustrate important, qualitative transformations in the operational meaning of state sovereignty with reference primarily to the twentieth century. One of the best ways to track important changes in the meaning of sovereignty is by examining the criteria explicitly articulated by

states when they decide to recognize other states as sovereign. As will be evident from the discussion that follows, the practices of recognition show important variation over the course of the twentieth century.

In order to be recognized as a sovereign state, effective control over territorial space is essential. Article I of the 1933 Montevideo Convention on Rights and Duties of States identifies a defined territory, along with a permanent population, government and a capacity to enter into relations with other states as minimal criteria for statehood under international law (Shaw, 1997: 140). Although there can be important differences in the criteria for recognition across different states – including differences between countries sharing fairly similar legal traditions like the United Kingdom and the United States – a brief case study of changes in US recognition criteria well illustrates important changes in the operational meaning of sovereignty over time.

Thomas Jefferson, the first American Secretary of State, employed a conception of legitimacy borrowed from the work of Jean-Jacques Rousseau, when he was first confronted with the question of the new republic's criteria for the recognition of another state. In response to an inquiry from the American Minister to Paris in 1792 about recognition during the course of the French Revolution, Jefferson wrote: 'It accords with our principles to acknowledge any Government to be rightful which is formed by the will of the nation, substantially declared' (Hackworth, 1931: 120). In practice, the particular form of governance did not matter, and the United States recognized monarchies, as well as fledgling democracies. The crucial point for recognition purposes was that the state maintain effective territorial control and that it be accorded some form of popular legitimacy.

By the beginning of the twentieth century, an additional criterion was added to the list of recognition criteria. States were recognized as legitimate if they were capable of fulfilling their international commitments and obligations, especially as they related to property rights. This criterion was applied to Colombia in 1900, to Honduras and the Dominican Republic in 1903 and to Haiti in 1911 (Hackworth, 1931: 122–3). The addition of this criterion is an important illustration of American convergence with established European criteria and is indicative of changing American concerns once the United States began to emerge as a major power on the world stage, with substantial economic interests of its own. The concern with a state's capacity to fulfill international commitments and obligations was especially prominent in the 1920s debate over the recognition of the revolutionary regime that had assumed control in Russia. The revolutionary ideology of the new regime was not viewed as consistent with the standards of the major powers of the time and is one of the reasons it took the United States until the 1930s to recognize the new state of the Soviet Union.

During the 1920s, the United States experimented with the idea of adding the criterion of democratic governance (and explicit rejection of non-constitutional changes of regime), at least with regard to five Central American states. This principle was not generalized to the rest of the world, however, until after the end of the Cold War. During the immediate post-Second World War period, the United States generally followed the lead of the former European colonial powers when it came to granting of recognition to the new states formed out of the process of decolonization.

During the Cold War, the United States appears to have lost sight of Jefferson's relatively tolerant practice of following the general will. Recognition became one of the tools of Cold War politics. A semblance of territorial control, fulfillment of international obligations and Cold War alignment mattered more than the presence of a democratic regime when it came to the recognition of the Congo, South Korea and South Vietnam. Democracy was more important in the discursive justifications for recognition than in the practices of recognition.

By the end of the twentieth century, particularly following the end of the Cold War, democratic governance increasingly became a prerequisite for state recognition. In its 1991 declaration on 'Guidelines on the Recognition of New States in Eastern Europe and in the Soviet Union', the European Community noted that recognition required commitments with regard to the rule of law, democracy and human rights, as well as guarantees for the rights of ethnic minorities (Shaw, 1997: 301). These ideas were also adopted by the United States in the 'new world order' statements of the elder Bush's administration and by the rhetorical and diplomatic practices of the Clinton administration throughout the 1990s. Even more significant is the fact that when Croatia and Bosnia were first recognized in 1991, neither possessed firm, territorial control. Not only did this provide a new vehicle for external intervention (using diplomatic recognition to influence developments on the ground), but it also suggests a potentially profound departure from practices that had prevailed throughout the course of the twentieth century. However, the controversy generated by the practice of recognition in these two cases raises questions about whether it will be sustained in the twenty-first century.

Changes in recognition criteria have been, and will continue to be, contested and challenged by states. It is best to think of the meaning of sovereignty in terms of a continual contestation of practices, with some agents pushing the boundaries and frontiers of legitimate practice, and others resisting and countering at every point. The important point

here is that the norms of recognition have changed significantly over time, again, even over the course of a single century. Whether they are moving in one particular direction is less important than the fact that they are not fixed in meaning in time and place. There is, however, some evidence that the international community has become increasingly more intrusive into what was once assumed to be under the domain of the domestic affairs of states.[3] That is, there is some evidence of a progression in recognition criteria over time.

At the outset, elements of the territorial state are basic to recognition (from territorial control, to Weberian ideas about legitimate means of coercion and an ability to extract resources). This is a limited, 'Weberian' form of sovereignty. If we add to this the Rousseauian ideal that a recognized state must be an expression of the general will, it is reasonable to expect that this ideal is likely to secure the territorial control. States that are a genuine expression of the general will are also likely to be better able to fulfill their international obligations, both in financial and in alliance terms. This was critical during the middle part of the twentieth century, during the heyday of the period of 'state' sovereignty. The establishment of democratic forms has only recently become a global norm for recognition, but it reinforces the likelihood that the state is an expression of the general will and it may also be associated with the fulfillment of international obligations. Finally, the recent relaxation of the requirement of firm, territorial control in certain instances suggests a potentially significant departure from historical practices of recognition (as well as a new means of external intervention), should it be sustained. Thus, by the end of the twentieth century, sovereignty increasingly appeared to be 'conditioned' sovereignty.

Thus, when we examine the history of changes in recognition criteria over the course of the past century, there is some evidence to suggest that there has been a general progression, direction, or ratcheting up of intrusion into the domestic affairs of states. The path has been uneven, inconsistent, resisted and occasionally reversed. Chilean claims about the status of General Pinochet, Russian assertiveness over Chechnya, Chinese resistance to World Bank claims, and US Senator Jesse Helms's declarations of the primacy of US sovereignty at the end of the twentieth century were all illustrations of efforts to reassert elements of traditional state sovereignty. Nevertheless, there appears to have been not only important qualitative change in the operational meaning of sovereignty over time (as indicated by changing recognition criteria), but there is also a certain directionality to that change.

Like the discussion of changing forms of state, this change in states of sovereignty is not restricted to change over time. There are also important differences in the operational meaning of sovereignty in different places on the globe at the same moment in time. It is no accident that those who have historically borne the brunt of external intervention in the developing world are the most ardent defenders of traditional conceptions of state sovereignty, the inviolability of state borders and the importance of the principle of non-intervention (Sha, 1995). China, Malaysia and Russia are reluctant to accept the presence of a democratic regime as an important criterion for state or regime recognition. In the contemporary period of conditioned sovereignty, only the remaining superpower, the United States, has the capability to resist most forms of self-restraint and assert an unconditioned form of sovereignty with some degree of credibility.

Like the discussion of changing forms of state, changing states (or forms) of sovereignty also have important implications for international relations. Because the norms of sovereign recognition determine who are allowed to be principal agents in international affairs, changes in these norms have important implications for the nature of the states themselves. It is no longer sufficient just to maintain territorial control and fulfill international obligations. To be recognized as a sovereign state, one increasingly has to possess democratic institutions (or a plan to consolidate them). Indeed, this may even be more important than territorial control in some instances. This changes the very definition of what it means to be sovereign.

Changes in the form of sovereignty also have significance for justifications for external intervention. Just as discursive justifications serve to define the meaning of sovereignty (Weber, 1995) so too do different forms of sovereignty enable (or undermine) different justifications for intervention. During the middle part of the twentieth century, the nature of the polity in control of territory generally did not matter, and non-democratic states were not only recognized as legitimate, but were also often protected by the institution of sovereignty. At the century's end, the maintenance of democratic institutions or the defense of universal human rights could be used to justify external intervention.

Finally, if the form of conditioned sovereignty prevalent at the end of the twentieth century remains in place for an extended period, along with the operational practices of recognition associated with it, there could be important systemic implications. This is particularly the case if the advocates of the democratic peace hypothesis are correct. That is, the prevailing practices of recognition could serve to extend the democratic form of state, hence transforming the nature of international politics and the likelihood of international conflict itself.

Conceptions of Territory

Border changes are neither new nor particularly out of the ordinary. From the age of the absolutist states of the seventeenth and eighteenth centuries, through the Napoleonic wars of the nineteenth century, the boundaries defining the great powers have shown dramatic changes (Kratochwil, 1986; Sahlins, 1989). The same is true if we glance at any map of Europe over the course of the twentieth century. We can readily see tangible evidence of the emergence and the disappearance of states, state forms and political entities over the course of the century. The decade of the 1990s alone witnessed the break up of the former Soviet Union, the former Yugoslavia, the division of the former Czechoslovakia and the unification of Germany. However, like forms of state and states of sovereignty, the salience of territory and even the meaning of 'the border' that separates territories are neither fixed nor constant across time and place. There are important variations both in the salience of physical territorial possession and in the degree of permeability of borders, the functions of borders (Kratochwil, 1986), or what some scholars have described as the degree of 'hardness' or 'softness' of boundaries (Mostov, 2000).

At the end of the nineteenth and the beginning of the twentieth century, there was an obsession with physical possession and control of territory, along with generally unchallenged assumptions about the benefits to be derived from that control. The nineteenth-century scholar of geopolitics Friedrich Ratzel developed the concept of the organic theory of the state, 'which treated states as competitive territorial entities vying with one another for control over parts of the earth's surface' (Murphy, 2001: 2). Control over physical territorial space was also vital for Sir Halford Mackinder (Mackinder, 1904), while for Captain A.T. Mahan, it was dominion of the seas that produced control of distant countries, the possession of colonies, and (dependent on these colonies) the potential for an increase of wealth. According to Mahan, even in instances where land forces were outnumbered, as was the case with the English forces in India during the eighteenth century,

the mysterious power ... was not in this or that man, king or statesman, but in that control of the sea which the French government knew forbade the hope of maintaining that distant dependency against the fleets of England. (Mahan, 1895: 278)

These assumptions about the virtues and benefits of territorial acquisition remained predominant until Norman Angell forcefully challenged them in 1910, with the publication of the first edition of *The Great Illusion*. Angell identified how widespread these views were at the turn of the century in both Britain and Germany, and he defined the 'great illusion' as the idea that territorial acquisition would provide a basis for prosperity and affluence (Angell, 1910: 30–1). For Angell, territorial conquest and acquisition were futile, since the conqueror acquired liabilities along with the assets of the conquered populace. He contended that the basis of wealth was not to be found in the physical possession of territory, but in the use to which that territory was put.

During the middle decades of the twentieth century, when the nation-state emerged as the predominant state form and the principle of non-intervention was widely proclaimed (if not always practiced), the boundaries between states became increasingly sharply drawn. The Covenant of the League of Nations (1919) bound its members to respect the territorial integrity of its members, while the Charter of the United Nations (1945) similarly asserted the principle of non-intervention in the affairs of member states (James, 1992). The movement of peoples, so widespread during the nineteenth century, became increasingly difficult, as state after state raised barriers to entry. In the economic realm, national capital controls and international monetary agreements protected national currencies from the destabilizing influences of international market forces (Ruggie, 1982). Elaborate alliance networks guaranteed the security and territorial integrity of their members, whether they were allied with the United States or the Soviet Union.

It was only after the advent of the nuclear age that states reluctantly began to recognize their strategic vulnerability, and their increased reliance on the symbolic territorial protection provided by nuclear deterrence. The change in thinking about the salience of territory is striking. Hans Morgenthau described the importance of having a large physical territory to guarantee the survival of a country from a potential nuclear attack. When he pointed out to a group of British military specialists that it would take only four well-placed nuclear weapons to destroy the United Kingdom, they strongly protested, insisting that it would actually take six (Morgenthau, 1970). Over the course of the past fifty years, major powers have grown accustomed to (if not comfortable with) this vulnerability. American efforts to develop a national missile defense shield could be interpreted as an attempt to reconstruct a hard, and a virtually physical boundary around the United States, a development that prompted strong objections from allies and potential adversaries alike.

By the end of the twentieth century, both the salience of physical territory and the significance of borders appeared to be on the decrease in most issue areas, with the only major exception involving the movement of people. There has been 'a subtle shift away from the state as the spatial unit within which problems are assumed to be most appropriately confronted' (Murphy, 1999: 235) and a belief that growing challenges to the state 'will direct attention to the nature and meaning of the changing spatial organization of politics' (Murphy, 2001: 18). Control of networks – of finance, of information, of raw material flows, of cyberspace – is increasingly more important than control of physical, territorial space. This is an observation made by geographers (Agnew and Knox, 1994; Murphy, 2001), and political scientists (Luke, 1991; Strange, 1996) alike. As sociologist Saskia Sassen reminds us, all transactions take place on some territorial space, but the precise location of those transactions is increasingly ambiguous, and they tend to be located in different places for different purposes (Sassen, 1996).

Following the end of the Cold War, the emerging European world order has been associated with a declining desire for territory (Tunander, 1997). Carl Schmitt's distinction between 'Friend' and 'Foe', where major powers are defined in terms of their conflicts with each other, no longer seems to prevail in a system 'characterized by all the major powers aiming for participation in the same system, none of them defining each other as an enemy in the radical sense' (Waever, 1997: 84). While there is plenty of differentiation and 'othering' going on, the 'other' as enemy has largely disappeared from great power politics in the post-Cold War world. 'The decreasing importance of territory hinges on whether states define the Other as enemy' (Waever, 1997: 84).

Beyond changes in the salience of territory, the meaning and significance of boundaries had also changed by the end of the twentieth century. With the expansion of interdependence, innovations in communications and information technologies, and the advent of globalization, political geographers started 'raising questions about the changing nature and function of boundaries' (Murphy, 2001: 13).

Political theorist Julie Mostov has distinguished between 'hard' and 'soft' boundaries to describe the phenomenon, arguing that a real alternative to the traditional discourse of external sovereignty and hard borders 'would be to "soften" the boundaries of the state and radically rethink notions of internal sovereignty, self-determination and citizenship rights' (Mostov, 2000: 6–7). Late twentieth-century increases in the flows of finance, of goods, of information, and in some employment sectors, even of people, have rendered boundaries increasingly porous or 'soft'. This development has been resisted by some state actors, and the tendency is by no means consistent or uniform across different activities. It is still much easier for finance to move across political boundaries than for people to move across them. Nevertheless, it is striking to observe the ways the states emerging out of East and Central Europe have been willing to forego some of the traditional territorial prerogatives of the sovereign state in exchange for the opportunity to join Europe. They appear eager to transfer authority to Brussels, accept greater institutional transparency and allow increasingly porous borders.

Changes in the organization of global finance have 'rendered ambiguous' the traditional territorial imagery of international political economy (Rosow, 1994), and some have suggested that we need to 'unbundle' our concept of territoriality

Table 8.1 *Historicizing conceptual change*

	Early 20th century	**Mid 20th century**	**Late 20th century**
State forms	Imperial state (great powers with colonies)	Nation-state (welfare state, national security state, developmental state)	Self-restrained state (neoliberal state, 'failed')
State of sovereignty	Weberian sovereignty	State sovereignty	Conditioned sovereignty
	Territorial control Fulfill international obligations	Territorial control Fulfill international obligations Political alignment	Territorial control? Fulfill international obligations Democracy
Territory	Physical control and occupation are paramount	Hard boundaries with nuclear vulnerability	Soft boundaries, control over networks, the 'region-state'

Table 8.2 *Contextualizing conceptual change in the contemporary era*

	Advanced, post-industrial states	**Developing states**
State forms	Self-restrained, neoliberal state	Neoliberal and failed states
States of sovereignty	Intervention is legitimate to secure democracy	Non-intervention in domestic affairs is inviolable
Territory	Control networks (soft borders)	Control physical territory (hard borders)

(Ruggie, 1993b: 171). Control over flows and over networks is becoming more important than hierarchical control over physical territorial space (Luke, 1991). The emergence of the 'region-state' – economic zones with integrated industrial investment and information systems that straddle national boundaries in an increasingly borderless world – is yet another manifestation of this blurring of traditional conceptions of territoriality (Ohmae, 1995: 79–82). This blurring of territoriality is apparent in the intense, and growing regional interdependence between the United States and Mexico. The recession in Mexico following the peso crisis in the mid-1990s had significant effects on the regional economy of the American southwest, and in many spheres of activity, what happens in Mexico City has become more important for Los Angeles than what happens in Boston.

Thus, as in the cases of forms of state and states of sovereignty, there have also been important changes in conceptions of territory – both in the salience of territorial possession and in the meaning of boundaries – over the course of the twentieth century. Once again, change over time is not the only important variation. There are also important differences in salience of territory and the meaning of boundaries across different locations on the globe at any particular moment. States lagging behind in the technological breakthroughs of the late twentieth century have tried to deny (or to retard) the shift to

the importance of control over networks and flows, rather than over physical territory. However, they are not well equipped to stem the flows of finance, goods or people across their frontiers.

Changes in the salience of territory and in the meaning of borders have important implications for international relations. The declining salience of direct, physical territorial possession and control has removed one of the principal sources of great power conflict. Symbolic attachments to specific places remain, but the means to hegemony is no longer believed to be through territorial acquisition, but through involvement in and control over networks, be they financial, informational or technological.

At the same time, the use of the border to protect and insulate a population from external influences has been replaced with the belief that, in many arenas, greater openness, rather than closure, may be the most effective way to advance the interests of a population. While there have been recurring efforts to reverse the radical acceptance of nuclear vulnerability (the ultimate in soft boundaries), the reintroduction of national missile defenses has yet to prove capable of restoring a hard boundary in the critical realm of national security.

Tables 8.1 and 8.2 provide a summary of the illustrations presented up to this point about important changes in meaning of the state, of sovereignty, and of territoriality over time and across place. The categories in the table should be considered as central tendencies, rather than absolutes. That is, there is not a perfect correspondence between the different periods and a particular state form, type of sovereignty (or set of criteria for the recognition of sovereignty), or conception of territoriality. The Portuguese Empire persisted until the mid-1970s, and there was early evidence of the phenomenon of a failed state in Lebanon during the same period. However, while the imperial state as a legitimate state form was the norm in 1900, it was universally delegitimated by the end of the century. The direction of change over the course of the twentieth century is fairly clear, but it is by no means irreversible. As already suggested above, there are plenty of resistances and efforts to reverse the trends, particularly when it comes to the variety of different ways in which states are constantly negotiating their sovereignty. It is also important to stress once again that this summary characterization is not intended to imply that we are moving inexorably in a single, irreversible direction or toward some certain goal or endpoint.

Implications of the Changing Meanings of Core Concepts for the Analysis of International Relations

Having illustrated some important, qualitative changes of meaning in some of our core concepts within international relations, how should we best go about incorporating these changes into our analyses of the subject? First, we should avoid making sweeping generalizations about our subject that are insensitive to either time (historicization) or place (contextualization). Second, as I will elaborate at greater length below, we should redirect our analytical attention to the practices that redefine our core concepts.

The changes in meaning of our core concepts of state, sovereignty and territory should make us cognizant of the limitations of sweeping generalizations about the state or the state system. It should also sensitize us to the pitfalls of relying on history as a uniform database for evaluating our theories and insights. This suggestion is not meant to imply that we should retreat entirely into history or that we should avoid evaluating hypotheses with empirical information derived from historical or comparative analysis. However, it is important that we do so with careful attention to when and how the meanings of some of our core concepts are undergoing important change and transformation. We should not assume uniformity across long expanses of time and place and need to take qualitative changes of meaning into consideration when we attempt to evaluate hypotheses and make valid statements about international relations.

Changes in meaning of our core concepts should also encourage us to redirect our focus to an analysis of the practices that produce different forms of state, states of sovereignty and conceptions of territoriality. Not only will this give us insight into the nature and direction of change, but it will also help us solve some of the persistent analytical deficiencies associated with some of our core concepts. In the section that follows, I will illustrate this general point with reference to the theoretical and conceptual literature on sovereignty.

The Westphalian *ideal* of state sovereignty – where states claim absolute and final authority over a wide range of issues, national identities are largely unproblematic, and boundaries are clear and unambiguous – was far from the actual meaning and practice of sovereignty during the final decades of the twentieth century. As already demonstrated, the criteria employed by states for the recognition of other states underwent important changes during the course of the twentieth century, enabling us to identify different operational meanings of what it takes to be sovereign at different points in time.

However, much of the theoretical and conceptual literature on the meaning of sovereignty has struggled with the significance of potential challenges to the Westphalian ideal of state sovereignty and concluded that sovereignty's central role as an organizing principle is essentially undiminished, see Hinsley, 1986; Jackson, 1990, 1999; James, 1986; Krasner, 1999. These authors are generally reluctant to accommodate qualitative changes or variation in the operational meaning of sovereignty into their analysis. However, by redirecting our focus to the practices of making and recognizing claims of authority, it is possible to gauge significant change in the meaning of sovereignty and to move beyond sterile debates about whether sovereignty is eroding. It also enables us to consider how to recognize when different types or forms of sovereignty have emerged.

It is helpful to begin with a conception of sovereignty as a social construct. Social construction links identity with practice (Biersteker and Weber, 1996: 278), and sovereignty is an inherently social concept. States' claims to sovereignty construct a social environment in which they can interact, 'the international society of states' (Bull, 1977), while at the same time the mutual recognition of each other's claims to sovereignty is an important element in the construction of states themselves. Moreover, each of the core components of sovereignty – authority, identity and territory – is also constructed socially.

Sovereignty entails the external recognition (by states) of claims of final authority made by other states. However, like the institution of private property, these claims are not absolute (Kratochwil, 1992). The authority claims made by states vary from one issue area to another and are not fixed over time. This is the key to understanding the changing meaning and forms of sovereignty. The question is not whether sovereignty exists as a unitary condition or state of being, but how claims of authority are issue-specific and change over time.

To come to terms with the changing meaning of sovereignty, we do not need to search for an alternative to the system of sovereign state authority that already exists, or is about to emerge. It is not necessary to identify a clearly defined, new global authority or imagine a return to the heteronomy of the Middle Ages, to comprehend emerging states of sovereignty. A more fruitful way to proceed is to focus on variation in claims of authority themselves.[4]

Power and authority are closely related, but authority is used here to refer to institutionalized or formal power. What differentiates authority from power is the legitimacy of the claim (implying both the rights of some superior or some location of authority and obligations on the part of subordinates or subjects of that authority). Legitimacy implies that there is some form of consent or recognition of authority on the part of the regulated or governed. This consent, itself, may be earned or it may be generated by the rhetorical practices of political leaders. Consent is the product of persuasion and trust, rather than overt coercion.

Sovereignty is variable in its meaning because the range of issues over which authority is claimed (and/or is recognized as legitimate by other states) is not fixed in space and time. Authority claims (and their recognition by others) vary, and this variance determines the change in the meaning of sovereignty itself. This approach allows us to move beyond static, essentialist notions about the timeless nature of sovereignty.

Many scholars interested in the study of sovereignty have long differentiated between the *internal* and the *external* dimensions of sovereignty. The internal dimension generally refers to the consolidation of the territory under a single authority and the recognition of that authority as legitimate by the population, while the external dimension generally refers to external recognition by other states. This distinction between the internal and external dimensions of sovereignty can be adapted to this argument about the issue-specific nature of sovereignty. That is, both the number and range of authority claims has changed (the traditional 'internal' dimension of sovereignty), as have the number and range of claims that are externally recognized as legitimate (the 'external' dimension).[5] The discussion about the changing criteria for recognition earlier in this chapter provides an illustration of change in the external dimension of sovereignty.

Since the range of authority claims is variable, where does the authority over specific issues previously claimed or recognized by states go? Does it disappear? If not, who or what inherits the authority that states no longer claim or are recognized by

others to possess? There has been a significant dispersal in the location of authority in the global system in recent years, or what Susan Strange labeled a 'diffusion of power in the world economy' (Strange, 1996). The state is no longer the predominant location of authority on a growing number of issues, and it faces challenges from other locations. In some cases, the state no longer claims to have authority, in other instances, it is no longer externally recognized by others as possessing authority in certain domains, and in still other cases, it faces competing claims and challenges from non-state actors. This can be illustrated by discussing, in turn, examples of each of these three types of challenges to traditional (or idealized) state authority claims.

Ceding Claims of Final Authority

First, states may cut back on the range of claims of final authority they make. The ceding of competences over certain issue domains from individual states to the European Union is a good example of reducing claims of authority. Similar, though far less extensive, transference of authority can be seen in the emergent dispute resolution mechanisms within the NAFTA.

Other international institutions have also been ceded legitimate authority. States created and willingly abide by the strictures of these institutions. For example, the United Nations has sanctioned humanitarian interventions in a growing number of instances. The operative issue is no longer one of whether these interventions are justified, but whether the UN can accommodate the large demand for action in so many different locations. There has also been a significant increase in the frequency, the extent and the apparent acceptability of conditionality by international financial institutions. This has ranged from the International Monetary Fund's enhanced surveillance, its demands for institutional reform during the Asian financial crisis, and its criticism of military spending in member countries, to the political conditionality of the World Bank and the European Bank for Reconstruction and Development and the World Bank's interest in environmental (or green) conditionality. The growing recognition and use of the dispute resolution mechanisms of the World Trade Organization provides yet another illustration. Similarly, the International Court of Justice has begun to hear cases that apply the principle of harms in transborder pollution cases, and international lawyers prosecuting international war crimes tribunals have pushed litigation well beyond the intentions and wishes of the major powers that initiated the proceedings. Issues that were once unambiguously 'inside' the realm of state responsibility have been delegated to 'outside' institutions. The boundary separating inside and outside has moved, and dramatically far, in some instances.

Changing Norms of External Recognition of Authority Claims

Second, there have been important changes in the external recognition, both by other states and by international institutions, of some of the claims previously made by states. For example, states are no longer recognized as legitimate final authorities when it comes to the violation of the human rights of individuals or groups located within their domains. Shortly after it was first promulgated in 1948, the Universal Declaration of Human Rights could be dismissed as just another United Nations proclamation, with no effective international enforcement mechanism. The influence of the declaration was contingent on the backing of major powers, primarily the US, which applied it when convenient during the Cold War, but ignored it when a critical alliance partner was involved. Today, however, ideas about the universalization of human rights have been institutionalized to the extent that they have begun to challenge some of the prerogatives of traditional state sovereignty. While there are important regional variations in conceptions of human rights (and a good deal of legitimate debate about their scope, from narrow applications to individuals to broader applications to groups) (Hurrell, 1995), there is a global acceptance of the discourse of human rights. That is, virtually everyone constructs their arguments in terms of a discourse of different forms of legitimate human rights (Sikkink, 1993). This is as significant for the global development of democracy as was the extension of suffrage throughout the world earlier in the twentieth century.

At the same time, as discussed extensively above, there have been important changes in the norms of recognition for new states. Until recently, the principal criteria for external recognition were associated with meeting the requirements of internal, Weberian sovereignty (physical control over the territorial space, acceptance by the subject population, clearly established lines of governmental authority, etc.). Increasingly important today, however, are requirements such as the establishment and consolidation of democratic institutions, the treatment of the rights of minority populations, and even the management of the economy.

International institutions have withheld recognition of some of the claims of states not just with regard to the actions of coercive agents of the state against subject populations, such as torture or fundamental violations of individual rights, but also with regard to the protection of other aspects of the lives of private individuals within states. The emergence of third party human rights law has extended the range of international law to issues like racial discrimination in housing, gender employment and relationships within the family (previously considered part of the domain of the 'private'). Other international institutions like the World Trade Organization have begun to extend their intrusiveness into the previously sacrosanct domain of the 'domestic' by criticizing some labor policies, consumer product safety standards and environmental accords as non-tariff barriers to free trade.

Emergence of Competing Locations of Authority

Third, and finally, competing claims of authority have started to emerge from non-state actors in the world system: from individuals, from firms, from non-governmental organizations, from private organizations, and even from markets. Individuals now have rights to challenge the actions of states and international institutions, as manifested in the European Court of Human Rights or the World Bank's Inspection Panel schema. In the case of the European Court, individuals have the right to appeal to a supranational institution with jurisdiction over nation-states. There are very specific circumstances under which individuals can appeal, but the arrangement establishes a competing location of authority to the state. In the case of the World Bank Inspection Panel, any two individuals who can claim a significant material harm from a World Bank project can initiate a quasi-independent review of investment decisions taken by the Bank. Although the Inspection Panel is located within the Bank, it is technically independent of it. Not only do individuals have the power to initiate a review of Bank decisions, but their intervention can lead to the termination of a project. The individuals who initiate the review do not need the sanction or backing of their own government for their actions, reinforcing the principle that individuals are recognized as legitimate agents by both states and by the intergovernmental institutions states have created.

Even more significant are the actions of transnational issue networks that operate most effectively in the domains of human rights and the global environment. Transnational issue networks have increasingly begun to constrain the actions of middle powers. The global acceptance of the discourse of human rights has been facilitated by the global reach of the media that has increased the visibility of state actions and increasingly exposed them to potential opinion sanctions from NGO networks operating across the globe. Traditional state claims of sovereign authority are increasingly competing with other sources of legitimate authority in the international system, especially the emerging moral authority of expertise represented by transnational issue networks, that some observers have described as evidence of the emergence of a global civil society (Lipschutz, 1996). NGO actors in global civil society set standards of international behavior that increasingly constrain the actions of individual states. The weight of global public opinion is such that states increasingly have to be concerned about the reactions of other states, of the publics of those states, and of non-governmental organizations, in order to avoid being labeled a pariah state, to gain entry into the society of states, to obtain access to conditional resources, or to enter regional common markets such as the European Union.

Transnational issue networks operate by drawing attention to issues, mobilizing their networks and placing issues on the global agenda. The practice of convening parallel meetings of NGOs alongside major UN-sponsored state congresses has become routine in recent years: from the human rights conference in Vienna to the conference on the environment in Rio, on women in Beijing, and on social development in Copenhagen. This has further legitimated the role of NGOs, as they put issues on the global agenda and even define the terms of the debate, in some instances.

Finally, the globalization of finance and the emergence of integrated global financial markets have increasingly begun to discipline all states, even the most powerful. There has been a major shift away from sharply demarcated national financial boundaries – with effective currency controls in place – toward increased financial liberalization, the elimination of currency controls, and the increased ease of cross-border financial transactions. This tendency toward financial liberalization has facilitated the emergence of new financial actors (bond traders, currency traders, portfolio investors, hedge fund managers) who have developed global strategies and operate on an around-the-clock and around-the-globe basis. As a result, the emerging world financial market 'is not comprised of linked national markets' but is 'a network integrated through electronic information systems that entails "… more than two hundred thousand electronic monitors in trading rooms all over the world that are linked together" ' (Kobrin, 1997: 20). This network has itself become a location of authority in the economic world, with an ability to reward (and to discipline) countries that pursue policies it deems prudent (or unsustainable). It operates, in effect, like a global 'hard budget constraint' on the behavior of economic and financial decision-makers who have ceded informal authority to the markets through both their public statements and their practices. When a finance minister or head of state begins to believe and publicly declare that markets have the power to discipline their actions, they signal their consent and participate in empowering markets as legitimate authorities within certain domains.

Each of these broad sets of practices – the ceding of final authority to other institutions, the changes in external recognition of final authority, and the emergence of competing locations of final authority – are indicative of, and participate in the construction of, important changes in the meaning of sovereignty. At some point, the cumulative impact of these incremental changes in practices could lead to a situation in which the authority claims of states become increasingly hollow. The indivisibility of the concept of state sovereignty may well remain, but its operational significance becomes increasingly empty. As that occurs, we may begin to be able to comprehend an alternative to sovereignty as an organizing principle of the international system. If we do not focus on changes of practices over time, we are not likely to comprehend the qualitative transformation of sovereignty as a generative principle of the international system, when it occurs.

We could extend this kind of analysis of changes in the meaning of sovereignty to the other conceptual changes considered earlier (forms of state and conceptions of territoriality), by looking for other kinds of practices that indicate and produce change. With regard to forms of state, the scope of state intervention in the economy and/or justifications for international intervention would indicate the sources of variation in state form. With regard to changing conceptions of territoriality, the degree of attention to physical control of territory and/or the porosity of borders would be indicative and constitutive of change.

AGENDAS FOR FUTURE RESEARCH

There are a number of issues raised, and left unresolved, by historicizing and contextualizing core concepts like state, sovereignty and territoriality. This chapter is intended to serve as a beginning, and as a stimulus to further reflection and work on the core concepts of international relations, rather than an attempt to reach closure on them. Thus, I would like to use this conclusion to begin to chart the course of some promising future research initiatives, and to suggest where some contemporary research is taking us.

Emerging Forms of State

As already suggested above, there is no consensus on how best to characterize the emerging form(s) of state. While the concept of 'failed state' has received a great deal of attention in recent years (Herbst, 2000), others have suggested the emergence of the 'postmodern state' (Harvey, 1989), the 'defective state' (Strange, 1995), or the 'self-restraining state' (Schedler et al., 1999). Some of the most creative efforts to think about contemporary state forms have been stimulated by efforts to characterize the polity emerging in the wake of the deepening of the European Union (Jorgensen, 1997; Schmitter, 1996; Wallace, 1999).

Another important area of contemporary research on the nature of the state is found in the globalization literature. In a return to many of the familiar issues associated with the debate over interdependence and the role of the state during the 1960s and 1970s (Nye and Keohane, 1977), the contemporary globalization debates pit those who emphasize the magnitude of the phenomenon and its implications for the changing role of the state (Dicken, 1992; Kobrin, 1997; Mittleman, 2000; Strange, 1996) against those who are highly skeptical about the significance of the phenomenon (Wade, 1996; and Hirst and Thompson, 1996; Pauly, 1997; Weiss, 1998). There are also important works that attempt to stake out a middle ground in the debate (Sassen, 1998).

Another of the most promising areas of contemporary research on the state is based on an effort to invert the pessimism of the 'failed state' literature and to begin to explore the domain of state capacity and/or incapacity. In many ways, this is a return to the classic literature on nation-building during the 1960s (Bendix, 1964), a literature that was initially driven by the practical needs and concerns stemming from the process of decolonization. It is also of great interest within international institutions concerned with development, like the United Nations and the World Bank. Twenty or thirty years ago, the subject of state-building would have seemed esoteric, applicable only to the few remaining colonial territories, trusteeships and to collapsed states like Lebanon. At the beginning of the twenty-first century, it is an agenda relevant to international interventions and to post-conflict reconstruction and development efforts in Liberia, Sierra Leone, Somalia, The Congo, Rwanda, Burundi, Cambodia, Afghanistan and Bosnia, as well as to regions like Kosovo and Chechnya. State-building is also central to the process under way in East Timor (arguably under a problematic and contested UN trusteeship).

Finally, there is important new work being done on emerging political forms of confederation within multi-ethnic states (which have become the modal form of state in the world today) (Koslowski, 2000). Creative work on the norms of recognizing claims of self-determination, and the construction of new institutional forms capable of addressing the legitimate interests of minorities within states, have important theoretical as well as practical significance (Lustick, 1993).

States of Sovereignty

The crisis in the Balkans and the failure or collapse of some states in Africa have led to controversial calls for the reinstitution of forms of trusteeship by the international community (Lyon, 1993). In a *de facto* sense, this has already begun to emerge in several post-conflict zones, ranging from Sierra Leone, to Kosovo and East Timor. However, many of the normative implications of this development have yet to be explored. It is also likely to be an extremely difficult undertaking, one that raises significant questions about the credibility, capability and legitimacy of international institutions. Moreover, while this may be an important development from a practical standpoint, it is likely to be only a temporary, or transitory phenomenon.

Not only is sovereignty a social construct, but so too are each of its constitutive elements (authority, identity and territory). Thus, there is a wealth of literature exploring the construction of identity and authority, as well as some important research under way on the emergence of non-state based (or private) forms of authority. Most of this research has been confined to the realm of the international political economy (Cutler et al., 1999), but there has also been some important research on the moral authority exercised by non-governmental organizations (Lipschutz, 1996). There is also some pioneering work on the emergence of the market itself as an authority (Hall, 2000).

The emergence of these potentially new locations of authority in the international system has given rise to significant concerns about the democratic accountability of these new forms of agency. There are serious, normative questions about the accountability of non-governmental organizations, institutions that are accountable to their members, but have an influence over (and make claims on behalf of) a far broader range of potential subjects. There are also under-examined normative issues raised by the extension of the global human rights regime, particularly about the extent to which values are universally shared, as well as the scope and domain of the international court of justice and the international criminal court. Within the realm of the international political economy, there are important questions about the accountability of private, market actors (and/or the lack of transparency in the manner in which authority has been transferred to some of them) (Sassen, 1998). This has led to increased calls for countervailing movements to bring public scrutiny and participation to bear on market actors.

Finally, there have been some important issues raised by theorists about the de-linking of state and sovereignty and moving beyond the concept of state sovereignty itself (Hoffman, 1998), research that has significant implications for both sovereignty and for political theory more generally. As already suggested, empirical research on the making, ceding and recognition of claims of authority (by states and non-states alike) holds great promise for our understanding of the changing meaning of sovereignty.

Conceptions of Territoriality

As control over physical territorial space has become less salient over the course of the past century, control over networks is increasingly important (Kobrin, 1997; Strange, 1996). However, much important research remains to be done on the operational meaning of networks within different domains. There is considerable variation in the scope and salience of networks, from financial to technological. There are also important questions about how networks emerge, how they function, how they are sustained, how they are regulated, and how they might be transformed (Deibert, 1997).

There are also a number of questions about how to conceptualize alternatives to the system of states. There is an important theoretical and conceptual debate about whether we are witnessing the emergence of a globalization or a regionalization of the world economy. For some scholars, the movement away from the nation-state as the principal market unit is leading to the rise of regional economies, rather than to an integrated, global one (Ohmae, 1995; Storper, 1997; Storper and Scott, 1992).

There is also a great deal of promising research on the salience and meaning of boundaries themselves (Andreas, 2000). The porosity of boundaries (soft versus hard) has already been discussed (Mostov, 2000). Anthropologists and students of literature have increasingly drawn our attention to the importance of understanding the phenomenon of border culture, a syncretic cultural conception that stresses the role of borders in constructing various forms of identity, as well as the multilayered nature of that identity (Donnan and Wilson, 1999).

CONCLUSION

No concept or analytical framework is ever complete, or entirely adequate for all situations or phenomena. Future research on the concepts of state, sovereignty and territoriality, like research of the past, will be driven by the dialectical interplay between events and theoretical efforts to interpret, comprehend and understand them. The limitations and contradictions contained within existing theoretical concepts, frameworks and explanations will be tested by their adequacy (or inadequacy) to explain contemporary events. At the same time, they will also play a role in the shaping of those events themselves. It is for this reason that it is so important to understand the origins, changes of meaning and transformations of the central concepts of state, sovereignty and territoriality in international relations.

Notes

I would like to thank Walter Carlsnaes, Helle Malmvig, Thomas Risse, Beth Simmons and John Tomasi for their insightful comments on an earlier draft of this chapter. I would also like to thank an anonymous reviewer for the Handbook, who made so many constructive suggestions and pushed me to clarify my arguments. Finally, I would like to acknowledge a long-standing intellectual debt to my colleagues on a related project, Hayward Alker, Tahir Amin and Takashi Inoguchi. Although they have not read this chapter in advance of its publication, they will understand that it could not have been written without our many discussions and debates over the years.

1 Wendt (1999) qualifies his state centrism on page 9 with the recognition of different state forms, and he makes the observation that the state should be seen as a 'project' in the Gramscian sense, 'an ongoing political program designed to produce and reproduce a monopoly on the potential for organized violence'. However, he concludes this passage with the premise that 'since states are the dominant form of subjectivity in contemporary world politics this means that they should be the primary unit of analysis for thinking about the global regulation of violence'. Thus, even if they are recognized to have changed form over time, they appear to be essentially the same in the contemporary period.

2 Some might be inclined to suggest that Henry Kissinger retained more than a little nostalgia for the absolutist state, something his critics would maintain Richard Nixon appeared at times intent on recreating.

3 It is worth noting here the basic ambiguity contained in the UN Charter on the issue of sovereignty. Note especially that Article II, Chapter 7 states that 'Nothing contained in the present Charter shall authorize the United nations to intervene in matters which are essentially within the domestic jurisdiction of any state …' While on the one hand, this statement can be interpreted as in keeping with the predominant form of the state during the middle of the twentieth century – the nation-state form – and conforming to the idea of the inviolability of firm state boundaries, on the other hand, the definition of 'matters which are essentially within the domestic jurisdiction of any state' is omitted, enabling both subsequent changes of interpretation and more far-reaching practices of intervention, of the sort we have seen since the end of the Cold War.

4 We need not restrict our analysis to authority, however. Identity is also crucial, because it defines a people over whom authority is exercised, as is territory, because it defines a physical domain within which authority is claimed to apply.

5 However, it is important not to reify this distinction between the internal and the external, because the boundary that separates them is a changing one.

Bibliography

Agnew, John (1998) *Geopolitics: Revisioning World Politics.* London and New York: Routledge.

Agnew, John and Knox, Paul (1994) *The Geography of the World Economy: An Introduction to Economic Geography.* New York: Routledge, Chapman & Hall.

Anderson, Perry (1974) *Lineages of the Absolutist State.* London: New Left Books.

Andreas, Peter (2000) *Border Games: Policing the U.S.– Mexico Divide.* Ithaca: Cornell University Press.

Angell, Norman (1910) *The Great Illusion: A Study of the Relation of Military Power in Nations to their Economic and Social Advantage.* New York and London: G.P. Putnam's Sons, The Knickerbocker Press.

Barraclough, Geoffrey (1967) *An Introduction to Contemporary History.* New York: Penguin Books.

Bartelson, Jens (1995) *A Geneology of Sovereignty.* Cambridge: Cambridge University Press.

Bendix, Reinhard (1964) *Nation-Building and Citizenship: Studies of Our Changing Social Order.* New York: Wiley.

Biersteker, Thomas J. (1992) 'The "Triumph" of Liberal Economic Ideas in the Developing World', in Barbara Stallings (ed.), *Global Change, Regional Response.* Cambridge: Cambridge University Press.

Biersteker, Thomas J. and Weber, Cynthia (1996) *State Sovereignty as Social Construct.* Cambridge: Cambridge University Press.

Bodin, Jean ([1576] 1962) *The Six Bookes of a Commonweale* (ed. Kenneth D. McRae). Cambridge, MA: Harvard University Press.

Bukovansky, Mlada (1997) 'American Identity and Neutral Rights from Independence to the War of 1812', *International Organization,* 51 (2): 209–43.

Bukovansky, Mlada (1999) 'The Altered State and the State of Nature – the French Revolution and International Politics'*, Review of International Studies,* 25 (2): 197–216.

Bull, Hedley (1977) *The Anarchical Society: A Study of Order in World Politics.* New York: Columbia University Press.

Carr, E.H. (1939) *The Twenty Years' Crisis, 1919–1939.* London: Macmillan .

Claude, Inis L. (1989) 'The Balance of Power Revisited'*, Review of International Studies,* 15 (2): 77–86.

Cox, Robert W. (1987) *Production, Power, and World Order: Social Forces in the Making of History.* New York: Columbia University Press.

Craig, Gordon A. and George, Alexander L. (1995) *Force and Statecraft: Diplomatic Problems of Our Time,* (3rd edn). New York and Oxford: Oxford University Press.

Cutler, A. Claire, Haufler, Virginia and Porter, Tony (1999) *Private Authority and International Affairs.* Albany: State University of New York Press.

Deibert, Ronald J. (1997) *Parchment, Printing, and Hypermedia: Communication in World Order Transformations.* New York: Columbia University Press.

Deudney, Daniel (1996) 'Binding Sovereigns: Authorities, Structures, and Geopolitics in Philadelphian Systems', in Thomas J. Biersteker and Cynthia Weber (eds), *State Sovereignty as Social Construct.* Cambridge: Cambridge University Press.

Deutsch, Karl W., Burrell, Sidney A., Kann, Robert A., Lee, Maurice Jr., Lichterman, Martin, Lindgren, Raymond E., Loewenheim, Francis L. and Van Wagenen, Richard W. (1957) *Political Community in the North Atlantic Area.* Princeton: Princeton University Press.

Dicken, Peter (1992) *Global Shift: The Internationalization of Economic Activity,* 2nd edn. London: Paul Chapman.

Donnan, Hastings and Wilson, Thomas M. (1999) *Borders: Frontiers of Identity, Nation and State.* Oxford and New York: Berg.

Evans, Peter B. (1979) *Dependent Development: The Alliance of Multinational, State, and Local Capital in Brazil.* Princeton: Princeton University Press.

Evans, Peter B., Rueschemeyer, Dietrich and Skocpol, Theda (1985) *Bringing the State Back In.* New York: Cambridge University Press.

Friedberg, Aaron (2000) *In the Shadow of the Garrison State: America's Anti-Statism and Its Cold War Grand Strategy.* Princeton: Princeton University Press.

Gerschenkron, Alexander (1962) *Economic Backwardness in Historical Perspective, A Book of Essays.* Cambridge: Belknap Press of Harvard University Press.

Giddens, Anthony (1985) *The Nation-State and Violence.* Berkeley: University of California Press.

Gilpin, Robert (1981) *War and Change in World Politics.* Cambridge and London: Cambridge University Press.

Haas, Ernst B. (1958) *The Uniting of Europe: Political, Social, and Economic Forces, 1950–1957.* Stanford: Stanford University Press.

Hackworth, Green H. (1931) 'The Policy of the United States in Recognizing New Governments during the Past Twenty-Five Years', *Proceedings of the American Society of International Law at its 25th Annual Meeting.* Washington, DC: published by the Society. pp. 120–37.

Hall, Rodney B. (1999) *National Collective Identity: Social Constructs and International Systems.* New York: Columbia University Press.

Hall, Rodney B. (2000) 'The Moral Authority of the Market? The Social Construction of Market Authority and Discursive Strategies in the Asian Financial Crisis', paper presented at the 41st annual conference of the International Studies Association, Los Angeles, California.

Harvey, David (1989) *The Condition of Postmodernity: An Enquiry into the Origins of Cultural Change.* Oxford: Blackwell.

Held, David (1983) *States and Societies*. New York: New York University Press.

Held, David (1995) *Democracy and the Global Order: From the Modern State to Cosmopolitan Governance.* Stanford: Stanford University Press.

Herbst, Jeffrey I. (2000) *States and Power in Africa: Comparative Lessons in Authority and Control.* Princeton: Princeton University Press.

Hinsley, F.H. (1986) *Sovereignty*, 2nd edn. Cambridge: Cambridge University Press.

Hirst, Paul Q. and Thompson, Grahame (1996) *Globalization in Question: The International Economy and the Possibilities of Governance.* Oxford: Blackwell.

Hobbes, Thomas ([1651], 1958), *Leviathan*, with an Introduction by Herbert W. Schneider. New York: Liberal Arts.

Hobson, J.A. (1902) *Imperialism: A Study*. New York: James Pott .

Hoffman, John (1998) *Sovereignty*. Minneapolis: University of Minnesota Press.

Hurrell, Andrew (1995) 'International Relations and the Promotion of Democracy and Human Rights' paper presented at the conference on 'The Third World After the Cold War: Ideology, Economic Development and Politics', Queen Elizabeth House, Oxford University, 5–8 July.

Jackson, Robert (1990) *Quasi-States: Sovereignty, International Relations and the Third World.* Cambridge: Cambridge University Press.

Jackson, Robert (1999) 'Sovereignty in World Politics: A Glance at the Conceptual and Historical Landscape', *Political Studies*, 47 (3): 431–56.

James, Alan (1986) *Sovereign Statehood: The Basis of International Society*. London and Boston: Allen & Unwin.

James, Alan (1992) 'The Equality of States: Contemporary Manifestations of an Ancient Doctrine', *Review of International Studies*, 18 (4): 377–91.

Jorgensen, Knud Erik (1997) *Reflective Approaches to European Governance*. London: Macmillan.

Kaplan, Morton A. (1962) *System and Process in International Politics*. New York: Wiley.

Katzenstein, Peter J. (1978) *Between Power and Plenty: Foreign Economic Policies of Advanced Industrial States*. Madison: University of Wisconsin Press.

Keohane, Robert O. (1984) *After Hegemony: Cooperation and Discord in the World Political Economy*. Princeton: Princeton University Press.

Kipling, Rudyard (1903) 'The White Man's Burden', in his collection of poetry, *The Five Nations*. New York: Charles Scribner's Sons.

Kobrin, Stephen J. (1997) 'Beyond Symmetry: State Sovereignty in a Networked Global Economy', in John Dunning (ed.), *Governments, Globalization and International Business*. Oxford: Oxford University Press.

Koslowski, Rey (2000) *Migrants and Citizens: Demographic Change in the European State System.* Ithaca: Cornell University Press.

Krasner, Stephen D. (1999) *Sovereignty: Organized Hypocrisy*. Princeton: Princeton University Press.

Kratochwil, Friedrich (1986) 'Of Systems, Boundaries, and Territoriality: An Inquiry into the Formation of the State System', *World Politics*, XXXIX (1): 27–52.

Kratochwil, Friedrich (1992) 'The Concept of Sovereignty: Sovereignty as Property', unpublished manuscript, University of Pennsylvania.

Lasswell, Harold D. (1941) 'The Garrison State', *American Journal of Sociology*, XLVI: 455–68.

Lenin, V.I. (1939) *Imperialism: The Highest Stage of Capitalism*. New York: International Publishers.

Lipschutz, Ronnie D. (1996) *Global Civil Society and Global Environmental Governance: The Politics of Nature from Place to Planet*. Albany: State University of New York Press.

Little, Richard (1989) 'Deconstructing the Balance of Power: Two Traditions of Thought', *Review of International Studies*, 15 (2): 87–100.

Luke, Timothy W. (1991) 'The Discipline of Security Studies and the Codes of Containment: Learning from Kuwait', *Alternatives*, 16 (3): 315–44.

Lustick, Ian S. (1993) *Unsettled States, Disputed Lands: Britain and Ireland, France and Algeria, Israel and the West Bank–Gaza*. Ithaca: Cornell University Press.

Lyon, Peter (1993*)* 'The Rise and Fall and Possible Revival of International Trusteeship', *Journal of Commonwealth and Comparative Politics*, 31 (1): 96–110.

Machiavelli, Niccolo (1965) *Chief Works and Others.* Durham, NC: Duke University Press.

Mackinder, Sir Halford J. (1904) 'The Geographical Pivot of History', *The Geographical Journal*, XXIII (4): 421–44.

Mahan, Captain A.T. (1895) *The Influence of Sea Power upon History: 1660–1783*. Boston: Little, Brown.

Mann, Michael (1988) *States, War, and Capitalism: Studies in Political Sociology*. New York: Blackwell.

Marx, Karl and Engels, Friedrich ([1848], 1978) 'Manifesto of the Communist Party' in Robert C. Tucker (ed.), *The Marx–Engels Reader*, 2nd edn. New York: W.W. Norton.

Mittelman, James H. (2000) *The Globalization Syndrome: Transformation and Resistance.* Princeton: Princeton University Press.

Morgenthau, Hans J. (1948) *Politics Among Nations.* New York: Alfred A. Knopf .

Morgenthau, Hans J. (1970) Class notes from the course, International Politics, taken at the University of Chicago by Thomas J. Biersteker.

Mostov, Julie (2000) 'Rethinking Sovereignty, Democracy and the Politics of National Identity', paper presented at the Watson Institute for International Studies conference on 'Whose Self-Determination: Agency and Amnesia in the Disintegration of Yugoslavia' Brown University, 4–5 February.

Murphy, Alexander B. (1999) 'International Law and the Sovereign State System: Challenges to the Status Quo', in George J. Demko and William B. Wood (eds), *Reordering the World: Geopolitical Perspectives on the Twenty-First Century*. Boulder: Westview.

Murphy, Alexander B. (2001) 'Political Geography', in N.D. Smelser and P.B. Baltes (eds), *International Encyclopedia of the Social and Behavioral Sciences*. Amsterdam: Pergamon.

North, Douglass C. (1981) *Structure and Change in Economic History*. New York: W.W. Norton.

Nye, Joseph S. and Keohane, Robert O. (1977) *Power and Interdependence: World Politics in Transition*. Boston: Little, Brown.

Ohmae, Kenichi (1995) *The End of the Nation State: The Rise of Regional Economies*. New York: The Free Press.

Pauly, Louis W. (1997) *Who Elected the Bankers? Surveillance and Control in the World Economy*. Ithaca: Cornell University Press.

Polanyi, Karl (1957) *The Great Transformation*. Boston: Beacon Press.

Poulantzas, Nicos A. (1975) *Classes in Contemporary Capitalism*. London: New Left Books.

Rosow, Stephen J. (1994) 'On the Political Theory of Political Economy: Conceptual Ambiguity and the Global Economy', *Review of International Political Economy*, 1 (3): 465–88.

Ruggie, John G. (1982) 'International Regimes, Transactions, and Change: Embedded Liberalism in the Postwar Economic Order', *International Organization*, 36 (2): 379–415.

Ruggie, John G. (1993a) *Multilateralism Matters: The Theory and Praxis of an Institutional Form*. New York: Columbia University Press.

Ruggie, John G. (1993b) 'Territoriality and Beyond: Problematizing Modernity in International Relations', *International Organization*, 47 (1): 139–74.

Russett, Bruce M. and Starr, Harvey (1985) *World Politics: The Menu for Choice*, 2nd edn. New York: W.H. Freeman.

Sahlins, Peter (1989) *Boundaries: The Making of France and Spain in the Pyrenees*. Berkeley: University of California Press.

Sassen, Saskia (1996) *Losing Control? Sovereignty in an Age of Globalization*. New York: Columbia University Press.

Sassen, Saskia (1998) *Globalization and its Discontents: Essays on the New Mobility of People and Money*. New York: New Press.

Schedler, Andreas, Diamond, Larry and Plattner, Marc F. (1999) *The Self-Restraining State: Power and Accountability in New Democracies*. Boulder and London: Lynne Rienner.

Schmitt, Carl (1985) *Political Theology: Four Chapters on the Concept of Sovereignty*. Cambridge, MA: MIT Press.

Schmitter, Philippe (1996) 'Imagining the Future of the Euro-Polity with the Help of New Concepts', in Gary Marks, Fritz Scharpf, Philippe Schmitter and Wolfgang Streeck (eds), *Governance in the European Union*. London: Sage.

Schroeder, Paul W. (1989) 'The Nineteenth Century System: Balance of Power or Political Equilibrium?', *Review of International Studies*, 15 (2): 135–54.

Sha Yang (1995) 'Sovereignty Reigns Supreme', *Beijing Review*, 38 (34): 4.

Shaw, Malcolm N. (1997) *International Law*, 4th edn. Cambridge: Cambridge University Press.

Sikkink, Kathryn (1993) 'Human Rights, Principled Issue Networks, and Sovereignty in Latin America', *International Organization*, 47 (3): 411–41.

Singer, J. David (1961) 'The Level-of-Analysis Problem in International Relations', in Klaus Knorr and Sidney Verba (eds), *The International System: Theoretical Essays*. Princeton: Princeton University Press.

Smith, Michael Joseph (1986) *Realist Thought from Weber to Kissinger*. Baton Rouge and London: Louisiana State University Press.

Storper, Michael (1997) *The Regional World: Territorial Development in a Global Economy*. New York: Guilford Press.

Storper, Michael and Scott, Allen J. (1992) *Pathways to Industrialization and Regional Development*. London: Routledge.

Strange, Susan (1995) 'The Defective State', *Daedalus*, 124 (2): 55–74.

Strange, Susan (1996) *The Retreat of the State: The Diffusion of Power in the World Economy*. New York: Cambridge University Press.

Tilly, Charles (1975) *The Formation of National States in Western Europe*. Princeton: Princeton University Press.

Tunander, Ola (1997) 'Post Cold War Europe: Synthesis of a Bipolar Friend–Foe Structure and a Hierarchic Cosmos–Chaos Structure?', in Ola Tunander, Pavel Baev and Victoria Ingrid Einagel (eds), *Geopolitics in Post-Wall Europe*. London: Sage.

Wade, Robert (1987) *Governing the Market: Economic Theory and the Role of Government in East Asian Industrialization*. Princeton: Princeton University Press.

Wade, Robert (1996) 'Globalization and its Limits: Reports of the Death of the National Economy are Greatly Exaggerated', in Suzanne Berger and Ronald Dore (eds), *National Diversity and Global Capitalism*. Ithaca: Cornell University Press.

Waever, Ole (1997) 'Imperial Metaphors: Emerging European Analogies to Pre-Nation-State Imperial Systems', in Ola Tunander, Pavel Baev and Victoria Ingrid Einagel (eds), *Geopolitics in Post-Wall Europe*. London: Sage.

Wallace, William (1983) 'Less than a Federation, More than a Regime: the Community as a Political System', in Helen Wallace, William Wallace and Carole Webb (eds), *Policy-Making in the European Community*, 2nd edn. Chichester: Wiley.

Wallace, William (1999) 'The Sharing of Sovereignty: The European Paradox', *Political Studies*, 47 (3): 503–21.

Waltz, Kenneth N. (1979) *Theory of International Politics*. Reading, MA: Addison–Wesley.

Watson, Adam (1992) *The Evolution of International Society: A Comparative Historical Analysis.* London: Routledge.

Weber, Cynthia (1995) *Simulating Sovereignty: Intervention, the State, and Symbolic Exchange.* Cambridge: Cambridge University Press.

Weber, Max (1949) 'Power. Part 2', in *From Max Weber: Essays in Sociology* (trans. and ed. Hans H. Gerth and C. Wright Mills). New York: Oxford University Press.

Weiss, Linda (1998) *The Myth of the Powerless State.* Ithaca: Cornell University Press.

Wendt, Alexander (1999) *Social Theory of International Politics*. Cambridge: Cambridge University Press.

Wight, Martin (1977) *Systems of States*. Leicester: Leicester University Press.

9

Power and International Relations

DAVID A. BALDWIN

Most definitions of politics involve power. Most international interactions are political or have ramifications for politics. Thus, it is not surprising that power has been prominent in discussions of international interaction from Thucydides to the present day. The long history of discussions of the role of power in international relations, however, has failed to generate much agreement. Scholars disagree not only with respect to the role of power but also with respect to the nature of power. One scholar notes that power is a key concept in realist theories of international politics, while conceding that 'its proper definition remains a matter of controversy' (Waltz, 1986: 333). Robert Gilpin describes the concept of power as 'one of the most troublesome in the field of international relations' (1981: 13) and suggests that the 'number and variety of definitions should be an embarrassment to political scientists' (1975: 24). There is, however, widespread consensus among international relations scholars on both the necessity of addressing the role of power in international interactions and the unsatisfactory state of knowledge about this topic (Guzzini, 2000).

Although it is often useful to distinguish among such power terms as power, influence, control, coercion, force, persuasion, deterrence, compellence, inducement and so on, it is possible to identify common elements underlying all such terms. Robert A. Dahl (1957) has suggested that underlying most such terms is the basic intuitive notion of A causing B to do something that B otherwise would not have done. (In the discussion that follows, 'A' refers to the actor having or exercising influence; while 'B' refers to the actor being influenced.) Although alternative definitions of power abound, none rivals this one in widespread acceptability. In the following discussion, the term

'power' will be used in a broad generic sense that is interchangeable with such terms as 'influence' or 'control' unless otherwise indicated. This usage is not intended to deny the validity or the utility of distinguishing among such terms for other purposes.

POWER AND THE STUDY OF INTERNATIONAL POLITICS

International politics has been defined in terms of influencing 'major groups in the world so as to advance the purposes of some against the opposition of others' (Wright, 1955: 130). Although the term 'power politics' has unsavory connotations for some, such a definition implies that the term is redundant (Carr, [1939]1946; Morgenthau, [1948]1960; Sprout and Sprout, 1945; Spykman, 1942; Wright, 1955). From this perspective, all politics is power politics in the sense that all politics involves power. This is not to say that politics is *only* about power.

Traditionally, the study of international politics assumed the existence of national states with conflicting policies, placing a high value on maintaining their independence, and relying primarily on military force. The states with the most military power were designated 'Great Powers', and the 'game' of international politics was 'played' primarily by them (Sprout and Sprout, 1945, 1962; Wight, 1946). Noting that only a few states possessed the military capabilities to support their foreign policies effectively, an influential text in the 1930s averred that 'these alone constitute the Great Powers' (Simonds and Emeny, 1937: 28).

In the eighteenth century, 'the power of individual states was conceived to be susceptible of measurement by certain well-defined factors' (Gulick, 1955: 24), including population, territory, wealth, armies and navies. In the ensuing years, this approach evolved into the 'elements of national power' approach to power analysis reflected in Hans J. Morgenthau's influential textbook *Politics Among Nations* ([1948] 1960 see also Sprout and Sprout, 1945).

States were depicted as seeking to maximize power relative to each other, thus producing a 'balance of power' or as seeking to produce a balance of power (Claude, 1962; Gulick, 1955; Haas, 1953; Morgenthau [1948] 1960). Each version of balance of power theory shared the assumption that it was possible to add up the various elements of national power, sometimes called 'power resources' or 'capabilities', in order to calculate the power distribution among the Great Powers. A modern version of this approach is found in Kenneth N. Waltz's *Theory of International Politics* (1979).

THE POWER ANALYSIS REVOLUTION

The 'elements of national power' approach depicted power as a possession or property of states. This approach was challenged during the last half of the twentieth century by the 'relational power' approach, developed by scholars working in several disciplines, including psychology, philosophy, sociology, economics and political science (Baldwin, 1989; Barry, 1976; Cartwright, 1965; Dahl, 1957, [1963, 1984] 1991; 1968; Frey, 1971, 1985, 1989; Harsanyi, 1962; Nagel, 1975; Oppenheim, 1981; Simon, 1957; Tedeschi and Bonoma, 1972). Some would regard the publication of *Power and Society* by Harold Lasswell and Abraham Kaplan (1950) as the watershed between the old 'power-as-resources' approach and the new 'relational power' approach, which developed the idea of power as a type of causation. This causal notion conceives of power as a relationship in which the behavior of actor A at least partially causes a change in the behavior of actor B. 'Behavior' in this context need not be defined narrowly, but may be understood broadly to include beliefs, attitudes, opinions, expectations, emotions and/or predispositions to act. In this view, power is an actual or potential relationship between two or more actors (persons, states, groups, etc.), rather than a property of any one of them.

The shift from a property concept of power to a relational one constituted a revolution in power analysis. Despite the ancient origins of the study of power, Dahl maintains that 'the systematic empirical study of power relations is remarkably new' (1968: 414). He attributes the 'considerable improvement in the clarity' of power concepts to the fact that 'the last several decades have probably witnessed more systematic efforts to tie down these concepts

than have the previous millennia of political thought' (Dahl, [1963, 1984] 1991: 27–8).

Dimensions of Power

Power was no longer viewed as monolithic and unidimensional, but rather as multidimensional. This allowed for the possibility that power could increase on one dimension while simultaneously decreasing on another. Among the more important dimensions of power were the following.

Scope Scope refers to the aspect of B's behavior affected by A. This calls attention to the possibility that an actor's power may vary from one issue to another. Thus, a country like Japan may have more influence with respect to economic issues than with respect to military issues.

Domain The domain of an actor's power refers to the number of other actors subject to its influence. In other words, how big is B; or how many Bs are there? Thus, a state may have a great deal of influence in one region of the world, while having little or no influence in other parts of the world.

Weight The weight of an actor's power refers to the probability that B's behavior is or could be affected by A (Dahl, 1957; see also Deutsch, [1968]1988; Lasswell and Kaplan, 1950). Thus, a country that has only a 30 per cent chance of achieving its aims in trade negotiations is less powerful than one with a 90 per cent chance, *ceteris paribus*. This dimension could also be labeled the 'reliability' of A's influence.

Costs Both the costs to A and the costs to B are relevant to assessing influence (Baldwin, 1989; Barry, 1976; Dahl, 1968; Harsanyi, 1962; Schelling, 1984: 268–90). Is it costly or cheap for A to influence B? Is it costly or cheap for B to comply with A's demands? Some have suggested that more power should be attributed to an actor that can exercise influence cheaply than to one for whom it is costly (Harsanyi, 1962). If A can get B to do something that is costly for B, some would contend that this is indicative of more power than if A can only get B to do things that are cheap for B. Even if A is unable to get B to comply with its demands, it may be able to impose costs on B for non-compliance. Some have argued that this should be viewed as a kind of power (Baldwin, 1985; Harsanyi, 1962; Schelling, 1984: 268–90).

Means There are many means of exercising influence and many ways to categorize such means. One scheme (Baldwin, 1985) for classifying the means of influence in international relations includes the following categories:

1 Symbolic means. This would include appeals to normative symbols as well as the provision of information. Thus one country might influence another either by reminding them that slavery is bad or by informing them that AIDS is caused by HIV.
2 Economic means. Augmenting or reducing the goods or services available to other countries has a long history in world politics.
3 Military means. Actual or threatened military force has received more attention than any other means in international relations.
4 Diplomatic means. Diplomacy includes a wide array of practices, including representation and negotiation.

Which dimensions of power should be specified for meaningful scholarly communication? There is no single right answer to this question. The causal concept of power, however, does imply a minimum set of specifications. The point is well put by Jack Nagel (1975: 14):

> Anyone who employs a causal concept of power *must* specify domain and scope. To say 'X has power' may seem sensible, but to say 'X causes' or 'X can cause' is nonsense. Causation implies an X and a Y – a cause and an effect. If power is causation, one must state the outcome caused. Stipulating domain and scope answers the question 'Power over *what*?'

The idea that a meaningful specification of a power relationship must include scope and domain is widely shared by power analysts committed to social scientific inquiry (Barry, 1976; Dahl, 1991, 1968; Deutsch, [1968] 1988; Frey, 1971, 1989; Lasswell and Kaplan, 1950).

The multidimensional nature of power makes it difficult to add up the various dimensions in order to arrive at some overall estimate of an actor's power. Although there are some similarities between political power and purchasing power (Baldwin, 1989), one important difference is the lack of a standardized measuring rod for the former. Whereas money can be used to measure purchasing power, there is no comparable standard of value in terms of which to add up the various dimensions of power so as to arrive at an overall total. For this reason, estimates of an actors 'overall power' are likely to be controversial.

Faces of Power?

One of the most famous debates in the literature on power during the last half of the twentieth century is known as the 'Faces of Power' debate (Bachrach and Baratz, 1962; Isaac, 1987; Lukes, 1974). Although this debate clarified some important points, its significance for international relations is sometimes misunderstood. The first issue was whether

control over agendas could be accommodated. And the second issue was whether control over the desires and thoughts of others could be taken into account. Whatever the shortcomings of various empirical analyses of power, it should be noted that the basic causal concept of power discussed earlier can easily accommodate either of these phenomena. A can cause B to do something that B would otherwise not do by controlling B's agenda (that is, B's options) or by affecting B's preferences, desires and thoughts. Brainwashing can be analyzed with the conventional relational concept of power. One does not need to reconceptualize power in order to treat such matters.

INTERNATIONAL POWER ANALYSIS

Although many political scientists have contributed to the power analysis revolution during the past fifty years, very few have been students of international relations (Baldwin, 1971b; Singer, 1963). Harold and Margaret Sprout, who had been proponents of the elements of national power approach in their early work (Sprout and Sprout, 1945), later repudiated that approach and were among the first international relations scholars to call for incorporation of the relational power approach into the study of international politics (Sprout and Sprout, 1956, 1962, 1965). Despite the efforts of the Sprouts and others, however, the elements of national power approach is still deeply embedded in the international relations literature (Waltz, 1979). This situation has given rise to several problems in the analysis of power in the international arena, some of which are discussed below.

The Potential Power Problem

The elements of national power approach to power analysis is a variant of the power-as-resources approach. In this approach, power resources are treated as if they were power itself. One problem with this approach is that what functions as a power asset in one situation may be a power liability in a different situation. Planes loaded with nuclear bombs may be worse than useless in a situation calling for planes with conventional weapons with insufficient time to unload the nuclear weapons and reload the planes with conventional ones. And the same stockpile of arms that is useful for deterring one country may trigger an arms race with another. Similarly, what constitutes a 'good hand' in card games depends on whether one is playing poker or bridge.

Discussions of the capabilities of states that fail to designate or imply a framework of assumptions about who is trying (or might try) to get whom to do what are comparable to discussions of what constitutes a good hand in cards without specifying which game is to be played. The Sprouts called this set of assumptions a 'policy-contingency framework' (1965, 1971). Focusing on the capabilities of states is simply a way of drawing attention to their potential power. It makes no more sense to talk about state capabilities in general than to talk about state power without (explicitly or implicitly) specifying scope and domain. If one wants to estimate the potential power of Guatemala, it helps to know, nay, it is imperative to know whether it concerns a border dispute with El Salvador or a trade agreement with the United States.

Although it is sometimes suggested that insistence on specification of the scope and domain of potential power relationships makes prediction and or generalization nearly impossible (Guzzini, 2000; Keohane, 1986), this is not true. Specification of scope and domain (or policy-contingency frameworks) need not imply atheoretical empiricism. Policy-contingency frameworks may be defined more or less broadly to suit the purpose of the analyst. As Nagel (1975: 14) observes, 'domain and scope need not be particularistic or unique. Depending on one's purpose and the limits imposed by reality, the outcome class may contain a few similar members or many diverse elements'. It is, of course, possible to make predictions or generalize about the potential power of Guatemala (or similar states) without reference to Guatemala's goals and without reference to the goals or capabilities of other states; but it is not clear why one would want to do so.

Power resources are the raw materials out of which power relationships are forged. Although it might seem that the predictive value of power resource inventories is impaired by insistence on prior specification of scope and domain, the opposite is true. The accuracy of one's estimate of whether an architect has adequate raw materials to complete his or her project is likely to improve if one first ascertains whether the architect plans to build a birdhouse or a cathedral.

The Fungibility Problem

'Fungibility' refers to the ease with which power resources useful in one issue-area can be used in other issue-areas. Money in a market economy is the prototypical fungible resource. Indeed, fungibility (that is, liquidity) is one of the defining characteristics of money.[1] In a market economy one does not usually need to specify the scope or domain of the purchasing power of money because the same euro (yen, dollar, etc.) can be used to buy a car, a meal, or a book.

It is sometimes suggested that power plays the same role in international politics that money does in a market economy (Deutsch, [1968] 1988; Wolfers,

1962). Political power resources, of course, do vary in degree of fungibility. Money, time and information tend to be more fungible than most other power resources in that they are useful in many different issue-areas. To the extent that the power–money analogy leads to ignoring the need to specify scope and domain, however, it can be quite misleading for the political power analyst (Baldwin, 1989).

Some scholars have suggested that the fungibility of power resources increases as the amount increases (Art, 1996; Waltz, 2000). Thus, power is said to be more fungible for powerful states than for weaker states. It is not clear what this means or why it might be true. It is, of course, true that more power resources allow one to do more things, that is, influence more actors and/or more issues. This implies nothing about the fungibility of any particular power resource. Fungibility refers to the uses of a *given* amount of a power resource, not to the uses of varying amounts. In the economic realm, rich people can buy more things than poor people; but this is not because a rich person's dollar is more fungible than a poor person's dollar. The contention that fungibility increases with the amount of power resources is based either on a confused concept of fungibility or on a logic that has yet to be spelled out (Baldwin, 1999; Guzzini, 1998).

The Problem of Intentions

Max Weber (1947: 152) defined power as 'the probability that one actor within a social relationship will be in a position to carry out his own will despite resistance, regardless of the basis on which this probability rests'. This definition clearly makes the intentions of actor A an important part of the concept of power. Many of the most interesting and important questions in international relations concern the ability or inability of governments to realize their goals. Can the Allies win the Second World War? Can the United States get other countries to join the United Nations? Can Japan get the members of the United Nations to let it join? Can China get the approval of member countries to join the World Trade Organization? Can the poor countries get trade preferences from the rich? All such questions involve the ability of countries to realize their goals.

But what about unintended effects? When the United States Federal Reserve system raises interest rates, it usually intends to affect the American domestic economy; but the actual effects are likely to reverberate around the world. There is no question about the reality or importance of unintended effects in international politics (Guzzini, 2000; Jervis, 1997; Strange, 1988). The question is whether the conventional concept of power can account for such phenomena. Although intentions are often built into the causal concept of power, for example, the Weberian version, they need not be. It is quite possible to differentiate between situations in which A intentionally causes a change in B's behavior and situations in which A does so unintentionally (Baldwin, 1989; Frey, 1989). Relational power analysis is historically indebted to the Weberian formulation, but it is not logically bound by it. Thus, there is no need for a fundamental reformulation of the concept of power in order to account for its unintended effects.

Those who call for more attention to the unintended effects of power tend to imply that these unintended effects are detrimental to the interests of those affected (Guzzini, 2000; Strange, 1988). This is not necessarily so. The unintended effects can also be beneficial to the interests of those affected. When the United States encourages trade with other countries, it does so primarily with the intention of improving its own economic welfare; but this may have the unintended effect of improving the welfare of its trading partners also. When the United States took steps to deter Soviet nuclear attack on North America during the Cold War, it did so primarily with the intention of providing for its own security; but this action had the unintended effect of providing for Canadian security also.[2] Whether the unintended effects of the actions (or inactions) of powerful states tends to be beneficial or detrimental to the interests of those affected is an empirical question. It should be answered by research, not by assertion.

The Measurement Problem

Before one can measure power, one must first have a concept of power. In the field of international relations, the desire to measure power on a single dimension that would allow states to be ranked often gets in the way of – or even precedes – conceptual analysis. Frey (1989) has pointed out that the difficulty of measuring power often leads researchers to redefine it so as to make operationalization easier. 'In this fashion, power has frequently been defined in terms of supposed resources – e.g., the ability to mobilize resources, possession of resources, and other forms of what Elster (1976: 252) calls "generalized fetishist theories," that is, theories that attempt to regard relations as properties' (Frey, 1989: 7–8).

As noted above, there is no political counterpart for money. There is no standardized measure that facilitates reducing the various dimensions of power to a single dimension. Yet the desire to measure power makes this an inconvenient fact:

> The search for an index of national power has been largely, ... based on the assumption that it is possible and desirable to find a *currency* of politics. As economists view economic transactions of all sorts and at all levels in terms of a standardized unit of currency, ... so, the assumption runs, must the political scientist find an absolute scale along which to evaluate the 'power' of nation-states. (Merritt and Zinnes, 1988: 142)

It is the desire of international relations scholars to rank the overall power of states from highest to lowest that generates the most difficult measurement problems. This requires comparing different dimensions of power relations without any agreed-upon way to do this. Some scholars contend that the question of 'Who's number one?' is as useful in international relations as it is in sports (Ray and Vural, 1986). It is not clear, however, that it is either meaningful or useful to ask this question even in the realm of sports. Assessing athletic ability without reference to a specified set of athletic activities is akin to assessing power without reference to scope and domain. How is one to compare a golfer, a swimmer, an archer, a runner and a weightlifter? As Dahl ([1963, 1984] 1991: 27) has pointed out, 'it is difficult enough to estimate relative influence within a particular scope and domain; it is by no means clear how we can "add up" influence over many scopes and domains in order to arrive at total, or aggregate, influence'. This is equally true of attempts to 'add up' and compare athletic accomplishments in different sports.

Most indices of overall national power rely primarily on GNP, but are sometimes supplemented with demographic and military measures (Merritt and Zinnes, 1988). The best known of these is that developed by the Correlates of War Project (Singer, 1988). The difficulty with all such measures, however, is that they treat power as a property rather than a relation. 'The escape through redefining power to be a property, though seductive, warps the very essence of what interests us' (Frey, 1985: 12). GNP is correlated not only with war-winning ability, but also with Olympic medals. No one, however, has suggested that GNP is a useful measure of athletic ability. Not every correlate of power (or Olympic medals) provides a useful operational definition of power (or athletic ability).

This is not to suggest that it is impossible to measure power. Power is difficult but not impossible to measure. Measures of the power of A with respect to B (domain) and with respect to C (scope) can be made on the following dimensions: (1) the probability of B's compliance; (2) the speed with which B complies; (3) the number of issues included in C; (4) the magnitude of the positive or negative sanction provided by A; (5) the costs to A; (6) the costs to B; and (7) the number of options available to B (Dahl, 1968; Frey, 1985, 1989). If international relations researchers were to give up the search for a universally valid measure of overall national power, much useful research could be focused on measuring the distribution of power within specified scopes and domains. What makes the

Correlates of War power index more useful than most such indices is that it was developed, and has usually been applied, in the context of the policy-contingency framework of war. Whether this index is equally applicable to other situations has yet to be established.

POWER IN INTERNATIONAL RELATIONS THEORY

'The proposition that the nature of international politics is shaped by power relations' is often listed as a 'defining characteristic of Realism' (Wendt, 1999: 96–7). As Wendt (1999: 97) points out, however, this is not a *unique* characteristic of realism. Neoliberals, Marxists, postmodernists, constructivists, dependency theorists, globalists and feminists all think power matters. No attempt will be made here to survey the treatments of power relations in all of these theories. The discussion will confine itself to two well-known and influential theories – the balance of power and neorealism.

Classic Balance of Power Theory

The 'balance of power' was used by Thucydides to explain the onset of the Peloponnesian War, was the subject of an essay by David Hume (1742) in the eighteenth century, and continues to fascinate international relations theorists even today (Claude, 1989; Guzzini, 2000; Little, 1989; Moul, 1989; Walt, 1987; Waltz, 1979). Although many different theories carry the 'balance of power' label, the term itself, 'implies that changes in relative political power can be observed and measured' (Wright, 1965: 743).

The question of precisely what was being observed and measured, however, has remained illusive. In the ninetteenth century Richard Cobden argued that the term 'balance of power' could 'be discarded as fallacious, since it gives no definition – whether by breadth of territory, number of inhabitants, or extent of wealth – according to which, in balancing the respective powers, each state shall be estimated' (quoted in Gulick, 1955: 27). Pollard (1923: 58) concluded that the term 'may mean almost anything; and it is used not only in different senses by different people, or in different senses by the same people at different times, but in different senses by the same person at the same time'. Morgenthau (1960: 167) discussed the balance of power at length, but admitted to using the term to mean four different things. One is tempted to despair when one writer dismisses the term as meaningless (Guzzini, 2000), while another contends that the problem is 'not that it has no meaning, but that it has too many meanings' (Claude,

1962: 13; Haas, 1953). It is beyond the limits of this chapter to attempt clarification of this conceptual morass.

No matter which version of balance of power theory one considers, the idea of power as a property rather than a relation is firmly embedded. It could hardly be otherwise, since any attempt to interpret balance of power theory using the relational concept of power would immediately encounter the difficulties flowing from the multidimensionality of power and the lack of a standardized measure of value in terms of which these dimensions could be expressed. Suppose a country drains resources from its domestic economy in order to increase its military strength, as the Soviet Union did. Its military power may be increasing at the same time, and partly because, its economic power is decreasing. How is one to calculate the net effect on the overall balance of power, given the difficulty of adding up various scopes and domains of power? It is precisely these difficulties that lead Guzzini (1998, 2000) to pronounce the term meaningless.

To the extent that balance of power theory has been meaningful, it has been based on a conception of power as a particular type of power resource used in a particular policy-contingency framework, that is, military force conceived in the context of war-winning ability (Claude, 1962; Gulick, 1955; Morgenthau, [1948] 1960; Walt, 1987; Wright, 1965: 743ff). The analytical perspective of relational power prompts one to ask, 'Power to get whom to do what?' One of the benefits of bringing this perspective to bear on balance of power theories is that it brings to light the underlying assumptions that: (1) military force is the measure of power; and (2) war-winning is what matters most. Only after these assumptions have been made explicit can fruitful debate as to their wisdom occur.

Neorealism

The theory of neorealism developed by Waltz (1979) dominated discussions of international relations theory during the last quarter of the twentieth century, much as Morgenthau's (1948) version of the theory of realism dominated discussions during the period between 1950 and 1975. Overall evaluation of neorealism is beyond the scope of this chapter. Instead, the focus is on the role of power and capabilities in the theory.

Waltz advances a structural theory of international politics. One of the defining characteristics of the structure of the international system is the distribution of capabilities. Since judgments must be made about how capabilities are distributed, Waltz must confront the issue of how to measure them. Realizing that his theory requires the rank ordering of states according to their capabilities, he resists the specification of scope and domain necessitated by a relational notion of power. Ranking the capabilities of states is much harder if power/capability is conceived as multidimensional. Thus, he asserts that 'the economic, military, and other capabilities of nations cannot be sectored and separately weighed' (1979: 131). He provides neither argument nor evidence to support the assertion that different kinds of capabilities *cannot* be measured separately; he simply asserts it. It may be that Waltz has in mind the constraints of his theory in the sense that permitting capabilities to be weighed separately could make ranking states excessively difficult. Waltz goes on to say that 'states are not placed in the top rank because they excel in one way or another. Their rank depends on how they score on *all* of the following items: size of population and territory, resource endowment, economic capability, military strength, political stability and competence. States spend a lot of time estimating one another's capabilities, especially their abilities to do harm' (1979: 131). The use of the term 'score' is revealing. It implies a measuring rod, or standard, in terms of which the various elements of national power can be evaluated; but there is no indication of what this standard is. The assertion that states devote 'a lot of time to estimating one another's capabilities' is unsupported and contestable. The defense ministries of states formulate contingency plans with respect to a variety of policy-contingency frameworks, but it is unlikely that they spend much time estimating each other's capabilities in general or without reference to actual or postulated situations. The idea that American policy-makers spend a lot of time calculating the capabilities of Canada or the United Kingdom in general, or in the abstract, seems rather far-fetched. Still, these are empirical questions and are, in principle, researchable.

Despite his admission that 'states have different combinations of capabilities which are difficult to measure and compare' (1979: 131), Waltz proclaims that 'ranking states … does not require predicting their success in war or in other endeavors. We need only rank them roughly by capability'. This assertion, of course, begs the question of how 'capabilities' are to be defined – a definition that Waltz never provides. We are told only that capabilities are 'attributes of units' (1979: 98). Clearly, the relational concept of power or capabilities is ruled out, since that concept of power depicts capabilities as potential relationships rather than as properties of a single state (or unit). The question of 'Capability to get whom to do what?' is simply begged; and the power as resources concept underlying Waltz's theory becomes apparent.

At some level, however, most international relations theorists recognize the wisdom of the Sprouts's contention that 'without some set of given undertakings (strategies, policies), actual or postulated, with reference to some frame of operational contingencies, actual or postulated, there can be no estimation of political capabilities' (1965: 215). In most treatments of the elements of national power in international politics an implicit set of policy-contingency assumptions can be identified, usually having to do with military power. Just as Morgenthau's discussion of the elements of national power implies that war-winning is the standard of judgment (Baldwin, 1993: 17–18), careful reading of Waltz generates a strong suspicion that war-winning ability is the unstated standard by which states are being ranked. Morgenthau's contention that 'nations active in international politics are continuously preparing for, actively involved in, or recovering from organized violence in the form of war' ([1948] 1960: 38) is remarkably similar to the outlook in Waltz's *Theory of International Politics*. 'The possibility that force will be used by one or another of the parties looms always as a threat in the background. In politics force is said to be the *ultima ratio*. In international politics force serves, not only as the *ultima ratio*, but indeed as the first and constant one' (Waltz, 1979: 113). 'The daily presence of force and recurrent reliance on it mark the affairs of nations. Since Thucydides in Greece and Kautilya in India, the use of force and the possibility of controlling it have been the preoccupations of international-political studies' (Waltz, 1979: 186). Given the absence of any explicit standard for 'scoring' the capabilities of states in Waltz's text, there is more than a little reason to suspect that war-winning is the implicit standard being applied.

Although the book is nearly devoid of references to the scholarly literature on relational power, at the end of *Theory of International Politics* (1979: 191–2), almost as an afterthought, Waltz launches a confusing and confused attack on the relational concept of power: 'We are misled by the pragmatically formed and technologically influenced American definition of power – a definition that equates power with control. Power is then measured by the ability to get people to do what one wants them to do when otherwise they would not do it.' This is a puzzling and misleading criticism. It is unclear why Waltz uses the phrases 'pragmatically formed,' 'technologically influenced,' or 'American'. The relational concept of power was developed by non-Americans as well as Americans (Barry, 1976; Weber, 1947) and has no intrinsically ethnocentric biases. And neither the meaning nor the significance of pragmatism and technology is self-evident or explained.

Waltz goes on to assert that 'the common relational definition of power omits consideration of how acts and relations are affected by the structure of action', which is not necessarily true, and that unintended effects are ruled out of consideration, which is true of some versions of relational power but not others – as noted above.

'According to the common American definition of power, a failure to get one's way is proof of weakness.' In a sense this is true. Actors that consistently try and fail to influence other actors are unlikely to be viewed as powerful. Indeed, Waltz himself appears to believe this, since he later observes that 'the stronger get their way – not always, but more often than the weaker' (Waltz, 1993).

Waltz then asks: 'What then can be substituted for the practically and logically untenable definition? I offer the old and simple notion that an agent is powerful to the extent that he affects others more than they affect him.' There are several remarkable aspects of this proposed definition of power. First, after rejecting both causal and relational concepts of power, he proposes a definition that is both causal and relational. Second, the notion proposed is similar to those espoused by Deutsch (1953, 1963) and Frey (1985), both of whom saw themselves as contributing to the development of the relational concept of power. Third, it is inconsistent with the statement in the very next paragraph that 'the extent of one's power cannot be inferred from the results one may or may not get'. And fourth, the proposed concept of power seems to have little or nothing to do with the concepts of power and capability used throughout the earlier sections of the book. If capability is defined as the potential power to affect others more than one is affected by others, it is no longer a property of a single actor.

Even the critics of neorealism credit it with having enhanced the clarity and rigor of the realist theoretical tradition (Keohane, 1986). With respect to its treatment of power and capability, however, *Theory of International Politics* seems to have introduced a considerable amount of confusion, and contradiction.

CURRENT ISSUES

The study of power in international relations has generated a number of issues in addition to those discussed above. Among these are the following: the role of military force, structural power and constructivism.

Military Power

Many writers have commented on the preoccupation with military force by students of international politics down through the ages (Art and Waltz, [1971] 1999; Baldwin, 1989; Osgood and Tucker, 1967; Sprout and Sprout, 1945, 1962, 1965; Waltz, 1979; Wright, 1955, [1942] 1965). Although war is an important phenomenon that international relations scholars regard as their special province, the field of international relations has paid a price for its preoccupation with military force. The importance of military force has been exaggerated; the role of non-military forms of power has been underestimated;

and the field of international relations has been impoverished by its insulation from studies of power in other realms.

The privileged place of military power in the study of international politics is demonstrated and reinforced by references to the 'centrality' of force to international politics (Art, 1996; Baldwin, 1999); to the study of power as 'a study of the capacity to wage war' (Cline, [1975] 1997); to force as 'the ultimate form of power' (Gilpin, 1975, 1981); or to international security studies as 'the study of the threat, use, and control of military force' (Walt, 1991: 212). Even Keohane and Nye ([1977] 2001: 15), who have criticized the traditional emphasis on military force, depict force as dominating other means of power.

The tendency to single out force as the ultimate measuring rod to which other forms of power should be compared is anathema to the approach advocated by Lasswell and Kaplan (1950: ix, 76, 85, 92, 94). Although they gave 'special consideration to the role of violence', they repeatedly denied that power rests 'always, or even generally, on violence'; and they maintained 'that power may rest on various bases'; that 'none of the forms of power is basic to all the others'; and that 'political phenomena are only obscured by the pseudosimplification attained with any unitary conception of power as always and everywhere the same'. Despite the vigorous efforts of Lasswell and Kaplan and the tradition of relational power analysis they spawned, the contemporary literature on international relations often exhibits the same tendencies to exaggerate the role of military power as did earlier works (Baldwin, 1995; Ray and Vural, 1986; Walt, 1991; Waltz, 1979).

The preoccupation with military force in the study of international politics has led to the neglect of nonmilitary forms of power, such as economic statecraft (Baldwin, 1985). In addition, it has ironically limited understanding of military statecraft itself. The question of when military force should be used cannot be answered without consideration of alternative instruments of statecraft (Baldwin, 1995; 1999/2000). Thus, the neglect of non-military forms of power has hampered understanding of the conditions under which military force should be used.

Structural vs. Relational Power

The relational power approach has been criticized both for neglecting the study of structural power and for its alleged inability to take account of structural power (Guzzini, 1993, 2000; Strange, 1988). To the extent that structural power is viewed as unrelated to human agency or based on a non-causal notion of power, it would be fair to say that relational power and structural power represent fundamentally different approaches to the study of power. Otherwise, the relational concept of power is quite capable of taking account of power structures.

If structural power refers to unintentional power or to power with respect to the creation and/or control of structures (Guzzini, 1993; Krasner, 1985; Strange, 1988), there is no need to seek an alternative to the relational concept of power. The first meaning can be taken care of by excluding intentionality from the concept of power, as noted above. And the second meaning of structural power can easily be accounted for by proper specification of scope and domain. The creation and/or control of structures is simply an instance of influence with a particular scope and domain.

The study of power structures does present difficulties for the relational notion of power if such structures are depicted as unidimensional and monolithic and unspecified as to scope and domain. Thus, the idea of a single power structure dominating all issue areas and all domains to an equal degree is difficult to reconcile with the relational power approach. Some discussions of 'hegemony' in international relations seem to imply this view. There is no reason, however, why structures, defined as persistent patterns of power relationships in specified scopes and domains, cannot be usefully studied using the relational concept of power (Frey, 1971). It is worth noting that Lasswell and Kaplan (1950) devoted a whole chapter to 'structures'.

Constructivism vs. Rationalism

How does the debate between constructivism and rationalism intersect with power analysis in the study of international relations? It depends on which of the many versions of constructivism one examines. If constructivism is viewed as rejecting human agency and causal concepts and theories, there is very little overlap. The postmodernist followers of Michel Foucault, for example, may find the relational power approach of little interest. Subscribers to Wendt's (1999) version of constructivism, however, will find much grist for their mill in the relational power literature. Wendt (1999: 97) divides international relations theories into those that emphasize 'brute material forces' as bases of power and those that view power as 'constituted primarily by ideas and cultural contexts'.

From its inception, the relational power approach has included both material and non-material bases of power. Lasswell and Kaplan (1950: 87) cited respect, rectitude, affection and enlightenment as base values of power and influence; and they devoted a whole chapter to 'symbols'. And Dahl ([1963, 1984] 1991: 35) includes information, friendship, social standing and the right to make laws in addition to threats of force and money in a list of political power resources.

In addition, norms, values, ideas and cultural contexts have figured prominently in the relational power approach. Among the factors that a power analyst might want to examine in explaining power relations, Dahl (1968: 412) included values, attitudes, expectations, decision-making rules, structures and constitutions. No constructivist is more emphatic about the importance of cultural context in power analysis than are Lasswell and Kaplan (1950: 85, 94):

> In particular, it is of crucial importance to recognize that power may rest on various bases, differing not only from culture to culture, but also within a culture from one power structure to another.
>
> None of the forms of power is basic to all the others. As patterns of valuation in a culture are modified, and changes come about in the social order and technology, now one form of power and now another, plays a fundamental role. Political analysis must be contextual, and take account of the power practices actually manifested in the concrete political situation.

In sum, far from being a battleground for the dueling forces of constructivism and rationalism, power analysis may be a point of convergence for at least some members of each camp.

POWER ANALYSIS AND POLICY RELEVANCE

The two dominant traditions in power analysis in international relations have been described above in terms of the elements of national power approach, which depicts power as resources, and the relational power approach, which depicts power as an actual or potential relationship. Which is more likely to be useful to policy-makers? Nye (1990: 26) suggests that the relational power approach is likely to seem 'too ephemeral' to 'practical politicians and leaders'. The idea of power as the 'possession of resources', he contends, holds more appeal for policy-makers because it 'makes power appear more concrete, measurable, and predictable' than does the relational definition. 'Power in this sense,' he notes, 'means holding the high cards in the international poker game.'

A case can be made, however, for the opposite conclusion. It is the elements of national power approach that has proved useful in the Correlates of War Project. Various studies based on this project of numerous wars during the past 500 years (Small and Singer, 1982; Stam, 1996; Wang and Ray, 1994) have produced useful knowledge about the causes and outcomes of war. Policy-makers, however, tend to have notoriously short time horizons. If they are considering going to war, it is not very helpful to point out that if they fight fifty wars during the next century, they are likely to win most of them. Nor are they likely to care much about what factors were important in most of the wars for the past 500 years. Most policy-makers are likely to be involved in only one war. They want to know whether their country is likely to win a particular war, fought in a particular context, during a particular time period, against a particular adversary. The gross inventory of American elements of national power was not only of little help in predicting the outcome of the Vietnam War, it was quite misleading. The United States may have been the greatest power in the history of the world, but it was ill- equipped to fight a guerilla war in a faraway land with language, culture and history that it understood poorly. In that situation, a relational power approach, setting the capability estimate in the context of a relevant policy-contingency framework, would probably have been more useful to American foreign policy-makers. Context matters, and policy-makers, as practical people, are likely to understand this more readily than academics. It is correct to depict the elements of power as holding the high cards in *the* international poker game, but it is incorrect to imply that there is only one kind of game in international politics. If the name of the game is bridge, the person with the good poker hand may be in big trouble. Policy-makers need to know the name of the game in order to evaluate the strength of their hands.

FUTURE RESEARCH DIRECTIONS

Power analysis intersects with almost every major research program in international relations. It would be impossible to identify all of the promising avenues of research for the power analyst during the next ten years or so. Those discussed here do not begin to exhaust the possibilities for fruitful research.

Power Relations as Dependent Variables

Power may be treated as either a dependent or an independent variable (Dahl, 1968). Dahl's (1961) classic study of community power was entitled *Who Governs?* In this study, power was treated as a dependent variable. The study began, as the title implies, with the assumption that power was being exercised by those who govern and proceeded to ask, 'By whom?'; 'On what issues?'; 'How?'; and so on. International relations scholars need to devote more attention to power as a dependent variable. Instead of focusing on how a given power distribution affects regime formation or war initiation, international relations scholars need to devote more attention to questions like 'Who has power with respect to which other actors, on which issues?' 'By what means is

this power exercised?' And 'What resources allow states to exercise this power?' A good example of this kind of research is Cox and Jacobson's (1973) study of influence in international organizations. They focus on the distribution of influence, different issue areas, and different time periods. They also examine the bases of power of various actors. Students of international relations need to devote more attention to treating power as a dependent variable and less to treating it as an independent variable (cf. Caporaso and Haggard, 1989).

Forms of Power

Preoccupation with military power has led students of international relations to neglect other forms of power.

Soft power   The term 'soft power' was introduced by Nye (1990). He used it to call attention to the ability to get 'others to want what you want' (Nye, 1990: 31–2). Noting that this ability to affect the preferences of others 'tends to be associated with intangible power resources such as culture, ideology, and institutions', he distinguished it from 'the hard command power usually associated with tangible resources like military and economic strength'. Insofar as this distinction calls attention to the need for students of international relations to direct attention to forms of power other than traditional military force, it has performed a useful service. The concept, however, needs clarification. Nye's discussion confuses power resources with scope. At times, the 'tangibility' of power resources seems to be the defining characteristic; while at other times, the use of those resources to control agendas or preferences seems to define soft power. It is also not clear what 'tangibility' means. Is a threat of military force tangible? Overall, soft power is a huge conceptual misstep in the right direction.

Further research would also be helped by recognition that there is little new in the idea of soft power from the standpoint of the literature on relational power. All of the forms of soft power discussed by Nye are familiar to relational power analysts. Further research on soft power should be more firmly rooted in that literature.

Positive sanctions   Positive sanctions are actual or promised rewards. Most of the research on power in international relations focuses on negative sanctions, i.e., actual or threatened punishments (Baldwin, 1971a). Despite a number of recent works on the role of positive sanctions (Cortwright, 1997; Crumm, 1995; J. Davis, 2000; P. Davis, 1999; Long, 1996; Newnham, 2000), the opportunities for further research are enormous.

Comparative influence techniques The instruments of statecraft – diplomatic, economic, military and symbolic – tend to be studied separately. This is a hindrance from the standpoint of both theory and policy relevance. Without comparative research on techniques of statecraft, theorists can say little about the utility of various policy instruments. If the success rate of economic sanctions is estimated at 34 per cent, should one conclude that policy-makers are fools for using an instrument with such a low rate of success? Or is this about the best that can be expected of any instrument of statecraft? There is little or no reliable data on comparative success rates of instruments of statecraft.

Policy-makers have little use for research findings regarding one technique of statecraft. Policy-makers need information that will help them choose among alternative policy options. Thus, what they want to know is: How successful is a given policy instrument likely to be, with respect to which goals and targets, at what cost, and in comparison with which policy alternatives? Without comparative studies of techniques of statecraft, it is hard to answer such questions (Baldwin, 1999/2000).

Military force Despite the emphasis on military force in the literature on international politics, much work remains to be done. Three problems are especially deserving of further research. First, the question of whether the utility of military force is declining needs attention. The groundwork for this research was provided by Knorr (1966: 5) long ago. The basic questions to be asked were identified as follows: 'How much has it [i.e., force] lost in utility, if there has been any loss at all? And utility for what purpose? And to whom? And under what, if not all, circumstances? And military power in all its forms and modes of employment, or only in some?' Utility for the economist Knorr, naturally, was a function of both costs and benefits. Recent studies that purport to say something about the utility of military power while devoting little or no attention to the costs of using force can be quite misleading (e.g., Art, 1996; Art and Waltz, [1971] 1999; Pape, 1996).

Second, the fungibility of military force needs further study. To what extent can military force be used to exercise influence in which situations? Although it is usually assumed that force is quite fungible with respect to military issues and conflicts, this assumption needs to be questioned. Wars and militarized conflicts come in a variety of sizes and shapes – guerilla war, civil war, limited conventional war, limited nuclear war, chemical and biological warfare, large scale nuclear warfare, deterrent situations, etc. It is not clear that the military power resources useful in one type of war can easily be transferred to another type. Thus, more studies of the use of particular types of military

power in different policy-contingency frameworks are needed.

The third problem concerns the question of how to define and measure military success (Baldwin, 1999/2000). Despite the voluminous literature on war, very little attention has been devoted to explicating the concept of success. The idea that 'every war has a winner' is deeply embedded in the literature on military force. The persistence of the zero-sum concept of military conflict is troublesome since it is incompatible with many of the topics dominating the scholarly research agenda during the past fifty years. As Schelling (1984: 269) notes: Deterrence …

> is meaningless in a zero-sum context. So is surrender; so are most limited-war strategies; and so are notions like accidental war, escalation, preemptive war, and brinkmanship. And of course so are nearly all alliance relationships, arms-race phenomena, and arms control. The fact that war hurts – that not all losses of war are recoverable – makes war itself a dramatically nonzero-sum activity.

Institutions and Power

Power can be exercised in the formation and maintenance of institutions, through institutions, within and among institutions. Institutions may reflect power relations, constrain them, or provide the basis for their existence. To what extent do the World Bank and the International Monetary Fund serve as instruments of American foreign policy? To what extent does the United Nations enhance the power of some countries and constrain the power of others? To what extent does the World Trade Organization constrain US power? To what extent does it strengthen US power? How is power distributed within the European Union (Garrett and Tsebelis, 1999; Holler and Widgren, 1999; Steunenberg et al., 1999)? To what extent do international institutions exercise power rather than merely reflecting it (Mearsheimer, 1994/95)? All of these questions provide a rich research agenda for the study of institutions and power relations.

Domestic Politics

How does domestic politics affect national power? Even classic elements of national power approaches included national morale, quality of government, public support and political stability among the determinants of a country's power (Morgenthau, [1948]1960). Does regime type matter? Are democracies at a disadvantage in international bargaining? How, if at all, does divided government affect a country's international bargaining position? Although the conventional realist wisdom has depicted democracy as hampering the efficient conduct of foreign policy, recent studies have called this view into question and opened new lines of research on the relationship between domestic politics and the exercise of international power (Fearon, 1994, 1998; Lake, 1992; Mansfield et al., 2000; Martin, 2000; Milner, 1997, 1998; Milner and Rosendorff, 1996; Mo, 1995).

Strategic Interaction and Bargaining

The bare-bones specification of power in terms of A causing a change in B's behavior is compatible with strategic interaction, but it neither calls attention to strategic interaction nor requires taking it into account. This is unfortunate, since most of what interests students of international politics involves strategic interaction. One of the most important research needs is linking the relational power literature with research on international strategic interaction (e.g., Martin, 2000; Milner, 1997, 1998; Mo, 1995).

This is not to suggest, however, that game theory is the only way to analyze strategic interaction. The work of Jervis (1997), Lake and Powell (1999), Larson (1998), Schelling (1984) and others has demonstrated the value of non-mathematical approaches to strategic interaction. Game theory is a useful tool for analyzing strategic interaction, but the analysis of international strategic interaction is too important to be left to game theorists alone. As Lake and Powell observe: 'The strategic-choice approach is theoretically inclusive. … [It] provides a foundation for integrating and synthesizing many otherwise competing theories of international relations' (1999: 6).

Distribution of Power

The question of how power is distributed needs to be studied using the relational power approach. The work of Frey (1971, 1985, 1989) is especially relevant to this line of research. Rather than striving to produce yet another global ranking of the so-called 'overall power' of every country in the world, scholars need to focus on power distributions within specified issue-areas and perhaps within specified regions. To the extent that persistent patterns are found, issue-relevant structures of power may be identified. Rather than trying to identify a single overall international power structure, scholars should strive to identify multiple structures of power in different issue areas. Admittedly, such research will not try to provide answers to the question of 'Who's number one in the game of international poker?' But simply redirecting attention away from that kind of question would, in itself, constitute progress in international power analysis.

CONCLUSION

Power has figured importantly in discussions of international interaction since the time of Thucydides. Despite the long tradition of power analysis in international politics, scholarly agreement on the nature of power and its role in international relations is lacking. The two principal approaches to power analysis in international interaction have been the 'power as resources' (or 'elements of national power') approach and the 'relational power' approach. The latter was developed during the last half of the twentieth century by scholars in philosophy and a variety of social science disciplines. Both approaches are evident in contemporary international relations scholarship.

Although power is an ancient focus in the study of international relations, there are many opportunities for further research. These include (1) the treatment of power as a dependent variable; (2) the forms of power; (3) institutions and power; (4) domestic politics and power; (5) strategic interaction; and (6) power distributions in different issue areas.

Although scholarly agreement on the nature and role of power in international interaction is unlikely in the near future, research along the lines suggested above may nevertheless enhance understanding of important dimensions of international behavior.

Notes

1 The terms 'liquidity', 'fungibility' and 'asset specificity' all refer to the same underlying concept of convertibility and can be used interchangeably. Money is high in liquidity and fungibility and low in asset specificity. The liquidity of a resource is a function of time, scope and domain (Baldwin, 1989). The difference between money and other resources is that money permits one to buy a greater variety of things from more people more quickly. It should be noted, however, that no resource is ever completely liquid. Even money, it is often noted, cannot buy love.

2 Although the degree to which the United States intended its nuclear deterrent to provide for Canadian security can be questioned, I would like to sidestep this issue for the purpose of illustrating the general point. The point is that Canadian security against nuclear attack was provided for regardless of the intentions of the United States.

Bibliography

Art, Robert J. (1996) 'American Foreign Policy and the Fungibility of Force', *Security Studies*, 5 (4): 7–42.

Art, Robert J. and Waltz, Kenneth N. (eds) ([1971] 1999) *The Use of Force: Military Power and International Politics*, 5th edn. New York: Rowman and Littlefield.

Bachrach, Peter and Baratz, Morton S. (1962) 'Two Faces of Power', *American Political Science Review*, 56: 947–52.

Baldwin, David A. (1971a) 'The Power of Positive Sanctions', *World Politics*, 24 (1): 19–38.

Baldwin, David A. (1971b) 'Inter-nation Influence Revisited', *Journal of Conflict Resolution*, 15 (4): 471–86.

Baldwin, David A. (1985) *Economic Statecraft*. Princeton: Princeton University Press.

Baldwin, David A. (1989) *Paradoxes of Power*. New York: Blackwell.

Baldwin, David A. (1993) 'Neoliberalism, Neorealism, and World Politics', in David A. Baldwin (ed.), *Neorealism and Neoliberalism: The Contemporary Debate*. New York: Columbia University Press. pp. 3–25.

Baldwin, David A. (1995) 'Security Studies and the End of the Cold War', *World Politics*, 48 (1): 117–41.

Baldwin, David A. (1999) 'Force, Fungibility, and Influence', *Security Studies*, 8 (4): 173–83.

Baldwin, David A. (1999/2000) 'The Sanctions Debate and the Logic of Choice', *International Security*, 24 (3): 80–107.

Barry, Brian (ed.) (1976) *Power and Political Theory: Some European Perspectives*. London: Wiley.

Caporaso, James A. and Haggard, Stephan (1989) 'Power in International Political Economy', in Richard D. Stoll and Michael D. Ward (eds), *Power in World Politics*. London: Lynne Rienner. pp. 99–120.

Carr, E.H. ([1939] 1946) *The Twenty Years' Crisis, 1919–1939*, 2nd edn. New York: St Martin's Press.

Cartwright, Dorwin (1965) 'Influence, Leadership, Control', in James March (ed.), *Handbook of Organizations*. Chicago: Rand McNally. pp. 1–47.

Claude, Inis L. (1962) *Power and International Relations*. New York: Random House.

Claude, Inis L. (1989) 'The Balance of Power Revisited', *Review of International Studies*, 15 (2): 77–85.

Cline, Ray S. ([1975] 1997) *World Power Assessment, 1997: A Calculus of Strategic Drift*. Boulder: Westview.

Cortwright, David (1997) *The Price of Peace: Incentives and International Conflict Prevention*. Lanham: Rowman and Littlefield.

Cox, Robert W. and Jacobson, Harold K. (1973) *The Anatomy of Influence: Decision Making in International Organization*. New Haven: Yale University Press.

Crumm, Eileen (1995) 'The Value of Economic Incentives in International Politics', *Journal of Peace Research*, 32: 313–30.

Dahl, Robert A. (1957) 'The Concept of Power', *Behavioral Science*, 2: 201–15.

Dahl, Robert A. (1961) *Who Governs?* New Haven: Yale University Press.

Dahl, Robert A. ([1963, 1984] 1991) *Modern Political Analysis*, 5th edn. Englewood Cliffs, Prentice Hall.

Dahl, Robert A. (1968) 'Power', in *International Encyclopedia of the Social Sciences*. New York: The Free Press.

Davis, James W. (2000) *Threats and Promises: The Pursuit of International Influence*. Baltimore: Johns Hopkins University Press.

Davis, Patricia A. (1999) *The Art of Economic Persuasion: Positive Incentives and German Economic Diplomacy*. Ann Arbor: University of Michigan Press.

Deutsch, Karl W. (1953) *Nationalism and Social Communication*. Cambridge, MA: MIT Press.

Deutsch, Karl W. (1963) *The Nerves of Government*. New York: The Free Press.

Deutsch, Karl W. ([1968] 1988) *The Analysis of International Relations*, 3rd edn. Englewood Cliffs: Prentice Hall.

Elster, Jon (1976) 'Some Conceptual Problems in Political Theory', in Brian Barry (ed.), *Power and Political Theory: Some European Perspectives*. Baltimore: Johns Hopkins University Press. pp. 245–70.

Fearon, James D. (1994) 'Domestic Political Audiences and the Escalation of International Disputes', *American Political Science Review*, 88: 577–92.

Fearon, James D. (1998) 'Domestic Politics, Foreign Policy, and Theories of International Relations', in Nelson Polsby (ed.), *Annual Review of Political Science*, vol. 1. Palo Alto: Annual Reviews. pp. 289–313.

Frey, Frederick W. (1971) 'Comment: On Issues and Nonissues in the Study of Power', *American Political Science Review*, 65 (4): 1081–101.

Frey, Frederick W. (1985) 'The Distribution of Power in Political Systems', paper presented at the World Congress of the International Political Science Association, Paris.

Frey, Frederick W. (1989) 'The Location and Measurement of Power: A Critical Analysis', paper presented at the International Studies Association Annual Meeting and Study Group on Power, International Political Science Association, London.

Garrett, Geoffrey and Tsebelis, George (1999) 'Why Resist the Temptation to Apply Power Indices to the European Union?', *Journal of Theoretical Politics*, 11 (3): 291–308.

Gilpin, Robert (1975) *US Power and the Multinational Corporation: The Political Economy of Foreign Direct Investment*. New York: Basic Books.

Gilpin, Robert (1981) *War and Change in World Politics*. New York: Cambridge University Press.

Gulick, Edward V. (1955) *Europe's Classical Balance of Power*. New York: W.W. Norton.

Guzzini, Stefano (1993) 'Structural Power: The Limits of Neorealist Power Analysis', *International Organization*, 47 (3): 443–78.

Guzzini, Stefano (1998) *Realism in International Relations and International Political Economy*. London: Routledge.

Guzzini, Stefano (2000) 'The Use and Misuse of Power Analysis in International Theory', in Ronen Palan (ed.), *Global Political Economy: Contemporary Theories*. London: Routledge. pp. 53–66.

Haas, Ernst B. (1953) 'The Balance of Power: Prescription, Concept, or Propaganda?', *World Politics*, 5: 442–77.

Harsanyi, John C. (1962) 'Measurement of Social Power, Opportunity Costs, and the Theory of Two-person Bargaining Games', *Behavioral Science*, 7: 67–80.

Holler, Manfred and Widgren, Mika (1999) 'Why Power Indices for Assessing European Union Decision-making?', *Journal of Theoretical Politics*, 11 (3): 321–30.

Hume, David ([1742] 1953) 'Of the Balance of Power', in Charles W. Hendel (ed.), *David Hume's Political Essays*. Indianapolis: Bobbs–Merrill.

Isaac, Jeffrey C. (1987) *Power and Marxist Theory: A Realist View*. Ithaca: Cornell University Press.

Jervis, Robert (1997) *System Effects: Complexity in Political and Social Life*. Princeton: Princeton University Press.

Keohane, Robert O. (1986) 'Theory of World Politics: Structural Realism and Beyond', in Robert O. Keohane (ed.), *Neorealism and Its Critics*. New York: Columbia University Press. pp. 158–203.

Keohane, Robert O. and Nye, Joseph ([1977] 2001) *Power and Interdependence*, 3rd edn. New York: Longman.

Knorr, Klaus (1966) *On the Uses of Military Power in the Nuclear Age*. Princeton: Princeton University Press.

Krasner, Stephen D. (1985) *Structural Conflict: The Third World Against Global Liberalism*. Berkeley: University of California Press.

Lake, David A. (1992) 'Powerful Pacifists: Democratic States and War', *American Political Science Review*, 86: 24–37.

Lake, David A. and Powell, R. (eds) (1999) *Strategic Choice and International Relations*. Princeton: Princeton University Press.

Larson, Deborah W. (1998) 'Exchange and Reciprocity in International Negotiation', *International Negotiation*, 3 (2): 121–38.

Lasswell, Harold D. and Kaplan, Abraham (1950) *Power and Society: A Framework for Political Inquiry*. New Haven: Yale University Press.

Little, Richard (1989) 'Deconstructing the Balance of Power: Two Traditions of Thought', *Review of International Studies*, 15 (2): 87–100.

Long, William J. (1996) *Economic Incentives and Bilateral Cooperation*. Ann Arbor: University of Michigan Press.

Lukes, Steven (1974) *Power: A Radical View*. London: Macmillan.

Mansfield, Edward H., Milner, H.V. and Rosendorff, B.P. (2000) 'Free to Trade: Democracies, Autocracies, and International Trade Negotiations', *American Political Science Review*, 94 (2): 305–22.

Martin, Lisa L. (2000) *Democratic Commitments: Legislatures and International Cooperation*. Princeton: Princeton University Press.

Mearsheimer, John J. (1994/95) 'The False Promise of International Institutions', *International Security*, 19 (3): 5–49.

Merritt, Richard L. and Zinnes, Dina A. (1988) 'Validity of Power Indices', *International Interactions*, 14 (2): 141–51.

Milner, H.V. (1997) *Interests, Institutions, and Information: Domestic Politics and International Relations*. Princeton: Princeton University Press.

Milner, H.V. (1998) 'Rationalizing Politics: The Emerging Synthesis of International, American, and Comparative Politics', *International Organization*, 52 (4): 759–86.

Milner, H.V. and Rosendorff, Peter B. (1996) 'Trade Negotiations, Information, and Domestic Politics', *Economics and Politics*, 8: 145–89.

Mo, Jongryn (1995) 'Domestic Institutions and International Bargaining: The Role of Agent Veto in Two-level Games', *American Political Science Review*, 89: 914–24.

Morgenthau, Hans J. ([1948] 1960) *Politics Among Nations: The Struggle for Power and Peace*, 3rd edn. New York: Alfred A. Knopf.

Moul, William B. (1989) 'Measuring the "Balances of Power": A Look at Some Numbers', *Review of International Studies*, 15 (2): 101–21.

Nagel, Jack H. (1975) *The Descriptive Analysis of Power*. New Haven: Yale University Press.

Newnham, Randall E. (2000) 'More Flies with Honey: Positive Economic Linkage in German *Ostpolitik* from Bismarck to Kohl', *International Studies Quarterly*, 44 (1): 73–96.

Nye, Joseph S. (1990) *Bound to Lead: The Changing Nature of American Power*. New York: Basic Books.

Oppenheim, Felix E. (1981) *Political Concepts: A Reconstruction*. Chicago: University of Chicago Press.

Osgood, Robert E. and Tucker, Robert W. (1967) *Force, Order, and Justice*. Baltimore: Johns Hopkins University Press.

Pape, Robert A. (1996) *Bombing to Win: Air Power and Coercion in War*. Ithaca: Cornell University Press.

Pollard, A.F. (1923) 'The Balance of Power', *Journal of the British Institute of International Affairs*, 2: 51–64.

Ray, James Lee and Vural, Ayse (1986) 'Power Disparities and Paradoxical Conflict Outcomes', *International Interactions*, 12 (4): 315–42.

Schelling, Thomas C. (1984) *Choice and Consequence: Perspectives of an Errant Economist*. Cambridge, MA: Harvard University Press.

Simon, Herbert (1957) *Models of Man*. New York: Wiley.

Simonds, F.H. and Emeny, B. (1937) *The Great Powers in World Politics*. New York: American Book.

Singer, J.D. (1963) 'Inter-nation Influence: A Formal Model', *American Political Science Review*, 57: 420–30.

Singer, J.D. (1988) 'Reconstructing the Correlates of War Dataset on Material Capabilities of States, 1816–1985', *International Interactions*, 14 (2): 115–32.

Small, Melvin and Singer, J.D. (1982) *Resort to Arms: International and Civil Wars, 1816–1980*. London: Sage.

Sprout, Harold and Sprout, Margaret (eds) (1945) *Foundations of National Power*. Princeton: Princeton University Press.

Sprout, Harold and Sprout, Margaret (1956) *Man–Milieu Relationship Hypotheses in the Context of International Politics*. Center of International Studies, Princeton University, Research Monograph.

Sprout, Harold and Sprout, Margaret (1962) *Foundations of International Politics*. New York: Van Nostrand.

Sprout, Harold and Sprout, Margaret (1965) *The Ecological Perspective on Human Affairs: With Special Reference to International Politics*. Princeton: Princeton University Press.

Sprout, Harold and Sprout, Margaret (1971) *Toward a Politics of the Planet Earth*. New York: Van Nostrand.

Spykman, Nicholas (1942) *American Strategy and World Politics: The United States and the Balance of Power*. New York: Harcourt, Brace.

Stam, Alan C. (1996) *Win, Lose, or Draw*. Ann Arbor: University of Michigan Press.

Steunenberg, Bernard, Schmidtchen, Dieter and Koboldt, Christian (1999) 'Strategic Power in the European Union: Evaluating the Distribution of Power in Policy Games', *Journal of Theoretical Politics*, 11 (3): 339–66.

Strange, Susan (1988) *States and Markets*. New York: Blackwell.

Tedeschi, James T. and Bonoma, Thomas V. (1972) 'Power and Influence: An Introduction', in James T. Tedeschi (ed.), *The Social Influence Processes*. Chicago: Aldine–Atherton. pp. 1–49.

Walt, Stephen M. (1987) *The Origins of Alliances*. London: Cornell University Press.

Walt, Stephen M. (1991) 'The Renaissance of Security Studies', *International Studies Quarterly*, 35 (2): 211–39.

Waltz, Kenneth N. (1979) *Theory of International Politics*. London: Addison–Wesley.

Waltz, Kenneth N. (1986) 'Reflections on *Theory of International Politics*: A Response to My Critics', in Robert O. Keohane (ed.), *Neorealism and Its Critics* . New York: Columbia University Press. pp. 322–45.

Waltz, Kenneth N. (1993) 'The Emerging Structure of International Politics', *International Security*, 18: 44–79.

Waltz, Kenneth N. (2000) 'Structural Realism after the Cold War', *International Security*, 25 (1): 5–41.

Wang, Kevin and Ray, James Lee (1994) 'Beginners and Winners: The Fate of Initiators of Interstate Wars Involving Great Powers since 1495', *International Studies Quarterly*, 38 (1): 139–54.

Weber, Max (1947) *The Theory of Social and Economic Organization*, (trans. A.M. Henderson and Talcott Parsons). New York: The Free Press.

Wendt, Alexander (1999) *Social Theory of International Politics*. Cambridge: Cambridge University Press.

Wight, Martin (1946) *Power Politics*. London: Royal Institute of International Affairs.

Wolfers, Arnold (1962) *Discord and Collaboration: Essays in International Politics*. Baltimore: Johns Hopkins University Press.

Wright, Quincy ([1942] 1965) *A Study of War*, 2nd edn. Chicago: University of Chicago Press.

Wright, Quincy (1955) *The Study of International Relations*. New York: Appleton–Century–Crofts.

10

International Organizations and Institutions

BETH A. SIMMONS AND LISA L. MARTIN

International institutions have become an increasingly common phenomenon of international life. The proliferation of international organizations (IOs) (Shanks et al., 1996), the growth in treaty arrangements among states (Goldstein et al., 2000) and the deepening of regional integration efforts in Europe all represent formal expressions of the extent to which international politics has become more institutionalized.

The scholarship on international institutions has burgeoned in response. Moreover, in the past decade theories devoted to understanding why institutions exist, how they function and what effects they have on world politics have become increasingly refined and the methods employed in empirical work more sophisticated. The purpose of this chapter is to draw together this divergent literature, to offer observations on the development of its various theoretical strands and to examine progress on the empirical front. We predict that a broad range of theoretical traditions – realist, rational functionalist, constructivist – will exist alongside one another for many years to come, and offer some suggestions on research strategies that might contribute to a better empirical base from which to judge more abstract claims.

The chapter proceeds as follows. The first section is concerned with defining international institutions.[1] The second section sketches four general clusters of institutional theorizing and characterizes how each views the questions of institutional creation, issues of institutional choice and design, institutional change and institutional effects. We do not offer these approaches as either exhaustive or mutually exclusive, but rather as representative, semi-permeable frameworks that share certain assumptions and diverge elsewhere. Indeed

a number of institutional scholars straddle or draw selectively from more than one approach.

The third section is devoted to an examination of the empirical literature on the effects of international institutions. Empirical research has developed significantly over the past decade as scholars have turned from the question of why institutions exist to whether and how they significantly impact governmental behavior and international outcomes. We examine these questions with respect to international cooperation generally and rule compliance specifically. We note, too, the few studies that have looked for broader institutional effects, some of which have been unanticipated.

The final section delineates some recent developments and directions for future research. We tentatively suggest that the study of international institutions might benefit from a close look at the general theoretical work on institutions that has been developed largely in the domestic context. We also suggest a research program that locates mechanisms for institutional effects at the transnational and domestic levels, opening up 'unified' state actors to a host of political influences.

INTERNATIONAL INSTITUTIONS: DEFINITIONS AND CONCEPTUALIZATIONS

Organizations

The term 'international institution' has been used over the course of the past few decades to refer to a broad range of phenomena. In the early post-war years, these words almost always referred to formal IOs, usually to organs or branches of the United Nations System. This is hardly surprising. Such organizations were the most 'studiable' (if not necessarily the most crucial) manifestations of what was 'new' about post-war international relations (see Martin and Simmons, 1998).

The best of the early work in this genre looked at the interplay between formal IOs, rules and norms, domestic politics and governmental decision-making – themes we would recognize today as being near the cutting edge of international institutional research. On the other hand, researchers focusing primarily on purely internal and formal aspects of the UN were travelling down roads increasingly removed from the central problems of world politics. The most clearly identifiable research program in this respect was that devoted to voting patterns and office seeking in the UN General Assembly (Alker and Russett, 1965; Ball, 1951; Keohane, 1967; Volgy and Quistgard, 1974).[2] This literature chose to focus on difficult to interpret behavior (what did these coalitions signify, anyway?) and imported methods uncritically from American studies of legislative behavior. Studies of the UN that focused on bureaucratic politics with links to transnational actors made more progress, since they opened up a research program that would ultimately lead to more systematic reflection on non-governmental actors (Cox and Jacobson, 1973: 214; Keohane and Nye, 1974).[3]

Formal organizations remain an important focus of research, especially in the post-Cold War setting. This is partially because organizations have agency; they make loans, send peacekeepers, inoculate babies. They have long been viewed as actors providing international collective or redistributive goods (Gregg, 1966; Kindleberger, 1951), but recently they have also come to regulate many of the social, political and economic problems traditionally within nation-states' purview (Smouts, 1993). Organization theorists point out that through the development of specific competencies, organizations can potentially transform agendas and goals (Cohen et al., 1972; Cyert and March, 1963). Moreover, these entities can function as creators of meaning and of identities (Olsen, 1997). Some have urged far greater attention to the sociology of IOs, as well as the ways in which intergovernmental organizations interact with nongovernmental organizations (De Senarclens, 1993; Jönsson, 1993). In a critical vein Barnett and Finnemore (1999) draw attention not only to IO autonomy, but also to the potential for pathological behavior when IOs become bureaucratized. These efforts represent a synthetic look at international organizational structures, normative standards, transnational actors and governmental decision-making.

In short, IOs deserve attention at least in part because they have agency, agenda-setting influence and potentially important socializing influences. Events in the early 1990s have lent plausibility to this assertion, although some periodicity to the centrality of IOs to world politics should be kept in mind. After all, it was the apparent irrelevance of formal organizations that gave rise to an alternative conception in the 1970s: the study of international 'regimes'.

International Regimes

The centrality of IOs to the study of international relations has waxed and waned. As the study of IOs progressed after the Second World War, the gulf between international politics and formal organizational arrangements began to open in ways that were not easy to reconcile. The major international conflict for a rising generation of scholars – the Vietnam War – raged beyond the formal declarations of the United Nations. Two decades of predictable monetary relations under the purview of the IMF were shattered by a unilateral decision of the United States in 1971 to close the gold window and later to float the dollar. For some, the proper normative response seemed to be to strengthen IOs to deal with rising problems of interdependence (Gosovic and Ruggie, 1976; Ruggie, 1972). Those writing from a public-choice perspective argued that the extension of property rights, under way in areas such as environmental protection, rather than a formal extension of supranational authority was the answer to solving problems of collective action (Conybeare, 1980). It became apparent that much of the earlier focus on formal structures and multilateral treaty-based agreements, especially the UN, had been overdrawn (McLin, 1979; Strange, 1978).

The events of the early 1970s gave rise to the study of 'international regimes', defined as rules, norms, principles and procedures that focus expectations regarding international behavior (Krasner, 1983; see Haggard and Simmons, 1987). The regimes movement represented an effort to theorize about international governance more broadly (e.g., Hopkins and Puchala, 1978: 598). It demoted the study of IOs as actors and began instead to focus on rules or even 'understandings' thought to influence governmental behavior. Research in this vein defined regimes for specific issue-areas (for which this approach had been criticized; see Hurrell, 1993; Junne, 1992; Kingsbury, 1998) and viewed regimes as focal points around which actors' expectations converge. Principles and norms provide the normative framework for regimes, while rules and decision-making procedures provide more specific injunctions for appropriate behavior.[4] The definition led to some debates that were of questionable utility, such as what exactly counted as a norm or a rule. But while the consensus definition offered by Krasner and his colleagues has been harshly criticized as imprecise and tendentious (De Senarclens, 1993: 456; Strange, 1983), efforts to improve on it have been marginal (see for example Levy et al., 1995: 274).

In spite of definitional problems, the study of international regimes made an important contribution by supplementing the technical aspects of formal IOs with the norms and rules governing state behavior. This move allowed a more unified framework for the analysis of formal and informal institutions.

International Institutions

The regimes literature gave rise to such definitional confusion that scholars in the 1990s have sought a simpler conception as well as a new label. The word 'institution' has now largely replaced 'regime' in the scholarly IR literature (but see Hasenclever, et al., 1997). Though a range of usages exists, most scholars have come to regard international institutions as sets of rules meant to govern international behavior. Rules, in turn, are often conceived as statements that forbid, require or permit particular kinds of actions (Ostrom, 1990: 139). John Mearsheimer (ironically a neorealist who does not believe that institutions are effective) provides a useful definition of institutions as 'sets of rules that stipulate the ways in which states should cooperate and compete with each other' (Mearsheimer, 1994/95).

This definition has several advantages. First, it eliminates the moving parts that lent so much confusion to regimes analysis. Underlying principles, while perhaps of analytical interest, are not included in the definition of an institution itself. Rules and decision-making procedures, referring respectively to substance and process, are both simply 'rules' in this conception. Nor are organizations included in this definition, since some informal institutions may not have organizations associated with them; and some organizations (such as the UN) may embody multiple institutions.

A second advantage of this definition is that it separates the definition of an institution from behavioral outcomes that ought to *be explained*. Regularized patterns of behavior – frequently observed in international relations for reasons that have nothing to do with rules – are excluded. Contrast this approach with other well-accepted definitions. Robert Keohane (1989: 3) defines institutions as 'persistent and connected sets of rules (formal and informal) that prescribe behavioral roles, constrain activity, and shape expectations', which makes it impossible to test for the impact of institutions on activities and expectations. Volker Rittberger (1990) has argued that an arrangement should only be considered a regime if the actors are persistently guided by its norms and rules, making inquiry into the effects of regimes on behavior tautological. Similarly, Krasner posits that '[t]he greater the conformity between behavior and institutional rules, the higher the level of institutionalization' (1999: 58), precluding institutionalization as a testable constraint on behavior. While it may be problematic in any given case to tell whether

particular patterns are rule-driven, such a project should be the subject of empirical research and not the result of an overly generous definition. The narrow definition strips institutions from posited effects and allows us to ask *whether* rules influence behavior.

Finally, this definition is relatively free from a particular theoretical perspective. There are no qualifying criteria about the social construction of rules, nor about whether rules are explicit or implicit, nor about their efficiency-enhancing characteristics.[5] This definition thus allows theorists writing from a range of perspectives to devise their own conditional statements as theoretically driven hypotheses. For example, it should be possible to test claims to the effect that rules are most effective when actors share intersubjective interpretations of what the rule requires, or that rules influence behavior if they lead to improved outcomes for governments. It therefore allows for the systematic evaluation of a broad range of theoretical claims using a single definition of institutions.[6]

In short, this definition allows for the analysis of both formal and informal sets of rules, although the difficulty of operationalizing informal rules is unavoidable. Institutions are viewed as explicitly normative – they specify what states *should* do. On the other hand, the definition we propose does not insist that institutions are effective; it leaves this question, as well as the mechanisms through which we might expect rules to operate, to empirical analysis. In the rest of this chapter we refer to institutions as sets of rules without drawing a distinction between institutions and regimes. While we recognize the distinction between institutions and organizations, many of our arguments apply to both. In the actual practice of research, the distinction between institutions and organizations is usually of secondary importance, unless the institution under study is especially informal.

THEORETICAL APPROACHES TO INTERNATIONAL INSTITUTIONS

Prelude to Institutionalism: Realist Schools of Thought

Theories of international institutions have had to contend with the dominant paradigm in international relations from at least the 1930s to the 1970s: realism. Traditional realists rarely referred explicitly to international institutions, but they did take explicit positions on the role of IOs and international law – the clearest example of what today we would consider to be an international institution – in foreign policy and international relations. Virtually all realists see the hand of power exerting the true influence behind the façade of international institutional structures. Hans Morgenthau attributed apparently rule-consistent behavior either to convergent interests or prevailing power relations, arguing that governments 'are always anxious to shake off the restraining influence that international law might have upon their foreign policies, to use international law instead for the promotion of their national interests ...' (Morgenthau, [1948]1985; see also Aron, 1981; Boyle, 1980; Hoffmann, 1960). For traditional realists, international institutions are epiphenomenal to state power and interests (Carr, [1939] 1964: 170–1).

Realist skepticism pervaded much of the literature on international institutions following the Second World War. The UN (Claude, 1963; Hoffmann, 1956), the General Agreement on Tariffs and Trade (Gorter, 1954) and the International Monetary Fund (Kindleberger, 1951; Knorr, 1948) all were the subject of highly critical review. A more fully articulated realist account of institutions developed in the 1970s and 1980s. Stephen Krasner introduced what he referred to as a 'basic force model' of international regimes (Krasner, 1983). A sub-set of scholars in the realist tradition found hegemonic stability theory an especially fruitful way to think about linking power distribution with the creation and stability of international institutions (Krasner, 1985; Strange, 1983).[7] According to this approach, international institutions were only likely to be established by dominant powers during periods of hegemony. Subsequently, empirical (Keohane, 1984; Rittberger, 1990; Young and Osherenko, 1993) as well as theoretical (Snidal, 1985) criticisms of this approach have encouraged institutionalists to look beyond the systemic distribution of power to explain the rise and especially the survival of international institutions.

Neorealists' most recent role in institutional analysis has been that of forceful critic. On the logical side, Joseph Grieco (1988) and John Mearsheimer (1994/95) argue that relative-gains concerns prevent states from intensive cooperation: since the benefits of cooperation can be translated into military advantages, concerns about the distribution of the gains impede substantial sustained cooperation (but see Powell, 1991; Snidal, 1991). Downs, Rocke and Barsoom (1996) embellish a familiar realist theme in their claim that *deep* cooperation – anything other than superficial policy adjustments about which states care little – requires enforcement. (However, they recognize that institutions are important in the process of enforcement.) Lloyd Gruber's work is a realist caution about assuming international institutions provide joint gains. Powerful states, in his view, often have the ability to present others with a *fait accompli* to which they are forced to adjust, sometimes making them worse off than they were before the agreement was made (Gruber, 2000).

In short, contemporary realist scholars of regimes would be reasonably comfortable with the view of Aron (1981), who was prepared to admit that 'the domain of legalized inter-state relations is increasingly large' but that 'one does not judge international law by peaceful periods and secondary problems'. And as realists have noted for decades, institutions reflect and enhance state power; in Evans and Wilson's words, they are 'arenas for acting out power relations' (Evans and Wilson, 1992; see also Carr, [1939] 1964: 189).

The strength of realist theorizing has been its insistence that international institutions be rooted in the interaction of power and national interest in the international system. This basic insight cannot be neglected by any theoretical approach that purports to explain international politics. It does pose one important puzzle, however: if governments are not likely to be constrained by the rules to which they agree, why do they spend time and other resources negotiating them in the first place?

Rational Functionalism

Rational functionalism developed in the early 1980s in response to precisely this puzzle. By the mid-1980s explanations of international regimes became intertwined with explanations of international cooperation more generally. The work of Robert Keohane (1984) drew from functionalist approaches that emphasized the efficiency reasons for agreements among regime participants. This research sought to show that international institutions provided a way for states to overcome problems of collective action, high transactions costs and information deficits or asymmetries. This approach has produced a number of insights, which we will discuss and extend below. But its analytical bite – derived from its focus on states as unified rational actors – was purchased at the expense of earlier insights relating to transnational coalitions and domestic politics. Furthermore, the strength of this approach has largely been its ability to explain the creation and maintenance of international institutions. It has been weaker in delineating their effects on state behavior, an issue to which we turn later in this chapter.

This rational/functionalist research agenda originated with Keohane's *After Hegemony* (1984) and Krasner's edited volume on international regimes. Their work was informed by a fundamentally important insight: individually rational action by states could impede mutually beneficial cooperation. Institutions would be effective to the degree that they allowed states to avoid short-term temptations to renege, thus realizing available mutual benefits. In particular, institutions could help to focus expectations on a cooperative solution, reduce transaction costs and provide a greater degree of transparency, through which it was expected that reputational concerns would come into play, thus rendering cooperative rules effective. In short, institutions could be explained as a solution to the problem of international collective action, providing a response to the puzzle posed by realism.

Once a basic functionalist explanation for international institutions was in place, researchers began to refine their conceptions of the strategic conditions that give rise to cooperative arrangements. Some authors, recognizing that the prisoners' dilemma was only one type of collective action problem, drew a distinction between collaboration and coordination problems (Martin, 1992a; Snidal, 1985; Stein, 1983). Collaboration problems are exemplified by the prisoners' dilemma. Coordination games are characterized by the existence of multiple Pareto-optimal equilibria. The problem states face in this situation is not to avoid temptations to defect, but to choose among equilibria. Choice may be relatively simple and resolved by identification of a focal point, if the equilibria are not sharply differentiated from one another in terms of the distribution of benefits (Garrett and Weingast, 1993). But some coordination games involve multiple equilibria over which the actors have divergent preferences. Initially, most authors argued that institutions would have little effect on patterns of state behavior in coordination games.

Some work in the rational functionalist vein has recognized the need to incorporate notions of bounded rationality and 'rules of thumb' (Keohane, 1984), sometimes based on normative expectations, in order to make meaningful empirical predictions. Thomas Gehring (1994), studying environmental regimes, brings together a rationalist model and attention to the role of norms in shaping expectations and behavior. He observes the complex reality of international affairs and the limited information-processing capacities of individuals. When governments interact in a complex situation, they will develop norms that shape ongoing expectations. These norms, as collective standards of behavior, then form the core of international institutions. Gehring's work attempts to bring together the insights of rationalist and constructivist models, discussed below, suggesting that a focus on the choice and influence of norms could provide a bridge between the two approaches.

German scholars have contributed to the further refinement of the basic functionalist logic. Rittberger and Zürn (1990) have argued that issue areas should be differentiated according to 'problem structural typologies'. One such typology distinguishes between 'dissentual' and 'consensual' conflicts. Consensual conflicts are ones in which every actor desires the same valued object but cannot fully be satisfied because there is not enough for everybody. Dissentual conflicts include conflicts over both values and means (Rittberger and Zürn, 1990: 1). Regime development will depend on whether the problems regimes address are dissentual or consensual in nature (see also List and Rittberger, 1992).

Closely related to the problem-structural approach is a situation-structural approach. This approach distinguishes among different types of games. Michael Zürn argues for an approach focusing on 'problematic social situations' which he defines as those in which the Pareto optimum on the one hand and the individually rational Nash equilibrium on the other are not congruent (Zürn, 1997: 295; see also Wolf and Zangl, 1996: 358–61). The logic is functionalist: states build institutions in order to achieve collectively desirable outcomes. These authors have emphasized that in order to identify the impact of institutions, it is important to understand the constellation of interests that underlie regime formation. Some constellations of interests are conducive to regime formation, while others are not. These logics have been explored empirically in the issue area of East–West relations, using case studies as well as quantitative analyses (List and Rittberger, 1992; Rittberger, 1990).

One of the major drawbacks of the approach, however, lies in accurate *ex ante* specification of games and interests. Empirical researchers wanting to test functional explanations often find it difficult to determine precisely what games are being played without observing the outcome of state interactions, leading to a lack of refutability and loss of explanatory power. While recognizing the need for independent measures of interests, researchers have found it difficult to construct them.

Rational functionalism has also made pioneering forays into an area that has received relatively little attention: explaining the *form* that institutional choice will take. While arguments linking problem structure with institutional form are not wholly new (Lipson, 1991; Little, 1949; Martin, 1992a; Oye, 1992), a number of scholars have recently placed rational functional explanations of institutional form at the center of their intellectual agenda. Koremenos, Lipson and Snidal (2002) explore how five dimensions of institutional design – membership, issue scope, centralization of tasks, rules for controlling the institution, and institutional flexibility – vary across institutions. The explanations for particular choices over form are hypothesized to be a response to distributional and enforcement problems arising from the number of actors relevant to the provision of joint-gains, as well as uncertainty about behavior or the state of the world. While findings to date are only suggestive, this research program rounds out the range of rational functional theorizing with respect to international institutions, their form and their development.

Others have located rational explanations for the choice of institutional form in domestic politics. Drawing from economic models of industrial organization, David Lake (1996) argues that the choice of institutional form[8] is driven by states' desire simultaneously to reduce the risk of opportunism and governance costs. The risk of opportunism generally decreases as the level of hierarchy in an institution increases; however, governance costs increase as the level of hierarchy increases. States will choose an institution that balances these two dynamics. So, for example, the Soviet Union faced lower governance costs within its sphere of influence during the Cold War than did the United States, leading it to choose institutions that had a higher level of hierarchy.

Rational institutional approaches have also been applied to questions of the level of governance – should we expect institutions to develop at the regional, national or supranational level in particular issue areas? Drawing from classic theories of subsidiarity (Oates, 1972; Tiebout, 1956), recent works have tried to match expectations about levels of governance with the degree of 'heterogeneity of tastes' with respect to the provision of public goods, often combining these explanations with attention to the nature and degree of externalities associated with a particular policy area (Seabright, 1996; Treisman, 1999). These approaches lead rational institutionalists to anticipate that the development of more integrative centralized governance structures should increase with externalities and decrease with heterogeneity.

This work on institutional form is notable because the method of analysis treats institutions both as environmental constraints and as objects that are consciously chosen and manipulated by actors, an assumption that has been challenged most directly by scholars working from sociological assumptions.

From the English School to Social Constructivism

Rational functionalist approaches have been roundly criticized by theorists that place prime analytical importance on the social context of state behavior. While rational functionalism focuses on explaining cooperation under anarchy, social constructivists have questioned the primacy of anarchy. They have sought to reassert social context into the understanding of international relations. While rational functionalism explains international institutions in terms of various forms of market failure, constructivists situate international institutions in their intersubjective social context.

Social explanations for international institutions have a venerable intellectual pedigree. The idea of an 'international society' is rooted in the classical legal tradition of Hugo Grotius, and his notion that an international community could be understood to exist among states participating in the international legal order. A number of scholars, frequently associated with English scholarship, have emphasized the importance of international society in maintaining international order. Bull and Watson (1984b: 1) define international society in state-centric terms, as a group of states that have 'established by dialog and consent common rules and institutions for the conduct of their relations, and recognize their common interest in maintaining these arrangements'. International society, in this conception, is the legal and political idea on which the concept of international institutions rests (Buzan, 1993: 350). Martin Wight's work emphasized the role of cultural unity in the identity of an international society (Wight, 1977: 33). Bull on the other hand saw the possibilities of international society for any group of states that shared coherent goals, such as limits on the use of force (Bull, 1977: 4–5). Others offer a subjective interpretation of international society that is echoed in contemporary constructivist assumptions: international society exists because those who speak and act in the name of states assume that it does (Evans and Wilson, 1992: 332).

The English School has offered a definition of institutions that is much broader than that of regimes in the American context, and that eschews reference to specific issue-areas. Institutions in this view are 'a cluster of social rules, conventions, usages, and practices … , a set of conventional assumptions held prevalently among society-members … [that] provide a framework for identifying what is the done thing and what is not in the appropriate circumstances' (Suganami, 1983: 2365). Theorists in this tradition have been concerned with 'institutions' as broad as the balance of power and the practice of diplomacy (Evans and Wilson, 1992: 338). The concern of the English School has traditionally been the problem of international order, and a central concern has been to investigate how shared purposes contribute to order (Bull, 1977). This school has clear organic links to international legal traditions, and draws especially from Grotian conceptions of law as constituting a community of those participating in a particular legal order. Regime theory in the United States, on the other hand, for the most part self-consciously shunned explicit connections with legal perspectives, and only recently has been willing to acknowledge international law as an important kind of international institution (Goldstein et al., 2000).

Scholars working from this perspective have urged researchers to analyze the social and political processes that underlie international society. Their work has tended to de-emphasize formal organizations (Crawford, 1996: 7), viewing these as important only to the extent that they 'strengthen and render more efficient the more basic institutions of diplomacy, international law, and the balance of power' (Evans and Wilson, 1992: 341). On the whole, scholars in this tradition have been less interested in economic issues and rather less taken by dilemmas of interdependence than have American scholars working in a more functionalist vein.

John Ruggie and Friedrich Kratochwil have done the most to advance the central insights of the English School and adapt them to the institutions that have been central to the American research agenda. At the center of their approach to institutions is their intersubjective meaning that explains the role that they play in international life. In a critique of the regimes literature as it was developing in the United States, these authors noted the inconsistencies of trying to describe a subjective world of norms and beliefs with a positivist epistemology based on observed behavior (Kratochwil and Ruggie, 1986). In Kratochwil's view (1988: 277), 'interpretations of actions by the actors are an irreducible part of their collective existence. We as observers therefore can go only as far as looking "at the facts" of their overt behavior; beyond that lies the realm of intersubjective rules which are constitutive of social practice and which an interpretive epistemology has to uncover.' It is crucial in this view to understand the ways in which specific institutions are embedded in larger systems of norms and principles, such as the liberal economic order of the post-war period (Ruggie, 1983).

Constructivist approaches are highly attentive to the framing of rules and norms as clues to a deeper understanding of their intended meanings. When a rule is embedded in the context of international law, for example, governments have to forgo idiosyncratic claims and make arguments based on rules and norms that satisfy at a minimum the condition of universality (Kratochwil, 1988: 279; see also Hurrell, 1993; Kingsbury, 1998). Indeed, most constructivist theorists would go further and insist on the mutually constitutive nature of institutions and actors' identities. International institutions define who the players are in a particular situation and how they define their roles, and thus place constraints on behavior. Constructivist scholars emphasize that international institutions can alter the identities and interests of states, as a result of their interactions over time within the auspices of a set of rules (Arend, 1999: 142–47; Onuf, 1989: 127). This gives rise to an analysis of international institutions that takes nothing for granted: the relevant actors, their interests and their understandings of the rules are all open to interpretation.

Social constructivist approaches have been especially appropriate for appreciating the ways in which international institutions create and reflect intersubjective normative understandings. Finnemore (1993, 1996) and Legro (1997) study specific examples of norm promotion in international politics, finding that institutions can play a crucial role in the systematic dispersion of beliefs and standards of appropriate behavior. Finnemore and Sikkink (1998) sketch out various stages of the norm 'life cycle' and note that international institutions (understood primarily as organizations) contribute to norm 'cascades' by 'pressuring targeted actors to adopt new policies and laws and to ratify treaties and by monitoring compliance with international standards'. In this way IOs can be 'chief socializing agents' pressuring violators to conform (Finnemore and Sikkink, 1998: 902).[9] Jeffrey Checkel (1999) has attempted to specify the domestic political structures that might prove differentially susceptible to such international normative diffusion.

Another body of work reverses the causal arrow, analyzing how domestic norms shape international regimes. A prominent example of such work is David Lumsdaine's (1993) examination of foreign-assistance policies of OECD states. He argues that it is impossible to explain foreign aid policies since 1940 without considering normative change. In Lumsdaine's view, 'national self-interests emerge from a social process of choice and self-definition whose character and objectives are influenced by people's basic values and views of life' (1993: 21). Because these social processes differ across countries, we see different sets of norms being transferred to the international arena: countries with generous domestic social welfare programs will also be generous foreign aid contributors.

As constructivism emphasizes feedback effects and the complexity of social interactions, it lends itself naturally to the view that institutions cannot be treated as simply exogenous or purely objects of choice. In a volume edited by John Ruggie (1992), a number of scholars argued explicitly for a normative understanding of multilateral regimes, based on a normative commitment among major states to multilateralism. Prevalent norms of collective action, in this view, account for the pervasive choice of multilateralist institutions in the post-war world. However, taking this constructivist insight to the empirical realm highlights the research-design issues it creates. Admitting numerous feedback effects and complex, iterative interactions makes the design of positivist research nearly impossible. The tendency has been to rely heavily on individual case studies and counterfactual analyses. While such work has contributed to our understanding of the varied roles that institutions play, it could usefully be supplemented by more traditional positivist research.

In short, the English School and the work of social constructivists have drawn attention to the intersubjective nature of international institutional arrangements. The former insists on understanding institutions in the context of the broader purposes of the major actors in world politics. Constructivists have incorporated the importance of social meanings into their analysis of institutions, and have more fully developed the notion that institutions and interests are mutually constitutive. Both approaches have provided ways to think about the links between norms and institutions. It is to institutional effects on state behavior that we turn in the following section.

INSTITUTIONAL IMPACT: EMPIRICAL STUDIES OF COOPERATION AND COMPLIANCE

The theories of international institutions reviewed above address both issues of institutional design and of the effects of institutions on state behavior. However, systematic empirical work in international relations has concentrated on the latter of these questions. In this section we survey empirical work on institutions. We identify areas where substantial empirical work exists, areas of active ongoing research, and suggest a few ideas about future directions for empirical studies of institutional effects.

Empirical studies of international cooperation, while subject to certain research-design flaws, have done much to establish that institutions can enhance cooperation.[10] Empirical research has found instances in which institutions led states to behave in a more cooperative manner than they otherwise might have. In many cases, researchers strive to establish a baseline pattern of state behavior in the absence of institutions. For example, Duffield's (1992) study of military force levels within NATO controlled for changes in the level of external threat. NATO has enhanced cooperation among its members, and between those states and democratizing Central and Eastern European states (Haftendorn et al., 1999). Martin's (1992c) research on cooperation on economic sanctions demonstrates that cooperation increases when sanctions are imposed in an institutionalized environment. Mitchell (1994) has shown that control of intentional oil pollution at sea took place only after institutional rules and technology changed. Wallander's (1999) work suggests that the existence of overarching institutions such as the OSCE has enhanced Russian–German cooperation even in the face of vastly changed circumstances after the end of the Cold War. The central methodological problem these studies face is how to identify regime effects. Rittberger offers a partial solution: he suggests that we ask whether regimes continue to influence behavior once overall relations have deteriorated between parties (Rittberger, 1990: 48). So, for example, the Baltic environmental regime was not affected by the downturn in US–Soviet relations in 1979–84 because of the presence of institutions.

Large collaborative projects offer broader opportunities to examine the impact of international rules on cooperation. Haas, Levy and Keohane (1993) offer specific causal mechanisms that they and their collaborators examine across a number of environmental case studies. Institutions are hypothesized to enhance cooperation by raising concern for the issue; improving the contractual environment as prescribed by functionalist theories; and improving domestic capacity for implementing agreements. Cases examining protection of the ozone layer, acid rain, water pollution and fisheries find general support for the efficacy of these causal mechanisms, although they also find that in general levels of cooperation are quite low. Some successful instances of cooperation do not seem to be explained by these mechanisms, instead relying on the power of 'shaming' or peer pressure (Levy, 1993). One mechanism often used to enhance cooperation with environmental institutions is the transfer of financial aid, and the dynamics of this mechanism have also received extensive analysis (Keohane and Levy, 1996; on factors that increase the effectiveness of environmental institutions see Sand, 1990).

Surprisingly, studies of military alliances have been more optimistic about the effect of institutions on patterns of cooperation (Haftendorn et al., 1999; Noehrenberg, 1995; Risse-Kappen, 1995), as have studies of East–West regimes during the Cold War. East–West regimes served to stabilize relations in particular issue-areas such as arrangements regarding Berlin by 'immunizing' them against repercussions from the deterioration of overall relations between superpowers (Rittberger, 1990: 6). These case studies also point to factors that enhance cooperation that lie outside the functionalist framework, such as the embeddedness of institutions (Peters, 1999).

Finally, one strand of research has concentrated on the constraining effects that international institutions can have on the development of new institutions. Vinod Aggarwal (1998) and others have examined the ways in which new institutions must be reconciled with the pre-existing institutional structure. When actors agree that a substantive case can be made for nesting one arrangement within a broader set of principles, appeals to existing norms and rules can be especially persuasive. Pre-existing institutions can facilitate the creation and maintenance of new institutional arrangements, as Steven Weber (1998) argues the EU did for the survival of the EMS when it was under stress. But in other cases, institutional innovation can be stymied by incompatible structures, as Benjamin Cohen (1998) has argued the IMF did in the case of the proposed OECD oil facility during the crisis of 1973–4. Aggarwal's (1985) work suggests that the nesting of specific agreements within a broader framework of principles (such as that of the Multifibre Agreement within the context of the GATT) helps to ensure a high degree of conformity among institutions and may contribute to their strength.

International institutions may also have effects because they facilitate learning, a point that Ernst Haas made in his pathbreaking work on regional integration in Europe (E. Haas, 1958). Many environmental regimes, for example, contain decision-making procedures that facilitate rule revision and therefore are likely to foster learning at the international level (P. Haas et al., 1993). Learning can also be facilitated in institutions that rely on the involvement of non-state actors (P. Haas, 1992). Learning may be either through the generation of new facts or through the reassessment of values and resulting redefinition of actor interests (Nye, 1987). These cognitive or ideational approaches emphasize how institutions diffuse information and values that can have the effect of enhancing international cooperation.

Compliance with the prescriptions and proscriptions of international institutions is a new research growth area (Chayes and Chayes, 1995; Simmons, 1998b; Victor et al., 1998; Weiss and Jacobson, 1998. See Raustiala and Slaughter Chapter 28 of this volume for a thorough review.) The explanatory work informing studies of compliance is virtually identical to that informing studies of cooperation. However, empirical studies of compliance have done somewhat more to uncover the conditions conducive to compliance (see, for example, Hasenclever et al., 1996; Levy et al., 1995: 295–308).

Just what constitutes compliance is an enduring conceptual and methodological difficulty (see Simmons, 1998b). Given actors' capacity to interpret the exact meaning of rules, and frequent existence of multiple sets of rules, determining the meaning of compliance in any given situation is not straightforward. As Nicholas Onuf (1989: 261) states, '[m]ost situations are bounded by a number of rules. At choice then is not just to follow a rule, but which one, to what extent, and so on.' Onuf's critique is related to a broader constructivist critique of the study of compliance (see Hurrell, 1993; Kingsbury, 1998). Kratochwil has articulated this critique most forcefully, as summarized above. Moreover, the problem of identifying compliance in a systematic manner has been compounded by possible conflicts between legal and political definitions of the term.

Unsurprisingly, empirical compliance studies suffer from some of the same threats to inference that have plagued the cooperation literature. A state may be legally 'in compliance' with an agreement, but this may tell us nothing about the impact of the agreement on state behavior. Downs, Rocke and Barsoom (1996) argue that studies of compliance are conceptually flawed for reasons like this. Focusing on the 'managerial' approach to compliance adopted by legal scholars such as Chayes and Chayes (1993, 1995), they note that research-design problems of selection bias and endogeneity make the results of many existing empirical studies of compliance highly suspect.

Some studies try to address these methodological difficulties by examining rule compliance under 'difficult' conditions. Harald Müller (1993) studies the role of the ABM treaty and finds that, in the face of pressure to 'break out' of treaty commitments in response to the Soviet radar at Krasnoyarsk, American decision-makers decided to abide by treaty arrangements. Beth Simmons (2000) adopts a similar strategy with a quantitative test of compliance with international monetary rules. Controlling for a range of pressures on the balance of payments, she finds that states that commit to keep their current account free from restrictions actually do so more often, even when facing unanticipated economic crisis.

While these empirical studies of cooperation and compliance contribute to the institutionalist research agenda, they suffer from a number of methodological flaws that lead skeptics to challenge their validity. When researchers look at only one or a few cases, analysis of what happens in the absence of institutions necessarily requires counterfactual reconstruction of events (this is noted explicitly by Wettestad and Andresen, 1991). Young and Levy (1999) suggest the use of 'thought experiments' (the use of counterfactuals) as well as 'natural experiments' (controlled comparisons across cases) to try to ferret out the causal effects of institutions. The latter strategy allows researchers to observe variation, rather than postulating it. Some studies of cooperation do not control adequately for alternative explanations, particularly changes in patterns of interests. Few empirical studies specify the conditions under which institutions should have the predicted effects. Few studies take the problem of institutional endogeneity seriously.

These failings, particularly the last, allow skeptics to argue that since institutions are obviously endogenous – they do change in response to changes in structural variables, and often serve as agents of state interests – they are epiphenomenal. In other words, the *causal* significance of institutions remains open to challenge (see Mearsheimer, 1994/95; for a response see Keohane and Martin, 1995). This identification between endogeneity and epiphenomenality is a mistake, but better research designs are necessary. Future research should concentrate on examining variation in the major explanatory variable (international institutions), consider problems of omitted variable bias, and control for alternative explanations. Explicit comparison of observed variation in levels of cooperation, rather than counterfactual analysis of individual cases, will be helpful in drawing sound inferences about the effects of institutions. The institutionalist research agenda cries out for alternative approaches to analyzing institutional effects, which we consider in the following section.

RECENT DEVELOPMENTS AND FUTURE DIRECTIONS

Insights Across Levels of Analysis

To what extent can insights into international institutions derive from concepts and methods developed in a domestic setting? Are there general approaches that might usefully inform our understanding of international institutions? We approach this issue cautiously, cognizant of the limitations of past efforts to borrow from the American literature on legislative behavior (discussed in Martin and Simmons, 1998). In this section, we briefly consider whether recent approaches are more likely to bear fruit.

One possibility is to draw on domestic conceptualizations of institutional stability to inform our studies at the international level. In his study of the Non-Proliferation Treaty (NPT), Roger Smith (1989) draws on Samuel Huntington's development of a measure of institutionalization in the domestic context (Huntington, 1968). Huntington proposed that institutionalization be conceptualized as having four dimensions: adaptability, complexity, autonomy and unity. Using this complex measure, Smith demonstrates that the NPT regime has gained in stability since its inception, despite the questionable behavior of a handful of states (Smith, 1989: 232). The regime has become more complex and its resilience has been enhanced by a fundamental unity of ultimate purposes. This approach shows promise for providing an alternative measure of regime stability to the problematic reliance on compliance.

Recent models of domestic institutions that have drawn on non-cooperative game theory may be useful for furthering a rationalist account of international institutions. The basic assumptions of non-cooperative game theory are that actors are rational, strategic and opportunistic, and that no neutral outside actor can be counted on to enforce agreements. Therefore agreements that will make a difference must be self-enforcing. These conditions are remarkably similar to the usual characterization of international politics as a situation of anarchy and self-help (Waltz, 1979). As long as models use the same basic assumptions about the nature of actors and their environment, the potential for learning across the level-of-analysis divide could be enormous.

As one example, consider what international relations scholars might learn from looking at current debates on the nature of legislative institutions.[11] These models treat legislators as self-interested actors whose mutual agreements cannot be enforced (Shepsle and Weingast, 1995) and ask how legislators under these conditions might construct institutions (committees, parties) that will allow them to reach goals such as re-election.[12] Similarly, international relations scholars are interested in how states design institutional forms (organizations, procedures, informal cooperative arrangements, treaty arrangements) that assist in the realization of their objectives. The point is *not*, as much of the earlier literature assumed, that 'legislative activity' at the international level is interesting *per se*. The analogy is powerful to the extent that it

rests on actors' strategies to cope with similar strategic environments: notably, those in which actors have mixed motives and cannot turn easily to external enforcement.

The debate about legislative organization may provide a useful analogy. Informational models concentrate on the ways in which legislative structures allow legislators to learn about the policies they are adopting, thus avoiding inefficient outcomes (Gilligan and Krehbiel, 1990; Krehbiel, 1991). Informational models can be used to extend and clarify arguments in the international literature that stress the role of institutions in the provision of information and in the learning process. They lead to predictions about the conditions under which international institutions can effectively provide policy-relevant information to states; about the kinds of institutions that can provide credible information; and about the effects of such information provision on patterns of state behavior. Such a model might be applicable to an analysis of international arms control, environmental, or financial institutions, where credible information on activities and conditions may be key to the success of an agreement (Simmons, 1993). Within the EU, for example, the Commission's role as a relatively independent collector of policy-relevant information is a plausible explanation for its ability to exercise influence over policy outcomes (see Bernauer, 1995; P. Haas, 1989). Empirically, informational models lead us to expect the development and use of relatively independent experts in promoting cooperation, especially where such information is scarce, asymmetric and valuable to governments.

Distributional models, on the other hand, assume that information is not all that problematic. They concentrate on the heterogeneity of legislators' tastes (Weingast and Marshall, 1988). Achieving mutual gains, in this framework, means cutting deals that will stick across different issues. Since exchanges of votes cannot always be simultaneous, legislators have developed structures such as committees and agenda-setting rules that allow them to put together majorities on the issues of most intense particularistic interest to them. Distributional models may be especially useful in exploring in a rigorous fashion the role of international institutions in facilitating or hampering issue linkages (Martin, 1992b; Stein, 1980). Empirically, they predict that institutions will be most successful in allowing for credible cross-issue deals when those states with the most intense interest in any particular issue dominate policy-making on that dimension; and when institutional mechanisms inhibit states from reneging on cross-issue deals. Institutions that try to cope with environmental protection and development needs in the same package (for example, UNCED and the Agenda 21 program) provide a plausible example. Our point is that rational models of institutions can be enriched by research at any level of analysis, as long as we are considering mixed-motive situations in which actors must cooperate without an external 'enforcer' in order to pursue their objectives.

Finally, we can turn to the domestic level of analysis to ask questions of normative significance. How and under what conditions can characteristics valued in domestic politics be preserved in governance structures at the international level? This concern has progressed furthest in the discussion of the 'democratic deficit' in the EU (Lodge, 1991). Critics of EU structure argue that the inability of national parliaments to deeply influence EU decision-making, combined with the weakness of the European Parliament, mean that the EU itself falls far short of the democratic standards it demands of its members. This concern has led to creative thinking about the meaning of 'democracy', and whether the procedures that assure legitimacy on the international level should mimic those on the domestic level (Weiler, 1995). Fritz Scharpf (1999) has cogently argued that the lack of a strong 'European identity' means that measures such as majority voting that ensure legitimacy within states cannot do so on the European level, and argues instead in favor of 'output oriented' mechanisms. Such discussions will have wide relevance, as demands for greater transparency and broader participation in the decisions of the WTO, the IMF and the World Bank have recently highlighted.

Exploring Institutional Mechanisms: The Link to Domestic Politics

The idea that international institutions can influence state behavior by acting through domestic political channels has been recognized by scholars since at least the mid-1950s (Matecki, 1956). But because American institutionalists have largely allowed their research agenda to be defined by responding to the neorealist challenge to show that 'institutions matter', they have generally neglected the role of domestic politics.[13] Rational functionalists tend to treat states as unitary actors, and assign them preferences and beliefs, as in neorealist theory. This framework has been productive in exploring the broad ways in which institutions can change patterns of behavior. But in privileging the state as an actor, they have neglected the ways in which other actors in international politics might use institutions (a central insight of earlier studies of transgovernmental organization).

One of the more fundamental ways in which international institutions can change international outcomes is by substituting for domestic practices. Under what conditions should we expect such substitution to take place? Functionalist logic might suggest delegation to an international institution will be beneficial if domestic institutions pose a barrier to the realization of benefits for society as a whole. Judith Goldstein's (1996) analysis of dispute settlement under the US–Canada Free Trade Act suggests that actors who have the most to gain from a pursuit of general welfare – such as executives elected by a national constituency – tend to show the most interest in turning to international institutions.

We can identify other incentives for domestic actors to transfer policy-making to the international level. One common problem with institutions that are under the control of political actors is that of time-inconsistent preferences. While generating an unexpectedly high level of growth today may bring immediate benefits to politicians up for re-election, for example, allowing monetary policy to be made by politicians will introduce a welfare-decreasing inflationary bias to the economy. Putting additional constraints on policy, for example by joining a system of fixed exchange rates, can provide a mechanism to overcome this time-inconsistency problem. In general, if pursuit of gains over time involves short-term sacrifices, turning to international institutions can be an attractive option for domestic policy-makers.

A second and related question about domestic politics is whether particular kinds of actors will regularly see an advantage in turning to the international level. At the simplest level, it seems likely that 'internationalist' actors – those heavily engaged in international transactions (Frieden, 1991), those who share the norms of international society (Sikkink, 1993), or those who have a stake in a transnational or global resource (Young, 1979) – will have an interest in turning to the international level. This may especially be the case when such groups are consistently in a minority position in domestic politics. Certain domestic institutional actors may also have a tendency to benefit from international-level policy-making. One such actor, which is just beginning to enter political scientists' analysis, is the judiciary. Increasingly, international agreements are legal in form. This means that they are interpreted by domestic courts, and that judges can use international law as a basis on which to make judgments (Alter, 1996; Conforti, 1993). Because international law provides this particular actor with an additional resource by which to pursue agendas, whether bureaucratic or ideological, we might expect that the judiciary in general tends to be sympathetic to international institutions.

Some scholars have suggested a normative argument for linking international institutions with domestic politics. Zürn (1993) introduces the idea of 'regime conducive foreign policy', characterized by its emphasis on economic and information resources and by 'an orientation towards reciprocity accompanied by the readiness to make one-sided concessions'. It is hypothesized to emerge in states with a corporatist domestic structure, after a change in domestic power constellations has taken place, and when 'the degree of routinization of the pre-established policy is not very high' (Underdal, 1995: 116). Conceiving of regime-conducive policy as a general foreign-policy orientation allows these authors to posit explanatory factors rooted in domestic politics and regime type (see also Cortell and Davis, 1996).

Broadening Measures of Institutional Effects

Tests of the effects of institutions have been plagued by the problems noted above: selection bias, simultaneity, inadequate specification of conditional expectations and variation, and heavy reliance on counterfactuals. These problems have needlessly undermined the promise of institutionalist theory.

Most existing empirical studies of institutional effects rely on a standard definition of cooperation, resolution of collective-action dilemmas. This assumption forces researchers to assume that all institutions are designed to confront similar problems of collective action and market failure. It thus sits uncomfortably with the notion, highlighted by those who consider variation in institutional design, that different institutions are designed to solve different problems. The focus on problems of collective action has directed our attention away from some explanatory issues, such as which states prevail in the attempt to establish their preferred standards as the international norm (Krasner, 1991). Furthermore, how do we understand institutions that are designed to be weak (Donnelly, 1986) or even to fail (Moe, 1991)? Finally, how do we think theoretically about possible unintended, even perverse, effects of institutions?[14] For example, governments that believed that human rights accords were nothing but meaningless scraps of paper found themselves surprised by the ability of transnational actors to use these commitments to force governments to change their policies (Sikkink, 1993). In the European Community, few anticipated that the European Court of Justice would have the widespread influence on policy that it has (Burley and Mattli, 1993). Prime Minister Thatcher was apparently quite surprised at the results of agreeing to change voting rules within the EC, such as the adoption of qualified-majority voting she accepted in the Single European Act (Moravcsik, 1991). Krebs (1999) argues that the provisions of NATO for security guarantees and transparency have unintentionally exacerbated conflict between Greece and Turkey. Functionalist logic and the language of 'cooperate', 'do not cooperate' does not provide us with the necessary tools to explore this darker side of possible institutional effects. The widespread presence of unanticipated effects presents a serious challenge to a rationalist approach (Gallarotti, 1991).

At a minimum, it would be useful to specify the conditions under which unanticipated consequences are most likely. This would at least suggest when it will be necessary to integrate the insights of other schools of thought. One hypothesis might be that changes in secondary rules – that is, rules about rules – are the changes most likely to work in unexpected ways. Changes in voting rules within an institution, for example, can give rise to new coalitions and previously suppressed expressions of interest, leading to unpredicted policy outcomes. Changes in decision-making procedures can have even more widespread and unexpected effects if they open the policy process to input from new actors, including non-governmental and transnational actors (Sikkink, 1993). Both as sources of new information and as strategic actors in their own right, such groups are often able to use new points of access to gain unexpected leverage over policy.

Rapid technological change or large economic shocks should also cause institutions to work in ways that governments could not originally anticipate. If the issue-area covered by the institution is one that exhibits increasing returns to scale, governments may be willing to put up with a high level of unexpected outcomes before they would seriously consider withdrawing from an institution. Sociologists have written extensively about 'competency traps' in which positive feedback 'locks in' a particular rule-based structure, strengthening the institution in the short run but rendering it less adaptable when faced with change (March and Olsen, 1998: 964). In these cases, historical or sociological approaches, which view institutions as deeply rooted and path-dependent, are likely to yield interesting insights (Pierson, 1996; Steinmo et al., 1992). These approaches are likely to be superior to traditional functional approaches for explaining obsolescing institutions in a range of contexts (Levinthal and March, 1993).

Studies of international institutions have gained sophistication, innovation and empirical accuracy by re-introducing non-state actors that had been central to the transnational relations literature of the 1970s (Keohane and Nye, 1974, 1977). International institutions can create new opportunities for non-state actors, often with important (if hard to predict) consequences for policy. For example, qualified majority voting in the EU has encouraged many European interest groups to open offices and intensify contacts with Brussels (Streeck and Schmitter, 1991). Studies of European integration have also highlighted the role of institutions in changing the attitudes of national officials, sometimes leading to the redefinition of national goals (E. Haas, 1958, 1990). International institutions can also have important redistributive effects at the national level, which can create domestic political realignments that were not fully expected by national leaders.

The major sustained effort at bringing together the analysis of non-state actors, particularly NGOs, and international institutions has been Keck and Sikkink's (1998). They find that transnational NGOs can work with institutions to promote respect for norms, changing state behavior in sometimes profound ways. Peter Haas (1989) finds that epistemic communities similarly interact with institutions to change international outcomes. Glennon and Stewart (1998) argue that US compliance with environmental treaties has been influenced by the participation of environmental groups. Jacobeit (1996) studies debt-for-nature swaps and finds that NGOs were the dominant actors in organizing and implementing them. The key question here is how non-state actors can use institutions as leverage to promote their agenda, and the conditions under which they can do so. While good individual case studies of examples of this dynamic are evident, research designs that allow for arguments about conditional effects and that precisely specify causal mechanisms are still lacking. Exactly why an NGO's influence on governments should increase when international institutions exist remains somewhat mysterious. Yet, the question is of obvious analytical and policy interest, as formal organizations like the UN increasingly allow for active participation in their deliberations by non-state actors.

A discussion of broadening our measures of institutional effects would not be complete without attention to distributive effects. International institutions are usually designed to address the problem of which among many possible outcomes on the Pareto frontier to institutionalize in a situation of multiple equilibria (Krasner, 1991). To be effective, institutions must provide a mechanism for resolving distributional conflict.[15] For example, institutions may construct focal points, identifying one possible equilibrium as the default or 'obvious' one. The role of institutions as diverse as the European Court of Justice (Garrett and Weingast, 1993) and the Basle Banking Committee (Simmons, 2001) is captured in part by constructed focal-point analysis. Where states fear that the benefits of cooperation are disproportionately flowing to others, institutions can provide reliable information about the realized benefits of cooperation to allay such fears. Institutions might also assist in mitigating distributional conflict by 'keeping account' of deals struck, compromises made, and gains achieved, particularly in complex multi-issue institutions. The networks created within the supranational institutions of the EU, for example, provide the necessary scope for issue-linkage and institutional memory to perform the function of assuring that all members, over time, achieve a reasonably fair share of the benefits of cooperation (Pollack, 1997). A distinct research tradition emphasizes the legitimizing role that international institutions can play in focal-point selection (Franck, 1990; Peck, 1996: 237). This

legitimacy, in turn, has important political consequences (Claude, 1966: 367).

There is, of course, a more normative point to be made about international institutions and their distributive consequences, and in this regard the European literature is more advanced than is the North American. Beyond the analytics of equilibrium analysis, it is important to inquire into the contribution of international regimes to social justice and sustainable development (see Rittberger et al., 1990: 277–97). The early regimes literature emphasized distributive consequences of international institutions, but this was lost in the rational functionalist line of theorizing that followed. In the late 1970s, a special issue of *International Organization* used regime language to analyze the 'ways in which the global food regime affects ... wealth, power, autonomy, community, nutritional well-being, ... and sometimes physical survival' (Hopkins and Puchala, 1978: 598). Little thought was given in this volume to the idea that regimes were somehow efficiency-improving, as later theorizing would imply; rather the food regime was characterized by 'broad and endemic inadequacies' that are the result of national policies that are 'internationally bargained and coordinated ... by multilateral agreement or unilateral dictate' (Hopkins and Puchala, 1978: 616, 615). More work could be done to recapture this original concern with the normative implications of institutional choice.

CONCLUSIONS

The political study of international institutions reveals a vibrant and diverse body of scholarship. In recent decades, research has turned from the study of formal IOs to the study of regimes and institutions, informal as well as formal. For the most part, this turn has been salutary, as it has reflected a broad interest not only in formal organizations but in the deeper role that rules and norms play in a system of formally co-equal states. Initially, this turn was instigated by the observation that much of what is interesting about world politics – especially during the Cold War period – seemed to take place among intensely interdependent actors but beyond the purview of formal inter-state organizations. This turn was furthered by a rational-functionalist approach to the study of institutions, which took up the puzzle of how we could understand international cooperation at all, given the assumptions of neorealism prevalent in the American international relations literature at the time. Meanwhile in European circles, theorists of international society worked from sociological assumptions on a parallel question: how can order be maintained in an anarchical international society?

These theoretical orientations have made for interesting theoretical fireworks, as we have seen in the broader debates between today's constructivists and rationalists. This debate is clearly reflected in the institutional literature as a distinction between those who view international institutions (including institutional form) as rational responses to the strategic situations in which actors find themselves, versus those who insist on a subjective interpretation of social arrangements (which may or may not be 'rational' and are unlikely to be understood through the use of positive methodologies). These approaches in turn have spawned sub-sets of coherent scholarship, such as the German School among the rationalists or those who give primacy of place to normative explanations among the constructivists. Each school has its more state-centric proponents: the English School among the contructivists; those whose mission it was to meet neorealism on its own terms among the rational functionalists.

Several positive developments in the institutional literature should be highlighted. First, scholars from a range of approaches are showing a greater willingness to drop the assumption of unitary state actors and to engage systematically with the world in which we live. For the rationalists, this has meant looking to domestic institutional conditions that make it rational to delegate authority to international institutions. For others working from a more sociological point of view, this has meant drawing in a wide array of transnational actors that have been empowered by democratization or international institutionalization itself. Much of the recent literature has furthered our understanding of the complex milieu in which institutions operate by systematically examining the relationship between governments, domestic coalitions, IOs and transnational actors.

Despite these gains, weaknesses remain. The major weakness we would point out is the lack of confidence we have in the ability to draw strong inferences from much of the research to date. Some scholars would, of course, deny that this is the point of the exercise, but we feel that more attention to the causal mechanisms advanced, as well as much greater attention to research designs that allow for systematic comparisons across time, across states, or across international institutions, would greatly enhance our ability to explain the world around us. A careful look at literatures that develop theories of domestic and transnational politics, for example, should be drawn upon more systematically if we are to understand the sources and effects of international institutionalization. We also advocate thinking conditionally about institutional effects, as some of the compliance literature has begun to do. Both the research completed so far and the directions we identify for future research suggest a promising and productive future for studies of international institutions.

Notes

1 We limit ourselves in this chapter to public international organizations and institutions, and leave the analysis of private authority structures to Thomas Risse (Chapter 13, in this volume).

2 For two systematic reviews of the quantitative research on the UN and IOs see Alger, 1970; Riggs et al., 1970.

3 For a critical assessment of the impact of such actors see Keohane, 1978; Russell, 1973.

4 Subsequently, some scholars have divided this definition and labeled the principles and norms underlying an international relationship the 'meta-regime' while reserving the term 'international regime' for specific rules and procedures in a given issue area (Aggarwal, 1998: 4).

5 This definition probably downplays but need not exclude 'constitutive rules' that have been central to constructivist theories (Ruggie, 1998). It is clearly consistent, however, with the 'regulative rules' that dominate empirical constructivist research (Finnemore and Sikkink, 1998).

6 Of course this definition is not neutral in one important sense: it embodies our preference for the testing of theoretical propositions using social-scientific methods.

7 The term 'neorealist institutionalist' is used by Vinod Aggarwal (1998) to distinguish these neorealists who were interested in explaining international institutions from those, such as Waltz (1979), who were not. Furthermore, a number of hegemonic theorists (Gilpin, 1981; Kindleberger, 1973) had little to say about international institutions *per se*.

8 Lake concentrates on a wider range of international institutions than typically studied by institutionalists, including hierarchical institutions such as empires.

9 This approach bears some affinity with sociological institutionalism, which emphasizes the role of 'world culture' in explaining institutional isomorphism across countries, but which might also account for growing participation in the network of international institutions that can result from such socialization. See Meyer and Rowan, 1977; Meyer et al., 1994; Thomas et al., 1987.

10 Underdal (1995: 232–3) highlights the difficulties of defining and measuring terms such as 'cooperation' or 'effectiveness,' issues which are beyond the scope of this chapter.

11 The work on legislative institutions is just one example of the application of non-cooperative game theory to domestic institutions. But since it is a particularly well-developed literature, we concentrate on it here, without wishing to imply that this is the only branch of research on domestic institutions that may have interesting analogies to international institutions.

12 While much of the work on legislative organization concentrates on the American context, recent years have seen creative efforts to develop such models in non-US settings. See Huber, 1996; Ramseyer and Rosenbluth, 1993; Shugart and Carey, 1992.

13 There has been a good deal of attention to the role of domestic politics in institutional creation. See for example, Wolf and Zangl, 1996.

14 It is important to differentiate between unintended and unanticipated effects. Effects may be anticipated but unintended. For example, it is generally expected that steps taken to lower the rate of inflation will lead to somewhat higher levels of unemployment. Thus, higher unemployment is an anticipated, although unintended, consequence of stringent monetary policies. It is best understood as a price actors are sometimes willing to bear to gain the benefits of low inflation. Such unintended but anticipated consequences of institutions present little challenge to a rationalist approach, since they fit neatly into a typical cost–benefit analysis. Genuinely unanticipated effects, however, present a greater challenge.

15 Hasenclever, Mayer and Rittberger (1996) have proposed to explain institutional robustness in terms of the institution's distributive characteristics.

Bibliography

Aggarwal, Vinod K. (1985) *Liberal Protectionism: The International Politics of Organized Textile Trade.* Berkeley: University of California Press.

Aggarwal, Vinod K. (ed.) (1998) *Institutional Designs for a Complex World: Bargaining, Linkages, and Nesting.* Ithaca: Cornell University Press.

Alger, Chadwick (1970) 'Research on Research: A Decade of Quantitative and Field Research on International Organization', *International Organization*, 23: 414–50.

Alker, Hayward and Russett, Bruce (1965) *World Politics in the General Assembly.* New Haven: Yale University Press.

Alter, Karen (1996) 'The European Court's Political Power', *West European Politics*, 19: 458–60.

Arend, Anthony C. (1999) *Legal Rules and International Society.* New York: Oxford University Press.

Aron, Raymond (1981) *Peace and War: A Theory of International Relations.* Malabar, FL: Kreiger.

Ball, M. Margaret (1951) 'Bloc Voting in the General Assembly', *International Organization,* 5 (1): 3–31.

Barnett, Michael N. and Finnemore, Martha (1999) 'The Politics, Power, and Pathologies of International Organizations', *International Organization*, 53 (4): 699–732.

Bernauer, Thomas (1995) 'The Effect of International Environmental Institutions: How Do We Learn More?', *International Organization*, 49 (2): 351.

Boyle, Francis A. (1980) 'The Irrelevance of International Law', *California Western International Law Journal*, 10 (2): 193–219.

Bull, Hedley (1977) *The Anarchical Society.* London: Macmillan.

Bull, Hedley (1984) *Justice in International Relations.* 1983–1984 Hagey Lectures. University of Waterloo.

Bull, Hedley and Watson, Adam (eds) (1984a) *The Expansion of International Society.* Oxford: Oxford University Press.

Bull, Hedley, and Watson, Adam (eds) (1984b) 'Introduction', in H. Bull and A. Watson (eds), *The Expansion of International Society.* Oxford: Oxford University Press. pp. 1–9.

Burley, Anne-Marie and Mattli, Walter (1993) 'Europe before the Court: A Political Theory of Legal Integration', *International Organization*, 47: 41–76.

Buzan, Barry (1993) 'From International System to International Society: Structural Realism and Regime Theory Meet the English School', *International Organization*, 47: 327–52.

Carr, Edward Haller ([1939] 1964) *The Twenty Years' Crisis, 1919–1939.* New York: Harper and Row.

Chayes, Abram and Handler Chayes, Antonia (1993) 'On Compliance', *International Organization*, 47: 175–205.

Chayes, Abram and Handler Chayes, Antonia (1995) *The New Sovereignty.* Cambridge, MA: Harvard University Press.

Checkel, Jeffrey T. (1999) 'Norms, Institutions, and National Identity in Contemporary Europe', *International Studies Quarterly*, 43 (1): 83–114.

Claude, Inis L. (1963) 'The Political Framework of the United Nations' Financial Problems', *International Organization*, 17 (4): 831–59.

Claude, Inis L. (1966) 'Collective Legitimization as a Political Function of the United Nations', *International Organization*, 20 (3): 367–79.

Cohen, Benjamin J. (1998) 'When Giants Clash: The OECD Financial Support Fund and the IMF', in Vinod K. Aggarwal (ed.), *Institutional Designs for a Complex World: Bargaining, Linkages, and Nesting.* Ithaca: Cornell University Press. pp. 161–94.

Cohen, M.D., March, J.G. and Olsen, J.P. (1972) 'A Garbage Can Model of Organizational Choice', *Administrative Science Quarterly*, 17: 1–25.

Conforti, Benedetto (1993) *International Law and the Role of Domestic Legal Systems.* Dordrecht: Martinus Nijhoff.

Conybeare, John (1980) 'International Organization and the Theory of Property Rights', *International Organization*, 34 (3): 307–34.

Cortell, Andrew P. and Davis, James W. Jr (1996) 'How Do International Institutions Matter? The Domestic Impact of International Rules and Norms', *International Studies Quarterly*, 40 (4): 451–79.

Cox, Robert and Jacobson, Harold (1973) *The Anatomy of Influence: Decisionmaking in International Organization.* New Haven: Yale University Press.

Crawford, Robert M.A. (1996) *Regime Theory in the Post-Cold War World.* Aldershot: Dartmouth Publishing.

Cyert, R.M. and March, James G. (1963) *A Behavioral Theory of the Firm.* Englewood Cliffs: Prentice Hall.

De Senarclens, Pierre (1993) 'Regime Theory and the Study of International Organizations', *International Social Science Journal*, 45 (4): 453–62.

Donnelly, Jack. (1986) 'International Human Rights: A Regimes Analysis', *International Organization*, 40 (3): 599–642.

Downs, George W., Rocke, David M. and Barsoom, Peter N. (1996) 'Is the Good News about Compliance Good News about Cooperation?', *International Organization*, 50 (3): 379–406.

Duffield, J.S. (1992) 'International Regimes and Alliance Behavior: Explaining NATO Conventional Force Levels', *International Organization*, 46: 819–55.

Evans, Tony and Wilson, Peter (1992) 'Regime Theory and the English School of International Relations: A Comparison', *Millennium: Journal of International Studies*, 21 (3): 330.

Finnemore, Martha (1993) 'International Organizations as Teachers of Norms: The United Nations Educational, Scientific, and Cultural Organization and Science Policy', *International Organization*, 47: 565–97.

Finnemore, Martha (1996) 'Norms, Culture, and World Politics: Insights from Sociology's Institutionalism', *International Organization*, 50 (2): 325–47.

Finnemore, Martha and Sikkink, Kathryn (1998) 'International Norm Dynamics and Political Change', *International Organization*, 52 (4): 887–918.

Franck, Thomas (1990) *The Power of Legitimacy among Nations*. New York: Oxford University Press.

Frieden, Jeffry A. (1991) 'Invested Interests: The Politics of National Economic Policies in a World of Global Finance', *International Organization*, 45: 425–51.

Gallarotti, G.M. (1991) 'The Limits of International Organization: Systematic Failure in the Management of International Relations', *International Organization*, 45: 183–220.

Garrett, Geoffrey and Weingast, Barry R. (1993) 'Ideas, Interests, and Institutions: Constructing the EC's Internal Market', in Judith Goldstein and Robert O. Keohane (eds), *Ideas and Foreign Policy*. Ithaca: Cornell University Press.

Gehring, Thomas (1994) *Dynamic International Regimes: Institutions for International Environmental Governance*. Frankfurt-am-Main: Peter Lang.

Gilligan, Thomas W. and Krehbiel, Keith (1990) 'Organization of Informative Committees by a Rational Legislature', *American Journal of Political Science*, 34: 531–64.

Gilpin, Robert (1981) *War and Change in World Politics*. New York: Cambridge University Press.

Glennon, Michael J. and Stewart, Alison L. (1998) 'The United States: Taking Environmental Treaties Seriously', in Edith Brown Weiss and Harold K. Jacobson (eds), *Engaging Countries: Strengthening Compliance with International Environmental Accords*. Cambridge, MA: MIT Press. ch. 6.

Goldstein, Judith (1996) 'International Law and Domestic Institutions: Reconciling North American "Unfair" Trade Laws', *International Organization*, 50: 541–64.

Goldstein, Judith, Kahler, Miles, Keohane, Robert and Slaughter, Anne-Marie (eds) (2000) 'Introduction: Legalization and World Politics', *International Organization*, 54 (3): 385–400.

Gorter, Wytze (1954) 'GATT after Six Years: An Appraisal', *International Organization*, 8 (1): 1–18.

Gosovic, Branislav and Ruggie, John Gerard (1976) 'On the Creation of a New International Economic Order: Issue Linkage and the Seventh Special Session of the UN General Assembly', *International Organization*, 30 (2): 309–45.

Gregg, Robert W. (1966) 'The UN Regional Economic Commissions and Integration in the Underdeveloped Regions', *International Organization*, 20 (2): 208–32.

Grieco, Joseph M. (1988) 'Anarchy and the Limits of Cooperation: A Realist Critique of the Newest Liberal Institutionalism', *International Organization*, 42 (3): 485–507.

Gruber, Lloyd (2000) *Ruling the World: Power Politics and the Rise of Supranational Institutions*. Princeton: Princeton University Press.

Haas, Ernst B. (1958) *The Uniting of Europe: Political, Social, and Economic Forces, 1950–1957*. Stanford: Stanford University Press.

Haas, Ernst B. (1990) *When Knowledge is Power*. Berkeley: University of California Press.

Haas, Peter M. (1989) 'Do Regimes Matter? Epistemic Communities and Mediterranean Pollution Control', *International Organization*, 43 (3): 377–405.

Haas, Peter M. (1992) 'Knowledge, Power, and International Policy Coordination', *International Organization*, 46 (1): Special issue.

Haas, Peter M., Levy, Marc A. and Keohane, Robert O. (eds) (1993) *Institutions for the Earth: Sources of Effective International Environmental Protection*. Cambridge, MA: MIT Press.

Haftendorn, Helga, Keohane, Robert O. and Wallander, Celeste A. (eds) (1999) *Imperfect Unions: Security Institutions Over Time and Space*. New York: Oxford University Press.

Haggard, Stephan and Simmons, Beth A. (1987) 'Theories of International Regimes', *International Organization*, 41 (3): 491–518.

Hasenclever, Andreas, Mayer, Peter and Rittberger, Volker (1996) *Justice, Equality, and the Robustness of International Regimes: A Research Design*. Tübinger Arbeitspapiere zur Internationalen Politik und Friedensforschung Nr 25, Tübingen, Germany.

Hasenclever, Andreas, Mayer, Peter and Rittberger, Volker (1997) *Theories of International Regimes*. Cambridge: Cambridge University Press.

Hoffmann, Stanley (1956) 'The Role of International Organization: Limits and Possibilities', *International Organization*, 10 (3): 357–72.

Hoffmann, Stanley (1960) *Contemporary Theory in International Relations*, Englewood Cliffs: Prentice Hall.

Hopkins, Raymond F. and Puchala, Donald J. (1978) 'Perspectives on the International Relations of Food', *International Organization*, 32 (3): 581–616.

Huber, John D. (1996) *Rationalizing Parliament: Legislative Institutions and Party Politics in France*. New York: Cambridge University Press.

Huntington, Samuel (1968) *Political Order in Changing Societies*. New Haven: Yale University Press.

Hurrell, Andrew (1993) 'International Society and the Study Regimes: A Reflective Approach', in Volker Rittberger (ed.), *Regime Theory and International Relations*. Oxford: Clarendon Press. pp. 49–72.

Jacobeit, Cord (1996) 'Nonstate Actors Leading the Way: Debt for Nature Swaps', in Robert O. Keohane and

Marc A. Levy (eds), *Institutions for Environmental Aid: Pitfalls and Promises*. Cambridge, MA: Harvard University Press. ch. 5.

Jönsson, Christer (1993) 'International Politics: Scandinavian Identity Amidst American Hegemony?', *Scandinavian Political Studies*, 16: 149–65.

Junne, Gerd (1992) 'Beyond Regime Theory', *Acta Politica*, 27: 9–21.

Keck, Margaret and Sikkink, Kathryn (1998) *Activists Beyond Borders: Advocacy Networks in International Politics*. Ithaca: Cornell University Press.

Keohane, Robert O. (1967) 'The Study of Political Influence in the General Assembly', *International Organization*, 21: 221–37.

Keohane, Robert O. (1978) 'The International Energy Agency: State Influence and Trans-Governmental Politics', *International Organization*, 32 (4): 929–51.

Keohane, Robert O. (1984) *After Hegemony: Cooperation and Discord in the World Political Economy*. Princeton: Princeton University Press.

Keohane, Robert O. (1989) 'Neoliberal Institutionalism: A Perspective on World Politics', in Robert O. Keohane (ed.), *International Institutions and State Power: Essays in International Relations Theory*. Boulder: Westview. pp. 1–20.

Keohane, Robert O. and Levy, Marc A. (eds.) (1996) *Institutions for Environmental Aid: Pitfalls and Promises*. Cambridge, MA: Harvard University Press.

Keohane, Robert O. and Martin, Lisa L. (1995) 'The Promise of Institutionalist Theory', *International Security*, 20: 39–51.

Keohane, Robert O. and Nye, Joseph S. (1974) 'Transgovernmental Relations and International Organizations', *World Politics*, 27: 1.

Keohane, Robert O. and Nye, Joseph S. (1977) *Power and Interdependence: World Politics in Transition*. Boston: Little, Brown.

Kindleberger, Charles P. (1951) 'Bretton Woods Reappraised', *International Organization*, 5 (1): 32–47.

Kindleberger, Charles P. (1973) *The World in Depression, 1929–1939*. Berkeley: University of California Press.

Kingsbury, Benedict (1998) 'The Concept of Compliance as a Function of Competing Conceptions of International Law', *Michigan Journal of International Law*, 19 (2): 345.

Knorr, Klaus (1948) 'The Bretton Woods Institutions in Transition', *International Organization*, 2 (1): 19–38.

Koremenos, Barbara, Lipson, Charles and Snidal, Duncan (2002) 'Rational International Institutions', *International Organization*, 55(4): Special issue.

Krasner, Stephen D. (ed.) (1983) *International Regimes*. Ithaca: Cornell University Press.

Krasner, Stephen D. (1985) *Structural Conflict: The Third World Against Global Liberalism*. Berkeley: University of California Press.

Krasner, Stephen D. (1991) 'Global Communications and National Power: Life on the Pareto Frontier', *World Politics*, 43: 336–56.

Krasner, Stephen D. (1999) *Sovereignty: Organized Hypocrisy*. Princeton: Princeton University Press.

Kratochwil, Friedrich (1988) *Millenium Journal of International Studies*, 17 (2): 263–84.

Kratochwil, Friedrich and Ruggie, John Gerard (1986) 'International Organization: A State of the Art on an Art of the State', *International Organization*, 40: 229–54.

Krebs, Ronald R. (1999) 'Perverse Institutionalism: NATO and the Greco-Turkish conflict', *International Organization*, 53 (2): 343–78.

Krehbiel, Keith (1991) *Information and Legislative Organization*. Ann Arbor: University of Michigan Press.

Lake, David (1996) 'Anarchy, Hierarchy, and the Variety of International Relations', *International Organization*, 50 (1): 1–34.

Legro, Jeffrey (1997) 'Which Norms Matter? Revisiting the "Failure" of Internationalism', *International Organization*, 51 (1): 31–64.

Levinthal, D.A. and March, James G. (1993) 'The Myopia of Learning', *Strategic Management Journal*, 14: 95–112.

Levy, Marc A. (1993) 'European Acid Rain: The Power of Tote-Board Diplomacy', in Peter Haas, Robert Keohane and Marc Levy (eds), *Institutions for the Earth: Sources of Effective International Environmental Protection*. Cambridge, MA: MIT Press. ch. 3.

Levy, Marc A., Young, Oran R. and Zürn, Michael (1995) 'The Study of International Regimes', *European Journal of International Relations*, 1 (3): 267–330.

Lipson, Charles (1991) 'Why Are Some International Agreements Informal?', *International Organization*, 45 (4): 495–538.

List, Martin, and Rittberger, Volker (1992) 'Regime Theory and International Environmental Management', in Andrew Hurrell and Benedict Kingsbury (eds), *The International Politics of the Environment*. Oxford: Clarendon Press. pp. 85–109.

Little, Virginia (1949) 'Control of International Air Transport', *International Organization*, 3 (1): 29–40.

Lodge, Juliet (1991) 'The Democratic Deficit and the European Parliament', Fabian Society Discussion Paper No. 4, January.

Lumsdaine, David Halloran (1993) *Moral Vision in International Politics: The Foreign Aid Regime, 1949–1989*. Princeton: Princeton University Press.

March, James G. and Olsen, Johan (1998) 'The Institutional Dynamics of International Political Orders', *International Organization*, 52 (4): 943–70.

Martin, Lisa L. (1992a) 'Interests, Power, and Multilateralism', *International Organization*, 46: 765–92.

Martin, Lisa L. (1992b) 'Institutions and Cooperation: Sanctions During the Falkland Islands Conflict', *International Security*, 16 (4): 143–77.

Martin, Lisa L. (1992c) *Coercive Cooperation: Explaining Multilateral Economic Sanctions*. Princeton: Princeton University Press.

Martin, Lisa and Simmons, Beth A. (1998) 'Theories and Empirical Studies of International Institutions', *International Organization*, 52 (4): 729–58.

Matecki, B.E. (1956) 'Establishment of the International Finance Corporation: A Case Study', *International Organization*, 10 (2): 261–75.

McLin, Jon (1979) 'Surrogate International Organization and the Case of World Food Security', *International Organization*, 33 (1): 35–55.

Mearsheimer, John J. (1994/95) 'The False Promise of International Institutions', *International Security*, 19 (3): 5–49.

Meyer, John W. and Rowan, Brian (1977) 'Institutionalized Organizations: Formal Structure as Myth and Ceremony', *American Journal of Sociology*, 83: 340–63.

Meyer, John W., Scott, Richard and associates (1994) *Institutional Environments and Organizations: Structural Complexity and Individualism*. Thousand Oaks: Sage.

Mitchell, Ronald B. (1994) *Intentional Oil Pollution at Sea: Environmental Policy and Treaty Compliance*. Cambridge, MA: MIT Press.

Moe, Terry (1991) 'Politics and the Theory of Organization', *Journal of Law, Economics, and Organization*, 7 (1): 106–29.

Moravcsik, Andrew (1991) 'Negotiating the Single European Act: National Interests and Conventional Statecraft in the European Community', *International Organization*, 45: 19–56.

Morgenthau, Hans J. ([1948] 1985) *Politics Among Nations: The Struggle for Power and Peace*, 6th edn. New York: Knopf.

Müller, Harald (1993) 'The Internationalization of Principles, Norms, and Rules by Governments: The Case of Security Regimes', in Volker Rittberger (ed.), *Regime Theory and International Relations*. Oxford: Clarendon Press. pp. 361–90.

Noehrenberg, Eric H. (1995) *Multilateral Export Controls and International Regime Theory*. Sinzheim, Germany: Pro Universitate Verlag.

Nye, Joseph S. (1987) 'Nuclear Learning and US Soviet Security Regimes', *International Organization*, 41 (3): 371–402.

Oates, Wallace E. (1972) *Fiscal Federalism*. New York: Harcourt Brace Jovanovich.

Olsen, Johan (1997) 'European Challenges to the Nation State', in Steunenberg and F. van Vught (eds), *Political Institutions and Public Policy*. Dordrecht: Kluwer. pp. 157–88.

Onuf, Nicholas (1989) *World of Our Making*. Columbia, SC: University of South Carolina Press.

Ostrom, Elinor (1990) *Governing the Commons: Evolution of Institutions for Collective Action*. Cambridge: Cambridge University Press.

Oye, Kenneth (1992) *Economic Discrimination and Political Exchange: World Political Economy in the 1930s and 1980s*. Princeton: Princeton University Press.

Peck, Connie (1996) *The United Nations as a Dispute Settlement System*. The Hague: Kluwer Law International.

Peters, Ingo (1999) 'The OSCE and German Policy: A Study in *How* Institutions Matter', in Helga Haftendorn, Robert O. Keohane and Celeste A. Wallander (eds), *Imperfect Unions: Security Institutions Over Time and Space*. New York: Oxford University Press. ch. 7.

Pierson, Paul (1996) 'The Path to European Integration: A Historical Institutionalist Analysis', *Comparative Political Studies*, 29: 2.

Pollack, Mark A. (1997) 'Delegation, Agency, and Agenda Setting in the European Community', *International Organization*, 51 (1): 99–134.

Powell, Robert (1991) 'Absolute and Relative Gains in International Relations Theory', *American Political Science Review*, 85 (4): 1303–20.

Ramseyer, J. Mark and Rosenbluth, Frances McCall (1993) *Japan's Political Marketplace*. Cambridge, MA: Harvard University Press.

Riggs, Robert E., Hanson, Karen, Heinz, Mary, Hughes, Barry and Volgy, Thomas (1970) 'Behavioralism in the Study of the United Nations', *World Politics*, 22: 197–236.

Risse-Kappen, Thomas (1995) *Cooperation Among Democracies. The European Influence on US Foreign Policy*. Princeton: Princeton University Press.

Rittberger, Volker (1990) *International Regimes in East–West Politics*. London and New York: Pinter Publishers.

Rittberger, Volker and Zürn, Michael (1990) 'Towards Regulated Anarchy in East–West Relations: Causes and Consequences of East–West Regimes', in Volker Rittberger (ed.), *International Regimes in East–West Politics*. London and New York: Pinter Publishers. pp. 9–63.

Rittberger, Volker, Efinger, M. and Mendler, M. (1990) 'Toward an East–West Security Regime: The Case of Confidence-Building and Security-Building Measures', *Journal of Peace Research*, 27 (1): 55–74.

Ruggie, John Gerard (1972) 'Collective Goods and Future International Collaboration', *American Political Science Review*, 66: 874–93.

Ruggie, John Gerard (1983) 'International Regimes, Transactions, and Change: Embedded Liberalism in the Postwar Economic Order', in Stephen D. Krasner (ed.), *International Regimes*. Ithaca: Cornell University Press. pp. 195–231.

Ruggie, John Gerard (1992) 'Multilateralism: The Anatomy of an Institution', *International Organization*, 46: 561–98.

Ruggie, John Gerard (1998) 'What Makes the World Hang Together? Neo-Utilitarianism and the Social Constructivist Challenge', *International Organization*, 52 (4): 855–86.

Russell, Robert W. (1973) 'Transgovernmental Interaction in the International Monetary System, 1960–1972', *International Organization*, 27 (4): 431–64.

Sand, Peter (1990) *Lessons Learned in Global Environmental Governance*. Washington, DC: World Resources Institute.

Scharpf, Fritz (1999) *Governing in Europe: Effective and Democratic?* New York: Oxford University Press.

Seabright, Paul (1996) 'Accountability and Decentralization in Government: An Incomplete Contracts Model', *European Economic Review*, 40: 61–89.

Shanks, Cheryl, Jacobson, Harold K. and Kaplan, Jeffrey H. (1996) 'Inertia and Change in the Constellation of International Governmental Organizations, 1981–1992', *International Organization*, 50 (4): 593–626.

Shepsle, Kenneth A., and Weingast, Barry R. (eds) (1995) *Positive Theories of Congressional Institutions*. Ann Arbor: University of Michigan Press.

Shugart, Matthew and Carey, John (1992) *Presidents and Assemblies: Constitutional Design and Electoral Dynamics*. New York: Cambridge University Press.

Sikkink, Kathryn (1993) 'Human Rights, Principled Issue-Networks, and Sovereignty in Latin America', *International Organization*, 47: 411–41.

Simmons, Beth A. (1993) 'Why Innovate? Founding the Bank for International Settlements', *World Politics*, 45 (2): 361–405.

Simmons, Beth A. (1998a) 'See You in "Court?" The Appeal to Quasi-Judicial Legal Processes in the Settlement of Territorial Disputes', in Paul F. Diehl (ed.), *A Roadmap to War: Territorial Dimensions of International Conflict*. Nashville: Vanderbilt University Press. ch. 8.

Simmons, Beth A. (1998b) 'Compliance with International Agreements', *Annual Review of Political Science*, 1: 75–93.

Simmons, Beth A. (2000) 'International Law and State Behavior: Compliance with the Public International Law of Money', *American Political Science Review*, 94 (4): 819–35.

Simmons, Beth A. (2001) 'The International Politics of Harmonization: The Case of Capital Market Regulation', *International Organization*, 55 (3): 589–620.

Smith, Roger K. (1989) 'Institutionalization as a Measure of Regime Stability: Insights for International Regime Analysis from the Study of Domestic Politics', *Millennium: Journal of International Studies*, 18 (2): 227–44.

Smouts, M.C. (1993) 'Some Thoughts on International Organizations and Theories of Regulation', *International Social Science Journal*, 45 (4): 443–51.

Snidal, Duncan (1985) 'Coordination versus Prisoners' Dilemma: Implications for International Cooperation and Regimes', *American Political Science Review*, 79: 923–42.

Snidal, Duncan (1991) 'Relative Gains and the Pattern of International Cooperation', *American Political Science Review*, 85: 701–26.

Stein, Arthur A. (1980) 'The Politics of Linkage', *World Politics*, 33 (1): 62–81.

Stein, Arthur A. (1983) 'Coordination and Collaboration: Regimes in an Anarchic World', in Stephen D. Krasner (ed.), *International Regimes*. Ithaca: Cornell University Press. pp. 115–40.

Steinmo, Sven, Thelen, Kathleen and Longstreth, Frank (1992) *Structuring Politics: Historical Institutionalism in Comparative Analysis*. New York: Cambridge University Press.

Strange, Susan (1978) 'The Management of Surplus Capacity: Or How Does Theory Stand Up to Protectionism 1970s Style?', *International Organization*, 33 (3): 303–34.

Strange, Susan (1983) 'Cave! Hic Dragones: A Critique of Regimes Analysis', in Stephen D. Krasner (ed.), *International Regimes*. Ithaca: Cornell University Press. pp. 337–54.

Streeck, W. and Schmitter, P.C. (1991) 'From National Corporatism to Transnational Pluralism: Organized Interests in the Single European Market', *Politics and Society*, 19 (2): 133–64.

Suganami, Hidemi (1983) 'The Structure of Institutionalism: An Anatomy of British Mainstream International Relations', *International Relations*, 7 (5): 2363–81.

Thomas, George M., Meyer, John W., Ramirez, Francisco O. and Boli, John (eds) (1987) *Institutional Structure: Constituting State, Society, and Individual*. Newbury Park: Sage.

Tiebout, Charles M. (1956) 'A Pure Theory of Local Expenditure', *Journal of Political Economy*, 64: 416–24.

Treisman, Daniel (1999) 'Political Decentralization and Economic Reform: A Game-Theoretic Analysis', *American Journal of Political Science'*, 43 (2): 488–517.

Underdal, Arid (1995) Review of 'Regime Theory and International Relations' by V. Rittberger, *Journal of Peace Research*, 32 (1): 113–19.

Victor, David G., Raustiala, Kal and Skolnikoff, E.B. (eds) (1998) *Implementation and Effectiveness of International Environmental Commitments: Theory and Practice*. Cambridge, MA: MIT Press.

Volgy, Thomas J. and Quistgard, Jon E. (1974) 'Correlates of Organizational Rewards in the United Nations: An Analysis of Environmental and Legislative Variables', *International Organization*, 28 (2): 179–205.

Wallander, Celeste A. (1999) *Mortal Friends, Best Enemies: German–Russian Cooperation After the Cold War*. Ithaca: Cornell University Press.

Waltz, Kenneth N. (1979) *Theory of International Politics*. Reading, MA: Addison–Wesley.

Weber, Steven (1998) 'Nested Institutions and the European Monetary System', in Vinod K. Aggarwal (ed.), *Institutional Designs for a Complex World: Bargaining, Linkages, and Nesting*. Ithaca: Cornell University Press. pp. 32–83.

Weiler, Joseph H.H. (1995) 'Does Europe Need a Constitution? Reflection on Demos, Telos, and the German Maastricht Decision', *European Law Journal*, 1: 219–58.

Weingast, Barry R. and Marshall, William (1988) 'The Industrial Organization of Congress', *Journal of Political Economy*, 96: 132–63.

Weiss, Edith Brown, and Jacobson, Harold K. (eds) (1998) *Engaging Countries: Strengthening Compliance with International Environmental Accords*. Cambridge, MA: MIT Press.

Wettestad, Jorgen and Andresen, Steinar (1991) *The Effectiveness of International Resource Cooperation:*

Some Preliminary Findings. Oslo: Fridtjof Nansen Institute.

Wight, Martin (1977) *Systems of States.* Leicester: Leicester University Press.

Wolf, Dieter and Zangl, Bernhard (1996) 'The European Economic and Monetary Union: "Two-level games" and the Formation of International Institutions', *European Journal of International Relations*, 2 (3): 355–93.

Young, Oran R. (1979) *Compliance with Public International Authority.* Baltimore: Johns Hopkins University Press.

Young, Oran R. and Levy, Marc A. (1999) 'The Effectiveness of International Environmental Regimes', in Oran R. Young (ed.), *Effectiveness of International Environmental Regimes: Causal Connections and Behavioral Mechanisms.* Cambridge, MA: MIT Press. pp. 1–32.

Young, Oran R. and Osherenko, Gail (eds) (1993) *Polar Politics: Creating International Environmental Regimes.* Ithaca: Cornell University Press.

Zürn, Michael (1993) 'Problematic Social Situations and International Institutions: On the Uses of Game Theory in International Politics', in Frank R. Pfetsch (ed.), *International Relations and Pan-Europe: Theoretical Approaches and Empirical Findings.* Munster: Lit.

Zürn, Michael (1997) 'Assessing State Preferences and Explaining Institutional Choice: The Case of Intra-German Trade', *International Studies Quarterly*, 41 (2): 295–320.

11

Diplomacy, Bargaining and Negotiation

CHRISTER JÖNSSON

International bargaining and negotiation constitute a relatively well-defined sub-field of international relations (IR) scholarship, with a rich and variegated literature and a respectable amount of middle-range theorizing. Paradoxically, diplomacy – the institutional framework within which much of international negotiation takes place – is a considerably less established field of study. Yet it provides the logical point of departure for this overview.

This chapter thus starts by scrutinizing the academic literature on diplomacy in terms of varying conceptualizations and a common core of themes. Then it goes on to trace the evolution of theoretically oriented studies of international negotiation from the 1960s onwards, and to identify accumulated insights and findings on a number of pertinent aspects, including the role of culture, symmetry/asymmetry, side-effects, mediation and multilateral negotiations, institutional embeddedness, and different understandings of negotiation dynamics.

DIPLOMACY

Diplomacy has been characterized as 'the master-institution' (Wight, 1978: 113) or, more prosaically, as 'the engine room' of international relations (Cohen, 1998). These and other labels point to diplomacy as an essential institution for the conduct of inter-state relations, as we know them. Moreover, diplomacy has proved to be a resilient institution; it is one of the few international institutions that have survived the challenges of popular sovereignty and nineteenth-century nationalism (Sharp, 1999: 56).

In view of its pivotal role, diplomacy has received surprisingly little attention among IR scholars. Practitioners rather than scientists have written the classic works on diplomacy, such as François de Callière's *De la manière de négocier avec les Souverains* (1716, 1919), Ernest Satow's *Guide to Diplomatic Practice* (1917) and Harold Nicolson's *Diplomacy* (1939).[1] The relatively few specialized academic studies of diplomacy that exist have tended to be 'marginal to and almost disconnected from' the rest of IR scholarship (Sharp, 1999: 34). As a result, diplomacy has not been the object of much theorizing (cf. Der Derian, 1987a: 91).

There are promising signs of change, however. In recent years, the academic study of diplomacy appears to have been revitalized. Specialized research centers have encouraged new projects and launched publication series. Prominent US and European examples include the Institute for the Study of Diplomacy at Georgetown University, which publishes *The Diplomatic Record* annually, and the Centre for the Study of Diplomacy at the University of Leicester, which issues monthly Discussion Papers and a book series, Studies in Diplomacy. The journal *Diplomacy and Statecraft* was founded in 1990 as a transdisciplinary complement to the older *Diplomatic History*. In addition, both the International Studies Association (ISA) and the British International Studies Association (BISA) have established diplomatic studies sections in the 1990s. And postmodern contributions to the study of diplomacy (Constantinou, 1996; Der Derian, 1987a, 1987b) have provided new impetus to theoretical debates.

Essence of Diplomacy

Given the undeveloped and fragmented nature of the field, it is not surprising that the study of diplomacy displays a variety of conceptualizations rather than scholarly consensus. The very definition of diplomacy is a bone of contention. Let us take two examples to illustrate some of the major controversies. One recent textbook defines diplomacy as 'the peaceful conduct of relations amongst political entities, their principals and accredited agents' (Hamilton and Langhorne, 1995: 1). The Portuguese diplomat José Calvet De Magalhães, who criticizes the existing conceptual confusion, offers his own 'pure concept' of diplomacy as 'an instrument of foreign policy for the establishment and development of peaceful contacts between the governments of different states, through the use of intermediaries mutually recognized by the respective parties' (Magalhães, 1988: 59).

One element, which these two definitions have in common but which has been questioned by others, concerns the peaceful character of diplomacy. Whereas these and many other authors regard diplomacy as the opposite to war or any use of force, several scholars are reluctant to draw such a clear-cut line. From a cross-cultural, historical perspective, the 'juxtaposition of diplomacy and war as polar opposites appears as a peculiarly Western notion not necessarily found in other traditions' (Cohen, 1999: 4). Alternatively, the blurring of the line between diplomacy and violence is seen as 'one of the developments of note distinguishing modern diplomacy' (Barston, 1988: 1). Students of contemporary international relations, the Cold War era in particular, have coined the phrase 'coercive diplomacy' to denote the use of threats or limited force to persuade opponents not to change the status quo in their favor or to call off or undo an encroachment (George, 1991; George and Simons, 1994). A compromise of sorts on this issue is provided by scholar-diplomat Adam Watson (1982: 60): 'Diplomacy is neither the simple casuistry of force, nor is it a guaranteed technique for solving by negotiation the conflicts of states without resort to it.'

This touches on another aspect, where the two illustrative definitions differ. While Magalhães delimits the term diplomacy to the activities of professional diplomats – 'intermediaries mutually recognized by the respective parties' – Hamilton and Langhorne include both 'principals and accredited agents' and thus equate diplomacy with statecraft. This reflects a perennial tension between broad and narrow definitions of diplomacy. In broad conceptions, diplomacy tends to become a synonym for foreign policy. This usage, claim Europeans (cf. James, 1993: 92; Sharp, 1999: 37), is especially common in the United States. In a narrower sense, diplomacy refers to the practices of professional diplomats. A comparison of two books with the same title is instructive in this regard. Henry Kissinger's *Diplomacy* (1994) covers broad themes of statecraft and international relations, whereas Harold Nicolson's *Diplomacy* (1939) is emblematic of a narrower conception.

Another difference in our two definitions opens up a broader perspective. In Magalhães's understanding, diplomacy is an institution of the modern state system. Hamilton and Langhorne, on the other hand, refer merely to 'political entities', and thus leave open the question whether diplomacy may exist among other actors than states and in other historical eras. In the former view, the word 'diplomacy' is reserved for the diplomatic system that originated in fifteenth-century Italy and was perfected by the French during the seventeenth and eighteenth centuries, central features of which remain at the core of today's diplomatic practices. Harold Nicolson (1939, 1954) is a prominent advocate of this view, which also finds expression in a more recent textbook (Berridge, 1995). Proponents of such a time-bound understanding may point to the fact that the word 'diplomacy' did not become current in the modern sense until the late eighteenth century.

On the other hand, a number of authors argue that diplomacy 'expresses a human condition that precedes and transcends the experience of living in the sovereign, territorial states of the past few hundred years' (Sharp, 1999: 51). Rather than restricting the concept to specific practices and specific actors, these authors understand diplomacy in terms of generic concepts, such as *representation* and *communication*.

That representation – in the sense of 'acting on behalf of' – is a key function of diplomacy is recognized by most observers, regardless of theoretical background. Paul Sharp (1999: 51), who is the most explicit advocate of an understanding of diplomacy in terms of representation, argues that its 'practice and context should be seen as responses to a common problem of living separately and wanting to do so, while having to conduct relations with others'. He proffers the following hypothesis:

> The less obvious or 'natural' the identities of the agents appear and the thinner the social context in which they operate, the more diplomacy is needed. Conversely, we would expect to see less diplomacy in the relations within a family, where identities appear self-evident, or within a religious or legal setting, where roles and rules are clearly marked and accepted. (Sharp, 1999: 50)

In addition to being a system of representation, diplomacy is also a system of communication. Authors who emphasize this aspect argue that communication is one of the logically necessary conditions for the existence of international relations.

Diplomacy can thus be understood as 'a regulated process of communication' (Constantinou, 1996: 25) or 'the communication system of the international society' (James, 1980: 942). The need to communicate is demonstrated, paradoxically, when diplomatic relations are broken and the parties almost always look for, and find, other ways of communicating (James, 1993: 96; cf. Berridge, 1994).

If we define diplomacy in terms of representation and communication, its origin obviously can be traced back further than fifteenth-century Italy. In fact, collections of cuneiform tablets from the Amarna period, lasting from about 1350 to 1220 BC, bear witness to a well-developed system of representation and communication in the ancient Near East, which deserves to be labeled diplomacy (see Cohen, 1996a; Westbrook and Cohen, 2000). Nor is diplomacy, in this perspective, limited to state agents but may exist wherever 'there are boundaries for identity and those boundaries of identity are crossed' (Constantinou, 1996: 113).

Postmodern interpretations of diplomacy go beyond representation and communication, and see the institution as a reflection of more existential aspects of the human condition. James Der Derian (1987a: 93; 1987b: 6) defines diplomacy as 'mediation between estranged individuals, groups or entities'. His key concept is 'alienation'. The primeval alienation of man, from the Judeo-Christian mythology of the Fall to the estranged relations between political entities, has required mediation; 'the form this mediation takes, as estranged relations change, constitutes a theoretical and historical base for the study of the origins of diplomacy' (Der Derian, 1987b: 6). Costas Constantinou (1996: 31), for his part, argues that 'the fable of diplomacy' is 'nothing less than the story of modernity', featuring 'a sovereign who enjoys the *ius legationis* and has the capacity to send embassies and messages representative of his thought'.

Aspects of Diplomatic Studies

Despite this bewildering array of definitions and conceptualizations, most texts on diplomacy have a common core. In varying proportions, they typically contain (1) an account of the history and pre-history of diplomacy, (2) typologies of diplomatic functions, modes and techniques, (3) information about the legal framework of diplomacy, and (4) a discussion of contemporary developments and problems.

History   An element in most, if not all, treatises on diplomacy, chronological narratives often figure predominantly in much-used texts (see, e.g., Anderson, 1993; Hamilton and Langhorne, 1995). As indicated above, authors have varying temporal scope, the main difference being between those who

set the beginning at fifteenth-century Italy and those who delve further back into the pre-history of modern diplomacy. The latter usually refer to diplomacy in ancient Greece, the Roman Empire and Byzantium, and less frequently to ancient Near East, Chinese and Indian diplomatic traditions. Regardless of scope, a prominent purpose of these accounts is to identify significant hereditary links and turning-points in the development of diplomacy.

The city-states of ancient Greece, while war-prone and passionately attached to their political independence, recognized the need to conduct a dialogue. Its rudimentary nature notwithstanding, the Greek diplomatic system may in a certain sense be seen as a harbinger of Renaissance diplomacy.

> The pattern which had been present much earlier in classical Greece was *mutatis mutandis* repeated in Renaissance Italy: an absence of outside threat, an equality of power among the states within the local system, sufficient proximity both to enable and compel communication, and a shared linguistic and cultural infrastructure which made such communication effective. (Hamilton and Langhorne, 1995: 31)

In view of its organization and longevity, the Roman Empire contributed surprisingly little to the development of diplomacy. Its most important legacy was the methods of regulating long-distance transactions, which can be seen as the first basis of a diplomatic law (Cohen, 1999: 11; Hamilton and Langhorne, 1995: 12–14).

Byzantine diplomacy had a more lasting impact. 'Byzantine' has become a synonym for labyrinthine and devious, and in its efforts to avoid war Byzantium used a broad range of instruments, including bribery, flattery, intelligence-gathering and ceremonial manifestations of its superiority (Cohen, 1999: 12; Hamilton and Langhorne, 1995: 14–20). 'The expansion of its techniques, its immensely long range and its persistence made it a forerunner of the modern system to a degree which its predecessors could not have been, and the close relationship between Byzantium and Venice provided a channel of transmission to the Western world' (Hamilton and Langhorne, 1995: 14).

Among non-European traditions, Amarna diplomacy, dating back more than three millennia, has received most attention among contemporary scholars (Cohen, 1996a; Westbrook and Cohen, 2000). Amarna diplomacy was underpinned by an elaborate code of protocol and customary law; it was facilitated by a *lingua franca*, Akkadian; and its unique feature was the tolerance of diversity, based on a myth of community transcending civilizational differences (Cohen, 1999; cf. Westbrooke and Cohen, 2000).

Around the same time as the ancient Greek system, India and China, which also consisted of a number of independent entities, developed complex patterns of communication and diplomatic practices.

In contrast to the Greek city-states, both the Indian and Chinese systems looked back to an idealized empire uniting all the fragmented territories (Cohen, 1999: 10–11; Watson, 1982: 89–92).

Irrespective of what historical precedences are adduced, there is general consensus that Renaissance Italy can claim the birthright of the modern system of diplomacy. The most important innovation was the introduction of permanent embassies and resident ambassadors, caused by the growing need not only to send messages but to gather information about neighbors among vulnerable yet ambitious Italian city-states (Berridge, 1995: 3; Hamilton and Langhorne, 1995: 32). A final break with the ambiguous legacy of the Middle Ages came by the end of the seventeenth century, when it was accepted that diplomatic representation was the prerogative of sovereigns alone (Anderson, 1993: 42). Interestingly, the development of diplomacy predated the introduction of foreign ministries. Only in 1626 did Richelieu institute the first foreign ministry, and England established its Foreign Office as late as 1782 (Anderson, 1993: 73–87; Hamilton and Langhorne, 1995: 71–75).

The 'old' or 'classic' diplomacy, which was advanced by the French in particular during the seventeenth and eighteenth centuries, was characterized by elaborate ceremonial, secrecy and gradual professionalization. The continuing sensitivity over ceremonial, procedure and precedence was a legacy of the past. Until the early nineteenth century endless crises were caused by intended or unintended slights between ambassadors or attempts by ambassadors to elevate their status and gain favors from the ruler to whom they were accredited. The eighteenth and nineteenth centuries saw the deveopment of procedural rules, or *protocol*, to avoid or minimize such conflicts (cf. Anderson, 1993: 56–68; Hamilton and Langhorne, 1995: 64–8). The concern about gathering and protecting information in combination with the established practice of conducting negotiations in secret tended to foster excessive secretiveness (Berridge, 1995: 9–10; Hamilton and Langhorne, 1995: 75–6).

The professionalization of diplomacy was a slow and fitful process. Well into the nineteenth century diplomacy remained an aristocratic pursuit. The European aristocracies were linked by ties of friendship, blood and marriage and were united by similarities in outlook and education, which created a sense among diplomats of belonging to a single 'cosmopolitan fraternity' or 'aristocratic international' (cf. Anderson, 1993: 121; Hamilton and Langhorne, 1995: 104). In fact, diplomats could easily change from one monarchical employer to another. French, the language of courts and aristocracies, naturally became the *lingua franca* of diplomacy as well (Anderson, 1993: 102). In the latter half of the nineteenth century most European governments were making efforts at tighter control of the recruitment and promotion of diplomats on the basis of merit rather than social rank, introducing nationality requirements, tests and training programs; and by the outbreak of the First World War diplomacy was a fairly well established profession (Anderson, 1993: 123; Berridge, 1995: 8).

In the wake of the First World War, the secretiveness of the 'old' diplomacy came under heavy criticism, and the entire diplomatic system was held responsible for the failure to prevent the outbreak of war. Demands for a 'new' diplomacy were widespread. US President Woodrow Wilson's call for 'open covenants, openly arrived at' epitomized the transition to a new, or some would say 'American' (Berridge, 1995: 10), diplomacy. This is where the historical account ends in most texts; the development and problems of this new diplomacy are then given special and more detailed treatment (see below).

Typologies If treatises on diplomacy are short on theory, as noted above, they are generally long on typologies. Typically, they distinguish the various *functions* of diplomacy. Even if the categories differ, there seems to be a modicum of convergence around a set of functions.[2] Almost all authors list representation as the primary function, and some identify sub-categories. Hans Morgenthau (1967: 522–5), for example, makes a distinction between symbolic, legal and political representation; whereas Sharp (1997: 612–18) offers a slightly different trichotomy of symbolic representation, representation of interests and power, and representation of ideas (such as the idea of peace and dialogue). Information exchange is usually listed next to representation. This includes being a listening post, clarifying intentions and trading valued information. Negotiation is a third broad type of diplomatic functions. A fourth category is protection of citizens and commercial and legal interests of the sending state in the receiving state. Fifth, promotion of economic, cultural and scientific relations is an increasingly important function of diplomacy. Policy preparation or policy advice is sometimes added as a sixth function (Barston, 1988: 2–3; Berridge, 1995: 39–44).

Other typologies may concern the *modes* of diplomacy – distinguishing, for instance, between bilateral diplomacy, multilateral diplomacy and summitry, or between secret and open diplomacy – or diplomatic *techniques* – be it outlining the difference between negotiation, mediation and good offices, or explicating various types of diplomatic correspondence, agreements and rules of protocol. The general point, to repeat, is that the literature on diplomacy displays an abundance of taxonomies, but a shortage of theories.

Legal framework From the time of its medieval origins, modern diplomacy has been subject to international regulation. 'Diplomatic law' was originally concerned primarily with the immunities, privileges and obligations of diplomats and was of a customary nature. Efforts to codify diplomatic law began in the late nineteenth century, but only in 1961 were they crowned with success. After more than a decade of negotiations within the International Law Commission of the United Nations, the Vienna Convention on Diplomatic Relations was then signed. By the early 1990s the Convention had been either ratified or acceded to by 165 states. As the legal framework of present-day bilateral diplomacy (excluding relations with international organizations and special missions), this Convention is commonly referred to, and sometimes treated at length, in texts on modern diplomacy (see, e.g., Berridge, 1995: 20–9; Wood and Serres, 1970).

Contemporary issues Two prominent themes emerge in the literature on recent developments of diplomacy: 'newness' and 'decline' (Hocking, 1999: 21). Several significant changes in the context and practice of diplomacy are identified, and the decline or crisis of diplomacy has become 'a well rehearsed proposition' (Hocking, 1997: 169). Diplomacy is sometimes suggested as a candidate for the endangered species list (Cooper, 1997: 174), and Zbigniew Brzezinski's quip in 1970 to the effect that if foreign ministries and embassies 'did not already exist, they surely would not have to be invented' is frequently quoted (Hamilton and Langhorne, 1995: 232; Hocking, 1999: 23; James, 1980: 933). On the other hand, there are voices questioning the amount of change and emphasizing instead the continuity of diplomatic practices. Magalhães (1988: 63), for example, considers the distinction between old and new diplomacy 'superficial', and Alan James (1980: 932) asks whether the new diplomacy may not be 'contemporary froth on top of a solid base of traditional ways'.

One way to approach this debate is to subsume the various arguments under the four factors which, according to Keith Hamilton and Richard Langhorne (1995: 238–9), shape the development of diplomacy: (1) the international order; (2) the threat, prevalence and changing nature of war; (3) the evolution of the state; and (4) advances in science and technology.

(1) The increasing number and types of international actors along with the expanding diplomatic agenda are usually identified as significant changes in the international order. Not only has the total number of states more than tripled since 1945, but new types of actors have come to participate in international relations. Multilateral diplomacy or conference diplomacy (Kaufmann, 1996) has become a hallmark of the twentieth century, and diplomats are increasingly engaged in building coalitions within international organizations or forming contact groups outside existing multilateral

fora (Leigh-Phippard, 1999). But the advent of new actors has also given rise to new, unconventional modes of diplomacy. Thus, R.P. Barston (1988: 108–16) uses the label 'associative diplomacy' to describe relations between regional organizations, and Brian Hocking (1999) has coined the term 'catalytic diplomacy' to denote the growing linkages and symbiotic relationships between governmental and non-governmental actors. Firms and enterprises are increasingly part of the diplomatic dialogue. Susan Strange (1992) identifies the emergence of a 'triangular' pattern of diplomacy, consisting of state–state, state–firm and firm–firm bargaining.

In short, dialogues between states and other types of international actors are today 'blurring the distinction between what is diplomatic activity and what is not, and who, therefore, are diplomats and who are not' (Hamilton and Langhorne, 1995: 3). The widening diplomatic agenda, which today encompasses anything from international debt management and telecommunications to refugee flows and the environment, has 'led professional diplomats into unfamiliar territory' (Melissen, 1999: xv) and has emphasized the need for expertise beyond that of diplomats. Participation by untraditional actors has been described in terms of 'paradiplomacy' – direct foreign contacts by government departments and agencies other than the foreign ministry (Meerts, 1999: 90; Melissen, 1999: xv) – 'unofficial', 'private' or 'citizen' diplomacy – the opportunity for non-state actors, groups and individuals to operate on the world stage (Hocking, 1999: 24) – and 'track-two' or 'multi-track' diplomacy – informal interaction between members of adversarial states as a complement to traditional diplomacy (McDonald, 1991; Montville, 1991; Rouhana, 1999: 113–14). To the extent that we are moving into an era of 'diplomacy without diplomats' (Kennan, 1997), diplomacy seems to be 'losing both its professional and conceptual identity' (Sharp, 1997: 630).

(2) The advent of nuclear weapons constituted a challenge to traditional diplomacy in several respects. Nuclear weapons were perceived as a threat to state sovereignty, the very pillar on which modern diplomacy rests. Moreover, the nuclear age seemed to herald a shift of influence away from diplomats to the military. Yet during the Cold War the superpowers developed a nuclear diplomacy of sorts, using the new weapons as signaling instruments in crisis management. With the end of the Cold War, the conventions of superpower crisis management no longer seem valid. On the other hand, traditional diplomacy, both bilateral and multilateral, is generally seen to have gained room for maneuver. Gradually, however, it has become evident that one important complication concerns the increasing incidence and significance of intra-state rather than inter-state conflicts in the post-Cold War world. The duty of

diplomats not to interfere in the internal affairs of the receiving state, codified in Article 41 of the 1961 Vienna Convention on Diplomatic Relations, sets obvious limits to traditional diplomacy in cases of ethnic conflicts and human rights violations, while prompting the evolution of new forms of unofficial intervention (Rouhana, 1999).

(3) The much-debated question of the future of the sovereign state reflects on diplomacy as well. To the extent that the state is in decline, as many argue, diplomacy – as an instrument of the state – is in trouble. Conversely, diplomacy appears to be an institution that is 'central to the social reproduction of the society of states' (Wolfe, 1998: 49). This is not the place to delve into that larger debate.

(4) Perhaps the most important factor affecting the evolution of diplomacy has been the revolution in communication and transportation technology. The speed and ease of transportation and communication have reduced the role of diplomats in several different ways. First, compared to earlier periods when it took a long time to relay instructions, the actions of diplomats are today much more circumscribed (Hamilton and Langhorne, 1995: 132). Moreover, direct contacts between political leaders have become frequent. George Ball, a senior US diplomat, lamented in the early 1980s that 'jet planes and telephones and the bad habits of Presidents, National Security Assistants and Secretaries of State had now largely restricted ambassadors to ritual and public relations' (quoted in Berridge, 1995: 52n). Summitry, the well-publicized meeting of national leaders, has been 'roundly anathematised by historians as well as professional diplomats' yet has been 'valued chiefly for its enormous symbolic or propaganda potential' (Berridge, 1995: 82; cf. Dunn, 1996). Finally, the rapid development of electronic media and information technology (IT) has reduced the importance of diplomats in information-gathering, and the contemporary emphasis on speed often forces decision-makers to react instantaneously to international events, bypassing traditional diplomatic channels. At the same time, diplomats are becoming engaged in 'media diplomacy', exploiting the media for their purposes (cf. Y. Cohen, 1986; Jönsson, 1996; McNulty, 1993).

It is impossible to draw any clear-cut conclusions as to whether the institution of diplomacy is in peril or not. Several authors point to its adaptability to changing circumstances in the past (see, e.g., Jönsson and Aggestam, 1999: 166; Sharp, 1999: 56), and one goes so far as to argue that 'contemporary diplomacy shows every sign of adapting vigorously to new conditions and participants' (Langhorne, 1997: 13).

In sum, diplomacy is a fragmented field of study, with a weak theoretical base. Its recent revival entails evolving dialogues across disciplines, between scientific approaches, and between scholars and practitioners. While students have been preoccupied with the 'nuts and bolts' of diplomatic practice and debates about the decline of traditional diplomacy in the contemporary age, there is today greater willingness to broaden the perspective and theorize. One common theme that pervades the entire literature is the emphasis on negotiation as the core of diplomacy. In fact, several sources define diplomacy in terms of negotiations. According to the *Oxford English Dictionary* diplomacy is 'the conduct of international relations by negotiation'; Adam Watson (1982: 33) defines diplomacy as 'negotiations between political entities which acknowledge each other's independence'; and G.R. Berridge's (1995: 1) more elaborate definition is 'the conduct of international relations by negotiation rather than by force, propaganda, or recourse to law, and by other peaceful means (such as gathering information or engendering goodwill) which are either directly or indirectly designed to promote negotiation'. The centrality of negotiation in diplomacy is paralleled by its centrality in the study of international relations, to which we will now turn.

BARGAINING AND NEGOTIATION

Negotiation can be regarded as one identifiable mode of joint decision-making, to be distinguished from coalition, when the choice is made by numerical aggregation (such as voting), and adjudication, when the choice is made hierarchically by a judge who aggregates conflicting values and interests into a single decision. In negotiations the parties are left to themselves to combine their conflicting points of view into a single decision (Zartman, 1977: 621–3). Regardless of formal decision rule, an element of negotiation usually precedes social decisions. In the international arena, dominated by sovereign states, negotiation is the primary and predominant mode of reaching joint decisions.

It is therefore not surprising that the study of international bargaining and negotiation has developed into a vital and productive sub-field of IR research. One bibliography, covering literature up to 1988 (Lakos, 1989), has more than 5,000 entries; and the rate of publication continues apace. Like diplomacy, international negotiation is a field occupied by academicians as well as practitioners; but unlike diplomacy, it is a field that has yielded a substantial body of middle-range theory.[3]

Negotiations are studied from a variety of disciplinary perspectives, and students of international negotiation have drawn on insights from diplomatic history, economics, management, sociology, anthropology, social psychology, law and other fields. To mention but one prominent example, an early work on labor negotiations (Walton and McKersie, 1965) is frequently cited in the literature on international negotiations. It should also be noted that the field has seen several fruitful transdisciplinary research projects. Negotiation theory in general has prescriptive as well as descriptive elements, and the study of international negotiation is no exception in that regard. Roger Fisher and William Ury's modern classic *Getting to Yes* (1981) has served as a source of inspiration to many authors who, like Fisher and Ury, aim at providing guidance to negotiators and mediators.

The words *bargaining* and *negotiation* are frequently used interchangeably in the literature. To the extent that a distinction is made, it goes in either of two directions. On the one hand, bargaining can be seen as the broader concept, including the exchange of verbal as well as non-verbal communication, formal as well as informal exchanges. Negotiation, in this view, refers to a formalized process relying on verbal communication; negotiation thus becomes a sub-class of bargaining (Jönsson, 1990: 2–3). On the other hand, bargaining can be understood as the exchange of offers and counter-offers, concessions and retractions; as bazaar-like haggling in contrast to joint problem-solving. Bargaining then becomes a sub-class of negotiation. In this perspective, bargaining and problem-solving can also refer to two different paradigms in the study of negotiations (Hopmann, 1995; cf. Murray, 1986).

In any event, there is broad agreement that a *bargaining situation* is characterized by the coincidence of cooperative and conflictual elements as well as interdependent decisions. 'Without common interest there is nothing to negotiate for, without conflict nothing to negotiate about' (Iklé, 1964: 2). Interdependence entails the need for mutual rather than unilateral action and renders the best course of action by individual actors dependent on the behavior of others. Far from all bargaining situations, thus understood, lead to negotiations. The parties may exchange non-verbal signals – bargain, in the first sense of the word – 'each aware that his own actions are being interpreted and anticipated, each acting with a view to the expectations that he creates' (Schelling, 1960: 21). Crisis management and signaling in limited war are cases in point. When negotiations occur, they may, in concordance with the definition of bargaining situations, be understood as 'a process in which explicit proposals are put forward ostensibly for the purpose of reaching an agreement on an exchange or on the realization of a common interest where conflicting interests are present' (Iklé, 1964: 3–4).

Even if treatises on international negotiations have been written by scholars and diplomats for centuries, systematic analysis and theory-building began only in the 1960s (cf. Hopmann, 1995: 25; 1996: 24). In 1960 two pioneering works were published: Thomas Schelling's *The Strategy of Conflict* and Anatol Rapoport's *Fights, Games and Debates*. Both were inspired by game theory, as it had been applied to social phenomena by economists. Neither author restricted himself to formal game theory, both aiming at a synthesis with other fields of knowledge. Schelling combined the game-theoretical basis with psychological insights, and Rapoport contrasted games with 'debates' – processes of developing mutual understanding and 'domains of validity' – which heralded the distinction between bargaining and problem-solving paradigms, alluded to above.

Since then several large-scale research projects on international negotiation have been launched. For example, the Harvard Negotiation Workshop of the 1970s has developed into a continuous, transdisciplinary Program on Negotiation. Its publications include the *Negotiation Journal* and cover a broad range of topics in the field of negotiation and dispute resolution, including several works bearing on international negotiations (see, e.g., Fisher and Ury, 1981; Fisher et al., 1994; Raiffa, 1982; Sebenius, 1984). In the late 1960s and early 1970s the Crisis Bargaining Project at the State University of New York at Buffalo engaged political scientists, historians, philosophers and psychologists (see Lockhart, 1979; Pruitt, 1981; Snyder and Diesing, 1977). In 1996 the Washington Interest in Negotiation (WIN) Group, based at the Johns Hopkins University School of Advanced International Studies (SAIS), launched a specialized journal, *International Negotiation*, complementing the *Journal of Conflict Resolution* and *Negotiation Journal* as a major outlet for research communication in the field. Under the auspices of the International Institute of Applied Systems Analysis (IIASA) in Laxenburg, outside Vienna, a project on Processes of International Negotiation (PIN) was initiated in 1986. Organized as a network of PIN groups in the sponsoring states of IIASA, the PIN Project has brought together scholars and practitioners of different nationalities and has resulted in a series of edited volumes (Faure and Rubin, 1993a; Kremenyuk, 1991a; Mautner-Markhof, 1989; Sjöstedt, 1993; Spector et al., 1994; Zartman, 1994a, 2000; Zartman and Rubin, 2000).

The game-theoretical heritage of negotiation studies may be less apparent today, as scholars have come to employ a variety of theoretical and methodological approaches, drawing on diplomatic history as well as legal, organizational, economic and psychological theories and using laboratory experiments and gaming as well as content analysis and interviews.[4] Yet game theory continues to be a benchmark of sorts, to which most analysts relate one way or another. First, they can draw on important developments within game theory itself. Robert Axelrod's (1984, 1997) innovative treatment of the prisoners' dilemma game, employing computer tournaments, has renewed interest in 'iterative games' and 'tit-for-tat' strategies. Steven Brams's (1990, 1994) applications of game theory to real-life episodes of international relations as well as recent refinements of 'non-cooperative game theory' and the analysis of games of incomplete information (Morrow, 1994, 1999) have served as sources of inspiration.

Second, several students of international negotiations seek eclectic syntheses of game theory and other approaches. Examples include Glenn Snyder and Paul Diesing's (1977) effort to build bridges between varieties of systems theory, bargaining theory and decision-making theory as well as James Sebenius's (1991) 'negotiation analysis' – focusing on interests, alternatives to agreement, creating and claiming value, and moves to change the game itself – and Terrence Hopmann's (1996) attempt at a comprehensive framework, adding layers of complexity to a game-theoretical foundation. Third, alternative approaches to international negotiations typically proceed from a critique of game theory. In these cases, it is the shortcomings rather than the accomplishments of game theory that stimulate new research.

In fact, some of the problematic aspects of game theory, as practiced in the 1950s and 1960s, provided impetus to independent theory-building regarding international negotiation and may thus serve as a vantage point for an overview of the present range of approaches to international negotiation. Specifically, early game theory tended to (1) homogenize actors, (2) assume symmetrical relations, (3) emphasize instrumentality, (4) favor bilateral encounters, (5) disregard context and institutions and (6) be static. In the following, I shall review attempts by negotiation analysts to overcome these limitations. It is worth noting that, even if more recent advances in game theory have addressed the same issues, the answers differ and the early parting of ways has entailed increased specialization and differentiation.

The Role of Culture

Early game theory was situation-specific, insofar as it assumed that all actors react similarly to any given situation, as reflected in a game structure, and use the same kind of rational calculus. Yet experience indicates that negotiation behavior is frequently actor-specific, insofar as actors with different cultural backgrounds prefer dissimilar negotiating strategies and react individually to the same kind of stimuli. Hence, a voluminous literature on national negotiating styles has appeared, often based on the experiences of professional negotiators. At the same time, the role of culture in international encounters is a perennial issue among negotiation theorists.

The notion that national cultures produce distinct negotiating styles has long been entertained by scholars and practitioners alike. After the Second World War, the negotiating styles of 'difficult' opponents, such as the Soviet Union (Dennett and Johnson, 1951; Kimura, 1999; Schecter, 1998; Sloss and Davis, 1986; Smith, 1989; Whelan, 1983), China (Lall, 1968; Pye, 1982, 1992: Solomon, 1999; Young, 1968) and Japan (Blaker, 1977; Graham, 1993), became popular objects of scrutiny. In parallel with the publications focusing on diplomatic negotiating behavior, a 'Negotiating With …' literature emerged in business circles, guiding novices through the intricacies of making deals in specific foreign cultures.[5] Both sets of works are typically written by practicing negotiators for the benefit of others in similar positions; they often focus on negotiation techniques and 'etiquette' rather than conflicting values; and they tend to overemphasize the uniqueness of each national negotiating style. Comparative studies of negotiating behavior are less common.[6]

The literature on national negotiating styles has been the target of much criticism. Strictly speaking, many of these works are not about Soviet/Russian, Chinese or Japanese negotiating behavior, but about *US perceptions* of distinct negotiating styles (cf. Cohen, 1993: 24). The authors seldom allow for variation in styles and behavior depending on opponent, issue-area or other contextual factors. The genre has tended to produce and reproduce stereotypes, which may ultimately serve as self-fulfilling prophecies. Cultural consistency and coherence are emphasized at the expense of the contradictions, tensions or dialectics that are usually embedded in national cultures (Janosik, 1987: 389–91). In addition, culture is not only associated with nationality. With growing complexity and specialization, professional cultures play an increasingly important role in international negotiations; and multilateralism and an emerging 'system of negotiations' (Kremenyuk, 1991b) have arguably spawned an international 'negotiation culture', socializing its members into similar behavior (cf. Lang, 1993).

An alternative approach to the culture–negotiations link has grown out of the tradition of intercultural communication (for pioneering works, see Fisher, 1980, 1988; Gulliver, 1979). Rather than trying to identify individual negotiating styles, this perspective highlights negotiation *encounters*. Instead of viewing culture as a simple determinant of behavior, it focuses on the meeting of different cultures in negotiations, which may create problems of relative, not absolute, values and meanings. While shared cultural background facilitates negotiations, intercultural dissonance renders verbal and non-verbal communication more difficult (Cohen, 1993: 22).

In particular, students of international negotiations have pointed to the problematic encounters between 'high-context' and 'low-context' cultures (Hall, 1976: 78–9). Representatives of high-context cultures communicate allusively rather than directly; they see language as a social instrument, dislike directness and contradiction, prefer inaccuracy to painful precision and are concerned with appearance and loss of face. In low-context cultures, by contrast, explicitness is the norm; language has an informational rather than socially lubricative function; contradiction is regarded as functional; and content takes precedence over outward appearance. US–Japanese and Israeli–Egyptian negotiations illustrate the problems associated with encounters between low-context and high-context cultures (cf. Cohen, 1990, 1997; Ting-Toomey, 1985a, 1985b).

Critics argue that culture is little more than a residual category accounting for negotiation failures (Faure and Rubin, 1993b: xii). Moreover, culture is a vague concept with no agreed definition. Cultural explanations are criticized as being tautological and epiphenomenal (Zartman, 1993). Advocates, on the other hand, are careful to emphasize that culture can never be the sole determinant of negotiation processes and outcomes, but insist that 'any reasonable explanation of what happens in international negotiation must include the cultural aspects of the negotiation relationship' (Faure and Rubin, 1993c: 212; cf. Faure, 1999).

Asymmetrical Negotiations

Prominent games, such as prisoners' dilemma and chicken, presume symmetrical relations and do not take power asymmetries into account. This game-theoretical heritage was reinforced by the overshadowing attention paid to US–Soviet negotiations during the Cold War. Yet it has become increasingly obvious that the relative symmetry brought about by the nuclear stalemate represents an exception rather than the rule in international negotiation. Therefore, the dearth of research into asymmetrical negotiation is surprising and bothering (Habeeb, 1988: 1; Zartman, 1985b: 122). Only recently have efforts been made to redress this imbalance (see Zartman and Rubin, 2000).

At issue is 'the power of the weak' – the observation that the 'stronger' party does not always 'win' in asymmetrical negotiation encounters. The answers that have been suggested to this paradox all go beyond the realist notion that aggregate structural power determines outcomes. For example, Hopmann (1996: 119) argues that parties 'with more attractive alternatives, and consequently with lower losses associated with the failure of negotiations, are more likely to be influential in claiming a larger share of the value being distributed within negotiations'. The significance of asymmetrical commitment or 'resolve' as a source of weak states' power is confirmed by Snyder and Diesing (1977: 190) in the context of crisis bargaining.

Mark Habeeb (1988) makes a distinction between issue-specific structural power and behavioral power. Issue-specific power, in his framework, is determined by available alternatives, commitment and control (the degree to which one side can unilaterally achieve its preferred outcome). Behavioral power refers to the actors' tactics to alter the issue-power balance, such as building coalitions or threatening to veto an agreement, and thus adds a dynamic element to the power calculus. The importance of behavioral power in compensating for structural weakness is echoed by other authors as well. William Zartman (1985b: 122) maintains that 'weak parties can often make use of procedural manipulations when substantive equality eludes them', citing fractioning and packaging of issues as well as the use of deadlines and withholding signature as examples. John Odell (1980, 1985) shows that weaker states, in bilateral trade negotiations with the United States, have taken advantage of the pluralist US system to mobilize allies within the United States to promote their cause; in addition, they have pursued a 'technological strategy', profiting from being more informed and coming better prepared to the negotiating table. Similarly, Habeeb (1988: 132–3) points to the 'asymmetry of attention' in enhancing the power of weak states.

Empirical studies of asymmetrical negotiations cover different actors and issues and reach varying conclusions. Robert Rothstein's (1979) and William Zartman's (1985b, 1987) studies of mostly unsuccessful North–South negotiations on economic issues emphasize the insufficiencies of the international bargaining system and make prescriptive suggestions as to how the negotiation process might be improved to the benefit of the weaker parties (Zartman, 1985b: 121). Ole Elgström (1990, 1992) shows that shared norms may increase the leverage of recipient countries in highly asymmetrical foreign aid negotiations. The pattern in the early phase (1973–5) of the Conference on Security and Cooperation in Europe (CSCE), according to Hopmann (1978), was that states with the least to lose from non-agreement were more influential as to what was included in the text than those with more to lose. From his analysis of the Panama Canal negotiations, US–Spanish bases negotiations and the three Anglo-Icelandic Cod Wars, Habeeb (1988: 130–1) concludes that issue-specific structural power is the best predictor of negotiation outcomes, and control the single most important component of issue power.

Negotiating for Side-Effects

Iklé defined negotiation, it will be recalled, in terms of an exchange of proposals 'ostensibly for the purpose of reaching an agreement'. His use of the word *ostensibly* indicates that he believes negotiations can be used for other purposes as well. Accordingly, Iklé (1964: 43–58) pioneered inquiries into various side-effects of negotiations – effects not concerning agreement that may arise either by accident or by design. This is an aspect disregarded by pure game theory and most other approaches that proceed from assumptions of instrumentality.

Negotiations may be a way to maintain contact with the opponent and establish a habit of communicating, which might be useful in case of crises or emergencies. Furthermore, they can serve as a substitute for violent action; a prevalent view in the West, according to Iklé, is that engaging the opponent in talks will prevent him from using force. Intelligence may be another side-effect of negotiations; the information obtained in the negotiation process is sometimes more important than the settlement of issues. The flip side is that negotiations can be exploited for purposes of deception, for instance to gain time to prepare for future use of force. Propaganda as a side-effect occurs when parties use negotiations to have a sounding-board, to gain prestige or publicity or to show Pharisaic rectitude. Governments know that refusal to participate in negotiations will impair the good will of important groups. States may also engage in negotiations in order to improve their bargaining position with third parties. Iklé proffers several historic examples of these various side-effects, and present-day realities – especially the many frustrating attempts at negotiating ethnic conflicts in the Balkans and elsewhere – testify to their continued relevance.

Mediation and Multilateral Negotiations

Bilateral encounters have provided the foundation for most negotiation theory. Additional parties entail increased complexity. Even if the interaction of three or more parties can logically be broken down into dyadic component sub-systems, the dynamics of tri- and multilateral negotiation cannot adequately be analyzed as a sequence of bilateral negotiations. Mediation – which transforms the negotiation structure from a dyad to a triangle – and multilateral negotiations have therefore given rise to studies and theorizing, which draw on other traditions than game theory.

The literature on *international mediation* usually proceeds from a conflict perspective. Mediation is framed as an instrument of conflict resolution, especially in intractable conflicts such as in the Middle East or the Balkans. Less attention is paid to 'unauthorized mediation' in multilateral negotiations (Stenelo, 1972). On the basis of statistical analysis of a large data set of international disputes from 1945 to 1990, mediation emerges as a vastly more common type of conflict management than direct negotiation between the parties (Bercovitch and Houston, 1996: 18). The significance of mediation has, if anything, been enhanced in recent years, when 'state leaders and international institutions can no longer hide behind the fig leaf of superpower rivalry as an excuse for their own inactivity or ineffectiveness' (Kleiboer, 1998: 2).

Mediation is a political form of third party intervention, to be distinguished from the legal procedures of arbitration and adjudication. In mediation the ultimate decision-making authority remains in the hands of the disputants and the outcome is not binding. Mediators, whether invited by the parties or offering their services, must be acceptable to both or all disputants. Identifiable varieties of informal intervention, such as conciliation, good offices and fact-finding, can be subsumed under mediation (cf. Touval and Zartman, 1985: 7; Kleiboer, 1998: 6–7).

With the expansion in the numbers and varieties of third party intervention in international conflicts in recent years, scholars have become increasingly interested in 'multiparty mediation'. The term refers to efforts by multiple mediators, whether sequential, simultaneous, or 'composite' actors such as international organizations. Multiparty mediation may entail benefits in terms of burden-sharing, complementary action and leverage, but also raises serious management issues of coordination, leadership, commitment and responsibility (Crocker et al., 1999).

Mediation analysts tend to agree that mediation outcomes are the result of the interaction of contextual and process variables. Contextual variables include the nature of the dispute, the contending parties and their relationships, and mediator characteristics. Process variables concern the strategies and tactics employed by mediators (cf. Bercovitch and Houston, 1996: 15; Kleiboer, 1998: 18). There is also some convergence concerning identifiable mediator roles and methods. Saadia Touval and William Zartman's (1985: 11–14) three-fold typology of the mediator as *communicator*, *formulator* and *manipulator* has been expanded on by others. Terrence Hopmann (1996: 231–7), for example, adds *process facilitator* (working on atmospherics and logistical support) and *facilitator of cognitive change* (inducing the parties to see the problem in a new light). And Raymond Cohen (1996b: 111–23) points to three specifically cross-cultural roles: acting as *interpreter* (decoding and explaining the parties' culturally encoded messages), as *buffer* (helping disputants to save face) and as *coordinator* (synchronizing discordant negotiating conventions).

However, there is more diversity than commonality among mediation studies. The theoretical foundation varies. Marieke Kleiboer (1998: 39–83) identifies four ideal-type models: international mediation is variably viewed as *power brokerage* (drawing on neorealism, this perspective posits major powers as the most plausible mediators); as *political problem-solving* (drawing on political psychology, this perspective emphasizes the mediator's knowledge, commitment to peace, analytical skills and ability to communicate); as *domination* (drawing on structuralism, this perspective sees mediation as an instrument used by élites and powerful states to defend the status quo); and as *restructuring relationships* (drawing on critical theory, this perspective points up the mediator's commitment to social change and the advantages of moving mediation efforts away from the usual diplomatic arena to more informal workshop settings). Similarly, mediation researchers have employed a variety of methods, ranging from single-case studies to laboratory experiments, computer simulations and statistical analyses of large data sets.

The lack of a common theoretical or methodological basis has entailed a number of scholarly disagreements and debates. Three prominent issues have concerned the assessment of mediation outcomes, the impartiality of mediators and the timing of mediation efforts. First, there are no agreed criteria, according to which a mediation effort can be judged successful or a failure, and there is a lack of normative consensus. Several analysts beg the normative question by avoiding any conceptualization of mediation success and failure. In the conceptualizations that can be found in the literature, mediation is variably considered successful: if it settles or makes a great difference to the dispute; if it initiates dialogue and avoids violence among the disputants; if it allows both parties to save face; if it creates a valuable precedent; if it fulfils the mediator's objectives; or if it resolves the underlying roots of conflict (cf. Kleiboer, 1998: 13–14).

Second, the impartiality of mediators, deemed pivotal by earlier analysts (see, e.g., Young, 1967: 81, 309), came under intensive debate in the 1970s and 1980s. One important impetus was the publicized use of mediation by high-ranking representatives of major powers, especially Henry Kissinger's shuttle diplomacy in the Middle East (Mitchell and Webb, 1988: 8). The notion of a disinterested, impartial mediator becomes difficult to uphold in an increasingly interdependent world. Most analysts today agree that mediators have a stake in the conflict they try to resolve and act out of self-interest as much as altruism. Moreover, there seems to be consensus that it is the mediators' resources and ability to effect change, rather than their perceived impartiality, that determine their acceptability and effectiveness (cf. Bercovitch, 1996a: 5; Zartman and Touval, 1985: 255). Some scholars argue that even 'biased' mediators – who have closer ties with one of the disputants, and are perceived as such by all parties – can be effective, when the bias adds to their capacity and motivation to influence (Carnevale and Arad, 1996; Smith, 1985; Touval, 1985). Thus, the United States can be accepted by Arab states as a mediator in the Middle East because of its ability to 'deliver Israel'.

A third debate zeroes in on the appropriate timing of mediation. The accepted wisdom is that third party roles are most relevant when the parties have reached an impasse; only after having exhausted all other possibilities – and themselves – will disputants be susceptible to outside help. The notion that a 'mutually hurting stalemate' (Zartman, 1985a; see below) precedes and facilitates mediation has been questioned by analysts who argue that this is a situation inviting failure: 'the relationship between the parties has deteriorated significantly, interests are often interfused with needs and appear nonnegotiable, and the respective positions have become intransigent through a series of past commitments' (Keashly and Fisher, 1996: 247). Instead, some claim, mediation is a particularly useful tool in conflict prevention (Bercovitch, 1996b).

Multilateral negotiations are less studied and theorized than either bilateral negotiations or mediation; in fact, they represent 'one of the least developed areas in negotiation theory' (Hopmann, 1996: 244). The principal reason is their bewildering complexity – 'a very messy affair, almost defying generalization' (Holsti, 1982: 160). Yet multilateral negotiations have become increasingly common and significant in the global arena. In fact, one might claim that there are no bilateral negotiations in international relations, since each side is always composite (Zartman, 1991: 74). Multilateral negotiations raise the problem of managing complexity (Winham, 1977a, 1977b) for practitioners and theorists alike. 'The more the messier' (Zartman, 1994b: 3) applies not only to the parties to multilateral negotiations, but to issues and roles as well. Methods to reduce complexity therefore include *coalition-building, issue aggregation and disaggregation*, and *role differentiation*. These aspects of multilateral negotiations are also highlighted in the scholarly literature.

First, coalitions reduce the number of negotiating actors to a manageable amount (see Dupont, 1996). Coalition-building, however, may be a double-edged sword. While simplifying the negotiation process by reducing the number of actors, coalition formation often entails intransigent negotiation positions, once consensus is reached within the coalition, and may thus intensify conflicts among members of opposing coalitions (Hopmann, 1996: 261). Hence, multilateral negotiations can be understood as a coalition-building, coalition-bridging and coalition-breaking exercise (Hampson with Hart, 1995: 20). Sequencing is important, since potential coalition partners' assessments of the returns of joining are influenced by knowledge of who has already joined, or decided not to join (Sebenius, 1996; Watkins and Rosegrant, 1996). In addition, several studies point to the importance of cross-cutting rather than reinforcing coalitions (cf. Hampson with Hart, 1995: 353; Hopmann, 1996: 264; Touval, 1989: 164).

Second, multilateral negotiations typically encompass several, complex issues. Two diametrically opposite techniques to handle this complexity are identified in the literature. One is issue disaggregation, also referred to as issue decomposition and sequencing (Hampson with Hart, 1995: 45–7; Hopmann, 1996: 81). This incremental approach, which involves negotiating each issue separately and sequentially, rests on the belief that half a loaf is better than none. It often entails organizing working groups to deal with specific issues or sub-issues (Midgaard and Underdal, 1977: 336–7). Issue aggregation or issue linkage represents another method of handling complexity (see, e.g., Hopmann, 1996: 81–4). This means combining sub-issues that would be non-negotiable if treated separately into package deals or tradeoffs.

Third, multilateral negotiations involve not only many parties and many issues, but also have a multi-role character (Zartman, 1994b: 5). Role differentiation is a trait of international conferences as well as other social groups (Touval, 1989: 161–2). The mediator role can be assumed by parties or groups of parties to multilateral negotiations. The difficulty of differentiating the role of 'mediator' from that of 'negotiator' then constitutes a problem for presumptive mediators as well as other parties (cf. Stenelo, 1972; Williams, 1988). Leadership roles are considered especially significant in multilateral negotiation (see Hermann, 1995; Malnes, 1995; Sjöstedt, 1999; Underdal, 1994; Young, 1991). Various modes of leadership have been identified in the literature, with a substantial degree of overlap. For example, Oran Young (1991) distinguishes between structural, entrepreneurial and intellectual leadership; Margaret Hermann (1995) between crusaders, salesmen, agents and fire fighters; Lance Antrim (1994) between inspirational, procedural and substantive leadership; and Arild Underdal (1994) between unilateral, coercive and instrumental leaders. Different modes of leadership may be required at different stages of the negotiations (Sjöstedt, 1999).

In sum, multilateral negotiation is an area of theoretical underdevelopment but of growing scholarly concern. The research focus is on the management of complexity, including 'reduction (simplification) to make complexity comprehensible, structuring to make it manageable, and direction to produce a result' (Zartman, 1994c: 220).

Context and Institutional Embeddedness

Game theory in its purest form operates in a context-free and institution-free environment. The choices of the interdependent parties are supposedly based on information about their own and the opponent's preferences and the game structure.[7] In real-life negotiations an endless variety of contextual factors may influence behavior and processes, and it matters whether the negotiation is embedded in an institutional framework or not. For instance, the current and past relationships between the negotiating actors obviously affect the negotiation climate. In the estimate of one experienced international negotiator (Brady, 1991), the most difficult negotiations are those between 'friends' – countries that share neither membership in a formal alliance nor an adversarial relationship.

One common notion is that bargaining behavior and processes may be issue-specific rather than situation-specific, as assumed by game theorists, or actor-specific, as in studies of negotiating styles and culture. Iklé (1964: 26–42) makes a distinction between negotiations aiming at extension, normalization, redistribution, innovation or side-effects with different negotiation patterns. Students of negotiations on different issues, such as arms control, trade, crisis management and environmental protection, have noted issue-specific traits. Odell (2000), for instance, points to sensitivity to changes in market conditions as the fundamental distinguishing trait of negotiations over economic issues as compared to other international negotiations.

Several international negotiations tend to become continuous. Arms control negotiations and trade talks in the context of GATT/WTO are cases in point. Then it becomes difficult to pinpoint the beginning and end of bargaining processes; the outcome of one round of negotiations creates a new bargaining situation, and the parties are continually in contact with each other. According to Axelrod's (1984) notion of the 'shadow of the future', this would make cooperation more likely, as the short-run gains of non-cooperation are outweighed by the long-run losses of mutual non-cooperation. Moreover, continuous negotiations tend to become institutionalized; they develop a culture, behavioral norms and a language of their own.

Students of international institutions or regimes have paid relatively little attention to negotiation processes. They have addressed questions of *why* states cooperate rather than *how* they cooperate, and have focused on the conditions of regime creation rather than its process. Yet it could be argued that the building and maintenance of regimes involve continuous negotiations and that 'regimes deserve greater attention as forums for bargaining' (Fearon, 1998). Among regime theorists, Oran Young (1989, 1994) is exceptional by having elaborated the notion of 'institutional bargaining', in which the participants seek to reach agreement on the terms of constitutional contracts.

The most prominent example of *institutionalized negotiations* in today's world is the European Union, which has been characterized as a 'permanent negotiation institute' (Bal, 1995: 1) or a 'multilateral inter-bureaucratic negotiation marathon' (Kohler-Koch, 1996: 367). Negotiations in the EU take place within an institutional framework, with norms and rules impinging on the negotiations, and persistent negotiation patterns over time. The main dividing line among students of EU negotiations runs between 'liberal intergovernmentalists', who maintain that all major agreements are in effect bargains between the most powerful states (Moravcsik, 1991), and network theorists, who emphasize the participation by state as well as non-state actors and the informal nature of EU negotiations (Jönsson et al., 1998; Pfetsch, 1998). The former approach focuses on 'history-making' negotiations; the latter on day-to-day negotiations. Although some studies point to the importance of institutional factors in EU negotiations (Jönsson et al., 1998; Pfetsch, 1999), the institutionalization of international negotiations is still insufficiently understood and deserves further research.

Negotiation Dynamics

While useful in revealing the nature of bargaining situations and available strategies, game theory originally offered less guidance to the analysis of negotiation *processes*. The back-and-forth communication, the exchange of proposals and signals, the tactics and techniques used, the patterns of concessions and retractions – in short, the dynamics of mutual persuasion attempts that we usually associate with negotiations – were insufficiently caught by early game theory.

No alternative, overarching theory of international negotiation processes was developed in response; instead, the literature today offers a variety of approaches, which highlight different dynamic aspects and have been used alone or in different combinations in studies of international negotiations. One may distinguish at least seven perspectives, according to which the essence of international negotiation processes is, respectively, (1) establishing a contract zone, (2) using tactical instruments, (3) reducing uncertainty, (4) balancing contradictory imperatives, (5) timing, (6) coordinating internal and external processes, and (7) communicating. These approaches can be placed along a continuum, with (1) being closest to, and (7) most removed from, the game-theoretical tradition. At the risk of oversimplification and streamlining, each perspective will be treated separately below.

Establishing a contract zone One central feature of our common understanding of negotiation is that the parties initially ask for more than they expect to get. If we add the assumption that the parties know how far they are willing to go in terms of concessions, we can, for each party, construct a continuum ranging from its maximum objective to its minimum acceptable outcome or 'resistance point'. The crucial problem then is to identify a

space where these continua overlap, that is, where both parties prefer an agreement to breaking off negotiations. This space is often called 'contract zone' – 'bargaining range' and 'settlement range' are other labels used. The exchange of proposals and other signals, in this conception, serves to gradually reveal whether a contract zone exists and, if so, where it is located.

This understanding of the negotiation process applies most readily to bilateral, distributive negotiations on single, easily measurable issues. The difficulties of identifying maximum objectives, resistance points and contract zones in multilateral negotiations on complex, abstract issues can be staggering to analysts and negotiators alike. Yet one notion, originating from this perspective, that has gained wide currency in the negotiation literature is that of BATNA (the Best Alternative to a Negotiated Agreement) (Fisher and Ury, 1981; Raiffa, 1982). Negotiators are supposed (and recommended) to determine their resistance points by comparing the value of an agreement at any stage of the negotiations with the value of no agreement; only if a negotiated solution is better than their BATNA will (or should) they agree.

Using tactical instruments Another perspective focuses on the attempts by each party to outwit the other by means of 'strategic moves', such as commitments, threats and promises, designed to constrain the opponent's behavior by affecting the opponent's expectations of one's own behavior. This 'manipulative' (Young, 1975: 317) conception of negotiation owes much to Thomas Schelling's (1960, 1966) pioneering work. His analysis of commitments, 'the power to bind oneself', through which bargaining parties eliminate some of the options open to them, has been especially influential. To be effective, Schelling argues, a commitment must not only be communicated and made intelligible to the other side, but has to be made credible as well.

Schelling's seminal treatment of the credibility problem has been followed up by other scholars. For instance, Robert Jervis (1970), drawing on Erving Goffman's (1969) analysis of 'expression games', has suggested a basic distinction between *signals* and *indices*. Signals are issued for manipulative purposes; they have no inherent credibility, as they can be used as easily by a deceiver as by an honest actor. Indices, by contrast, are less easily manipulated; they are believed to be inextricably linked to the actor's capabilities or intentions and to be untainted by deception. Indices, according to Jervis, are used by negotiators to verify or falsify the opponent's signals. Yet once the sender becomes conscious of the fact that the adversary perceives certain behavior as an index, possibilities of manipulation emerge. If the receiver, in turn, becomes conscious of the adversary's manipulation, 'multiple cycles of manipulation' may ensue (Jervis, 1970: 41–65).

The 'contract zone' and 'manipulative' perspectives share a view of the negotiation process as a battle of retreat. Agreement is seen to be the result of a series of incremental steps away from the parties' opening proposals; through mutual concessions convergence may be achieved. The two complementary perspectives are therefore sometimes referred to as the 'concession–convergence' approach to negotiation. The game-theoretical heritage is evident in their assumptions of rational choice and exogenously given interests as well as the primary focus on bilateral encounters. These assumptions are relaxed in the following approaches.

Reducing uncertainty   This approach proceeds from the structural uncertainty experienced by negotiating parties, especially – but not only – in multilateral negotiations; that is, 'the nature of the possible outcomes and not just the probability associated with different outcomes is unknown' (Winham, 1977a: 101). Trial-and-error search, information processing and uncertainty control are basic elements in this understanding of negotiations. The central focus of the joint decision-making process is to reduce the variety inherent in the complex and multidimensional bargaining situation. An important element in this process is the search for a *formula*, 'a shared perception or definition of the conflict that establishes terms of trade, the cognitive structure of referents for a solution, or an applicable criterion of justice' (Zartman and Berman, 1982: 95). A formula can be something akin to Schelling's (1960: 57–8) idea of 'focal points' – mutually recognized keys to coordinated solutions, based on prominence, conspicuousness and uniqueness. It may also be a captivating metaphor, such as 'the common heritage of mankind' formula guiding the Law of the Sea negotiations on the exploitation of the seabed. A formula, in short, 'helps give structure and coherence to an agreement on details, helps facilitate the search for solutions on component items, and helps create a positive, creative image of negotiation rather than an image of concessions and compromise' (Zartman and Berman, 1982: 93).

In this perspective, negotiation appears as a deductive exercise. Only after a formula has been established, can a structured search for solutions of more precise problems – the 'detail phase' – begin (Zartman and Berman, 1982: 147). One technique that has been identified as particularly helpful in the detail phase of multilateral negotiations is the use of a 'single negotiation text' (SNT) (Fisher and Ury, 1981: 118–22; Raiffa, 1982: 205–17). After listening to the stated positions of all the parties, one participant, in a mediator or leadership role (often a chairperson), drafts a text, which is then circulated for criticism, modifications and refinements. Successive rounds of redrafting and feedback may eventually produce an agreed document, as in the Camp David negotiations in 1978 and the Law of the Sea negotiations. In sum, a distinguishing feature of viewing negotiations as uncertainty reduction is that 'the development of common perceptions becomes more important than the exchange of concessions' (Winham, 1977a: 97). Creativity and reconceptualizations are considered more important than outwitting the opponents.

Balancing contradictory imperatives   One conceptualization of international negotiations that resonates among practitioners is that of a series of dilemmas with no fixed, invariably acceptable solution (cf. Snyder and Diesing, 1977: 207–56). The essence of the negotiation process is thus to find the appropriate mix of contradictory imperatives along several dimensions. One basic dilemma concerns firmness vs. flexibility. If you are too firm, you may invite hostility and stalemate; if you are too flexible, you may be exploited by the opponent. It has been suggested that 'early firmness followed by later flexibility' is the optimal mix (Druckman, 1995: 79). Notions of 'firm flexibility' or 'flexible rigidity' have been introduced to denote combinations of firmness with respect to ends and basic interests and flexibility with respect to means and tactics (Pruitt, 1995: 103–9; Pruitt and Lewis, 1977: 183–4; Pruitt and Rubin, 1986: 153).

Several dilemmas of this kind can be identified, be they openness and honesty vs. secrecy and deception; explicitness vs. ambiguity; manipulating risk vs. minimizing risk; or aggregating vs. disaggregating issues. The view of negotiations as a series of dilemmas implies an indeterminate process. Practitioners therefore frequently conclude that negotiation defies scientific generalizations. To use an analogy once suggested by star negotiator Richard Holbrooke, negotiation, like jazz, is based on skills of improvisation.

Timing   Another approach that finds strong support among practitioners emphasizes the importance of timing in negotiations. There are two variants of this perspective. One distinguishes *stages* in the negotiation process, the other focuses on *ripeness*. The notion that negotiations proceed through several identifiable stages, each with a pattern of characteristic and/or appropriate behavior, is common in the literature. Theorists adhering to the 'concession–convergence' paradigm typically postulate an early contentious stage and a later problem-solving phase, with varying numbers of stages in between (Pruitt and Rubin, 1986: 137). Those who see the reduction of uncertainty as the essence of negotiations distinguish three stages: a diagnostic, a formula and a detail phase (Zartman and Berman, 1982). The notion of stages is sometimes combined with efforts to identify turning points, 'events or processes that mark the passage of a negotiation from one stage to the next' (cf. Druckman, 1986; Druckman et al., 1991: 56).

Negotiation analysis has, in fact, extended beyond the negotiating table and identified pre-negotiation and post-agreement stages as well. The pre-negotiation phase has attracted increased attention (Saunders, 1985; Stein, 1989). In pre-negotiations, the parties attempt to identify the problem and ways to deal with it, produce a commitment to negotiate and set the parameters for the negotiations. At the other end, a post-agreement bargaining phase follows the conclusion of many agreements – the point where most negotiation analyses end. For instance, the Oslo and Dayton agreements marked the starting point rather than the end point of bargaining between the parties. 'Compliance bargaining' concerning the terms and obligations of international agreements (Jönsson and Tallberg, 1998: 372) takes place in such institutional settings as the European Union and the World Trade Organization (WTO).

A somewhat different approach to the question of timing proceeds from the concept of ripeness (Zartman, 1985a). Negotiation or mediation is most likely to bring results at a moment when the conflict or issue is ripe for solution. The definition of a ripe moment has two components. First, the parties experience a 'mutually hurting stalemate', that is, a realization that neither can benefit but will suffer from continued conflict or status quo. Second, they perceive the possibility of a way out by means of a negotiated solution.

The ripeness notion has intuitive appeal, and it has been built on, refined and criticized by a number of scholars and practitioners. Dean Pruitt (1997: 239), in his 'readiness theory', defines a 'motivationally ripe moment' in terms of the parties being motivated to achieve de-escalation as well as optimistic that the other party will reciprocate cooperation. Christopher Mitchell (1995) emphasizes the importance of an 'enticing opportunity', the prospect of future gains, in assessing ripeness. On the basis of a study of international mediation efforts in Zimbabwe, Stephen Stedman (1991: 235–42) concludes that it is not necessary for all actors in a conflict to perceive a mutually hurting stalemate and that ripeness, paradoxically, can come from a situation where both sides believe that a settlement will produce a victory for them. Like Jo Husbands (1991), he points to the significance of domestic political processes and cycles in the determination of a ripe moment. Louis Kriesberg (1991: 1–2) and Jeffrey Rubin (1991: 239) caution that claims about timing and ripeness can be used to attempt to manipulate the pace and direction of negotiations. In short, efforts to apply and specify ripeness have tended to emphasize the subjective aspects of a concept that may seem to connote an objective condition (see, e.g., Aggestam and

Jönsson, 1997: 772–4; Kleiboer, 1994; Mooradian and Druckman, 1999).

Coordinating external and internal processes
It is sometimes said that every bilateral international negotiation encompasses at least three bargaining processes: the external one between the two parties, and two internal ones within each of the parties. Practitioners, in particular US negotiators, usually emphasize the problems of internal bargaining, arguing they spend as much or even more time achieving consensus within their own side (cf. Martin, 1988: 49–50; Winham, 1979: 116–19; Zartman and Berman, 1982: 207). Although practitioners often accuse theorists of neglecting the internal aspect of international negotiation, the nexus between internal and external negotiations has been a perennial theoretical concern. For instance, a recurring game-theoretical idea holds that a bilateral negotiation might be represented as one main game with a number of sub-games or 'auxiliary games', the playing of which influences the playing and outcome of the main game (Midgaard, 1966). Similarly, the notion of 'intraorganizational bargaining' in labor negotiations can be translated into intra-alliance and internal bargaining in the international arena (Walton and McKersie, 1965: 281–351, 389–91; cf. Jönsson, 1979).

Robert Putnam's (1988) conceptualization of 'two-level games' has gained wide currency and has been applied to a number of international negotiations (Evans et al., 1993). Internal bargaining concerning 'ratification', broadly understood, parallels inter-state negotiations. The 'win-set' in any international negotiation is thus determined not only by strategies at the inter-state level, but by preferences and coalitions as well as institutions at the national level. A narrow win-set internally (due, for example, to varying interests and opposing views in a vital democracy) may be an asset externally, whereas a broad win-set internally (due, for example, to lack of opposition in an authoritarian state) may be a liability. The side that can credibly point to domestic conditions that limit its bargaining range – be they the parliamentary situation, strong interest groups or public opinion – has an advantage over the side that cannot in the same way narrow down the win-set. Some international negotiations have the character of 'multi-level' rather than two-level games. Thus, changes in EU agricultural policy have been analyzed as the result of a 'three-level game' – parallel negotiations within GATT with the EU as one party, among the EU member states, and between various interests within key member states (Patterson, 1997).

Communicating   Bargaining and negotiation can be seen as sub-classes of social communication. One might argue that 'without communication there is no negotiation' (Fisher and Ury, 1981: 33) or that 'in essence, international negotiation is communication' (Stein, 1988: 222). Yet the linguistic or nonlinguistic aspects of communication in international negotiations have received scant attention; in fact, 'much of the existing literature derives from theoretical approaches that are particularly insensitive to language and communication' (Bell, 1988: 233). Both verbal and non-verbal messages are exchanged in international negotiations. Diplomatic 'body language' ranges from the venue and the format of the negotiations or the level of delegations to the mobilization and movement of military troops and hardware. Indeed, activity as well as inactivity and words as well as silence may be perceived as messages in bargaining situations.

Diplomatic signaling (Cohen, 1987; Jönsson and Aggestam, 1999) thus seems a pertinent yet not sufficiently explored area of research. One study (Jönsson, 1990), which draws on attribution theory and semiotics in analyzing inherently ambiguous communication in international bargaining, characterizes negotiators as 'intuitive semioticians'. There are recent efforts to apply semantics (Cohen, 2000) and Jürgen Habermas's critical theory of communicative action (Risse, 2000) to the argumentative processes of international negotiations. Shared meanings (or the lack thereof) and 'the power of the better argument' then become foci of attention. On the whole, however, the communication aspects of bargaining warrant more research.

LESSONS LEARNED AND UNANSWERED QUESTIONS

Bargaining and negotiation as well as diplomacy represent vital and variegated research areas. While efforts at generalizations and theory-building have been considerably more advanced in the study of international negotiations, neither area has a firm, generally accepted theoretical foundation. Game theory originally promised to provide such a basis for bargaining and negotiation. Yet, game theory – its indisputable heuristic value notwithstanding – has perhaps been more important because of its shortcomings than because of its success. The rewards of game theory have thus been indirect, as was the case with the sons who were told by their father to dig for buried treasures in the vineyard: they found no treasures, but they improved the soil (Rapoport, 1960: xii, 360).

This chapter has tried to chronicle the accomplishments as well as the shortcomings of scholarship in diplomacy and international bargaining and negotiation. The study of diplomacy has provided us with a detailed picture of the evolution of diplomatic practice. Recent research has traced the roots of diplomacy far back into history and beyond the European perimeters of earlier writing. At the same time, students have explored the peculiar problems of diplomacy in the post-Cold War era of revolutionized communications technology and globalization. Postmodern authors, framing diplomacy as a reflection of more fundamental problems of alienation or modernity, have posed the challenge of formulating a general theory of diplomacy. Representation and communication have been suggested as the conceptual foundation of such a theory, which should also take into account the role of diplomacy in reproducing sovereign states.

Students of diplomacy and international negotiation have joined forces to a surprisingly limited degree. Yet there would seem to be synergetic dividends from collaboration between the two branches of scholarship. Diplomacy represents the institutional framework of inter-state negotiations, an aspect largely neglected by negotiation theorists. Multilateralism constitutes a common research concern. The notion of a global diplomatic culture, an aspect frequently mentioned but seldom explored by students of diplomacy, is closely related to the equally unexplored idea of a common negotiation culture, found in the negotiation literature. This represents another promising area of joint research efforts. Comparative studies of the significance of the diplomatic culture relative to national cultures and negotiating styles are warranted, as are systematic comparisons of national diplomatic and negotiating styles.

Students of international bargaining and negotiation, in their search for useful middle-range theory, have largely eschewed the grand theoretical debates between various 'isms'.[8] Yet a bargaining perspective offers valuable correctives to both neorealism and neoliberalism. On the one hand, it admonishes realists that power is more than material resources and that interests are malleable; on the other hand, it advises liberals that international cooperation does not necessarily ensue when facilitating background factors are present. Whereas realism focuses on explaining conflict and is worse at handling cooperation, and liberalism focuses on explaining cooperation and is worse at handling conflict, bargaining theory highlights the conjunction of cooperation and conflict in most international relations.

Empirical findings and theoretical ideas related to bargaining processes abound. The range of available negotiation techniques has been explored in considerable detail. Increasing efforts are put into the study of multilateral negotiations and mediation, as opposed to the previous emphasis on bilateral encounters. Transdisciplinary research is flourishing. Despite all these positive developments, there is still a dearth of efforts to combine insights from different approaches and perspectives. To that extent, the field can be said to represent an archipelago of conceptual and theoretical islands. The lack of bridges concerns two areas in particular.

First, research has so far failed to reconcile strategic-choice perspectives and perspectives emphasizing cognitive and social processes. Whereas the strategic-choice perspective posits purposive and instrumental actors, furthering their own interests while taking the actions of others into account, cognitive and social process perspectives highlight information processing, joint search for commonalities and socialization. These are often construed as rival, mutually exclusive approaches. Yet, to the extent that international negotiations encompass elements of both – as several scholars and practitioners maintain – they would seem to be complementary. A second shortcoming concerns the neglect of the ongoing structure–agent discussion in IR. The prevalent actor-oriented perspectives have largely neglected the structural parameters of international negotiations, be they institutions, norms or varying international systems. Frameworks that explicitly and theoretically combine agent and structure are needed to provide a fuller view of international bargaining and negotiation.[9]

Notes

For helpful comments I would like to thank Alexander George, Raymond Cohen, Jan Melissen, William Zartman and colleagues at the Department of Political Science, Lund University, as well as the editors of this volume. A grant from the Royal Society of Letters at Lund made possible a two-month visit at Stanford University, where the Department of Political Science generously granted me office space and library privileges. The Centre for the Study of Diplomacy at Leicester University circulated an earlier draft of this chapter as a discussion paper.

1 For a guide to these and other classic works, see Craig, 1979.

2 Typologies of diplomatic functions can be found in Barston, 1988: 2–3; Berridge, 1995: 34–50; Holsti, 1983: 168–73; Magalhães, 1988: 101–26; Wood and Serres, 1970: 9–13.

3 The label 'middle-range theory' should not be taken to imply that negotiation theory does not relate to 'grand theory', such as realism or liberalism, but rather that it is seldom explicitly grounded in it. For an attempt to relate negotiation theory to realism and liberalism, see Hopmann, 1995: 28–39.

4 For early attempts to draw on social-psychological experiments in studying international negotiations, see Druckman, 1973, 1977; Sawyer and Guetzkow, 1965.

5 For a bibliography of this literature, see Salacuse, 1991: 174–83.

6 Exceptions include Binnendijk, 1987 and Weiss and Stripp, 1985. A Cross-Cultural Negotiation Project, aiming at comparisons of national negotiating styles, is in progress at the United States Institute of Peace.

7 For an example of game-theoretical analysis that takes context and institutions into account, see Fearon, 1998.

8 John Odell (2000: 6) is unusually explicit about this, as he denies that his work will 'fit easily into familiar IR molds such as realism or liberalism or constructivism', and argues that 'horse-races between their partisans have distracted us … from the development of useful middle range theory'.

9 Aggestam, 1999 and Odell, 2000 represent rare efforts to combine agent and structure in the analysis of international negotiations.

Bibliography

Aggestam, Karin (1999) *Reframing and Resolving Conflict: Israeli–Palestinian Negotiations 1988–1998.* Lund: Lund University Press.

Aggestam, Karin and Jönsson, Christer (1997) '(Un)ending Conflict: Challenges in Post-War Bargaining', *Millennium*, 26 (3): 771–93.

Anderson, M.S. (1993) *The Rise of Modern Diplomacy 1450–1919.* London and New York: Longman.

Antrim, Lance (1994) 'Dynamics of Leadership in UNCED', in Bertram I. Spector, Gunnar Sjöstedt and I. William Zartman (eds), *Negotiating International Regimes: Lessons Learned from the United Nations Conference on Environment and Development (UNCED).* London: Graham & Trotman; Boston: Martinus Nijhoff.

Axelrod, Robert (1984) *The Evolution of Cooperation.* New York: Basic Books.

Axelrod, Robert (1997) *The Complexity of Cooperation.* Princeton: Princeton University Press.

Bal, Leendert Jan (1995) 'Decision-Making and Negotiations in the European Union', University of Leicester, Centre for the Study of Diplomacy, Discussion Paper No. 7.

Barston, R.P. (1988) *Modern Diplomacy.* London and New York: Longman.

Bell, David V.J. (1988) 'Political Linguistics and International Negotiation', *Negotiation Journal*, 4 (3): 233–46.

Bercovitch, Jacob (1996a) 'Introduction: Thinking About Mediation', in Jacob Bercovitch (ed.), *Resolving International Conflicts: The Theory and Practice of Mediation.* Boulder: Lynne Rienner.

Bercovitch, Jacob (1996b) 'Understanding Mediation's Role in Preventive Diplomacy', *Negotiation Journal*, 12 (3): 241–58.

Bercovitch, Jacob and Houston, Allison (1996) 'The Study of International Mediation: Theoretical Issues and Empirical Evidence', in Jacob Bercovitch (ed.), *Resolving International Conflicts: The Theory and Practice of Mediation.* Boulder: Lynne Rienner.

Berridge, G.R. (1994) *Talking to the Enemy: How States without 'Diplomatic Relations' Communicate.* London: Macmillan.

Berridge, G.R. (1995) *Diplomacy: Theory and Practice*. London: Prentice Hall; Harvester Wheatsheaf.

Binnendijk, Hans (ed.) (1987) *National Negotiating Styles*. Washington, DC: Center for the Study of Foreign Affairs, Foreign Service Institute, US Department of State.

Blaker, Michael (1977) *Japanese International Negotiating Style*. New York: Columbia University Press.

Brady, Linda P. (1991) *The Politics of Negotiation: America's Dealings with Allies, Adversaries, and Friends*. Chapel Hill, NC and London: University of North Carolina Press.

Brams, Steven J. (1990) *Negotiation Games: Applying Game Theory to Bargaining and Arbitration*. New York and London: Routledge.

Brams, Steven J. (1994) *Theory of Moves*. Cambridge: Cambridge University Press.

de Callières, François (1716) *De la manière de négocier avec les Souverains*. Paris: M. Brunet.

de Callières, François (1919) *On the Manner of Negotiating with Princes*. Boston and New York: Houghton Mifflin.

Carnevale, Peter J. and Arad, Sharon (1996) 'Bias and Impartiality in International Mediation', in Jacob Bercovitch (ed.), *Resolving International Conflicts: The Theory and Practice of Mediation*. Boulder: Lynne Rienner.

Cohen, Raymond (1987) *Theatre of Power: The Art of Diplomatic Signalling*. London and New York: Longman.

Cohen, Raymond (1990) *Culture and Conflict in Egyptian-Israeli Relations: A Dialogue of the Deaf*. Bloomington: Indiana University Press.

Cohen, Raymond (1993) 'An Advocate's View', in Guy Olivier Faure and Jeffrey Z. Rubin (eds), *Culture and Negotiation*. Newbury Park: Sage.

Cohen, Raymond (1996a) 'On Diplomacy in the Ancient Near East: The Amarna Letters', *Diplomacy and Statecraft*, 7 (2): 245–70.

Cohen, Raymond (1996b) 'Cultural Aspects of International Mediation', in Jacob Bercovitch (ed.), *Resolving International Conflicts: The Theory and Practice of Mediation*. Boulder: Lynne Rienner.

Cohen, Raymond (1997) *Negotiating Across Cultures: International Communication in an Interdependent World*, revised edn. Washington, DC: United States Institute of Peace Press.

Cohen, Raymond (1998) 'Putting Diplomatic Studies on the Map', *Diplomatic Studies Programme Newsletter*, Leicester University, 4 May.

Cohen, Raymond (1999) 'Reflections on the New Global Diplomacy: Statecraft 2500 BC to 2000 AD', in Jan Melissen (ed.), *Innovation in Diplomatic Practice* London: Macmillan; New York: St Martin's Press.

Cohen, Raymond (2000) 'Meaning, Interpretation and International Negotiation', *Global Society*, 14 (3): 317–35.

Cohen, Yoel (1986) *Media Diplomacy: The Foreign Office in the Mass Communication Age*. London: Frank Cass.

Constantinou, Costas M. (1996) *On the Way to Diplomacy*. Minneapolis: University of Minnesota Press.

Cooper, Andrew F. (1997) 'Beyond Representation', *International Journal*, 53 (1): 173–8.

Craig, Gordon A. (1979) 'On the Nature of Diplomatic History: The Relevance of Some Old Books', in Paul Gordon Lauren (ed.), *Diplomacy: New Approaches in History, Theory, and Policy*. New York: The Free Press.

Crocker, Chester A., Hampson, Fen Osler and Aall, Pamela (eds) (1999) *Herding Cats: Multiparty Mediation in a Complex World*. Washington, DC: United States Institute of Peace Press.

Dennett, Raymond and Johnson, Joseph E. (eds) (1951) *Negotiating with the Russians*. New York: World Peace Foundation.

Der Derian, James (1987a) 'Mediating Estrangement: A Theory for Diplomacy', *Review of International Studies*, 13 (2): 91–110.

Der Derian, James (1987b) *On Diplomacy*. Oxford: Blackwell.

Druckman, Daniel (1973) *Human Factors in International Negotiations: Social-Psychological Aspects of International Conflict*. Sage Professional Paper in International Studies 02–020. Beverly Hills: Sage.

Druckman, Daniel (1977) 'Social-Psychological Approaches to the Study of Negotiation', in Daniel Druckman (ed.), *Negotiations: Social-Psychological Perspectives*. Beverly Hills and London: Sage.

Druckman, Daniel (1986) 'Stages, Turning Points, and Crises: Negotiating Military Base Rights, Spain and the United States', *Journal of Conflict Resolution*, 30 (2): 327–60.

Druckman, Daniel (1995) 'Situational Levers of Position Change: Further Explorations', *Annals of the American Academy of Political and Social Science*, 542: 61–80.

Druckman, Daniel, Husbands, Jo L. and Johnston, Karin (1991) 'Turning Points in the INF Negotiations', *Negotiation Journal*, 7 (1): 55–67.

Dunn, David H. (ed.) (1996) *Diplomacy at the Highest Level: The Evolution of International Summitry*. London: Macmillan.

Dupont, Christophe (1996) 'Negotiation as Coalition Building', *International Negotiation*, 1 (1): 47–64.

Elgström, Ole (1990) 'Norms, Culture, and Cognitive Patterns in Foreign Aid Negotiations', *Negotiation Journal*, 6 (2): 147–59.

Elgström, Ole (1992) *Foreign Aid Negotiation: The Swedish–Tanzanian Aid Dialogue*. Aldershot: Avebury.

Evans, Peter B., Jacobson, Harold K. and Putnam, Robert D. (eds) (1993) *Double-Edged Diplomacy: International Bargaining and Domestic Politics*. Berkeley: University of California Press.

Faure, Guy Olivier (1999) 'Cultural Aspects of International Negotiation', in Peter Berton, Hiroshi Kimura and I. William Zartman (eds), *International Negotiation: Actors, Structure/Process, Values*. New York: St Martin's Press.

Faure, Guy Olivier and Rubin, Jeffrey Z. (eds) (1993a) *Culture and Negotiation*. Newbury Park: Sage.

Faure, Guy Olivier and Rubin, Jeffrey Z. (1993b) 'Preface', in Guy Olivier Faure and Jeffrey Z. Rubin (eds), *Culture and Negotiation*. Newbury Park: Sage.

Faure, Guy Olivier and Rubin, Jeffrey Z. (1993c) 'Lessons for Theory and Research', in Guy Olivier Faure and Jeffrey Z. Rubin (eds), *Culture and Negotiation*. Newbury Park: Sage.

Fearon, James D. (1998) 'Bargaining, Enforcement, and International Cooperation', *International Organization*, 52 (2): 269–305.

Fisher, Glen (1980) *International Negotiation: A Cross-Cultural Perspective*. Chicago: Intercultural Press.

Fisher, Glen (1988) *Mindsets*. Yarmouth, ME: Intercultural Press.

Fisher, Roger and Ury, William (1981) *Getting to Yes: Negotiating Agreement Without Giving In*. Boston: Houghton Mifflin.

Fisher, Roger, Kopelman, Elizabeth and Kupfer Schneider, Andrea (1994) *Beyond Machiavelli: Tools for Coping with Conflict*. Cambridge, MA: Harvard University Press.

George, Alexander L. (1991) *Forceful Persuasion: Coercive Diplomacy as an Alternative to War*. Washington, DC: United States Institute of Peace Press.

George, Alexander L. and Simons, William E. (eds) (1994) *The Limits of Coercive Diplomacy*. Boulder: Westview.

Goffman, Erving (1969) *Strategic Interaction*. Philadelphia: University of Pennsylvania Press.

Graham, John L. (1993) 'The Japanese Negotiation Style: Characteristics of a Distinct Approach', *Negotiation Journal*, 8 (2): 113–23.

Gulliver, P.H. (1979) *Disputes and Negotiations: A Cross-Cultural Perspective*. New York: Academic Press.

Habeeb, William Mark (1988) *Power and Tactics in International Negotiation: How Weak Nations Bargain with Strong Nations*. Baltimore and London: Johns Hopkins University Press.

Hall, Edward T. (1976) *Beyond Culture*. New York: Anchor.

Hamilton, Keith and Langhorne, Richard (1995) *The Practice of Diplomacy: Its Evolution, Theory and Administration*. London and New York: Routledge.

Hampson, Fen Osler with Hart, Michael (1995) *Multilateral Negotiations: Lessons form Arms Control, Trade, and the Environment*. Baltimore and London: Johns Hopkins University Press.

Hermann, Margaret G. (1995) 'Leaders, Leadership, and Flexibility: Influences on Heads of Government as Negotiators and Mediators', *Annals of the American Academy of Political and Social Science*, 542: 148–67.

Hocking, Brian (1997) 'The End(s) of Diplomacy', *International Journal*, 53 (1): 169–72.

Hocking, Brian (1999) 'Catalytic Diplomacy: Beyond "Newness" and "Decline" ', in Jan Melissen (ed.), *Innovation in Diplomatic Practice*. London: Macmillan; New York: St Martin's Press.

Holsti, Kalevi J. (1982) 'Bargaining Theory and Diplomatic Reality: The CSCE Negotiations', *Review of International Studies*, 8 (3): 159–70.

Holsti, Kalevi J. (1983) *International Politics: A Framework for Analysis*, 4th edn. Englewood Cliffs: Prentice Hall.

Hopmann, P. Terrence (1978) 'Asymmetrical Bargaining in the Conference on Security and Cooperation in Europe', *International Organization*, 32 (1): 141–77.

Hopmann, P. Terrence (1995) 'Two Paradigms of Negotiation: Bargaining and Problem Solving', *Annals of the American Academy of Political and Social Science*, 542: 24–7.

Hopmann, P. Terrence (1996) *The Negotiation Process and the Resolution of International Conflict*. Columbia, SC: University of South Carolina Press.

Husbands, Jo L. (1991) 'Domestic Factors and De-escalation Inititatives: Boundaries, Process, and Timing', in Louis Kriesberg and Stuart J. Thorson (eds), *Timing the De-escalation of International Conflicts*. Syracuse: Syracuse University Press.

Iklé, Fred Charles (1964) *How Nations Negotiate*. New York: Praeger.

James, Alan (1980) 'Diplomacy and International Society', *International Relations*, 6 (6): 931–48.

James, Alan (1993) 'Diplomacy', *Review of International Studies*, 19 (1): 91–100.

Janosik, Robert J. (1987) 'Rethinking the Culture-Negotiation Link', *Negotiation Journal*, 3 (4): 385–95.

Jervis, Robert (1970) *The Logic of Images in International Relations*. Princeton: Princeton University Press.

Jönsson, Christer (1979) *Soviet Bargaining Behavior: The Nuclear Test Ban Case*. New York: Columbia University Press.

Jönsson, Christer (1990) *Communication in International Bargaining*. London: Pinter.

Jönsson, Christer (1996) 'Diplomatic Signaling in the Television Age', *Harvard International Journal of Press/Politics*, 1 (3): 24–40.

Jönsson, Christer and Aggestam, Karin (1999) 'Trends in Diplomatic Signalling', in Jan Melissen (ed.), *Innovation in Diplomatic Practice*. London: Macmillan; New York: St Martin's Press.

Jönsson, Christer and Tallberg, Jonas (1998) 'Compliance and Post-Agreement Bargaining', *European Journal of International Relations*, 4 (4): 371–408.

Jönsson, Christer, Bjurulf, Bo, Elgström, Ole, Sannerstedt, Anders and Strömvik, Maria (1998) 'Negotiations in Networks in the European Union', *International Negotiation*, 3 (3): 319–44.

Kaufmann, Johan (1996) *Conference Diplomacy: An Introductory Analysis*, 3rd edn. London: Macmillan.

Keashly, Loraleigh and Fisher, Ronald J. (1996) 'A Contingency Perspective on Conflict Interventions: Theoretical and Practical Considerations', in Jacob Bercovitch (ed.), *Resolving International Conflicts: The Theory and Practice of Mediation*. Boulder: Lynne Rienner.

Kennan, George F. (1997) 'Diplomacy Without Diplomats?' *Foreign Affairs*, 76 (5): 198–212.

Kimura, Hiroshi (1999) 'Russian Negotiating Behavior', in Peter Berton, Hiroshi Kimura and I. William Zartman (eds), *International Negotiation: Actors, Structure/ Process, Values*. New York: St Martin's Press.

Kissinger, Henry A. (1994) *Diplomacy*. New York: Simon and Schuster.

Kleiboer, Marieke (1994) 'Ripeness of Conflict: A Fruitful Notion?', *Journal of Peace Research*, 31 (1): 109–16.

Kleiboer, Marieke (1998) *The Multiple Realities of International Mediation*. Boulder: Lynne Rienner.

Kohler-Koch, Beate (1996) 'Catching Up with Change: The Transformation of Governance in the European Union', *Journal of European Public Policy*, 3 (3): 359–80.

Kremenyuk, Victor A. (ed.) (1991a) *International Negotiation: Analysis, Approaches, Issues*. San Francisco: Jossey–Bass.

Kremenyuk, Victor A. (1991b) 'The Emerging System of International Negotiation', in Victor A. Kremenyuk (ed.), *International Negotiation: Analysis, Approaches, Issues*. San Francisco: Jossey–Bass.

Kriesberg, Louis (1991) 'Introduction: Timing Conditions, Strategies, and Errors', in Louis Kriesberg and Stuart J. Thorson (eds), *Timing the De-escalation of International Conflicts*. Syracuse: Syracuse University Press.

Lakos, Amos (1989) *International Negotiations: A Bibliography*. Boulder: Westview.

Lall, Arthur S. (1968) *How Communist China Negotiates*. New York: Columbia University Press.

Lang, Winfried (1993) 'A Professional's View', in Guy Olivier Faure and Jeffrey Z. Rubin (eds), *Culture and Negotiation*. Newbury Park: Sage.

Langhorne, Richard (1997) 'Current Developments in Diplomacy: Who Are the Diplomats Now?' *Diplomacy and Statecraft*, 8 (2): 1–15.

Leigh-Phippard, Helen (1999) 'The Influence of Informal Groups in Multilateral Diplomacy', in Jan Melissen (ed.), *Innovation in Diplomatic Practice*. London: Macmillan; New York: St Martin's Press.

Lockhart, Charles (1979) *Bargaining in International Conflicts*. New York: Columbia University Press.

McDonald, John W. (1991) 'Further Exploration of Track Two Diplomacy', in Louis Kriesberg and Stuart J. Thorson (eds), *Timing the De-escalation of International Conflicts*. Syracuse: Syracuse University Press.

McNulty, Timothy J. (1993) 'Television's Impact on Executive Decision-making and Diplomacy', *Fletcher Forum of World Affairs*, 17 (1): 67–83.

Magalhães, José Calvet De (1988) *The Pure Concept of Diplomacy*. New York: Greenwood Press.

Malnes, Raino (1995) '"Leader" and "Entrepreneur" in International Negotiations: A Conceptual Analysis', *European Journal of International Relations*, 1 (1): 87–112.

Martin, Geoffrey R. (1988) 'The "Practical" and the "Theoretical" Split in Modern Negotiation Literature', *Negotiation Journal*, 4 (1): 45–54.

Mautner-Markhof, Frances (ed.) (1989) *Processes of International Negotiations*. Boulder: Westview.

Meerts, Paul W. (1999) 'The Changing Nature of Diplomatic Negotiation', in Jan Melissen (ed.), *Innovation in Diplomatic Practice*. London: Macmillan; New York: St Martin's Press.

Melissen, Jan (1999) 'Introduction', in Jan Melissen (ed.), *Innovation in Diplomatic Practice*. London: Macmillan; New York: St Martin's Press.

Midgaard, Knut (1966) 'Auxiliary Games and the Modes of a Game', *Cooperation and Conflict*, 1 (1): 64–81.

Midgaard, Knut and Underdal, Arild (1977) 'Multiparty Conferences', in Daniel Druckman (ed.), *Negotiations: Social-Psychological Perspectives*. Beverly Hills and London: Sage.

Mitchell, Christopher (1995) 'The Right Moment: Notes on Four Models of "Ripeness" ', *Paradigms: The Kent Journal of International Relations*, 9 (2): 35–52.

Mitchell, C.R. and Webb, K. (1988) 'Mediation in International Relations: An Evolving Tradition', in C.R. Mitchell and K. Webb (eds), *New Approaches to International Mediation*. New York: Greenwood Press.

Montville, Joseph V. (1991) 'Transnationalism and the Role of Track Two Diplomacy', in W. Scott Thompson and Kenneth M. Jensen (eds), *Approaches to Peace: An Intellectual Map*. Washington, DC: United States Institute of Peace Press.

Mooradian, Moorad and Druckman, Daniel (1999) 'Hurting Stalemate or Mediation? The Conflict over Nagorno-Karabakh, 1990–95', *Journal of Peace Research*, 36 (6): 709–27.

Moravcsik, Andrew (1991) 'Negotiating the Single European Act: National Interests and Conventional Statecraft in the European Community', *International Organization*, 45 (1): 19–56.

Morgenthau, Hans J. (1967) *Politics among Nations: The Struggle for Power and Peace*, 4th edn. New York: Alfred A. Knopf.

Morrow, James D. (1994) *Game Theory for Political Scientists*. Princeton: Princeton University Press.

Morrow, James D. (1999) 'The Strategic Setting of Choices: Signaling, Commitment, and Negotiation in International Politics', in David A. Lake and Robert Powell (eds), *Strategic Choice and International Relations*. Princeton: Princeton University Press.

Murray, John S. (1986) 'Understanding Competing Theories of Negotiation', *Negotiation Journal*, 2 (2): 179–86.

Nicolson, Harold (1939) *Diplomacy*. Oxford: Oxford University Press.

Nicolson, Harold (1954) *The Evolution of Diplomatic Method*. London: Constable.

Odell, John S. (1980) 'Latin American Trade Negotiations with the United States', *International Organization*, 34 (2): 207–8.

Odell, John S. (1985) 'The Outcome of International Trade Conflicts: The US and South Korea, 1960–1981', *International Studies Quarterly*, 29 (3): 263–86.

Odell, John S. (2000) *Negotiating the World Economy*. Ithaca, NY: Cornell University Press.

Patterson, Lee Ann (1997) 'Agricultural Policy Reform in the European Community: A Three-Level Game Analysis', *International Organization*, 51 (1): 135–65.

Pfetsch, Frank P. (1998) 'Negotiating the European Union: A Negotiation-Network Approach', *International Negotiation*, 3 (3): 293–317.

Pfetsch, Frank P. (1999) 'Institutions Matter: Negotiating the European Union', in Peter Berton, Hiroshi Kimura and I. William Zartman (eds), *International Negotiation: Actors, Structure/Process, Values*. New York: St Martin's Press.

Pruitt, Dean G. (1981) *Negotiation Behavior*. New York: Academic Press.

Pruitt, Dean G. (1995) 'Flexibility in Conflict Episodes', *Annals of the American Academy of Political and Social Science*, 542: 100–15.

Pruitt, Dean G. (1997) 'Ripeness Theory and the Oslo Talks', *International Negotiation*, 2 (2): 237–50.

Pruitt, Dean G. and Lewis, Steven A. (1977) 'The Psychology of Integrative Bargaining', in Daniel Druckman (ed.), *Negotiations: Social-Psychological Perspectives*. Beverly Hills and London: Sage.

Pruitt, Dean G. and Rubin, Jeffrey Z. (1986) *Social Conflict: Escalation, Stalemate, and Settlement*. New York: Random House.

Putnam, Robert D. (1988) 'Diplomacy and Domestic Politics: The Logic of Two-Level Games', *International Organization*, 42 (3): 428–60.

Pye, Lucian W. (1982) *Chinese Commercial Negotiating Style*. Cambridge, MA: Oelgeschlager, Gunn & Hain.

Pye, Lucian W. (1992) *Chinese Negotiating Style: Commercial Approaches and Cultural Principles*. Westport: Quorum Books.

Raiffa, Howard (1982) *The Art and Science of Negotiation*. Cambridge, MA: Harvard University Press.

Rapoport, Anatol (1960) *Fights, Games and Debates*. Ann Arbor: University of Michigan Press.

Risse, Thomas (2000) ' "Let's Argue!" Communicative Action in World Politics', *International Organization*, 54 (1): 1–39.

Rothstein, Robert L. (1979) *Global Bargaining: UNCTAD and the Quest for a New International Economic Order*. Princeton: Princeton University Press.

Rouhana, Nadim N. (1999) 'Unofficial Intervention: Potential Contributions to Resolving Ethno-national Conflicts', in Jan Melissen (ed.), *Innovation in Diplomatic Practice*. London: Macmillan; New York: St Martin's Press.

Rubin, Jeffrey Z. (1991) 'The Timing of Ripeness and the Ripeness of Timing', in Louis Kriesberg and Stuart J. Thorson (eds), *Timing the De-escalation of International Conflicts*. Syracuse: Syracuse University Press.

Salacuse, Jeswald W. (1991) *Making Global Deals: Negotiating in the International Market Place*. Boston: Houghton Mifflin.

Satow, Ernest (1917) *Guide to Diplomatic Practice*. London and New York: Longmans, Green & Co.

Saunders, Harold H. (1985) 'We Need a Larger Theory of Negotiation: The Importance of Pre-negotiating Phases', *Negotiation Journal*, 1 (3): 249–62.

Sawyer, Jack and Guetzkow, Harold (1965) 'Bargaining and Negotiation in International Relations', in Herbert

C. Kelman (ed.), *International Behavior: A Social-Psychological Analysis*. New York: Holt, Rinehart & Winston.

Schecter, Jerrold L. (1998) *Russian Negotiating Behavior: Continuity and Transition*. Washington DC: United States Institute of Peace Press.

Schelling, Thomas C. (1960) *The Strategy of Conflict*. Cambridge, MA: Harvard University Press.

Schelling, Thomas C. (1966) *Arms and Influence*. New Haven and London: Yale University Press.

Sebenius, James K. (1984) *Negotiating the Law of the Sea: Lessons in the Art and Science of Reaching Agreement*. Cambridge, MA: Harvard University Press.

Sebenius, James K. (1991) 'Negotiation Analysis', in Victor A. Kremenyuk (ed.), *International Negotiation: Analysis, Approaches, Issues*. San Francisco: Jossey–Bass.

Sebenius, James K. (1996) 'Sequencing to Build Coalitions: With Whom Should I Talk First?', in Richard J. Zeckhauser, Ralph L. Keeney and James K. Sebenius (eds), *Wise Choices: Decisions, Games and Negotiations*. Boston: Harvard Business School Press.

Sharp, Paul (1997) 'Who Needs Diplomats? The Problem of Diplomatic Representation', *International Journal*, 52 (4): 609–34.

Sharp, Paul (1999) 'For Diplomacy: Representation and the Study of International Relations', *International Studies Review*, 1 (1): 33–57.

Sjöstedt, Gunnar (ed.) (1993) *International Environmental Negotiation*. Newbury Park: Sage.

Sjöstedt, Gunnar (1999) 'Leadership in Multilateral Negotiations: Crisis or Transition?', in Peter Berton, Hiroshi Kimura and I. William Zartman (eds), *International Negotiation: Actors, Structure/Process, Values*. New York: St Martin's Press.

Sloss, Leon and Davis, M. Scott (eds) (1986) *A Game for High Stakes: Lessons Learned in Negotiating with the Soviet Union*. Cambridge, MA: Ballinger.

Smith, Raymond (1989) *Negotiating with the Soviets*. Bloomington and Indianapolis: Indiana University Press.

Smith, William P. (1985) 'Effectiveness of the Biased Mediator', *Negotiation Journal*, 1 (4): 363–72.

Snyder, Glenn H. and Diesing, Paul (1977) *Conflict among Nations: Bargaining, Decision Making, and System Structure in International Crises*. Princeton: Princeton University Press.

Solomon, Richard H. (1999) *Chinese Negotiating Behavior: Pursuing Interests Through 'Old Friends'*. Washington, DC: United States Institute of Peace Press.

Spector, Bertram I., Sjöstedt, Gunnar and Zartman, I. William (eds) (1994) *Negotiating International Regimes: Lessons Learned from the United Nations Conference on Environment and Development (UNCED)*. London: Graham & Trotman; Boston: Martinus Nijhoff.

Stedman, Stephen John (1991) *Peacemaking in Civil War: International Mediation in Zimbabwe, 1975–1980*. Boulder and London: Lynne Rienner.

Stein, Janice Gross (1988) 'International Negotiation: A Multidisciplinary Perspective', *Negotiation Journal*, 4 (3): 221–31.

Stein, Janice Gross (ed.) (1989) *Getting to the Table: The Processes of International Prenegotiation*. Baltimore: Johns Hopkins University Press.

Stenelo, Lars-Göran (1972) *Mediation in International Negotiations*. Lund: Studentlitteratur.

Strange, Susan (1992) 'States, Firms and Diplomacy', *International Affairs*, 68 (1): 1–15.

Ting-Toomey, Stella (1985a) 'The "Root Metaphors" Orientations: Implications for Intercultural Communication Researchers', in Sari Thomas (ed.), *Culture and Communication: Methodology, Behavior, Artifacts, and Institutions*. Norwood: Ablex.

Ting-Toomey, Stella (1985b) 'Toward a Theory of Conflict and Culture', in William B. Gudykunst, Lea P. Steward and Stella Ting-Toomey (eds), *Communication, Culture, and Organizational Processes*. Beverly Hills: Sage.

Touval, Saadia (1985) 'The Context of Mediation', *Negotiation Journal*, 1 (4): 373–8.

Touval, Saadia (1989) 'Multilateral Negotiation: An Analytical Approach', *Negotiation Journal*, 5 (2): 159–73.

Touval, Saadia and Zartman, I. William (1985) 'Introduction: Mediation in Theory', in Saadia Touval and I. William Zartman (eds), *International Mediation in Theory and Practice*. Boulder: Westview.

Underdal, Arild (1994) 'Leadership Theory: Rediscovering the Art of Management', in I. William Zartman (ed.), *International Multilateral Negotiations: Approaches to the Management of Complexity*. San Francisco: Jossey–Bass.

Walton, Richard E. and McKersie, Robert B. (1965) *A Behavioral Theory of Labor Negotiations*. New York: McGraw-Hill.

Watkins, Michael and Rosegrant, Susan (1996) 'Sources of Power in Coalition Building', *Negotiation Journal*, 12 (1): 47–68.

Watson, Adam (1982) *Diplomacy: The Dialogue Between States*. London: Eyre Methuen.

Weiss, Stephen E. and Stripp, W. (1985) *Negotiating with Foreign Businesspersons: An Introduction for Americans with Propositions on Six Cultures*. New York: Graduate School of Business Administration, New York University, Working Paper No. 1.

Westbrook, Raymond and Cohen, Raymond (eds) (2000) *Amarna Diplomacy: The Beginnings of International Relations*. Baltimore: Johns Hopkins University Press.

Whelan, Joseph G. (1983) *Soviet Diplomacy and Negotiating Behavior: The Emerging New Context for US Diplomacy*. Boulder: Westview.

Wight, Martin (1978) *Power Politics*. Leicester: Leicester University Press.

Williams, Andrew (1988) 'The Role of Third Parties in the Negotiation of International Agreements', in C.R. Mitchell and K. Webb (eds), *New Approaches to International Mediation*. New York: Greenwood Press.

Winham, Gilbert R. (1977a) 'Negotiation as a Management Process', *World Politics*, 30 (1): 87–114.

Winham, Gilbert R. (1977b) 'Complexity in International Negotiation', in Daniel Druckman (ed.), *Negotiations: Social-Psychological Perspectives*. Beverly Hills and London: Sage.

Winham, Gilbert R. (1979) 'Practitioners' Views of International Negotiation', *World Politics*, 32 (1): 111–35.

Wolfe, Robert (1998) '*Still* Lying Abroad? On the Institution of the Resident Ambassador', *Diplomacy and Statecraft*, 9 (2): 23–54.

Wood, John R. and Serres, Jean (1970) *Diplomatic Ceremonial and Protocol*. New York: Columbia University Press.

Young, Kenneth T. (1968) *Negotiating with the Chinese Communists*. New York: McGraw–Hill.

Young, Oran R. (1967) *Intermediaries: Third Parties in International Crises*. Princeton: Princeton University Press.

Young, Oran R. (1975) *Bargaining: Formal Theories of Negotiation*. Urbana: University of Illinois Press.

Young, Oran R. (1989) 'The Politics of International Regime Formation: Managing Natural Resources and the Environment', *International Organization*, 43 (3): 349–75.

Young, Oran R. (1991) 'Political Leadership and Regime Formation: On the Development of Institutions in International Society', *International Organization*, 45 (3): 281–308.

Young, Oran R. (1994) *International Governance: Protecting the Environment in a Stateless Society*. Ithaca: Cornell University Press.

Zartman, I. William (1977) 'Negotiation as a Joint Decision-Making Process', *Journal of Conflict Resolution*, 21 (4): 619–38.

Zartman, I. William (1985a) *Ripe for Resolution*. New York: Oxford University Press.

Zartman, I. William (1985b) 'Negotiating from Asymmetry: The North–South Stalemate', *Negotiation Journal*, 1 (2): 121–38.

Zartman, I. William (1987) *Positive Sum: Improving North–South Negotiations*. New Brunswick: Transaction Books.

Zartman, I. William (1991) 'The Structure of Negotiation', in Victor A. Kremenyuk (ed.), *International Negotiation: Analysis, Approaches, Issues*. San Francisco: Jossey–Bass.

Zartman, I. William (1993) 'A Skeptic's View', in Guy Olivier Faure and Jeffrey Z. Rubin (eds), *Culture and Negotiation*. Newbury Park: Sage.

Zartman, I. William (ed.) (1994a) *International Multilateral Negotiations: Approaches to the Management of Complexity*. San Francisco: Jossey–Bass.

Zartman, I. William (1994b) 'Introduction: Two's Company and More's a Crowd: The Complexities of Multilateral Negotiation', in I. William Zartman (ed.), *International Multilateral Negotiations: Approaches to the Management of Complexity*. San Francisco: Jossey–Bass.

Zartman, I. William (1994c) 'The Elephant and the Holograph: Toward a Theoretical Synthesis and a

Paradigm', in I. William Zartman (ed.), *International Multilateral Negotiations: Approaches to the Management of Complexity*. San Francisco: Jossey–Bass.

Zartman, I. William (ed.) (2000) *Preventive Negotiation: Avoiding Conflict Escalation*. Lanham: Rowman and Littlefield.

Zartman, I. William and Berman, Maureen R. (1982) *The Practical Negotiator*. New Haven and London: Yale University Press.

Zartman, I. William and Rubin, Jeffrey Z. (eds) (2000) *Power and Negotiation*. Ann Arbor: University of Michigan Press.

Zartman, I. William and Touval, Saadia (1985) 'Conclusion: Mediation in Theory and Practice', in Saadia Touval and I. William Zartman (eds), *International Mediation in Theory and Practice*. Boulder: Westview.

12

From Interdependence to Globalization

MICHAEL ZÜRN

The literature on interdependence in the 1970s and on globalization in the 1990s reveals remarkable similarities, of which two are especially striking. The first is that the interest in both interdependence and globalization can be seen as an expression of a 'poorly understood but widespread feeling that the very nature of world politics is changing' (Keohane and Nye, 2000: 104). The second is that both concepts never reached the status of a sound theory of world politics. While most users of these concepts realize that they challenge conventional theories of world politics and have pointed to, and in a sense created, new research agendas in international relations (IR), endeavors to formulate an interdependence or globalization theory of international relations have so far not succeeded.

Not least because of these commonalities, the more recent literature on globalization is confronted with questions like 'What's new?' and 'So what?' In the United States at least, theorists of international relations seem to have adopted this point of view. As an example, the special issue 'International Organization at Fifty: Exploration and Contestation in the Study of World Politics' contains no articles on the effects of interdependence or, for that matter, the effects of globalization on the constitution of world politics. That globalization studies are suspected of being nothing more than a revival of interdependence literature, however, is only one way to interpret the common attributes of the interdependence literature and recent works on globalization. Another way would be to argue that interdependence theorists of earlier times – a first wave of literature was published before and after the First World War, a

second wave in the 1970s – were right and it just took us some time to realize it and learn from it. When the First World War broke out, Sir Norman Angell commented: 'No, we have not been successful. We have been merely right' (cited after de Wilde, 1991: 92).

In this chapter I want to defend a third position, which emphasizes two differences between interdependence and globalization research. On the one hand, the notion of globalization differs from that of interdependence in that it refers to qualitatively different conditions. Whereas the notion of interdependence refers to a growing sensitivity and vulnerability between separate units, globalization refers to the merging of units. Evidence indeed suggests that the driving force of change itself has changed. Nevertheless, the causal mechanisms mentioned in connection with the driving forces and the ongoing change in world politics are quite similar in both fields. Therefore, a reassessment of those propositions made by both interdependence and globalization literature is called for. In addition, to the extent that the notion of globalization refers to much more than just interdependence between distinct units, it can come as no surprise that the propositions about change in world politics go much further in the current debate on globalization. While some of these conclusions may indeed be overstated, debates on themes such as the end of sovereignty and the end of democracy certainly indicate the need for a theory of world politics that re-evaluates the notion of distinct territorial units – be they ontologically given as in realism or socially constructed as in constructivism – as theoretical buildings blocks.

THE DRIVING FORCE: DIFFERENT FORMS OF INTERCONNECTEDNESS AND SOCIAL SPACES

Interdependence

In its most general form, dependence can be described as a situation in which a system is contingent upon external forces. The analysis of dependence in the social sciences focuses on activities of social groups as the external forces. Interdependence describes a situation of mutual dependence between social actors. Thus defined, interdependence relates to specific kinds of actions in specific issue areas (see Morse, 1976: 118). Based on the distinction between the types of social actors that figure as external forces, interdependence in international relations can be due to two factors. On the one hand, nation-states and national societies are dependent upon the activities of other states (*state interdependence*). In this sense, states have been dependent upon each other since the Westphalian system of states emerged. National security has always been dependent upon the decisions of governments in neighboring states – for instance, whether or not to wage war. On the other hand, the effects of given actions by a government may depend on societal developments that take place outside of its jurisdiction (*societal interdependence*). For instance, the effectiveness of a national environmental regulation may easily be undermined by increased emissions from outside that country. Moreover, the development of national economies and societies themselves cannot be understood without taking into account what happens elsewhere. State interdependence is constitutive for the Westphalian system of states. Without state interdependence there can be no society of states (Bull, 1977). Societal interdependence is not constitutive for the Westphalian state system, it is rather a (mostly unintended) side-effect of the growing interconnectedness between societies.

Social interconnectedness can lead to quite different forms of societal interdependence. While there are countless distinctions made in the literature (see Caporaso, 1978; Senghaas, 1994; de Wilde, 1991), some of these distinctions are especially important. The most consequential but also the most contested distinction is the one between 'sensitivity interdependence', defined in terms of mutual effects, and 'vulnerability interdependence', defined in terms of the opportunity costs of disrupting the relationship (Keohane and Nye, 1977: 12–15). Vulnerability implies more than sensitivity in that whereas vulnerability interdependence presupposes mutual effects, sensitivity interdependence implies nothing about the cost of altering the relationship. The difference as such is widely accepted and can easily be used to structure the history of thought on interdependence (Baldwin, 1980).

The concept of interdependence in IR therefore refers mainly to societal interdependence. Despite the common use of the term that is close to vulnerability interdependence, interdependence in IR is most often understood as mutual sensitivity, that means that events and actions taking place in one unit of the international system affect other units of it. Most importantly, the interdependence literature rests on a concept of social actors (most often governments) being structurally affected by the behavior of others (most often societies in other countries), but nevertheless autonomous. In this sense, each state 'decides for itself how it will cope with its internal and external problems, including whether or not to seek assistance from others' (see Keohane, 1993: 93). Such a notion of interdependence still implies a choice between unilateral and multilateral strategies, even if a unilateral strategy is less effective in terms of the degree to which the actor's intentions have been fulfilled than a successful multilateral endeavor.

Globalization and Societal Denationalization

Globalization goes further than interdependence. Richard Cooper argues that 'the internationalized economy of the 1960s was characterized by a sensitivity of economic transactions between two or more nations to economic developments within those nations' (1986: 1). By contrast, the process of economic globalization describes a movement towards one integrated world market in which 'buyers and sellers are in such free intercourse with one another that the prices of the same goods tend to equality easily and quickly' (Cooper, 1986: 71). This distinction between an internationalized economy and the global integration of markets can be taken *pars pro toto*. When generalized to include all societal relations, it highlights the most important difference between interdependence and globalization. Globalization thus describes a process of transition towards one integrated global society and away from a cluster of merely internationalized societies. Accordingly, globalization can also be seen as a process which reduces the significance of national societies thus calling into question the distinction between domestic and foreign relations. In this view, the living conditions of people and local communities have changed through globalization; distant events of all sorts have immediate consequences not only for states but for individuals' daily lives (Held et al., 1999: ch. 1; Hirst and Thompson, 1996: 7; Holm and Sørensen, 1995: 4–5; Rosenau, 1990: 78). This notion of globalization refers to a measurable process of *social change* which, in turn, may or may not have causal effects on *political developments*. Globalization is thus neither identical with nor does it *necessarily* lead to the extension of political space and governance beyond the nation-state. Nor does it necessitate the formation of a world society[1] or transnational identities.[2] In this respect, this societally based understanding of globalization is similar to predominant notions of interdependence. It also facilitates a distinction between different issue areas and runs counter to notions of globalization that are restricted to the economic (Altvater and Mahnkopf, 1996) or the cultural sphere (Robertson, 1992).

While the term 'interdependence' refers to a condition, 'globalization' includes the notion of a process. In this context it is helpful to contrast the terms 'interdependence' and 'globalism' (Keohane and Nye, 2000: 104). The data, however, do not justify the use of the term globalism. Globalism may only be appropriate to sketch some exceptional cases such as the financial markets and some global dangers, but it is inappropriate for most other fields. Moreover, in some areas a process towards globalism, that is, globalization as a process leading to global social spaces, does not seem to be taking place at all. Many economic indicators suggest that a gradual development towards an OECD zone is taking place, but at the same time this is accompanied by an uncoupling of this zone from other regions in the world (Goldgeier and McFaul, 1992; Singer and Wildavsky, 1993). Against this background, I prefer the term 'societal denationalization' (Zürn, 1992, 1995). The question that then arises is whether intensified transboundary social interactions that are already at a relatively high level signify a further decline in the importance of nationally defined borders. The condition of a society can be described as denationalized when transactions within national borders are no denser than transnational transactions.[3] The term societal denationalization – as a process – thus has the advantage that it defines a starting point (national society) of the process but leaves the end point indeterminate. Moreover, if cases can be singled out that show a clear trend towards globalization, there is no problem in interpreting them as special instances of a more general trend towards societal denationalization. Seen thus, the transboundary pollution of the Rhine is just as much a phenomenon of societal denationalization as global warming, although only the latter is genuinely global.[4]

Measurement

What indicates a transition from interdependence to globalization or societal denationalization? The measurement of interdependence has always been contested and this also holds true for globalization. While the interconnectedness of societies is a direct measure of neither interdependence nor globalization, it has often been used as an indicator. The interconnectedness of societies can be measured by the rise of transboundary transactions relative to transactions that take place within a national territory (see Beisheim et al., 1999; Deutsch and Eckstein, 1961; Garrett, 1998b; Held et al., 1999; Hirst and Thompson, 1996; Katzenstein, 1975; Reinicke, 1998; Rosecrance and Stein, 1973; Rosecrance et al., 1977). While the increased ratio of transboundary transactions on a low level is assumed to indicate a rise in interdependence between different units, the notion of globalization refers to societal connectedness to the extent that societal borders lose importance or even dissolve, indicating the merging of formerly nationally defined units. In the words of K.W. Deutsch, societal borders dissolve when there is no more critical reduction in the frequency of social transactions (1969: 99).

The objection raised now and again by economists to this approach to measurement is that by observing these transactions little can be said about real interdependence or, for that matter, globalization. For instance, changes in flow values may be due to market volatility, i.e. changes in the attractiveness of economic locations, and perfectly integrated spaces may even be characterized by lower flow values (see Garrett, 1998a: ch. 3). For this reason, economists often propose the analysis of transaction costs and convergent prices, which they claim more closely approximate the theoretical conception of integrated spaces (Frankel, 1993; Garrett, 1998a). For instance, between 1939 and 1990 average prices for air travel dropped from around 60 cents to about 10 cents per mile; international telecommunication costs have sunk by about 8 per cent per year since the late 1960s, and the price for one computer capacity unit has plummeted by 99 per cent over the past thirty years (Zacher with Sutton, 1996: 129). To a certain extent, these developments are indeed indications for growing societal interdependence.

Nevertheless, more differentiated evidence based on the direct measurement of these transactions is necessary. First, it is by no means certain that low transaction costs are a more reliable indication of integrated social spaces than the intensification of transactions. A reduction in the price of international phone calls, for instance, tells us much less about transboundary communication than an actual increase in the number of phone calls. It is not the facilitation of communication, but communication itself that constitutes the relevant social action. Second, the argument that perfectly integrated spaces do not necessarily show evidence of an increase in transactions is theoretically correct, yet of little practical significance. There are in effect no perfect, totally stable markets, but only approximations. Real-world approximations such as national markets are indeed characterized by extremely high transaction flows. Furthermore, if transaction flows are monitored over longer periods, temporary volatilities should be negligible as random noise created by periodic political events and spasmodic competitive shifts. Third, the measurement of transaction costs is technically very problematic, especially if specific national differences are taken into consideration. As a result, when it comes to operationalization, researchers who for theoretical reasons opt for measuring transaction costs ultimately have to resort to measuring the transactions themselves. As Milner and Keohane, for example, put it: 'An exogenous reduction in the costs of international transactions (...) can be empirically measured by the growth in the proportion of international economic flows relative to domestic ones' (1996: 4).

Against this background, empirical studies on levels of interdependence and globalization can be summarized as follows.

- Early propositions about decreasing interdependence among highly industrialized countries (Deutsch and Eckstein, 1961) and between great powers (Waltz, 1979) have proved, at least in their generalized versions, to be wrong. While it is correct that levels of economic interdependence were lower in the 1950s and 1960s than in the decades prior to 1929, economic interdependence grew again in the industrialized world in the decades after the Second World War (Katzenstein, 1975; Rosecrance and Stein, 1973; Rosecrance et al., 1977). In the 1970s, the low levels of economic and communicative interdependence between the Superpowers increased as well (Frei and Ruloff, 1988). And as early as the late 1950s and 1960s there was a dramatic surge in both the expansion of long-distance systems and the proliferation of weapons of mass destruction. As a result, any war in which weapons of mass destruction are deployed will have an impact that by far exceeds the actual area of combat.
- Whereas with respect to some indicators such as trade quotas and the proportion of international telephone calls, the growth rates leveled out slightly in the early 1980s, the latter part of the 1980s and most of the 1990s brought a sharp increase in transborder transactions in many areas such as trade, foreign direct investments and other capital flows, but also human mobility, the volume of transborder information and communication and the exchange of cultural products (Beisheim et al., 1999: 39–320). This surge led to the use of the term globalization. In most areas, the level of interconnectedness today clearly surpasses the levels of 1914.[5]
- Many social transactions today transcend national borders, but they are neither global nor can a general tendency towards globality be observed. In fact, new social boundaries are

becoming visible at the periphery of the OECD world. This is particularly evident in the economic sphere. Transborder trade primarily takes place within the three large trade blocks of the EU/EFTA, NAFTA and ASEAN. This is followed by trade between the large trade blocks, with only a small share finally left for the rest of the world. The OECD focus is even more evident if one looks at foreign direct investments. Over 91 per cent of all foreign direct investments between 1980 and 1991 went to the OECD countries and the ten leading threshold countries (Hirst and Thompson, 1996: 67; see also Reinicke, 1998: ch. 2). Communication flows indicate a similar concentration on OECD countries. A world map showing the distribution of Internet connections is particularly illustrative. It shows that even within the OECD world there are clear gravitational centers, the borders of which, however, do not coincide with national borders. Even in the USA there are only extensive networks along the two coastlines, including parts of Canada (Beisheim et al., 1999: 65).
- Within the OECD, substantial cross-national differences in market integration remain (see Garrett, 1998b). The levels of market integration are significantly higher in smaller countries than in larger ones. Moreover, a comparison of larger economies (G7) reveals that the integration of the British and German economies into the world market is higher for most economic indicators than in other G7 countries. These national differences become even more accentuated when other fields of globalization such as culture, environment, mobility etc. are taken into account.
- The spatial scope of dense transactions varies significantly between different fields and issues. While the proportion of transborder postal deliveries, cross-border phone calls and foreign direct investments, to name but a few indicators, is still below 10 per cent in all G7 countries, the proportion of foreign trade, foreign travel, foreign e-mails and the consumption of foreign culture is often above 50 per cent (Beisheim et al., 1999: 39–320).
- A completely new development is the transboundary production of some goods and bads (as opposed to the transboundary exchange of goods), which suddenly took off in the mid-1980s. One can justifiably say that these phenomena – the Internet, international crime, global climate changes and other global environmental dangers as well as the global financial markets – represent a new departure. It is these – still relatively rare – cases to which references of de-territorialization or even de-borderization (Agnew and Duncan, 1989; Albert, 1996; Appadurai, 1996; Brock and Albert, 1995; Harvey, 1989) are most pertinent and the term globalization most justifiably

applies. Multinational corporations (MNCs) are often seen as the primary agents of the transnational production of goods. Indeed, trade with intermediate products has risen sharply over the past decades. At the same time, MNCs are less footloose than usually assumed, and seem to be shaped to a remarkable extent by traits of the national economy in which the head office is located (Pauly and Reich, 1997).

In spite of these findings, the academic debate on the extent of interdependence and globalization reveals several weaknesses. First, measured against the tremendous changes in world politics that are ascribed to interdependence and globalization, systematic data on the driving forces behind these phenomena are still remarkably scarce. In particular, statistics other than those on the ratio of trans-border transactions to national transactions do not exist in such detail as allows systematic comparisons across time, countries and fields. Moreover, there is a clear lack of data on other possible sources of change such as the dematerialization of the economy (see Albert et al., 1999), changes in people's values and attitudes (see Hughes, 1999; Inglehart, 1997) and individualization processes (see Beisheim et al., 1999).

This deficit itself points to another weakness: we know little about the causes and origins of interdependence and globalization. While some, in a somewhat apolitical fashion, overemphasize the role of technology (see Wriston, 1986), others highlight the role of political decisions. Among those who focus on political decisions, three arguments deserve special attention. First, the role of the Bretton Woods institutions and embedded liberalism as the background against which globalization was able to evolve is emphasized (Ruggie, 1983). Second, the decision of the US and British governments to abolish capital controls and deregulate capital markets was identified as a particularly important move (Helleiner, 1994). Third, the notion of a transnational élite that has more or less deliberately challenged the Keynesian élites is sometimes put forward as an explanation for globalization (van der Pijl, 1998). Another, more structural strand of thinking sees economic globalization as the inherently necessary outcome of an economic organization that is permanently seeking and creating larger markets. The change from a Fordist to a post-Fordist mode of production is in this view crucial for accounting for economic globalization (Jessop, 1994). While all these studies certainly contribute to a better understanding of the causes of globalization, an all-encompassing explanation is still lacking. A thorough conceptualization of globalization as an unintended and unanticipated side-effect of the interplay of technological developments and political decisions is certainly a theoretically attractive, but little studied option. In addition, different processes of globalization may have different causes: the rise of global financial markets probably needs to be explained in other ways than the 'world risk society', that is, the globalization of industrially produced risks as identified by Ulrich Beck (1999). At all events, we have little systematic knowledge on the causes of globalization. In that sense Rosenau's (1986) critique of an underdeveloped knowledge of the driving force of interdependence applies to globalization studies as well.

HOW DO INTERDEPENDENCE AND GLOBALIZATION GIVE RISE TO POLITICAL CHANGE?

Structure

Structural effects can be separated into two categories. The first refers – from an outside perspective – to a *reduction of distance and difference*. While increased contact and the convergence of consumption patterns often lead to a heightened emphasis of difference and conflict on the side of the actors (Elkins, 1995; Holsti, 1980), the increase in transborder transactions 'objectively' increases transnational contacts and thus the density of transnational relations. In a material sense, people of different societies grow closer to each other and get to know each other better. Transparency between societies increases. In addition, increased transnational transactions necessarily create an economic interest in the maintenance of good transnational relations. The interest of strengthened export capital is one reason for the stability of free trade since the Second World War (Milner, 1988).

The other direct effect is best conceived as a *challenge* regarding the capacity of the nation-state to unilaterally reach its processual and material governance targets. Effective governance depends upon the *spatial congruence* of political regulations with socially integrated areas and the absence of significant externalities. As societal interconnectedness increases, national governments are increasingly confronted with difficulties in the implementation of their policies. That is to say that policies are strongly affected by externalities insofar as they are still only valid within their own national borders and do not extend over the whole socially integrated territory (Reinicke, 1998: 65). It is possible to distinguish four specific challenges to the achievement of national governance goals as a result of interdependence and societal denationalization.

As national borders no longer encompass sufficient territory to function as self-contained markets for large companies, all national legislation aimed to protect the domestic economy is challenged. Any national measure that is not harmonized at the international level separates markets and creates a barrier for the efficient development, purchase and sale of goods and services. As the barriers between different markets dissolve, R&D costs rise and product cycles grow shorter. Larger markets and unhindered cooperation with other enterprises are then deemed essential to remain competitive. In other words, in a denationalized world the 'static efficiency costs of closure' increase (Frieden and Rogowski, 1996: 35). If, due to tariffs, imports are more expensive in one country than in another country with a more liberal trade policy, manufacturers who need to import parts from foreign countries will be at a significant (comparative) disadvantage and will press for liberalization. In general, economic integration will increase demands for the harmonization of national policies, or for common rules that prohibit national state intervention, in order to overcome the disadvantages of political segmentation and maximize the gains from economic exchange. These demands are due to *efficiency pressures* and express a desire for non-discrimination in the markets.

Political regulations may have little impact if they cover only a part of the relevant social space. A national regulation implemented by Australia alone would do little to prevent rising cancer rates due to the depletion of the atmospheric ozone layer. Along the same lines, Germany – for good reasons – has more severe restrictions on the distribution of racist propaganda material than many other countries. However, if someone residing in the United States feeds such material into the Internet, authorities in Germany cannot legally prohibit, let alone effectively prevent these activities. One may label these challenges to the effectiveness of national policies *externality problems*.

Policies that may still be effective at the national level may become too costly if they do not apply to all social actors within an integrated social space. In particular, policies that create costs for the production of goods may turn out to be self-defeating in terms of competitiveness for the area to which the policy applies. Manufacturers' associations throughout the industrialized world complain at every opportunity that the social and environmental costs of production are too high. In their view, it is essential to cut wages, social policies, environmental regulations and corporate taxes. Against this background, the widespread fear of a downward spiral of national social and environmental standards is not surprising. In the national context, this discourse about *competitiveness* benefits those groups in particular who are not in favor of cost-intensive market-correcting or re-distributive policies.

Effective participation depends on the spatial congruence between the rulers (the nation-*state*) and the ruled (the national *society*). Yet this notion becomes problematic as soon as the nature of the relevant community is contested, as happens in the course of societal denationalization (see Held, 1995). The rise of cross-border transactions infringes on the normative dignity of political borders and national identities. If there is no congruence, then a group affected by a decision but not participating in its making can be considered as being subject to foreign determination rather than self-determined. This new form of foreign determination tends to be mutual (yet not symmetrical), and derives from the manifold externalities that result from many political decisions having if not unlimited, at least transboundary effects. Any national decision that leads to transboundary pollution affects people who live outside the political system responsible for the decision. The specific challenge in this case arises out of *representational deficits*.

Agency

The structural changes cited above have not remained unanswered. These direct effects and challenges to the effectiveness of national policies do not directly translate into a decline of national society and the nation-state. The effects and challenges are serious, yet the outcome is largely determined by the political choices made by agents. Governments and other political organizations are able to respond to these challenges in a number of different ways.

Political actors may *passively await the decline in effectiveness* of national schemes, partly because they lack institutional imagination and prefer to stick to the institutional status quo, and partly because they can use the pretext of international pressure to further their own domestic goals such as deregulation and de-democratization. Many employers' associations and liberal-minded governments, for instance, pursue international free-trade policies which they can instrumentalize for the purposes of national deregulation. This response is quite different from that of groups and governments which even under pressure focus on the maintenance of traditional national regulations (see Zürn et al., 2000). At the same time, one can interpret the willingness of many governments to selectively engage in intergovernmental agreements as an attempt to gain the autonomy of the executive from society (Wolf, 2000).

A second principal response can be described as *fragmentative political restructuring* (Holsti, 1980). Regionalist political actors may push for decentralization or even secession from nation-states in order to be able to respond as flexibly as possible in the new denationalized environment. The rise of the Lega Norte in Northern Italy and other regionalist movements elsewhere can thus be interpreted as a fragmentative political response (Woods, 1992). Alternatively, nationalist political actors may attempt to reassert the importance of national borders, especially by pushing for protectionist policies in areas like trade, culture and migration (Zürn, 1998: ch. 9).

Governments and other political organizations may also opt for *integrative political restructuring* in response to interdependence and societal denationalization. The incongruence between national political regulations and denationalized areas of social transactions calls into question the capacity of the nation-state to provide the very goods that made it the dominant political institution in the first place. In this predicament, governments and other political actors may endeavor to regain control by establishing new international and transnational or even supranational regimes, networks and organizations for the coordination and harmonization of their policies, that is, they may endeavor to establish legitimate governance beyond the nation-state.

WHAT DO INTERDEPENDENCE AND GLOBALIZATION EXPLAIN?

'What are the characteristics of world politics under conditions of extensive interdependence?' (Keohane and Nye, 1977: 19). Having described the rise of interdependence and globalization and discussed the causal mechanism the question now arises whether or not the assumed effects really take place. In this section I shall discuss two assumed effects that are ascribed to both growing interdependence and globalization.

Peace and Cooperation

The promise of early interdependence theorists was nothing less than 'peace'. Sir Robert Angell (1969) and Ramsey Muir (1932) emphasized the reduction of distance and difference as the mechanism through which rising interdependence would directly, though unintentionally, change world politics (see de Wilde, 1991). Angell's prediction – made on the eve of the First World War – that war among industrialized nations had become unlikely, has frequently been ridiculed. However, a closer look at his and Muir's work shows that both put forward highly advanced arguments with a good sense of their limitations. Czempiel (1986) elegantly framed this kind of thinking in terms of 'peace through trade' as one of the three most important peace strategies at hand. Although it is contested to what extent there is any direct association between interdependence and peace, empirical studies show at least indirect effects. Accordingly, the pacifying effects of trade depend on the symmetry and the extent of the ensuing interdependence and other factors (Barbieri, 1996; Dorusen, 1999; Polachek et al., 1999; Reuveny and Kang, 1998; Russett et al., 1998).

Keohane and Nye (1977: ch. 2) have discussed related issues using a more developed framework. In their view, interdependence does not lead to the disappearance of conflicts, but rather conflicts will take on new forms. In this context the responses of political actors are more important for an understanding of the effects of interdependence than the direct structural effects. Their model of 'complex interdependence' implies the hypothesis that growing interconnectedness may lead to political processes that differ from those typically described by realism. Instead of an international politics being dominated by states that focus on security as their goal and the armed forces as the means, in a situation of complex interdependence actors also include international organizations. Moreover, security and the armed forces lose relevance as a goal and as an instrument of international politics. Today it can safely be stated that in those regions of the world that are very closely interconnected, complex interdependence indeed seems to comprehend processes and outcomes of world politics much better than realism. It is hard to deny that the relative importance of issues other than security, especially economic and ecological issues, has increased over the past three decades. In addition, the role and importance of the armed forces has declined in the conduct of foreign policy between those industrialized nations that are most closely connected.

Most importantly, over the past three decades the role of international institutions has been enhanced more or less parallel to the rise of interdependence. While the number of international organizations, which is only a very rough measure for the development of international governance, has remained more or less constant (see Rittberger and Zangl, 1995; Shanks et al., 1996), the overall number of multilateral treaties deposited at the United Nations shows linear growth from less than 150 in 1960 to well over 400 in 1998. The same applies to the annual ratification of multilateral treaties (Hirschi et al., 1999: 40). The increase in international agreements is accompanied by a growing intensity of transgovernmental relations. Various state agencies – regulatory agencies, courts, executives and increasingly also legislatures – now network with their counterparts abroad (Slaughter, 1997: 190). In contrast to earlier interdependence writers, the theorists of the 1960s and 1970s thus emphasized two 'peace strategies' induced by rising interdependence: the reduction of difference and the rise of international institutions in response to the need to manage interdependence.

The current globalization literature is remarkably tacit on the issue of international peace and security. Relevant statements are mostly of a very general nature. Whenever the challenges and the problems of globalization are emphasized, a general picture of violence-prone chaos in a globalized world is evoked (see Horsman and Marshall, 1995). In contrast, those neoliberals who triumphantly observe the retreat of the state – which, after all, was always the instigator of inter-state wars – prophesy the end of all such wars. By emphasizing the pressures that globalization puts on authoritarian states to foster liberalization, however, some writers – more implicitly than explicitly – have also connected globalization with the third peace strategy identified by Czempiel (1986): the 'democratization' of authoritarian societies. In this sense, globalization may be helpful in supporting three processes that are conducive to the absence of war between states. These are the direct effects of the reduction of difference, that is, a diminished role for the armed forces (peace through trade), a liberalization of society brought about by the pressure to improve efficiency (peace through democracy) and the strengthening of international institutions as a political response (peace through international organization) (Russett et al., 1998). The evolving patterns resemble what Karl Deutsch once described as the conditions and the processes leading to a pluralistic security community (Deutsch, 1957).

The association of peace with globalization must be qualified for several reasons. First, it applies only to those areas in the world in which interconnectedness is highly prevalent and in which the effect of smaller differences is accompanied by the rise of international institutions and liberal societies. Whereas the OECD world may be described as a zone of peace, this certainly cannot be said of the rest of the world, which again proves the point that the concept of globalization, if taken literally and assessed on a global scale, is misleading (Singer and Wildavsky, 1993). The degree of interdependence and societal denationalization not only varies across issue areas but also across nations and regions, and this variance is extremely important when taking account of the effects. Second, only figures in the category of 'inter-state wars' have clearly decreased, while intra-state or civil wars have not. While the rise of societal interdependence and new social spaces may indeed have reduced the capacity of the nation-state to mobilize people for inter-state wars, this does not imply a decline in general willingness to participate in instances of organized collective violence. A denationalized world may give rise to additional conflicts leading to complex cleavages and numerous 'small' wars instead of large-scale wars.

Deregulation and Convergence

The second major issue in the interdependence literature is the autonomy of nation-states. As a result of the incongruence between economic and political spaces, nation-states are less able to control markets and to meet their governance targets through national policies. The growing ineffectiveness of national policies was the major theme of Richard Cooper's (1968) contribution on the economics of interdependence. With the integration of markets, so the argument goes, growing numbers of national policies no longer work. Empirical studies on the effect of economic interdependence however did not support this expectation. On the contrary, work on national adaptation to external economic challenges demonstrated convincingly that domestic structures are decisive for an understanding of national political responses (see Cameron, 1978; Gourevitch, 1978; Katzenstein, 1978, 1985). Quite contrary to the original hypothesis, this literature was instrumental in bringing the state back into (Anglo-Saxon) political science (Evans et al., 1985).

Nevertheless, Cooper's analysis has experienced a revival. Most of the current literature on the effects of globalization takes up the argument and diagnoses 'the end of the social democratic era' (Scharpf, 1987), the 'retreat of the state' (Strange, 1996), the 'misery of politics' (Narr and Schubert, 1994), the 'globalization trap' (Martin and Schumann, 1997), a 'race to the bottom' or at least a 'competition of the obsessed' (Krugman, 1995), a competitive state (Hirsch, 1995), a Schumpeterian workfare state (Jessop, 1994) or a residual state (Cerny, 1996). For similar reasons, Ohmae (1993) goes as far as to predict the end of the state itself. Common to these studies is the notion that efficiency pressures, congruence problems and above all problems of competitiveness induce a rapid deterioration in the effectiveness of national regulations. As a result, the state retreats and gives way to economic and social deregulation. Two empirical trends should corroborate this argument. First, to the extent that changes in state intervention have external causes, we should see a convergence of different national policies. Second, to the extent that efficiency pressures and competitiveness problems dominate, we should see a downward movement, that is a general trend towards deregulation.

A number of important objections have so far been raised that challenge both elements of this hypothesis. First, higher levels of economic openness increase the demand for policies to buffer the less desirable effects of world market integration. In this sense, social policies and state intervention can be seen not only as cost-intensive burdens for efficient production, but also as a form of risk insurance in the face of increased economic openness (Garrett, 1998a; Rieger and Leibfried, 1997; Rodrik, 1997). Moreover, new growth theory suggests that many state interventions are still economically efficient and thus effective, even and especially in times of global competition (Barro, 1996; Krugman, 1994). Under certain circumstances, integrated markets may even trigger a race to the top (Vogel, 1995). Hence, higher levels of economic interdependence and globalization may well lead to more, rather than less state intervention. Finally, the way external challenges are mediated is still the single most important factor for understanding national policies. The mediation process is determined by a number of different, mainly institutional factors (Kitschelt et al., 1999; Vogel, 1996; Weiss, 1998). In addition, ideas determine 'what states make of globalization' (Clark, 1999). Convergence – be it downward or upward – can thus not be expected to take place. The evidence produced in these studies clearly demonstrates that neither the convergence nor the deregulation trend exist in a strong and dominant sense. The level of state expenditures has not fallen parallel to the rise of economic interdependence and globalization, nor can clear convergence processes be observed (see Bernauer, 2000 for an excellent overview). In addition, a broad-scale redistribution of state expenditures from the welfare sector to the security and R&D sectors, as predicted by the notion of a competitive state, cannot be observed (Zürn, 1998: 153–7).

The debate and evidence produced so far, however, are still inconclusive for a number of reasons.

- If it is at all possible to identify a threshold that marks the step from interdependence to globalization, it is the late 1980s and early 1990s. The data of most studies utilizes statistics on state expenditures and social expenditures and, for practical reasons, now end in the early 1990s. This is still very early, especially since quite recent data seem to show first signs of a change in trends (Kittel et al., 2000). Moreover, the importance of institutional inertia is emphasized by the data problem. For instance, although Sweden made extensive cuts in social benefits, expenditures initially grew faster than in states offering less generous benefits, because the sudden rise in unemployment activated the welfare state. In such a case, figures on state expenditure indicate neither convergence nor deregulation, in spite of a significant development in this direction.
- The absence of convergence processes cannot be equated with an absence of constraints. Case studies on current political processes in many welfare states show that constraints imposed on social policies are strongly felt and translate into uneasy compromises (Seeleib-Kaiser, 2000). While the level of unemployment expenditure did grow, the amount of money received by the individual beneficiaries dropped in almost all G7 countries.
- Studies focusing on specific policy areas could easily demonstrate a strong convergent trend towards deregulation. Deregulation in the postal and telecommunication services is a strong case in point (Grande and Schneider, 1991; Vogel, 1996). It thus seems necessary to focus much more on issue area-specific differences in order to understand the dynamics triggered by globalization (see Bernauer, 2000: ch. 8 and Scharpf, 1999: ch. 3).

- It is conceivable that challenges to the effectiveness of national policies exist and that, the absence of any political response, would lead to a downward convergence. In order to maintain or even step up a given level of intervention, states may cooperate and build common policy-making institutions. Some studies on environmental regulations exemplify this process (see Héritier et al., 1996; Jänicke, 1998; Vogel, 1995); however, most studies fail to take the international response into account.

On the aggregate level, the growth in economic interdependence in the 1970s did not lead to a convergence of national policies. In fact, quite the contrary, states proved to be relatively powerful in the face of interdependence problems. Economic and societal denationalization in the late 1980s and 1990s certainly increased efficiency pressures and accentuated the problems of congruence and competitiveness. So far, however, there is little indication that structural constraints led to generalized patterns of downward convergence. In order to have a better understanding of the challenges to the effectiveness of national policies, it seems necessary to re-focus studies on at least two counts.

First, the mode of most of the studies referred to here is mainly macro-correlative. Propositions about political changes are tested by establishing the extent to which a rise in social interconnectedness has led to new political *outcomes*. By contrast, the study of the way in which interdependence and societal denationalization affect political *processes* has been neglected. An examination of this aspect of the politics of interdependence could be extremely useful for a more accurate understanding of and predictions about policy changes, as it is rather unlikely that denationalization directly affects policies. Indeed, it seems much more plausible to assume that policy outcomes are mediated by political institutions, political actors and political struggles (Cowles et al., 2001). A much better understanding of the effects of the process can be gained by looking at 'the politics of denationalization' rather than policy changes, and by examining processes instead of outcomes (see Zürn et al., 2000).

Second, most studies are implicitly built on the assumption that interdependence and/or societal denationalizaton give rise to similar political processes independent of the issue under investigation, although there are in fact no a priori reasons for doing so. On the one hand, different states have, for institutional reasons, different strengths and weaknesses in adapting to external pressures. In a slightly different context, Krasner noted many years ago: 'One state may be able to alter the structure of its medical system but be unable to construct an efficient transportation network, while another can deal relatively easily with getting its citizens around but cannot get their illnesses cured'

(1978: 58). On the other hand, the opportunity for international regulation in response to increasingly ineffective national policy measures depends on a number of conditions that vary from one issue to another, that is, according to the type of challenge. Political dynamics initiated by globalization may vary greatly depending on whether the problems we are dealing with concern efficiency, competition or congruence.

Research that focuses on peace and cooperation or on convergence and deregulation as functions of increasing societal interdependence never fundamentally challenged the theory of international relations. It essentially builds on given assumptions, for instance that national societies are separable units and state executives are agents who act rationally in the name of their principals, as well as some basic economic theorems. The same applies to most of the research that falls under the 'globalization' heading and aims at establishing the impact of accelerated world market integration on national regulation. These studies also use existing theoretical assumptions and theorems in order to assess the effects of interdependence on national policies and world politics. In this sense, they were never intended to culminate in an interdependence theory (writ large) of world politics. They did, however, have a theoretical impact in that they constituted a serious challenge to realism on a number of counts. Since the emergence of interdependence, research in international politics can no longer be reduced to the study of security and military issues, of peace and war. World politics today is much more than that. Moreover, interdependence research brought non-state actors and, above all, international institutions to the fore. In this sense, interdependence research can be seen as the forerunner of New Institutionalism in international relations.

THE DEEPER EFFECTS OF GLOBALIZATION ON (GLOBAL) GOVERNANCE

The transition from interdependence to globalization research is not only due to different values of interconnectedness. It also indicates a significant increase in conceived effects. There is hardly a modern political institution which is not allegedly challenged, transformed or undermined by globalization. Globalization is not only said to be curbing the autonomy of nation-states and enforcing a convergence of national policies, but also disabling democracy and with it the legitimacy of national political systems, altering the nature of sovereignty and thus ultimately transforming the fundamental structures of the international system (see Beisheim and Walter, 1997; Rosenau, 1997). Globalization has intensified interdependence by the creation of new social spaces, and thus raised issues like

transnational participation and transnational networks as well as the merging and interplay of political institutions that once were conceived as separable units (Keohane and Nye, 2000). In my view, the issues of democracy, transnational civil society (see Risse et al., 1999 and Chapter 13 by Thomas Risse in this volume), political fragmentation and multi-level governance are the most fascinating in this context. So far, none of these fields of debate and research has come up with conclusive results, but they do highlight interesting fields of research for the future.

Democracy

Through which mechanism does globalization or societal denationalization affect democracy? A growing incongruence between social and political spaces does indeed bear upon the democratic principle according to which every individual affected by a political decision should have the chance to have a say in this decision (Held, 1995: 16; Scharpf, 1993). For a long time, the notion of a nation-state consisting of a more or less contained national society, a clearly demarcated territory and an administrative apparatus designed to provide services for that society within that territory, led political theorists to treat congruence as given. The notion of a territorially defined nation-state was hence used as a shortcut to ensure the spatial congruence between rulers (the nation-*state*) and subjects (the national *society*). Yet this notion becomes problematic as soon as the nature of the relevant community is contested, as has happened in the course of societal denationalization. The increase in cross-border transactions infringes on *the normative dignity* of political borders (Schmalz-Bruns, 1998: 372; see also Linklater, 1998; McGrew, 1998).

For the purposes of democracy, spatial congruence is necessary at two critical points. First, congruence between the people who are affected by a decision and their representatives in the decision-making system (input congruence) is required. If there is no *input congruence*, then a group affected by a decision but not participating in its making can be considered to have been determined by others rather than self-determined. All environmental externalities are cases in point. Congruence between the space for which regulations are valid and the boundaries of the relevant social transactions – that is, *output incongruence* – is also significant for democratic legitimacy. In a denationalized world ruled by a system of formally independent nation-states, there is a danger that political communities cannot reach a desired goal due to conditions outside their jurisdiction. For instance, a social policy desired by the majority of the population of a given political community can become unaffordable for reasons of international competitiveness. Of course, political systems have always had to take external restraints into account, but from a critical perspective it is equally vital not to simply resign and adjust normative standards to political reality.

Viewing globalization as the underlying problem of democracy challenges the still somewhat dominant view that the problem is actually constituted by moving decisions to the international level. At present – and this is where analysts are almost unanimous – this legitimacy is clearly inadequate. There are two strands of thought among those who identify a democratic deficit in the way international institutions work. One strand points to institutional deficits of international institutions that can be adjusted through reforms, provided there is the right political will. Another strand considers these suggestions as naïve and even questions the *mere possibility* of democratic processes beyond the nation-state because the EU and other international institutions cannot meet the social prerequisites for democracy. According to skeptics, democratic legitimacy is only possible within the framework of a demos, that is, a political community with the potential for democratic self-governance as expressed in the concept of the modern nation. Beyond the nation-state, the social prerequisite for a democratic political community – the political space – is missing. Peter Graf Kielmannsegg eloquently summarizes this point of view with respect to Europe: 'Collective identities develop, become stable and are passed into tradition in communities of communication, of experiences and of memory. Europe, even within the narrower scope of Western Europe, has no communication community, hardly any common memory and only limited common experiences' (1994: 27; translation by M.Z.). Hence, the connection between nation and democracy is not a historical coincidence but systematic and indissoluble. A demos as exemplified in the modern nation-state requires cultural homogeneity, and without a demos there is no democracy.[6]

To the extent that for pragmatic reasons skeptics accept the need for decisions through international institutions, globalization leads to the uncomfortable choice between 'effective problem-solving through international institutions' or 'democractic political processes.' (see Dahl, 1994). This is not, however, a particularly convincing theoretical perspective (Grande, 2000; Zürn, 2000). In democratic terms, international institutions are a sensible response to the problems facing democracy in times of societal denationalization, as they help to redress the incongruence between social and political spaces. Theoretically, the rise of international institutions in a transnational setting, that is, the 'emergence of denationalized governance structures' (Joerges, 1996), helps to bring all those who are affected by a political decision into the decision-making system, thus observing the principle of 'no taxation without representation'. What is more, international institutions help to increase the factual freedom of political communities. Governance beyond the nation-state can therefore improve both social welfare *and* democracy in the face of societal denationalization. In this sense, international institutions are not the problem, but part of the solution to the problems of modern democracy.

This debate raises a number of issues that require further normative reflection and much more empirical study to be resolved. On the empirical side there are two salient issues. First, what exactly are the socio-cultural prerequisites for the application of what kind of democratic procedures? Second, to what extent are these prerequisites systematically intrinsic to the nation, and to what extent can they be generated on a transnational scale as intended or unintended side-effects of societal denationalization and as endeavors to further the development of democratic procedures in effective international institutions? The debate on the relationship between globalization (global economy) and (national) democracy has stimulated some very promising research that, however, has not yet developed far enough for results to be conclusive (see Schmalz-Bruns, 1999; Wiener, 1998, 1999; Wolf, 2000).

Political Fragmentation

Interdependence and globalization can lead to both political integration and political fragmentation. Kalevi Holsti (1980: 23) has adequately described the approach of most interdependence theorists to this double movement: 'Analysts have been so impressed by growing interdependence that they have ignored a simultaneous and parallel process that results in increased international fragmentation.' On the contrary, analysts of globalization have often pointed to an inherent relationship between globalization and fragmentation (see Menzel, 1998), most eloquently expressed in the formula 'Jihad vs. McWorld' (Barber, 1995). Nevertheless, solid empirical work concerned with identifying the causal pathways between globalization and political fragmentation has remained scarce.

It is possible to distinguish at least three different fragmentative responses to societal denationalization. First, Robert Cox (1997) and others have identified so-called anti-systemic movements that organize against globalization and the accompanying loss in substance for national democracy. In this view, Chiapas's resistance against the Mexican state, the strikes that paralyzed Paris and much of France in 1995, and protests that halted WTO negotiations in Seattle are part of a double movement in which the deregulation of markets produces social forces that struggle for re-regulation. In this view, current developments are somehow similar to what has been analyzed by Karl Polanyi (1944) with respect to the marketization and the regaining of political control in England after the Industrial Revolution.

Second, an ominous factor accompanying the decline of public confidence in traditional political authority in many OECD countries is a resurgence of right-wing extremism. Societal and political denationalization has led to a nationalist response, especially among young men who feel threatened by immigration, the decline of welfare policies and national political authority in general (Betz, 1994; Cox, 1997; Zürn, 1998: ch. 9). In a similar vein, anti-modernist movements have gained strength in parallel to globalization outside of the OECD world, too. Fears of a resulting clash of civilizations and a broad, cross-cultural Jihad movement are, however, unfounded (Senghaas, 1998).

Third, the most interesting and probably best studied case of political fragmentation in response to globalization is the rise of bottom-up regionalism, including all patterns of endeavors toward political decentralization from within the particular region. At least three causal mechanisms connecting globalization and bottom-up regionalism have been identified.

- *Welfare regionalism*: In a denationalized economy each region endeavors to increase its attractiveness for foreign direct investment and to increase the productivity of its economy through the *reduction of national policy costs*. Therefore, rich regions in countries with regional disparities may see an opportunity to pursue their own economic strategies without having to provide for the interests of other, poorer regions within that nation-state. This kind of welfare regionalism, the most prominent example being the Lega Norte in Northern Italy (Schmidtke, 1996), is most likely to emerge in regions which form part of the economic core, but not the political centre of the nation-state (Woods, 1992: 58).
- *Functionality of regions*: The *growing ineffectiveness of national intervention into markets* restricts the states' capacity for territorial management, which is crucial to the integration of peripheral regions in the national project. In addition, the advantages of small units in an integrating world market are increasingly emphasized in concepts like 'flexible specialization' (Piore and Sabel, 1989), and popularized in the debate on a 'Europe of the Regions'.
- *Diminishing risks*: The *rise of market-making international institutions* diminishes the risks of regionalism, since one of the central tasks of the nation-state was the establishment of a large market, to which they granted the various

regions access that they in turn did not wish to risk losing. In the past, the fear of losing markets used to be one of the main obstacles to regionalist mobilization. In the light of the high degree of economic integration within the OECD and regional economic blocs such as the EU and NAFTA, the role of the nation-state in granting accessibility to markets has diminished (Zürn and Lange, 2000).

In sum, the political consequences of globalization change the logic of some variables used to explain regionalism. It is no longer only the political actions of the nation-state that provoke regionalist responses, but also the undermining of some traditional functions of the nation-state through globalization and political internationalization. In an increasingly competitive world market, rich regions want to rid themselves of their national commitments, while at the same time the development of market-enhancing international institutions has reduced the risks of secession and even increased incentives to organize regionally in order to be eligible for supranational resources. The evolving complexity of governance beyond the nation-state in turn creates desires to emphasize cultural differences at the regional level and to represent regional interests directly, no longer via the nation-state. Studies on the regionalist movements in Québec and Scotland have produced some evidence in favor of such mechanisms (Bernauer, 2000: ch. 7; Lange, 2000).

Transformation of the Westphalian System and the Rise of Supranationalism

Societal denationalization over the past two or three decades has led to a rise in international institutions that in effect may change the constitution of world politics. At first sight, the quantitative growth of governance with government does not seem to affect the national constellation in qualitative terms. The *constitutional principles* of the Westphalian system of sovereign states are intergovernmental in that governments mutually acknowledge each other as governments, thus laying the foundation for international society (see Bull, 1977). It is therefore true that since the early nineteenth century – many see the Congress of Vienna subsequent to the Napoleonic Wars as the point of departure – international institutions have assisted states in meeting their own governance targets. What is new about more recent developments is not only the sheer amount of governance with governments, but also the types and objects of regulation.

Traditionally, international institutions regulated the interaction between states, be it in the field of security (for instance alliances, arms treaties etc.) or in the economy (reduction of tariffs). The purpose of those international institutions currently emerging is mainly to assist states in *regulating societal actors*. Most international environmental regimes exemplify this development. Their aim is to reduce external and internal threats to the security of human beings and their environment, and the ultimate target of these regulations is society. For this purpose, they rely increasingly not only on negative regulations (i.e. regulations that prohibit states from taking certain measures), but also on *positive regulations* (i.e. regulations that require states to take certain measures; see Corbey, 1995; Scharpf, 1996). In addition, new issues have been taken on board by these institutions. The development of the GATT Regime in the field of economics is a case in point. The early GATT removed government restrictions at the borders, that is, tariffs on manufactured goods. Over time this increased the importance of non-tariff barriers, thus inducing demands for regulations that focus on *behind-the-border issues*. The Tokyo Round of negotiations (1973–9) began to deal with non-tariff barriers such as anti-dumping measures, government subsidies, government procurement and customs and licensing procedures. The results of the Uruguay Round (1986–94) were a major step forward in this direction (see Kahler, 1995). International institutions have thus changed in character in response to societal denationalization. Increasingly, their aim is to regulate not only the actions of state actors but also those of societal actors, and not only at the border, but also behind-the-border issues. In doing so, positive regulations have gained importance relative to negative regulations. The extent and the objects of international governance no longer easily match the notion of a sovereign state in the Westphalian system.

Supranational governance even more clearly contradicts the notion of a sovereign state in the national constellation. Supranational institutions develop rules that are considered superior to national law and involve servants who have some autonomy from national governments. The demand for supranational governance increases as the density and scope of international governance grows. As international governance covers more and more issue areas, overlaps and collisions between the jurisdictions of international regulations and other international or national regulations becomes more likely. Supranational bodies are a logical response to avoid such collisions. Moreover, the more international regimes address behind-the-border issues, which are especially difficult to monitor and have significant impacts on societal actors, the more the question of credibility arises. A logical way to increase the credibility of commitments is to develop supranational bodies that monitor regulations and resolve conflicts (see Moravcsik, 1998: 73–7).

To be sure, beyond Europe – the area in which both societal and political denationalization have moved furthest – supranational institutions are still rare. However, even here there have been some notable recent developments. First of all, the section of the new WTO on the manufactured goods trade brought in new monitoring and dispute settlement procedures to deal more effectively with behind-the-border issues which to some extent resemble the supranational role of the European Court of Justice. Moreover, the establishment of the Rome Statute of the International Criminal Court as a permanent institution in 1998 also indicates a move in the direction of supranationality. This court 'shall have the power to exercise its jurisdiction over persons for the most serious crimes of international concern ....' (Article 1; see http://www.un.org/law/icc/index.htm). Finally, insofar as infringements of rights can be brought directly before independent bodies by individuals, as in the case of the 'Civil Covenant', the 'Race Discrimination Convention' and the 'Convention against Torture', one may also speak of an element of supranationality. Given these very recent developments and the effects these agreements may have on other issue areas, it is fair to conclude that the extent to which institutions with supranational elements have emerged in global politics is much greater than was expected ten years ago.

The shape of more recent inter-, trans- and supranational institutions is hardly compatible with the traditional notion of state sovereignty in the national constellation. Governments and other political organizations do not merely sit back and watch globalization and the decline in the effectiveness of unilateral policies. They respond to the challenges by setting up new institutions, and this should not be neglected in the analysis and understanding of statehood and the constitution of world politics. The national constellation, that is the convergence of resources, recognition and the realization of governance goals in one political organization – the nation-state – seems to be in a process of transformation into a post-national constellation. The nation-state is no longer the only site of authority and the normativity that accompanies it.

This transformation process itself can be separated into different stages. The first stage can be regarded most plausibly as a more or less *unintended outcome* of political responses to (perceived) functional demands. The steady progression of some international regimes to the point that they now deal with positive interventions into society and behind-the-border issues is part of this first stage. The same appears to hold for the need for credibility in the design of these more ambitious regimes and the development of supranational bodies to deal with collisions between different regulations.[7] The second stage of the transformation is much more *reflective*. When society and political actors begin to comprehend the change, they begin to put issues of transboundary identity and transboundary ethics onto the agenda. Pressures to improve living conditions for people of another nationality and race that live in countries thousands of miles away, as well as the debate on European identity and democracy, are first signs of this reflective stage in the transformation process.

CONCLUSION: SOVEREIGNTY AND IR THEORY AT BAY?

Interdependence and globalization studies so far hardly constitute a theory of world politics. In many ways, both these strands of literature speculate and hypothesize about the political effects of increasing societal interconnectedness using already existing theories. The globalization literature differs from interdependence studies in that it assumes a qualitatively higher level of interconnectedness and, more importantly, broadens the range of themes which may be affected by it.

In a very subtle sense, however, the interdependence literature has structured the theoretical debate in international relations (IR) over the past three decades. Waltz's (1979) theory of international politics and other realist writings can be seen as a deliberate attempt to rescue IR as an independent discipline from the logic of interdependence. In realist thinking, it was possible not only to understand IR without taking domestic politics and international institutions into consideration; the notion was reconfirmed, moreover, that national societies and their respective states can be conceptualized as utterly separate entities. Thus the interaction of those entities was declared a field of the discipline of IR. This reconfirmation put interdependence writers on the defensive. Their counter-attack was directed at a different target: the issue of international institutions. In this way, they indirectly reconfirmed the strict notions of distinctly separate national societies and traditional notions of sovereignty. In a sense, the debate as a whole accepted the analytical shackles of 'methodological nationalism'.

Methodological nationalism considers nation-states as the basic unit of all politics. It assumes that humankind is naturally distributed among a limited number of nations, which organize themselves internally as nation-states and delimit themselves externally from other nation-states (see Beck, 2000; Smith, 1979). In addition, it assumes that the external delimitation and the subsequent competition between nation-states are the most fundamental concepts of political organization. Methodological nationalism is distinct from normative nationalism, according to which each nation has the inalienable right to organize itself in its own culturally specific way. Methodological nationalism sees national self-determination as ontologically given and as the most important cleavage in the political sphere.

This double premise pre-determines empirical observations, as can be seen for example in the case of aggregate statistics, which are almost exclusively categorized in national terms. It locates and restricts the political sphere to the national level.

Globalization studies that focus on issues like transnational civil society and the transformation of the Westphalian state system are now beginning to question methodological nationalism. Again, the realist response is strong and intellectually challenging, but quite defensive this time. Krasner (1999) defends the realist notion of unchanged sovereignty by arguing that it has always been wrong, that is, it has always been full of loopholes and never existed in any pure sense. Whereas this analysis is on the one hand historically rich and convincing, it downplays the effects of the institution of sovereignty on the Westphalian state system. Sovereignty has indeed never been a constraining norm, but a regulative idea like democracy or equality. The effectiveness of *regulative ideas*, however, cannot be rejected by pointing to internal contradictions or imperfections, as is possible when discussing constraining norms. Regulative ideas by definition cannot be flawless, and they comprise of different components that need to be evenly balanced. In the case of democracy, the mere claim to have perfected it would be considered as proof of the opposite. Krasner's analysis fails to conceptualize sovereignty as a regulative idea, and thus overlooks the change that the content and the relative importance of sovereignty are undergoing – a change that affects the constitution of world politics in that methodological nationalism is becoming increasingly inappropriate for analysis.

This critique of methodological nationalism must not be confused with the thesis of the end of the nation-state. Nation-states will persist and will remain of central importance. Relaxing methodological nationalism rather means that the nation as the dominant organizing principle of politics can no longer be presumed, but must be given an empirical status. As the significance of governance beyond the nation-state increases, the separation of political issues into nationally defined territorial units must be conceptualized as a variable – dependent and independent – rather than a conceptual premise.

Governance beyond the nation-state extends the realm of the political beyond national borders and sovereign states. We must therefore develop a notion of a global polity which cannot only be seen as a substitute for nation-states at a higher level. All forms of governance beyond the nation-state lack a central authority or a 'world state' equipped with a legitimate monopoly of the use of force. Thus, governance beyond the nation-state cannot take the form of governance by government, rather, it needs to be a form of governance with governments such as we see in international institutions, or governance without governments[8] as in transnational institutions, or in supranational governance. The interplay of different forms of governance beyond the nation-state produces polities of a new quality, as certainly attested by the European Multi-Level Governance System (see Jachtenfuchs and Kohler-Koch, 1996; Marks et al., 1996). Others also speak of an emerging global polity (see Ougaard and Higgott, 2001). Such conceptualizations do not need to rely on utopian thinking about a world state or world federalism. It seems more promising to recall the tradition of historical macro-sociology upheld by Stein Rokkan, Charles Tilly and others. As early as the 1960s and 1970s they aimed at overcoming the dominant approach of treating nation-states as logically independent cases. Instead, they advocated a more complete map of one interdependent system (Tilly, 1984: 129). It is hard to understand why these attempts to conceive of nation-states as parts of a larger polity have declined to the extent that globalization and interdependence have increased.

What are the features of such an emerging polity? What makes governance beyond the nation-state special and separates it from the framework of methodological nationalism? Contrary to many national political systems, such a post-national polity is characterized by (1) members that are corporate actors in highly organized and specialized sub-systems instead of individual citizens. The notion of individual representatives and personally influential politicians of states that we know from the analyses of national political systems loses importance. In such a system of multiple corporate actors, nation-states would then be a territorial form of interest organization within a functionally segmented system, existing side by side with functional forms of interest organization. The membership's participation is motivated by (2) an interest in problem-solving, not so much in the political organization of a common identity. Members share the notion of upgrading the common interest rather than pursuing the common good. The organizing principle of a post-national polity is (3) the absence of a central authority that can impose rules and regulations and, therefore, the dominance of a decision-mode which is closer to unanimity than to majority rule, thus favoring bargaining and deliberation over voting as decision-making mechanisms (Eising and Kohler-Koch, 1999). The notion of a post-national polity requires the introduction of concepts such as functional differentiation and the conceptualization of world politics as a sphere in which not all actors, and not even all states have similar functions (see Buzan et al., 1993). It implies the acceptance of many forms of association located somewhere between hierarchy and anarchy, and of some elements of authority in world politics (Hurd, 1999; Rosenau, 1997). It also means conceiving world politics less as a struggle for survival in a brutish environment than

as a struggle over appropriate forms of governance in a given polity (Reinicke, 1998; Zürn, 1998). Such a theory of complex governance in a denationalized world would devalue not only the borders between societies, but also the border between comparative politics and IR. In one of the most imaginative contributions in the special issue of *International Organization*, Helen Milner writes: 'The degree of divergence between IR and the rest of political science has waxed and waned over the years, but in the past decade it seems to have lessened' (1998: 760). The move from interdependence to globalization is one driving force behind this change.

Notes

For their support and helpful comments, I wish to thank the editors of this volume as well as Peter Arnhold, Marianne Beisheim, Andrea Liese, Hans-Henrik Holm, Robert O. Keohane, Vicki May, Gregor Walter and Bernhard Zangl.

1 This, of course, depends on the notion of world society. I use a definition that requires more than just transactions. For major contributions to the question of world society see Luhmann, 1971, the contributions to Beck, 1998 and Albert et al., 2000.

2 Thus, globalization is *not* defined here as an all-encompassing process of epochal proportions. According to this latter understanding, globalization not only implies a growth in transnational interactions, but also comprises political processes and 'the stretching and deepening of social relations and institutions across space and time' (see Elkins, 1995; Giddens, 1990; Held, 1995: 20; Held and McGrew, 1993: 263; Rosenau, 1997). Globalization thus understood denotes all (individual as well as the sum total of) globally oriented practices and patterns of thought as well as the epochal transformation which is constituted by them (Albrow, 1996: 89). These general notions of de-territorialization underestimate the extent to which politics is spatially bound. Politics tends to be more particularistic than, for example, economics, since, as Michael Walzer writes, 'communities must have boundaries' (1983: 50).

3 The denationalized condition is still rare. Helliwell (1998) demonstrates that even between the US and Canada the national border still has an impact on reducing trade between cities and provinces in North America.

4 In the remainder I use globalization and societal denationalization interchangeably. The term denationalization goes back to the classic works of Karl W. Deutsch (1969) and Eric Hobsbawm (1992) on nationalism, according to which a nation is a political community for which dense societal transactions within the national territory and a sharp reduction in the frequency of social transactions at the borders are constitutive components. In this view, a nation stands in a mutually constitutive relationship to the nation-state. Consequently, societal denationalization is an indication of the weakening link between 'nation-states

and [their] corresponding national societies' (Beck, 1997: 44; see also Kaufmann, 1997: 119).

5 Still, Zevin concludes in a comprehensive literary review of international financial systems that '... every available descriptor of financial markets in the late nineteenth and early twentieth centuries suggests that they were more fully integrated than they were before or have been since' (1992: 51–2). It may be contested whether this statement still holds true for financial markets today. More importantly, it neglects that in the nineteenth century European imperialism structured openness and the speed of financial transactions was still much slower.

6 See Greven and Pauly, 2000 and Offe, 2000 as well as Scharpf, 1998 for important contributions representing this point of view.

7 See especially Burley and Mattli, 1993 and Alter, 1998 for convincing accounts of how the European Court of Justice was not the outcome of intergovernmental design.

8 The meaning of this term differs from Rosenau's (1992: 5) governance without government, which refers to all politics without a central authority.

Bibliography

Agnew, John A. and Duncan, James S. (1989) *The Power of Place: Bringing Together Geographical and Sociological Imaginations*. Boston: Unwin Hyman.

Albert, Mathias (1996) *Fallen der (Welt-)Ordnung. Internationale Beziehungen und ihre Theorien zwischen Moderne und Postmoderne*. Opladen: Leske & Budrich.

Albert, Mathias, Brock, Lothar and Menzel, Ulrich (1999) *Die neue Weltwirtschaft: Entstofflichung und Entgrenzung der Ökonomie*. Frankfurt-on-Main: Suhrkamp.

Albert, Mathias, Brock, Lothar and Wolf, Klaus-Dieter (eds) (2000) *Civilizing World Politics. Society and Community Beyond the State*. Lanham: Rowman and Littlefield.

Albrow, Martin (1996) *The Global Age. State and Society Beyond Modernity*. Cambridge: Polity.

Alter, Karen J. (1998) 'Who Are the "Masters of the Treaty"? European Governments and the European Court of Justice', *International Organization*, 52 (1): 121–47.

Altvater, Elmar and Mahnkopf, Birgit (1996) *Grenzen der Globalisierung. Ökonomie, Ökologie und Politik in der Weltgesellschaft*. Münster: Westfälisches Dampfboot.

Angell, Robert Cooley (1969) *Peace on the March: Transnational Participation* (New Perspectives in Political Science). New York: van Nostrand Reinhold.

Appadurai, Arjun (1996) *Modernity at Large. Cultural Dimensions of Globalization*. Minneapolis: University of Minnesota Press.

Baldwin, David (1980) 'Interdependence and Power. A Conceptual Analysis', *International Organization*, 34: 471–506.

Barber, Benjamin R. (1995) *Jihad vs. McWorld. How the Planet Is Both Falling Apart and Coming Together and What This Means for Democracy*. New York: Random House.

Barbieri, Katherine (1996) 'Economic Interdependence. A Path to Peace or a Source of Interstate Conflict?', *Journal of Peace Research*, 33 (1): 29–49.

Barro, Robert J. (1996) *Getting it Right: Markets and Choices in a Free Society*. Cambridge, MA: MIT Press.

Beck, Ulrich (1997) *Was ist Globalisierung?*. Frankfurt-on-Main: Suhrkamp.

Beck, Ulrich (ed.) (1998) *Politik der Globalisierung*. Frankfurt-on-Main: Suhrkamp.

Beck, Ulrich (1999) *World Risk Society*. Cambridge: Polity Press.

Beck, Ulrich (2000) *Translegale Herrschaft*. Frankfurt-on-Main: Suhrkamp.

Beisheim, Marianne and Walter, Gregor (1997) '"Globalisierung" – Kinderkrankheiten eines Konzeptes', *Zeitschrift für Internationale Beziehungen*, 4 (1): 153–80.

Beisheim, Marianne, Dreher, Sabine, Walter, Gregor, Zangl, Bernhard and Zürn, Michael (1999) *Im Zeitalter der Globalisierung? Thesen und Daten zur gesellschaftlichen und politischen Denationalisierung*. Baden-Baden: Nomos.

Bernauer, Thomas (2000) *Staaten im Weltmarkt*. Opladen: Leske & Budrich.

Betz, Hans-Georg (1994) *Radical Right-Wing Populism in Western Europe*. Basingstoke: Macmillan.

Brock, Lothar and Albert, Mathias (1995) 'Entgrenzung der Staatenwelt. Zur Analyse weltgesellschaftlicher Entwicklungstendenzen', *Zeitschrift für Internationale Beziehungen*, 2 (2): 259–85.

Bull, Hedley (1977) *The Anarchical Society. A Study of Order in World Politics*. Basingstoke: Macmillan.

Burley, Anne-Marie and Mattli, Walter (1993) 'Europe before the Court: A Political Theory of Legal Integration', *International Organization*, 47 (1): 41–76.

Buzan, Barry, Jones, Charles and Little, Richard (1993) *The Logic of Anarchy. Neorealism to Structural Realism*. New York: Columbia University Press.

Cameron, David R. (1978) 'The Expansion of the Public Economy: A Comparative Analysis', *American Political Science Review*, 72: 1243–61.

Caporaso, James A. (1978) 'Dependence, Dependency, and Power in the Global System. A Structural and Behavioral Analysis', *International Organization*, 32: 13–43.

Cerny, Philip G. (1996) 'What Next for the State?', in Eleonore Kofman and Gillian Youngs (eds), *Globalization: Theory and Practice*. London: Pinter. pp. 123–37.

Clark, Ian (1999) *Globalization and International Relations*. Oxford: Oxford University Press.

Cooper, Richard (1968) *The Economics of Interdependence*. New York: McGraw-Hill.

Cooper, Richard (1986) *Economic Policy in an Interdependent World*. Cambridge, MA: MIT Press.

Corbey, Dorette (1995) 'Dialectical Functionalism: Stagnation as a Booster of European Integration', *International Organization*, 49 (2): 253–84.

Cowles, Maria Green, Risse, Thomas and Caporaso, James (eds) (2001) *Transforming Europe: Europeanization and Domestic Change*. Ithaca: Cornell University Press.

Cox, Robert W. (1997) 'Democracy in Hard Times. Economic Globalization and the Limits to Liberal Democracy', in Anthony McGrew (ed.), *The Transformation of Democracy*. Cambridge: Polity. pp. 49–72.

Czempiel, Ernst-Otto (1986) *Friedensstrategien. Systemwandel durch internationale Organisationen, Demokratisierung und Wirtschaft*. Paderborn: Schöningh.

Dahl, Robert A. (1994) 'A Democratic Dilemma: System Effectiveness versus Citizen Participation', *Political Science Quarterly*, 109 (1): 23–34.

Deutsch, Karl W. (1957) *Political Community and the North Atlantic Area*. Princeton: Princeton University Press.

Deutsch, Karl W. (1969) *Nationalism and its Alternatives*. New York: Alfred A. Knopf.

Deutsch, Karl W. and Eckstein, Alexander (1961) 'National Industrialization and the Declining Share of the International Economic Sector, 1890–1959', *World Politics*, 13 (2): 267–72.

Dorusen, Han (1999) 'Balance of Power Revisited: A Multi-Country Model of Trade and Conflict', *Journal of Peace Research*, 36 (4): 443–62.

Eising, Rainer and Kohler-Koch, Beate (1999) 'Governance in the European Union. A Comparative Assesment', in Beate Kohler-Koch and Rainer Eising (eds), *The Transformation of Governance in the European Union*. London: Routledge. pp. 266–84.

Elkins, David J. (1995) *Beyond Sovereignty. Territory and Political Economy in the Twenty-First Century*. Toronto: University of Toronto Press.

Evans, Peter B., Rueschemeyer, Dietrich and Skocpol, Theda (eds) (1985) *Bringing the State Back In*. Cambridge: Cambridge University Press.

Frankel, Jeffrey A. (1993) *On Exchange Rates*. Cambridge, MA: MIT Press.

Frei, Daniel and Ruloff, Dieter (1988) 'Reassessing East–West Relations: A Macroquantitative Analysis of Trends, Premises and Consequences of East–West Cooperation and Conflict', *International Interactions*, 15 (1): 1–23.

Frieden, Jeffry A. and Rogowski, Ronald (1996) 'The Impact of the International Economy on National Policies: An Analytical Overview', in Robert O. Keohane and Helen V. Milner (eds), *Internationalization and Domestic Politics*. Cambridge: Cambridge University Press. pp. 25–47.

Garrett, Geoffrey (1998a) *Partisan Politics in the Global Economy*. Cambridge: Cambridge University Press.

Garrett, Geoffrey (1998b) 'Global Markets and National Politics: Collision Course or Virtuous Circle?', *International Organization*, 52 (4): 787–824.

Giddens, Anthony (1990) *The Consequences of Modernity*. Stanford: Stanford University Press.

Goldgeier, James M. and McFaul, Michael (1992) 'A Tale of Two Worlds: Core and Periphery in the Post-Cold War Era', *International Organization*, 46 (1): 467–92.

Gourevitch, Peter (1978) 'The Second Image Reversed: The International Sources of Domestic Politics', *International Organization*, 32 (4): 881–912.

Grande, Edgar (2000) 'Postnational Democracy in Europe', in Michael Th. Greven and Louis W. Pauly (eds), *Democracy Beyond National Limits. The European Dilemma and the Emerging Global Order*. Lanham: Rowman and Littlefield. pp. 115–38.

Grande, Edgar and Schneider, Volker (1991) 'Reformstrategien und staatliche Handlungskapazitäten. Eine vergleichende Analyse institutionellen Wandels in der Telekommunikation in Westeuropa', *Politische Vierteljahresschrift*, 32 (3): 452–78.

Greven, Michael Th. and Pauly, Louis W. (eds) (2000) *Democracy Beyond National Limits. The European Dilemma and the Emerging Global Order*. Lanham: Rowman and Littlefield.

Harvey, David (1989) *The Condition of Postmodernity. An Enquiry into the Origins of Cultural Change*. Oxford: Blackwell.

Held, David (1995) *Democracy and the Global Order. From the Modern State to Cosmopolitical Governance*. Cambridge: Polity.

Held, David and McGrew, Anthony G. (1993) 'Globalization and the Liberal Democratic State', *Government and Opposition*, 28 (2): 261–85.

Held, David, McGrew, Anthony, Goldblatt, David and Perraton, Jonathan (1999) *Global Transformations. Politics, Economics and Culture*. Cambridge: Polity.

Helleiner, Eric (1994) *States and the Reemergence of Global Finance. From Bretton Woods to the 1990s*. Ithaca: Cornell University Press.

Helliwell, John F. (1998) *How Much Do National Borders Matter?*, Washington, DC: Brookings Institution.

Héritier, Adrienne, Knill, Christoph and Mingers, Susanne (1996) *Ringing the Changes in Europe: Regulatory Conception and Redefinition of the State. Britain, France, Germany*. Berlin and New York: de Gruyter.

Hirsch, Joachim (1995) *Der nationale Wettbewerbsstaat. Staat, Demokratie und Politik im globalen Kapitalismus*. Berlin and Amsterdam: Edition ID-Archiv.

Hirschi, Christian, Serdült, Uwe and Widmer, Thomas (1999) 'Schweizerische Außenpolitik im Wandel', *Schweizerische Zeitschrift für Politikwissenschaft*, 5 (1): 31–56.

Hirst, Paul and Thompson, Grahame (1996) *Globalization in Question. The International Economy and the Possibilities of Governance*. Cambridge: Polity.

Hobsbawm, Eric J. (1992) *Nations and Nationalism since 1780. Programme, Myth, Reality*, 2nd edn. Cambridge: Cambridge University Press.

Holm, Hans-Henrik and Sørensen, Georg (1995) 'Introduction: What has Changed?', in Hans-Henrik Holm and Georg Sørensen (eds), *Whose World Order? Uneven Globalization and the End of the Cold War*. Boulder: Westview. pp. 1–17.

Holsti, Kalevi J. (1980) 'Change in the International System: Interdependence, Integration and Fragmentation', in Ole R. Holsti, Randolph M. Siverson and Alexander L.

George (eds), *Change in the International System*. Boulder: Westview. pp. 23–53.

Horsman, Mathew and Marshall, Andrew (1995) *After the Nation-State. Citizens, Tribalism and the New World Order*. London: HarperCollins.

Hughes, Barry (1999) *International Futures. Choices in the Face of Uncertainty*. Boulder: Westview.

Hurd, Ian (1999) 'Legitimacy and Authority in International Politics', *International Organization*, 53 (2): 379–408.

Inglehart, Ronald (1997) *Modernization and Post-modernization. Cultural, Economic, and Political Change in 43 Societies*. Princeton: Princeton University Press.

Jachtenfuchs, Markus and Kohler-Koch, Beate (1996) 'Regieren im dynamischen Mehrebenensystem', in Markus Jachtenfuchs and Beate Kohler-Koch (eds), *Europäische Integration*. Opladen: Leske and Budrich. pp. 15–44.

Jänicke, Martin (1998) 'Umweltpolitik: Global am Ende oder am Ende global? Thesen zu ökologischen Determinanten des Weltmarktes', in Ulrich Beck (ed.), *Perspektiven der Weltgesellschaft*. Frankfurt-on-Main: Suhrkamp. pp. 332–44.

Jessop, Bob (1994) 'Post-Fordism and the State', in Ash Amin (ed.), *Post-Fordism. A Reader*. Oxford: Blackwell. pp. 251–79.

Joerges, Christian (1996) 'The Emergence of Denationalized Governance Structures and the European Court of Justice', ARENA Working Paper No. 16, Oslo.

Kahler, Miles (1995) *International Institutions and the Political Economy of Integration*. Washington, DC: Brookings Institution.

Katzenstein, Peter J. (1975) 'International Interdependence: Some Long-term Trends and Recent Changes', *International Organization*, 29: 1021–34.

Katzenstein, Peter J. (ed.) (1978) *Between Power and Plenty. The Foreign Economic Policies of Advanced Industrial States*. Madison: University of Wisconsin Press.

Katzenstein, Peter J. (1985) *Small States in World Markets. Industrial Policy in Europe*. Ithaca and London: Cornell University Press.

Kaufmann, Franz-Xaver (1997) *Herausforderungen des Sozialstaates*. Frankfurt-on-Main: Suhrkamp.

Keohane, Robert (1993) 'Sovereignity, Interdependence and International Institutions', in Linda B. Miller and Michael Joseph Smith (eds), *Ideas and Ideals. Essays on Politics in Honor of Stanley Hoffmann*. Boulder: Westview. pp. 91–107.

Keohane, Robert O. and Nye, Joseph S. (1977) *Power and Interdependence. World Politics in Transition*. Boston and Toronto: Little, Brown.

Keohane, Robert O. and Nye, Joseph S. (2000) 'Globalization: What's New? What's Not? (And so What?)', *Foreign Policy*, 118: 104–19.

Kielmannsegg, Peter Graf (1994) 'Läßt sich die Europäische Gemeinschaft demokratisch verfassen?', *Europäische Rundschau*, 22 (2): 23–33.

Kitschelt, Herbert, Lange, Peter, Marks, Gary and Stephens, John D. (eds) (1999) *Continuity and Change in Contemporary Capitalism*. Cambridge: Cambridge University Press.

Kittel, Bernhard, Obinger, Herbert and Wagschal, Uwe (2000) 'Die "gezügelten" Wohlfahrtsstaaten im Vergleich. Politisch-Institutionelle Faktoren der Entstehung und Entwicklungsdynamik', in Herbert Obinger and Uwe Wagschal (eds), *Der gezügelte Wohlfahrtsstaat. Sozialpolitik in reichen Ländern*. Frankfurt and New York: Campus. pp. 329–64.

Krasner, Stephen D. (1978) *Defending the National Interest. Raw Material Investments and US Foreign Policy*. Princeton: Princeton University Press.

Krasner, Stephen D. (1999) *Sovereignty. Organized Hypocrisy*. Princeton: Princeton University Press.

Krugman, Paul R. (1994) *Peddling Prosperity*. New York: W.W. Norton.

Krugman, Paul R. (1995) 'Growing World Trade. Causes and Consequences', *Brookings Papers on Economic Activity*, (1): 327–62.

Lange, Niels (2000) *Globalisierung und regionaler Nationalismus. Schottland und Québec im Zeitalter der Denationalisierung*. Baden-Baden: Nomos.

Linklater, Andrew (1998) *The Transformation of Political Community: Ethical Foundations of the Post-Westphalian Era*. Cambridge: Polity.

Luhmann, Niklas (1971) 'Die Weltgesellschaft', in Niklas Luhmann, *Soziologische Aufklärung, vol. 2, Aufsätze zur Theorie sozialer Systeme*. Opladen: Westdeutscher Verlag. pp. 51–71.

Marks, Gary, Hooghe, Liesbet and Blank, Kermit (1996) 'European Integration from the 1980s: State Centric vs. Multi-level Governance', *Journal of Common Market Studies*, 34 (3): 341–78.

Martin, Hans-Peter and Schumann, Harald (1997) *Die Globalisierungsfalle. Der Angriff auf Demokratie und Wohlstand*. Reinbek: Rowohlt.

McGrew, Anthony (ed.) (1998) *The Transformation of Democracy*. Cambridge: Polity.

Menzel, Ulrich (1998) *Globalisierung versus Fragmentierung*. Frankfurt-on-Main: Suhrkamp.

Milner, Helen V. (1988) *Resisting Protectionism*. Princeton: Princeton University Press.

Milner, Helen V. (1998) 'Rationalizing Politics: The Emerging Synthesis of International, American, and Comparative Politics', *International Organization*, 52 (4): 759–86.

Milner, Helen V. and Keohane, Robert O. (1996) 'Internationalization and Domestic Politics: An Introduction', in Robert O. Keohane and Helen V. Milner (eds), *Internationalization and Domestic Politics*. Cambridge: Cambridge University Press. pp. 3–24.

Moravcsik, Andrew (1998) *The Choice for Europe. Social Purpose and State Power from Messina to Maastricht*. Ithaca, NY: Cornell University Press.

Morse, Edward L. (1976) *Modernization and the Transformation of International Relations*. New York: The Free Press.

Muir, Ramsey (1932) *The Interdependent World and its Problems*. London: Constable.

Narr, Wolf-Dieter and Schubert, Alexander (1994) *Weltökonomie. Die Misere der Politik*. Frankfurt-on-Main: Suhrkamp.

Offe, Claus (2000) 'The Democratic Welfare State in an Integrating Europe', in Michael Th. Greven and Louis W. Pauly (eds), *Democracy Beyond National Limits. The European Dilemma and the Emerging Global Order*. Lanham: Rowman and Littlefield. pp. 63–89.

Ohmae, Kenichi (1993) 'The Rise of the Regional State', *Foreign Affairs*, 72 (2): 78–87.

Ougaard, Morten and Higgott, Richard (eds) (2001) *Towards a Global Polity*. London: Routledge.

Pauly, Louis W. and Reich, Simon (1997) 'National Structures and Multinational Corporate Behavior: Enduring Differences in the Age of Globalization', *International Organization*, 51 (1): 1–30.

Pijl, Kees van der (1998) *Transnational Classes and International Relations*. London: Routledge.

Piore, Michael J. and Sabel, Charles F. (1989) *Das Ende der Massenproduktion. Studie über die Requalifizierung der Arbeit und die Rückkehr der Ökonomie in die Gesellschaft*. Frankfurt-on-Main: Fischer.

Polachek, Solomon W., Robst, John and Chang, Yuan Ching (1999) 'Liberalism and Interdependence: Extending the Trade-Conflict Model', *Journal of Peace Research*, 36 (4): 405–22.

Polanyi, Karl (1944) *The Great Transformation. The Political and Economic Origins of Our Time*. Boston: Rinehart.

Reinicke, Wolfgang (1998) *Global Public Policy. Governing without Government?* Washington, DC: Brookings Institution.

Reuveny, Rafael and Kang, Heejon (1998) 'Bilateral Trade and Political Conflict/Cooperation. Do Goods Matter?', *Journal of Peace Research*, 35 (5): 581–602.

Rieger, Elmar and Leibfried, Stephan (1997) 'Sozialpolitische Grenzen der Globalisierung. Wohlfahrtsstaatliche Gründe außenwirtschaftlicher Schließung und Öffnung', *Politische Vierteljahresschrift*, 38 (4): 771–96.

Risse, Thomas, Ropp, Stephen C. and Sikkink, Katheryn (eds) (1999) *The Power of Human Rights. International Norms and Domestic Change*. Cambridge: Cambridge University Press.

Rittberger, Volker and Zangl, Bernhard (1995) *Internationale Organisationen. Politik und Geschichte*, 2nd edn. Opladen: Leske & Budrich.

Robertson, Roland (1992) *Globalization. Social Theory and Global Culture*. London and Beverly Hills: Sage.

Rodrik, Dani (1997) *Has Globalization Gone too Far?* Washington, DC: Institute for International Economics.

Rosecrance, Richard, Alexandroff, Alan, Koehler, Wallace, Kroll, John, Laqueur, Shlomit and Stocker, John (1977) 'Whither Interdependence?', *International Organization*, 31 (3): 425–72.

Rosecrance, Richard and Stein, Arthur (1973) 'Interdependence: Myth or Reality?', *World Politics*, 26 (1): 1–27.

Rosenau, James N. (1986) 'Before Cooperation. Hegemons, Regimes and Habit-Driven Actors in World Politics', *International Organization*, 40 (4): 849–94.

Rosenau, James N. (1990) *Turbulence in World Politics. A Theory of Change and Continuity*. Princeton: Harvester Wheatsheaf.

Rosenau, James N. (1992) 'Governance, Order and Change in World Politics', in James N. Rosenau and Ernst Otto Czempiel (eds), *Governance without Government: Order and Change in World Politics*. Cambridge: Cambridge University Press. pp. 1–29.

Rosenau, James N. (1997) *Along the Domestic–Foreign Frontier. Exploring Governance in a Turbulent World*. Cambridge: Cambridge University Press.

Ruggie, John Gerard (1983) 'International Regimes, Transactions, and Change: Embedded Liberalism in the Postwar Economic Order', in Stephen Krasner (ed.), *International Regimes*. Ithaca: Cornell University Press. pp. 195–231.

Russett, Bruce, Oneal, John and Davis, David R. (1998) 'The Third Leg of the Kantian Tripod for Peace: International Organizations and Militarized Disputes, 1950–1985', *International Organization*, 52 (3): 441–67.

Scharpf, Fritz W. (1987) *Sozialdemokratische Krisenpolitik in Europa*. Frankfurt-on-Main and New York: Campus.

Scharpf, Fritz W. (1993) 'Legitimationsprobleme der Globalisierung. Regieren in Verhandlungssystemen', in Carl Böhret and Göttrik Wewer (eds), *Regieren im 21. Jahrhundert – Zwischen Globalisierung und Regionalisierung. Festgabe für Hans Hermann Hartwich*. Opladen: Leske & Budrich. pp. 165–85.

Scharpf, Fritz W. (1996) 'Negative and Positive Integration in the Political Economy of European Welfare States', in Gary Marks, Fritz W. Scharpf, Philippe C. Schmitter and Wolfgang Streeck (eds), *Governance in the European Union*. London: Sage. pp. 15–39.

Scharpf, Fritz W. (1998) 'Demokratische Politik in der internationalisierten Ökonomie', in Michael Th. Greven (ed.), *Demokratie – eine Kultur des Westens? 20. Wissenschaftlicher Kongreß der Deutschen Vereinigung für Politische Wissenschaft*. Opladen: Leske and Budrich. pp. 81–103.

Scharpf, Fritz W. (1999) *Governing in Europe*. Oxford: Oxford University Press.

Schmalz-Bruns, Rainer (1998) 'Grenzerfahrungen und Grenzüberschreitungen: Demokratie im integrierten Europa', in Beate Kohler-Koch (ed.), *Regieren in entgrenzten Räumen* (PVS Sonderheft 29/1998). Opladen: Westdeutscher Verlag. pp. 369–80.

Schmalz-Bruns, Rainer (1999) 'Deliberativer Supranationalismus. Demokratisches Regieren jenseits des Nationalstaats', *Zeitschrift für internationale Beziehungen*, 6 (2): 185–245.

Schmidtke, Oliver (1996) *Politics of Identity. Ethnicity, Territories, and the Political Opportunity Structure in Modern Italian Society*. Sinzheim: Pro Universitate.

Seeleib-Kaiser, Martin (2000) 'Globalisierung, politische Diskurse und Wohlfahrtssysteme. Die Bundesrepublik Deutschland, Japan und die USA im Vergleich'. Habilitationsschrift, Universität Bremen.

Senghaas, Dieter (1994) 'Interdependenzen im Internationalen System', in Gert Krell and Harald Müller (eds), *Frieden und Konflikt in den internationalen Beziehungen*. Frankfurt-am-Main: Campus. pp. 190–222.

Senghaas, Dieter (1998) *Zivilisierung wider Willen*. Frankfurt-on-Main: Suhrkamp.

Shanks, Cheryl, Jacobson, Harold K. and Kaplan, Jeffrey H. (1996) 'Inertia and Change in the Constellation of International Governmental Organizations, 1981–1992', *International Organization*, 50 (4): 593–629.

Singer, Max and Wildavsky, Aaron (1993) *The Real World Order*. Chatham: Chatham House Publication.

Slaughter, Anne-Marie (1997) 'The Real New World Order', *Foreign Affairs*, 76 (5): 183–97.

Smith, Anthony D. (1979) *Nationalism in the Twentieth Century*. Oxford: Martin Robertson.

Strange, Susan (1996) *The Retreat of the State. The Diffusion of Power in the World Economy*. Cambridge: Cambridge University Press.

Tilly, Charles (1984) *Big Structures, Large Processes, Huge Comparisons*. New York: Russell Sage Foundation.

Vogel, David (1995) *Trading up. Consumer and Environmental Regulation in a Global Economy*. Cambridge, MA: Harvard University Press.

Vogel, Steven K. (1996) *Freer Markets, More Rules: Regulatory Reform in Advanced Industrial Countries*. Ithaca: Cornell University Press.

Waltz, Kenneth N. (1979) *Theory of International Politics*. New York: McGraw–Hill.

Walzer, Michael (1983) *Spheres of Justice*. New York: Basic Books.

Weiss, Linda (1998) *The Myth of the Powerless State. Governing the Economy in a Global Era*. Cambridge: Polity.

Wiener, Antje (1998) *European Citizenship Practise – Building Institutions of a Non-State*. Boulder: Westview.

Wiener, Antje (1999) 'The Constructive Potential of Citizenship: Building the European Union', *Policy and Politics*, 27 (4): 271–93.

Wilde, Jaap de (1991) *Saved from Oblivion: Interdependence Theory in the First Half of the 20th Century. A Study on the Causality Between War and Complex Interdependence*. Aldershot: Dartmouth.

Wolf, Klaus Dieter (2000) *Die neue Staatsräson – Zwischenstaatliche Kooparation als Demokratieproblem in der Weltgesellschaft*. Baden- Baden: Nomos.

Woods, Dwayne (1992) 'The Centre No Longer Holds: The Rise of Regional Leagues in Italian Politics', *West European Politics*, 15 (2): 56–76.

Wriston, Walter (1986) *Risk and Other Four Letter Words*. New York: Harper & Row.

Zacher, Mark W. with Brent A. Sutton (1996) *Governing Global Networks. International Regimes for Transportation and Communication*. Cambridge: Cambridge University Press.

Zevin, Robert B. (1992) 'Are World Financial Markets More Open? If So, Why and With Which Effects?', in Tariq Banuri and Juliet B. Schor (eds), *Financial Openness and National Autonomy*. Oxford: Clarendon Press. pp. 43–83.

Zürn, Michael (1992) 'Jenseits der Staatlichkeit', *Leviathan*, 20 (4): 490–513.

Zürn, Michael (1995) 'The Challenge of Globalization and Individualization: A View From Europe', in Hans-Henrik Holm and Georg Sørensen (eds), *Whose World Order*. Boulder: Westview. pp. 43–68.

Zürn, Michael (1998) *Regieren jenseits des Nationalstaates. Denationalisierung und Globalisierung als Chance*. Frankfurt-on-Main: Suhrkamp.

Zürn, Michael (2000) 'Democracy Beyond the Nation State', *European Journal of International Relation*, 6 (2): 183–221.

Zürn, Michael and Lange, Niels (2000) 'Regionalism in the Age of Globalization', InIIS-Working Paper 16/99, Bremen.

Zürn, Michael, Walter, Gregor, Dreher, Sabine and Beisheim, Marianne (2000) 'Postnationale Politik? Über den politischen Umgang mit den Denationalisierungsherausforderungen Internet, Klima und Migration', *Zeitschrift für Internationale Beziehungen*, 7 (2): 297–329.

13

Transnational Actors and World Politics

THOMAS RISSE

The end of the Cold War and globalization processes have led to renewed interest in the study of transnational relations and the impact of non-state actors on world politics. Some authors praise the emergence of a global transnational civil society (Boli and Thomas, 1999; Florini, 2000; Held et al., 1999), while others denounce an increasing transnational capitalist hegemony (Gill, 1995). Both positions ascribe to non-state actors quite an extraordinary influence on outcomes in international politics. It is certainly true that transnational actors – from multinational corporations (MNCs) to International Non-Governmental Organizations (INGOs) – have left their mark on the international system and that we cannot even start theorizing about the contemporary world system without taking their influence into account. But there is little systematic evidence to sustain claims that the transnational 'society world' has somehow over-taken the 'state world' (see Czempiel, 1991, on these notions). Rather than analyzing transnational and inter-state relations in zero-sum terms, it is more useful to study their interactions and inter-penetration. As Reinicke put it, 'governing the global economy *without* governments is not an option. Yet for global governance to succeed, governments will also have to enlist the active cooperation of nonstate actors' (Reinicke, 1998: 219). The following review of the literature tries to substantiate this point.

'Transnational relations' is a rather elusive concept. If we take the 1971 definition by Keohane and Nye referring to 'regular interactions across national boundaries when at least one actor is a non-state agent …' (Keohane and Nye, 1971b: xii–xvi), the concept encompasses anything as long

as human agency is involved. Yet, cross-border capital flows, international trade, CNN media broadcasts, international migration, cross-border tourism, the diffusion of values and norms, trans-national social movements, INGOs and MNCs are quite different phenomena. It is impossible to theo-rize about them in any systematic sense. This chapter does not deal with transnational relations in general, but more specifically with transnational organizations and actors with a particular purpose. This refinement still comprises a wide range of regularized transnational relationships, from infor-mal networks exchanging material and/or ideational resources to INGOs and large organizations such as MNCs. Some transnational actors operate globally, for example, the Catholic Church, the International Committee of the Red Cross (ICRC), Amnesty International, Daimler–Chrysler, while others are confined to specific regions of the world (such as the European Environmental Bureau, Asia Watch, or the European Trade Union Confederation). Some transnational actors concentrate on a single issue (such as the transnational campaign to ban land-mines), while others follow a multipurpose mission, such as religious organizations.

This chapter distinguishes among transnational actors along two dimensions. The first dimension concerns their internal structure. Some transnational actors are formal organizations (from multinational corporations to INGOs). Others are connected in a far more loose fashion for which I use the term 'net-work', defined as 'forms of organization character-ized by voluntary, reciprocal, and horizontal patterns of communication' (Keck and Sikkink, 1998: 8).[1] Some networks simply consist of groups of indivi-duals, others comprise formal organizations.

'Epistemic communities', for example, are networks of individuals and/or organizations based on authoritative claims to consensual knowledge (Haas, 1992b). Advocacy networks comprise actors who share specific values, principled beliefs and a common discourse (Keck and Sikkink, 1998: 2).

The second dimension which is relevant for this chapter differentiates between the motivations of various types of transnational actors. Some, such as MNCs or transnational special interest groups, are primarily motivated by *instrumental* goals and try to promote the well-being of the organization itself or the members of the group. Others, such as INGOs, epistemic communities or advocacy networks are primarily motivated by promoting a perceived 'common good'. This differentiation roughly coincides with the distinction between the 'for profit' and the 'not for profit' sector as frequently found in the literature. However, it is useful to think of this distinction as a continuum rather than sharply divided classes of actors. The business-sponsored Global Climate Coalition certainly proclaims that it promotes the international public good, while some (I)NGOs seek to make a profit in the humanitarian action sector.

This chapter proceeds in the following steps. I begin with a brief intellectual history of theorizing about transnational relations in world politics. I conclude from this survey that constructing dichotomies between a society-centered and a state-dominated view of international relations is misleading and distracts from interesting research questions. The main parts of the chapter examine the mutual relationship and interaction between the inter-state world, on the one hand, and the transnational world, on the other. I next deal with transnational actors and networks as 'dependent variables'. How do states, their institutional structures, as well as their international relations, affect transnational actors, their characteristics and their strategies? The following section changes perspective and looks at the impact of transnational actors and networks on world politics. This is the realm where most empirical research has been carried out in recent years and where we can make some empirically informed theoretical statements. The chapter concludes with some remarks on emerging public–private governance structures comprising states, international organizations and transnational actors.

INTERNATIONAL RELATIONS AND TRANSNATIONAL ACTORS: AN INTELLECTUAL HISTORY

Neither transnational relations nor theorizing about them started in the post-Second World War era. Multinational corporations with dispersed investments and productions across several political

jurisdictions date back at least to the medieval era. During the Renaissance era, 'family businesses' such as the Medicis in Florence or the Fuggers in Augsburg held huge investments and production facilities across Europe and had agents in India and China by the end of the sixteenth century (Krasner, 1999: 221). From the sixteenth century onwards, the trading companies of the imperial powers such as the British East India Company and the Hudson Bay Company operated across continents (Held et al., 1999: 238–9). Similar observations hold true for advocacy groups bound together by principled ideas and values. Precursors to modern transnational networks in the human rights and women's rights areas include the campaign to end slavery in the United States during the early to mid-1900s (Kaufmann and Pape, 1999), the international suffrage movement to secure the vote for women in the late nineteenth century, as well as the campaigns by Western missionaries and Chinese reformers to end the practice of footbinding in China during the same period (Keck and Sikkink, 1998: ch. 2). While these early transnational movements did not enjoy modern communications technologies such as the Internet, their strategies were remarkably similar and sometimes no less effective than those of their modern successors. Krasner concludes, therefore, that rulers 'have always operated in a transnational environment; autarky has rarely been an option; regulation and monitoring of transborder flows have always been problematic' (Krasner, 1999: 223).

If the phenomenon of transnational actors is not particularly new, theorizing about them also has its precursors. Yet, scholarship on transnational relations during the eighteenth and nineteenth centuries was much more normative and prescriptive than analytical and descriptive. Take Immanuel Kant, for example. His 1795 'Perpetual Peace', which has become the mantra of today's literature on the democratic peace, contains ideas on transnational relations (Kant, [1795] 1983). His statement that the 'spirit of trade cannot coexist with war, and sooner or later this spirit dominates every people' (Kant, [1795] 1983: 125 [368]) has been among the first claims about the causal relationship between economic interdependence and world peace. Long before modern human rights treaties proclaimed individuals as subjects of international law, Kant postulated a right of foreigners to hospitality against the government of their host state. Kant's cosmopolitanism was rather common among liberal intellectuals during the late eighteenth and nineteenth centuries. The modern literature on the democratic peace has largely lost this connection between a democratic society, transnationalism and peace. Yet, liberals such as Tocqueville argued that transnational relations, that is, links among democratic societies of different countries and its citizens, constituted a primary tool to prevent wars: 'As the spread of equality, taking place in several countries at once, simultaneously draws the inhabitants into trade and industry, not only do their tastes become to be alike, but their interests become so mixed and entangled that no nation can inflict on others ills which will not fall back on its own head' (Tocqueville, 1994: 660).

While these scholars related the democratic organizations of polities, transnationalism and peace, liberal writers of the nineteenth century such as Adam Smith or John Stuart Mill took up Kant's ideas about free trade and peace. Yet, the First World War, which was fought among highly interdependent nations, discredited the idea that economic interdependence alone is a sufficient condition for peace in the absence of democracy. Schumpeter's *Sociology of Imperialism* constitutes perhaps the most elaborate statement of the interwar period on the causal relationship between liberal capitalism, economic interdependence and peace. He argued that the essence of capitalism is anti-imperialist, but recognized that capitalist states might pursue aggressive foreign policies if they are usurped by particular economic interests (Schumpeter, [1919] 1953). Schumpeter reacted primarily to Marxist theories of imperialism, particularly Lenin's writings, who claimed exactly the opposite, namely that imperialist wars resulted from the externalization of the internal class struggles toward the outside world and the eternal capitalist striving for new markets and profit-making. Lenin argued that wars among capitalist states were inevitable in a stage of development 'in which the dominance of monopoly and finance capital has established himself' (Lenin, [1917] 1939: 89). The controversy about the precise relationship between economic interests, capitalism and economic interdependence, on the one hand, and aggressive/imperialist foreign policies as well as peace and war, on the other, continues until today.

With the emergence of international relations as a social science discipline, scholars increasingly employed analytical rather than purely normative arguments. Mitrany, the founder of modern functionalism and integration theories, argued, in 1943 that technology and technical issues confronting the industrialized democracies in the twentieth century necessitated international cooperation along functional lines. Organizations for functional collaboration would eventually overcome the political institutions of the past including the nation-state (Mitrany, [1943] 1966). After the Second World War, regional integration theory and, particularly, neofunctionalism (Haas, 1958) reformulated the argument claiming that rational economic behavior not only leads to transnational interdependence, but also to the creation of supranational institutions as stable peace orders such as the European Community. It is important to note here that (neo)functionalism never fell into the trap of later theorizing about transnational relations

which created a dichotomy and adverse relationship between a 'society-centered' and 'state-dominated' perspective on world politics. Rather, the argument was about – in today's terms – the emergence of international institutions and supranational governance structures resulting from, responding to, and facilitating transnational interactions of private actors.

This also holds true for another version of integration theory, one of the most important predecessors of today's constructivism, the analysis of transnational and supranational community-building by Karl W. Deutsch and his colleagues (Deutsch et al., 1957). Deutsch argued that increasing transaction flows and crossborder communication as facilitated by trade, migration, tourism, educational exchanges and the like, lead to a sense of community among people and to collective identification processes. 'Pluralistic security communities', while retaining the legal sovereignty of their member states, possess a 'compatibility of core values derived from common institutions, and mutual responsiveness – a matter of mutual identity and loyalty, a sense of "we-ness", and are integrated to the point that they entertain "dependable expectations of peaceful change"' (Adler and Barnett, 1998b: 7, quoting Deutsch et al., 1957: 5). In line with the behavioralist orientation of the time, Deutsch and his colleagues measured transnational transactions quantitatively and compared them to the transaction flows inside the countries in order to determine the degree of international community-building. Deutsch's work in this area was largely ignored until recently when constructivist scholars picked up and reformulated his insights (see, e.g., Adler and Barnett, 1998a).

In the meantime, the question of transnational relations was relegated to the sidelines of theorizing on either side of the Atlantic. Explicit analytical work on transnational actors and relations started during the late 1960s and early 1970s, both in the United States and in Europe (Cooper, 1968; Vernon, 1971). In 1969, the flagship journal of the German Political Science Association *Politische Vierteljahresschrift* published a special issue entitled '*Die anachronistische Souveränität*' (anachronistic sovereignty) which contained an essay on 'transnational politics' (Kaiser, 1969). Two years later, the journal *International Organization* followed suit with a special issue edited by Keohane and Nye on 'Transnational Relations and World Politics' (Keohane and Nye, 1971a; see also Huntington, 1973; Keohane and Nye, 1977; Rosenau, 1980). These and other works challenged the state-dominated view of world politics. Rosenau in particular attacked the state-centered paradigm of international relations theory promoting the 'transnationalization of world politics', a subject to which he came back ten years later (Rosenau, 1990).

This early literature was theoretically inspired by a broader critique of the concept of the state in political theory and in comparative politics. Liberal pluralist theories defined political systems functionally in terms of the authoritative allocation of values in a given society. Societal interest groups and organizations substantially constrained political actors and the political process was largely conceptualized by conflict and bargaining among these societal groups. The work on transnational relations of the late 1960s and early 1970s transposed pluralist theory to the level of international affairs. But this work did not produce a theory of transnational politics in the sense of testable propositions. It focused on the international political economy, in particular the rise of multinational corporations in the post-Second World War era. INGOs and other transnational actors were not yet the subject of systematic inquiry (see, however, Huntington, 1973; Vallier, 1971). One of the first volumes explicitly dealing with INGOs used the term 'pressure groups' suggesting an analysis commensurate with the study of interest groups (Willetts, 1982).

The 1970s also saw a revival of critical political economy attacking transnational economic relations in general and the role of multinational corporations in particular with regard to the North–South relationship. Dependency theory argued against liberal free trade economists that underdevelopment results from the structural dependency and the integration of the developing world in the world economy. MNCs in particular were seen as the main agents preventing the development of an endogenous industry in Southern countries, transferring their profits from the South to the North and exploiting cheap labor in the developing world (see, for example, Amin, 1977; Emmanuel, 1972; Frank, 1967). Dependency theory constituted the first major contribution to the subject of transnational relations by Latin American, African and Asian scholars, even though most of its propositions could not be confirmed empirically (see, for example, Caporaso, 1978; Menzel, 1992; see also Maxfield, Chapter 24 in this volume).

But liberal arguments about transnational relations of the 1960s and 1970s claiming an end of the state-centered view of world politics, did not survive the counter-attack of realism, either. In the 1971 'Transnational Relations and World Politics' volume, Gilpin had already argued against the liberal grain that MNCs were primarily an instrument of American foreign policy and power, not the other way round (Gilpin, 1971, 1975). The late 1970s and early 1980s then saw a revival of (neo)realist theory (Waltz, 1979). Hegemonic stability theory was the realist response to the liberal interdependence arguments.

The result was rather profound, particularly in the United States. Ruggie, Keohane and Nye had originally theorized about international regimes by arguing that economic interdependence led to increased inter-state conflicts to be regulated by international institutions (Keohane and Nye, 1977; Ruggie, 1975). This connection between transnationalism and international institution-building was mostly lost during the early 1980s when regime analysis and neoliberal institutionalism took off. The main controversy between neorealism and neoliberal institutionalism concerned the prospects of 'cooperation under anarchy', that is, of cooperation among states (cf. Baldwin, 1993). In Europe, a state-of-the-art volume of the German-speaking international relations community did not bother to deal with transnational relations, except for a sharp critique of the disappointing accomplishments of the interdependence literature (Kohler-Koch, 1990; see also Zürn, Chapter 12 in this volume).

Two developments of the late 1980s re-opened intellectual space for theorizing about the cross-border activities of non-state actors in the United States and Europe. First, the late 1980s saw the beginning of what would later be called constructivism or sociological institutionalism in international relations (Kratochwil, 1989; Kratochwil and Ruggie, 1986; Wendt, 1987). Kratochwil, Ruggie and Wendt drew attention to the social and ideational rather than simply material structure of international relations (for the most comprehensive statement see Wendt, 1999). Second, the end of the Cold War should not be underestimated in its impact on international relations theorizing. The failure of traditional international relations theory to at least recognize some underlying trends, pushed many scholars away from structuralist theories such as realism and state-centered institutionalism to a renewed appreciation of domestic politics, on the one hand, and of transnational relations, on the other.

As a result of these two developments, the 1990s saw a revival of theorizing about transnational actors, a trend that was further enhanced by the debate on 'globalization'. First, Rosenau's book on 'Turbulence in World Politics' constituted a sweeping statement on post-international politics marked by a 'bifurcation in which the state-centric system now coexists with an equally powerful, though more decentralized, multi-centric system' characterized by transnational 'sovereignty-free actors' (Rosenau, 1990: 11; also Rosenau, 1997). Second, a 1992 special issue of *International Organization* elaborated the notion of transnational 'epistemic communities', defined as networks among professionals with an authoritative claim to policy-relevant knowledge (Haas, 1992c). The authors used constructivist work on socialization, cognitive evolution and learning in order to theorize about the relationship between consensual knowledge and power (Adler and Haas, 1992). Third, a 1995 volume (Risse-Kappen, 1995b) argued that the impact of transnational actors on outcomes depends on the domestic structures of the polity to be affected and the extent to which transnational actors operate in an environment regulated by international institutions. Fourth, Keck and Sikkink elaborated the concept of transnational advocacy networks and explored their impact in the human rights and environmental spheres (Keck and Sikkink, 1998). Finally, Reinicke's book on 'global public policy' represents one of the first attempts to systematically analyze governance networks involving public and private actors on the international level (Reinicke, 1998).

Compared to the attempts of the 1970s, these latest moves at thinking about non-state actors in world politics share three characteristics:

1 While the empirical literature on transnational relations of the 1970s largely concentrated on MNCs, this focus on the international political economy is now taken over by the literature on globalization (see Chapter 12 by Zürn in this volume). The new transnationalism of the 1990s concentrates more thoroughly on the transnational non-profit sector, such as 'epistemic communities', value-based advocacy networks, INGOs and cross-border social movements.
2 The recent literature is much more about the *inter-action* between states and transnational society than about *replacing* a state-centered view with a society-dominated perspective. One indicator of this trend is the increasing replacement of traditional regime analysis with its focus on inter-state institutions by a 'governance without government' perspective emphasizing non-hierarchical networks among public and transnational actors (see, for example, Cutler et al., 1999; Czempiel and Rosenau, 1992; Kaul et al., 1999; Kohler-Koch, 1998b; O'Brien et al., 2000).
3 As mentioned above, constructivism and sociological institutionalism have influenced recent work on transnational relations. This has resulted in work focusing on transnational actors promoting and diffusing causal knowledge (epistemic communities) and norms (advocacy networks). As to critical theory, neo-Gramscianism and its contribution to the literature on the international political economy has to be mentioned (e.g. Cox and Sinclair, 1996; Gill, 1993).

In the following, I discuss the recent work on transnational actors (TNAs) in more detail. I begin with the impact of the 'inter-state world' on the 'transnational society world'.

THE IMPACT OF THE INTER-STATE WORLD ON TNAs

The nation-state system and its structuration of the world along territorially defined boundaries has a profound impact on both the nature and the activities of TNAs. The very concept of *transnational* relations implies an international system composed of nation-states as well as the distinction between state and societal actors within a given nation-state. It makes little sense to talk about transnational actors in a world of empires or in a medieval world of cross-cutting authority structures. However, most empirical work on TNAs remains rather unidirectional by looking at the impact of TNAs on inter-state relations, international organizations and international institutions in general. We know rather little about states and international organizations enabling and/or constraining TNA activities.

TNAs as Instruments of National Governments and International Organizations

On the one end of the theoretical spectrum are those (realists) for whom the growth of transnational relations in the contemporary international system essentially reflects the interests of the most powerful states. Gilpin developed this argument most eloquently, namely that it was US post-war foreign policy and the US hegemony in the international political economy that enabled the rise of MNCs and economic interdependence in the first place (Gilpin, 1971, 1975). To ask the counterfactual, would we still experience economic globalization if Adolf Hitler had won the Second World War?

Gilpin's argument shows some similarities with the claims by critical theorists such as Cox, even though the causal mechanism is different. Cox argued that post-Second World War American hegemony arose from a confluence of three factors, the hegemony of US capitalism and its particular mode of production, the power of the US state, and the consensual nature of Western liberal ideas (Cox, 1987; Cox and Sinclair, 1996). Cox concluded that US hegemony enabled the rise of transnational (economic) relations in the post-war era in the first place. From a liberal perspective, Nye argued in a similar fashion that the days of American hegemony in the world system are far from over, even though its economic preponderance has gone. US 'soft' power and the hegemony of US economic, political and cultural ideas continue to secure the current world order (Nye, 1990).

One could develop this argument further and point out that the international free trade order – from the GATT to the World Trade Organization (WTO) – and other international institutions which are ultimately based on inter-state agreements both enable and constrain transnational interactions by regulating them. The legal framework provided by states and international institutions has, thus, constitutive effects on transnational actors and relations. The international refugee regime, for example, defines refugees and their rights in the first place.

While Gilpin's work focuses on the international political economy, a similar argument has emerged in security studies. Thomson argued in a historical study that state rulers in thirteenth century Europe began authorizing the international use of force by private armies (privateers, mercenaries etc.) in order to accumulate power and wealth (Thomson, 1994). When the unintended consequences of this privatization of international violence became obvious, rulers of the eighteenth and nineteenth centuries struggled against pirates and mercenaries in order to (re)gain the monopoly of the international use of force. The modern state monopoly over the means of internal and external violence did not fall from heaven, but resulted from a sustained conflict between states and TNAs which the states ultimately won (see, however, the rise of global terrorism, of piracy in East Asia and of private armies in 'failed states').

In sum, these authors share the view that state power and state foreign policies gave rise to contemporary transnational relations (and globalization, one might add) where it suited their interests, but viciously fought these transnational forces when it did not. Realists would conclude that, when powerful states are pitched against transnational actors, even mighty ones, the former usually win over the latter (overview in Krasner, 1995b: 267–76). This latter assertion, however, does not follow from recognizing state power and international institutions as enabling transnational relations and has been challenged by the recent literature on TNAs.

The question concerning TNAs as instruments of state power must also be asked with regard to the non-profit sector of INGOs and transnational advocacy networks. Unfortunately, there is little empirical work available in this area. Some preliminary observations can be made, though. First, INGOs by and large originated in the Western industrialized world and they are extremely unevenly spread across the world regions. 'The global stratification structure is clearly reproduced in INGO participation. Residents of resource-rich, technically developed, older, formally democratic Anglo-European countries participate the most; residents of poor, less developed, newer, less democratic countries participate the least' (Boli et al., 1999: 69). Does the INGO world then represent a 'global civil society' (Wapner, 1996) or does it merely reproduce Western enlightenment values such as universalism, individualism, progress and cosmopolitanism? INGOs as part and parcel of a 'world culture' dominated by Western liberal hegemony?

Second, many INGOs are more directly dependent on the 'state world' than many of them would admit. Particularly in the issue-areas of international development and humanitarian aid, funding for the grassroot activities of INGOs originates to a large extent from public sources. According to the World Bank, public funding for development

(I)NGOs increased from 1.5 per cent of their total income in the early 1970s to 30 per cent in the mid-1990s. Some scholars estimate that the dependency of Southern NGOs on public funding by states or International Organizations reaches 80–90 per cent (according to Hulme and Edwards, 1997a: 6–7). The percentage of EU relief aid channeled through INGOs rose from 47 to 67 per cent from 1990 to 1994. Even in the human rights area where one would expect most INGOs to be heavily critical of state policies, more than half of the organizations claimed to have received public funding (Smith et al., 1998). In the context of the European Union (EU), it has been frequently pointed out that the European Commission both created and funded many transnational organizations in order to be able to deal with societal interests on a European rather than on the various national levels (Greenwood and Aspinwall, 1998; Kohler-Koch, 1994).

TNA dependence on the resources of states and international organizations suggests that it would be preposterous to claim that the INGO world simply represents global civil society *against* the interstate system. Transnational advocacy groups and epistemic communities often perform tasks that states and international organizations either cannot or do not want to carry out. In the issue-areas of foreign and humanitarian aid, states and International Organizations often subcontract (I)NGOs, because these groups are less bureaucratic, more flexible and can reach those in need of assistance more easily. The World Bank and other organizations have long recognized that strengthening civil society in the developing world through INGO networks contributes to political, economic and social development. In the human rights and environmental areas, transnational actors provide monitoring capacities and supply information to states and international organizations which would otherwise not be available because of concerns about sovereignty rights. In the international economy, states have delegated regulatory authority to transnational private actors, for example, in international standard setting, because they can carry out these tasks more efficiently (Cutler et al., 1999). Last but not least, taking the concerns of INGOs on board also increases the legitimacy of international institutions such as the World Bank or the International Monetary Fund (O'Brien et al., 2000). As Forsythe argued in the mid-1970s with regard to the International Committee of the Red Cross (ICRC), it cooperates with and, therefore, stabilizes the state system in war-making (see Forsythe, 1976).

In sum, transnational advocacy groups and INGOs should not be seen as necessarily in opposition to the inter-state system. Rather, their work often conforms to the interests of states and international organizations. But little is known as to how the increasing role of the INGO world in global governance affects these groups themselves in terms of their institutional structures, and strategies (see the contributions in Edwards and Hulme, 1996; Hulme and Edwards, 1997b). For example, the growing involvement of INGOs in partnerships with IOs might alienate them from their own social base in civil society (Finger, 1994). INGOs working with the World Bank, the IMF, or the WTO, for example, need to moderate their goals considerably, since they have to accept the principal goal of liberalization in order to promote human rights and environmental concerns effectively (O'Brien et al., 2000: 224). This might then lead to increasing tension between more radical transnational social movements and more 'professional' and moderate INGOs.

Institutional Similarities Between TNAs and Structures of Governance

The works discussed so far adopt an actor-centered perspective to discuss the influence of state governments and international institutions on TNAs. The question was how state actors impact upon transnational actors and how the latter actually perform functions which states or international organizations cannot or are unwilling to carry out. A second, though even less-developed argument takes a more structural perspective and asks how institutional features of states or international regimes and organizations – that is, domestic and international 'structures of governance' – impact upon institutional characteristics of transnational actors. Krasner, for example, took a sociological institutionalist perspective and argued that the 'institutional structures of transnational actors must reflect the institutional environment within which they function' (Krasner, 1995b: 260). Domestic laws, for example, constitute a strong tool forcing transnational actors to adjust their institutional structures to the country in which they operate. As a result, US Honda looks different from its Japanese mother company, even though it is still institutionally different from General Motors or Ford. While the Catholic Church constitutes a quintessential transnational organization which preceded the modern state system, it still had to adjust to the domestic structure of the state in which it operates (see Vallier, 1971). Church–state relations in, say, Germany where the churches enjoy quasi-public status, differ profoundly from the United States where the Catholic Church is treated like any private organization.

Doremus and others have carried this line of argument further (Doremus et al., 1998) by investigating the internal structure and activities of MNCs operating out of Germany, Japan and the United States (see also Pauly and Reich, 1997). They claim that the current talk of 'global corporations' and 'global players' constitutes an, albeit powerful, myth: 'Despite intensifying international competition, MNCs are not promoting the ineluctable convergence and integration of national systems of innovation, trade, and investment, nor are they forcing deep convergence in the national economies in which they are embedded. They cannot do so because they themselves are not converging toward global behavioral norms' (Doremus et al., 1998: 3). Globally operating MNCs do not at all look alike, but maintain distinct institutional features pertaining to their organizational structure and culture which originate from the national institutional environment in which the mother company operates.

If these claims hold true for private transnational actors such as MNCs that command powerful economic resources, similar arguments should be relevant for INGOs and the transnational non-profit sector. To begin with, states and national governments control access to a territory. Moreover, transnational actors operate in institutional environments which are largely determined by the domestic structures of nation-states. Amnesty International in the United States has to abide by different laws than, say, Amnesty International in Germany. As a result, their internal organizational structures are likely to diverge, at least to some extent.

International institutions are also likely to shape organizational features of transnational actors. The EU, for example, represents an international governance structure which has given rise to particular forms of transnational interest organization. The European Commission has actively encouraged the formation of transnational organizations in Brussels, both traditional interest groups and not-for-profit INGOs. The result is a rather pluralist structure of interest organization at the EU level, in contrast to more corporatist structures with strong peak organizations in some member states (see, for example, Kohler-Koch, 1994; Greenwood and Aspinwall, 1998).

Finally, international rule structures such as norms embedded in treaties and international regimes provide an enabling environment for transnational network activities. Take the human rights area, for example. The emerging legalization of the international human rights regime went hand in hand with an increasing professionalization and even bureaucratization of INGOs such as Amnesty International or Human Rights Watch. They changed their character from transnational social movements to professional organizations employing a large staff of lawyers, media experts and country specialists. Yet, the empirical evidence on how institutional structures of the polities – both national and international – in which TNAs operate shapes the latter's organizational structures and cultures remains sketchy at best. Most of the empirical work so far has concentrated on the question of how and under what conditions TNAs of various sorts have managed to affect the nation-state, international institutions and international organizations. The realist and state-centered legacy in international relations theory required that scholars first established that TNAs mattered before they could study how domestic and international institutions shaped the organizational structures of INGOs and the like. Such work could, for example, draw on the literature on 'political opportunity structures' which originated from scholarship on social movements, but has reached work on transnational actors rather recently (e.g. Thomas, 2002; on 'political opportunity structures' see Kitschelt, 1986; Tarrow, 1996).

THE IMPACT OF TNAs ON WORLD POLITICS

So far, I have discussed the literature with regard to how the 'state world' impacts upon the transnational 'society world'. As mentioned above, however, most of the empirical work poses the question the other way around and asks what effects, if any, TNAs have on structures and processes of world politics. There is one important difference between scholarly controversies of the 1990s as opposed to the 1970s and 1980s. Most of the contemporary work in international affairs no longer disputes that TNAs influence decisions and outcomes (compare, for example, Waltz, 1979 with Krasner, 1995b, 1999). Rather, current scholarship focuses on the *conditions* under which these effects are achieved and most of the controversies center around the significance of these intervening factors (e.g. Kaufmann and Pape, 1999; Moravcsik, 2000).

However, a body of literature mostly concerned with studying 'globalization' (see Zürn's Chapter 12 in this volume) goes much further and claims that the transnational 'society world' has not only profoundly changed the 'state world' but has made obsolete the current order of international relations as an inter-state system (see, for example, Amin, 1997; Gill, 1995; Strange, 1996). We do not live in a borderless world, but political, social and economic boundaries cease to coincide and to be confined to the nation-state (e.g. Brock and Albert, 1995; Ferguson and Mansbach, 1996; Ruggie, 1993; Wolf, 2000). Even talking about transnational as opposed to state actors becomes problematic, the more we accept that the current 'Westphalian' system of nation-states is coming to an end and that political authority is increasingly structured along functional rather than territorial lines (Caporaso, 2000). In the following, however, I bracket this discussion, which is taken up elsewhere in this volume (see, for example, Chapter 8 by Bierstekker and Chapter 12 by Zürn). I take a more 'pedestrian' and actor-centered approach and ask how and under which conditions specific TNAs such as multinational

corporations and 'non-profit' INGOs affect outcomes in world politics. I put somewhat more emphasis on the non-profit sector, since the impact of MNCs is treated elsewhere in this handbook (see Chapters 12, 22 and 23).

Globalization and MNCs: 'Global Players' as Sources of Policy Convergence?

As mentioned above, both the liberal and the critical-Marxist literature on transnational relations of the 1970s focused on the role of MNCs in world politics. At the time, the main controversies centered around the question of whether MNCs contributed to or hindered economic development (overview in Gilpin, 1987: chs 6, 7; see also Chapter 24 by Maxfield in this volume). Realists argued that MNCs were irrelevant for developments, since national government remained largely in control of development policies, even in the less developed world (e.g., Krasner, 1978). Liberals and modernization theory claimed that MNCs had an overall positive effect on economic modernization by guaranteeing an open world economy based on free trade and by exporting capital, know-how and modern values into less developed countries (for an early statement see Huntington, 1968). Critical theorists, particularly 'dependentistas', maintained that, on the contrary, MNCs were among the main culprits of uneven development by essentially extracting resources from developing countries that were desperately needed for economic development (e.g., Amin, 1977; Frank, 1967).

Twenty years later, this controversy has largely disappeared, for two reasons. First, as Menzel claimed, *the* Third World has ceased to exist (Menzel, 1992). The differentiation process among developing countries led to functionally equivalent paths to economic development (compare, for example, the Latin American experience with South East Asia). As a result, it is impossible to sustain a unifying theory of MNC impact on economic development such as claimed by either modernization or dependency theorists. MNC impact on development varies enormously depending on social, political and cultural structures in target countries (Clark and Chan, 1995).

Second, accounts ascribing an enormous influence of MNCs on less developed countries usually overstate their significance for the local economies. On a worldwide scale, overseas production of firms as a percentage of world GDP has risen from 4.5 per cent in 1970 to 7.5 per cent in 1995, while the sales of foreign affiliates of MNCs have doubled to about one-quarter of world GDP in the meantime (according to Held et al., 1999: 246). These figures already challenge some exaggerated arguments about 'globalization', at least in production.

Interestingly enough, the significance of MNCs and their local affiliates is even lower for the developing world, as concerns production as percentage of GDP (6.3 per cent in 1995). While the developing world and Eastern Europe since the end of the Cold War have taken part in the boom of Foreign Direct Investments (FDI) starting in the late 1980s, most FDIs still take place within the industrialized world. In fact, the proportion of FDI stocks in developing economies as compared to the OECD world has fallen from 32.3 per cent in 1960 to 25.3 per cent in 1994 (Held et al., 1999: 249). In sum, FDI and MNC activities are largely concentrated within the industrialized world, both intra- and inter-regional.

As a result of these patterns, the debate about MNC impact on world politics in the 1990s largely concentrated on the developed world in the context of discussions about 'globalization' and internationalization (for a useful overview see Held et al., 1999: ch. 5). This controversy is far from over, since the very notion of 'globalization' is heavily contested in the literature, let alone the impact of so-called 'global players' such as MNCs (see the excellent review in Beisheim and Walter, 1997; also Keohane and Milner, 1996; see also Chapter 12 in this volume). The debate largely concentrates on the effects of MNCs and other transnational market forces on the nation-states, in particular the ability of industrialized countries to conduct their own 'autonomous' economic and monetary policies (see also Chapter 22 in this volume).

The 'convergence hypothesis' holds that 'the authority of the governments of all states, large and small, strong and weak, has been weakened as a result of technological and financial change and of the accelerated integration of national economies into one single global market economy' (Strange, 1996: 13–14; see also Stopford and Strange, 1991). There is widespread agreement that the MNCs' ability to shift production elsewhere and their capacity as transnational actors to allocate financial and other resources to places promising the highest profit rates severely circumscribe the autonomy of national governments to take economic decisions. The more a national economy is integrated into global markets, the higher the costs of a national economic policy which is not oriented toward liberalizing markets, but toward expansionary monetary and fiscal policies to create full employment. Since the latter policies are usually identified with center-left rather than center-right governments, the former should be more severely constrained in their policies than the latter (Milner and Keohane, 1996: 17–18). The result is a growing convergence of national economic policies toward neoliberalism and monetarism.

Critical theory in the neo-Gramscian tradition agrees with the overall description of recent trends, but explains it differently. Gill and others see an emerging transnational 'historic bloc' establishing the hegemony of transnationally mobile capital and relevant capitalist classes. The industrialized nation-states have not been passive by-standers of these trends, but have actively encouraged and contributed to them through, for example, the liberalization of capital markets and the encouragement of FDIs. At the same time and with the demise of Keynesianism, neoliberalism became the dominant ideology of how to run a national economy shaping the world-views of transnational elites, policy-makers and other actors (Gill, 1995; Gill and Law, 1993). In the neo-Gramscian view, it is this confluence of modes of production (transnational), international and national institutions and dominant ideas which constitutes transnational global hegemony. What is less clear in this rather sweeping argument, is how it can be disconfirmed, that is, how do we know transnational hegemony when we see it? Van Apeldoorn has recently applied the neo-Gramscian argument which takes constructivist work on the role of ideas into account, to the European Roundtable (ERT) of businesspeople and CEOs from major European MNCs (Van Apeldoorn, 1999). He claims that the ERT has successfully shaped the economic agenda of the EU toward the neoliberal paradigm, starting with the Single European Act and culminating in the Economic and Monetary Union (EMU). His point is not so much that the ERT lobbied for particular policies, but that it moved the dominant ideology toward an, albeit 'embedded', neoliberal agenda.

The emerging literature on globalization, internationalization and the role of MNCs in the international economy has only started to tackle these questions (see Chapter 12). The more empirical evidence becomes available about the domestic effects of the internationalization of production, the more it becomes clear that generalizations such as the 'convergence' hypothesis miss the mark. First, we can observe a transformation of national economic policies rather than a broad 'retreat of the state'. Second, the scholarly discussion moves toward specifying the conditions under which nation-states are more or less able to face the challenges of internationalization without giving up social and democratic values. Similar trends toward differentiated arguments can be observed when we look at the literature on the other type of transnational actors to be discussed here, namely advocacy networks and INGOs.

The Power of Principles and Knowledge: Transnational Advocacy Networks and INGOs

There is a growing consensus in the literature that INGOs and other non-profit TNAs make a difference in world politics. Scholars have collected evidence that advocacy networks, epistemic communities and other TNAs can have a substantial impact on state policies, on the creation of international norms and on the diffusion of these norms into domestic practices (e.g., Boli and Thomas, 1999; Checkel, 1997; Evangelista, 1999; Finnemore, 1996a; Florini, 2000; Haas, 1992c; Keck and Sikkink, 1998; Klotz, 1995; Litfin, 1994; O'Brien et al., 2000; Price, 1998; Princen and Finger, 1994; Risse-Kappen, 1995a; Risse et al., 1999; Smith et al., 1997; Willetts, 1996). While these and other works provide evidence that the power of knowledge and of principled beliefs matters in world politics, the more interesting question is why and under what conditions? But many studies do not lead to generalizable conclusions, since they suffer from methodological problems such as case selection on the dependent variable. There are many single-case studies of successful transnational campaigns, while we know much less about failed campaigns (see, however, Cortright and Pagnucco, 1997; Evangelista, 1999). The propositions emerging from the literature can be grouped under the following categories:

- International material and institutional conditions.
- Domestic conditions.
- Complex models linking the international and domestic levels.
- TNA strategies and socialization processes.

International conditions for TNA impact
Realist-inspired authors essentially argue that the more TNAs and coalitions succeed in changing the preferences and policies of the most powerful states, the greater their impact in international affairs becomes. Only great powers enjoy the ability and capacity of affecting outcomes in world politics as a result of which TNAs need to influence their decisions and policies in order to make a difference (e.g. Krasner, 1993, 1995a). The proposition no longer claims to account for state preferences in the international system and, thus, does not explain why great powers sometimes promote INGO goals in international relations. A stronger version of the argument would have to maintain that great powers only promote 'soft norms' such as human rights or environmental concerns, if it suits their security and/or economic interests. In this latter formulation, TNA impact becomes more or less epiphenomenal.

Whether in its stronger or in its weaker form, a systematic evaluation of the argument in the human rights area has not shown much evidence for the proposition that TNAs had first to convince great powers in order to influence outcomes and decisions in international affairs (Risse et al., 1999). While it certainly helps if the governments of great powers start promoting the goals of transnational advocacy networks, this is neither a necessary nor a sufficient condition for TNA impact. This work on the impact of transnational networks on the domestic implementation of human rights norms in various regions of the world shows that great powers are rarely decisive in promoting these norms, because they rarely pursue consistent human rights policies. Realism might well explain that great powers do not promote human rights when it does not suit their strategic or economic interests, but precisely for this reason it cannot account for the substantial TNA influence on the implementation of human rights in domestic practices across the world regions.[2]

While the realist proposition has not yet been systematically tested in other issue-areas of world politics, there is circumstantial evidence to challenge it. INGO impact despite great power resistance has been amply documented in the environmental area (e.g. Keck and Sikkink, 1998: ch. 4; Lipschutz and Mayer, 1996; Princen and Finger, 1994), but also in international security. In the case of the international treaty banning landmines, for example, transnational advocacy networks succeeded, even though they were pitched against the fierce opposition of several great powers, including the United States (Price, 1998).

But structure is not confined to the material realm. We need to take the social structure of international politics into account. I argued in my earlier work (Risse-Kappen, 1995a) that TNAs are expected to increase their political influence, the more they act in an international environment which is heavily structured by international institutions. International organizations, for example, provide arenas enabling regular interactions between transnational and state actors. In some cases, they actively encourage (and even finance) INGOs and other transnational coalitions. The European Commission, the World Bank and the developmental sector are cases in point (see, for example, Chabbott, 1999; Imig and Tarrow, 2001). The more international organizations and Western states realized that their developmental policies and foreign aid had to be targeted to the civil societies in Third World countries, the more they came to rely on the INGO world linking the local and the global. The strong collaboration between the World Bank and the INGO world did not result in a less contentious relationship between the two, even though sharp divisions among INGOs emerged concerning how far one should cooperate with the World Bank (O'Brien et al., 2000). The United Nations system provides another arena for INGO participation. The UN world conferences in particular have served as important focal points for the activities of transnational advocacy networks (Clark et al., 1998; see also Weiss and Gordenker, 1996). Moreover, the UN and its various organizations increasingly serve as fora where transnational actors and state officials regularly meet and interact (see for example, Finger, 1994; Willetts, 1996).

It is one thing to argue that international institutions provide arenas in which the activities of TNAs are allowed to flourish. It is quite different to conclude that, therefore, they should have a policy impact on international organizations, international regimes and state policies. The above proposition probably needs refinement. International governance arenas such as the UN system or regional organizations such as the EU certainly provide TNAs with regular *access* to policy-making. But access does not guarantee *impact*. As Clark and others showed, NGO influence on policy outcomes of UN world conferences varied significantly according to subject area and countries involved (Clark et al., 1998).

We probably need to differentiate among various phases in the international policy cycle, such as agenda-setting, international norm creation and norm implementation. It is safe to argue that *ceteris paribus* the influence of transnational advocacy networks has always been greatest during the agenda-setting or 'norm emergence' phase of a 'norm life cycle' (Finnemore and Sikkink, 1998). Since TNAs provide moral authority and knowledge about causal relationships, they are particularly crucial when it comes to paradigm shifts on the international agenda. One can probably go as far as to argue that there has rarely been a new normative issue on the international agenda which has not been advocated by transnational advocacy coalitions, INGOs or epistemic communities. In the international political economy, for example, an epistemic community put Keynesian ideas of 'embedded liberalism' on the international agenda during the negotiations establishing the Bretton Woods system and the GATT (Ikenberry, 1993). In the environmental area, examples include the protection of the ozone layer, global warming, deforestation, wildlife conservation and other questions (Haas, 1992a; Hurrell, 1992; Keck and Sikkink, 1998: ch. 4; Litfin, 1994; Princen, 1995; Raustiala, 1997; Ringus, 1997). Concerning human rights, the origins of almost every single post-Second World War international human rights agreement can be found in the activities of transnational advocacy networks (Keck and Sikkink, 1998: ch. 2; Korey, 1998 see also Chapter 27 by Schmitz and Sikkink in this volume). Examples from international security include the Geneva Conventions, the nuclear test ban debate and – most recently – the treaty banning landmines (Adler, 1992; Finnemore, 1996b: ch. 3; Price, 1998).

Yet, agenda-setting does not equal norm creation. When it comes to international rule-creation and international treaty-making, national governments and IOs assume center-stage again. During this stage of the process, INGOs and transnational advocacy networks need to work through governments or international organizations. Moreover, while the agenda-setting phase might be dominated by well-organized transnational networks and INGOs, they are likely to counter considerable opposition when it comes to transforming principled beliefs or knowledge into concrete norms and rules prescribing appropriate behavior enshrined in treaties and other instruments of international governance and accepted by the international community. As a result, the requirements to build 'winning coalitions' with and among state actors usually become extensive and, thus, TNA impact appears to be less pronounced. There are few comparative case studies varying the conditions under which TNAs have an impact on treaty-making or regime creation. The available evidence points to three potential pathways by which TNAs influence multilateral negotiations:

- through lobbying activities in the domestic society of powerful states such as the United States, thus exploiting 'two level game' mechanisms and changing state preferences;
- through coalitions with international organizations thus pressuring states 'from above' and 'from below'; this particular pathway seems to be pronounced in the EU;
- through coalition-building with smaller states providing the latter with knowledge and 'informational power'.

Once international rules and norms are created and international regimes have emerged, these normative commitments need to be implemented in the domestic practices of states and societies. This is by no means an automatic process as numerous studies about rule compliance (or lack of), and rule effectiveness reveal (see, for example, Keohane et al., 1993; Victor et al., 1998). While we still lack systematic comparative studies across issue-areas, the available evidence suggests that transnational advocacy networks and epistemic communities once again assume center-stage in the process by which states and their societies internalize international rules in their domestic practices. There are two reasons for this. First, the legalization process of international norms drastically increases the legitimacy of those actors who demand compliance with them. International institutions and the rules emanating from them empower both domestic and transnational actors in a differential way, thereby enhancing their moral and knowledge power.

Second, international organizations and state agencies must often rely on the monitoring and information capacities of transnational networks and INGOs, because the former are bound by rules of sovereignty and of 'non-interference in internal affairs', while the latter can move more freely. This reliance on TNA expertise and information-gathering capacities is particularly pronounced in issue-areas such as human rights and environment (probably less so in international security and international economy) and probably most relevant concerning international regimes that lack adequate, detailed and intrusive verification procedures (see, for example, Haas, 1992c; Korey, 1998; Peterson, 1997; Smith, 1997).

Domestic conditions for TNA impact   So far, I have concentrated on discussing effects of transnational activities mainly on the international level. Many transnational advocacy networks focus on influencing national policies and national governments in conjunction with international institutions and organizations. One proposition claims that differences in domestic structures explain the variation in TNA policy influence:

> Domestic structures mediate, filter, and refract the efforts by transnational actors and alliances to influence policies in the various issue-areas. In order to affect policies, transnational actors have to overcome two hurdles. First, they have to gain access to the political system of their 'target state'. Second, they must generate and/or contribute to 'winning' policy coalitions in order to change decisions in the desired direction. ... Domestic structures are likely to determine both the availability of access points into the political systems and the size of and requirements for 'winning coalitions'. (Risse-Kappen, 1995a: 25)

This argument resembles to some extent the suggestions in the social movement literature that 'political opportunity structures' constitute an important factor in explaining the success of new social movements (Kitschelt, 1986; Tarrow, 1996). The domestic structure hypothesis has been evaluated empirically with regard to a variety of countries with diverging institutional setups (case studies in Risse-Kappen, 1995b).

This proposition posits a somewhat inverse relationship between TNA access and TNA impact on the domestic policy-making processes. The more open and the less centralized a political system, on the one hand, and the more pluralist the society, on the other, the easier it should be for TNAs to gain access to decision-makers. The United States probably represents the best approximation of such a domestic structure. Yet, easy access does not equal policy impact. In fact, the coalition-building requirements in open political systems and societies such as the United States are quite formidable. On the other end of the spectrum are extremely centralized political systems such as the former Soviet Union which also dominate state-society relations. Evangelista's book on the impact of transnational networks on Soviet and Russian security and arms control policies (Evangelista, 1999) confirms the argument that TNA access to the Soviet policy-making structure was extremely difficult to achieve for transnational networks of advocacy and expert groups. Once Soviet leaders were prepared to listen, however, the transnational coalitions exercised an almost immediate policy impact. This explains the

variation between the Khrushchev and Gorbachev eras, on the one hand, and the situation under Brezhnev and Andropov, on the other, when access to the top leadership was extremely limited. By contrasting Gorbachev's Soviet Union with Yeltsin's Russia, Evangelista also shows that the opening of the Soviet/Russian system multiplied the access points for TNAs, but severely circumscribed their policy impact (Evangelista, 1995). This work constitutes one of the few examples whereby case selection on the independent variable (domestic structure) and keeping other factors constant allows for valid causal inferences on TNA impact.

But, as Keck and Sikkink point out, emphasizing domestic institutional arrangements does not tell the whole story of TNA impact: 'They cannot tell us why some transnational networks operating in the same context succeed and others do not' (Keck and Sikkink, 1998: 202). Human rights groups were more successful in changing US policies under Presidents Carter and even Reagan than environmental groups. Their objection points to a weakness of the domestic structure argument. It has so far mainly emphasized formal aspects of political and social institutions rather than the substantive content of ideas and norms embedded in them. Constructivist insights might help to solve the puzzle why some TNAs successfully influence changes in state policies, while other fail, despite similar institutional conditions. A 'resonance' hypothesis has been developed by students of international norms trying to explain the differential diffusion in domestic practices (e.g. Checkel, 1997; Cortell and Davis, 2000; Ulbert, 1997): the more new ideas promoted by transnational coalitions resonate or are compatible with pre-existing collective identities and beliefs of actors, the more policy influence they might have.

This proposition can be applied to efforts by transnational coalitions promoting international norms to affect domestic change. A comparison of human rights changes in the Philippines and Indonesia shows, for example, that the arguments by transnational networks resonated well with the Westernized political discourse in the Philippines under Marcos, while similar networks failed for quite a long time to pry open political space for human rights in Indonesia, since their arguments were not compatible with the prevailing nationalist discourse (Jetschke, 2000). In both cases, the domestic structure was strikingly similar during the 1970s (authoritarian rule). The 'resonance' argument would also explain the variation in transnational influence on Soviet security policy under Brezhnev as compared with Gorbachev (Evangelista, 1999). Litfin's critique of the 'epistemic community' literature and its application to the case of ozone depletion points in a similar direction (Litfin, 1994). She argues that Ernst and Peter Haas's conceptualization of consensual knowledge emphasizes too much apolitical and 'objective' scientific knowledge. Rather, the claims by scientific communities must be framed in such a way that they are compatible with the prevailing political discourse. Otherwise, they fall by the wayside.

But the 'resonance hypothesis' is not unproblematic (see the discussion in Cortell and Davis, 2000). First, assessing the compatibility between transnationally diffused ideas and given domestic identities and collective beliefs must strictly concentrate on the discourses rather than on the behavioral practices of actors so as to avoid circular reasoning. Second, if there is a complete match between the new transnational norms and the ideas embedded in a given domestic culture, we do not need conscious efforts by transnational actors to make the norms stick. In other words, a certain degree of cultural misfit or incompatibility is necessary to ascribe causal weight to the activities of transnational actors. Most TNAs, INGOs and epistemic communities alike are in the business of strategic construction (Finnemore and Sikkink, 1998: 269–75). In other words, they deliberately make new ideas and principled beliefs 'resonate' with pre-existing and embedded norms and collective understandings. It is very hard to predict beforehand which of these new ideas carry the day. The argument about ideational (in)compatibility is still underspecified in the literature.

Toward complex models of TNA impact   Most recently, scholars have advanced complex models of TNA impact integrating international and domestic levels. This work is particularly relevant for the study of TNA impact on norm implementation and compliance. Scholars have started specifying the conditions and causal mechanisms by which transnational advocacy networks manage to link the 'global' and the 'local' levels (on norms socialization in general see Checkel, 1999a). Keck and Sikkink have developed the so-called 'boomerang effect' model to show how domestic and transnational social movements and networks unite to bring pressure 'from above' and 'from below' on authoritarian governments to accomplish human rights change (Keck and Sikkink, 1998: 12–13; see also Brysk, 1993; Klotz, 1995). A 'boomerang' pattern of influence exists when domestic groups in a repressive state bypass their government and directly search out international allies to bring pressure on their states from outside. National opposition groups and social movements link up with TNAs who then convince international human rights IOs and Western states to pressure norm-violating states. Transnational networks provide access, leverage, information and often money to struggling domestic groups. International contacts can amplify the demands of domestic groups, pry open space for new issues, and then echo these demands back into the domestic arena.

Risse, Ropp and Sikkink have developed a five-phase dynamic model of human rights change consisting of several 'boomerang throws' (Risse et al., 1999) and specifying the conditions under which links between domestic opposition groups and transnationally operating networks produce change toward domestic norm implementation and compliance. The 'spiral model' of human rights change claims that the mobilization activities of transnational advocacy networks are particularly significant in early stages of the process when domestic groups in the repressive state are too weak or too oppressed to constitute a serious challenge to the regime. At this stage, the information and monitoring capacities of transnational networks as agents of norms change are particularly relevant to mobilize the international community. The more the government is under pressure 'from above' and 'from below' and forced to make tactical concessions to its critics, the more the center of activities shifts from the transnational to the domestic level. During these later phases of the process, a major effect of transnational network activities is to empower and to strengthen domestic civil society. The spiral model has been successfully evaluated for the human rights area, but there is not yet systematic research for other issue-areas of international relations.

TNA strategies and communicative processes Structural conditions need to be complemented by agency-centered approaches to account for TNA impact. Work focusing on INGOs and transnational advocacy networks which is largely inspired by moderate social constructivism and sociological institutionalism points to three relevant factors in this context:

1   TNA characteristics, particularly network density, material resources and organizational capacities, but also ideational resources such as moral authority and legitimate knowledge.
2   Target characteristics, such as vulnerability to transnational pressures and uncertainty about cause–effect relationships.
3   Communication processes such as shaming, learning and arguing.

As to the first factor, Keck and Sikkink point out that transnational advocacy networks 'operate best when they are dense, with many actors, strong connections among groups in the network, and reliable information flows' (Keck and Sikkink, 1998: 28, see also 206–7). One should add that material resources and organizational capacities of networks and INGOs also contribute to their effectiveness. But the example of Transparency International (TI), a tiny INGO with initially only few professional staff members, which almost single-handedly put corruption on the international agenda, indicates that ideational resources and knowledge might overcome a lack of material power and organizational capacities, at least initially (Galtung, 2000). Within a few years, TI acquired both moral and knowledge power in the area of corruption. The effectiveness of TI and other INGOs depends on ideational resources, particularly moral authority in terms of legitimate claims of representing some international 'common good' as well as informational capacities and knowledge. This ability to convert moral authority and excellent knowledge of the issue-area into ideational power explains to a large degree why transnational advocacy networks sometimes win against materially more powerful actors such as MNCs and national governments.

TNA impact not only depends on their own resources and capacities, but also on the vulnerability of their 'targets' – states, international organizations, or multinational corporations – to network pressures (Keck and Sikkink, 1998: 29, 208–9). Such sensitivity might concern vulnerability to material pressures such as economic sanctions or the cutoff of foreign aid in the cases of many Third World countries. But 'target vulnerability' might also imply reputational concerns and normative commitments. States or international organizations might be vulnerable to TNA pressures, because they want to be members of the international community 'in good standing'. In other words, the more these actors have committed themselves and their collective identities to the norms advocated by the networks, the more they should be vulnerable to TNA pressures in cases of norm violation. Finally, 'target vulnerability' to network pressures might include uncertainty about the situation and about cause–effect relationships. This point has been particularly emphasized by the literature on epistemic communities (particularly Haas, 1992c). In many cases, policy-makers recognize a collective action problem in international life, but simply lack the knowledge to tackle it. Such uncertainty provides a window of opportunity for knowledge-based epistemic communities to exert influence.

Transnational networks as moral and knowledge entrepreneurs use various communication strategies to achieve their goals, the third group of factors to be mentioned here. INGOs rely on social mobilization, protest and pressure. They use strategic constructions such as the re-framing of issues or shaming in order to mobilize people around new principled ideas and norms (Meyer and Tarrow, 1998). Shaming strategies remind actors such as national governments of their own standards of appropriateness and collective identities and demand that they live up to these norms (Keck and Sikkink, 1998: 23–4; Liese, 1999). Advocacy networks and epistemic communities also rely on the 'power of the better argument'. They need to justify their claims and to use various communication strategies in order to persuade their audiences to change their interests and policies. Shaming and the re-framing of issues is usually not sufficient to convince others and overcome opposition. INGOs and other transnational actors must engage their audiences in an argumentative process in order to achieve their goals. As 'teachers of norms' (Finnemore, 1993), they need to start a reasoned discourse justifying their claims in front of various public audiences.

Work on these micro-mechanisms and TNA strategies has just begun. It usually involves detailed process-tracing in (comparative) case studies research. Many case studies are methodologically problematic, however, since they focus on single cases and/or 'success stories' of transnational pressures without specifying the scope conditions of their arguments. As a result, we still lack testable propositions on the conditions under which such strategies succeed and when they fail (see, however, Checkel, 1999b). This area certainly deserves further scholarly exploration.

CONCLUSIONS: TOWARD TRIPARTITE 'GLOBAL GOVERNANCE'?

This survey of more than thirty years of scholarship on transnational actors demonstrates that the significance of cross-border interactions involving non-state actors – multinational corporations, INGOs, epistemic communities and advocacy networks – is no longer seriously contested in an age of globalization. But it would be premature to proclaim the end of the inter-state world as we knew it. The picture emerging from the literature reveals instead complex interactions between transnational actors, on the one hand, and corporate actors on all levels of supranational, international, national, regional and local governance, on the other. Unfortunately, most of the literature is still primarily concerned with proving against a state-centered picture of world politics that TNAs matter. As a result, the more interesting questions – when and under what conditions do they matter? – are rarely asked. Moreover, most research on TNAs focuses on their direct policy impact rather than the structural implications of their activities on international society. This is particularly regrettable, since the goal of many transnational advocacy networks and INGOs is not so much geared to directly shape policies, but to engage in consciousness-raising and, thus, changing societies and building a transnational civil society (Lipschutz and Mayer, 1996; Wapner, 1996). While research on MNCs has always included the structural dimension in evaluating their impact, particularly in the developing world, this aspect is largely missing in studies concerning the non-profit sector.

There is no lack of propositions on TNA impact concentrating on institutional conditions (both domestic and international), coalition-building abilities, organizational capacities and resources, and actors' strategies. Research on transnational advocacy networks and epistemic communities appears to be a fruitful area for probing competing as well as complementary assumptions derived from rational choice liberalism and institutionalism, on the one hand, and sociological and constructivist approaches on the other. But we are still in the early stages of a research program that concentrates more on hypothesis-generating than hypothesis-testing through systematic and comparative case studies. Future research on TNAs should evaluate competing explanations and specify the conditions of TNA impact on the various levels of governance. We also need more studies that turn the 'dependent variable' around and investigate the effects of increasing TNA influence in world politics on these non-state actors themselves.

Most important, future research on TNAs needs to take into account that these actors – whether MNCs or principled INGOs – have lost their 'innocence' and have become part and parcel of international governance structures. Most previous scholarship has concentrated on the question how transnational actors affect national governments and international organizations through the various channels of exerting influence. Yet, international governance seems to be increasingly characterized by cooperative partnerships involving governmental as well as transnational actors, both MNCs and INGOs (see Cutler et al., 1999; Kaul et al., 1999; O'Brien et al., 2000; Reinicke, 1998; Reinicke and Deng, 2000). Examples include regulations in the financial services sector (Reinicke, 1998: ch. 4), private regimes in the insurance sector (Haufler, 1993), and the Transatlantic Business Dialogue (TABD) initiated by the European Commission and the US government (Cowles, 2000). The UN system is replete with cooperative arrangements including international organizations, national agencies and the NGO community (e.g.Weiss and Gordenker, 1996; Willetts, 1996).

Empirical research on global (or regional) governance by tripartite networks including state actors, firms and advocacy groups has just begun. The evidence is still sketchy and has not yet yielded testable propositions regarding the conditions under which such network structures emerge and how effective they are in international problem-solving. On the one hand, network governance might increase information capacities of both private and public actors as well as lead to new participation and learning possibilities. On the other hand, tripartite governance networks might lead to overly complex negotiation systems and to decision blockages.

Last not least, there is the problem of *democratic* and *legitimate* governance beyond the nation-state (see also Chapter 12 in this volume). How can global governance by increasingly complex tripartite networks solve the dual problems of insuring 'input legitimacy' through participation of those

concerned by the regulations and of 'output legitimacy' through effective and enhanced problem-solving? (On these distinctions see Scharpf, 1999: 16–28; for general reviews see Kohler-Koch, 1998a; Wolf, 2000.) This debate has a long history, starting with the first liberal thinkers on transnational relations for whom transborder interactions were an unproblematic ingredient of liberal democracy and a guarantee for peaceful international relations. But, as Kaiser pointed out already in 1971 (Kaiser, 1971), it constitutes a problem for democratic accountability if transnational governance structures include private actors – be it MNCs or INGOs – who are not elected by and, therefore, not accountable to anybody except, say, shareholders, and members of the transnational organizations. Claims by transnational advocacy networks to represent the international 'common good' and 'global civil society' have to be taken with a grain of salt when it comes to democratic accountability, representativity and participation.

Two positions can essentially be distinguished in the emerging debate about the 'democratic deficit' of global governance. The first set of arguments is represented by Scharpf's work on the EU (Scharpf, 1999) and is rather pessimistic about overcoming the democratic deficit of multi-level governance. Increasing democratic participation in international governance networks ('input legitimacy') faces the problem that there is no transnational 'demos', no transnational collective identity and no international public sphere as we know them from the nation-states. Thus, 'output legitimacy' has to overcome the democracy problem in international governance. But there are limits to increasing the effectiveness and problem-solving capacity of international governance, since it requires positive collaboration among actors with diverging interests ('positive integration'), while market liberalization ('negative integration') tends to be much easier.

The second position is more optimistic. Held's concept of a 'cosmopolitan democracy' (Held, 1995) goes probably furthest in suggesting the strengthening of parliamentarian representation on the level of the United Nations and elsewhere and, the systematic inclusion of transnational civil society and the INGO world into governance mechanisms. The concept of 'deliberative democracy' assumes center-stage among those who argue that the problems of democratic accountability in global governance and tripartite network structures can be overcome (see, for example, Schmalz-Bruns, 1999; Wolf, 2000: 213–42). It rests on the assumption that the legitimacy of the political process can be strengthened through public debate and deliberation and through the open exchange of arguments among citizens. The more tripartite networks of global governance are inclusive, their procedures and decisions transparent and subject to public deliberation, the more the democratic deficit of transnational governance can be tackled. Public deliberation might also increase the problem-solving capacity of multi-level governance, that is 'output legitimacy'. At least, the concept of deliberative democracy offers a way out to tackle the legitimacy problems of global governance by networks, since it does not require a global 'demos' in terms of a strong supranational collective identity.

Notes

For helpful comments and suggestions on the draft of this chapter, I thank my two co-editors, Beth Simmons and Walter Carlsnaes, and an external reviewer, as well as Tanja Börzel, Ralf Leiteritz and Michael Zürn.

1 Strictly speaking, of course, networks are not actors, but informal structures coordinating the activities of their members.

2 I owe this thought to Anja Jetschke.

Bibliography

Adler, Emanuel (1992) 'The Emergence of Cooperation: National Epistemic Communities and the International Evolution of the Idea of Nuclear Arms Control', *International Organization*, 46 (1): 101–45.

Adler, Emanuel and Barnett, Michael (eds) (1998a) *Security Communities*. Cambridge: Cambridge University Press.

Adler, Emanuel and Barnett, Michael (1998b) 'Security Communities in Theoretical Perspective', in E. Adler and M. Barnett (eds), *Security Communities*. Cambridge: Cambridge University Press. pp. 3–28.

Adler, Emanuel and Haas, Peter (1992) 'Conclusion: Epistemic Communities, World Order, and the Creation of a Reflective Research Program', *International Organization*, 46 (1): 367–90.

Amin, Samir (1977) *Imperialism and Unequal Development*. New York: Monthly Review Press.

Amin, Samir (1997) *Capitalism in the Age of Globalization*. London: Zed Press.

Baldwin, David A. (ed.) (1993) *Neorealism and Neoliberalism: The Contemporary Debate*. New York: Columbia University Press.

Beisheim, Marianne and Walter, Gregor (1997) '"Globalisierung" – Kinderkrankheiten eines Konzeptes', *Zeitschrift für Internationale Beziehungen*, 4 (1): 153–80.

Boli, John and Thomas, George M. (eds) (1999) *Constructing World Culture. International Nongovernmental Organizations since 1875*. Stanford: Stanford University Press.

Boli, John, Loya, Thomas A. and Loftin, Teresa (1999) 'National Participation in World-Polity Organization', in J. Boli and G.M. Thomas (eds), *Constructing World Culture. International Nongovernmental Organizations since 1875*. Stanford: Stanford University Press. pp. 50–77.

Brock, Lothar and Albert, Mathias (1995) 'Entgrenzung der Staatenwelt. Zur Analyse weltgesellschaftlicher Entwicklungstendenzen', *Zeitschrift für Internationale Beziehungen*, 2 (2): 259–85.

Brysk, Alison (1993) 'From Above and From Below: Social Movements, the International System, and Human Rights in Argentina', *Comparative Political Studies*, 26 (3): 259–85.

Caporaso, James A. (1978) 'Dependence and Dependency in the Global System', *International Organization*. Special Issue, 32 (1).

Caporaso, James A. (ed.) (2000) *Continuity and Change in the Westphalian Order. Special Issue of International Studies Review*. Oxford: Blackwell.

Chabbott, Colette (1999) 'Development INGOs', in J. Boli and G.M. Thomas (eds), *Constructing World Culture. International Nongovernmental Organizations since 1875*. Stanford: Stanford University Press. pp. 222–48.

Checkel, Jeffrey T. (1997) 'International Norms and Domestic Politics: Bridging the Rationalist-Constructivist Divide', *European Journal of International Relations*, 3 (4): 473–95.

Checkel, Jeffrey T. (1999a) 'International Institutions and Socialization', Working Paper No. 5. Oslo: ARENA, University of Oslo, February.

Checkel, Jeffrey T. (1999b) 'Social Construction and Integration', *Journal of European Public Policy*, 6 (4): 545–60.

Clark, Ann Marie, Friedman, Elisabeth J. and Hochstetler, Kathryn (1998) 'The Sovereign Limits of Global Civil Society. A Comparison of NGO Participation in UN World Conferences on the Environment, Human Rights, and Women', *World Politics*, 51 (1): 1–35.

Clark, Cal and Chan, Steve (1995) 'MNCs and Developmentalism: Domestic Structure as an Explanation for East Asian Dynamism', in T. Risse-Kappen (ed.), *Bringing Transnational Relations Back In. Non-State Actors, Domestic Structures and International Institutions*. Cambridge: Cambridge University Press. pp. 112–45.

Cooper, Richard N. (1968) *The Economics of Interdependence: Economic Policy in the Atlantic Community*. New York: McGraw–Hill.

Cortell, Andrew P. and Davis, James W. Jr (2000) 'Understanding the Domestic Impact of International Norms: A Research Agenda', *International Studies Review*, 2 (1): 65–87.

Cortright, David and Pagnucco, Ron (1997) 'Limits to Transnationalism: The 1980s Freeze Campaign', in J. Smith, C. Chatfield and R. Pagnucco (eds), *Transnational Social Movements and Global Politics. Solidarity Beyond the State*. Syracuse: Syracuse University Press. pp. 159–74.

Cowles, Maria Green (2000) 'Private Firms and US–EU Policymaking: The Transatlantic Business Dialogue', in E. Philippart and P. Winand (eds), *Policy-Making in the US–EU Relationship*. Manchester: Manchester University Press.

Cox, Robert W. (1987) *Production, Power, and World Order*. New York: Columbia University Press.

Cox, Robert W. and Sinclair, Timothy J. (1996) *Approaches to World Order*. Cambridge: Cambridge University Press.

Cutler, Claire A., Haufler, Virginia and Porter, Tony (eds) (1999) *Private Authority and International Affairs*. Albany: State University of New York Press.

Czempiel, Ernst-Otto (1991) *Weltpolitik im Umbruch. Das internationale System nach dem Ende des Ost-West-Konflikts*. Munich: Beck.

Czempiel, Ernst-Otto and Rosenau, James (eds) (1992) *Governance Without Government: Order and Change in World Politics*. Cambridge: Cambridge University Press.

Deutsch, Karl W. et al. (1957) *Political Community and the North Atlantic Area: International Organization in the Light of Historical Experience*. Princeton: Princeton University Press.

Doremus, Paul N., Keller, William W., Pauly, Louis W. and Reich Simon (1998) *The Myth of the Global Corporation*. Princeton: Princeton University Press.

Edwards, Michael and Hulme, David (eds) (1996) *Beyond the Magic Bullet: NGO Performance and Accountability in the Post-Cold War World*. West Hartford: Kumarian Press.

Emmanuel, Arghiri (1972) *Unequal Exchange: A Study of the Imperialism of Trade*. New York: Monthly Review Press.

Evangelista, Matthew (1995) 'The Paradox of State Strength: Transnational Relations, Domestic Structures, and Security Policy in Russia and the Soviet Union', *International Organization*, 49: 1–38.

Evangelista, Matthew (1999) *Unarmed Forces. The Transnational Movement to End the Cold War*. Ithaca: Cornell University Press.

Ferguson, Yale H. and Mansbach, Richard W. (1996) *Polities – Authority and Change*. Columbia, SC: University of South Carolina Press.

Finger, Matthias (1994) 'Environmental NGOs in the UNCED Process', in T. Princen and M. Finger (eds), *Environmental NGOs in World Politics. Linking the Local and the Global*. London: Routledge. pp. 186–213.

Finnemore, Martha (1993) 'International Organization as Teachers of Norms: The United Nations Educational, Scientific, and Cultural Organization and Science Policy', *International Organization*, 47 (4): 565–97.

Finnemore, Martha (1996a) 'Constructing Norms of Humanitarian Intervention', in P.J. Katzenstein (ed.), *The Culture of National Security. Norms and Identity in World Politics*. New York: Columbia University Press. pp. 153–85.

Finnemore, Martha (1996b) *National Interests in International Society*. Ithaca: Cornell University Press.

Finnemore, Martha and Sikkink, Kathryn (1998) 'International Norm Dynamics and Political Change', *International Organization*, 52 (4): 887–917.

Florini, Ann (ed.) (2000) *The Third Force. The Rise of Transnational Civil Society*. Tokyo and Washington,

DC: Japan Center for International Exchange and Carnegie Endowment for International Peace.

Forsythe, David P. (1976) 'The Red Cross as Transnational Movement: Conserving and Changing the Nation-State System', *International Organization*, 30 (4): 607–30.

Frank, Andre Gunder (1967) *Capitalism and Underdevelopment in Latin America: Historical Studies of Chile and Brazil*. New York: Monthly Review Press.

Galtung, Fredrik (2000) 'A Global Network to Curb Corruption: The Experience of Transparency International', in A. Florini (ed.), *The Third Force: The Rise of Transnational Civil Society*. Tokyo and Washington, DC: Japan Center for International Exchange and Carnegie Endowment for International Peace. pp. 17–47.

Gill, Stephen (ed.) (1993) *Gramsci, Historical Materialism, and International Relations*. Cambridge: Cambridge University Press.

Gill, Stephen (1995) 'Globalization, Market Civilization, and Disciplinary Neoliberalism', *Millennium: Journal of International Studies*, 24 (3): 399–423.

Gill, Stephen and Law, David (1993) 'Global Hegemony and the Structural Power of Capital', in S. Gill (ed.), *Gramsci, Historical Materialism, and International Relations*. Cambridge: Cambridge University Press. pp. 93–124.

Gilpin, Robert (1971) 'The Politics of Transnational Economic Relations', in R.O. Keohane and J.S.J. Nye (eds), *Transnational Relations and World Politics*. Cambridge, MA: Harvard University Press. pp. 48–69.

Gilpin, Robert (1975) *US Power and the Multinational Corporation: The Political Economy of Foreign Direct Investment*. New York: Basic Books.

Gilpin, Robert (1987) *The Political Economy of International Relations*. Princeton: Princeton University Press.

Greenwood, Justin and Aspinwall, Mark (eds) (1998) *Collective Action in the European Union: Interests and the New Politics of Associability*. London: Routledge.

Haas, Ernst B. (1958) *The Uniting of Europe: Political, Social, and Economic Forces 1950–57*. Stanford: Stanford University Press.

Haas, Peter M. (1992a) 'Banning Chlorofluorocarbons: Epistemic Community Efforts to Protect Stratospheric Ozone', *International Organization*, 46 (1): 187–224.

Haas, Peter M. (1992b) 'Introduction: Epistemic Communities and International Policy Coordination', *International Organization*, 46 (1): 1–36.

Haas, Peter M. (ed.) (1992c) 'Knowledge, Power and International Policy Coordination', *International Organization*, 46 (1): Special Issue.

Haufler, Virginia (1993) 'Crossing the Boundary between Public and Private: International Regimes and Non-State Actors', in V.M. Rittberger (ed.), *Regime Theory and International Relations*. Oxford: Clarendon Press. pp. 94–111.

Held, David (1995) *Democracy and the Global Order.
From the Modern State to Cosmopolitan Governance*.
Cambridge: Cambridge University Press.

Held, David, McGrew, Anthony, Goldblatt, David and
Perraton, Jonathan (1999) *Global Transformations.
Politics, Economics, and Culture*. Stanford: Stanford
University Press.

Hulme, David and Edwards, Michael (1997a) 'NGOs,
States and Donors: An Overview', in D. Hulme and
M. Edwards (eds), *NGOs, States and Donors. Too Close
for Comfort?* London: Macmillan and Save the
Children Fund. pp. 3–22.

Hulme, David and Edwards, Michael (eds) (1997b)
NGOs, States and Donors. Too Close for Comfort?
London: Macmillan and Save the Children Fund.

Huntington, Samuel P. (1968) *Political Order in
Changing Societies*. New Haven: Yale University
Press.

Huntington, Samuel P. (1973) 'Transnational
Organizations in World Politics', *World Politics*,
25 (April): 333–68.

Hurrell, Andrew (1992) 'Brazil and the International
Politics of Amazonian Deforestation', in A. Hurrell and
B. Kingsbury (eds), *The International Politics of the
Environment*. Oxford: Clarendon Press. pp. 398–429.

Ikenberry, G. John (1993) 'Creating Yesterday's New
World Order: Keynesian "New Thinking" and the Anglo-
American Postwar Settlement', in J.R.O.K. Goldstein
and Judith Goldstein (eds), *Ideas and Foreign Policy –
Beliefs, Institutions and Political Change*. Ithaca:
Cornell University Press.

Imig, Doug and Tarrow, Sidney (2001) *Contentious
Europeans: Politics and Protest in a Composite Polity*.
Lanham: Rowman and Littlefield.

Jetschke, Anja (2000) 'International Norms, Transnational
Human Rights Networks, and Domestic Political
Change in Indonesia and the Philippines, PhD disserta-
tion, European University Institute, Florence.

Kaiser, Karl (1969) 'Transnationale Politik', in
E.-O. Czempiel (ed.), *Die anachronistische Souveränität*.
Köln-Opladen: Westdeutscher Verlag. pp. 80–109.

Kaiser, Karl (1971) 'Transnational Relations as a Threat
to the Democratic Process', in R.O. Keohane and J.S.
Nye Jr (eds), *Transnational Relations and World
Politics*. Cambridge, MA: Harvard University Press.
pp. 356–70.

Kant, Immanuel ([1795]1983) 'To Perpetual Peace. A
Philosophical Sketch', in T. Humphrey (ed.), *Immanuel
Kant. Perpetual Peace and Other Essays on Politics,
History, and Morals*. Indianapolis: Hackett. pp. 107–43.

Kaufmann, Chaim D. and Pape, Robert A. (1999)
'Explaining Costly International Moral Action: Britain's
Sixty-year Campaign Against the Atlantic Slave Trade',
International Organization, 53 (4): 631–68.

Kaul, Inge, Grunberg, Isabelle and Stern, Marc A. (eds)
(1999) *Global Public Goods. International Cooperation
in the 21st Century*. Oxford: Oxford University Press.

Keck, Margaret and Sikkink, Kathryn (1998) *Activists
Beyond Borders. Transnational Advocacy Networks in
International Politics*. Ithaca: Cornell University Press.

Keohane, Robert O. and Milner, Helen (eds) (1996)
Internationalization and Domestic Politics. Cambridge:
Cambridge University Press.

Keohane, Robert O. and Nye, J.S. Jr (eds) (1971a)
Transnational Relations and World Politics.
Cambridge, MA: Harvard University Press.

Keohane, Robert O. and Nye, J.S. Jr (1971b)
'Transnational Relations and World Politics: An
Introduction', in R.O. Keohane and J.S. Nye (eds),
Transnational Relations and World Politics.
Cambridge, MA: Harvard University Press.
pp. ix–xxix.

Keohane, Robert O. and Nye, J.S. Jr (1977) *Power and
Interdependence*. Boston: Little, Brown.

Keohane, Robert O., Haas, Peter M. and Levy, Marc A.
(1993) 'The Effectiveness of International Environ-
mental Institutions', in P.M. Haas, R.O. Keohane and
M.A. Levy (eds), *Institutions for the Earth. Sources of
Effective International Environmental Protection*.
Cambridge, MA: MIT Press. pp. 3–26.

Kitschelt, Herbert P. (1986) 'Political Opportunity
Structures and Political Protest: Anti-Nuclear
Movements in Four Democracies', *British Journal of
Political Science*, 16 (1): 57–85.

Klotz, Audie (1995) *Norms in International Relations.
The Struggle against Apartheid*. Ithaca: Cornell
University Press.

Kohler-Koch, Beate (1990) 'Interdependenz', in
V. Rittberger (ed.), *Theorien der internationalen
Beziehungen*. Opladen: Westdeutscher Verlag.
pp. 110–29.

Kohler-Koch, Beate (1994) 'Changing Patterns of Interest
Intermediation in the European Union', *Government
and Opposition*, 29 (2): 166–80.

Kohler-Koch, Beate (1998a) 'Einleitung. Effizienz und
Demokratie. Probleme des Regierens in entgrenzten
Räumen', in B. Kohler-Koch (ed.), *Regieren in
entgrenzten Räumen. PVS-Sonderheft 29*. Opladen:
Westdeutscher Verlag. pp. 11–25.

Kohler-Koch, Beate (ed.) (1998b) *Regieren in entgrenzten
Räumen. PVS-Sonderheft*. Opladen: Westdeutscher
Verlag.

Korey, William (1998) *NGOs and the Universal
Declaration of Human Rights. 'A Curious Grapevine'*.
New York: St Martin's Press.

Krasner, Stephen (1978) *Defending the National Interest*.
Princeton: Princeton University Press.

Krasner, Stephen D. (1993) 'Sovereignty, Regimes, and
Human Rights', in V.M. Rittberger (ed.), *Regime
Theory and International Relations*. Oxford: Clarendon
Press. pp. 139–67.

Krasner, Stephen D. (1995a) 'Minority Rights and the
Westphalian Model', Stanford: Department of Political
Science. Unpublished Manuscript.

Krasner, Stephen D. (1995b) 'Power Politics, Institutions,
and Transnational Relations', in T. Risse-Kappen (ed.),
*Bringing Transnational Relations Back In. Non-State
Actors, Domestic Structures and International
Institutions*: Cambridge: Cambridge University Press.
pp. 257–79.

Krasner, Stephen D. (1999) *Sovereignty. Organized Hypocrisy*. Princeton: Princeton University Press.

Kratochwil, Friedrich (1989) *Rules, Norms, and Decisions*. Cambridge: Cambridge University Press.

Kratochwil, Friedrich and Ruggie, John G. (1986) 'International Organization: A State of the Art on an Art of the State', *International Organization*, 40 (4): 753–75.

Lenin, Vladimir I. ([1917] 1939) *Imperialism: The Highest Stage of Capitalism*. New York: International Publishers.

Liese, Andrea (1999) 'Compliance and Noncompliance with International Norms against Torture and Ill-Treatment'. Conference paper, Mannheim, ECPR Joint Sessions of Workshops, 26–31 March 1999.

Lipschutz, Ronnie D. and Mayer, Judith (1996) *Global Civil Society and Global Environmental Governance*. Albany: State University of New York Press.

Litfin, Karen (1994) *Ozone Discourses. Science and Politics in Global Environmental Cooperation*. New York: Columbia University Press.

Menzel, Ulrich (1992) *Das Ende der Dritten Welt und das Scheitern der Großen Theorie*. Frankfurt-am-Main: Suhrkamp.

Meyer, David S. and Tarrow, Sidney (1998) 'A Movement Society: Contentious Politics for a New Century', in D.S. Meyer and S. Tarrow (eds), *The Social Movement Society. Contentious Politics for a New Century*. Lanham: Rowman and Littlefield. pp. 1–28.

Milner, Helen V. and Keohane, Robert O. (1996) 'Internationalization and Domestic Politics: An Introduction', in R.O. Keohane and H.V. Milner (eds), *Internationalization and Domestic Politics*. Cambridge: Cambridge University Press. pp. 3–24.

Mitrany, David ([1943] 1966) *A Working Peace System. An Argument for the Functional Development of International Organization*. Chicago: Chicago University Press.

Moravcsik, Andrew (2000) 'The Origins of Human Rights Regimes: Democratic Delegation in Postwar Europe', *International Organization*, 54 (2): 217–52.

Nye, Joseph S. Jr (1990) *Bound to Lead: The Changing Nature of American Power*. New York: Basic Books.

O'Brien, Robert, Goetz, Anne Marie, Scholte, Jan Art and Williams, Marc (2000) *Contesting Global Governance. Multilateral Economic Institutions and Global Social Movements*. Cambridge: Cambridge University Press.

Pauly, Louis W. and Reich, Simon (1997) 'National Structures and Multinational Corporate Behavior: Enduring Differences in the Age of Globalization', *International Organization*, 51 (1): 1–30.

Peterson, M.J. (1997) 'International Organizations and the Creation of Environmental Regimes', in O.R. Young (ed.), *Global Governance. Drawing Insights from the Environmental Experience*. Cambridge, MA: MIT Press. pp. 115–51.

Price, Richard M. (1998) 'Reversing the Gun Sights: Transnational Civil Society Targets Land Mines', *International Organization*, 52 (3): 613–44.

Princen, Thomas (1995) 'Ivory, Conservation, and Environmental Transnational Coalitions', in T. Risse-Kappen (ed.), *Bringing Transnational Relations Back In Non-State Actors, Domestic Structures and International Institutions*, Cambridge: Cambridge University Press. pp. 227–53.

Princen, Thomas and Finger, Matthias (1994) *Environmental NGOs in World Politics: Linking the Local and the Global*. London: Routledge.

Raustiala, Kal (1997) 'States, NGOs, and International Environmental Institutions', *International Studies Quarterly*, 41 (4): 719–40.

Reinicke, Wolfgang H. (1998) *Global Public Policy. Governing without Government?* Washington, DC: Brookings Institution.

Reinicke, Wolfgang H. and Deng, Francis (2000) *Critical Choices. The United Nations, Networks, and the Future of Global Governance*. Ottawa: International Development Research Centre.

Ringus, Lasse (1997) 'Environmental NGOs and Regime Change: The Case of Ocean Dumping of Radioactive Waste', *European Journal of International Relations*, 3 (1): 61–104.

Risse, Thomas, Ropp, Stephen C. and Sikkink, Kathryn (eds) (1999) *The Power of Human Rights: International Norms and Domestic Change*. Cambridge: Cambridge University Press.

Risse-Kappen, Thomas (1995a) 'Bringing Transnational Relations Back In: Introduction', in T. Risse-Kappen (ed.), *Bringing Transnational Relations Back In: Non-State Actors, Domestic Structures and International Institutions*. Cambridge: Cambridge University Press. pp. 3–36.

Risse-Kappen, Thomas (ed.) (1995b) *Bringing Transnational Relations Back In: Non-State Actors, Domestic Structures and International Institutions*. Cambridge: Cambridge University Press.

Rosenau, James N. (1980) *The Study of Global Interdependence. Essays on the Transnationalization of World Affairs*. London: Frances Pinter.

Rosenau, James N. (1990) *Turbulence in World Politics. A Theory of Change and Continuity*. Princeton: Princeton University Press.

Rosenau, James N. (1997) *Along the Domestic-Foreign Frontier. Exploring Governance in a Turbulent World*. Cambridge: Cambridge University Press.

Ruggie, John G. (1993) 'Territoriality and Beyond: Problematizing Modernity in International Relations', *International Organization*, 47 (1): 139–74.

Ruggie, John Gerard (1975) 'International Responses to Technology', *International Organization*, 29: 557–84.

Scharpf, Fritz W. (1999) *Regieren in Europa*. Frankfurt-am-Main: Campus.

Schmalz-Bruns, Rainer (1999) 'Deliberativer Supranationalismus. Demokratische Regieren jenseits des National-staates', *Zeitschrift für Internationale Beziehungen*, 6 (2): 185–244.

Schumpeter, Josef (1919/1953) 'Zur Soziologie der Imperialismen', in *Aufsätze zur Soziologie*. Tübingen: Mohr.

Smith, Jackie (1997) 'Building Political Will after UNCED: EarthAction International', in J. Smith, C. Chatfield and R. Pagnucco (eds), *Transnational Social Movements and Global Politics: Solidarity Beyond the State*. Syracuse: Syracuse University Press. pp. 175–91.

Smith, Jackie, Chatfield, Charles and Pagnucco, Ron (eds) (1997) *Transnational Social Movements and Global Politics: Solidarity Beyond the State*. Syracuse: Syracuse University Press.

Smith, Jackie, Pagnucco, Ron and Lopez, George A. (1998) 'Globalizing Human Rights: The Work of Transnational Human Rights NGOs in the 1990s', *Human Rights Quarterly*, 20 (2): 379–412.

Stopford, John and Strange, Susan (1991) *Rival States, Rival Firms. Competition for World Market Shares*. Cambridge: Cambridge University Press.

Strange, Susan (1996) *The Retreat of the State. The Diffusion of Power in the World Economy*. Cambridge: Cambridge University Press.

Tarrow, Sidney (1996) 'States and Opportunities: The Political Structuring of Social Movements', in D. McAdam, J.D. McCarthy and M.N. Zald (eds), *Comparative Perspectives on Social Movements. Political Opportunities, Mobilizing Structures, and Cultural Framings*. Cambridge: Cambridge University Press. pp. 41–61.

Thomas, Daniel C. (2002) *The Helsinki Effect*. Princeton: Princeton University Press.

Thomson, Janice E. (1994) *Mercenaries, Pirates, and Sovereigns. State-Building and Extraterritorial Violence in Early Modern Europe*. Princeton: Princeton University Press.

Tocqueville, Alexis de (1994) *On Democracy in America*. London: Fontana Press.

Ulbert, Cornelia (1997) *Die Konstruktion von Umwelt. Der Einfluss von Ideen, Institutionen und Kultur auf (inter-) nationale Klimapolitik in den USA und der Bundesrepublik*. Baden-Baden: Nomos.

Vallier, Ivan (1971) 'The Roman Catholic Church: A Transnational Actor', in R.O. Keohane and J.S. Nye Jr. (eds), *Transnational Relations and World Politics*. Cambridge, MA: Harvard University Press.

Van Apeldoorn, Bastian (1999) 'Transnational Capitalism and the Struggle Over European Order', PhD dissertation, European University Institute, Florence.

Vernon, Raymond (1971) *Sovereignty at Bay*. New York: Basic Books.

Victor, David G., Raustiala, Kal and Skolnikoff, Eugene B. (eds) (1998) *The Implementation and Effectiveness of International Environmental Commitments*. Cambridge, MA: MIT Press.

Waltz, Kenneth (1979) *Theory of International Politics*. Reading, MA: Addison–Wesley.

Wapner, Paul (1996) *Environmental Activism and World Civic Politics*. New York: State University of New York Press.

Weiss, Thomas G. and Gordenker, Leon (eds) (1996) *NGOs, the UN, and Global Governance*. Boulder: Lynne Rienner.

Wendt, Alexander (1987) 'The Agent–Structure Problem in International Relations Theory', *International Organization*, 41 (3): 335–70.

Wendt, Alexander (1999) *Social Theory of International Politics*. Cambridge: Cambridge University Press.

Willetts, Peter (ed.) (1982) *Pressure Groups in the Global System. The Transnational Relations of Issue-Orientated Non-Governmental Organizations*. London: Pinter.

Willetts, Peter (ed.) (1996) *The Conscience of the World. The Influence of Non-Governmental Organisations in the UN System*. London: Hurst & Co.

Wolf, Klaus Dieter (2000) *Die Neue Staatsräson – Zwischenstaatliche Kooperation als Demokratieproblem in der Weltgesellschaft*. Baden-Baden: Nomos.

14

Feminist Perspectives on International Relations

J. ANN TICKNER

Compared to the other social sciences, feminist perspectives entered the discipline of international relations (IR) relatively late – at the end of the 1980s. Asking why IR remained immune to gender for so long, Margot Light and Fred Halliday have suggested that IR scholars have tended to view gender as an intra-national problem, irrelevant to international relations; international relations have been seen as 'gender neutral', which means that they can no more be about women than they are about men (Light and Halliday, 1994: 45). With its focus on the 'high' politics of war, the discipline has privileged issues that grow out of men's experiences; we are socialized into believing that war and power politics are spheres of activity with which men have a special affinity and special expertise and that their voices in describing and prescribing for this world are, therefore, likely to be more authentic (Tickner, 1992: 4–5).

It is not coincidental that feminist perspectives entered the discipline at the same time as the end of the Cold War and the consequent lessening in the predominance of military security issues that had tended to dominate IR since its founding. Previously obscured by the East–West rivalry, a variety of issues such as ethnic conflict, economic globalization, democratization and human rights began to occupy the IR agenda in the late 1980s. While international politics has never been just about relations between states, increasingly it has been defined in terms of relationships between international organizations and non-state actors such as transnational corporations, social movements and international non-governmental organizations.

This broad set of issues and a more comprehensive definition of global politics offered an entry point for feminist approaches. While women have always

been players in international politics their voices have rarely been heard in the halls of state power. Therefore, their international political participation, which has more often taken place in non-governmental settings such as social movements, fits better into these broader frameworks.

FEMINIST BEGINNINGS IN IR

Much of the early work in feminist IR was generated by a series of conferences in the United States and the United Kingdom. Papers given at a conference held at the London School of Economics in 1988 were published in a special issue of *Millennium* the same year; many of the articles were reprinted in *Gender and International Relations*, edited by Rebecca Grant and Kathleen Newland; several of the authors came from the development studies field, others from IR. Conferences attended by IR and feminist scholars were held at the University of Southern California in 1989 and Wellesley College in 1990, the latter of which resulted in the volume *Gendered States*, edited by Spike Peterson. In 1989, one of the first courses on women and international relations was introduced into the MA program at the London School of Economics; Fred Halliday, one of the founders of the course, noted that, at that time, there was very little literature in the area to assign to students (Halliday, 1991: 167). In the early 1990s, the British and North American International Studies Associations established gender studies research sections.

Since the early 1990s, publications and panels at professional meetings have proliferated. There is now a substantial body of literature on gender and IR and courses in the field have multiplied. Certain introductory IR texts are including feminist approaches in their overview of the field and edited volumes and anthologies sometimes contain a chapter on feminist perspectives (see for example, Art and Jervis, 1996; Goldstein, 1994; Rourke, 1993; Smith et al., 1996). Special issues on feminist IR have appeared in *Alternatives* and the *Fletcher Forum* edited by Christine Sylvester (1993), and Eric Giordano and Kimberly Silver (1993) respectively. In 1998, *Millennium* published a ten-year anniversary issue, 'Gendering the "international"'. In 1999, the first IR feminist journal, *The International Feminist Journal of Politics* began publication.

Why the Take-Off?

Besides the newly recognized developments in world politics referred to earlier, I believe that the rapid growth of feminist perspectives was also due to the ferment in the discipline in the early 1990s. It is not coincidental that feminist theory came to IR at the same time as a fundamental questioning of its epistemological foundations that called for rethinking the ways in which we explain or understand world politics. Constructivists suggested that ideational as well as material forces could explain international politics and the 'third debate' proclaimed the beginning of a 'post-positivist era' in international relations (Lapid, 1989); these developments marked the appearance of a substantial body of scholarship, associated with critical theory, historical sociology and postmodernism, that challenged both the epistemological and ontological foundations of a field dominated, in the United States at least, by rationalist methodologies. Like feminist theory, much of this critical scholarship is interdisciplinary, drawing from fields such as sociology, history and political philosophy. Also like feminist theory, many scholars on the critical side of the third debate have been skeptical of 'conventional' scholars' quests for objective, universal explanations, typical of positivist methodologies;[1] asking in whose interests and for what purpose knowledge is constructed, post-positivist scholars have examined the intersection between knowledge and power (Walker, 1993).

Even though scholars on both sides of the third debate have been slow to introduce gender into their analyses, these epistemological critiques opened up space for feminist perspectives in a way that previous IR debates did not. Coming out of hermeneutic, historically based and humanistic methodologies, many IR feminist theorists, like critical scholars, have drawn on philosophical traditions outside the social sciences. Rather than generalized rationalist explanations about the behavior of asocial states and anarchic structures, typical of conventional methodologies, feminist theories are based on an ontology of social relations. By revealing and analyzing socially constructed gender hierarchies, feminist perspectives attempt to understand women's subordination, which is seen as variable across time and place.[2] Asking different questions from conventional IR and motivated by different normative concerns, feminists often employ bottom-up analyses which start at the micro-level and attempt to understand how individuals, embedded in social relations, impact and are impacted by international politics at the highest level.

Like scholars on the critical side of the third debate, feminists have frequently gone outside the discipline to seek answers to their questions. Drawing on earlier literatures on women and war, and women and development, feminist approaches are rooted in a long tradition of feminist theory. First-generation IR feminist theory was primarily concerned with bringing to light and critiquing the gendered foundations of the discipline. More recently, IR feminists have begun to develop their own research programs – extending the boundaries of the discipline, asking different questions, and listening to unfamiliar voices from the margins. Besides shedding new light on traditional topics, such as conflict and security, these investigations are taking IR feminists far from the discipline in terms of both subject matter and ways of understanding.

FEMINIST THEORIES

Feminist perspectives also entered IR at about the same time as a debate was taking place within feminist theory itself. The key concern for all types of feminist theory has been to explain women's subordination or the unjustified asymmetry between women and men's social and economic position and to seek prescriptions for ending it. Sandra Whitworth (1994: 2) has claimed that contemporary feminist theory has its roots in social movements directed at transforming the unequal power relationships between women and men. Therefore, a key goal for feminist theory is to understand how the existing social order, one many feminists believe is marked by discrimination and oppression, came into being and how this knowledge can be used to work toward its transformation. Claiming that knowledge emerges from political practice, many feminists do not believe in, nor see the need for, the separation between theory and practice. However, feminists disagree on what they believe constitutes women's subordination as well as how to explain and overcome it.

Feminist theories have been variously described as liberal, Marxist, radical, socialist, psychoanalytic, standpoint, post-colonial and postmodern

(Tong, 1998). Generally committed to a positivist epistemology, typical of the analytic and empiricist tradition of knowledge, liberal feminists believe that the removal of legal obstacles can overcome women's subordination. Most women's political movements in the United States have been and continue to be motivated by liberal feminism. However, post-liberal approaches or 'second-wave' feminisms, see deeply rooted structures of patriarchy that cannot be overcome by legal remedies alone. While psychoanalytic traditions have looked for causes of women's subordination in socialization practices of early childhood, radicals, Marxists and socialists have looked for explanations in structures of patriarchy that 'naturalize' women's subordination, or in the labor market with its gender discriminations and divisions between public (paid) and private (unpaid/domestic) work. Rather than seeking equality with men, radical perspectives, which were strongly influenced by the consciousness-raising movements of the 1960s, have celebrated women's 'feminine' characteristics, and postulated feminist utopias.

In the 1990s, the introduction of postmodern and post-colonial perspectives generated a debate within feminist theory that has had important implications for feminist IR. Postmodernism has viewed with suspicion any mode of feminist thought that has tried to provide *the* feminist explanation as to why women are oppressed (Tong, 1998: 193). Challenging arbitrary boundaries between reason and emotion, mind and body, and self and other, feminist postmodernism has criticized the entire conceptual scheme of Western dualistic thinking and its gendered implications. Emphasizing plurality, multiplicity and difference among women, postmodernism has questioned radical feminism's notion of an essentialized women's standpoint.[3] Emphasizing the connection between knowledge and power and skeptical of the social scientific quest for 'objectivity', postmodern feminists seek to uncover in whose interests existing theories have been constructed. They express skepticism with respect to explanations associated with knowledge from which women have frequently been excluded as knowers and subjects. Postmodern feminism is interested in the problematic of 'otherness' and new forms of subjectivity (Zalewski and Parpart, 1998: 29). Writing in 1994, Christine Sylvester suggested that all feminists can, in some way, be thought of as postmodern because most women have been outsiders in the intellectual life of modernity (Sylvester, 1994: 16).

According to Marianne Marchand and Jane Parpart, whose edited volume *Feminism/Postmodernism/Development* has put the debate about postmodernism in the context of its utility for studying development, feminists have responded to postmodernism in a number of ways. The strongest opposition has come from liberal and Marxist feminist traditions, both of which claim that postmodernism denies the liberal promise of modernity and progress as well as the overarching theories of patriarchy, racism and capitalism upon which Marxist and socialist feminisms have been constructed. Given its skepticism about all forms of knowledge, many feminists believe that postmodernism threatens feminism's emancipatory agenda; its anti-essentialism and refusal to speak of women as an undifferentiated category can lead to political fragmentation and the dissipation of feminist activism (Marchand and Parpart, 1995: 4–7).

However, a growing number of feminists, including many IR feminists, believe postmodernism has much to offer feminist theorizing; one of its most appealing aspects has been its focus on difference, which has been particularly empowering for women of color (Marchand and Parpart, 1995: 4–7). Strongly influenced by Black feminist critiques (Collins, 1990), postmodern feminists have emphasized the need to take into account a variety of structures of oppression associated with race and class as well as gender. Stressing the importance of producing their own knowledge and recovering their own identities, Third World feminists, speaking out of the historical experiences of colonial oppression, offer further evidence of the multiplicity of oppressions (Mohanty, 1991).

FEMINIST THEORIES MEET IR

IR feminists have drawn from all these theoretical traditions. While there is an established liberal literature within feminist IR, much of which focuses on foreign policy, decision-making, voting and public opinion, to which I return later, many IR feminists would identify themselves as post-liberals in that they challenge the claim that women can simply be added to existing theoretical frameworks; they also acknowledge the centrality of gender as a category of analysis. Although many would deny the label 'postmodern', most have been influenced by postmodern and post-colonial approaches and their emphasis on difference among women. Writing on issues such as rape, trafficking, prostitution, domestic service and homework, issues that are far from conventional IR agendas, many IR feminists have focused on individuals and groups at the margins of world politics (Chin, 1998; Moon, 1997; Pettman, 1996; Prügl, 1999a, 1999b). They have shown how the lives of marginalized people are multiply positioned in terms of race, class and culture as well as gender and how the social relations within which individuals' lives are embedded impact on and are impacted by global politics.

Writing in 1991, Rebecca Grant and Kathleen Newland claimed that this diversity of feminist thought should not be a handicap nor stand in the way of conducting research on the gendered nature of international relations (Grant and Newland, 1991: 4). Generally committed to what they term a 'celebration of diversity', IR feminists have followed a variety of different approaches in their explorations. Working across knowledge frameworks, feminists challenge the 'disciplining' effects of disciplinary boundaries. Many of those whose work I discuss are not IR scholars in the disciplinary sense; some would deny affiliation with any traditional disciplinary label. Thus, it is hard to speak of the emergence of a canonized body of knowledge or even the state of the art. Indeed, many feminists would vigorously resist such categorizations of their work. Jill Steans (1998: 15) has suggested that, rather than try to identify the essence of feminism, or establish a set of core feminist beliefs, it is more useful to demonstrate the richness and variety in feminist theories and practices.

In spite of this diversity of thought, debates between IR feminists have been muted and there has not been a great deal of self-criticism among them. This may be due in part to the relative newness of the approach; it may also be due to the fact that, in spite of its rapid growth, feminist IR is still quite marginalized. Since IR feminists, whatever their theoretical orientation, are still struggling to be heard by the wider discipline they may be reluctant to engage in self-criticism. Nevertheless, in summarizing some of the questions and issues with which IR feminists have been concerned, I will attempt to identify some of the debates between them.

Feminist Questions

A question with which IR feminists have often begun their research is, 'where are the women?' Acknowledging that we need to look in unconventional places not normally considered within the boundaries of IR to answer this question, Cynthia Enloe has asked whether women's roles, as secretaries, clerical workers, domestic servants and diplomats' wives, are relevant to the business of international politics (Enloe, 1989: 8). While Enloe believes they are significant, she notes that it is difficult to imagine just what these questions would sound like in the arena of international politics and whether they would be taken seriously (Enloe, 1989: 5).

Locating women has included placing them within gendered structures. Typically, feminist research questions have to do with investigating how the international system and the global economy contribute to the subordination of women and other marginalized groups. Investigating how global structures and processes constrain women's security and economic opportunities requires asking how the types of power necessary to keep unequal gender structures in place are perpetuated. Does it makes any difference to states' behavior that their

foreign and security policies are generally conducted by men and often legitimated through appeals to various types of 'hegemonic' masculinity? Feminists believe that answering questions such as these may enable us to see that what is so often taken for granted in how the world is organized is, in fact, legitimating certain social arrangements that contribute to the subordination of women and other disadvantaged groups.

Questioning the way we have come to understand the world, as well as the forms of power necessary to sustain dominant forms of interpretation, demands different methodologies. In order to answer the kinds of questions outlined above, feminist research has looked both up and down; looking up enables the investigation of how structures of political and economic power as well as dominant forms of knowledge are created, upheld and legitimated. Looking down involves investigations based on the lives of those not normally considered as bearers of knowledge – looking in strange places for people and data or 'lower than low politics' (Sylvester, 1996: 264). Critical of IR's Western centricity, IR feminists have attempted to include the voices and experiences of Third World women in their investigations. Questioning how structural power is legitimated and recovering the experiences of subjugated people demands methods more typical of discourse, anthropology and sociology than political science.

IR feminists have engaged a wide variety of international issues including security, the global economy, development, human rights, global governance and democratization. In order to illustrate some of the paths that feminist IR has taken over the past ten years and some of the emergent debates, I focus on three of these issues – development, the global economy and international security – and discuss some exemplary literature from each.[4] While development is not an issue normally considered in IR, the development debate has been an important locus of the evolution of IR feminist approaches. While international political economy (IPE) and international security have been central to IR, feminist approaches to these topics are quite different; in both the cases, they focus on the security of individuals, particularly those at the margins of global politics.

GENDER IN DEVELOPMENT

During the 1950s and 1960s, development theory and practice was based on the idea that, with Western assistance accompanied by a Western definition about what it meant to be modern, newly independent states in the South could 'take off' into self-sustained economic growth. The early literature on development paid little attention to women in the development process and, for the most part, ignored the contributions that women were making to development.

A separate literature on women and development illustrates the evolution of feminist theories outlined above. Early writings, in the 1970s, were informed by liberal feminism; their goal was to make women visible in the development process. In the 1980s, emphasis shifted to an understanding of gender relations and how they impacted women's lives. Most recently, due to the influence of postcolonial and postmodern feminisms, this literature has emphasized local and particularized knowledge with which to challenge the hegemony of Western orthodoxy. Emanating from women in postcolonial societies, it has contributed significantly to the contemporary feminist epistemological debates discussed earlier; it has also been an important arena for feminist attempts to expand the boundaries and subject matter of IR.

One of the early books which broke the silence about women was Ester Boserup's *Women's Role in Economic Development*, published in 1970. Boserup pointed out that early development models not only overlooked women's contributions but also devised projects that were frequently harmful to women. While Boserup's work has been criticized for ignoring women's reproductive roles as well as hierarchical gender relations that uphold women's subordination more generally (Beneria and Sen, 1986), her book succeeded in making women visible and stimulated calls for women to be integrated into the development process.

Paralleling critiques of liberalism more generally, the Women in Development (WID) approach was criticized for ignoring gender. In her contribution to the Grant and Newland volume, Anne Marie Goetz claimed that international development organizations were engaged in a misleading strategy of integrating women into a process in which they were already fully participating and of which their unremunerated labor was an essential part (Goetz, 1991: 138). Moreover, the WID literature tended to see women as separate from men; it did not deal with the more radical issue as to how gender relations and triple burdens of paid, household and community work decrease women's economic security. An emergent critical literature, much of which is summarized in *Feminism/Postmodernism/ Development*, an edited volume that includes authors from a variety of geographical regions and theoretical perspectives, began to focus on the gendered dimensions of global restructuring and the value of postmodernism for generating new thinking about women, gender and development. It investigated how development processes are embedded in power structures related to ethnicity, race and class as well as gender (Parpart and Marchand, 1995; see also Marchand, 1996a; Pettman, 1996). The gender and development

(GAD) literature has focused on both women and men and how relations between them must be changed if women are to be empowered. This has led to a fundamental re-examination of social structures, a rethinking of hierarchical gender relations, and an acknowledgement of the fact that the situation of women is not homogeneous but a function of multiple power relations (Rathgeber, 1995).

The shift from women to gender occurred not only in the literature but also in development policy circles; this move has not been without its critics, however. In certain cases, the 'mainstreaming' of gender, that has taken place as international governmental organizations have begun to adopt the term, has created a disjuncture between feminist intent, which was to focus on hierarchical and unequal social relations, and the way it is being used in certain policy circles to talk only about women's issues. This has the effect of minimizing the political and contested character of relations between women and men. When gender is used descriptively to refer to women rather than analytically to underscore unequal relations between women and men, questions of power can easily be removed; Sally Baden and Annemarie Goetz (1998: 25) have suggested that it is ironic that a term intended to carry a political message has been so depoliticized in many policy arenas. This has the effect of removing from debate any radical restructuring of political, economic and social relations, an emancipatory goal to which many post-liberal IR feminists are committed.

Recent feminist perspectives on development, as in feminist IR more generally, have emphasized the importance of knowledge emanating from the South. An important feminist critique of Western development models, that has claimed as one of its goals the empowerment of women, has taken place within DAWN (Development Alternatives for Women for a New Era); DAWN is a network that links women researchers from the South to provide guidelines for action based on research and analysis growing out of Southern women's experiences. DAWN's research methodology differs from economistic approaches in that it is bottom-up; starting from analyses of micro-level experiences of poor women and linking these experiences to the macroeconomic level, it works from the assumption that knowledge at each level should inform the other. It claims to promote a new science of empathy that uses intuition and reason simultaneously (Braidotti et al., 1994: 146; Sen and Grown, 1987).

Given their skepticism about the universalism of Western theories and their call for local, specific and historically informed analyses, post-colonial and postmodern approaches have made important contributions to the development debate. Braidotti et al. (1994: ch. 3) argue that postmodernism, with its stress on difference and locality, can make an important contribution to generating new types of knowledge. Since it respects difference and thinks beyond dualism and hierarchy, postmodernism can contribute to dismantling power relations implicit in the production of knowledge; it offers important new ways to critique scientific rationality and technological development.

These claims are highly contested, however. Supporting WID's role in giving voice to women and putting gender onto the agenda of international aid agencies, Mridula Udayagiri has asked whether postmodernism can lead the way to political activism through textual analysis that is decipherable for the most part only by erudite academic feminists (Udayagiri, 1995). Arguing that it is not only postmodernism that can effectively study difference, she claims that the political nature of feminist studies derives from the Enlightenment goal of universalizing experiences that bind us together in order to build effective coalitions (Udayagiri, 1995: 166, 169).

Braidotti et al. propose an alliance between Northern and Southern women built on mutual respect and a recognition of multiple positionality. Based on an interchange of local knowledge arising out of specific situations, this type of model is very different from Western models that rely on elite knowledge emanating only from the North (Braidotti et al., 1994: 120–1). This type of knowledge, informed by political and social practice, is often advocated by feminist theorists and practitioners.

Evolution of the literature on women and development illustrates some important trends in feminist IR more generally. The move from women to gender has allowed IR feminists to investigate how hierarchical structures of inequality between women and men are responsible for women's subordination. A focus on local knowledge has led feminists to different methodologies, such as narrative and ethnography, when designing and conducting their research projects. Debates on the advisability of the shift from women to gender continue, however. While acknowledging that women's lives must be seen in the context of a variety of hierarchical social, political and economic structures, certain feminists believe that losing sight of 'woman' threatens the normative goal of working for women's emancipation (Zalewski, 1998).

GENDER IN THE GLOBAL ECONOMY

While there are obviously enormous differences in the socioeconomic status of women depending on their race, class, nationality and geographic location, women share a certain commonality in that they are disproportionately located at the bottom of the socioeconomic scale in all societies. While figures vary from state to state, on an average, women earn three-quarters of men's earnings even though they work longer hours, many of which are spent in unremunerated reproductive and caring tasks. Of the 1.3 billion people estimated to be in poverty, 70 per cent are women: the number of rural women living in absolute poverty rose by nearly 50 per cent from the mid-1970s to the mid-1990s (United Nations, 1995: 36).[5]

Feminist perspectives on IPE have investigated the extent to which these disturbing figures are attributable to the gendered effects of recent trends in the restructuring of the global economy. Women who work in the wage sector are generally the most poorly paid and women make up a disproportionate number of those working in the informal sector or in subsistence agriculture, areas of the economy that are often ignored by conventional economic analysis. Echoing feminist critiques of the development literature, Marianne Marchand has suggested that women have not been left outside global restructuring; they are participating while remaining invisible (Marchand, 1996a: 585). IR feminists have investigated the reasons for this invisibility that exists not only in the global economy itself but also in the field that studies it. Silence about gender occurs because it is invisible in the concepts used for analysis, the questions that are asked, and the preference for state levels of analysis typical of conventional IPE (Marchand, 1996b: 257).

While *Gendered States*, one of the early volumes in feminist IR, took a state-centric perspective (Peterson, 1992), many of the subsequent feminist analyses of the global economy have relied on a different ontology, one which is closer to that of critical theory. Just as critical theorists have focused on global class structures rather than states (Cox with Sinclair, 1996; Gill, 1995), feminists have examined how hierarchical structures of class, race and gender cross and intersect with state boundaries as well as the interactive effects of these hierarchies on the workings of the global economy (Krause, 1996; Peterson, 1996). Given their interest in understanding how culture, norms and values shape and are shaped by material structures, most IR feminists have rejected rational choice methodologies that focus on calculation of interest. For many IR feminist theorists, adding women to the liberal literature on the global economy is equally problematic because it hides the gendered power structures that feminists believe are the cause of women's disadvantaged position. Working within a variety of postliberal modes of analysis, IR feminists have focused on the global gendered division of labor and how it contributes to women's subordination (Marchand and Runyan, 2000).

A Gendered Division of Labor

As they seek to explain women's disproportionate representation at the bottom of the socioeconomic scale in all societies, feminists have drawn attention to a gendered division of labor that had its origins in seventeenth-century Europe when definitions of male and female were becoming polarized in ways that were suited to the growing division between work and home required by early capitalism. Spike Peterson tells us that the notion of 'housewife' began to place women's work in the private domestic sphere as opposed to the public world of the market inhabited by 'rational economic man', the unit of analysis in liberal economics (Peterson, 1992: 43). Even though women have always worked outside the home, the association of women with gendered roles, such as housewife, caregiver and mother, has become institutionalized and even naturalized, thereby decreasing women's economic security and autonomy.[6] While post-colonial feminists have cautioned against imposing these Western categories on women in the South (Mohanty, 1991), Western forms of patriarchy spread to much of the rest of the world through imperialism where 'civilized' behavior was often equated with the behavior of Western men and women, particularly behavior based on appropriate gender roles.

When women enter the workforce they are disproportionately represented in the caring professions or in 'light' manufacturing industries, vocations, or occupations that are chosen not on the basis of market rationality and profit maximization alone as liberal economic theory assumes, but because of values and expectations that are often emphasized in female socialization. Expectations about appropriate roles for women help to explain why women are disproportionately represented in the caring professions such as education, nursing and social work. Cynthia Enloe has claimed that a 'modern' global economy requires traditional ideas about women, ideas that depend on certain social constructions of what is meant by femininity and masculinity (Enloe, 1989: 174). However, in spite of these assumptions about appropriate gender roles that characterize women as supplemental wage earners, estimates suggest that one-third of all households are headed by women, about half of which are in the South, a fact that is frequently obscured by role expectations based on the notion of male breadwinners (Holcomb and Rothenberg, 1993: 55).[7]

Socialist feminists, particularly, have emphasized how gender ideologies and structures, as well as market forces, lead to low wages and double burdens. They claim that women provide an optimal labor force for contemporary capitalism because, since they are defined as housewives rather than workers, they can be paid lower wages on the assumption that their wages are supplemental to their family's income. In the export processing zones (EPZs) of Asia, Africa and Latin America in the 1980s, more than 70 per cent of the workforce was female (Enloe, 1989: 162).[8] Companies favor hiring young unmarried women who can achieve a high level of productivity at a lower wage; these women are frequently fired if they get married or pregnant. Because of expectations associated with traditional gender roles there is a belief that women possess 'nimble fingers', have patience for tedious jobs, and sew 'naturally'; thus, this kind of work is not seen as skilled and is remunerated accordingly.

How disadvantaged women are by a division of labor that has evolved simultaneously with global capitalism is a subject of debate, however. Not all feminist scholars believe that the increase in employment of women in low-paying factory jobs is detrimental. Linda Lim has argued that negative stereotyping of women in export manufacturing in the South has been based on outworn assumptions and generalizations from data collected in the 1970s during the earliest stages of the establishment of export factories. Lim claims that wages, hours and conditions in factories in EPZs are generally better than in their domestic counterparts and, therefore, are much desired. She also suggests that women workers in these industries tend to be better educated than average workers in their countries and that there is considerable diversity in terms of age and marital status (Lim, 1990: 101–19). Even if it is underremunerated relative to men or to wages in the North, many argue that this type of work may be the best option for women and better than no work at all. It also gives women more financial independence and higher status.

In her study of African women, April Gordon has claimed that paid work is an important source of power for women; like Lim, she sees no necessary connection between capitalism and the exploitation of women. Citing the African case, she suggests that a transition to capitalism that, she predicts, is leading to the increased participation of women in the waged sector, will actually enhance women's position relative to men and break the hold of African patriarchy that predates both capitalism and colonialism. For Gordon, therefore, it is patriarchy, not capitalism that is the real source of women's oppression (Gordon, 1996).

Ruth Pearson has suggested that the only way to assess the validity of these competing arguments is by conducting empirical case studies; such studies are indeed demonstrating that women's experiences of employment vary between marginality, inclusion and exploitation. In some places women's share of the industrial workforce is declining because of upgrading of levels of technology whereas in others they are emerging as multi-skilled workers. Pearson claims that it is necessary to recognize that we are not talking about structurally determined processes but gender identities that are open to reconstruction by women workers themselves (Pearson, 1998: 171–6). Many of these empirical case studies have been conducted by scholars outside IR as traditionally defined. I elaborate on two whose authors explicitly draw on IR constructivist and critical approaches as bases for their research. They are both concerned with labor issues that complicate the public/private divide and with the ways in which gender can be deployed as a strategy for improvement as well as repression.

Women workers on the margins: two IR feminist case studies Gender enters into the issue of home-based work. As companies have moved toward a more 'flexible' labor force in all parts of the world, cost-saving has included home-based work which is easily hired and fired. Exempt from any national labor standards that may exist, 'domesticated' workers are outside the working class and its regulations; they are generally paid lower wages than factory workers and are not paid at all when there is no work. Since women, often of necessity, prefer work that more easily accommodates to family responsibilities, home-based workers are predominantly women. Traditional notions of the division of labor which defines women as housewives, a category with expectations that labor is free, legitimizes wages at below subsistence levels (Prügl, 1999b: 198).

In her study of home-based work and the International Labor Organization (ILO), Elisabeth Prügl investigates how the ILO finally came to adopt the 1996 convention setting international standards for home-based work (Prügl, 1999a). Prügl positions her research in the context of the IR constructivist literature; she argues that since the constructivist approach assumes that life is social and social relations are variably constructed, it is a useful framework for analyzing gender. She draws on Nicholas Onuf's (1989) characterization of rules to suggest that 'gender is an institution that codifies power, a constellation of rules and related practices that distributes privilege in a patterned way and is reproduced in communication' (Prügl, 1999a: 13). The goal of the study is to demonstrate how social activists, lobbying for ILO protection for home workers, deployed various definitions of gender to pressure the ILO to adopt the convention. The discourse of separate worlds of male 'breadwinners' and female 'dependants' had to be challenged and the gender ideology that separates public and private had to be broken down before standards for homework were eventually put in place in 1996.

Acknowledging the current emphasis in feminist research on local knowledge, Prügl defends her research design and its focus on global rules (Prügl, 1999a: 148). Given the divorce of space from territory and place, typical of the modern economy, Prügl claims that the distinction between the global and the local have become problematic as global networks are constructed among distant agents. Since activists, in their efforts to work for protective legislation at the local level, employ global claims to effect particular

outcomes, she argues for the emancipatory potential of 'practical knowledge' that focuses at both levels.

While they have paid considerable attention to women's unpaid reproductive labor, feminists have been reluctant to take on the question of paid domestic service, an issue that is becoming increasingly internationalized due to recent economic restructuring. Since it is women who usually employ and often exploit other women, paid domestic service is an arena where issues of colonialism, class and race are particularly acute. In a case study of the employment of Philippine and Indonesian domestic servants in Malaysia, Christine Chin (1998) dates the inflow of overseas domestic workers back to the 1970s when the Malaysian government instituted the New Economic Policy designed to promote growth through modernization of the economy. Chin claims that domestic service, a 'pre-modern' labor form that has traditionally been thought of as a private issue beyond the reach of the state, is actually shaped by state policies. She uses a critical theory perspective to demonstrate how domestic service, rather than being a personal, private issue as is often assumed, is one that involves the state and the political economy of the East Asian region. Reinforcing the feminist claim of the interpenetration of the personal and the political, she investigates the multi-causal linkages between region, state and household. While previous analyses have examined class and racial dimensions of what she calls the repressive developmental state, little work has been done on its gendered dimensions.

Chin describes her work as multi-method ethnographic research; she describes analysis of her interviews as a study of narrativity. Narrative is a method employed by some feminists to further their goal of constructing knowledge that comes out of people's everyday life experiences. Chin claims that such knowledge is important for reaching a level of self-understanding that can enable people to comprehend hierarchical structures of inequality or oppression within which their lives are situated and thereby move toward overcoming them. Like Prügl, her emphasis is on practical, emancipatory knowledge.

Most feminists working on global economic issues believe that women continue to be disadvantaged relative to men by a global division of labor that relegates them disproportionately to unremunerated subsistence and household tasks or to low-paying waged jobs – roles that are based on traditional notions of the public/private divide but that are being reinterpreted to respond to new demands for flexible labor. As these case studies demonstrate, feminists are particularly interested in the local/global dynamic; they have examined the extent to which global economic forces penetrate as far down as the household and how activities in the local arena sustain and support the global economy, often at the expense of those on the margins.

Suspicious of universal arguments about economic rationalization, feminists working in this area have drawn on local knowledge and analyses that take social as well as economic relations into account. They claim that the negative effects of the gendered division of labor on women cannot be understood without an analysis of the complex social relations in which the lives of all individuals are embedded; women's subordination is caused not by impersonal market forces alone, but by processes that result from conscious political, economic and social choices, choices that are often based on changing assumptions about gender. Feminists writing about the contemporary global economy claim, therefore, that only when these processes are revealed and understood can progress be made toward substantially reducing these gendered boundaries of inequality.

GENDERING INTERNATIONAL SECURITY

Feminist perspectives on security have raised different issues, engaged in different debates and used different methodologies from traditional international security studies. Feminists have questioned the foundational stories of IR on which explanations about the 'security dilemma' have been built. Using discourse analysis, they have analyzed the 'masculinity' of strategic discourse and its consequences for strategic policy. Examining the effects of war on women, they have challenged the claim that women are a 'protected' category. They have also entered into the long-standing debate as to whether women are more peaceful than men; recently, an emergent empirical literature is linking this debate to the issue of the democratic peace.

National Security: A Gendered Discourse

In her feminist re-analysis of what she calls the 'creation myths' of international relations, on which realist assumptions about states' behavior are built, Rebecca Grant has claimed that these stories depend on male representations of how individuals function in society. While the parable of man's amoral, self-interested behavior in the state of nature, made necessary by the lack of restraint on the behavior of others, is taken by realists to be a universal model for explaining states' behavior in the international system, Grant asserts that it is male rather than universal. If life were to go on in the state of nature for more than one generation, other activities, such as childbirth and child-rearing, typically associated with women, must have been taking place. Grant suggests that, when women are absent from these foundational myths, a source of gender bias is created that extends into international relations theory (Grant, 1991: 9–17).

For similar reasons, feminists have also questioned the use of rational choice theory based on the instrumentally rational behavior of individuals in the marketplace that neorealists have used to explain states' security-seeking behavior. According to this model, states are unproblematically assumed to be instrumental profit maximizers pursuing power and autonomy in an anarchic international system. When international cooperation exists, it is explained not in terms of community, but rather in terms of enlightened self-interest. Feminists have suggested that rational choice theory is also based on a partial representation of human behavior which, since women in the West have historically been confined to reproductive activities, has been more typical of certain men (Tickner, 1992: 82). The instrumentally competitive behavior of states, that results in power-balancing, is similar to equilibrium theory or the market behavior of 'rational economic man'. Therefore, it tends to privilege certain types of behaviors over others. While states do indeed behave in these ways, these models offer us only a partial understanding of their behavior.

For example, does the fact that states' national security policies are often legitimated by appealing to 'hegemonic' masculine characteristics, such as power and self-help, mean that certain types of foreign policy behaviors – standing tall rather then wimping out – are seen as more legitimate than others? Carol Cohn has asked whether it could it be that men who, in the role of defense experts, must employ tough 'masculine' language and suppress any 'feminized' thoughts when constructing strategic options, come to regard more cooperative choices as unthinkable and cooperative behavior as unlikely. Motivated by her claim that the power of language shapes how and what people think, Cohn uses discourse analysis and ethnography to answer some of these questions in her study of defense intellectuals (Cohn, 1993). Her analysis suggests that the masculine gendered discourse of American security experts is the only permissible way of speaking about national security if one is to be taken seriously by the strategic community. This rational, disembodied language precludes discussion of the death and destruction of war, issues that can only be spoken of in emotional terms stereotypically associated with women. In other words, Cohn claims that the limits on what can be said with the language of strategic discourse constrains our ability to think fully and well about national security.

Challenging the Myth of Protection

Despite the widespread myth that wars are fought, mostly by men, to protect 'vulnerable' people, a category to which women and children are generally assigned, women and children constitute a significant proportion of casualties in recent wars. There has been a sharp increase in the proportion of civilian casualties of war – from about 10 per cent at the beginning of the century to 90 per cent in the mid-1990s (United Nations, 1995: 45). Women and children constitute about 90 per cent of the total refugee population, a population whose numbers increased from 3 million to 27 million between 1970 and 1994, mainly due to military conflict, particularly ethnic conflicts (United Nations, 1995: 14). Feminists also draw our attention to issues of rape in war. As illustrated by the war in the former Yuogoslavia, where it is estimated that 20,000 to 35,000 women were raped during the war in Bosnia and Herzegovina (Pettman, 1996: 101), rape is not just an accident of war but often a systematic military strategy. Cynthia Enloe has described social structures in place around most US army bases where women are kidnapped and sold into prostitution; this system of militarized sexual relations has required explicit American policy-making (Enloe, 1993: 19–20).

In her study of prostitution around US military bases in South Korea in the 1970s, Katharine Moon has shown how these people-to-people relations were actually matters of security at the international level. Clean-up of prostitution camps by the South Korean government through policing of sexual health and work conduct of prostitutes was part of its attempt to prevent withdrawal of American troops that had begun under the Nixon Doctrine of 1969. Thus, military prostitution interacted with US–Korean security politics at the highest political level. Crossing levels of analysis, Moon demonstrates how the weakness of the Korean state, in terms of influencing the US government, resulted in authoritarian sexist control at the domestic level. In other words, national security translated into social insecurity for these women (Moon, 1997: 151–60). Describing her fieldwork in Korea as an attempt to lift the curtains of invisibility that have shrouded Korean prostitutes' existence, Moon's stories, based on ethnographic research, locate women in places not normally considered relevant to IR and link their experiences to wider processes and structures crucial to national security.

Feminists believe that by looking at the effects of war on women, a better understanding of the unequal gender relations that sustain military activities can be gained. Given the belief of many feminists that knowledge has the potential for emancipation, revealing social practices that support war and that are variable across societies suggests that war is a cultural construction rather than an inevitability. Evidence about women in conflict situations severely strains the protection myth; yet, such myths have been important in upholding the legitimacy of war and the impossibility of peace. Looking more deeply into these gendered constructions can help understand not only some of the causes of war, but how certain ways of thinking about security have been legitimized at the expense of others both in the discipline of IR and in political practice.

Gendering War

The association between masculinity and war has been central to feminist investigations. While the manliness of war is rarely denied, militaries must work hard to turn men into soldiers through misogynist training thought necessary to teach men to fight. Importantly, such training depends on the denigration of anything that could be considered feminine; to act like a soldier is not to be 'womanly'. 'Military manhood', a type of heroic masculinity that goes back to the Greeks, attracts recruits and maintains self-esteem in institutions where subservience and obedience are the norm (Segal, 1987: 187).

Another image of a soldier is a just warrior, self-sacrificially protecting women, children and other vulnerable people (Elshtain, 1987). The notion that young males fight wars to protect vulnerable groups, such as women and children, who cannot be expected to protect themselves, has been an important motivator for the recruitment of military forces. As discussed earlier, the concept of the 'protected' is essential to the legitimation of violence; it has been an important myth that has sustained support for war by both women and men. In wartime, the heroic just warrior is sometimes contrasted with a malignant often racialized masculinity attributed to the enemy; this serves as further justification for protection.

These images of the masculinity of war depend on rendering women invisible. The recent acceptance of women into the armed forces of certain states complicates this issue however. By the end of the 1980s, 430,000 women were serving as uniformed personnel in the world's regular military units, although this has not changed the masculinized culture of states' militaries. The military remains largely a male institution and the presence of women stirs deep currents, particularly with respect to combat. The image of female soldiers fighting and dying in wars, as was evidenced in the Gulf War of 1991, is deeply disturbing to public opinion. While placing women in combat is motivated by the liberal principle of equality, it is in strong tension with the myth of protection and with the culturally embedded view of what it means to be a warrior; in certain cases, it has been strongly resisted by the military itself with claims of its negative effect on combat readiness. It has also generated a debate within feminism; while liberal feminists support women's equal participation in the military, many radical feminists believe that women should reject fighting in men's wars. In fact, certain radical feminists have claimed that women have a special affinity with peace.

Gendering Peace

If women have been largely absent from the world's militaries, they have been well represented in a variety of peace movements. All-women peace groups have frequently drawn upon maternal imagery to relay their message. Drawing on feminine characteristics, such as caregiving and connectedness, many women in these movements see themselves as different from men. Such movements have ranged from protesting the nuclear confrontation between the great powers during the Cold War to organizing against the repressive activities of states on their own populations. The Women's Strike for Peace in the United States in the early 1960s drew attention to what its members believed was an alarming escalation of the Cold War. Although pre-dating radical feminism, these women defended their right as mothers to influence the course of government in its support for nuclear containment, a course which they claimed was not protecting but threatening the American family. Stressing that nuclear war was the greatest threat to families, they challenged the notion that war is waged by men to protect women (Swerdlow, 1990: 8).

The association of women with peace is a major debate in feminist IR. The suffrage movement at the beginning of the century argued that, if women were given the vote and allowed more influence over foreign policy, peace would follow. Many women in peace groups and peace research today have similar beliefs. For example, feminist peace researcher Betty Reardon has argued for the need for 'feminine' values which she sees as morally superior in a nuclear world (Reardon, 1985). Drawing on psychoanalytic object relations theory and influenced by the work of Carol Gilligan (1982), Sara Ruddick has argued for the affinity of a politics of peace with maternal thinking. While Ruddick is careful not to say that women are more peaceful than men, she does claim that there is a contradiction between mothering and war (Ruddick, 1989: chs 4, 5). While Ruddick believes that the association of women with peace is the result of female socialization, other feminists, particularly radical feminists, believe that this association is biologically rooted in the ability of women to bear children.

While maternal thinking has often been quite successful in motivating women's peace movements, it has made many feminists, including many IR feminists, uncomfortable. The association of men with war and women with peace reinforces gender hierarchies and false dichotomies that contribute to the devaluation of both women and peace (Sylvester, 1987). Assumptions about peaceful women and warlike men lead to antagonisms that threaten the credibility of feminist projects. In their study of women foreign policy decision-makers, Nancy McGlen and Meredith Sarkees (1993) set out to test the relationship between women and peace. Characterizing the debate as one between 'minimizers', who minimize differences between women and men, and 'maximizers', who support the special affinity of women with peace, they interviewed women in high level positions in the US Departments of Defense and State. Relying on data from their interviews and anonymous questionnaires, they found that, while there was some indication of different styles of leadership, there was little evidence of different attitudes; thus, they concluded that more women in leadership positions would not result in significant changes in policy. Asking the question to both women and men as to whether more women in the departments of Defense and State would have an impact on US foreign policy, 75 per cent replied in the negative (McGlen and Sarkees, 1993: 303).

The broader evidence for the association of women with peace is inconclusive (Light and Halliday, 1994: 48). Jean Elshtain (1987), Cynthia Enloe (1993) and others have documented both women's roles in various peace movements as well as their support for, and participation in, war. McGlen and Sarkees (1993: 5) and others have claimed that the association of women with peace is a liability because it has been used to keep women out of politics. While peace movements, that have relied on maternal images, may have had some success, they do nothing to change existing gender relations; this allows men to remain in control and to continue to dominate the agenda of world politics while women's voices are often seen as inauthentic and 'idealistic' in matters of defense and foreign policy-making.

An example of the negative consequences of associating women with peace is Francis Fukuyama's discussion of the biological roots of human aggression and its association with war that appeared in the journal *Foreign Affairs* in 1998. Fukuyama claimed that women are more peaceful than men, a fact that, he believes, for the most part is biologically determined. Therefore, a world run by women would be a more peaceful world. However, Fukuyama claimed that only in the West is the realization of what he calls a 'feminized' world likely, since he believes that areas outside the West will continue to be run by young aggressive men; therefore, Western men, who can stand up to threats posed by dangers from outside, must remain in charge, particularly in the arena of international politics (Fukuyama, 1998).

Arguments such as these are, in reality, deeply conservative; given the dangers of an aggressive world, they imply that women must be kept in their place and out of international politics (Tickner, 1999). And, as many IR scholars have claimed, the leap from aggressive men to aggressive states is problematic. Moreover, there is little evidence to suggest that men are 'naturally' aggressive or that women are always peaceful; many feminists believe that traditional socially constructed concepts of masculinity and femininity that, as I have suggested, sustain war require an exercise of power; therefore, they are not inevitable and can be changed (Enloe, 1989: 3).

Certain scholars have also begun to outline a possible relationship between the claim that democracies do not fight each other and gender. Robert Keohane (1998: 197) has suggested that a research program that links gender hierarchies with war and peace could be fruitful. One such study (Caprioli, 2000) has investigated whether gender equality correlates with fewer military solutions to resolve international disputes. Testing whether high levels of gender equality yield low levels of militarization, Mary Caprioli finds that states with a long history of female suffrage, a high percentage of women in parliaments, and relatively high economic and social status for women, are more likely to settle disputes peacefully.

Since there are very few states in which women are in positions of power in significant numbers it is difficult to say whether gender equality accounts for the relative peacefulness of certain states. While there is little evidence to suggest that the influence of women has predisposed states against entering wars, it is true, however, that, in certain cases, a gender gap does exist when measuring support for war. Nancy Gallagher (1993) has demonstrated that women in the United States have consistently shown less support for forceful means of pursuing foreign policy goals than men and that this gender gap continues to grow. It was widest at the time of the Gulf War of 1991 although it closed somewhat once the fighting had begun.[9] There was evidence to suggest that those who opposed military intervention were amongst those most likely to support feminist goals, a claim also supported by an analysis of attitudes toward the peace process in the Middle East.

A study of Israeli, Egyptian, Palestinian and Kuwaiti attitudes toward the Arab/Israeli conflict broken down by sex found that men and women did not have different attitudes and there was no evidence of women being less militaristic. Using data collected between 1988 and 1994, it did, however, find a strong positive correlation between attitudes toward support for equality of women and support for diplomacy and compromise. Therefore, the authors saw a connection between feminism and positive attitudes about international conflict resolution (Tessler and Warriner, 1997).

These examples are instructive; they suggest that reducing unequal gender hierarchies could make a positive contribution to peace and social justice; such a goal is more 'realistic' than idealized notions of an unattainable 'feminine' peace. Offering a counter position that rejects both the masculinity of war and a feminine peace, Mary Burguieres has argued for building a feminist security framework on common ungendered foundations. She claims that women have no superior moral claim to being bearers of peace (Burguieres, 1990: 8). She has suggested a role for feminism in dismantling the imagery that underlies patriarchy and militarism and a joint effort in which both women and men would be responsible for changing existing structures.

Much of the feminist work on international security, in addition to these empirical studies, has been concerned with analyzing various constructions of masculinity and femininity and examining how they have upheld the legitimacy of war and the devaluation of peace. Increasingly, the study of masculinity is being included on the feminist IR agenda more generally. Feminists are beginning to examine not only the masculinity of war, but also how various types of masculinity play out in the global economy and in the construction of IR theory more generally. A 1998 volume entitled *The 'Man' Question in International Relations*, included contributions from a number of male scholars in the field writing about masculinity (Zalewski and Parpart, 1998). This type of work is important if feminism is to successfully engage with and have a future in the broader discipline.

WHAT IS THE FUTURE FOR FEMINIST IR?

In *Gendered States*, Spike Peterson (1992: 11–15) challenged IR to open up space for feminist conversations. She encouraged the discipline to question the empirical adequacy of knowledge claims that exclude knowledge about women and to think about the implications of taking gender seriously. Through discussion of some scholarship in development, the global economy, and international security, I have shown why feminists believe that it is important to take women and gender seriously. Yet, for the most part, IR has been slow to include women or gender in its investigations.

Ten years after the introduction of the graduate course on gender and international relations at the London School of Economics, Fred Halliday saw little progress in integrating gender into the wider discipline. In 1998 he claimed that most IR departments, journals and conferences still paid scant attention to feminist IR (Halliday, 1998: 843). Although she thinks this may be changing, Marianne Marchand notes a lack of engagement with critical IR also (Marchand, 1998: 202).[10] While the third debate and the introduction of constructivist approaches more generally have engaged critical and conventional scholars to some degree, there has been little discussion of feminism.

In the few cases where critiques of IR feminism have occurred, they have usually been at a fairly abstract level of generality; they have focused on feminists' lack of 'rigor' or of an adequate explanatory framework (Genest, 1996: 511). Feminists have also been criticized for claiming that women are more peaceful and cooperative than men, a claim many would deny as discussed earlier.[11]

What are some of the reasons for this lack of engagement? Robert Keohane has claimed that it may be because the politicization of the debate on issues related to feminist scholarship has meant that IR scholars fear that if they engage seriously, they will become targets for attacks on their motives (Keohane, 1998: 612). I would argue, however, that, particularly with respect to conventional IR, it may be due to the very different onto-logical and epistemological commitments of each approach (Tickner, 2001). IR scholars see a world of states which they portray as rational unitary actors; feminists de-emphasize state boundaries and focus on hierarchical social relations notably, but not exclusively, gender relations. Joya Misra sees a similar disjuncture between feminism and world systems theory. She claims that feminism focuses on individuals' lives as its unit of analysis while world systems theory focuses on the world system (Misra, 2000: 120). As they move on from revealing and critiquing the gendered foundations of the discipline toward establishing their own research programs, IR feminists are drawing on tools, such as discourse analysis and ethnography, more typical of history, sociology and anthropology than of political science. These are methodologies not typical of IR as conventionally defined. Frequently, this type of research is dismissed as 'not IR' or 'not science'; these epistemological differences are probably the most serious barriers to engagement.

The lack of conversation works in both directions. Fred Halliday (1998: 843) has faulted feminist scholarship more generally for its lack of recognition of the international. He has also criticized feminists for their 'celebration of diversity' which, he claims, runs the risk of slipping into fruitless discourses that do little to address policy issues or help students understand these issues (Halliday, 1998: 844). Halliday's remarks were published in the 1998 *Millennium* anniversary special issue which was intended to 'revisit gender in IR ten years on'. The volume began with an article by a post-colonial feminist, Gayatri Spivak. Contributors included scholars from a variety of disciplines such as area studies, cultural studies, literary criticism and philosophy, and theorists and practitioners from non-governmental organizations (NGOs). The editors' introduction stated that the goal of the conference, which formed the basis of the articles, was to expand the ways and means of analysis in international studies beyond those considered legitimate by state-centric IR – to show that it is possible to think about 'the international' without being trapped in the traditional framework of IR. The editors rejected the strategy of those IR feminists who are still trying to engage the IR mainstream on the importance of gender (Odysseos and Seckinelgin, 1998: iii–iv).

Several of the articles in the *Millennium* special issue represented views of feminists in international studies broadly defined who reject or ignore the discipline of IR and who are venturing out to create new definitions of international studies and new ways of analyzing them. The attempts to engage with a discipline that they see as lacking an understanding of and interest in gender and feminist theory is regarded as fruitless. It is indeed instructive to note that a number of the early founders of feminist IR have moved on to other professional lives.[12] Then there are scholars, such as Cynthia Enloe and Jean Elshtain, who have written extensively about women, gender and international politics, but who frame their arguments without addressing the discipline directly.[13]

There are also those feminists who continue to call for conversations (Locher and Prügl, 2001; Marchand, 1998; Tickner, 1997) and, as I have described, continue to write within the analytical frameworks of the discipline. In spite of the difficulties of conversation, I believe that it is important that IR feminists stay connected to the discipline. Nevertheless, it is important to recognize that power differences have played an important role in the marginalizing of gender issues and feminist scholarship. Inequalities between mainstream and feminist IR allow for greater ignorance of feminist approaches on the part of the mainstream than is possible for feminists with regard to the broader discipline if they are to be accorded any legitimacy within the profession. For those feminists not working with methodologies considered acceptable by much of the discipline, efforts to delegitimate their work on epistemological grounds will continue. This will not change until these methodologies are awarded equal legitimacy in political science departments where most IR graduate training takes place.

While feminist IR cannot tell us all we need to know about global politics, it does allow us to see new issues in new ways as well as to reconsider how we view traditional ones. Listening to the voices of those on the margins has allowed feminists to uncover different worlds and begin to build the kind of practical knowledge necessary to construct a more democratic global politics. Moving toward a global politics, built on foundations where gender is no longer a system of oppression, is a goal to which such knowledge can contribute. Critical questioning of the founding assumptions of IR and the raising of the kinds of issues discussed in this chapter are crucial if IR is to contribute to building a more peaceful and just world, goals which have motivated the discipline since its founding.

Notes

This chapter draws from Tickner (1997) and Tickner (2001). I would like to thank Craig Murphy and the volume editors for their helpful comments.

1 I define 'conventional' in the methodological sense – as scholars in realist, neorealist, neoliberal, behavioral and empiricist traditions who are committed to data-based methods of testing. I define positivism broadly – as a belief that the same methodologies can be applied in the natural and social worlds; that the social world, like the natural world, has regularities; that there can be a distinction between facts and values; and that truth statements can be determined by appeal to neutral facts (Smith, 1997: 168).

2 Throughout this chapter, I define gender, as do most feminists, as a set of culturally defined, socially constructed characteristics. (Gender is distinct from sex, which is the biological aspect of what it means to be a man or a woman.) Power, autonomy, public and reason are characteristics stereotypically associated with masculinity, while their opposites, weakness, dependence, private and emotion, are associated with femininity. The masculine characteristics are generally regarded more favorably by men and women alike; they correspond to an idealized form of masculinity, or 'hegemonic masculinity', to which, obviously, not all men conform. (This carries particular implications for minorities.) Importantly, gender is relational; masculinity and femininity depend on each other for their definitions which vary across history and culture. Gender is a hierarchical relationship of power and inequality between men and women. For a comprehensive analysis of gender as a lens for viewing world politics see Peterson and Runyan, 1999: ch. 2.

3 The term 'standpoint' comes from the Marxist notion of a privileged political and epistemological standpoint. Standpoint feminism has been defined as a vision produced by the political conditions and distinctive work of women (Hartsock, 1983). Given feminist concerns with difference, the question of a single feminist standpoint has been much debated.

4 For some examples of literatures that summarize feminist perspectives on human rights, global governance and democratization see Charlesworth, 1994; Meyer and Prügl, 1999; and Waylen, 1994, respectively.

5 While not the most recent issue, I draw on the 1995 edition of the *Human Development Report* because its focus was specifically on women and gender issues.

6 For further elaboration of the origins of the gendered division of labor see Mies, 1986: ch. 2.

7 Note, however, that statistics on the number of female-headed households in the world are notoriously unreliable. For an analysis that disputes the assumption that women-headed households are necessarily poor see Jackson, 1998: 44.

8 Evidence suggests that this percentage may be declining as automation increases and women are replaced by more technically skilled males. See Runyan, 1996: 240.

9 In December 1990, men were evenly divided, 48 per cent for and 48 per cent against attacking Iraqi forces:

73 per cent of women were opposed and 22 per cent were supportive (Gallagher, 1993: 29).

10 Marchand cites exceptions to this lack of engagement; they include George, 1994; Scholte, 1993; and Zalewski and Parpart, 1998.

11 One IR scholar who has engaged more specifically with feminist IR is Adam Jones. Jones disagrees that IR feminists are constructing new theories; he has also faulted feminism for not paying sufficient attention to male victims of international and inter-ethnic violence (Jones, 1996).

12 Both Rebecca Grant and Kathleen Newland have left academic IR for more policy-oriented work.

13 One of Elshtain's early pieces (1985) did offer a feminist critique of realism but she has since moved away from engaging directly with IR as a discipline.

Bibliography

Art, Robert and Jervis, Robert (1996) *International Politics: Enduring Concepts and Contemporary Issues*, 5th edn. New York: Longman.

Baden, Sally and Goetz, Anne Marie (1998) 'Who Needs [Sex] When You Can Have [Gender]? Conflicting Discourses on Gender at Beijing', in Cecile Jackson and Ruth Pearson (eds), *Feminist Visions of Development: Gender Analysis and Policy*. New York: Routledge.

Benerai, Lourdes and Sen, Gita (1986) 'Accumulation, Reproduction and Women's Role in Economic Development: Boserup Revisited', in Eleanor Leacock and Helen I. Safa (eds), *Women's Work: Development and the Division of Labor by Gender*. South Hadley, MA: Bergin and Garvey.

Boserup, Ester (1970) *Women's Role in Economic Development*. London: Allen & Unwin.

Braidotti, Rosi, Charkiewicz, E., Hausler, S. and Wieringa, S. (1994) *Women, the Environment and Sustainable Development: Towards a Theoretical Synthesis*. London: Zed Books.

Burguieres, Mary (1990) 'Feminist Approaches to Peace: Another Step for Peace Studies', *Millennium: Journal of International Studies*, 19 (1): 1–18.

Caprioli, Mary (2000) 'Gendered Conflict', *Journal of Peace Research*, 37 (1): 51–68.

Charlesworth, Hilary (1994) 'What are "Women's International Human Rights"?', in Rebecca J. Cooke (ed.), *Human Rights of Women: National and International Perspectives*. Philadelphia: University of Pennsylvania Press.

Chin, Christine B.N. (1998) *In Service and Servitude: Foreign Female Domestic Workers and the Malaysian 'Modernity Project'*. New York: Columbia University Press.

Cohn, Carol (1993) 'Wars Wimps and Women: Talking Gender and Thinking War', in Miriam Cooke and Angela Wollacott (eds), *Gendering War Talk*. Princeton: Princeton University Press.

Collins, Patricia Hill (1990) *Black Feminist Thought*. New York: Routledge.

Cox, Robert W. with Sinclair, Timothy J. (1996) *Approaches to World Order*. Cambridge: Cambridge University Press.

Elshtain, Jean Bethke (1985) 'Reflections on War and Political Discourse: Realism, Just War, and Feminism in the Nuclear Age', *Political Theory*, 13 (1): 39–57.

Elshtain, Jean Bethke (1987) *Women and War*. New York: Basic Books.

Enloe, Cynthia (1989) *Bananas, Beaches, and Bases: Making Feminist Sense of International Politics*. Berkeley: University of California Press.

Enloe, Cynthia (1993) *The Morning After: Sexual Politics at the End of the Cold War*. Berkeley: University of California Press.

Fukuyama, Francis (1998) 'Women and the Evolution of World Politics', *Foreign Affairs*, 77 (5): 24–40.

Gallagher, Nancy (1993) 'The Gender Gap in Popular Attitudes Toward the Use of Force', in Ruth Howes and Michael Stevenson (eds), *Women and the Use of Military Force*. Boulder: Lynne Rienner.

Genest, Mark A. (1996) *Conflict and Cooperation: Evolving Theories of International Relations*. New York: Harcourt Brace.

George, Jim (1994) *Discourses of Global Politics: A Critical (Re)Introduction to International Relations*. Boulder: Lynne Rienner.

Gill, Stephen (1995) 'Globalisation, Market Civilisation, and Disciplinary Neoliberalism', *Millennium: Journal of International Studies*, 24 (3): 399–423.

Gilligan, Carol (1982) *In a Different Voice: Psychological Theory and Women's Development*. Cambridge, MA: Harvard University Press.

Giordano, Eric and Silver, Kimberly (1993) 'Special Issue: Gender in International Relations: Evolving Perspectives', *Fletcher Forum*, 17 (1): 1–131.

Goetz, Ann Marie (1991) 'Feminism and the Claim to Know: Contradictions in Feminist Approaches to Women and Development', in Rebecca Grant and Kathleen Newland (eds), *Gender and International Relations*. Indianapolis: Indiana University Press.

Goldstein, Joshua (1994) *International Relations*. New York: Harper Collins.

Gordon, April A. (1996) *Transforming Capitalism and Patriarchy: Gender and Development in Africa*. Boulder: Lynne Rienner.

Grant, Rebecca (1991) 'The Sources of Gender Bias in International Relations Theory', in Rebecca Grant and Kathleen Newland (eds), *Gender and International Relations*. Indianapolis: Indiana University Press.

Grant, Rebecca and Newland, Kathleen (eds) (1991) *Gender and International Relations*. Indianapolis: Indiana University Press.

Halliday, Fred (1991) 'Hidden from International Relations; Women and the International Arena', in Rebecca Grant and Kathleen Newland (eds), *Gender and International Relations*. Indianapolis: Indiana University Press.

Halliday, Fred (1998) 'Gender and IR: Progress, Backlash, and Prospect', *Millennium: Journal of International Studies*, 27 (4): 833–46.

Hartsock, Nancy C.M. (1983) *Money, Sex and Power: Toward a Feminist Historical Materialism*. New York: Longman.

Holcomb, Briavel and Rothenberg, Tamar Y. (1993) 'Women's Work and the Urban Household Economy in Developing Countries', in Meredith Turshen and Briavel Holcomb (eds), *Women's Lives and Public Policy: The International Experience*. Westport: Greenwood.

Jackson, Cecile (1998) 'Rescuing Gender from the Poverty Trap', in Cecile Jackson and Ruth Pearson (eds), *Feminist Visions of Development: Gender Analysis and Policy*. New York: Routledge.

Jones, Adam (1996) 'Does "Gender" Make the World Go Round? Feminist Critiques of International Relations', *Review of International Studies*, 22 (4): 405–29.

Keohane, Robert O. (1998) 'Beyond Dichotomy: Conversations Between International Relations and Feminist Theory', *International Studies Quarterly*, 42 (1): 193–8.

Krause, Jill (1996) 'Gender Inequalities and Feminist Politics in a Global Perspective', in Eleonore Kofman and Gillian Youngs (eds), *Globalization: Theory and Practice*. London: Pinter.

Lapid, Yosef (1989) 'The Third Debate: On the Prospects of International Theory in a Post-Positivist Era', *International Studies Quarterly*, 33 (3): 235–54.

Light, Margot and Halliday, Fred (1994) 'Gender and International Relations', in Margot Light and Fred Halliday (eds), *Contemporary International Relations: A Guide to Theory*. London: Pinter.

Lim, Linda (1990) 'Women's Work in Export Factories: The Politics of a Cause', in Irene Tinker (ed.), *Persistent Inequalities: Women and World Development*. Oxford: Oxford University Press.

Locher, Birgit and Prügl, Elisabeth (2001) 'Feminism and Constructivism: Worlds Apart or Sharing the Middle Ground?', *International Studies Quarterly*, 45 (1): 111–29.

Marchand, Marianne H. (1998) 'Different Communities/ Different Realities/Different Encounters: A Reply to J. Ann Tickner', *International Studies Quarterly*, 42 (1): 199–204.

Marchand, Marianne H. (1996a) 'Reconceptualising "Gender and Development" in an Era of Globalisation', *Millennium: Journal of International Studies*, 25 (3): 577–603.

Marchand, Marianne H. (1996b) 'Selling NAFTA: Gendered Metaphors and Silenced Gendered Implications', in Eleonore Kofman and Gillian Youngs (eds), *Globalization: Theory and Practice*. London: Pinter.

Marchand, Marianne H. and Parpart, Jane (eds) (1995) *Feminism/Postmodernism/Development*. London: Routledge.

Marchand, Marianne H. and Runyan, Anne Sisson (eds) (2000) *Gender and Global Restructuring: Sightings, Sites and Resistances*. New York: Routledge.

McGlen, Nancy E. and Sarkees, Meredith Reid (1993) *Women in Foreign Policy: The Insiders*. New York: Routledge.

Meyer, Mary K. and Prügl, Elisabeth (eds) (1999) *Gender Politics in Global Governance*. Lanham: Rowman and Littlefield.

Mies, Maria (1986) *Patriarchy and Accumulation on a World Scale*. London: Zed Books.

Misra, Joya (2000) 'Gender and the World-System: Engaging the Feminist Literature on Development', in Thomas D. Hall (ed.), *A World-Systems Reader: New Perspectives on Gender, Urbanism, Cultures, Indigenous Peoples, and Ecology*. Lanham: Rowman and Littlefield.

Mohanty, Chandra (1991) 'Under Western Eyes: Feminist Scholarship and Colonial Discourses', in Chandra Mohanty, Ann Russo and Lourdes Torres (eds), *Third World Women and the Politics of Feminism*. Indianapolis: Indiana University Press.

Moon, Katharine H.S. (1997) *Sex Among Allies: Military Prostitution in U.S.–Korean Relations*. New York: Columbia University Press.

Odysseos, Louiza and Seckinelgin, Hakan (eds) (1998) Editors' Introduction in 'Anniversary Special Issue: Gendering "the International"', *Millennium: Journal of International Studies*, 27 (4): iii–iv.

Onuf, Nicholas G. (1989) *Worlds of our Making: Rules and Rule in Social Theory and International Relations*. Columbia: University of South Carolina Press.

Parpart, Jane L. and Marchand, Marianne H. (1995) 'Exploding the Canon: An Introduction/Conclusion', in Marianne H. Marchand and Jane L. Parpart (eds), *Feminism/Postmodernism/Development*. London: Routledge.

Pearson, Ruth (1998) ' "Nimble Fingers" Revisited: Reflections on Women and Third World Industrialisation in the Late Twentieth Century', in Cecile Jackson and Ruth Pearson (eds), *Feminist Visions of Development: Gender Analysis and Policy*. Boulder: Lynne Rienner.

Peterson, V. Spike (ed.) (1992) *Gendered States: Feminist (Re)Visions of International Relations Theory*. Boulder: Lynne Rienner.

Peterson, V. Spike (1996) 'The Politics of Identification in the Context of Globalization', *Women's Studies International Forum*, 19 (1/2): 5–15.

Peterson V. Spike and Runyan, Anne Sisson (1999) *Global Gender Issues*, 2nd edn. Boulder: Westview.

Pettman, Jan Jindy (1996) *Worlding Women: A Feminist International Relations*. London: Routledge.

Prügl, Elisabeth (1999a) *The Global Construction of Gender: Home-Based Work in the Political Economy of the 20th Century*. New York: Columbia University Press.

Prügl, Elisabeth (1999b) 'What is a Worker? Gender, Global Restructuring and the ILO Convention on Homework', in Mary K. Meyer and Elisabeth Prügl (eds), *Gender Politics in Global Governance*. Lanham: Rowman and Littlefield.

Rathgeber, Eva M. (1995) 'Gender and Development in Action', in Marianne H. Marchand and Jane L. Parpart (eds), *Feminism/Postmodernism/Development*. London: Routledge.

Reardon, Betty (1985) *Sexism and the War System*. New York: Teachers College Press.

Rourke, John (1993) *International Politics on the World Stage*, 4th edn. Guilford, CT: Dushkin Publishing Group.

Ruddick, Sara (1989) *Maternal Thinking: Toward a Politics of Peace*. Boston: Beacon Press.

Runyan, Anne Sisson (1996) 'The Places of Women in Trading Places', in Eleonore Kofman and Gillian Youngs (eds), *Globalization: Theory and Practice*. London: Pinter.

Scholte, J.A. (1993) *International Relations of Social Change*. London: Open University Press.

Segal, Lynne (1987) *Is The Future Female? Troubled Thoughts on Contemporary Feminism*. London: Virago.

Sen, Gita and Grown, Caren (1987) *Development, Crises and Alternative Visions: Third World Women's Perspectives*. New York: Monthly Review Press.

Smith, Steve (1997) 'New Approaches to International Theory', in John Baylis and Steve Smith (eds), *The Globalization of World Politics: An Introduction to International Relations*. Oxford: Oxford University Press.

Smith, Steve, Booth, Ken and Zalewski, Marysia (eds) (1996) *International Theory: Positivism and Beyond*. Cambridge: Cambridge University Press.

Steans, Jill (1998) *Gender and International Relations*. Cambridge: Polity.

Swerdlow, Amy (1990) 'Motherhood and the Subversion of the Military State: Women's Strike for Peace Confronts the House Committee on Un-American Activities', in Jean Bethke Elshtain and Sheila Tobias (eds), *Women, Militarism and War: Essays in History, Politics and Social Theory*. Savage: Rowman and Littlefield.

Sylvester, Christine (1987) 'Some Dangers in Merging Feminist and Peace Projects', *Alternatives*, 12 (4): 493–509.

Sylvester, Christine (ed.) (1993) 'Special Issue: Feminists Write International Relations', *Alternatives*, 18 (1): 1–118.

Sylvester, Christine (1994) *Feminist Theory and International Relations in a Postmodern Era*. Cambridge: Cambridge University Press.

Sylvester, Christine (1996) 'The Contributions of Feminist Theory to International Relations', in Steve Smith, Ken Booth and Marysia Zalewski (eds), *International Theory: Positivism and Beyond*. Cambridge: Cambridge University Press.

Tessler, Mark and Warriner, Ina (1997) 'Gender, Feminism, and Attitudes Toward International Conflict: Exploring Relationships with Survey Data from the Middle East', *World Politics*, 49 (2): 250–81.

Tickner, J. Ann (1992) *Gender in International Relations: Feminist Perspectives on Achieving Global Security*. New York: Columbia University Press.

Tickner, J. Ann (1997) 'You Just Don't Understand: Troubled Engagements between Feminists and IR Theorists', *International Studies Quarterly*, 41 (4): 611–32.

Tickner, J. Ann (1999) 'Why Women Can't Run the World: International Politics According to Francis Fukuyama', *International Studies Review*, 1 (3): 3–11.

Tickner, J. Ann (2001) *Gendering World Politics: Issues and Approaches in the Post-Cold War Era*. New York: Columbia University Press.

Tong, Rosemarie Putnam (1998) *Feminist Thought: A More Comprehensive Introduction*, 2nd edn. Boulder: Westview.

Udayagiri, Mridula (1995) 'Challenging Modernization', in Marianne H. Marchand and Jane Parpart (eds), *Feminism/Postmodernism/Development*. London: Routledge.

United Nations (1995) *Human Development Report*. Oxford: Oxford University Press.

Walker, R.B.J. (1993) *Inside/Outside: International Relations as Political Theory*. Cambridge: Cambridge University Press.

Waylen, Georgina (1994) 'Women and Democratization: Conceptualizing Gender Relations in Transition Politics', *World Politics*, 46 (3): 327–54.

Whitworth, Sandra (1994) *Feminism and International Relations*. New York: St Martin's Press.

Zalewski, Marysia (1998) 'Where is Woman in International Relations? "To Return as a Woman and Be Heard" ', *Millennium: Journal of International Studies*, 27 (4): 847–67.

Zalewski, Marysia and Parpart, Jane (eds) (1998) *The 'Man' Question in International Relations*. Boulder: Westview.

15

Psychological Explanations of International Conflict

JANICE GROSS STEIN

International conflict can be conceived as a set of interactive and interdependent decision problems that arise within the context of world politics. The context shapes, but does not determine, the choices leaders make and, indeed, through their choices, leaders change the context and structures of world politics. Individual and collective theories of choice, the focus of systematic research in cognitive and social psychology, become relevant to international politics insofar as we accept the proposition that leaders of collectivities – states or groups – acting alone or as part of a group, make decisions that have consequences not only for themselves but for others. The choices of one leader can have a powerful effect on the structure of the decision-problem itself and on the choices available to others.

Psychological approaches are useful in establishing boundary conditions for on-going arguments within structural explanations of systemic patterns. They help as well to specify theories built on identity formation and change and on system-wide norm creation and observance. Psychological theories are also useful in explaining the bounded choices political leaders make to escalate – and to de-escalate – conflict, and in the analysis of patterns of interaction that are the result of linked series of choices.

In international conflict, important decision-problems are typically ill-structured. The definition of the problem is often contested among the parties and there is little agreement on the nature of the stakes or their value. Even when the representation of the problem is not contested, the environment often does not provide timely and accurate feedback nor do leaders have the opportunity to engage in repeated trials over time to generate robust probability distributions (Newell and Simon, 1972; Simon, 1973;

Voss and Post, 1988; Voss et al., 1983; Voss et al., 1991). Leaders are consequently often uncertain about the problem, stakes, the values and intentions of others, and the constraints that define the problem. Abstract values must be constructed, interpreted and reformulated as precise objectives in the light of specific contingent circumstances. Often, the options themselves are not known and leaders must identify the options as well as their consequences. At times, the structure of a problem emerges only through the process – individual or collective – of constructing the representation of the problem. Leaders' representations of decision problems have a significant impact on their construction of preferences and identification of options, as well as on their choices.

Psychological theories are especially useful in the explanation of international conflict when representations of problems are contested, when these problems are not routine, the stakes are high to the choosers, and when the environment offers sufficient degrees of freedom to permit a range of choice. Under these conditions, institutional routines are often not considered adequate and the role of leaders, acting alone or collectively, is critical. In the first part of the chapter, I begin by reviewing the contribution of cognitive psychology to the explanation of processes of problem representation in ill-structured problems typical of non-routine conflict environments in international politics. I examine next the contribution of prospect theory, the leading alternative to theories that model choice as subjectively expected maximizing decisions. I then move from the individual level to explore the contribution of social psychology to the explanation of small group decisions. Many foreign policy decisions are made in the context of a small group, functioning either as a collective chooser, or as advisers to a leader with final executive responsibility. In the second part of the chapter, I move beyond choice as the focus of explanation to examine the contribution of social psychology to the analysis of mass ethnic conflict, where identity and group dynamics are important drivers of conflict in the international system.

Psychological Explanations of Choice

Cognitive Approaches to Individual Choice

Cognitive psychology has identified a series of systematic deviations from the norms of rational choice. Deviations from rational-actor assumptions about judgement, estimation and choice are explained by the need for simple rules that permit timely responses to the complex, often ill-structured problems and the uncertain environments of the kind political leaders typically face in international relations. These responses are adaptive in routine, well-structured environments but can produce significant distortions in complex poorly structured environments. There is no single cognitive theory of choice, and cognitive psychologists have identified no dominant decision rule (Mintz and Geva, 1995). Instead, they have specified and categorized the filters through which people process information, and the simplifying mechanisms they employ to help them make sense of the world. Political psychologists, drawing on research done in cognitive psychology, see leaders of collectivities facing choices about conflict as cognitive managers struggling to manage inherent uncertainties and complexities through typical cognitive 'short-cuts'. Although cognitive psychology provides no unified theory of choice, it explains why people deviate from ideally rational choice and alerts the analyst of international politics both to the importance of identifying leaders' representation of their problems, and to a menu of systematic strategies of simplification leaders are likely to use.

Cognitive Stability: Beliefs, Schema, Heuristics, Biases and Information Processing

Cognitive psychology has demonstrated that people's prior beliefs strongly affect information processing (Grayson and Schwartz, 1999; Larson, 1997; Sanbonmatsu et al., 1997; Wegener and Petty, 1998). Theories of cognitive consistency postulate that individuals seek to maintain the consistency of their 'belief systems' against discrepant information in ways that lead them to depart from norms of rational inference and choice. Indeed, exposure to contradictory information frequently results in the strengthening of beliefs. The strengthening of beliefs after exposure to contradictory information results from the processes of reasoning people use to explain the apparent inconsistency. The discount rate of information that is inconsistent with organizing beliefs is systematically higher than rational norms would dictate and people tend to choose options whose anticipated outcomes are consistent with established beliefs.

In international politics, leaders can be expected to discount systematically new information and resist change in fundamental beliefs (Little and Smith, 1988). President George Bush, for example, required a consistent stream of evidence over a protracted period of time before he changed his belief about Mikhail Gorbachev. Indeed, even a consistent stream of evidence was insufficient; it took the destruction of the Berlin Wall to overcome his resistance. Discounting has also been used to explain the success of strategies of deception and the consequent strategic surprise experienced by intelligence officials. The failure by American intelligence to detect Japanese intentions before the attack on Pearl Harbor, the failure of Israel's intelligence to predict the Egyptian and Syrian attack in 1973, and the failure to predict Iraq's invasion of Kuwait in 1990 have all been explained not by the absence of good evidence but rather by the tendency of officials to discount systematically evidence that was inconsistent with prevailing beliefs. Analyses of a wide range of political leaders, working in divergent political systems, suggest very similar processes of discounting information is incompatible with belief systems are at work.

Attribution theorists have emphasized the importance of 'schema', or individuals' concepts and their defining attributes. A schema is a working hypothesis about some aspect of the environment, and may be a concept of the self (self-schema), other individuals (person schema), groups (role-schema), or sequences of events in the environment (scripts) (Fiske, 1986; Fiske and Taylor, 1984: 140; Lau and Sears, 1986; Walker, 1988). People use schema to organize their interpretation of their environment and develop scripts – a working hypothesis about the environment – to prepare for action. Unlike theories of cognitive consistency, attribution theories do not assume that an individual's collection of schema form a coherent system. But like theories of cognitive consistency, they too assume that schema, once formed, are resistant to change.

The well-established tendency to discount information that is discrepant with existing schema contributes significantly to cognitive stability. The postulate that schema are resistant to change can be interpreted as consistent with statistical logic if people assign a low variance estimate to their expectations. Psychological research contradicts this interpretation through repeated observations that exposure to discrepant information strengthens rather than undermines existing schema.

Common heuristics and biases can impair processes of rational revision and judgement as well (Kahneman et al., 1982; Nisbett and Ross, 1980; Suedfeld and Tetlock, 1997; Von Winterfeldt and Edwards, 1986). Heuristics are rules people use to test the propositions embedded in their schema, and may be thought of as convenient short-cuts or rules-of-thumb for processing information. Three of the best documented heuristics are *availability, representativeness* and *anchoring*. The availability heuristic refers to people's tendency to interpret ambiguous information in terms of what is most easily remembered (Ross and Sicoly, 1979; Taylor, 1982; Tversky and Kahneman, 1973). The heuristic of representativeness refers to people's proclivity to exaggerate similarities between one event and a prior class of events, typically leading to significant errors in probability judgements or estimates of frequency (Kahneman and Tversky, 1972, 1973; Tversky and Kahneman, 1982). The heuristic of anchoring refers to an estimation of magnitude or degree by comparing it with an 'available' initial value (often an inaccurate one) as a reference point and making a comparison (Fiske and Taylor, 1984: 250–6, 268–75).

All three heuristics help explain crucial errors in estimation and judgement by mapping the effects of prior mental states. Availability and representativeness provide a convincing account for the tendency of Israel's leaders to relate Arab threats to the Nazi holocaust, despite differences in capacity and context. These heuristics affect not only estimates of probability but also the representation of the problem Israel's leaders use. Anchoring accounts in part for Arafat's failure to recognize the significant differences between the offer made by Prime Minister Barak in the autumn of 2000 – one which included a return of approximately 90 per cent of the West Bank to Palestinian sovereignty as well as all the Palestinian neighborhoods in Jerusalem – and the far more limited offers made by earlier leaders.

Cognitive biases also lead to errors in attribution. The egocentric bias, which leads people to exaggerate the likelihood that the actions of others are the result of their own prior behavior and to overestimate the extent to which they are the target of those actions, contributes to an escalation spiral in a conflict environment. When people exaggerate the importance of dispositional over situational factors in explaining the behavior of others, and attribute greater coherence and meaning to others' behavior, and to stimuli in general, than reality warrants, they commit the fundamental attribution error (Fiske and Taylor, 1984: 72–9; Kahneman et al., 1982; Nisbett and Ross, 1980). The fundamental attribution error makes it more likely that the leaders will attribute hostile intentions to others and that they will discount the situational constraints other leaders face. This kind of reasoning can fuel mutual perception of intentional hostility that is unwarranted by

behavior, exacerbate security dilemmas, and spur arms races and escalation to violence.

Research suggests that the fundamental attribution error is most likely to occur when the observed behavior is consistent with prior beliefs about the actor (Kulik,1983). Consistent behavior is especially likely to be attributed to dispositional factors even when there are compelling situational explanations. Dispositional attributions are likely to be highly accessible for consistent behavior and the readily available belief that the actor is 'just the kind of person' who would engage in such behavior may make people insensitive to situational factors that might have evoked consistency. The representative bias may therefore help to explain the occurrence of fundamental attribution errors when observed behavior is consistent with prior beliefs. This kind of reasoning can sustain and deepen hostile representations of others' intentions, and make conflict escalation more likely and conflict resolution more difficult.

Impact of Embedded Enemy Images on Conflict

Once schema are embedded, they are extraordinarily difficult to change. This is particularly true of hostile imagery. An image refers to a set of beliefs, or the hypotheses and theories that an individual or group is convinced are valid. An image includes both experience-based knowledge and values, or beliefs about desirable behavior (Vertzberger, 1990: 114–27.) Insofar as enemy images contain an emotional dimension of strong dislike, there is little incentive to seek new information (Druckman, 1994: 50, 63). Stereotyped images generate behavior that is hostile and confrontational, and increase the likelihood that an adversary will respond with hostile action. A cycle of reciprocal behavior then reinforces adversary images by providing allegedly confirming evidence of hostile intentions. Adversarial images tend to become self-fulfilling and self-reinforcing and can fuel spirals of international conflict (Chen and Bargh, 1997: 541–60; Pruitt and Rubin, 1986: 117–18).

Research has established at least three different schemas of enemies: imperials, barbarians and degenerates (Herrmann and Fischerkeller, 1995). Throughout the Cold War, the Soviet leadership saw the United States as an 'imperial' enemy, Chinese leaders have at times stereotyped others as 'barbarians', and the Ayatollah Khomeini in Iran described Western leaders as 'degenerates'. These schemas informed the representation of problems that leaders in the Soviet Union, China and Iran constructed, and influenced the way they processed information and estimated probabilities, and the choices they made.

Cognitive processes tend to support stereotypical images and biases once they are established. People make heavy use of social stereotypes in predicting one another's personal characteristics and behavior. Drawing on stereotypes, they also tend to make social predictions with greater subjective certainty or confidence than can be justified by their objective accuracy (Brodt and Ross, 1998). Behavioral memory retrieval processes operate differently when judging ingroup and outgroup members, contributing to a perpetuation of social biases. Implicit theories of others were linked to individual differences in evaluative processing (Hong et al., 1997; Sherman et al., 1998). Attribution processes also influence judgements of discriminatory behavior (Burgess and Borgida, 1999). All these processes work to reinforce rather than mitigate international conflict (Little and Smith, 1988).

Mitigating Factors

Although these are systematic errors and biases, their impact can be mitigated in part by the institutional and group setting in which decision-making takes place. The group context of the decision may mitigate or accentuate individual biases. Group processes can reinforce and strengthen the tendency to discount inconsistent information, by appealing to group solidarity, or deliberately structure processes that allow and indeed encourage early challenges to prevailing beliefs (t'Hart et al., 1997). I return to this argument when I examine the dynamics of collective choice. At a more general level, transparent systems, which allow for scrutiny and accountability, can help to reduce the impact of some of these biases by forcing inconsistent information into the system in a timely manner (Lerner and Tetlock, 1999; Tetlock and Lerner, 1999). A political system where powers are shared helps to reduce these kinds of biases by leaders while the kind of isolation characteristic of leaders of authoritarian states – Hafez al-Asad in Syria and Saddam Hussein in Iraq – reinforces biases. *Ceteris paribus*, democratic and pluralist systems can better mitigate these kinds of biases than closed authoritarian political systems.

Revision of Schemas, Inference and Estimates

Stability in enemy images is the default and change the exception. Yet conservatism does not hold unconditionally. Schema do change, although they generally tend to change gradually over time, rather than undergo quick and far-reaching conversion. Schema theory has not yet developed an integrated set of propositions about why schema change. In large part because schema theories focus on whole schemas, they are relatively static (Kuklinski et al., 1991). The centrality of schema, their refutability, the diagnosticity of discrepant information, the pattern of attribution and cognitive complexity have

all been identified as predictors of the likelihood of revision and, by extension, of change in judgement.

Change is in part a function of the rate at which discrepant information occurs, and how diagnostic leaders and officials consider the information. Contradictory evidence dispersed across many instances should have a greater impact on schema than a few isolated examples (Crocker et al., 1983). As people consider information inconsistent with previous knowledge, they incorporate into their schema the conditions under which the schema does not hold, permitting gradual change and adjustment (Higgins and Bargh, 1987: 386). Important schema are challenged only when there is no other way to account for contradictory data that people consider diagnostic. Greater change will occur when information arrives in large batches, rather than bit by bit. President George Bush, as I noted, did not change his image of Gorbachev even though the Soviet leader made a series of unilateral gestures to the United States. Only when information about large changes arrived in a rush, did he finally alter his well-established image. Even the strongest schema cannot withstand the challenge of strongly incongruent information or a competing schema that fits the data better (Markus and Zajonc, 1985).

Significant change in schema about another also occurs when subjects are exposed to incongruent information and are persuaded that the behavior is not arbitrary, but reflects the nature of the target. Croatian and Muslim leaders, for example, did not change their image of Serbians because they attributed the change in Serbian policy to the military setback they suffered at the hands of the Croatian forces in Krajina. Change occurs when inconsistent information is attributed to dispositional rather than situational factors. The general tendency to prefer situational rather than dispositional attributions for incongruent behavior explains why change occurs so infrequently.

Change is also a function of cognitive complexity, or the intricacy of the cognitive rules used to process information about objects and situations. Cognitive complexity refers to the structure or the organization of cognition rather than to the content of thought. Complexity has somewhat contradictory effects on schema change. The more complex the cognitive system, the more capable is the decision-maker of making new or subtle distinctions when confronted with new information (Tetlock, 1985). Experts with highly complex cognitive schema are more sensitive to new information than novices with low cognitive complexity, whose schema are likely to be fixed and rigid (Conover and Feldman, 1984). Those who possess multiple judgement dimensions also tend to possess rules of abstraction that facilitate the integration and comparison of information. They tend to produce alternative interpretations of new information, but by using their capacity for abstraction and integration, are able to resolve these ambiguities

(Vertzberger, 1990: 134–7). Experts who have more relevant information can more easily incorporate inconsistent information as exceptions and special cases. Incongruent data therefore have less impact on their schema than they would have on those of novices (Higgins and Bargh, 1987). Paradoxically, experienced leaders are more likely to be conservative in their judgements than are novice leaders with little experience in foreign policy.

Framing Effects and Prospect Theory

Cognitive psychology has identified a series of systematic biases that are likely to distort the judgements leaders make when they construct representations of high-stakes international conflict. An important stream of research relates framing not to the individual but to the situation, and predicts strong effects on choice. Prospect theory – the most important corrective to the subjective expected utility variant of rational choice theory – maintains that choice is influenced by how a decision-problem is framed (Kahneman and Tversky, 1979). Framing describes the way in which a choice can be influenced simply by the order in which options are presented or the language that is used to describe the options. Research suggests strongly counter-intuitive results: choice can be manipulated by the order and presentation of the options available, without changing the substance of the problem. That simple frame changes can elicit changes in preferences violates one of the most fundamental axioms of rational choice. The policy implications for the management of international conflict are obvious and strong. When, for example, Secretary of State James Baker had tried, with no success, to persuade Prime Minister Yitzhak Shamir of Israel to join the Madrid Process in 1991, he finally cautioned him to think not about what he would gain if he came to the table, but what he would lose if he stayed away. Shamir agreed to participate.

Baker intuitively recognized an important proposition put forward by prospect theorists. People frame problems around a reference point and consider options from its vantage. When the options they identify are in the domain of gain, people tend to be risk-averse, and when the options they identify are in the domain of loss, people tend to choose the risky option. Risk is consequently not a function of individual predisposition, but of the framing of problems (Bazerman, 1986; Farnham, 1990, 1992; Levy, 1992; Stein and Pauly, 1989; Tversky and Kahneman, 1981).

Prospect theory identifies situational conditions that promote risk-aversion and risk-acceptance. Leaders are especially likely to be more risk-prone than rational choice would suggest when they have not normalized for a (recent) loss, and when they treat small probabilities as the equivalent to certainty. They are likely to be more risk-averse when they are in the domain of gain or have normalized for gain, when they overweigh small probabilities of failure by focusing on salient examples of failure, and when they systematically undervalue large probabilities of success.

Evidence in support of prospect theory is robust across a wide variety of experiments in a broad range of cultures. Prospect theory has been extensively applied to the analysis of foreign policy decision-making (Levy, 1992; Farnham, 1997; McDermott, 1998), and provides a convincing explanation, for example, of President Sadat's decision to go to war in 1973; he had not normalized for the loss of the Sinai seven years earlier. A threat-based strategy of deterrence by Israel only pushed him further into the domain of loss. It also explains Arafat's decision to escalate the violence in October 2000; he was in the domain of loss and underweighted the probability of loss from a return to violence in comparison to the certain loss of full sovereignty over East Jerusalem. Here too threat-based strategies appear to have reinforced risk propensity and contributed to escalation.

Prospect theory provides a decision rule embedded within the cognitive frames leaders construct and suggests propensities to risk-acceptance that can have serious consequences for escalation and dampening effects on bargaining and negotiation. When leaders view their own concessions as losses, and those of their opponent as gains, they will tend to overvalue their own concessions and underestimate those of their opponents (Jervis, 1989). This kind of dynamic makes negotiated agreements more rather than less difficult and is one candidate explanation of why leaders engaged in international conflict so often leave value on the table when they are bargaining. Similarly, when leaders fear loss, they are more likely to choose options that risk escalation (Levy, 1992).

The predisposition to loss aversion under specified conditions is a powerful explanation of the escalation of international conflict and can be usefully integrated into the systematic design of strategies of conflict prevention. It holds promise especially because it locates risk-taking propensity in attributes of the situation as well as in characteristics of the individual leader. An emphasis on leaders' framing of the problem complements the expected consequences of the fundamental attribution error where leaders tend to overweight personality and undervalue situational determinants of choice (McDermott, 1998: 165–86).

Mitigating Factors

Cognitive psychology developed in the laboratory. Biases and heuristics were discovered in the course of experiments in a highly controlled environment, but the laboratory differs from the real world in a number of significant ways. This raises important questions about whether concepts tested in the laboratory can be transposed to and made operational in naturalistic settings.

Attribution studies typically ask subjects explicitly to determine why an event occurred, whereas most events occur in the absence of specific causal questions. The elicitation procedure of structuring the problem and defining the tradeoffs may systematically bias the results of the studies (Enzle and Shopflocher, 1978; Pyszczynki and Greenberg, 1981: 31). Moreover, the tasks subjects are asked to perform in most prospect theory experiments are generally trivial and highly structured. They are also unrelated to other tasks and judgements the subjects are likely to perform outside the laboratory. Judgements made by political leaders on foreign policy issues, by contrast, are often interrelated and deal with issues that are significant and highly valued. People's recognition of the importance of a decision may influence their thoroughness in collecting and evaluating information and choice of decision-making rules (Jervis, 1986). Some cognitive psychologists, however, dispute the proposition that important judgements will encourage the adoption of more explicit and articulated cognitive processes. They argue that laboratory procedures often result in an underestimation of the magnitude of inferential failings (Nisbett and Ross, 1980: 220–2, 250–4).

Biases may matter less in foreign policy decision-making than they do in the laboratory because the continuous environment of foreign policy decision-makers gives them some feedback that often permits them to approach decisions incrementally, repeatedly correcting for past mistakes. Change is most likely when decision-makers receive timely feedback from competitive markets (Tetlock, 1998: 880). This kind of structured environment and timely feedback is, as I have argued, unlikely in the high stakes, complex and uncertain environments characteristic of high value international conflict. My arguments suggests that, other things being equal, systematic psychological biases are likely to be more rather than less important in an explanation of high value international conflict.

Social and political conditions may also work to minimize biases. When controlled political systems become more open, for example, leaders may learn more about the intentions and the range of choices available to others and, consequently, shift their reference points and give greater weight to attributes of others in explaining change. Again, *ceteris paribus*, democratic pluralist political systems are most likely to mitigate these kinds of biases.

PSYCHOLOGICAL EXPLANATIONS OF COLLECTIVE CHOICE

Group Decision-Making

Social psychology, through its analysis of small group dynamics, helps, under specified conditions, to explain important decisions about international conflict. These kinds of explanations are useful when problems are ill-structured, when a single small group is at the apex of the policy-making process, or when policies develop out of the interplay among a number of groups (t'Hart et al., 1997).

Of particular interest is how groups arrive at a collective representation of a decision problem. Groups may tend toward 'simple conformity', where collective discussion works to minimize differences in order to construct a shared representation of a problem and undifferentiated analysis of the advantages and disadvantages of alternatives. They may do so, for example, through a process of 'anticipatory compliance', the tendency of those lower down in the political or administrative hierachy to adopt problem representations that conform to the real or perceived predispositions of senior decision-makers (Stern and Sundelius, 1997). They may also do so to preserve group solidarity and maximize group cohesiveness.

This kind of collective decision-making is especially likely to occur when policy-makers feel threatened and are under stress. It produces pathologies in policy-making: inadequate attention to alternative problem representations, unduly short search for information and discounting of inconsistent information. Pressures to conform within groups reduce their capacity to develop differentiated representations of problems, debate values and resolve conflict. Although key explanatory variables are frequently difficult to operationalize and measure in real-world policy-making systems, the expected 'flawed' processes have been widely documented across a variety of crisis decision-making contexts, in diverse political systems, across cultures.

Mitigating Factors

Not all groups develop these kinds of tendencies toward conformity. A central differentiator is whether or not leaders intervene actively to establish norms and processes that actively promote debate about alternative representations of a problem and, more generally, signal their tolerance of dissent, especially at the early stages of decision-making. A culture of deliberation and argument flourishes only when leaders actively promote debate and differentiation. Generally, balanced critical deliberation tends to be associated with more open, pluralistic, and facilitative leadership styles that are more likely to be found in democratic cultures that emphasize norms of accountability. These kinds of deliberations are especially likely to occur when there is a rough balance of power and policy-making resources among group members. When access to and control of information is roughly evenly distributed, group membership is heterogeneous rather than homogeneous, and expertise is not the monopoly of one or two members, pressures to conformity are likely to be less (t'Hart et al., 1997).

SOCIAL PSYCHOLOGICAL EXPLANATIONS OF CONFLICT

Group Identity and Conflict

International conflict grows not only out of the interaction among states and their leaders, but also increasingly out of the violence among ethnic groups that spills across international borders. In the past ten years far more people have been killed in civil wars than in inter-state wars, and it is civil wars that have provided the greatest challenge to international institutions struggling to manage conflict. Social psychology addresses the dynamics of conflict among groups and processes of conflict management, reduction and resolution. It pays particular attention to incompatible group identities as a permissive context of conflict.

Two important bodies of scholarship in international relations challenge the importance of inter-group differences and incompatible group identities as significant contributors to violent conflict. Structural explanations of conflict generally give little attention to the processes that mediate between attributes of the environment and behavior. Realist explanations that focus on competition for scarce resources or changes in patterns of alignment assume that conflict can be explained independently of the collective identities of contending groups. They treat collective identities as epiphenomenal.

A second body of scholarship uses rational choice models to explain the resort to violence as an optimal response to collective fears of the future (Fearon and Laitin, 2000; Lake and Rothchild, 1996; Posen, 1993). As groups begin to fear for their safety, strategic dilemmas arise that are exacerbated by information failures and problems of credible commitment, and, fueled by political entrepreneurs, conflict explodes into violence. Violence becomes a rational response to strategic dilemmas fueled by fear. Here, rational choice explanations are compatible with psychological explanations insofar as they develop the intervening mechanism that transforms fear into violence. Lake and Rothchild argue, for example, that ethnic activists deliberately play on fears of collective insecurity, which are in turn magnified by political memories and anxieties.

Social psychology addresses the origins and triggers to the collective fears that prepare the ground for violence. Converging streams of evidence from social psychology, cultural anthropology, international relations and comparative politics suggest that individuals and groups are motivated to form and maintain images of an enemy as part of a collective identity even in the absence of solid, confirming evidence of hostile intentions.

Enemy images can be a product of the need for identity and the dynamics of group behavior. Social psychologists have identified a fundamental human need for identity – the way in which a person is, or wishes to be known by others; it is a conception of self in relation to others. One important component of individual identity is social identity, or the part of an individual's self-concept which derives from knowledge of his or her membership in a social group or groups, together with the value attached to that membership (Tajfel, 1981: 255). Social psychologists suggest that people satisfy their need for positive self-identity, status or reduction of uncertainty by identifying with a group (Hogg and Abrams, 1993: 173). These needs lead to bolstering and favorable comparison of the 'in-group' with 'out-groups' (Brewer and Schneider, 1990: 169–84; Hogg, 1992; Messick and Mackie, 1989; Tajfel, 1982; Tajfel and Turner, 1986: 7–24). Membership in a group leads to systematic comparison and differentiation, and often to derogation of other groups.

The most striking finding of social psychologists is that social differentiation occurs even in the absence of material bases for conflict. This need for collective as well as individual identity leads people to differentiate between 'we' and 'they', to distinguish between 'insiders' and 'outsiders', even when scarcity or gain is not at issue. In an effort to establish or defend group identity, groups and their leaders identify their distinctive attributes as virtues and label the distinctiveness of others as vices. This kind of 'labeling' responds to deep social-psychological needs and can lead to the creation of enemy stereotypes. An examination of massive state repression leading to group extinction, for example, concluded that genocides and politicides are extreme attempts to maintain the security of one's 'identity group' at the expense of other groups (Harff and Gurr, 1988).

Ethnocentrism draws on myths that are central to group culture and breeds stereotyping and a misplaced suspicion of others' intentions (Booth, 1979; Eberhardt and Fiske, 1996; Fiske, 1998). Strong feelings of self-group centrality and superiority, however, do not necessarily culminate in extreme or violent behavior. The critical variables are the kinds of environments in which groups seek to satisfy their needs and the norms that they generate and accept. Certain kinds of international and domestic conditions facilitate the collective formation of enemy images (Taylor and Moghaddam, 1987).

Mediating Factors

Social identity and differentiation do not lead inevitably to violent conflict (cf. Mercer, 1995). If they did, conflict would occur at all times, under all conditions. First, personal and social identities are often in tension with one another. By identifying strongly with a group, people inevitably de-emphasize their individual identity, and those with a strong sense of individual identity give less weight to their group identities. Human rights activists, for example, characteristically identify less with a particular group and more with norms of individual responsibility. Second, people also generally identify with several groups and typically identify with a group whose importance is salient in a given situation (Turner et al., 1987). Which group identity is activated is situationally specific.

The critical question is under what conditions identity and violent conflict are related. Why are relationships among some groups so much more competitive – and violent – than among others? Hutus and Tutsis have engaged in violent conflict six time since 1962 while Quebecois and Anglophones in Canada, despite important and deep differences between the two groups, have not fought for over two hundred years. Moreover, substantial numbers of Quebecois also share multiple identities, including strong and positive identification with Canada. What explains why strong group identity precipitates violent conflict only in some situations?

The answer may lie partly in the stability of democratic pluralist systems where citizens have internalized norms of conflict resolution. Canada is a stable democratic system whereas the successor states to the former Yugoslavia were not. Even stable democratic systems, however, have experienced violent conflict. Much depends on the variability of identity. Social identity is not given; social learning theorists and constructivists argue that it is constructed through membership in a group and through interaction with others (Bandura, 1973; Harre, 1986). The patterns of identity formation and mapping are critical. Conflict does not develop when the sources of identities or the identities themselves are compatible. When the identity an individual chooses is incompatible with the identity imposed by others or the social context in which identity is constantly being recreated, conflict can develop. Muslims living in Bosnia–Herzegovina, for example, defined themselves as Serbs or Croats until the 1970s, when the Serb and Croat identities began to be recreated to exclude Muslims. Only then did they begin to define themselves as Bosnian Muslims with a distinct political identity. Even then, however, incompatible political identities may not be sufficient to create violent conflict. To return again to the Canadian example, some Quebecois see fundamental incompatibilities between being Quebecois and Canadian, but do not consider a resort to force. They do not because they are committed to norms of fairness and due process, and they expect that these commitments will be reciprocated by their counterparts in English Canada (Stern, 1995).

Several important conditions have been identified that sharpen identity and prepare the terrain for violent conflict. The first set of factors operate between groups within incompatible identities, while the second set is internal to the groups. Ethnic or national identity intensifies during periods of social, economic, or political crisis, when uncertainty grows and the mechanisms in place to protect one group from another lose their credibility (Lake and Rothchild, 1996: 43). As central authority declines in the context of socio-economic or political crisis, fears about physical security grow, and groups invest in measures to protect themselves, making the violence they fear more likely (Posen, 1993). State weakness, its perceived incapacity to protect one group from the anticipated violence of another, is an important trigger of violence among groups with incompatible identities.

Identity conflict is often a competition for ownership of the state and control of its resources. States can stand above and attempt to mediate conflict – by, for example, giving representation to different groups as in Belgium – or be the creature and the instrument of one exclusive group, as in Nigeria where the Hausa Fulani dominate the military regime (Brass, 1995; Gurr, 1993). The expropriation of the identity, symbols and resources of the state by one group to the exclusion of others is a strong predictor of the likelihood of violence.

Conflict can trigger violence among groups under conditions of scarcity. Some evidence suggests that culturally and physically similar groups can generate hostility and aggression toward one another due to competition for scarce resources (Sherif, 1966). Some analyses of civil violence similarly conclude that relative deprivation is the most important condition for participants in collective violence (Gurr, 1970: 12–13). As the gap grows between material expectations and assets, aggression toward those perceived as the cause of relative deprivation grows and intensifies. The competition for scarce resources is exacerbated when the state actively controls the distribution of important resources. In the former Yugoslavia, for example, Slovenians and Croatians actively resented federal redistribution of resources to poorer regions of the country. Loss aversion is likely to intensify when groups compete for scarce resources in a context of decline: when expectations remain stable, but capabilities decline, prospect theory expects that people who are experiencing a decline in their assets or 'loss', are especially likely to make risky choices (Gurr, 1970: 46–50; Stein and Pauly, 1989). Yet, the Czechs and Slovaks competed for scarce resources and divided assets without a resort to violence. Competition for resources and relative deprivation, a sharpened version of competition, cannot satisfactorily account for violence among groups with differentiated and competing identities.

Conflicts of identity are likely to escalate to violence when group members consider that recognition of another's identity can compromise their own, when they perceive the granting of rights to the other as an abdication of their own identity, and when they fear that the other group may move pre-emptively to make gains at their expense. Throughout much of its history, the Israeli–Palestinian conflict has been this kind of existential conflict; because both identities are tied to the same territory, leaders on both sides long felt that acknowledgement of the other's identity would fundamentally compromise their own (Kelman, 1982: 61). When one or the other group has attempted, for example, to seize territory and establish a presence on contested ground, violence has resulted. When the state is too weak or unwilling to constrain pre-emptive action by one group, the other becomes more fearful, loses confidence in institutional arrangements, deepens the perception of the hostility of their ethnic rival, and prepares for violence. The intense violence between Palestinians and Israelis in 2000 did not erupt after the failure of bargaining, but when the Palestinian leadership perceived that Israel was tangibly asserting sovereignty over holy places in East Jerusalem. It had never normalized for the loss of sovereignty, and Israel's position accentuated the Palestinian sense of loss.

Leaders of ethnic groups manipulate group fears to solidify their positions within their own ethnic community. Ethnic activists, with a strong need to identify with their ethnic group, manipulate identities and fears to produce a rapid and spontaneous process of social polarization that magnifies hostility and fear among groups (Fearon and Laitin, 2000). As polarization proceeds, members of an ethnic group are pressured by their leaders – and by the reciprocal intensification of hostility in the other group – to identify only with their ethnic group and to break any cross-cutting ties. In the former Yugoslavia, for example, despite a high degree of social integration among Croats and Serbs, ethnic activists were able to initiate a process that broke apart families and forced members to self-identify with a single group. In a related process, 'political entrepreneurs', who see opportunities for political gain, may take advantage of a process of social polarization to achieve political ends. They deliberately reinterpret histories and traditions to sharpen ethnic differentiation, heighten grievance and increase fear (Ranger, 1983). Slobodan Milosevic was both an ethnic activist and a political entrepreneur: he exaggerated Croatian violence against Croatian Serbs and the Muslim threat to Serbia in Kosovo as a pretext to consolidate and expand the political power of the Serbs when the state structure of Yugoslavia weakened following Tito's death.

'Spoilers', or militant ethnic activists have also fomented social polarization when new political arrangements that would cut across ethnic cleavages seem likely. After the moderate Hutu and Tutsi reached a painful compromise on new arrangements for political leadership in Rwanda, the militant Hutus, anticipating their exclusion from political power and marginalization, deliberately planned the assassination of the moderate Hutu leadership and a genocidal campaign of violence against Tutsis. The Rwandan genocide is often mistakenly explained as the result of competition for scarce resources, or the weakening of the state structures, or a primordial rivalry between the two dominant ethnic groups. None of these is a sufficient explanation of the outburst of genocidal violence. Militant leaders who feared marginalization and loss from institutional arrangements that would have dampened polarization chose to execute others rather than to accept a diminished political status. They were able, however, to mobilize support for genocidal action because they expertly played on long-standing ethnic fears.

Entrepreneurial leaders or elites whose domestic support is uncertain or threatened can manipulate identities to bolster political loyalty. A leading non-governmental observer of human rights concluded that 'time after time, a proximate cause of violence is governmental exploitation of communal differences ... The "communal card" is frequently played, for example, when a government is losing popularity or legitimacy, and finds it convenient to wrap itself in the cloak of ethnic, racial, or religious rhetoric' (Human Rights Watch, 1995: viii).

To gain public support, parochial interest groups that benefit from militarist or imperialist policies create strategic rationalizations or 'myths'. Over time, some elites come to believe the myths that they have learned, making these images extraordinarily resistant to change. A process of myth-making that perpetuates hostile imagery is most likely when concentrated interest groups trade and log-roll (Snyder, 1991: 2–6, 31–49). The salience and intensity of identity myths are closely tied to the perceived stakes of ethnic relations (Esman, 1986, 1994). The greater the gap between expectations and capabilities, the more important the values that are endangered by declining capabilities, and the smaller the range of other satisfactions that can compensate for the loss in assets, the more receptive populations are to elite attempts to manipulate identities (Gurr, 1970: 59).

Differences in domestic political conditions make some kinds of populations more receptive to elite manipulation than others. In controlled political regimes, leaders and elites who dominate the instruments of communication can more easily manipulate identities and mass images. Not only the kind of regime but also the organization of society has an impact on the creation of hostile imagery. The hallmark of a deeply divided society, that is likely to sustain significant hostile imagery and experience violent conflict, is the presence of separate structures, organized on the basis of identity, that infuse every aspect of society. In Lebanon, for example, political office from the center to local levels traditionally has been allocated on the basis of religious identity. In these kinds of societies, creation and maintenance of ethnic stereotypes and enemy images is easily done.

This analysis suggests that differentiated identities are not themselves a cause of violent conflict. Even when incompatible identities are present, violence is likely only when it is triggered by the exclusionary acts of leaders, either by monopolizing the resources of the state against groups within their own societies, or to press claims against those within others. Leaders and elites evoke threats to political identity that then provoke stereotyping and contribute to violence.

PSYCHOLOGICAL EXPLANATIONS AND CONFLICT RESOLUTION

Hostile imagery must change if enduring conflict is to be reduced and resolved. Inter-state conflict has been managed and routinized without modification in elite, much less public images, but recurrent civil violence as well as bitter inter-state conflict cannot be resolved unless images change and leaders and publics learn. The process must also be reciprocated. Once leaders or groups begin to change their image of their adversary and are interested in attempting to resolve their conflict, they must change the image their adversary has of them if conflict reduction is to make any progress.

Strategies of conflict resolution that focus only on competing interests will likely not be sufficient to provoke the learning that is fundamental to the change of hostile imagery and identity conflict. In both enduring inter-state rivalries and bitter ethnic conflict, interests are shaped by images and beliefs that in turn are partially shaped by identity. What we see as a threat is a function in large part of the way we see the world and who we think we are.

If threatened identities facilitate the creation of hostile imagery and contribute to violent conflict, then securing these identities must be a fundamental component of conflict resolution. If they are to be effective, peace-makers who confront bitter civil wars or enduring state rivalries must address interests in the broader context of images and identity. In the former Yugoslavia, the conflict could at best be managed temporarily by territorial partition and safe havens. The conflict can be resolved only if the parties recognize the legitimacy and the permanence of the others' identities. President Sadat's recognition of Israel's legitimacy was the critical key that unlocked the long and difficult peace process between Israel and its neighbors.

In conflict between states, reciprocal recognition of legitimacy and renunciation of the use of force can most directly secure threatened identities and reshape images. Civil conflicts may be more difficult to resolve, in part because of the proximity of clashing identities and the intensity of fear and emotion (Crawford, 2000: 150; Stedman, 1988). Fractured states can be reconstructed through political separation and mutual recognition of competing identities, through a 'consociational' or group building-block approach, where elite leaders accommodate and groups remain distinct with constitutional guarantees, or through an integrative approach, which seeks to forge multi-ethnic coalitions with cross-cutting ties (Sisk, 1995).

Mutual recognition and political separation is the most far-reaching strategy of conflict reduction. In 1989, after a brutal civil war that lasted over a decade, leaders of Lebanese religious groups modified the fundamentals of their pre-war consociational bargain. Instead of privileging the Maronite Christian community, Muslims and Christians now share power equally. The bargain still provides for a Maronite Christian president, a Sunni Muslim prime minister, and a Shi'a president of the National Assembly. Political decisions are still made by leaders at the top while their communities remain distinct.

The forging of multi-ethnic coalitions with cross-cutting ties is yet another strategy. This was the principal demand of the Muslim leadership of Bosnia–Herzegovina. The agreement reached in Dayton honors a multi-ethnic Bosnia in principle, but in its political arrangements provides for *de facto* separation of Bosnian Serbs from Muslims and Croats. Kosovo simmers unresolved as Kosovars press for formal independence and Serbia insists on integration. In all these cases, conflict reduction required more than reciprocation of small concessions in a gradually building process. The core of the solution lies in the often difficult decision by senior leaders to acknowledge, respect and accommodate different identities and share political power.

All these strategies assume that identities and images are fixed and that they must be accommodated as they are. Such a pessimistic assumption is unwarranted. Research in social psychology suggests that individual stereotyping can be overcome, but at times educational and social processes can inadvertently reinforce bias (Fiske, 1998; Lopez et al., 1998; Malo and Olson, 1998; Petty et al., 1998; Slomczynski and Shabad, 1998). Others argue that identity is not given, but that it is socially reconstructed as interactions develop and contexts evolve (Teske, 1997). Benedict Anderson (1991) observed that nations, unlike families and clans where individuals can know the others, are 'imagined communities', whose past, tradition and connections are interpreted and reinterpreted through time. Political identities similarly depend on imagined communities whose traditions are constructed and reinterpreted. Identities can consequently be reshaped and reconfigured as leaders and communities restructure their relationships.

Identities are complex structures, with components that emphasize shared communitarian traditions and norms that usually include emphasis on protection of the weak, social responsibility, generosity, fairness and reciprocity as well as honor, reputation and vengeance. Emphasis given to these different norms varies with the situation. Skilled mediators can emphasize the positive values of responsibility, fairness and compassion as important elements of honor and reputation. Appeal to the 'best' in the tradition of an identity may shift the emphasis within an 'imagined community' to create the space for fairness and reciprocity which can ultimately change images, reshape interests and culminate in tolerance and recognition of others' identities.

PSYCHOLOGICAL EXPLANATIONS AND INTERNATIONAL RELATIONS THEORIES: THE SCOPE OF ANALYSIS

The evidence of systematic patterns of deviation from norms of rational choice is robust. Although much of the evidence grows out of controlled laboratory experiments, political psychologists have documented these patterns across a wide range of institutional settings and political cultures in the analysis of decisions about high value international conflict. Yet, the dominant theories in international relations use much more limited assumptions about choice and motivation: realists treat states as unitary security maximizers and liberals and neoliberal institutionalists conceive of states as wealth maximizers. Both accept the representation of a problem as given and establish the contours of the decision problem from attributes of the payoff matrix; in this sense, they reason backward. Constructivists do problematize the representation of choice but focus on states as creators of norms. The theoretical – and empirical – gaps among these theoretical constructions and between psychological analyses seem very wide. The gaps may be less than they seem, however, when the boundary conditions of different theoretical approaches are examined more carefully.

A central challenge is to identify the scope conditions of analysis. Under what conditions can psychological tools be used in combination with leading theoretical approaches to increase explanatory power and enrich the analysis? Are psychological analyses competitors to the prevailing theories, or can they be useful complements under specified conditions? How can psychological approaches best be embedded within the structural analyses of the dominant approaches?

Rational and Psychological Explanations of Choice: the Scope of Analysis

Realist and liberal approaches embed rational choice at their core. Psychological approaches and rational choice have different comparative advantages. Rational choice is theoretically elegant while psychological approaches provide descriptive accuracy of processes of decision-making. Each has different disadvantages: the evidence from psychological studies is now robust that people are not 'rational actors', except in the most trivial and uninteresting situations, yet psychologists have not yet developed powerful general theories that explain choice. Theorists of rational choice who accept concepts of 'bounded rationality' find it easier to engage in conversation with cognitive psychologists.

Rational choice provides a transposable deductive apparatus for the formal analysis of interstate interactions. Rational choice theorists forego descriptive accuracy in specific cases and insist that treating states as if they were unitary rational actors yields dividends in explanatory and predictive power if predictions of the model match behavior. Through simplified representations of strategic interactions, rational choice theories claim to provide powerful explanation and prediction of state behavior that would otherwise be obscured by empirical detail (Morrow, 1995). Rational choice analysis is most successful when decision-problems typically concern examples of well understood classes of events that are formally identical to large numbers of other events. In the analysis of competitive markets, or large organizational systems, rational choice can provide elegant, powerful and at times counter-intuitive explanations.

International conflict occurs in a relatively small universe, however, with small numbers. It is therefore difficult for analysts and decision-makers alike to identify among historical antecedents a significant number of 'like' cases on crucial dimensions from which to tease out generic problem representations, probability distributions and metrics of value across dimensions of options. Much rational-choice scholarship on international conflict deals with the apparent complexity and indeterminacy of decision problems in international conflict through a strategy of simplified representation. Such simplified representations are often analytically tractable, in the sense that equilibrium solutions to games, when they exist, yield determinate predictions of behavior (Snidal, 1986). A strategy of simplified representation assumes that the abstraction captures the essence of a decision problem for states or group leaders, notwithstanding their confusion and uncertainty about stakes, options, costs, benefits, likelihoods and the interests, goals and intentions of the adversary. The claim is *prima facie* plausible when reality and representation are isomorphic, and becomes less plausible as the isomorphisms break down (Green and Shapiro, 1994; Moe, 1979). While simplified representation might be a useful analytical strategy in well-structured decision problems, it is unlikely to help in the analysis of international conflict where problems are almost always ill-structured. In ill-structured decision problems, the choice of game to use as a representation of a strategic interaction (and the specification of players' preference orderings) represents an arbitrary stipulation that undermines the analytical utility of the representation as an explanatory tool.

Cognitive and social psychology explain how leaders cope with this uncertainty and complexity. They commonly interpret ambiguous situations in the light of personally salient historical experiences, or employ behavioral rules of thumb that reflect idiosyncratic 'lessons of history' (Khong, 1992; Lebow, 1981; Neustadt and May,1986). Since these are idiosyncratic variables that none the less strongly influence problem representation, judgement and estimation, they greatly complicate rational choice analysis. Problem representation is a significant variable in any international conflict and, consequently, it is difficult to justify formal abstractions from real-world decision-problems of the kind rational choice theorists seek. The concepts and methods of cognitive psychology are comparatively well suited to understanding problem representation (George and George, 1956; Hermann, 1974, 1980; Holsti, 1989; Holsti and George, 1975; Janis, 1982; Jervis, 1976; Jervis et al., 1985; Lebow, 1981; Mandel, 1986; Stein, 1992; Stein, 1994).

Analyses of the debates between modelers of deterrence and spirals of escalation illustrate the complementarities between the two approaches. The debate can be better formulated as a problem of scope conditions. Rational choice theorists model deterrence as a set of interdependent rational choices, and have identified counter-intuitive strategic choices to resolve the dilemmas they design. Psychological explanations have focused on problem representation, judgement, motivation and fear, have specified how leaders as cognitive managers cope with ambiguous information in threatening environments, and have argued that the strategies deduced from rational models can be counterproductive and culminate in dangerous escalatory spirals (Achen and Snidal, 1989; Downs, 1989; Fearon, 1993; Huth and Russett, 1990, 1984; Jervis, 1989; Jervis et al., 1985; Lebow and Stein, 1989, 1990a, 1990b, 1994).

Prospect theory helps to resolve these seemingly contradictory findings. When states are fundamentally satisfied with the status quo, they can be considered in the domain of gain, and as appropriate targets for deterrence threats, since they are likely to be risk-averse with respect to gains. Under these conditions, except at the extremes of the probability distribution, rational choice is likely to provide a parsimonious explanation. When, however, states have experienced significant loss, and have not normalized for the loss, deterrence threats are likely to provoke escalation by leaders who are risk-acceptant with respect to losses.

Cognitive psychology and rational choice can be complementary, once the critical scope conditions are established. After the representation of the problem is identified, rather than assumed, scholars can examine the complexity of the environment, the scope of uncertainties, and the attributes of the situation. They can then establish whether leaders are in the domain of gain or loss and assess the likelihood that the calculus will be utility-maximizing, satisficing, or approximate the systematic deviations from rational norms that psychologists expect.

Constructivism and Psychological Explanations

There is a much more natural fit between constructivist explanations of international conflict and psychological analyses. While the conversation with rational choice centers on cognitive psychology, the dialogue of constructivists is with social psychology. Constructivists develop a concept of choice that is deeply informed by leaders' identity – how they define their state or group, who they are, and how they see themselves in relation to others. Constructivists have expanded the repertoire of psychological explanations of international relations – that traditionally focused on beliefs, images, and judgement of leaders – to include the collective or shared beliefs that constitute a common identity, and processes of norm creation and norm observance. Unlike realists and liberals, constructivists do not take identities and interests as given, but rather as created largely through interaction with others. They build into the concept of identity not only interests but attention to norms as a constitutive element (Finnemore and Sikkink, 1998; Price, 1997; Ruggie, 1998; Tannenwald, 1999).

This emphasis on constructed identities as the explanation of choice makes possible a useful dialogue with social psychological theories that examine the conditions under which norms become the criteria for choice. Social psychology explores the conditions under which criteria of equity, fairness and justice override the maximization of interest as the decision rule. Social identity theory in psychology emphasizes how identity changes a critical component of constructivist arguments.

Social identity theory can enrich and broaden arguments about identity change. Social identity is created not only through interaction with others, as constructivists suggest, but as social psychologists argue, through processes of identification with a group. Whether people identify with a particular social group is a matter of choice and, in choosing an identity, people struggle between the contradictory imperatives of inclusion and differentiation (Brewer, 1993; Brewer and Schneider, 1990). Canada, for example, is part of the larger North American trading system while seeking to protect its cultural distinctiveness. The cognitive mechanisms that produce group identification – or social identity – are categorization and social comparison (Abrams and Hogg, 1990). Categorization sharpens inter-group boundaries and produces stereotyping (Hogg and Abrams, 1988: 19–20).

As I have argued earlier, however, stereotyping does not always lead to conflict. Groups and states have a choice of strategies to deal with identity conflict: they may seek to assimilate to a more favorable identity, they may choose to redefine the value of their identity, or finally, they may choose to compete (Tajfel and Turner, 1979). Some states currently excluded from the European Union emphasize their identity as democratic states observing norms of human rights and respect for legal processes. Their leaders have chosen to assimilate to an identity that they regard as more favorable; identity change becomes a strategy of entry and opportunity. ASEAN members have chosen to emphasize the value of their distinctiveness by creating a group that is defined by the 'Asian way'. At the extreme, when groups feel that their identity is threatened, and barriers to inclusion are insuperable, they choose to compete. Social identity theory helps to explain why leaders select from a repertoire of available social representations, and by examining the thickness of barriers to inclusion, helps to identify the conditions under which states and groups are likely to choose one or another strategy of identity change.

Psychology and Theories of International Conflict

Critics of psychological approaches to international politics contend that these approaches may be relevant to individual choice but they are both too limited, too under-determined, too messy, and situated at an inappropriate level of analysis to explain the large systemic patterns of world politics. Proponents argue that evidence of systematic patterns of thinking and choice, both at the individual and the group level, are robust, and that broad deductive arguments, premised on flawed assumptions that violate much of what we now know about how individuals and collectivities define themselves and choose, are unlikely to provide valid foundations for powerful explanations of international and inter-group conflict. This has largely been a dialogue of the deaf.

Psychological approaches are useful in establishing boundary conditions for on-going arguments within structural explanations of systemic patterns. They help to refine and inform explanations that rely implicitly on theories of choice that are unlimited by varying conditions. The 'messiness' of psychological theories and evidence can give specificity – and rigor – to big debates about the dynamics of international conflict and its prevention. Psychological approaches also help to specify

theories built on identity formation and change and on norm creation and observance.

Psychological theories are also useful in explaining the bounded choices political leaders make to escalate – and to de-escalate – conflict, and in the analysis of patterns of interaction that are the result of linked series of choices. The recurrent puzzle of why bargaining processes, for example, leave value on the table, or fail to produce the agreements that are transparently obvious to the disinterested omniscient observer, is often powerfully explained by psychological theories of choice. A related puzzle – the repeated failure of one set of leaders to read and interpret accurately the signals of another set – is also well explained by psychological theories. Theoretical and empirical progress in the explanation of escalation and de-escalation of conflict can benefit by embedding psychological theories within the dominant rational and constructivist traditions and by carefully examining their complementarities and their relative purchase.

Bibliography

Abrams, D. and Hogg, M.A. (1990) 'An Introduction to the Social Identity Approach', in D. Abrams and M.A. Hogg (eds), *Social Identity Theory: Constructive and Critical Advances*. New York: Harvester Wheatsheaf. pp. 1–9.

Achen, C. and Snidal, D. (1989) 'Rational Deterrence Theory and Comparative Case Analysis', *World Politics*, 41: 143–69.

Anderson, B. (1991) *Imagined Communities*, 2nd edn. London: Verso.

Bandura, A. (1973) *Aggression: A Social Learning Analysis*. Englewood Cliffs: Prentice Hall.

Bazerman, M.H. (1986) *Judgement in Managerial Decision Making*. New York: Wiley.

Booth, K. (1979) *Strategy and Ethnocentrism*. London: Croom Helm.

Brass, P. (1995) *Ethnic Groups and the State*. Towota: Barnes and Noble Books.

Brewer, M.B. (1993) 'The Role of Distinctiveness in Social Identity and Group Behaviour', in M. Hogg and D. Abrams (eds), *Group Motivation: Social Psychological Perspectives*. New York: Harvester Wheatsheaf. pp. 1–16.

Brewer, M.B. and Schneider, S.K. (1990) 'Social Identity and Social Dilemmas: A Double-Edged Sword', in M. Hogg and D. Abrams (eds), *Social Identity Theory: Constructive and Critical Advances*, London: Harvester Wheatsheaf. pp. 169–84.

Brodt, S.E. and Ross, L.D. (1998) 'The Role of Stereotyping in Overconfident Social Prediction', *Social Cognition*, 16: 225–52.

Burgess, D. and Borgida, E. (1999) 'Refining Sex-Role Spillover Theory: The Role of Gender Subtypes and Harasser Attributions', *Social Cognition*, 15: 332–65.

Chen, M. and Bargh, J.A. (1997) 'Nonconscious Behavioral Confirmation Processes: The Self-Fulfilling Consequences of Automatic Stereotype Activation', *Journal of Experimental Social Psychology*, 33: 541–60.

Conover, P.J. and Feldman, S. (1984) 'How People Organize the Political World: A Schematic Model', *American Journal of Political Science*, 28: 95–126.

Crawford, N.C. (2000) 'The Passion of World Politics: Propositions on Emotion and Emotional Relationships', *International Security*, 24: 116–56.

Crocker, J. Hannah, D.B. and Weber, R. (1983) 'Person Memory and Causal Attributions', *Journal of Personality and Social Psychology*, 44: 55–66.

Downs, G.W. (1989) 'The Rational Deterrence Debate', *World Politics*, 41: 225–38.

Druckman, D. (1994) 'Nationalism, Patriotism, and Group Loyalty: A Social Psychological Perspective', *Mershon International Studies Review*, 38: 43–68.

Eberhardt, J.L. and Fiske, S.T. (1996) 'Motivating Individuals to Change: What Is a Target To Do?', in C.N. Macrae, C. Stangor and M. Hewstone (eds), *Stereotypes and Stereotyping*. New York: Guilford pp. 369–418.

Enzle, M.E. and Shopflocher, D. (1978) 'Instigation of Attribution Processes by Attributional Questions', *Personality and Social Psychology Bulletin*, 4: 595–9.

Esman, M.J. (1986) 'Ethnic Politics and Economic Power', *Comparative Politics*, 19: 395–418.

Esman, M.J. (1994) *Ethnic Politics*. Ithaca Cornell University Press.

Farnham, B. (1990) 'Political Cognition and Decision Making', *Political Psychology*, 11: 83–112.

Farnham, B. (1992) 'Roosevelt and the Munich Crisis: Insights from Prospect Theory', *Political Psychology*, 13: 205–35.

Farnham, B. (1997) *Roosevelt and the Munich Crisis: A Study of Political Decision-Making*. Princeton: Princeton University Press.

Fearon, J.D. (1993) 'Selection Effects and Deterrence', In K. Oye (ed.), *Deterrence Debates: Problems of Definition, Specification, and Estimation*. Ann Arbor: University of Michigan Press.

Fearon, J.D. and Laitin, D.D. (2000) 'Violence and the Social Construction of Identity', *International Organization*, 54: 845–77.

Finnemore, M. and Sikkink, K. (1998) 'International Norm Dynamics and Political Change', *International Organization*, 52 (4): 887–918.

Fiske, S.T. (1986) 'Schema-Based versus Piecemeal Politics: A Patchwork Quilt, but Not a Blanket, of Evidence', in R. Lau and D. Sears (eds), *Political Cognition*. Hillsdale: Lawrence Erlbaum and Associates. pp. 41–53.

Fiske, S.T. (1998) 'Stereotyping, Prejudice, and Discrimination', in D.T. Gilbert, S.T. Fiske and G. Lindzey (eds), *Handbook of Social Psychology*. New York: McGraw–Hill. pp. 357–411.

Fiske, S.T. and Taylor, S.E. (1984) *Social Cognition*. Reading, MA: Addison–Wesley.

George, A.L. and George, J.L. (1956) *Woodrow Wilson and Colonel House: A Personality Study*. New York: John Day.

Grayson, C.E. and Schwartz, N. (1999) 'Beliefs Influence Information Processing Strategies: Declarative and Experiential Information in Risk Assessment', *Social Cognition*, 17: 1–18.

Green, Donald P. and Shapiro, I. (1994) *Pathologies of Rational Choice: A Critique of Applications in Political Science*. New Haven: Yale University Press.

Gurr, T.R. (1970) *Why Men Rebel*. Princeton: Princeton University Press.

Gurr, T.R. (1993) *Minorities at Risk: A Global View of Ethnopolitical Conflict*. Washington, DC: United States Institute of Peace Press.

Harff, B. and Gurr, T.R. (1988) 'Toward Empirical Theory of Genocides and Politicides: Identification and Measurement of Cases since 1945', *International Studies Quarterly*, 32: 359–71.

Harre, R. (1986) *The Social Construction of Emotions*. Oxford: Blackwell.

Hermann, M.G. (1974) 'Leader Personality and Foreign Policy Behavior', in J.N. Rosenau (ed.), *Comparing Foreign Policies: Theories, Findings, and Methods*. New York: Sage. pp. 201–34.

Hermann, M.G. (1980) 'Explaining Foreign Policy Behavior Using the Personal Characteristics of Political Leaders', *International Studies Quarterly*, 24: 7–46.

Herrmann, R. and Fischerkeller, M.P. (1995) 'Beyond the Enemy Image and Spiral Model: Cognitive-Strategic Research after the Cold War', *International Organization*, 49: 415–50.

Higgins, E.T. and Bargh, J.A. (1987) 'Social Cognition and Social Perception', in M.R. Rosenzweig and L.W. Porter (eds), *Annual Review of Psychology*. Palo Alto: Annual Reviews. 38: 369–425.

Hogg, M. (1992) *The Social Psychology of Group Cohesiveness: From Attraction to Social Identity*. New York: New York University Press.

Hogg, M. and Abrams, D. (1988) *Social Identifications: A Social Psychology of Intergroup Relations and Group Processes*. London: Routledge.

Hogg, M. and Abrams, D. (1993) 'Toward a Single-Process Uncertainty-Reduction Model of Social Motivation in Groups', *Group Motivation: Social Psychological Perspectives*. London: Harvester Wheatsheaf. pp. 173–190.

Holsti, O.R. (1989) 'Crisis Decision-Making', in P. Stern, J.L. Husbands, R. Axelrod, R. Jervis and P. Tetlock (eds), *Behavior, Society, and Nuclear War*. New York: Oxford University Press.

Holsti, O.R. and George, A.L. (1975) 'The Effects of Stress on the Performance of Foreign Policy-Makers', in C.P. Cotter (ed.), *Political Science Annual: An International Review*. Indianapolis: Bobbs–Merrill.

Hong, Y., Chiu, C., Dweck, C.S. and Sacks, R. (1997) 'Implicit Theories and Evaluative Processes in Person Cognition', *Journal of Experimental Social Psychology*, 33: 296–323.

Human Rights Watch (1995) *Playing the Communal Card: Communal Violence and Human Rights*. New York: Human Rights Watch.

Huth, P. and Russet, B. (1984) 'What Makes Deterrence Work? Cases from 1900 to 1980', *World Politics*, 36: 496–526.

Huth, P. and Russet, B. (1990) 'Testing Deterrence Theory: Rigor Makes a Difference', *World Politics*, 42: 466–501.

Janis, I. (1982) *Groupthink: Psychological Studies of Policy Decisions and Fiascoes*. New York: Houghton Mifflin.

Jervis, R. (1976) *Perception and Misperception in International Politics*. Princeton: Princeton University Press.

Jervis, R. (1986) 'Cognition and Political Behavior', in R.R. Lau and D.O. Sears (eds), *Political Cognition*. Hillsdale: Lawrence Erlbaum and Associates.

Jervis, R. (1989) 'Rational Deterrence Theory', *World Politics*, 41: 183–207.

Jervis, R., Lebow, R.N. and Stein, J.G. (1985) *Psychology and Deterrence*. Baltimore: Johns Hopkins University Press.

Kahneman, D. and Tversky, A. (1972) 'Subjective Probability: A Judgement of Representativeness', *Cognitive Psychology*, 3: 430–54.

Kahneman, D. and Tversky, A. (1973) 'On the Psychology of Prediction', *Psychological Review*, 80: 237–51.

Kahneman, D. and Tversky, A. (1979) 'Prospect Theory: An Analysis of Decision Under Risk', *Econometrica*, 47: 263–91.

Kahneman, D., Slovic, P. and Tversky, A. (1982) *Judgement under Uncertainty: Heuristics and Biases*. Cambridge: Cambridge University Press.

Kelman, H.C. (1982) 'Creating the Conditions for Israeli–Palestinian Negotiations', *Journal of Conflict Resolution*, 26: 39–76.

Khong, Y.F. (1992) *Analogies at War: Korea, Munich, Dien Bien Phu, and the Vietnam Decisions of 1965*. Princeton: Princeton University Press.

Kuklinski, J.H., Luskin, R.C. and Bollard, J. (1991) 'Where is the Schema? Going Beyond the "S" Word in Political Psychology', *American Political Science Review*, 85: 1341–56.

Kulik, J.A. (1983) 'Confirmatory Attribution and the Perpetuation of Social Beliefs', *Journal of Personality and Social Psychology*, 44: 1171–81.

Lake, D.A. and Rothchild, D. (1996) 'Containing Fear: The Origins and Management of Ethnic Conflict', *International Security*, 21: 41–75.

Larson, D.W. (1997) 'Trust and Missed Opportunities in International Relations', *Political Psychology*, 18: 701–34.

Lau, R.R. and Sears, D.O. (1986) 'Social Cognition and Political Cognition: The Past, Present, and Future', in R. Lau, and D. Sears (eds), *Political Cognition*. Hillsdale: Lawrence Erlbaum and Associates.

Lebow, R.N. (1981) *Between Peace and War: The Nature of International Crisis*. Baltimore: Johns Hopkins University Press.

Lebow, R.N. and Stein, J.G. (1989) 'Rational Deterrence Theory: I Think, Therefore I Deter', *World Politics*, 61: 208–34.

Lebow, R.N. and Stein, J.G. (1990a) 'Deterrence: The Elusive Dependent Variable', *World Politics*, 42: 336–69.

Lebow, R.N. and Stein, J.G. (1990b) *When Does Deterrence Succeed and How Do We Know?* Canadian Institute for International Peace and Security. Ottawa: Monograph Series, CIIPS.

Lebow, R.N. and Stein, J.G. (1994) *We All Lost the Cold War*. Princeton: Princeton University Press.

Lerner, J. and Tetlock, P.E. (1999) 'Accounting for the Effects of Accountability', *Psychology Bulletin*, 124: 255–75.

Levy, J.S. (1992) 'An Introduction to Prospect Theory', *Political Psychology*, 13: 171–86.

Little, R. and Smith, S. (eds) (1988) *Belief Systems and International Relations*. Oxford: Blackwell.

Lopez, G.E., Gurin, P. and Nagda, B.A. (1998) 'Education and Understanding Structural Causes for Group Inequalities', *Political Psychology*, 19: 305–29.

Malo, G.R. and Olson, J.A. (1998) 'Attitude Dissimulation and Persuasion', *Journal of Experimental Social Psychology*, 34: 1–26.

Mandel, R. (1986) 'Psychological Approaches to International Relations', in M.G. Hermann (ed.), *Political Psychology*. San Francisco: Jossey–Bass. pp. 251–78.

Markus, H. and Zajonc, R.B. (1985) 'The Cognitive Perspective in Social Psychology', in G. Lindzey and E. Aronson (eds), *Handbook of Social Psychology*, vol. 1, 3rd edn. New York: Random House.

McDermott, R. (1998) *Risk Taking in International Relations*. Michigan: University of Michigan Press.

Mercer, J. (1995) 'Anarchy and Identity', *International Organization*, 49: 229–52.

Messick, D. and Mackie, D. (1989) 'Intergroup Relations', *Annual Review of Psychology*, 40: 45–81.

Mintz, A. and Geva, N. (1995) 'The Poliheuristic Theory of Foreign Policy Decision Making', in A. Mintz and N. Geva (eds), *Decision Making on War and Peace: The Cognitive-Rational Debate*. Boulder: Lynne Rienner.

Moe, T.M. (1979) 'On the Scientific Status of Rational Models', *Journal of Political Science*, 23: 215–43.

Morrow, J.D. (1995) 'A Rational Choice Approach to International Conflict', in A. Mintz and N. Gava (eds), *Decision Making on War and Peace: The Cognitive-Rational Debate*. Boulder: Lynne Rienner .

Neustadt, R.E. and May, E.R. (1986) *Thinking in Time: The Uses of History for Decision-Makers*. New York: The Free Press.

Newell, A. and Simon, H.A. (1972) *Human Problem Solving*. Englewood Cliffs: Prentice Hall.

Nisbett, R. and Ross, L. (1980) *Human Inference: Strategies and Shortcomings of Social Judgement*. Englewood Cliffs: Prentice Hall.

Petty, R.E., Wegener, D.T. and White, P.H. (1998) 'Flexible Correction Processes in Social Judgement: Implications for Persuasion', *Social Cognition*, 16: 93–113.

Posen, B.R. (1993) 'The Security Dilemma and Ethnic Conflict', in M.E. Brown (ed.), *Ethnic Conflict and International Security*. Princeton: Princeton University Press. pp. 103–24.

Price, R. (1997) *The Chemical Weapons Taboo*. Ithaca: Cornell University Press.

Pruitt, D.G. and Rubin, J.Z. (1986) *Social Conflict*. New York: McGraw–Hill.

Pyszczynski, T.A. and Greenberg, J. (1981) 'Role of Disconfirmed Expectancies in the Instigation of Attributional Processing', *Journal of Personality and Social Psychology*, 40: 31–8.

Ranger, T. (1983) *The Invention of Tradition*. Cambridge: Cambridge University Press.

Ross, M. and Sicoly, F. (1979) 'Egocentric Biases in Availability and Attribution', *Journal of Personality and Social Psychology*, 37: 322–36.

Ruggie, J. (1998) *Constructing the World Polity: Essays on International Institutionalization*. London: Routledge.

Sanbonmatsu, D.M., Posavac, S.S. and Stasnye, R. (1997) 'The Subjective Belief Underlying Probability Estimation', *Journal of Experimental Social Psychology*, 33: 276–95.

Sherif, M. (1966) *In Common Predicament: Social Psychology of Intergroup Conflict and Cooperation*. Boston: Houghton Mifflin.

Sherman, J.W., Klein, S.B., Laskey, A. and Wyer, N.A. (1998) 'Intergroup Bias in Group Judgement Processes: The Role of Behavioral Memories', *Journal of Experimental Social Psychology*, 34: 51–65.

Simon, H.A. (1973) 'The Structure of Ill-Structured Problems', *Artificial Intelligence*, 4: 181–201.

Sisk, T.D. (1995) *Living Together: International Mediation to Promote Power Sharing in Ethnic Conflicts*. New York: Carnegie Commission on Preventing Deadly Conflict.

Slomczynski, K.M. and Shabad, G. (1998) 'Can Support for Democracy and the Market be Learned in School? A Natural Experiment in Post-Communist Poland', *Political Psychology*, 19: 749–79.

Snidal, D. (1986) 'The Game Theory of International Politics', in K. Oye (ed.), *Cooperation Under Anarchy*. Princeton: Princeton University Press.

Snyder, J. (1991) *Myths of Empire: Domestic Politics and International Ambition*. Ithaca: Cornell University Press.

Stedman, S.J. (1988) *Peacemaking in Civil War: International Mediation in Zimbabwe, 1974–1980*. Boulder: Lynne Rienner.

Stein, J.G. (1992) 'Deterrence and Compellence in the Gulf, 1990–91: A Failed or Impossible Task?', *International Security*, 17: 147–79.

Stein, J.G. (1994) 'Political Learning by Doing: Gorbachev as an Uncommitted Thinker and a Motivated Learner', *International Organization*, 48: 155–83.

Stein, J.G. and Pauly, L. (1989) *Choosing to Cooperate: How States Avoid Loss*. Baltimore: Johns Hopkins University Press.

Stern, E.K. and Sundelius, B. (1997) 'Understanding Small Group Decisions in Foreign Policy: Process, Diagnosis and Research Procedure', in P. t'Hart, E.K. Stern and B. Sundelius (eds), *Beyond Group Think: Political Group Dynamics and Foreign Policy Making*. Ann Arbor: University of Michigan Press. pp. 123–50.

Stern, P. (1995) 'Why do People Sacrifice for Their Nations?', *Political Psychology*, 16: 217–35.

Suedfeld, P. and Tetlock, P. (1997) 'Integrative Complexity of Communication in International Crisis', *Journal of Conflict Resolution*, 21: 168–84.

Tajfel, H. (1981) *Human Groups and Social Categories*. Cambridge: Cambridge University Press.

Tajfel, H. (1982) *Social Identity and Intergroup Relations*. New York: Cambridge University Press.

Tajfel, H. and Turner, J.C. (1979) 'An Integrative Theory of Intergroup Conflict', in W.G. Austin, and S. Worchel (eds), *The Social Psychology of Intergroup Relations*. Monterey: Brooks/Cole. pp. 33–47.

Tajfel, H. and Turner, J.C. (1986) 'The Social Identity Theory of Intergroup Behavior', in S. Worchel and W.G. Austin (eds), *Psychology of Intergroup Relations*. Chicago: Nelson Hall. pp. 7–24.

Tannenwald, N. (1999) 'The Nuclear Taboo: The United States and the Normative Basis of Nuclear Non-Use', *International Organization*, 53: 433–68.

Taylor, D.M. and Moghaddam, F.M. (1987) *Theories of Intergroup Relations: International and Social Psychological Perspectives*. New York: Praeger.

Taylor, S.E. (1982) 'The Availability Bias in Social Perception and Interaction', in D. Kahneman, P. Slovic and A. Tversky (eds), *Judgement Under Uncertainty: Heuristics and Biases*. New York: Cambridge University Press.

Teske, N. (1997) 'Beyond Altruism: Identity-Construction as a Moral Motive in Political Explanation', *Political Psychology*, 18: 71–91.

Tetlock, P.E. (1985) 'Integrative Complexity of American and Soviet Foreign Policy Rhetorics: A Time-Series Analysis', *Journal of Personality and Social Psychology*, 49: 1565–85.

Tetlock, P.E. (1998) 'Social Psychology and World Politics', in D.T. Gilbert, S.T. Fiske and G. Lindzey (eds), *The Handbook of Social Psychology*. Boston: McGraw–Hill. pp. 868–912.

Tetlock, P.E. and Lerner, J. (1999) 'The Social Contingency Model: Identifying Empirical and Normative Boundary Conditions on the Error-and-Bias Portrait of Human Nature', in S. Chaiken and Y. Trope (eds), *Dual Process Models in Social Psychology*. New York: Guilford Press. pp. 571–85

t'Hart, P., Stern, E.K. and Sundelius, B. (1997) 'Foreign Policy Making at the Top: Political Group Dynamics', in P. t'Hart, E.K . Stern and B. Sundelius (eds), *Beyond Group Think: Political Group Dynamics and Foreign Policy Making*. Ann Arbor: University of Michigan Press. pp. 3–34.

Turner, J.C., Hogg, M.A., Oakes, P.J., Reicher, S.D. and Wetherwell, M.S. (1987) *Rediscovering the Social*

Group: A Self-Categorization Theory. Oxford: Blackwell.

Tversky, A. and Kahneman, D. (1973) 'Availability: A Heuristic for Judging Frequency and Probability', *Cognitive Psychology*, 5: 207–32.

Tversky, A. and Kahneman, D. (1981) 'The Framing of Decisions and the Psychology of Choice', *Science*, 211: 453–8.

Tversky, A. and Kahneman, D. (1982) 'Judgements of and by Representativeness', in D. Kahneman, P. Slovic and A. Tversky (eds), *Judgement Under Uncertainty: Heuristics and Biases.* Cambridge: Cambridge University Press. pp. 84–98.

Vertzberger, Y.Y. (1990) *The World in Their Minds: Information Processing, Cognition, and Perception in Foreign Policy Decision-Making.* Stanford: Stanford University Press.

Von Winterfeldt, D. and Edwards, E. (1986) *Decision Analysis and Behavioral Research.* New York: Cambridge University Press.

Voss, J.F. and Post, T.A. (1988) 'On the Solving of Ill-Structured Problems', in M.H. Chi, R. Glaser and M.J. Farr (eds), *The Nature of Expertise.* Hillsdale: Lawrence Erlbaum Associates. pp. 1261–85.

Voss, J.F., Greene, T.R., Post, T.A. and Penner, B.C. (1983) 'Problem-Solving Skill in the Social Sciences', in G.H. Bower (ed.), *The Psychology of Learning and Motivation: Advances in Research and Theory.* New York: Academic Press. pp.165–213

Voss, J.F., Wolfe, C.R., Lawrence, J.A. and Engle, R.A. (1991) 'From Representation to Decision: An Analysis of Problem Solving in International Relations', in R.J. Sternberg and P.A. Frensch (eds), *Complex Problem Solving: Principles and Mechanisms.* Hillsdale: Lawrence Erlbaum. pp. 158–99.

Walker, S.G. (1988) 'The Impact of Personality Structure and Cognitive Processes upon American Foreign Policy Decisions', paper delivered at the Annual Meeting of the American Political Science Association. Washington, DC .

Wegener, D.T. and Petty, R.E. (1998) 'The Naive Scientist Revisited: Naive Theories and Social Judgement', *Social Cognition*, 16: 1–7.

16

Domestic Politics and International Relations

PETER GOUREVITCH

Did the Soviet Union and the United States struggle for fifty years because one was communist, the other capitalist? Or was it because of their situation in the world, as the two major powers of the global system, inescapably locked into a classic security dilemma? If all countries were democracies, would there be peace, as Woodrow Wilson predicted? Are democracies developing in Latin America and East Asia because of forces internal to each country, or are their political systems shaped by international forces? These questions show the centrality of domestic politics to any understanding of the strategic interactions in the world, that is, of international relations (Bueno de Mesquita, 2000; Lake and Powell, 1999).

That international relations and domestic politics interact quite profoundly no longer seems to be a controversial statement (Kahler, 2001; Keohane and Milner, 1996; Müller and Risse-Kappen, 1993; Zürn, 1993). Appreciation of domestic politics in understanding international relations has certainly risen over the past two decades. Putnam's (1988) metaphor of two-level games is widely cited to inspire and legitimate work on domestic politics. A very substantial literature examines the role of interest groups, domestic institutions, ideas, non-governmental organizations, civil society transnational relations and 'the second image reversed' (Gourevitch, 1978), a phrase used by this author to express the impact of international pressures on domestic politics, and the consequences that has back on international relations.

For many decades discourse has been structured around the notion of 'levels', or, in Waltz's (1959) language, 'images' – system (third image,

characterized by anarchy), state (second image, characterized by institutions and socio-economic structures) and individual (first image, characterized by individual psychology). These distinctions no longer capture intellectual life in our field, as indeed they have for many years not captured reality. Anarchy and institutionalization are important distinctions but they are endpoints on a continuum and they do not differentiate domestic from international politics (Lake, 1998). Various aspects of international life are highly institutionalized – the European Union, the postal and telephone regime, the rules of diplomatic exchange. Many domestic situations are anarchic – gangs in urban slums, warlords in countries torn by civil strife. International and domestic are both 'politics'. They can be understood by the same categories and concepts. The real question is not whether the two 'levels' are distinct, but how to study their unmistakable interaction.

Seeing the domestic and international dimensions as part of a whole does not ease the challenge of understanding. Indeed, it may make it harder, for it raises difficult problems of endogeneity. That issue has been handled in three ways. First, system-level theorizing holds domestic politics constant and explores variance in the international arena. This approach flattens the role of domestic politics to zero in order to see whether changes in the environment within which states operate alters their behavior. This is, of course, the central premise of realism: assuming a unitary, rational state in order to examine variance within the international system. It is as well the central premise of any system approach, including neoliberal institutionalism (NLI) and system constructivism, which retain assumptions of unitary actors while challenging realism's account of their interactions. NLI (Keohane, 1984) says states can cooperate in anarchy if there are institutions; system constructivism (Wendt, 1992) says states operate according to a code derived from the international arena. Neither includes domestic politics.

The second level of theorizing holds the system relatively constant and looks at the aspects of domestic politics which shape how a country responds to its environment. The core of any argument about the importance of domestic politics lies with the degree of freedom countries have in how they interpret their situation in the world. The system may indeed have 'imperatives' but these are rarely wholly determinative of a country's choices. The system has many dimensions, with multiple, often conflicting incentives, confusing signals, complex information. Disagreement within countries over policy leads to a politics of choice among alternatives.

If nations have choices, we need theories and research that explains how countries make these choices. An important branch of domestic politics theorizing looks within the country to find factors that shape its choices. It reverses system theorizing: instead of seeing how the system induces behavior in its units, it looks at aspects within the units that shape its behavior outward. This is the classic version of second-image reasoning.

A third level of analysis about domestic politics seeks to explore interactions: of levels (system and unit), of countries with each other and of transnational forces. This approach stresses strategic interaction of all elements. Countries evaluate each other's domestic political situation; actors derive their preferences from a pattern of influences involving other actors and the internal politics of other countries. Institutions, interests and ideas within countries are constantly influencing the same factors in other countries. This third body of work, the interaction of domestic and international, is the least well developed, and the place that particularly requires further analysis.

This chapter will focus on the second and third programs of research. The first model, focusing on system, is examined in other chapters of this volume. Since theorizing arises out of the problem to be examined, the discussion is organized around issue areas.

THE POLITICS OF TRADE DISPUTES: INTEREST GROUPS, INSTITUTIONS, IDEAS

The most highly articulated body of work exploring domestic/international interaction has arisen from international political economy. Foreign economic policy inherently links the two by seeking the causes behind a nation's choices. Schattschneider (1935) developed one of the most widely accepted concepts in politics – that concentrated interests defeat diffuse ones – to explain the passage of the Smoot Hawley tariff. Olson (1982) applied his concept of collective action to economic policy with the idea of 'all-encompassing' coalitions or institutions, those that aggregate at a high level versus those that induce fragmentation to explain why the former produce more 'general welfare enhancing' policies than the latter. A number of significant writings helped advance the analysis of trade relationships: Gerschenkron's (1962) study of the iron–rye coalition in Germany, Hirschman's (1945) analysis of the use of state power to promote economic dependencies, Kindleberger's (1951) look at interest groups in trade, Bauer, de Sola Pool and Dexter's (1963) study of public opinion, interest groups and institutions, Gilpin's (1975) and Vernon's (1971) arguments about the role of multinational corporations.

By the 1960s and 1970s, these ideas had generated a sustained attack on unitary system models. Writers in the emerging field of international political economy disaggregated the state, exploring how its internal processes explained policy. They dislocated security issues from their primacy and challenged as well the interest in ideas or national culture as explanations of foreign policy (Hoffmann, 1960). A number of works emerged to examine interest groups, institutions and the patterns of their interaction (Gourevitch, 1977, 1986; Katzenstein, 1978; Keohane and Nye, 1977; Krasner, 1978; Kurth, 1979). That literature has strongly influenced the way the field deals with the interaction among preferences (or interests), institutions and ideas; the building blocks of most debates in international relations.

Arguing from Preferences

What explains a country's choice between free trade and protectionism? The general logic of a preferences argument is familiar to everyone: interests within a country are differentially impacted by trade according to their competitive position in the world and the national economies; they lobby the government to get the policies that fit their preferences (Frieden, 1999). The controversies arise over specifying the interests and then linking these to decision-making processes.

By the 1980s, descriptive accounts of economic cleavages gave way to deductively derived ones, drawing on economic models, and such models are now required of any serious work in this field. The fights here have turned on class versus factor as the basis of cleavages. Rogowski's (1989) quite important book uses Stoper-Samuelson models of trade to predict that those whose factor endowment was scarce within their country would prefer protectionism, while those whose factors were abundant would support free trade. In applying this logic to historical cases, Rogowski was careful not to say that the explanation of preference cleavages was sufficient to explain the choice of country policy – but his account is frequently taken as the standard bearer of that logic. The most extensive version of the preferences approach has become known as 'endogenous' macro theory, for which the work of Magee, Brock and Young (1989) is among the most important statements.

The sectors argument draws on Ricardo–Viner trade theory to stress factor specificity. Frieden (1991a) argues that as some force (technology, geography) inhibits the mobility of factors of production, these become tied to a particular industry. All the participants of that industry then have an interest in its preservation and growth, and will ally despite the difference in their class position.

Hiscox (1999, 2001) argues that the two theories should be read as empirical alternatives. Both are deductively valid, but apply to different historical moments. Factor specificity is not a constant, but an attribute that can change over time. Policy preferences shift as the degree and location of factor specificity shifts. Hiscox measures changes in asset specificity and finds that changes in that parameter do correlate with patterns of class (when asset specificity is low) and sectoral conflict (when it is high).

The logic of the preference approach invites researchers to investigate other principles of cleavage, or incentives for a particular policy position, and apply them to a range of policy areas. Milner (1997) argues that the concentration of interests is not exclusive to protectionists: there are groups who benefit strongly from exports and can lead a fight against the protectionists (see also Destler and Odell, 1987). Frieden (1991b) looks at capital markets, Bernhard and Leblang (1999) at banking policy, Henning (1994) at financial institutions.

Interest groups are not the only source of pressure on politicians. Public opinion can be an important factor, directly in democratic elections, indirectly in authoritarian regimes. Understanding mass preferences of individual voters deductively requires better economic models than we have (Frieden and Martin, 2000). Inductive approaches (surveys, interviews) provide important information on economic policy concerning European economic and monetary integration (Gabel, 2000) and on trade policy (Scheve, 1999; Scheve and Slaughter, 2001).

Preferences need not be economic, or based solely on economic interest. Voters and interest groups may have ideological preferences on economic issues arising from a value system about

justice and equality or about nationalism. Goldstein (1993) has applied this reasoning to US trade policy. And many issues may influence foreign policy which are not economic: ethnic attachments; irridentist claims of territory from an adjacent country; religious difference – all of these can be seen as preferences by members of society which influence the decision-making of their leaders. Some constructivist arguments can be read this way: ideational foundations of preferences which put pressure on politicians.

What unifies all preferences arguments, then, is the logic of looking to the goals of political actors, to assume that institutions arise themselves from preferences, and that how institutions work turns on who uses them.

Institutions

The institutionalist critique of the preferences approach is in its general form familiar; a statement of preferences by itself does not tell us how they are aggregated into an outcome. Outcomes can be varied by altering the procedures of aggregation. Policy choices are thus a function of institutional arrangements. The major quarrels within this part of the field lie in specifying which institutions matter and how.

The analysis of reciprocal trade legislation in the United States has been particularly fruitful for these debates. The shift in American policy from protectionism to free trade in the mid-twentieth century coincided with the growth of presidential power. One branch of institutionalists suggest the one caused the other (Haggard, 1988). With smaller constituencies, Congress reflects the particularism of its electors, while the President faces a larger more diverse constituency which he must integrate with a broader appeal. Congress is vulnerable to protectionist log-rolling while the Presidency is able to articulate the larger gains from free trade. Thus the growth of Presidential power produces a shift in policy away from protectionism.

A contrary line of reasoning reverses the causality. Congress supports reciprocal trade legislation because a majority there wants it, not because the President pushes them toward it. Free traders understood that foreign countries would not negotiate with the executive if any agreements reached could be amended on the floor of Congress (Lohmann and O'Halloran, 1994). To enable international negotiations, the majority protected its members from the temptations of protectionist log-rolling by imposing a self-binding rule which authorizes the President to negotiate without possibility of amendment (see Chapter 23 on the political economy of trade in this volume). Thus, the growth of presidential power on trade is not the cause of a shift in power, but a reflection of a change in policy preference, by a Congress that can revoke the authorization or fail to renew it, as happened after 1994 (Bailey et al., 1997; Epstein and O'Halloran, 1999; Gilligan, 1997; O'Halloran, 1994). Evidence from other periods of history and countries shows as well that trade policies have shifted without changes in institutions, and different systems have produced similar policies (Gourevitch, 1986).

While much of the thinking about institutions arose in the exploration of the relationship between the American Congress and Presidency, these ideas have been extended to a wider ranger of countries and situations, exploring the role of legislative–executive relations, the relationship between elected leaders and their constituencies, and voting rules and party systems (Cox and McCubbins, 1993, 2001; Rogowski, 1999). Proportional representation systems were adopted in the European countries, Rogowski (1987) argues, as a way of orchestrating compromises on policy questions those countries needed to deal with foreign trade pressures. The voting system in Japan has favored the representation of producer groups who feel threatened by trade, thereby exacerbating Japan's conflict with the United Sates (Cox, 1997; Ramseyer and Rosenbluth, 1993). Cowhey (1995) explores the way differences in the political systems of the United States and Japan shape their policy disagreements. Andrew MacIntyre (2001) shows the ways difference in political systems influences East Asian responses to the Asian financial crisis of 1997. The choice between presidential and parliamentary systems can have significant consequences for the pattern of power (Laver and Shepsle, 1994; Shugart and Carey, 1992; Shugart and Haggard, 2001). Lijphart (1999) provides an impressive foundation for further research about institutional structures by carefully specifying the arrangements in many countries on a wide variety of dimensions, and he provides some application to policy.

This literature on institutional design derives largely from the rationalist model of institutions. While these approaches are important, significant work is done in other traditions (Hall and Taylor, 1996; Weber, 1997). Historical institutionalist work seeks to provide process tracing of major events and patterns in the formation of patterns of power (Steinmo et al., 1992). A concern with norms leads to an interest in the normative and cultural foundations of cooperation and conflict (Kratochwil, 1989). Sociological approaches explore structures of social reproduction and control (Mayer, 1959; Powell and DiMaggio, 1991). Eising (2002) explores the interaction of rationalist models with notions of policy learning. Levy (2001) shows the way in which the French state is constrained in policy options by the weakness of social institutions in French society, a theme also explored by Putnam, Leonardi and Nanetti (1993) and Zeigler (1997).

Much of the debate about institutions revolves around explaining and debating structures rather than the linkage between these and policy outcomes. IPE could benefit from further integration of comparative, international and institutionalist work with public policy outcomes in economic issue areas other than trade (for example, social welfare, education, health and safety, environment), and from research that explores the interactive effects between preferences and institutions.

Problemtizing Interests and Institutions

Much of the research on preferences and institutions has sought to understand the importance of each by holding the other constant. This is a necessary research ploy, but needs also to be questioned. Where do interests come from and where do institutions come from? Rationalists tend to be take interests as given, as somehow primordial. Rationalists tend to be materialists, seeing interests as arising from some structural logic of situation, usually economic, but interests could also derive from beliefs, which shape a preference, thus an interest. Interests drive preferences, which in turn drive the creation of institutions: since everyone understands that institutional arrangements influence outcomes, everyone will work to get the institutional pattern that increases their chances of victory.

Once institutions are established, they themselves structure debates about changing institutions. In the case of reciprocal trade noted above, those who favor and oppose free trade will fight over the institution of delegation to the President, but this takes place in the framework of a stable set of rules (Congress) about how to resolve the disagreement. Where there are no institutions or weak ones (as in the formation of many international institutions such as the United Nations) there are no rules to govern an argument about them, so they are shaped by non-institutional processes – military power, bargaining, ideology etc. (Gourevitch, 1999).

Preferences and institutions cannot be modeled independent of politics. Either can change if the opportunity to do so exists. Verdier (1994) argues that in competitive capitalist democracies, preferences are shaped by the politically defined probability of success or failure in attaining policy goals, and not by a purely economic logic. In choosing among options, political actors consider not only what they want but the costs of getting each option and the probability of getting it. Economic position, the presumed driver of preferences in trade issues, cannot be ascertained outside of property relations and these in turn derive from politics: the definition of property, the rules of competition, the structure of markets can all be seen as derived from political authority, as politics can change them. Since institutions shape the probability of policy outcomes, and institutions can be changed by politics, then a shift in institutions can lead to a change in desired options.

This leads to a difficult analytic point. If we observe a shift in policy position, do we classify it as a change of preferences? It could be understood instead as a change not in core preferences (the desire to maximize profit, for example) but rather a change in tactics (modifying a regulation in order to get the profits). Altering institutions shifts power relationships and thus alters incentives, provides new information and a number of other things which can change policy position. This is different from a change in preference deriving from a change in identity. Operationalizing the difference is a challenge to constructivists and materialist rationalists alike (Eising, 2002; Frieden, 1999). If a worker shifts from free trade to protectionism because of decisions made by the European Union, this will most likely be agreed to be a change of tactics. If an individual who expressed him- or herself politically as a worker now does so as a Catalan, is this a change in identity or in tactics (the Catalan parties can provide more)?

The core of a constructivist critique of interest lies in the notion of constituted identity. Prior to interests and institutions lies the formation of an identity and a framework of discourse. Debates about interests, institutions and tactics can only take place in a framework of shared assumptions, understanding and 'common language'. These are the primordial elements, socially constructed as a cultural force, not a hard material fact. Other chapters of this volume explore constructivism (Chapters 3 and 5). The relevant point here relates to research strategy concerning domestic politics. In challenging the rationalist versions of the interest and preferences approaches, the constructivists seek more work on the formation of 'interest' identities. To sharpen the debate, alternative accounts of classic political economy dependent variables are needed.

GLOBALIZATION AND DOMESTIC POLITICS: THE CONVERGENCE–DIVERGENCE DEBATE

Globalization has made international relations important to scholars of comparative politics, and issues about the internal workings of countries relevant to IR scholars. That trade influences countries is not a new idea. Wallerstein (1974) and Anderson (1974) take it back to the emergence of Holland in the sixteenth century. The claim for originality in current trends lies in the intensity,

extent and reach of global markets: a profoundly deeper division of labor, no longer just trade of primary products for manufactured goods, but trade of components through international production networks; coverage of the whole globe in a world economic system; and penetration of the system into culture, the movement of peoples and social institutions. The virtues and vices of globalization are hotly contested, but these are not the primary concern here.

The central issue for our purposes concerns the implications of convergence–divergence arguments for the linkage between domestic and international relations. Does globalization constrain all countries to become alike, or at least significantly more similar, in their economic policies, institutions, political economy, culture and social structure (Friedman, 1999)? If so, globalization acts as a system, constraining the units in it; it works like the system modeled by realists, a force that shapes profoundly the actions of its members, even internally. Or is there a substantial amount of slack allowed by the international economic system, so that countries can integrate into the world economy but none the less differ substantially in a wide range of policies, institutions and practices? If so, we then again need theories that explain what options countries actually chose to take (Berger and Dore, 1996).

On the side of convergence lie many examples of governments abandoning programs under the pressure of world markets: Mitterrand's socialist government of the early 1980s; the requirement by the European Monetary Union to reduce deficits and debts; World Bank and IMF demands on Mexico, East Asia, Russia, Ecuador and other countries in recent years. How do these pressures work? The answer may appear obvious from the preferences pressure model noted above. Equity investors move against a currency, withdraw assets, or fail to invest in a country whose economic policy they dislike. This is obvious in a crisis situation such as a falling currency, hyperinflation or political instability (Haggard and Kaufman, 1995).

In crisis or non-crisis situations, what is it exactly that investors look for in defining good from bad policy (Goldstein et al., 2000; Mosely, 2000)? Political variables can be quite important, Simmons (1994) shows, as indicators of policy; in the interwar years, markets feared governments with ties to left parties and trade unions. In recent years, analysis has come to understand the role of regulatory patterns that structure market relationships. For example, Shinn (2001) argues that investors demand a premium for buying shares in the 'closed corporate' governance model of Germany and Japan over shares in countries like the United States with more open models that protect external shareholders (Gourevitch, 2001; Roe, 1994).

Against the convergence hypothesis is a rapidly growing literature showing quite substantial country differences in a number of policy areas. Comparing OECD countries, Iversen and Wren (1998) demonstrate that despite substantial commonality of economic pressures from the European and global economies, countries do differ significantly in the policy choices they make, picking different combinations of trade-offs among equality, growth and stability: a Christian Democratic model, which stresses stability, a Social Democratic model, which stresses equality, and a neoliberal model, which stresses growth. Garrett and Lange (1991; also Garrett, 1998) agree that there has been policy divergence. They provide an explanation based on partisan conflict – left vs. right strategies for dealing with international trade. Esping-Andersen (1999) stresses path dependence in shaping divergent responses to common pressures: previous choices interact with new trends in labor markets and family patterns to shape current developments. Streeck (1997) calls attention to the role of worker training systems in accounting for divergence. Scharpf and Schmidt (2000) and their collaborators examine vulnerabilities and capabilities of countries and provide case studies on such issues as women in the labor market, retirement systems, tax competition, as well as employment and equality. Kitschelt et al. (1999), Hall and Soskice (2001) and Stephens and Huber-Stephens (2001) all explore the importance of variance in micro-institutions interacting with political and macro-economic variables. Some older work by Cameron (1978) and Katzenstein (1985), focusing on the small countries in Europe have higher levels of government spending than large ones, has been extended by Rodrik (1997) and Bates (1997).

An important theme in much of this literature is an interaction affect among variables. Some analysts argue that making central banks truly independent from political influence produces a 'technology' that prevents inflation through strict monetary policy (Alesina and Grilli, 1993; Grilli et al., 1991). Conversely, the effect of central bank independence, Hall and Franzese (1998) argue, is strongly mediated by other institutions in society: strong trade unions, industry-wide bargaining, agreement on wage increases tied to productivity are all institutional features of German economic life which condition the impact of bank policy. Soskice and Iversen (2000) show that the validity of rational expectations models turns on institutional features of the economy; the models' predictions are correct with perfectly fluid factor markets, but wrong when there is stickiness in those markets, such as trade unions, oligopolies or corporatist practices. Iversen (1999) develops a model that shows the need to integrate the autonomy of the bank with the character of the labor market. Drawing on concepts of delegation, it can be argued central bank autonomy relies on political support for the policies and outcomes they generate. Autonomy given is autonomy that can be withdrawn.

Hall and Soskice (2001) extend this embeddedness concept to find strong connections among many dimensions of policy and the economy. The United States and other neoliberal economies have fluid labor markets, generalized systems of education and training, fluid mechanisms of price and wage determination, stockholder highly competitive mechanisms of corporate control, and quite varied welfare systems. Germany and other countries in a 'continental model' in contrast have highly structured labor markets, education and training that link workers to specific jobs, structured mechanisms of price and wage determination, interlocking ownership patterns with weak shareholder involvement and no market for control, and highly structured welfare systems. There is a logic to the bundling: the German system provides incentives for investment in specific assets, which it needs to protect by highly structured institutions; the United States model rewards generalized investments by individuals and investors. If tightly bundled, the pieces of the system do not change separately; they are in some kind of equilibrium; changes in one will either be contained, or be quite destabilizing. Each system has its own strengths and weaknesses, its own comparative advantage.

This argument has quite substantial implications for the globalization debate. If quite different systems can operate effectively, there is more than one way to be efficient. Economic competition will thus not produce convergence, but rewards to specialization (Gourevitch, 2001). The division of labor will intensify, rewarding the specific features of national production systems. The convergence logic requires the assumption that there really is only way to do things, and the market has the capacity to reward those countries which do that, whatever the political resistance to doing so.

The existence of divergence, in turn, highlights the importance of domestic politics. External pressures do not translate themselves into policy automatically. Some political actors within a country must decide that accepting the dictates of the pressure is better than resistance. Evans (1979) analyzed 'compradors', the domestic allies of foreign capital. Allies or not, policies do require domestic support, which leads us right back to the issues of interest group power, institutional aggregation and ideology noted above. The notion of embeddedness suggests the need for research strategies that do not isolate variables, but explore their relationships.

The Domestic Politics
of Security Issues

If the boundary between international and domestic seems to be fading, so is the one between security and political economy. These two branches of work have generated contrasting research and theoretical traditions. There is good reason to think that behavior varies with issue areas: for example, it may be easier to cooperate on trade issues because there are so many more interactions. At the same time, both economic and security concerns involve politics. Both entail the making of choices in a situation of strategic interaction, and both can be analyzed from a common theoretical framework – the example just noted can be explained from a single logic, the impact of frequent iterations on cooperation (Axelrod, 1984).

While security studies and realist views of system and unitary actors are quite intermingled, the security field has its own rich tradition of domestic politics explanations of policy choices. Military budgets and policy have long been explored by the same logic of interest groups and institutions noted above in discussing trade. Where realists explain Germany's decision to build a navy before the First World War as part of systemic rivalry with Britain, others see it as a response to domestic lobbies seeking to link a steel industry facing weak demand to military groups wanting bigger budgets (Kehr, 1977; Kurth, 1971; Snyder, 1991).

Recent work extends this type of analysis by looking at the domestic elements of strategic doctrine. Papayoanou (1999) shows the British were hindered in sending clear signals to Germany in 1914 about their course of action in case of war because domestic economic interests were divided between those with strong ties to Germany and those with ties to the Empire and other countries. Brooks (2000) links the ability of a country to develop comprehensive strategic doctrine to the structural relationships between the military and civilian institutions.

An important locus of work on security deals with historical memory in shaping expectations about future behavior. Public opinion among Japan's neighbors protests when Japanese textbooks minimize Japan's role in the Second World War and wartime atrocities (Buruma, 1994). Germany faced more muted reactions to unification, but there was concern none the less. Are these countries safely peaceful? The system answer is of course to look at the balance of power arrayed to deter aggression, while an international institutionalist would point to Germany's integration into the European Union and NATO, and Japan's treaty commitments. Domestic politics approaches look inside the country. Japan prohibits war in its constitution, limits the size of the military, and subjects the military to extensive civilian control by placing representatives of other civilian ministries on the bureaucratic structures that supervise it (Katzenstein, 1996). Germany now makes clear that the armed forces are subject to democratic civilian control.

Emphasis on interest groups would call attention to profound social change in each country: land reform in Japan; the elimination of the Junkers as a social class in Germany. Emphasis on culture would stress pacifism and anti-militarist sentiment in each country. Berger (1993) shows how arguments over the causes of the war in Japan correlate with political positions: there is widespread agreement on the role of the military, but not on the other causes – *zaibatsu* interested in expanding investment in Korea, Manchuria, China; social groups aligned with the military, repression of democratic forces, Japanese culture.

Another line of research on security issues applies interest in institutions to civil–military relations. Where realists interpret military structure and behavior in terms of system threats, a domestic view sees the armed forces as having their own internal interests and political role. As comparativists study democratization processes, a vital element is the changing relationship of the military to the formal political system and to society. Studies of Latin America frequently portray a military active in internal politics far more than one defending national borders or projecting force outside the country. The military regards itself as an arbiter of domestic political struggles, a guarantor of goals it regards civilian forces as unable to attain or protect, and often demands institutional guarantees of that role (Loveman, 1993; Stepan, 1988). Thus Pinochet overturned the Chilean constitution to stop Allende; one example of many military coups. Argentina provides an example of an old idea in this field of study: that foreign policy adventures are used to cover up political weakness at home. The Argentine generals used the Malvinas/Falklands crisis for this purpose, but lost their bet to UK prime minister Thatcher, for whom it did provide a political rebound (Richardson, 1996).

The study of culture, never wholly absent from security studies (Benedict, 1946; Leites, 1950; Osgood, 1953), has attracted increasing attention, in part from the theoretical advances of constructivism and in part from the explosion of ethnic conflicts around the world. Huntington's *The Clash of Civilizations* (1996) unleashed a storm of criticism, and heightened interest in the issue. The main criticism is not so different from the ones levied by domestic politics experts against unitary actor models: countries and cultures are complex constructs of many elements, capable of supporting a wide range of actions. The ideas that triumph may indeed have an influence over policy, but one needs a political explanation for that triumph rooted in institutions, interest, politics and conflicting ideas.

European considerations of culture in the security field focus more on the structure of communication and discussion, of which Habermas is the most famous theoretician. This has influenced a substantial literature (Risse, 2000), much of it theoretical, which appears to be generating much needed application to empirical cases. It could be promising to link this line of work to research drawing on cognition, learning, information cost theory – a range of material dealing with how people think about policy issues and communicate with each other (Jervis, 1976).

The resurgence of ethnic conflicts in recent years provides ground for new work on culture. Within countries, these can lead to civil war – a breakdown of authority which swiftly erases the boundary between international and domestic politics. (See the section below on 'Composing and Decomposing States'.)

POLITICAL FORMS: DEMOCRACY AND AUTHORITARIANISM

How do democratic institutions influence foreign policy and strategic interaction? If democratization continues to spread, this becomes an increasingly important question. The discussion of the democratic peace literature is treated elsewhere in this volume. Our concern here is with the way the fact of democratization influences international relations.

In a number of ways theorists argue democracies are able to make more credible commitments to other countries because of their institutions. Forced by democratic rules to operate publicly, leaders have to worry about 'audience costs' (Fearon, 1994), the price leaders pay to constituencies for going against their wishes. One audience is the foreign power, who judges intention, resolve and capacity. Another audience is a domestic one, those publics that have the capacity to remove leaders from office or prevent them from attaining desired objectives. Public accountability in a democracy limits the range of likely behaviors that happen in an autocracy, where the rulers have fewer immediate constraints. External observers can thus evaluate the future in connection to the cost they think leaders will avoid paying. It is harder in a democracy to shift policy quickly, hence they are more credible in commitments they make (Schultz, 1999). Democracies may take longer to make decisions, but these have more stability because they have required a broader engagement of society in the approval process (Martin, 2000).

It is often argued that the problem of audience costs makes democracies less effective in foreign policy (Crozier et al., 1975). Conversely, it can be argued that audience costs may strengthen a government in negotiating cooperation. Because open political processes reveal the domestic political game, leaders are able to show convincingly their costs to making concessions (Cowhey, 1995; Schultz, 1999). An agreement may be more difficult to reach but more credible once signed. Martin (1994) argues open processes of ratification in the European Union give greater strength to the agreements than was the case when they were done by executives behind closed doors.

Do democracies make 'better' decisions? The need for open debate may yield better information, since rulers are not able fully to limit the boundary of acceptable discussion. The extent of pollution and health hazards was for example quite hidden in the Soviet bloc since there was no ability to object. The ability to have voice and power shapes the considerations that enter a decision. Sen (1981) argues that since the eighteenth century famines have occurred not because there was insufficient food but because the poor lacked the voice or power to make their needs felt, thus to have food made available to them. Women, he argues, are poorly treated in many countries again because they are disenfranchised. Mass publics may be more averse to the loss of life in war than are leaders, not less belligerent or xenophobic, but more ready to abandon costly projects (Lake, 1992).

Can mass publics in a democracy really understand the issues? Information theory gives new answers to this old question. Foreign policy is by no means the only issue area that poses great requirements on individuals for information and analysis: health, environment, science policy, safety standards for products all involve complexity beyond the reach of most people, and, for the wide range of issue areas, beyond the scope of even the brightest well-educated person. Voters find ways of simplifying their information tasks by looking for shorthands, or heuristic indicators. These often consist of individuals or groups whose expertise they trust, whose values are similar to theirs: thus an environmentally concerned voter looks to the Sierra Club for advice, or a human rights voter to Amnesty International (Lupia and McCubbins, 1998). In this way, the public is able to monitor its agents without the kind of deep investment in every issue which no person can do. In this regard, foreign policy is no different than any other issue area of complexity.

Democracies do of course vary substantially in their institutions. In addition to voting rules, legislative executive relations and party systems, there is a rich tradition of examining bureaucratic structures and organizational processes. Allison's (1971) famous account of the Cuban missile crisis remains quite appropriately a classic, both for its introduction of alternatives to unitary models of the state, and its strategy of presenting alternative explanations of the same event. Its weakness is that the power of the bureaucracies and organizations themselves cannot be understood outside the context of the political system itself. Having shown that a fight among bureaucracies occurs, the bureaucratic politics model does not tell us how the fight is resolved, why one ministry coalition defeats another. Having shown us the consequences of organizational process, that model does not tell us why that process was selected, or why the agency in question had the power to apply its procedures. As Bendor and Hammond (1992) argue, the presidency sits at the top of an internal hierarchy whose character influences the President's power resources. A model of the political system must therefore lie at the core of any institutional analysis of foreign policy. During the Cuban missile crisis, it was in the end the President who made the final choice for moderation (Evans et al., 1993; Pastor, 1980; Welch, 1992).

Another famous example comes from the mobilization plans of the European powers in 1914 and Germany's Schlieffen Plan, which together helped turn a crisis into full-scale war (Craig, 1955; Keegan, 1998; Miller et al., 1991). Posen (1984) argues the military prefer offense-oriented strategic doctrines, largely because this demands more resources and puts them centrally into decision-making, while the civilians are more cautious, fiscally prudent and thus inclined toward defense-oriented doctrines. Kier (1997), by contrast, argues the choice of doctrines turns on military culture and its relationship to domestic politics. In Japan, it was the army that favored expansion into Manchuria, then into China; the navy was more cautious about the ability to project force in competition with the navies of the other great powers (Sagan, 1989). Richardson (1996) shows how these processes influenced conflict between the United States and the UK in the Falklands, Suez, and the Skybolt missile cases.

Trade policy shows bureaucratic politics at work. The US Commerce Department and trade-related agencies push Japan for trade concessions, while the State and Defense Departments favor deference to Japan's importance as an ally on Asian security considerations. The disagreement is mirrored in Japan's internal debates on how to respond to trade pressures: Japan's Ministry of Foreign Affairs often favors concessions to the United States while the Ministry of International Trade and Industry often takes a tougher stand (Destler, 1995; Schoppa, 1997).

If democracies are less warlike and make better decisions, should promoting democracy be a goal in foreign policy? The peace–efficiency arguments add an instrumental dimension to the moral one, that democracy is a value in itself. The United States

and other democracies may find it preferable to deal with other democracies – would a democratic China be a more cooperative one? China may not agree with the obverse: that a democratic United States is a better ally than an authoritarian one. Preferring democracy is not the same as expending costs to get one.

The question of democracy, long associated with issues of security, has increasingly entered the political economy field. The older argument comparing democracy and authoritarianism toward prospects for economic growth continues to stimulate research (Haggard and Kaufman, 1995). It has shifted now toward concerns with institutional design and effective governance, in which democratization is one component.

North and Weingast (1989) argued in a well-known paper that constitutionalism gave the British an economic advantage over their absolutist continental counterparts. Because Parliament could monitor the Crown, loans to the government were less likely to be renounced, reassuring lenders, giving seventeenth-century England lower interest rates than the Sun King's France and the other absolute monarchies of Europe. The limited state was thus a stronger state (Brewer and Echhart, 1999). This line of reasoning turns on its head an earlier discussion about strong and weak states, which saw the centralized states as strong, and highly constitutionalized and pluralist ones like the United States as weak (Katzenstein, 1985). Constitutional governments may work more slowly, but because they must mobilize consent, they are more consistent and reliable.

This debate has taken a new turn in the past decade, with a widespread interest in transparency and effective governance. The rapid growth of East Asia and Japan in the post-war years undermined quite substantially the dependencia notion of world systems theorizing about growth: the idea that countries were confined to a particular location in the global division of labor from which they could not move. Clearly countries could move, if they made certain choices. The countries of rapid growth were frequently not democratic or if so, as in Japan, held to be state-centered in development model, and bureaucracy-dominated in policy formation (Haggard, 1990; Wade, 1990).

The Asian Financial Crisis of 1997, the slow growth of the Japanese economy, and gradual rejection of the import substituting and state-led policy model in Latin America altered the debate quite substantially. The developmental state was now called corrupt crony capitalism, vulnerable to moral hazard. The solution, in the so-called Washington consensus, was transparency which required greater democratization. International and domestic economic policy-making institutions developed a strong interest in the institutional foundations of policy-making, long absent from these circles. Policy-makers now speak of the problem of good governance, of how to design institutions in developing countries capable of making effective decisions, capable of providing public goods rather than particularistic pork barrel (Haggard and McCubbins, 2001).

As policy-makers seek advice from institutionalists on the design of good governance institutions, they find, MacIntyre (2001) argues, conflicting advice. One branch of institutionalists thinks democracy, with its multiple 'veto-gates', inhibits decisive action, so that authoritarian governments have an advantage; the other approach thinks the veto-gates build consensus and commitment, so that democratic governments have the ability to be consistent (Lijphart, 1999; Shugart and Haggard, 2001; Tsebelis and Money, 1997). MacIntyre (2001) integrates the two lines of reasoning into a U-shaped curve; countries having one extreme or another on each dimension behave less well than governments having a blend of the two. International pressures and domestic political-processes and institutions blend well in this issue area. Haggard and Kaufman explore the ways democracy influences the adjustment countries make to international economic pressures in developing countries (Haggard and Kaufman, 1995). Further progress on the role of institutions requires more work integrating institutional analysis with ideas about interests and ideas for countries and regions where institutions have not received much attention, particularly the developing ones.

A particularly great challenge lies in modeling authoritarian regimes. These are no longer modeled as unitary states, expressing the will of a dominant leader. Experts on the USSR and Nazi Germany long ago introduced ideas of competing forces within these regimes, struggles for dominance involving a kind of politics. It has been none the less difficult to import all of the tools of institutionalist analysis because of the need to find a clear utility function for leaders and a stable account of their constituencies and incentives. In democracies, leaders can be assumed to seek re-election. For authoritarian leaders, the functional equivalent of the electorate and open voting systems must be found in order to define the leaders' objective utility function. Roeder (1993) and Shirk (1993) have used the concept of 'selectorate' to solve this problem and apply it to the Soviet Union and China, respectively. Authoritarian leaders do not have to win public elections, but they do need to maintain the support of key élites and figures in a society to remain in office (Bueno de Mesquita, et al., 1999a, 1999b).

It remains none the less difficult to provide fully satisfying accounts of authoritarian regimes from an institutionalist's point of view. Leaders appear to have substantial discretion, despite the constraints of a selectorate. They can shift institutions and their selectorate with greater ease than in a democracy, which leaves a more fluid game. None the less, this appears to be a rich area for further work, linking together insights from institutionalism, advances in the modeling of interests in the open world economy, and the evolution of ideas about appropriate models of institutions and development models.

CONSTRUCTIVISM, CULTURE AND DOMESTIC POLITICS

Constructivists have helped bring about a revival of interest in ideas. The portion of the debate relevant for this chapter is to explore the implications of constructivist approaches for research on domestic politics. Ideas have been taken seriously before in the study of both domestic politics and international relations, but it is fair to say that the major literatures of political economy and institutionalism do not give them much scope. Discussions of norms, discourses and constitutive understandings all require considerable research into the actions of individuals and groups within society and their dialogue with counterparts elsewhere.

Several lines of investigation can be observed. One approach engages in careful historical reconstruction of the emergence of norms by examining the statements or speech acts of leading figures and comparing these to patterns of behavior. In this way, Tannenwald (1999) looks at the norm against the use of nuclear weapons, and Lynch (1999) examines the writings of peace movements prior to the Second World War to challenge the realist treatment of them as ineffectual and naïve. Another approach looks at law as a generator and distributor of norms and the institutions that could enforce them (Finnemore and Toope, 2001); this leads to examination of courts and 'law-like' institutions, such as international regulatory bodies (Alter, 1998; Mattli and Slaughter, 1998). Discourse analysis looks very carefully at speech acts. Other work looks carefully at survey research on public opinion (Herrmann and Shannon, 2001). Tarrow's (1998) work on the general phenomena of movements provides a basis for understanding those that advocate various value concerns in politics.

How are norms taken up in domestic politics? Norms shape preferences. As with any other variable involving preferences such as economic interest, the study of norms requires an analysis of why one or another normative orientation predominates. Ideas, understandings, discourse have a political sociology to them: groups who advocate or oppose them, institutions which favor or hinder them, prior cultural commitments that encourage or oppose their adoption. The political sociology of understandings can be non-ideational (looking at interest groups and institutions, in which case see the discussion above) or it can itself be culturalist in its causal mechanism. Integrative work on norms explores these dimensions: Kaufmann and Pape (1999) examine the social characteristics of the anti-slavery activists in Britain, how they organized for political action, how they made alliances with other groups, and how they were able to operate in the political institutions of the day. Keck and Sikkink (1998) show how NGO groups put pressures on governments to assist groups in other countries seeking to defend human rights; they need to mobilize voters, make allies, influence elections and work through political institutions. In studying Japan, Katzenstein (1996) seeks to locate norms in specific institutions; the purveyors of norms act instrumentally to design an institution that will favor a particular outcome (in this case to limit the autonomy of the Japanese military).

These arguments differ from more system-oriented constructivist research, which focus on international interactions. Wendt (1992, 1999) is a major example. He speaks of states constructing understandings of the world, how they are socialized into accepting rules. This sort of reasoning implies a unitary way of thinking which downplays the arena of domestic politics. It draws us away from examining the processes within a country that lead to the absorption (or opposition) of these international norms. The cutting edge of constructivist research has got away from proving the importance of norms by positing two alternatives, realism or constructivism, and then proving the latter by showing flaws in the former. Instead, it has moved toward the integrative task of showing how ideas merge with material and institutional power through domestic political processes (Checkel, 1997; Katzenstein, 1996; Kaufmann and Pape, 1999; Keck and Sikkink, 1998).

The theoretical and research issues raised by constructivist concerns are quite significant for analyzing the range of issues arising over values in international relations: human rights, democratization, gender and related normative concerns on areas like the environment, abortion, the death penalty and cultural autonomy. Are such values universal or local/regional? This issue poses some considerable analytic problems in the treatment of domestic politics. How are we to know whether ideas are 'alien imports' 'imposed?' In particular, how are we to know this in political systems which are themselves not democratic? The 'alien import' argument is frequently made by authoritarian leaders in regimes where there is no possibility of autonomous debate; how are we to

know if they speak for their people (Neier, 1993; Sen, 1981)?

Debates on norms in international relations lead therefore straight to domestic politics, to an analysis of why norms are supported or opposed in any given country, which in turn links this discussion to all the debates on how to explain domestic outcomes.

NON-STATE PROCESSES AND DOMESTIC POLITICS – THE INTERNATIONALIZATION OF NGOS

In the challenge to unitary state/system theories, the study of transnational relations and international civil society were in the forefront. Both decentered the state as the only relevant unit of international relations, and both disaggregated the state, opening it up to political analysis of contending views of the national interest. Recent work on NGOs (non-governmental organizations) builds on this earlier work in advancing arguments about new types of transnational groups, the role of norms and new forms of civil society. NGOs act across national borders to push for various goals: the environment, human rights, equality for women, working conditions for children (Evangelista, 1999; Keck and Sikkink, 1998; see Chapter 13 in this volume).

Theorists in the English School situate NGOs in the framework of transnational forces as comprising a kind of 'civil society' at the international level (Bull, 1977). These ideas resonate with a revival of interest in civil society by comparativists interested in democratization (Pérez-Díaz, 1993; Putnam et al., 1993). In terms of domestic politics, this leads methodologically to a shift away from the centrality of formal processes of the state in shaping policy outcomes, and toward the study of social institutions. Consumer boycotts are an interesting example: consumers force countries to comply with child labor or environmental rules without formal government legislation by refusing to buy products that have not received approval by the NGO (Spar, 1998).

Alternatively, NGOs, along with other aspects of civil society and transnational forces, can be located in domestic political processes. Risse-Kappen (1995) argues that variance in the impact of transnational forces turns on differences in domestic structures. Keck and Sikkink (1998) show this in 'boomerang' effect. Protesters in country A are blocked by authoritarian institutions from the capacity effectively to pressure their government. They link up with sympathetic NGOs in country B, who are able to pressure their government to put pressure on the government of country A. If country B has leverage over A, that pressure can be effective. The power of the NGOs turns on their ability to persuade citizens in the democratic country to sanction their government unless it follows their suggestions.

In this perspective, NGOs can be analyzed as interest groups, operating like others, to influence public policy by mobilizing pressures on governments. What makes them distinctive is their transnational scope of activity and the use of new instruments of communication. When NGOs mobilize international pressure, we need to know who it is within the state that 'feels' this pressure, and acts to demand a policy response from their own government. In that regard, the argument is similar to that used in political economy. Japan is more likely to comply with US pressure ('*ghaitsu*') concerning trade imbalances, Schoppa (1997) argues, if there are domestic forces who agree with the complaint made by the Americans, forces that are sympathetic to the changes being proposed; where there are no such sympathetic domestic forces, Japan resists. Thus the impact of international pressure, be it from civil society, NGOs, or open state diplomacy, requires some understanding of the domestic debate about compliance – a model of what Kahler (2000b) calls the 'compliance constituencies' and the political process around them.

STATE FORMATION AND DECOMPOSITION: NATIONS, FEDERATIONS, CIVIL WARS, EVOLUTION

States may not be the only players, but they are important ones. Yet international relations theory has generally ignored the problem of where states come from or why they fall apart. The emergence of the European Union, the decomposition of the USSR and the spread of ethnic conflict has brought these issues forward.

New Entities

The European Union has profoundly altered the study of the domestic–international interaction. By joining a number of countries, many historic enemies, into a highly developed international institution it raises all the theoretical issues of the domestic politics interaction being explored here – the role of institutions, interest groups, ideas; the importance of democracy, civil society and the formation of identity; concepts of delegation, agency, international institutions and system. The very definition of the EU shows the degree of thematic interaction: is the EU an international institution or a country, or something else

altogether? That question leads to a number of others.

How does the European Union obtain compliance from its members? The system-centric approach of neoliberal institutionalist theory locates the causal mechanism to the utility of an institution to lower transaction costs among its participants (Keohane and Martin, 1995). By itself, that view says nothing about domestic politics; it only requires that countries have an interest in cooperation, but allows these to be unitary. The power of the EU lies in the desire of countries to continue the cooperation, the costs to them of leaving or having the union break up.

If we assume countries have internal debates about cooperation, then it is necessary to examine the politics that causes one or the other side to prevail. Cooperation turns on the success or failure of 'compliance coalitions'. The interesting debate there lies in modeling the impact on domestic politics of involvement in the EU. Moravcsik's (1998) intergovernmentalism model has two steps to it: first, a domestic politics produces a definition of national interest; then, the agents of the nation bargain at the European level. The impact of the EU itself lies in the way its institutions influence the bargaining process between agents of the national governments, a classic institutionalist model. Cowles et al. (2001) seek to reverse the causal flow, from the European level downward: being in Europe alters interests, preferences and identities (Banchoff, 1999). Political actors reach different conclusions about what they want from being in Europe than they would if it did not exist. Those opinions do get refracted through national governments, but they are still different (Evangelista, 1997; Risse-Kappen, 1991). This interactive model is surely correct; its problems lie in the difficulties of operationalizing the differences between interest, preferences and identities, as these can easily be confused.

Questions of identity in relation to institutions arise in analysis of the 'democratic deficit'. The more the reach of the EU grows, the greater the problem of popular commitment to its goals (Scharpf, 1999). Since national governments are represented, not people, the public feels some disconnection from the EU's decisions. To increase the role of directly elected representatives undermines the national foundations of the EU. Can such a system of representation be created without a cultural foundation of identity with the Union rather than with nations? Haas doubted spillover could create a nation (Haas, 1958; Deutsch, 1953). It remains a serious question as to whether one can move from customs union to country without powerful nation-building experiences that transform identity as well as interests and institutions. From a methodological point of view, it is hard to define and test the movement from economic union to nation. If the EU is more than the average international institution, but not a nation, what is it? Perhaps we need new categories.

The study of the EU's institutions shows how concepts drawn from domestic politics are being applied to an international process: the application of institutional design concepts from formal modeling on the decision-rules of the Union, the debates about reform and expansion (Tsebelis and Money, 1997); the role of the European Court of Justice, its ability to strengthen the Union through its rulings and the internalization of these rulings in each country (Alter, 1998; Mattli and Slaughter, 1998); the negotiation of Union-wide standards and regulations governing commerce, finance, safety and health are some examples (Scharpf and Schmidt, 2000); the spread of norms and cultural elements of cooperation (Sandholtz, 1993).

The European Union provokes comparisons of great theoretical interest. It is surely the most advanced contemporary case of integration. Can the same happen in other regions? Or do they lack some critical ingredient, and if so, what? An external threat, economic interdependence, a common culture or identity, geographical proximity (Kahler, 2000a)?

Disintegration

While new states emerge, others fall apart, changing the constituent elements of the international system. Civil wars push analytic boundaries quite forcefully. The breakdown of national authority often draws international actors into the domestic politics of the warring country. Morally, should outsiders enter a domestic quarrel? Sovereignty has been, as Krasner (1999) shows, an inconsistently applied principle, but it can be used to defend local autonomy, independence and culture. Domestic issues influence the probability of internal conflict, but international forces are usually an influence as well and almost always a player in the struggle (Walter, 1997). Governments face the same challenges as social scientists: what are effective means of nation-building?

Civil wars often arise from the assertion of cultural distinctions, such as religion, language, ethnicity. How do peoples living peacefully for many decades suddenly begin killing each other? A vigorous literature has arisen on this topic, blending game theory with careful ethnographic description seeking to understand the incentive situation that leads to rapid 'tipping', where a new piece of information about possible dangers induces rapid change by a large number of people

in their strategic evaluation of the 'rewards' to peace and violence (Fearon and Laitin, 1996; Laitin, 1998). A neighbor seen as friendly is now suddenly seen to be dangerous. A similar line of reasoning has been applied to the collapse of the regimes of Eastern Europe (Hirschman, 1993; Lohmann, 1994).

All of the concepts discussed so far about the creation or disintegration of states assumes some degree of conscious agency at work. A relatively new and interesting way of thinking about these issues, an evolutionary approach, draws on biological models, to analyze states as unconscious respondents to forces that push them one way or another (Kahler, 1999). The mechanism is adaptation to pressures from other units, themselves responding to overriding forces such as technology, war and markets (Downing, 1992; Ertman, 1997; Spruyt, 1994).

Most of these discussions blur old analytic boundaries. The emergence of new structures such as the European Union blurs the distinction between anarchy and institutionalization. Civil wars show that domestic politics can include anarchy. Evolutionary models blur the issues of choice and agency, and play down the role of domestic politics. Lake argues we should place states and anarchy as end points on a continuum of political forms, ranging empire (direct control from the center of sub-units), to federations, to voluntary confederations, regimes, alliances and finally anarchy; in his book, this allows him to examine the forces that shape one form of relationship over another (Lake, 1998).

CONCLUSION

The great challenge confronting the domestic politics research agenda is to model the interaction of countries with each other and with the system. We have developed strong research traditions that hold either system or country constant. We do not have very good theories to handle what happens when both are in play, when each influences the other, when the domestic politics of one country interacts with the domestic politics of another, an interaction which itself helps define a system that reverberates back on the parts.

We have good metaphors, but not clear research programs. Putnam's (1988) 'two-level games' paper struck a very strong, and welcome, chord. It has been widely used to inspire and legitimize an exploration of domestic politics. Yet most writers evoke it rather than follow it as a formulated research program. Milner (1997) is the most careful application, but one sees there the difficulty predicting, hence testing, clear interactions. It is hard to specify the objectives of all the players and the results produce multiple equilibria, rather than a clear resolution. The general formulation does not, moreover, actually model interaction of the domestic politics of different countries. It asks what the win set in one country does to the likelihood of cooperating with another, but does not include the domestic politics of the second country.

Gourevitch's (1978) 'second image reversed' has also been more of a metaphor than a guide to a research program. It helped introduce the idea that country institutions and internal interests were influenced by international forces, rather than being only the shaper of such forces. Often cited, the phrase evokes the idea of interaction between levels, more than a research strategy of how to study that interaction.

To develop interactive models, we need to avoid the reappearance of unitary actor assumptions, which often occurs. Endogenous macro theory appears to say that interests are shaped by a position in the global division of labor, but does not include the role of domestic politics in specifying world markets. In contrast to Rogowski's account of governments as the relatively passive registrants of societal pressure, Simmons and Elkins (2001) develop a model that has governments as self-aware strategic actors. This makes much sense, but it does risk being unitary in its logic. NLI writing speaks of the state's interests in the institutions, not of the support constituencies in each country that shape the determination of state interests. Constructivists speak of discourses or understandings between countries constituting their interests, but frequently do not explore why one or another discourse prevails in a particular country.

Waltz's (1959) three images remain powerful and useful tools for organizing our thinking, but the thrust of work in recent years has been to break down these boundaries, to integrate anarchy and domestic politics, to integrate individualist perspectives with theorizing about states and institutions. Domestic politics has become central to most discussions of international relations.

If, as Lake and Powell (1999) write, strategic interaction lies at the core of the study of politics, the elements involved in shaping that interaction are indeed rather vast. They include the many branches of domestic politics interacting across boundaries through many different mechanisms (markets, culture, force). The integration of domestic politics with international, and the integration of international with a generalized study of politics gives us a language. It does not make our task easier as the integration of concepts is indeed difficult. It remains to be seen whether the field accepts this reworking of its categories – perhaps we will know more at the next edition of the Handbook.

Notes

Thanks to Miles Kahler, David Lake, Andrew MacIntyre and the editors of this volume for comments on an earlier draft, and to Naoko Kada for research assistance.

Bibliography

Alesina, Alberto and Grilli, Vittorio (1993) 'The European Central Bank: Reshaping Monetary Policy in Europe', in Matthew Canzoneri, Vittorio Grilli and Paul Masson (eds), *Establishing a Central Bank: Issues in Europe and Lessons from the United States*. Cambridge: Cambridge University Press. pp. 49–77.
Allison, Graham T. (1971) *Essence of Decision: Explaining the Cuban Missile Crisis*. Boston: Little, Brown.
Alter, Karen J. (1998) 'Who Are the "Masters of the Treaty"?: European Governments and the European Court of Justice', *International Organization*, 52 (1): 121–47.
Anderson, Perry (1974) *Lineages of the Absolutist State*. London: New Left Books.
Axelrod, Robert (1984) *The Evolution of Cooperation*. New York: Basic Books.
Bailey, M.A., Goldstein, J. and Weingast, B.R. (1997) 'The Institutional Roots of American Trade Policy', *World Politics*, 49 (3): 309–38.
Banchoff, Thomas (1999) 'German Identity and European Integration', *European Journal of International Relations*, 5 (3): 259–89.
Bates, Robert H. (1997) *Open-Economy Politics: The Political Economy of the World Coffee Trade*. Princeton: Princeton University Press.
Bauer, Raymond A., de Sola Pool, Ithiel and Dexter, Lewis Anthony (1963) *American Business and Public Policy: The Politics of Foreign Trade*. New York: Atherton Press.
Bendor, Jonathan and Hammond, Thomas H. (1992) 'Rethinking Allison's Models', *American Political Science Review*, 86 (2): 301–22.
Benedict, Ruth (1946) *The Chrysanthemum and the Sword: Patterns of Japanese Culture*. Boston: Houghton Mifflin.
Berger, Suzanne and Dore, Ronald (eds) (1996) *National Diversity and Global Capitalism*. Ithaca: Cornell University Press.
Berger, Thomas (1993) 'From Sword to Chrysanthemum: Japan's Culture of Anti-Militarism', *International Security*, 17 (4): 119–50.

Bernhard, William and Leblang, David (1999) 'Democratic Institutions and Exchange-rate Commitments', *International Organization*, 53 (1): 71–97.

Brewer, John and Echhart, Hellmuth (eds) (1999) *Rethinking Leviathan: The Eighteenth-Century State in Britain and Germany.* London: German Historical Institute; Oxford: Oxford University Press.

Brooks, Risa A. (2000) 'Institutions at the Domestic/International Nexus: The Political-Military Origins of Strategic Integration, Military Effectiveness and War', PhD dissertation, University of California, San Diego.

Bueno de Mesquita, Bruce (2000) *Principles of International Politics: People's Power, Preferences and Perceptions.* Washington, DC: CQ Press.

Bueno de Mesquita, Bruce, Morrow, James D., Siverson, Randolph M. and Smith, Alastair (1999a) 'An Institutional Explanation of the Democratic Peace', *American Political Science Review*, 93 (4): 791.

Bueno de Mesquita, Bruce, Morrow, James D., Siverson, Randolph M. and Smith, Alastair (1999b) 'Policy Failure and Political Survival: The Contribution of Political Institutions', *Journal of Conflict Resolution*, 43 (2): 147.

Bull, Hedley (1977) *The Anarchical Society: A Study of Order in World Politics.* New York: Columbia University Press.

Buruma, Ian (1994) *The Wages of Guilt: Memories of War in Germany and Japan.* New York: Farrar, Straus, Giroux.

Cameron, David R. (1978) 'The Expansion of the Public Economy', *American Political Science Review*, 72 (4): 1243–61.

Checkel, Jeffrey (1997) 'International Norms and Domestic Politics: Bridging the Rationalist Constructivist Divide', *European Journal of International Relations*, 3 (4): 473–95.

Cowhey, Peter F. (1995) in Peter F. Cowhey and Mathew D. McCubbins (eds), *Structure and Policy in Japan and the United States.* New York: Cambridge University Press.

Cowles, Maria Green, Caporaso, James and Risse, Thomas (eds) (2001) *Transforming Europe.* Cornell: Cornell University Press.

Cox, Gary W. (1997) *Making Votes Count: Strategic Coordination in the World's Electoral Systems.* Cambridge: Cambridge University Press.

Cox, Gary W. and McCubbins, Mathew D. (1993) *Legislative Leviathan: Party Government in the House.* Berkeley: University of California Press.

Cox, Gary W. and McCubbins, Mathew D. (2001) 'The Institutional Determinants of Public Policy', in Stephan Haggard and Mathew D. McCubbins (eds), *Presidents, Parliaments and Policy.* Cambridge: Cambridge University Press.

Craig, Gordon (1955) *The Politics of the Prussian Army, 1640–1945.* New York: Clarendon.

Crozier, Michael, Huntington, Samuel P. and Watanuki, Joji (1975) *The Crisis of Democracy: Report on the Governability of Democracies to the Trilateral Commission.* New York: New York University Press.

Destler, I.M. (1995) *American Trade Politics.* Washington, DC: Institute for International Economics; New York: Twentieth Century Fund, 3rd edn.

Destler, I.M. and Odell, John S. (1987) *Anti-Protection: Changing Forces in United States Trade Politics.* Washington, DC: Institute for International Economics.

Deutsch, Karl Wolfgang (1953) *Nationalism and Social Communication: An Inquiry into the Foundations of Nationality.* Cambridge, MA: Technical Press; New York: Wiley.

Downing, Brian M. (1992) *The Military Revolution and Political Change.* Princeton: Princeton University Press

Eising, Rainer (2002) 'Bounded Rationality and Policy Learning in EU Negotiations: The Liberalization of the Electricity Supply Industry', *International Organization*, 56 (1).

Epstein, David and O'Halloran, Sharyn (1999) *Delegating Powers: A Transaction Cost Politics Approach to Policy-Making under Separate Powers.* Cambridge, and New York: Cambridge University Press.

Ertman, Thomas (1997) *Birth of the Leviathan: Building States and Regimes in Medieval and Early Modern Europe.* Cambridge: Cambridge University Press.

Esping-Andersen, Gosta (1999) *Social Foundations of Postindustrial Economies.* Oxford and New York: Oxford University Press.

Evangelista, Matthew (1997) 'Domestic Structure and International Change', in Michael Doyle and John Ikenberry (eds), *New Thinking in International Relations Theory.* Boulder: Westview. pp. 202–28.

Evangelista, Matthew (1999) *Unarmed Forces: The Transnational Movement to End the Cold War.* Ithaca: Cornell University Press.

Evans, Peter B. (1979) *Dependent Development: The Alliance of Multinational, State, and Local Capital in Brazil.* Princeton: Princeton University Press.

Evans, Peter B., Jacobson, Harold K. and Putnam, Robert D. (eds) (1993) *Double-Edged Diplomacy: International Bargaining and Domestic Politics.* Berkeley: University of California Press.

Fearon, James D. (1994) 'Domestic Political Audiences and the Escalation of International Disputes', *American Political Science Review*, 88 (3): 577–92.

Fearon, James D. and Laitin, David D. (1996) 'Explaining Interethnic Cooperation', *American Political Science Review*, 90 (4): 715–35.

Finnemore, Martha and Toope, Stephen J. (2001) 'Alternatives to "Legalization": Richer Views of Law and Politics', *International Organization*, 55 (3): 743–58.

Frieden, Jeffry A. (1991a) *Debt, Development, and Democracy: Modern Political Economy and Latin*

America, 1965–1985. Princeton: Princeton University Press.

Frieden, Jeffry A. (1991b) 'Invested Interests: The Politics of National Economic Policies in a World of Global Finance', *International Organization*, 45 (4): 425–51.

Frieden, Jeffry A. (1999) 'Actors and Preferences in International Relations', in David A. Lake and Robert Powell (eds), *Strategic Choice and International Relations*. Princeton: Princeton University Press. pp. 39–76.

Frieden, Jeffry A. and Martin, Lisa L. (2000) 'International Political Economy: The State of the Sub-Discipline'. Cambridge, MA: Harvard Univeristy, mimeo.

Friedman, Thomas L. (1999) *The Lexus and the Olive Tree.* New York: Farrar, Straus, Giroux.

Gabel, Matthew (2000) 'European Integration, Voters, and National Politics', *West European Politics*, 23: 52–72.

Garrett, Geoffrey (1998) *Partisan Politics in the Global Economy.* New York: Cambridge University Press.

Garrett, Geoffrey and Lange, Peter (1991) 'Political Responses to Interdependence: What's "Left" for the Left?' *International Organization*, 45 (4): 539–64.

Gerschenkron, Alexander (1962) *Economic Backwardness in Historical Perspective.* Cambridge, Belknap Press of Harvard University Press.

Gilligan, Michael J. (1997) 'Lobbying as a Private Good with Intra-industry Trade', *International Studies Quarterly*, 41 (3): 455–74.

Gilpin, Robert (1975) *US Power and the Multinational Corporation: The Political Economy of Foreign Direct Investment.* New York: Basic Books.

Goldstein, Judith (1993) *Ideas, Interests and American Trade Policy.* Ithaca: Cornell University Press.

Goldstein, Morris, Kaminsky, Graciela L. and Reinhart, Carmen M. (2000) *Assessing Financial Vulnerability: An Early Warning System for Emerging Markets.* Washington, DC: Institute for International Economics.

Gourevitch, Peter A. (1977) 'International Trade, Domestic Coalitions and Liberty: Comparative Responses to the Crisis of 1873–1896', *Journal of Interdisciplinary History*, 8 (2): 281–313.

Gourevitch, Peter A. (1978) 'The Second Image Reversed: International Sources of Domestic Politics', *International Organization*, 32 (4): 881–911.

Gourevitch, Peter A. (1986) *Politics in Hard Times: Comparative Responses to International Economic Crises.* Ithaca: Cornell University Press.

Gourevitch, Peter A. (1999) 'The Governance Problem in International Relations', in David A. Lake and Robert Powell (eds), *Strategic Choice and International Relations*. Princeton: Princeton University Press. pp. 137–64.

Gourevitch, Peter A. (2001) 'Comparative Capitalism in the Globalized Economy: Understanding National

Production Systems', University of California, San Diego, mimeo draft.

Grilli, Vittorio, Masciandaro, Donato and Tabellini, Guido (1991) 'Political and Monetary Institutions and Public Financial Policies in the Industrialized Countries', *Economic Policy*, 13: 42–92.

Haas, Ernst B. (1958) *The Uniting of Europe: Political, Social, and Economic Forces, 1950–1957.* Stanford, CA: Stanford University Press.

Haggard, Stephan (1988) 'The Institutional Foundations of Hegemony: Explaining the Reciprocal Trade Agreements Act of 1934', *International Organization*, 42 (1): 91–119.

Haggard, Stephan (1990) *Pathways from the Periphery: The Politics of Growth in the Newly Industrializing Countries.* Ithaca: Cornell University Press.

Haggard, Stephan and Kaufman, Robert R. (1995) *The Political Economy of Democratic Transitions* Princeton: Princeton University Press.

Haggard, Stephan and McCubbins, Mathew D. (eds) (2001) *Presidents, Parliaments and Policy.* Cambridge: Cambridge University Press.

Hall, Peter A. and Franzese, Robert J. (1998) 'Mixed Signals: Central Bank Independence, Coordinated Wage Bargaining, and European Monetary Union', *International Organization*, 52 (3): 505–35.

Hall, Peter A. and Soskice, David (2001) *Varieties of Capitalism: The Institutional Foundations of Comparative Capitalism.* Oxford: Oxford University Press.

Hall, Peter A. and Taylor, Rosemary (1996) 'Political Science and the Three New Institutionalisms', *Political Studies*, 44 (5): 936–57.

Henning, C. Randall (1994) *Currencies and Politics in the United States, Germany, and Japan.* Washington, DC: Institute for International Economics.

Herrmann, Richard K. and Shannon, Vaughn P. (2001) 'Defending International Norms: The Role of Obligation, Material Interest, and Perception in Decision Making', *International Organization*, 55 (3): 621–54.

Hirschman, Albert O. (1945) *National Power and the Structure of Foreign Trade.* Berkeley and Los Angeles: University of California Press.

Hirschman, Albert O. (1993) 'Exit, Voice, and the Fate of the German Democratic Republic: An Essay in Conceptual History', *World Politics*, 45 (2): 173–202.

Hiscox, Michael J. (1999) 'The Magic Bullet? The RTAA, Institutional Reform, and Trade Liberalization', *International Organization*, 53 (4): 669–98.

Hiscox, Michael (2001) 'Class versus Industry Cleavages: Inter-industry Factor Mobility and the Politics of Trade', *International Organization*, 55 (1): 1–46.

Hoffmann, Stanley (1960) *Contemporary Theory in International Relations.* Englewood Cliffs: Prentice Hall.

Huntington, Samuel P. (1996) *The Clash of Civilizations and the Remaking of the World Order.* New York: Simon and Schuster.

Iversen, Torben (1999) *Contested Institutions.* New York: Cambridge University Press.

Iversen, Torben and Wren, Anne (1998) 'Equality, Employment, and Budgetary Restraint – the Trilemma of the Service Economy', *World Politics*, 50 (4): 507–46.

Jervis, Robert (1976) *Perception and Misperception in International Politics.* Princeton: Princeton University Press.

Kahler, Miles (1999) 'Evolution, Choice and International Change', in David A. Lake and Robert Powell (eds), *Strategic Choice and International Relations.* Princeton: Princeton University Press. pp. 165–96.

Kahler, Miles (2000a) 'Legalization as Strategy: The Asia Pacific Case', *International Organization*, 54 (3): 549–72.

Kahler, Miles (2000b) 'Conclusion: The Causes and Consequences of Legalization', *International Organization*, 54 (3): 661–83.

Kahler, Miles (2001) 'The State of the State in World Politics'. University of California, San Diego: Graduate School of International Relations and Pacific Studies, unpublished mimeo.

Katzenstein, Peter J. (ed.) (1978) *Between Power and Plenty: Foreign Economic Policies of Advanced Industrial States.* Madison: University of Wisconsin Press.

Katzenstein, Peter J. (1985) *Small States in World Markets: Industrial Policy in Europe.* Ithaca: Cornell University Press.

Katzenstein, Peter J. (1996) *Cultural Norms and National Security: Police and Military in Postwar Japan.* Ithaca: Cornell University Press.

Kaufmann, Chaim D. and Pape, Robert A. (1999) 'Explaining Costly International Moral Action: Britain's Sixty-year Campaign against the Atlantic Slave Trade', *International Organization*, 53 (4): 631–68.

Keck, Margaret E. and Sikkink, Kathryn (1998) *Activists Beyond Borders: Advocacy Networks in International Politics.* Ithaca: Cornell University Press.

Keegan, John (1998) *The First World War.* London: Hutchinson.

Kehr, Eckart (1977) *Economic Interest, Militarism, and Foreign Policy: Essays on German History.* Berkeley: University of California Press.

Keohane, Robert O. (1984) *After Hegemony: Cooperation and Discord in the World Political Economy.* Princeton: Princeton University Press.

Keohane, Robert O. and Martin, Lisa L. (1995) 'The Promise of Institutionalist Theory', *International Security*, 19 (7): 39–51.

Keohane, Robert O. and Milner, Helen V. (eds) (1996) *Internationalization and Domestic Politics.* Cambridge: Cambridge University Press.

Keohane, Robert O. and Nye, Joseph (1977) *Power and Interdependence: World Politics in Transition.* Boston: Little, Brown.

Kier, Elizabeth (1997) *Imagining War: French and British Military Doctrine between the Wars.* Princeton: Princeton University Press.

Kindleberger, Charles P. (1951) 'Group Behavior and International Trade', *Journal of Political Economy*, 59 (1): 30–46.

Kitschelt, Herbert, Marks, Gary, Lange, Peter and Stephens, John (eds) (1999) *Continuity and Change in Contemporary Capitalism.* Cambridge and New York: Cambridge University Press.

Krasner, Stephen D. (1978) *Defending the National Interest: Raw Materials Investments and US Foreign Policy.* Princeton: Princeton University Press.

Krasner, Stephen D. (1999) *Sovereignty: Organized Hypocrisy.* Princeton: Princeton University Press.

Kratochwil, Friedrich V. (1989) *Rules, Norms, and Decision: On the Conditions of Practical and Legal Reasoning in International Relations and Domestic Affairs.* Cambridge and New York: Cambridge University Press.

Kurth, James (1971) 'The Widening Gyre: The Logic of American Weapons Procurement', *Public Policy*, 19 (3): 373–404.

Kurth, James R. (1979) 'The Political Consequences of the Product Cycle: Industrial History and Political Outcomes', *International Organization*, 33 (1): 1–34.

Laitin, David D. (1998) *Identity in Formation: The Russian-Speaking Populations in the Near Abroad.* Ithaca: Cornell University Press.

Lake, David A. (1992) 'Powerful Pacifists: Democratic States and War', *American Political Science Review*, 86 (1): 24–37.

Lake, David A. (1998) *Entangling Relations: American Foreign Policy in Its Century.* Princeton: Princeton University Press.

Lake, David A. and Powell, Robert (1999) 'International Relations: A Strategic-choice Approach', in David A. Lake and Robert Powell (eds), *Strategic Choice and International Relations.* Princeton: Princeton University Press. pp. 3–38.

Laver, Michael and Shepsle, Kenneth A. (eds) (1994) *Cabinet Ministers and Parliamentary Government.* Cambridge and New York: Cambridge University Press.

Leites, Nathan (1950) *Operational Code of the Politburo.* Santa Monica: Rand.

Levy, Jonah D. (2001) *Tocqueville's Revenge: State, Society, and Economy in Contemporary France.* Cambridge, MA: Harvard University Press.

Lijphart, Arend (1999) *Patterns of Democracy: Government Forms and Performance in Thirty-Six Countries.* New Haven: Yale University Press.

Lohmann, Susanne (1994) 'The Dynamics of Informational Cascades: The Monday Demonstrations in Leipzig, East Germany, 1989–91', *World Politics*, 47 (1): 42–101.

Lohmann, Susanne and O'Halloran, Sharyn (1994) 'Divided Government and US Trade Policy: Theory and Evidence', *International Organization*, 48 (4): 595–632.

Loveman, Brian (1993) *The Constitution of Tyranny: Regimes of Exception in Spanish America*. Pittsburgh: University of Pittsburgh Press.

Lupia, Arthur and McCubbins, Mathew D. (1998) *The Democratic Dilemma: Can Citizens Learn What They Need to Know?* New York: Cambridge University Press.

Lynch, Cecilia (1999) *Beyond Appeasement: Interpreting Interwar Peace Movements in World Politics*. Ithaca: Cornell University Press.

MacIntyre, Andrew J. (2001) 'Institutions and Investors: The Politics of the Economic Crisis in Southeast Asia', *International Organization*, 55 (1): 81–122.

Magee, Stephen P., Brock, William A. and Young, Leslie (1989) *Black Hole Tariffs and Endogenous Policy Theory: Political Economy in General Equilibrium*. Cambridge: Cambridge University Press.

Martin, Lisa L. (1994) 'The Influence of National Parliaments on European Integration'. Working paper no. 94–10, Cambridge, MA: Center for International Affairs, Harvard University.

Martin, Lisa L. (2000) *Democratic Commitments: Legislatures and International Cooperation* Princeton: Princeton University Press.

Mattli, Walter and Slaughter, Anne-Marie (1998) 'Revisiting the European Court of Justice', *International Organization*, 52 (1):177–209.

Mayer, Arno J. (1959) *Political Origins of the New Diplomacy, 1917–1918*. New Haven: Yale University Press.

Miller, Steven E., Lynn-Jones, Sean M. and Van Evera, Stephen (1991) *Military Strategy and the Origins of the First World War*, rev. edn. Princeton: Princeton University Press.

Milner, Helen V. (1997) *Interests, Institutions, and Information: Domestic Politics and International Relations*. Princeton: Princeton University Press.

Moravcsik, Andrew (1998) *The Choice for Europe: Social Purpose and State Power from Messina to Maastricht*. Ithaca: Cornell University Press.

Mosely, Layna (2000) 'Room to Move: International Financial Markets and National Welfare States', *International Organization*, 54 (4): 737–73.

Müller, Harald and Risse-Kappen, Thomas (1993) 'From the Outside in and the Inside Out: International Relations, Domestic Policy and Foreign Policy', in Valerie Hudson and David Skidmore (eds), *The Limits of State Autonomy: Societal Groups and Foreign Policy Formulation*. Boulder: Westview.

Neier, Aryeh (1993) 'Asia's Unacceptable Standard', *Foreign Policy*, 92: 42–51.

North, Douglass C. and Weingast, Barry R. (1989) 'Constitutions and Commitment: The Evolution of Institutions Governing Public Choice in Seventeenth-Century England', *Journal of Economic History*, 49 (4): 803–32.

O'Halloran, Sharyn (1994) *Politics, Process, and American Trade Policy*. Ann Arbor: University of Michigan Press.

Olson, Mancur (1982) *The Rise and Decline of Nations*. New Haven: Yale University Press.

Osgood, Robert E. (1953) *Ideals and Self-Interest in America's Foreign Relations: The Great Transformation of the Twentieth Century*. Chicago: University of Chicago Press.

Papayoanou, Paul A. (1999) *Power Ties: Economic Interdependence, Balancing, and War*. Ann Arbor: University of Michigan Press.

Pastor, Robert A. (1980) *Congress and the Politics of US Foreign Economic Policy, 1929–1976*. Berkeley: University of California Press.

Pérez Díaz, Víctor (1993) *The Return of Civil Society: The Emergence of Democratic Spain*. Cambridge, MA: Harvard University Press.

Posen, Barry (1984) *The Sources of Military Doctrine: France, Britain, and Germany between the World Wars*. Ithaca: Cornell University Press.

Powell, Walter W. and DiMaggio, Paul J. (eds) (1991) *The New Institutionalism in Organizational Analysis*. Chicago: University of Chicago Press.

Putnam, Robert D. (1988) 'Diplomacy and Domestic Politics: The Logic of Two-level Games', *International Organization*, 42 (3): 427–60.

Putnam, Robert D. with Leonardi, Robert and Nanetti, Raffaella Y. (1993) *Making Democracy Work: Civic Traditions in Modern Italy*. Princeton: Princeton University Press.

Ramseyer, J. Mark and Rosenbluth, Frances McCall (1993) *Japan's Political Marketplace*. Cambridge, MA: Harvard University Press.

Richardson, Louise (1996) *When Allies Differ: Anglo-American Relations during the Suez and Falkland Crises*. New York: St Martin's Press.

Risse-Kappen, Thomas (1991) 'Public Opinion, Domestic Structure and Foreign Policy in Liberal Democracies', *World Politics*, 43 (4): 479–512.

Risse-Kappen, Thomas (1995) 'Bringing Transnational Relations Back In: Introduction', in Thomas Risse-Kappen (ed.), *Bringing Transnational Relations Back In*. Cambridge: Cambridge University Press. pp. 3–36.

Risse, Thomas (2000) '"Let's Argue!": Communicative Action in World Politics', *International Organization*, 54 (1): 1–39.

Rodrik, Dani (1997) *Has Globalization Gone Too Far?* Washington, DC: Institute for International Economics.

Roe, Mark J. (1994) *Strong Managers, Weak Owners: The Political Roots of American Corporate Finance*. Princeton: Princeton University Press.

Roeder, Philip G. (1993) *Red Sunset: The Failure of Soviet Politics*. Princeton: Princeton University Press.

Rogowski, Ronald (1987) 'Trade and the Variety of Democratic Institutions', *International Organization*, 41 (2): 203–23.

Rogowski, Ronald (1989) *Commerce and Coalitions: How Trade Affects Domestic Political Alignments.* Princeton: Princeton University Press.

Rogowski, Ronald (1999) 'Institutions as Constraints on Strategic Choice', in David A. Lake and Robert Powell (eds), *Strategic Choice and International Relations.* Princeton: Princeton University Press. pp. 115–36.

Sagan, Scott (1989) 'The Origins of the Pacific War', in Robert Rotberg and Theodore Rabb (eds), *The Origin and Prevention of Major Wars.* New York: Cambridge, University Press. pp. 323–52.

Sandholtz, Wayne (1993) 'Choosing Union: Monetary Politics and Maastricht', *International Organization,* 47 (2): 1–39.

Scharpf, Fritz (1999) *Governing in Europe.* Oxford: Oxford University Press.

Scharpf, Fritz and Schmidt, Vivien (2000) *Welfare and Work in the Open Economy,* 2 vols. Oxford: Oxford University Press.

Schattschneider, E.E. (1935) *Politics, Pressures and the Tariff: A Study of Free Private Enterprise in Pressure Politics, as Shown in the 1929–1930 Revision of the Tariff.* New York: Prentice Hall.

Scheve, Kenneth (1999) 'European Economic Integration and Electoral Politics in France and Great Britain'. Paper prepared for presentation at the 1999 Annual Meetings of the American Political Science Association.

Scheve, Kenneth and Slaughter, Matthew J. (2001) 'What Determines Individual Trade-policy Preferences?', *Journal of International Economics.*

Schoppa, Leonard (1997) *Bargaining with Japan: What American Pressure Can and Cannot Do.* New York: Columbia University Press.

Schultz, Kenneth A. (1999) 'Do Democratic Institutions Constrain or Inform?: Contrasting Two Institutional Perspectives on Democracy and War', *International Organization,* 53 (2): 233–66.

Sen, Amartya (1981) *Poverty and Famines: An Essay on Entitlement and Deprivation.* Oxford: Clarendon Press.

Shinn, James (2001) 'Globalization, Governance and the State', Princeton University, PhD dissertation.

Shirk, Susan L. (1993) *The Political Logic of Economic Reform in China.* Berkeley: University of California Press.

Shugart, Matthew Soberg and Carey, John M. (1992) *Presidents and Assemblies: Constitutional Design and Electoral Dynamics.* New York: Cambridge University Press.

Shugart, Matthew Soberg and Haggard, Stephan (2001) 'Institutions and Public Policy in Presidential Systems', in Matthew D. McCubbins and Stephan Haggard (eds), *Structure and Policy in Presidential Democracies* New York: Cambridge University Press.

Simmons, Beth (1994) *Who Adjusts? Domestic Sources of Foreign Economic Policy During the Interwar Years.* Princeton: Princeton University Press.

Simmons, Beth and Elkins, Zachary (2001) 'Globalization and Policy Diffusion: Explaining Three Decades of Liberalization', University of California, Berkeley, mimeo.

Snyder, Jack L. (1991) *Myths of Empire: Domestic Politics and International Ambition.* Ithaca: Cornell University Press.

Soskice, David and Iversen, Torben (2000) 'The Non Neutrality of Monetary Policy with Large Price or Wage Setters', *Quarterly Journal of Economics,* 115 (1): 265.

Spar, Deborah L. (1998) 'The Spotlight and the Bottom Line', *Foreign Affairs,* 77 (2): 7–12.

Spruyt, Hendrik (1994) *The Sovereign State and Its Competitors: An Analysis of Systems Change.* Princeton: Princeton University Press.

Steinmo, Sven, Thelen, Kathleen and Longstreth Frank (eds) (1992) *Structuring Politics: Historical Institutionalism in Comparative Analysis.* Cambridge: Cambridge University Press.

Stepan, Alfred C. (1988) *Rethinking Military Politics: Brazil and the Southern Cone.* Princeton: Princeton University Press.

Stephens, John and Huber-Stephens, Evelyn (2001) *Development and Crisis of the Welfare States: Parties and Policies in Global Markets.* Chicago: Chicago University Press.

Streeck, Wolfgang (1997) 'German Capitalism: Does it Exist? Can it Survive?', in Colin Crouch and Wolfgang Streeck (eds), *The Political Economy of Modern Capitalism: Mapping Convergence and Diversity.* London: Sage pp. 33–54.

Tannenwald, Nina (1999) 'The Nuclear Taboo: The United States and the Normative Basis of Nuclear Non-use', *International Organization,* 53 (3): 433–68.

Tarrow, Sidney (1998) *Power in Movement: Social Movements and Contentious Politics,* 2nd edn. Cambridge and New York: Cambridge University Press.

Tsebelis, George and Money, Jeannette (1997) *Bicameralism.* Cambridge and New York: Cambridge University Press.

Verdier, Daniel (1994) *Democracy and International Trade: Britain, France, and the United States, 1860–1990.* Princeton: Princeton University Press.

Vernon, Raymond (1971) *Sovereignty at Bay: The Multinational Spread of US Enterprises.* New York: Basic Books.

Wade, Robert (1990) *Governing the Market: Economic Theory and the Role of Government in East Asian Industrialization.* Princeton: Princeton University Press.

Wallerstein, Immanuel (1974) *The Modern World-System.* New York: Academic Press.

Walter, Barbara F. (1997) 'The Critical Barrier to Civil War Settlement', *International Organization,* 51 (3): 335–64.

Waltz, Kenneth (1959) *Man, the State, and War: A Theoretical Analysis.* New York: Columbia University Press.

Weber, Steven (1997) 'Institutions and Change', in Michael Doyle and John Ikenberry (eds), *New Thinking in International Relations Theory*. Boulder: Westview. pp. 229–65.

Welch, David A. (1992) 'The Organization Process and Bureaucratic Politics Paradigms', *International Security*, 12 (2): 112–41.

Wendt, Alexander (1992) 'Anarchy is What States Make of It: The Social Construction of Power Politics', *International Organization*, 46 (2): 391–425.

Wendt, Alexander (1999) *Social Theory of International Politics*. New York: Cambridge University Press.

Ziegler, J. Nicholas (1997) *Governing Ideas: Strategies for Innovation in France and Germany*. Ithaca: Cornell University Press.

Zürn, Michael (1993) 'Bringing the Second Image (Back) in: About Domestic Sources of Regime Formation', in Volker Rittberger (ed.), *Regime Theory and International Relations*. Oxford: Oxford University Press. pp. 282–311.

Part Three

SUBSTANTIVE ISSUES IN INTERNATIONAL RELATIONS

17

Foreign Policy

WALTER CARLSNAES

Taking the broad historical perspective is often a suggestive strategy for gauging the current state of a field of study. The chapter on 'Foreign Policy' in the magisterial eight-volume *Handbook of Political Science*, published in 1975, is in this regard insightful for at least two reasons. The first is its tone, which is guardedly optimistic about the future of foreign policy analysis despite deep-rooted disagreements within the field regarding both its conceptual boundaries and the most appropriate manner to analyze its substance. There is, the two authors write, a 'sense of movement at last, akin to one's first responses as a traffic jam unlocks and cars begin, hesitantly and tentatively, to pick up forward speed' (Cohen and Harris, 1975: 381). The second reason is the unquestioned assumption that the subject matter of foreign policy belongs naturally to the empirical domain of public policy rather than of international relations – so much so that Cohen and Harris' chapter was published in the volume on 'Policies and Policymaking' rather than that on 'International Politics'. To most readers today, a quarter of a century later, both of these characterizations will undoubtedly raise more than a few puzzled eyebrows. The first due to its misplaced (if admittedly guarded) optimism about the future disciplinary development of the field; and the second because if there is anything which all foreign policy analysts today can and do agree on (and there is not much else), it is that they belong squarely to the scholarly domain of International Relations (IR) rather than to any of the policy sciences.

This is not to say, however, that the study of foreign policy currently enjoys an undisputed professional domicile within IR. This uneasy state of affairs is due at least in part to the failure of foreign policy researchers, during the past twenty-five years, to consolidate their field in the manner once envisioned. Instead, their practice has to a considerable degree become one of eclecticism and defensiveness within a larger scholarly milieu which, on the whole, is not especially engaged with the issues at the head of the agenda of foreign policy analysis. A quick perusal of the table of contents of the major IR journals published during the past decade or so is quite clear on this score: very few contain titles in which the concept of 'foreign policy analysis' plays a prominent role. At the same time interest in the development of IR theory itself has grown exponentially, but for the most part with little or no reference to 'foreign policy', either as an integral part of such theory or as a separate but important approach in its own right. On the contrary, most of the time it is simply ignored in these debates and discussions, or politely dismissed with reference to the distinction between system level and unit level theories, the former pertaining to international politics proper, the latter 'merely' to the behaviour of individual states. 'Theory development at this level', a recent review of theories of foreign policy thus states laconically, 'has received comparatively little attention' (Rose, 1998: 145). Alexander Wendt's declaration of (a lack of) interest is equally symptomatic: 'Theories of international politics are distinguished from those that have as their object explaining the behaviour of individual states, or "theories of foreign policy"... Like Waltz, I am interested in international politics, not foreign policy' (Wendt, 1999: 11). Perhaps of equal significance, foreign policy analysts themselves seem to have lost heart. Hence, as a British scholar noted in 1999, 'These are testing times for foreign policy analysts. At issue is whether their area of study remains a major sub-field of International Relations or whether it has become anachronistic, either subsumed or replaced by other approaches to understanding and explaining state behaviour' (White, 1999: 37). Similarly, a German colleague has noted that despite a plethora of publications on the topic in his home country, the study of foreign policy itself is currently in the throes of a conceptual crisis and theoretically at a standstill (Schneider, 1997).

However, let me already at this point signal that although there is some justification for the bleak picture of the sub-field of foreign policy analysis adumbrated above, it by no means represents the whole picture. It reflects a disciplinary development during the past two to three decades which has put a strong structuralist-systemic stamp on IR, and hence also an effective damper on approaches – such as foreign policy analysis – premised not primarily on the international system as the generator of behaviour but on the importance of unit-level factors and actors for understanding and explaining state behaviour. But this structuralist-systemic perspective has never been totally hegemonic even in North America, and in Europe it has failed to achieve the same grip on the scholarly imaginations of its mostly small, eclectic and not equally 'scientistic' or 'rationalistic' IR communities. More importantly, since at least the end of the Cold War – and perhaps to a considerable extent as a result of it – this dominant perspective has increasingly had to provide space for a view of the substance of interstate interactions which is more in tune with some of the basic premises of foreign policy approaches. In other words, a case can be made for why a focus on foreign policy is once again regaining ground within IR, and why it should indeed do so.

The way I intend to proceed is as follows. In the next section an intellectual history of foreign policy analysis will be presented, primarily covering developments during the past half-century. After that a conceptual and analytical overview of the field itself will be provided, in which I will first very briefly discuss fundamental definitional issues and present four rock-bottom types of explanatory frameworks defined not in terms of 'schools', 'grand debates' or 'contending approaches' but with reference to two fundamental meta-theoretical dimensions within the philosophy of social science. On the basis of these four generic perspectives, my intention in the subsequent and core part of the chapter is to highlight and briefly discuss some of the more prominent contemporary attempts to structure and to pursue analysis within the field. After this the question will be raised – and a brief answer suggested – whether a synthetic or integrated approach to foreign policy analysis is at all feasible. The concluding section will pinpoint a few current and contentious issues straddling the various approaches discussed, indicating some areas of potential development within the field.

INTERNATIONAL RELATIONS AND FOREIGN POLICY ANALYSIS: A SHORT INTELLECTUAL HISTORY

As is the case with IR itself, most historical accounts of foreign policy analysis – and there are not many available – tend to suffer from a Whig interpretation of this history, or from what Brian C. Schmidt, in the opening chapter of this *Handbook*, has called the problem of 'presentism': 'the practice of writing a history of the field for the purpose of making a point about the present character of the field'. These accounts are also to a considerable degree infused with parochialisms of various shades, both of a geographic, scholarly and sub-disciplinary nature. The combination of these two characteristics makes for interesting reading but hardly for a fully illuminating overview of this historical development. In other words, they have on the whole contributed to conventional images of the progression and hence identity of the field that need to be challenged and corrected.

As suggested above, the conception of foreign policy as an academic subject matter has had strong roots in the broader domain of public policy, especially in the United States. However, this is not where the field originated but is, rather, a reaction to the earlier tradition – primarily of a European provenance, with origins in the seventeenth century and the rise of the modern state thereafter – of viewing foreign policy as a distinct domain differing in fundamental respects from all other spheres of public policy. 'The leading assumption', Bernard C. Cohen thus noted some years ago, 'is that foreign policy is "more important" than other policy areas because it concerns national interests, rather than special interests, and more fundamental values' (Cohen, 1968: 530). A further consequence of this doctrine of the 'primacy of foreign policy' was, of course, that being distinct in this manner, political elites demanded that it be treated differently from all other areas of public policy, that is, beyond democratic control and public scrutiny. However, the experiences leading up to, and the consequences of, the First World War convinced some influential statesmen – in particular Woodrow Wilson – that an end should be put to the traditional secretive practices of statecraft and diplomacy.

Despite the subsequent failure of the Wilsonian project, the study of foreign policy was deeply affected – especially in the United States – by this liberal and democratic ideology, with the result that much of its activities subsequent to the Second World War, when foreign policy analysis first came to be firmly established academically, was concerned with the study of two major implications of these beliefs (Cohen, 1968). The first was to focus on how the governmental institutions responsible for the formulation and implementation of foreign policy could be made more efficient in the pursuit of their tasks. The second had a more ideological thrust, essentially involving a plea for the democratization of foreign policy – of why and how public values and interests should be introduced to every stage in the formulation and execution of such policy.

However, concomitant with this institutionally focused and policy-oriented tradition in the academic study of foreign policy, which enjoyed its American heyday during the two decades following the Second World War, we also find a second major tradition, and one which has left a much stronger and seemingly indelible imprint on the subsequent development of the field. I here have in mind the induction into American thinking of a powerful European influence, and one that stands in marked contrast to the indigenous strands of the liberal Wilsonian project. Realism is its name, and Hans Morgenthau was for decades its undisputed high priest (Morgenthau, 1948). As argued by Stefano Guzzini in his comprehensive sociological analysis of the history of realism, Morgenthau's main concern, as that of realists more generally, was to resuscitate an older tradition by translating 'the maxims of [the] nineteenth century's European diplomatic practice into more general laws of an American social science' (Guzzini, 1998: 1; see also Dunne, 1998; Kahler, 1997). To summarize a complex argument, he did this by claiming 'that the inherent and immutable self-interested nature of human beings, when faced with a structure of international anarchy, results in states maximizing one thing, power' (Smith, 1986: 15). By linking this view of power to the concept of the national interest, he believed that he could provide a universal explanation for the behaviour of particular states.

The behaviouralist turn in American social science in the 1950s and 1960s had a decisive effect on both of these approaches to the study of foreign policy. Its impact on the institutionally oriented research tradition was perhaps the more deep-going in the sense that it changed its character altogether from being an essentially idiographic and normative enterprise – analysing particular forms of policy or prescribing better means for its formulation and implementation – to one which now aspired to generate and to test hypotheses in order to develop a cumulative body of empirical generalizations. The main outgrowth of this fundamental theoretical and methodological reorientation was a movement, starting in the late 1960s, which became known as the comparative study of foreign policy, or CFP for short. Its strong behaviouralist character is manifested in its focus on explaining foreign policy in terms of discrete acts of 'behaviour' rather than in the form of 'purposive' state actions in the realist mode; and taking its cue from how American behavioural political science focused on the 'vote' as its fundamental unit of

analysis, it posited the 'event' as its dependent variable. In this view foreign policy is seen as the exercise of influence in international relations, with 'events' specifying 'who does what to whom, and how' (Hudson and Vore, 1995: 215). As a consequence the task of collecting data on and analysing such events, with the aim of generating and accumulating empirical generalizations about foreign policy behaviour, became a major industry within CFP (Brecher, 1972; East, 1978; McGowan and Shapiro, 1973; Rummel, 1972; Wilkenfeld et al., 1980). It was also an activity generously funded by a federal government fully in tune with these ambitions (Andriole and Hopple, 1984).

However, it is generally acknowledged by friend and foe alike that this programme of establishing a truly 'scientific' approach to the analysis of foreign policy was, on the whole, a significant if commendable failure. The empirical results of the major research programmes which had been launched during these years turned out to be disappointing (Hudson and Vore, 1995: 215–16), and it became increasingly evident that the aim of a unified theory and a methodology based on aggregate analysis had to be rejected as empirically impracticable and analytically unfruitful (Caporaso, et al., 1987; East, 1978; Kegley, 1980; Munton, 1976; Smith, 1987).

The CFP programme did not, however, eclipse the type of foreign policy analysis which all along had focused mainly on the processes involved in foreign policy decision-making, or on contextual or sociopsychological factors influencing such behaviour (Hudson and Vore, 1995: 216–19). The former, with roots going back the pioneering work on decision-making by Snyder, Bruck and Sapin (1954), developed into extensive research exemplified by, for example, studies focusing on small group dynamics (C. Hermann, 1978; Janis, 1982; Tetlock, 1979), the 'bureaucratic politics' approach made famous by the publication in 1971 of Graham Allison's study of the Cuban crisis, as well as Steinbruner's attempt to present foreign policy-making as analogous to cybernetic processes (Steinbruner, 1974). The latter type of research focus, concentrating on more particular aspects of the decision-making process, produced a number of distinguished studies ranging from Michael Brecher's (1972) work on Israel, Robert Jervis's (1976) book on perceptions and misperceptions, and a long series of studies – continuing to the present time, as we shall see below – on the role of cognitive and psychological factors in the explanation of foreign policy actions (Axelrod, 1976; Cottam, 1977; M. Hermann, 1974, 1980a, 1980b; Holsti et al., 1968).

What can be said generally about this broad tradition is that whereas there was perhaps a brief moment in time when it could be asserted that foreign policy analysis was self-consciously in the process of achieving an identity of its own ('all the evidence', James N. Rosenau thus proclaimed in 1974, in a statement that was soon and forever after to cause him considerable chagrin, 'points to the conclusion that the comparative study of foreign policy has now emerged as a *normal* science'), this is certainly not the case at the beginning of the new millennium (quoted in Smith, 1986: 20). Instead, if anything is typical of its practitioners at present, it is the almost total lack of such a sub-disciplinary identity. In the words of one of its contemporary chroniclers, the attitude today is instead one of allowing 'a hundred flowers to bloom' (Hudson and Vore, 1995: 22); or as another reviewer has put it (in a slightly more upbeat locution), of opening 'conversational space' to the multiple perspectives and 'new vistas' of foreign policy analysis (Neack et al., 1995: 12).

Turning to the development of realism in the face of the behaviouralist challenge we are presented with an intriguing paradox in the history of foreign policy analysis. On the one hand, it was believed by many that given the centrality in Morgenthau's approach of power defined in terms of the innate, unobservable but crucial notion of a fixed human nature, it would not be able to withstand this confrontation. Yet, this is precisely what it did, insofar as the behaviouralists never really challenged the underlying assumptions of realism, only its methodology (Vasquez, 1983). Nevertheless, while continuing to be the major intellectual force defining IR itself (Guzzini, 1998; Hollis and Smith, 1990), realism became methodologically divided as a consequence of the debate on its scientific status, and suffered a setback – by no means permanent – with the publication of Allison's in-depth penetration of the Cuba crisis in terms primarily of an analysis of unit-level rather than systemic factors (Allison, 1971). Since the celebrated appearance of Kenneth Waltz's *Theory of International Politics* (1979), an even clearer bifurcation within realism has occurred, particularly in response to the strong stand against all forms of reductionist approaches – typified by most theories of foreign policy – which lies at the core of his structuralist reformulation of realism.

In summation of half a century of foreign policy analysis one can thus say that two broad traditions have played a major role in it, and that they continue to do so. The first is the more difficult to label, insofar as it contains a host of different and disparate approaches, including work on cognitive and psychological factors, bureaucratic and neoinstitutional politics, crisis behaviour, policy implementation, group decision-making processes, and transnational relations, to name some of the most important (see Hudson and Vore, 1995: 222–8). If only for lack of a better term, we can refer to this tradition in terms of the primacy allocated within it to the role of *Innenpolitik* – of domestic factors – in the explanation of foreign policy. As recently noted, although there 'are many variants of this approach, each favouring a different specific domestic independent variable … they all share a common assumption – that

foreign policy is best understood as the product of a country's internal dynamics' (Rose, 1998: 148). Juxtaposed against its explanatory logic we find realism broadly conceived, and for the sake of simplicity (and linguistic consistency) we can refer to this tradition as that of *Realpolitik*. Although not averse to allowing for the play of domestic factors in the pursuit of foreign policy, the major explanatory weight is here given to material systemic-level factors in one form or another.

However, although this characterization in terms of the classical divide between domestic and international politics has a long historical pedigree, it does have at least one major drawback as a criterion for classifying contemporary foreign policy analysis. For while many scholars continue to think of this analytical boundary as the major line of division within the field, and one that continues to be conceptually fruitful in analysis, it is nevertheless based on an assumption which is highly questionable as both an empirical and a theoretical proposition: that it is indeed feasible to determine the nature and function of such a boundary, and to do so without begging a fundamental question in the study of international relations. Thus, while it can be argued that this characterization of the field in terms of these two broad traditions continues to reflect a sub-disciplinary self-understanding of its development, it will not be used below when discussing the current state of affairs in foreign policy analysis. Instead of a criterion based specifically on the *substantive* nature of foreign policy (and one of dubious value), the discussion will proceed from two *meta-theoretical* dimensions – one ontological, the other epistemological – which are entirely neutral with regard to the substance of foreign policy itself.

CONCEPTUALIZING THE DOMAIN

'There is a certain discomfort in writing about foreign policy,' we are forewarned in the first lines of the *Handbook of Political Science* chapter on foreign policy, 'for no two people seem to define it in the same way, disagreements in approach often seem to be deep-seated, and we do not yet know enough about it to be able to say with confidence whether it may be differentiated from all other areas of public policy' (Cohen and Harris, 1975: 318). What its two authors point to here is a twin *problematique* which has occupied a central place in the history of foreign policy analysis, and which needs to be addressed as much today as in the past. The first of these concerns the crucial issue of what constitutes the particular explanandum of the study of foreign policy: what it is that is to be explained. For while this definitional issue may on first sight seem trivial, it in fact goes to the core of what distinguishes this field of study from that of both domestic and international politics, and hence lies at the heart of the long-standing issue of where and how to draw the analytical boundary between a sub-field that willy-nilly straddles these two major disciplinary foci of political science. Secondly, this issue is also crucial to the choice of theoretically feasible instruments of analysis, since the nature of a given explanandum has obvious and fundamental implications for the types of explanans, that is, explanatory factors, which in principle are appropriate and in practice fruitful. Although there is today (in contrast to a generation ago) a relatively stable consensus with regard to the explanandum, which therefore need not detain us for long, this is not the case with respect to the considerably more contentious meta-theoretical issue.

This consensus boils down to a specification of the *unit of analysis* that emphasizes the purposive nature of foreign policy actions, a focus on policy and the crucial role of state boundaries. The following stipulation is intended to capture these definitional aspects: foreign policies consist of those actions which, expressed in the form of explicitly stated goals, commitments and/or directives, and pursued by governmental representatives acting on behalf of their sovereign communities, are directed toward objectives, conditions and actors – both governmental and non-governmental – which they want to affect and which lie beyond their territorial legitimacy.

As a starting point for discussing the types of *explanatory factors* that have characterized foreign policy analysis, it is necessary to consider two fundamental issues that have dominated current meta-theoretical debate within social theory (and IR). The first concerns the ontological foundation of social systems: the type of issue exemplified by the claim, reputedly made by Margaret Thatcher, that there is 'no such thing as a society', but 'only individuals'. Essentially, it revolves around the question of where the dynamic foundations of social systems are located. This dynamism either has its origin in 'the effects, intended or not, of individual action; or from the slowly evolving rules of the self-reproducing structure' (Guzzini, 1998: 197). This classic distinction in social theory is usually expressed in terms of the dichotomy between 'individualism' and 'holism', the former holding 'that social scientific explanations should be reducible to the properties or interactions of independently existing individuals', while holism stands for the view 'that the effects of social structures cannot be reduced to independently existing agents and their interactions' (Wendt, 1999: 26).

This ontological polarity between individualism and holism should be clearly distinguished from the epistemological issue of whether social agency is to be viewed through an 'objectivistic' or an 'interpretative' lens. Using a different metaphor, two choices are available here: to focus on human agents and their actions either from the 'outside' or from the 'inside', corresponding to the classical Weberian distinction between *Erklären* (explaining) and *Verstehen* (understanding). As argued by Martin Hollis and Steve Smith, these two approaches tell two different types of 'stories' about international relations, each with its own view of human nature and a concomitant range of 'appropriate' theories (Hollis and Smith, 1990). The choice is thus between an approach that models itself on the natural sciences, and one premised on the independent existence of a social realm constituted by social rules and intersubjective meanings. Whereas the former is based on a 'naturalistic' epistemology self-consciously replicated on that of the natural sciences, the latter – and the epistemological notion of *Verstehen* – is based on Weber's claim that 'The science of society attempts the interpretative understanding of social action' (quoted in Hollis and Smith, 1990: 71). This means that 'action must always be understood from within', and this in a double sense: the investigator must both get to 'know the rules, conventions, and context governing the action', and 'to know what the agent intended by and in performing the action' (Hollis and Smith, 1990: 72). Although not uncontroversial and hence in need of further discussion (which cannot be provided here), this epistemological distinction will in the present context concern us only by virtue of its implications when combined with the two ontological choices presented above.

The individualistic answer to the ontological question reduces the epistemological issue to a choice between either treating actors from the 'outside' as rational or cognitive agents in social systems, or from the 'inside' as interpretative or reflexive actors in an intersubjective world of meaning. In either case, the individual is viewed as the primary source of social order, and hence all conceptions of the link between agents and social structures are ultimately reduced to explanations in terms of individual action. Explanations proceeding from a holistic approach to social order treat action either as a function of structural determination in some sense or other, or with reference to processes of socialization broadly defined. In both cases the relationship between actors and social structures is tendered in terms of some form of structural determination in which individual action is conceived as a function of a pre-established social order.

On the basis of these two dimensions we can now summarize their implications for foreign policy approaches in the following fourfold matrix (Figure 17.1) (see also Dunne, 1995: 370–2; Guzzini, 1998: 190–210; Hollis, 1994: 183–260; Hollis and Smith, 1990: 155–9, 214–16; Wendt, 1999: 22–40). I shall now proceed to discuss prominent examples of each of the four types of rock-bottom perspectives in the study of foreign policy identified in Figure 17.1. Given the space available, the ambition here is to be illustrative rather than comprehensive or exhaustive.

ONTOLOGY	EPISTEMOLOGY	
	Objectivism	**Interpretativism**
Holism	*Structural perspective*	*Social-institutional perspective*
Individualism	*Agency-based perspective*	*Interpretative actor perspective*

Figure 17.1   *Four types of rock-bottom perspectives in the study of foreign policy*

CURRENT APPROACHES IN FOREIGN POLICY ANALYSIS

Approaches Based on a Structural Perspective

Realism   Although, as we shall see below, there are other structurally oriented approaches to foreign policy analysis as well, there is no doubt that most contemporary forms of realism fit this bill best. It is also the case that despite the massive attacks which neorealism has experienced as a consequence of its reputed inability either to predict or to explain the end of the Cold War, it continues not only to be alive and well (especially in North America), but also to contribute to the contemporary analysis of foreign policy. For although Waltz has repeatedly claimed that neorealism is a theory of international politics and hence not a theory of foreign policy (Waltz, 1996), strong counter-arguments have been made that this is essentially an untenable position, and hence that nothing prevents neorealists from formulating a theory of foreign policy of their own (Elman, 1996a, 1996b). It has also been noted that despite such denials, neorealists in actual fact frequently engage in the analyses of foreign policy (Baumann et al., 2001: 37–67).

However, there are different variants of (neo)realism, of which at least the following play important roles in the contemporary debate. First of all, a distinction should be made between 'aggressive' and 'defensive' types (Snyder, 1991: 11–12; see also Lynn-Jones and Miller, 1995: xi–xii; Rose, 1998). During the past decade *aggressive neorealism* has been pre-eminently represented by John Mearsheimer, who has argued that whereas the Cold War, based on bipolarity, military balance and nuclear weapons, produced peace in Europe for 45 years, its demise will – contrary to the conventional wisdom – perforce have deleterious effects in the long run. This pessimistic scenario follows from a strict application of neorealist tenets, especially of the view that insofar as the international system invariably fosters conflict and aggression, rational states are compelled to pursue offensive strategies

in their search for security (Mearsheimer, 1995: 79–129; see also Layne, 1995: 130–76). It also emphazises the role of the polarity of the international system – bipolarity being more conducive to peace than multipolarity – as well as the effects of changes in the relative power of states.

Defensive neorealists, on the other hand, do not share this pessimistic and essentially Hobbesian view of the international system, instead arguing that although systemic factors do have causal effects on state behaviour, they cannot account for all state actions. Instead of emphasizing the role played by the distribution of power in the international system, scholars such as Stephen Walt and Charles L. Glaser thus instead pointed to the importance of the source, level and direction of *threats*, defined primarily in terms of technological factors, geographic proximity, offensive capabilities and perceived intentions (Glaser, 1995; Walt, 1995; see also the references in Rose, 1998: 146, fn. 4). The picture presented here is that states pursuing security in a rational manner can on the whole afford to be relatively relaxed except in rare instances; and that security can generally be achieved by balancing against threats in a timely way, a policy that will effectively hinder most forms of actual conflict. 'Foreign policy activity', Rose thus explains, 'is the record of rational states reacting properly to clear systemic incentives, coming into conflict only in those circumstances when the security dilemma is heightened to fever pitch' (Rose, 1998: 150; see also Glaser, 1995; Lynn-Jones and Miller, 1995: xi; Snyder, 1991; Van Evera, 1990/91: 11–17; Walt, 1995; Zakaria, 1995: 475–81).

Neoclassical realists should be distinguished from both offensive and defensive neorealists. They share with neorealists the view that a country's foreign policy is primarily formed by its place in the international system and in particular by its relative material power capabilities. However, and here the classical roots of this approach come to the fore, they also argue that the impact of systemic factors on a given country's foreign policy will be indirect and more complex than neorealists have assumed, since such factors can effect policy only through intervening variables at the unit level (Rose, 1998:

146). This view is clearly contrary to the whole tenor of offensive neorealism, but neoclassical realists also fault defensive neorealists, mainly because it is claimed that their systemic argument fails to explain much of actual foreign policy behaviour and hence needs to be augmented by the *ad hoc* introduction of unit-level variables (see, for example, Schweller, 1996: 114–15; Zakaria, 1995). As a consequence of the stress on the role of both independent (systemic) and intervening (domestic) variables, research within neoclassical realism is generally conducted in the form of theoretically informed narratives – ideally supplemented by counterfactual analysis – that trace how different factors combine to forge the particular foreign policies of states (Rose, 1998: 153). More specifically, this has yielded extensive narrative case studies of how twentieth century great powers – especially the United States, the Soviet Union and China – have reacted to the material rise or decline of their relative power in the international system (Christensen, 1996; Schweller, 1998; Wohlforth, 1993; Zakaria, 1998).

Neoliberal institutionalism Although not generally touted as an approach to the analysis of foreign policy, it is obvious that the type of focus that usually goes under the name of neoliberal institutionalism is as relevant to the study of foreign policy as are realism and neorealism in their various configurations. Indeed, insofar as this school of thought is posited as an alternative to realism (and, the view of some, as the only one), it also *pari passu* entails an alternative approach to foreign policy analysis (see Baldwin, 1993).

Neoliberal institutionalism is a structural, systemic and 'top-down' view for some of the same reasons that realism constitutes such an approach. It assumes that states are the primary actors in the international system; that they behave like egoistic value maximizers; and that the international system is essentially anarchic (Baldwin, 1993: 8–14; Grieco, 1993). It is also for this reason that Andrew Moravcsik has claimed that 'neoliberal institutionalism' is a misnomer insofar as it essentially constitutes a variant of realism (Moravcsik, 1997: 537).

What then is distinctive about the neoliberal institutionalist approach to foreign policy analysis? Very briefly, the following: whereas both realists and neoliberals view foreign policy-making as a process of constrained choice by purposive states, the latter understand this constraint not primarily in terms of the configurations of power capabilities facing policy-makers, but in terms of an anarchic system which, while it fosters uncertainty and hence security concerns, can nevertheless be positively affected by the institutional provision of information and common rules in the form of functional regimes. The result is that international cooperation under anarchy *is* possible in the pursuit of given state preferences (Oye, 1985); and hence certain specific features of an international setting can explain state outcomes in the form of cooperative foreign policies (Axelrod and Keohane, 1993; Keohane, 1993).

Organizational process approaches While both realism and neoliberal institutionalism are structural approaches of a systemic kind, foreign policy analysis can be pursued 'structurally' on a lower level of analysis as well, in which the structural factor driving foreign policy behaviour is not external but internal to the state. As argued by Hollis and Smith, a 'top-down' approach on the sub-systemic level either focuses on the causal relationship between the state and its agencies – how the latter conform to the demands of the former – or between agencies and individuals; on this level a structural view would imply that individual decision-makers do not act independently but generally in conformity with the dictates of the agencies employing them (Hollis and Smith, 1990: 8–9, 196–202).

The latter type of claim has become known as the organizational process approach ever since the celebrated publication of Allison's *Essence of Decision* in 1971. With roots in organizational theory, it focuses on decisions not in terms of instrumental rationality but as *outputs* of large organizations functioning according to regular patterns of behaviour, usually referred to as standard operating procedures. The most prominent recent research in which organizational theory has been used in foreign policy analysis has focused on decision-making in general, and on the role of decision-making units – particularly small groups – in this process. This has been the case, for example, in recent work reconsidering and going beyond Irving Janis's notion of 'groupthink', focusing on the interplay between group dynamics and the role of broader organizational cultures and socialization in foreign policy decision-making (Beasley, 1998; 't Hart et al., 1997; Ripley, 1995). This type of research points to the applicability of recent organizational theory (see, e.g., March and Olsen, 1998), in particular the celebrated (if not entirely transparent) distinction between the logic of 'consequences', defining the type of action appropriate within both realist and neoliberal thinking, and the logic of 'appropriateness', which – as Allison and Zelikow have claimed in their recent and substantial updating of the organizational model – is very much at the heart of the organizational process approach to decision-making (Allison and Zelikow, 1999: 146).

Approaches from an Agency-Based Perspective

Cognitive and psychological approaches Although research on the cognitive and psychological characteristics of individual decision-makers has been viewed with considerable scepticism in some quarters, this has in fact been one of the growth areas within foreign policy analysis over the past quarter of a century (see, for example, Hudson, 1997; Renshon and Larson, 2001; Rosati, 2000; Singer and Hudson, 1992; Sylvan and Voss, 1998). As against the rational choice assumption – common to both realism and neoliberal institution-alism – that individuals are in principle open-minded and adaptable to the dictates of structural change and constraints, it is based on the contrary assump-tion that they are to a considerable degree imper-vious to such effects due to their underlying beliefs, the way they process information as well as a number of other personality and cognitive traits.

From having in its earliest years focused essen-tially on the study of attitudes and attitudinal change, and more specifically on theories of cognitive con-sistency, including cognitive dissonance, congruity and balance theory (Rosati, 1995: 52), psychological analysis underwent a 'cognitive revolution' in the 1970s. Instead of the conception of the passive actor underlying previous work, a new view emerged stressing the individual as problem-solver rather than malleable agent (Rosati, 1995: 52–4; Young and Shafer, 1998). The most significant of these have been the application of 'operational codes' (George, 1979; Walker, 1990, 1995; Walker et al., 1998), 'cognitive mapping' (Axelrod, 1976; Bonham et al., 1997; Young, 1996), 'attribution theory' (Heradstveit and Bonham, 1986) and 'image theory' (Herrmann and Fischerkeller, 1995).

Important book-length work done during the 1980s and onwards include Deborah Larson's study of changes in the attitude of major American decision-makers between 1944 and 1947 (Larson, 1985), her more recent analysis of Cold War mistrust between the two superpowers (Larson, 1997), Richard Herrmann's (1985) study of perceptions and behaviour in Soviet foreign policy, Jerel A. Rosati's (1987) cognitive study of the Carter administration, Yuen Foong Khong's (1992) study of the role of his-torical analogies in foreign policy decision-making, and Martha Cottam's (1994) work on Latin America. In this context mention must also be made of Yaacov Y.I. Vertzberger's magisterial *The World in their Minds* (Vertzberger, 1990), which not only provides a very useful summary of much of the work done within this genre by the end of the 1980s, but also propounds a comprehensive and multicausal frame-work for analysing information processing, cognition and perception in foreign policy decision-making. This was also a period when studies of how the char-acteristics of leadership – beliefs, motivations, deci-sional and interpersonal styles – affected the pursuit of foreign policies first received serious attention, a focus which has continued to this day (M. Hermann, 1993; Hermann and Preston, 1998).

To this list one must also add prospect theory, not least because it reputedly 'has evoked the most interest among students of foreign policy-making' (Kahler, 1998: 927). This approach, pioneered by

Kahneman and Tversky more than twenty years ago (Kahneman and Tversky, 1979), holds that decision-makers frame – that is, identify – their choices not in terms of maximizing their expected utility (as assumed in rational choice models) but, rather, with regard to a so-called reference point (often the status quo), in terms of which they are risk-averse with respect to gains, and risk-acceptant with respect to losses (Farkas, 1996: 345; Kahler, 1998; Levy, 1997; McDermott, 1998). In other words, it claims that people are more sensitive to gains and losses from a given reference point than to changes in net asset levels; and that they tend to overvalue losses relative to gains (Levy, 1997: 89).

Finally, a review of cognitive and psychological approaches to foreign policy analysis would be incomplete without touching upon the issue of learning in foreign policy. The literature here is sub-stantial and growing, and to some extent overlap-ping with some of the cognitive approaches mentioned above (although some of these have a holistic rather than individualist thrust). Fortunately, Jack S. Levy has written an excellent overview of this field, and hence – taking heed also of his characterization of it as a minefield – I will not elaborate on this theme here; he has already swept much of it for us (Levy, 1994).

Bureaucratic politics approach   Although the so-called bureaucratic politics – or governmental – approach to the analysis of foreign policy, first popularized by Allison in his study of the Cuban crisis, is often assumed to be closely similar to the organizational process model discussed above (and sometimes conflated with it), it is premised on an agency-oriented rather than a structural view of the field (Allison, 1971). Insofar as it focuses on inter-action among organizational players involved in bargaining games and competing preferences, it does not aim to explain in terms of organizational outputs but on the basis of the actual 'pulling and hauling that is politics' (Allison and Zelikow, 1999: 255). At the same time, although in a certain sense akin to rational choice thinking insofar as its main rationale is to explain why decisions often take the form of 'resultants' as distinct from what any person or group intended, it does this not in terms of given preferences and strategic moves but 'accord-ing to the power and performance of proponents and opponents of the action in question' (Allison and Zelikow, 1999: 256). The power in question is not in the firsthand personal but bureaucratic, inso-far as the actors involved in these bargaining games represent sectional or factional rather than individual interests. Hence the famous apothegm (reputedly minted by Don Price, but also known as Miles's law) which encapsulates this bureaucratic link between individual actors and their organizational anchorage: where you stand depends on where you sit (Hollis, 1994; Stern and Verbeek, 1998: 206).

Although explicitly theorized on the basis of the empirical realities of how governments actually work (at least in the United States), this view of foreign policy decision-making has over the years received considerable criticism both with reference to conceptual confusion and poor empirical performance (see, for example, Bendor and Hammond, 1992; Bernstein, 2000; Rhodes, 1994; Welch, 1998). Nevertheless, it continues to stimulate research on foreign policy, and although earlier claimed to be excessively US-centred in its empirical applicability, it is slowly finding its way to Europe as well (see, for example, the contributions in Stern and Verbeek, 1998). Allison (with his co-author) has also upgraded the chapter on governmental politics in the second edition of his study, including in it a host of empirical examples postdating the Cuban crisis (Allison and Zelikow, 1999: 255–378; see also Karbo, 1998).

Liberal approach   Although it has roots going back to the early Rosenau (Rosenau, 1969) and prominent European scholars of foreign policy (Czempiel, 1981; Hanrieder, 1967), as well as to research on the role of domestic structures in foreign policy analysis pioneered by Peter Katzenstein (Katzenstein, 1976, 1978) and subsequently developed by Matthew Evangelista, Thomas Risse-Kappen and others (Evangelista, 1988, 1995; Risse-Kappen, 1991; Snyder, 1991), Andrew Moravcsik must nevertheless be given primary credit for having put the liberal approach squarely on the contemporary IR agenda (Moravcsik, 1997; but see also Doyle, 1997). In his view, three core assumptions underlie this challenge to neorealism and neoliberalism: the primacy of societal actors over political institutions, the implication of which is that being based on a 'bottom-up' view of the political system, individual and social groups are treated as prior to politics, insofar as they define their interests independently of politics and then pursue these through political exchange and collective action; state preferences represent the interests of a subset of society, in the sense that state officials define state preferences and act purposively in world politics in terms of these interests; and state behaviour in the international system is determined by the configuration within it of interdependent state preferences, that is, by the constraints imposed on a given state by the preferences of other states (Moravcsik, 1997: 520). Each of these core assumptions, Moravcsik argues, supports a specific variant of liberal theory, that is, ideational, commercial and republican liberalism, respectively. The first pertains to the generation of domestic social demands, the second to the causal mechanisms by means of which these are transformed into state preferences, and the third to the resulting patterns of national preferences in international settings (Moravcsik, 1997: 524–33).

Approaches Based on a Social-Institutional Perspective

Social constructivism   Although 'social constructivism' (or simply 'constructivism'), like 'rational choice', is essentially a meta-theoretical standpoint in the study of social phenomena, and hence is foundational to political analysis rather than being a specific analytical or 'theoretical' approach within IR, it will here – following most constructivist scholars (Adler, 1997; Dunne, 1995; Guzzini, 2000; Hopf, 1998; Ruggie, 1998; Wendt, 1999: 31) – be used to designate a more or less coherent and emerging body of thought in IR, including foreign policy analysis. Although it has roots going back to Grotius, Kant and Hegel, and was embedded already in some of the classic contributions by Karl Deutsch, Ernst Haas and in particular the English School (Bull, 1977; Deutsch, 1954; Haas, 1964, 1990; see also Dunne, 1995), it is nevertheless regarded by most IR scholars today as a relative newcomer to the sub-discipline; the term itself was first introduced to IR by Nicholas Onuf as recently as 1989 (Onuf, 1989). At the same time, however, it has quickly established itself as perhaps the main contender to a mainstream perspective in IR usually designated as 'rationalist' (see Katzenstein, 1996; and Fearon and Wendt in this volume).

This is not the place to go into the details of social constructivism, since this is done elsewhere in this *Handbook* (see Chapter 5, as well as Guzzini, 2000). However, it is fruitful to distinguish between essentially 'thinner' and 'thicker' versions, since constructivism incorporates – rather uneasily – an increasingly broad spectrum of views. The former is quintessentially represented by Wendt in his recent treatise on international politics (Wendt, 1999), but also by other 'modernist' constructivists, including Emanuel Adler and Michael Barnett (1998), Jeff Checkel (1999), John Ruggie (1998), Peter Katzenstein (1996), Thomas Risse-Kappen (1995b) and Martha Finnemore (1996b). Followers of 'thicker' versions range from what Adler terms 'modernist linguistic' (or 'rule-oriented') constructivists such as Friedrich Kratochwil (1989) and Nicholas Onuf (1989), the 'discursive' group to be discussed below, to the 'postmodernists' such as Richard Ashley (1984) and Rob Walker (1993), in addition to a number of feminist scholars, particularly Spike Peterson (1992), J. Ann Tickner (1993; see also Chapter 14 in this volume) and Christine Sylvester (1994). Since Wendt's type of constructivism is explicitly not designed for the analysis of foreign policy (Wendt, 1999: 11), I will not discuss it further here. Similarly, insofar as postmodernist versions are difficult to incorporate within a foreign policy framework as defined here, these too will be left aside. The specifically discursive approach will, however, be discussed below.

This leaves us here with contributions to the study of foreign policy from within the 'modernist' type of constructivism. This stream can be said to consist, first of all, of a normative and ideational strand, which emphasizes that the world of international relations does not exist independently of human action and cognition but, rather, that it is an intersubjective and meaningful world whose rules and practices are made and reproduced by human interactions. A second strand, often intertwined with the first, emphasizes the role of identities in international relations, and does this by pointing to the 'constitutive' role that norms and ideas play in defining identities and hence prescribing proper behaviour on the part of given types of actors.

Both these strands are exemplified in the various chapters of the influential volume on *The Culture of National Security* (1996), edited by Peter J. Katzenstein. Although it by no means cuts its roots to mainstream social science (see Ruggie, 1998: 38), it takes issue with the rationalism of both neorealism and neoliberalism with regard to the role of both norms and identities in world politics. In particular, it 'makes problematic the state interests that predominant explanations of national security often take for granted', as Katzenstein writes in his introduction (1996: 1). In this volume two studies in particular exemplify a constructivist analysis of foreign policy. The first, by Richard Price and Nina Tannenwald, shows that while a rationalist analysis of the non-use of both nuclear and chemical weapons cannot account for such policies, a constructivist view, emphasizing the socially constructed nature of deterrence and deterrence weapons, shows that the non-use of these weapons can only be understood if one takes 'into account the development of prohibitionary norms that shaped these weapons as unacceptable "weapons of mass destruction"' (Price and Tannenwald, 1996: 115). Similarly, Martha Finnemore has focused on another form of foreign policy behaviour which cannot be adequately explained by either realist or liberal theories: humanitarian interventions which have no geostrategic and/or economic importance to the interveners in question (Finnemore, 1996a; see also Finnemore, 1996b). Instead, she argues, this type of behaviour, and the manner in which it has changed and developed since the nineteenth century, cannot be understood apart from the changing normative context in which it occurs, insofar as 'international normative context shapes the interests of international actors and does so in both systematic and systemic ways' (Finnemore, 1996a: 154). A third study which also exemplifies a constructivist analysis of foreign policy along these lines is Audie Klotz's analysis of the role of international norms in the international embargo against the *apartheid* regime in South Africa (Klotz, 1995). She argues that the emergence of an international norm of racial equality led states – such as the United States – to redefine

their foreign policy interests despite a lack of material incentives for so doing.

Discursive approaches   Following the so-called linguistic turn in philosophy and social theory, a second holistic-interpretative approach, focusing on the role of language in social inquiry, is slowly but determinedly making inroads into foreign policy analysis. One strand of this movement – belonging to the so-called Copenhagen School (see, for example, Buzan et al., 1998) – has as its starting point a critique of the use of psychological and cognitive factors in the explanation of the role of belief systems in foreign policy, in particular a tendency to focus exclusively on individual decision-makers, viewing and analysing beliefs in positivists terms, and an assumption that language is a transparent medium without an inner dynamic of its own (Larsen, 1997: 1–10). Instead of analysing the belief systems of individual decision-makers in this conventional manner, the emphasis is here put on viewing the discourse characterizing the foreign policy domain as a powerful structural constraint, on a high level of generality, shaping the foreign policy of the state in question. More specifically, drawing on social constructivist premises, Henrik Larsen has argued that 'the framework of meaning within which foreign policy takes place is seen as the basis of the way in which interests and goals are constructed' (Larsen, 1999: 453). However, contrary to 'thinner' constructivists, the assumption in this type of discursive approach is that intersubjective meaning cannot be apprehended in or by itself but, rather, that it is constituted by language. As a consequence, discourses 'provide the basis on which policy preferences, interests and goals are constructed' (Larsen, 1999: 453; Waever, 1998). Along similar lines, Ole Waever has argued for a conceptualization of security – as 'securitization' – based not on the 'objective' measures of traditional security studies but on speech act theory and its emphasis on language as a privileged vehicle for gaining and exercising social power. In this view, he writes, 'security is not of interest as a sign that refers to something more real; the utterance *itself* is the act', and hence 'something is a security problem when elites declare it to be so' (Waever, 1995: 55, 54).

A second, different and broader strand has recently been presented and discussed by Jennifer Milliken (Milliken, 1999: 225, 228–30; see also 2001). She characterizes discourse theorists as crossing over and mixing 'divisions between post-structuralists, postmodernists and some feminists and social constructivists', sharing at least the following three commitments: viewing discourses as systems of signification that construct social realities (see, for example, Milliken, 1996; Mutimer, 1999; Weldes and Saco, 1996); the claim that discourses are productive of the things defined by the discourse, such as common sense and policy practices (see, for example, Campbell, 1993; Doty,

1996; Huysmans, 1998; Waever, 1995; Weber, 1995; Weldes, 1999; Weldes and Saco, 1996); and 'studying dominating or hegemonic discourses, and their structuring of meaning as connected to implementing practices and ways of making these intelligible and legitimate' (see, for example, Bartelson, 1995; Fierke, 1998; Neumann, 1998; Sylvester, 1994). Discourse analysts thus focus on significative practices and the knowledge systems underlying them, and are as such not only concerned with meta-theoretical critique but also with critical theorizing about the knowledge/power nexus (on the latter, see also Guzzini, 2000; Neufeld, 1993).

Approaches Based on an Interpretative Actor Perspective

In their book-length discussion of core meta-theoretical issues in IR, Martin Hollis and Steve Smith have described individualist interpretative approaches to foreign policy as follows:

> Understanding proceeds by reconstructing at an individual level. This Weberian line has been much used in International Relations, especially in the sub-field known as Foreign Policy Analysis. Here the concern is to understand decisions from the standpoint of the decision-makers by reconstructing their reasons. The foreign policy behaviour of states depends on how individuals with power perceive and analyse situations. Collective action is a sum or combination of individual actions. (Hollis and Smith, 1990: 74)

In addition, they make the distinction within hermeneutics – which the above approach exemplifies – between understanding individual actions through social rules and collective meanings (a top-down procedure), and understanding collective policy through their individual elements (bottom-up). Inasmuch as the top-down view is quintessentially the one discussed above in terms of social-institutional approaches, we are here left with the latter type of focus, which also happens to be the least utilized today in the study of foreign policy.

The historical antecedents of this approach go back to the pioneering work of Richard C. Snyder and his associates, focusing on a systematic empirical analysis of the actual deliberations of foreign policy decision-makers (Snyder et al., 1962; see also Paige, 1968). Insofar as the focal point in studies of this kind are the *reasoned* – rather than *rational* – choices made by decision-makers, certain aspects of role theory also exemplify this approach, at least insofar as the analysis of particular role conceptions puts the focus on the reasoning of individual national foreign policy-makers and their understanding of the international system and the perceived role of their own states within this larger system (see, for example, Holsti, 1987; Hyde-Price, 2000: 42–7; and the discussion of 'role-players' in Hollis and Smith,

1990: 155–9, 214–16). The same goes for more classical understandings of the role of the 'national interest' in foreign policy decision-making, based on individual interpretations of this much maligned but exceedingly flexible concept, as well as to the study of the role of crucial decision-makers during crises (see, for example, Bernstein, 2000: 161–4).

However, a more illustrative and contemporary exemplar of this type of analysis is Philip Zelikow and Condoleezza Rice's detailed study of German reunification (Zelikow and Rice, 1995). It offers an insider's view of the innermost workings of the top elites of the United States, the Soviet Union, West Germany, East Germany, Britain and France in the creation of a united Germany. The logic of explanation is to determine the thinking of these elites – the reasoning behind their choices – and then to proffer it in explanation of the immense changes that occurred during the year following the collapse of the Berlin Wall. This is 'thick description' at its best; and although they have been chided for eschewing theory altogether in following this strategy (see, for example, Risse, 1997), it should at the same time be emphasized that although no causal analysis (or theorizing) in the conventional sense is provided, the focus is most certainly not simply on 'what' occurred, but also on the 'why' and 'how' aspects of this process. The assumption underlying this type of analysis is the counter-factual argument that had not the main actors in this historical process reasoned and made choices the way they actually did, the history of this period would have been different. In any case, insofar as 'why' issues can have both a 'because of' and an 'in order to' implication, and since there are strong philosophical arguments in favour of imputing some form of causality also to purposive behaviour (see Carlsnaes, 1986: 32–8), there is no justification for off-hand denigrating this type of an approach for being 'descriptive' rather than 'explanatory'. In this connection it should also be noted that despite a deep concern with its lack of theoretical anchorage, Risse has been able to utilize this descriptive-analytic study to illustrate the role of 'communicative action' and 'friendly persuasion' in international relations (Risse, 2000). Indeed, insofar as the 'logic of arguing' – as distinct from the logics of 'consequentialism' and 'appropriateness' – aims at achieving a reasoned consensus on the part of real life decision-makers (such as Kohl and Gorbachev), this approach seems to be ideally suited for analysis from within the interpretative actor perspective.

IS A SYNTHETIC APPROACH TO FOREIGN POLICY ANALYSIS FEASIBLE?

This rich flora – indeed, surfeit – of alternative approaches to foreign policy analysis raises the question whether it is possible to synthesize or integrate at least some of these, or if we are willy-nilly obliged to choose between them. Hollis and Smith, for example, have claimed that there are always two stories to tell – that of 'explanation' versus 'understanding', corresponding to the distinction above between 'objectivism' and 'interpretativism' – and that they cannot be combined into one type of narrative (Hollis and Smith, 1990). Similarly, 'holism' and 'individualism' have most often been assumed to be in principle mutually exclusive categories, forcing us into either a 'top-down' or 'bottom-up' mode of analysis. However, other scholars – often with a less pronounced meta-theoretical bent – have argued for the feasibility of such analytical integration, usually combining this with empirical research that has lent strong support for such an integrative view of foreign policy analysis.

Perhaps the most notable recent example of such an ambition is provided by a number of studies that have focused on the link between domestic structures and foreign policy actions. Peter Katzenstein's early work (1976, 1978) has played a pioneering role in paving the way for studies of this kind, which have often had the added advantage of being comparative and hence reaching back – albeit without the same 'scientistic' ambitions – to earlier work within CFP. Significant research stimulated by this approach has included studies by Matthew Evangelista (1988, 1995), Risse-Kappen (1991, 1994, 1995a) and Jack Snyder (1991; see also the discussion in Evangelista, 1997). Some of this work has also taken its cue from Peter Gourevitch's notion of the 'second-image reversed', focusing on how international institutions affect foreign policy change via its effects on domestic publics and hence on state actions (Gourevitch, 1978; Checkel, 1999; Keck and Sikkink, 1998; Risse et al., 1999).

However, the main problem with 'domestic structure' as an integrative bridge is that it assumes and hence reinforces the divide between domestic and international politics which, as I have suggested above, is highly questionable as a feasible foundational baseline for a sub-discipline that needs to problematize this boundary rather than positing it by assumption. Furthermore, this argument has various strands that are not necessarily mutually compatible as explanations. Thus, it can refer to an essentially holistic structural view, as in Katzenstein's work on the role of weak versus strong societies (Katzenstein, 1976), or in the 'democratic peace' argument (Russett, 1993); to an agency-based view in terms of which domestic structures act as intervening factors between societal actors and state action (Checkel, 1997; Risse-Kappen, 1991); or to more recent constructivist approaches emphasizing the impact of ideas and norms – either domestic or international – as sources of foreign policy change (Checkel, 1997; Finnemore and Sikkink, 1998; Reus-Smit, 1999). Given these contending uses to which the domestic structure argument has been put, as well as the

more fundamental criticism raised above, it is difficult to see how it can sustain a central role as a 'theoretical bridge' (Evangelista, 1997: 204) in foreign policy analysis.

My own view is that a synthetic framework for analysing foreign policy is indeed possible, but that it has to be on a level of abstraction that does not substantively prejudge explanation in favour of any particular type or combination of empirical factors (such as 'domestic structure'). Since I have elaborated on it elsewhere, I will here simply give a skeletal outline of the explanatory logic of such a suggested synthetic framework of analysis (Carlsnaes, 1986, 1992, 1993, 1994). The starting point is the claim that while the meta-theoretical matrix used above is specifically designed for the purpose of classifying approaches to foreign policy analysis in terms of their most fundamental ontological and epistemological presuppositions, it is less suitable for *empirical* analysis itself as distinguished from *meta-theoretical* dissection. Arguably, in the 'games real actors play' (Scharpf, 1997) action is always a combination of purposive behaviour, cognitive-psychological factors and the various structural phenomena characterizing societies and their environments, and hence explanations of actual foreign policy actions must perforce be able to give accounts that do not by definition exclude or privilege any of these types of explanans. Insofar as the matrix used above does have such implications (albeit for good analytical-cum-pedagogical reasons), it simply will not be able to deliver the goods in this respect. Indeed, an ironic implication of this way of conceptualizing and understanding the foundational issues underlying foreign policy analysis is that it is only when we succeed in *overriding* the logic exemplified in this chapter – the four generic perspectives, which by definition are mutually exclusive – that there will be a real chance of achieving this ambition.

Thus, rather than thinking in terms of a logic of mutual exclusion, I suggest that we instead conceptualize such an analytic framework in terms of a tripartite approach consisting of an *intentional*, a *dispositional* and a *structural* dimension of explanation, as follows:

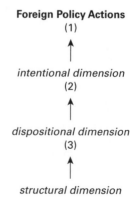

Foreign Policy Actions
(1)

↑

intentional dimension
(2)

↑

dispositional dimension
(3)

↑

structural dimension

Although analytically autonomous, these three dimensions are conceived as closely linked in the sense that they can be conjoined in a logical, step-by-step manner to render increasingly exhaustive explanations of foreign policy actions qua explanandum as defined earlier. This means, first of all, that a teleological explanation (1) in terms solely of the intentional dimension is fully feasible, based either on strict rationality assumptions or on more traditional modes of intentional analysis. It also means, however, that one can choose to 'deepen' the analysis by providing a causal determination (2) of policy – as opposed to an explanation wholly in terms of given goals and preferences – in which the factors characterizing the intentional dimension are themselves explained in terms of underlying psychological-cognitive factors which have disposed a given actor to have this and not that preference or intention. The distinction between these two levels can also be described in terms of an 'in order to' and a 'because of' dimension, the former referring to the intentional sphere, the latter constituting the link between this intention and the having of it: how a particular intention has become a particular actor's intention. Finally, the third layer is based on the assumption that in so far as intentional behaviour is never pursued outside the crucible of structural determination, factors of the latter kind must always be able to figure causally (3) in our accounts of the former. As conceived here, this link between structure and agency can be conceived as both of a constraining and of an enabling kind, causally affecting policy actions via its effects on the dispositional characteristics of the agents of policy. (Although not indicated in the figure, foreign policy actions can in turn affect – either by intention or unintentionally in the form of outcomes – both the structural and dispositional dimensions, providing for the dynamic interaction over time between agential and structural factors, thus invoking the agency–structure issue, to be discussed briefly below.)

Although this type of an integrative framework eschews the dichotomization of approaches discussed above, it does not as such negate the applicability of any of these – as long as they are used when and if analytically appropriate. Indeed, approaches from all the four types of rock-bottom perspectives discussed above can be fully utilized: the 'structural' and 'social-institutional' when analysing causal links between the structural and dispositional dimensions; 'agency-based' perspectives when tracing causal patterns between the dispositional and the intentional dimension; and the 'interpretative actor' perspective when the purpose is to penetrate the teleological links between intentions and foreign policy actions.

CONCLUDING REMARKS

To round up this overview I would like to conclude by briefly pointing to three theoretical issues that cut across the perspectives discussed above and which, in my opinion, will continue to remain topical and controversial in the study of foreign policy (as in the social sciences in general).

The first of these pertains to explaining the dynamics of foreign policy *change*, both in terms of actor and policy characteristics. Except for a short burst of interest in the early 1980s (Buzan and Jones, 1981; Gilpin, 1981; Goldmann, 1982; Holsti, 1982; Holsti et al., 1980; see also Goldmann, 1988), this was not a topic that attracted much attention until the profound transformations occurring at the end of that decade. These developments revealed the embarrassing fact that not only were many of these changes unanticipated, but also that the events in question were difficult to explain even *ex post facto* in terms of existing theories, models or analytic approaches. Although this theoretical dearth led to a renewed interest in the analysis of foreign policy change (Carlsnaes, 1993; Gustavsson, 1998, 1999; Hermann, 1990; Rosati et al., 1994; see also Koslowski and Kratochwil, 1995), there is little consensus on the best way of doing so. Given the eclectic nature of the field as such, as well as the fundamental differences between the types of perspectives presented above, some of which are inherently more amenable to the study of change than others, this should of course not come as a surprise. At the same time, this issue is seminal to the future of the field as a whole, given the increased globalization of international relations – a process arguably undermining the relative *autonomy* of the state qua foreign policy actor – as well as the emergence of new types of foreign policy actors, such as the EU, claiming not only foreign policy competencies of their own but also as representing their member states, hence eroding the *sovereignty* of the latter (see, for example, White, 2001).

A second contentious and topical concern within the field pertains to the role of *ideas* in the explanation of foreign policy. For long banished from mainstream social science explanations, the ideational factor finally gained full admission in the early 1990s with the publication of the edited volume on *Ideas and Foreign Policy* (Goldstein and Keohane, 1993). Underlying this introduction lay the realization that explanations based solely on rational actors maximizing a utility function rooted in material interests were often inadequate to account fully for the foreign policy behaviour of states. Instead, it was suggested, ideas too can have an independent causal effect on foreign policy 'even when human beings behave rationally to achieve their ends' (Goldstein and Keohane, 1993: 5; see also Checkel, 1997; Jacobsen, 1995; Risse-Kappen, 1994; Yee, 1996). Although welcomed by scholars on the interpretative side of the epistemological fence, this admission of the causal efficacy of ideas has nevertheless led to considerable controversy within the field (see, for example, Koslowski and Kratochwil, 1995; Laffey and Weldes, 1997). The basic criticism is that 'rationalists' continue to think in terms of 'naturalistic' factors even when conceptualizing ideas (viewing them as cognitively and individually held 'beliefs' with causal effects, as well as being distinct from 'interests'), whereas the social constructivist view is that 'ideational factors relate to social action in the form of constitutive rules', as Ruggie notes (Ruggie, 1998: 38). In the light of this view, to speak of 'ideational variables' is tantamount to perpetrating an oxymoron – a begging of the whole question of what ideas are and are not, and hence how they are affected by and affect social interaction. Clearly, this debate is only at its beginning and will continue to be a focal point for critical discussion.

Finally, a third issue, and one that has received considerable theoretical attention during the past decade, and continues to do so today, is the *agency-structure problematique* in foreign policy analysis. For all practical purposes Wendt put it on the agenda in a much-quoted article published in 1987, and since then it has been hotly debated but hardly resolved to the satisfaction of all concerned (Bieler and Morton, 2001; Carlsnaes, 1992, 1994; Dessler, 1989; Doty, 1997; Friedman and Starr, 1997; Guzzini, 1993; Hollis and Smith, 1991, 1992, 1994; Patomäki, 1996; Suganami, 1999; Wight, 1999). At the heart of this problem lies the increasingly widespread recognition that, instead of being antagonistic partners in a zero-sum relationship, human agents and social structures are in a fundamental sense dynamically interrelated entities, and hence that we cannot account fully for the one without invoking the other. The 'problem' is that although such views of reciprocal implication suggest that the properties of both agents and social structures are relevant to a proper understanding of social behaviour (including the study of change), we nevertheless (as Wendt noted in his original article) 'lack a self-evident way to conceptualize these entities and their relationship' (Wendt, 1987: 338).

This is also, perhaps, an appropriate issue and tone of voice with which to put an end to this overview of the vicissitudes and current condition of foreign policy analysis, since it touches on the central core of the field itself: the fact that foreign policy actions are located at the very centre of the international relations of states, incorporating a multitude of influences – structural and agential, as well as international, societal and individual – that continually impinge on them and on their decision-makers. To capture these complex and reciprocal processes, and to do so well, is the challenge that will persist in energizing this field of study as long as states continue to remain viable actors within the international system.

Note

The author would like to thank the following colleagues (as well as an anonymous reviewer) for commenting on earlier versions of the chapter: Stefano Guzzini, Valerie Hudson, Jennifer Milliken, Thomas Risse, Jerel Rosati, Beth Simmons and Colin Wight. The author also thanks participants at various seminars in Uppsala, Oslo and Gothenburg.

Bibliography

Adler, Emanuel (1997) 'Seizing the Middle Ground: Constructivism in World Politics', *European Journal of International Relations*, 3: 319–63.

Adler, Imanuel and Barnett, Michael (eds) (1998) *Security Communities*. Cambridge: Cambridge University Press.

Allison, Graham T. (1971) *Essence of Decision: Explaining the Cuban Missile Crisis*. Boston: Little, Brown.

Allison, Graham and Zelikow, Philip (1999) *Essence of Decision: Explaining the Cuban Missile Crisis*. New York: Longman.

Andriole, Stephen J. and Hopple, Gerald W. (1984) 'The Rise and Fall of Events Data: From Basic Research to Applied Use in the US Department of Defense', *International Interactions*, 11: 293–309.

Ashley, Richard (1984) 'The Poverty of Neorealism', *International Organization*, 38: 225–86.

Axelrod, Robert (ed.) (1976) *Structure of Decision: The Cognitive Maps of Political Elites*. Princeton: Princeton University Press.

Axelrod, Robert and Keohane, Robert O. (1993) 'Achieving Cooperation Under Anarchy: Strategies and Institutions', in David A. Baldwin (ed.), *Neorealism and Neoliberalism: The Contemporary Debate*. New York: Columbia University Press.

Baldwin, David A. (1993) 'Neoliberalism, Neorealism, and World Politics', in David A. Baldwin (ed.), *Neorealism and Neoliberalism: The Contemporary Debate*. New York: Columbia University Press.

Bartelson, Jens (1995) *A Genealogy of Sovereignty*. Cambridge: Cambridge University Press.

Baumann, Rainer, Rittberger, Volker and Wagner, Wolfgang (2001) 'Neorealist Foreign Policy Theory', in Volker Rittberger (ed.), *German Foreign Policy Since Unification: Theories and Case Studies*. Manchester: Manchester University Press.

Beasley, Ryan (1998) 'Collective Interpretations: How Problem Representations Aggregate in Foreign Policy Groups', in Donald A. Sylvan and James F. Voss (eds), *Problem Representation in Foreign Policy Decision Making*. Cambridge: Cambridge University Press.

Bendor, Jonathan and Hammond, Thomas H. (1992) 'Rethinking Allison's Models', *American Political Science Review*, 86: 301–22.

Bernstein, Barton J. (2000) 'Understanding Decision-making, U.S. Foreign Policy, and the Cuban Missile Crisis', *International Security*, 25: 134–64.

Bieler, Andreas and Morton, Adam David (2001) 'The Gordian Knot of Agency–Structure in International Relations', *European Journal of International Relations*, 7: 5–35.

Bonham, G. Matthew, Sergeev, Victor M. and Parshin, Pavel (1997) 'The Limited Test-Ban Agreement: Emergence of New Knowledge Structures in International Negotiation', *International Studies Quarterly*, 41: 215–40.

Brecher, Michael (1972) *The Foreign Policy System of Israel: Setting, Images, Process*. London: Oxford University Press.

Bull, Hedley (1977) *The Anarchic Society*. New York: Columbia University Press.

Buzan, Barry and Jones, J. Barry (1981) *Change and the Study of International Relations*. London: Pinter.

Buzan, Barry, Waever, Ole and Wilde, Jaap de (1998) *Security: A New Framework for Analysis*. Boulder: Lynne Rienner.

Campbell, David (1993) *Politics without Principle: Sovereignty, Ethics, and the Narratives of the Gulf War*. Boulder: Lynne Rienner.

Caporaso, James A., Hermann, Charles F. and Kegley, Charles W., Jr (1987) 'The Comparative Study of Foreign Policy: Perspectives on the Future', *International Studies Notes*, 13: 32–46.

Carlsnaes, Walter (1986) *Ideology and Foreign Policy: Problems of Comparative Conceptualization*. Oxford: Blackwell.

Carlsnaes, Walter (1992) 'The Agency–Structure Problem in Foreign Policy Analysis', *International Studies Quarterly*, 36: 245–70.

Carlsnaes, Walter (1993) 'On Analysing the Dynamics of Foreign Policy Change: A Critique and Reconceptualization', *Cooperation and Conflict*, 28: 5–30.

Carlsnaes, Walter (1994) 'In Lieu of a Conclusion: Compatibility and the Agency–Structure Issue in Foreign Policy Analysis', in Walter Carlsnaes and Steve Smith (eds), *European Foreign Policy: The EC and Changing Perspectives in Europe*. London: Sage.

Checkel, Jeffrey T. (1997) *Ideas and International Political Change: Soviet/Russian Behavior at the End of the Cold War*. New Haven: Yale University Press.

Checkel, Jeffrey T. (1999) 'Norms, Institutions, and National Identity in Contemporary Europe', *International Studies Quarterly*, 43: 83–114.

Christensen, Thomas J. (1996) *Useful Adversaries: Grand Strategy, Domestic Mobilization, and Sino-American Conflict, 1947–1958*. Princeton: Princeton University Press.

Cohen, Bernard C. (1968) 'Foreign Policy', in David L. Sills (ed.), *International Encyclopedia of the Social Sciences*. New York: Macmillan and The Free Press.

Cohen, Bernard C. and Harris, Scott A. (1975) 'Foreign Policy', in Fred I. Greenstein and Nelson W. Polsby (eds), *Handbook of Political Science*, vol. 6: *Policies and Policymaking*. Reading, MA: Addison–Wesley.

Cottam, Martha (1994) *Images and Intervention: US Policies in Latin America*. Pittsburgh: University of Pittsburgh Press.

Cottam, Richard (1977) *Foreign Policy Motivation: A General Theory and a Case Study*. Pittsburgh: University of Pittsburgh Press.

Czempiel, Ernst-Otto (1981) *Internationale Beziehungen: Ein Konfliktmodell*. Munich: UTB.

Dessler, David (1989) 'What's at Stake in the Agency–Structure Debate?', *International Organization*, 43: 441–73.

Deutsch, Karl (1954) *Political Community at the International Level*. Garden City, NY: Doubleday .

Doty, Roxanne Lynn (1996) *Imperial Encounters*. Minneapolis: University of Minnesota Press.

Doty, Roxanne Lynn (1997) 'Aporia: A Critical Examination of the Agent–Structure Problematique in International Relations Theory', *European Journal of International Relations*, 3: 365–92.

Doyle, Michael (1997) *Ways of War and Peace: Realism, Liberalism, and Socialism*. New York: W.W. Norton.

Dunne, Timothy (1995) 'The Social Construction of International Society', *European Journal of International Relations*, 1: 367–89.

Dunne, Timothy (1998) 'International Theory and the Mirror of History', *European Journal of International Relations*, 4: 347–62.

East, Maurice A. (1978) 'National Attributes and Foreign Policy', in Maurice A. East, Stephen A. Salmore and Charles F. Hermann (eds), *Why Nations Act*. Beverly Hills: Sage.

Elman, Colin (1996a) 'Horses for Courses: Why No Realist Theories of Foreign Policy?', *Security Studies*, 6: 7–53.

Elman, Colin (1996b) 'Cause, Effect, and Consistency: A Response to Kenneth Waltz', *Security Studies*, 6: 58–61.

Evangelista, Matthew (1988) *Innovation and the Arms Race: How the United States and the Soviet Union Develop New Military Technologies*. Ithaca: Cornell University Press.

Evangelista, Matthew (1995) 'The Paradox of State Strength: Transnational Relations, Domestic Structures, and Security Policy in Russia and the Soviet Union', *International Organization*, 49: 1–38.

Evangelista, Matthew (1997) 'Domestic Structure and International Change', in Michael W. Doyle and G. John Ikenberry (eds), *The New Thinking in International Relations Theory*. Boulder: Westview.

Farkas, Andrew (1996) 'Evolutionary Models in Foreign Policy Analysis', *International Studies Quarterly*, 40: 343–61.

Fierke, Karin (1998) *Changing Games, Changing Strategies: Critical Investigations in Security*. Manchester: Manchester University Press.

Finnemore, Martha (1996a) 'Constructing Norms of Humanitarian Intervention', in Peter J. Katzenstein (ed.), *The Culture of National Security: Norms and Identity in World Politics*. New York: Columbia University Press.

Finnemore, Martha (1996b) *National Interests in International Society*. Ithaca: Cornell University Press.

Finnemore, Martha and Sikkink, Kathryn (1998) 'International Norm Dynamics and Political Change', *International Organization*, 52: 887–917.

Friedman, Gil and Starr, Harvey (1997) *Agency, Structure, and International Politics: From Ontology to Empirical Inquiry*. London: Routledge.

George, Alexander L. (1979) 'The Causal Nexus Between Cognitive Beliefs and Decision Making Behavior: The "Operational Code" Belief System', in L.S. Falkowski (ed.), *Psychological Models in International Politics*. Boulder: Westview.

Gilpin, Robert (1981) *War and Change in World Politics*. Cambridge: Cambridge University Press.

Glaser, Charles L. (1995) 'Realists as Optimists: Co-operation as Self-Help', in Michael E. Brown, Sean M. Lynn-Jones and Steven E. Miller (eds), *The Perils of Anarchy: Contemporary Realism and International Security*. Cambridge, MA: MIT Press.

Goldmann, Kjell (1982) 'Change and Stability in Foreign Policy: Détente as a Problem of Stabilisation', *World Politics*, 34: 230–66.

Goldmann, Kjell (1988) *Change and Stability in Foreign Policy: The Problems and Possibilities of Détente*. New York: Harvester Wheatsheaf.

Goldstein, Judith and Keohane, Robert O. (eds) (1993) *Ideas and Foreign Policy: Beliefs, Institutions, and Political Change*. Ithaca: Cornell University Press.

Gourevitch, Peter (1978) 'The Second Image Reversed: The International Sources of Domestic Politics', *International Organization*, 32: 881–912.

Grieco, Joseph M. (1993) 'Anarchy and the Limits of Cooperation: A Realist Critique of the Newest Liberal Institutionalism', in David A. Baldwin (ed.), *Neorealism and Neoliberalism: The Contemporary Debate*. New York: Columbia University Press.

Gustavsson, Jakob (1998) *The Politics of Foreign Policy Change*. Lund: Lund University Press.

Gustavsson, Jakob (1999) 'How Should We Study Foreign Policy Change?', *Cooperation and Conflict*, 34: 73–95.

Guzzini, Stefano (1993) 'Structural Power: The Limits of Neorealist Power Analysis', *International Organization*, 47: 443–78.

Guzzini, Stefano (1998) *Realism in International Relations and International Political Economy*. London: Routledge.

Guzzini, Stefano (2000) 'A Reconstruction of Constructivism in International Relations', *European Journal of International Relations*, 6: 147–82.

Haas, Ernst (1964) *Beyond the Nation-State*. Stanford: Stanford University Press.

Haas, Ernst (1990) *Knowledge is Power*. Berkeley: University of California Press.

Hanrieder, Wolfram F. (1967) 'Compatibility and Consensus: A Proposal for the Conceptual Linkage of External and Internal Dimensions of Foreign Policy', *American Political Science Review*, 61: 971–82.

Hart, Paul 't, Stern, Eric K. and Sundelius, Bengt (eds) (1997) *Beyond Groupthink: Political Dynamics and Foreign Policy-Making*. Ann Arbor: University of Michigan Press.

Heradstveit, Daniel and Bonham, G. Matthew (1986) 'Decision-Making in the Face of Uncertainty: Attributions of Norwegian and American Officials', *Journal of Peace Research*, 23: 339–56.

Hermann, Charles F. (1978) 'Decision Structure and Process Influences on Foreign Policy', in Maurice A. East, Stephen A. Salmore and Charles F. Hermann (eds), *Why Nations Act*. Beverly Hills: Sage.

Hermann, Charles F. (1990) 'Changing Course: When Governments Choose to Redirect Foreign Policy', *International Studies Quarterly*, 34: 3–21.

Hermann, Margaret G. (1974) 'Leader Personality and Foreign Policy Behavior', in James N. Rosenau (ed.), *Comparing Foreign Policies: Theories, Findings, and Methods*. New York: Sage–Halsted.

Hermann, Margaret G. (1980a) 'Assessing the Personalities of Members of the Soviet Politburo', *Personality and Social Psychology Bulletin*, 6: 332–52.

Hermann, Margaret G. (1980b) 'Explaining Foreign Policy Behavior Using Personal Characteristics of Political Leaders', *International Studies Quarterly*, 24: 7–46.

Hermann, Margaret G. (1993) 'Leaders and Foreign Policy Decision Making', in Dan Caldwell and Timothy McKeown (eds), *Diplomacy, Force, and Leadership: Essays in Honor of Alexander George*. Boulder: Westview.

Hermann, Margaret G. and Preston, Thomas (1998) 'Presidents, Leadership Style, and the Advisory Process', in Eugene R. Wittkopf and James M. McCormick (eds), *Domestic Sources of American Foreign Policy*. New York: Rowman and Littlefield.

Herrmann, Richard K. (1985) *Perceptions and Behavior in Soviet Foreign Policy*. Pittsburgh: University of Pittsburgh Press.

Herrmann, Richard K. and Fischerkeller, Michael (1995) 'Beyond the Enemy Image Spiral Model: Cognitive-Strategic Research After the Cold War', *International Organization*, 49: 415–50.

Hollis, Martin (1994) *The Philosophy of Social Science*. Cambridge: Cambridge University Press.

Hollis, Martin and Smith, Steve (1990) *Explaining and Understanding International Relations*. Oxford: Clarendon Press.

Hollis, Martin and Smith, Steve (1991) 'Beware of Gurus: Structure and Action in International Relations', *Review of International Studies*, 14: 393–410.

Hollis, Martin and Smith, Steve (1992) 'Structure and Action: Further Comments', *Review of International Studies*, 18: 187–8.

Hollis, Martin and Smith, Steve (1994) 'Two Stories about Structure and Agency', *Review of International Studies*, 20: 241–51.

Holsti, K.J. (1982) *Why Nations Realign: Foreign Policy Restructuring in the Postwar World*. London: Allen & Unwin.

Holsti, K.J. (1987) 'National Role Conceptions in the Study of Foreign Policy', in Stephen Walker (ed.), *Role Theory and Foreign Policy Analysis*. Durham, NC: Duke University Press.

Holsti, Ole R., North, Robert and Brody, Richard (1968) 'Perception and Action in the 1914 Crisis', in J. David Singer (ed.), *Quantitative International Politics: Insights and Evidence*. New York: The Free Press.

Holsti, Ole R., Siverson, Randolph M. and George, Alexander L. (1980) *Change in the International System*. Boulder: Westview.

Hopf, Ted (1998) 'The Promise of Constructivism in International Relations Theory', *International Security*, 23: 171–200.

Hudson, Valerie M. (ed.) (1997) *Culture and Foreign Policy*. Boulder: Lynne Rienner.

Hudson, Valerie M. and Vore, Christopher S. (1995) 'Foreign Policy Analysis Yesterday, Today, and Tomorrow', *Mershon International Studies Review*, 39: 209–38.

Huysmans, Jef (1998) 'Security! What Do You Mean? From Concept to Thick Signifier', *European Journal of International Relations*, 4: 226–55.

Hyde-Price, Adrian (2000) *Germany and European Order: Enlarging NATO and the EU*. Manchester: Manchester University Press.

Jacobsen, John Kurt (1995) 'Much Ado about Ideas: The Cognitive Factor in Economic Policy', *World Politics*, 47: 283–310.

Janis, Irving J. (1982) *Groupthink: Psychological Studies of Policy Decisions and Fiascoes*. Boston: Houghton Mifflin.

Jervis, Robert (1976) *Perception and Misperception in International Politics*. Princeton: Princeton University Press.

Kahler, Miles (1997) 'Inventing International Relations: International Relations Theory After 1945', in Michael W. Doyle and G. John Ikenberry (eds), *The New Thinking in International Relations Theory*. Boulder: Westview.

Kahler, Miles (1998) 'Rationality in International Relations', *International Organization*, 52: 919–41.

Kahneman, D. and Tversky, A. (1979) 'Prospect Theory: An Analysis of Decision Under Risk', *Econometrica*, 47: 263–91.

Karbo, Juliet (1998) 'Power Politics in Foreign Policy: The Influence of Bureaucratic Minorities', *European Journal of International Relations*, 4: 67–97.

Katzenstein, Peter J. (1976) 'International Relations and Domestic Structures: Foreign Economic Policies of Advanced Industrial States', *International Organization*, 30: 1–45.

Katzenstein, Peter J. (1978) *Between Power and Plenty: Foreign Economic Policies of Advanced Industrial States*. Madison: University of Wisconsin Press.

Katzenstein, Peter J. (1996) 'Introduction: Alternative Perspectives on National Security', in Peter J. Katzenstein (ed.), *The Culture of National Security: Norms and Identity in World Politics*. New York: Columbia University Press.

Keck, Margaret E. and Sikkink, Kathryn (1998) *Activists Beyond Borders: Advocacy Networks in International Politics*. Ithaca: Cornell University Press.

Kegley, Charles W., Jr (1980) 'The Comparative Study of Foreign Policy: Paradigm Lost?', published by Institute of International Studies, University of South Carolina, Essay Series No. 10.

Keohane, Robert O. (1993) 'Institutional Theory and the Realist Challenge After the Cold War', in David A. Baldwin (ed.), *Neorealism and Neoliberalism: The Contemporary Debate*. New York: Columbia University Press.

Khong, Yuen Foong (1992) *Analogies at War: Korea, Munich, Dien Bien Phu, and the Vietnam Decisions of 1965*. Princeton: Princeton University Press.

Klotz, Audie J. (1995) *Protesting Prejudice: Apartheid and the Politics of Norms in International Relations*. Ithaca: Cornell University Press.

Koslowski, Rey and Kratochwil, Friedrich V. (1995) 'Understanding Change in International Politics: The Soviet Empire's Demise and the International System', in Richard Ned Lebow and Thomas Risse-Kappen (eds), *Internatiuonal Relations Theory and the End of the Cold War*. New York: Columbia University Press.

Kratochwil, Friedrich (1989) *Rules, Norms, and Decisions*. Cambridge: Cambridge University Press.

Laffey, Mark and Weldes, Jutta (1997) 'Beyond Belief: Ideas and Symbolic Technologies in the Study of International Relations', *European Journal of International Relations*, 3: 193–237.

Larsen, Henrik (1997) *Foreign Policy and Discourse Analysis: France, Britain and Europe*. London: Routledge.

Larsen, Henrik (1999) 'British and Danish European Policies in the 1990s: A Discourse Approach', *European Journal of International Relations*, 5: 451–83.

Larson, Deborah W. (1985) *Origins of Containment: A Psychological Explanation*. Princeton: Princeton University Press.

Larson, Deborah W. (1997) *Anatomy of Mistrust: U.S.–Soviet Relations during the Cold War*. Ithaca: Cornell University Press.

Layne, Christopher (1995) 'Kant or Cant: The Myth of the Democratic Peace', in Michael E. Brown, Sean M. Lynn-Jones and Steven E. Miller (eds), *The Perils of Anarchy: Contemporary Realism and International Security*. Cambridge, MA: MIT Press.

Levy, Jack S. (1994) 'Learning and Foreign Policy: Sweeping a Conceptual Minefield', *International Organization*, 48: 279–312.

Levy, Jack S. (1997) 'Prospect Theory, Rational Choice, and International Relations', *International Studies Quarterly*, 41: 87–1121.

Lynn-Jones, Sean M. and Miller, Steven E. (1995) 'Preface', in Michael E. Brown, Sean M. Lynn-Jones and Steven E. Miller (eds), *The Perils of Anarchy: Contemporary Realism and International Security*. Cambridge, MA: MIT Press.

March, James G. and Olsen, Johan P. (1998) 'The Institutional Dynamics of International Political Orders', *International Organization*, 52: 943–69.

McDermott, Ross (1998) *Risk-Taking in International Politics: Prospect Theory in American Foreign Policy*. Ann Arbor: University of Michigan Press.

McGowan, Patrick J. and Shapiro, Howard B. (1973) *The Comparative Study of Foreign Policy: A Survey of Scientific Findings*. Beverly Hills: Sage.

Mearsheimer, John J. (1995) 'Back to the Future: Instability in Europe After the Cold War', in Michael E. Brown, Sean M. Lynn-Jones and Steven E. Miller (eds), *The Perils of Anarchy: Contemporary Realism and International Security*. Cambridge, MA: MIT Press.

Milliken, Jennifer (1996) 'Prestige and Reputation in American Foreign Policy and American Realism', in Francis Beer and Robert Hariman (eds), *Post-Realism: The Rhetorical Turn in International Relations*. East Lansing: Michigan State University Press.

Milliken, Jennifer (1999) 'The Study of Discourse in International Relations: A Critique of Research and Methods', *European Journal of International Relations*, 5: 225–54.

Milliken, Jennifer (2001) *Conflict Possibilities: The Social Construction of the Korean War*. Manchester: Manchester University Press.

Moravcsik, Andrew (1997) 'Taking Preferences Seriously: A Liberal Theory of International Politics', *International Organization*, 51: 513–53.

Morgenthau, Hans J. (1948) *Politics Among Nations: The Struggle for Power and Peace*. New York: Alfred A. Knopf.

Munton, Don (1976) 'Comparative Foreign Policy: Fads, Fantasies, Orthodoxies, and Perversities', in James N. Rosenau (ed.), *In Search of Global Patterns*. New York: The Free Press.

Mutimer, David (1999) *The Weapons State: Proliferation and the Imagination of Security*. Boulder: Lynne Rienner.

Neack, Laura, Hey, Jeanne A.K. and Haney, Patrick J. (1995) 'Generational Change in Foreign Policy Analysis', in Laura Neack, Jeanne A.K. Hey and Patrick J. Haney (eds), *Foreign Policy Analysis: Continuity and Change in Its Second Generation*. Englewood Cliffs: Prentice Hall.

Neufeld, Mark (1993) 'Reflexivity and International Theory', *Millennium: Journal of International Studies*, 22: 53–76.

Neumann, Iver (1998) *Uses of the Other: The 'East' in European Identity Formation*. Minneapolis: University of Minnesota Press.

Onuf, Nicholas (1989) *World of Our Making*. Columbia: University of South Carolina Press.

Oye, Kenneth (ed.) (1985) *Cooperation Under Anarchy*. Princeton: Princeton University Press.

Paige, Glenn D. (1968) *The Korean Decision*. New York: The Free Press.

Patomäki, Heikki (1996) 'How to Tell Better Stories about World Politics', *European Journal of International Relations*, 2: 105–33.

Peterson, V. Spike (ed.) (1992) *Gendered States*. Boulder: Lynne Rienner.

Price, Richard and Tannenwald, Nina (1996) 'Norms and Deterrence: The Nuclear and Chemical Weapons Taboo', in Peter J. Katzenstein (ed.), *The Culture of National Security: Norms and Identity in World Politics*. New York: Columbia University Press.

Renshon, S.A. and Larson, Deborah W. (eds) (2001) *Good Judgement in Foreign Policy*. Lanham, MD: Rowman and Littlefield.

Reus-Smit, Christian (1999) *The Moral Purpose of the State: Culture, Social Identity, and Institutional Rationality in International Relations Theory*. Princeton: Princeton University Press.

Rhodes, Edward (1994) 'Do Bureaucratic Politics Matter? Some Disconfirming Findings from the Case of the US Navy', *World Politics*, 47: 1–41.

Ripley, Brian (1995) 'Cognition, Culture, and Bureaucratic Politics', in Laura Neack, Jeanne A.K. Hey and Patrick J. Haney (eds), *Foreign Policy Analysis: Continuity and Change in Its Second Generation*. Englewood Cliffs: Prentice Hall.

Risse, Thomas (1997) 'The Cold War's Endgame and German Unification', *International Security*, 21: 159–85.

Risse, Thomas (2000) '"Let's Argue!": Communicative Action in World Politics', *International Organization*, 54: 1–39.

Risse, Thomas, Ropp, Steven and Sikkink, Kathryn (eds) (1999) *The Power of Principles: International Human Rights Norms and Domestic Change*. Cambridge: Cambridge University Press.

Risse-Kappen, Thomas (1991) 'Public Opinion, Domestic Structures, and Foreign Policy in Liberal Democracies', *World Politics*, 43: 479–512.

Risse-Kappen, Thomas (1994) 'Ideas Do Not Float Freely: Transnational Coalitions, Domestic Structures, and the End of the Cold War', *International Organization*, 48: 185–214.

Risse-Kappen, Thomas (ed.) (1995a) *Bringing Transnational Relations Back In: Non-State Actors, Domestic Structures, and International Institutions*. Cambridge: Cambridge University Press.

Risse-Kappen, Thomas (1995b) *Cooperation among Democracies: The European Influence on US Foreign Policy*. Princeton: Princeton University Press.

Rosati, Jerel (1987) *The Carter Administration's Quest for Global Community: Beliefs and Their Impact on Behavior*. Columbia: University of South Carolina Press.

Rosati, Jerel A. (1995) 'A Cognitive Approach to the Study of Foreign Policy', in Laura Neack, Jeanne A.K. Hey and Patrick J. Haney (eds), *Foreign Policy Analysis: Continuity and Change in Its Second Generation*. Englewood Cliffs: Prentice Hall.

Rosati, Jerel A. (2000) 'The Power of Human Cognition in the Study of World Politics', *International Studies Review*, 2: 45–75.

Rosati, Jerel, Hagan, Joe D. and Sampson, Martin W. (eds) (1994) *Foreign Policy Restructuring: How Governments Respond to Global Change*. Columbia, SC: University of South Carolina Press.

Rose, Gideon (1998) 'Neoclassical Realism and Theories of Foreign Policy', *World Politics*, 51: 144–72.

Rosenau, James N. (ed.) (1969) *Linkage Politics: Essays on the Convergence of National and International Politics*. New York: Free Press.

Ruggie, John Gerard (1998) *Constructing the World Polity*. London: Routledge.

Rummel, Rudolph J. (1972) *The Dimensions of Nations*. Beverly Hills: Sage.

Russett, Bruce (1993) *Grasping the Democratic Peace: Principles for a Post-Post-Cold War World*. Princeton: Princeton University Press.

Scharpf, Fritz W. (1997) *Games Real Actors Play: Actor-Centered Institutionalism in Policy Research*. Boulder: Westview.

Schneider, Gerald (1997) 'Die bürokratische Politik der Aussenpolitikanalyse: Das Erbe Allisons im Licht der gegenwärtigen Forschungspraxis', *Zeitschrift für Internationale Beziehungen*, 4: 107–23.

Schweller, Randall L. (1996) 'Neorealism's Status Quo Bias: What Security Dilemma?', *Security Studies*, 5: 90–121.

Schweller, Randall L. (1998) *Deadly Imbalance: Tripolarity and Hitler's Strategy of World Conquest*. New York: Columbia University Press.

Singer, Eric G. and Hudson, Valerie M. (eds) (1992) *Political Psychology and Foreign Policy*. Boulder: Wesview Press.

Smith, Steve (1986) 'Theories of Foreign Policy: An Historical Overview', *Review of International Studies*, 12: 13–29.

Smith, Steve (1987) 'CFP: A Theoretical Critique', *International Studies Notes*, 13: 47–8.

Snyder, Jack (1991) *Myths of Empire: Domestic Politics and International Ambition*. Ithaca: Cornell University Press.

Snyder, Richard C., Bruck, H.W. and Sapin, B. (1954) 'Decision-Making as an Approach to the Study of International Politics', *Foreign Policy Analysis Project Series No. 3*. Princeton: Princeton University Press.

Snyder, Richard C., Bruck, H.W. and Sapin, B. (eds) (1962) *Foreign Policy Decision Making: An Approach to the Study of International Politics*. New York: Free Press.

Steinbruner, John D. (1974) *The Cybernetic Theory of Decision*. Princeton: Princeton University Press.

Stern, Eric and Verbeek, Bertjan (1998) 'Whither the Study of Governmental Politics in Foreign Policy-making? A Symposium', *Mershon International Studies Review*, 42: 205–55.

Suganami, Hidemi (1999) 'Agents, Structures, Narratives', *European Journal of International Relations*, 5: 365–86.

Sylvan, Donald A. and Voss, James F. (eds) (1998) *Problem Representation in Foreign Policy Decision Making*. Cambridge: Cambridge University Press.

Sylvester, Christine (1994) *Feminist Theory and International Relations in a Postmodern Era*. Cambridge: Cambridge University Press.

Tetlock, Philip E. (1979) 'Identifying Victims of Groupthink from Public Statements of Decision Makers', *Journal of Personality and Social Psychology*, 37: 1314–24.

Tickner, J. Ann (1993) *Gender in International Relations*. New York: Columbia University Press.

Van Evera, Stephen (1990/91) 'Primed for Peace: Europe After the Cold War', *International Security*, 15: 7–57.

Vasquez, John (1983) *The Power of Power Politics: A Critique*. New Brunswick: Rutgers University Press.

Vertzberger, Yaacov Y.I. (1990) *The World in Their Minds: Information Processing, Cognition, and Perception in Foreign Policy Decisionmaking*. Stanford: Stanford University Press.

Waever, Ole (1995) 'Securitization and Desecuritization', in Ronnie Lipschutz (ed.), *On Security*. New York: Columbia University Press.

Waever, Ole (1998) 'Explaining Europe by Decoding Discourses', in Anders Wivel (ed.), *Explaining European Integration*. Copenhagen: Copenhagen Political Studies Press.

Walker, R.B.J. (1993) *Inside/Outside: International Relations as Political Theory*. Cambridge: Cambridge University Press.

Walker, Stephen G. (1990) 'The Evolution of Operational Code Analysis', *Political Psychology*, 11: 403–17.

Walker, Stephen G. (1995) 'Psychodynamic Processes and Framing Effects in Foreign Policy Decision-Making: Woodrow Wilson's Operational Code', *Political Psychology*, 16: 697–717.

Walker, Stephen G., Schafer, Mark and Young, Michael D. (1998) 'Operational Codes and Role Identities: Measuring and Modeling Jimmy Carter's Operational Code', *International Studies Quarterly*, 42: 173–88.

Walt, Stephen M. (1995) 'Alliance Formation and the Balance of World Power', in Michael E. Brown, Sean M. Lynn-Jones and Steven E. Miller (eds), *The Perils of Anarchy: Contemporary Realism and International Security*.

Waltz, Kenneth (1979) *Theory of International Politics*. Reading, MA: Addison–Wesley.

Waltz, Kenneth N. (1996) 'International Politics is not Foreign Policy', *Security Studies*, 6: 54–7.

Weber, Cynthia (1995) *Simulating Sovereignty: Intervention, the State and Symbolic Exchange*. Cambridge: Cambridge University Press.

Welch, David A. (1998) 'A Positive Science of Bureaucratic Politics?', *Mershon International Studies Review*, 42: 210–16.

Weldes, Jutta (1999) *Constructing International Interests*. Minneapolis: University of Minnesota Press.

Weldes, Jutta and Saco, Diana (1996) 'Making State Action Possible: The United States and the Discursive Construction of "The Cuban Problem", 1960–1994', *Millennium*, 25: 361–98.

Wendt, Alexander (1987) 'The Agency–Structure Problem in International Relations', *International Organization*, 41: 335–70.

Wendt, Alexander (1999) *Social Theory of International Politics*. Cambridge: Cambridge University Press.

White, Brian (1999) 'The European Challenge to Foreign Policy Analysis', *European Journal of International Relations*, 5: 37–66.

White, Brian (2001) *Understanding European Foreign Policy*. London: Palgrave.

Wight, Colin (1999) 'They Shoot Horses Don't They? Locating Agency in the Agent–Structure Problematique', *European Journal of International Relations*, 5: 109–42.

Wilkenfeld, Jonathan, Hopple, Gerald W., Rossa, Paul J. and Andriole, Stephen J. (1980) *Foreign Policy Behavior: The Interstate Behavior Analysis Model*. Beverly Hills: Sage.

Wohlforth, William (1993) *The Elusive Balance: Power and Perceptions during the Cold War*. Ithaca: Cornell University Press.

Yee, Albert S. (1996) 'The Causal Effect of Ideas on Politics', *International Organization*, 50: 69–108.

Young, Michael D. (1996) 'Cognitive Mapping Meets Semantic Networks', *Journal of Conflict Resolution*, 40: 395–414.

Young, Michael D. and Shafer, Mark (1998) 'Is There Method in Our Madness? Ways of Assessing Cognition in International Relations', *Mershon International Studies Review*, 42: 63–96.

Zakaria, Fareed (1995) 'Realism and Domestic Politics: A Review Essay', in Michael E. Brown, Sean M. Lynn-Jones and Steven E. Miller (eds), *The Perils of Anarchy: Contemporary Realism and International Security*. Cambridge, MA: MIT Press.

Zakaria, Faheed (1998) *From Wealth to Power: The Unusual Origins of America's World Role*. Princeton: Princeton University Press.

Zelikow, Philip and Rice, Condoleezza (1995) *Germany Unified and Europe Transformed*. Cambridge, MA: Harvard University Press.

18

War and Peace

JACK S. LEVY

Ever since Thucydides's account of the Peloponnesian War over 2,400 years ago (Strassler, 1996), scholars from a wide range of disciplines have studied war in the hope of facilitating efforts to prevent its occurrence, reduce its frequency, or mitigate its consequences. Political science is absolutely central to this task. Clausewitz's ([1832] 1976) influential conceptualization of war as a 'continuation of politics by other means', an instrument to advance political interests, suggests that war is intrinsically *political*, so that if we want to understand war we must understand why decision-makers choose military force rather than other means to achieve their desired ends.

The study of war in political science varies enormously in theoretical orientation, methodological approach, ontological assumptions and empirical domain, and there is now greater diversity in the study of war and in the international relations field as a whole than at any time in recent memory. The old 'great debate' between realists and liberals continues, but scholars have increasingly recognized significant variations within each contending paradigm, and new debates have arisen among rational choice theorists, constructivists and critical theorists. Scholars continue to use the influential levels-of-analysis framework (Singer, 1961) that emerged from Waltz's (1959) three 'images' of international politics, but they have shifted from asking which level has the greatest causal impact to constructing multi-level theories and examining the interaction effects between variables at different levels. International relations scholars have also engaged in increasingly productive dialogues with economists, sociologists, psychologists and diplomatic historians (Elman and Elman, 2001). Finally, there has been a growing interest in the conditions of

peace as well as the causes of war, and a growing belief that the study of war and the study of peace are inseparable.

In some respects all of these efforts have yielded little tangible progress. We have few law-like propositions, limited predictive capacities and no consensus as to what the causes of war are, what theories and what methodologies are most useful for identifying and validating those causes, what criteria are appropriate for evaluating competing theories, and whether it is possible to generalize about anything as complex and context-dependent as war. In other respects, however, we have made enormous progress. The field of international relations (and the sub-field of peace, war and security studies) is more rigorous in its theorizing, more sophisticated in the use of statistical methods, more theoretically and methodologically self-conscious in the use of qualitative methods, more willing to utilize multi-method research designs, and more willing to think critically about the meta-theoretical assumptions underlying theoretical and empirical research. A social science orientation is more entrenched than ever in the field, but the conception of social science has broadened. Those in the broad 'mainstream' engage in meta-theoretical debates with each other as well as with critical theorists about the logic of inference (King et al., 1994), the meaning of causality (Nicholson, 1996; Braumoeller and Goertz, 2000), the proper relationship between theory and evidence (Lichbach and Lebow, 2001), and the criteria for evaluating scientific progress (Elman and Elman, 2002). While some meta-theoretical discussions only paralyze theoretical and empirical research, these debates have enriched it.

I begin by examining some general trends in the study of war and peace. I then distinguish among three different things that we want to explain: the constant recurrence of war, variations in war and peace, and the origins of particular wars. I argue that these different questions or perspectives on war lead to different theoretical frameworks and different methodologies. I then examine some leading realist and liberal theories of the causes of war and conditions of peace, and conclude by emphasizing the utility of multi-method research programs.

Any essay of this kind must be selective. Given other reviews in the literature (Levy, 1989; Vasquez, 1993, 2000; Cashman, 1993; Doyle, 1997; Midlarsky, 2000), and given the division of labor in this volume, I focus in some detail on leading realist and liberal theories of the causes of war and the conditions for peace rather than attempting to cover the entire field. The most notable exclusions from this chapter are intra-state and ethnonational wars, cognitive and psychological models, and feminist approaches, which are discussed in the chapters by Lars-Erik Cederman, Janice Stein and J. Ann Tickner, respectively, and an important new class of rationalist bargaining models, which are discussed in the chapter by Lilach Gilady and Bruce Russett. I make only brief references to constructivist approaches (Giddens, 1979; Katzenstein, 1996; Wendt, 1999), which are discussed in Part One of this volume.

GENERAL TRENDS IN WAR AND IN THE STUDY OF WAR

International relations scholars generally define war as large-scale organized violence between politically defined groups (Bull, 1977: 184; Vasquez, 1993: 21–9). War has been a recurring and persistent pattern of behavior among peoples since the beginning of recorded history, but it has also varied enormously in its frequency and seriousness over time and space. The past five centuries of the modern system have witnessed an average of one great power war per decade, but the frequency of great power wars has declined significantly over time (Levy, 1983).[1] We have experienced only three such wars in the twentieth century and arguably none in the period since the Second World War[2] and this constitutes the longest period of great power peace in 500 years. For many centuries war was disproportionately concentrated in the hands of the great powers in Europe (Wright, 1965) but the twentieth century, and the second half-century in particular, marked a significant shift in warfare from the major powers to minor powers, from Europe to other regions, and from inter-state warfare to intra-state wars (Levy et al., 2001).

The steady decline in the frequency of great power war has been accompanied by a steady increase in the severity of war (generally defined in terms of the number of battle-related deaths, either in absolute terms or relative to population). The rising severity of war is evidenced by the enormous destructiveness of the two world wars of the twentieth century, and, more generally, by the increasing severity of 'general' or 'hegemonic' wars, which have occurred at least once or twice a century since 1500 (Thompson, 1988; Levy, 1989). Inter-state wars have demonstrated no significant secular trend over the past century, while civil wars have increased in frequency. Vivid media images of ethnonational conflicts may have led to the impression that the severity of civil wars has continued to increase in the past half century or even in the past ten years, but deaths from civil wars have actually been declining since the Second World War and even since the end of the Cold War (Holsti, 1996; Wallensteen and Sollenberg, 1999; Marshall, 1999; Gurr, 2000).

The changing nature of warfare over the past century, and over the last two decades of that century in particular (Keegan, 1984; Bond, 1986; Van Creveld, 1991) has, along with new analytic developments, led to important changes in the way international relations scholars have approached the study of war. The nuclear revolution led to the analyses of the conditions for strategic stability and of the hypothesized obsolescence of war (Schelling, 1966; Jervis, 1989; Mueller, 1989; Mandelbaum, 1998–9), and the information revolution has led to discussions of the 'revolution in military affairs' (Biddle, 1998; Freedman, 1998). Political changes have been equally important. The end of the Cold War, the collapse of the Soviet Union, and the rise of ethnonational conflicts have contributed to a shift in focus away from a longstanding emphasis on the behavior of the great powers and on inter-state wars more generally,[3] and toward intra-state wars.

We have also witnessed a shift from a nearexclusive focus on the causes of war to a greater interest in the termination of war (King, 1997; Goemans, 2000). The analysis of the termination of war is now closely linked to analyses of the relationship between war and conditions for statebuilding and democratization (Zartman, 1995; Licklider, 1998), which has some parallels in the study of the role of war in state-building in early modern Europe (Mann, 1986; Tilly, 1990). This is related to the more general question of the conditions under which peace settlements are most likely to persist. Conflict theorists have traditionally defined peace as the absence of war (or perhaps the absence of militarized disputes) and have focused more on explaining war than explaining peace. Theorists have recently begun to give more attention to the conditions for peace (Wallensteen, 1984; Holsti, 1991; Vasquez, 1993: ch. 8), and some have begun to distinguish between peace and stable peace, or between cold peace and warm peace (Kacowitz and Bar-Siman-Tov, 2000; Miller, 2000).

The rise of regional and ethnonational wars has also contributed to increasing attention to the impact of domestic variables, long neglected by a field that has focused primarily on the role of structural systemic sources of conflict (Waltz, 1979) and secondarily on individual-level beliefs and misperceptions (Jervis, 1976; George, 1979; Holsti, 1989) and on bureaucratic/organizational factors (Allison and Zelikow, 1999).[4] The new emphasis on domestic sources of conflict includes a variety of research programs, ranging from the democratic peace, diversionary theory, cultural approaches and signaling theories based on variations in the credibility of commitments across different regime types and institutional arrangements. There has also been a shift in the level (or unit) of phenomenon to be explained, as evidenced by the diminished attention to systemic patterns and greater attention to dyadic-level behavior. This shift derives in part from the explanatory power of the dyadic-level democratic peace hypothesis and the hope that its success could be duplicated elsewhere, the growing interest in international rivalries (Thompson, 1999; Diehl and Goertz, 2000) and from the emphasis on bargaining in rational choice theory (Fearon, 1995; Powell, 1999; Wagner, 2000).

The spread of ethnonational conflicts has also led to serious reconsideration of the best way to define and operationalize war. Traditional conceptualizations of warfare are grounded in Clausewitz's ([1832] 1976) emphasis on states and their organized armies, assume a sharp distinction between international and intranational conflict, and generally operationalize war in terms of a minimum threshold of 1,000 battle-deaths severity (Singer and Small, 1972). This conceptualization works well for most inter-state wars, but much less so for many contemporary conflicts, whether they be 'low-intensity conflicts' or 'identity wars' between communal groups. The recognition of this conceptual problem has led to the generation of several new data sets designed to better capture the new forms of armed conflict (Marshall, 1999; Wallensteen and Sollenberg, 1999; Gurr, 2000).

THREE PERSPECTIVES ON WAR

The earlier summary of patterns of warfare over time suggests two ways of looking at war. In one sense war has been a constant – a persistent, pervasive and recurring pattern of violent conflict between peoples since the beginning of recorded history. Some war is going on somewhere almost all of the time, particularly if we include internal as well as external wars. At the same time, however, war has varied enormously in terms of its frequency, severity, location, participants, and social and political consequences. Some scholars

focus on the first theme and treat war as a non-zero *constant* in international politics, while others treat war as a *variable*. Still others focus neither on the general phenomenon of war nor variations in wars but instead on *particular wars*.[5]

These three perspectives on the question of what causes war are clearly related, yet they generate fundamental differences in the kinds of methodologies, research designs, conceptions of causation and more general epistemological orientations that scholars bring to bear on the question of what causes war. Explanations for war as a constant (based on 'human nature' or international anarchy, for example) cannot explain either variations in war and peace or the outbreak of particular wars; explanations for particular wars cannot be generalized to explanations for variations in war and peace without empirical tests of those generalizations against a broader empirical domain; and the idea of using explanations for variations in war and peace to explain individual wars – by subsuming explanations for particular events under 'covering laws' (Hempel, 1942) – is something that most historians reject (Dray, 1957).

While political scientists give some attention to each of these questions, the most influential work in the discipline focuses on the second question, explaining variations in war and peace. This orientation is more pronounced in the United States, where positivistic social science is most dominant, than in Europe or elsewhere (Hill, 1985; Waever, 1998). True, many political scientists focus on explaining particular wars, not only as a vehicle for constructing or testing more general propositions about war, but sometimes also for the primary purpose of understanding those wars as an end in itself, as illustrated by studies of the First World War or the Cold War. Many of these studies – especially those that use well-developed theoretical frameworks to guide historical case studies – have made important contributions to our understanding of individual wars or rivalries. Given prevailing social science norms and current reward structures in the discipline, however, this is not the kind of work that has the greatest impact on the study of international relations, at least in the United States (Levy, 2001).

REALIST THEORIES OF WAR

The realist tradition has long dominated the study of war, and includes intellectual descendants of Machiavelli, Hobbes and Rousseau (Doyle, 1997).[6] All share a common set of assumptions: the key actors in world politics are sovereign states who act rationally to advance their security, power and wealth in an anarchic international system, defined as the absence of a legitimate governmental authority to regulate disputes and enforce agreements between states or other actors. Given uncertainties regarding the current and future intentions of the adversary, political leaders focus on short-term security needs, adopt worst-case thinking, engage in a struggle for power and security, and utilize coercive threats to advance their interests, influence the adversary and maintain their reputations.[7]

Following Waltz's (1979) development of neorealism (or structural realism), most contemporary realists begin with the proposition that international anarchy is an important permissive condition for war. For Rousseau and other system-level theorists, 'wars occur because there is nothing to prevent them' (Waltz, 1959: 232). While realist arguments based on anarchy provide an important alternative to explanations for the recurrence of war based on human nature, anarchy is generally treated as a structural constant (except for rare instances of non-anarchic systems such as the Roman Empire) and consequently it cannot account for variations in war and peace (Milner, 1991). Waltz recognizes this and concedes that 'Rousseau's analysis explains the recurrence of war without explaining any particular war' (1959: 232), and that 'although neorealist theory does not explain why particular wars are fought, it does explain war's dismal recurrence through the millennia' (1988: 620).[8] Ironically, then, Waltz's (1959) compelling critique of 'first image' theories on the grounds that one cannot explain a variable with a constant applies to the neorealist focus on anarchy as well.

If constants (or variables with limited variation) cannot explain variations in war and peace, can they explain the constant recurrence of war? The problem here is that it is not clear how to empirically test explanations of the constant recurrence of war (whether based on anarchy, human nature, or perhaps the patriarchal and gendered nature of all human societies) or to adjudicate among competing theories. If a permissive condition allows war to happen but does not make war happen, then whether wars occur or not, or the frequency with which they occur, has no bearing on the validity of the theoretical argument.[9] In addition, because there can be more than one necessary condition for an outcome, and because there is no logical basis for preferring one necessary condition over another, it is difficult to assess the relative validity of contending explanations for the recurrence of war unless they generate additional testable implications besides the recurrence of war. This suggests that for a theory of the recurrence of war to be meaningful and useful, it would have to generate a series of implications or predictions about variations in war and peace.

In an important sense, this is what realist theory has done. Anarchy is not a causal variable but instead an analytical primitive or point of departure, from which a theoretical system is constructed and hypotheses are generated. It is these hypotheses, not anarchy, that carry the explanatory power in neorealism, and what they attempt to explain is not 'war's dismal recurrence through the millennia', but the conditions under which war is most likely to occur.

The core realist proposition is that variations in the distribution of power, and polarity in particular, help to explain variations in the frequency of war and other important aspects of international behavior (Waltz, 1988: 620). As many critics have argued, however, the distribution of power alone does not explain enough of the variance in war and peace across time and space, much less broader changes in international systems, and in this sense war is underdetermined in neorealist theory (Keohane, 1986; Ruggie, 1998).

Realists have increasingly come to acknowledge this limitation, and have begun to incorporate other variables – including the offensive – defensive balance (Lynn-Jones, 1995; Van Evera, 1999) and even domestic institutional and cultural variables (Van Evera, 1990; Snyder, 1991) – in an attempt to explain more of the variation in international conflict. Whether these additional variables explain enough variation for realism to constitute an empirically adequate theory, and whether the addition of domestic variables is consistent with the 'hard core' assumptions of the realist research program, thus constituting a 'theoretically progressive problem shift' (Lakatos, 1970), are subjects of ongoing debate (Vasquez and Elman, 2002).

Paths to War in Realist Theory

Realists often distinguish between status quo and revisionist states and use this distinction as the basis for identifying two alternative paths to war. One path involves a direct conflict of interests between two states and calculations by at least one side that this conflict is better resolved by war than by peace. Ancient imperial conquests like those of Alexander, or more modern cases of aggression by Hitler's Germany in the Second World War and Saddam's Iraq in 1990, come immediately to mind, though each of these cases is usually more complex than first appears.

A second path to war involves two or more security-seeking states, each of whom is more interested in maintaining its current position than in extending its influence. The explanation of the conditions and processes through which such security-seeking states can still end up in war is a distinctive contribution of realist theory. Because the absence of a higher authority requires states to depend on their own actions (or perhaps those of allies) for their security, because of the uncertainty regarding the present and future intentions of other states, and because of the dire consequences of the failure to be prepared for possible predatory actions of others, certain actions (armaments, alliances, ~~ireats~~, etc.) to protect themselves against ~~l~~ future threats. Because of the inherent regarding the intentions underlying the actions of others, the offensive as well as defensive potential of most weapons systems, and the tendency toward worst case analysis in the context of extreme uncertainty, even defensively motivated actions are perceived as threats to the security of others (the 'security dilemma'). The threatened state responds with measures to protect itself, these are perceived as threatening by the other, and the ensuing action–reaction cycle often leads to conflict spirals that can escalate to war (Jervis, 1978; Glaser, 1997).

Realists debate how compelling anarchic structures and the security dilemma actually are, or how often status quo states without expansionist motivations get locked in conflict spirals that end up in war. 'Offensive realists' argue that the international system is so hostile and unforgiving that uncertainty about the future intentions of the adversary combined with extreme worst-case analysis lead states to adopt offensive strategies, which often lead to war (Mearsheimer, 1990, 2001; Zakaria, 1992; Labs, 1997). 'Defensive realists', on the other hand, argue that security is not as scarce as offensive realists suggest, that international anarchy does not in itself force states into conflict and war, and that moderate behavior and defensive strategies work to provide security. If states behave aggressively, it is not because of systemic pressures but instead because of domestic pressures and pathologies. Defensive realists argue that war will not arise in a world of purely security-seeking states in the absence of domestically induced revisionist goals or extreme misperceptions of external threats (Snyder, 1991; Schweller, 1996; Glaser, 1997; Van Evera, 1999).

One possible causal mechanism in the 'pure security' path to war involves a 'pre-emptive strike' by a state motivated only by the fear that its adversary is about to attack and by the belief that if war is inevitable it is better to initiate it. Reiter (1995) makes a persuasive case that such wars rarely happen, and identifies only the First World War and the 1967 Arab–Israeli War as cases of preemptive wars. The First World War has traditionally been interpreted as one that leaders did not seek but that was the inadvertent result of a combination of blunders, misperceptions, miscalculations and overreactions that spiraled out of control (Tuchman, 1962), but an important line of argument suggests that Germany did in fact seek war in 1914, just not a world war involving British intervention (Fischer, 1975; Levy, 1990/1; Van Evera, 1999).[10]

The hypothesis of a German preference for some kind of war in 1914, even a war against Russia and France, if true, would not settle the question of predation versus security fears, or revisionist versus status quo motivations. If a state faces a rising adversary, anticipates a 'power transition' and initiates a 'preventive war' to maintain the status quo (a standard interpretation of Germany in 1914, given the rising power of Russia), or if it initiates war to recover territory lost in a previous war and re-establish the earlier status quo, is this predation or security-seeking? Thus the analytical distinction between predation and security-seeking is not always clear, and in fact the two can mutually reinforce each other. As Snyder and Jervis (1999: 21) argue, 'the security dilemma gives rise to predators, and predation intensifies the security dilemma'.

A pure 'preventive war' – one motivated only by the anticipation of a negative power shift and the fear of its consequences – is another path through which anarchic structures alone might induce war. Although the anticipation of negative power shifts often plays a significant role in the processes leading to war,[11] whether the combination of power shifts and uncertainty about the future is ever jointly sufficient for war, apart from more specific conflicts of interests, is open to question. The clearest case of military action induced almost exclusively by a negative power shift was Israel's 1981 attack against the Iraqi nuclear reactor. Even here, however, if Peres rather than Begin had been in power, or if Egypt rather than Iraq was building a nuclear reactor, it is unlikely that Israel would have responded militarily (Perlmutter, 1982: 35; Levy and Gochal, 2000). As Kydd (1997: 48) argues, 'preventive wars sparked by fears about the future motivations of currently benign states almost never happen'. The preventive motivation leads to war only in conjunction with existing hostilities or conflicts of interest, and most wars involve some combination of security-seeking and predatory motivations.[12]

Balance of Power and Hegemonic Realism

Another important but underemphasized debate within realist theory is between 'balance of power realism' and 'hegemonic realism' (Levy, 1994). Balance of power approaches include both classical theories as reformulated by Morgenthau (1948), Gulick (1955), Claude (1962) and Aron (1973), and the more systematic structural realism of Waltz (1979). Hegemonic realism includes power transition theories, hegemonic stability theory (Gilpin, 1981; Keohane, 1984), and long cycle theories (Thompson, 1988; Rasler and Thompson, 1994).

Balance of power theories posit that the avoidance of hegemony is the primary goal of states (or at least of the great powers) and that the maintenance of an equilibrium of power in the system is an essential means to that end. The theory predicts that states, and particularly great powers, will build up their arms and form alliances to balance against those who constitute the primary threats to their interests and particularly against any state which threatens to secure a hegemonic position over the system.[13] Balance of power theorists argue that the balancing mechanism almost always works successfully to avoid hegemony, either because potential hegemons are deterred by their anticipation of a military coalition forming against them or because they are defeated in war after deterrence fails.

Hegemonic theories share realist assumptions but de-emphasize the importance of anarchy while emphasizing system management within a hierarchical order. The most influential hegemonic theory is power transition theory (Organski and Kugler, 1980; Kugler and Lemke, 1996). Hegemons commonly arise and use their strength to create a set of political and economic structures and norms of behavior that enhances the stability of the system at the same time that it advances their own security. Differential rates of growth lead to the rise and fall of hegemons (Organski and Kugler, 1980; Gilpin, 1981; Kennedy, 1987), and the probability of a major war is greatest at the point when the declining leader is being overtaken by the rising challenger. Either the challenger initiates a war to bring its benefits from the system into line with its rising military power, or the declining leader initiates a preventive war to block the rising challenger while the opportunity is still available.

Because balance of power theory posits that concentrations of power are destabilizing and that hegemony never occurs, while power transition theory posits that hegemony frequently occurs and is stabilizing, the two appear to be diametrically opposed. Indeed, power transition theory grew directly out of Organski's critique of balance of power theory (Organski and Kugler, 1980).[14] What is rarely recognized, however, is that most applications of the two theories define key concepts differently. Most balance of power theories have a strong Eurocentric bias and implicitly conceive of power in terms of land-based military power and of hegemony in terms of hegemony over Europe. They predict balancing coalitions against threats of European hegemony (the Habsburgs under Charles V, France under Louis XIV and then Napoleon, Germany under Wilhelm and then Hitler). They do not necessarily predict balancing against rich naval powers that have small armies and that are geographically separated from the European continent (nineteenth-century Britain or the twentieth/twenty-first-century United States), which pose little direct threat to the territorial integrity of other great powers (Levy, 1994, 2002; Mearsheimer, 2001). Most applications of hegemonic theories generally define hegemony in terms of dominance in global finance, trade and naval power, and indeed most versions of 'hegemonic stability theory' (Keohane, 1984) are theories of the stability of the international political economy and say little about war and peace.

Given these different conceptions of the nature of the system and of the basis of power in the system, it is possible that both theories are correct. It is conceivable, for example, that the European system has been most stable under an equilibrium of military power and that hegemonies rarely if ever form, whereas the global system is most stable in the presence of a single dominant economic and naval power (which occurs frequently). These two systems interact, of course, but exactly how they interact has been undertheorized. The most destabilizing situation would be one characterized by the combination of the diffusion of global power (and particularly an impending global power transition) with the increasing concentration of power in Europe (Rasler and Thompson, 1994). In fact, many of history's 'hegemonic wars' fit this pattern: the two world wars of this century, the French Revolutionary and Napoleonic wars (1792–1815), and the wars of Louis XIV (1672–1713) – the first two pairs following the decline of Britain's global dominance and the third following the decline of Dutch global economic supremacy. Although scholarship has been shifting away from systemic-level analyses, studies of the interaction of the global system with the dominant continental system – and of other nested systems as well – is a particularly fruitful area for further research.

LIBERAL THEORIES OF WAR AND PEACE

Liberals have always questioned the realist perspective on international politics and argued that under certain domestic and international conditions and with appropriate state strategies the violent-prone character of world politics can be ameliorated and levels of warfare significantly reduced. Although the liberal theory of the international political economy is fairly well-developed, until recently there was no coherent liberal theory of peace and war. With the development of the democratic peace research program, renewed interest in the hypothesis that economic interdependence promotes peace, the development of a theory of international institutions, and preliminary attempts to combine these into a single integrated theory, we now have the outlines of a liberal *theory* of peace and war. For some (Russett and Oneal, 2001) this represents the systematization and empirical testing of Kant's ([1795] 1949) conception of perpetual peace based on democratic institutions, free trade, and international law and institutions.

Here I focus on the hypotheses that economic interdependence and democratic institutions each promotes peace. I leave aside theories of the peaceful effects of law and institutions. Institutionalists have constructed theories about the effects of international law and institutions on cooperation between states, particularly in the international political economy and on environmental issues (Keohane, 1984; Archibugi, 1995; Keohane and Martin, 2002; see also Chapters 10 and 28 in this volume). They have also applied institutionalist approaches to collective security systems (Kupchan and Kupchan, 1991), regional security communities (Deutsch et al., 1957) and alliances (Haftendorn et al., 1999). Some have taken a constructivist approach to the study of institutions, alliances and security communities and emphasized the role of norms and collective identity (Schroeder, 1994; Risse-Kappen, 1996; Adler and Barnett, 1998). But analyses of the impact of institutions on war and peace are still in an early stage of development, raise important analytic and historical questions, and have yet to be empirically tested (Betts, 1992; Mearsheimer, 1994/5; Keohane and Martin, 1995).

Economic Interdependence and Peace

The idea that trade and other forms of economic interdependence promote peace was a central theme in nineteenth-century liberal economic theory, and was expressed most famously by Norman Angell when he argued in *The Great Illusion* (1912) that the economic costs of a great power war would be so devastating that such a war was unthinkable. Angell's argument was discredited within two years by a very thinkable world war, but was resurrected after the Second World War as a cornerstone of American liberal internationalist ideology. It is now the basis for optimistic (but qualified) forecasts about the beneficial effects of globalization on international security (Friedman, 1999).

Liberal theorists advance a number of inter-related theoretical arguments in support of this proposition, but the greatest emphasis is on the economic deterrence argument: because trade generates economic benefits for both parties, the anticipation that war will disrupt trade and lead to a loss or reduction of the gains from trade deters political leaders from taking actions that are likely to lead to war against key trading partners (Polachek, 1980; Oneal and Russett, 1999).

Liberals also advance domestic-level causal arguments in support of the trade-promotes-peace hypothesis (Veblen, [1915] 1966; Schumpeter, [1919] 1951; Aron, 1958). Trade increases prosperity, and prosperity lessens the domestic problems that sometimes lead to war, either through external scapegoating by élites to solidify their domestic political support, or through pressures for protectionism that can lead to countermeasures, increase hostilities and trigger conflict spirals. As Wilson (1978: 150) argues, 'economic depression [is] particularly favorable to war hysteria'. Prosperity can also generate a culture of acquisitiveness that dampens the martial spirit and diverts resources away from the military sector, as reflected in the view of the nineteenth century that 'Men were too busy growing rich to have time for war' (Blainey, 1988: 10).[15]

Some researchers argue that trade alters the domestic balance of power within states by increasing the influence of groups who benefit from trade and who have a vested interest in maintaining a peaceful environment for trade (Rogowski, 1989), and others suggest, from a sociological perspective, that trade increases contact, communication, familiarity and understanding, which in turn reduce the hostilities and misperceptions that contribute to war (Deutsch et al., 1957). Finally, some argue that while trade promotes peace, the link is indirect: trade promotes prosperity, prosperity promotes democracy and democracy promotes peace (Weede, 1995).

The commercial liberal hypothesis suffers from a number of analytic problems. The argument that leaders' fears of the economic costs of war deters them from taking actions that might lead to war attempts to explain a dyadic outcome (peace) with state-level variables (foreign policy preferences) and ignores strategic interaction. It is possible that if a dispute arises between trading partners, each of whom prefers peace, both will refrain from belligerent actions in order to preserve the benefits of trade. It is also possible that one side might interpret the other's conciliatory actions as a lack of resolve and lead it to believe that it can exploit the adversary's fear of war by standing firm and thereby improving its own strategic or economic position. In the absence of additional information about expectations regarding the economic benefits of trade, the impact of war on trade and each side's risk orientation and domestic sensitivity to those costs, the outcome – and hence the impact of economic interdependence on peace within a dyad – is theoretically indeterminate (Morrow, 1999; Gartzke et al., 2001). The neglect of the impact of inter-state bargaining is a serious deficiency of most empirical research on the trade-promotes-peace hypothesis.[16]

Strategies of coercion rather than cooperation with the trading partner are more likely if one side believes that it is more resolved than the other, whether because of differing risk orientations or perhaps different sensitivities to the domestic economic and political costs of a cutoff of trade. It is also more likely if economic interdependence is asymmetrical rather than symmetrical (Hirschman, [1945] 1980; Barbieri, 1996), in which case the least dependent state may be tempted to resort to economic coercion to exploit the adversary's vulnerabilities and influence its behavior relating to security as well as economic issues.

The potential for exploitation of the weak by the strong in a situation of asymmetrical interdependence is the basis of the argument, advanced by both realists and Marxist-Leninists, that interdependence, and particularly asymmetrical interdependence, increases rather than decreases the probability of militarized conflict. While some realists concede that symmetrical interdependence may create mutual incentives to maintain the peace (Barbieri and Schneider, 1999), even symmetrical interdependence is no guarantee of restraint if the two sides have different risk orientations and/or different sensitivities to domestic costs. Just as analysts of crisis bargaining have begun to incorporate the risk orientations and domestic cost-sensitivity of political leaders into their models (Fearon, 1995; Wagner, 2000), those who study the political economy of war and peace must do the same.

Another basis for the realist argument that trade can increase rather than decrease the likelihood of militarized conflict involves relative gains concerns. Realists argue that political leaders are less influenced by the possibility of gains from trade in an absolute sense than by the fear that the adversary will gain more from trade and convert those gains into further gains, political influence and military power (Grieco, 1990; Gowa, 1994). Realists are not always clear, however, about the precise causal mechanisms leading from relative gains to war. To the extent that relative rather than absolute gains are important, they should have a greater impact on decisions to engage in trade (particularly with adversaries) than on the likelihood of conflict once trade is under way. If states are extremely worried about a particular adversary making relative gains they will have minimal trade with that adversary, and if states are already trading with each other they have presumably already discounted relative gains concerns. If diplomatic relations between trading partners begin to deteriorate, however, relative gains concerns may lead states to cut back on trade, which may exacerbate existing tensions and contribute to a conflict spiral.

Not all realists argue that trade significantly increases the likelihood of war. Some concede that trade and other forms of economic interdependence might have pacifying effects, but argue that these effects are negligible relative to the effects of military and diplomatic considerations (Buzan, 1984; Levy, 1989: 261–2). Other realists acknowledge that periods of trade might be peaceful, but question the *causal* impact of trade on peace. They argue that the causal arrow often points in the opposite direction: it is peace that creates the conditions under which trade flourishes, as Blainey (1988) argues with respect to nineteenth-century Europe. The more general argument is that politics determines trade, or that 'trade follows the flag', rather than trade shaping politics (Pollins, 1989; Gowa, 1994).

It is also possible that the inference that trade promotes peace is spurious, because the conditions that facilitate trade simultaneously promote peace. States with common interests tend to trade with each other (Morrow et al., 1998) and also to be less inclined to fight, so the association between trade and peace may be explained in part or in full by the commonality of interests. Similarly, there is more trade between allies than between adversaries (Gowa, 1994), and allies are less likely to go to war with each other (Ray, 1990), so alliances may account for part of the association between trade and peace. Democratic dyads trade more than other pairs of states (Mansfield et al., 2000), so that studies of trade and peace must parcel out the effects of the democratic peace (Russett and Oneal, 2001). Finally, hegemonic stability theorists argue that one of the primary conditions facilitating trade is the existence of a liberal economic hegemon able and willing to maintain a stable political economy, and they strongly imply that liberal economic hegemony also promotes peace (Gilpin, 1981; Keohane, 1984), so the link between trade and peace might be spurious and explained primarily by economic hegemony.

A similar problem arises in analyses of the relative efficiency of commerce and conquest as strategies for accumulating wealth (Rosecrance, 1986). Although many formulations of the trade-promotes-peace hypothesis implicitly assume that trade is always more efficient than military coercion in expanding markets and investment opportunities and in promoting state wealth, realists are almost certainly right that this assumption is historically contingent rather than universal. Trade may be economically efficient and peace-promoting in the Western world in the contemporary era, at least for advanced industrial states, because the foundations of wealth and power have historically shifted from territory to industrialization and now to knowledge-based forms of production, and because the economic value of territorial conquest has diminished while the military and diplomatic costs of territorial conquest have significantly increased (Van Evera, 1990). In many historical eras, however, military force has been a useful instrument to promote state wealth as well as power. In the mercantilist era of the seventeenth and eighteenth centuries, for example, war was a profitable enterprise for both merchants and kings. War also increased the political influence of those merchants who benefited from war; which generated additional political support for war (Howard, 1976; Wilson, 1978).

How much causal weight to attribute to trade in this equation is a more difficult analytic question. If underlying conditions make conquest more efficient than trade as a strategy for acquiring wealth, those conditions will simultaneously decrease trade and increase the use of force, while conditions under which trade is more efficient may simultaneously and independently promote peace. If this is true, trade has no independent impact on conflict.

Whether the deterrent effects of the gains from trade outweigh the potentially destabilizing effects of economic asymmetries and economic competitions, whether the latter escalate to trade wars and militarized conflicts, and whether the magnitude of these economic effects is outweighed by strategic considerations are ultimately empirical questions that analysts have only recently begun to analyze systematically. Although there is a growing consensus that trade is associated with peace, both at the dyadic (Polachek, 1980; Oneal and Russett, 1999; Russett and Oneal, 2001) and systemic levels (Mansfield, 1994), some find that trade is associated with war (Barbieri, 1996). Because few of these studies have dealt with possible endogeneity effects and explored the simultaneous impact of trade on conflict and conflict on trade (Reuveny and Kang, 1996), because of questions regarding the sensitivity of these relationships to the precise operationalization of interdependence (Barbieri and Schneider, 1999), and because a number of prominent historical cases (the First World War, for example) appear to run counter to the liberal hypothesis (Copeland, 1996; Ripsman and Blanchard, 1996/7; Papayoanou, 1999), the current evidence in support of the liberal economic theory of peace must be treated as provisional. Further research needs to focus as much on the *conditions* under which trade promotes peace as on the aggregate relationship between trade and peace.

One important informational condition relates to the beliefs of political leaders and of key economic actors regarding the likely impact of war on trade, both in the short term and in the long term. There is ample evidence that trade often continues even after the outbreak of war (Barbieri and Levy, 1999), though the frequency of trading with the enemy, in what kinds of goods, and with what impact on the economy and the war effort has yet to be established. If leaders anticipate that war will not significantly suppress trade, their economic incentives to avoid war will be diminished. There is also a strategic dimension: for bargaining purposes leaders may have incentives to threaten to cut off trade in the event of war. Once war occurs, however, those same leaders may have incentives to allow their firms to continue to trade, either for the good of the economy as a whole or to gain the political and economic support of key domestic groups. The anticipation of this undercuts the credibility of earlier threats to cut off trade. This credibility depends on alliance ties as well as other variables (Dorussen, 1999).

Most explanations of the trade-promotes-peace hypothesis focus on the dyadic level. Scholars have overlooked the systemic context of dyadic trade in general and diplomatic alignments in particular. Trade between A and B may deter a dyadic war between A and B. If A is aligned with C and B threatens C, however, A's trade ties with B may prevent A from attempting to deter B's attack on C, which may actually increase the probability of a war between B and C. This is one causal mechanism through which high levels of economic interdependence contributed to the First World War: the British failure to make a formal commitment to join France and Russia if they were attacked by Germany was a critical factor leading to German aggression (Fischer, 1975; Levy, 1990/1), and Britain's failure to do so derived in part from her strong economic ties with Germany (Papayoanou, 1999).

This brief overview suggests the relationship between interdependence and peace is shaped by factors associated with both liberal and realist international theories. A satisfactory theory of interdependence and conflict theory must incorporate 'liberal' concerns about the opportunity costs of the loss of trade, the influence of domestic actors who have an interest in maintaining and expanding trade and the political power to influence state decisions, and the constraints imposed on firms by state structures and actions. Such a theory must also incorporate 'realist' concerns about the strategic consequences of trade at both the dyadic and systemic levels, but the theory must be sensitive to whether these considerations affect the level and kinds of trade between countries or the impact of that trade on the likelihood of war. More generally, empirical research designs must do more to reflect the complex causal linkages among trade, security and war that theorists have begun to identify. They must also give more attention to the dependent variable and distinguish between war and militarized conflict more generally. It is possible that trade ties might have a pacifying effect on war but not on militarized disputes.

The Democratic Peace

Liberals have long argued that democracies are more peaceful than are other states, but the 'democratic peace' did not become a coherent and quite visible research program in international relations until a number of studies in the mid-1980s offered systematic and compelling evidence that democracies rarely if ever go to war with each other (Ray, 1995; Doyle, 1997). Researchers then demonstrated that this empirical regularity cannot be explained by the geographic separation of democratic states, by extensive trade among democratic dyads, by the role of American hegemonic power in suppressing potential conflicts between democracies in the period since the Second World War, or by other economic or geopolitical factors correlated with democracy (Ray, 1995, 2000; Doyle, 1997; Maoz, 1997; Oneal and Russett, 1999; Russett and Starr, 2000; Russett and Oneal, 2001).[17]

Although some still argue that the hypothesized impact of democracy on peace is spurious or that causality runs from peace to democracy rather than from democracy to peace (Brown et al., 1996; Gowa, 1999), there is a growing consensus that the pacifying effects of joint democracy are real. While some say that it goes too far to claim that the absence of war between democracies 'comes as close as anything we have to an empirical law in international relations' (Levy, 1989: 270), no one has identified a stronger empirical regularity, and many make the law-like claim that joint democracy is a sufficient condition for peace (Gleditsch, 1995; Chan, 1997; Russett and Starr, 2000; Braumoeller and Goertz, 2000).

Research has uncovered other patterns involving the behavior of democratic states with respect to war and peace – though none as strong as the near absence of war between democracies. At a minimum, any explanation for the dyadic peace between democracies must not contradict these other patterns, and ideally it should explain them. Most analysts have found that, contrary to Kant, democracies are not significantly more peaceful than other kinds of states. Democracies are as likely as authoritarian states to get involved in wars; they frequently fight imperial wars; in wars between democracies and autocracies they are more likely to be the initiators than targets; and they occasionally use covert action against each other (Ray, 1995, 2000; Bennett and Stam, 1998; Russett and Oneal, 2001). In addition, democratic-authoritarian dyads are more war-prone than are pure authoritarian dyads.

Some recent research suggests than democracies may be more peaceful than authoritarian states after all (Rummel, 1995; Benoit, 1996; Ray, 2000). The differences are only modest, however, and this is unlikely to change with future research. Consequently, any explanation for the democratic peace that implies that democracies are *significantly* more peaceful than other states, in terms of the frequency of their involvement in wars or in their tendency to initiate wars, will probably not be viable.

An explanation for the democratic peace must also be consistent with evidence that democracies almost never end up on opposing sides in multilateral wars, win a disproportionate number of the wars they fight, suffer fewer casualties in the wars they initiate (Reiter and Stam, forthcoming), and engage in more peaceful processes of conflict resolution when they get into disputes with other democracies (Dixon, 1994). Although some argue that states involved in transitions to democracy are more likely to end up in war than are other states (Mansfield and Snyder, 1995), most evidence suggest that democratizing states are not more warlike (Ward and Gleditsch, 1998; Russett and Oneal, 2001) and that democracies do not fight shorter wars than other states do (Reiter and Stam, forthcoming). It is important to distinguish, however, between the early stages of transitions away from authoritarian rule and later stages when democratic institutions have begun to consolidate. Recent evidence suggests that war is significantly more likely only in these early transitional stages (Mansfield and Snyder, forthcoming).

The growing consensus that democracies rarely if ever fight each other is not matched by any agreement as to how best to explain this strong empirical regularity. Theorizing about the democratic peace is in its early stages, and new theories will undoubtedly be proposed, but at the present time there are several alternative explanations.

The 'democratic culture and norms' model (Owen, 1997; Russett and Oneal, 2001) suggests that democratic societies are inherently averse to war because (as Kant argued) citizens will not vote to send themselves off to war. In addition, democracies share norms of bounded political competition and peaceful resolution of disputes; and these internal democratic norms are extended to relations between democratic states. Democracies shed norms of peaceful conflict resolution in relations with non-democratic states, however, because they fear being exploited.[18]

The plausibility of the normative model of the democratic peace is undercut by the fact that such norms have not precluded democratic states from initiating imperial wars against weaker opponents despite the absence of any threat of exploitation by the latter, or from fighting wars against autocracies with an intensity disproportionate to any plausible security threat. These concerns lead some to supplement a democratic culture argument with a constructivist emphasis on shared identity and perceived distinction between self and other (Risse-Kappen, 1995), which provides a more plausible explanation for democratic hostility toward culturally dissimilar, non-democratic states. Yet democracies do engage in covert action against each other (James and Mitchell, 1995), and they occasionally use low levels of military force against each other (Bueno de Mesquita and Lalman, 1992), which is not consistent with the idea of a shared identity of democratic states.[19]

The 'institutional constraints model' emphasizes checks and balances, the dispersion of power and the role of a free press. These institutions preclude political leaders from taking unilateral military action, ensure an open public debate and require leaders to secure a broad base of public support before adopting risky policies. As a result, leaders are risk-averse with respect to decisions for war and can take forceful actions only in response to serious immediate threats (Morgan and Campbell, 1991; Siverson, 1995). Although the institutional constraints model provides a plausible explanation for the relative absence of wars between democracies, like the democratic norms model it fails to explain why democracies frequently fight imperial wars despite the absence of serious threats. It also fails to explain why democracies get involved in wars just as frequently as do non-democratic states.[20] In addition, most versions of the institutional model assume that leaders have more warlike preferences than do their publics, which is why leaders need to be constrained. This is not always true, and in fact belligerent publics sometimes push their leaders into wars those leaders prefer to avoid (the United States in the Spanish-American War, for example), and politically insecure leaders engage in diversionary action in order to trigger 'rally round the flag' effects that bolster their domestic political support (Levy, 1989; Smith, 1996; Gelpi, 1997).

Many of these anomalies are explained by Bueno de Mesquita et al. (1999) in an alternative institutional explanation of the democratic peace based on a game-theoretic model that more fully incorporates strategic interaction between democracies and their adversaries. The model emphasizes political survival as the primary goal of political leaders. It suggests that the political survival of leaders with larger winning coalitions (usually characteristic of democracies) depends on successful public policies, whereas the political survival of leaders with smaller winning coalitions (authoritarian states) depends on their ability to satisfy their core supporters through the distribution of private goods. This implies that democratic leaders are more sensitive to the outcome of wars than are authoritarian leaders, which in fact is consistent with the finding that democratic leaders are more likely than their authoritarian counterparts to be removed from office after an unsuccessful war (Bueno de Mesquita and Siverson, 1995). Because of the political benefits of successful wars and the political costs of unsuccessful wars, democratic leaders tend to initiate only those wars they are confident of winning and, once in war, to devote enormous resources to win those wars. Autocratic leaders devote fewer resources to war because the costs of failure in war are less and because they need those resources to distribute to their key supporters at home.[21]

In a war between democracies, both sides would invest enormously in the war effort, which would result in a war that is economically costly to both sides as well as politically costly to the loser. Democratic leaders understand this and have strong incentives to seek a negotiated peace rather than to fight, which explains the dyadic democratic peace. The model also accounts for the fact that democracies frequently get involved in wars as well as other empirical regularities regarding democratic war behavior. Because democratic leaders benefit from successful wars, especially those involving low casualties, they will not hesitate to initiate imperial wars and wars against weaker autocracies. The model also explains why strong democracies sometimes initiate low levels of force against a much weaker democracy (few domestic political risks), why the target capitulates immediately (anticipating that leaders in the stronger state have strong incentives to win the war), and thus why militarized disputes between democracies do not escalate to war.

In the Bueno de Mesquita et al. (1999) model, the willingness of democracies to invest heavily in the war effort makes them unattractive targets of aggression, but autocrats also take greater gambles in war because the outcome of war has less of an impact on their political survival. Autocracies will initiate wars against weak democracies but rarely against strong democracies. If *ex ante* military capabilities are approximately equal, the likelihood of a democratic-autocratic war depends on the specific values of key variables in the model. Democratic leaders will consider war if they believe that their greater investment in the war effort guarantees victory, while autocratic leaders' greater willingness to gamble might lead them to consider war if the democratic effort advantage is modest.

Schultz (1998) provides an alternative explanation of the democratic peace, one based on a signaling game and the transparency of democratic institutions and processes. The basic argument is that because a free press guarantees transparency and because the political opposition has different incentives than the government and some influence over the government, democracies are better able than non-democracies to send credible signals of their resolve in crises, and this reduces the dangers of crisis escalation due to misperceptions.

More specifically, the transparency of the democratic process makes it obvious whether democratic political leaders involved in international crises have the support of the political opposition and the public in an international crisis. In the absence of domestic support the government cannot stand firm in a crisis because it cannot implement its threats, and the adversary knows this and adopts a harder line in crisis bargaining. Democratic leaders anticipate their adversary's resolve and refrain from getting involved in crises in the first place.

If leaders expect public support, however, they will initiate disputes knowing they will be able to stand firm if the adversary resists, and the anticipation of this leads the adversary to behave more cautiously. As a result, crises involving democratic states are less likely to be characterized by misperceptions regarding the adversary's resolve and less likely to escalate to war because of misperceptions. This is critical because misperceptions based on private information and incentives to misrepresent that information play a central role in the outbreak of war (Jervis, 1976; Blainey, 1988; Fearon, 1995). In jointly democratic dyads, misperceptions are reduced even further, though whether this reduction is enough to account for the near-absence of wars between democracies is problematic.[22]

The democratic peace research program has evolved from the description of empirical regularities to controlling for spurious influences, exploring anomalous cases and constructing models to explain observed regularities. Another important development is the effort to use these models to generate a new set of predictions about a wide range of other types of behavior (conflict resolution, intervention, covert action, the conduct and outcome of war, perceptions of the adversaries, etc.), and to subject these predictions to empirical test (Russett and Starr, 2000). This last step is a particularly welcome one, as the generation and empirical confirmation of new testable implications is a critical requirement of a progressive research program (Lakatos, 1970; King et al., 1994).

One distinctive feature of the democratic peace research program is that it has engaged scholars from several different research communities sharing rather different methodological orientations – large-*n* statistical methods, small-*n* case study methods, and formal modeling. Each has made a distinctive contribution to our understanding of the security policies and strategic interaction of democratic states, and the democratic peace research program has benefitted enormously from the combination of their efforts.

Quantitative methods were indispensable in establishing the empirical regularity that propelled the research program, demonstrating that the extraordinarily strong association between joint democracy and peace was not spurious, and identifying other empirical regularities that constrain any theoretical explanation of the democratic peace. Qualitative case studies were indispensable for exploring potentially anomalous cases, helping to resolve debates about whether states did or did not satisfy the definitional requirements for democracy, and assessing whether the inference of a causal connection between joint democracy and peace was valid or spurious in that particular case. Finally, applications of formal modeling helped in exploring possible causal paths leading from joint democracy to peace, incorporating a theory of strategic interaction as well as the domestic sources of foreign policy, and in the process generating some very plausible theoretical explanations of the democratic peace and associated empirical regularities.

Each of these methodological approaches has been essential in the evolution of the democratic peace research program, and their synergistic effects have added much to our understanding of the pacifying effects of joint democracy. Although the literature on the democratic peace was driven largely by evidence in its early stages (the 1980s) – by the unprecedented level of empirical support for the dyadic democratic peace proposition – it is now driven by a genuine dialectic of theory and evidence. This particular temporal sequence of approaches (quantitative, case study and formal) may not follow the textbook model of theory, hypotheses and empirical test, but it has unquestionably been effective in the accumulation of knowledge about the democratic peace. It is also a useful reminder that different methodologies can be combined in different sequences and that there are multiple paths to knowledge about the empirical world.[23]

CONCLUSIONS

Having emphasized the advantages of the multimethod character of research on the democratic peace, let me end by noting that multi-method approaches are beginning to benefit other research communities as well. The analysis of the relationship between interdependence and conflict is a good example. In response to the very general theoretical argument that trade promotes peace, scholars attempted to operationalize this hypothesis and test it statistically over a large number of cases (Barbieri, 1996; Russett and Oneal, 2001), and at the same time others explored the trade-promotes-peace hypothesis through more intensive case studies of individual cases (Ripsman and Blanchard, 1996/7). Other scholars followed with the application of insights from formal models to help identify logical problems in early theories of commercial liberalism and to suggest new causal linkages (Morrow, 1999; Dorussen, 1999), and case studies in turn have been helpful in illuminating some of these derived causal linkages (Papayoanou, 1999). Some of the testable implications of hypotheses on trade and peace are best examined by large-*n* statistical methods, while other implications are more easily examined through case study methods. One example of the latter involves hypotheses about the impact of leaders' expectations regarding the duration and severity of an anticipated war and their expectations of the impact of war on trade.

Just as multi-method approaches have potentially significant benefits, the reluctance of scholars to cross methodological divisions and build on the work of those in other research communities is a serious limitation of some research programs. One example is the old realist debate on the relative stability of bipolar and multipolar systems. Although neorealists rely heavily on polarity as a key explanatory variable (Waltz, 1979; Mearsheimer, 1990), their analyses are primarily deductive in character and not informed by systematic empirical investigation. They overgeneralize from the Cold War experience, where bipolarity is confounded with the existence of nuclear weapons and other key variables, and fail to demonstrate the validity of their arguments with respect to earlier historical eras.

Although multipolarity is more common than bipolarity, there are surely enough instances of the latter to warrant empirical investigation,[24] but there has been no serious effort to do this. Neorealists also ignore a number of quantitative studies that generally show no significant and systematic relationship between polarity and war (Sabrosky, 1985; Kegley and Raymond, 1994). In addition, formal modeling perspectives question the logical links between the basic assumptions of neorealist theory and the hypothesis of bipolar stability (Bueno de Mesquita, 2002). The opportunity costs of failing to build upon important research on polarity in different research communities is particularly serious because the bipolar stability hypothesis is one of the central testable hypotheses in the neorealist research program.

For the most part, however, scholars have increasingly come to recognize the benefits of a multi-method orientation towards research and to inform their own work with the insights and findings of scholars working in other research communities. This methodological pluralism is yet another reason for optimism about progress in the study of war and peace and of international relations more generally.

Notes

The author thanks Jon DiCicco, Carmela Lutmar, Ed Rhodes, Tom Walker, the Editors of this volume and an anonymous reviewer for helpful comments.

1 A great (or major) power war involves at least one great power on each side of the conflict. Historians generally date the origins of the modern system, which until the middle of the twentieth century was centered in Europe, to 1500.

2 There would be five great power wars in the twentieth century if we included the short and limited Russo-Japanese War of 1939 (the Nomonhan War) and classified China as a great power before the Korean War.

3 Just as diplomatic history has often focused on the history of the relations between the (European) great powers (von Ranke, [1833] 1973; Taylor, 1954: xix), many of the leading theories of international relations are essentially theories of great power behavior (Levy, 1989: 215). This great power bias has begun to diminish, not only with the development of theories of regional wars (Miller, 2000) and ethnonational wars (Holsti, 1996; Brown et al., 1997; Lake and Rothchild, 1998; Walter and Snyder, 1999; Snyder, 2000), but also with applications of balance of power theory and power transition theory to regional systems (Walt, 1987; Lemke, 1996; DiCicco and Levy, 1999).

4 Although international relations theorists have always given some attention to Marxist-Leninist theories of imperialism and war, which focus primarily on the societal level, that attention has waned with the end of the Cold War and the collapse of communist political systems in the Soviet Union and the Soviet bloc. Marxist-Leninist theories focus on the domestic economic structure of capitalist societies and posit that the inequitable distribution of wealth generates 'underconsumption', inadequate domestic investment and stagnant economies. This leads to expansionist and imperialist foreign policies to secure external markets for surplus products, external investment opportunities for surplus capital, outlets for surplus population and access to raw materials at stable prices, and also to high levels of military spending to stabilize and stimulate the economy. The result is arms races, conflict spirals and war. See Lenin, 1939; Hobson, 1965; Brewer, 1980; Semmel, 1981.

5 This is a modification of Suganami's (1990) distinction between the questions of '(1) What are the conditions in the absence of which war could not happen at all? (2) Under what sorts of circumstances have wars occurred more frequently? (3) How did this particular war come about?' Similarly, Jeremy Black (1998: 13) distinguishes among the causes of war, wars and specific wars.

6 Many claim that Thucydides was the first realist, but his conception of international politics was sufficiently complex that scholars from different theoretical perspectives have all claimed Thucydides as their own. See Doyle, 1997 and Lebow, 2001.

7 This is a standard conception of realism, but the importance of anarchy is de-emphasized by hegemonic realists, and the state-centric assumption is relaxed by the application of the ethnic security dilemma to intrastate communal conflicts (Posen, 1993; Snyder and Jervis, 1999).

8 As Suganami (1990: 22) argues, 'international anarchy does not in fact make war recur, but only makes the recurrence of war possible'. See also Suganami (1996).

9 Nearly everyone who attempts to explain the constant recurrence of war strongly implies that the magnitude of the constant is quite high – that war is frequent. But the proper baseline for evaluating the frequency of war is not clear. At the aggregate level there may be more years characterized by war than by peace, but most states are usually at peace, especially when one considers the number of dyadic opportunities for war, and in this sense war is a rare event (Bremer, 1992).

10 Others argue that Germany was so eager for war that it was indifferent about British intervention (Trachtenberg, 1990/1; Copeland, 2000).

11 The importance of the preventive motivation for war is suggested by A.J.P. Taylor's (1954: 166) statement that 'Every war between Great Powers [in the 1848–1918 period] started as a preventive war, not a war of conquest', and by Michael Howard's (1983: 18) argument that 'The causes of war remain rooted, as much as they were in the pre-industrial age, in perceptions by statesmen of the growth of hostile power and the fears for the restriction, if not the extinction, of their own.'

12 Similarly, Snyder and Jervis (1999: 16) argue that few contemporary civil conflicts are driven purely by security fears.

13 Whereas defensive realists generally argue that states balance against threats, not just against power (Walt, 1987), offensive realists argue that because of uncertainty power is inherently threatening and that states balance against power.

14 At the dyadic level 'power preponderance theory' is always contrasted with 'power parity theory', and the evidence strongly supports the former (Kugler and Lemke, 1996).

15 Prosperity can also increase the size of war chests and thus increase the ability of states to wage war (Blainey, 1988).

16 From a signaling game perspective, one possible path through which interdependence might promote peace is by providing states with additional instruments through which they can credibly signal commitment during a crisis (since a loss of trade is a costly signal), which increases the efficiency of signaling and hence reduces the dangers of crisis escalation driven by misperception of the other's resolve (Morrow, 1999).

17 Criteria for war include a military conflict involving at least 1,000 battle-deaths, and criteria for democracy include regular fair elections, tolerance of opposition parties and a parliament that at least shares powers with the executive. Possible exceptions to this 'law' include the American Civil War and the Spanish-American War, among other cases (Ray, 1995).

18 Many argue that democratic culture precludes democratic leaders from fighting 'preventive wars' for the sole purpose of suppressing rising adversaries (Schweller, 1992), and that (at least in the United States) 'the public mood inclines to support really bold action only in response to great anger or great fright. The fright must be something more than a sudden new rise in [the adversary's] capability' (Brodie, 1965: 237–9). Evidence suggests, however, that democracies occasionally fight preventive wars (Levy and Gochal, 2000).

19 Notions of a shared identity of democratic states would not necessarily preclude some democratic states being left outside such a community, being classified as 'other', and hence being the targets of violent actions. For such an analysis to be meaningful it would have to identify the boundaries of the shared community independently of its hypothesized consequences, and also to generate new predictions in order to avoid being ad hoc (Lakatos, 1970).

20 Because most of the wars between democratic and non-democratic states are initiated by democracies (Reiter and Stam, forthcoming), and because pre-emptive wars are rare (Reiter, 1995), this eliminates the hypothesis that democracies fight autocracies only in defense against aggression.

21 Much of the Bueno de Mesquita et al. (1999) argument hinges on the assumption that democratic leaders are more sensitive to the political costs of a military defeat than are authoritarian leaders. It may be true that democratic leaders are more likely than authoritarian leaders to be removed from office after an unsuccessful war, but authoritarian leaders often suffer a greater personal cost, and leaders undoubtedly base their calculations on the potential costs of negative outcomes as well as their probabilities (Goemans, 2000). Bueno de Mesquita et al. (1999) focus on the probability of being removed from office but ignore the personal costs and risks (and hence the expected utility) associated with those outcomes.

22 Schultz's (1998) model begins with the decision by a democracy whether or not to initiate a crisis. Crisis dynamics may be different if an authoritarian state makes the first move. For a critique of Schultz's model and for an alternative model of the relationship between leaders, political oppositions and adversaries, see Mabe and Levy, 1998.

23 This sequence is the reverse of the one advocated by Russett (1970) and Lijphart (1971), who each suggest the use of comparative methods for refining hypotheses followed by statistical methods to test them.

24 These include the rivalry between Athens and Sparta in the fifth century BC, the rivalry between Rome and Carthage in the third century BC, and the rivalry between Habsburgs and Valois in the early sixteenth century, among others.

Bibliography

Adler, Emannuel and Barnett, Michael (eds) (1998) *Security Communities*. New York: Cambridge University Press.

Allison, Graham T. and Zelikow, Philip (1999) *Essence of Decision: Explaining the Cuban Missile Crisis*. New York: Longman.

Angell, Norman (1912) *The Great Illusion*. London: Heinemann.

Archibugi, Daniele (1995) 'Immanuel Kant, Cosmopolitan Law and Peace', *European Journal of International Relations*, 1 (4): 429–56.

Aron, Raymond (1958) 'War and Industrial Society', in Leon Bramson and George W. Goethals (eds), *War*. New York: Basic Books. pp. 359–402.

Aron, Raymond (1973) *Peace and War* (trans. by Richard Howard and Annette Baker Fox). Garden City, NY: Doubleday/Anchor Press.

Barbieri, Katherine (1996) 'Economic Interdependence: A Path to Peace or Source of Interstate Conflict?', *Journal of Peace Research*, 33 (1): 29–49.

Barbieri, Katherine and Levy, Jack S. (1999) 'Sleeping With the Enemy: Trade Between Adversaries During Wartime', *Journal of Peace Research*, 36 (4): 463–79.

Barbieri, Katherine and Schneider, Gerald (1999) 'Globalization and Peace: Assessing New Directions in the Study of Trade and Conflict', *Journal of Peace Research*, 36 (4): 387–404.

Bennett, D. Scott and Stam, Allan C., III (1998) 'The Declining Advantages of Democracy: A Combined Model of War Outcomes and Duration', *Journal of Conflict Resolution*, 42 (3): 344–66.

Benoit, Kenneth (1996) 'Democracies Really Are More Pacific (in General)', *Journal of Conflict Resolution*, 40 (4): 309–41.

Betts, Richard K. (1992) 'Systems for Peace or Causes of War: Collective Security, Arms Control, and the New Europe', *International Security*, 17 (1): 5–43.

Biddle, Stephen (1998) 'The Past as Prologue: Assessing Theories of Future Warfare', *Security Studies*, 8 (1): 1–74.

Black, Jeremy (1998) *Why Wars Happen*. New York: New York University Press.

Blainey, Geoffrey (1988) *The Causes of War*, 3rd edn. New York: The Free Press.

Bond, Brian (1986) *War and Society in Europe, 1870–1970*. New York: Oxford University Press.

Braumoeller, Bear and Goertz, Gary (2000) 'The Methodology of Necessary Conditions', *American Journal of Political Science*, 44 (4): 844–58.

Bremer, Stuart A. (1992) 'Dangerous Dyads: Conditions Affecting the Likelihood of Interstate War, 1816–1965', *Journal of Conflict Resolution*, 36 (2): 309–41.

Brewer, Anthony (1980) *Marxist Theories of Imperialism*. London: Routledge & Kegan Paul.

Brodie, Bernard (1965) *Strategy in the Missile Age*. Princeton: Princeton University Press.

Brown, Michael E., Lynn-Jones, Sean M. and Miller, Steven E. (eds) (1996) *Debating the Democratic Peace*. Cambridge, MA: MIT Press.

Brown, Michael E., Cote, Owen R., Jr, Lynn-Jones, Sean M. and Miller, Steven E. (eds) (1997) *Nationalism and Ethnic Conflict*. Cambridge, MA: MIT Press.

Bueno de Mesquita, Bruce (2002) 'Neorealism's Logic and Evidence: When Is a Theory Falsified?', in John A. Vasquez and Colin Elman (eds), *Realism and the Balancing of Power: A New Debate*. Englewood Cliffs, NJ: Prentice Hall.

Bueno de Mesquita, Bruce, and Lalman, David (1992) *War and Reason*. New Haven: Yale University Press.

Bueno de Mesquita, Bruce and Siverson, Randolph M. (1995) 'War and the Survival of Political Leaders: A Comparative Study of Regime Types and Political Accountability', *American Political Science Review*, 89 (4): 841–55.

Bueno de Mesquita, Bruce, Morrow, James D., Siverson, Randolph M. and Smith, Alastair (1999) 'An Institutional Explanation of the Democratic Peace', *American Political Science Review*, 93 (4): 791–808.

Bull, Hedley (1977) *The Anarchical Society*. New York: Columbia University Press.

Buzan, Barry (1984) 'Economic Structure and International Security: The Limits of the Liberal Case', *International Organization*, 38 (44): 597–624.

Cashman, Greg (1993) *What Causes War?* New York: Macmillan/Lexington.

Chan, Steven (1997) 'In Search of Democratic Peace: Problems and Promise', *Mershon International Studies Review*, 41 (1): 59–91.

Claude, Inis L., Jr (1962) *Power and International Relations*. New York: Random House.

Clausewitz, Carl von ([1832] 1996) *On War* (ed. and trans. by Michael Howard and Peter Paret). Princeton: Princeton University Press.

Copeland, Dale C. (1996) 'Economic Interdependence and War: A Theory of Trade Expectations', *International Security* 20 (4): 5–41.

Copeland, Dale (2000) *The Origins of Major Wars*. Ithaca: Cornell University Press.

Deutsch, Karl W., Burrell, Sidney A., Kann, Robert A., Lee, Maurice Jr, Lichterman, Martin, Lindgren, Raymond E., Lowenheim, Francis L., Van Wagenen, Richard, W.(1957) *Political Community and the North Atlantic Area*. Princeton: Princeton University Press.

DiCicco, Jonathan M. and Levy, Jack S. (1999) 'Power Shifts and Problem Shifts: The Evolution of the Power Transition Research Program', *Journal of Conflict Resolution*, 43 (6): 675–704.

Diehl, Paul F. and Goertz, Gary (2000) *War and Peace in International Rivalry*. Ann Arbor: University of Michigan Press.

Dixon, William J. (1994) 'Democracy and the Peaceful Settlement of International Conflict', *American Political Science Review*, 88 (1): 14–32.

Dorussen, Han (1999) 'Balance of Power Revisited: A Multi-Country Model of Trade and Conflict', *Journal of Peace Research*, 36 (4): 443–62.

Doyle, Michael W. (1997) *Ways of War and Peace*. New York: W.W. Norton.

Dray, William H. (1957) *Laws and Explanation in History*. London: Oxford University Press.

Elman, Colin and Elman, Miriam Fendius (eds) (2001) *Bridges and Boundaries: Historians, Political Scientists, and the Study of International Relations*. Cambridge: MIT Press.

Elman, Colin and Elman, Miriam Fendius (eds) (2002) *Progress in International Relations Theory: Metrics and Methods of Scientific Change*. Cambridge, MA: MIT Press.

Fearon, James D. (1995) 'Rationalist Explanations for War', *International Organization*, 49 (3): 379–414.

Fischer, Fritz (1975) *War of Illusions* (trans. Marian Jackson). New York: W.W. Norton.

Freedman, Lawrence (1998) *The Revolution in Strategic Affairs*. International Institute for Strategic Studies, Adelphi Paper 318.

Friedman, Thomas L. (1999) *The Lexus and the Olive Tree*. New York: Farrar, Straus, Giroux.

Gartzke, Erik, Li, Quan and Boehmer, Charles (2001) 'Investing in the Peace: Economic Interdependence and International Conflict', *International Organization*, 55 (2): 391–438.

Gelpi, Christopher (1997) 'Democratic Diversions: Governmental Structure and the Externalization of Domestic Conflict', *Journal of Conflict Resolution*, 41 (2): 255–82.

George, Alexander L. (1979) 'The "Operational Code": A Neglected Approach to the Study of Political Leaders and Decisionmaking', *International Studies Quarterly*, 13 (2): 190–222.

Giddens, Anthony (1979) *The Nation-State and Violence*. Berkeley: University of California Press.

Gilpin, Robert (1981) *War and Change in World Politics*. New York: Cambridge University Press.

Glaser, Charles L. (1997) 'The Security Dilemma Revisited', *World Politics*, 50 (1): 171–201.

Gleditsch, Nils Petter (1995) 'Geography, Democracy, and Peace', *International Interactions*, 20: 297–323.

Goemans, H.E. (2000) *War and Punishment: The Causes of War Termination and the First World War*. Princeton: Princeton University Press.

Gowa, Joanne (1994) *Allies, Adversaries, and International Trade*. Princeton: Princeton University Press.

Gowa, Joanne (1999) *Ballots and Bullets*. Princeton: Princeton University Press.

Grieco, Joseph M. (1990) *Cooperation Among Nations*. Ithaca: Cornell University Press.

Gulick, Edward V. (1955) *Europe's Classical Balance of Power*. Ithaca: Cornell University Press.

Gurr, Ted Robert (2000) *People Versus States: Minorities at Risk in the New Century*. Washington, DC: United States Institute of Peace.

Haftendorn, Helga, Keohane, Robert O. and Wallander, Celeste A. (eds) (1999) *Imperfect Unions: Security Institutions over Time and Space*. Oxford: Oxford University Press.

Hempel, Carl G. (1942) 'The Function of General Laws in History', *Journal of Philosophy*, 39: 35–48.

Hill, Christopher (1985) 'History and International Relations', in Steve Smith (ed.), *International Relations: British and American Perspectives*. Oxford: Blackwell. pp. 126–45.

Hirschman, Albert O. ([1945] 1980) *National Power and the Structure of Foreign Trade*. Berkeley: University of California Press.

Hobson, J.A. (1965) *Imperialism*. Ann Arbor: University of Michigan Press.

Holsti, K.J. (1991) *Peace and War: Armed Conflicts and International Order, 1648–1989*. New York: Cambridge University Press.

Holsti, K.J. (1996) *The State, War, and the State of War*. New York: Cambridge University Press.

Holsti, Ole R. (1989) 'Crisis Decision-Making', in Philip E. Tetlock, Jo L. Husbands, Robert Jervis, Paul C. Stern and Charles Tilly (eds), *Behavior, Society, and Nuclear War*, vol. 1. New York: Oxford University Press. pp. 8–84.

Howard, Michael (1976) *War in European History*. Oxford: Oxford University Press.

Howard, Michael (1983) *The Causes of Wars*. Cambridge, MA: Harvard University Press.

James, Patrick and Mitchell Glenn E., II (1995) 'Targets of Covert Pressure: The Hidden Victims of the Democratic Peace', *International Interactions*, 21 (1): 85–107.

Jervis, Robert (1976) *Perception and Misperception in International Politics*. Princeton: Princeton University Press.

Jervis, Robert (1978) 'Cooperation under the Security Dilemma', *World Politics*, 30 (2): 186–213.

Jervis, Robert (1989) *The Meaning of the Nuclear Revolution*. Princeton: Princeton University Press.

Kacowicz, Arie Marcelo and Bar-Siman-Tov, Yaacov (2000) *Stable Peace Among Nations*. Lanham: Rowman and Littlefield.

Kant, Immanuel (1795/1949) 'Eternal Peace', in C.J. Frederich (ed.), *The Philosophy of Kant*. New York: Modern Library, 1949. pp. 430–76.

Katzenstein, Peter J. (ed.) (1996) *The Culture of National Security: Norms and Identity in World Politics*. New York: Columbia University Press.

Keegan, John (1984) *A History of Warfare*. New York: Vintage.

Kegley, Charles W. and Raymond, Gregory A. (1994) *A Multipolar Peace?* New York: St Martin's Press.

Kennedy, Paul (1987) *The Rise and Fall of the Great Powers*. New York: Random House.

Keohane, Robert O. (1984) *After Hegemony: Cooperation and Discord in the World Political Economy*. Princeton: Princeton University Press.

Keohane, Robert O. (ed.) (1986) *Neorealism and Its Critics*. New York: Columbia University Press.

Keohane, Robert O. and Martin, Lisa L. (1995) 'The Promise of Institutionalist Theory', *International Security*, 20 (1): 39–51.

Keohane, Robert O. and Martin, Lisa L. (2002) 'Institutional Theory as a Research Program', in Colin Elman and Miriam Fendius Elman (eds), *Progress in International Relations Theory*. Cambridge, MA: MIT Press.

King, Charles (1997) *Ending Civil Wars*. International Institute for Strategic Studies, Adelphi Paper 308.

King, Gary, Keohane, Robert O. and Verba, Sidney (1994) *Designing Social Inquiry*. Princeton: Princeton University Press.

Kugler, Jacek and Lemke, Douglas (eds) (1996) *Parity and War*. Ann Arbor: University of Michigan Press.

Kupchan, Charles A. and Kupchan, Clifford A. (1991) 'Concerts, Collective Security, and the Future of Europe', *International Security*, 16 (1): 114–61.

Kydd, Andrew (1997) 'Sheep in Sheep's Clothing: Why Security Seekers Do Not Fight One Another', *Security Studies*, 7 (1): 114–54.

Labs, Eric J. (1997) 'Beyond Victory: Offensive Realism and the Expansion of War Aims', *Security Studies*, 6 (4): 1–49.

Lakatos, Imre (1970) 'Falsification and the Methodology of Scientific Research Programmes', in Imre Lakatos and Alan Musgrave (eds), *Criticism and the Growth of Knowledge*. New York: Cambridge University Press. pp. 91–196.

Lake, David A. and Rothchild, Donald (eds) (1998) *The International Spread of Ethnic Conflict: Fear, Diffusion, and Escalation*. Princeton: Princeton University Press.

Lebow, Richard Ned (2001) 'Thucydides the Constructivist', *American Political Science Review*, 95 (3): 547–60.

Lemke, Douglas (1996) 'Small States and War: An Expansion of Power Transition Theory', in Jacek Kugler and Douglas Lemke (eds), *Parity and War*. Ann Arbor: University of Michigan Press. pp. 77–92.

Lenin, V.I. (1939) *Imperialism*. New York: International Publishers.

Levy, Jack S. (1983) *War in the Modern Great Power System, 1495–1975*. Lexington: University Press of Kentucky.

Levy, Jack S. (1989) 'The Causes of War: A Review of Theories and Evidence', in Philip Tetlock, Jo L. Husbands, Robert Jervis, Paul C. Stern and Charles Tilly (eds), *Behavior, Society, and Nuclear War*, vol. 1. New York: Oxford University Press. pp. 209–333.

Levy, Jack S. (1990/1) 'Preferences, Constraints, and Choices in July 1914', *International Security*, 15 (3): 151–86.

Levy, Jack S. (1994) 'The Theoretical Foundations of Paul W. Schroeder's International System', *International History Review*, 16 (4): 715–44.

Levy, Jack S. (2001) 'Explaining Events and Testing Theories: History, Political Science, and the Analysis of International Relations', in Colin Elman and Miriam Fendius Elman (eds), *Bridges and Boundaries: Historians, Political Scientists, and the Study of International Relations.* Cambridge, MA: MIT Press. pp. 39–83.

Levy, Jack S. (2002) 'Do Great Powers Balance Against Hegemonic Threats?', in John A. Vasquez and Colin Elman (eds), *Realism and the Balancing of Power: A New Debate.* Englewood Cliffs, NJ: Prentice Hall.

Levy, Jack S. and Gochal, Joseph R. (2000) 'When Do Democracies Fight Preventive Wars?', paper presented at the annual meeting of the International Studies Association.

Levy, Jack S., Walker, Thomas C. and Edwards, Martin S. (2001) 'Continuity and Change in the Evolution of War', in Zeev Maoz and Azar Gat (eds), *War in a Changing World.* Ann Arbor: University of Michigan Press. pp. 15–48.

Lichbach, Mark and Lebow, Richard Ned (eds) (2001) *Theory and Evidence in Comparative and International Politics.* Unpublished book manuscript.

Licklider, Roy (1998) 'The Consequences of Negotiated Settlements in Civil Wars, 1945–1993', *American Political Science Review*, 89 (3): 681–90.

Lijphart, Arend (1971) 'Comparative Politics and the Comparative Method', *American Political Science Review*, 65 (3): 682–93.

Lynn-Jones, Sean M. (1995) 'Offense–Defense Theory and Its Critics', *Security Studies*, 4 (1): 660–91.

Mabe, William, Jr and Levy, Jack S. (1998) 'Politically-Motivated Opposition to War: A Comparative Study of the US in the Quasi-War and the War of 1812', paper presented at the annual meeting of the American Political Science Association.

Mandelbaum, Michael (1998–9) 'Is Major War Obsolete?', *Survival*, 40 (4): 20–38.

Mann, Michael (1986) *The Sources of Social Power*, 2 vols. New York: Cambridge University Press.

Mansfield, Edward D. (1994) *Power, Trade, and War.* Princeton: Princeton University Press.

Mansfield, Edward D. and Snyder, Jack (1995) 'Democratization and the Danger of War', *International Security* 20 (1): 5–38.

Mansfield, Edward D. and Snyder, Jack (forthcoming) 'Democratic Transitions, Institutional Strength, and War', *International Organization*.

Mansfield, Edward D., Milner, Helen V. and Rosendorf, B. Peter (2000) 'Free to Trade: Democracies, Autocracies, and International Trade', *American Political Science Review*, 94 (2): 305–21.

Maoz, Zeev (1997) 'The Debate Over the Democratic Peace: Rearguard Action or Cracks in the Wall?', *International Security*, 32: 162–98.

Marshall, Monty G. (1999) *Third World War.* Lanham: Rowman and Littlefield.

Mearsheimer, John J. (1990) 'Back to the Future: Instability in Europe after the Cold War', *International Security*, 15 (1): 5–56.

Mearsheimer, John J. (1994/5) 'The False Promise of International Institutions', *International Security*, 19 (3): 5–49.

Mearsheimer, John J. (2001) *The Tragedy of Great Power Politics.* New York: W.W. Norton.

Midlarsky, Manus I. (ed.) (2000) *Handbook of War Studies II.* Ann Arbor: University of Michigan Press.

Miller, Benjamin. (2000) 'Explaining Variations in Regional Peace: Three Strategies for Peacemaking', *Cooperation and Conflict*, 35 (2): 155–91.

Milner, Helen (1991) 'The Assumption of Anarchy in International Relations Theory', *Review of International Studies*, 17 (1): 67–85.

Morgan, T. Clifton and Campbell, Sally Howard (1991) 'Domestic Structure, Decisional Constraints, and War: So Why Can't Democracies Fight?', *Journal of Conflict Resolution*, 35 (2): 187–211.

Morgenthau, Hans J. (1948) *Politics Among Nations.* New York: Alfred A. Knopf.

Morrow, James D. (1999) 'How Could Trade Affect Conflict?', *Journal of Peace Research*, 36 (4): 481–9.

Morrow, James D., Siverson, Randolph M. and Tabares, Tressa E. (1998) 'The Political Determinants of Trade: The Major Powers, 1907–1990', *American Political Science Review*, 92 (3): 649–61.

Mueller, John (1989) *Retreat from Doomsday: The Obsolescence of Major War.* New York: Basic Books.

Nicholson, Michael (1996) *Causes and Consequences in International Relations Theory.* London: Pinter.

Oneal, John R. and Russett, Bruce (1999) 'The Kantian Peace: The Pacific Benefits of Democracy, Interdependence, and International Organizations, 1885–1992', *World Politics*, 52 (1): 1–37.

Organski, A.F.K. and Kugler, Jacek (1980) *The War Ledger.* Chicago: University of Chicago Press.

Owen, John, IV (1997) *Liberal Peace Liberal War: American Politics and International Security.* Ithaca: Cornell University Press.

Papayoanou, Paul A. (1999) *Power Ties: Economic Interdependence, Balancing, and War.* Ann Arbor: University of Michigan Press.

Perlmutter, Amos (1982) 'The Israeli Raid on Osiraq: A New Proliferation Landscape', *Strategic Review*, Winter: 34–43.

Polachek, Soloman W. (1980) 'Conflict and Trade', *Journal of Conflict Resolution*, 24 (1): 55–78.

Pollins, Brian (1989) 'Does Trade Still Follow the Flag?', *American Political Science Review*, 83 (2): 465–80.

Posen, Barry R. (1993) 'The Security Dilemma and Ethnic Conflict', *Survival*, 35: 103–24.

Powell, Robert (1999) *In the Shadow of Power.* Princeton: Princeton University Press.

Ranke, Leopold von ([1833] 1973) 'The Great Powers', in Leopold von Ranke, *The Theory and Practice of History* (ed. by George G. Iggers and Konrad von Moltke). Indianapolis: Bobbs–Merrill. pp. 65–101.

Rasler, Karen A. and Thompson, William R. (1994) *The Great Powers and Global Struggle, 1490–1990.* Lexington: The University Press of Kentucky.

Ray, James Lee (1990) 'Friends as Foes: International Conflict and Wars between Formal Allies', in Charles S. Gochman and Alan Ned Sabrosky (eds), *Prisoners of War?* Lexington: D.C. Heath. pp. 73–91.

Ray, James Lee (1995) *Democracy and International Conflict.* Columbia: University of South Carolina Press.

Ray James Lee (2000) 'Democracy: On the Level(s), Does Democracy Correlate with Peace', in John A. Vasquez (ed.), *What Do We Know about War?* Lanham: Rowman & Littlefield. pp. 299–316.

Reiter, Dan (1995) 'Exploding the Powder Keg Myth: Preemptive Wars Almost Never Happen', *International Security*, 20 (2): 5–34.

Reiter, Dan and Stam, Allan C., III (forthcoming) *Search for Victory: Understanding the Sources of Democratic Military Power.* Princeton: Princeton University Press.

Reuveny, Rafael and Kang, Heejoon (1996) 'International Trade, Political Conflict/Cooperation and Granger Causality', *American Journal of Political Science*, 40 (3): 943–70.

Ripsman, Norrin M. and Blanchard, Jean-Marc F. (1996/7) 'Commercial Liberalism under Fire: Evidence from 1914 and 1936', *Security Studies*, 6 (2): 4–50.

Risse-Kappen, Thomas (1995) 'Democratic Peace – Warlike Democracies? A Social Constructivist Interpretation of the Liberal Argument', *European Journal of International Relations*, 1 (4): 491–517.

Risse-Kappen, Thomas (1996) 'Collective Identity in a Democratic Community: The Case of NATO', in Peter J. Katzenstein (ed.), *The Culture of National Security.* New York: Columbia University Press. pp. 357–99.

Rogowski, Ronald (1989) *Commerce and Coalitions: How Trade Affects Domestic Political Alignments.* Princeton: Princeton University Press.

Rosecrance, Richard (1986) *The Rise of the Trading State: Commerce and Conquest in the Modern World.* New York: Basic Books.

Ruggie, John Gerard (1998) *Constructing the World Polity.* New York: Routledge.

Rummel, R.J. (1995) 'Democracies ARE Less Warlike Than Other Regimes', *European Journal of International Relations*, 1 (4): 457–79.

Russett, Bruce M. (1970) 'International Behavior Research: Case Studies and Cumulation', in Michael Haas and Henry S. Kariel, (eds), *Approaches to the Study of Political Science.* Scranton: Chandler. pp. 425–43.

Russett, Bruce and Oneal, John R. (2001) *Triangulating Peace: Democracy, Interdependence, and International Organization.* New York: W.W. Norton.

Russett, Bruce M. and Starr, Harvey (2000) 'From the Democratic Peace to Kantian Peace: Democracy and Conflict in the International System', in Manus I. Midlarsky (ed.), *Handbook of War Studies II.* Ann Arbor: University of Michigan Press. pp. 93–128.

Sabrosky, A. (ed.) (1985) *Polarity and War.* Boulder: Westview.

Schelling, Thomas C. (1966) *Arms and Influence.* New Haven: Yale University Press. pp. 221–39.

Schroeder, Paul W. (1994) *The Transformation of European Politics, 1763–1848.* New York: Oxford University Press.

Schultz, Kenneth A. (1998) 'Domestic Opposition and Signaling in International Crises', *American Political Science Review*, 92 (4): 829–44.

Schumpeter, Joseph A. (1919/51) *Imperialism and Social Classes.* Oxford: Oxford University Press.

Schweller, Randall L. (1992) 'Domestic Structure and Preventive War: Are Democracies More Pacific?', *World Politics*, 44 (2): 235–69.

Schweller, Randall L. (1996) 'Neorealism's Status Quo Bias: What Security Dilemma?', *Security Studies*, 5 (3): 90–121.

Semmel, Bernard (ed.) (1981) *Marxism and the Science of War.* New York: Oxford University Press.

Singer, J. David (1961) 'The Level-of Analysis Problem in International Politics', in Klaus Knorr and Sidney Verba (eds), *The International System: Theoretical Essays.* Princeton: Princeton University Press. pp. 77–92.

Singer, J. David and Small, Melvin (1972) *The Wages of War, 1816–1965.* New York: Wiley.

Siverson, Randolph M. (1995) 'Democracies and War Participation: In Defense of the Institutional Constraints Argument', *European Journal of International Relations*, 1 (4): 481–9.

Smith, Alastair (1996) 'Diversionary Foreign Policy in Democratic Systems', *International Studies Quarterly*, 40 (1): 133–53.

Snyder, Jack (1991) *Myths of Empire: Domestic Politics and International Ambition.* Ithaca: Cornell University Press.

Snyder, Jack (2000) *From Voting to Violence: Democratization and Nationalist Conflict.* New York: W.W. Norton.

Snyder, Jack and Jervis, Robert (1999) 'Civil War and the Security Dilemma', in Barbara F. Walter and Jack Snyder (eds), *Civil Wars, Insecurity, and Intervention.* New York: Columbia University Press. pp. 15–37.

Strassler, Robert B. (ed.) [Thucydides] (1996) *History of the Peloponnesian War. In The Landmark Thucydides.* New York: The Free Press.

Suganami, Hidemi (1990) 'Bringing Order to the Causes of War Debates', *Millennium*, 19 (1): 19–35.

Suganami, Hidemi (1996) *On the Causes of War.* New York: Oxford University Press.

Taylor, A.J.P. (1954) *The Struggle for Mastery in Europe, 1848–1918.* Oxford: Oxford University Press.

Thompson, William R. (1988) *On Global War.* Columbia: University of South Carolina Press.

Thompson, William R. (ed.) (1999) *Great Power Rivalries.* Columbia: University of South Carolina Press.

Tilly, Charles (1990) *Coercion, Capital, and European States, AD 990–1990.* Cambridge, MA: Blackwell.

Trachtenberg, Marc (1990/1) 'The Meaning of Mobilization in 1914', *International Security*, 15 (3): 120–50.

Tuchman, Barbara W. (1962) *The Guns of August*. New York: Dell.

Van Creveld, Martin (1991) *The Transformation of War*. New York: The Free Press.

Van Evera, Stephen (1990) 'Primed for Peace', *International Security*, 15 (3): 7–57.

Van Evera, Stephen (1999) *Causes of War*. Ithaca: Cornell University Press.

Vasquez, John A. (1993) *The War Puzzle*. New York: Cambridge University Press.

Vasquez, John A. (ed.) (2000) *What Do We Know about War?* Lanham: Rowman and Littlefield.

Vasquez, John A. and Elman, Colin (eds.) (2002) *Realism and the Balancing of Power: A New Debate*. Englewood Cliffs, NJ: Prentice Hall.

Veblen, Thorstein ([1915] 1966) *Imperial Germany and the Industrial Revolution*. Ann Arbor: University of Michigan Press.

Waever, Ole (1998) 'The Sociology of a Not So International Discipline: American and European Developments in International Relations', *International Organization*, 52 (4): 687–727.

Wagner, R. Harrison (2000) 'Bargaining and War', *American Journal of Political Science*, 44 (3): 469–84.

Wallensteen, Peter (1984) 'Universalism vs. Particularism: On the Limits of Major Power Order', *Journal of Peace Research*, 21 (3): 243–57.

Wallensteen, Peter and Margareta Sollenberg (1999) 'Armed Conflict, 1989–98', *Journal of Peace Research*, 36 (5): 593–606.

Walt, Stephen M. (1987) *The Origins of Alliances*. Ithaca: Cornell University Press.

Walter, Barbara and Snyder, Jack (eds) (1999) *Civil Wars, Insecurity, and Intervention*. New York: Columbia University Press.

Waltz, Kenneth N. (1959) *Man, the State, and War*. New York: Columbia University Press.

Waltz, Kenneth N. (1979) *Theory of International Politics*. Reading, MA: Addison–Wesley.

Waltz, Kenneth N. (1988) 'The Origins of War in Neorealist Theory', *Journal of Interdisciplinary History*, 18 (4): 615–28.

Ward, Michael D. and Gleditsch, Kristian S. (1998) 'Democratizing for Peace', *American Political Science Review*, 92 (1): 51–62.

Weede, Eric (1995) 'Economic Policy and International Security: Rent-Seeking, Free Trade and Democratic Peace', *European Journal of International Relations*, 1 (4): 519–37.

Wendt, Alexander (1999) *Social Theory of International Politics*. New York: Cambridge University Press.

Wilson, Charles. (1978) *Profit and Power: A Study of England and the Dutch Wars*. The Hague: Martinus Nijhoff.

Wright Quincy (1965) *A Study of War*, 2nd edn, rev. Chicago: University of Chicago Press.

Zakaria, Fareed (1992) 'Realism and Domestic Politics', *International Security*, 17 (1): 177–98.

Zartman, I. William. (1995) *Elusive Peace: Negotiating an End to Civil Wars*. Washington, DC: Brookings. Institution.

19

Security Cooperation

HARALD MÜLLER

This chapter starts with definitions of the meaning and scope of the term security. It then gives an overview of the types of security cooperation in international relations. The third section defines puzzles that emerge from these cooperative endeavors among actually or potentially mutually hostile actors. The main body of the chapter tries to disentangle the puzzle from the perspectives of the major theoretical approaches in international relations. It describes how the theories explain the phenomena of states cooperating in the security field, and what opportunities and limits the theory would set for such cooperation. Each section also discusses the shortcomings – in the view of the author – of the respective explanation.

SECURITY

The understanding of security[1] as the absence of existential threats to the state emerging from another state is under heavy fire from two directions. First, it has been stated that the state is not the correct, or at least not the single, subject of security. Social, ethnical, religious or otherwise cultural minorities ('societal security') (see Waever et al., 1993), individuals with their basic needs ('human security') (Suhrke, 1999) or else the world community or humankind ('global or world security') (Klare and Thomas, 1994), have been proposed as carriers of security needs of equal rights with states. Second, it has been emphasized that the exclusive attention devoted to the physical – or political – dimension of security of territorial entities is misplaced, at least in an age of complex interdependence. Other aspects relating to human life are as important in security terms: the availability of economic resources, stability, institutions and relations to provide for an adequate level of welfare ('economic security') (Borrus et al., 1992; B. Crawford, 1993, 1994; Kapstein, 1992; Orme, 1997/8; Sen, 1990), the integrity of the systems that supply and process information on which modern society is dependent ('information security') (Feaver, 1998; Keohane and Nye, 1998; Soo Hoo et al., 1997) and the natural environment as the basis for all life, but also the supplier of resources on which societies and states thrive ('environmental security'). (Among countless contributions on this subject, consult Homer-Dixon, 1994; Levy, 1995.) It has been argued that this debate on the meaning of security is a reflection of new conditions of global politics engendered by increasing globalization (Cha, 2000).

The generalization and universalization of the term security has been criticized. What is the *differencia specifica,* and thus the analytical utility, of this term if it covers everything on earth? (See, for example, Deudney, 1990.) For the sake of argumentation economy, the chapter applies a rather conventional understanding of security: security between states, and related mainly to the organized instruments for applying force – the military in the first instance (Betts, 1997; Buzan, 1987). Even so, it must be noted that the concept is not simple. States are not unitary objects. Barry Buzan differentiates between the idea of the state, its physical base and its institutional representation. Security risks may apply to each of these three incarnations (Buzan, 1991: 65).

SECURITY COOPERATION

Cooperation among Friends and Cooperation among Rivals

Security cooperation is usually understood as collaboration between conflictuous parties; this is the reason why alliances are usually dealt with as entities *sui generis*. This distinction, however, is not completely convincing. If international relations are seen as anarchy wherein conflict is principally possible between any pair of actors, then alliances tend to be problematic. If the temporary security cooperation, undertaken to fend off an imminent threat, emboldens the transient partner too much, cooperation may end in less security rather than more, and in loss of sovereignty or extinction in the worst case. In other words, if we look at alliance partners of today as potential enemies of tomorrow, the latent conflict dimension becomes visible. The difference to other forms of security cooperation, for example the nonproliferation regime is then more one of latency versus visibility, and thus more gradual than principal.

Security cooperation implies relying for an essential objective, national survival, on the resources, intentions and activities of other states, which is hard to reconcile with the notion of security being guaranteed exclusively by self-help. In addition, security cooperation entails some loss of freedom of action, some constraint on one's ability to accumulate as much military power as resources permit, some sacrifice in options; for instance, enhanced transparency may mean reduced chances of achieving surprise, a premium value in most strategic writings. Arms control, for instance, aims at reducing offensive, destabilizing options. In wartime alliances, the mutual dependency can be extremely high. Since in war the existence of a state is easily at stake, relying on someone else is an existential issue; strategic choices have to be most closely coordinated, freedom of action might be entirely lost. Peacetime alliances can be much more relaxed and may be hardly more than token promises that might be broken in the first second of the hour of truth. But they may also entail intimate structural cooperation or integration. The degree of mutual knowledge, transparency and dependence within NATO was and is breathtaking when seen from the perspective of potential hostilities in the future. In that sense, NATO member states put much more on the line than participants in average arms control or non-proliferation agreements. If there is a puzzle to be solved in explaining security cooperation, it concerns alliances as well.

Post-war Security Arrangements, Concerts and Collective Security

There are three more variants of security cooperation that merit a brief discussion. The first is the relation former enemies must establish after a postwar settlement. The enemy is suddenly turned into a partner, but memories of past hostilities are still vivid, the risk of reversal looms large, and personal animosities and grievances overlap with genuine concerns over cheating, hidden weapons and the like.

A different type of security cooperation is the work of the United Nations Security Council, notably its permanent members. The Charter has invested considerable responsibilities and rights in this body. The idea was to create an institutional framework wherein the big powers could sort out their problems with each other and join their considerable clout to prevent others from stirring up trouble. Historically, the performance of the UNSC fell short of expectations most of the time. Yet cooperation has occurred; given the differences in geopolitical interests, this remains a remarkable fact.

Finally, collective security is a normative proposition to replace the dangers and uncertainty of balancing. The states belonging to a collective security system promise to come to the aid of the attacked victim if one of them would dare to start an aggression: Note that the attacker is presumed to be a member of the community, not an outsider (in which case it would be an alliance, not a collective security system) and that the aggressor is not known in advance. Both the League of Nations and the UN Charter have tried to incorporate elements of collective security, with limited success so far (see Betts, 1992; Claude, 1971; Downs, 1994; Kupchan and Kupchan, 1991; for surprising positive results of a computer simulation, see Cusack and Stoll, 1994).

The Puzzle

Security cooperation has been in existence and continues to exist. During the East–West conflict, the growth of cooperative endeavors was impressive even while the rivalry was continuing (George et al., 1988). The end of that conflict resulted in an unprecedented intensification of that collaboration, and was influenced and accelerated by it. From the mid-1990s on, the dynamic slowed down, without, however, grinding to a halt. Meanwhile, global cooperation such as the Nuclear Nonproliferation Treaty, the Biological and Chemical Weapons Convention, the Conventional Arms Register, or the Anti-Personnel Mines Convention had long since elevated security cooperation from the narrow confines of the East–West conflict. Peacekeeping has usually brought together countries from all parts of the world. Also, regional efforts have grown. Nuclear weapon-free zones have been agreed in Latin America, South Pacific, Africa, Southeast Asia. Regional activities to deal with small arms have become a major topic for cooperation in such different places as the OSCE, West Africa and Latin

America. Different types of confidence-building measures have been or are being tried in the Middle East, Central Asia and through the ASEAN Regional Forum. The list is not exhaustive, but illustrative.

The puzzle that theories try to solve is the possibility of future hostility confronting today's partners in security cooperation. This poses a challenge of virtual schizophrenia for security collaborators. Security cooperation does not come cost-free, as shown above. States opting for security cooperation sacrifice a security asset to gain higher security by obtaining another asset that, they believe, helps them better to provide for their security: the collaboration of their potential enemies and the pursuant agreements and organizations. How states develop interests, interpretations and perceptions that permit them to jump into security cooperation is the challenge that all explanations are facing.

INTERNATIONAL RELATIONS THEORY AND SECURITY COOPERATION

Realist Accounts

Realism sends us into confusion. Its reformulation by Kenneth Waltz (Waltz, 1979) has claimed pride of place for this theory because it follows the standards of natural science (never mind that it is Newton's physics rather than Einstein's or Planck's). We thus expect the coherence of axioms and strict deduction, only to discover that realists deduce contradictory hypotheses from the same body of abstract theory.

Classical realists analyze state behavior as built upon the innate human striving for cumulating power. Competitive cumulation in an anarchical environment creates inevitable problems for state survival, for which, in turn, accumulating further power is the obvious solution. Neorealists waive the anthropological assumption in favor of a systemic imperative: the need to survive in anarchy where no sovereign grants security means that states are on their own for providing the necessary means to ensure their continued existence. While the starting assumptions vary between classical and neorealism, the theory-relevant consequences, the character of the system as anarchic and dangerous, and the formation of states' preferences are very similar.

The Problem of relative gains In its parsimonious formulation by Kenneth Waltz, and the ensuing interpretations by Joseph Grieco (Grieco, 1990) and Mearsheimer (Mearsheimer, 1990, 1994/5), realism is pessimistic about the prospects for cooperation beyond that based on hegemonic guarantee, persuasion and/or imposition because of the preferences states are assumed to hold as a consequence of the imperative of survival in anarchy (for example, Frankel, 1993; for a critical analysis compare Grunenberg, 1990). The problem lies in the shifting course of history. New polarities emerge from changes in capabilities, a new system structure evolves, and this may make our friend, ally and cooperation partner of today our competitor, rival or enemy of tomorrow. Neither do we know what another government really wants; we can know even less about its intentions tomorrow. We have therefore to take care that the spoils from cooperation are not distributed in a way that may disadvantage us – however marginally – since the margin might be used by today's cooperation partner to impose his will upon us tomorrow. It is not that we can extract gains from cooperation which is the controlling factor influencing our strategic choice, but the distinct risk that the other could gain more: this is, in short, the problem of 'relative gains' that minimizes neorealists' expectations for security cooperation. Of course, equality of relative gains does not require symmetric distribution among asymmetric partners mathematically; but the point is moot in security cooperation among rivals, where denying the other a superiority of resources that may pose dangers tomorrow is imperative. Since symmetric distributions are extremely hard to calculate reliably, and even harder to execute, the opportunities for successful cooperation are naturally very limited. Institutions do not help much; they are epiphenomena that wax and wane with the interest of the primary actors, the states. They have no remarkable influence on their own on these interests and the ensuing behavior (Waltz, 1986: 336).

Alliances The one type of security cooperation that plays a major role in realist accounts is the alliance. The alliance is a necessary tool of balancing when states' own resources are insufficient to create an appropriate counterweight to the hegemonial endeavors of one state or a group of states. Alliances are problematic under the 'relative gain' assumption as well, but they are inevitable tools of convenience if the alternative – succumbing to the risk of an overwhelming power – is clear and immediate. Stephen Walt has modified the 'balancing-against-capabilities' hypothesis by proving that states usually balance against threat (see Walt, 1987) since threat is both a behavioral and a perceptual variable rather than a material one. Realist theory is stretched to the limits here. From another realist perspective, Randall Schweller has shown that bandwagoning – joining the stronger side rather than balancing it – is compatible with realist premises if we assume that the objective of this type of alliance policy is not security, but gain (see Schweller, 1994).

The most elaborate and elegant body of security cooperation theory within the realist paradigm is Glenn Snyder's theory of alliances (Snyder, 1984, 1997). It stays well within the basic realist assumptions and creates a couple of dynamic 'laws of alliance' that catch well the contradictory impulses that mutual security dependence produces. According to Snyder, there is an intra-alliance equivalent of the security dilemma. Since the interests of allies are never completely congruent, a state allied to another will quickly face the choice between supporting its ally in a conflict where the state itself has no real interest, or keeping out of this conflict. Opting for support may drag that state into a deadly contest it may wish to avoid. Staying out may risk the defection of the ally. And vice versa, in the conflict in which the state's national interest is most intimately involved, confronting the enemy very hard may scare the ally away, while accommodating the enemy may induce the ally to pursue its own version of appeasement. As Snyder has shown, even within the basic assumptions of realism, allying is far from being the straightforward and uncomplicated balancing act that simplified and popular versions of the theory would have it. Rather, it is a complex set of relations, fraught with contradictions and dilemmas. Interestingly enough, Snyder, though writing in realist terms most of the time, finds it necessary to introduce, ad hoc, the intrinsic binding quality of norms as a factor persuading states to enter alliances and live up to their commitments, a notion hardly compatible with basic realist assumptions (G. Snyder, 1997: 8, 35, 350, 355).

Optimist realists and the disappearance of the relative gains problem   Security cooperation among allies is certainly the easier part of the realist account of security cooperation. Dealing with cooperation among enemies is more challenging. Charles Glaser has refined the realist argument further, creating a new brand of defensive realism that claims to account better for the cooperation we observe in the real world (Glaser, 1994/5, 1997). Defensive realism does not refute the possibility of long-term security cooperation even under the assumption that anarchy is the structure of the international system and that the state actors, relying on self-help, strive to pursue their security as the overriding national interest. Glaser starts by defining cooperation as an instrument of self-help rather than its opposite; this definition, though, remains problematic as cooperation is always reliant on somebody else's assets, intentions and behavior, which does not fit well with a common-sense notion of self-help. Self-help, it should be recalled, is put up as insurance against the uncertainties of an anarchic environment. Security cooperation does not eliminate the uncertainty about the present and future intentions of the partner(s). As far as a state's security depends critically on the cooperation of others, the certainties of autarchic self-help are replaced by the uncertainties inherent in anarchy, as long as we accept the basic premises of realist theory.

Glaser argues further that the risks of cooperation must be weighed against the risks of non-cooperation, such as risky arms races that could be lost. He does not note, though, that this is a view that can be ascribed readily to weaker parties in highly asymmetrical races. A strong party can be confident to outrace its competitor(s), while in close calls an incremental investment might suffice to stay even and thus not to lose. Glaser notes – correctly – that what counts for security in the first place is not power as such, but how power translates into military capabilities. However, this reformulation of the balancing needs in an anarchic world helps cooperation only marginally. For one, 'reserve power resources' can always be transformed into additional military capabilities – if we believe in the universal fungibility of power resources, as realism does. And secondly, as balances of military capabilities are precarious, rational actor governments will wish to have a margin of insurance against a possible miscalculation of the balance, a margin that might look threatening from the other side. If all other realist assumptions hold, renouncing this insurance margin for the sake of cooperation might look very risky indeed.

Glaser opens another front against the conventional realist argument that uncertainty about intentions works as a show-stopper for cooperation in maintaining that signaling of defensive intentions is possible by foregoing offensive options and sacrificing offensive capabilities. He agrees that this supposes a clear distinction between offensive and defensive, and that, while the signal will become all the clearer the more advantages the military technology of the day gives to the offensive – because the more options the signaler would actually forego – giving the signals would become ever riskier, as the clearest signals would probably mean serious risks to the signaler if the other side would not join the cooperation train (also Van Evera, 2000; Christensen, 1997). The major problem, however, is the intrinsic difficulty in sending signals that will be read correctly. For one, the distinction between offensive and defensive is never really clear, and interpretations may deviate considerably from reality – see the outset of the First and Second World Wars. What is meant as an unequivocally defensive move – for example, NATO's renunciation of conventional parity in Europe and the introduction of short-range tactical nuclear weapons as a stopgap measure – may be interpreted by the other side as outrageously offensive. We witness exactly this process presently in the context of the planning for theater missile defense in East Asia. Secondly, particularly in hostile relationships, the common ground for interpretation may be lacking. The West did not at all understand Khruschev's bold attempt to reduce the Red Army, and did not respond in kind, a factor that accelerated the Secretary-General's fall from power (see Grinevsky, 1996). In contrast, it learned to understand Gorbachev's signaling, but how much did it take to reach this effect? Gorbachev not only reduced unilaterally Soviet offensive capabilities, he opened up Soviet society, freed dissidents and stopped competition in troublespots around the world. Even so, Chancellor Kohl reacted to his moves by calling him 'another Goebbels', and NATO came close to another round of nuclear deployments as late as 1989. The crucial point theoretically is that the receiver can never be certain that there is not a piece of private information retained by the sender which might discard the benign interpretation, such as unknown priorities, different standards for evaluation, or hidden assets.

In summary, while 'defensive realism' is certainly much better suited to come up with more convincing explanations why major powers succeed in cooperating in the field of security, it appears to – almost invisibly – introduce change into basic realist assumptions about actors and structure that are somehow alien to the realist creed: to view cooperation as a self-help strategy takes it for granted that the mutual compliance by agreed rules is a viable model of behavior in international relations. In the end, betting on compliance would rely on trust in the exclusion of risks by deception, strategic cheating, lulling and surprise. Likewise, the assumption that signaling will succeed must rest on a notion of common language and common interpretative culture which is non-trivial and certainly not part and parcel of the realist model of international relations: to the contrary, it could be read as drawing constructivist elements into realism through the back door.

Are realists still realists? A particular puzzle for the realist creed is the considerable robustness of the nuclear non-proliferation regime (Davis, 1993). The quest for nuclear weapons as the 'ultimate insurance' against unforeseeable or uncertain threats should still be the primary choice for states acting in such an environment. If one sees the risk emerging from unwanted escalation, rather than from conscious power policies of actual or potential rivals, one breaks out significantly from the sort of calculus both classical and structural realism view as the rule for prudent statesmen. Relying on nuclear guarantees from others begs the question whether these others may be reliable, or shy away from making good on alliance promises, or may turn their superiority into blackmailing policies in the future. All these arguments are not just hypothetical. They have influenced states' choices in practice: 'Deterring the uncertain' is very much French and British nuclear doctrine today; the reliability of allies has haunted NATO throughout the Cold War, and has influenced French and Israeli nuclear choices. Being subject to an ally's nuclear blackmail was very much in de Gaulle's mind. It is hard to see how non-proliferation can be accounted

for within the realist theoretical body without borrowing elements such as trust, the intrinsic binding force of norms, and the like, from other theories.

Joseph Grieco himself, initially an impressive 'pessimist', has later modified realist theory so as better to accommodate the growing reality of cooperation. He has specified the conditions under which the 'relative gains' orientation may be relaxed, and thus cooperation may have a better chance of being realized. The most original, and also most problematic, deviation from standard realist theory is the admittance that the past – whether the other state has been for an extended period friend or foe – influences threat perception, and, consequently, the inclination to measure the relationship against the standard of relative gains or against some more relaxed referential system (Grieco, 1988). The crucial point here is that perception, interpretation of experience and the transfer thereof from one generation of policy-makers to the rest are arguments outside the realm of realism proper. They bear no causal relation to anarchy, the distribution of capabilities and polarity. They look breathtakingly like elements from a constructivist handbook. There is little doubt that they help to account better for variations in political reality, but clearly at the cost of consistency at the paradigmatic level.

The same verdict would apply to Randall Schweller's 'motivational realism'. He finds that the security dilemma does not rest in structure, but in the existence of predatory states, thereby moving the causes of insecurity from the system to the unit level and thereby, consequently, opening the road to problem-free security cooperation among non-predatory powers (Schweller, 1996). Correspondingly, Andrew Kydd argues that 'security seekers' create peaceful environments and thereby conditions for security cooperation (Kydd, 1997).

Even more compromising with other – neoinstitutionalist and liberal – approaches, Robert Jervis, whose 'Cooperation under the Security Dilemma' is the classic statement of the realist cooperation problematic (Jervis, 1978), and who has enumerated the formidable obstacles that anarchy puts in the way of security cooperation (Jervis, 1983, 1985, 1988), has recognized the capability of institutions to change preferences over outcomes, a strong break with the realist creed that states preferences, fixed by the survival imperative in anarchy, are virtually unchangeable (Jervis, 1999: 58–62).

The contradiction with regard to our subject divides 'pessimistic' and 'optimistic' realists (for the debates within the realist approach, see Brooks, 1997; Schweller and Priess, 1997). To assign sympathies to these different schools remains a difficult task. Pessimists deserve distinction as they preserve an optimum of theoretical coherence. Yet optimists, heroically sacrificing a measure of coherence, at least are able to explain some of the empirical security cooperation that we see every day (Legro and Moravcsik, 1999).

Neoinstitutionalist Accounts

Realist and, even more so, neorealist thinking can be modeled in rational choice terms, even though the origins of that theory did not emerge from the rational choice paradigm. Neoinstitutionalist analysts are firmly rooted in that paradigm; its most important foundational texts start from rational choice (Keohane, 1984; Oye, 1986), and in the academic debate, rational choice has clearly preserved dominance in the neoinstitutionalist discourse (Lake and Powell, 1999). Like realists, they start from the assumption of self-interested actors working in an international structure of anarchy. However, their assumption about the consequences of anarchy are more forgiving and less fixed on the imperative of survival in an environment of danger. Consequently, their assumptions about states' preferences are also not fixed on the relative gain assumption; they admit easily the desire of states to achieve absolute gains in welfare and security. Some confusion emerges from the neoinstitutionalist claim that their assumptions were identical with those of realism; they are not. In what follows it is shown that, if the harsh propositions of realism are adopted, neoinstitutionalist reasoning has a hard time explaining the emergence of cooperation, while if those assumptions are relaxed, it can contribute well to such an explanation.

Situation structure and problem structure as constraints on cooperation Institutionalists have identified factors that influence the propensity of given constellations of interactions for the creation or not of international cooperation, security cooperation included. In particular, the 'Tübingen school' in Germany has devised two relevant typologies. First, the type of 'situation structure', that is, the game that is played, influences the likelihood that cooperation will emerge. The game 'leader', in which a player will always earn its best payoff from cooperation, the moves of that player's partner notwithstanding, is obviously most favorable to cooperation. Prisoners' dilemma is at the center, while 'Rambo', where one player always reaps his best payoff by defecting, is least probable to engender cooperation. The second typology is the value at stake in the conflict at hand. Where parties struggle for absolutely assessed goods, cooperation is relatively easy. Next is conflict about means to achieve an objective appreciated by either player. Third is conflict about relatively assessed goods, and least favorable to cooperation is conflict about values. Since security falls normally in the third category, it is obvious that cooperation is not easily achieved (Rittberger, 1990; Zürn, 1992).

Communication in neoinstitutionalism The first neoinstitutionalist argument why cooperation in the security field is not only possible, but even likely under conditions of anarchy is that rational actors are not prevented from communicating as long as the exchange of information does not involve prohibitive cost. In indicating to their interlocutor their own interpretation about the situation both parties find themselves in, and in enlightening each other about their preferences, they may approach an outcome that is close to a Pareto-optimum and which neither has difficulties of accepting, since it serves the security interests of both parties well (Kydd and Snidal, 1993; Morrow, 1994).

The problem here is that security talk is not cheap in a realist world. Since Sun Tzu, the great classical Chinese strategist, it has been part and parcel of strategic thinking that surprise is the key to victory – and, conversely, falling victim to surprise may be the beginning of annihilation – while deception is a most useful instrument to achieve surprise in the first place. If this is so, then listening to information from somebody who is supposed to be a potential enemy is a treacherous endeavor. The intention might be sincere. But the intention might also be to filter in false information about the situation – for example to pretend to be weaker (or stronger) than one really is; this may lull the 'cooperation partner' into complacency before an onslaught; or it may intimidate the 'partner' into virtual surrender and the acceptance of an unequal distribution of whatever spoils the security cooperation might offer. Now countries considering security cooperation know of this danger; and they know the other side knows; and they know the other side knows they know, and so on ad infinitum. It is very hard to see, as long as we assume acute survival risks within anarchy, how cheap talk that is not really cheap helps us to arrive at cooperation (Johnson, 1993).

In another use of the communication argument, neoinstitutionalists explain that the gap from cooperation motivation to actual agreement can be overcome exactly if the partners can prove credibly their commitment to cooperation by giving signals that are costly to themselves; Sadat's speech before the Knesset is a vivid example (Fearon, 1997; Kydd, 2000; Morrow, 1999: 87–9). However, two questions arise: first, how would a rational actor give such a signal first, not knowing if the other side reciprocates, but having to pay the heavy costs anyway? The willingness to do that, for sure, enhances credibility. But the calculus for making this move remains unclear: as George Downs and David Rocke have proved, uncertainty about a prospective partner's responsiveness and a short time horizon make an initial cooperative step inadvisable under rational choice assumptions (Downs and Rocke, 1990: 201–5). Secondly, successful signaling in this sense presumes a common reference system for evaluating the content of this signal (compare the reasoning about 'defensive realism'). This condition is by no means sure, as research about security cultures (see below) has revealed, and the emergence of such an ideational superstructure appears to be exogeneous to neoinstitutionalist theory based on rational choice.

The shadow of the future   A second argument is the shadow of the future (Axelrod, 1984; Axelrod and Keohane, 1986; Goldstein, 1995). The prospect of repeated games relaxes the risks of the first round; the higher the net present value of the future, the less imposing the value of 'defecting' will appear at present. Three problems arise here: first, even if the game is sure to be continued into the distant future, getting a good deal becomes even more important and may induce negotiators to bargain harder, leading to standoff rather than to cooperation (Fearon, 1998). Second, because survival is at stake, the future is heavily discounted; this diminishes the expected payoff of cooperation and thus reduces the incentive to cooperate (Stein, 1990: ch. 4). Third, it is rather uncertain how many further rounds of the game will take place; if the security stakes are high – as they usually are – then the risk of the 'partner's' defection with asymmetrical gains in its pocket loom very large indeed (Lipson, 1984). A leading proponent of neoinstitutionalism has countered that what is needed is not absolute certainty that the game will be played in future rounds, but only a 'certain' probability that this will be the case, and that in more benign situations – certain alliance types, for example – an expectation iteration is not needed at all (Keck, 1997: 50–2). Unfortunately, the threshold for this probability was not quantified; but even if it were, the solution begs more questions than it answers. If there is a 'certain' probability (p) that a further round will be played, then there is the complementary probability $(1–p)$ that it will not. My expected utility is then diminished by exactly that probability times the expected damage which a defection will cause. A rational actor, desiring to neutralize this risk, will look for insurance against it. But incidentally, the assumption of anarchy eliminates also the practical institution of a neutral insurance company. The two insurance possibilities remaining are either to provide for an ally in case of defection of the 'partner' or to set aside some resources to make up for the loss. These two options, however, push us back into the well-known vicious cycle of the security dilemma: either enhances my own capabilities and must look somehow ominous to my *partner-in-spe*. Will not the enhancement of my capabilities – at the outset of security cooperation! – look like a preparation for defection? And if so, would not the partner feel compelled to reciprocate?

In fact, the partner would feel compelled to take some measures even before he discovered my own insurance moves. Being in exactly the same situation, and being a rational actor, the partner would as well have to consider insurance action before entering security cooperation for good. In other words, the evil $1–p$ probability of defection, however small or big p might be, propels us back into the security dilemma which we desired to leave through the door of security cooperation in the first place.

The relativity of the relative gains problem   A third argument put forward by rational choice institutionalists is that the problem of relative gains does not kill the possibility of cooperation as long as the asymmetries of gains are so small that they cannot be translated into decisive military advantage (Powell, 1991, 1994; Snidal, 1991a, 1991b). This sounds reasonable. It echoes the famous dictum of Henry Kissinger in the heated debates, about the SALT I Interim Agreement: 'What in heaven is nuclear superiority?' Nevertheless, we have to note that in this debate the other side believed that the small inequalities inbuilt in the marginally higher upper limits for the Soviet Union were relevant indeed; the partisans of this view, led by the late Senator Henry 'Scoop' Jackson, prevailed in inserting the prescription into the ratification resolution that no future nuclear arms control treaty must establish lower limits for US forces. This episode serves as a reminder that the asymmetry problem is anything but trivial.

The problem is twofold. First, it is intrinsically hard to quantify cooperation gains in the first place. Given the fluid situation in international politics, the permanent possibility of allies changing sides, the evolution of military technology and the virtually insuperable difficulties of assessing their meaning (see above), distributing the spoils of security cooperation in an equal way is close to impossible; this was discussed in some detail in connection with realism. The argument applies here as well.

Second, the future consequence of a present distribution of gains remains bogged down in uncertainty. Every investment can carry enhanced profits. Small asymmetries may be amplified through smart use by the better winner, and used to secure even more unequal distribution outcomes in later rounds. A slightly stronger party may be able to press its advantage, either against immediate rivals, or to force a weaker party to bandwagon. It is all very well to maintain that relative gains only matter if they accumulate in the future to dangerous levels (Matthews, 1996, 112–46), but how can a state be sure they will not? In other words, the shadow of the future, usually seen as a benevolent element for security cooperation, may turn upside down and impede, rather than foster, collaboration among self-interested parties that behave strictly within the rules of rational choice textbooks. Even if we assume that there is somewhere a threshold between small and big gains in asymmetries, small asymmetries are still good enough to make governments nervous as long as the rational choice paradigm is ruling within a 'realist' type of anarchic environment. Only if we relax the assumption about the threat of survival and/or introduce common knowledge about the persistence of non-threatening preferences among the states can institutionalist assumptions help explain the emergence of security cooperation.

The perseverance of cooperative regimes

Rational choice institutionalism is in a much better position to analyze and explain the perseverance of security cooperation once it has been established in the first place (Keohane, 1984). Security institutions are a tool to reduce transaction costs among parties. They open communication channels with established rules: parties are told what they have to report, what they can expect to receive from their partners in terms of relevant information, and they are given standards of evaluation to review and scrutinize that information (Mitchell, 1998). Games played over extended rounds within the framework of an established institution prolong the shadow of the future considerably and positively. Means are available to clarify ambiguities – an evil problem in an unregulated security environment. In multilateral frameworks, parties can rely on the solidarity of regime communities if ambiguities turn out to be real and effective breaches of the rules. Lowered transaction costs, provision of information and institutionalized enforcement are important incentives to cooperate (on enforcement, see Downs et al., 1996). In comparison with the 'standing alone' posture in an uninstitutionalized world, these are tangible advantages. They explain why countries most of the time abide by institutions' rules – even if in their absence they would have pursued different policies – and support them as long as the overwhelming majority of their partners do the same (for example Duffield, 1992, 1994).

Another rationalist–institutionalist argument helps us understand why institutions show an astonishing robustness despite challenging changes in the international structures that existed when they were created. For instance, the Nuclear Non-proliferation Treaty has survived the breakdown of bipolarity, the structure instrumental in bringing it to life, the rule-breaking by both Iraq and the Democratic People's Republic of Korea, and the defiance by India and Pakistan demonstrating their nuclear weapons status, and thus the failure of the NPT to achieve the objective of full universality. A second impressive example is the Treaty on Conventional Forces in Europe (CFE), concluded to establish a balance of forces between the two alliances of the East–West conflict. The conflict has gone, one alliance has disappeared, the other one has swallowed part of the former's membership. One could surmise that the CFE Treaty had outlived its mission, and yet member states have worked with enthusiasm to adapt this apparently obsolete instrument to the new circumstances! Finally, the perseverance of NATO even after the enemy against which this alliance was established had disappeared is comprehensible in an institutionalist framework much better than in a realist one (Hellmann and Wolf, 1993; Lepgold, 1998; McCalla, 1996; Skalnes, 1998).

Rationalist institutionalists tell us that governments calculate the utility of existing institutions against the investment costs for new ones. This calculation, in most cases, results in unequivocal support for the – however imperfect – institutional structures that are there. To summarize, neoinstitutionalism, built upon the rational choice paradigm, gives a good explanation why countries should wish to cooperate in the security sector (Keohane and Martin, 1995). Their rigorous models force us to think through thoroughly our assumptions about actors' preferences and the constellations they create.[2] It is also apt to overcome the domestic/international divide by constructing two-level games (Evans et al., 1993; Zangl, 1994) or to model national leaders as replaceable 'principal-agent' of domestic politics (Bueno de Mesquita and Siverson, 1995; Morrow, 1991). However, it has great difficulties in explaining convincingly how actors can overcome the considerable barriers that the structural constraints rationalism buys from realism – unfettered anarchy, self-interested actors – pose to the jump from the mere motivation to cooperate to real cooperation. The call for including cognitive factors into rationalist cooperation theory has thus been heard repeatedly, including in one of the most meticulous rationalist case studies on security regime formation (Bernauer, 1993: ch. 7; see also Hasenclever et al., 1997, ch. 6).

Liberal Accounts

Liberal theory seeks the roots and causes of external behavior in domestic structures and processes.[3] Accordingly, different domestic structures will cause different preferences in security policy, notably variations in the inclination to enter security cooperation. At the most general level, then, liberal theory would analyze security cooperation as the result of a convergence of benign, cooperation-prone national preferences, engendered by domestic coalitions for which such cooperation obtains priority (Risse-Kappen, 1991).

Liberal cooperation theory: democratic peace

There is a particular branch of liberalism that has developed substantive hypotheses about preference-formation in democracies bearing on security cooperation: this is the theory of 'democratic peace', first developed by Immanuel Kant, but now with a very solid body of IR theorizing behind it.[4] In its 'monadic' variant, based more on the Lockean and commercial foundations, it is hypothesized that democracies prefer peace to war because of citizens' basic interests in self-preservation and welfare and wish to avoid costly (and sinful) external violent adventures. Another root cause is the value orientation of the democratic citizen, which prefers non-violent means of conflict management and solution to the decision by the sword, because he and she appreciate the value of human life. In the same vein, democracies and their citizens are disinterested in the costs of maintaining highly armed standing armies, preferring the minimalist defense posture of militias instead (Russett, 1990, 1993).

It is not the objective here to discuss the contribution of democracy to peace, but what follows for security cooperation. Deducing from democratic peace argumentation, we would expect democracies to seek understandings with potential enemies – democracies or not – to provide for procedures to settle conflicts peacefully, externalizing the internal modes of conflict management, and to find ways to agree on minimalist military postures in order to prevent costly arms races. Kant himself, and consequently the modern version of the theory, has proposed international organization as a way to frame the international interactions between the republics (B. Crawford, 1994; for a promising variant compare Deudney, 1995; more critical on this point is Remmer, 1998). But the theory is ambivalent on whether this mode of cooperation is also appropriate for relations between democracies and non-democracies. However, since their intrinsic peacefulness would compel democracies to seek ways to settle their problems with non-democratic states also in a non-violent manner, it would appear that in the monadic version of this theory organized security cooperation and arms control/disarmament in a heteronomous setting would be a logical deduction (Russett et al., 1998; for additional empirical evidence see Leeds and Davis, 1999). In other words, what appears a puzzle for other theories – the alliance version of security cooperation as well as cooperative efforts to come to collaborate with rivals and enemies – liberal theory sees as the inevitable and consequent outgrowth of a particular form of internal rule. The reasoning would allow for all forms of security cooperation we know of, be it alliance (among democracies), arms control, broader security regimes and collective security arrangements.

The dyadic variant maintains that the 'peacefulness' argument applies only to relation among democracies. Initially, this insight was forced upon theorists by empirical findings that the warlikeness of democracies was not so different statistically from that of non-democracies, but that 'democratic wars' were fought almost exclusively against non-democratic states, while among democracies a 'zone of peace' prevailed. However, there are voices – and some empirical support – suggesting that democracies may be generically less war-prone than other systems (Ray, 1995). There is some debate on the causes of this difference. One school argues for institutional affinity: open, welfare-orientated societies are more prone to develop patterns of cooperation with each other than other types of political systems. Cooperation intensifies and extends its scope, ultimately into the security area – a neofunctionalist argument. In addition, transparency, an essential condition for deep and intense security collaboration, is an attribute of democracy, but not of autocratic or totalitarian states. Consequently, democracies lose much less in opening up their military sector to the eyes of their partners than these other states, and feel more comfortable as transparency rises. We should thus expect security cooperation in all forms to be much stronger among democracies than between them and non-democracies.

Another school argues with the mechanism of mirror-image empathy embedded in political culture. Democracies have an image of themselves as peaceful and rational; they project this image onto fellow democracies. Being democratic is interpreted as a valid marker for peaceful intentions. As a consequence, the security dilemma shrinks, and the risk of being cheated or of getting unequal gains out of cooperation is seen as negligible (Owen, 1994; Risse-Kappen, 1995a; Weart, 1994, 299–316). Democracies are thus not only able to develop far-reaching regimes of cooperation among each other across the security sector, or to enter long-term military alliances, but to take serious steps at integration, such as joint commands, joint procurement, joint planning or even joint services (such as the integrated navy of the Benelux states). Democracies have much better prospects to develop long-lasting, intimate alliances (Risse-Kappen, 1995b; Starr, 1997; more critical on the joint democratic organization thesis are Lai and Reiter, 2000) and even security communities, an advanced type of security cooperation that will be described in more detail in the next section.

As a pragmatic consequence of liberal theory, democratization appears as the necessary tool to extend the zone of peace over the globe. If democracies are more cooperation-prone and peaceful than others, or if at least security cooperation can be taken for granted as the prevailing mood within and among democratic states, then the more democracies, all the better for security cooperation! In fact, this conclusion has long trespassed across the boundary of academic discussion and has become the creed of Western security policy, providing a powerful self-image – and ideology – for the Western alliance (Muravchik, 1991).

Empirical evidence gives a first-cut confirmation of aspects of both versions of liberal theory. For monadic liberalism, the growth of security cooperation – bilateral, regional and global – has seen democracies in the driver's seat. The most essential attempts at providing security jointly, the League of Nations and the United Nations, emerged from concepts developed in democratic countries (notably the United States). Equally, arms control and nonproliferation were 'invented' in the United States and quickly picked up by other democratic states who persuaded others to follow suit. The dyadic version finds some affirmation in the fact that security cooperation is much broader in scope and more intense and deep between democracies than between them and non-democracies, not to mention security relations among non-democratic states (Mousseau, February 1997, 73–87). NATO and the EU are the cases in point. Indeed, it is plausible that the transfer of the structural and normative principles that guide conflict management inside democracies to the security cooperation institutions of the Western world are primary causes for both their relatively smooth operation and their longevity (Ikenberry, 1998/9).

Why do democracies behave differently in security cooperation?   Nevertheless, liberal theory leaves open some very important questions. To start with, one should assume – on the basis of the theoretical argument and the causal chains assumed by either version – that the behavior of democracies in security cooperation should be rather similar, and that variations for the same democracy over time should be limited. This, however, is not the case. If we compare the present inclination of democratic states to expand the realm of security cooperation in ways that imply further constraints on national sovereignty, we find countries like Canada, Sweden, the Netherlands or Germany in the forefront, the United Kingdom somewhere in the middle, and France, and even more the United States, towards the end. For the United States, the commitment to security cooperation evolves through waves, with the early 1980s and the late 1990s showing particularly strong unilateralism, and the early 1970s and early 1990s displaying determined efforts to cooperate.

Within liberal theory itself, we find some clues to explain this deviation from standard expectation. Democratic peace theory is a particular mode of liberal theory that predicts conclusions on expected behavior from fundamental system attributes. However, other variations of liberal theory rely on more detailed differentiations between various types of democratic society and their relation to the political system, or between different types of democratic institutions. If we take this as a starting point, we may expect variations in security cooperation depending on the strengths and weaknesses of

countervailing forces within a democratic country: the pluralistic structure of policy-making gives various interests different chances of access and influence, and the outcome then depends on the balance of chances of the pro- and contra-security cooperation forces within a country (for the argument and additional empirical studies, compare Risse-Kappen, 1994 and Knopf, 1998).

An example for such a preference-biasing factor might be the 'military–industrial complex'. This socio-political formation is thought to present a coalition of the defense industry, the military services, security think-tanks, military research and development establishments, defense-dependent local or regional governments and their representatives in national parliaments. While this formation is not necessarily opposed in principle to all forms of security cooperation, it would request constraints on it if it threatened priority armament projects, the financial resources allocated to defense, or research and development options. To preserve a considerable degree of freedom of choice in defense is thus a basic interest of the MIC that would tend to keep security cooperation limited unless more cooperation-minded forces were to overwhelm the collective MIC influence.

Can democracies cooperate with non-democracies?   There is another difficulty for the dyadic democratic peace strand of liberal theory in both versions: to come up with explanations as to how security cooperation is possible with non-democracies. This appears so easy to the monadic version, as democracies are supposed to pursue collaboration 'tous azimuts'(all directions). However, since this theory bases the roots and prerequisites of cooperative behavior so exclusively in the structure of the political system of democracy, it can hardly explain where motivations to reciprocate should emerge from in non-democratic systems. It must thus be assumed that democracies are offering such outrageously asymmetrical deals in their own disfavor that the asymmetrical gains accruing from such agreements satisfy the nasty interest calculus of the non-democratic governments; but then it is difficult to understand how such cooperation results could resonate well in an enlightened electorate.

The dyadic version is facing a different problem with similar results. The increasing in-group feeling of democratic states – facilitated through their extraordinary inclination to join together in international organizations, including security alliances, an important pillar of the democratic peace – produces a commensurately growing aversion against the non-democratic 'other'. Personification of this hostility and demonization of the chosen personality (Saddam Hussein, Slobodan Milosevic) creates the image of a dangerous and powerful, alien enemy who must be vanquished before he can do too much damage to the democracies and their security environment. This explains well why democratic states gang up together to solve conflicts with non-democracies – Iraq, Yugoslavia – by force if needed. It falls short of a convincing explanation of how this aversion can be overcome so that collaboration is possible with the loathed 'other'; however, as we have seen, such collaboration has been seen and begs explanation. Again, the most obvious answer is a rational choice calculus; another would be customs or cultural habits. None of these answers are really rooted in liberal theory. The first intrudes into rationalism, the second into constructivism. It thus appears that it would be difficult for liberalism to stand alone in the battle for good explanations as to why security cooperation is possible.

Antinomies within the theory Three further puzzles and contradictions deserve mentioning. The first concerns an internal contradiction between norm dynamics in democratic systems and the requirements of security cooperation. Privacy and ownership rights count among important normative prescriptions and proscription in democracies. Transparency requirements, however, cut deeply into these rights of private actors. The difficulties to arrive at a consensus in the endgame of the Chemical Weapons Convention negotiations, the reservations introduced by the US Senate into the ratification decisions which, *inter alia*, prohibit taking chemical samples from US industry outside US borders (in strict contradiction to the stipulations of the CWC verification system) and the barriers to a successful negotiation of a transparency and verification protocol for the Biological Weapons Convention pay witness to this fundamental problem.

The second concerns a vicious dynamic that applies to both monadic and dyadic democratic peace theory. If democracies are shy to risk their citizens' lives in war, and bear sympathetic feelings even to the subjects of an enemy – having internalized the value of human rights and human lives – but still regard the possibility of being attacked as real, then an important conclusion emerges for their armament policy: they must try to develop weapons technologies that would be capable of protecting their own country while limiting victims on both sides in war, and helping to finish war very quickly. Unfortunately, such arms technology providing superiority runs counter to the requirements of security cooperation through arms control regimes and is powerfully feeding the security dilemma. In other words, the very motivations that are an important drive for democratic peace may tend to cause an armament research, development and procurement policy that prevents security cooperation. The prominence of National Missile Defense and the Revolution in Military Affairs fits this hypothesis well.

Finally, there might be a last contradictory dynamic that is both part of democratic peace-driven

security cooperation while at the same time obviating it. The extension of the zone of democratic peace is, by the logic of the theory, the only secure way to work towards eternal global peace. However, an increasing number of democratic states working together intimately in the security field may look very threatening for those non-democratic states who are not – or much less intensely – participating in security cooperation with the community of democratic countries. Feeling overwhelmed, these countries may then seek their security in increasingly unilateralist armament moves. Again, some statements coming from Moscow in response to NATO enlargement, and echoed in Beijing, may point to such a vicious mechanism.

Constructivist Accounts

Constructivists do not believe in fixed, quasi-natural structures or individual preferences that give way to quasi-mechanic laws of system development and actor behavior. They see agents' preferences as being in eternal development, and structures as historically evolved and thus malleable. However, malleability at both the agent and structure sides is not limitless. Structures change usually only slowly, and what agents think and do is influenced by constraints on and opportunities for action that structures afford. Nevertheless, there are leeways. Situations where action is required retain a degree of indeterminacy. Several options are open, and if agents opt continuously for options at the limit of what structure admits, structure will be subject to change. As Alexander Wendt has shown, this theoretical model for agent–structure change can be applied to the security dilemma. Since the environment is not depicted, as in realism, as necessarily survival-threatening, states are in a position to choose non-aggressive, defensive options for national security policy and cooperative options for inter-state security interactions. By continuing this choice over time, state-agents are capable of changing their security environment – with little risk to come – from highly competitive (and deadly dangerous) to highly cooperative (and much more forgiving).

In the constructivist paradigm, the emergence of security cooperation, thus, rests on two requirements:

- A structure that permits to an actor moderate, non-aggressive moves without the immediate risk of perishing; this requirement, one can boldly state, was given throughout the 'Westphalian' age, and more and more so as the twentieth century approached its close.
- Agents that would discover such options and choose them as better alternatives to a perpetual rivalry for superiority, with all the unpleasant risks such a course of behavior entails.

The malleability of security concerns
Structures in the constructivist paradigm are not primarily material. Matter can only contribute to structural features if it acquires social meaning. If it does, it becomes part of the structure. The primary quality of structure, however, consists of the meaning ascribed to it by the agents whose perpetual practice reproduces and changes it. This explains why the normative and the habitual dimensions loom so large in constructivist thinking. Habits tell actors what to do in most unproblematic and problematic situations in which they find themselves. Norms tell them how to consider possible courses of actions in situations where mere habits are of no help. But as said before, norms and habits are not necessarily determining behavior in all and every situation. Indicators of where actors are and stand may be ambiguous or blurred. A residual creativity is thus always implied in any new action, and this means that habits and norms are by themselves changeable. In this, constructivist theory is analogous to international law that maintains that legal rules change if states show deviant behavior in large numbers over a considerable span of time.

On this ontological basis, security cooperation is less of a puzzle than for some other approaches. It is, in principle, a plausible and thus possible mode of interaction (Ruggie, 1998). Constructivist theory can take two approaches to inquire into the subject: it can reconstruct, in the abstract, the conditions in the structure–actor interface that can bring cooperation about and maintain it; and it can analyze, in empirical history, how cooperation actually did develop, persist and decay.

In his seminal article 'Anarchy is what states make of it', Alexander Wendt (1992) elaborated the first approach. He constructed a hypothetical interaction between two actors and described how a collaborative structure would emerge from it. He positions two actors into a not-yet-structured environment; their first encounter, incidentally, emerges through a series of mutual, more or less amicable, moves. He then shows how, as a result of a couple of such encounters, mutual expectations develop that the partner will behave in a cooperative way, and that a norm to behave cooperatively ensues. What was spontaneous reciprocity in the first place becomes mutually expected habit. A normative structure that fosters cooperation develops, rather than prescriptions for extremely cautious behavior driven by fear, as in the classical security dilemma among states.

Security cooperation has, of course, not emerged in a no-man's land, but in a very violent and competitive international environment. Constructivists put much emphasis on change; individual and collective learning, defined as a change of basic ideas about security, and an ensuing adaptation of the constitutive and regulative norms that shape the environment, is the basic mechanism by which change emerges. The constructivist ontology, in which neither structure nor agency are unchangeably fixed, but mutually modifiable and changeable, supports this emphasis (Koslowski, and Kratochwil, 1994; Lebow, 1994; Stein, 1994). The dynamic relation between material and ideational factors has been shown by Steve Weber's analysis of *détente*. Nuclear weapons, in his view, changed the international structure by eliminating concerns about relative gains. The first *détente*, however failed because the two antagonists developed different understandings of what it meant. Only when ideas converged on the notion of 'joint custodianship' could broad security cooperation evolve (Weber, 1990; similar results are reported by Bonham et al., 1997).

Initiation of a change in the normative structure   The initiation of learning and change needs ideational/normative entrepreneurs who offer an alternative discourse to pure power politics. Much of the empirical work by constructivists has been devoted to identifying such initiators and to analyzing the type of activities by which they succeeded in persuading decision-makers to adopt their suggestions.

Frequently, ideas for cooperation did not originate with governments – supposed to calculate cooly national interests – but from non-governmental individuals and organizations. The model of the 'epistemic community' – a transnational group of experts who come to share specific ideas about a policy field and derive action programs for cooperation from these ideas – has been applied to the evolution of arms control regimes in the East–West contexts (Adler, 1992): security experts from the United States and the Soviet Union, starting from quite different positions, developed a common framework for regulating the risky arms competition. This epistemic arms control community succeeded in establishing a new paradigm on security thinking (mutual assured destruction stabilized by agreements) as the leading – if not uncontested – norm for the two superpowers (Checkel, 1998; Evangelista, 1995, 146–89; Risse-Kappen, 1994). From there, important agreements such as the SALT Treaties or the ABM Treaty emerged (Kubbig, 1996); such experts, on the Soviet side, later became close advisors to Mikhail Gorbachev and helped shape his 'New Thinking', the basis for the growth in security cooperation in the late 1980s and early 1990s.

A second source for initiating security cooperation is disarmament-specialized non-governmental organizations. Such organizations follow a logic of action different from that of government. Almost universally, they start from a humanistic value orientation that leads them to demand and support disarmament steps (Keck and Sikkink, 1998; Smith et al., 1997). An outstanding success by such a nongovernmental movement was the landmine campaign (Price, 1998, 613–44). Joining more than 2,000 organizations across the globe, the campaign managed to persuade a group of governments to take the lead for an international convention on anti-personnel landmines, and retained their influence throughout the negotiations with a view to resisting the watering down of a full prohibition of those weapons. Non-governmental organizations, thus, not only initiated a new agenda, but helped shape the emerging cooperative norm even in detail (for several case studies compare Risse-Kappen, 1995c).

A third initiator is the benevolent individual. Martha Finnemore has traced the origins of modern humanitarian law of war – one of the most striking civilizational projects in security cooperation – back to the efforts of a single person, Henri Dunant, the founder of the Committee of the Red Cross (Finnemore, 1996). With immense energy and commitment, Dunant managed to project his ideas on limiting carnage in wartime and excessive cruelty into high politics; concerns by the military and deep skepticism in various governments were overcome. A self-sustaining process was started which led to a continuing broadening and deepening of the norms up to the present system of the Geneva Conventions and the Convention on Certain Conventional Weapons. Remarkably for such a value-driven project, transcultural boundaries were easily broken, as proven by the existence and growth of the Red Crescent, the Red Cross's Islamic partner organization. Humanitarian law of war regimes have changed profoundly our understanding of right and wrong in a conflict situation, and have equally changed our definition of who is counted as a legitimate state in international affairs and who falls into the category of a 'rogue'.

Identity and the process of preference-shaping This points to an important difference between rationalist and constructivist approaches to security regimes. For constructivists, regimes are not just instrumental systems of rules designed to regulate issue-specific state behavior with a view to enhance all participants' interests, with preferences and identities given. Rather, they tend to reshape preferences themselves. The norms they contain tell states not only what they should do but what they are supposed to wish; at an even deeper level, it impacts upon what states believe they should be. A decent actor in international affairs is one that does not even think of employing atrocities in war for the sake of victory, one that supports the strengthening and sharpening of the respective international rules, and one that does not have too amiable a relationship with states whose compliance with these rules is not assured. Norms that have become generally accepted and have enjoyed validity over an extended period of time will thus shape states' identities (Wendt, 1994). As an example, the embracing of the idea of democracy and human rights by the

CSCE in its Paris Charter in 1990 established the democratic state as the ideal identity in this region, depicted the non-democratic state as a security concern and opened a new practice – hitherto seen as illegitimate or at least contested – that interference in non-democratic internal affairs was not only desirable, but necessary to overcome possible risks to security and peace (Flynn and Farrell, 1999).

Germany's relationship to the Nuclear Non-proliferation Treaty is a case in point. Germany felt initially target and victim of this regime. It did its best to restrict the scope and impact of the rules and behaved initially accordingly. Over time, Germany came to tolerate, then to determinedly apply the rules. When reunification occurred, Germany had unlearned its opposition and instead understood non-nuclear status as part and parcel of its own identity. This explains why the parliament voted unanimously to support indefinite extension of the Treaty (and thus infinite perpetuation of Germany's 'lower status'), helping to eliminate a weakness of the Treaty that German diplomats had worked hard to insert some twenty-five years before. German non-proliferation policy, in the late 1990s, was devised and executed not from the role of a grudging anti-regime rebel, but from an identity of committed non-nuclear weapon state; acting within the regime had profoundly changed the way in which German political élites looked upon the identity of their own state (Berger, 1998; Duffield, 1999; Müller, 1999; Müller and Kötter, 1990).

Security cultures and subcultures Under normal circumstances, policy aims at making the international and the domestic discourse on security compatible, while being shaped by both. The stabilizing structure that emerges over time from the interaction of the two discourses is 'security culture', a set of values, norms, rules and practices with regard to security that gives thinking and acting in the security field of a specific state a particular, sometimes singular, pattern; states in a given region may share a set of cultural values or a security culture as a whole. Security cultures define identity and thereby shape preferences. Thus they frame action and reaction in specific situations and help explain the considerable variation in security policies among states that may share the same security environment and/or are endowed with fairly similar domestic institutions (Katzenstein, 1996; Krause, 1998).

Even specific sub-cultures may influence the capability of states to enter and maintain cooperative relationships. Traditions, value-orientations and deep-seated priorities by the military can take a particular impact upon security policy and facilitate or impede security cooperation (Farrell, 1998; Johnston, 1995; Klein, 1991; J. Snyder, 1990). Either the military as the decisive expert group can exert a virtual veto over decisions for or against cooperating in the security area (Legro, 1995), or their views may spread over society as to influence the whole security culture of a country, such as in the 'cult of the offensive' so popular at the outset of the First World War (J. Snyder, 1984; Van Evera, 1990).

When benign security cultures converge, interests are interpreted in a similar way and cooperative institutions abound, states may form security communities as specific institutions for security cooperation. The concept of the security community, initially originating from the functionalist approach (Deutsch et al., 1957), has been appropriated by constructivists as entities uniquely fit for studying the institutional effects of converging interpretations, values and security cultures, that is, of variables emphasized by constructivism (Adler and Barnett 1998). Members of such communities develop mutual images of each other that make the thought of violent conflict unthinkable; in addition, the 'other' is represented within one's own mind. Perpetual, dense communication helps in addition to include the partners' interests, wishes and preferences within one's own decision-making (Risse-Kappen, 1995a). Research has shown that democratic countries have displayed a strong inclination to form such communities – this may be the most important contribution so far by constructivism to the debate on the 'democratic peace'. Yet it appears that cultural affinity is another variable that helps to bring about at least a weaker form of security communities, such as in Latin America or the Gulf Cooperation Council, thus putting considerable weight on the cultural variable.

Constructivism contributes strong arguments for explaining both stability and change, not only in policy outcomes but, more importantly, in preference formation and – at a deeper level – identity. It thereby makes up for some blind spots in rationalist theories. Its weakness, however, is that it has not yet managed to specify the contexts in which one or the other set of identity/preferences is more likely. This may not be intrinsic to either the epistemology or the ontology of constructivism, but it has not been done. The approach is thus lacking predictive power, and some of its interpretations of past events may appear to a skeptical observer arbitrary.

Postmodernist Accounts

While constructivists pay due attention to security discourses, they are also interested in how these discourses relate to the observable material reality of power relations 'out there'. In contrast, postmodernism focuses on discourses exclusively. While the existence of a reality 'out there' is not denied, its intelligibility is refuted. Since the 'out there' is represented for us in perception and interpretation through language only, we cannot deal with it other than through these representational artifacts. We can describe and analyze discourses only, without the vain hope of discovering behind the words the real thing: there is no corresponding theory of truth. Nevertheless, concepts that are central to mainstream international relations, and particularly the security debates, take pride of place in postmodernist theory, too: power and hegemony. However, these concepts do not address the relationship between states, classes, or individuals 'out there', but the subordination and domination relationships between the discourses themselves. Postmodernists ask for the history of present interpretations and understandings ('archeology', 'genealogy'), trying to dismantle the aura of necessity and incontradictability that surrounds them. In the course of this, they identify alternative views of the issue in question that have been suppressed – silenced – as the presently hegemonic discourse made its way to ascendancy (Foucault, 1973, 1980).

Given the prioritization and the sense of urgency that common security discourses contain, they are a natural target for postmodern analysis: since a security discourse integrates, explicitly or implicitly, the notion of fear and the threat of force, it is uniquely placed to function in a discursive practice of power and hegemony (Walker, 1986).

Securitization   The deconstruction of the security discourse has been developed into a sophisticated theory as well as methodology of analysis by the Copenhagen School, notably Ole Waever (Waever et al., 1993).[5] In line with the core postmodernist argument, objective analysis of a constellation with a view to identify security threats to a given actor is refuted. Since a given constellation can motivate a set of very different, equally legitimate interpretations, since the world 'out there' is always perceived and analyzed through the lenses of language-bound cultural filters, the only object of analysis can be the discourse of the actors. This is in full agreement with the postmodernist argument: 'Danger is not an objective condition. It is not a thing which exists independently of those to whom it may become a threat. ... Danger is an effect of interpretation' (Campbell, 1992: 1–2).

Security analysis has thus to focus on discourses of 'securitization'. Constellations are not a security problem by themselves; they become one by the application of specific speech acts by actors. The speech act of securitization consists of identifiable components. These are (a) the declaration of an existential threat to a given community to which the speaker belongs, requiring priority attention for dealing with this situation and (b) the request for extraordinary, non-routine measures to cope with the threat identified in (a). The process of securitization is only complete, however, if the performative effect intended by the speaker obtains: the speech act is directed to an audience and is only successful if the audience accepts the validity of

(a) and (b), consequently putting (b) into action (Waever, 1989). The move is all but interest-free. Since it gives the state the legitimate claim to go beyond the limits of routine political behavior, and since securitization claims are most frequently made by the power-holders of the state, the act serves to reaffirm their rule over society. By invoking the extraordinary measures for defending against the alleged threat, securitization opens the specter of enhanced fears abroad; the dangerous spiral of the security dilemma, at its core, is thus not a matter of accumulating hardware, but of applying specific terms of language to interpretable situations.

The way out of the dilemma cannot be sought in ever more 'national security policies' with the big apparatuses of military defense, intelligence and so on at its core that tend to perpetuate the securitization process. Rather, desecuritization helps to overcome it. To remove issues out of the realm of security language, and submitting it to the normal (non-extraordinary) instruments of everyday politics, is the only way out of the trap created by the securitization speech act. Only if we have stopped talking (or even thinking) in security terms have we become truly secure. The job of the researcher is thus to identify securitization processes, to analyze and reveal the consequences, and to point to desecuritization as the alternative path (Waever, 1995).

No doubt the securitization approach is, again, a most useful tool to deal with the risks embedded in setting security agendas. It creates a clear operational standard with which security discourses can be analyzed. Yet it begs two questions that, as an exclusive approach to the field, make it less than satisfactory.

For one, we cannot be satisfied with exclusively analyzing speech acts and their consequences. If we want to predict the consequences of securitization, we must have a model for how the ensuing action affects the relation with other actors in the field. For this, we need also an image of these actors. This amounts to nothing less than a fairly comprehensive analysis of structures and processes 'out there' with which our discourse is supposed to interact.

The second criticism is that security cooperation cannot be analyzed properly with the securitization approach. The opposite to securitization is desecuritization, removing an issue from the language of security (Buzan et al., 1997). But this is not what partners in security cooperation do. Rather, they recognize that an issue is security-relevant, containing risks to the existence of all of them; nuclear weapons is the most obvious example. It is the mutual recognition that the existential risks existed in the interaction system created by hair-trigger ready nuclear arms on both sides that motivated the astonishing series of negotiations and agreements which established the field of nuclear arms control. These were indeed 'extraordinary measures', namely close cooperation with the rival in the most

sensitive field. The field was not desecuritized at all, but repeated speech acts of securitization were used to continue to motivate further steps towards cooperatively disentangling the nuclear stand-off, as they were used by the critics to request the end of arms control.

Inclusion/exclusion According to postmodernist analysis, the notion of security has to rely on a sharp polar differentiation between 'self' and 'other'. This distinction is very central to the whole deconstructivist endeavor in postmodernism, particularly in the version going back to Derrida. The insistence on the centrality of the subject, the hard core of modernist philosophy and everyday thinking and talking, can only be upheld if that subject, the self, is sharply separated from the alien 'other' against which it defines and defends its subjective identity. This distinction is one of inclusion – that which belongs – and exclusion – that which is alien. The same process evolves at the collective level of the state (Walker, 1988).

The state itself, as an artificial construct of identity, cannot exist without this discursive mechanism of inclusion and exclusion. It is the determined exclusion of the 'other' that construes the bounds between those included in the territorially enshrined boundaries of the construct. And it is the ascription of danger (threat, disorder, anarchy) to the excluded 'other' that produces the necessary discipline to subordinate the inhabitants of that territory to the prevailing identity discourse centered on the state (Ashley, 1998; Campbell, 1992). In fact, human beings could adopt many identities, and the permanent risk of defection from the hegemonic one has to be contained; the security discourse emerging from the self–other distinction serves that very function.

The inclusion–exclusion scheme applies to agent as well as to structure. And in both cases, it is not just a value-free description of different entities, but it contains heavy ascriptions of positive and negative values. The included is seen in a positive light: the internal structure offers order, stability, safety, security. The external disorder – anarchy in realist parlance – vibrates with threat, risk and danger. The security discourse thus is instrumental to rally strong support around the state, and to direct defensive energies against that which is outside.

The deconstructivist approach along the self/other, inclusion/exclusion border is a powerful and useful tool to uncover the origins of enemy images, and to reveal the abuse of propaganda and public influence in order to exaggerate threats and risks. It has, however, serious shortcomings. It is ill-equipped to look for, and find, polarities containing more than two poles, overlapping identities, partial compatibilities though all these are theoretical possibilities and can be found in practice and are indeed the foundation on which security cooperation is built. For example, Simon Dalby analyses the process by which the Committee of the Present Danger established a security discourse that became hegemonic over, and eventually destroyed, the *détente* discourse that prevailed previously (Dalby, 1990). But it is hard to explain from the same vantage point how the *détente* discourse could emerge from the Cold War in the first place. If the self/other divide is necessarily dominating the statist security discourse – being the precondition for the existence of the state – how could a 'third area', that of common interest, ever be recognized, codified and even expanded? For the area of cooperation rests on a (partial) amalgamation of self and other into a 'we', even though, in other respects, the distinction continued as sharply as before in the still unregulated spheres of international competition. It appears from this discussion that postmodernist deconstructivism contains an inbuilt bias that makes it difficult to account for inter-state security cooperation at all; significantly, Campbell's study of US foreign policy identifies all possible exclusions and constructions of enemies; it contains not a single word on the panoply of cooperative relationships in which the American state has been involved – and has quite frequently initiated – in the course of its foreign policy history (Campbell, 1992).

Does postmodernism recognize cooperation when it reads it?   Reading through postmodern security studies one discovers a virtual complete lacuna of analysis of the many instances of states cooperating in the security sector. The few that we find are problematic in their application of the inclusion/exclusion and hegemony/subordination schemes. Given the basic orientation of postmodernist analysis it is perhaps not incidental that certain types of security regimes that are ostensibly more symmetric than the hegemony/subordination divide would permit are not found, such as the Latin American Nuclear Weapon Free Zone, the Berlin Four Powers Agreement, CSCE, the CFE Treaty or superpower arms control.

Richard Price has tackled the genealogy of the Chemical Weapons Taboo as the growth and finally successful imposition of an image developed from what behavior is appropriate for a (Western) civilized country (Price, 1997). 'Belonging' to the included 'inside' means to behave according to the rules of this taboo. For all the sophisticated analysis that brings out this result, though, the question remains open why countries that have shown considerable resistance to Western attempts to impose a civilizational model, embrace the taboo in its ultimate form, the Chemical Weapons Convention; countries such as Iran, India, Indonesia or China.

The discriminatory nature of the nuclear non-proliferation regime has motivated postmodernist analysts to devote some attention to its analysis. It is seen by James Keeley as a hegemonic imposition

of a proliferation discourse over an alternative – but suppressed – discourse emphasizing nuclear disarmament. This hegemony, obviously, serves the power interests of the nuclear weapon states and is reproduced through the practices of regime members (Keeley, 1990).

Along very much similar lines (but curiously unaware of Keeley's study), David Mutimer has reconstructed the non-proliferation regime (Mutimer, 2000). While Keeley emphasizes directly its roots in the power hierarchy, Mutimer traces it back to an image of self-spreading technology. Technology, in his view, is thus at the heart of the – academic and political – 'proliferation discourse', and the inside/outside division is thus provided by the membership or non-membership in the various suppliers' groups; this, in turn, reveals the discourse as hegemonic along a North–South divide. Mutimer proposes a disarmament discourse as a dissenting alternative. Both accounts are seriously flawed. For one, the disarmament discourse has been dominant in international diplomacy (though not in nuclear weapon states' activities) throughout the existence of the NPT, and it became clearly dominant in the 1990s, as the discursive contests during the 1995 and 2000 Extension and Review Conferences revealed (Johnson, 2000). Secondly, while parts of US academia and the various administrations overemphasized the technical aspects, there is an abundance of scholarly analysis of nuclear proliferation and non-proliferation that focuses on the political factors and requests addressing them as first priority (for example Goldblat, 1985; Müller, 1987; Reiss, 1988; Snyder and Wells, 1985). Indeed, non-proliferation diplomacy has made continuous efforts to deal with the political issues; however, in some regions they proved intractable to the diplomatic instruments at hand. Third, some of the most difficult controversies about nuclear supplies arose within the members of the suppliers groups themselves – for example, between the United States and the European Union – for the simple reason that this group does not succumb easily to a dichotomic divide: all suppliers are recipients as well. Fourth, there is no fixed dichotomy between the 'non-proliferation' and 'disarmament' discourses. Countries with an impeccable disarmament pedigree such as Sweden, Ireland, New Zealand, South Africa or Brazil participate actively in the suppliers group. The participation of the two latter countries also shows that the North–South dichotomy has long become blurred. Mutimer's attempt to identify the 'proliferation discourse' as defined by him in other regimes as well is even less convincing. The Chemical Weapons Convention is emphatically a disarmament treaty, requesting in the first place the notification and dismantlement under strict verification of existing chemical arsenals. The same applies to one of his other examples, the Ottawa Convention banning antipersonnel landmines. That either Convention contains stipulations on verification and export surveillance is inevitable given the goals of disarmament: parties to such a convention want to make sure that those who have not signed cannot get easy access to the prohibited weapons and related technologies, and they want to assure that those subscribing to the rules abide by them and, if not, the rest get an early warning. Without verification and export controls, these goals cannot be satisfied.

The conclusion is very clear: the scheme of discursive inquiry, consisting of two dichotomies – inclusion/exclusion and hegemony/subordination – leads analysts to overlook those aspects of the discourses which don't fit: symmetries, compromises, cross-cutting identities, ambivalences, tri- or multipolar discourse structures, which are all more or less conducive to security cooperation – and therefore found in the respective regimes – than the structures postmodernists look for.[6] Rescue from the security quagmire in which the reification of the modern state has put mankind is not expected from state discourse and related actions, but from the ascendancy of the alternative discourse promoted by the postmodernists and for which they seek societal carriers in, *inter alia*, civil society (Dalby, 1997; Klein, 1988). If highest state representatives carry out such a changed discourse themselves – as Mikhail Gorbachev did – postmodernist analysis can at best describe it; how it could happen cannot be explained on the basis of the postmodernist approach, except by simply appointing Mikhail Gorbachev a 'critical strategic theorist'![7] Very ironically, the structures that poststructuralist analysis has claimed to find as typical in modernist discourses are used to construct a world of discourses that looks awfully similar to the world as constructed by realists: a world of sharp and dangerous hostility between 'we' and 'them', and a world of hegemony, suppression and struggle against it.[8] What remains on the positive side is the deconstructive method that is very useful to disentangle the ideologies of national security policy and their academic analysis.

Conclusion

None of the theoretical perspectives on security cooperation discussed in the previous paragraphs gives full satisfaction. Realism is useful by warning against well-minded illusions about cooperative possibilities in the light of the barriers posed by power politics, but is short on explaining why, under the circumstances, security cooperation has been relatively successful if not abundant. Its counterpart at the other end of the spectrum, postmodernism, mirrors curiously that skepticism. It supplies us with useful tools to uncover the ideological roots of much of present security policy, but – as realism – puts so much emphasis on hostility (that is, the inclusion/exclusion divide) that real cooperative relationships can be hardly seen as anything else but hegemony imposed on the carriers of suppressed discourses. Rational choice informs us about the constellations of preferences that are more or less favorable to security cooperation, and about the useful role of institutions in reducing uncertainty and transaction costs. But it leaves us wondering how the states, despite these prospects, can overcome the profound impediments to engaging in those institutions under the dire circumstances of the struggle for survival in anarchy in the first place. Liberalism, in the form of democratic peace theory, offers a rich theory of how security cooperation is motivated and maintained. But its one (dyadic) version falls short of explaining how democracies come to cooperate with non-democracies, and both versions have difficulties in accounting for the vast variation in cooperative behavior among democracies. Finally, constructivism, with its emphasis on ideas and the cultural grounding of behavior, its treatment of the interplay between material and ideational factors and between structure and agency, may be best fitted to explain security cooperation. But it does so only in hindsight; the theory is much too indeterminate at present to allow for the development of distinct hypothesis, let alone prediction. Attempts at synthesizing various strands of theory are in too early a stage to be fairly assessed (Hasenclever et al., 1997: ch. 6 and Deudney, 2000).

Notes

1 Among many accounts of security, compare Baldwin, 1995; Betts, 1997; N. Crawford, 1991; Croft and Terriff, 1999; Gray, 1992; Haftendorn, 1991; Kolodziej, 1992; Mathews, 1989; Prins, 1998; Walt, 1991.

2 For a vigorous discussion of the merits of rational choice model building, consult Walt (1999b) and the ensuing debate between Bueno de Mesquita and Morrow (1999), Martin (1999), Niou and Ordeshook (1999), Powell (1999), Walt (1999a) and Zagare (1999).

3 The best-known formulation of this theory is Moravczik, 1997. However, Czempiel (1981), had provided the first comprehensive, book-length elaboration of IR liberalism, widely ignored by the US IR community, some sixteen years earlier.

4 Doyle (1997) gives a detailed account of the argument in its different versions. Doyle rescued Kant's theory in his famous articles 'Kant, Liberal Legacies, and Foreign Affairs' (1983a) and 'Kant, Liberal Legacies, and Foreign Affairs, Part 2' (1983b). However, Czempiel (1972) had proposed Kant's theory eleven years before Doyle – again without the US IR community taking notice.

5 The author is aware that Ole Waever and the Copenhagen School have made many contributions to the

security debate based on non-postmodernist epistemology
(for example, Waever et al., 1993).

6 A remarkable exception is Fierke's (1999) analysis of
how NATO became captured by its own effort to expand
a hegemonic dialogue to Eastern Europe.

7 Fierke, 1997: 223–52; Klein, 1994: 130. Significantly, the Index of Klein's book does not contain the
following entries: arms control, disarmament, confidence-building, non-proliferation, ABM Treaty, SALT,
START.

8 In fact, a neorealist analysis of the non-proliferation
regime is strikingly similar to Mutimer's (Bradley,
1995: esp. 506–7).

Bibliography

Adler, Emanuel (1992) 'The Emergence of Cooperation:
National Epistemic Communities and the International
Evolution of the Idea of Nuclear Arms Control', in
Peter M. Haas (ed.), *Knowledge, Power, and Inter-
national Policy Coordination: International Organi-
zation*, Special Issue, 46 (1): 101–46.

Adler, Emanuel and Barnett, Michael (eds) (1998)
Security Communities. Cambridge: Cambridge University Press.

Ashley, Richard K. (1998) 'Untying the Sovereign State:
A Double Reading of the Anarchy Problematique',
Millennium: Journal of International Studies, 17 (2):
227–62.

Axelrod, Robert (1984) *The Evolution of Cooperation*.
New York: Basic Books.

Axelrod, Robert and Keohane, Robert O. (1986)
'Achieving Cooperation under Anarchy: Strategies and
Institutions', in Kenneth A. Oye (ed.), *Cooperation
under Anarchy*. Princeton: Princeton University Press.
pp. 226–54.

Baldwin, David A. (1995) 'Security Studies and the End
of the Cold War', *World Politics*, 48 (1): 117–41.

Berger, Thomas U. (1998) *Cultures of Antimilitarism:
National Security in Germany and Japan*. Baltimore:
Johns Hopkins University Press.

Bernauer, Thomas (1993) *The Chemistry of Regime
Formation: Explaining International Cooperation for a
Comprehensive Ban on Chemical Weapons*. Aldershot:
Dartmouth Publishing.

Betts, Richard K. (1992) 'Systems for Peace or Causes of
War? Collective Security, Arms Control, and the New
Europe', *International Security*, 17 (1): 5–43.

Betts, Richard K. (1997) 'Should Strategic Studies
Survive', *World Politics*, 50 (1): 7–33.

Bonham, Matthew G., Sergeev, Victor M. and Parshin,
Pavel B. (1997) 'The Limited Test-Ban Agreement:
Emergence of New Knowledge Structures in
International Negotiation', *International Studies
Quarterly*, 41 (2): 215–40.

Borrus, Michael, Conca, Ken, Sandholtz, Wayne,
Stowsky, Jay, Weber, Steven and Zysman, John (1992)
*The Highest Stakes: Technology, Economy and Security
Policy*. New York: Oxford University Press.

Bradley, A. (1995) 'Thayer, the Causes of Nuclear
Proliferation and the Utility of the Nuclear Nonproliferation Regimes', *Security Studies*, 4 (3): 463–519.

Brooks, Stephen G. (1997) 'Dueling Realisms', *International Organizations*, 51 (3): 445–77.

Bueno de Mesquita, Bruce and Morrow, James D. (1999)
'Sorting Through the Wealth of Notions', *International
Security*, 24 (2): 56–73.

Bueno de Mesquita, Bruce and Siverson, Randolph M.
(1995) 'War and the Survival of Political Leaders: A
Comparative Study of Regime Types and Political
Accountability', *American Political Science Review*,
89: 841–55.

Buzan, Barry (1987) *An Introduction to Strategic Studies:
Military Technology and International Relations*.
Basingstoke: Macmillan.

Buzan, Barry (1991) *People, States and Fear: An Agenda
for International Security Studies in the Post Cold War
Era*, 2nd edn. New York: Harvester Wheatsheaf; and
Boulder: Lynne Rienner.

Buzan, Barry, Waever, Ole and de Wilde, Jaap (1997)
Security: A New Framework for Analysis. Boulder:
Lynne Rienner.

Campbell, David (1992) *Writing Security. United States
Foreign Policy and the Politics of Identity*.
Minneapolis: University of Minnesota Press.

Cha, Victor D. (2000) 'Globalization and the Study of
International Security', *Journal of Peace Research*,
37 (3): 391–403.

Checkel, Jeff (1998) *Ideas and International Political
Change: Soviet/Russian Behavior and the End of the
Cold War*. New Haven: Yale University Press.

Christensen, Thomas J. (1997) 'Perceptions and Alliances
in Europe, 1865–1940', *International Organization*,
51 (1): 65–98.

Claude, Inis Lo, Jr (1971) *Swords Into Ploughshares*,
4th edn. New York: Random House.

Crawford, Beverly (1993) *Economic Vulnerability in
International Relations: The Case of East–West Trade,
Investment and Finance*. New York: Columbia
University Press.

Crawford, Beverly (1994) 'The New Security Dilemma',
Millenium, 23 (1): 345–85.

Crawford, Neta C. (1991) 'Once and Future Security
Studies', *Security Studies*, (2): 283–316.

Crawford, Neta C. (1994), 'A Security Regime among
Democracies: Cooperation among Iroquois Nations',
International Organization, 48 (3): 25–55.

Croft, Stuart and Terriff, Terry (eds) (1999) 'Critical
Reflections on Security and Change', *Contemporary
Security Policy*, Special Issue, 20 (3).

Cusack, Thomas R. and Stoll, Richard J. (1994) 'Collective
Security and State Survival in the Interstate System',
International Studies Quarterly, 38 (1): 33–59.

Czempiel, Ernst-Otto (1972) *Schwerpunkte und Ziele der
Friedensforschung*. Mainz: Grünewald.

Czempiel, Ernst-Otto (1981) *Internationale Beziehungen.
Ein Konfliktmodell*. Munich UTB.

Dalby, Simon (1990) *Creating the Second Cold War. The
Discourse of Politics*. London: Pinter.

Dalby, Simon (1997) 'Contesting an Essential Concept: Reading the Dilemmas in Contemporary Security Discourse', in Keith Krause and Michael C. Williams (eds), *Critical Security Studies. Concepts and Cases.* London: UCL Press. pp. 3–32.

Davis, Zachary S. (1993) 'The Realist Nuclear Regime', *Security Studies*, 2 (3/4): 79–99.

Deudney, Daniel (1990) 'The Case Against Linking Environmental Degradation and National Security', *Millennium: Journal of International Studies*, 19 (3): 461–76.

Deudney, Daniel (1995) 'The Philadelphian System: Sovereignty, Arms Control, and Balance of Power in the American States-Union, circa 1787–1861', *International Organization*, 49 (2): 191–228.

Deudney, Daniel (2000) 'Geopolitics as Theory: Historical Security Materialism', *European Journal of International Relations*, 6 (1): 77–107.

Deutsch, Karl W., Burrell, Sidney A., Kann, Robert A. et al. (1957) *Political Community and the North Atlantic Area: International Organization in the Light of Historical Experience.* Princeton: Princeton University Press.

Downs, George W. (ed.) (1994) *Collective Security Beyond the Cold War.* Ann Arbor: University of Michigan Press.

Downs, George W. and Rocke, David M. (1990) *Tacit Bargaining, Arms Races, and Arms Control.* Ann Arbor: University of Michigan Press.

Downs, George W., Rocke, David M. and Barsoom, Peter N. (1996) 'Is the Good News About Compliance Good News About Cooperation?', *International Organization*, 50 (3): 379–406.

Doyle, Michael W. (1997) *Ways of War and Peace. Realism, Liberalism, and Socialism.* New York and London: W.W. Norton.

Doyle, Michael W. (1983a) 'Kant, Liberal Legacies, and Foreign Affairs', *Philosophy and Public Affairs*, 12: 205–35.

Doyle, Michael W. (1983b) 'Kant, Liberal Legacies, and Foreign Affairs, Part 2', *Philosophy and Public Affairs*, 12.

Duffield, John S. (1992) 'International Regimes and Alliance Behavior: Explaining NATO Conventional Force Levels', *International Organization*, 46 (4): 819–55.

Duffield, John S. (1994) 'Explaining the Long Peace in Europe: The Contributions of Regional Security Regimes', *Review of International Studies*, 20 (4): 369–88.

Duffield, John S. (1999) 'Political Culture and State Behavior: Why Germany Confounds Neorealism', *International Organization*, 53 (4): 765–804.

Evangelista, Matthew (1995) 'Transnational Relations, Domestic Structures, and Security Policy in the USSR and Russia', in Thomas Risse-Kappen (ed.), *Bringing Transnational Relations Back In: Non-State Actors, Domestic Structures, and International Institutions.* Cambridge: Cambridge University Press. pp. 146–89.

Evans, Peter B., Jacobson, Herold K. and Putnam, Robert D. (eds) (1993) *Double-Edged Diplomacy: International Bargaining and Domestic Politics.* Berkeley: University of California Press.

Farrell, Theo (1998) 'Culture and Military Power', *Review of International Studies*, 24, 3.

Fearon, James D. (1997) 'Signaling Foreign Policy Interests: Tying Hands versus Sinking Costs', *Journal of Conflict Resolution*, 41 (1): 68–90.

Fearon, James D. (1998) 'Bargaining, Enforcement and International Cooperation', *International Security*, 52 (2): 269–306.

Feaver, Peter D. (1998) 'Blowback: Information Warfare and the Dynamics of Coercion', *Security Studies*, 7 (4): 88–120.

Fierke, Karin M. (1997) 'Changing Worlds of Security', in Keith Krause and Michael C. Williams (eds), *Critical Security Studies. Concepts and Cases.* London: UCL Press. pp. 223–52.

Fierke, Karin M. (1999) 'Dialogues of Manoevre and Entanglement: NATO, Russia, and the CEECs', *Millennium*, 28 (1): 27–52.

Finnemore, Martha (1996) *National Interests in International Society.* Ithaca: Cornell University Press.

Flynn, Gregory and Farrell, Henry (1999) 'Piecing Together the Democratic Peace: The CSCE, Norms, and the "Construction" of Security in Post-Cold War Europe', *International Organization*, 53 (3): 505–35.

Foucault, Michel (1973) *The Order of Things: An Archaeology of the Human Sciences.* New York: Vintage.

Foucault, Michel (1980) *Power/Knowledge.* Brighton: Harvester.

Frankel, Benjamin (1993) 'The Brooding Shadow: Systemic Incentives and Nuclear Weapons Proliferation', *Security Studies*, 2 (3/4): 37–78.

George, Alexander, Farley, Philip J. and Dallin, Alexander (eds) (1988) *U.S–Soviet Security Cooperation. Achievements, Failures, Lessons.* New York and Oxford: Oxford University Press.

Glaser, Charles (1994/5) 'Realists as Optimists. Cooperation as Self-Help', *International Security*, 19 (3): 50–90.

Glaser, Charles (1997) 'The Security Dilemma Revisited', *World Politics*, 50 (1): 171–201.

Goldblat, Jozef (1985) *Non-Proliferation: The Why and the Wherefore.* London: Taylor and Francis.

Goldstein, Joshua S. (1995) 'Great-Power Cooperation Under Conditions of Limited Reciprocity: From Empirical to Formal Analysis', *International Studies Quarterly*, 39 (4): 453–77.

Gray, Colin S. (1992) 'New Directions for Security Studies? How Can Theory Help Practice?', *Security Studies*, 1 (4): 610–35.

Grieco, Joseph M. (1990) *Cooperation among Nations: Europe, America and Non-Tariff Barriers to Trade.* Ithaca: Cornell University Press.

Grieco, Joseph M. (1988) 'Realist Theory and the Problem of International Cooperation: Analysis with an Amended Prisoners' Dilemma', *Journal of Politics*, 50: 600–24.

Grinevsky, Oleg (1996) *Tauwetter: Entspannung, Krisen und neue Eiszeit*. Berlin: Siedler.

Grunenberg, Isabelle (1990) 'Exploring the "Myth" of Hegemonic Stability', *International Organization*, 44, (4): 431–79.

Haftendorn, Helga (1991) 'The Security Puzzle: Theory-Building and Discipline-Building in International Security', *International Studies Quarterly*, 35 (1): 3–17.

Hasenclever, Andreas, Mayer, Peter and Rittberger, Volker (1997) *Theories of International Regimes*. Cambridge: Cambridge University Press.

Hellmann, Gunther and Wolf, Reinhard (1993) 'Neorealism, Neoliberalism and the Future of NATO', *Security Studies*, 3 (1): 3–43.

Homer-Dixon, Thomas F. (1994) 'Environmental Scarcities and Violent Conflict: Evidence from Cases', *International Security*, 19 (1): 5–40.

Ikenberry, John G. (1998/9) 'Institutions, Strategic Restraint, and the Persistence of American Postwar Order', *International Security*, 23 (3): 43–78.

Jervis, Robert (1978) 'Cooperation under the Security Dilemma', *World Politics*, 20: 167–214.

Jervis, Robert (1983) 'Security Regimes', in Stephen Krasner (ed.), *International Regimes*. Ithaca: Cornell University Press. pp. 173–94.

Jervis, Robert (1985) 'From Balance to Concert: A Study of International Security Cooperation', *World Politics*, 18 (1): 58–79.

Jervis, Robert (1988) 'Realism, Game Theory, and Cooperation', *World Politics*, 40 (3): 317–49.

Jervis, Robert (1999) 'Realism, Neoliberalism, and Cooperation. Understanding the Debate', *International Security*, 24 (1): 42–63.

Johnson, James (1993) 'Is Talk Really Cheap? Prompting Conversation Between Critical Theory and Rational Choice', *American Political Science Review*, 87 (1): 74–86.

Johnson, Rebecca (2000) 'The 2000 NPT Review Conference: A Delicate, Hard-Won Compromise', *Disarmament Diplomacy*, 46: 2–21.

Johnston, Alastair Iain (1995) 'Thinking About Strategic Culture', *International Security*, 19 (4): 32–64.

Kapstein, Ethan B. (1992) *The Political Economy of National Security: A Global Perspective*. Columbia: University of South Carolina Press.

Katzenstein, Peter (ed.) (1996) *The Culture of National Security: Norms and Identities in World Politics*. New York: Columbia University Press.

Keck, Margaret E. and Sikkink, Kathryn (1998) 'Activists Beyond Borders. Advocacy Networks', *International Politics*. Ithaca: Cornell University Press.

Keck, Otto (1997) 'Der Beitrag rationaler Theorieansätze zur Analyse von Sicherheitsinstitutionen', in Helga Haftendorn and Otto Keck (eds), *Kooperation jenseits von Hegemonie und Bedrohung. Sicherheitsinstitutionen in den internationalen Beziehungen*. Baden–Baden: Nomos. pp. 35–56.

Keeley, James F. (1990) 'Toward a Foucauldian Analysis of International Regimes', *International Organization*, 44 (1): 83–105.

Keohane, Robert O. (1984) *After Hegemony: Cooperation and Discord in the World Political Economy*. Princeton: Princeton University Press.

Keohane, Robert O. and Martin, Lisa L. (1995) 'The Promise of Institutionalist Theory', *International Security*, 20 (1): 39–51.

Keohane, Robert O. and Nye, Joseph S., Jr (1998) 'Power and Interdependence in the Information Age', *Foreign Affairs*, 77 (5): 81–94.

Klare, Michael T. and Thomas, Daniel C. (1994) *World Security – Challenges for a New Century*. New York: St Martin's Press.

Klein, Bradley S. (1994) *Strategic Studies and World Order. The Global Politics of Deterrence*. Cambridge: Cambridge University Press.

Klein, Bradley S. (1988) 'After Strategy: The Search for a Post-Modern Politics of Peace', *Alternatives*, 13: 293–318.

Klein, Yitzhak (1991) 'A Theory of Strategic Culture', *Comparative Strategy*, 10 (1): 3–23.

Knopf, Jeffrey W. (1998) *Domestic Society and International Cooperation*. Cambridge: Cambridge University Press.

Kolodziej, Edward (1992) 'What is Security and Security Studies?', *Arms Control*, 13(1): 1–31.

Koslowski, Rey and Kratochwil, Friedrich V. (1994) 'Understanding Change in International Politics: The Soviet Empire's Demise and the International System', *International Organization*, 48 (2): 215–48.

Krause, Keith (ed.) (1998) 'Culture and Security. Multilateralism, Arms Control and Security Building', *Contemporary Security Policy*, Special Issue, 19.

Krause, Keith and Latham, Andrew (1998) 'Constructing Non-Proliferation and Arms Control: The Norms of Western Practice', in Keith R. Krause (ed.), *Culture and Security. Multilateralism, Arms Control and Security Building*. London: Frank Cass. pp. 23–54.

Kubbig, Bernd W. (1996) *Kommunikatoren im Kalten Krieg. Die Pugwash-Konferenzen, die US-Sowjetische Studiengruppe und der ABM-Vertrag. Ein Kapitel in der Geschichte der Naturwissenschaft(ler) als politische Erfolgsgeschichte – Lehren für die zukünftigen Aktivitäten*. Frankfurt-am-Main: HSFK-Report 6.

Kupchan, Charles A. and Kupchan, Clifford A. (1991) 'Concerts, Collective Security, and the Future of Europe', *International Security*, 16 (1): 114–61.

Kydd, Andrew (1997) 'Sheep in Sheep's Clothing: Why Security Seekers Do not Fight Each Other', *Security Studies*, 7 (1): 114–54.

Kydd, Andrew (2000) 'Trust, Reassurance, and Cooperation', *International Organization*, 54 (2): 323–57.

Kydd, Andrew and Snidal, Duncan (1993) 'Progress in Game-Theoretical Analysis of International Regimes', in Volker Rittberger (ed. with the assistance of Peter Mayer), *Regime Theory and International Relations*. Oxford: Clarendon Press. pp. 112–35.

Lai, Brian and Reiter, Dan (2000) 'Democracy, Political Similarity, and International Alliances, 1816–1992', *Journal of Conflict Resolution*, 44 (2): 203–27.

Lake, David A. and Powell, Robert (eds) (1999) *Strategic Choice and International Relations*. Princeton: Princeton University Press.

Lebow, Richard Ned (1994) 'The Long Peace, the End of the Cold War, and the Failure of Realism', *International Organization*, 48 (2): 249–77.

Leeds, Brett Ashley and Davis, David R. (1999) 'Beneath the Surface: Regime Type and International Interaction, 1963–1978', *Journal of Peace Research*, 36 (1): 5–23.

Legro, Jeffrey W. (1995) *Cooperation under Fire. Anglo-American Restraint During World War II*. Ithaca: Cornell University Press.

Legro, Jeffrey W. and Moravcsik, Andrew (1999) 'Is Anybody Still a Realist?', *International Security*, 24 (2): 5–55.

Lepgold, Joseph (1998) 'NATO's Post-Cold War Collective Action Problem', *International Security*, 23 (1): 78–106.

Levy, Marc A. (1995) 'Is the Environment a National Security Issue?', *International Security*, 20 (2): 35–62.

Lipson, Charles (1984) 'International Cooperation in Economic and Security Affairs', *World Politics*, 39 (1): 1–23.

Martin, Lisa L. (1999) 'The Contributions of Rational Choice: A Defense of Pluralism', *International Security*, 24 (2): 74–83.

Mathews, Jessica Tuchman (1989) 'Redefining Security', *Foreign Affairs*, 68 (2): 162–77.

Matthews John C. (1996) 'Current Gains and Future Outcomes: When Cumulative Relative Gains Matter', *International Security*, 21 (1): 112–46.

McCalla, Robert (1996) 'NATO's Persistence After the Cold War', *International Organization*, 50 (3): 445–75.

Mearsheimer, John J. (1990) 'Back to the Future. Instability in Europe After the Cold War', *International Security*, 15 (1): 5–56.

Mearsheimer, John J. (1994/5) 'The False Promise of International Institutions', *International Security*, 19 (3): 5–49.

Mitchell, Ronald B. (1998) 'Sources of Transparency: Information Systems in International Regimes', *International Studies Quarterly*, 42 (1): 109–30.

Moravczik Andrew (1997) 'Taking Preferences Seriously: A Liberal Theory of International Politics', *International Organization*, 51 (4): 513–53.

Morrow, James D. (1991) 'Electoral and Congressional Incentives and Arms Control', *Journal of Conflict Resolution*, 35 (2): 245–65.

Morrow, James D. (1994) 'Modeling the Forms of International Cooperation: Distribution versus Information', *International Organization*, 48 (3): 387–8.

Morrow, James D. (1999) 'The Strategic Setting of Choices: Signaling, Commitment, and Negotiation in International Politics', in David A. Lake and Robert Powell (eds), *Strategic Choice and International Relations*. Princeton: Princeton University Press. pp. 77–114.

Mousseau, Michael (1997) 'Democracy and Militarized Interstate Collaboration', *Journal of Peace Research*, 34 (1): 73–87.

Müller, Harald (ed.) (1987) *European Non-Proliferation Policy. Prospects and Problems*. Oxford: Clarendon Press.

Müller, Harald (1999) *Kernwaffen und deutsche Interessen: Versuch einer Neubestimmung*. Frankfurt-am-Main: HSFK, HSFK-Report No. 5–99.

Müller, Harald and Kötter, Wolfgang (1990) *Germany and the Bomb. Nuclear Policies in the Two German States, and the United Germany's Nonproliferation Commitments*. Frankfurt-am-Main: HSFK, PRIF Report No. 14.

Muravchik, Joshu (1991) *Exporting Democracy. Fulfilling America's Destiny*. Washington, DC: American Enterprise Institute.

Mutimer, David (2000) *The Weapons State. Proliferation and the Framing of Security*. Boulder: Lynne Rienner.

Niou, Emerson M.S. and Ordeshook, Peter C. (1999) 'Return of the Luddites', *International Security*, 24 (2): 84–96.

Orme, John (1997/8) 'The Utility of Force in a World of Scarcity', *International Security*, 22 (3): 138–67.

Owen, John M. (1994) 'How Liberalism Produces Democratic Peace', *International Security*, 19 (2): 87–125.

Oye, Kenneth A. (ed.) (1986) *Cooperation under Anarchy*: Princeton: Princeton University Press.

Powell, Robert (1991) 'Absolute and Relative Gains in International Relations Theory', *American Political Science Review*, 85: 1303–20.

Powell, Robert (1994) 'Anarchy in International Relations Theory: The Neorealist–Neoliberal Debate', *International Organization*, 48 (2): 313–44.

Powell, Robert (1999) 'The Modeling Enterprise and Security Studies', *International Security*, 24 (2): 97–106.

Price, Richard (1997) *The Chemical Weapons Taboo*. Ithaca: Cornell University Press.

Price, Richard M. (1998) 'Reversing the Gun Sights: Transnational Civil Society Targets Land Mines', *International Organization*, 52 (4): 613–44.

Prins, Gwyn (1998) 'The Four-Stroke Cycle in Security Studies', *International Affairs*, 74 (4): 781–808.

Ray, James Lee (1995) *Democracy and International Conflict. An Evaluation of the Democratic Peace Proposition*. Columbia: University of South Carolina Press.

Reiss, Mitchell (1988) *Without the Bomb. The Politics of Nuclear Nonproliferation*. New York: Columbia University Press.

Remmer, Karen L. (1998) 'Does Democracy Promote Interstate Cooperation? Lessons from the Mercosur Region', *International Studies Quarterly*, 42 (1): 25–52.

Risse-Kappe, Thomas (1991) 'Did "Peace Through Strength" End the Cold War? Lessons from INF', *International Security*, 16 (1): 162–88.

Risse-Kappen, Thomas (1994) 'Ideas Do not Float Freely: Transnational Coalitions, Domestic Structures, and the End of the Cold War', *International Organization*, 48 (2): 185–214.

Risse-Kappen, Thomas (1995a) 'Democratic Peace – Warlike Democracies? A Social Constructivist Interpretation of the Liberal Argument', *European Journal of International Relations*, 1 (4): 491–517.

Risse-Kappen, Thomas (1995b) *Cooperation Among Democracies. The European Influence on US Foreign Policy*. Princeton: Princeton University Press.

Risse-Kappen, Thomas (ed.) (1995c) *Bringing Transnational Relations Back In: Non-State Actors, Domestic Structures, and International Institutions*. New York: Cambridge University Press.

Rittberger, Volker (ed.) (1990) *Regimes in East–West Politics*. London: Pinter.

Ruggie, John G. (1998) *Constructing the World Polity: Essays on International Institutionalization*. London: Routledge.

Russett, Bruce (1990) *Controlling the Sword*. Cambridge, MA: Harvard University Press.

Russett, Bruce (1993) *Grasping the Democratic Peace. Principles for a Post-Cold War World*. Princeton: Princeton University Press.

Russett, Bruce, Oneal, John and Davis, David R. (1998) 'The Third Leg of the Kantian Tripod for Peace: International Organization and Militarized Disputes, 1950–1985', *International Organization*, 52 (3): 441–68.

Schweller, Randall L. (1994) 'Bandwagoning for Profit: Bringing the Revisionist State Back In', *International Security*, 19 (1): 72–107.

Schweller, Randall L. (1996) 'Neorealism's Status-Quo Bias: What Security Dilemma?', *Security Studies*, 5 (3): 90–121.

Schweller, Randall L. and Priess, David (1997) 'A Tale of Two Realisms: Expanding the Institutions Debate', *Mershon International Studies Review*, 41, Suppl. I: 1–32.

Sen, Somnath (1990) 'Debt, Financial Flows and International Security', in *SIPRI Yearbook: World Armaments and Disarmament*. Oxford: Oxford University Press. pp. 203–18.

Skalnes, Lars S. (1998) 'From the Outside In, From the Inside Out: NATO Expansion and International Relations Theory', *Security Studies*, 7 (4): 44–87.

Smith, Jackie G., Chatfield, Charles and Paglucco, Ron (eds) (1997) *Transnational Social Movements and World Politics: Solidarity Beyond the State*. Syracuse: Syracuse University Press.

Snidal, Duncan (1991a) 'International Cooperation Among Relative Gains Maximizers', *International Studies Quarterly*, 35 (4): 701–26.

Snidal, Duncan (1991b) 'Relative Gains and the Pattern of International Cooperation', *American Political Science Review*, 85 (3): 387–402.

Snyder, Glenn H. (1984) 'The Security Dilemma in Alliance Politics', *World Politics*, 36 (4): 461–95.

Snyder, Glenn H. (1990) 'Alliance Theory: A Neorealist First Cut', *Journal of International Affairs*, 44 (1): 103–24.

Snyder, Glenn H. (1997) *Alliance Politics*. Ithaca: Cornell University Press.

Snyder, Jack (1984) *Ideology of the Offensive*. Ithaca: Cornell University Press.

Snyder, Jack (1990) 'The Concept of Strategic Culture: Caveat Emptor', Carl Jacobsen (ed.), *Strategic Power: USA/USSR*. New York: St Martin's Press.

Snyder, Jed C. and Wells, Samuel F. (eds) (1985) *Limiting Nuclear Proliferation*. Cambridge, MA: Ballinger.

Soo Hoo, Kevin, Goodman, Seymour and Greenberg, Lawrence (1997) 'Information Technology and the Terrorist Threat', *Survival*, 39 (3): 135–55.

Starr, Harvey (1997) 'Democracy and Integration: Why Democracies Don't Fight Each Other', *Journal of Peace Research*, 34 (2): 153–62.

Stein, Arthur (1990) *Why Nations Cooperate. Circumstance and Choice in International Relations*. Ithaca and London: Cornell University Press.

Stein, Janice Gross (1994) 'Political Learning by Doing: Gorbachev as uncommitted Thinker and Motivated Learner', *International Organization*, 48 (2): 155–84.

Suhrke, Astri (1999) 'Human Security and the Interest of States', *Security Dialogue*, 30 (3): 265–76.

Van Evera, Stephen (1990) 'The Cult of the Offensive', *International Security*, 15 (3): 7–57.

Van Evera, Stephen (2000) *Causes of War. Power and the Roots of International Conflict*. Ithaca: Cornell University Press.

Waever, Ole (1989) *Security the Speech Act: Analyzing the Politics of a Word*. Copenhagen: Centre for Peace and Conflict Research, Working Paper No. 19.

Waever, Ole (1995) 'Securitization and Desecuritization', in Ronnie D. Lipschutz (ed.), *On Security*. New York: Columbia University Press. pp. 46–86.

Waever, Ole, Buzan, Barry, Kelstrup, Morton and Lemaitre, Pierre (1993) *Identity, Migration and the New Security Agenda in Europe*. London: Pinter.

Walker, R.B.J. (1986) 'Culture, Discourse, Insecurity', *Alternatives*, 11 (4): 485–504.

Walker, R.B.J. (1988) *The Concept of Security and International Relations*. California: University of California, Institute of Global Conflict and Cooperation, Working Paper No. 3.

Walt, Stephen M. (1987) *The Origins of Alliances*. Ithaca: Cornell University Press.

Walt, Stephen M. (1991) 'The Renaissance of Security Studies', *International Security Quarterly*, 35 (2): 211–39.

Walt, Stephen M. (1999a) 'A Model Disagreement', *International Security*, 24 (2): 115–30.

Walt, Stephen M. (1999b) 'Rigor or Rigor Mortis? Rational Choice and Security Studies', *International Security*, 23 (4): 5–48.

Waltz, Kenneth N. (1979) *Theory of International Politics*. New York: Random House.

Waltz, Kenneth N. (1986) 'Reflections on Theory of International Relations. A Response to My Critics', in Robert O. Keohane (ed.), *Neorealism and Its Critics*. New York: Columbia University Press. pp. 322–46.

Weart, Spencer R. (1994) 'Peace among Democratic and Oligarchic Republics', *Journal of Peace Research*, 31 (3): 299–316.

Weber, Steve (1990) 'Realism, Détente, and Nuclear Weapons', *International Organization*, 44 (1).

Wendt, Alexander (1992) 'Anarchy is What States Make of It: The Social Construction of Power Politics', *International Organization*, 41: 391–425.

Wendt, Alexander (1994) 'Collective Identity Formation and the International State', *American Political Science Review*, 88.

Zagare, Fred C. (1999) 'All Mortis, No Rigor', *International Security*, 24 (2): 107–14.

Zangl, Bernhard (1994) 'Politik auf zwei Ebenen: Hypothesen zur Bildung internationaler Regime', *Zeitschrift für Internationale Beziehungen*, 1: 279–312.

Zürn, Michael (1992) *Interessen und Institutionen in der Internationalen Politik: Grundlegung und Anwendung des situationsstrukturellen Ansatzes*. Opladen: Leske and Budrich.

20

Peacemaking and Conflict Resolution

LILACH GILADY AND BRUCE RUSSETT

The modern study of international relations originates in the twentieth-century experience of global war and the desire to avoid subsequent wars. This normative impetus still operates, but much of the literature is dedicated to the study of war rather than the study of peace, and even less is dedicated to the study of peacemaking. In this chapter we seek to return peacemaking to the heart of theoretical discussion by analyzing this literature, first within the context of the Kantian study of peace and then by reviewing it using the increasingly influential framework of the rationalist bargaining approach to the study of conflict. To do so we focus on mediation.

Whereas the analysis of bargaining is currently the citadel of the rationalist school, mediation and peacemaking are still strongholds of practitioners who rely mainly on psychological and sociological approaches. In this chapter we prefer not to view these approaches as incompatible alternatives, but rather to focus on overlapping and complementing dimensions of the rational choice school and the psychological-sociological approaches. We are aware that deep differences in the philosophy of science stand at the heart of these approaches, yet believe that some complementarities call for a closer dialogue between them. Social-psychological theories sketch the limits and boundaries of rationality. They provide tools to help us define cases in which rationality assumption may not apply, and to help us reach generalizations even under such circumstances. In this sense they are pivotal companions to any rational choice endeavor. By emphasizing the value of linking these approaches, we try to establish productive dialogues between different issue-areas, between theory and practice, and between different theoretical schools within international relations theory.

Third-party dispute resolution is one of the most common behaviors in international politics. Most violent or potentially violent conflicts in the twentieth century experienced mediation attempts, often multiple ones (Princen, 1992: 5). States, international organizations and private individuals are involved in numerous attempts to resolve international disputes without violence, or at least to minimize the level of violence resulting. A unified framework for the study of mediation in particular, and peacemaking in general, should interest practitioners and theorists alike. For practitioners, such a framework can offer new insights and more rigorous prescriptions; for theorists it can help fill a theoretical lacuna and offer pathways toward future research. We use the bargaining approach as a platform for a more unified review of the existing mediation literature in the hope of ultimately reaching such a framework. We open with a broad discussion locating peacemaking within recent developments in the more general study of peace. We then discuss some major problems and shortcomings of the peacemaking literature. We provide a short overview of both the bargaining and mediation literatures, and proceed to review and analyze the mediation literature, employing a taxonomy of conflicts suggested by theorists of the bargaining approach.

PEACEMAKING AND THE KANTIAN STUDY OF PEACE

If one simply equates peace with the absence of war, then the study of peace is just the mirror image of the study of war. In this sense, deterrence theorists are part of the study of peace since they are concerned with preventing the outbreak of war. However, the perspective that 'to have peace one must have justice' rejects any simple equation of peace with non-war, and is concerned with the distributional implications of policy for the expectation of a stable and non-coercive peace. In this perspective, nuclear deterrence or imperial dominance at best achieve a kind of 'negative peace' of structural violence rather than a stable or 'positive peace' of mutual conflict resolution (Boulding, 1979; Galtung, 1969).

Peacemaking, especially in the literature on third-party contributions to dispute resolution, is concerned especially with the conditions whereby mutually acceptable settlement of disputes can be achieved. Yet there are circumstances under which coercive settlement can be useful. Dominance by one party may actually help propel movement toward a settlement, as can the power of a third-party intervenor who is not neutral. This understanding informs recent developments in the role of United Nations peacekeeping, shifting away from traditional peacekeeping (impartial, largely nonviolent, with consent of the parties, only after a ceasefire has been achieved) to more active and vigorous efforts to enforce peace.[1]

The possibility of a serious military confrontation or war is inherent in international relations. Theories of peace need not contest the basic realist conception of international politics as occurring in a state of anarchy. Kant ([1795] 1970: 165) did not, saying that nations, 'like lawless savages, exist in a condition of ... war'. But Kant and other liberals insist that not all states are equally in this condition with each other. In particular, those that share democratic institutions, are economically interdependent and cooperate through international law and institutions are constrained from fighting each other. Such states are in a state of peace with one another, constrained by norms and institutions from resorting to military violence and rarely even threatening to use violence against each other. For pairs of states where democracy, interdependence and joint international organization all are at fairly high levels, the chance of a militarized dispute arising between them is more than 70 per cent lower than for the average pair of states. This pattern of constraint on the probability of conflict held quite constant throughout the twentieth century. Even in relations with states where ties of shared democracy and interdependence are not strong, states that are themselves democratic and have open economies are somewhat more peaceful than the average member of the international system. Democracies are less likely to experience wars than are most kinds of autocracies, and – though there are obvious exceptions – less likely to intervene militarily in other countries to change their form of government (Russett and Oneal, 2001). R.J. Rummel (1997)

concludes that in addition to relative peacefulness abroad, democracy is characterized by a 'method of nonviolence' at home.[2] Therefore, when we look at peacemaking we need to consider what types of actors tend to select themselves into conflictual situations, under what conditions and to what extent the characteristics of the actors and conditions that led to the conflict affect third-party intervention. Different types of actors operate under different sets of normative and institutional constraints that affect their responses to various forms of peacemaking.

Third-party dispute resolution methods constitute one set of those normative and institutional constraints, and international organizations are some of the principal actors attempting to create those constraints and produce a positive peace. International organizations, a key part of this Kantian understanding, may play a legal role, adjudicating and arbitrating disputes. In doing so they reduce the cost of enforcing contracts, encourage their creation and promote exchange of concessions (Stone Sweet and Brunell, 1998). This in turn facilitates interdependence. Institutions like the European Court of Justice or the Permanent Court of Arbitration may incorporate a degree of voluntarism in states' participation, and rarely is enforcement carried out by the threat or use of military force. IGOs can also mediate disputes or provide diplomatic 'good offices', where the capability of enforcing settlements is explicitly absent (Abbott and Snidal, 1998; Bercovitch and Langley, 1993; Haas, 1993; Miall, 1992; Young, 1967). Manlio Brosio, as Secretary-General of NATO, helped mediate the dispute between Greece and Turkey over Cyprus in 1967 and was able to avert widening of the war. Even while caring for refugees fleeing across inter-state borders from civil wars, as in Rwanda, IGOs may provide useful services of mediation.

The Kantian emphasis on democracy and nonviolent means of conflict resolution is also very relevant. Democratic government entails both cultural practices of non-violence and institutions to facilitate the peaceful settlement of conflicts of interest, in external relations as well as domestic politics. Pairs of democratic states more frequently seek third-party mediation (including adjudication and arbitration) for their disputes (Dixon, 1993, 1994; Raymond 1994), and were more likely to take their trade disputes to GATT panels for adjudication (Busch, 2000). The study of third-party participation in dispute resolution thus becomes an important next step in a Kantian research program, asking how dangerous disputes, or already violent ones, can be settled and the threat of violence sharply reduced.

We restrict our discussion here to those mechanisms for third-party assistance in dispute settlement – peacemaking – that do not depend on military coercion, and which seek to achieve some degree of actual resolution of the underlying conflicts. Thus we differentiate between peacemaking and other types of third-party intervention such as peacekeeping and peace enforcement. While in practice these categories are hard to identify and are sometimes employed simultaneously, ignoring their substantial differences obscures variance in the conditions under which they can most usefully be employed and conceals trade-offs between them. For example, if the Security Council has authorized a peace enforcement operation, the UN Secretary General may have great difficulty in retaining credibility as an impartial mediator (Skjelsbaek, 1991).

While research on peacemaking seems like one of the natural next steps for the Kantian research agenda, its application is yet to be realized in a satisfactory way. To do so requires overcoming some deep-rooted problems of the peacemaking literature.

PROBLEMS IN THE PEACEMAKING LITERATURE

Many theorists of international relations neglect peacemaking, leaving it to practitioners and to proponents of psychological and sociological approaches. The result is a literature with a relatively prescriptive and *ad hoc* case study approach that leaves a wide gap between it and mainstream concerns in international relations theory. That gap hampers dialogue and pushes the topic to the periphery, far from its real importance in the day-to-day practice of international relations. Theory regarding it has not evolved into coherent schools of thought with clear direction or a generally accepted framework. Indeed, recognizable theory of any sort is often lacking. How-to-do-it books of advice abound, but disparate propositions or hypotheses rarely cohere in a logical structure.

The reasons for these deficiencies are many. For some analysts the need for peacemaking already suggests a failure of the theoretical endeavor because war was not averted. They therefore direct their efforts toward means to release us from the need for peacemaking by preventing conflicts altogether. Yet peacemaking techniques are often employed to avert war: preventive diplomacy, mediation, arbitration and adjudication can take place before a single bullet is fired. Thus the notion of peacemaking need not imply the existence of an active war, but rather a conflict of interest that might deteriorate into war. Mediation in such circumstances is often quiet and unobtrusive, with little external manifestation of any sense of crisis, thus making it virtually impossible to bound the universe of cases and especially to identify successes. Nevertheless, third-party intervention is also widely employed long after violence has become

intense, as a means to bring about a ceasefire and, ultimately, a peaceful settlement.

These distinctions in stages of the process of peacemaking alert us to a general problem in international relations theory – the analytical and empirical dangers of selection bias (Fearon, 1994a; Smith, 1996) – that is especially serious here. At each stage in the development and escalation of a conflict, any empirical evaluation of the benefits of third-party dispute resolution requires considering not just the success and failures of intervention at that stage, but the circumstances under which intervention was *attempted* as compared to those under which no effort was made. The conditions and influences that contribute to success at one stage may be very different from those at an earlier stage (Kriesberg, 1998). One might imagine that mediation at an early stage in a dispute would be most successful if undertaken by a recognizably neutral third party, but that once the conflict had become violent a third party who was partisan, but nevertheless prepared to enforce a settlement even on its favored side, would have more success. Or one might hypothesize just the opposite. The point is that to ignore these distinctions is to risk making empirical generalizations that could be extremely misleading.

For example, Raymond (1994) finds that democracies are more likely than dictatorships to seek international arbitration of their disputes, but not more likely (Raymond, 1996) to abide by the arbitrator's decision. Selection bias, in the form of a difference in the type of disputes democracies and dictatorships are willing to submit to arbitration, seems a likely explanation. Busch (2000) found democracies more likely to take their trade disputes to GATT panels for adjudication, but no more likely to make concessions at that stage, perhaps because democratic governments might then incur high audience costs with their publics. The farther back one can go in the chain of causation the less the danger of distorting the results at the final stage. Simmons (1999) and Reinhardt (2001) also present analyses of arbitration outcomes that are sensitive to selection bias problems, as does Dixon (1996) for a wide range of third-party intervention techniques.

Our ability to understand peacemaking depends largely on our ability to understand the underlying processes of conflict the peacemaking is trying to overcome. While the study of war and conflict does show progress, we are still far from producing a coherent approach to the study of conflicts, and thus the peacemaking literature lacks a clear baseline in international relations theory to rely upon. In her review of the mediation literature, Marieke Kleiboer reaches a similar conclusion. She finds it to be suffering from conceptual confusion, over-determination and a difficulty in differentiating between evidence and conjectures. For her the source of these shortages lies elsewhere:

The three difficulties of current research on international mediation mentioned above are, in fact, caused by a more fundamental problem: the absence of more explicitly articulated theories on international conflict and its management of which mediation theory is a part. (Kleiboer, 1996: 376; also Kleiboer, 1998)

Kleiboer's focus on peacemaking directs her to search for a better explanation for the origins of conflict. By contrast, Geoffrey Blainey, whose work on the causes of war is an important stepping-stone in the development of the rationalist bargaining approach, claims that our ability to understand the onset of wars depends on our ability to explain their termination (Blainey, 1988; also Wittman, 1979). Thus researchers of both conflict initiation and conflict resolution recognize the interdependence of these issues. Progress in the study of peace depends on a close dialogue with those who study war and *vice-versa*.

The remainder of this chapter follows Kleiboer's and Blainey's lead in connecting the study of peacemaking with recent developments in the study of conflict as part of international relations. The development of rationalist models of war, and especially progress in applying bargaining models from economics to the study of war, is one of the most interesting developments in the study of international conflicts (Banks, 1990; Kreps, 1990; Meyerson, 1991; Rubinstein, 1982). A bargaining approach offers a new analytical framework to the study of war, and the basis for a new reading of the peacemaking literature. Although we make some reference to the full range of third-party dispute resolution – from diplomatic good offices, through mediation, to the more coercive practices of arbitration and adjudication – we concentrate on mediation, as probably the best-developed body of work within the peacemaking literature. We also largely restrict ourselves to violent conflicts between states, ignoring most intra-state conflicts and conflicts with little potential to become violent. This limitation makes theoretical as well as substantive sense. For example, in civil wars the stakes are more nearly indivisible than in international ones (Pillar, 1983: 24), since civil wars are about which side will control the state's coercive institutions, and there are no comparable institutions in the anarchic inter-state system. We re-examine the international mediation literature by highlighting some prominent debates and asking whether we can achieve new insights for international relations by analyzing them within a bargaining framework.

Rarely do we encounter serious dialogue between rationalist approaches and psychological, sociological, or even simply prescriptive ones. As the following analysis shows, these approaches often attempt to answer similar questions and in many cases could provide complementing elements for understanding peacemaking and war. The next section opens with a short overview of major debates in the mediation literature, followed by a basic review of the bargaining approach. The rest of the chapter is devoted to analyzing ways in which mediation can address rationalist explanations of war. Currently the bargaining literature suggests three possible explanations for war. Each poses different problems to the mediator and might affect the efficiency of certain mediation strategies.

THE STUDY OF MEDIATION

Bercovitch and Houston (2000: 171) define mediation as a

> process of conflict management, related to but distinct from the parties' own efforts, whereby the disputing parties or their representatives seek the assistance, or accept an offer of help from an individual, group, state or organization to change, affect or influence their perceptions or behavior, without resorting to physical force, or invoking the authority of law.

For Touval and Zartman (1989: 177) mediation is

> an intervention acceptable to the adversaries, who cooperate diplomatically with the intervenor ... it is not based on direct use of force and it is not aimed at helping one of the participants to win. Like good offices, mediation is concerned with helping the adversaries communicate, and like conciliation it emphasizes changing the parties' images and attitudes toward one another – but it also performs additional functions. Mediators suggest ideas for a compromise and they negotiate and bargain directly with the adversaries ... mediation is basically a political process without advance commitment of the parties to accept the mediators ideas.

The literature focuses on the study of variables that affect the probability of successful mediation. Researchers try to define the interaction between the structure of the conflict, the identity and characteristics of the mediator, the mediation strategies the mediator chooses to apply, and the success of mediation in managing and even resolving the conflict. Assessing the extent of mediation's success is problematic since it is not always clear what constitutes success. Criteria may range from reducing the violence to endemic rather than acute levels, to ending the violence, to the ambitious goal of creating a political solution that effectively ends the expectation of future violence. For example, are UN efforts in Cyprus a success because they seem to have prevented a new outbreak of war? Cyprus could be considered a failure since the underlying conflict persists and would likely return to violence in the absence of peacekeepers.[3] One must distinguish reaching an agreement from its subsequent implementation (Dixon, 1996). Nor is it often clear whether success or failure can be directly attributed to the mediation or to more structural characteristics of the conflict and adversaries. Does the outcome of mediation in Cyprus result from the mediation strategies, the identity and capabilities of the mediator, or the relations and relative capabilities of the Turkish and Greek Cypriots?

Kleiboer (1998) counts at least a dozen different variables suggested in the literature as preconditions for successful mediation. If this inflation of preconditions is not enough, a lively debate surrounds the effects and the necessity of each variable, a debate usually supported by conflicting empirical results. Our analysis can address only a few of these dozen variables, so we limit ourselves to those most common in the literature: the effects and characteristics of mediation strategies, the mediator's minimal required level of leverage and power, the effects of impartiality vs. partiality of the mediator, and the effects of asymmetry in the balance of power between adversaries. The literature is largely fragmented into separate debates on each. But as we will show, in most cases the mediation literature is working with highly complex and non-linear causal links. For example, there is no simple relation between impartiality and mediation success. The effects of partiality interact with characteristics of the mediator and the amount of leverage it enjoys, and all this in turn depends on such structural characteristics of the conflict as the level of symmetry between the adversaries. To make sense of it we need rigorous analysis of the effects of these variables under different conditions and structures of conflict. Our analysis shows that the effects of the mediator's partiality vary across the three categories of conflict we examine.

Much of the mediation literature relies on the anecdotal use of case studies without a rigorous research design. The relatively few large-n studies often produce inconsistent results. When we add these traits to the theoretical problems listed above we should be wary of selection bias effects that may obscure causal links and produce inconsistencies. Many researchers control for type of conflict by dividing all conflict into categories according to their content; for example, territorial, religious and ethnic (Bercovitch and Houston, 2000; Regan, 1996). These taxonomies often fail to address the analytical characteristics underlying these conflictual situations. Israel finds it hard to resolve its territorial dispute with Syria mainly because it fears the territory will be used as a strategically advantageous base for future attacks. In Northern Ireland the IRA long held up the peace process by refusing to disarm, mostly because it mistrusted its opponents and feared their future policies. Whereas the first is an international territorial dispute and the second a domestic religious one, both share similar analytical characteristics. For both the main impediment to conflict resolution is the inability of the

adversaries to credibly commit to keeping the peace agreement and not defecting at some future time, so the mediator's role is to devise mechanisms to guarantee future enforceability of present commitments. To define an optimal mediation process we need to understand the mechanisms of conflict and match the right remedy to each conflict. In the threefold analytical taxonomy offered by the bargaining approach, both the Irish and the Syrian–Israeli cases fall under the 'conflicts of credible commitments' category. The following section reviews this taxonomy and the logic behind it.

THE BARGAINING APPROACH: RATIONALIST EXPLANATIONS FOR WAR

The basic reasoning behind the bargaining approach has been with us since the works of Schelling (1966) and Blainey (1988). Yet only in recent years, especially following James Fearon's (1994a, 1995) work, has this literature started to come into a coherent framework. The main intuition is that if the outcome of a war were obvious from the start, then the war itself could be avoided and this outcome could be instituted by peaceful means, avoiding the suffering and destruction of war. Force is used as a costly signal to reveal information on actors' preferences and relative capabilities. Thus uncertainty and lack of information serve as preconditions for war. Analysts then move to define the conditions under which actors would fail to reach an agreement and would prefer to use force.[4]

This game theory literature is generally dyadic, like much recent work in international relations. Introducing a mediator into the picture breaks the dyadic structure of the game into a triadic one (Bercovitch, 1991; Touval and Zartman, 1989). One aspect of the bargaining literature that makes it especially amenable to a synthesis with the mediation literature is its emphasis on war as a continuous bargaining process instead of an 'all-or-nothing' lottery (Wagner, 2000). Rarely if ever do we encounter an absolute war in which total victory or total defeat are the only two options facing the actors. If they were, there would be no need for mediators. Mediation is the art of compromise. Successful mediation requires a solution somewhere between victory and defeat. Bargaining incorporates this notion by modeling war outcomes as mutually agreed-upon bargains that can only be found in a mutually acceptable bargaining space. Absolute wars are but a small and rare sub-set of cases that is not relevant to the mediation literature, and is residual to the bargaining literature as well. Therefore the following discussion revolves around what Clausewitz, and Wagner (2000: 472), define as 'real wars': wars that can be terminated by a negotiated settlement.

In this context the mediator can play several roles. On the most basic level, the mediator can help solve coordination problems between the conflicting parties and help them reach a mutually accepted point within their bargaining space. Another role is helping the adversaries to identify the bargaining space by supplying them with information and/or correcting misperceptions. In more complicated cases the mediator would have to broaden the bargaining space or even create one in order to facilitate an agreement. Manipulations of the bargaining space can be material, such as the use of side-payments or deterrence, or they can be social-psychological, such as trying to reconstruct the conflict or reorder the preferences of the adversaries in terms that could create a bargaining space. The bargaining space is dynamic and thus can be manipulated by the mediator. Yet affecting the bargaining space is a complicated, tasking and possibly expensive venture. Hence, mediators seek prescriptions that could help them match the right mediation strategy to the type of conflict and adversaries they are facing.

Fearon (1995) counts three major rationalist explanations for war: conflicts originating in lack of information, conflicts fought over indivisible resources, and conflicts arising from the inability of actors to credibly commit themselves to upholding the terms of the current agreement in the future. In the following section we identify optimal approaches to mediation for each of these analytical prototypes.

We examine how this rationalist framework affects our reading of the mediation literature. We use each of the three explanations for war as a platform to review the mediation literature, focusing on the specific implications of each explanation for the role of the mediator and then surveying its implications for the main variables discussed by mediation scholars.[5] Our analysis cannot resolve all the shortcomings in the fragmented mediation literature, but by reviewing it under a unified theoretical framework we highlight certain themes and interactions.

MEDIATING CONFLICTS OF INCOMPLETE INFORMATION

The explanation that concentrates on information is probably the most innovative and has gained most attention. International relations becomes a great game of signaling in which information is the most valuable resource. Actors reveal some pieces of information, hide others, signal their capabilities and intentions with varied degrees of credibility and success, try to bluff their way out of uncomfortable situations, and in general are involved in a huge and risky game of poker (Gartzke, 1999). Research following this line of argument has followed the Kantian intuition and moved on to examine the effects of domestic structures on actors' ability to collect and transmit information in an efficient way, and their ability to reorder their preferences in light of new information (Fearon, 1994a; Goemans, 2000; Guisinger and Smith, 2002; Schultz, 1999; Smith, 1998a). Another branch of research uses these insights to improve our understanding of war termination (Goemans, 2000; Werner, 1998).

The notions of misperception, lack of information and miscalculation appear frequently in the literature (for example, Jervis, 1976; Van Evera, 1999). Fearon (1995) differs by providing a rationalist explanation for these phenomena. For him, information consists of information about actors' capabilities and information on the intensiveness and ordering of actors' preferences. At first glance it seems that, in a perfectly rational world, actors who wish to avoid war should reveal their preferences and capabilities so that the probable outcome of the war could be determined and a peaceful agreement designed along its lines. Thus information should be accessible to all and we should not witness any wars. Nevertheless, actors typically choose not to reveal this type of information, hoping to bluff their way to a better outcome than warranted by their objective capabilities and the relative intensiveness of their preferences. Another disincentive to disclose private information is awareness that other actors in the system might misuse it in future conflicts. A third actor might choose to mount a challenge if it learns that one of the adversaries is much weaker than previously thought. Thus the incentive to provide public information is mitigated by incentives to protect private information so as to improve one's bargaining position by misrepresenting the intensity of one's preferences and capabilities. With incomplete and sometimes intentionally misleading information the actors cannot derive accurate calculations, and thus may end up fighting avoidable wars.

If the lack of information is the main factor contributing to the onset of such conflicts, then the best way to approach them is by confronting these information issues. From this perspective, the main role of a mediator is to supply information – an idea which is hardly new to the mediation literature. In their taxonomy of mediators, Touval and Zartman (1989) identify the role of mediator-as-communicator as one of their three prototypes of mediation strategies. Bercovitch sees the provision and collection of information as the main role of a 'reflective mediation behavior' or as strategies of 'communication-facilitation' (Bercovitch, 1984; Bercovitch and Houston, 2000; also Sheppard, 1984). This type of mediator 'tries to achieve some convergence of expectations by reducing distortion, ignorance, misperception or unrealistic intentions' (Kleiboer, 1996: 374). Burton, a pioneer in applying psychological approaches to the study of conflict resolution in the international arena, sees providing information as the most important role of the mediator (Burton, 1969; also Fisher, 1983: 325).

The bargaining approach gives theoretical reasoning to this intuition. War is part of a signaling game. Every battle reveals more information and the outcome is a signal of the 'real' balance of capabilities and preferences. In this context, mediation is another step in this process of revealing information. Perhaps this is why Dixon (1996) finds that mediation and a separate category of communication show the highest success rates in both limiting conflict escalation and promoting peaceful settlements of any type of third-party intervention in international relations.

The introduction of a mediator is supposed to increase the amount of information shared by the conflicting parties, thus correcting misinformation and miscalculations that lead to war. This does not mean the mediator has complete and accurate information regarding the situation and therefore can automatically solve any deficiencies of information. Yet one of the main roles of the mediator is to collect information and to provide it to both parties. Furthermore, the mediation process itself allows the parties to continue their signaling game through peaceful means instead of signaling each other only through their actions on the battlefield.

Once the parties to the conflict accept a mediator's help they may lose control over their own private information. A mediator is more than a simple message carrier. Mediators can collect information, reach independent assessments and gain better access to informal information sources. The mediator then decides what pieces of this information to transmit to the other side. This implies that adversaries who accept mediation to some degree value the provision of more public information, and the probability of conflict resolution, more than they fear that some of their private information would be 'declassified' against their will. It implies some degree of impartiality to the mediator, or at least an understanding that the mediator is committed to achieving some settlement fully within their bargaining space.

If the mediator is to solve problems of information, then success depends on the quality and credibility of the information the mediator can gather and transmit. So, when assessing the characteristics of an optimal mediator we should examine their effects on the mediator's ability to collect and supply credible information. This insight can help us to sift through the mediation literature and to reassess the effects of such characteristics that are commonly cited as preconditions for mediation's success.

The role of providing information and facilitating communication is usually perceived as the least demanding level of a mediator's intervention. Information is the only good that the mediator is expected to supply, and its provision does not depend on the mediator's size, strength, or what the mediation literature describes as leverage. Successful mediation in this type of conflict is possible even when a mediator – for example, a private individual like Jimmy Carter in his post-presidential role (Troester, 1996), a small state like one of the Nordic countries, or the representative of an international organization (see Bercovitch, 1992a) – lacks the kind of power and leverage that comes with great power status. Although access to technology may improve a mediator's ability to gather certain kinds of information, in general it is hard to see clear relations between the credibility and quality of the information and the size of the mediator. On the contrary, smaller, more distant mediators may find it easier to convince the adversaries to disclose information. In such cases disclosure is less threatening since there is only a remote chance that the mediator would be involved in any future conflict and be able to abuse this information for its own benefit. The mediator's past reputation as a credible supplier of information and its current relations with the adversaries probably play more important roles than size in successfully mediating this type of conflict. Any 'leverage' such a mediator can exert must derive from a reputation for fairness and impartiality.

All mediators – even 'neutral' ones – have some interests of their own. Small states can try to enhance their status and influence in the international arena by 'specializing' in mediation (Touval and Zartman, 1989: 119–20). A reputation as successful and trustworthy mediators enhances the credibility assigned to the information they supply and thus improves their ability to mediate successfully in future conflicts. As a specialized actor of this type derives status and influence from a reputation as a successful mediator, any breach of this reputation might be costly for the mediator, which therefore has an incentive to supply only reliable information – an incentive that enhances the mediators's credibility. While keeping one's good reputation may be an incentive for all actors, it is more necessary for actors that do not enjoy the luxury of power as an almost automatic guarantee of influence and prestige. Adopting a permanent position of neutrality is a way to institutionalize the role of the specialized mediator.

The presence of specialized actors guarantees a supply of trustworthy and efficient mediators, a supply of interest to all actors because all could potentially find themselves involved in a conflict and in need of mediation. These actors play a functional role in the international system by framing themselves as 'professional' mediators and offering their services whenever those are needed. Neutrality, impartiality and active participation in conflict resolution are often costly behaviors. These are repaid by the willingness of other actors to assign status to states that function as specialized mediators, and a willingness to respect their neutrality.[6]

For Touval and Zartman (1989: 127), mediators who provide information should be 'neutral hyphens in a dyadic relationship'. Impartial mediators' influence depends on their success in gathering information, which in turn depends on trust from both sides. The role of a mediator is a dynamic one; the ability to provide information brings a mediator leverage to affect the adversaries' pay-off structures (Princen, 1992). Yet once mediators gain information and influence, they risk losing their impartial status.

While the advantages of an impartial mediator as supplier of information are obvious, sometimes a partial mediator can also reach a high level of credibility. A mediator who is close to one of the adversaries may possess access to private information. Actors may be less hesitant to reveal information to mediators they perceive as allies. However, the same reasoning may reduce the quality of information the mediator can obtain from the other adversary in the dispute. It is safe to assume that a partial mediator would supply credible information to the adversary it supports. The credibility of the information it supplies to the other side may be questionable. It can raise its credibility by choosing to reveal information that is disadvantageous to its protégé. Such disclosure is a costly signal of the mediator's commitment to the mediation process. Partiality enables the mediator to attach costs to its signals and so to enhance the credibility and effectiveness of those signals. Costly disclosure of information might be abused by the adversaries, so a partial mediator who decides to use this strategy must be sure it can protect its ally from such risks. Hence a partial mediator has to be more powerful than an impartial one. Power allows the partial mediator to reach some credibility, and to make some side-payments to both parties. Consequently, in conflicts that revolve around questions of information successful mediation requires either impartiality or a partiality backed by power.

In either version the mediator's acts are those of an assistant in a process of information-gathering. As noted above, war itself reveals information on the true capabilities and preferences of the adversaries. If the rationalist analysis is correct in viewing wars as means of information-gathering then we should expect most wars to be relatively short. Once the actors start examining the consequences of the war they can reassess their positions and strike a deal that represents the 'true' balance of capabilities between them. By contrast to Zartman's (1985, 1995) emphasis on waiting much longer, for the conflict to 'ripen', into a 'hurting stalemate', or Bercovitch's (1997: 145) prescription to act 'roughly halfway' in the conflict process, a rationalist perscription should imply that intervention in this type of dispute should come early. It

would be relatively short, and would require only low levels of mediators' intervention. In their research on the relation between the timing of mediation and conflict duration, Regan and Stam (2000) do find that mediators often enjoy a window of opportunity for success very early on in the conflict (see also Northedge and Donelan, 1971).[7] This is not surprising if we take into account the implications of information in mediation. Early intervention supplies the required information before domestic coalitions have time to reorganize themselves and work for a new ordering of preferences (Goemans, 2000; Mitchell and Nicholson, 1983). Domestic structures affect information-gathering, the ability to signal capabilities and intentions credibly, and the process of preference aggregation and preference ordering (Fearon, 1994b; Schultz, 1999).

If the lack of information and high levels of uncertainty are at the heart of this type of conflict, how does the introduction of a mediator who plays the role of a 'communicator' affect them? A rationalist analysis of war anticipates rising levels of certainty as the war and/or the mediation process progress, because war and mediation are methods of 'objective' revelation of information to the adversaries.[8] A mediator may facilitate agreement not only by supplying information in the strict sense, but by helping the parties clarify and improve their interpretation of already available information. In the bounded rationality (Dawes, 1988; Simon, 1982) of actors' search for options, the values they attach to different outcomes are influenced by the order in which the outcomes are presented and compared on the agenda. A mediator can call attention to such differences, advise which alternatives may be relevant and which irrelevant, ask whether the parties are fully using the information already available to them, and if necessary urge re-evaluation.

In prospect theory as applied to simulations of international politics (Boettcher, 1995; McDermott, 1998; Tetlock, 1998) actors' subjective estimates of the probabilities of various outcomes are affected by how those outcomes are framed. For example, the certain loss of a piece of territory may appear worse than even odds on avoiding the loss of twice as much – even though the rational expected utility calculations are identical. In general, losses are perceived as having greater negative utility than the positive utility of objectively equivalent gains. Both utilities and probability estimates contain large subjective elements; a good mediator can point out those subjective elements, and their consequences, without pretending that some fully objective measure exists.

Yet the introduction of a mediator into the game also raises levels of uncertainty. A mediator breaks some of the dyadic nature of the bargaining process, adding its own preferences and capabilities as an additional source of uncertainty. This could have a positive effect on some aspects of conflict resolution. One example is the positive effect such uncertainty has when it comes to concession-making. Psychologists have noticed that adversaries find it easier to make concessions to a mediator than directly to their opponent (Podell and Knapp, 1969; Touval, 1994: 51). When an actor makes concessions that actor reveals information on its capabilities and intensity of its preferences. This information might convince the other side that it can raise its demands in the future. Podell and Knapp (1969: 512) define this problem as the 'bargainer's dilemma', or, in other words, 'how to yield without seeming to yield'. The mediator helps concession-making precisely by adding uncertainty. When a concession is made it is not easy to determine whether it is pushed forward by the mediator or by the other actor, whether it reflects the balance of capabilities and preferences of all three actors or only of the two adversaries. The same uncertainty limits the ability of other actors to use the disclosed information against the adversaries, thus mitigating one of the fears that motivates concealment of information. Therefore concession-making is cheaper in a mediated conflict because it reveals less information.

It is also made cheaper because the first actor to make a concession puts itself in a dangerous position since its adversary may refuse to accept it. In the prisoners' dilemma this is the situation in which one cooperates while the other defects. For the cooperating actor it is the worst possible outcome. A failed concession is costly both domestically and internationally. The fear of being caught in such a disadvantageous position creates incentives to defer concession-making and prolongs the conflict. A mediator may alleviate this problem by controlling the timing of information disclosure. A concession would be made public only when both sides have agreed to cooperate. Thus the danger of making a first move is reduced. By controlling and protecting the flow of information the mediator can manipulate the adversaries and minimize the pay-offs for intra-negotiations defection.

When a conflict derives from a lack of information, the mediator's role is to help both parties identify an already existing bargaining space (Pillar, 1983). Once this bargaining space is revealed and a deal is concluded, the conflict is resolved. If this deal indeed reflects the true balance of capabilities and interests, and so then discourages attackers, at least theoretically both parties could be satisfied with it. Therefore most such conflicts require peacemaking efforts, but not peacekeeping.

Another issue in the mediation literature is the effect of symmetry of power between the adversaries on the prospects for successful mediation. Conflicts that revolve around questions of information can get out of control despite the existence of a bargaining space. When the adversaries are

balanced (the difference in power is marginal) high uncertainty about their relative power may make it hard to identify the bargaining space between them. The balance of capabilities is often estimated from the publicly known military strength of the actors. With an unbalanced dyad this accessible and relatively 'objective' information could suffice to allow the actors to reach reliable estimates of the results they would be likely to achieve in war. Missing pieces of information would not be crucial, because the objective asymmetry would dictate an easily expected outcome. But when the actors are almost balanced, any piece of information becomes crucial for the ability to correctly estimate which has the better chance to improve its position by opting for war. Any new piece of evidence might tilt the calculation one way or another. Under these conditions it is logical to assume that a larger proportion of the required information would be part of actors' private information and thus not available. Decision-makers may also need to include 'subjective' or 'soft' factors in their calculations because, faced with symmetry of capabilities, they cannot treat any such variable as marginal. This opens the door to more misperceptions, inconsistent estimates and miscalculations – and therefore raises the probability of violence or war (Wagner, 2000: 479).

Thus symmetry is probably a conducive environment for the onset of conflicts of misinformation. It is less common to see this type of conflict originating from an unbalanced dyad even though there can still be misperception of intentions and preferences. Therefore discussion of the effects of symmetry on the efficiency of mediation is problematic because there should be a strong selection bias toward conflicts between symmetric dyads, as is consistent with recent empirical research (see Russett and Oneal, 2001, ch. 3). If an asymmetric dyad does end up in violent conflict, the likely outcome should be quite clear and thus the work of the mediator should be easier. Major violence in an asymmetric dyad usually signals that the adversaries are involved in a bargaining war in which the weaker party is trying to improve its position by forcing the stronger one to reassess its estimate of costs (Wagner, 2000). This insight can direct the mediator to the type and quality of information that may most contribute to conflict resolution.

This argument follows that behind the power transition school of international relations (Organski and Kugler, 1980), and joins a classic realist debate between supporters and critics of balance of power theory. That debate assumes that the relative distribution of power is known to both actors – but the bargaining approach assumes that information about a near-symmetrical power distribution is often inadequate. Furthermore, Wagner (2000) claims that even under perfect information actors might disagree on the implications of the balance of power and how it could be translated into 'real' military power. Wittman (1979) goes even further, claiming that in 'real wars' the balance of capabilities does not affect the probability of war. Still, we can assume that problems of information and miscalculation increase after periods of rapid change or sudden shocks that change the distribution of power without providing enough information or time for the actors to adjust their calculations.

This category of conflicts highlights the importance of information both as a goal and a technique of mediation. While the mediation literature refers to many implications of information, explicitly addressing the underlying theme of information structures can link many fragments of that literature together in a way that could offer a more coherent research agenda.

MEDIATING CONFLICTS OF INDIVISIBILITY

Conflicts of indivisibility – where the adversaries perceive the disputed resource as a unit they cannot divide between them – are hard to solve, and may lead actors to choose the destructive path that leads to total war. The only possible outcomes seem to be all or nothing, a zero-sum game with no bargaining space. Unlike in disputes arising from insufficient information, the mediator's role in the indivisibility category is not to help the parties locate themselves in an already perceived bargaining space, but to convince the adversaries that such a space does exist or to devise one. This type of conflict requires a more creative and resourceful mediator: one who can make substantive proposals that can affect the outcome and who has the will and the ability to reach higher levels of intervention in the conflict. Here the mediator is a problem-solver, even a power-broker (Kleiboer, 1998). A mediator may even find ways to distribute seemingly indivisible goods (Young, 1994). This is the most 'artful' and dynamic type of mediation.

Conflicts of indivisibility are likely to be protracted and intractable. New information would have little effect if any concession means total surrender of the resource under dispute. Actors would continue to fight so long as the value of holding the resource, or of capturing it, exceeds the cost of losing it altogether. New information must pass quite a high threshold in order to move one's preferences from fighting for 'all' to conceding to 'nothing'.

The willingness to fight depends on how the disputed resource is valued. The more valuable the resource, the less amenable the conflict is to mediation. Some resources have more symbolic than 'real' value to both sides; that is, the costs of conflict exceed the value of holding the resource and the main problem is one of how to make concessions and preserve reputation (O'Neill, 2000). This

may be especially serious when the domestic audience is seen as more hawkish than the state's leadership.[9] A mediator must be fully aware of the domestic political constraints on a state's leadership. Whether the leaders are faced with a democratic opposition or factions within an oligarchy, they are inevitably engaged in bargaining and negotiation over side-payments with that opposition as well as with the leaders of the other state. The mediation literature addresses three principal methods to help mediators overcome the indivisibility problem: creating divisibility by 'enlarging the pie', creating divisibility by fractionating the resource, and creating divisibility by separating values from interests through a problem-solving approach (Burton, 1986; Druckman et al., 1988; Fisher, 1971; Fisher, 1983; Oye 1985; Rubin, 1981).

With the first strategy, enlarging the pie, mediators can solve indivisibility by creating linkages between the disputed resource and other issues. This expands the scope of topics under consideration, allows for more complexity and flexibility, creates trade-offs, and moves the actors from a zero-sum game to a positive-sum condition. In bargaining language, the goal of this strategy is to turn the game from unidimensional to multidimensional. The logic of enlargement stands behind the common practice of side-payment compensation offered to the adversaries as an incentive for conflict resolution. While the disputed resource might be lost, compensation by a third party may create a new balance that pushes actors toward an agreement. In the Camp David negotiations of his presidency, Jimmy Carter played this role with the resources of a superpower by offering different types of compensations to both parties (Raiffa, 1982: ch. 14).

The second strategy is one of fractionation, disaggregating problems into smaller, more specific issues. In this approach negotiations should start with less important issues on which both sides can agree and then move toward more complicated core issues, creating positive inertia toward a successful resolution process. By the time the parties reach the problematic issues they may enjoy higher levels of mutual trust and might find the aggregation of the issues that were already concluded as having a value to counter-balance the costs of concessions that still lie ahead. Fractionation as a diplomatic strategy was especially identified with the tactics of Henry Kissinger in Arab–Israeli relations (Rubin, 1981; for more recent applications see Massoud, 2000).

Divisibility by problem-solving, the third strategy, relies mainly on psychological theories of conflict resolution. Conflicts are resolved only when the underlying problems that generate them are confronted. The commitment of actors to satisfying their own preference structure may lead to ignoring the other's perspectives, and require a third party to understand and express the interests of both. Some basic values are indeed indivisible. States translate basic values such as security into a language of interests such as borders, armament and control over natural resources. Territory may appear divisible, but it often taps powerful emotions of identity and security, rooted in historical traumas of the conflicting societies. Identity conflicts, expressed in hostile images of the other as enemy, are typically blind to the other's perception of threat (White, 1965) and resistant to contrary information (Festinger, 1957; Heider, 1958), and may be the most difficult to moderate. Yet the mediator's role is to help both sides to separate interests and values and find creative ways to address conflicting values by a new set of complementary interests (Burton, 1986; Druckman et al., 1988). For example, in the Israeli–Egyptian conflict, control over the Sinai desert was motivated by security needs on the Israeli side, and by identity concerns on the Egyptian. The Camp David accords solved this problem without dividing the disputed territory itself. Sinai was returned to Egypt, thus solving the identity and sovereignty issues, while demilitarization and deployment of an international peacekeeping force alleviated Israeli security concerns. Values can be achieved through a set of interests. By identifying the values that stand behind interests, the mediator can suggest alternative ways to maintain values while allowing compromise.

In effect this strategy requires reordering or restructuring the preferences of the adversaries. It does not rely as much on material factors as on re-constructing the conflict. A successful mediation of this type affects the preferences of the parties to the extent that they are no longer fighting a 'conflict of indivisibility'. Since most rational choice models take the preferences of actors as granted, they have relatively few insights to offer for mediation strategies that focus on reordering actors' preferences as the key to successful mediation. Side-payments from the mediator may alleviate fears and produce immediate compliance, but the mediator must also try to change actors' beliefs about the long-term threat each side poses to the other (Kelman, 1997).

The degree to which substantial resources and leverage at the disposal of the mediator become preconditions for successful mediation differs across these strategies. The first strategy requires a powerful or prestigious mediator, perhaps indicating why the United States and the United Nations are, respectively, by far the most frequent mediators among countries and international organizations (Bercovitch and Schneider 2000). For the second and third strategies, however, skill, reputation and experience may be more important. Therefore, small states can play a role in mediating conflicts of indivisibility. In practice all three strategies are not mutually exclusive, and in most cases mediators combine them depending on the context (Bercovitch, 1992b). Fractionation might dictate a more active involvement of the mediator and a supply of compensations to convince the parties to move forward toward core issues. Problem-solving might dictate expensive solutions requiring active investment by the mediator.

Unlike leverage, the effect of partiality depends not only on the mediation strategy but on the structure of the conflict itself: who holds the disputed resource at the time of mediation, who does the partial mediator support, which of the three strategies does the mediator choose as a solution for indivisibility, and the proposed solution; that is, who ends up keeping the good? Assessing the effects of partiality is complicated because there is no clear linear relation between partiality and mediation success. When the mediator supports the status quo actor (who currently holds the disputed resource) and the proposed solution is that the status quo should not be altered, partiality damages the mediator's legitimacy. The mediation process would not improve the mediator's relations with the adversary and it is unlikely that this mediation would solve the problem of indivisibility. A strategy of enlargement is problematic because it is not clear whether the mediator would want to commit resources to compensate its less favored party. If compensations are offered by a powerful though biased mediator, the mere possibility of improved relations in the future might create an incentive to concede to an unfavorable outcome. Nevertheless, a biased mediator may not always be able to promise compensation in a credible way, because some of the compensations could be contradictory to the interests of its protégé.

For this set of cases, the credibility of the mediator as a future compensator depends on the time frame of the agreement and the degree to which the mediator's reputation is connected to the success of the mediation in general and to fulfilling its commitments in particular. The analysis above suggests that compensations are credible if offered within a short time frame. When the structure of triangular relations between the mediator and the adversaries prevents creation of a self-enforcing agreement, the mediator's reputation becomes the only incentive to continue compensation over time. If the mediator's sensitivity to damage to its reputation was in doubt, actors would push harder for immediate compensation.

Since fractionation and problem-solving require more trust and openness, a lack of impartiality might be more problematic. Most psychological approaches to mediation view neutrality as an important precondition for successful mediation (Burton, 1969; Fisher, 1983; Kelman and Cohen, 1979; Walton, 1969). Whereas in theory this strategy is most useful when applied by an impartial mediator, in practice a viable solution usually needs to be backed by some compensation and investment on the side of the mediator, and a mediator so neutral as to be disinterested – and perhaps therefore uninterested – might not be willing to make such an investment.

Partiality can play an interesting role when the mediator supports the actor who is supposed to give up the disputed resource. In these conflicts the mediator can credibly commit to both sides and its legitimacy would probably not be contested (Carnevale and Arad, 1996). All three strategies might be effective in this situation. By contrast, a biased mediator will face problems if it opposes the side holding the good at the time of mediation. The mediator then enjoys little leverage over that side, with little ability to convince it to make concessions. Furthermore, intervention by such a mediator might in itself reduce the willingness of such an actor to make any concession, and the legitimacy of the mediation itself might be contested. Since a biased mediator finds it hard to commit credibly to compensating the party it does not support, it cannot pretend to 'understand its needs' as the more psychological approaches prescribe.

This analysis exemplifies the complex and non-linear relations between impartiality and mediation success. Similar problems hinder our ability to find clear and simple relations between symmetry and mediation success, which would explain a divergence in empirical conclusions between Bercovitch (1991) and Miall (1992) about the effects of asymmetry. Nevertheless, both theory and some empirical findings suggest that asymmetry between adversaries may help resolve conflicts of indivisibility (Kacowicz, 1994; Zartman, 1995). Here the argument is straightforward: stronger parties find it easier to make concessions because asymmetry assures them that even after they concede an indivisible good they can retain their predominance.

As this review shows, the mediation literature acknowledges and discusses strategies that are meant to overcome issues of indivisibility, but as in other cases it does so in an isolated way without connecting it to other dimensions of mediation. To optimize the effects of the mediation strategy chosen by the mediator one has to acknowledge its interaction with issues of leverage, symmetry and impartiality.

MEDIATING CONFLICTS OF CREDIBLE COMMITMENTS

The final rationalist explanation for war relies on the inability of states credibly to commit themselves to future policies, especially in times of power shifts. A rising power cannot promise not to challenge other actors once it has gained more power. Therefore, actors who anticipate power shifts to their disadvantage have an incentive to use their current power superiority to launch a pre-emptive war that could delay or prevent future challenges. The rationalist approach thus views shifts in the distribution of power as a source of instability. In so doing it echoes the reasoning of power transition theory while embedding it in a wider framework of analysis (Gilpin, 1981; Kugler and Lemke, 2000; Organski and Kugler, 1980; Powell, 1999).

The problem of power shifts is connected to problems of indivisibility. Once an indivisible resource is left in the hands of one actor, that actor cannot credibly commit not to use it to alter the distribution of goods in the future. In fact, almost any current asymmetric redistribution of resources creates a power shift that might later be abused. Thus the problem of credible commitments inhabits agreements involving asymmetric redistribution. Solving the problem of credible commitments requires external intervention because no self-enforcing solution is available. The role of the mediator becomes one of constructing a mechanism to constrain the instability by offering credible external enforcement. In other words, this type of conflict requires a much higher level of intervention and investment by the mediator because in most cases it would have to play the role of enforcer. To provide credible enforcement the mediator must demonstrate enough resources and interest to satisfy adversaries' anxieties. The bigger the issues at stake, the more power the mediator must be prepared to exert.

A role of enforcement requires high levels of intervention in the mediation process. It is not enough to supply information, or even to devise creative solutions. This mediator must actively change the calculations of the adversaries by exercising its own power. Touval and Zartman (1989: 128–9) characterize this mediation strategy as that of a manipulator. Bercovitch and Houston (2000) put it in their 'directive strategies' category; they find that although it is used in only 35 per cent of mediation attempts, it tends to be the most successful. Directive strategies succeeded in 42 per cent of their cases whereas communication-facilitation strategies scored only a 31 per cent success rate (also see Bercovitch, 1984; Kleiboer, 1996: 374–5). To evaluate this success rate however, would require careful attention to selection bias: what kinds of disputes emerge as plausible candidates for directive settlements?

A more psychological analysis reaches similar prescriptions. The notion of power shifts suggests that one of the adversaries views itself as losing ground. Typically the situation is one of escalating conflict and a self-perpetuating dynamic of fear driven in part by social-psychological variables. To make concessions in exchange for short-term compensations could leave a party open to subsequent vulnerabilities (Kelman, 1997). In terms of prospect theory, such an actor feels that it is operating in the realm of losses. When the actor looks forward it sees an even grimmer future and so is willing to try risky measures to subvert the process of deterioration. This again suggests that power shifts create an inherently unstable situation. A mediator should strive to affect the reference point of the 'losing' actor in a way that shifts it back into the realm of gains. This can be done by strategies that involve side-payments and binding commitments that create clear boundaries to the realm of losses and thus minimize the extent of a worst case scenario.

Nevertheless, the mediator suffers from a related problem of credibility. How can the adversaries be sure that the mediator will enforce the agreement in the future? In an anarchic international system the mediator cannot authoritatively bind itself to expensive enforcement obligations. Hence, conflicts of vital national security that involve problems of credible commitments call for a partial mediator, preferably one who supports the actor that must make concessions. Such a mediator would have more incentives to come to its associate's help should the other side defect, without igniting the other side's fears so long as it had no intention to defect. Consideration of the mediator's reputation and prestige alone may not be enough to assure the adversaries that their future wellbeing is protected. Nevertheless, the past record of the mediator may help to establish its credibility and the value of its commitments. Its domestic political structure should also matter to both adversaries, to the extent that it affects the durability of the regime and the commitment of future regimes to old commitments.

While the prescription may seem quite straightforward, it is problematic. The mediator is assumed to press for an outcome that at least in the short run seems disadvantageous to the actor it supports, and which might drag the mediator itself into expensive future commitments. The mediator has to be able to push its own protégé toward painful concessions. This requires a high level of leverage and a high level of interest in the resolution of the conflict to justify risky commitments that bind the mediator to an unstable dyad. The mediator has to see beyond the immediate interests of its protégé and to consider the stability of the region or the system as a value in its own right. An optimal mediator in this type of conflict needs a combination of demanding preconditions: capabilities, leverage and high levels of interest both in the conflict itself and in the stability of the system. It calls for mediation by a big power (Touval, 1992), not a small or even medium state.

The mediator's credibility is affected by the way in which its commitments are incorporated into the mediated solution. It matters whether the commitments are made officially or unofficially, and whether they are an integral part of the peace agreement and thus have a triadic character or are part of a dyadic agreement. Also relevant is the time horizon within which the agreement is supposed to be carried out. With uncertainty rising the more we gaze ahead, the credibility of actors' commitments decreases as we move further into the future.

If power shifts generate the problem of credible commitments, then asymmetry is inherent to this category of conflicts. As with partiality, the main question is who needs more guarantees. The mediator must offer protection to the actor who expects to be on the losing side of the power shift. This is not an empirically easy or clean distinction, but it matters when analyzing a specific case and when constructing an optimal mediation structure. The structure of symmetry obviously influences the direction in which partiality affects the chances of successful mediation.

This last category addresses a problem inherent to almost every cooperative interaction in international relations. For realists the fear of future defection stands at the heart of the infeasibility of stable cooperative relations. Kantians recognize the existence of constraints and incentives that can limit the effects of this fear and facilitate stable peaceful cooperation. Any mediation attempt that must deal with problems of credible commitments seeks to establish such constraints and incentives in a dyad that otherwise lacks them. Therefore this type of conflict demands a high level of commitment by the mediator, a level usually more appealing to great powers who can afford it.

CONCLUSIONS

The study of mediation is an example of the peacemaking literature, which falls more broadly within a Kantian perspective on the causes and constraints affecting international conflict. In examining it we have incorporated perspectives from the bargaining approach to the study of conflict, which itself can be seen as relevant both to a Kantian perspective on peaceful conflict resolution and a realist emphasis on bargaining throughout even violent struggle. Our analysis offers a framework to foster productive dialogue within the literature on third-party dispute resolution and between different theoretical schools. The attempt to link psychological and rationalist approaches shows many of their findings are complementary. This review asks researchers of mediation to conduct more theoretically driven and rigorous research that takes selection biases, nonlinearity and possible interactions into consideration. At the same time it challenges rationalists to extend their analysis to include third-party intervention and construct it in a way that generates testable hypotheses.

One of the main shortcomings of the bargaining approach is its inability to predict which point on the bargaining space will be chosen as the mutually accepted solution. This opens a complementing role for mediation literature that deals directly with such questions. While the bargaining framework may help us identify all possible solutions that are part of the bargaining space, the mediation literature may help us understand the process by which one of those solutions is picked as the final outcome. In this sense, even this rationalist analysis leaves space for the 'art of negotiation' (Raifa, 1982).

We opened this chapter by identifying an insufficiency in the quantity and quality of theoretical work on peacemaking, and by discussing some shortcomings of the existing literature that does try to deal with this topic. Our analysis indeed suggests that peacemaking in general, and mediation in particular, are highly complex. Whereas the rationalist literature struggles to explain conflicts, the introduction of third-party intervention adds another tier to the analysis and with it more complexities from a larger number of actors, incentives and possible configurations. It is therefore not surprising that the peacemaking literature has produced little consensus and is still dealing with severe problems of conflicting empirical results. The effects of mediation, for example, depend on the structural character of the conflict and therefore the same variable can show different outcomes under different conditions. In general, most of the variables show a high level of interdependence, and the relations between them are complex and non-linear. Thus an isolated analysis of a single variable – a method often employed in the study of mediation and peacemaking – is misleading and highly dependent on the selection of cases.

These problems, however, should not deter the study of peacemaking. By being aware of selection biases, non-linearity and interdependence of variables we can construct better research designs to overcome some of these problems and reach some real progress in the study of peacemaking. This chapter does not offer many clear hypotheses that can be easily operationalized. Yet even this initial analytical exercise suggests that further analysis along these lines might offer new insights into the mechanisms of mediation in particular, and third-party intervention in general. Issues of time frame of the agreement, the effects of different structures of partiality, variation in the requirements for mediator's levels of leverage across different types of conflicts, and the role of the mediator as supplier of information illustrate possible lines for further inquiry. They have prescriptive as well as analytical value. Our understanding of international relations cannot be complete if we continue to marginalize such an important part of day-to-day practice from our theoretical debate. We hope this review is a step toward strengthened interest in a rigorous study of peacemaking, thus putting peacemaking back under the spotlights of our research agenda.

Notes

We thank the Carnegie Corporation of New York and the Ford Foundation for financial support, and Allan C. Stam and Alexandra Guisinger for their insights.

1 Compare the recommendations of UN Secretary General Boutros-Ghali (1995) in his *An Agenda for Peace* with his subsequent thoughts; also see Daniel and Hayes, 1995.

2 Also see Jack Levy's discussion of the democratic peace in this volume (Chapter 18).

3 On multiple criteria of success, see Bercovitch and Houston, 1996; Druckman and Stern, 1997; Jett, 2000: 12–20; Kleiboer, 1998.

4 Wagner (2000) adds an important caveat to Fearon's analysis by differentiating between force used to reveal information about relative capabilities and force used to affect capabilities by targeting the enemy's military, territory and resources. A state can choose to go to war if it believes it can fight its opponent in a way that would improve its position to reach a more favorable settlement in the next bargaining round.

5 As noted above, we concentrate on the characteristics of mediation strategies, the mediator's minimal required level of leverage and power, impartiality vs. partiality of the mediator, and asymmetry in the balance of power between the adversaries.

6 Examples of such 'specialized mediators' include Sweden and Norway, which invest much effort in mediation attempts in many conflicts around the world.

7 It is not clear how early in the conflict this must be, since Regan and Stam's variable for time is simply from the beginning of the militarized dispute as indicated by the first threat or use of force, without distinguishing the level or duration of conflict prior to the violence.

8 This assumption becomes more problematic when we allow for a more dynamic model since the war itself can affect the balance of capabilities and the ordering of preferences in each stage. Thus any information revealed by the war is an indication of what used to be the situation before the last battle and might not be relevant to the balance of capabilities and preferences at its end (Goemans, 2000; Wagner, 2000).

9 Theoretically, such situations might be especially amenable to arbitration or adjudication. Both parties prefer conceding to fighting but need to find a way to save face, and to tie their hands so they will not reflexively end up fighting. Arbitration or adjudication by a legitimate third party could offer a way out of this deadlock. It is interesting that such revolutionary regimes as Libya and Iran are among the most frequent users of arbitration by the International Court of Justice. None the less, if even one of the adversaries puts a high value on the resource under dispute, voluntary arbitration or adjudication are unlikely to be acceptable, leaving only mediation as a possible type of third-party intervention (Bilder, 1997).

Bibliography

Abbott, Kenneth and Snidal, Duncan (1998) 'Why States Act Through Formal International Organizations', *Journal of Conflict Resolution*, 42 (1): 3–32.

Banks, Jeffrey (1990) 'Equilibrium Behavior in Crisis Bargaining Games', *American Journal of Political Science*, 34 (4): 599–614.

Bercovitch, Jacob (1984) *Social Conflicts and Third Parties: Strategies of Conflict Resolution*. Boulder: Westview.

Bercovitch, Jacob (1991) 'International Mediation and Dispute Settlement: Evaluating the Conditions for Successful Mediation', *Negotiation Journal*, 7 (1): 17–30.

Bercovitch, Jacob (ed.) (1992a) *Mediation in International Relations: Multiple Approaches to Conflict Management*. New York: St Martin's Press.

Bercovitch, Jacob (1992b) 'Mediators and Mediation Strategies in International Relations', *Negotiation Journal*, 8 (2): 99–112.

Bercovitch, Jacob (1997) 'Mediation in International Conflict: An Overview', in I. William Zartman and J.L. Rasmussen (eds), *Peacemaking in International Conflict: Methods and Techniques*. Washington, DC: US Institute of Peace. pp. 125–53.

Bercovitch, Jacob and Houston, Allison (1996) 'Influence of Mediator Characteristics and Behavior on the Success of Mediation in International Relations', in Jacob Bercovitch (ed.), *International Conflicts: The Theory and Practice of Mediation*. Boulder: Lynne Rienner.

Bercovitch, Jacob and Houston, Allison (2000) 'Why Do They Do It Like This? An Analysis of the Factors Influencing Mediation Behavior in International Conflicts', *Journal of Conflict Resolution*, 44 (2): 170–202.

Bercovitch, Jacob and Langley, Jeffrey (1993) 'The Nature of Dispute and the Effectiveness of International Mediation', *Journal of Conflict Resolution*, 37 (4): 670–91.

Bercovitch, Jacob and Schneider, Gerald (2000) 'Who Mediates? The Political Economy of International Conflict Management', *Journal of Peace Research*, 37 (2): 145–65.

Bilder, Richard B. (1997) 'Adjudication: International Arbitral Tribunals and Courts', in I. William Zartman and J. Lewis Rasmussen (eds), *Peacekeeping in International Conflict: Methods and Techniques*. Washington, DC: US Institute of Peace. pp. 155–89.

Blainey, Geoffrey (1988) *The Causes of War*, 3rd edn. New York: The Free Press.

Boettcher, William (1995) 'Context, Methods, Numbers and Words: Prospect Theory in International Relations', *Journal of Conflict Resolution*, 39 (3): 561–84.

Boulding, Kenneth (1979) *Stable Peace*. Austin: University of Texas Press.

Boutros-Ghali Boutros (1995) *An Agenda for Peace*, 2nd edn, with new supplement (1st edn, 1992). New York: United Nations.

Burton, J.W. (1969) *Conflict and Communication: The Use of Controlled Communication in International Relations*. London: Macmillan.

Burton, J.W. (1986) 'The History of International Conflict Resolution', in E.E. Azar and J.W. Burton (eds), *International Conflict Resolution: Theory and Practice*. Boulder: Lynne Rienner. pp. 40–56.

Busch, Marc (2000) 'Democracy, Consultation, and the Paneling of Disputes under GATT', *Journal of Conflict Resolution*, 44 (4): 425–46.

Carnevale, Peter and Arad, Sharon (1996) 'Bias and Impartiality in International Negotiation', in Jacob Bercovitch (ed.), *Resolving International Conflicts: The Theory and Practice of Mediation*. Boulder: Lynne Reinner. pp. 39–54.

Daniel, Donald and Hayes, Brad (1995) *Beyond Traditional Peacekeeping*. New York: St Martin's Press.

Dawes, Robyn (1988) *Rational Choice in an Uncertain World*. New York: Harcourt Brace.

Dixon, William (1993) 'Democracy and the Management of International Conflict', *Journal of Conflict Resolution*, 37 (1): 42–68.

Dixon, William (1994) 'Democracy and the Peaceful Settlement of International Conflict', *American Political Science Review*, 88 (1): 14–32.

Dixon, William (1996) 'Third-party Techniques for Preventing Conflict Escalation and Promoting Peaceful Settlement', *International Organization*, 40 (3): 653–81.

Druckman, Daniel and Stern, Paul (1997) 'Evaluating Peacekeeping Missions', *Mershon International Studies Review*, 41 (1): 151–65.

Druckman, Daniel, Broome, Benjamin and Kroper, Susan (1988) 'Value Differences and Conflict Resolution', *Journal of Conflict Resolution*, 32 (3): 489–510.

Fearon, James (1994a) 'Signalling vs. the Balance of Power and Interests', *Journal of Conflict Resolution*, 38 (2): 236–69.

Fearon, James (1994b) 'Domestic Political Audiences and the Escalation of International Disputes', *American Political Science Review*, 88 (3): 577–92.

Fearon, James (1995) 'Rationalist Explanations for War', *International Organization*, 49 (3): 379–414.

Festinger, Leon (1957) *A Theory of Cognitive Dissonance*. Stanford: Stanford University Press.

Fisher, Roger (1971) 'Fractionating Conflict', in Joan V. Bondurant (ed.), *Conflict: Violence and Nonviolence*. Chicago: Aldine–Atherton. pp. 135–45.

Fisher, Ronald J. (1983) 'Third Party Consultation as a Method of Intergroup Conflict Resolution', *Journal of Conflict Resolution*, 27 (2): 301–34.

Galtung, Johan (1969) 'Violence, Peace, and Peace Research', *Journal of Peace Research*, 5 (3): 67–91.

Gartzke, Erik (1999) 'War is in the Error Term', *International Organization*, 53 (3): 567–88.

Gilpin, Robert (1981) *War and Change in World Politics*. Cambridge: Cambridge University Press.

Goemans, H.E. (2000) *War and Punishment: The Causes of War Termination and the First World War*. Princeton: Princeton University Press.

Guisinger, Alexandra and Smith, Alastair (2002) 'Honest Threats: The Interaction of Reputation and Political

Institutions in International Crises', *Journal of Conflict Resolution*, 46 (2).

Haas, Ernst B. (1993) 'Collective Conflict Management: Evidence for a New World Order', in Thomas Weiss (ed.), *Collective Security in a Changing World Order*. Boulder: Lynne Rienner.

Heider, Fritz (1958) *The Psychology of Interpersonal Relations*. New York: Wiley.

Jervis, Robert (1976) *Perception and Misperception in International Politics*. Princeton: Princeton University Press.

Jett, Douglas (2000) *Why Peacekeeping Fails*. New York: St Martin's Press.

Kacowicz, Arie M. (1994) *Peaceful Territorial Changes*. Columbia: University of South Carolina Press.

Kant, Immanuel ([1795]1970) 'Perpetual Peace: A Philosophical Stretch', in Hans Reiss (ed.), *Kant's Political Writings*. Cambridge: Cambridge University Press.

Kelman, Herbert (1997) 'Social-psychological Dimensions of International Conflict', in I. William Zartman and J. Lewis Rasmussen (eds), *Peacemaking in International Conflict: Methods and Techniques*. Washington, DC: US Institute of Peace. pp. 191–237.

Kelman, H.C. and Cohen, S.P. (1979) 'Reduction of International Conflict: An Interactional Approach', in W.G. Austin and S. Worchel (eds), *The Social Psychology of Intergroup Relations*. Belmont: Wadsworth. pp. 288–303.

Kleiboer, Marieke (1996) 'Understanding Success and Failure of International Mediation', *Journal of Conflict Resolution*, 40 (2): 360–89.

Kleiboer, Marieke (1998) *The Multiple Realities of International Mediation*. Boulder: Lynne Reinner.

Kreps, David (1990) *Game Theory and Economic Modeling*. Oxford: Oxford University Press.

Kriesberg, Louis (1998) 'The Phases of Destructive Conflicts', in David Carment and Patrick James (eds), *Peace in the Midst of Wars: Preventing and Managing International Ethnic Conflicts*. Columbia: University of South Carolina Press. pp. 33–60.

Kugler, Jacek and Lemke, Douglas (2000) 'The Power Transition', in Manus Midlarsky (ed.), *Handbook of War Studies*, 2nd edn. Ann Arbor: University of Michigan Press.

Massoud, Tansa George (2000) 'Fair Division, Adjusted Winner Procedure (AW), and the Israeli–Palestinian Conflict', *Journal of Conflict Resolution*, 44 (3): 333–58.

McDermott, Rose (1998) *Risk-Taking in International Politics: Prospect Theory in American Foreign Policy*. Ann Arbor: University of Michigan Press.

Meyerson, Roger (1991) *Game Theory: Analysis of Conflict*. Cambridge, MA: Harvard University Press.

Miall, Hugh (1992) *The Peacemakers: Peaceful Settlement of Disputes since 1945*. New York: St Martin's Press.

Mitchell, C.R. and Nicholson, Michael (1983) 'Rational Models and the Ending of Wars', *Journal of Conflict Resolution*, 27 (3): 495–520.

Northedge, F.S. and Donelan, M.D. (1971) *International Disputes: The Political Aspects*. London: Europa.

O'Neill, Barry (2000) *Honor, Symbols, and War*. Ann Arbor: University of Michigan Press.

Organski, A.F.K. and Kugler, Jacek (1980) *The War Ledger*. Chicago: University of Chicago Press.

Oye, Kenneth A. (1985) 'Explaining Cooperation under Anarchy: Hypotheses and Strategies', *World Politics*, 38 (1): 1–24.

Pillar, Paul (1983) *Negotiating Peace: War Termination as a Bargaining Process*. Princeton: Princeton University Press.

Podell, Jerome, E. and Knapp, William M. (1969) 'The Effect of Mediation on the Perceived Firmness of the Opponent', *Journal of Conflict Resolution*, 13 (4): 511–20.

Powell, Robert (1999) *In the Shadow of Power: States and Strategies in International Politics*. Princeton: Princeton University Press.

Princen, Thomas (1992) *Intermediaries in International Conflict*. Princeton: Princeton University Press.

Raiffa, Howard (1982) *The Art and Science of Negotiation*. Cambridge, MA: Belknap.

Raymond, Gregory A. (1994) 'Democracies, Disputes, and Third Party Intermediaries', *Journal of Conflict Resolution*, 38 (1): 24–42.

Raymond, Gregory A. (1996) 'Demosthenes and Democracies: Regime-Types and Arbitration Outcomes', *International Interactions*, 22 (1): 1–20.

Regan, Patrick M. (1996) 'Conditions of Successful Third-Party Intervention in Intrastate Conflicts', *Journal of Conflict Resolution*, 40: 336–59.

Regan, Patrick and Stam, Allan C. (2000) 'In the Nick of Time: Conflict Management, Mediation Timing and the Duration of Interstate Disputes', *International Studies Quarterly*, 44 (2): 239–60.

Reinhardt, Eric (2001) 'Adjudication without Enforcement in GATT Disputes', *Journal of Conflict Resolution*, 45 (1): 174–95.

Rubin, Jeffrey Z. (ed.) (1981) *Dynamics of Third Party Intervention: Kissinger in the Middle East*. New York: Praeger, in cooperation with the Society for Psychological Study of Social Issues.

Rubinstein, Ariel (1982) 'Perfect Equilibrium in a Bargaining Model', *Econometrica*, 50 (1): 97–109.

Rummel, R.J. (1997) *Power Kills: Democracy as a Method of Non-Violence*. New Brunswick: Transaction.

Russett, Bruce and Oneal, John R. (2001) *Triangulating Peace: Democracy, Interdependence, and International Organizations*. New York: W.W. Norton.

Schelling, Thomas C. (1966) *Arms and Influence*. New Haven: Yale University Press.

Schultz, Kenneth A. (1999) 'Do Democratic Institutions Constrain or Inform? Contrasting Two Institutional Perspectives on Democracy and War', *International Organization*, 53 (2): 233–66.

Sheppard, B.H. (1984) 'Third Party Conflict Intervention: A Procedural Framework', *Research in Organizational Behavior*, 6: 141–90.

Simmons, Beth (1999) 'Capacity, Commitment and Compliance: International Institutions and Territorial

Disputes'. Manuscript, Political Science Department, University of California at Berkeley.

Simon, Herbert (1982). *Models of Bounded Rationality.* Cambridge, MA: MIT Press.

Skjelsbaek, Kjell (1991) 'The UN Secretary-General and the Mediation of International Disputes', *Journal of Peace Research*, 28 (1): 99–115.

Smith, Alastair (1996) 'To Intervene or Not to Intervene: A Biased Decision', *Journal of Conflict Resolution*, 40 (1): 16–40.

Smith, Alastair (1998) 'International Crises and Domestic Politics', *American Political Science Review*, 92 (3): 623–38.

Stone Sweet, Alec and Brunell, Thomas L. (1998) 'Constructing a Supranational Constitution: Dispute Resolution and Governance in the European Community', *American Political Science Review*, 91 (1): 63–82.

Tetlock, Philip (1998) 'Social Psychology and World Politics', in D. Gilbert, S. Fiske and G. Lindzey (eds), *Handbook of Social Psychology*, vol. 2, 4th edn. New York: McGraw–Hill. pp. 868–914.

Touval, Saadia (1992) 'The Superpowers as Mediators', in Jacob Bercovitch and Jeffrey Z. Rubin (eds), *Mediation in International Relations: Multiple Approaches to Conflict Management.* New York: St Martin's Press. pp. 232–48.

Touval, Saadia (1994) 'Why the UN Fails', *Foreign Affairs*, 73 (5): 44–57.

Touval, Saadia and Zartman, I. William (1989) 'Mediation in International Conflicts', in Kenneth Kressel and Dean Pruitt (eds), *Mediation Research: The Process and Effectiveness of Third-Party Intervention.* San Francisco: Jossey–Bass. pp. 115–37.

Troester, Rod (1996) *Jimmy Carter as Peacemaker.* Westport: Praeger.

Van Evera, Stephen (1999) *Causes of War: Power and the Roots of Conflict.* Ithaca: Cornell University Press.

Wagner, R. Harrison (2000) 'Bargaining and War', *American Journal of Political Science*, 44 (3): 469–84.

Walton, R.E. (1969) *Interpersonal Peacemaking: Confrontation and Third Party Consultation.* Reading, MA: Addison–Wesley.

Werner, Suzanne (1998) 'Negotiating the Terms of Settlement: War Aims and Bargaining Leverage', *Journal of Conflict Resolution*, 42 (3): 321–43.

White, Ralph K. (1965) 'Images in the Context of International Conflict: Soviet Perceptions of the US and the USSR', in Herbert Kelman (ed.), *International Behavior: A Social-Psychological Analysis.* New York: Holt, Rinehart & Winston. pp. 236–76.

Wittman, Donald (1979) 'How a War Ends: A Rationalist Model Approach', *Journal of Conflict Resolution*, 21: 741–61.

Young, H. Peyton (1994) *Equity in Theory and Practice.* Princeton: Princeton University Press.

Young, Oran (1967) *The Intermediaries: Third Parties in International Crises.* Princeton: Princeton University Press.

Zartman, I. William (1985) *Ripe for Resolution: Conflict and Intervention in Africa.* Oxford: Oxford University Press.

Zartman, I. William (1995) 'Dynamics and Constraints in Negotiations in Internal Conflicts', in I. William Zartman (ed.), *Elusive Peace: Negotiating an End to Civil Wars.* Washington, DC: Brookings Institution. pp. 3–29.

21

Nationalism and Ethnicity

LARS-ERIK CEDERMAN

Today, at the dawn of the twenty-first century, most international relations (IR) specialists accept that ethnicity and nationalism are highly relevant to their field. Yet, only a decade ago, IR studies on these topics were few and far between. It was only with considerable delay that the IR literature vindicated Donald Horowitz's (1985) comment in the mid-1980s about ethnicity's having 'fought and bled and burned its way into public and scholarly consciousness'. In fact, it took an extraordinary amount of nationalist activity in the early 1990s for scholars to begin to grapple with the challenge posed by these topics. The decade that followed after the collapse of communism has indeed been marked by remarkable outbursts of nationalist violence, most notably, but far from exclusively, in the former Yugoslavia and Rwanda. Despite the Gulf War, it is becoming increasingly clear that the importance of inter-state war is declining while that of nationalist conflict is increasing (Wallensteen and Sollenberg, 1999).[1]

This chapter explores primarily the response to these recent events for the simple reason that not much else exists to review in the IR literature. A quick glance at recently published textbooks and handbooks speaks a clear language.[2] Indeed, one of the few political-science experts in the area summed up the situation in the mid-1980s by referring to the study of politics and culture as 'moribund' (Laitin, 1986: 171).[3]

Granted the sustained relevance of ethnic and nationalist conflict since the French Revolution, this silence calls for an explanation. With the exception of the decolonization process which ended by the late 1970s, the *Zeitgeist* of the post-Second World War period triggered a scholarly rejection of nationalist themes: 'Nationalism was

blamed for the onset of war in 1939; as statesmen paid no attention to national self-determination when dividing Germany and Korea, so scholars in their turn ignored nationalism' (Hall, 1998b: 1). Furthermore, the strong impact of economics on the social sciences has tended to obscure topics such as culture and collective identity formation. Finally, as a result of its state-centric focus, IR theory has become strangely 'depopulated' as a result of ignoring the role of individuals and non-state groups (though see Wolfers, 1962). Fortunately, this is beginning to change.

Yet it would be a mistake to limit the scope to the first decade following the fall of the Berlin Wall. Because the scholarly output appeared as late as it did, and mainly focused quite narrowly on the post-Cold War situation, it is necessary to cast a wider net. First, the IR treatments of these topics constitute a very small fraction of a broader and more mature, interdisciplinary literature on nationalism. At any rate, border-transgressing phenomena such as nationalism make a mockery of any attempt to demarcate IR as a distinct field separate from comparative politics. But even this widening of the disciplinary scope remains insufficient, for most of our knowledge of nationalism and ethnicity stems from academic writings located entirely outside political science. This burgeoning literature brings together a motley collection of disciplinary perspectives, including history, historical sociology, cultural anthropology, social psychology and social theory.

Far from being historical constants, ethnic and nationalist processes antedate the current era by a wide margin. To argue that the post-Cold War cases of conflict along nationalist lines represent a profoundly novel development in world politics would thus be tantamount to a glaring anachronism

(Ayres, 2000; Fearon and Laitin, 1996; Gurr, 1993). Such a post hoc rationalization squanders a valuable opportunity to engage in reconstructive theorizing of the discipline's conceptual foundations. As I will argue, such a need for conceptual reconstruction relates to widespread terminological confusion that has even turned the name of the sub-field into a misnomer, for the actual practice of 'international relations' would be better characterized as 'inter-*state* relations' (Connor, 1972).

Rather than merely summarizing the recent work in IR, then, I adopt a wider, interdisciplinary approach as a way to put the IR literature in its proper theoretical and macro-historical perspective. This opening will facilitate the assessment of its strengths and weaknesses and help us identify future avenues to a deeper understanding of the complex processes underpinning the phenomena under scrutiny.

To my knowledge, there have been few, if any, attempts comprehensively to take stock of the structure and insights of the IR literature on nationalism and ethnicity. Because of the relative scarcity of studies in IR, previous reviews of these topics that have appeared in political science publications have tended to focus on extra-disciplinary work (Haas, 1986; Waldron, 1985). In addition to these useful, but now somewhat dated, reviews, Brubaker and Laitin (1998) provide an excellent survey of the literature in sociology and political science (see also Calhoun, 1993, 1997; Hall, 1995; Smith, 1991, 1995). The current chapter complements their insightful, stock-taking exercise by focusing primarily on IR applications. Yet, as opposed to Brubaker and Laitin's methodological classification, this chapter follows a distinctly theoretical outline that classifies the literature according to the ontological status of the key concepts.[4]

While I have made an effort to encompass as much of the recent IR literature as possible, the current wealth of writings has forced me to limit the scope to:

- explanatory and analytical research, at the expense of normative studies and practical prescriptions (e.g. Beiner, 1999; Brown, 1997: Part II; Lake and Rothchild, 1998a: Part 4);
- predominantly theoretical and analytical studies, rather than purely empirical ones, with the exception of such texts that elucidate general analytical points;
- mostly conflictual cases due to their impact on the international system;[5]
- political science writings, whereas other fields receive attention to the extent they elucidate the IR problems under scrutiny; and
- primarily, but not exclusively, US scholarship, because of the relative lack of publications in the non-American IR literature.[6]

This chapter is organized as follows. The next section attempts to bring some clarity to the thorny issue of conceptualization. The following section introduces an ontological 3 × 3 table, which will serve as the main taxonomic device used in this chapter, followed by four sections, each one covering a 'field of construction'. A concluding section evaluates the main trends characterizing IR work on nationalism and ethnicity, and comments on the general direction of future research.

DEFINING THE MASTER CONCEPTS: THE STATE, THE NATION AND NATIONALISM

It has become a cliché to characterize the key concepts relating to ethnicity and nationalism as hopelessly elusive. Nevertheless, despite some signs of improvement, observations to this effect remain pertinent. What is more, political science seems curiously resistant to repeated attempts at clarification of the fundamental ontology.[7] I will therefore start by discussing the two most serious misconceptions (cf. Miller, 1995: ch. 2).

The most acute one pertains to two central concepts, namely the state and the nation. To disentangle these terms, it is helpful to start with Max Weber's (1946) classical definition of the *state* as a territorial organization exercising legitimate control over its own bounded territory, unchallenged by internal power competition or external intervention. Against this conceptualization, Weber pits the *nation*, which he defines as 'a community of sentiment which would adequately manifest itself in a state of its own' and hence 'tends to produce a state of its own' (176; see also Alter, 1989; Cederman, 1997: 16–19; Haas, 1986: 726; 1997: ch. 2).

This preliminary definition of the nation calls for several remarks. First, although the nation sometimes coincides with the state, such a coincidence should be treated as a historical contingency rather than as a case of conceptual unity (Connor, 1972, 1978). Where the state and the nation do coincide, it is legitimate to refer to the *nation-state*. Second, Weber's definition requires the presence of an inter-subjective understanding of belonging. This is precisely what Benedict Anderson (1991) aptly labels an 'imagined community'. In addition, the nation must be a bounded community defining citizenship for the masses. Third, Weber's nation concept depends directly on the state. By definition, there can be no nations independently of the state system (though see Smith, 1991: 14, for a cultural definition). Since some nations do not fight for full sovereignty but instead claim wide-ranging powers, it makes sense to relax Weber's demanding definition by including self-defined communities that pursue autonomy within a state framework (e.g. Brubaker, 1998: 276; Snyder, 2000: 19).

The last remark highlights a second pernicious terminological blurring characterizing much of the

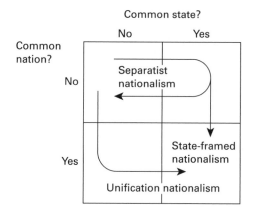

Figure 21.1 *Three historical types of nationalism*

political science literature, namely the failure to separate nationalism from ethnicity. Too often the two are treated as if they were synonymous. To enhance conceptual precision, it is therefore preferable to define an *ethnic group* or an *ethnie* as a cultural community based on a common belief in real or putative descent (Weber, 1978; cf. Smith, 1991: 21). Although nations sometimes correspond closely to ethnic groups, in which case they are usually referred to as nations' 'ethnic cores', other nations contain many ethnic groups and may in some cases be devoid of any sense of ethnic belonging (cf. Barrington, 1997: 731). Ethnic groups, in turn, differ from *ethnic categories*, which are based on cultural markers imposed by outside observers without the members necessarily attaching any importance to the characteristics (Brass, 1976: 226). Sometimes kinship is also differentiated from ethnicity, but this will not concern me in this chapter (cf. Calhoun, 1997: 39–40).

Having defined the basic units, I now turn to the notion of *nationalism*. Again there is a plethora of definitions to choose from (see Calhoun, 1997: 4–5; A.D. Smith, 1991: 72), but I will limit the use of the term to a specific ideology with European origins stating that each nation should possess its own state or at least some degree of territorial self-determination. This definition is somewhat wider than Gellner's (1983: 1) terse formula stating that 'nationalism is primarily a political doctrine, which holds that the political and the national unit should be congruent' (cf. Haas, 1997). Viewed as a corollary, this conceptualization implies (1) that the world is divided into nations, (2) that the nation is the source of all political power, and (3) that national loyalty overrides all other allegiances as a 'trump card' (cf. Calhoun, 1993, 1997; Smith, 1991: 72).

To put the pieces together, I propose a simple, historically inspired taxonomy that will help to identify the main types of nationalism. Following

up the distinction between the state and the nation given above, Figure 21.1 introduces a two-dimensional scheme depicting stylized historical situations. Logically speaking, such situations can be characterized by either the presence or absence of a *common* state and/or nation.

Starting with the anarchical configuration in the upper left quadrant, where neither entity dominates the entire area, I sketch three developmental paths that can, but do not have to, lead to the formation of a nation-state in the lower right corner. This dynamic categorization draws on Theodor Schieder's (1991) three ideal types of nationalism (cf. Alter, 1989; Cederman, 1997: ch. 6; Gellner, 1997: ch. 6). Depending on the initial geo-cultural configuration, either a common state emerges before the nation or nation-building precedes state-formation. The former 'Western European' possibility leads to *state-framed nationalism* (Brubaker, 1998: 300). In Germany and Italy, the order was arguably reversed, such that a cultural nation preceded the state thus generating *unification nationalism*. Finally, when the East European empires collapsed, *separatist nationalism* appeared in their wake. While originally associated with European cases, these three trajectories are quite general, and could be applied to both decolonization and post-communist nationalism.

Since nationalism requires national and territorial units to coincide, pressures will be exerted on existing state frameworks where this is not the case, that is, in the 'mixed situations' corresponding to the upper right and the lower left cells. In a very simplified way, the diagram thus illustrates that nationalist activity can both produce political integration and territorial fragmentation.

CONTEXTUALIZING THE IR LITERATURE: FIELDS OF CONSTRUCTION

The remainder of this chapter considers to what extent the territorial and popular dimensions of world politics are problematized. A few words are in order to justify the use of 'fields of construction' as an ontological map since it may be less familiar to an IR audience used to the traditional levels-of-analysis scheme.

While Waltz's (1959) three images have been used to explain ethnic conflict (e.g. Kaufman, 1996), such applications are problematic. For one, it is unclear how to fit ethnic groups and nations into the traditional state-centric scheme. Moreover, the levels-of-analysis model usually entails a one-shot and level-against-level notion of causation that would fail to do full justice to the complex processes under scrutiny. Third, given the importance of identities, a classification of theories of nationalism should be able to represent different 'levels of construction' (Wendt, 1999: 244).

Here three levels of analytical problematization will be considered. Logically speaking, theoretical frameworks can view social actors as either being *absent, reified,* or *constructed.* Absence means that the theory in question ignores the unit or presupposes it implicitly. Reification corresponds to the practice of treating actors as if they were objects, that is, given entities that are held constant throughout the analysis (Berger and Luckmann, 1966). Not only assumptions, but also independent variables and parameters, belong to this category. Finally, I consider a collective actor to be constructed to the extent that its identity plays the role of a dependent variable or at least varies with time. In short, it has to be a 'moving part' of the explanatory machinery even if it is not fully explained.

The two-dimensional exposition thus allows me to discern different meanings of constructivism in IR. While the term is often reserved for theories that endogenize states' identities, constructivist theories can also endogenize both national and ethnic identities. Applied to such identities, the construction–reification dichotomy has the advantage of circumventing the potentially pejorative term primordialism. Scholars often use this label as a description of nationalists' ideological efforts to convince others (and themselves) that their own nations are naturally given entities. But they also employ it as a characterization of social science research. Yet, while many analysts engage in 'methodological reification' for pragmatic rather than ideological reasons, it would be wrong to assume that they accept the nationalists' argumentation (although in some cases this cannot be excluded).[8]

Neither the reified nor the constructivist perspective on national identities follows a single logic. Indeed, there is considerable variance on both sides of the ontological divide. The assumption of nations' invariance in reifying approaches can be justified by references to biology (e.g. van den Berghe, 1982), cultural stability over long time periods (e.g. Smith, 1986), or analytical convenience for a shorter period not exhibiting identity change (e.g. Kaufmann, 1996). Constructivist approaches differ even more widely. There are many ways to explain how national identities form, change, dissipate, or remain stable. The last explanatory task may seem to be the turf of reifying theories, but these assume identities to be constants rather than explaining *why* they fail to vary (Wendt, 1999: 238). Furthermore, two distinct logics drive constructivist explanations. Whereas some analysts view identity-formation in exclusively instrumentalist terms, thus following March and Olsen's (1998) 'logic of consequences', others emphasize rule-following and identity-reproducing institutions, that is, 'the logic of appropriateness'. Although this analytical distinction does not always coincide with the question of

identity malleability, instrumentalists typically assume identities to be fluid and subject to relatively free individual choice. Sociological institutionalists, by contrast, are more prone to regard identity as being ascribed rather than chosen, and if an element of choice is involved, it is heavily embedded in an interpretative frame of constitutive rules locking individuals into a path-dependent collective identification process (Calhoun, 1997: 30–3). Thus, it would be a mistake to treat rationalist and constructivist approaches to identity-formation as inherently competing perspectives (Brubaker, 1998: 291).

Together the distinctions relating to actor type and levels of construction open up a two-dimensional landscape of theoretical possibilities consisting of nine cells (see Figure 21.2), ranging from theories in which both states and national (or ethnic) identities are absent (type A) to those that attempt to problematize them both (type 4). Without confusing ethnicity and nationalism, cells D and E in the first column refer to ethnic groups rather than nations because the latter cannot by definition exist in the absence of the state.

Rather than defining self-contained 'paradigms', the figure depicts analytical combinations adopted by various approaches, some of which cover more than one cell. Since their utility depends on the substantive goal of the research, none can be said to be better than the other without specifying the substantive task at hand. Nevertheless, the highlighted four cells in the lower right corner correspond closely to the topic of this chapter (types 1–4). *In the following, I limit the scope to studies that render both state and national identities explicit.* Since states figure in all these combinations, the main focus will be on nationalism rather than on ethnicity in its own right.

With respect to national identities, analytical approaches can be either reifying or constructivist. The second question pertains to the analytical status of state identities. Whereas the nation-reifying perspectives freeze state identities as well (type 1), or endogenize these (type 2), those that adopt a constructivist approach to national identities either limit their constructivist outlook to nations while treating states as if they were fixed objects (type 3) or embrace 'double constructivism' with respect to both states and nations (type 4).

The remaining combinations correspond to 'contiguous' fields that constitute the intellectual context of this chapter's main area of focus (types A–E). The type A category is silent about both the state and the nation. Despite attempts to 'bring the state back in' (Evans et al., 1985), students of domestic politics have frequently resorted to this analytical starting point, as for example in pluralist studies of interest groups and other societal actors (see references in Nettl, 1968). Type-1 research also includes analysis of historical periods during which neither the state nor the nation was present.

State identities? National (or ethnic)* identities?	Absent	Reified	Constructed
Absent	A Pluralism and pre-modern IR	B State essentialism (mainstream IR)	C State-centric constructivism
Reified	D Essentialist anthropology	**1** **Double** **essentialism**	**2** **Systemic** **nation-** **essentialism**
Constructed	E Constructivist anthropology	**3** **Comparative** **nation-** **constructivism**	**4** **Systemic** **nation-** **constructivism**

**Literature on state and
national identities**

Figure 21.2   *Classifying analytical perspectives: nine fields of construction*
In cells D and E, the vertical axis refers to ethnic groups rather than nations.

Type-B research combines an explicit but reified treatment of the state with no, or minimal, references to ethnic or nationalist actors in their own right. Most mainstream IR writings fit comfortably in this state-essentialist cell since both neorealism and neoliberalism tend to represent states as given and unchanging entities while ignoring nationalism and ethnicity. Relaxing this position, type-C studies problematize state identities while still bracketing nationalism and ethnicity. While social constructivism has secured a safe position on the state-centric IR agenda, they continue to pay surprisingly little attention to other actor types, such as ethnic or national communities. Ironically enough, while arguably better placed to break new ground in analyzing nationalism than any other meta-theoretical paradigm within IR, 'conventional' constructivism has had little to say about this important phenomenon. The strong focus on the purely intra-scientific goal of criticizing and surpassing neorealism has detracted from the more important theoretical objective of analyzing major substantive developments in world politics (e.g. Wendt, 1999).

Reifying ethnic groups while bracketing states, type-D research corresponds to traditional, 'pre-Barthian' approaches to anthropology, especially those that analyze primitive, pre-modern communities as objectified collections of cultural traits (Neumann, 1999: 4). While often misclassified as a primordialist theory of nationalism, Clifford Geertz's (1973) approach to ethnicity does reify ethnic groups (Calhoun, 1997: 31–2). Reacting to such reified conceptions of ethnicity, Fredrik Barth

(1969) shifted the attention from cultural 'essences' to ethnogenesis through boundary formation, thus pioneering the type-E research. According to this type of constructivist anthropology, groups do not consist of objective cultural traits but need to be viewed through the self-categorization of its members. Although recent anthropological studies also stress 'cultural contents', contemporary anthropology is deeply indebted to Barth's formal boundary approach.

REIFYING BOTH STATES AND NATIONS: 'DOUBLE ESSENTIALISM' (TYPE 1)

Since so little 'native' theorizing of nationalism existed in IR at the beginning of the 1990s, it is hardly surprising that most analysts started by extending their type-B frameworks. While retaining a reified notion of the state, studies of this type incorporate nations and/or ethnic groups as equally objectified entities, either encapsulated within states or plugging cultural units into the slot previously held by states. Recently, some studies have tried to disaggregate ethnic groups. Each possibility will be explored in turn.

Explaining Inter-state Behavior

In the years that followed immediately upon the collapse of communism, most IR scholars retained their state-centric and state-reifying frameworks.

Viewed through this rather narrow lens, nationalism appears to be primarily a popularity-enhancing device reinforcing states' internal cohesion and external power projection. For instance, Barry Posen (1993a) investigates the spread of nationalism in the nineteenth century as a means to enhance states' extractive and mobilizing power. Drawing on Waltz's (1979) arguments about competition and socialization inducing unit likeness, Posen explains the post-Napoleonic spread of mass armies.

But not all behavior fits into the matrix of *raison d'état*. Committed to rationalistic assumptions, some realist scholars resort to the term 'hypernationalism' for episodes of what they consider to be nationalist over-reactions. Defined as an artificially generated 'belief that other nations or nation-states are both inferior and threatening', hypernationalism is thought to undermine carefully calibrated balance of power calculations (Mearsheimer, 1992: 221; see also Van Evera, 1990/1). Yet, it is tempting to use hypernationalism in order to explain away whatever does not fit neorealist rationalism (Lapid and Kratochwil, 1996b: 112). Indeed, the definitional section above has shown that nationalism does not always strengthen the state or its policies.

In a dramatic and highly publicized departure from the neorealist tradition, Samuel Huntington (1993a, 1996) claims that state behavior in the post-Cold War period will no longer reflect primarily power calculations or ideology but, rather, civilizational affiliations. It is along the 'fault lines' between the world religions that conflict will be most prone to erupt. In particular, the 'kin-group syndrome' prompts intervention by distant cultural relatives, as illustrated by Russian and Greek nationalists aligning themselves with Serbia. Needless to say, Huntington's thesis, with its overtly normative overtones, has come in for fervent criticism because of its attempt to reify civilizations as large-scale ethnic categories (see Huntington's, 1993b rebuttal to the critiques in the same issue).

Explaining the Behavior of Given Ethnic/Nationalist Groups

In the post-Cold War period, a number of scholars have abandoned the exclusive focus on the state system and applied the unitary rational actor assumption to ethnic groups. There are four clusters of analyses: first, some studies explain inter-group conflict as a direct consequence of long-standing antipathies among ethnic groups. Second, rejecting this view as too culturally deterministic, others draw on the 'security dilemma'. Third, rational-choice theorists have joined these efforts. Finally, statistics on ethnic minority groups have been collected and analyzed.

We start by considering conflict-reifying studies. Reacting to the painful images broadcast from the former Yugoslavia and Rwanda, politicians and journalists have tended to attribute the appalling acts of violence to longstanding, 'century-old' hatreds between the ethnic groups. This argument assumes that conflict erupts as soon as the state's power wanes: once the lid is lifted the 'seething cauldron' boils over (see critique in Brubaker, 1998: 281–5).

Although most academic commentators disagree with this version of events, a minority of scholars have followed similar lines. These studies rely heavily on culture as the main factor perpetuating the animosities. In an often-cited interpretation of the Yugoslav conflict, Robert Kaplan (1993) attributes the violence to specific traits characterizing the entire region's allegedly belligerent culture. Similarly, Huntington's (1993a) civilizational thesis not only applies to inter-state exchanges, but can also be seen as a theory of culturally defined groups. In particular, Islamic culture allegedly provokes more conflicts than other civilizations.

The tendency to reify conflict, together with the cultural units perpetrating it, is also strongly present in an article by Chaim Kaufmann (1996), who recommends partition as a solution to ethnic civil wars (see also Mearsheimer and Van Evera, 1995). Contending that such conflicts differ fundamentally from ideological contests, Kaufmann asserts that ethnic divisions render conflict resolution next to impossible. Once started, violent exchanges quickly harden ethnic identities to such an extent that reification presumably becomes a fully justifiable analytical assumptions. In fact, Kaufmann even thinks that ethnic boundaries are inert (1996: 269) and that 'atrocity histories cannot be reconstructed' (1996: 283).

Nevertheless, outside the security literature, most political scientists appear to reject these perspectives as over-simplified (cf. Laitin, 1998: ch. 12; Snyder, 2000: ch. 1). Unfortunately, some of the rebuttals are quite overstated. From the rejection of conflict-reifying determinism it does not follow that all arguments involving culture are tantamount to primordialism. Indeed, it cannot be excluded that specific cultural types of discourse are violence-inducing (Brubaker, 1998: 283), nor does it seem implausible that violence often hardens group boundaries (Simmel, 1955). Nevertheless, recent statistical evidence appears to contradict the effectiveness of partition as a policy, thus undermining the credibility of essentialist theorizing in general (Sambanis, 2000).

The fact that the most violent conflicts usually cannot be traced back to 'century-old' conflict seriously undermines 'ancient hatred' accounts. To illustrate, most Yugoslavs lived peacefully side by side until shortly before the violence erupted (Gagnon 1994/5; Ignatieff, 1994; Sekulic et al., 1994; Woodward, 1995). In order to resolve this anomaly, some IR theorists have attempted to account for conflictual outcomes by replacing the strong assumptions of long-standing hatred by weaker postulates.

For example, Barry Posen (1993b) suggests that the ethnic conflict in post-communist Europe should be seen as a situation of 'emerging anarchy'. Using the same logic as in a traditional inter-state setting, Posen contends that belligerent ethnic groups, such as Croats and Serbs in the early 1990s, are subject to a security dilemma (Jervis, 1978), because without stable state-led enforcement, they cannot trust each other and commit to liberal policies. On this view, ethnic conflict erupts due to offensive strategies and high degrees of uncertainty.

Especially when used as an alternative to conflict-reifying interpretations of ethnic conflict, security-dilemma analysis usefully highlights action–reaction effects locking the participants into an escalating process of increasing radicalism and violence.[9] These insights come at a high price, however, since questionable assumptions are carried over from type-B theorizing. For example, Posen's interpretation of the Yugoslav case reifies the ethnic groups while 'neglecting both the role of the state in constructing these identities and the cynical rewriting of history that is taking place to fit present political purposes' (Lapid and Kratochwil, 1996b: 115). Moreover, the substitution of ethnic groups for states confuses the fundamental nature of the units and exaggerates the cohesion of ethnic groups (cf. Crawford, 1998; Gagnon, 1994/5; Laitin, 1998: ch. 12). Statistical work casts further doubt on the viability of 'security dilemma' applications (Sambanis, 2000).

Formal modelers have not been lagging far behind their qualitative colleagues in reacting to the changes following the Cold War. Most of the initial modeling effort formalized and elaborated on the security-dilemma logic at the level of ethnic groups. Viewed more broadly, this rationalistic literature highlights information failures and problems of credible commitments (Lake and Rothchild, 1998b).

James Fearon's (1994) paper represents one of the first systematic efforts to use game-theoretic tools to model ethnic conflict in IR. Inspired by Posen's theory of the ethnic security dilemma, Fearon provides an alternative to the 'ancient hatred' explanation of the ethnic conflict between Serbs and Croats. Subsequently published in revised form, Fearon's (1998) model features a government and an ethnically distinct minority group. Once the geopolitical situation shifts from hierarchy to anarchy, inter-ethnic contracts can no longer be expected to hold. Faced with this structural transformation, both actors now face a serious commitment problem (see also Bates et al., 1998 and Weingast, 1998).

In a more philosophical essay, Russell Hardin (1995) proposes a qualitative rational-choice framework as an antidote to 'primordialist' explanations of ethnic conflict. Following rationalistic principles, Hardin comes to the conclusion that ethnicity can solve collective-action problems *within* groups while creating sub-optimal outcomes *between* them driven by pre-emption and a lack of centralized control: 'Even people of good will can be panicked into escalating moves by the fear of failing to respond to an aggressive adversary, especially when pre-emptive responses might be vastly more beneficial than later responses' (1995: 160).

As Posen's interpretation, these rational-choice models usefully highlight the strategic aspects of ethnic politics. Due to the strong isomorphism with the security-dilemma setup, however, the formal approach suffers from the same structural weaknesses as the qualitative version.[10] First, the reification of ethnic groups as unitary rational actors is problematic, because, in the absence of centralized enforcement, it is unclear how such loosely aggregated communities could exist in the first place despite free-riding at the individual level. This problem does not disappear by moving the strategic analysis up to the group level (e.g. Hardin, 1995: 144). Second, because of the commitment to non-cooperative game theory, ethnification of politics and the breakdown of trust remain outside the scope of rational-choice analysis.[11] Third, while formal approaches of this type go beyond qualitative theorizing in offering causal micro-mechanisms, it does not mean that they are empirically accurate or even particularly plausible (Elster, 2000).

Compared to the small number of statistical studies exploring the impact of ethnicity on inter-state war, the quantitative literature on ethnic minorities within states has advanced much further. These advances are due to Ted Gurr's (1993) massive data collection effort entitled *Minorities at Risk*. As its title suggests, the project contains data on the relations between states and their culturally distinct minorities. Rather than trying to summarize the rather complicated causal model that Gurr proposes, however, I will here turn directly to Fearon and Laitin (1999), who improve and reinterpret Gurr's original data set. Applying a simple multivariate model to the modified data, Fearon and Laitin conclude that violence tends to increase robustly with economic indicators, such as GDP per capita and growth, settlement patterns including a rural base, and the presence of rough terrain. In addition, they report less robust results on minority size and the presence of nearby co-ethnic states. More importantly though, they fail to find a relationship between ethnic violence on the one hand, and the size of the cultural differences, the degree of the state's discrimination, and democracy on the other hand (though see Vanhanen, 1999).

While providing useful information about large-scale conflict patterns, quantification also poses problems. Apart from obvious difficulties of measurement and observability (cf. Gurr and Harff, 1994: 93), there are tricky conceptual issues associated with the operationalization of culture and identity. For example, Yee (1996: 102) suggests that the behaviorists' 'commitment to empirical analyses of observable behavior that can be tested and falsified renders them reluctant and ill-equipped to analyze the intersubjective meanings and symbolic discourses that give ideas their causal effects'. More specifically, hypotheses linking 'cultural difference' to political action, such as nationalist warfare, implicitly accept an essentialist notion of culture and thus cannot problematize 'politically relevant identities' (Crawford, 1998: 18; see also Barth, 1969). Thus, it is necessary to complement these studies with qualitative process tracing. Selection bias is another serious problem haunting projects relying on the data set, for it is far from clear what 'at risk' really means (Fearon and Laitin, 1999). Other tricky problems pertain to the absence of 'majority' groups, such as Russia within the former Soviet Union, as well as the failure to consider the endogeneity due to historical path-dependence and action 'spilling over' state boundaries (see types 2 and 4 below).

Explaining the Behavior of Individuals in Inter-ethnic Relations

Not all type-2 studies treat ethnic groups as unitary rational actors. A technically sophisticated solution is to let the individual group members act strategically. While keeping the macro-identities reified, Fearon and Laitin (1996, 1999) propose models that disaggregate micro-behavior. In these cases, individuals belonging to either of two groups do the acting. Attacking the puzzle of inter-ethnic cooperation, Fearon and Laitin (1996) model group interaction as a series of pairwise encounters in a 'matching game'. They show that such a setup yields two equilibria, one leading to conflictual spirals and the other supporting decentralized, in-group policing. In addition, Fearon and Laitin (1999) attempt to explain the empirical regularities measured at the group-level by pitting a unitary state against an n-member minority.

Though representing an advance over the group-reifying models, these papers still fail to problematize the groups themselves, since their boundaries are imposed exogenously by the initial labeling of the individual actors. Furthermore, like other reasonably complex game-theoretic models, they assume high levels of rationality without proving an intuitively plausible mechanism tracing how the equilibria can actually be reached. In that sense, neither the creation of trust nor its breakdown is explained.

PROBLEMATIZING STATES WHILE REIFYING NATIONS: 'SYSTEMIC NATION-ESSENTIALISM' (TYPE 2)

One way of relaxing the double reification assumed by type-1 approaches is to let state identities vary while national identities remain fixed. In many ways, this category of work follows the example of IR constructivism (type C). Due to the state-centric assumptions, however, these scholars have endogenized state identities rather than national or ethnic ones. For example, Wendt (1994: 387) states that 'nationalism may be in part "primordial" and thus inherent to societies' self-conception as distinct groups' (see Pasic, 1996 for a critique).[12]

To find nation-reifying studies that endogenize states' boundaries, it is necessary to turn to scholarship that has normally not been associated with IR constructivism. While exogenizing national identities, these perspectives focus on disintegration and irredentism.[13]

Disintegration

Analyses of this type explain the presence or lack of states' fragmentation in reified cultural terms. Simply put, territorial rule is assumed to require ethnic cohesion, implying that in its absence state collapse becomes likely (Collins, 1986: ch. 8). Disintegration comprises a spectrum of possibilities ranging from weak types of decentralization, such as separatist claims for cultural autonomy, to full-fledged secession (Horowitz, 1985: 231). Empirical evidence shows that while many secessionist attempts were made during the Cold War period, before the last wave of imperial dissolution, secession has rarely been successful (e.g. Hechter, 1992), though this has changed in this post-Cold War period.

The main debate concerns the role of cultural identities as a driving force in secessionist projects. While some theorists emphasize the non-instrumental nature of secession (e.g. Connor, 1994: ch. 6), others are more prone to stress material factors (e.g. Gourevitch, 1979; Hechter, 1992). Despite the elegance of parsimonious explanations, however, mixed ones probably provide a better account of the underlying processes than more one-sided explanations. Offering an interpretation that draws on both cultural and rationalist reasoning, Donald Horowitz (1985) suggests that while advanced groups engage in interest-based calculations, their backward counterparts are more likely to secede regardless of the costs.

Irredentism

The concept of irredentism stems from the Italian state's claim to 'redeem' its ethnic brethren in the

Habsburg provinces Venice and Trento at the end of the nineteenth century. It can be defined as the attempt to break loose and integrate a territory populated by a 'kin' population into the state of its ethnic 'homeland' (e.g. Chazan, 1991b). Either the homeland state already exists (as in the case of newly unified Italy) or it has yet to be created (as in the Kurdish case). Thus, irredentism can be seen as a combination of nationalist secession and integration: 'Irredentism involves subtracting from one state and adding to another state, new or already existing; secession involves subtracting alone' (Horowitz, 1991: 10).

The differences between irredentism and secession do not imply that the two phenomena are unconnected (Horowitz, 1985, 1991). Indeed, a successful bid for irredentism must include secession. The question, however, is whether the process ends there or whether nationalist integration ensues. The decision to secede and unify hinges on a chain of conditions, including power-related considerations. For example, it could be that the diaspora minority's leaders are unwilling to give up power to the homelands' politicians or that the latter are reluctant to upset the domestic balance (Chazan, 1991b).

The factors governing the spread of irredentism are typically both regional and systemic. Regional explanations attribute irredentist pressures to a discrepancy between the cultural and political maps in a particular area. The more 'stranded diasporas' there are, the more likely secessionist campaigns become (Chazan, 1991b; Van Evera, 1994). Systemic accounts trace the spread of secessionism from one state to the other. Whereas some analysts warn against the risk of diffusion (e.g. Halperin, 1998; Heraclides, 1990; Kuran, 1998), others are less alarmed (e.g. Fearon, 1998; Saideman, 1998).

Diffusion of irredentist politics can be attributed to several mechanisms. First, ethnic conflict may proliferate due to physical externalities through the spread of violence and refugees from one state to the other. While the particularist logic of ethnic nationalism is to some extent 'self limiting' (Fearon, 1998), the possibility of imagining large pan-national units should not be entirely discounted. Second, behavioral demonstration effects may also drive diffusion. Both minority élites and homeland politicians could get inspiration from successful irredentism elsewhere (cf. Kuran, 1998).

Despite this list of explanations, culturally reified approaches overlook one of the most important sources of diffusion, namely demonstration effects pertaining to the very principle of nationalism. Once the direct link between cultural 'raw material' and political identities is broken, it becomes possible to imagine a mobilization effect spreading the 'modular' idea of nationalism (Anderson, 1991) to unmobilized areas where it had not previously been present. While further discussion of this topic will have to be postponed to the survey of type-4 studies, the approaches described in the next section take an important step in this direction.

Problematizing Nations While Reifying States: 'Comparative Nation-Constructivism' (Type 3)

Given their close interest in societal dynamics, it is unsurprising that comparativists have got farther than IR specialists on the 'long road from primordialism to a more constructed view of nations' (Laitin, 1998: 334). Due to the emphasis on country comparisons, however, these contributions usually reify the states as cases:

> The boundaries of states are territorially defined, and despite border wars, remain fixed over time. Classic theories of international relations assume fixed boundaries. But the boundaries of nations are defined by the cultural stocks of people, and these boundaries are forever ambiguous. (Laitin, 1998: 340)

As opposed to reified perspectives that resort to 'groupism' (Brubaker, 1998: 292), this 'sociational' focus on the very existence of national collective identities forces the analyst to consider the puzzle of how nationalism ties together large numbers of people, spans over long time periods and vast territories (Simmel, [1908] 1992).[14] The best theoretical solution to this puzzle remains Ernest Gellner's (1964) classic analysis in *Thought and Change*. Gellner asserts that, in contrast to pre-modern society which was based on direct interpersonal relationships, the large scale of the nation requires abstract categorization: 'In modern societies, culture does not so much underline structure: rather it replaces it' (Gellner, 1964: 155; see also Anderson, 1991; Calhoun, 1991; Gellner, 1983). As opposed to illiterate peasants, modern citizens need to possess a modular communicative capacity that can only be acquired through formal education in a high language.

Thus, modern national identities should not be confused with pre-modern, ethnic cores: 'Nationalism is not the awakening of nations to self-consciousness: it invents nations where they do not exist – but it does need some pre-existing differentiating marks to work on, even if ... these are purely negative' (Gellner, 1964: 168). This fundamental constructivist point shows that there is no simple one-to-one correspondence between ancient, cultural groups and modern political identities (Calhoun, 1997: 48; cf. Barth, 1969: 14; Cederman, 2001a).

Following the seminal conceptualization of Gellner's compatriot Mroslav Hroch (1985, 1993), nationalization projects can be divided into three consecutive phases: cultural manipulation, nationalist politicization and nationalist mass mobilization, each of which will be discussed in turn.

Cultural Manipulation

Since high culture seldom comes in pre-fabricated bundles ready to be politically employed, the cultural 'raw material' first needs to be 'engineered'. This is what Hroch (1985) calls the period of 'scholarly interest'. The typical situation features cultural fragmentation that is overcome through centralized assimilation or 'horizontal' standardization (Miller, 1995: 33). Either one culture is chosen and then promoted through more or less coercive means, or an entirely new conglomerate of pre-existing bits and pieces are fitted together (as exemplified by the Norwegian linguist Åsen's invention of the new high language *Nynorsk*, an amalgam of various dialects). In the case of cultural differentiation, new cultural barriers are erected, such as seemingly arbitrary linguistic rules emphasizing the distinction between the Serb and Croat communities (for more examples, see Smith, 1991).[15]

Both integrative and disintegrative projects require a fair amount of intellectual work. Although diffuse political purposes may figure in the background, this phase is usually the responsibility of historians, linguists and other humanists (Hroch, 1985). Mythological historiography is of particular importance since cultural standardization calls for not just remembering but also selective forgetting (Connor, 1972; Renan, [1882] 1996).

Nationalist Politicization

Culture can be politicized in two ways: either it develops as a state-framed project or its role is state-seeking. The latter case includes both unification nationalism and national mobilization in opposition to a pre-existing, multinational state. Whether the state plays an opposing or supporting role, type-3 theories view it as an exogenous factor influencing nationalist activities.

In most scholarly texts, nationalist mobilization starts with a small élite of politicians who turn the cultural agenda into a political one (though see Kaufman, 1996 for a bottom-up account). Ideal-typically, the key actors are either intellectuals extending their cultural projects or political opportunists who use cultural identities for their own instrumental purposes. Most nationalist movements contain a mix of both nationalist activists and political entrepreneurs (Lake and Rothchild, 1998a: 19; see also Snyder, 2000). Exemplified by Garibaldi and Cavour respectively, romantic activism or cynical élite manipulation complement each other (Brubaker, 1998; Bunce, 1999).

In addition to conscious attempts to politicize culture, the explicitly political phase of nationalist mobilization is sometimes triggered inadvertently by a central state's mobilizing for other purposes than national identity formation. State leaders may opt for assimilation policies in the name of political participation, or economic and administrative efficiency (Deutsch, 1961) while overlooking the identity repercussions of such projects (Cederman, 1997: ch. 7). Wherever such mobilization processes outpace cultural assimilation, counter-state nationalism is likely to follow (Deutsch, 1953a, 1953b). The classic case involves the introduction of the dominant nation's language as a standardized lingua franca in a multi-ethnic setting, as illustrated by Vienna's attempt to replace Latin with German as the standard administrative language within the Habsburg Empire (Breuilly, 1982). Other examples include the inadvertently Russifying effects of Gorbachev's political reforms (e.g. Bunce, 1999; Gitelman, 1992) and the colonial powers' self-defeating exploitation of the Third World territories (Breuilly, 1982; Mayall, 1990).

According to Gellner's (1964, 1983) original theory, a state's centralized mobilization will trigger centrifugal nationalism in the cases where the minority élite's access to the dominant high culture is blocked (see also Deutsch, 1953b). While some cultural traits are harder to change than others, ultimately what matters is not so much the cultural differences themselves, as the political selection of the traits to be included in a national identity. Applying this Gellnerian logic to nationalism in the post-Soviet republics, Laitin (1998) argues that, to a large degree, the form of nationalist activity in these areas reflected the Soviet Union's nationalist policies.

Nationalist Mass Mobilization

The need to conceptualize national identities as abstract categories becomes particularly acute once the question of mass mobilization is addressed. Rather than being based exclusively on a tight network of interpersonal communication among élites, the nation acquires its cohesion thanks to institutional mechanisms that bring together large groups of people most of whom have never met each other and never will (Anderson, 1991).

As in the process of politicization, much hinges on whether the nationalist movement controls state institutions or not. If the nationalist élite controls territorially based organizations, the task of reaching out to large numbers of people obviously becomes much simpler than without such resources. These instruments include state policies in a broad set of areas. As stressed by Gellner (1964, 1983), education is the most obvious of these. The nation-state presupposes a mechanism 'generating citizens', and no other state institution contributes as intensively to political and cultural socialization as universal schooling (Boli, 1989).

As we have seen, such a project requires a medium. Thus, few nationalizing states can do without a language policy (Brass, 1974). From a historical standpoint, the commercial printing press dominated the earlier phases of nationalism (Anderson, 1991). Today, modern mass media, especially radio and TV stations, contribute to national identity formation (Schlesinger, 1991). In addition, party systems both reflect and channel cultural affiliations within civil society (Rokkan, 1999). Less obviously identity-conferring projects, such as road building, legal unification and bureaucratic and monetary standardization, may also enhance mobility considerably and thus accelerate national mass mobilization (Deutsch, 1953a, 1953b; Weber, 1979).

In addition to the internal mechanisms covered so far, there is a set of external ones (Simmel, 1955). Historical evidence shows that many nation-states unified internally mainly through inter-state war (Colley, 1992; Mann, 1992, 1993). Beyond violence, other types of interaction may encourage nationalism, including commerce and immigration (Brubaker, 1992). It should be noted that internal and external institutional mechanisms depend on each other. For example, creating a national enemy may require negative stereotyping in school curricula.

Counter-state nationalists have to operate under much tougher conditions than those movements that enjoy the support of their 'own' state. Therefore, state-opposing mobilization tends to rely primarily on ethnic rather than civic mobilization, such as oral tradition, extended kinship networks, and autonomous churches. Yet, as noted above, multinational state élites sometimes unwittingly generate separatist nationalism by improving the infrastructural conditions for nationalist activity (Brass, 1980: 47; Olzak, 1983: 359). Even more ironically, state-led repression itself sometimes has a long-time disintegrating effect by creating a tougher selection environment in which only more inclusive, and thus more powerful, peripheral nationalist platforms survive (Cederman, 1997: ch. 8; Hannan, 1979). Concessions to nationalists equipping them with 'ethno-federal' institutions that attempt to buy short-term ethnic peace often compromise long-term integration, as illustrated by the Soviet and Yugoslav break-ups (Brubaker, 1996; Bunce, 1999; Motyl, 1990: ch. 6; Roeder, 1991).

The three-step logic of national mobilization begs the question how the nationalization process shifts from one step to the other. It would be a mistake to view Hroch's scheme as a deterministic sequence that all national movements have to traverse. To be sure, some nationalist campaigns never make it to the last, mass-based stage. Others skip over the cultural construction phase thanks to pre-existing cultural identities.

In spite of these differences, however, it is possible to identify general mechanisms that drive the transition from politicization to mass mobilization. As we have seen above, Russell Hardin (1995) suggests that nationalist coordination may help overcome collective-action dilemmas. Unlike pre-modern rebellions that can be more easily dealt with by the state's repressive institutions through a strategy of 'divide and conquer', national mobilization coordinates the resistance thus setting the 'snow ball' of collective action in motion. Once the critical threshold is reached, the process 'tips over' so that the expectation of more protest begets even more activity, and so forth (Granovetter, 1978; Schelling, 1978; see also Kuran, 1998; Laitin, 1998).

As it extends to the masses, nationalist mobilization depends crucially on categorical, abstract identification connecting the nationalist and activist entrepreneurs with the entire population. Thus this macro process cannot be reduced to interpersonal 'games' featuring conscious 'choices' of identity. In general, exclusive reliance on such a voluntarist approach underestimates the structural framing effects embedding identity-formation (Horowitz, 1975: 121). More nuanced, partly extra-rational explanations are thus needed to show how participants are 'reprogrammed' through media, educational systems, and other identity-conferring mechanisms and how the 'selection environment' favors certain identities over others.[16]

PROBLEMATIZING BOTH STATES AND NATIONS: 'SYSTEMIC NATION-CONSTRUCTIVISM' (TYPE 4)

Our ontological exploration has finally reached the most general ontological position that calls for a doubly constructivist perspective, endogenizing not only nations but also states. Very few political scientists have ventured this far in the quest for theoretical flexibility. As shown by the last section, most constructivist theories of nationalism analyze the emergence of national consciousness and its political repercussions within a given state. Gellner's theory is no exception from this tendency: 'Its explanatory capacities are implicitly limited to nationalist conflicts within states; it has little to say about nationalist conflicts between states' (O'Leary, 1998: 61).

Nevertheless, in situations characterized by drastic boundary transformations, it makes little sense to talk about 'domestic' and 'international' realms. As the former Yugoslavia broke up, what was literally 'inside' became 'outside' and vice versa. Theoretical schemes and disciplinary categorizations that 'hard-wire' the internal–external distinction into units of analysis and causal explanations, rule out change of territorial and national boundaries by assumption.

Endogenization is not an end in itself for it carries with it conceptual costs due to the analytical framework's many moving parts. Nevertheless, a sound research strategy needs to confront substantive puzzles with as few preconceived notions about the ontological status of the basic units as possible. Type-4 constructivism becomes indispensable when studying periods characterized by tumultuous and far-reaching change during which both states and national communities co-evolve (Cederman, 2000; Waever, 1993). It is also the most sensible theoretical choice for general macro-historical IR theories featuring changes of the basic actor types (Gilpin, 1981).

Explaining Turbulent Periods Marked by Co-evolving States and Nations

While transformation periods can be marked both by integration and disintegration, space constraints prevent me from covering the latter.[17] The discussion of systemic nation-essentialism (type 2) illustrated that nation-reifying theories suggest candidate explanations of separatism and secession. But the leap from cultural diversity to polity-destroying action is far from automatic. Some of the nation-constructivist frameworks (type 3) discussed above go beyond intra-state mobilization by explicitly explaining secession. For example, rather than viewing the national components of the communist empires as pre-given units, Bunce (1999) suggests that the central regime itself contributed to creating these counter-state identities, and that together with historically contingent opportunity structures, the communist parties and the state's culturally decentralizing and identity-reifying institutions paved the way for secession (see also Brubaker, 1996).

While enlightening, this constructivist core–periphery logic does not go far enough in cases where the disintegration process affects an entire system of states. In a pioneering article introducing the notion of the 'Macedonian syndrome', Myron Weiner (1971) showed that nationalization often spills over state borders. This realization highlights a triad of actor types including nationalizing states, national minorities and national homelands (see also Brubaker, 1996: ch. 3). Inspired by this Balkan analogy, Weiner sketches a stylized scenario in which an irredentist claim by homeland or minority leaders unleashes a dynamic that radicalizes politics along national lines in the entire region thus either creating or reinforcing the three community types. Because of the emotional polarization, democracy and territorial moderation usually fall victim to processes of this kind. In the end, violence and, ultimately, secession typically follows.

In some particularly conflict-prone situations, there is not just one irredentist state but two, as illustrated by the recent case of Serbia and Croatia in the early 1990s. Such cases of 'competing nationalization' are hard to square with security-dilemma accounts, not merely because of these perspectives' dyadic actor typology, but also because of the conflict-seeking preferences on both sides. In the Yugoslav case, both Serb and Croatian élites preferred conflict as a way to reconfigure the ethno-political map.

Most dramatically, 'ethnocidal jerrymandering' features authoritarian power-holders threatened by sudden democratization, and unsurprisingly has represented some of the worst human rights abuses since the Second World War. In Rwanda, the Kigali government's meticulously planned genocide served to reshape the nation by simply murdering the Tutsi ethnic group and the entire political opposition whether Tutsi or Hutu (Prunier, 1995). Indeed, even in the most extreme cases, there is a perversely 'constructive' aspect of violence that can be exploited by ruthless leaders: 'Genocide, after all, is an exercise in community building. ... Killing Tutsis was a political tradition in postcolonial Rwanda. It brought people together' (Gourevitch, 1998: 95–6).

In the Yugoslav case, Milosevic's notorious decision in 1990–91 to combine nationalization of his own federation with its territorial 'amputation' in order to vindicate the principle of ethnic nationalism illustrates the same point (Gagnon, 1998). Despite the ensuing warfare, these priorities suited the late Croatian president Tudjman as well. Thus, explanations that reify state and national boundaries cannot provide an accurate description of these strategies. More ominously, treating groups' corporate identities as if they were unproblematic even risks playing into the hands of the perpetrators of genocide by retroactively legitimizing their preferred group boundaries (Gagnon, 1998; Lapid and Kratochwil, 1996b).

Macro-historical IR Theory

Having so far considered theories of 'the middle range', it is appropriate to end this chapter on a more ambitious note. Rather than attempting to capture 'covering laws' supposedly governing interactions between nicely compartmentalized, ahistorical units of analysis, a focus on nationalism invites us to view IR in broadly macro-historical terms: 'The study of international relations, like much of social science, is a branch of history' (March and Olsen, 1998: 969).

Expressed schematically, the challenges involve capturing three macro-historical transitions in state–nation space (see Figure 21.3). As opposed to Figure 21.2, the quadrants here describe world-historical configurations rather than regional cases of nationalism. This holistic schema allows us to sketch the evolution of world politics since the Middle Ages in terms of actor types. Thanks to steadily improving communication technology and administrative and organizational innovations, the infrastructural reach of power centers gradually improved during this period (Mann, 1986).

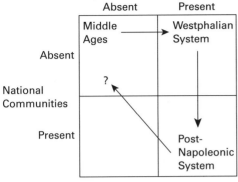

Figure 21.3 *Three macro-historical transitions in state–nation space*

This gigantic process began with a medieval situation in which neither the state nor the nation existed in their modern forms (Ferguson and Mansbach, 1996). The first transition saw the birth of the modern, territorial state in Western Europe led by absolutist monarchs and finally justified by the doctrine of territorial sovereignty as enshrined in the Westphalian Peace (e.g. Spruyt, 1994; Strayer, 1970; Tilly, 1990; though see Krasner, 1999). The next major transition featured the move from territorial to popular sovereignty (e.g. Hinsley, 1986; Holsti, 1991). The American and French Revolutions irrevocably reversed the descending logic of dynastic legitimacy into an ascending notion vesting sovereign power in the nation (Calhoun, 1997: 4–7) and created the doctrine of national self-determination (Mayall, 1990; Neuberger, 1995). Partly implementing these historical novelties, the state system since the Napoleonic wars has developed in acute tension between territorial and national sovereignty (Barkin and Cronin, 1994).

By explicitly endogenizing both states and nations, perhaps Otto Hintze ([1902] 1975: 161) provides the most concise summary of this co-evolutionary two-stage process:

> States are created by war, colonization, conquest and peaceful settlement, through amalgamation of different parts and through their separating from each other; and all this is bound up with an alternating process of intermingling and separation of races and civilizations, and languages. The European peoples have only gradually developed their nationalities; they are not a simple product of nature but are themselves a product of the creation of states.

Is world history moving out of the post-Napoleonic constellation? It is not just representative democracy and the welfare state that are arguably being threatened by globalization and supranational integration, but the principle of nationalism itself. These trends could generate a reversal to a 'neo-medieval' situation devoid of states and nations (Bull, 1977; Ruggie, 1993). Since nationalist ideology serves as the prime legitimation of the system's constitutive unit, the nation-state (Meyer et al., 1997), it seems unlikely that systems change will ever be properly understood without a macro-theory of nationalism.

Yet, very few IR scholars have attempted to place nationalism in its world-historical context. Karl Deutsch and Ernst Haas belong to the most important exceptions. Karl Deutsch's (1953b) essay 'The Growth of Nations' remains equally refreshing more than half a century later (see also Deutsch, 1953a, 1969). Unlike much of the contemporary literature, Deutsch not only distinguishes between national communities and states, he also investigates their historical co-evolution. For example, the article traces the slow unfolding of cultural assimilation prior to the age of nationalism, and the subsequent acceleration of mobilization after this threshold. Moreover, Deutsch explicitly relates this development to geopolitics by emphasizing the mobilizational impact of nationalism on power politics without losing sight of the potentially centrifugal consequences of supra-national mobilization projects. This is a useful reminder that nationalism can lead to both integration and disintegration of states, a fact evidenced by the end of the Cold War.

Similarly analyzing competing centralizing and decentralizing processes, the first volume of Haas's (1997) magisterial study explores nationalism in five countries. As would be expected from Haas's previous work on nationalism and integration, his recent book follows Weberian lines and adopts an instrumental-constructivist perspective. His main argument is that while different forms of nationalism can lead to political integration, progress is only possible on the basis of liberal nationalism. Citing examples such as India and Switzerland, Haas downplays the role played by cultural cohesion as the key to state-building.[18]

Yet it is hard to avoid the conclusion that IR theory remains curiously ill-equipped to describe, let alone explain, 'systems change', defined by Gilpin (1981: 40) as the most fundamental type of historical transformation affecting the very nature of the actors of the international system. Based on this terminology, the nationalist transformation of the state system following the French Revolution constitutes a macro-historical process that could be labeled *nationalist systems change*. Due to their rigid assumptions of actor-type invariance, structural approaches such as Waltz's neorealism are incapable of tracing systems change in general, and nationalist systems change in particular (cf. Cederman, 1997; Ruggie, 1983: ch. 6). Despite its focus on dynamics, even Gilpin's (1981) book refrains from systematically exploring systems change. By classifying the German unification process as a case of 'systems change at the level of intra-German politics' (1981: 40), he loses sight of the long-term geopolitical consequences triggered by the French revolution.

By contrast, a 'sociational' rewriting of IR theory that problematizes both states and nations as general actor types and specific historical entities promises to cast new light on events that have so far been viewed as mere inter-state exchanges unrelated to nationalism (Simmel, [1908] 1992). For instance, rather than viewing the world wars as failures of a culturally neutral balance of power mechanism, they could be interpreted as reactions to the entire state system's nationalization with the disruptive collapse of the Austrian-Hungarian Empire together with the emergence of Germany as a newly unified nation-state at the very center of the system (cf. Holsti, 1991; Schroeder, 1972).

CONCLUSION

What can be concluded from this inventory of recent IR literature on nationalism and ethnicity? Given these topics' under-theorized status at the end of the Cold War, the current situation offers more reasons for optimism. After a somewhat hesitant start in the early 1990s, IR scholarship on these topics has begun to show signs of maturity. The general tendency of the intellectual development is pointing away from reified and imprecise terminology and toward a more flexible ontology problematizing both territorial and cultural units whenever theoretically fruitful. This marks a potential break from the last decades' inter-paradigmatic debates that were driven primarily by intra-scientific assumptions. But there is still plenty of room for improvement.

Conceptual wrangles continue to haunt the discipline. While treating states and nations as synonyms and mixing nationalism with ethnicity may make little difference in many situations, this practice causes serious problems where these phenomena do not coincide. Mistaking the Soviet Union for a nation-state, for example, may have contributed to the failure not just to predict, but more fundamentally to *imagine*, the end of the Cold War (Kratochwil, 1993). Although it would be both utopian and pedantic to expect IR scholars to replace references to the 'national interest' by the 'state interest' wherever they mean the latter rather than former, increased awareness of the distinctions would prevent unnecessary confusion.

Compared to rationalist and realist scholars, IR constructivists have been surprisingly slow to address nationalism and ethnicity. This is all the more ironic given the obvious relevance of constructivist approaches to nationalism and ethnicity.

The reason for this unfortunate delay appears to be yet another inter-paradigmatic distraction that has diverted much of the IR constructivists' attention toward combating their 'theoretical others' rather than worrying about substantive puzzles. This is obviously not just the constructivists' fault, but is also due to the efforts to establish constructivism as a legitimate approach in IR, which in itself is a precondition for making progress in studying nationalism. Now that it is finally becoming acceptable to use concepts such as identity in mainstream IR, however, constructivists should be able join forces with constructivist colleagues outside IR thus liberating themselves from arbitrary, self-imposed ontological restrictions.

Rationalist studies of ethnicity and nationalism have much to offer, especially because they serve as an antidote to the cultural determinism that has plagued parts of the qualitative literature. More often than not, however, the rational-choice approach has been framed in narrowly voluntarist and utilitarian terms, thus exerting an unfortunate, constraining influence on theory-building. All the same, some of the most advanced rational-choice work acknowledges the relevance of constructivist thinking and strives for tighter conceptual integration of the two perspectives (e.g. Fearon and Laitin, 2000). What is still missing, however, are models that embed both calculative and norm-driven behaviors in a macro-historical framework with explicit representations of endogenized collective identities.

Apart from elucidating the topics themselves, future IR research on nationalism and ethnicity could serve as an analytical wedge breaking up the ontological closure that still characterizes mainstream IR theory (see type B). Few theorists have realized what a fundamental challenge nationalist and ethnic processes pose to standard conceptualizations of world politics. An explicit focus on nationalism, viewed as a macro-historical family of processes featuring abstractly mediated collective categorizations and boundaries, forces the analyst to consider not only the creation and dissipation of collective identities, but also their continued maintenance. Instead of conceiving of the state system as a passive theoretical backdrop, then, comprehensive theories have to trace the historical emergence and interactions of states and national communities.

Finally, the preceding points have direct consequences for policy-making. Whether the issue is supra-statist democratic governance or prevention of nationalist violence, future policy solutions hinge critically on an understanding of the underlying politico-cultural processes. Those who believe that national identities are both inert and ethnic are reduced to recommending conflict-building methods or even drastic separation of groups. If, however, it is assumed that political identities are at least in principle detachable from the cultural 'raw material', identity change might become more than an academic possibility. Even under the assumption of 'sticky identities', explicit analysis of the processes responsible for the creation and maintenance of national identities could help identify realistic ways to manage multicultural polities and to prevent and overcome nationalist conflict. Without tighter conceptual integration of nationalism and ethnicity as central ingredients of IR theory, the discipline will remain hopelessly incapable of identifying future policy challenges.

As a postscript, it could be noted that there are two ways of conceptualizing nationalism and ethnicity within a handbook of IR: either as yet another 'issue area' deserving a chapter or as a part of the field's theoretical core. I leave to the reader to decide which way to approach the topic. IR scholars, whether they wish it or not, will be grappling with these issues over the coming decades.

Notes

I am indebted to Ron Jepperson, Chip Gagnon, Iver Neumann, Willfried Spohn, Jack Snyder, Sidney Tarrow, Ben Valentino, the editors of this handbook and an anonymous reviewer, for their useful advice. The responsibility for the final text, however, remains mine.

1 The number of intra-state wars is not a perfect indicator of nationalist violence since there are nationalist inter-state wars and non-nationalist inter-state wars. See also Byman and Van Evera (1998), who conclude that 'communal hegemonism' will be pervasive in the future.

2 Despite covering international politics in a separate section, *A New Handbook of Political Science*, edited by Goodin and Klingemann (1996), contains no specific chapter on the topic. Likewise, there was no article focusing on nationalism in *International Organization*'s fiftieth anniversary issue in 1998.

3 Quantitative data drawn from databases indicate that political science in general, and IR in particular, have lagged behind other disciplines in their coverage of ethnic and nationalist phenomena. For example, there was no single (non-review) article with title words related to nationalism or ethnicity in the leading IR journals *World Politics* and *International Organization* throughout the 1980s (see JSTOR). However, based on a broader sample of journals listed in *Current Contents*, it can be shown that the number of articles with such keywords rose from close to zero in the late 1980s to significant numbers in IR journals toward the mid-to-late 1990s. Apart from the literature on the decolonization process and a few volumes that appeared in the UK at the very end of the Cold War (e.g. Bloom, 1990; Mayall, 1990; Ryan, 1990), there were few exceptions from this trend in book publishing.

4 For general introductions to nationalism and ethnicity, see Calhoun, 1993, 1997; Hall, 1995; Smith, 1991, 1995.

5 Obviously, nationalism is neither inherently conflict-inducing (Calhoun, 1993) nor limited to dramatic events (Billig, 1995).

6 While much has been written on nationalism outside the United States – in fact, the general field of study originated in Europe – non-American IR researchers have produced surprisingly little on this topic. An informal inquiry among European colleagues yielded surprisingly few results. In sociology and history, however, the European coverage of nationalism is much stronger.

7 This is probably due to political scientists' almost exclusive focus on explanation as a scientific task at the expense of conceptual and descriptive analysis. For exceptions, see e.g. Barrington, 1997; Brass, 1991; Connor, 1994; Haas, 1986, 1997.

8 In addition, there is a disturbing tendency to dismiss sophisticated work as 'primordialist' just because it highlights the inertia of cultural constructs. Scholars such as Walker Connor and Anthony D. Smith are routinely referred to as 'primordialists' (e.g. Lake and Rothchild, 1998b; Roeder, 1991) despite their having forcefully argued against this position (Connor, 1994: 103–6; Smith, 1986: 12–13; cf. also Calhoun, 1997).

9 While Posen introduced his security-dilemma interpretation as an attempt to transcend conflict-reifying arguments, the latter can be combined with the former (see Kaufman, 1996; Kaufmann, 1996; Van Evera, 1994). Note, however, that the dilemma-based reasoning plays a conflict-reinforcing, rather than a conflict-initiating, role in those cases.

10 Claiming that his model differs fundamentally from Posen's security dilemma, Fearon (1998: 120) tries to escape the critique leveled at security-dilemma explanations. True, the formal framework allows Fearon to draw precise inferences about the factors influencing the seriousness of the strategic dilemma. However, because of his commitment to the unitary rational actor assumption, Fearon's model is every bit as reified as Posen and Hardin's frameworks (Cederman, 1996; Laitin, 1998: 327). Though see Fearon and Laitin's (1996) attempt to circumvent this difficulty discussed at the end of this section.

11 For example, Weingast's (1998) attempt to explain the construction and deconstruction of trust is entirely instrumental and cannot therefore capture situations in which the use of violence becomes unthinkable (Deutsch et al., 1957; Kaysen, 1990).

12 Similarly, in distinguishing between internal and external identities, Kowert (1999) associates the former with nations and the latter with states, thus deliberately treating these actor types as if they were equivalent.

13 Integration is another possibility, but there is no room to cover it here. Elsewhere I have applied theories of nationalism to European integration (Cederman, 2001a, 2001b). For a discussion of pan-nationalism, see Snyder, 1984 and Smith, 1995 for an essentialist approach to supranational integration.

14 Some constructivist scholars content themselves with endogenizing 'social' rather than 'corporate' identities (Wendt, 1994: 385). In these cases, the focus is less on the constitution and boundaries of nations but on attitudes and role complexes (see e.g. Arfi, 1998; Gagnon, 1994/5; Snyder and Ballentine, 1996).

15 Sigmund Freud coined the expression 'narcissism of small differences' for such boundary phenomena (see e.g. Ignatieff, 1994). This phenomenon undermines type-1 attempts to explain behavior in terms of objective 'cultural distance'.

16 State élites carried out dehumanizing 'programming' during the period leading up to the genocides in Rwanda and the former Yugoslavia. In the former case, government-sanctioned radio stations depicted the Tutsi population as 'cockroaches' (Gourevtich, 1998; Prunier, 1995). Cf. also Gagnon, 1994/5 and Snyder, 2000.

17 Elsewhere I have applied constructivist theories of nationalism to European integration (Cederman, 2001a, 2001b). Such theories predict a 'post-national' outcome characterized by the decline of the nation-state (e.g. Haas, 1958; Habermas, 1992; Hobsbawm, 1990), or they could be classified as approaches to 'bounded integration' that emphasize the resilience of this organization form, though without reifying it (e.g. Lepsius, 1991).

18 At the moment of writing this text, a second volume had been announced but had not yet appeared. Recently, Rodney Bruce Hall (1999) has attempted to delineate explicitly the first two transitions of Figure 21.3 while reinterpreting standard IR topics. Although Hall's book is marred by less-than-clear constructivist jargon, it is right in placing nationalism at the very heart of general IR theory.

19 Similarly overlooking nationalist systems change, Fearon and Laitin (2000: 850) suggest that '[i]n explaining World War I, we do not typically demand an account of why France and Germany were separate countries in 1914'.

Bibliography

Alter, Peter (1989) *Nationalism*. London: Edward Arnold.

Anderson, Benedict (1991) *Imagined Communities: Reflections on the Origin and Spread of Nationalism.* London: Verso.

Arfi, Badredine (1998) 'Ethnic Fear: The Social Construction of Insecurity', *Security Studies*, 8: 151–203.

Ayres, R. William (2000) 'A World Flying Apart? Violent Nationalist Conflict and the End of the Cold War', *Journal of Peace Research*, 37: 105–17.

Barkin, J. Samuel and Cronin, Bruce (1994) 'The State and the Nation: Changing Norms and the Rules of Sovereignty in International Relations', *International Organization*, 48: 107–30.

Barrington, Lowell W. (1997) '"Nation" and "Nationalism": The Misuse of Key Concepts in Political Science', *PS: Political Science and Politics*, 30: 712–16.

Barth, Fredrik (1969) 'Introduction', in Fredrik Barth (ed.), *Ethnic Groups and Boundaries: the Social Organization of Culture Difference*. Boston: Little, Brown.

Bates, Robert H., deFigueiredo, R.J.P. and Weingast, Robert (1998) 'The Politics of Interpretation: Rationality, Culture, and Transition', *Politics and Society*, 26: 603–42.

Beiner, Ronald (ed.) (1999) *Theorizing Nationalism.* Albany: State University of New York Press.

Berger, Peter L. and Luckmann, Thomas (1966) *The Social Construction of Reality: A Treatise in the Sociology of Knowledge.* Harmondsworth: Penguin Books.

Billig, Michael (1995) *Banal Nationalism.* London: Sage.

Bloom, William (1990) *Personal Identity, National Identity and International Relations.* Cambridge: Cambridge University Press.

Boli, John (1989) *New Citizens for a New Society: The Institutional Origins of Mass Schooling in Sweden.* Oxford: Pergamon.

Brass, Paul R. (1974) *Language, Religion, and Politics in North India.* Cambridge: Cambridge University Press.

Brass, Paul R. (1976) 'Ethnicity and Nationality Formation', *Ethnicity*, 3: 225–41.

Brass, Paul R. (1980) 'Ethnic Groups and Nationalities: The Formation, Persistence, and Transformation of Ethnic Identities', in Peter F. Sugar (ed.), *Ethnic Diversity and Conflict in Eastern Europe*. Santa Barbara: ABC-Clio.

Brass, Paul (1991) *Ethnicity and Nationalism: Theory and Comparison.* Newbury Park: Sage.

Breuilly, John (1982) *Nationalism and the State.* Chicago: University of Chicago Press.

Brown, Michael E. (1997) *Nationalism and Ethnic Conflict.* Cambridge, MA: MIT Press.

Brubaker, Rogers (1992) *Citizenship and Nationhood in France and Germany.* Cambridge, MA: Harvard University Press.

Brubaker, Rogers (1996) *Nationalism Reframed: Nationhood and the National Question in the New Europe.* Cambridge: Cambridge University Press.

Brubaker, Rogers (1998) 'Myths and Misconceptions in the Study of Nationalism', in John A. Hall (ed.), *The State of the Nation: Ernest Gellner and the Theory of Nationalism.* Cambridge: Cambridge University Press.

Brubaker, Rogers and Laitin, David D. (1998) 'Ethnic and Nationalist Violence', *Annual Review of Sociology*, 24: 423–52.

Bull, Hedley (1977) *The Anarchical Society.* London: Macmillan.

Bunce, Valarie (1999) *Subversive Institutions: The Design and the Destruction of Socialism and the State.* Cambridge: Cambridge University Press.

Byman, Daniel and Van Evera, Stephen (1998) 'Why They Fight: Hypotheses on the Causes of Contemporary Deadly Conflict', *Security Studies*, 7: 1–50.

Calhoun, Craig (1991) 'Indirect Relationships and Imagined Communities: Large-Scale Social Integration and the Transformation of Everyday Life', in Pierre Bourdieu and James S. Coleman (eds). *Social Theory for a Changing Society.* Boulder: Westview.

Calhoun, Craig (1993) 'Nationalism and Ethnicity', *Annual Review of Sociology*, 19: 211–39.

Calhoun, Craig (1997) *Nationalism.* Minneapolis: University of Minnesota Press.

Cederman, Lars-Erik (1996) 'From Primordialism to Constructivism: The Quest for More Flexible Models of Ethnic Conflict', paper presented at the Annual Convention of the American Political Science Association, San Francisco.

Cederman, Lars-Erik (1997) *Emergent Actors in World Politics: How States and Nations Develop and Dissolve*. Princeton: Princeton University Press.

Cederman, Lars-Erik (2000) 'The Co-Evolution of States and Nations: Modeling Nationalist Conflict as a Side-Effect of Macro-Historical Change', paper presented at the Annual Convention of the American Political Science Association, Washington, DC.

Cederman, Lars-Erik (2001a) 'Political Boundaries and Identity Tradeoffs', in Lars-Erik Cederman (ed.), *Constructing Europe's Identity: The External Dimension*. Boulder: Lynne Rienner.

Cederman, Lars-Erik (2001b) 'Nationalism and Bounded Integration: What it Would Take to Construct a European Demos', *European Journal of International Relations*, 7: 139–74.

Chazan, Naomi (ed.) (1991a) *Irredentism and International Politics*. Boulder: Lynne Rienner.

Chazan, Naomi (1991b) 'Introduction: Approaches to the Study of Irredentism', in Naomi Chazan (ed.), *Irredertism and International Politics*. Boulder: Lynne Rienner.

Colley, Linda (1992) *Britons: Forging the Nation, 1707–1837*. London: Pimlico.

Collins, Randall (1986) *Weberian Sociological Theory*. Cambridge: Cambridge University Press.

Connor, Walker (1972) 'Nation–Building or Nation-Destroying', *World Politics*, 24: 319–55 (reprinted in Connor, 1994).

Connor, Walker (1978) 'A Nation is a Nation, is a State, is an Ethnic Group is a …', *Ethnic and Racial Studies*, 1: 377–400 (reprinted in Connor, 1994).

Connor, Walker (1994) *Ethnonationalism: The Quest for Understanding*. Princeton: Princeton University Press.

Crawford, Beverly (1998) 'The Causes of Cultural Conflict: An Institutionalist Approach', in Beverly Crawford and Ronnie D. Lipschutz (eds), *The Myth of 'Ethnic Conflict': Politics, Economics, and 'Cultural' Violence*. Berkeley: University of California Press.

Deutsch, Karl W. (1953a) *Nationalism and Social Communication: An Inquiry Into the Foundations of Nationality*. Cambridge, MA: MIT Press.

Deutsch, Karl W. (1953b) 'The Growth of Nations: Some Recurrent Patterns of Political and Social Integration', *World Politics*, 5: 168–95.

Deutsch, Karl W. (1961) 'Social Mobilization and Political Development', *American Political Science Review*, 60: 493–514.

Deutsch, Karl W. (1969) *Nationalism and Its Alternatives*. New York: Alfred A. Knopf.

Deutsch, Karl W., Burrell, Sidney, A., Kann, Robert A., Lee, Maurie Jr, Lichterman, Martin, Lindgren, Raymond E., Loewnheim, Francis L. and Van Wagenen, Richard W. (1957) *Political Community and the North Atlantic Area*. Princeton: Princeton University Press.

Elster, Jon (2000) 'Rational-Choice History: A Case of Excessive Ambition', *American Political Science Review*, 94: 685–95.

Evans, Peter, Rueschemeyer, Dietrich and Skocpol, Theda (eds) (1985) *Bringing the State Back In*. Cambridge: Cambridge University Press.

Fearon, James D. (1994) 'Ethnic War as a Commitment Problem', paper presented at Annual Meeting of the American Political Science Association in New York, NY.

Fearon, James D. (1998) 'Commitment Problems and the Spread of Ethnic Conflict', in David A. Lake and Donald Rothchild (eds), *The International Spread of Ethnic Conflict: Fear, Diffusion, and Escalation*. Princeton: Princeton University Press.

Fearon, James D. and Laitin, David D. (1996) 'Explaining Interethnic Cooperation', *American Political Science Review*, 90: 715–35.

Fearon, James D. and Laitin, David D. (1999) 'Weak States, Rough Terrain, and Large-Scale Ethnic Violence since 1945', paper presented at the Annual Meetings of the American Political Science Association, Atlanta.

Fearon, James D. and Laitin, David D. (2000) 'Violence and the Social Construction of Ethnic Identity', *International Organization*, 54: 845–77.

Ferguson, Yale H. and Mansbach, Richard (1996) *Polities: Authority, Identities, and Change*. Columbia: University of South Carolina Press.

Gagnon, V.P., Jr (1994/5) 'Ethnic Nationalism and International Conflict: The Case of Serbia', *International Security*, 19: 130–66.

Gagnon, V.P., Jr (1998) '"Bosnian Federation" and the Institutionalization of Ethnic Division', paper presented at the workshop Nationalism, Federalism, and Secession, Cornell University.

Geertz, Clifford (1973) *The Interpretation of Cultures*. New York: Basic Books.

Gellner, Ernest (1964) *Thought and Change*. London: Weidenfeld & Nicolson.

Gellner, Ernest (1983) *Nations and Nationalism*. Ithaca: Cornell University Press.

Gellner, Ernest (1997) *Nationalism*. New York: New York University Press.

Gilpin, Robert (1981) *War and Change in World Politics*. Cambridge: Cambridge University Press.

Gitelman, Zvi (1992) 'Development and Ethnicity in the Soviet Union', in Alexander J. Motyl (ed.), *The Post-Soviet Nations: Perspectives on the Demise of the USSR*. New York: Columbia University Press.

Goodin, Robert E. and Klingemann, Hans-Dieter (eds) (1996) *A New Handbook of Political Science*. Oxford: Oxford University Press.

Gourevitch, Peter A. (1979) 'The Re-Emergence of "Peripheral Nationalisms": Some Comparative Speculations on the Spatial Distribution of Political Leadership and Economic Growth', *Comparative Studies in Society and History*, 21: 303–22.

Gourevitch, Philip (1998) *We Wish to Inform You that Tomorrow We Will Be Killed with Our Families: Stories from Rwanda*. New York: Farrar, Straus and Giroux.

Granovetter, Mark (1978) 'Threshold Models of Collective Behavior', *American Journal of Sociology*, 83: 1420–43.

Gurr, Ted Robert (1993) *Minorities at Risk: A Global View of Ethnopolitical Conflicts.* Washington, DC: United States Institute of Peace Press.

Gurr, Ted Robert and Harff, Barbara (1994) *Ethnic Conflict in World Politics.* Boulder: Westview.

Haas, Ernst B. (1958) *The Uniting of Europe: Political, Economic and Social Forces.* Stanford: Stanford University Press.

Haas, Ernst B. (1986) 'What is Nationalism and Why Should We Study It?', *International Organization*, 40: 707–44.

Haas, Ernst B. (1997) *Nationalism, Liberalism, and Progress.* Ithaca: Cornell University Press.

Habermas, Jürgen (1992) 'Citizenship and National Identity: Some Reflections on the Future of Europe', *Praxis International*, 12: 1–19.

Hall, John A. (1995) 'Nationalisms, Classified and Explained', in Sukumar Periwal (ed.), *Notions of Nationalism.* Budapest: Central European University Press.

Hall, John A. (ed.) (1998a) *The State of the Nation: Ernest Gellner and the Theory of Nationalism.* Cambridge: Cambridge University Press.

Hall, John A. (1998b) 'Introduction', in *The State of the Nation: Ernest Gellner and the Theory of Nationalism.* Cambridge: Cambridge University Press.

Hall, Rodney Bruce (1999) *National Collective Identity: Social Constructs and International Systems.* New York: Columbia University Press.

Halperin, Sandra (1998) 'The Spread of Ethnic Conflict in Europe: Some Comparative-Historical Reflections', in David A. Lake and Donald Rothchild (eds), *The International Spread of Ethnic Conflict: Fear, Diffusion and Escalation.* Princeton: Princeton University Press.

Hannan, Michael T. (1979) 'The Dynamics of Ethnic Boundaries in Modern States', in John W. Meyer and Michael T. Hannan (eds), *National Development and the World System.* Chicago: University of Chicago Press.

Hardin, Russell (1995) *One For All: The Logic of Group Conflict.* Princeton: Princeton University Press.

Hechter, Michael (1992) 'The Dynamics of Secession', *Acta Sociologica*, 35: 267–83.

Heraclides, Alexis (1990) 'Secessionist Minorities and External Involvement', *International Organization*, 44: 341–78.

Hinsley, F.H. (1986) *Sovereignty.* Cambridge: Cambridge University Press.

Hintze, Otto ([1902] 1975) 'The Formation of States and Constitutional Development: A Study in History and Politics', in *The Historical Essays of Otto Hintze* (ed. and transl. Felix Gilbert). New York: Oxford University Press.

Hobsbawm, Eric J. (1990) *Nations and Nationalism since 1780.* Cambridge: Cambridge University Press.

Holsti, Kalevi J. (1991) *Peace and War: Armed Conflicts and International Order, 1648–1989.* Cambridge: Cambridge University Press.

Horowitz, Donald L. (1975) 'Ethnic Identity', in Nathan Glazer and Daniel P. Moynihan (eds), *Ethnicity: Theory and Experience.* Cambridge, MA: Harvard University Press.

Horowitz, Donald L. (1985) *Ethnic Groups in Conflict.* Berkeley: University of California Press.

Horowitz, Donald L. (1991) 'Irredentas and Secesssions: Adjacent Phenomena', in Naomi Chazan (ed.), *Irredentism and International Politics.* Boulder, Westview.

Hroch, Miroslav (1985) *Social Preconditions of National Revival in Europe: A Comparative Analysis of the Social Composition of Patriotic Groups among the Smaller European Nations.* Cambridge: Cambridge University Press.

Hroch, Miroslav (1993) 'From National Movement to the Fully-formed Nation', *New Left Review*, 198: 3–20.

Huntington, Samuel P. (1993a) 'The Clash of Civilizations?', *Foreign Affairs*, 72: 22–49.

Huntington, Samuel P. (1993b) 'If Not Civilizations, What? Paradigms of the Post-Cold War World', *Foreign Affairs*, 72: 186–94.

Huntington, Samuel P. (1996) *The Clash of Civilizations and the Remaking of World Order.* New York: Simon & Schuster.

Ignatieff, Michael (1994) *Blood and Belonging: Journeys into the New Nationalism.* London: Vintage.

Jervis, Robert (1978) 'Cooperation Under the Security Dilemma', *World Politics*, 30: 167–214.

Kaplan, Robert D. (1993) *Balkan Ghosts: A Journey Through History.* New York: St Martin's Press.

Kaufman, Stuart J. (1996) 'An "International Theory" of Inter-Ethnic War', *Review of International Studies*, 22: 149–71.

Kaufmann, Chaim (1996) 'Possible and Impossible Solutions to Ethnic Civil Wars', *International Security*, 20: 136–75.

Kaysen, Carl (1990) 'Is War Obsolete? A Review Essay', *International Security*, 14: 42–64.

Kowert, Paul A. (1999) 'National Identity: Inside and Out', *Security Studies*, 8: 1–34.

Krasner, Stephen D. (1999) *Sovereignty: Organized Hypocracy.* Princeton: Princeton University Press.

Kratochwil, Friedrich (1993) 'The Embarrassment of Change: Neorealism as the Science of Realpolitik without Politics', *Review of International Studies*, 19: 63–80.

Kuran, Timur (1998) 'Ethnic Dissimilation and Its International Diffusion', in David A. Lake and Donald Rothchild (eds), *The International Spread of Ethnic Conflict: Fear, Diffusion and Escalation.* Princeton: Princeton University Press.

Laitin, David D. (1986) *Hegemony and Culture: Politics and Religious Change among the Yoruba.* Chicago: University of Chicago Press.

Laitin, David D. (1998) *Identity in Formation: The Russian-Speaking Populations in the Near Abroad.* Ithaca: Cornell University Press.

Lake, David A. and Rothchild, Donald (eds) (1998a) *The International Spread of Ethnic Conflict: Fear,*

Diffusion, and Escalation. Princeton: Princeton University Press.

Lake, David A. and Rothchild, Donald (1998b) 'Spreading Fear: The Genesis of Transnational Ethnic Conflict', in *The International Spread of Ethnic Conflict: Fear, Diffusion and Escalation.* Princeton: Princeton University Press.

Lapid, Yosef and Kratochwil, Friedrich (eds) (1996a) *The Return of Culture and Identity in IR Theory.* Boulder: Lynne Rienner.

Lapid, Yosef and Kratochwil, Friedrich (1996b) 'Revisiting the "National": Toward an Identity Agenda in Neorealism?', in *The Return of Culture and Identity in IR Theory.* Boulder: Lynne Rienner. pp. 105–27.

Lepsius, M. Rainer (1991) 'Nationalstaat oder Nationalitätenstaat als Modell für die Weiterentwicklung der Europäischen Gemeinschaft', in Rudolf Wildenmann (ed.), *Staatswerdung Europas.* Nomos: Baden–Baden.

Mann, Michael (1986) *The Sources of Social Power: A History of Power from the Beginning to AD 1760,* vol. 1. Cambridge: Cambridge University Press.

Mann, Michael (1992) 'The Emergence of Modern European Nationalism', in John A. Hall and Ian Jarvie (eds), *Transition to Modernity: Essays on Power, Wealth and Belief.* Cambridge: Cambridge University Press.

Mann, Michael (1993) *The Sources of Social Power: The Rise of Classes and Nation-States, 1760–1914,* vol. 2. Cambridge: Cambridge University Press.

March, James G. and Olsen, Johan P. (1998) 'The Institutional Dynamics of International Political Orders', *International Organization,* 52: 943–69.

Mayall, James (1990) *Nationalism and International Society.* Cambridge: Cambridge University Press.

Mearsheimer, John (1992) 'Disorder Restored', in Graham Allison and Gregory F. Treverton (eds), *Rethinking America's Security.* New York: W.W. Norton.

Mearsheimer, John J. and Van Evera, Stephen (1995) 'When Peace Means War: The Partition that Dare Not Speak its Name', *New Republic,* 213: 16–19.

Meyer, John W., Boli, John, Thomas, George M. and Ramirez, Francisco O. (1997) 'World Society and the Nation-State', *American Journal of Sociology,* 103: 144–81.

Miller, David (1995) *On Nationality.* Oxford: Oxford University Press.

Motyl, Alexander J. (1990) *Sovietology, Rationality, Nationality: Coming to Grips with Nationalism in the USSR.* New York: Columbia University Press.

Nettl, J.P. (1968) 'The State as a Conceptual Variable', *World Politics,* 20: 559–92.

Neuberger, Benjamin (1995) 'National Self-Determination: Dilemmas of a Concept', *Nations and Nationalism,* 1 (3): 297–325.

Neumann, Iver (1999) *Uses of the Other: 'The East' in European Identity Formation.* Minneapolis: University of Minnesota Press.

O'Leary, Brendan (1998) 'Ernest Gellner's Diagnoses of Nationalism: A Critical Overview, or, What Is Living and What is Dead in Ernest Gellner's Philosophy of Nationalism', in John A. Hall (ed.) *The State of the Nation: Ernest Gellner and the Theory of Nationalism.* Cambridge: Cambridge University Press.

Olzak, Susan (1983) 'Contemporary Ethnic Mobilization', *Annual Review of Sociology,* 9: 355–74.

Pasic, Sujata Chakrabarti (1996) 'Culturing International Relations Theory: A Call for Extension', in Yosef Lapid and Friedrich Kratochwil (eds), *The Return of Culture and Identity in IR Theory.* Boulder: Lynne Rienner.

Posen, Barry R. (1993a) 'Nationalism, the Mass Army, and Military Power', *International Security,* 18: 80–124.

Posen, Barry R. (1993b) 'The Security Dilemma and Ethnic Conflict', in Michael E. Brown (ed.), *Ethnic Conflict and International Security.* Princeton: Princeton University Press.

Prunier, Gérard (1995) *The Rwanda Crisis: History of a Genocide.* New York: Columbia University Press.

Renan, Ernest ([1882] 1996) 'What Is a Nation?' (transl. from French), in Geoff Eley and Ronald Grigor Suny (eds), *Becoming National: A Reader.* Oxford: Oxford University Press.

Roeder, Philip G. (1991) 'Soviet Federalism and Ethnic Mobilization', *World Politics,* 43: 196–232.

Rokkan, Stein (1999) *State Formation, Nation-Building, and Mass Politics in Europe: The Theory of Stein Rokkan* (ed. Peter Flora). Oxford: Oxford University Press.

Ruggie, John Gerard (1983) 'Continuity and Transformation in World Polity: Toward a Neorealist Synthesis', *World Politics,* 35: 261–85.

Ruggie, John Gerard (1993) 'Territoriality and Beyond: Problematizing Modernity in International Relations', *International Organization,* 47: 139–74.

Ryan, Stephen (1990) *Ethnic Conflict and International Relations* (2nd edn 1995). Brookfield, VT: Dartmouth.

Saideman, Stephen M. (1998) 'Is Pandora's Box Half Empty or Half Full? The Limited Virulence of Secessionism and the Domestic Sources of Disintegration', in David Lake and Donald Rothchild (eds), *The International Spread of Ethnic Conflict: Fear, Diffusion and Escalation.* Princeton: Princeton University Press.

Sambanis, Nicholas (2000) 'Partition as a Solution to Ethnic War: An Empirical Critique of the Theoretical Literature', *World Politics,* 52: 437–83.

Schelling, Thomas C. (1978) *Micromotives and Macrobehavior.* New York: W.W. Norton.

Schieder, Theodor (1991) *Nationalismus und Nationalstaat: Studien zum nationalen Problemen im modernen Europa.* Göttingen: Vandenhoeck and Ruprecht.

Schlesinger, Philip (1991) *Media, State and Nation: Political Violence and Collective Identities.* London: Sage.

Schroeder, Paul W. (1972) 'World War I as Galloping Gertie: A Reply to Joachim Remak', *Journal of Modern History,* 44: 319–45.

Sekulic, Dusko, Hodson, Randy and Massey, Garth (1994) 'Who Were the Yugoslavs? Failed Sources of a

Common Identity in the Former Yugoslavia', *American Sociological Review*, 59: 83–97.

Simmel, Georg ([1908] 1992) *Soziologie: Untersuchungen über die Formen der Vergesellschaftung.* Frankfurt-am-Main: Suhrkamp.

Simmel, Georg (1955) *Conflict and The Web of Group-Affiliations.* (transl K.H. Wolff). New York: The Free Press.

Smith, Anthony D. (1986) *The Ethnic Origins of Nations.* Oxford: Blackwell.

Smith, Anthony D. (1991) *National Identity.* Harmondsworth: Penguin Books.

Smith, Anthony D. (1995) *Nations and Nationalism in a Global Era.* Cambridge: Polity.

Snyder, Jack (2000) *From Voting to Violence: Democratization and Nationalist Conflict.* New York: W.W. Norton.

Snyder, Jack and Ballentine, Karen (1996) 'Nationalism and the Marketplace of Ideas', *International Security*, 21: 5–40.

Snyder, Louis (1984) *Macro-Nationalisms: A History of the Pan-Movements.* Westport: Greenwood.

Spruyt, Hendrik (1994) *The Sovereign State and Its Competitors: An Analysis of Systems Change.* Princeton: Princeton University Press.

Strayer, Joseph R. (1970) *On the Medieval Origins of the Modern State.* Princeton: Princeton University Press.

Tilly, Charles (1990) *Coercion, Capital, and European States, AD 990–1990.* Oxford: Blackwell.

Van den Berghe, Pierre L. (1982) *The Ethnic Phenomenon.* New York: Elsevier.

Van Evera, Stephen (1990/1) 'Primed for Peace: Europe after the Cold War', *International Security*, 15: 7–57.

Van Evera, Stephen (1994) 'Hypotheses on Nationalism and War', *International Security*, 18: 5–39.

Vanhanen, Tatu (1999) 'Domestic Ethnic Conflict and Ethnic Nepotism: A Comparative Analysis', *Journal of Peace Research*, 36: 55–73.

Waever, Ole (1993) 'Societal Security: The Concept', in Ole Waever, Barry Buzan, Morten Kelstrup and Pierre Lemaitre (eds), *Identity, Migration and the New Security Agenda in Europe.* London: Pinter.

Waldron, Arthur N. (1985) 'Theories of Nationalism and Historical Explanation', *World Politics*, 37: 416–33.

Wallensteen, Peter and Sollenberg, Margareta (1999) 'Armed Conflict, 1989–1998', *Journal of Peace Research*, 36: 593–606.

Waltz, Kenneth N. (1959) *Man, the State and War.* New York: Columbia University Press.

Waltz, Kenneth N. (1979) *Theory of International Politics.* New York: McGraw–Hill.

Weber, Eugen (1979) *Peasants into Frenchmen.* London: Chatto & Windus.

Weber, Max (1946) *From Max Weber: Essays in Sociology.* New York: Oxford University Press.

Weber, Max (1978) *Economy and Society: An Outline of Interpretative Sociology.* Berkeley: University of California Press.

Weiner, Myron (1971) 'The Macedonian Syndrome: An Historical Model of International Relations and Political Development', *World Politics*, 23: 665–83.

Weingast, Barry R. (1998) 'Constructing Trust: The Political and Economic Roots of Ethnic and Regional Conflict', in Karol Soltan, Eric M. Uslaner and Virginia Haufler (eds), *Institutions and Social Order.* Ann Arbor: University of Michigan Press.

Wendt, Alexander (1994) 'Collective Identity Formation and the International State', *American Political Science Review*, 88: 384–96.

Wendt, Alexander (1999) *Social Theory of International Politics.* Cambridge: Cambridge University Press.

Wolfers, Arnold (1962) *Discord and Collaboration: Essays on International Politics.* Baltimore: Johns Hopkins University Press.

Woodward, Susan L. (1995) *Balkan Tragedy: Chaos and Dissolution After the Cold War.* Washington, DC: Brookings Institution.

Yee, Albert S. (1996) 'The Causal Effects of Ideas on Politics', *International Organization*, 50: 69–108.

22

International Finance

BENJAMIN J. COHEN

Once relegated to the 'low politics' of technical economic analysis, international finance is now recognized as a core substantive element of the field of international relations (IR) and a fertile source of inspiration for the development and testing of theory. Monetary and financial issues figured prominently in many of the field's most important debates of the final third of the twentieth century. As they continue to evolve, the institutions and practice of international finance will persist in raising new challenges to old understandings about world politics and the nature of the global system and are sure to remain a major influence on research agendas in the twenty-first century as well.

The aim of this chapter is to provide both a retrospective and prospective overview of critical thinking about international finance in the IR field, with particular emphasis on interactions between theory and practice and between economics and politics. Coverage is necessarily selective. Contributions that are strictly institutional in nature or policy discussions that are not systematically informed by theory will not be directly considered. The focus, rather, will be on analyses that build on or contribute directly to the intellectual development of the IR field.

To set the context, discussion will begin with a brief historical narrative tracing the evolution of the international monetary system since the Second World War. The research literature has continually adjusted to the changing structure of financial relations. Key has been the gradual resurrection of global currency and capital markets, an accelerating trend which over time has greatly widened the range of actors with power to influence outcomes. Earlier in the post-war period, international finance was mainly a matter of interactions between

states – the traditional *dramatis personae* of world politics. Today, by contrast, the cast of characters has expanded to include a multitude of non-state actors as well – the newer agents of what has come to be called the increasing 'globalization' of economic affairs.

These changes are reflected in the related literature, which has developed greatly since the rebirth of international political economy as a systematic area of study in the 1960s.[1] Broadly speaking, two overlapping generations of scholarship may be distinguished. The first was state-centric and focused mainly on issues of policy and statecraft in monetary affairs. Most influential were pioneering works by American economists such as Richard Cooper (1968) and Charles Kindleberger (1970, 1973), together with Benjamin Cohen (1971, 1977) and, especially, the late Susan Strange (1971, 1976), a British subject trained in IR. The second generation, by contrast, has put more stress on the growing role of markets and non-state actors, cast as a direct challenge to the authority and capacity of governments. Here too Strange helped lead the way, with books like *Casino Capitalism* (1986) and *States and Markets*, first published in 1988 (second edition, 1994). Other early contributions came from Cohen (1981, 1986) and Robert Gilpin (1987). The two generations have proceeded in almost dialectical fashion, the first asserting (or assuming) the primacy of the state, the second posing states and markets as distinct and opposing principles. Following the historical narrative in the next section of this chapter, each of the two approaches will be examined in turn.

The key questions for future research involve prospects for the relationship between states and markets in the new century. How serious is the

challenge to state authority, and what can governments do about it? More fundamentally, who now
governs in the world of international finance? Are
states and markets necessarily in opposition to one
another? Or, after the thesis of state-centrism and
the antithesis of market forces, is a new research
synthesis needed or even possible? Our understanding of the political economy of international finance
is still far from complete.

For the purposes of this chapter, international
finance is understood to encompass all the main
features of monetary relations between states – the
processes and institutions of financial intermediation (mobilization of savings and allocation of
credit) as well as the creation and management of
money itself. As Strange wrote in *States and
Markets* 'The financial structure really has two
inseparable aspects. It comprises not just the structures of the political economy through which credit
is created but also the monetary system or systems
which determine the relative values of the different
moneys in which credit is denominated' (1994: 90).
Both aspects of international finance have attracted
intense scrutiny.

THE EVOLUTION OF INTERNATIONAL FINANCE

The key feature that distinguishes international
finance from purely domestic monetary analysis is
the existence of separate national currencies.
Legally, the concept of state sovereignty has long
been understood to include an exclusive right to
create and manage money. Within national frontiers
no currency but the local currency is expected,
normally, to serve the traditional functions of
money: medium of exchange, unit of account, and
store of value. Formally, there is no money for the
world as a whole (though selected national currencies have informally played important international
roles). Hence when we speak of the international
monetary system (or, synonymously, the global
financial structure), we are talking of a universe of
diverse national monetary spaces, not one homogenous entity – a Westphalian world, in short, where
the nation-state, still the world's basic unit of formal governance, remains the core (though far from
exclusive) actor.

The existence of separate national currencies
has both economic and political implications.
Economically, monetary sovereignty means that
currencies that are legal tender in one place are
unlikely, with few exceptions, to be fully usable
elsewhere. From that tradition stems the need for
mechanism, and arrangements, such as foreign
exchange and other financial markets, to facilitate
transactions and interchanges between national
moneys and credit systems. Politically, monetary

sovereignty means that governments, in principle,
each enjoy sole authority within their own borders.
From that stems the need for mechanisms and
arrangements, concerning such matters as currency
values and access to finance, to minimize frictions
and, if possible, to facilitate cooperation in financial
management. It is in the interaction of these twin
economic and political imperatives – the ever-
shifting relations among states and between states
and markets – that the modern history of international finance is written, from the Bretton Woods
system of the first decades after the Second World
War to what many call the 'non-system' of today.

From Bretton Woods to 'Non-System'

The Bretton Woods system is commonly understood
to refer to the monetary regime that prevailed from
the end of the Second World War until the early
1970s. Taking its name from the site of the 1944
conference that created the International Monetary
Fund and World Bank, the Bretton Woods system
was history's first example of a fully negotiated
financial order intended to govern monetary relations among sovereign states. Based on a formally
articulated set of principles and rules, the regime
was designed to combine binding legal obligations
with multilateral decision-making conducted
through an international organization, the IMF,
endowed with limited supranational authority.

Central to the Bretton Woods system was an
exchange rate regime of 'adjustable pegs'. Countries
were obligated to declare a par value (a 'peg') for
their national money and to intervene in currency
markets to limit exchange rate fluctuations within
certain limits (a 'band'); though they also retained
the right, in accordance with agreed procedures, to
alter their par value when needed to correct a 'fundamental disequilibrium' in their external payments. The IMF was created to assure governments
of an adequate supply of financing, if and when
needed, as well as to provide a permanent institutionalized forum for inter-state cooperation on monetary matters. International liquidity was to consist
of national reserves of gold or currencies convertible, directly or indirectly, into gold – the so-called
'gold exchange standard' – later supplemented by
Special Drawing Rights (SDRs), a negotiated form
of 'paper gold'. The main component of liquidity
was the US dollar, the only currency at the time
that was directly convertible into gold for central-
bank holders.

The history of the Bretton Woods system is generally divided into two periods: the era of dollar
'shortage', lasting roughly until the late 1950s,
when world liquidity needs were fed primarily by
deficits in the US balance of payments; and a
subsequent period of dollar 'glut', culminating in
termination of the greenback's gold convertibility

in 1971 and collapse of the par value system in 1973. With the closing of Washington's gold window, the gold exchange standard passed into history, to be succeeded by a polyglot collection of national currencies, gold and SDRs in the reserves of central banks. Likewise, with the end of par values, the exchange rate regime was transformed into a mixed bag of choices, some governments continuing to peg to a single currency like the dollar or to some form of 'basket' of anchor currencies while others opted for more flexible arrangements, up to and including free floating.

Some elements of the old system survived, of course – not least, the IMF itself, which has continued to perform vital roles as a source of finance and a forum for inter-state cooperation. Moreover, new albeit less formal mechanisms of monetary management gradually emerged to cope with subsequent threats to stability such as the oil shocks of the 1970s, the debt crisis of the 1980s and the financial market eruptions of the 1990s. Exchange rate policies remain subject to 'multilateral surveillance' by the Fund. Access to liquidity can still be secured, though without the degree of assurance promised at Bretton Woods. And new procedures for consultation and policy coordination have been developed and regularized, not only through the IMF but also in such now well established bodies as the Group of Seven (G-7) and the Bank for International Settlements (BIS). Still there is no question that, on balance, the system has become more decentralized and diffuse. As compared with the elaborate rule-based design laboriously negotiated at Bretton Woods, what has evolved since the early 1970s seems both less restrictive and more rudderless. In the eyes of some, it is little more than a 'non-system' bordering on anarchy if not chaos.

From Hegemony to 'Privatization'

Dominating the evolution of international finance over the past half century have been two major trends in the distribution of influence over monetary outcomes. The first is a redistribution of power among states, principally involving a relative decline in the overwhelming pre-eminence once enjoyed by the United States. The second is a redistribution of power from states to markets, involving a relative increase in the role of non-state actors in deciding such fundamental matters as currency values or access to credit. Simultaneously, the system has become less hegemonic and more market-determined – less centralized and more 'privatized', to recall an earlier phrase (Cohen, 1981, 1983). Together, these two trends have largely defined the research agenda for finance specialists in the IR field.

That US dominance of finance has declined, especially in relation to Europe and Japan, is widely accepted. Washington can no longer exercise quite the same degree of autonomy as during the era of dollar shortage, when the United States was effectively freed from all external constraint to spend as liberally as deemed necessary to promote national objectives. Other countries have also gained an influential voice on monetary matters. The only question is empirical: *How much* has US dominance declined? At one extreme is the view, particularly common in the 1970s and 1980s, that the day of American hegemony is irretrievably over. We are faced with the challenge of living in a world 'after hegemony', wrote Robert Keohane in 1984 (Keohane, 1984). The United States, echoed Gilpin, 'had forfeited its role of monetary leadership' (1987: 142). At the other extreme are scholars like Strange, who even in her last books continued to maintain that the supposed loss of American hegemony was little more than a 'myth' ([1988] 1994, 1996, 1998). Most observers today would acknowledge that reality, as is so often the case, undoubtedly lies somewhere between these two polar views.

Likewise, that the role of non-state actors in finance has increased is also widely accepted. In fact, the transformation has been dramatic. A half century ago, after the ravages of the Great Depression and the Second World War, currency and credit markets everywhere (with the notable exception of the United States) were generally weak, insular and strictly controlled, reduced from their previously central role in the world economy to offer little more than a negligible amount of trade financing. Starting in the late 1950s, however, private lending and investment once again began to gather momentum, generating a phenomenal growth of cross-border capital flows and an increasingly close integration of national markets. While it is yet premature to speak of a single world financial market, it is by no means an exaggeration to speak of 'financial globalization' – a genuine resurrection of global finance (Cohen, 1996). By the end of the century, the process had proceeded to the point where the authority of governments seemed directly threatened. Again the main question is *how much?* At a minimum states have been thrown on the defensive, no longer able to enforce their will without constraint. At a maximum states appear on the verge of total emasculation, with monetary sovereignty soon to be transferred in its entirety from national governments to 'stateless' markets. Here too we shall see that reality more likely lies somewhere in between.

EXPLAINING STATE BEHAVIOR

Consider, first, the politics of financial relations between states. As in IR theory generally, it seems natural to start with governments, still the core unit in a Westphalian world. So long as national sovereignty remains the basic principle of world politics, as it has since the seventeenth-century Peace of Westphalia, the state will remain central to analysis, treated as an endogenous and purposive actor. Two broad sets of questions have traditionally been addressed by IR theorists. One has to do with *actor behavior*. What motivates government behavior in international affairs, and how is that behavior best explained and analyzed? The other has to do with *system governance*. What determines the standards for behavior in international affairs, and how do states manage (or fail to manage) their policy conflicts? Both sets of questions have been addressed in the finance literature as well, though with far more serious attention paid to the latter than to the former. Whereas discussions of monetary governance have made real contributions to the broader IR field, analysis of state motivations has tended to rely most heavily – and often simplistically – on paradigms borrowed from others.

I begin in this section with the issue of actor behavior and take up system governance in the following section.

Levels of Analysis

In trying to understand state behavior, IR theory has long distinguished among three broad levels of analysis, each a general theoretical orientation in the rationalist tradition corresponding to one of Kenneth Waltz's well-known images of international relations (Waltz, 1959). Most enduring is the familiar *systemic level* (or structural level) of analysis, analogous to Waltz's 'third' image, which focuses on the constraints and incentives for policy associated with alternative global structures. Explanations, in Waltz's terms (1979), are 'outside-in', accounting for the behavior of individual states on the basis of attributes of the system as a whole. Next is the *domestic level* (or unit level), analogous to Waltz's 'second' image, which addresses attention to the internal characteristics of states rather than to their external environment. Explanations are 'inside-out', concentrating on the political and institutional basis at home for policy preferences abroad. And finally there is the *cognitive level*, analogous to Waltz's 'first' image, which focuses on the base of ideas and consensual knowledge that legitimate governmental policy-making.

In earlier years, the most vigorous debates in IR theory were between various systemic and domestic approaches – in particular, between realism and its variants (neorealism, etc.) on the one hand, stressing the primacy of structural variables, and liberalism and its variants (neoliberal institutionalism, etc.) on the other, with their greater emphasis on unit-level considerations. More recently, as noted elsewhere in this volume, discourse has shifted to a newer debate between rationalist theories of all kinds (including both

realism and liberalism) – labeled 'neo-utilitarianism' by John Ruggie (1999) – and constructivism, highlighting the role of first-image cognitive variables in shaping conceptions of identity and interest. Constructivism, as Ruggie (1999) points out, goes beyond neo-utilitarianism by asking not only what role ideational factors play in the policy-making process but also where 'intersubjective beliefs' come from and how they become transformed into 'social facts'. The IR field's rich diversity of analytical approaches is well reflected in the finance literature, though more as consumer than producer. Alternative orientations have been borrowed wholesale from more general discussions of world politics, with few insights added to help resolve overarching meta-theoretical debates.

For many scholars writing on international finance, the temptation to simplify by 'black-boxing' the state, as in the traditional systemic-level approach of IR, has been overwhelming. This tendency is especially evident in studies of monetary diplomacy and negotiation, most of which derive their inspiration directly from the parsimonious logic of game theory and microeconomic analysis. For economists, nothing seems more natural than to treat the state as the equivalent of an atomistic firm, taking policy preferences as given in order to concentrate on the pivotal role of a small number of structural variables. Typical are the formal game models of Koichi Hamada (1985), which elegantly explore diverse aspects of policy strategy in a context of monetary interdependence. The same path has also been followed by many political scientists, albeit with more attention to institutional and historical detail. One example is Kenneth Oye's (1986) study of monetary statecraft in the interwar period, which attributes much of the blame for the breakdown of great power cooperation in the 1930s to changes in the global financial structure. Another example is Vinod Aggarwal's monumental survey of two centuries of international debt reschedulings, aptly titled *Debt Games* (1996), which focuses explicitly on structural characteristics of different 'epochs' to explain bargaining outcomes.

Only in the 1980s did a small number of scholars begin to open up the black box to explore in more systematic fashion where policy preferences might come from. Notable early contributions include studies of US international monetary policy by John Odell (1982) and Joanne Gowa (1983), both of which *inter alia* highlighted the role of domestic politics – inside-out explanations – to account for governmental behavior. Their lead has since been followed most prominently by Jeffry Frieden in a series of influential papers (e.g., 1991, 1994) exploring in more generalized terms the links between international finance and domestic interests. Varying degrees of capital mobility or different exchange rate regimes, Frieden argues, have a direct impact on the material interests of specific segments of society; in turn, distributional implications systematically shape group preferences and political coalitions affecting policy. The effect of interest groups or institutions on external monetary policy is now widely affirmed and figures prominently in a number of later studies, including Randall Henning (1994), Helen Milner (1997) and Beth Simmons (1994). All can be cited as evidence of the emerging synthesis of IR and the related fields of American politics and comparative politics that was suggested recently by Milner (1999).

Cognitive variables, on the other hand, have until recently played little formal part in the finance literature, perhaps because they are so difficult to operationalize for analytical purposes. As one recent source comments, 'the role of ideas in monetary affairs ... has not been sufficiently addressed to this point' (Kirshner, 2000: 422). Odell, in his early study (1982), did stress shared ideologies and subjective perceptions as influences on America's post-war monetary behavior. Likewise, more recently, John Ikenberry (1993) has highlighted the importance of 'new thinking' in helping to account for US and British agreement on the terms of the post-war monetary regime negotiated at Bretton Woods. Most suggestions, however, tend to be impressionistic at best, rarely backed by systematic testing or argument, and rest squarely in the neo-utilitarian tradition. Even less has constructivism, as a formal analytical approach, yet begun to enter the mainstream of research on financial issues. The most serious effort to date is by Kathleen McNamara (1998), who carefully explores the 'currency of ideas' as a driving force in the process of monetary integration in Europe.[2]

Thus we are still very far from anything that might be described as a commonly agreed or standard theory of state behavior in international finance (just as we are still far from a standard theory of state behavior in general). Various influences at all three levels, as in the broader IR literature, are now typically acknowledged. But their relative utility and the relationships among them remain, to say the least, unclear. Most recent discussions, understandably wary of monocausal interpretations of motivation, rightly emphasize multiple factors but seem tempted to fudge, either by analyzing explanatory variables in sequence, highlighting one and then adding others to account for residual differences; or else by simply listing them more or less indiscriminately. What is needed is more effort to integrate the separate levels of analysis, with particular focus on underlying linkages and how and why they may change over time – perhaps along the lines of Robert Putnam's 'two-level game' (1988) or the more elaborate frameworks proposed by Frieden and Rogowski (1996) and Garrett and Lange (1996) to analyze connections between economic internationalization and domestic politics. Formal unification of the

three levels of analysis is a central epistemological challenge for all of IR theory, not just for monetary studies in particular.

Money and Power

Whatever motivates state behavior, policy is bound to be conditioned heavily by considerations of power. This is as true in finance as in any other aspect of international relations. The meaning of power, however, is no better understood in monetary scholarship than it is in the broader IR literature.

At its most general, power in international relations may be defined as the ability to control, or at least influence, the outcome of events. Two dimensions are important: internal and external. The internal dimension corresponds to the dictionary definition of power as a capacity for action. A state is powerful to the extent that it is insulated from outside influence or coercion in the formulation and implementation of policy. A common synonym for the internal dimension of power is 'autonomy'. The external dimension corresponds to the dictionary definition of power as a capacity to control the behavior of others; to enforce compliance. A state is also powerful to the extent that it can influence or coerce outsiders. Such influence need not be actively exercised; it need only be acknowledged by others, implicitly or explicitly, to be effective. It also need not be exercised with conscious intent; the behavior of others can be influenced simply as a by-product of 'powerful' acts (or potential acts). A useful synonym for the external dimension of power is 'authority'.[3]

Of most interest to students of international finance is the external dimension: the authority that one state can exert over others. Yet remarkably few scholars have even tried to explore monetary power in formal theoretical terms. As Jonathan Kirshner has noted, the topic is in fact 'a neglected area of study' (1995: 3). Kindleberger offered a few pioneering observations in his early essay on *Power and Money* (1970), followed a few years later by Cohen in *Organizing the World's Money* (1977). Most influential to date have been Strange's contributions in her first book, *Sterling and British Policy* (1971), and especially in *States and Markets* (1994).

For Strange, the key to authority in economic affairs lay not in tangible resources – territory, population and the like – but rather in structures and relationships. Who depends on whom, and for what? Power could be understood to operate at two levels, structural and relational. *Relational power*, echoing more conventional treatments in the IR literature, was the familiar 'power of A to get B to do something they would not otherwise do' ([1988] 1994: 24). *Structural power* was 'the power to shape and determine the structures of the global political economy. ... the power to decide how things will be done, the power to shape frameworks within which states relate to each other' ([1988] 1994: 24–5). Four key structures were identified: security, production, finance and knowledge. Of most relevance here of course is the financial structure: 'the sum of all the arrangements governing the availability of credit plus all factors determining the terms on which currencies are exchanged for each other' ([1988] 1994: 90).

Strange's distinction between relational and structural power was critical, even inspired.[4] In the crudest terms, one refers to the ability to gain advantage under the prevailing rules of the game, the other to the ability to create advantage by defining (or redefining) the rules of the game. Regrettably, though, there is little here that could be described as genuine theory, in the sense of a formal, systematic analysis of either the sources or the use of power at either level of operation. Strange's approach was essentially taxonomic in nature. So too is Kirshner's in his more recent *Currency and Coercion* (1995), which uses a wealth of historical material to catalog the diverse ways that money can be used in inter-state relations as an instrument of coercion. Theory calls for more than just a set of categories. The familiar challenge of theory is to provide reasonably parsimonious and well-specified set of propositions about behavior – statements that are both logically true and, at least in principle, empirically falsifiable. Neither Strange nor Kirshner meet that test. In this sense no true theory of monetary power may be said, as yet, to exist. Progress in meeting that challenge could make a contribution to power analysis well beyond the specific issue-area of finance.

SYSTEM GOVERNANCE

Reduced to its essence, governance is about rules – how rules are made for the allocation of values in society and how they are implemented and enforced. Rules may be formally articulated in statutes or treaties outlining specific prescriptions or proscriptions for action. Or they may be expressed more informally, as implicit norms defining behavioral standards in terms of understood rights and obligations. Either way, what matters is that they exercise some degree of authority: some degree of influence over the behavior and decisions of actors. The rules of the game rule.

And who makes the rules? In analytical discussions of monetary relations, two principles of governance have received the most attention. One is *hegemony*, a structure organized around a single dominant country with acknowledged leadership responsibilities (as well as privileges). The other is *cooperation*, a structure of shared responsibilities and decision-making.[5] Here, unlike in discussions of actor behavior, the finance literature has been as

much producer as consumer, providing insights of significance not only for students of monetary affairs but also for the study of world politics in general.

Hegemony

Of all the diverse theories that have captured attention in the IR field over the years, few have achieved the prominence, not to say notoriety, of the so-called theory of hegemonic stability – the familiar argument, as first summarized by Keohane, that 'hegemonic structures of power, dominated by a single country, are most conducive to the development of strong international regimes whose rules are relatively precise and well obeyed' (1980: 132). Specialists in finance can take a sort of pride in the fact that hegemonic stability theory found its first inspiration in the history of the monetary system. Writing after the breakdown of Bretton Woods, observant scholars like Kindleberger (1973) and Gilpin (1975) remarked on what seemed a striking correlation between great power dominance and financial stability both in the late nineteenth century, the era of the classical gold standard, and during the Bretton Woods period. The first period was led by Britain (a financial *Pax Britannica*), the second by the United States (a *Pax Americana*). Both Kindleberger and Gilpin found it reasonable to attribute causation to the relationship. Furthermore, given the apparent decline of US hegemony, it also seemed reasonable to fear a growing instability of monetary relations, possibly even a crash on the model of what happened in the interwar period. The basic argument has since been extended to address most other aspects of inter-state relations as well, political as well as economic, and has given rise to whole new areas of inquiry in IR, such as regime theory and theories of international cooperation and institutions. Yet for all its ubiquity, the proposition remains highly controversial – even in the issue-area of finance, where it was born.

The central issue is whether monetary leadership really matters all that much. The historical correlation noted by Kindleberger and Gilpin is a broad one that does not stand up well to detailed analysis, as Barry Eichengreen (1989) has ably demonstrated. Eichengreen considers separately the role of hegemony at three distinct stages in the evolution of an international monetary system – genesis, operation and disintegration – and compares three different experiences: the classical gold standard, the interwar period and Bretton Woods. What he finds is that 'the relationship between the market power of the leading economy and the stability of the international monetary system is considerably more complex than suggested by simple variants of hegemonic stability theory' (1989: 258). Hegemony appears to be neither necessary nor sufficient to explain the rise or fall of past financial orders.[6]

But that is not the same thing as saying that hegemony thus matters not at all. Leadership is hardly inconsequential, as Eichengreen goes on to insist. Though the theory fails to explain all stages of each of the three experiences he examines, it is 'helpful for understanding' many of them (1989: 287). Moreover, other scholars continue to find a significant role for hegemony in diverse monetary arrangements, particularly at the regional level. Garrett (2001), for instance, makes a strong case for the leadership part that Germany played in bringing about agreement on the terms of Economic and Monetary Union (EMU) in Europe, embodied in the Maastricht Treaty of 1991. But for German initiative and concessions, it seems, the euro might never have been created. Along similar lines, Cohen argues, on the basis of a comparative historical study of monetary unions past and present, that local hegemony is a key determinant of whether an experiment like EMU, once established, is apt to prove sustainable over time (Cohen, 2001).

Such observations have led David Lake (1993) to offer a useful distinction between two different strands of hegemonic-stability theory: *leadership theory*, which builds upon the theory of public goods and focuses on the production of international stability, redefined as the 'international economic infrastructure'; and *hegemony theory*, which seeks to explain patterns of international economic openness by focusing on national trade preferences. Only the former is directly relevant to the study of international finance where, following Kindleberger (1973), Lake summarizes the key components of the infrastructure that must be provided. These include first and foremost a stable medium of exchange and store of value as well as sufficient liquidity to support both short-term stabilization and longer-term growth. Recasting analysis in terms of public-goods theory is critical because it helps explain the diverse empirical findings of Eichengreen and others – why hegemony seems critical at some moments and yet neither necessary nor sufficient at other times.

The reason, by now well understood, is that there is nothing in public-goods theory that limits leadership to a single state. Infrastructure can also be provided collectively by so-called 'privileged groups' in Mancur Olson's terminology (or 'k' groups, in Thomas Schelling's terminology) – a point confirmed empirically by Eichengreen, who found that

> even when individual countries occupied positions of exceptional prominence in the ... international monetary system, that system was still fundamentally predicated on international collaboration. ... The international monetary system has always been 'after hegemony' in the sense that more than a dominant economic power was required to ensure the provision and maintenance of international monetary stability. (1989: 287)

A narrow preoccupation with hegemony thus is really beside the point. The more basic question, as Lake suggests, has to do with the conditions that either facilitate or inhibit production of needed public goods, whether by one country or several. Future research, therefore, should concentrate on such issues as the cost of producing the different components of financial infrastructure and the efficacy of state power in negotiating and maintaining agreements. That is where the real challenge to system governance lies.

Cooperation

That brings us to the problem of cooperation, which has also attracted a great deal of attention from specialists in international finance. Here too money has been a particularly strong inspiration for broader theorizing about world politics; and here too much controversy remains to occupy future scholars.

In international finance as in the IR field generally cooperation among states is identified, following Keohane (1984), with a mutual adjustment of policy behavior achieved through an implicit or explicit process of negotiation. Practically speaking, cooperation may vary greatly in intensity, ranging from simple consultation or occasional crisis management to partial or even full collaboration in the formulation and implementation of policy. Cooperation may also take many forms, ranging from informal 'networks of bargains' of the sort envisioned by Strange ([1988] 1994) to the more formally structured procedures of bodies like the G-7 or IMF. Whatever its intensity or form, the key to cooperation is shared responsibility and decisionmaking. Related terms such as 'coordination' or 'collaboration' may be treated as essentially synonymous.

The theoretical case for monetary cooperation is clear. In financial relations, any one government's actions can generate significant 'spillover' effects – foreign repercussions and feedbacks – that may influence its own ability, as well as that of others, to achieve preferred objectives. That will be true whether the policies at issue involve interest rates or exchange rates, international lending or external debt. The result of these 'externalities' is 'market failure' – a situation where policies that are chosen unilaterally, even if seemingly optimal from the individual country's point of view, will almost certainly turn out to be sub-optimal globally. Decision-making becomes inextricably enmeshed in a context of strategic interdependence. The basic rationale for cooperation is that it can correct the market failure by *internalizing* the externalities. If each government can claim a degree of control over the behavior of others, it is possible to move policy collectively closer to what might be considered a Pareto optimum. In other words, everyone potentially can gain from an outward movement toward the Pareto frontier. Nowhere has the case for monetary cooperation been developed so forcefully as in the formal models of Hamada (1985) cited earlier. Using a methodology borrowed directly from game theory, Hamada makes a persuasive case for the mutual benefits of overt policy coordination.

The practical impediments to monetary cooperation, however, are equally clear. Much attention has been devoted, by economists and political scientists alike, to explaining why incentives for collaboration may be diluted in the real world, even among rational policy-optimizing governments. On the economics side, several factors have been cited.[7] First, in practical terms, potential gains might be too small, or the costs of coordination too large, to make the effort seem worthwhile. Second is the so-called time-inconsistency problem: the chance that agreements, once negotiated, will later be violated by governments tempted by changing circumstances to renege on their commitments. Among sovereign states, compliance mechanisms are by definition imperfect at best. And third is the possibility, quite serious in the opinion of many, that cooperation might actually prove to be counterproductive, shifting countries away from rather than toward the Pareto frontier. One possibility is that governments may choose policies that are more politically expedient than economically sound. In an early and influential article Kenneth Rogoff (1985) pointed out that formal coordination of monetary policies could, perversely, lead to higher inflation if authorities all agreed to expand their money supplies together in order to escape the external payments constraint that would discipline any country trying to inflate on its own. Another possibility is that officials may simply not understand how their policies operate and interact. In a more recent study, Keisuke Iida (1999) found much evidence to suggest that the principal cause of counterproductive cooperation is 'model-uncertainty' – the difficulty of making firm cause–effect inferences about highly contingent events.

Political scientists, on their side, focus on the time-inconsistency and expediency issues and ask why governments might cheat on commitments or might seemingly jeopardize their own best interests.[8] At the systemic level, the main question is whether governments are more interested in absolute or relative gains – the familiar debate kicked off by Joseph Grieco's notorious neorealist attack on neoliberal institutionalism (Grieco, 1988). Are states primarily concerned with market failure or with distributional conflicts? In reality, it is most likely that they worry about both. As Stephen Krasner (1991) has noted, the challenge of cooperation is twofold: not just to reach the Pareto frontier but also to choose some mutually satisfactory point along that frontier, an issue that cannot be easily resolved in a world of many jealous 'defensive positionalists'.

At the domestic level, the main question is how interest groups and institutional structures interact to determine policy preferences and strategies. Politics at home will influence not only the willingness of governments to enter into commitments abroad but also their ability to abide by such agreements over time. Putnam and Henning (1989) make a critical distinction between *voluntary* and *involuntary* defection. In practice, even if policy-makers rationally calculate that it is not in their interest to abandon Pareto-optimizing cooperation (voluntary defection), they may none the less be forced to do so because of resistance by key domestic actors (involuntary defection). Conversely, following Rogoff's logic, it is also possible that dominant interest groups might exploit the process to promote particularist or even personal ambitions at the expense of broader collective goals.

How, then, can productive monetary cooperation be promoted? For many, the solution lies in the creation of international organizations with the capacity to constrain and shape behavior by facilitating agreements and enforcing rules. That was what governments had in mind at Bretton Woods when they created the IMF; and it is of course what others have in mind today when they call for something more or less approximating a world central bank. In practice, however, it has never been clear to what extent any international organization may realistically be regarded as an autonomous actor rather than simply a forum for the playing out of inter-state politics. The Fund is a case in point. The IMF plainly does exercise supranational authority over at least some of its members, by determining access to credit and by the policy conditions attached to its loans. But the question remains: Where does that authority come from, and on whose behalf is it exercised? One view, long espoused by radical analysts such as Cheryl Payer (1974), holds that the Fund is little more than a crude instrument for advancing the interests of its most powerful members. Formal evidence to support that view has recently come from Strom Thacker (1999), who finds that a key determinant of access to IMF credit appears to be a country's political relationship with the United States, the Fund's largest power. A more subtle view, best represented by the work of Louis Pauly (1997, 1999), sees the IMF as a promoter of behavioral norms reflecting a consensus of views among its stronger participating governments. The risk, according to Pauly, is that if this norm structure is then imposed upon the weak, even though they have little role in its design, the political legitimacy of the Fund will eventually be eroded, impeding rather than promoting cooperation. But as insightful as these contributions may be, we still do not have a satisfactory answer to the question. Miles Kahler gets it right when he writes that as an agent of rule enforcement, 'the role of the IMF … remains unclear' (1995: 49). Much room yet remains for research on the Fund's role, or that of related bodies, in governance of the monetary system.

A more practical solution to the cooperation issue, as Martin and Simmons (1999) emphasize in an important discussion, lies in finding some way to agree on rules that can become effectively self-enforcing. A key is provided by Arthur Stein's (1990) critical distinction between what he calls 'dilemmas of common aversions' and 'dilemmas of common interests'. Dilemmas of common aversions, otherwise known as coordination games, exist when all actors share a concern to avoid a particular outcome. The only question is how to establish a common 'norm', or focal point, around which behavior may coalesce. Beyond agreeing to play by some standard set of rules (for example, driving on the right-hand side of the road), no compromise of underlying preferences is called for. This is in contrast to dilemmas of common interests, so-called collaboration problems, where reciprocal concessions are indeed required to avoid sub-optimal outcomes.[9] Cooperation in such situations will obviously be more difficult to achieve or sustain.

Happily, in many dimensions of international finance, states do find themselves confronted more with common aversions than with fundamentally divergent interests. This is especially true in such matters as supervision and regulation of financial markets, where effective cooperation has indeed proved feasible (Kapstein, 1994; Porter, 1993; Underhill, 1995). Moreover, even in more conflictual situations, the temptation to behave selfishly in the short term will be tempered by the fact that governments must factor in potential consequences over the longer term – the long 'shadow of the future', which puts a premium on considerations of reputation and credibility. As Martin and Simmons remind us, 'repetition transforms collaboration problems into coordination problems' (1999: 105). Separately, Simmons (2000) has demonstrated empirically the degree to which reputational concerns appear to encourage governments to comply with their legal commitments under the IMF's Articles of Agreement.

The real challenge, therefore, would seem to be to find ways to construct focal points on which all states can agree, even where preferences might otherwise be expected to conflict – standard rules that would serve the role of the international infrastructure spoken of by Lake. How to construct relevant focal points, in practical political terms, was the implicit agenda of the old theories of international regimes that flourished in the 1980s. It is also the intent of the newer theories of international institutions that emerged in the 1990s, which explicitly address the issue of how to make agreements not only mutually acceptable but also sustainable. Martin and Simmons (1999) list a number of ways in which institutions can be structured to 'lock in' patterns of cooperation. The IMF provides only one possible model among many. The task for students of international finance, relatively neglected until now, is to look seriously at how the Fund or other multilateral organizations might be reformed with these specific principles in mind, in order to produce the public goods needed for effective governance of money and credit.

STATES AND MARKETS

Complicating analysis, of course, is the fact that in finance, as in every area of political economy, states are not the only actors involved. Governments must contend not only with each other but also with *markets* – more specifically, with the myriad of non-state actors that make up the increasingly integrated markets for currency and credit across the globe. Recent decades, as indicated, have witnessed a remarkable revival of global finance, which in turn has directly challenged the authority and capacity of state actors to manage monetary affairs. Capital mobility has soared, and national financial markets have become integrated to a degree not seen since the end of the nineteenth century – all part of the wider trend toward globalization of international affairs that has become a cliché of the IR literature. Theory, however, has yet to catch up with the implications of these developments for world politics and the nature of the international system.

As in the more general IR literature, three core questions are suggested. The first has to do with *causes*: How did financial globalization happen? The remaining two have to do with *consequences* – first, for individual countries; and second, for the structure and operation of the state system as a whole. All three questions have been hotly debated in the second generation of international finance scholarship, with answers that hold promise of contributing to broader discussions of the globalization phenomenon.

Causes of Financial Globalization

What has caused the dramatic revival of global finance since the Second World War? Clearly at the center of the process is government policy: a gradually accelerating trend toward deregulation and liberalization of markets, in advanced industrial countries and developing economies alike. But what accounts for this conduct? A wide variety of explanations have been offered in the literature, with little consensus overall. Hypotheses generally break down along the lines of the three traditional levels of analysis of actor behavior in IR theory.[10]

At the systemic level, two classes of causal interpretation can be identified, stressing the contrasting roles of market forces and state rivalries. The first class, with roots in standard neoclassical economics, points to the powerful effects of competition and innovation in the financial marketplace – particularly advances in communications and information technologies – that have literally swept away institutional barriers to market integration and the free flow of capital. This approach, not surprisingly, is the personal favorite of most economists. Typical is Ralph Bryant, a well known international monetary specialist, who confidently asserts that 'technological nonpolicy factors were so powerful ... that they would have caused a progressive internationalization of financial activity even without changes in government separation fences' (1987: 69). On the political-science side the case has been put most firmly by David Andrews (1994), who emphasizes both the degree to which increases in capital mobility appear to have taken place independently of changes in state regulatory frameworks and also the degree to which liberalization at the national level has seemingly occurred in response to market pressures at the systemic level.

The second class of systemic explanations, more consistent with rationalist traditions in IR theory, stresses the determining role of policy rivalry among national governments, each calculating how best to use its influence and capabilities to promote state interests in an insecure world. A prime example is provided by Eric Helleiner (1994) in an admirably detailed historical study. Rejecting interpretations that highlight 'unstoppable technological and market forces rather than state behavior and political choices', Helleiner contends that 'the contemporary open global financial order could never have emerged without the support and blessing of states' (1994: vii, 1). Most pivotal, in his view, was a process of 'competitive deregulation' by governments maneuvering unilaterally to attract the business of mobile financial traders and investors. From the 1960s onward, inter-state rivalry was reinforced by policy initiatives from the two leading monetary powers of the day, the United States and Britain, both with a strong interest in promoting a more open financial system.

At the domestic level, emphasis is placed on constituency politics – inside-out explanations of government behavior rather than outside-in. Representative is Andrew Sobel who, focusing on industrial countries, highlights 'competition between organized interests within domestic political economies' (1994: 16) as the driving force behind financial globalization. 'The primary motivation for regulatory change rests within the domestic political economy', he asserts. 'The international outcome is solidly rooted in domestic policy dilemmas and distributional debates' (1994: 16, 19). A parallel argument is offered by Haggard and Maxfield (1996) to explain liberalization in developing countries, stressing the effects of increased economic openness on the preferences and capabilities of policy-relevant economic interests. Expanding foreign trade and investment ties, they argue, 'increase interest group pressures for financial internationalization ... while decreasing the effectiveness of government controls' (1996: 214). Both sources place particular emphasis on the pivotal role of large financial intermediaries, corporate borrowers and institutional investors.

Finally, at the cognitive level, attention is directed to the part played by belief systems and consensual knowledge as catalysts for policy change. Helleiner (1994) himself, even while stressing structural factors and inter-state rivalries, acknowledges as well the possible importance of the dramatic ideological shift that has occurred in so many countries, from Keynesian activism to a more permissive neoliberal framework. Central has been a gradual loss of faith in the efficacy of capital controls as a conventional instrument of public policy, despite much evidence and argument to the contrary (Bhagwati, 1998). Andrews, similarly, speaks of the critical role of 'widely shared ideological commitments' and 'mindsets' (1994: 200–1) – a constellation of views labeled by Philip Cerny (1993) the new 'embedded financial orthodoxy'.

Out of this variety of interpretations, however, no common view has emerged to account for the globalization trend – confirming once again how far we remain from anything that might be described as a standard theory of state behavior in international finance. To what extent might the three levels of analysis be linked? The possibility of interactions between explanatory variables is occasionally acknowledged but only rarely explored systematically. One exception is Cerny, who directly ties the widespread embrace of 'embedded financial orthodoxy' to competitive pressures at the systemic level which, in his words, have 'undermined the structures of the Keynesian state' (1993: 80). Another is Stephen Gill (1995), who stresses what he sees as the conjoined role of neoliberal ideology and the influence of dominant class interests in driving national policies. But to date these remain relatively isolated contributions. In this context as in other dimensions of world politics, there is still a need for more systematic effort to link and integrate the separate levels of analysis.

Consequences for States

Even less consensus exists concerning the consequences of financial globalization, whether for individual countries or for the state system as a whole. That governments are challenged by the rising tide of capital mobility is undoubted. But questions remain about how serious the challenge is or what, if anything, policy-makers may be able to do about it. At issue is the task of governance: the respective roles of states and markets in the management of monetary affairs. Research is only beginning to sort out the nature of the evolving state–market relationship in international finance.

From the perspective of individual countries, the core issue is best summarized by what has elsewhere been labeled the 'Unholy Trinity' (Cohen, 1993) – the fundamental incompatibility of the three desiderata of exchange rate stability, free movement of capital and autonomy of national monetary policy. The logic of the Unholy Trinity is based on the so-called Mundell–Fleming model, long familiar to economists, which Paul Krugman has called the 'standard, workhorse model' of open-economy macroeconomics (1993: 2). Reduced to its essence, the model asserts that states are faced with a stark trade-off. In an environment of pegged exchange rates and integrated financial markets, a government loses all control over domestic money supply and interest rates. To regain monetary autonomy, policy-makers must either sacrifice currency stability (that is, float) or limit capital mobility (via capital controls of some kind). Governments unwilling or unable to do either must learn to live without an independent monetary policy, raising serious questions of political legitimacy (Cohen, 1998; Pauly, 1995; Underhill, 1995).

Given the stringent logic of the Unholy Trinity, it is not surprising that as capital mobility has increased, so too has concern about its implications for governmental authority. Strange set the tone of debate with her vivid denunciations of *Casino Capitalism* (1986) and *Mad Money* (1998). For her, as for many others inspired by her (Cerny, 1993, 1994b; Gill and Law, 1989), global finance has become something akin to a structural feature of world politics: an exogenous international attribute that, very much in the spirit of realist or neorealist IR theory, systematically constrains state behavior, rewarding some actions and punishing others. The ever-present threat of capital flight creates irresistible pressures for a convergence of national policies. Andrews calls this the Capital Mobility Hypothesis (CMH): 'The central claim associated with the capital mobility hypothesis is that financial integration has increased the costs of pursuing divergent monetary objectives, resulting in structural incentives for monetary adjustment' (1994: 203).

The CMH underlies the conclusion of Goodman and Pauly, in a notable discussion of financial liberalization, that 'systemic forces are now dominant in the financial area and have dramatically reduced the ability of governments to set autonomous economic policies' (1993: 81). It also underlies the work of Michael Webb (1995), who examines monetary coordination in the Group of Seven. The nature of cooperation by G-7 governments, Webb observes, changed greatly after the end of the Bretton Woods period. Whereas, previously, collaboration consisted mainly of 'external' measures designed to manage payments imbalances generated by incompatible national policies, more recently the focus has turned 'internal' to address national policies themselves – a significant increase in the depth of the coordination process. The reason for the shift, Webb argues, is nothing other than the great increase of international capital mobility. Financial globalization has intensified cooperation by making it more difficult for individual governments to pursue substantially divergent monetary or fiscal policies.

Is the CMH correct? There is nothing wrong with its reasoning, of course, just as there is nothing wrong with the fundamental logic of systemic theories more generally. Global finance clearly has become a significant structural constraint on the ability of states to control activities within and across their borders – what Krasner (1999) calls their 'interdependence sovereignty'. Capital mobility effectively limits the range of choice available to governments by altering the relative costs and benefits of alternative policy options. At one level, the constraint operates through the effect of globalization on the allocation of credit. Privatization of international finance means, in the words of Randall Germain, that 'private monetary agents, organized through markets, [now] dominate the decisions of who is granted access to credit and on what terms' (1997: 163). Both Maxfield (1997) and Sobel (1999) document the extent to which governments today feel compelled to tailor their policies to the preferences of international lenders. At a second level, the constraint operates through effects on the balance of payments. Openness of the capital account affords investors the option of exit whenever governments' behavior fails to live up to their expectations. In effect, financial markets operate as a sort of perpetual opinion poll – a kind of 'automatic, nonpolitical system for grading [policy] performance', as one source puts it (Meigs, 1993: 717). There is in fact no lack of anecdotal evidence to buttress the CMH's view of global finance as a structural feature of world politics, albeit one that tends often to be both late and exaggerated in its evaluations of policy behavior.[11]

None the less it is clear that the proposition, like broader systemic theory, is really something of a simplification. Upon reflection, in fact, the CMH has come to be seen as little more than a caricature, an initial over-reaction to the revival of global finance that seriously misrepresents the true degree of the challenge to governments today. It is one matter to suggest that states can no longer (if they ever could) ignore the signals of the marketplace, but quite another to suggest that, as a result, public officials have been wholly deprived of their capacity to make and implement policy. As thinking about the CMH has been refined, it has become clear that the discipline imposed on governments by mobile capital is rather less than first imagined, for at least three reasons. All three factors provide grist for the mill of future research.

First is the fact that national financial markets remain very far from fully integrated internationally, despite the unmistakable increase of capital mobility in recent decades (Simmons, 1999). This is certainly true of markets for equities, which have always tended to be sharply segmented. It is also still true, albeit to a lesser extent, of most long- and even short-term debt instruments, which even today remain imperfect substitutes due to differing currency denominations and country risk factors. The Mundell–Fleming model, strictly speaking, holds only for a world of *perfect* capital mobility. Insofar as borders and currencies continue to be impediments to trade in financial claims, governments will retain some room for maneuver to pursue independent monetary targets.

Researchers have only begun to develop useful measures of financial openness in today's increasingly globalized marketplace. Some rely on indirect behavioral indicators – such as interest-parity relationships, estimations of capital costs, or savings-investment correlations[12] – while others focus more directly on existing restrictions on capital movements (Haggard and Maxfield, 1996; Quinn, 1997). All the evidence to date confirms the persistence of significant limitations on international investment flows, albeit with much variation across countries and across different categories of capital. In the future, more work will be needed to extend these diverse measures of integration to differentiate among various types of flows that may be more or less sensitive to government policy choices. As Sylvia Maxfield (1998) points out, investor motivations tend to vary considerably, suggesting that different classes of market actors will constrain states in different ways. Monetary policy may yet be effective depending on the *composition* of cross-border movements of capital.

Second, it is important to recall that, even within the tight limits of the Unholy Trinity, governments still have choices. In principle, trade-offs remain possible between monetary autonomy, on the one hand, and currency stability or financial openness on the other. Even if capital flight does develop, policy-makers need not abandon their domestic targets – not so long as they are willing, in practice, to consider instead the alternative options of either floating or some variety of capital controls. The question, presumably, involves calculations of relevant gains and losses, political as well as economic. Here too research has only begun to provide useful insights.

One strand of the literature concentrates on the choice between fixed and flexible exchange rates. Earlier discussions, dominated mainly by economists, naturally focused on implications for economic welfare of alternative currency regimes, using the familiar theory of optimum currency areas as a guide (Cohen, 1998: 62–3). More recent studies stress straightforward political considerations grounded in domestic politics and institutions. For some analysts, working the vein pioneered by Frieden (1994), what matters most are interest-group preferences and pressures on policy-makers. Producers of internationally traded goods and international investors, for instance, might be expected to prefer stable exchange rates, while producers of non-tradables and labor unions are more likely to favor flexible rates because of the leeway provided for an autonomous monetary policy. A prime example of this approach is provided by Thomas Oatley (1997), who explains currency cooperation in the European Union during the 1970s and 1980s mainly in terms of partisan conflict and capital–labor struggles over the distribution of income.[13] Though the CMH correctly highlights general systemic pressures for convergence, Oatley contends, it is unable to account for the specific choices that individual governments made in attempting to stabilize exchange rates.

For other analysts, it is more a question of the structural characteristics of politics at work. Research along these lines has concentrated in particular on developing economies. Sebastian Edwards (1996, 1999a), for instance, considers a government's traditional ability to finance its own expenditures via the printing press, otherwise known as seigniorage. The seigniorage privilege, Edwards notes, tends to be most attractive to states plagued by unstable or divided polities, where tax collection is difficult. Yet a government's ability to support spending via money creation clearly depends on maintenance of an autonomous monetary policy, which is easiest when the exchange rate is allowed to float. Consistent with these observations, he finds empirically that resistance to pegging tends to be greatest in states with a high degree of political instability. Similarly, David Leblang (1999) demonstrates a close relationship in developing countries between exchange rate choices and domestic political institutions. Floating rates are more likely in democratic than authoritarian polities; and in democratic polities, are more likely in systems of proportional representation than in majoritarian electoral systems.

The importance of domestic structural variables is also affirmed for industrial countries in a study by Bernhard and Leblang (1999) stressing the persistent tension governments face between promoting credibility of policy and preserving flexibility for policy-makers (the rules vs. discretion issue). In this context domestic political institutions, particularly electoral and legislative arrangements, can be expected to play a critical role in shaping policy incentives. Statistical analysis suggests that in systems where the cost of electoral defeat is high and electoral timing is exogenous, politicians tend to be less willing to forgo discretion over monetary policy by choosing a fixed exchange rate. In an alternative approach, stressing the interchangeability of fixed exchange rates and an independent central bank as 'monetary commitment mechanisms', Lawrence Broz (2000) finds, like Leblang (1999), that floating rates (with an independent central bank) are more likely in democratic polities and fixed rates more likely in autocracies.[14]

Another strand of the literature, meanwhile, addresses the option of capital controls as a means to improve monetary independence. Why should governments tie one hand behind their back, it is asked, when by restoring some kind of limits on financial flows they might gain more leverage over domestic monetary conditions? For many analysts, the notion of capital mobility as a structural constraint is a red herring that unavoidably obscures the still powerful role of states in setting the parameters of market activity. What states have created, via deregulation and liberalization, they might also reverse if they so choose. The view has been promoted most vigorously by Helleiner (1996, 1999), who argues that since 'financial globalization [was] heavily dependent on state support and encouragement. ... a reversal of the liberalization trend is more likely than is often assumed' (1996: 193–4). Others, however, attack the implication, insisting instead on a kind of hysteresis in financial markets, owing in particular to the inexorable advance of technology which, in Cerny's words, 'allows the markets to stay ahead of the regulators' (1994a: 326). Says Cerny, bluntly: 'Financial globalization has become irreversible' (1994b: 226). Reality, once again, most likely lies somewhere between, depending on how governments reckon the costs, economic or political, associated with any attempt to reduce capital mobility – what Frieden and Rogowski call the 'opportunity cost of economic closure' (1996: 33). This issue too is rightly attracting increasing attention from specialists.[15]

Finally, we must not forget *fiscal policy* – the state's own budget – which is also available to governments to carry out their objectives. The trade-offs imposed by the Unholy Trinity involve only *monetary policy*; and as the original Mundell–Fleming model made clear, the implications of alternative combinations of currency regime and capital mobility for the effectiveness of each of the two types of policy are really very different. The same conditions that erode the effectiveness of monetary policy – fixed exchange rates and integrated financial markets – actually strengthen the impact of fiscal policy on macroeconomic performance. What governments cannot achieve via the money supply and interest rates, they can, in principle, attain via changes of public spending and/or taxation. Conversely, with floating exchange rates and capital mobility, it is monetary policy that gains leverage while fiscal policy is weakened.

Early formulations of the CMH tended to blur the distinction between monetary and fiscal policy, speaking simply (and simplistically) of 'the declining authority of states' (Strange, 1996: 4). Only recently have studies begun to differentiate more clearly between the two in order to highlight how much capacity still remains for public officials to exercise practical influence, depending on circumstances. Both William Clark and colleagues (Clark and Hallerberg, 2000; Clark and Reichert, 1998) and Oatley (1999) find evidence that while governments remain as motivated as ever to intervene in the economy for partisan or electoral purposes, the choice of policy instrument appears very much a function of the exchange rate regime. Fiscal policy is actively used when the exchange rate is fixed, and monetary policy when currencies are floating, just as the Mundell–Fleming model would predict. Parallel empirical studies (Garrett, 1998, 1999; Mosley, 2000; Rodrik, 1997) reinforce the impression that even with a high degree of capital mobility, fiscal policy remains a potent tool for the implementation of purposive political programs, at the microeconomic as well as the macroeconomic level. Further research should clarify other conditions conducive to an effective fiscal policy.

For all three reasons, therefore, the CMH as originally formulated must be treated with caution. Much like broad systemic theory, it is a useful starting point for thinking but hardly the last word. The world is actually a good deal more complex than the proposition suggests – more nuanced, more ambiguous and certainly more contingent. As Garrett concludes: 'There are good reasons to believe that the policy constraints generated by [market integration] are weaker and less pervasive than is often presumed' (1999: 165). Specialists in international finance have made considerable progress in analyzing the true nature of globalization's challenge for governments, with lessons that should prove useful to students of IR more generally. None the less, much work remains to be done before we can claim to fully understand the consequences of financial globalization at the state level.

Systemic Consequences

The same is also true at the systemic level, where the implications of globalization seem even less well understood. Students of IR sense that something significant may be happening as markets and societies become increasingly integrated, transcending the frontiers of the traditional territorial state – something fundamental to the structure and operation of world politics. But what, precisely? Central, once again, is the issue of governance: a growing disjuncture between a political system based on sovereign territory and a world economy that is increasingly global in scope. Who (or what) makes the rules? Are governments still in charge, or markets, or perhaps no one at all? Here too opinions divide sharply, no less among specialists in international finance than in other areas of IR.

Perhaps most extreme is the view expressed by Strange in her penultimate book, *The Retreat of the State* (1996), where she argued that the erosion of state authority had already gone so far that it had, in effect, left no one in charge. In her words: 'At the heart of the international political economy, there is *a vacuum*. ... What some have lost, others have not gained. The diffusion of authority away from national governments has left *a yawning hole of non-authority, ungovernance* it might be called' (1996: 14, emphasis added). But such a bold claim, while not uncommon, is based on a serious misconception of the meaning of authority in social relations. Though authority is inseparable from power, in the sense of influence over outcomes, it is in fact quite separable from the state, which is by no means the only agent capable of making and enforcing rules. Governance can also originate in a variety of other social institutions, some of which may be far less visible to the naked eye than the formal offices of the sovereign state – 'governance without governments', to use an increasingly popular phrase (Rosenau and Czempiel, 1992). Thus the 'retreat of the state', such as it is, does not necessarily mean that a 'vacuum' of 'ungovernance' has been created. Allegations about *Mad Money* notwithstanding, the fact is that much order remains in the monetary system, as in other dimensions of world politics – too much order to suggest that we are condemned to nothing more than a 'yawning hole of non-authority'.

What more is there? Three distinct perspectives can be distinguished in the finance literature, each with its own champions. Some analysts (e.g., Porter, 1996), concurring with Helleiner (1996, 1999), point to the still powerful role of the state, all appearances to the contrary notwithstanding. The 'retreat of the state', it is contended, is more illusion than reality. Global finance operates at the tolerance of governments and is no more a threat to state authority than governments, collectively, permit it to be. As Pauly puts it: 'Capital mobility constrains states, but not in an absolute sense. ... States can still defy markets' if they wish (1995: 373). The argument takes us back to the problem of intergovernmental cooperation and the challenge of constructing the public goods needed for effective management of money and credit. States can still make the rules if they are able to agree among themselves on the needed infrastructure.

For others, by contrast, more persuaded of the basic validity of the Capital Mobility Hypothesis, appearances are indeed reality. The state really has retreated, and in its place markets now rule. The only question, in this perspective, is how that dominion is effectuated. Some studies speak abstractly, if obscurely, of market structures reified as a distinct principle in opposition to traditional state authority. Cerny, for instance, describes a 'new hegemony of financial markets' (1994a: 320) – a 'transnational financial structure' (1994b: 225) that reduces governments to little more than rivals for market favor. This is Cerny's notion of the *competition state*, struggling to make itself as attractive as possible to international investors. Likewise, Germain talks of an increasingly decentralized 'international organization of credit [that] has robbed the international monetary system of a single dominant locus of power' (1997: 26).

Insightful though these arguments may be, however, they remain too vague about who or what actually exercises authority – about *agency*, in contrast to structure – to provide much guidance for practical analytical purposes. More useful are discussions that emphasize specific groups of market actors capable of exercising effective authority in their respective spheres of activity. An early example is provided by Timothy Sinclair (1994a, 1994b), who highlights the role of credit-rating agencies in the management of offshore lending markets. Another comes from Virginia Haufler (1997), who describes how insurance firms have historically been able to create private regulatory regimes for international risks insurance and reinsurance. Systematic study of the role of private authority in international affairs is just beginning (Cutler et al., 1999).

Finally, there is a third perspective, which stresses neither states nor markets alone but rather *both*, acting together to make the rules and set standards for behavior. Why treat the public and private sectors as necessarily in opposition to one another? one may ask. Instead, why not seek to understand how authority might be exercised by the two sides jointly in various hybrid combinations? That is the underlying logic of the newly fashionable concept of Global Governance, which over the past decade has attracted increasing attention from IR scholars, particularly in Europe. As a recent survey puts it, Global Governance 'offers one way beyond [a] dualistic and restrictive perspective on globalization. ... [It] highlights a shifting of the location of authority in the context of both integration and fragmentation' (Hewson and Sinclair, 1999: 4–5). It is also the logic of scholars like Wolfgang Reinecke, who call for a new Global Public Policy, in the sense of new forms of governance that 'decouple the operational aspects of internal sovereignty (governance) from its territorial foundation (the nation-state) and its institutional environment (the government). ... Traditional lines of demarcation between the public and the private spheres are not only being redefined but becoming increasingly blurred' (Reinecke, 1998: 8–9).

Applications of this third perspective are just starting to enter the literature of international finance. Among the first was Geoffrey Underhill (1997, 2000), who contended that states and markets are best seen 'as part of the same, integrated ensemble of governance, not as contrasting principles of social organization' (2000: 4). Another example is Cohen's *The Geography of Money* (1998), where he argues that the accelerating growth of cross-border competition among currencies – a phenomenon described as the 'deterritorialization' of money – has created a new structure of monetary governance comprised of private and public sector actors alike, 'interacting together ... in the social spaces created by money's transactional networks' (1998: 5). More work along these lines would surely be useful. As we look to the future of political-economy research on financial issues, there is much to be said for an analytical approach that moves beyond the 'either/or' of traditional treatments of the state–market relationship.

CONCLUSION

Scholarship in international finance has obviously come a long way over the past third of a century. The first generation of research taught us much about the motivations of state behavior and the opportunities and limitations of intergovernmental cooperation; the second, in turn, has greatly illuminated implications of the revival of global finance for state capacity and the management of monetary affairs. Yet it is equally clear that much remains to be done to gain a full comprehension of developments in this critical issue-area of world politics. After the thesis of state-centrism and the antithesis of market forces, a new synthesis seems needed – a new generation of research exploring in detail just how it is that states and markets interact in practice and how their relationship reacts and evolves over time. Finance has by no means exhausted its challenges for students of IR theory.

Notes

1 A number of useful reviews of different parts of the literature have appeared in recent years, including Andrews and Willett, 1997; Cohen, 1996; Dombrowski, 1998; Kirshner, 2000; Lukauskas, 1999; Watson, 1997. What distinguishes this chapter is the effort to survey the subject of international finance as a whole with particular reference to its reciprocal interaction with broader IR theory.

2 See also Marcussen (1999), who emphasizes a process of learning in European policy circles that he labels the 'ideational life-cycle'. The role of ideas also figures prominently in a collective research project directed by Kirshner, still ongoing as this chapter goes to press, on 'Power, Ideology, and Conflict: The Political Foundations of Twenty-First Century Money'.

3 See Cohen, 1998: ch. 7. In fact, there is much controversy among scholars about the precise meaning of authority in social relations. The use of the term suggested

here is consistent with the position of Hannah Arendt, who contended that authority falls somewhere between the contrasting modalities of coercion and persuasion. In her words: 'If authority is to be defined at all ... it must be in contradistinction to both coercion by force and persuasion through arguments' (Arendt, 1968: 93). Legitimacy is implied by the absence of a need to resort to either violence or reasoning to gain compliance.

4 Cohen had made the same distinction even earlier, labeling the two levels 'process power' and 'structure power' (1977: 53–7). But Strange's treatment was more fully developed. For more discussion, see Cohen, 2000a.

5 In *Organizing the World's Money* (1977) Cohen listed a total of four possible 'organizing principles' for monetary relations, not just two. In addition to hegemony and cooperation, these included the alternatives of automaticity (a self-disciplining structure of rules and norms binding for all states) and supranationality (a structure founded on collective adherence to the decisions of an autonomous international organization – a world central bank, in effect). Although elements of both automaticity and supranationality have long existed in the design and practices of the IMF, hegemony and/or cooperation have always been regarded as the more politically realistic for purposes of analysis.

6 A similar conclusion was reached earlier by Gowa (1984) in a more narrowly focused paper examining the failed effort by the major financial powers in the late 1970s to negotiate establishment of a so-called substitution account for excess dollar reserves. The outcome of that episode, she suggested, demonstrated that in key respects hegemonic-stability theory rests on assumptions 'that can easily be challenged' (Gowa, 1984: 662).

7 For useful surveys, see Cohen, 1993; Kenen, 1989; Willet 1999.

8. Political theories of international cooperation have been ably surveyed by Milner, 1992. For an economist's take on the political economy of cooperation, see Willett, 1999.

9 The difference between the two classes of dilemma is reflected in the distinction economist Peter Kenen (1988) draws between two types of cooperation – the 'policy-optimizing' approach, where governments seek to bargain their way from sub-optimality to something closer to a Pareto optimum; and the 'regime-preserving' or 'public-goods' approach, where mutual adjustments are agreed for the sake of defending existing arrangements or institutions against the threat of economic or political shocks.

10 For a review, see Cohen, 1996.

11 Willett (2000) labels this the 'too much, too late hypothesis'. For a variety of reasons inherent in the structure of financial markets, he points out, market agents generally fail to provide discipline early; and then, when crisis hits, tend to be overreactive in their response.

12 For reviews, see von Furstenberg, 1998; Simmons, 1999.

13 Other examples include Hefeker, 1997; Ruland and Viaene, 1993; Stephan, 1994.

14 Broz's paper is part of an ongoing research project on 'Exchange Rates, Central Bank Independence, and

Politics: Monetary Credibility in an Open Economy', directed by Broz together with William Bernhard and William Clark.

15 See, e.g., Cohen, 2000b; Cooper, 1999; Edwards, 1999b; Kirshner, 1999.

Bibliography

Aggarwal, Vinod K. (1996) *Debt Games: Strategic Interaction in International Debt Rescheduling.* New York: Cambridge University Press.

Andrews, David M. (1994) 'Capital Mobility and State Autonomy: Toward a Structural Theory of International Monetary Relations', *International Studies Quarterly*, 38 (2): 193–218.

Andrews, David M. and Willett, Thomas D. (1997) 'Financial Interdependence and the State: International Monetary Relations at Century's End', *International Organization*, 51 (3): 479–511.

Arendt, Hannah (1968) 'What Is Authority?', in *Between Past and Future: Eight Exercises in Political Thought.* New York: Viking Press. pp. 91–141.

Bernhard, William and Leblang, David (1999) 'Democratic Institutions and Exchange-Rate Commitments', *International Organization*, 53 (1): 71–97.

Bhagwati, Jagdish (1998) 'The Capital Myth', *Foreign Affairs*, 77 (3): 7–12.

Broz, J. Lawrence (2000) 'Political Institutions and the Transparency of Monetary Policy Commitments', paper presented at the annual meeting of the American Political Science Association, Washington, DC.

Bryant, Ralph C. (1987) *International Financial Intermediation.* Washington, DC: Brookings Institution.

Cerny, Philip G. (1993) 'The Deregulation and Re-regulation of Financial Markets in a More Open World', in Philip G. Cerny (ed.), *Finance and World Politics: Markets, Regimes and States in the Post-Hegemonic Era.* Brookfield, VT: Edward Elgar. pp. 51–85.

Cerny, Philip G. (1994a) 'The Dynamics of Financial Globalization: Technology, Market Structure, and Policy Response', *Policy Sciences*, 27 (4): 319–42.

Cerny, Philip G. (1994b) 'The Infrastructure of the Infrastructure? Toward "Embedded Financial Orthodoxy" in the International Political Economy', in Ronan P. Palan and Barry Gills (eds), *Transcending the State–Global Divide: A Neostructuralist Agenda in International Relations.* Boulder: Lynne Rienner. pp. 223–75.

Clark, William R. and Hallerberg, Mark (2000) 'Mobile Capital, Domestic Institutions, and Electorally Induced Monetary and Fiscal Policy', *American Political Science Review*, 94 (2): 323–46.

Clark, William R. and Reichert, Usha N. (1998) 'International and Domestic Constraints on Political Business Cycles in OECD Economies', *International Organization*, 52 (1): 87–120.

Cohen, Benjamin J. (1971) *The Future of Sterling as an International Currency.* London: Macmillan.

Cohen, Benjamin J. (1977) *Organizing the World's Money: The Political Economy of International Monetary Relations.* New York: Basic Books.

Cohen, Benjamin J. (1981) *Banks and the Balance of Payments: Private Lending in the International Adjustment Process.* Montclair, NJ: Allenheld, Osmun.

Cohen, Benjamin J. (1983) 'Balance-of-Payments Financing: Evolution of a Regime', in Stephen D. Krasner (ed.), *International Regimes.* Ithaca: Cornell University Press. pp. 315–36.

Cohen, Benjamin J. (1986) *In Whose Interest? International Banking and American Foreign Policy.* New Haven: Yale University Press.

Cohen, Benjamin J. (1993) 'The Triad and the Unholy Trinity: Lessons for the Pacific Region', in Richard Higgott, Richard Leaver and John Ravenhill (eds), *Pacific Economic Relations in the 1990s: Cooperation or Conflict?* Boulder: Lynne Rienner. pp. 133–58.

Cohen, Benjamin J. (1996) 'Phoenix Risen: The Resurrection of Global Finance', *World Politics*, 48 (2): 268–96.

Cohen, Benjamin J. (1998) *The Geography of Money.* Ithaca: Cornell University Press.

Cohen, Benjamin J. (2000a) 'Money and Power in World Politics', in Thomas C. Lawton, James N. Rosenau, and Amy C. Verdun (eds), *Strange Power: Shaping the Parameters of International Relations and International Political Economy.* London: Ashgate. pp. 91–113.

Cohen, Benjamin J. (2000b) 'Taming the Phoenix: Monetary Governance after the Crisis', in Greg Noble and John Ravenhill (eds), *The Asian Financial Crisis and the Structure of Global Finance.* Cambridge. Cambridge University Press. pp. 192–212.

Cohen, Benjamin J. (2001) 'Beyond EMU: The Problem of Sustainability', in Barry Eichengreen and Jeffry Frieden (eds), *The Political Economy of European Monetary Unification*, 2nd edn. Boulder: Westview. pp. 179–204.

Cooper, Richard N. (1968) *The Economics of Interdependence.* New York: McGraw–Hill.

Cooper, Richard N. (1999) 'Should Capital Controls be Banished?', *Brookings Papers on Economic Activity*, 1: 89–141.

Cutler, A. Claire, Haufler, Virginia and Porter, Tony (eds) (1999) *Private Authority and International Affairs.* Albany: State University of New York Press.

Dombrowski, Peter (1998) 'Haute Finance and High Theory: Recent Scholarship on Global Financial Relations', *Mershon International Studies Review*, 42 (1): 1–28.

Edwards, Sebastian (1996) 'Exchange Rates and the Political Economy of Macroeconomic Discipline', *American Economic Review*, 86 (2): 159–63.

Edwards, Sebastian (1999a) 'The Choice of Exchange Rate Regime in Developing and Middle Income Countries', in Takatoshi Ito and Anne O. Krueger (eds), *Changes in Exchange Rates in Rapidly Developing Countries.* Chicago: University of Chicago Press. pp. 9–27.

Edwards, Sebastian (1999b) 'How Effective are Capital Controls?', *Journal of Economic Perspectives*, 13 (4): 65–84.

Eichengreen, Barry (1989) 'Hegemonic Stability Theories of the International Monetary System', in Richard N. Cooper, Barry Eichengreen, Gerald Holtham, Robert D. Putnam and C. Randall Henning (eds), *Can Nations Agree? Issues in International Economic Cooperation*. Washington, DC: Brookings Institution. pp. 255–98.

Frieden, Jeffry A. (1991) 'Invested Interests: The Politics of National Economic Policies in a World of Global Finance', *International Organization*, 45 (4): 425–52.

Frieden, Jeffry A. (1994) 'Exchange Rate Politics: Contemporary Lessons from American History', *Review of International Political Economy*, 1 (1): 81–103.

Frieden, Jeffry A. and Rogowski, Ronald (1996) 'The Impact of the International Economy on National Policies: An Analytical Overview', in Robert O. Keohane and Helen V. Milner (eds), *Internationalization and Domestic Politics*. New York: Cambridge University Press. pp. 25–47.

von Furstenberg, George M. (1998) 'From Worldwide Capital Mobility to International Financial Integration: A Review Essay', *Open Economies Review*, 9: 53–84.

Garrett, Geoffrey (1998) *Partisan Politics in the Global Economy*. New York: Cambridge University Press.

Garrett, Geoffrey (1999) 'Global Markets and National Politics: Collision Course or Virtuous Circle?', in Peter J. Katzenstein, Robert O. Keohane and Stephen D. Krasner (eds), *Exploration and Contestation in the Study of World Politics*. Cambridge, MA: MIT Press. pp. 147–84.

Garrett, Geoffrey (2001) 'The Politics of Maastricht', in Barry Eichengreen and Jeffry Frieden (eds), *The Political Economy of European Monetary Unification*, 2nd edn. Boulder: Westview. pp. 111–30.

Garrett, Geoffrey and Lange, Peter (1996) 'Internationalization, Institutions, and Political Change', in Robert O. Keohane and Helen V. Milner (eds), *Internationalization and Domestic Politics*. New York: Cambridge University Press. pp. 48–75.

Germain, Randall D. (1997) *The International Organization of Credit: States and Global Finance in the World-Economy*. New York: Cambridge University Press.

Gill, Stephen R. (1995) 'Globalisation, Market Civilisation and Disciplinary Neoliberalism', *Millennium*, 24 (3): 399–423.

Gill, Stephen R. and Law, David (1989) 'Global Hegemony and the Structural Power of Capital', *International Studies Quarterly*, 33 (4): 475–99.

Gilpin, Robert (1975) *US Power and the Multinational Corporation*. New York: Basic Books.

Gilpin, Robert (1987) *The Political Economy of International Relations*. Princeton: Princeton University Press.

Goodman, John B. and Pauly, Louis W. (1993) 'The Obsolescence of Capital Controls? Economic Management in an Age of Global Markets', *World Politics*, 46 (1): 50–82.

Gowa, Joanne (1983) *Closing the Gold Window: Domestic Politics and the End of Bretton Woods*. Princeton: Princeton University Press.

Gowa, Joanne (1984) 'Hegemons, IOs, and the Market: The Case of the Substitution Account', *International Organization*, 38 (4): 661–83.

Grieco, Joseph M. (1988) 'Anarchy and the Limits of Cooperation: A Realist Critique of the Newest Liberal Institutionalism', *International Organization*, 42 (3): 485–507.

Haggard, Stephan and Maxfield, Sylvia (1996) 'The Political Economy of Financial Internationalization in the Developing World', in Robert O. Keohane and Helen V. Milner (eds), *Internationalization and Domestic Politics*. New York: Cambridge University Press. pp. 209–39.

Hamada, Koichi (1985) *The Political Economy of International Monetary Interdependence*. Cambridge, MA: MIT Press.

Haufler, Virginia (1997) *Dangerous Commerce: Insurance and the Management of International Risk*. Ithaca: Cornell University Press.

Hefeker, Carsten (1997) *Interest Groups and Monetary Integration: The Political Economy of Exchange Regime Choice*. Boulder: Westview.

Helleiner, Eric (1994) *States and the Reemergence of Global Finance: From Bretton Woods to the 1990s*. Ithaca: Cornell University Press.

Helleiner, Eric (1996) 'Post-Globalization: Is the Financial Liberalization Trend Likely to be Reversed?', in Robert Boyer and Daniel Drache (eds), *States Against Markets: The Limits of Globalization*. New York: Routledge. pp. 193–210.

Helleiner, Eric (1999) 'Sovereignty, Territoriality, and the Globalization of Finance', in David A. Smith, Dorothy J. Solinger and Steven C. Topik (eds), *States and Sovereignty in the Global Economy*. London: Routledge. pp. 138–57.

Henning, C. Randall (1994) *Currencies and Politics in the United States, Germany, and Japan*. Washington, DC: Institute for International Economics.

Hewson, Martin and Sinclair, Timothy J. (1999) 'The Emergence of Global Governance Theory', in Martin Hewson and Timothy J. Sinclair (eds), *Approaches to Global Governance Theory*. Albany: State University of New York Press. pp. 3–22.

Iida, Keisuke (1999) *International Monetary Cooperation Among the United States, Japan, and Germany*. Boston: Kluwer Academic.

Ikenberry, G. John (1993) 'Creating Yesterday's New World Order: Keynesian "New Thinking" and the Anglo-American Postwar Settlement', in Judith Goldstein and Robert O. Keohane (eds), *Ideas and Foreign Policy: Beliefs, Institutions, and Political Change*. Ithaca: Cornell University Press. pp. 57–86.

Kahler, Miles (1995) *International Institutions and the Political Economy of Integration*. Washington, DC: Brookings Institution.

Kapstein, Ethan B. (1994) *Governing the Global Economy: International Finance and the State*. Cambridge, MA: Harvard University Press.

Kenen, Peter B. (1988) *Managing Exchange Rates.* New York: Council on Foreign Relations.

Kenen, Peter B. (1989) *Exchange Rates and Policy Coordination.* Ann Arbor: University of Michigan Press.

Keohane, Robert O. (1980) 'The Theory of Hegemonic Stability and Changes in International Economic Regimes, 1967–1977', in Ole R. Holsti, Randolph M. Siverson and Alexander L. George (eds), *Change in the International System.* Boulder: Westview. pp. 131–62.

Keohane, Robert O. (1984) *After Hegemony: Cooperation and Discord in the World Political Economy.* Princeton: Princeton University Press.

Kindleberger, Charles P. (1970) *Power and Money: The Politics of International Economics and the Economics of International Politics.* New York: Basic Books.

Kindleberger, Charles P. (1973) *The World in Depression, 1929–1939.* Berkeley and Los Angeles: University of California Press.

Kirshner, Jonathan (1995) *Currency and Coercion: The Political Economy of International Monetary Power.* Princeton: Princeton University Press.

Kirshner, Jonathan (1999) 'Keynes, Capital Mobility, and the Crisis of Embedded Liberalism', *Review of International Political Economy,* 6 (3): 313–37.

Kirshner, Jonathan (2000) 'The Study of Money', *World Politics,* 52 (3): 407–36.

Krasner, Stephen D. (1991) 'Global Communications and National Power: Life on the Pareto Frontier', *World Politics,* 43 (3): 336–66.

Krasner, Stephen D. (1999) *Sovereignty: Organized Hypocrisy.* Princeton: Princeton University Press.

Krugman, Paul (1993) *What Do We Need to Know about the International Monetary System?*, essay in International Finance 190. Princeton: International Finance Section.

Lake, David A. (1993) 'Leadership, Hegemony, and the International Economy: Naked Emperor or Tattered Monarch with Potential?', *International Studies Quarterly,* 37 (4): 459–89.

Leblang, David A. (1999) 'Domestic Political Institutions and Exchange Rate Commitments in the Developing World', *International Studies Quarterly,* 43 (4): 599–620.

Lukauskas, Arvid (1999) 'Managing Mobile Capital: Recent Scholarship on the Political Economy of International Finance', *Review of International Political Economy,* 6 (2): 262–87.

Marcussen, Martin (1999) 'The Dynamics of EMU Ideas', *Cooperation and Conflict,* 34 (4): 383–411.

Martin, Lisa L. and Simmons, Beth (1999) 'Theories and Empirical Studies of International Institutions', in Peter J. Katzenstein, Robert O. Keohane and Stephen D. Krasner (eds), *Exploration and Contestation in the Study of World Politics.* Cambridge, MA: MIT Press. pp. 89–117.

Maxfield, Sylvia (1997) *Gatekeepers of Growth: The International Political Economy of Central Banking in Developing Countries.* Princeton: Princeton University Press.

Maxfield, Sylvia (1998) 'Effects of International Portfolio Flows on Government Policy Choice', in Miles Kahler (ed.), *Capital Flows and Financial Crises.* Ithaca: Cornell University Press. pp. 69–92.

McNamara, Kathleen R. (1998) *The Currency of Ideas: Monetary Politics in the European Union.* Ithaca: Cornell University Press.

Meigs, A. James (1993) 'Eurodollars: A Transition Currency', *Cato Journal,* 12 (3): 711–27.

Milner, Helen V. (1992) 'International Theories of Cooperation among Nations: Strengths and Weaknesses', *World Politics,* 44 (3): 466–96.

Milner, Helen V. (1997) *Interests, Institutions, and Information: Domestic Politics and International Relations.* Princeton: Princeton University Press.

Milner, Helen V. (1999) 'Rationalizing Politics: The Emerging Synthesis of International, American, and Comparative Politics', in Peter J. Katzenstein, Robert O. Keohane and Stephen D. Krasner (eds), *Exploration and Contestation in the Study of World Politics.* Cambridge, MA: MIT Press. pp. 119–46.

Mosley, Layna (2000) 'Room to Move: Financial Markets and National Welfare States', *International Organization,* 54 (4): 737–73.

Oatley, Thomas H. (1997) *Monetary Politics: Exchange Rate Cooperation in the European Union.* Ann Arbor: University of Michigan Press.

Oatley, Thomas H. (1999) 'How Constraining is Mobile Capital? The Partisan Hypothesis in an Open Economy', *American Journal of Political Economy,* 43 (4): 1003–27.

Odell, John S. (1982) *US International Monetary Policy: Markets, Power, and Ideas as Sources of Change.* Princeton: Princeton University Press.

Oye, Kenneth A. (1986) 'The Sterling–Dollar–Franc Triangle: Monetary Diplomacy 1929–1937', in Kenneth A. Oye (ed.), *Cooperation Under Anarchy.* Princeton: Princeton University Press. pp. 173–99.

Pauly, Louis W. (1995) 'Capital Mobility, State Autonomy and Political Legitimacy', *Journal of International Affairs,* 48 (2): 369–88.

Pauly, Louis W. (1997) *Who Elected the Bankers? Surveillance and Control in the World Economy.* Ithaca: Cornell University Press.

Pauly, Louis W. (1999) 'Good Governance and Bad Policy: The Perils of International Organizational Overextension', *Review of International Political Economy,* 6 (4): 401–24.

Payer, Cheryl (1974) *The Debt Trap: The International Monetary Fund and the Third World.* New York: Monthly Review Press.

Porter, Tony (1993) *States, Markets, and Regimes in Global Finance.* New York: St Martin's Press.

Porter, Tony (1996) 'Capital Mobility and Currency Markets: Can They be Tamed?', *International Journal,* 51 (4): 669–89.

Putnam, Robert D. (1988) 'Diplomacy and Domestic Politics: The Logic of Two-Level Games', *International Organization,* 42 (3): 427–60.

Putnam, Robert D. and Henning, C. Randall (1989) 'The Bonn Summit of 1978: A Case Study in Coordination', in Richard N. Cooper, Barry Eichengreen, Gerald

Holtham, Robert D. Putham and C. Randall Henning (eds), *Can Nations Agree? Issues in International Economic Cooperation*. Washington, DC: Brookings Institution. pp. 12–140.

Quinn, Dennis (1997) 'The Correlates of Change in International Financial Regulation', *American Political Science Review*, 91 (3): 531–51.

Reinicke, Wolfgang H. (1998) *Global Public Policy: Governing without Government?* Washington, DC: Brookings Institution.

Rodrik, Dani (1997) *Has Globalization Gone Too Far?* Washington, DC: Institute for International Economics.

Rogoff, Kenneth (1985) 'Can International Monetary Policy Cooperation be Counterproductive?', *Journal of International Economics*, 18 (3/4): 199–217.

Rosenau, James N. and Czempiel, Ernst-Otto (eds) (1992) *Governance without Government: Order and Change in World Politics*. New York: Cambridge University Press.

Ruggie, John Gerard (1999) 'What Makes the World Hang Together? Neo-Utilitarianism and the Social Constructivist Challenge', in Peter J. Katzenstein, Robert O. Keohane and Stephen D. Krasner (eds), *Exploration and Contestation in the Study of World Politics*. Cambridge, MA: MIT Press. pp. 215–45.

Ruland, L.J. and Viaene, J.-M. (1993) 'The Political Choice of the Exchange Rate Regime', *Economics and Politics*, 5 (3): 271–84.

Simmons, Beth A. (1994) *Who Adjusts? Domestic Sources of Foreign Economic Policy During the Interwar Years*. Princeton: Princeton University Press.

Simmons, Beth A.(1999) 'The Internationalization of Capital', in Herbert Kitschelt, Peter Lange, Gary Marks and John D. Stephens (eds), *Continuity and Change in Contemporary Capitalism*. New York: Cambridge University Press. pp. 36–69.

Simmons, Beth A. (2000) 'The Legalization of International Monetary Affairs', *International Organization*, 54 (3): 573–602.

Sinclair, Timothy (1994a) 'Between State and Market: Hegemony and Institutions of Collective Action under Conditions of International Capital Mobility', *Policy Sciences*, 27 (4): 447–66.

Sinclair, Timothy (1994b) 'Passing Judgment: Credit Rating Processes as Regulatory Mechanisms of Governance in the Emerging World Order', *Review of International Political Economy*, 1 (1): 133–60.

Sobel, Andrew C. (1994) *Domestic Choices, International Markets: Dismantling National Barriers and Liberalizing Securities Markets*. Ann Arbor: University of Michigan Press.

Sobel, Andrew C. (1999) *State Institutions, Private Incentives, Global Capital*. Ann Arbor: University of Michigan Press.

Stein, Arthur A. (1990) *Why Nations Cooperate: Circumstance and Choice in International Relations*. Ithaca: Cornell University Press.

Stephan, Joerg (1994) *A Political-Economic Analysis of Exchange Rate Movements*. Konstanz: Hartung-Gorre Verlag.

Strange, Susan (1971) *Sterling and British Policy: A Political Study of a Currency in Decline*. London: Oxford University Press.

Strange, Susan (1976) 'International Monetary Relations', in Andrew Shonfield (ed.), *International Economic Relations of the Western World, 1959–1971*, vol. 2. London: Oxford University Press. pp. 18–359.

Strange, Susan (1986) *Casino Capitalism*. Oxford: Blackwell.

Strange, Susan ([1988] 1994) *States and Markets*, 2nd edn. London: Pinter.

Strange, Susan (1996) *The Retreat of the State: The Diffusion of Power in the World Economy*. Cambridge: Cambridge University Press.

Strange, Susan (1998) *Mad Money*. Manchester: Manchester University Press.

Thacker, Strom C. (1999) 'The High Politics of IMF Lending', *World Politics*, 52 (1): 38–75.

Underhill, Geoffrey R.D. (1995) 'Keeping Governments Out of Politics: Transnational Securities Markets, Regulatory Cooperation, and Political Legitimacy', *Review of International Studies*, 21: 251–78.

Underhill, Geoffrey R.D. (ed.) (1997) *The New World Order in International Finance*. London: Macmillan.

Underhill, Geoffrey R.D. (2000) 'Conceptualizing the Changing Global Order', in Richard Stubbs and Geoffrey R.D. Underhill (eds), *Political Economy and the Changing Global Order*. New York: Oxford University Press. pp. 3–24.

Waltz, Kenneth N. (1959) *Man, the State and War*. New York: Columbia University Press.

Waltz, Kenneth N. (1979) *Theory of International Politics*. Reading, MA: Addison–Wesley.

Watson, Alison M.S. (1997) 'The Politics of Exchange Rates: Domestic Politics and International Relations', *Review of International Political Economy*, 4 (4): 762–72.

Webb, Michael C. (1995) *The Political Economy of Policy Coordination: International Adjustment Since 1945*. Ithaca: Cornell University Press.

Willett, Thomas D. (1999) 'Developments in the Political Economy of Policy Coordination', *Open Economies Review*, 10: 221–53.

Willett, Thomas D. (2000) *International Financial Markets as Sources of Crises or Discipline: The Too Much, Too Late Hypothesis*. Princeton: International Finance Section.

23

International Trade

HELEN V. MILNER

International trade has become one of the most potent issues in both domestic and international politics these days. Under the rubric of globalization, international trade has become a contentious issue in domestic politics, as the recent WTO conference in Seattle showed. In international politics, trade is today a premiere instrument of statecraft, as witnessed by the US–China trade agreement and the EU's accession negotiations with the countries of East and Central Europe. How can we explain the trade policy choices that states make? What theories do we possess that illuminate the nature of countries' trade relations?

It is important to note that trade has become such a critical issue largely because countries' economies are now more than ever open to trade flows. This has occurred both because of technological changes as well as government policies. Since the 1970s countries across the globe have adopted freer trade policies. Many lesser developed countries, like Mexico, India, Poland, Turkey, Ghana and Morocco, have chosen to unilaterally liberalize their trade policies.[1] In addition, the successful conclusion in 1994 of the multilateral trade negotiations under the GATT (the Uruguay Round) further liberalized trade among many developed countries and between them and developing ones. This global 'rush to free trade', as Rodrik (1994) has called it, is important because it has helped further integrate countries into the world economy.[2] But it has also increased their exposure to the pressures of quickly changing global markets, thus upsetting domestic politics at times.

The scholarly literature on international trade is vast. Both economists and political scientists have contributed much to it, as recent surveys by economists such as Reizman and Wilson (1995) and

Rodrik (1995) and political scientists such as Cohen (1990) and Lake (1993) demonstrate. This chapter will focus more on the contributions of political scientists, but will include the research of economists where it is particularly important.

Much of the research by economists in international trade has dealt with topics that political scientists have not examined. By and large economists remain very interested in the three issues: the composition and direction of trade flows and the welfare effects of trade. Why certain countries import and export particular goods or services to certain other countries has been a central question for them. Much theory in international trade addresses this question; for instance, one of the central theorems in trade theory, the Heckscher–Ohlin one, explains trade flows. Economists have also devoted attention to the issue of trade barriers. The central theoretical conclusion of the field, of course, has been that free trade is the best policy for most countries most of the time. Thus economists have puzzled over why, given this finding, countries invariably employ at least some protectionist policies. They have tended to ask why countries protect certain of their industries, when free trade would be better economically. By and large their answer has focused on the preferences of domestic actors for protection. Using the Stolper–Samuelson theorem and other economic theories, they have explored why certain domestic groups would prefer protection and why they would expend resources to lobby for it. A large part of this debate involves whether specific-factors models of trade perform better than Stolper–Samuelson type models depending on factor endowments. This has resulted in a large empirical literature examining levels of protection across industries and recently in the development of models of such protection. Ultimately, then, economists have been pushed into studying the politics of trade. But a great deal of this literature explains why protectionist policies should never change, which is anomalous given the dramatic changes in trade we have seen (e.g., Drazen, 1996; Fernandez and Rodrik, 1991).

In contrast, political scientists have rarely focused on explaining the composition or pattern of trade flows, and they have been less concerned with the welfare consequences of trade. Only some recent work has explored the political roots of import and export flows among countries. But like economists they have been interested in the issue of protectionism. However, they have tended to see trade protection as more of the norm and have puzzled more over why a country would ever liberalize its trade policy or adopt free trade. Politically, protectionism seems eminently reasonable. Explaining both protectionist and free trade policies and changes in them over time have occupied political scientists.

There are at least four sets of factors that political scientists refer to when trying to understand trade politics. In this chapter I will survey how these four factors have been discussed in the literature. First, some focus on the *preferences* of domestic groups for protection or free trade. These scholars see trade policy as ultimately being shaped by the preferences of strongest groups in domestic politics. The questions of central import here are why do some groups favor protection, and some free trade. Do these preferences change over time? And if so, why? Which groups have a greater ability to have their preferences heard and translated into policy?

Second, political *institutions* may affect the formation of trade policy. Much as in the macroeconomic issue area where independent central banks are an important factor, political institutions may matter for trade. They may shape the ways in which the preferences of actors are translated into policy. They may affect which domestic groups have the most access and voice in policy-making. Generally, institutions may be important for aggregating preferences and implementing policy. Changes in institutions may provide a natural way to examine their impact.

Third, some claim that factors at the international level shape trade policy choices. The nature of relations among countries and the structure of the *international system* may affect domestic choices about trade. Hegemonic stability theory was an early structural theory of trade. Finally, some scholars have asked whether and how *international trade* itself affects states and the international political system. They use trade as an independent variable. The debate on globalization is especially relevant here. Some claim that rising trade flows produce important changes in domestic preferences, institutions and policies. The rest of this chapter asks how political scientists have addressed these four central issues about trade politics.

WHAT DO WE KNOW ABOUT TRADE AND TRADE POLICY?[3]

Since the Second World War, the main instrument of trade policy, tariffs (which are taxes on imports), among advanced industrial countries have been reduced to insignificant levels. After the latest round of international trade negotiations sponsored by the GATT – the Uruguay Round, completed in 1994 – the average tariff for the developed countries was reduced from 6.3 per cent to 3.8 per cent (World Trade Organization, 1996: 31). Non-tariff barriers (NTBs), which include quantitative restrictions, price controls, subsidies, voluntary export restraints (VERs), etc., on the other hand, have proliferated, in part countering the decline in tariffs. But again the Uruguay Round slowed or reversed this, helping to reduce quotas, subsidies and VERs across a wide range of industries and to convert these barriers into more transparent tariffs (World Trade Organization, 1996: 32). Nevertheless, while tariffs have declined for advanced industrial countries, NTBs still make up an important arsenal of barriers to trade. For these countries close to 20 per cent of all categories of imports are subject to some form of NTBs (Laird and Yeats, 1990).

For most of the postwar period, LDCs have used trade barriers extensively, many for the explicit purpose of import-substituting industrialization (ISI). But from the late 1970s, many developing countries began to liberalize trade and adopt an outward, export-orientation (International Monetary Fund, 1992). The conclusion of the Uruguay Round promoted this by reducing trade barriers in many areas of key interest to the LDCs, such as textiles and agriculture; it also brought many new developing countries into the international trade organization, the WTO (World Trade Organization), inducing them to follow its rules. In addition, the transition from command or communist economies to market-based ones by many countries in the 1990s further accelerated the trend toward trade liberalization globally. All of these changes have resulted in one striking fact about the period since 1980: there has been a far-reaching liberalization of trade barriers across the globe (Rodrik, 1994, World Trade Organization, 1996).

Concomitantly and in part a product of this, the growth of world trade has surged. For most of postwar period, the growth of trade has outpaced growth in world output. Also important are changes in the nature of global trade: there has been tremendous growth in intra-industry trade (IIT) and in intra-firm trade (IFT). IIT, which involves the exchange of goods from within the same industry, say Toyotas for BMWs, now accounts for between 55 and 75 per cent of trade in advanced industrial countries (Greenaway and Milner, 1986: Table 5–3); for the United States, this figure was 83 per cent in

1990 (Bergsten and Noland, 1993: 66). IFT, which involves transfers of goods within one company across national boundaries, has also grown; it now accounts for over 40 per cent of total US imports and 30 per cent of US exports (Encarnation, 1992: 28). These two types of trade are important because they tend to have different effects than standard, inter-industry trade. Generally, they are associated with fewer displacement effects and less conflict. As Lipson (1982: 453) argues, 'intra-industry trade provides a powerful new source of multilateral interest in the liberal trade regime: diminished adjustment costs in some sectors, and higher net gains from trade as a result.'

Finally, there has been a significant regionalization of trade. Intraregional trade flows within the European Union, East Asia, North America and Latin America especially have become more important as a share of total trade. This is partially a result of the regional integration agreements signed by these countries in the past two decades – for example, the single market in Europe, NAFTA, ASEAN, APEC and Mercosur (WTO, 1996: 17–22). Also indicative of regionalism's growth are the increasing rates at which preferential trade agreements (PTAs) formed and states joined them throughout the post-Second World War period (Mansfield, 1998). The number of regional agreements notified to the General Agreement on Tariffs and Trade (GATT) from 1948 to 1994 has waxed and waned. Few PTAs were established during the 1940s and 1950s; then a surge in preferential agreements occurred in the 1960s and 1970s, and the incidence of PTA creation again tailed off in the 1980s (de Melo and Panagariya, 1993: 3). But there has been a significant rise in such agreements during the 1990s; and more than 50 per cent of all world commerce is currently conducted within regional trade arrangements (Serra et al., 1997: 8). Indeed, PTAs have become so pervasive that all but a few parties to the WTO now belong to at least one (World Trade Organization, 1996: 38). This regionalization of the trading system has been treated as evidence both of increasing protectionism and of increasing liberalization. The key issue is whether these agreements, which lower barriers between participants, also lower barriers with non-members. If so, then they might foster greater trade liberalization globally; if not, then they may be a force for undermining the integrated world economy, creating exclusive trading blocs.

TRADE POLICY PREFERENCES AND DOMESTIC POLITICS

Some of the earliest models explaining trade policy have focused on 'pressure group politics'. That is, they explain the trade policy choices by governments as a function of the demands made by domestic interest groups. Domestic groups seek protection or liberalization because such policies increase their incomes. The distributional consequences of trade policy thus become the explanation for its causes. Adam Smith ([1776] 1937) may have been one of the first to recognize this, when he noted that the subversion of the national interest in free trade is the frequent outcome of collusion among businessmen. Schattschneider (1935) was another early proponent of the view that special economic interests were mainly responsible for the choice of protectionism; he showed how these pressure groups hijacked the American Congress in 1929–30 and via a logroll produced one of the highest tariffs ever in American history, the Smoot–Hawley tariff.

Since then, development of the pressure group model has attempted to delineate more specifically the groups who should favor and oppose protection and the conditions under which they may be most influential. One motive for this has been the observation that the extent of protection and the demands for it vary both across industries and across countries. If all domestic groups always favored protection, then such variance should not exist. Explaining this variance has been a key feature of the literature. It has depended on theories about two factors: the sources of trade policy preferences and the nature of political influence of these interest groups.

The former area has been a more prolific research topic and a highly divisive one. The main divide over the sources of trade policy preferences has been between so-called factoral versus sectoral (or firm-based) theories of preferences. In both cases, preferences are deduced as a result of the changes in income that accrue to different actors when policy changes from free trade to protection or vice versa. These types of theories focus on the distributional effects of trade; they associate preferences for protection with those who lose (income or assets) from greater trade flows and preferences for liberalization with those who gain. Factoral theories rely on the Stopler–Samuelson theorem, which shows that when factors of production, like labor and capital, can move freely among sectors, a change from free trade to protection will raise the income of factors in which a country is relatively scarce and lower it for factors that are relatively abundant. Thus scarce factors will support protection, while abundant ones will oppose it. Rogowski (1989) has developed one of the most interesting political extensions of this, claiming that increasing (decreasing) exposure to trade sets off either increasing class conflict or urban–rural conflict according to the factor endowments of different countries.

In contrast, sectoral and firm-based theories of trade preferences follow from the Ricardo–Viner model of trade – also called the specific-factors model. This model claims that because at least one factor is immobile, all factors attached to import-competing sectors lose from trade liberalization while those in export-oriented sectors gain. Conflict over trade policy thus pits labor, capital and landowners in sectors besieged by imports against those who export their production. How tied factors are to their sectors – that is, the degree of factor specificity – is the key difference between these two models (Alt et al., 1996).

A number of studies have tested these two models, sometimes singly and sometimes simultaneously. Frieden (1990), Irwin (1994, 1996), Magee, Brock and Young (1989), have found evidence in support of the specific-factors model; in contrast, Balestreri (1997), Beaulieu (1996), Midford (1993), Rogowski (1989) and Scheve and Slaughter (1998) find support for the Stolper–Samuelson type factoral models. Despite such differences, most agree that domestic pressures from industry and labor play a significant role in both increasing protection and in preventing it (e.g., Milner, 1988).

In addition to these models of trade preferences, others have looked at how particular characteristics of industries affect patterns of protection. Anderson (1980), Baldwin (1986), Caves (1976), Marvel and Ray (1983), Pincus (1975), Ray (1981) and Trefler (1993) have shown how specific characteristics make an industry more likely not only to desire protection but also to be able to induce policy-makers to provide it. These regression analyses tend to straddle the debate between sectoral and factoral models of trade politics. Their comparison across industries suggests a sectoral type of model, but many of their findings do not disagree with those resulting from a more factoral view of the world. For example, they tend to demonstrate that in advanced industrial countries low-skill, labor-intensive industries with high and rising import penetration are frequently associated with high protection. In addition, many have shown that export-oriented industries and multinationals tend to favor freer trade and be associated with less protection (Milner, 1988). This attention to anti-protectionist groups is particularly interesting given the global move toward trade liberalization; one question is whether this movement has been due to the growth in importance of these types of groups domestically.

Can these models of societal preferences explain trade policy? As noted above, many of these theories are fairly good at explaining variance across industries in any one country. But in terms of explaining overall directions in national trade policy and crossnational differences these theories have a number of weaknesses. First, they have no theory of how preferences are aggregated at any level, let alone the national one. If firms in an industry are divided over trade policy, how does the sector choose a policy to advocate? If some industries are opposed to liberalization and some support it, how can we predict whether political leaders will

agree to international negotiations to reduce trade barriers? The issue of which groups are able to influence policy and which are not depends much on political factors, such as the clout of the industry or how institutions shape its access to policy-makers. Second, might not these differences in preferences give policy-makers a great deal of leeway to implement their own preferred policies, thus weakening the influence of interest groups? Political leaders could simply pick and choose the groups that they wanted to 'represent' and then build coalitions around their own preferences, rather than being driven by industry pressures. The literature on interest groups in trade policy-making continues to wrestle with these issues.

The preferences of other domestic actors have also been the focus of some attention. Many assume that individual voters take their preferences from their role as consumers. Since consumers gain from free trade, they should favor it (e.g., Grossman and Helpman, 1994). Other models of individual preferences contradict this. Mayer (1984), for example, introduces an electoral component into the determination of trade policy. Trade policy is determined by the median voter's preferences, which depend on that voter's factor endowments. The more well endowed he (or she) is in the factor used intensively for production of import-competing goods, the more protectionist he will be. Scheve and Slaughter (1998) add a new component by asking how asset-ownership is affected by trade policy. They show that the preferences of individual voters will depend on how trade affects their assets. Individuals living in regions with a high concentration of import-competing industries will be more favorable to protection because as imports rise economic activity in the region will fall causing their housing assets to fall in value. Some surveys have also shown that voters respond positively toward protection out of sympathy for workers who lose their jobs because of import competition. Thus, whether individual voters favor protection or free trade is an area demanding further research, especially in democracies where elections are often linked to trade policy decisions. Moreover, understanding changes in these preferences may help us account for the recent push to liberalize trade.

A number of scholars have argued that the preferences of interest groups and voters are less important in determining trade policy than are those of the policy-makers themselves. Bauer, Pool and Dexter (1972) were among the first to make this point. From their surveys, they showed that constituents rarely had strong preferences about trade policy and even more rarely communicated these to their political representatives. Trade policy depended much on the personal preferences and ideas of politicians. Baldwin (1986) and Goldstein (1988) have also argued that it is the ideas that policy-makers have about trade policy that matter most. Rather than material factors determining preferences, ideational ones are paramount. Interestingly, Krueger (1997), an economist, claims that it is ideas that have mattered most in trade policy-making in the lesser developed countries lately. She argues that it is 'ideas with regard to trade policy and economic development [that] are among those [factors] that have changed most radically' from 1950 to the 1990s, helping to explain the recent rush to free trade. Many suggest that the failures of ISI policy and the glaring success of the export-oriented newly industrializing Asian countries in the 1980s forced policy-makers to adopt new ideas about trade policy. A key example of this is Fernando Henrique Cardoso, who co-authored one of the most important books in dependency theory in the 1970s, arguing for the continuation of ISI policies to shelter LDCs from the capitalist world economy (Cardoso and Faletto, 1979). In the 1990s, of course, Cardoso was elected president of Brazil and initiated a major economic reform program, including extensive trade liberalization. Changes in the ideas that policy-makers have about trade policy may then, as this example suggests, play a large role in affecting trade policy choices.

Economic conditions may also affect the preferences of actors and lead to changes in trade policies. While Krueger and others, such as Bates and Krueger (1993), Haggard and Kaufman (1995), and Rodrik (1995), attribute leaders' decisions to initiate trade policy reform to crises and economic downturns, another strand of literature on the macroeconomics of trade policy concludes in the opposite direction. For many scholars, bad economic times are a prelude to rising demands for protection and increasing levels of protection. Cassing, McKeown and Ochs (1986), Gallarotti (1985), Magee and Young (1987), Takacs (1981) and Wallerstein (1987) all find that declines in economic growth or capacity utilization and/or increases in unemployment and imports tend to increase the demand and supply of protection. This earlier literature then sees policy-makers responding increasingly to the rising demands for protection from domestic groups in bad economic times.

The more recent literature, however, implies that bad economic times allow policy-makers more freedom to maneuver, so that they can overturn existing protectionist policies by blaming them for the bad times. For example, Rodrik (1992: 88–9) notes that

It is paradoxical that the 1980s should have become the decade of trade liberalization in the developing countries. Thanks to the debt crisis, the 1980s have also been a decade of intense macroeconomic instability. Common sense would suggest that the conventional benefits of liberalization become muted, if not completely offset, under conditions of macro instability.

But he (1992: 89) claims that 'a time of crisis occasionally enables radical reforms that would have been unthinkable in calmer times'. He argues that the prolonged macroeconomic crises of the 1980s were so bad that 'the overall gain from restoring the economy's health [in part via trade liberalization] became so large that it swamped distributional considerations [raised by such reforms]' (1994: 79).

On the other hand, others, especially Haggard (1995), have argued that crises reduce the room for maneuver of political leaders. They suggest that in the 1980s these leaders were almost forced to liberalize trade (and make other reforms) because of the lack of options and international pressures. Noting the difference between the 1930s and 1980s crises, Haggard (1995: 16–19) points out that

why external shocks and corresponding macroeconomic policy adjustments might also be associated with trade and investment liberalization … is puzzling. In the 1930s, balance of payments and debt crises spurred the substitution of imports … and gave rise to a more autarchic and interventionist policy stance. In the 1980s, by contrast, an inward-looking policy seemed foreclosed. … The opportunities for continued import substitution were limited, and ties to the world economy had become more varied, complex and difficult to sever.

The effect of economic crises on a country's decisions to liberalize trade thus seems contingent on a number of other factors, such as the prevailing ideas about trade, the extent of openness existing at the time and the influence of international factors.

A similar debate exists concerning the impact of the exchange rate on trade policy. Appreciation of the exchange rate may increase protectionist pressures because it increases imports and decreases exports, thus affecting the balance of trade preferences domestically (Mansfield and Busch, 1995). Others suggest that the effects of an exchange rate change may have little impact. For instance, Rodrik (1994: 73) shows that a devaluation, which is the opposite of an appreciation, increases the domestic price of all tradables – imports and exports, thereby allowing both import-competing and export-oriented sectors to benefit. But under certain conditions – for example, when foreign exchange is rationed, devaluations can work just like trade liberalization, prompting demands for new protection from import-competing sectors. Some studies reveal such an association between periods of currency devaluations and rising tariffs; Simmons (1994) points out that many of the same conditions – but not all – that drove states to devalue also pushed them to increase tariffs in the interwar period. Both policies were intended to increase demand for domestic output, thus counteracting the effects of the depression. Much debate continues over the macroeconomic conditions that produce increasing domestic pressures for protection and/or that induce policy-makers to relent to or resist such pressures.

Can these preference-based theories explain trade policy? These theories seem best at explaining the domestic sources of opposition to and support for trade liberalization. The role of interest groups, voters and policy-makers are obviously important in sketching the domestic politics of trade. But how far can these theories go? Without a concomitant theory of which groups are able to organize and exert influence, theories about interest groups and voters are best able to explain the demand for trade policy domestically. The preferences of policy-makers may play a different role. They may be more likely to explain the supply-side of trade policy; that is, they may indicate the willingness of political leaders to supply protection or liberalization, as separate from the demand for it. But our models of such preferences seem the most under-specified and *post hoc*. Why are some policy-makers more favorable to protectionism than others? Why and when do their preferences change? Theories about the conditions under which policy-makers will abandon ideas that produce 'bad' results and what ideas they will adopt in their stead are largely unavailable. In sum, theories of trade preferences seem to provide an initial level of explanation for the supply and demand for trade policy. But they cannot as of yet provide a complete explanation of this process.

POLITICAL INSTITUTIONS

Can theories that focus on political institutions do better at explaining trade policy-making? A number of scholars have argued that political institutions, rather than preferences, play a major role in explaining trade policy. While preferences play a role in these arguments, the main claim is that institutions aggregate such preferences. Different institutions do so differently, thus leading to distinct policies. Understanding institutions is necessary to explain the actual supply of protection, rather than simply its demand (Nelson, 1988). On the domestic side, different institutions empower different actors. Some institutions, for example, tend to give special interest groups greater access to policy-makers, rendering their demands harder to resist. For example, many believe that the fact that the US Congress controlled trade policy exclusively before 1934 made it very susceptible to protectionist pressures from interest groups (Baldwin, 1986; Destler, 1986; Goldstein, 1993; Haggard, 1988).

Other institutions insulate policy-makers from these demands, allowing them more leeway in setting policy. Thus, some argue that giving the executive branch greater control over trade after the Reciprocal Trade Act of 1934 made trade policy less susceptible to these influences and more free trade-oriented. In general, concentrating trade policy-making capabilities in the executive's hands seems to be associated with the adoption of trade

liberalization in a wide variety of countries (e.g., Haggard and Kaufman, 1995: 199). As Haggard and Webb (1994: 13) have noted about trade liberalization in numerous LDCs, 'In every successful reform effort, politicians delegated decisionmaking authority to units within the government that were insulated from routine bureaucratic processes, from legislative and interest group pressures, and even from executive pressure'.

Other aspects of political regimes may make them more or less insulated from societal pressures. Rogowski (1987), for example, has argued that policy-makers should be most insulated from domestic pressures for protection in countries having large electoral districts and proportional representation (PR) systems. Mansfield and Busch (1995), however, find that such institutional insulation does indeed matter, but often in exactly the opposite direction: greater insulation (that is, larger districts and a PR system) leads to more protection. Similarly, Rodrik (1998) shows that 'political regimes with lower executive autonomy and more participatory institutions handle exogenous shocks better', and this may include their response to shocks via trade policy. Thus it is not clear that greater insulation of policy-makers always produces policies that promote trade liberalization; the preferences of those policy-makers also matter.

The administrative capacity of the state is also seen as an important factor shaping trade policy. It is well-established that developed countries tend to have fewer trade barriers than do lesser developed countries (Conybeare, 1982, 1983; International Monetary Fund, 1992; Magee et al., 1989: 230–41; Rodrik, 1995: 1483). Part of the reason is that taxes on trade are fairly easy to collect and thus in LDCs where the apparatus of the state is less well developed such taxes may account for a substantial portion of total state revenues (between a quarter and a half, according to Rodrik, 1994: 77). As countries develop, their institutional capacity may also grow, thus reducing their need to depend on import taxes for revenue.[4] Thus the introduction of the personal income tax in 1913 in the United States made trade taxes much less important for the government, thereby permitting their later reduction. Hence political institutions and changes in them may help explain trade policy.

Large institutional differences in countries' political regime types also may be associated with different trade policy profiles. Some have argued that democratic countries are less likely to be able to pursue protectionist policies. Wintrobe (1998) claims that autocratic countries will be more rent-seeking, and protection is simply one form of rent-seeking. Mansfield, Milner and Rosendorff (1998, 2000) also show that democratic pairs of countries tend to be less protectionist and more likely to sign trade liberalizing agreements than are autocratic ones. Many of the countries that have embraced trade liberalization have also democratized. Mexico is a prime case here. The growth of political competition and the decline of the hegemonic status of the governing party, the PRI, seem to have gone hand-in-hand with the liberalization of trade policy beginning in the 1980s.

In contrast, others point out that trade reform in many LDCs occurred before the transition to democracy and was often more successful when it did occur this way (Haggard and Webb, 1994). Chile, Turkey, Taiwan and South Korea all began their trade liberalization processes before their democratic transitions. Rodrik argues more generally that any change in political regime is likely to induce trade reforms: 'Historically sharp changes in trade policy have almost always been preceded (or accompanied) by changes in the political regime. ... Not all political transformations result in trade reform, but sharp changes in trade policy are typically the result of such transformations' (Rodrik, 1994: 69). None the less, Milner and Kubota (2001) find evidence that democracy in general and democratization have contributed to the lowering of trade barriers in a number of LDCs since the 1970s. Thus it may be that the character of political regimes has a direct effect on trade policy choices.

On the other hand, Verdier (1998) argues that because of the political conflict engendered by trade, democracies may be less likely to pursue free trade and more likely to adopt protection against each other, except when intra-industry trade dominates their trade flows.

> The postwar democratic convergence among OECD countries did not hurt trade because similarity in endowments, combined with the presence of scale economies, allowed these countries to engage in intra-industry trade – a form of trade with few, if any, wealth effects ... The current wave of democratization endangers trade. Only in the presence of scale economies [and thus intra-industry trade] can democratic convergence sustain trade. (Verdier, 1998: 18–19)

Haggard and Kaufmann (1995) are more circumspect, arguing that the presence of crises and the form of autocracy may have more to do with the ability to adopt economic reforms, like trade liberalization, than does regime type alone. Debates over the impact of regime type on trade policy have just begun.

The structure of the government and the nature of the party system have also been seen as an important institutional factor shaping trade policy. Parties very often take specific stands on trade policy, and their movement in and out of government may explain trade policy changes, as many have contended about the United States (e.g., Epstein and O'Halloran, 1996). In general, partisanship as a source of trade policy had been unexplored except in the United States. But theory suggests that partisanship and the nature of the political party system may matter greatly. For example, countries with highly polarized party systems, in which the main parties are separated by large ideological differences, may experience dramatic swings in policy and generally produce unsustainable trade reforms. On the other hand, countries with large numbers of parties may experience coalition governments frequently, which may be unable to change the status quo. Haggard and Kaufman (1995: 170) predict that countries with fragmented and/or polarized party systems will be unable to initiate economic policy reforms, including trade liberalization, let alone to sustain them. In general, these perspectives suggest that fragmented political systems are similar to ones with many veto players, and like them are resistant to change (Tsebelis, 1995).

Party systems also interact with the structure of the government. For example, Lohmann and O'Halloran (1994) and O'Halloran (1994) have argued that when government in presidential systems, like the United States, is divided – that is, one party controls the legislature and the other controls the executive branch – protectionism is likely to be higher. Milner and Rosendorff (1996) also argue that divided government in any country is likely to make the lowering of trade barriers either domestically or internationally harder in most cases. In sum, 'political systems with weak executives and fragmented party systems, divided government, and decentralized political structures responded poorly to crises' and were unable to mobilize the support necessary for the initiation of economic reforms, like trade liberalization (Haggard and Kaufman, 1995: 378). In all of these cases, however, the trade policy preferences of the parties matter for the outcome. Political institutions tend to affect whose preferences will become dominant in policy-making.[5]

Many of these institutional arguments thus depend on prior claims about actors' preferences. For instance, many of the arguments about insulation assume that the policy-makers (usually executives) who are insulated from societal demands are free traders. But as Mansfield and Busch (1995) show they may actually be protectionist, in which case insulation allows greater protection than otherwise. The arguments about divided government, party systems and democracies also rest to some extent on assumptions about each actor's preferences. Divided government matters most when preferences of the parties differ, and differences in the preferences of autocratic leaders and democratic ones may be important for the implications of different regime types. Thus having theories that bring together both preferences and institutions seems most valuable, since we know that both matter. Very few studies, however, try to bring together theories of both preference formation and institutional influence; Gilligan (1997) and Milner (1997) are examples. Moreover, the matter of which comes first, preferences or institutions, is far from settled. Those who focus on preferences tend to argue that institutions are often shaped by the preferences of those in power; in contrast, those who emphasize institutions argue that they may actually shape actors' preferences. The growing consensus is that both matter and are jointly determined, but parsimoniously modeling and testing this is an area for future research.

INTERNATIONAL POLITICS

Trade policy is not just affected by domestic forces. A number of factors about the international system have been connected to a country's trade policy choices. A favored argument among realists has been that the distribution of capabilities in the international system has a fundamental effect on trade. The so-called theory of hegemonic stability (HST) posited that when the international system or economy was dominated by one country, a hegemon, then free trade would be most likely (Gilpin, 1987; Gowa, 1994; Krasner, 1976; Lake, 1988). A large number of critics have challenged this claim both theoretically and empirically (Lake, 1993; Keohane, 1998). Conybeare (1984) has shown that large countries should favor optimal tariffs, not free trade, even if others retaliate; Snidal (1985) and others have claimed that small numbers of powerful countries could maintain an open system, just as well as a single hegemon could. The theory has also faced empirical challenges that imply that a hegemon is neither necessary nor sufficient for an open trading system (e.g., Krasner, 1976; Mansfield, 1994). In light of these results, the theory has been modified as scholars examine more closely the dynamics of interaction among countries in the trading system.

Perhaps the most interesting point about this theory is that it has tried to explain change over time in the overall level of openness in the trading system; that is, it looks at the sum of countries' trade policy choices. The main claim of this theory is that changes in the distribution of capabilities over time should provide clues to changes in the openness of the international trading system. In the 1980s, many argued that the decline of American hegemony from its zenith after the Second World War would lead to a rise in protectionism and perhaps the fragmentation of the international economy into rival blocs (e.g., Gilpin, 1987). This prediction, however, would not seem to explain well the rush to free trade witnessed since the mid-1980s.

One possible retort, however, is that US hegemony has risen, not declined, since 1980, as Russett (1985) and Strange (1987) have argued. Thus the renewal of American preeminence in the international system explains the turn away from protectionism. This type of argument would fit well with a broader claim about the dominance of American ideas about free markets and trade, and their impact on other countries' trade policy choices. After all, the package of market-oriented reforms including trade liberalization that have been proposed for the LDCs and ex-communist countries is called the 'Washington consensus'. Others have also argued that American hegemony matters, but more through the direct pressure it may exert on lesser developed countries. Haggard (1995), for example, argues that changes in United States trade policy in the 1980s help explain the move toward free trade. The United States began exerting strong bilateral pressure on LDCs to liberalize their economies or face closure of the American market to their exports. American hegemony and its renewed will to exert influence may help explain recent changes in trade policy.

Other scholars have felt that aspects of the international security environment best explain the pattern of trade. Gowa (1994) has argued that countries which are military allies trade more with each other, and that is especially the case for those within the same alliance in the bipolar system. That is, when countries are allies in a system featuring one other major opposing alliance group, such as that during the Cold War, they will tend to trade the most freely among themselves. The security externalities of trade will drive their behavior, inducing them to help their allies while also punishing their enemies. Gowa and Mansfield (1993) and Mansfield and Bronson (1997) provide strong evidence for this effect. In terms of this argument, there should be a direct link between trade policy and the end of the Cold War and the dissolution of the Eastern bloc. Predictions from this model seem to be incomplete. The argument appears to suggest that protectionism should rise, not decline, with the demise of bipolarity and the emergence of multipolarity. A description of the current structure of the international system might be one of either multipolarity, or unipolarity, in which case the theory seems to have no single prediction.

Another aspect of the international system that scholars have noted for its effect on trade policy is the presence and influence of international institutions. Although a long debate has occurred over whether international institutions matter, many scholars now conclude that the fact that countries have been willing to set up and participate in such institutions would seem to imply that states feel that they matter (e.g., Keohane, 1984; Ruggie, 1983). In the trade area, a number of institutions provide support for an open, multilateral trading system; these include the GATT and its successor the WTO, as well as the International Monetary Fund (IMF) and World Bank. While regional trade institutions may have a more ambiguous effect on the multilateral system (Mansfield and Milner, 1999), some of them, including the EU, NAFTA and ASEAN, seem to have positive effects on lowering trade barriers and reinforcing unilateral moves toward freer trade.

These institutions are postulated to have a number of different effects on countries' trade policy choices. Some suggest that their main role is to provide information about other countries' behavior and compliance with the rules of the game (e.g., Keohane, 1984). Others see these institutions as providing a forum for dispute resolution so that partners in trade can feel more secure and thus more likely to trade (e.g., Yarbrough and Yarbrough, 1992). Others view such international institutions as encapsulating the norms by which countries agree to play the trading game, which again provides a common framework for sustaining trade flows (e.g., Ruggie, 1983). All of these arguments hypothesize that the presence of these institutions should be associated with a freer trade environment; moreover, they imply that the depth and breadth of these institutions should be positively related to trade liberalization and the expansion of trade.

Certainly the presence of institutions like the GATT and IMF have added leverage to arguments for trade liberalization; the IMF and World Bank have for instance often made loans conditional on trade policy reform. Some have argued that when countries are in severe economic crisis and need external financing, then these institutions may be especially powerful. As Rodrik (1992: 89) points out, 'The 1980s were a decade of great leverage for these institutions [i.e., the IMF and World Bank] vis-à-vis debtor governments, especially where poorer African governments are concerned. The trade policy recommendations of the World Bank were adopted by cash-starved governments frequently with little conviction of their ultimate benefits.' Others tend to argue that international institutions help lock in such domestic reforms. For example, Mexican unilateral trade liberalization seems much more secure now that Mexico is part of NAFTA and the WTO.

Finally, the creation of the WTO out of the GATT Uruguay Round represents a step toward the deeper institutionalization of an open trading system. The influence of these international institutions may depend either on the economic condition of debtors or on changing domestic preferences and ideas about trade. While there is little doubt that these institutions helped support trade liberalization globally, it seems likely that their influence varies over time and across countries (Haggard and Kaufman, 1995: 199). But, as with domestic political factors, these institutions may be an important element of the trade policy-making environment.

EFFECT OF TRADE ON COUNTRIES AND THE INTERNATIONAL SYSTEM

A final area of interest in the political economy of trade policy is the reciprocal effect of international trade on domestic and international politics. Once countries have liberalized or protected their economies, what might be the subsequent effects of such choices? Scholars have examined this question with attention to at least three aspects of the domestic political economy. First, some have argued that trade liberalization can in its wake change domestic preferences about trade. As countries liberalize, the tradables sector of the economy should grow in size along with exposure to international economic pressures. Rogowski (1989) has argued that this should lead to heightened or new political cleavages and conflicts between scarce and abundant factors domestically. These new cleavages in turn will alter domestic politics, as for example new parties arise to represent these groups or new coalitions form. Milner (1988) also argues that increasing openness to trade changes preferences domestically. Openness raises the potential number of supporters of free trade as exporters and multinational firms multiply; it may also reduce import-competing firms as they succumb to foreign competition. Hathaway (1998) presents a dynamic model that shows that trade liberalization changes industry structure in ways so that future demands for protection are reduced. 'Trade liberalization has a positive feedback effect on policy preferences and political strategies of domestic producer groups. As industries adjust to more competitive market conditions, their characteristics change in ways that reduce the likelihood that they will demand protection in the future' (1998: 606). James and Lake (1989) suggest an ingenious argument about how repeal of the protectionist Corn Laws in the UK created the necessary conditions for the creation of a successful coalition for free trade in the United States. Each of these arguments in distinct ways suggests that increasing exposure to trade leads to increasing pressure against protection, thus creating a virtuous cycle of rising demand for freer trade. As an explanation for trade policy in the advanced industrial countries over the past few decades, this type of argument seems plausible since these countries were increasingly exposed to trade. For the developing countries, their abrupt rejection of ISI and protectionism seems less explicable in these terms.

A second aspect of domestic politics that may be affected by increased trade flows involves the character of national political institutions. Among the advanced industrial countries, Cameron (1978) long ago noted the relationship between those that were very open to international trade and those with large governments. He and Katzenstein (1985) attributed this to the need for governments with open economies to provide extensive domestic compensation to the losers from trade and to employ flexible adjustment strategies for their industries. Rodrik (1997) has found strong evidence of this relationship around the globe. He claims that greater exposure to external risk, which trade promotes, increases the volatility of the domestic economy and thus that 'societies that expose themselves to greater amounts of external risk demand (and receive) a larger government role as shelter from the vicissitudes of global markets' (1997: 53). Increasing exposure to international trade may thus create demands for more government intervention and a larger welfare state, which in turn are necessary to sustain public support for an open economy.[6]

Rogowski (1987: 212) has argued that as countries become more open to trade, they will find it increasingly advantageous to devise institutions that maximize 'the state's insulation, autonomy and stability'. For him, this implies parliamentary systems with strong parties, proportional representation (PR) and large districts. He finds a strong relationship especially between openness and PR systems. Hadenius (1992) also finds that trade may have effects on domestic institutions. He argues that exposure to international trade brings higher rates of economic growth, which through the development process may translate into better conditions for the emergence of democracy. Thus trade liberalization may over time foster conditions conducive to political liberalization. This again suggests a virtuous cycle: trade liberalization fosters democratization and democracy in turn may promote more trade liberalization, and so on.

Besides its effects on preferences and institutions, trade may constrain the policy choices available to decision-makers. The recent literature on internationalization, or globalization, suggests this constraining influence. Rodrik (1997) provides some of the most direct evidence of how greater openness may force governments to relinquish the use of various policy instruments. In particular, he notes that openness often makes governments cut spending on social programs and reduce taxes on capital. In order to maintain competitiveness, governments are prevented from using many of the fiscal policy measures they once could.[7] Whether such constraints are good or bad depends on the value one places on government intervention in the economy. For some, like Rodrik (1997), this constraint is worrisome since it reduces the government's ability to shelter its citizens from external volatility and thus may erode the public's support for openness. Here the impact of trade liberalization may not be benign. It may produce a backlash, undermining societal support for openness and creating pressures for protection and closure.

In terms of international politics, trade liberalization may also have important effects. As countries become more open to the international economy, it may affect their political relations with other countries. In particular, scholars have asked whether increased trade promotes peace between countries or increases their chances of conflict. A number of scholars, such as Polachek (1980), Gasioworski (1986) and Russett, Oneal and Davis (1998), have found that increases in trade flows among countries (or between pairs of them) decrease the chances that those countries will be involved in political or military conflicts with each other. Others such as Waltz (1979) and Barbieri (1996) argue that increased trade and the interdependence it creates either increase conflict or have little effect on it. One way that trade policy might affect the international political system then is by increasing or decreasing the level of political-military conflicts. There are a variety of different feedback mechanisms that might exist. For instance, if trade promotes pacific relations among trading nations, then such a pacific environment is likely to stimulate further trade liberalization and flows; on the other hand, if increasing trade produces more conflict, then we might expect more protectionism and less openness as a result.

These more dynamic models of how international trade and domestic politics interact are an important area of research. They may tell us a good deal about what affects trade policy choices. For example, will the global liberalization process bring increasing pressures for more openness and for democracy? Or will it undermine itself and breed demands for closure and a backlash against the governments and international institutions which support openness, as O'Rourke and Williamson (1999) have shown happened in the early twentieth century? Will openness produce a peaceful international system or one prone to increasing conflict? The answers to these questions will in turn tell us much about the future direction of trade policy globally.

CONCLUSION

I have examined preeminent theories of trade policy and see how they explain trade policy and changes in it. The point of this conclusion is to assess how well they have done and where future research might be useful.

What factors drive trade policy and changes in it? Existing theories suggest several answers to this question. The first involves preferences about trade policy among domestic actors. Economic theory suggests that domestic groups may have clear preferences about trade policy. If groups are rational and prefer profit maximization, then policies that increase profits should be favored. Whether factors endowments or sectors or firms are the correct unit of analysis, these models suggest that the demand for trade policy should follow clear patterns domestically. It is probable that these groups recognize their interests as well, since they are more likely to be organized and to receive large, concentrated benefits from policy. For voters the question is more difficult. Voters are consumers but they may also be workers and asset-owners as well; hence their preferences for trade may be torn in different directions. Moreover, voters' capacity to organize is not well developed, as collective action theory suggests us.

Political leaders, on the other hand, may be able to take action, but it is harder to deductively derive their preferences for trade policy. Should we conceive of them as benign leaders intent on maximizing national social welfare or as politically motivated leaders dependent on special interests for support and often maximizing their own personal interests? The former might lead us to attribute to them preferences for free trade, while the latter view would incline us to see them as protectionists. Under what circumstances, should we expect which behavior?

This question leads to a discussion of political institutions and their role in shaping trade policy. Both the influence of domestic groups and the preferences of leaders may depend on the political institutions in place. Some argue that democracy makes a difference. Political leaders may be forced to concern themselves more with the national interest than with just special interests, according to one theory; others claim the opposite: that in democracies the relentless search for political support makes politicians more sensitive to the needs of and subservient to the demands of special interest groups. We need more research on these issues before we can conclude.

Other features of political institutions may also matter. Whether institutions – democratic or not – insulate policy-makers from special interest pressures may matter. After all, some non-democratic countries in Asia, such as Hong Kong and Singapore, have long had fairly liberal trade policies. Electoral rules, the nature of the party system and other institutional features may also affect which interest groups can exert the most influence. Institutions that can internalize the costs of protection so that all members bear them can make protection much more difficult for political leaders to choose. The role of political institutions is underexplored. We need more cross-national studies of trade policy.

As for international factors, they have also only received a small amount of attention. Hegemonic Stability theory remains the central explanation for trade policy at the systemic level. Security concerns also seem important. The gains from trade do pose security externalities. How in the new international system do such factors affect states? How should we expect trade policy to change in the wake of the collapse of socialist and communist economies and the end of the Cold War? One might anticipate that the lack of direct threats globally should lead all to adopt freer trade. On the other hand, some suggest that the end of bipolarity and the decline of American hegemony might lead to the fragmentation of the world economy into rival trading blocs, centered on the United States, Europe and Japan.

Some claim that this is what the growing role of regional trade agreements is leading to. Others see such PTAs as fostering the extension of a multilateral trading system. The impact of security concerns and the balance of capabilities and threats on trade policy is another area demanding empirical research.

The role of international institutions is also of importance. The creation of the GATT/WTO, the EU and a slew of regional organizations like Mercosur make it plain that such institutions play an important role in trade. But what exactly is this role? Can they alter states' behavior or preferences? Do they just provide information and hence help prevent cheating? Or are they simply the instruments of the most powerful states in them? And how do such institutions act to change the behavior of the weaker states in the grouping? Research on the role of international institutions in trade is a growing topic for both economists and political scientists (e.g., Bagwell and Staiger, 1999).

None of our existing theories appears to do very well in explaining trade policy. A better understanding of how political leaders form their trade preferences and how these preferences are connected to societal ones is essential. Moreover, theories about the relationship between democracy and trade are in their infancy. And knowledge of the conditions under which international institutions are able to exert greater (or lesser) influence over countries is necessary. Hence, although we have many theories of trade policy, none can provide a complete explanation of the trade policy process. Most are also too centered on the American political system and economy to provide convincing explanations of other countries' policies. Moreover, more empirical studies examining these theories are needed.

Finally, we need to be able to theorize about the possible future direction of trade policy. Will the recent moves toward freer trade around the globe be sustained or reversed? Will trade barriers remain as low as they are and keep declining, or will protectionism return? Again, the factors discussed above should give us some bearing on this issue. If leaders' or social groups' preferences for free trade are maintained or grow, then we might expect liberalization to remain in place. Factors, such as economic crises, that cause actors to question these preferences will limit their sustainability. We might also expect that the return of authoritarian governments would be associated with the return to protection, but democracy itself is not a sufficient condition for liberalization. Finally, the role of international institutions seems to be heightened by the severity of domestic economic crises. This suggests that as good times return political leaders who do not favor free trade may reject the policies forced on them by their lenders and turn protectionist. These and other factors will be important for understanding the sustainability of trade liberalization. But again these factors only give us some preliminary clues about where to look for the forces that may influence trade policy in the future.

Notes

I wish to thank David Baldwin, Jeffry Frieden, Stephan Haggard, Robert Jervis, Dani Rodrik and Beth Simmons for their very helpful comments on earlier versions of this chapter.

1 Many of these trade liberalizations occurred within the context of larger economic reform packages. Here I discuss only the trade liberalization component.

2 As he describes it (Rodrik 1994: 62), 'Since the early 1980s, developing countries have flocked to free trade as if it were the Holy Grail of economic development. ... Together with the historic transformation and opening of the Eastern European economies, these developments represent a genuine revolution in policy-making. The puzzle is why is it occurring now and why in so many countries all at once?'

3 Trade policies refers to all policies that have a direct impact on the domestic prices of tradables, that is, goods and services which are traded across national boundaries as either imports and/or exports. Such policies include not just import tariffs, which are taxes on imports, but also export taxes, which under certain conditions have identical effects as import taxes. Likewise, import and export subsidies also count. Exchange rate policy also affects trade flows, but it is a subject I leave for others to discuss.

4 Political leaders may also favor trade liberalization simply because it increases government revenues. Liberalization may generate more revenues because of the increased economic activity and higher volumes of trade it produces, even at lower tariff rates.

5 For a wide-ranging review of the effects of different political institutions on the probability of large-scale economic reform, including trade liberalization, see Haggard 1998.

6 Recent work by Iversen and Cusack (2000), however, shows that changes in economic structure rather than trade openness account for the growth of the welfare state.

7 Many have noted that in the presence of high capital mobility – another condition of globalization – governments also lose control of their monetary policy, especially if they desire to fix their exchange rates (e.g. Garrett, 1998).

Bibliography

Alt, James, Frieden, Jeffry, Gilligan, Michael, Rodrik, Dani and Rogowski, Ronald (1996) 'The Political Economy of International Trade', *Comparative Political Studies*, 29: 689–717.

Anderson, Kym (1980) 'The Political Market for Government Assistance to Australian Manufacturing Industries', *The Economic Record*, 56: 132–44.

Bagwell, Kyle and Staiger, Robert (1999) 'An Economic Theory of GATT', *American Economic Review*, 89: 215–48.

Baldwin, Robert (1986) *The Political Economy of US Import Policy*. Cambridge, MA: MIT Press.

Balestreri, Edward (1997) 'The Performance of the Heckscher–Ohlin–Vanek Model in Predicting Endogenous Policy Forces at the Individual Level', *Canadian Journal of Economics*, 30: 1–17.

Barbieri, Kathleen (1996) 'Economic Interdependence', *Journal of Peace Research*, 33: 29–49.

Bates, Robert and Krueger, Anne (eds) (1993) *Political and Economic Interactions in Economic Policy Reform*. Cambridge, MA: Blackwell.

Bauer, Robert, Pool, Ithiel and Dexter, Louis (1972) *American Business and Public Policy*. Chicago: Aldine Atherton.

Beaulieu, Eugene (1996) 'Who Supported the Canada–US Free Trade Agreement?', unpublished ms. November, Columbia University.

Bergsten, C. Fred and Noland, Marcus (1993) *Reconcilable Differences?* Washington, DC: Institute for International Economics.

Cameron, David (1978) 'The Expansion of the Public Economy', *American Political Science Review*, 72: 1243–61.

Cardoso, F. Henry and Faletto, E. (1979) *Dependency and Development in Latin America*. Berkeley, CA: University of California Press.

Cassing, James, McKeown, Timothy and Ochs, John (1986) 'The Political Economy of the Tariff Cycle', *American Political Science Review*, 80: 843–62.

Caves, Richard (1976) 'Economic Models of Political Choice', *Canadian Journal of Economics*, 9: 278–300.

Cohen, Benjamin J. (1990) 'The Political Economy of International Trade', *International Organization*, 44: 261–81.

Conybeare, John (1982) 'The Rent-seeking State and Revenue Diversification', *World Politics*, 35: 25–42.

Conybeare, John (1983) 'Tariff Protection in Developed and Developing Countries', *International Organization*, 37: 441–63.

Conybeare, John (1984) 'Public Goods, Prisoner's Dilemma and the International Political Economy', *International Studies Quarterly*, 28: 5–22.

de Melo, Jaime and Panagariya, Arvind (1993) 'Introduction', in Jaime de Melo and Arvind Panagariya (eds), *New Dimensions in Regional Integration*. New York: Cambridge University Press. pp. 3–21.

Destler, I.M. (1986) *American Trade Politics*. Washington, DC: Institute for International Economics.

Drazen, Alan (1996) 'The Political Economy of Delayed Reform', *Policy Reform*, 1: 25–46.

Encarnation, Dennis (1992) *Rivals Beyond Trade*. Ithaca: Cornell University Press.

Epstein, David and O'Halloran, Sharyn (1996) 'The Partisan Paradox and the US Tariff, 1877–1934', *International Organization*, 50: 301–24.

Fernandez, Rachel and Rodrik, Dani (1991) 'Resistance to Reform', *American Economic Review*, 81: 1146–55.

Frieden, Jeffry (1990) *Debt, Development and Democracy*. Princeton: Princeton University Press.

Gallarotti, Guilio (1985) 'Toward a Business Cycle Model of Tariffs', *International Organization*, 39: 155–87.

Garrett, Geoffrey (1998) *Partisan Politics in the Global Economy*. New York: Cambridge University Press.

Gasioworski, Mark (1986) 'Economic Interdependence and International Conflict', *International Studies Quarterly*, 30: 23–38.

Gilligan, Michael (1997) *Empowering Exporters*. Ann Arbor: University of Michigan Press.

Gilpin, Robert (1987) *The Political Economy of International Relations*. Princeton: Princeton University Press.

Goldstein, Judith (1988) 'Ideas, Institutions and American Trade Policy', *International Organization*, 42: 179–218.

Goldstein, Judith (1993) *Ideas, Interests and American Trade Policy*. Ithaca: Cornell University Press.

Gowa, Joanne (1994) *Allies, Adversaries, and International Trade*. Princeton: Princeton University Press.

Gowa, Joanne and Mansfield, Edward (1993) 'Power Politics and International Trade', *American Political Science Review*, 87: 408–20.

Greenaway, David and Milner, Chris (1986) *The Economics of Intraindustry Trade*. Oxford: Blackwell.

Grossman, Gene M. and Helpman, Elhanan (1994) 'Protection for Sale', *American Economic Review*, 84: 833–50.

Hadenius, Axel (1992) *Democracy and Development*. New York: Cambridge University Press.

Haggard, Stephan (1988) 'The Institutional Foundations of Hegemony: Explaining the Reciprocal Trade Agreements Act of 1934', *International Organization*, 42: 91–120.

Haggard, Stephan (1995) *Developing Nations and the Politics of Global Integration*. Washington: Brookings Institution.

Haggard, Stephan (1998) 'Interests, Institutions and Policy Reform', unpublished paper, University of California in San Diego.

Haggard, Stephan and Kaufman, Robert (1995) *The Political Economy of Democratic Transitions*. Princeton: Princeton University Press.

Haggard, Stephan and Webb, Steven (eds) (1994) *Voting for Reform: Democracy, Political Liberalization, and Economic Adjustment*. New York: Oxford University Press.

Hathaway, Oona (1998) 'Positive Feedback', *International Organization*, 52: 575–612.

International Monetary Fund (1992) *Issues and Developments in International Trade Policy*. Washington, DC: IMF.

Irwin, Douglas (1994) 'The Political Economy of Free Trade', *Journal of Law and Economics*, 37: 75–108.

Irwin, Douglas (1996) 'Industry or Class Cleavages over Trade Policy?', in Robert Feenstra, Gene Grossman and Douglas Irwin (eds), *The Political Economy of Trade Policy*. Cambridge, MA: MIT Press. pp. 53–75.

Iversen, Torben and Cusack, Thomas (2000) 'The Causes of Welfare State Expansion: Deindustrialization or Globalization?', *World Politics*, 52: 313–49.

James, Scott and Lake, David (1989) 'The Second Face of Hegemony', *International Organization*, 43: 1–30.

Katzenstein, Peter (1985) *Small States in World Markets*. Ithaca: Cornell University Press.

Keohane, Robert (1984) *After Hegemony*. Princeton: Princeton University Press.

Keohane, Robert (1998) 'Problem Lucidity: Stephen Krasner's "State Power and the Structure of International Trade"', *World Politics*, 50: 150–70.

Keohane, Robert and Milner, Helen V. (eds) (1996) *Internationalization and Domestic Politics*. New York: Cambridge University Press.

Krasner, Stephen (1976) 'State Power and the Structure of International Trade', *World Politics*, 28: 317–47.

Krueger, Anne (1997) 'Trade Policy and Economic Development: How We Learn', *American Economic Review*, 87: 1–22.

Laird, Sam and Yeats, Alexander (1990) *Quantitative Methods for Trade Barrier Analysis*. Houndmills: Macmillan.

Lake, David (1988) *Power, Protection and Free Trade*. Ithaca: Cornell University Press.

Lake, David (1993) 'Leadership, Hegemony and the International Economy', *International Studies Quarterly*, 37: 459–89.

Lipson, Charles (1982) 'The Transformation of Trade', *International Organization*, 36: 417–56.

Lohmann, Susanne and O'Halloran, Sharyn (1994) 'Divided Government and US Trade Policy: Theory and Evidence', *International Organization*, 48: 595–632.

Magee, Steven and Young, Leslie (1987) 'Endogenous Protection in the US', in R. Stern, (ed.), *US Trade Policies in a Changing World Economy*. Cambridge, MA: MIT Press. pp. 145–95.

Magee, Steven, Brock, William and Young, Leslie (1989) *Black Hole Tariffs and Endogenous Policy Theory*. New York: Cambridge University Press.

Mansfield, Edward (1994) *Power, Trade and War*. Princeton: Princeton University Press.

Mansfield, Edward (1998) 'The Proliferation of Preferential Trading Arrangements', *Journal of Conflict Resolution*, 42 (5): 523–43.

Mansfield, Edward and Bronson, Rachel (1997) 'Alliances, Preferential Trading Arrangements, and International Trade', *American Political Science Review*, 91: 94–107.

Mansfield, Edward and Busch, Marc (1995) 'The Political Economy of Nontariff Barriers: A Cross-National Analysis', *International Organization*, 49: 723–49.

Mansfield, Edward and Milner, Helen V. (1999) 'The New Wave of Regionalism', *International Organization*, 53: 589–627.

Mansfield, Edward, Milner, Helen V. and Rosendorff, B. Peter (1998) 'Why Do Democracies Cooperate More: Electoral Control and International Trade Negotiations', paper prepared for the 1998 American Political Science Association conference.

Mansfield, Edward, Milner, Helen V. and Rosendorff, B. Peter (2000) 'Free to Trade: Democracies and International Trade Negotiations', *American Political Science Review*, 94: 305–21.

Marvel, Howard and Ray, Edward (1983) 'The Kennedy Round', *American Economic Review*, 73: 190–7.

Mayer, Wolfgang (1984) 'Endogenous Tariff Formation', *American Economic Review*, 74: 970–85.

Midford, Paul (1993) 'International Trade and Domestic Politics', *International Organization*, 47: 535–64.

Milner, Helen V. (1988) *Resisting Protectionism*. Princeton: Princeton University Press.

Milner, Helen V. (1997) *Interests, Institutions, and Information*. Princeton: Princeton University Press.

Milner, Helen V. and Kubota, Keiko (2001) 'Why the Rush to Free Trade? Democracy and Trade Policy', prepared for the APSA meeting.

Milner, Helen V. and Rosendorff, B. Peter (1996) 'Trade Negotiations, Information and Domestic Politics', *Economics and Politics*, 8: 145–89.

Nelson, Douglas (1988) 'Endogenous Tariff Theory: A Critical Survey', *American Journal of Political Science*, 32: 796–837.

O'Halloran, Sharyn (1994) *Politics, Process and American Trade Policy*. Ann Arbor: University of Michigan Press.

O'Rourke, Kevin and Williamson, Jeffrey (1999) *Globalization and History*. Cambridge, MA: MIT Press.

Pincus, Jonathan (1975) 'Pressure Groups and the Pattern of Tariffs', *Journal of Political Economy*, 83: 757–78.

Polachek, Solomon W. (1980) 'Conflict and Trade', *Journal of Conflict Resolution*, 24: 55–78.

Ray, Edward (1981) 'Determinants of Tariff and Non-tariff Restrictions in the US', *Journal of Political Economy*, 89: 105–21.

Reizman, David and Wilson, James (1995) 'Politics and Trade Policy', in J. Banks and E. Hanuschek (eds), *Modern Political Economy*. New York: Cambridge University Press.

Rodrik, Dani (1992) 'The Limits to Trade Policy Reform in LDCs', *Journal of Economic Perspectives*, 6: 87–105.

Rodrik, Dani (1994) 'The Rush to Free Trade in the Developing World. Why so Late? Why Now? Will it Last?', in S. Haggard and S. Webb (eds), *Voting for Reform: Democracy, Political Liberalization, and Economic Adjustment*. New York: Oxford University Press. pp. 61–88.

Rodrik, Dani (1995) 'Political Economy of Trade Policy', in G. Grossman and K. Rogoff (eds), *Handbook of International Economics*, vol. 3. Netherlands: Elsevier Science Press. pp.1457–94.

Rodrik, Dani (1997) *Has Globalization Gone Too Far?* Washington, DC: Institute for International Economics.

Rodrik, Dani (1998) 'Democracy and Economic Performance', unpublished paper, Harvard University.

Rogowski, Ronald (1987) 'Trade and the Variety of Democratic Institutions', *International Organization*, 41: 203–24.

Rogowski, Ronald (1989) *Commerce and Coalitions*. Princeton: Princeton University Press.

Ruggie, John (1983) 'International Regimes, Transactions and Change', in Stephen Krasner (ed.), *International Regimes*. Ithaca: Cornell University Press. pp. 196–232.

Russett, Bruce (1985) 'The Mysterious Case of Vanishing Hegemony; or is Mark Twain Really Dead?', *International Organization*, 39: 207–32.

Russett, Bruce, Oneal, John and Davis, D. (1998) 'The Third Leg of the Kantian Tripod for Peace', *International Organization*, 52: 441–68.

Schattschneider, E.E. (1935) *Politics, Pressures and the Tariff*. Englewood Cliffs: Prentice Hall.

Scheve, Kenneth and Slaughter, Matthew (1998) 'What Determines Individual Trade Policy Preferences?', *National Bureau of Economic Research*, working paper no. 6531.

Serra, Jaime, Aguilar, Guillermo, Cordoba, Jose, Grossman, Gene, Hills, Carla, Jackson, John, Katz, Julius, Noyola, Pedro and Wilson, Michael (1997) *Reflections on Regionalism*. Washington, DC: Brookings Institution.

Simmons, Beth (1994) *Who Adjusts?* Princeton: Princeton University Press.

Smith, Adam ([1776] 1937) *An Inquiry into the Nature and Causes of The Wealth of Nations*. New York: Modern Library.

Snidal, Duncan (1985) 'The Limits of Hegemonic Stability Theory', *International Organization*, 39: 579–614.

Strange, Susan (1987) 'The Persistent Myth of Lost Hegemony', *International Organization*, 41: 551–74.

Takacs, Wendy (1981) 'Pressures for Protection', *Economic Inquiry*, 19: 687–93.

Trefler, Daniel (1993) 'Trade Liberalization and the Theory of Endogenous Protection', *Journal of Political Economy*, 101: 138–60.

Tsebelis, George (1995) 'Decision-Making in Political Systems: Veto Players in Presidentialism, Parliamentarism, Multicameralism and Multipartism', *British Journal of Political Science*, 25: 289–325.

Verdier, Daniel (1998) 'Democratic Convergence and Free Trade?', *International Studies Quarterly*, 42: 1–24.

Wallerstein, Michael (1987) 'Unemployment, Collective Bargaining and the Demand for Protection', *American Journal of Political Science*, 31: 729–52.

Waltz, Kenneth (1979) *Theory of International Politics*. Reading, MA: Addison–Wesley.

Wintrobe, Ronald (1998) *The Political Economy of Dictatorship*. New York: Cambridge University Press.

World Trade Organization (1996) *Annual Report 1996: Trade and Foreign Direct Investment*, vol. 1. Geneva: WTO.

Yarbrough, Beth V. and Yarbrough, Robert (1992) *Cooperation and Governance in International Trade: The Strategic Organizational Approach*. Princeton: Princeton University Press.

24

International Development

S Y L V I A   M A X F I E L D

As long ago as 1978 prominent scholars of international relations lamented that 'the field of development is in disarray' (Caporaso, 1978: 606). But observing development studies as an interdisciplinary, epistemologically rent and often politicized exercise it should not be surprising to find the field 'untidy' at best.

If it was disorderly in 1978, more than twenty years later development studies, as a coherent social science, is dead. 'Once upon a time,' writes Paul Krugman, 'there was a field called development economics … That field no longer exists' (Krugman, 1996: 7). 'Development studies no longer exists as a body of knowledge with a coherent identity,' writes Hoogvelt (1997: x). Today development studies encompasses sub-specialties in far-flung corners of our university campuses including medicine, public health, biology, environmental sciences, engineering and anthropology as well as the more traditional history, political science, economics and public policy. This diversity is more likely to place successful new courses of study in development at professional schools where they are promoted by practitioner-scholars than in discipline-bound faculties of arts or sciences.[1] Observers lament a theoretical impasse; development studies, they claim, replaced development theory because of this morass (Schuurmann, 1993).

This chapter argues that there have been important continuities and some points of convergence in development theory. Key founding themes of development theory, such as the interaction of international circumstances and domestic political economy, have been very long-lived in the social sciences. Dependency ideas, for example, comprised a startlingly original mode of inquiry focused on the interaction between international markets and domestic political economy. 'Second-wave' dependency theory in particular, and later literature on transnationalism and interdependence, examined themes such as the impact of international economic relations on the nature of the state that are still a central focus of international political economy. Through successive iterations beginning in the 1960s, development theory came to focus more and more on the role of global and non-governmental actors.

A second continuity in the intellectual history of development theory focuses on the appropriate role of the state. Several schools of development theory pointed, in different ways and for varying reasons, to potential benefits of a 'strong' state. For the original development economists market mechanisms alone would not propel development; development required state intervention in the economy. There was emphasis on the state in modernization theory as well; modernization required a technocratic bureaucracy. Dependency theory's view of the state is less clear. Developing countries' international economic relations could spur government repression. But, dependency theorists also credited these repressive states with overseeing development, although it was the less-than-ideal version called 'dependent development'. In contrast, neoclassical economists emphasized the damage wreaked by state intervention in the economy.

Two important points of convergence are evident looking ahead at the future of development studies. One set of development scholars is concerned with the dilemmas of decision-makers who operate nationally but must react to global problems beyond their control. These students of development are tackling questions also important in orthodox international political economy (IPE). The collapse of the Bretton Woods international monetary regime and rising international capital mobility make 'development' a 'universal problem faced by all states and areas of the world' (Payne, 1998: 265). Another perhaps more controversial convergence is between rational choice political economy and historicist area studies approaches. As it is more frequently used by non-US scholars, rational choice political economy is becoming more situationally specific. A careful study of economic decentralization in Brazil, for example, might employ rational choice methods to gain new insights into how the process varies across Brazil but not claim generalizable results for countries other than Brazil.

Few scholars acknowledge these continuities and points of convergence. In the United States development studies became a politicized, interdisciplinary, policy-oriented, practitioner-defined field, lamented, if not eschewed by the social scientists pursuing theoretical innovation from positions in leading departments of politics and economics. In the Americas, at least, politics and method limited collaboration and cross-fertilization between development studies and international relations.[2] For example, many international relations scholars saw in the dependency framework methodological proclivities and political views they could not accept. Although scholars of orthodox IPE pursued the basic thrust of dependency analysis, it was not called such. For their part dependency theorists failed to recognize aspects of dependence in 'core' countries and too quickly dismissed 'first world' scholarship.[3] Given some of the continuities and points of convergence highlighted in following pages, this less-than-perfect consort is disappointing.

This chapter proceeds in two parts. The following section outlines the intellectual history of development studies, moving from development economics through modernization and dependency theory to neoclassicism. To shed light on sources of discord in the field the outline evaluates dominant literatures according to three criteria. These are the extent to which dominant literatures were interdisciplinary, exhibited a normative bias and/or made universal claims for their theories. The literatures that were more interdisciplinary and politicized, such as modernization and dependency theory, undermined development studies' potential as a coherent social science discipline but broadened its general appeal. The review also stresses points of continuity and notes how theory changed with world events.

The second part briefly evaluates three contemporary strands of development studies: pragmatic, eclectic, practitioner-oriented; postmodern; and rational positivist political economy. Here there are also strong normative and epistemological issues dividing students of development. Yet in two (mostly) hidden ways development studies and political economy may converge.

DEVELOPMENT STUDIES: INTELLECTUAL ARCHAEOLOGY

Development studies began after the Second World War as the study of growth in newly decolonized nations around the globe. But developing countries experienced highly varied growth. This empirical reality posed a challenge for development economists. The Cold War also put political organization of developing countries high on the Western world's agenda. Overlapping and eventually overtaking development economics at the center of development studies in the 1960s and 1970s were political scientists loosely grouped under the moniker 'modernization' theorists. For modernization theorists, development involved synergies between democratization and economic growth. The social unrest of the 1960s hastened the demise of modernization theory. By the early 1970s dependency theory took center stage in development studies, gradually giving way in the 1980s to neoclassicism embodied in the 'Washington Consensus'.

Development Economics: 'Third World' Countries are Different

The connection between economists evaluating growth in developing nations after the Second World War and international organizations was close.[4] Considerable impetus for the field came from the United States's commitment to aid and technical assistance articulated in President Truman's Point Four program. This program complemented the United States's overarching foreign policy goal of rebuilding the post-Second World War world in its own liberal, democratic image.

As a scholarly endeavor, development economics is notable in the history of development studies for its view that the economic circumstances of developing countries were qualitatively different from those of already industrialized countries. The rationale for a separate sub-field of economics was that 'normal' economic relationships and theories might not adequately explain growth in 'new' nations. In contrast to some later approaches to development studies, development economics rejected universalism, meaning that one theory could fit all economies.

The notion that different methods and theories might apply to different types of economies had roots in Keynes's separate analysis of full employment and non-full employment economies. Generally speaking, mainstream development economists did not follow neoclassical economics. Their theoretical reference points were Keynes, Schumpeter and Marshall. Their models focused more on economic structures rather than individuals as the unit of analysis. They built on Schumpeter's insight into economics as a process of structural change more than simple growth or capital accumulation. Food analogies illustrate the difference between the neoclassical and structural view. Streeton says the neoclassical view paints the economy as toothpaste or syrup in which factors of production, prices and whatever else flow and change easily (Streeton, 1984). Structuralists view developing country economies as toffee, full of hard-to-move pieces of capital equipment and individuals with specific skills each tied to certain geographic areas. Many development economists also shared confidence in the value of government intervention in the economies of poor countries.

Development economists differed according to their relative emphasis on domestic or international structures, few, if any, looked to integrate international and domestic models. One group of North American and European development economists stressed domestic obstacles to growth such as surplus labor or economic dualism (Lewis, 1955; Rostow, 1960). Much of the early debate centered on whether growth was best achieved via a 'big push' of investment toward one particular sector or through balanced investments across multiple sectors (Hirschman, 1958; Nurkse, 1953; Rosenstein-Rodan, 1943). Parallel to this literature, other development economists stressed external conditions – uneven terms of trade, for example. Latin American and European scholars were more likely to stress international circumstances than US economists, probably because these forces exerted more influence outside the United States (Prebisch, 1950; Seers, 1959; Singer, 1950).

Carving out their own methods and models of the growth experience in developing countries fully absorbed these development economists. Those who pursued the links between international and domestic circumstances in the 1950s and 1960s were more likely to be political scientists. An article by Margaret Bates (1956) asks about the domestic impact of international organizations supervising Tanganyika in the 1950s. This mirrored a focus in US and European international relations scholarship on international organizations, administration and governance. Where development economists' models focused on technological weaknesses inhibiting growth, for example, political scientists would study the international administration of technical assistance (Sharp, 1953). Bates was an exception because very few political scientists tried to extend the main themes of the decade (international administration, voting patterns in international organizations) to the domestic political economy.[5]

In the 1950s both political science and economics failed to address questions of distribution and equity in the development process.[6] Development economists failed in another way. They did not accurately predict cross-national variation in growth among developing countries. Critics reproached development economists for missing the political and social aspects of development. The Cold War threw into relief political circumstances in developing countries. For these reasons, the intellectual excitement and practitioners' taste for development economics waned. In the social sciences the terms 'development' or 'modernization', meaning economic, social and political growth, superseded use of the term economic development.

Modernization Theory: Interdisciplinary and Normative

The shift from development economics to modernization theory as the central framework of development studies was the first of many changes in the field. With this shift development studies became more interdisciplinary and more explicitly normative. Modernization theory was also intensely universal. According to its adherents, one model of development could explain all of world history. One of the key attributes of modernization theory was to see development in stages that were at once political, economic and social. Rostow's work exemplifies the growing disciplinary breadth, universalism and explicitly normative thrust of development studies. He worked on his ideas in the 1950s but did not publish his seminal book until 1960. The book was titled *The Stages of Growth: An Anti-Communist Manifesto*. All countries begin with traditional societies, Rostow observed. Traditional society enjoys little economic production, has an agricultural economy, and a rigid, hierarchical social structure. Thought is not scientific. According to Rostow, societies move through three more stages where the economy becomes less localized, trade improves, communications improve, investment as a proportion of national income rises, political and social institutions are reshaped, and science and technology expand. Finally nations reach the *age of mass consumption* where the masses benefit from economic growth.

The modernization literature revolved around notions of traditional and modern societies (Levy, 1966; McClelland, 1961). Development studies encompassed debate about the attributes of backward or traditional and modern conditions. Traditional societies had religious authority, rigid social structures, no incentives for innovation and efficiency, few controls on arbitrary political authority and revolved around agricultural production and rural life. Modern societies were secular, science-oriented, urban, had an extensive division of labor, encouraged innovation and efficiency, protected private property through rule of law and built a liberal 'nightwatchman' state. Such broad and sweeping categories mandated a multidisciplinary approach spanning economics, political science and sociology. Modernization also propelled the social sciences in an interdisciplinary direction by linking change in different social arenas. Modernization theory explicitly linked industrialization with political development and these in turn with social rationalization and secularization.

A hallmark of modernization theory within political science was a series of country studies sponsored by the United States' Social Sciences Research Council. These studies focused on how democracy and political development would follow from economic growth. For many the 'intervening variable' was a changing political culture (Lapalombara, 1963; Pye, 1967).

Not only was modernization more multidisciplinary and universal than its predecessor at the center of development studies, development economics, but the Cold War engendered more explicit political discussion and judgement of what was right and wrong in the development debate. Modern societies looked like Europe and North America. All countries should be on a unilinear path toward the European and North American model. Breaking down barriers of tradition would set any country off on the route leading to North American-style economy, society and policy. Later scholars strongly criticized modernization theory for its universal, unilinear, Western-oriented bias (Cardoso and Faletto, 1979). Implicit in this theory were seeds of demise for development studies. If all countries moved through history on a linear course from backward to modern there was ultimately no need for a special field to study contemporary developing countries separately from developed countries.

Pregnant in modernization theory was the importance of non-governmental actors in the development process. The shift away from government as the unit of analysis mirrored political scientists' break with the legal-formalism that dominated the early rise of their field. Modernization also hinted at the theoretical importance of linking international relations with development studies. Exposure to the economies and cultures of the 'First World' could help to break down traditional social structures and values. Trade, foreign investment, cultural penetration were all-important vehicles of modernization. But this idea remained latent within the modernization literature.[7]

By the mid-1960s the Cuban revolution, growing Communist influence in developing countries and social unrest and political criticism in cities across the globe invaded the modernization theory paradise. One article notes a shift of emphasis in international development institutions from technical assistance, to human capital and institutions. 'This was sparked partly by a worry over ... [y]oung people unsettled by education but frustrated by their inability to find productive and satisfying jobs in their societies' (Millikan, 1968: 9). Social unrest and political turmoil around the world spurred a revolutionary new idea emerging in modernization

circles. Samuel Huntington turned modernization theory's happy claim that 'all good things go together' on its head. Economic growth and development of stable, robust democracy went hand in hand according the modernization theorists. But Huntington argued convincingly in a landmark book published in 1968 that economic growth might cause political decay. Ted Gurr (1970) added to this view with an analysis of how the rising expectations created by economic growth might be 'why men rebel'.

Modernization theory declined for many reasons. By the late 1960s international relations scholars began to suggest that international organizations were not successful facilitators of modernization as had been supposed. Developing countries, frustrated with Cold War international politics, formed an international group of non-aligned nations. From a comparative politics perspective, trouble in many developing countries substantiated the Huntington critique of modernization theory. In many cases political chaos did seem to follow on the heels of economic growth.

Academic critics faulted modernization for failing to stipulate the sources and processes of evolution from the traditional to modern condition. Caporaso took a more philosophical view, attributing modernization theory's demise to its pluralism. Modernization theorists, Caporaso suggests, failed to agree on what is important in development: mass participation, democracy, capacity of the government to direct social change, structural differentiation etc. (1978: 606). By 1976 dependency theory sympathizer Immanuel Wallerstein could publish an article entitled 'Modernization: Requiescat in Pace'.

Dependence, Transnationalism and Interdependence: Linking International and Domestic Political Economy?

While some development economists had studied how international economic flows effected development, and modernization theory hinted at the role of international relations as an impetus for evolution from backward to modern, neither placed the international–domestic interaction at the center of their theory. But in the early 1970s two books stressing the growing global importance of international economic actors garnered great attention among social scientists internationally. These were Keohane and Nye's special issue of *International Organization*, later published as *Transnational Relations and World Politics* (1971), and Cardoso and Faletto's *Dependency and Development in Latin America* (1979).

Modernization theory failed adequately to address the process of change from a traditional to modern nation. To fill this lacuna these two books pointed both to the role of non-governmental actors and to the international economy. Both books reflected growing criticism of international organizations as they had operated in the first two decades after the Second World War. Both tried seriously to combine political and economic analysis and both carried a normative message. Cardoso's work complemented a burgeoning Latin American criticism of contemporary development policy. In their introduction to *Transnational Relations*, Keohane and Nye (1971: 3) stated the intent to 'describ[e] patterns of interaction in world politics and then ask what role international institutions ... *should play*'.[8] But the two books differed greatly in methodology. Keohane and Nye worked in the positivist tradition while dependency theorists eschewed positivism for a more historical approach.

Latin American and African nations had been increasingly critical of the development policies promoted by multilateral agencies and international organizations in the 1950s and 1960s. Latin Americans were increasingly dismayed by the heavy-handed yet ineffective, or even malevolent, role of the US government, multilateral agencies such as the IMF and multinational corporations. Tensions between North and South were building. By the mid-1960s even international relations scholars began to recognize this tension. A special 1965 issue of *International Organization* commemorating the UN Charter's twentieth anniversary includes an article on economic development that notes the following with regard to 'the difference between North and South views on development':

> Less developed countries (LDCs) want more international aid and favorable trade policies, while the north imposes conditions saying the south must deliver stable governments and fair treatment of foreign direct investment. While the south focuses on protecting infant industry ... the north emphasizes agricultural efficiency. (Blough, 1965: 565)

Although dependency literature had not yet received attention by mainstream economists or political scientists, scattered English-language articles appeared that complemented the largely non-English dependency literature. One director of international studies at a US university picked up the southern criticism of international development agencies. 'International institutions', he wrote, 'have been built up for many reasons other than development, and nations pursue their development activities to only a minor extent through international institutions' (1968: 3). There, Millikan was simply reflecting what LDC leaders had been arguing for several years. GATT, for example, focused so heavily on advanced industrial countries that developing country leaders pushed for a separate forum, the United Nations Conference on Trade and Development, in which to pursue their trade concerns.

Against a backdrop of rising criticism for international organizations and the Bretton Woods monetary system's is demise, both the dependency and transnational relations frameworks pointed attention to international economic processes and their influence on politics. But these two approaches differed in their relationship to modernization theory. The literature on transnationalism grew more or less naturally from the modernization approach. Growing transnational connections propelled modernization. Modern nations were transnational nations. Edward Morse, a leading author in this school, argued that, 'Modern societies are interdependent ones ... All modern societies in interdependent situations acquire certain common political characteristics such as strong welfare pressures, bureaucratization ...'[9] International economic relations were salutary for developing nations.

The dependency framework broke explicitly with modernization theory. Dependency theory argued that developing countries had much to lose and little to gain from furthering international economic relations. Another issue for leading dependency theorist Cardoso was modernization theory's ahistorical, mechanical view of development (Cardoso and Faletto, 1979: 173).

Dependency literature is notoriously diverse.[10] Early dependency literature is typically considered overly focused on the (negative) consequences of international economic integration while later literature, of which Cardoso, Evans and O'Donnell are leading examples, is more nuanced.[11] This later variant of dependency theory diverged from early development paradigms (economic development, modernization) and the transnationalism literature in an important way. It included a relatively balanced consideration of internal and external influences on the state and political development. Caporaso's comment about traditional development literature could also be applied to international relations until the incorporation of dependency ideas, '... theory has had a tendency to offer one-sided interpretations of the sources of development – showing a blind spot to either internal or external factors. While other studies focus primarily on domestic causes of development, dependency focuses on internal and external forces (including their interactions)' (Caporaso, 1978: 613).

Caporaso notes how big a break the later dependency theory is with past theories of development. 'In terms of its intellectual genealogy, evolutionary coherence, working assumptions, research programs, and policy goals it stands on its own,' Caporaso wrote (1978: 613). He calls dependency theory 'a qualitatively new departure', closer to the Gerscenkronian comparative political economy tradition than any other. Based on study of Germany, Russia and other countries, Gerschenkron (1963) concluded that a country's relative international development status determined the extent of state involvement in the economy. A government that deemed its country backward relative to others in the world intervened to push the economy ahead as fast as possible. According to Caporaso (1978: 614), Cardoso and Faletto's 'primary task is to show how foreign capital interacts with domestic society to produce different alliances of social groups, and, in turn, how these alliances attempt to use the state to further their own interests'. 'To the extent that dependencia theorists pay attention to internal forces … and the Gershcenkronians stress external ones, the boundary between the two camps disintegrates' (Gourevitch, 1978: 891).

The dependency and transnationalism literatures share some important similarities. They both emphasize non-state actors and the role of international markets in politics. They both combine international economics and political science and look for explanations of the change in national political economies. Dependency theory certainly had an explicitly normative thrust and Keohane and Nye, at least, were more explicitly normative than students of international organization had been previously. But they differed in important ways also. Dependency broke openly with modernization theory while transnationalism and interdependence did not. At issue were two things: whether international economic relations played a positive role for developing countries and if positivist methodology was appropriate to political economy. As the two literatures evolved over time they diverged further. The interdependence literature remained focused on international relations while dependency's descendents emphasized the interaction between international market forces and domestic political economy. Transnationalism gave way to an emphasis on international regimes, their origins, rise and fall, and impact on national foreign policy while the dependency literature continued to search for patterns in the interaction of international and domestic political economy.

Hidden Continuity: Dependency Ideas and International Political Economy in the 1980s

Dependency had its hearing in English-language international relations journals and faded quickly from the mainstream. Cardoso and Faletto's 1967 book was not translated and published in English until 1979, but *International Organization* published a special issue on dependency theory in 1978. This followed an English-language generalist introduction to dependency theory by Osvaldo Sunkel in *Foreign Affairs* in 1972. Prior to this journal issue there was one English-language edited volume including pieces by dependentistas and a growing analysis of Canadian dependency, but relatively little discussion of dependency theory in the mainstream political science forum.[12] Given this limited airing, it is odd to read Gilpin's statement in 1975 that dependencia 'has now become legend' (1975: 40).

An opportunity for cross-fertilization between development studies and international relations was lost in the late 1970s as the world and academics struggled to understand the post-Bretton Woods international monetary system and its implications for national economies. Keohane's 1978 review of the McCracken Report hints at the 'potential for a general theory of the interaction of international economic forces and domestic politics' (Casaburi, 1993). In reviewing the McCracken Report, Keohane is impressed by its emphasis on how '[T]he internationalization of capital, as reflected in the rapid growth of international financial markets …' led to a situation in which international markets took over functions previously under the preview of government authorities. 'Dependence of governments', continues Keohane in a strikingly dependentista vein, 'on private financial markets – which is to a great extent the result of increases in oil prices – creates additional pressures for conservative economic policies that are deferential to the interests of capital' (1978: 120). Had the gap between Atlanticists and dependentistas been narrower, this statement could have been read as an invitation to use the rudimentary analytical tools of dependency theory to evaluate a loss of government autonomy to international economic forces. Such an endeavor, while new to Keohane and his colleagues, was old hat for the likes of Cardoso and Faletto.

Although several strands of dependency literature were pursued aggressively by successful mainstream political scientists, including Katzenstein, Gourevitch and many of their students, these authors did not emphasize the intellectual continuity between their work and that of the dependency scholars. Because or in spite of becoming a legend in their own time, dependency ideas were subsumed in an influential literature focused on the interaction of international markets with domestic structures.

Katzenstein's (1985) careful study of small states in world markets analyses industrial policy in diminutive European states. He understands national economic policy, particularly industrial strategy, as the outcome of national élites' attempts to meet structural change in the world economy (1985: 23). His conclusion summarizes the argument that small European states' policies are profoundly affected by 'historically shaped domestic structures and the pressures of the world economy' (1985: 207). This overall approach bears a striking similarity to how Cardoso sets up his investigation of Latin American political economy. Indeed Katzenstein suggests one could compare small European states and developing countries using the framework he outlines (1985: 203). Because the pressures of world markets are more intense for developing countries, Katzenstein speculates, they tended to adopt even stronger forms of central government than the strong corporatist structures of the small European states. In fact, this is similar to O'Donnell's (1973) argument about the emergence of bureaucratic authoritarian regimes in Latin America.[13] Cameron (1978) narrows the argument considerably so he can test it quantitatively. He discovers that for a set of advanced industrial countries, the more trade-open an economy, the higher government expenditure.

Of five categories of theory, Gourevitch's book on policy choice in times of international economic crisis gives 'pride of place to explanation based on the international economic situation' (1986: 66). Gourevitch cites dependency work and finds affinity with what he calls the 'weak' form, by which he means the later, more nuanced dependency ideas typified by Cardoso and Faletto. The key for Gourevitch is that early dependency does not allow for national choice; the international system so tightly shapes development trajectories that states do not have any choice regarding economic policy. But, as Gourevitch himself notes, it is not hard to find fault with the most sweeping version of this argument. He does find harmony with 'the line of reasoning based on the study of development patterns' and organizes his historical study by asking 'how and through what mechanisms ... the international system shapes domestic politics' (1986: 64–5). This was a more or less direct extension of work second-wave dependency theorists had begun two decades earlier.

Dependency also found a peculiar affirmation in the work of another great international political economist of the 1980s. 'A dependency orientation can be used to supplement ... arguments that have been put forth by conventional analysts ...' states Krasner. 'The penetration of domestic structures emphasized by dependency theory thus aggravates the difficulties of adjustment already imposed on central political institutions in developing countries by the rigidity of their own domestic social structures' (1985: 44). Although Krasner suggests complementarities between dependency theory and 'conventional' analysis, this is not the main thrust of his book. For him dependency ideas are an explanatory variable. As an ideology they help explain the ability of Third World states to create or sustain international regimes that shift from market-oriented to administrative forms of resource allocation. For Krasner dependency ideas helped inform the Third World's critique of First World foreign economic policy. They also helped diverse nations of the Third World unify. Dependency was a movement of thought, states Krasner, 'the subjective complement to the objective conditions of domestic and international weakness' (1985: 90). Krasner

depicts the dependency framework as an ideology that added fuel to the fire of conflict in North–South relations but says explicitly that dependency ideas are not 'social analysis' (1985: 85).[14]

Social analysis by the late 1980s was increasingly oriented toward rational choice theory, a field dominated by economists. Dependency theory had been at once dismissed and enveloped in orthodox political economy. Katzenstein, Gourevitch and others paved the way for a generation of political scientists who mastered vast quantities of economics literature and whose studies of development were increasingly informed by both the neoclassical revival and game theory.

The Neoclassical Revival and the Role of the State in Development Theory

Krasner's book *Structural Conflict* 'exposed' the role of the dependency 'ideology' in the developing countries' international campaign against market allocation mechanisms. Debt crisis brought an abrupt end to this campaign in the 1980s. A host of imbalances in international capital markets in the 1970s gave way to a round robin of developing country defaults in the 1980s. Developing countries found themselves prostrate before the International Monetary Fund and other exponents of what was dubbed the 'Washington Consensus' on appropriate economic policy for developing countries. Where development economics, modernization and the dependency/transnationalism/interdependence literature engaged in analysis that at least implicitly pointed to potential benefits of a 'strong' state, the Washington Consensus boiled down to 'shrink the state'!

For the original development economists market mechanisms alone would not propel development. 'Development economics concentrated', Wade notes,

> on showing how the special circumstances of developing countries including low private saving, dependence on primary product exports, declining prices of exports in relation to imports, small internal markets, limited skills, few entrepreneurs adept at large-scale organization, and pervasive underemployment, required an even bigger role for the state than in the more developed countries. (1990: 8)

There was a central emphasis on the state in modernization theory as well. The transition from traditional society to modern nation required a technocratic bureaucracy. This and democracy were part of political development.[15] Huntington took the focus on the state one step further, arguing that economic development required a strong state. And from this insight grew the 'developmental state' literature. This literature praised Japan's 'market-conforming' state intervention (Johnson, 1982).

Dependency theory's view of the state is more opaque. For many dependency thinkers developing countries' international economic relations aggravated a propensity for 'predatory' state behavior. On the stunted path of modernization economic failures bred bureaucratic authoritarianism. But, to varying degrees, these strong states oversaw development, albeit the less-than-ideal version Evans (1979) called 'dependent development' and exemplified in the Brazilian case. The transnationalism/interdependence theorists saw increasing challenge but no less need for states capable of negotiating international rules to govern the growing global economy.

But neoclassical economists emphasized the damage wreaked by state intervention in the economy. They make odd bedfellows with dependency-inspired scholars, who also saw the state playing a perverse role in the economy. The difference between neoclassical views and those of dependency-inspired scholars is that for the dependentistas international economic circumstances accentuated the state's negative impact (Frieden, 1981). The dependency theorist's critique of the state was interdisciplinary and internationally contextualized where the neoclassical critique was not.

In any case, the state's failures as direct producer and regulator were abundant by the late 1970s, not only in developing countries but developed ones as well. Keynes's criticisms of the neoclassical paradigm held great sway in global economic leadership circles during the 1960s and 1970s. But the poor performance of so many national economies in the 1970s and seeming ineffectiveness of Keynesian policy tools paved the way for neoclassicism's resurrection. Almost at the same time changes of government in the United States, United Kingdom and Germany brought to favor economic advisers preferring monetarist recipes for macroeconomic management and neoclassical microeconomists. The neoclassicists asserted that, with the exception of a very few instances of market failure, free competition and market mechanisms, in all countries and under all circumstances, would bring about a more optimal allocation of economic resources than a regulated economy with administrative control and central planning. The lemma was 'get the prices right' (i.e. allow the market to set prices) instead of get the policies right (Martinussen, 1997: 263). Several authors articulated the neoclassical view of development during the 1970s (Little et al., 1979) but the 'changing of the guard' or 'counter-revolution' did not occur until around 1980, when the World Bank, IMF and governments of major world powers thrust the neoclassical paradigm on the world stage. When a major debt crisis hit the developing countries in 1982, the IMF and World Bank were ready with a strong policy prescription based on the newly hegemonic neoclassical paradigm.

Anne Krueger, one of the leading neoclassical development scholars, delineated the government failures of the 1960s and 1970s. These include 'exceptionally high-cost public sector enterprises, engaged in … economic activities not traditionally associated with the public sector' such as distribution, manufacturing, banking and even tourism. Government investment was inefficient and wasteful, argued the neoclassicists (Krueger, 1990: 10). Pervasive controls on private sector activity were costly, with both investment and controls contributing to large government fiscal deficits. All together, these led to inflation and poor patterns of resource allocation and very low savings rates. Krueger also notes failures including poor maintenance of public infrastructure, exaggerated commitment to fixed exchange rates buttressed by exchange controls and import licenses, and government credit-rationing. The more state intervention, the greater the temptation for corruption, another highly visible example of government failure.

The so-called Washington Consensus was the prescription for these ills in developing countries. According to Williamson (1990) the consensus in 'the political Washington' of Congress and the executive branch and the 'technocratic Washington' of the international financial institutions, the Federal Reserve Board and think-tanks included ten policy instruments. Among these were: reduce fiscal deficits to roughly 2 per cent of GDP or less; redistribute public expenditure by eliminating subsidies but protect spending on education; health and efficient infrastructure projects; broaden the tax base; allow the market to determine interest and exchange rates; liberalize trade and foreign direct investment; privatize state-owned enterprises, de-regulate and safeguard property rights.

The neoclassical view is narrow in a disciplinary sense yet universal in its claims. In stark contrast to development economics the neoclassicists saw little need for a separate theory of developing economies. Neoclassical economic principles could be applied universally. Fundamental assumptions about consumers' utility maximization, producers' profit seeking and the market's central role determining the economic behavior of individuals, households and firms are applied indiscriminately across national contexts. The literature was obviously normative with clear policy prescriptions.

In the political science literature there was a concomitant focus on the international and domestic politics of economic reform. Although this literature was explicitly interdisciplinary, it was not normative. Scholars sought not to judge policies or outcomes but to explain the path of policy choice in developing countries. Why, how, when and where were international financial institutions successful in imposing these reforms in exchange for loans? Projects framed this way sometimes picked up directly on dependency theory ideas, although in more concrete and detailed fashion (Haggard, 1985). The government was an important intermediary in the reform process. Although the recommended reforms had broadened to include a number of institutional changes, by the 1990s one dominant strand of development literature encompassed economists and political scientists who explored how governments could overcome opposition to reform. Gradually post-dependency international political economy, as pursued in academia, gave way to a more universal, more rigorous approach relying on deductive analysis/quantitative empiricism.

Summarizing the Evolution of Development Studies Through 1990

The pre-1990s history of development studies begins and ends with the hegemony of economists; neither the early development economists nor the neoclassicists pursued an interdisciplinary approach. In between the 1950s hegemony of the development economists and the 1990s predominance of the neoclassicists development studies were much more interdisciplinary. Modernization and dependency took an explicitly interdisciplinary tack only to fail in sustaining a coherent presence at the center of any discipline.

Through time, the field of development studies became more political. Separating modernization and dependency were clearly strong political differences reflecting the tensions and pressures of the Cold War. Modernization theory in some guises was explicitly anti-Communist. At minimum it was clearly biased toward a version of economic and political liberalism definitely modeled on the United States. In a sense the transnationalism literature extended the political liberalism of modernization theory to the international arena. Growth and development of international markets, in the view of the interdependence theorists, engendered liberal international governance procedures called regimes. Modernization and interdependence were, respectively, the domestic and international sides of the same liberal coin.

Integrated analysis of international circumstances and domestic politics or domestic political economy was not a goal of the interdependence literature. But this was the main analytical focus of 'second-stage' dependency theory. In the history of development studies dependency theory made the first attempts to bridge the divide between international and domestic political economy, to try to focus attention equally on both the international and domestic spheres. Generations of successful political scientists took up the torch, eclipsing dependency theory with new language, more quantitative empiricism/rigorous deductive thinking, but more political opacity. Meanwhile, regime theory remained concerned primarily with international relations but escaped intense criticism and slowly converged with a more rational positivist approach to political science.

Hand-in-hand with the rise of rational choice approaches came universalism, the notion that one set of fundamental principles applies to most situations. Over time development studies clearly became more universal. The development economists felt that less developed economies were qualitatively different from more developed ones and that only a distinct set of theoretical ideas would improve our understanding of these countries. Modernization theory was universal in its tenet that all countries were moving along the same path toward the Anglo-Saxon model. But modernization theory *did* pause to examine the characteristics of traditional society in contrast to modern nationhood. Post-dependency international political economy tended to share an intensely universalistic approach with the neoclassicists. For the neoclassicists and many rationalist political economists one set of basic principles about the interests and behavior of individuals, households and firms undergirds any and all social choice situations.

Differences across these literatures on such fundamental issues as universalism and their often interdisciplinary reach and normative content hindered continuity in development studies. None the less, two common themes stand out. These are the central importance of state behavior and the growing focus on the interaction of international circumstances and domestic political economy.

DEVELOPMENT STUDIES AT THE START OF A NEW MILLENNIUM

Contemporary development studies operates in three different arenas that parallel different strands of international relations theory: the pragmatic-eclectic world of practitioner-oriented technical development training; the ideological and historicist area of postmodernist philosophizing; and the universal, interdisciplinary, rational positivist science of political economy.[16] The pragmatic-eclectic approach, consistent with the realist international relations paradigm, predominates. The postmodernist approach draws strong links to constructivist international relations theory.

Three Strands of Development Studies

The eclectic, policy-oriented arena where scholars and practitioners explore issue-specific topics ranging from biodiversity to aids to ethnic conflict dominates the field of development studies in the early years of the new millennium. In this arena the literature does not linger over theoretical debates but focuses on challenges confronting developing countries and how to solve them. By nature this is a cross-disciplinary endeavor. It is not necessarily interdisciplinary; development studies programs typically draw in faculty from different departments across the university campus. These individuals may or may not combine disciplines in their own research and writing. For example, a public health project on transmissions of HIV via breastfeeding among rural Brazilian women might be oriented toward a public health and sociology or cultural anthropology audience. Alternatively it might be defined squarely within the field of epidemiology. A school of forestry or environmental studies project on deforestation in Brazil might be framed politically or fall strictly within the fields of biology/environmental science.

A second area of development studies is the postmodernist theoretical exercise seeking to evaluate 'development as discourse'. Cooper and Packard, co-editors of a seminal book in 'postmodernist' development studies, outline the battle lines drawn in contemporary development studies. The 'postmodernists', they note, are wary of 'imposing an undesired modernity', while 'the people working in the trenches of development projects insist they do practical work ... and that the problems of sickness and poverty which they address' will not melt away under 'sweeping evocations of community values' (1997: 4). In defense of their postmodern position, Cooper and Packard argue that 'all have something to gain by a more introspective, contingent view of the terrain ...'. Falling under this rubric is also 'reflectivist' political economy flourishing in Europe and inspired by Robert Cox (1987).

The third arena of development studies falls under the liberal appellation in international relations theory. Here are the rational-choice guided scholars, evaluating how everything from property rights to electoral laws and any imaginable 'rule' in between shapes behavior. This is a highly developed interdisciplinary field spanning political science and economics. These political economists make theoretically universal claims; work in this field was not originally applied but it is increasingly empirical. When these political economists look for empirical validation of their deductive models they do not necessarily turn to developing countries. For a long time rational choice theorists were more likely to seek empirical validation in OECD countries than any other group because data were available and reliable. Also in this third grouping of social science scholarship relevant to development studies are those political economists concerned with globalization. In this literature the hidden continuity with dependency/interdependence ideas continues.

Across these different arenas in both praxis and scholarship the less-than-perfect collaboration between those focused on international relations and on domestic circumstances continues. For the pragmatic development studies practitioner, international cooperation may be key to solving development problems but it may also be too utopian. For some in this field the lemma is 'think global, act local'. For the post-development theorists, global cooperation on development issues is hugely suspect. There are two trends in rationalist positivist political economy: one is for work to become more situationally specific while the other pursues ambitious questions about the interaction of international circumstances and domestic political economy very similar to those put on the table in the 1960s by dependency theorists. But with a few notable examples rational positivist political economists do not see themselves as students of development. Instead, they are looking for universal truths about the interaction of politics and economics across all nations.

Pragmatic, Eclectic Development Studies

This practitioner, policy-oriented definition of international development studies dominates, especially in university/college programs. Still, few universities or colleges offer degrees in development studies. Most existing development studies programs operate at the graduate training level and are professionally focused.[17] European and Canadian universities and colleges boast a disproportionate number of international development programs compared with the United States. Slowly the number of higher education institutions offering degrees in development studies should increase, especially as developing countries improve their own college and university systems. But the United States may increasingly take a back seat in the global production of development scholars and practitioners.[18]

Each of the many policy issues tackled under the rubric of development studies in its practitioner-oriented guise has its own complexity. Many, such as population studies, environmental studies and public health, are major fields in their own right. From an international relations perspective some of these international development issues may be more relevant than others. International action is needed to solve many of the issues central to development studies as a practitioner field. But it is more nearly a reality in some cases than in others. In the issue area of environmental protection, for example, there are (at least) three topics governed to varying degrees by international regimes. These are ozone layer protection, hazardous waste trading and biodiversity (Miller, 1995). Human rights and building effective democracy are important development themes that are less amenable to international discussion than environmental degradation, for example, because they raise the specter of foreign intervention more than discussions over ozone emissions. Labor migration and refugee treatment are international issues that also tend to become politicized, making international cooperation difficult. For example, Mexicans were frustrated that during the North American Free Trade negotiations the United States demanded Mexicans completely liberalize capital flows while labor flows remained blocked. Later the Mexican government recognized the huge Mexican population living illegally in the United States by allowing them to vote in Mexican elections while the US government continued to increase border control efforts. In another area, the health problems of developing countries are certainly global issues but international cooperation is building only slowly, partly because funding is short.

Gaps between OECD and non-OECD country endowments of technology and capital are a major world problem from a developing country perspective yet international cooperation on this issue is also a long way off. Although debt forgiveness reached the international agenda in the 1990s the criteria were stringent and the overall relief meager.[19] Among the unorthodox economists explicitly or implicitly advocating a global extension of the Keynesian ideas that imbued early post-Second World War international relations, and early development theory, are loud calls for greater debt relief (Roodman, 2001). Streeton (2000) went a step further in the late 1990s, advocating a for-profit international trust that would recycle surpluses from heavily industrialized countries to less industrialized ones.[20] Although a twenty-first-century upswell of global Keynesianism is possible, at the turn of the millennium it does not seem likely (Greider, 1997).

Many students and teachers in the practitioner-oriented arena of development are skeptical of international cooperation and quick to denounce an idealistic utopia. The more common lemma is 'think globally, act locally'. In this sense, international development studies may be increasingly concerned with issues such as urbanization that arise in parallel across many countries but are addressed in specific, local contexts. This is another sign that the less-than-perfect collaboration between scholars of international relations and development studies may persist.

Post-Structural (Anti-) Development Studies

This awkward phrase refers to a body of literature harshly critical of development studies. The main point of this literature is that 'development is a disabling and archly Western discourse' that 'has brought disenchantment to many parts of the world' (Corbridge, 1998: 138–9). Development studies has failed to deliver on its promises, contend the post-developmentalists, and we must therefore jettison its discourse. The lemma of this school might well be 'development is the problem, not the solution'.

This strand of development studies stands in stark contrast to the practitioner-oriented development studies arena just analyzed. The notion of thinking globally is anathema to the post-developmentalists. For example, in *Grass-Roots Post-Modernism*, Esteva and Prakash denounce the notion of human rights for its insensitivity to local ideas of justice, truth and fulfillment (1998: 137–8). Western discussions of human rights, they argue, are too individualistic. Post-development authors reject pragmatic development studies completely. They denounce universities for perpetuating the notion that we can train development technicians. The post-development scholars universally reject development as either a pragmatic or social scientific endeavor. According to one post-developmentalist, 'development' as it has been taught is the transformation of Western liberal thought into 'a science for action' (Gupta, 1998). Postmodern development literature takes issue with 'Third World' education projects; they are a form of cultural defoliation. Public health projects fail to recognize hybrid meanings of medicine (Pigg, 1997). Applied to developing countries, neoclassical economics is 'planned poverty' (Illich, 1997). The post-development remedy is 'the simple life'.

Postmodern writing about development attracts many criticisms. First, as Corbridge points out, postmodern, reflectivist development draws unwittingly on the economic assumptions of dependency theory, particularly its early variant. In that literature international economic consort was evil and the remedy was isolation or only South–South intercourse. As early dependency theory did before it, postmodernization theory underestimates the costs of delinking from the world economy. Second, for all its effort to historically contextualize development studies as a field, post-development ignores important aspects of history in its effort to dismiss all that is modern and scientific. Life expectancy, for example, has risen dramatically for most of the world since the middle of the twentieth century. Third, postmodern research focuses on ideology in a purposive effort to downgrade the importance of material forces. Yet it is difficult in developing countries to ignore the weight of international capital markets on national, even sometimes local, circumstances. Fourth, among the ironies inherent in the post-development approach is that the social scientific method, particularly its emphasis on falsification, should teach humility rather than arrogant certainty. Postmodernists do the endeavor of development studies little service with their intense attack on other approaches. One comes away from reading this literature, writes one reviewer, 'with the impression that liberal development professionals and their academic allies are worse than slumlords, car salesmen, property speculators or even lawyers!' (Peet, 1997: 345).[21]

Although this literature may seem extreme, it might continue to grow. It will find fuel in globalization protesters so increasingly evident since 1999 at world economic forums such as the World Trade Organization and Davos meetings. Its links to constructivist international relations theory will also draw interest.

Development Studies and Rational Positivist Political Economy

The postmodern critique sees little difference between development as a field of technical practitioners and development as the domain of political economists. While they may converge in important ways,[22] there are crucial differences between development studies as a problem-solving field and the vestiges of development studies in contemporary, orthodox, political economy. In fact many political economists would not consider themselves part of the development studies field. But their scholarship often addresses the same questions asked decades earlier by development studies and their methods and models have broadened the neoclassical economic approach to comparative political economy and also heavily influenced the field of comparative politics. The defining characteristic of this literature is its epistemology. Epistemology identifies criteria for deciding 'how we know what we know'. Rational positivist political economy is, in the words of one of its leading practitioners, 'guided almost exclusively by the cannons of ... the Western Rationalist Tradition ...'. It uses, Krasner continues, 'the standard epistemological methodology of the social sciences which ... simply means stating a proposition and testing it against external evidence' (1996: 108–9).

There are several strands of positivist political economy scholarship relevant for the future of development studies. Most fall into the category of 'new' or rationalist political economy according to Saint-Paul's (2000) criteria.[23] He defines 'new' political economy by two features. These are the effort to explain economic policy choices and the inclusion of political mechanisms. By a tighter definition, the 'new political economy' applies rational choice theory to the study of institutions, broadly defined. It shares an important intellectual heritage with neoclassical economics. Applied to developing countries this rational choice political economy, while stunningly universalistic, is at the same time increasingly situationally specific. In this latter way rational choice political economy applied to developing countries may be converging with area studies and even historicist international political economy.

Reviewed below is also a slightly different strand of political economy relevant to development studies in the early years of the new millennium and defined more by large sample empirical studies concerned with universal features of globalization. This work is typically either implicitly or explicitly consistent with the rational choice models central to the new political economy but employs mathematics for inductive empirical exercises more often than for deductive modeling exercises. This literature on the political economy of globalization asks many of the same questions asked by second-wave dependency theorists and 1970s and 1980s liberal international political economy. What is the weight of international economic competition on domestic politics? Does it engender a 'race to the bottom' in wages, regulatory standards, etc.? Does it tend to increase inequality across nations/within nations?

The rationalist political economy focuses on institutions defined as any formal or informal system of rules, procedures or norms guiding individual and group behavior. These institutions range from bureaucracies and markets to kinship systems and religions. Choice-theoretic political economy derives from the new institutional economics, cousin to the neoclassical approach exemplified in the development studies world by the Washington Consensus. The new institutional economics is, in turn, closely related to the theory of industrial organization born in 1937 with Ronald Coase's inquiry into the existence of firms.[24] The new political economy adds greater sensitivity to politics than is evident in the other literatures' focus on imperfect information, property rights and transactions costs.

This body of scholarship first sought empirical confirmation in advanced industrial countries, probably to minimize data problems. But soon a handful of development studies specialists began to explore applications of choice-theoretic political economy to the countries they studied. In 1988 Bates published an edited collection that heralded the arrival of choice-theoretic political economy in the field of development. The title, 'Toward a Political Economy of Development', is somewhat misleading because Bates admits he has purposefully failed to cover 'established forms of political economy' (1988: 2). The hallmarks of the new political economy he trumpets are familiar. He highlights use of economic reasoning to explain how political processes and institutions affect individuals' choices and how these, in turn, shape development outcomes. Although this edited volume covered many countries and development issues, much of the early choice-theoretic work on developing countries focused on agriculture (Bates, 1981; Popkin, 1979).

This approach makes universal claims and is genuinely interdisciplinary. It is also, in Colin Leys words, 'politically anaesthetized' (1996b: 101). It can be applied to a vast multitude of issues and situations. These are tremendous strengths that are helping the literature flourish in the US university setting.

But the approach suffers several shortcomings, both generally and from a development studies perspective. First and foremost both theoretical progress and constructive critique emanate from political economists not directly concerned with development studies. Producers of the great works of new political economy are scholars searching for the limits of their models' universality, with a focus on how much of the world their models can explain rather than what they cannot. Two works destined to be foundational textbooks for choice-theoretical political economy, Drazen's *Political Economy in Macroeconomics* (2000) and Persson and Tabellini's *Political Economy: Explaining Economic Policy* (2000), provide good examples. Students of developing countries will find much in these books to 'consume' and apply but they could not replace an eclectic, practitioner-oriented text such as Todaro's *Economic Development in the Third World* (1989) as a guide to development studies issues.

Development studies scholars are not even well represented among those penning constructive critiques of rational choice theory. One early critique was that rational choice theorists employed scattered examples and 'stylized facts' to support their claims rather than systematic empirical investigation. Green and Shapiro developed this critique in an extensive, and soon canonized, review of rational choice literature (1994). But ironically their influential book does not mention the work of Bates or any other scholar who had applied rational choice theory to the study of development. In fact Bates and other rational choice-inspired development scholars may have been more immune to the Green/Shapiro criticism than most rational choice theorists. Their careful case studies may point the way of the future in rational choice development studies.

An emerging view within the rational choice school of development studies posits that the institutions operating to influence behavior and allocate resources may be unique to certain situations. The rational choice mode of inquiry may be best applied to intensive case studies of specific aspects of single countries.[25] For example, Saint-Paul paints a picture of rationality in political economy as situationally specific. Reforms, a common subject of rational choice development studies, are according to Saint-Paul 'unique and in many cases they are the response to a crisis which is itself unique' (2000: 917).

A related complaint about rational choice political economy is that 'theory is well ahead of measurement' (Saint-Paul, 2000: 919). Careful research of specific cases can help mitigate this problem. The future of development studies may see the convergence of traditional area studies approaches to comparative politics with rational choice applications. Payne (1998) also identifies potential for convergence between area studies and political economy but he focuses on the narrowing gap between 'Coxian' political economy and 'Third World' area studies. His is a weaker claim because Cox's brand of international political economy and area studies are typically both historicist. My claim is stronger. It is that there is an increasingly historicist furture

for rational choice scholarship that, without abandoning rationalist positivism, will partially converge with area studies.

A second strand of new political economy literature focuses on the political economy of globalization. This literature typically includes quantitative studies, of as large a number of cases as possible, designed to evaluate how globalization shapes the domestic political economy. The many questions arising under this rubric are extraordinarily germane to development studies at the beginning of the millennium. As with rational choice political economy, these studies aim to uncover universal phenomena.[26] Their findings shed light on questions that have been a mainstay of development studies since the birth of dependency theory. But the impetus for this research agenda was not dependency theory's unanswered questions. Scholars of advanced industrial countries rediscovered these questions as globalization engulfed their countries of interest. Does global economic integration force national governments to adopt similar economic policies? Is there room for social welfare in a global marketplace (Garett, 1998)? Does competition for economic resources in a global economy force a 'race to the bottom' in taxes, wages and regulatory standards (Fishlow and Parker, 1999)? Does this mean inequality will rise, either across or within nations (Quinn, 1997)? These are the central questions in literature on the political economy of globalization. They were central questions, in different form, to dependency theorists and they will continue to be central questions of development studies.

Unfortunately, literature on the political economy of globalization suffers from poor measurement and model specification. For example, findings about the impact of globalization on government spending by two leading international political economists differ. Rodrik (1998) draws a conclusion similar to that of Katzenstein and Cameron decades earlier, that trade openness and government spending are correlated. Garrett (1999) finds the opposite. They use different measures, data and specifications complicating efforts to draw conclusions about the contrasting results. Two very plausible hypotheses lie behind the differing results. First is the 'compensation' hypothesis following Katzenstein and arguing that trade exposure induces governments to spend money on programs that compensate for shocks emanating from global markets. Second is the 'efficiency' hypothesis claiming that internationally mobile capital will not locate in countries with interventionist governments, thus forcing policies to converge around minimal government spending. But proponents of each view fail to carefully specify and test the *mechanisms* whereby globalization either forces compensation or efficiency. Simmons and Elkins (2000) take a step forward in this regard by designing ways to test for different mechanisms of policy convergence. Of course, to focus on transmission mechanisms they trade away an opportunity to weigh in on the debate over the character and consequences of convergence. Notwithstanding its pitfalls, this field is wide open for research relevant to development studies and international political economy.[27]

Orthodox international political economy scholars working in this vein at the beginning of the new millennium perpetuated their mentors' mistakes. Somehow both generations saw development studies remain ghettoized outside the inner sanctum of US international relations, political science and economics. While the dependency theorists of the 1970s failed to see the relevance of their work for advanced industrial countries in the post-Bretton Woods era, early twenty-first-century development scholars champion their shared agenda with international relations scholars. They emphasize that many economic and political management problems in developing areas are problems for all states and areas of the world (Payne, 1998: 265). US international relations scholarship has an in-built bias against questions of development.[28] By redefining development problems as global problems, maybe development scholars hope to be let in from the cold!

This hidden continuity and point of convergence around the interaction of economic globalization and national political economy highlights a central question for development studies and international relations. Development studies derived from the unusual protection afforded national economies by the Keynes-inspired Bretton Woods regime. As that regime degenerated, so did development studies. Now we must ask, how much 'development' is possible in an era of ever-growing international capital markets and mobility (Leys, 1996a: 56)?

CONCLUSION

Development studies has seen more than its share of paradigmatic shifts and changing emphases. In more interdisciplinary guises it has struggled to find an institutional anchor in discipline-bound universities.[29] Even in its less interdisciplinary phases, particularly as development economics, development studies' normative bias and rejection of universal economic theory helped push it to the margins of economics. Political discord and methodological wars hid continuity and stymied cross-fertilization between Third World and Atlanticist political economists, between development theory and international political economy, between US and European development scholars.

But the disciplines of political science and economics have made strides toward a literature which could provide a long-lived paradigm for development studies. To the extent that rationalist political economy moves toward intensive case studies

illustrating the deductive logic of choice-theoretic analysis applied to developing countries, it offers a model that could fuel research on developing countries for decades. As choice-theoretic political economy finds application in intensive case studies reminiscent of traditional area studies scholarship in comparative politics, rational political economy's universalism might even become more palatable to those scholars of development studies who reject the idea that any single set of theoretical principles could explain such a vast variety of circumstances. As first world scholars increasingly focus on the national dilemmas posed by globalization, perhaps communication across orthodox international relations and development studies will improve. But for a long time to come students of development are likely to feel they are consumers of someone else's theory, that they are trespassing in disciplines were they don't fully belong.

There is little hope for a resilient, coherent development studies literature that forms a universal theoretical backbone for burgeoning development studies programs. But we need not lament this. Those who want to give their lives over to fighting for a universal notion of physical well-being and justice are probably best served by eclecticism and diversity.

Notes

1 The Master's Program in Administration and International Development at Harvard University's John F. Kennedy School of Government is a prominent example. While approval, design and development of this program moved forward at lightning speed, a dedicated group of Harvard Undergraduates labored tirelessly and unsuccessfully (to date) to find a modicum of support for an undergraduate development studies major.

2 In 1995 the International Studies Association formed a new working group on international relations and development.

3 In a speech to hundreds of New York financiers in 1996 Brazil's then-President spoke eloquently of the daily dilemmas he and his advisers confronted navigating between the rhythm of global financial markets and the Brazilian political stage. As he laid out a general argument about the tensions between globalization and social welfare, Cardoso, the most widely read author of dependency theory, sounded as though he had just finished surveying prominent contemporary contributions to IPE.

4 One international affairs journal even published an article directed at preparing economists for life in an international organization (Kindleberger, 1955).

5 In the 1950s legal-formalism dominated political science generally (Hawley and Dexter, 1952).

6 Meier (1964), the standard development economics text of the 1960s and 1970s, did not include a section on equity and redistribution.

7 One example is in the huge literature on regional integration, Haas and Schmitter (1964) note in passing the

role of 'tecnicos' within LDC governments as agents of change and proponents of integration. They highlight the cross-national and longitudinal variation in tecnicos power and speculate that it correlates with the nature of tecnico alliances with different political actors and groups. This foreshadows the convergence of international relations and development studies in the 1970s.

8 For his part, when Keohane became editor of *International Organization* in 1975 he called for submissions of more explicitly normative work.

9 This is Gourevitch's (1978: 893) interpretation of Morse.

10 Pioneering dependency theorists such as Andre Gundar Frank took inspiration from Marxist work on economic growth, notably by Baran's (1957) book. Later dependency literature diverged in many directions, including Marxist contributors to the dependency debate such as Amin (1974), Emmanuel (1972) and Kay (1975), on the one hand, and more 'bourgeois' authors such as Cardoso and Faletto (1979), on the other. Geopolitical events fostered this latter tradition. Latin American scholars threatened by their countries' military regimes found support in the United States. This probably helped pull Latin American neo-Marxism closer to liberal social analysis. Another author frequently included under the general rubric of dependency theory is Wallerstein (1976). Working from a neo-Marxist base, Wallerstein penned a grand theory of global capitalism based on the relationship among 'peripheral', 'semi-peripheral' and 'core' countries.

11 Caporaso wrote an extraordinarily intelligent review of dependency theory as represented in the work of Cardoso and Faletto and Peter Evans, published in 1980. 'It is a sad irony that recent interest in dependency theory in the United States and in the English-speaking world in general has taken place without access to most of the important Latin American works ...' (1980: 606). Caporaso goes on to argue that this created a misimpression of dependency theory as one-sidedly focused on external factors. Caporaso cites Tony Smith's work (1979) as an example of misinterpretation.

12 See Stepan, 1973 and, representative of the Canadian literature, Levitt, 1970.

13 Of course Katzenstein also outlines important differences between small European states and developing countries. His text is open to two interpretations. One is that Katzenstein's framework ought to apply to a continuum of countries running from developing countries to small European states, with the degree of political centralization rising as one moves along the continuum. Because he also outlines differences between developing countries and small European states, the text also leaves open the interpretation that developing countries are qualitatively different form small European states thus requiring entirely different theories of economic policy choice and strategy.

14 The first oil price rise made the role of developing countries, as a bloc, in the international arena a topic of interest. One interesting article presaged part of Krasner's study. 'MNCs and the Third World' evaluates claims that LDCs have emerged from their subordinate status in international relations. The author concludes, on the contrary, 'despite a modest shift in power toward the undeveloped countries, the changes which seem likely in the near future fall far short of the drastic transformation [argued by others]' (Weinstein, 1976: 3).

15 There was little fear that more specialization and technocracy could be inconsistent with democracy. Half a century later this was a great concern (UNRISD, 2000).

16 This categorization streamlines Leys's five-fold breakdown (Leys, 1996a).

17 UCLA's undergraduate international development studies major exemplifies this policy-oriented branch of development studies. The program defines its mission in response to the 'overall widening gap between highly industrialized nation-states and underdeveloped ones'. The programs' students confront policy problems corresponding to a wide range of international development issues. These include international aid, urbanization, population, migration and refugee relief, public health and education, environmental protection, conflict resolution, hunger, human rights, technological innovation and survival of indigenous societies.

18 Governments of the world's richest countries may also increasingly take on the challenge of training development practitioners. The Scandinavian countries have always excelled among OECD countries in their commitment to foreign aid. In 1998 Britain created a Department for International Development (DFID). The Overseas Development Office, a unit of the Department of State, gained autonomy and its director attained a cabinet seat. The DFID's mission is to 'mobilize the international political will' to halve the proportion of the global population living in abject poverty and to provide all children with basic education by 2015. Furthermore, the DFID aims to push for global access to basic health care, clean water and sanitation and sustainable development plans under implementation in every country (Short, 1998: 457). The Japanese government is also an increasingly important international development proponent, especially in funding public health initiatives.

19 The World Bank launched the Highly Indebted Poor Countries (HIPC) initiative in 1997. By 2001 only 20 countries had qualified for relief and the process is cumbersome. Qualifying countries typically had to wait for several years before their debt was finally written off. The 22 qualifying countries comprised only 20 per cent of the population of the world's 52 most-indebted countries. Their total debt reduction amounted to only 3.4 per cent of the total annual debt service payment of the 52 most-indebted nations. The 22 countries with debt relief packages were: Benin, Bolivia, Burkina Faso, Cameroon, Gambia, Guinea-Bissau, Guyana, Honduras, Madagascar, Malawi, Mali, Mauritania, Mozambique, Nicaragua, Niger, Rwanda, Saõ Tome and Principe, Senegal, Tanzania, Uganda and Zambia.

20 The system recalls the Clearing Union idea Keynes unsuccessfully proposed to the international framers of the Bretton Woods international monetary regime.

21 Post-dependency exhorts a critical response, particularly because its attack is so personal for scholars

identifying with Western liberalism/social science. 'We personally know ordinary men and women who share our daily predicaments', begins one book's introduction, 'who refuse to uncritically believe what is manufactured for the consumption of TV set owners, or what is considered "publishable" by editorial boards, constituted by "experts", of the "top journals"' (Estevea and Prakash, 1998: 7).

22 For example, the rational choice work on public infrastructure, including Ostrom et al., 1993.

23 The title 'new' political economy is also claimed by the unorthodox international political economists working in the tradition of Robert Cox (Payne, 1998: 256).

24 For an overview see Putterman (ed.), 1990.

25 Jones, 1997 is an example of this trend.

26 Rodrik is a notable exception. Much of his work focuses specifically on developing nations, (Rodrik, 1999).

27 Efforts in the 1970s to quantitatively test some of the international–domestic linkages proposed in dependency theory using comprehensive data for a large number of developing countries failed, despite generous National Science Foundation funding.

28 Although this is true more of US scholars than European, European scholars and journals also voice this complaint (Dickson, 1998: 364).

29 US institutions of higher education have arguably clung harder to traditional disciplines than their European counterparts.

Bibliography

Amin, Samir (1974) *Accumulation on a World Scale.* New York: Monthly Review Press.

Baran, Paul A. (1957) *The Political Economy of Growth.* New York: Monthly Review Press.

Bates, Margaret L. (1956) 'Tanganyika: The Development of a Trust Territory', *International Organization*, 9 (1): 32–51.

Bates, Robert H. (1981) *Markets and States in Tropical Africa.* Berkeley: University of California Press.

Bates, Robert H. (1988) *Toward a Political Economy of Development.* Berkeley: University of California Press.

Blough, Ray (1965) 'The Furtherance of Economic Development', *International Organization*, 19 (3): 562–80.

Cameron, David (1978) 'The Expansion of the Public Economy', *American Political Science Review*, 72 (December): 1243–61.

Caporaso, James (1978) 'Dependency and Dependencia in the Global System', *International Organization*, 32 (1): 13–43.

Caporaso, James (1980) 'Dependency Theory: Continuities and Discontinuities in Development Studies', *International Organization*, 34 (4): 605–25.

Cardoso, Fernando Henrique and Faletto, Enzo (1979) *Dependency and Development in Latin America.* Berkeley: University of California Press

Casaburi, Gabriel (1993) 'International Political Economy and Dependency Theory', mimeo, Yale University Department of Political Science.

Cooper, Frederick and Packard, Randall (eds) (1997) *International Development and the Social Sciences.* Berkeley: University of California Press.

Corbridge, Stuart (1998) 'Beneath the Pavement Only Soil: The Poverty of Post Development', *Journal of Development Studies*, 34 (6): 138–48.

Cox, Robert (1987) *Production, Power and the World Order.* New York: Columbia University Press.

Dickson, Anna (1998) 'Development and International Relations', *Review of International Political Economy*, 5 (2): 362–77.

Drazen, Allan (2000) *Political Economy in Macroeconomics.* Princeton: Princeton University Press.

Emmanual, Arghiri (1972) *Unequal Exchange.* New York: Monthly Review Press.

Esteva, Gustavo and Prakash, Madhu Suri (1998) *Grassroots Post-Modernism.* London: Zed Books.

Evans, Peter (1979) *Dependent Development.* Princeton: Princeton University Press.

Fishlow, Albert and Parker, Karen (eds) (1999) *Growing Apart.* New York: Council on Foreign Relations.

Frieden, Jeffry (1981) 'Third World Indebted Industrialization', *International Organization*, 35 (4): 603–31.

Frieden, Jeffry, Pastor, Manuel, Jr and Tomz, Michael (eds) (2000) *Modern Political Economy and Latin America.* Boulder: Westview.

Garrett, Geoffrey (1998) *Partisan Politics in the Global Economy.* New York: Cambridge University Press.

Garrett, Geoffrey (1999) 'Globalization and Government Spending Around the World', paper prepared for the Annual Meetings of the American Political Science Association, Atlanta, GA, 1–5 September.

Gerschenkron, Alexander (1963) *Economic Backwardness in Historical Perspective.* Cambridge, MA: Harvard University Press.

Gilpin, Robert (1975) 'Three Models of the Future', *International Organization*, 39 (1): 37–60.

Gourevitch, Peter (1978) 'The Second Image Reversed', *International Organization*, 32 (4): 881–912.

Gourevitch, Peter (1986) *Politics in Hard Times: Comparative Responses to International Economic Crises.* Ithaca: Cornell University Press.

Green, Donald P. and Shapiro, Ian (1994) *Pathologies of Rational Choice.* New Haven: Yale University Press.

Greider, William (1997) *One World Ready or Not.* New York: Simon & Schuster.

Gupta, Akhil (1998) *Postcolonial Developments.* Durham: Duke University Press.

Gurr, Ted Robert (1970) *Why Men Rebel.* Princeton: Princeton University Press.

Haas, Ernest B. and Schmitter, Phillipe (1964) *International Organization*, 18 (4): 705–37.

Haggard, Stephan (1985) 'The Politics of Adjustment: Lessons from the IMF's Extended Fund Facility', in Miles Kahler (ed.), *The Politics of International Debt.* Ithaca: Cornell University Press.

Hawley, Claude E. and Dexter, Lewis A. (1952) 'Recent Political Science Research in American Universities', *American Political Science Review*, 46 (2): 470–85.

Hirschman, Albert O. (1958) *The Strategy of Economic Development*. New Haven: Yale University Press.

Hoogvelt, Ankie (1997) *Globalization and the Post Colonial World*. Basingstoke: Macmillan.

Huntington, Samuel (1968) *Political Order in Changing Societies*. New Haven: Yale University Press.

Illich, Ivan (1997) 'Development as Planned Poverty', in Majid Rahnema and Victoria Bawtree (eds), *The Post-Development Reader*. London: Zed Books. pp. 179–98.

Johnson, Chalmers (1982) *MITI and the Japanese Miracle*. Stanford: Stanford University Press.

Jones, Mark P. (1997) 'Federalism and the Number of Parties in Argentine Congressional Elections', *Journal of Politics*, 59 (2): 538–49.

Katzenstein, Peter J. (1985) *Small States in World Markets*. Ithaca: Cornell University Press.

Kay, Geoffrey (1975) *Development and Underdevelopment*. London: Macmillan.

Keohane, Robert (1978) 'Economics, Inflation and the State', *International Organization*, 31(1): 108–28.

Keohane, Robert O. and Nye, Joseph S. (1971) *Transnational Relations and World Politics*. Cambridge, MA: Harvard University Press.

Kindleberger, Charles P. (1955) 'Economists in International Organizations', *International Organization*, 9 (3): 338–52.

Krasner, Stephen D. (1985) *Structural Conflict: The Third World Against Global Liberalism*. Berkeley: University of California Press.

Krasner, Stephen D. (1996) 'The Accomplishments of International Political Economy', in Steve Smith, Ken Booth and Marysia Zalewski (eds), *International Theory: Positivism and Beyond*. Cambridge: Cambridge University Press. pp. 102–11.

Krueger, Anne O. (1990) 'Government Failures in Development', in Jeffry Frieden, Manuel Pastor and Michael Tomz (eds) (2000), *Modern Political Economy and Latin America*. Boulder: Westview.

Krugman, Paul (1996) *Development, Geography and Economic Theory*. Cambridge, MA. MIT Press

Lapalombara, Joseph (ed.) (1963) *Bureaucracy and Political Development*. Princeton: Princeton University Press.

Lerner, Daniel (1958) *The Passing of Traditional Society*. Glencoe, IL: Free Press.

Levitt, Kari (1970) *The Silent Surrender*. Toronto: Macmillan.

Levy, Marion (1966) *Modernization and the Structure of Society*. Princeton: Princeton University Press.

Lewis, Arthur (1955) *The Economic Theory of Growth*. London: Allen, Unwin.

Leys, Colin (1996a) 'The Crisis in "Development Theory"', *New Political Economy*, 1 (1): 41–58.

Leys, Colin (1996b) *The Rise and Fall of Development Theory*. Oxford: James Currey.

Little, Ian M.D., Scitovsky, T. and Scott, M. (1979) *Industry and Trade in Some Developing Countries*. London: Oxford University Press.

Martinussen, John (1997) *Society, State and Market*. London: Zed Books.

McClelland, David (1961) *The Achieving Society*. Princeton: Van Nostrand.

Meier, Gerald (1964) *Leading Issues in Economic Development*. New York: Oxford University Press.

Meier, Gerald and Seers, Dudley (1984) *Pioneers in Development*. New York: Oxford University Press for the World Bank.

Miller, Marian A.L. (1995) *The Third World in Global Environmental Politics*. Buckingham: Open University Press.

Millikan, Max (1968) 'An Introductory Essay', *International Organization*, 32 (1): 1–16.

Nurkse, Ragnar (1953) *Problems of Capital Formation in Underdeveloped Countries*. London: Blackwell.

O'Donnell, Guillermo (1973) *Modernization and Bureaucratic Authoritarianism*. Berkeley: University of California Press.

Ostrom, Elinor, Schroer, Larry and Wynne, Susan (1993) *Institutional Incentives and Sustainable Development: Infrastructure Policies in Perspective*. Boulder: Westview.

Payne, Anthony (1998) 'The New Political Economy of Area Studies', *Millennium: Journal of International Studies*, 27 (2): 253–73.

Peet, Richard (1997) 'Feature Review', *New Political Economy*, 2 (2): 341–7.

Persson, Torsten and Tabellini, Guido (2000) *Political Economy: Explaining Economic Policy*. Cambridge, MA: MIT Press.

Pigg, Stacy Leigh (1997) '"Found in Most Traditional Societies": Traditional Medical Practitioners between Culture and Development', in Frederick Cooper and Randall Packard (eds), *International Development and the Social Sciences*. Berkeley: University of California Press. pp. 259–90.

Popkin, Samuel (1979) *The Rational Peasant*. Berkeley: University of California Press.

Prebisch, Raul (1950) 'The Economic Development of Latin America', reprinted in Stephan Haggard (ed.) (1995) *The International Political Economy and Developing Countries,* vol. I. Aldershot: Elgar.

Putterman, Louis (ed.) (1990) *The Economic Nature of the Firm*. Cambridge: Cambridge University Press.

Pye, Lucian (ed.) (1967) *Communications and Political Development*. Princeton: Princeton University Press.

Quinn, Dennis (1997) 'The Correlates of Changes in International Financial Regulation', *American Political Science Review*, 91: 531–51.

Rahnema, Majid and Bawtree, Victoria (eds) (1997) *The Post-Development Reader*. London: Zed Books.

Rodrik, Dani (1998) 'Why Do More Open Economies Have Bigger Government?', *Journal of Political Economy*, 106: 997–1032.

Rodrik, Dani (1999) *The New Global Economy and Developing Countries*. Washington, DC: Overseas Development Council.

Roodman, David Malin (2001) *Still Waiting for the Jubilee*. Washington, DC: Worldwatch Institute.

Rosenstein-Rodan, Paul (1943) 'Problems of Industrialization in Eastern and South-Eastern Europe', reprinted in Stephan Haggard (ed.) (1995) *The International*

Political Economy and Developing Countries. Aldershot: Elgar.

Rostow, Walt (1960) *The Stages of Growth. An Anti-Communist Manifesto.* Cambridge: Cambridge University Press.

Saint-Paul, Gilles (2000) 'The "New Political Economy": Recent Books', *Journal of Economic Literature*, 37 (December): 915–25.

Schuurmann, Frans J. (1993) *Beyond the Impasse: New Directions in Development Theory.* London: Zed Books.

Schuurmann, Frans J. (2000) 'Paradigms Lost, Paradigms Regained?', *Third World Quarterly*, 21 (7): 7–20.

Seers, Dudley (1959) 'An Approach to the Short-Period Analysis of Primary-Producing Economies', *Oxford Economic Papers*, February: 1–36.

Sharp, Walter L. (1953) 'The Institutional Framework for Technical Assistance', *International Organization*, 7 (3): 342–79.

Short, Clare (1998) 'The Meaning of Globalization for Development Policy', *Social Policy and Administration*, 32 (5): 456–63.

Simmons, Beth and Elkins, Zachary (2000) 'Globalization and Policy Diffusion: Explaining Three Decades of Liberalization', paper prepared for the Conference on Globalization and Governance, University of California, San Diego, 22–25 June.

Singer, Hans (1950) 'The Distribution of Gains Between Investing and Borrowing Countries', in Stephan Haggard (ed.) (1995) *The International Political Economy and Developing Countries.* Aldershot: Elgar.

Smith, Tony (1979) 'The Underdevelopment of the Development Literature: The Case of Dependency Theory', *World Politics*, 31 (2): 247–88.

Stephan, Alfred (1973) *Authoritarian Brazil.* New Haven, CT: Yale University Press.

Streeton, Paul (1984) 'Development Dichotomies' in Gerald Meier and Dudley Seers (eds), *Pioneers in Development.* New York: Oxford University Press for the World Bank.

Streeton, Paul (2000) 'Global Institutions for an Interdependent World', in Stuart Corbridge (ed.), *Challenges for Development.* London: Routledge. pp. 321–54.

Sunkel, Osualdo (1972) 'Big Business and Dependencia', *Foreign Affairs,* 50: 517–31.

Todaro, Michael P. (1989) *Economic Development in the Third World.* New York: Longman.

UNRISD (2000) *What Choices do Democracies Have?* Geneva: UNRISD.

Wade, Robert (1990) *Governing the Market.* Princeton: Princeton University Press.

Wallerstein, Immanuel (1976) 'Modernization: Requiescat in Pace', in Lewis A. Coser and Otto N. Larsen (eds), *The Uses of Controversy in Sociology.* New York: The Free Press. pp. 131–5.

Weiner, Myron (ed.) (1996) *The Dynamics of Growth.* New York: Basic Books.

Weinstein, Franklin B. (1976) 'MNCS and the Third World', *International Organization*, 30: 3.

Williamson, John (1990) 'What Washington Means by Policy Reform', in Jeffry Frieden, Manuel Pastor and Michael Tomz (eds), *Modern Political Economy and Latin America.* Boulder: Westview. ch. 3.

25

Comparative Regional Integration

YOUNG JONG CHOI AND JAMES A. CAPORASO

One of the most striking facts about the modern global political economy is that it is organized so strongly on a regional basis. For all the talk of globalization, many indicators of globalization (for example, trade, foreign direct investment, international institutions) are directed toward regional partners. In Western Europe, imports and exports increasingly have an origin and destination within the same area, and much the same can be said for North America and East Asia. From a global and national viewpoint, the regionalization of economic and political activity presents a puzzle. From a global vantage point, regional trade institutions are clearly sub-optimal and may even pose severe obstacles to wider integration (Bhagwati, 1992). If market enlargement, specialization and exchange are good (that is, efficient), why don't global solutions clearly trump regional ones? From a national standpoint, if security is considered along with economic exchange, then diversification of trade partners would seem valuable, and in some sense the further away one's partners the better. The spatial (regional) concentration of economic activity runs against prudent security concerns. Distant partners tend not to be security threats. Both neoclassical economics and realism would seem to hesitate about regional organization. Yet economic and political activities increasingly cluster in regional patterns.

Three regions (Western Europe, North America and East Asia) constitute the most prominent zones of global economic integration. There are other regions of importance, for example, southern Africa, Central Europe (increasingly drawn into the West), the Middle East, the Pacific Rim, South America, and sub-regional economic zones ('natural economic territories') like the Greater South China

Economic Zone (Hong Kong, Macao, Guangdon, Fujian Provinces, Taiwan) and the Growth Triangle including Singapore, Batam Island in Indonesia, and Johor Province in Malaysia (Haggard, 1995: 66). Regions, like nations, can be created and destroyed. Northeast Asia is more of a region today than it was thirty years ago, in large part due to the powerful role of Japan and Korea in stimulating economic growth in the region. By the same token, for nearly a half century of the Cold War, the term 'Mitteleuropa' all but disappeared from our geopolitical vocabulary. The tight bipolarity in Europe from 1945 to 1990 eroded the middle as gradually most countries were assimilated into the Eastern or Western bloc. Since 1990, we can speak once again of Central Europe and Mitteleuropa, though in a different way from before 1945 (Ash, 1999; Kundera, 1984).

Regional integration is a widespread phenomenon that transpires in almost every part of the world. The GATT received 124 notifications of regional trading arrangements (RTAs) in the period 1948–94, and from 1995 onwards 90 additional arrangements have been notified. Among them, about 134 RTAs are in force at present (WTO, 1999: 4). Currently, almost every member of the World Trade Organization (WTO) is a member of at least one such an arrangement (if APEC is included). However, few regional trading arrangements, except the European Union (EU), have moved in substantial ways beyond the stage of free trade area and customs union. Most of the free trade areas (FTAs) have not been able to achieve even their stated goal, that is, free trade among member countries. The proliferation of regional organizations, as well as their uneven success and longevity, prompts us to inquire further.

Quantitative increases in the number of regional organizations have gone along with increased diversification of membership. The early integration initiatives in the 1950s and 1960s were either among the advanced countries (North–North integration) or among the developing countries of the South (South–South integration).[1] In the mid-1980s a new breed of integration emerged among countries with different levels of economic development (North–South integration). The North American Free Trade Agreement (NAFTA), which includes Mexico, Canada and the United States, provides a good example. In addition, we could also mention integration attempts between Japan and other Asia–Pacific countries, such as the Asia Pacific Economic Cooperation (APEC) and the East Asian Economic Caucus (EAEC).

The growing diversity of regional integration efforts provides fertile ground on which to examine integration theories, which rely heavily on the European experience. Indeed, earlier integration research, during the 1950s, 1960s and partly into the 1970s, was much more comparative in scope than recent scholarship, in which Europe has become the conceptual universe and not just the practical site of applied research. Ernst Haas and Philippe Schmitter (1964), Sidney Dell (1966) and Miguel Wionczek (1970) all wrote about Latin American integration. Schmitter also made contributions to the study of Central American integration as well as integration in Western Europe (1969, 1970). Amitai Etzioni's *Political Unification* (1965) was organized around a comparison of the United Arab Republic, the Federation of West Indies, the Nordic Association and the European Economic Community. His book stands out not only for its comprehensive coverage and comparative scope but also for its astute sense of design. Etzioni examined two failed unions, one stable union and a growing one. Many of the variables that we have placed in the background today (security context, type of societies that are integrating, relation of countries to external powers) were taken as problematic by Etzioni. In the same vein, Joseph Nye (1966, 1970) wrote about economic integration in East Africa and did comparative work on the Arab League, the Organization of American States (OAS) and the Organization of African Unity (OAU). Others, such as Andrew Axline (1977), carried out extensive research on the less developed world and paid particular attention to distributional issues as causes of success and failure. By contrast, research today has become more heavily concentrated in Western Europe, North America and Asia, with little communication across the three areas, producing studies of multiple regions that are in a fundamental way not comparative.

The rest of this chapter is organized in the following way. The first section defines several key concepts related to regional integration and reviews the linkages among them. The second section provides a brief overview of regional integration efforts in recent decades. The third section attempts to take stock of our theoretical knowledge of regional integration. It both reviews these theories and evaluates them. In the fourth section, we examine some important issues relevant to integration efforts in Western Europe, East Asia and North America. The issues we bring into focus have to do with the relationship between regional integration and globalism, the variable link between economic integration and political institutions, and the relationship between regional integration and democratic control. Finally, we offer some conclusions and thoughts about integration research in the future.

DEFINITION OF REGIONAL INTEGRATION

In his book *International Regions and the International System* (1967), Bruce Russett proposed three criteria for the definition of regions: physical proximity and separateness, interdependence and homogeneity. Indicators of physical proximity and separateness were relied on most heavily by geographers before improvements in transportation and communication made physical barriers such as rivers and mountains less important. Even today, when the meaning of physical boundaries is considerably diminished, it does not follow automatically that the political and cultural patterns shaped by geography have been eroded. Strong contrasts may still exist on different sides of the Pyrenees, the Apennines and the Mediterranean, despite the fact that it is much easier to traverse these boundaries today. Still, spatial definitions of regions are not enough.

The second way of defining a region is to ask how interconnected a set of entities is, especially in economic terms. Do countries in Latin America, Europe or South Asia have high levels of economic transactions in trade, production of goods, tourism, labor flows etc.? A region in this sense is a zone where there is a high density of economic transactions relative to other units. In other words, since a region is partial (it is not global), it must shade off into another region or neutral zone. Countries in the EU may have very high levels of economic interaction with one another, but one should ask if these interactions are higher than with the rest of the world. The index of relative acceptance, developed by Richard Savage and Karl Deutsch (1960), was intended specifically to identify regions as groupings of countries that interact well beyond what is expected on the basis of countries' relative contributions to world imports and exports.[2] If regions have boundaries, these boundaries are usually vast gray areas that vary in tones and shades rather than black and white. On the other hand, sometimes the boundaries are sharp, as between Eastern and Western Europe during the Cold War. There could hardly have been a clearer boundary than the wall between East and West Germany, important not only in physical terms but also in political, social and psychological terms.

The third criterion for identifying regions is homogeneity. A large number of variables fit within this framework: similarity of values, of economic systems, of political systems, of way of life, of level of economic development and so on. The difficulty with the homogeneity criterion is that so many things can be assessed from this vantage point and it is not clear which ones count in terms of external criteria. Is Europe a homogenous entity, more so than say Latin America which has notable similarities in terms of language, religion and ethnic backgrounds? For many centuries, Europe was considered a common civilization. Yet, if we were interested in the degree to which this homogeneity predicted violent behavior toward one another, we would find that wars were relatively common occurrences among European countries.

Physical indicators of separateness are inadequate for defining regions because pure physical space and physical boundaries are less important in today's world. Interaction patterns are limited as a measure of regions in that political factors may control the direction of causality (that is, interactions such as trade may be endogenous to political choices). Homogeneity can be faulted as a general approach because there is a huge gap between attributes (even similarity of attributes among countries) and behavior among countries. To take just one example, whether or not two countries trade a lot with one another may be due less to attribute similarities than to a pattern of complementary differences in domestic production structure and comparative cost structures. Indeed, this proposition was advanced by Lipsey (1960) as central to the success of customs unions. In short, no one single approach is likely to work. All we can do is to keep an eye on the three criteria and use them as working hypotheses.

When Russett wrote his book in 1967, he emphasized economics (interdependence), culture (homogeneity of values) and geography (natural boundaries affecting human connections). Neither Russett nor many of his contemporaries accented political institutions. While it may have been possible to write about European integration during the 1960s as a process that was primarily economic, geographic and cultural, such a view would look bizarre today. Indeed, what seems most distinctive about the last several decades of European integration is the huge role played by political-institutional factors, for example, the grand bargains analyzed by Moravcsik (1998), the movement from a decentralized inter-state system towards an institutionalized supranational polity analyzed by Stone Sweet and Sandholtz (1998), the important Treaty amendments of Maastricht and Amsterdam, and the everyday role of Community institutions such as the Court of Justice, the Commission and the Council of Ministers. Political factors are arguably important in North America and Asia also, though less so than in Europe.

While political institutions and the public policies associated with them are undoubtedly important, a more difficult question is how to theorize their role. The literature on institutions has accommodated all viewpoints. Everything from informal understandings to rigidly hierarchical formal organizations has been labeled an institution. A definition that cannot decide what to leave out is not of much help. Stone Sweet and Sandholtz (1998: 8–9) have provided a useful place to start by suggesting a developmental continuum running from intergovernmental politics to supranational politics, both pure ideal types. As we move from intergovernmentalism to supranationalism, we move from a decentralized system of bargaining and coordination to a more centralized system of governance in which supranational organizations have some jurisdiction and decision-making power. Whether one sees institutions as transforming the nature of inter-state politics à la Stone Sweet and Sandholtz (1998) or as playing a more modest role in a larger system of delegated authority as Moravcsik (1998) sees it, it would be impossible to omit institutions from the list of criteria for judging regional integration today.

What are the alternatives to regionalism? It is usually assumed that globalism is the most important alternative. However, there are other alternatives, including functionalism and bilateralism. Functionalism may be taken as an approach to regionalism, or it may be taken as an approach completely at odds with the territorial principle, whether at the national or regional level. David Mitrany, often considered the father of functionalism (prior to Jean Monnet), warned against the logic of territorial organization at the regional level (Mitrany, 1968: 44–5). For Mitrany, functionalism represented an approach to collective problem-solving along lines suggested by the task, not along territorial lines. In contrast, bilateralism is a method of dealing with other countries on a one-for-one basis. The newly industrialized countries, so noted for their successes during the 1960s through to the 1980s, did not form a regional bloc, either in territorial terms or in terms of political organization. Indeed, most of these countries and provinces (South Korea, Taiwan, Singapore, Hong Kong) dealt with the international system on a bilateral basis, attempting to find a niche without exercising bargaining power (Yoffie, 1983).

Is regional integration a developmental process, that is, one in which a set of integrating units moves through numerous phases in orderly fashion, or is it more haphazard and non-linear? Economists have identified a set of stages, starting from free trade area and moving through customs union, common market, economic union to full economic integration (Balassa, 1961). However, even this neat typology is not strictly cumulative (one could have a common external tariff without a free trade area), nor is it clear that one must start with a free trade area, for example, a group of nations could begin with a common market. At best we have a set of labels that may be useful for categorizing the path of members undergoing regional integration, rather than a natural sequence through which all integrating states must pass.

Is there an analogous sequence, however imperfect, for political integration? We can identify several stages of political integration but caution in advance that one does not have to crawl in order to walk. The least integrated form of relationship is unilateral adjustment to the actions of others. This requires no coordination at all. In essence, it simply involves a series of best responses to the actions of others, perhaps suitable to a highly decentralized world with scarce (and abysmally low) information. Above this baseline we can identify simple forms of coordination and collaboration. They involve making rules of the road to smooth out relationships and devising institutions to solve collective action problems. Beyond this we have cooperation to remove obstacles to market integration, or negative integration according to Scharpf (1999). At a more advanced level, we can identify rule-making to foster positive integration. If policy integration is sufficiently advanced, political institutions may be required to structure and routinize decision-making, reflecting a still more advanced level of integration. Finally, once these political institutions are in place, they could work according to consensus or majority decision-making rules. The most deeply integrated political institutions operate according to majority decision-making rules and involve issues of distribution and redistribution, not just regulatory politics and control of international externalities. With majority decision-making, it is possible for states to lose out, that is, to be in the minority when policies are made. The delegation of sovereignty to international institutions involves a ceding of sovereignty, however contingent and retractable.

CURRENT STATE OF REGIONAL INTEGRATION

Economic integration is concentrated in three major regions, that is, Europe, the Americas and East Asia (broadly the Asia–Pacific region). While the broad patterns are similar, there are also wide divergences in terms of the institutional basis of associations, scope of activities covered, and the level of institutional authority.[3] The European Union (EU) has consolidated its status as the champion of regional integration in Europe over the past four decades. The EU currently has fifteen members, and it is poised to expand to include most of what used to be Central and Eastern Europe over the next decade. The scope of activity (the EU's competence) has expanded from coal and steel in the European Coal and Steel Community (ECSC) to trade and investment, agriculture, transport, environment, some aspects of social policy, and finally to economic and monetary union. Some progress has even been made in the difficult area of common foreign and security policy, as the Treaty on European Union (the Maastricht Treaty) shows. The European Commission has substantial power to make proposals and shape legislation that affects member states (Ludlow, 1991). The Council of Ministers, composed of representatives of each of the member states, has the power to pass regulations that are directly effective in the member states (Wessels, 1991). For some issues, the Council acts by unanimity and for others by qualified majority vote. The European Court of Justice (ECJ) is spearheading the integration of the economy by rendering judgments that implement the four freedoms of the Treaty, that is, goods, services, capital and labor (Burley and Mattli, 1993; Stone Sweet and Caporaso, 1998). The European Monetary Union (EMU) is in its final phase and is complete for all practical purposes. A European Central Bank (ECB) exists as well as a common currency, the euro (Cameron, 1998; McNamara, 1998). At that point, the member states will have delegated to the European level monetary powers previously exercised at the national level.

Regional integration in the Americas started in the 1950s with the failed attempt to create a Latin America Free Trade Area (LAFTA). A second wave of integration started in 1988 with the Canada–US Free Trade Agreement (CUSTA), which became the North American Free Trade Agreement (NAFTA) in 1993. Another attempt was the Common Market of the South (MERCOSUR), established in 1991 by Argentina, Brazil, Paraguay and Uruguay. The MERCOSUR aims at completing a customs union at the current stage, and its ultimate goal is a common market.

The NAFTA is a preferential trade arrangement, and thus its scope of activity remains largely limited to trade and investment, although it has also been used as a forum for discussing and implementing standards for labor and the environment. NAFTA has an institutional basis for dispute settlement. Chapter 20 of NAFTA sets forth a generally applicable procedure for dispute settlement, in which the third party's ruling is non-binding and without proper enforcement authority. In addition, Chapter 19 establishes a separate dispute settlement mechanism regarding anti-dumping and countervailing duties. Panel decisions are binding and have 'direct effect' in domestic laws, creating

Table 25.1   *Institutionalization of major regions*

	Institutional basis (type of institution)	Scope of activity	Level of institutional authority in dispute settlement (third-party review, bindingness, enforcement)
Europe	European Union (economic union)	Comprehensive	High (third-party review, binding ruling, direct effect in domestic law)
Americas	NAFTA (free trade area)	Trade and investment	Medium (Ch. 20: third-party review, non-binding, sanctions; Ch. 19: third-party review, binding ruling, direct effect in domestic law)
	MERCOSUR (projected customs union)	Trade and investment	Medium (third-party review, binding ruling, sanctions)
Asia and the Pacific	AFTA (free trade area)	Trade and investment	Low (third-party review, non-binding ruling, self-help)
	APEC (projected free trade area)	Consultation on numerous issues	None

a binding obligation under national law (Abbott, 2000: 535–43).

The MERCOSUR has so far concentrated on reducing intra-regional trade barriers. It also emphasizes foreign policy coordination geared toward presenting a united front on various economic issues such as debt management, multilateral trade negotiations and other regional economic affairs (Pereira, 1999). MERCOSUR has a provision for arbitration by a specially constituted tribunal or expert panel under the Brasilia Protocol of 1991 that makes binding rulings on disputes. However, it has no proper enforcement authority, and the enforcement is largely up to self-help or unilateral sanctions (Smith, 2000: 157). In practice, trade disputes are usually settled by negotiation (Laird, 1997: 5).

East Asia lags far behind even the Americas, not to mention Western Europe, in terms of institutionalization. A group of countries located in the south-eastern part of the region, excluding major economic and/or military powers such as Japan and China, formed a sub-regional grouping called the Association of the Southeast Asian Nations (ASEAN) in 1967.[4] ASEAN has proven to be the only sustainable regional cooperation organization in the region. Emerging out of security concerns in the Indo-China region, ASEAN began intra-regional economic cooperation only in the mid-1970s. Its widely pronounced free trade agreement (AFTA) has so far failed to live up to its name. It has many loopholes and lags well behind schedule. The ASEAN governments are extremely reluctant to create a supranational body with a binding authority (Ravenhill, 1995). In spite of a low level of legalism in its institutional structure, however, ASEAN has achieved a remarkable institutional development in the early 1990s in terms of the scope of cooperation and organizational ability to

monitor the implementation of agreements (Kahler, 2000: 553–5).

The East Asian Economic Caucus (EAEC), initiated by Malaysian Prime Minister Mahatir, is a weaker variant of the East Asian Economic Grouping (EAEG) aimed at forming a regional economic bloc. EAEC had to overcome internal opposition from ASEAN, as well as from outside, such as from the United States and Australia. EAEC has yet to win Japan's recognition and support. A note of promise is the gathering of East Asian leaders (ASEAN 10 plus Japan, China and South Korea), started in 1998 at the annual ASEAN summit meeting. Until then, the Asia Pacific Economic Cooperation (APEC) had been the sole regional organization in which all the willing East Asian countries participated in regional economic cooperation.

APEC deals with a broad range of issues rather thinly, relegating its role to only information-gathering and exchange. By emphasizing an informal, bottom-up approach to regional cooperation, reflecting the preferences of Japan and ASEAN, APEC has avoided becoming a legalistic institution. It has retained this character in spite of US efforts to push APEC in the direction of legalization and institutionalization. It maintains only a small secretariat, which relies heavily on numerous working groups to come to a consensus, and informal advisory groups play a prominent role in agenda-setting and research. APEC's commitment to trade liberalization is up to the voluntary, unilateral action of each member and peer pressure. As expected from its non-legalistic nature, there is no formal dispute settlement mechanism in APEC (Kahler, 2000: 556–9).

As summarized in Table 25.1, the three major regions of the world, that is (Europe, the Americas and East Asia) have shown a wide divergence in the degree of institutionalization as measured by the existence and the power of the regional authority presiding over the integration process. The strongest variation lies in the existence of a third party to make binding and enforceable decisions. This divergence, especially the institutional under-development in East Asia (or broadly the Asia–Pacific region), is one of the key topics to be dealt with throughout this chapter.

THEORIES OF REGIONAL INTEGRATION

The field of regional integration displays a wide range of theories, but few sharply formulated hypotheses to discriminate among them. As a result, scholars often engage in broad meta-theoretical debates emphasizing programmatic statements with selective illustrations designed to show why one approach is superior, rather than comparative theory-testing in light of systematic evidence. Since the data are sufficiently abundant and flexible to illustrate any meta-theoretical position, this approach does not result in the selective winnowing of alternative theories. In this section, we focus on some of the most important theories, inevitably omitting others. We discuss neofunctionalism, real-ism, liberal intergovernmentalism, constructivism and multi-level governance.

Neofunctionalist Approaches

Functionalism and neofunctionalism were the prog-enitors of the field of regional integration. These approaches contain two key insights or research foci. The first has to do with the power of trans-national society, the role of interest groups, profes-sional associations, producer groups and labor unions, as well as cultural and scientific organiza-tions. Jean Monnet argued that individuals and groups, engaged in practical problem-solving across borders, provided the push (or the demand-side) for regional integration. Without this demand side, regional integration could not succeed. It would have no popular motivation. Rulers and statespersons might bring together governments in international conferences, but without a supporting societal base regional integration would lack a broad appeal. Understood in this way, functionalism represents a type of social pluralism. It points to society as the engine of politics. Just as it would be impossible to understand domestic politics without understanding the strategies and demands of domes-tic interest groups, it is difficult to comprehend regional politics without taking into account indus-trialists, workers, consumers and special interests.

The second principle has to do with the role of supranational institutions. Social and economic interests, no matter how intense, may be lacking in organization, knowledge of group predicament,

capacity to mobilize interests and access to policy-making influence. A well-developed demand side is necessary for integration, but it is not sufficient. Without political mechanisms to provide leader-ship, aggregate interests and convert them into policy, even the most intense interests may not lead to policy consequences. Thus, international institu-tions and political leadership are required. Neo-functionalists in Western Europe placed great faith in the European Commission as the institution most likely to create initiatives, provide leadership and translate social demands into policy with a European scope.

It is best to think of neofunctionalism as a composite theory that has three components: back-ground conditions, process conditions and condi-tions that are likely to encourage or discourage task expansion (Haas and Schmitter, 1964). With regard to background conditions, neofunctionalism argued that integration was most likely to emerge first among countries with a certain type of domestic environment: liberal democratic countries with advanced capitalist economies, differentiated social structures, and highly pluralistic interest group structures. In these societies, class conflicts were to be muted, ethnic rivalries less intense, and warfare an obsolescent institution (Haas, 1968). Such coun-tries would have much to gain from an expansion of capitalism to the regional level. The process condi-tions entail dense networks of economic exchange, trade, labor migrations, tourism and free flows of productive factors. The third phase involves spillover. Once integration begins in initial settings (presumably the least controversial ones), there are prospects for expanding cooperative habits into other areas. This process of task expansion is labeled spillover. Spillover could be purely func-tional, with linkages among different sectors serv-ing as the transmission belts of integration (trade might imply increasing coordination of monetary policy for example), or it could rely on tactical link-ages among sectors by agents in a bargaining process (for example, tying together the move to the single market with structural policy) (Caporaso and Keeler, 1995: 31).

Two of the broadest neofunctional treatments of integration are provided by Haas and Schmitter (1964) and Nye (1968). Haas and Schmitter present nine variables – four background conditions (that is, size of units, rate of transactions, pluralism and élite complementarity), two conditions at time of economic union (that is, government purposes and the independence of regional institutions), and three process conditions (that is, decision-making style, rate of transactions and adaptability of govern-ments) that are related to political union (1964: 720). If a group of countries maintains a high degree of economic and social transactions, and at the same time shares pluralist domestic institutions with similar economic size and similar level of development, it will have a good chance of achieving political union.

Is functionalism dead? While few scholars explicitly carry out research under the banner of functionalism, it is best to see it as a proto-theory with continuous (though not one for one) lineage to contemporary theories. Part of the appeal of Moravcsik's work (1993, 1998) is that he captures the elemental appeal of socioeconomic forces in both domestic and transnational society and transmutes Monnet's raw materials into a theory of preference formation.[5] In contrast to Monnet, Moravcsik relies on tools from economics, political economy and collective action theory to derive preferences of key actors. Still, the problematic addressed by functionalism (that is, the construction of interests and the role they play in regional integration) is present.

The edited volume by Stone Sweet and Sandholtz, *European Integration and Supranational Governance* (1998), also develops some of functionalism's themes. They ask about the conditions under which political institutions emerge at the international level. In answering their question, they rely heavily on preferences in domestic and transnational society to generate the demand for regional integration, including the policies and political institutions needed to overcome the transaction costs associated with different regimes in different countries. A first-cut hypothesis is that as economic exchange goes up, so too will the demand for common rules and rule-adjudication. Since Stone Sweet and Sandholtz locate the main obstacle to regional integration in the differences among the rules and norms at the national level, it follows that political integration implies either eliminating these discrepancies or finding some other principle to coordinate the differences (1998: 11). Movement toward higher levels of institutionalization comes from the constant pressure exerted by the conflicts surrounding economic exchange and the ongoing arbitrage resulting from the attempts to devise rules as well as to escape them. Stone Sweet argues that third-party dispute resolution emerges as a credible way to solve conflicts. One increasingly powerful form of third-party dispute resolution involves judicialization (Stone Sweet, 1999).

In 'Choosing Union: Monetary Politics and Maastricht' (1993) and 'Membership Matters: Limits of the Functionalist Approach to European Institutions' (1996), Sandholtz continues the functionalist research program while at the same time redirects it to take into account changes in preferences due to membership. He criticizes the intergovernmentalist approach for assuming that preferences are exogenous to institutional membership, formed by some sort of 'hermetic process' and then transported to Brussels to be negotiated (1993: 3). He argues that interests of social actors, as well as negotiating positions adopted by states,

are affected not only by economic facts but also by the experience of membership in international institutions itself. Sandholtz's argument, while designed to point out a limitation of functionalism, provides a theoretical bridge between international institutions and domestic preferences.

In sum, while functionalism is still important today, it exists less as a separate research program and more as an influence on other theories. The functionalist message has been absorbed into theories of institutions as well as theories of preference formation that are based in asset ownership, leading sectors and the distribution of economic capabilities. Insofar as functionalism allows (even urges) a strong autonomous role for international institutions and provides a space for domestic actors to influence regional organizations and policies directly (rather than via national capitals), it provides a rival to realist explanations.

Realist Approaches

A realist theory of regional integration may sound like an oxymoron. Realism presents itself as a triumph of politics over economics, of power and security over economic exchange, of conflict over cooperation, and of the state over transnational economic and social processes. In addition, in stark contrast to functionalism and liberal intergovernmentalism, realist theory argues that the preferences of states (including preferences for integration) are determined by their position in the international system, that is, their position within the international distribution of power. Thus, the nature and composition of societal groups, attributes of states and similarities among countries do not matter so much as placement in the international distribution of power. Yet when states join a regional union, they presumably commit to cooperation with a stable membership over a long period of time. Durable membership with the same partners focused on mutual absolute gains implies the antithesis of realist expectations (frequently changing allies based on shifts of power and preoccupation with relative gains). So, is a realist theory of regional integration a non-starter?

As one of the leading theories of international relations, realism does have something to say about regional integration. Realists start by reasoning that two key elements of systemic structure are anarchy and the international distribution of power. Anarchy produces distrust and makes each country vulnerable to the deceits of others. Since economic exchange can make one's partners stronger in their military capacity, trade takes place only at severe risk to one's security, since one country may gain more than another or may deploy its share of gains from trade for security purposes. Yet anarchy by itself is not sufficient in explaining why some countries integrate regionally and others do not. After all, anarchy is a global property of the international system in realist theory, and it is not differentiated by region. Thus anarchy cannot explain variations in cooperative exchange or why some countries are devoured by a fixation on relative gains while others pursue absolute gains.

One approach to reconciling regional integration with realism is provided by Joanne Gowa in 'Bipolarity, Multipolarity and Free Trade' (1989). Gowa argues that the Cold War shifted the focus of European countries to the United States and the Soviet Union. Gowa recognizes the security externalities generated by trade, and she approaches this issue by parsing the effects of different kinds of power distributions (chiefly bipolarity and multipolarity) on the incentives for trade. Since bipolar systems are more stable than multipolar systems, Gowa predicts that countries will exploit this longer time horizon by deepening cooperative exchanges among them. Thus, the bipolar distribution of power after the Second World War encouraged deep integration within Europe. The incentives were all the stronger since all the members of the European Economic Community (EEC) were also members of the North Atlantic Treaty Organization (NATO) (Caporaso, 1993: 463–4).

When the Cold War ended in the early 1990s, the question immediately emerged of what effect this would have on integration in Western Europe. Mearsheimer (1990) provided the response most consistent with realist theory. In short, he argued that with the end of the Cold War and collapse of the Soviet Union, the United States was likely to pull back from NATO and tensions increase among European countries. Multipolar power balancing was likely to increase, and the problem of containing Germany was likely to be more pronounced. While the results of the end of the Cold War may not be in, a decade has elapsed and European integration seems even stronger. The Maastricht Treaty (1993), the Treaty of Amsterdam (1997), EMU, increased powers of the European Parliament, and a continuing strong role of the ECJ, all point to a strengthened EU.

The scholar who has most seriously considered the value of realism as an explanation of European integration after the Cold War is Joseph Grieco (1993, 1995, 1996). Focusing on the Treaty of Maastricht (1993) and EMU, Grieco asks how and why governments have committed to these agreements, which severely restrict their autonomy. His argument, in short form, is that countries (particularly the 'secondary states' that are weaker but still influential partners) bargain to increase their influence by binding powerful members into international institutions and policies. Grieco calls this the 'voice opportunity thesis', reflecting the political influence that states try to exert to enhance their role in international organizations, and to decrease

and manage the burdens coming from being part of an interconnected market with larger countries (Grieco, 1995: 24, 34).

Let us assume that this is an accurate description of secondary states' behavior within the negotiations over EMU. Then several questions remain. Why did the strongest country (Germany) choose to bind itself? Can an answer be derived based on the logic of anarchy and balance of power? Did weaker states, including Italy, Belgium, the Netherlands and others, choose to join out of power balancing considerations, lack of a viable alternative produced by the altered status quo (Gruber, 2000) or domestic considerations? To take just one example, it appears that in Italy's case joining EMU was in good part a matter of avoiding the worst faults of its own domestic political processes and providing an external stimulus to the reform of its pension system (Sbragia, 2001).

But the main question is simply this: can the voice opportunity thesis be derived from the systemic logic of realist theory? Grieco's voice opportunity thesis argues that states, faced with high levels of interdependence, prior thick institutions and policy externalities, will try to cut the best bargain in terms of the rule-based system they adopt for monetary affairs. Some states fear Germany's market hegemony more than its political power. Thus, for some, it is wise to push into a more rule-based arena an issue-area previously dominated by the market.

This argument affirms the importance of states, their varying national interests and the importance they attach to negotiations. If anyone believes that membership in the EU homogenizes interests or leads to the erosion of bargaining in favor of a Brussels consensus, Grieco's argument is a healthy corrective. However, it does little to affirm the realist (or neorealist) core. There is next to nothing in Grieco's argument about structure-induced preferences, about preoccupation with relative gains, and about shifting allies. What it does affirm is the importance of domestic politics, the weight of past institutions (the European Monetary System, Single European Market, the institutional acquis), and the continued relevance of power bargaining. But continued bargaining in the EU cannot be taken as evidence (let alone distinctive evidence) for realism. Bargaining is characteristic of nearly all theories of politics, from pluralism to varieties of institutionalism, so the presence of bargains can hardly be used to provide leverage in favor of one or another theory.

Liberal Intergovernmentalism

While neofunctionalism starts with transnational society and supranational institutions, liberal intergovernmentalism places states (central governments, usually executives) at the center of analysis.

This is not to say that interest groups are unimportant. However, the force of these groups is felt as part of a causal chain in which economic and social interests are funneled through the domestic political process and are affected by domestic institutions. Crucial to this approach to integration are the processes of interest aggregation, intergovernmental bargaining and enforcement of decisions. The most important exponent, indeed founder, of the liberal intergovernmental view of regional integration is Andrew Moravcsik. In 'Preferences and Power in the European Community: A Liberal Intergovernmental Approach' (1993), Moravcsik lays out a two-step process of preference formation and bargaining which he extends (1998) to a three-step process: preference-formation, intergovernmental bargaining and institutional lock-in of bargains.

The basic idea is that economic and social interests provide the raw material of politics but that these interests have to be recognized and mobilized before they become active in politics. Pluralist interest group theory, as well as the logic of collective action, helps to explain the formation of groups pursuing their interests. Some of these interests lie in the domestic arena and some in the transnational arena. At this level, the intergovernmental model is not state-centric. After interests are formed, they must pass through the political process. One of the telling lessons of modern institutional theory is that identical constellations of interests can produce very different results in terms of political outcomes. The political system is not simply an adding machine that translates economic demands into political results. Procedures for aggregating interests vary considerably from country to country. Leaders of countries must then take societal interests (as well as their own) into the international negotiating forum and bargain to achieve favorable results, that is, results that are acceptable to both foreign counterparts and domestic constituencies in all affected countries. Once agreement and ratification take place, institutions are devised to lock-in, monitor and enforce the agreements.

The liberal intergovernmental approach provides a more sophisticated theory of preference formation than neofunctionalism. This theory is based in part on the logic of collective action and the new institutionalism. Without institutions present as part of the theoretical specification of preferences, neofunctionalism risks providing an inaccurate account of the role of social and economic forces. In addition, there is now a central role for power in the process of international negotiation. The introduction of states, representing both their own institutional interests as well as the interests of their constituents, provides a more accurate picture of regional integration than one exclusively based on social forces and supranational entrepreneurs.

The intergovernmental approach is vulnerable on several grounds.[6] Moravcsik limits his focus to celebrated intergovernmental bargains or 'grand bargains'. There is, of course, nothing wrong with this focus *per se*. However, we want to ask how robust the theory of regional integration is, that is, how sensitive it is to departures from its own initial assumptions. As we look at less central issues or the not-so-grand bargains, does the same theory hold or do we need to devise a new one? Good case selection implies that we look at the full continuum or attempt to sample cases from different locations along the continuum. The main reason for such sampling is not to achieve representativeness but simply to build in the required variation for hypothesis-testing. If concern for sovereignty, minimum common denominator bargaining, and use of state power are factors that vary with the importance of the issue, then we would only know this if we have some variation on the underlying issues dealt with by governments.

A second problem, best stated in the form of a question, is more theoretical than methodological. What is the relationship between grand bargains and day-to-day politics in regional organizations? Intergovernmental theory implies that political agreements, with their accompanying institutions, provide a kind of equilibrium, until acted upon by outside forces. New economic demands will occur, as they are continuously generated in the domestic and transnational economy. However, the stimulus to these demands seems exogenous to the three-step process. Governments can monitor, enforce and rein in agents who go astray, and they can do so either directly or through delegating power to agents. However, as Pierson (1996) shows, this assumption is questionable. Agents often have considerable slack and access to resources, as well as enough asymmetric information about context to implement policy considerably at odds with the wishes of government principals. Also, as Joseph Jupille (2000) has demonstrated, day-to-day politics in regional organizations is about procedural manipulation or the choice of rules, rather than bargaining over grand constitutional structures. There is considerable discretion for international or supranational agents to engage in decision-making at odds with the outlines conceived by chiefs of governments.

The core of neofunctional theory rests on the power of unintended consequences, that is, unintended from the standpoint of the goals of the principal. If EU actors, particularly the Commission, develop independent goals, have access to inside information, and have considerable slack to influence policies, they may well both go beyond what states mandate and are capable of monitoring. The short- and long-term consequences of the interplay between state and regional actors have not been adequately explored.

Constructivist Approaches

A newer approach to regional integration, but again limited mostly to Western Europe, is constructivism. The core of the constructivist research program concerns the role of ideas, norms and identities, as opposed to material factors, in the integration process. Ruggie has argued that '... at bottom, constructivism concerns the issue of human consciousness' (1998: 33). Onuf, who has offered the most comprehensive statement of constructivism in *World of Our Making* (1989), sees human thought, ideas and agency as crucial to the explanation of the international order. Insofar as this is the core, the theoretical foundations for constructivism lie in social psychology and sociology. Berger and Luckmann's *The Social Construction of Reality* (1966) may be taken as a classic statement, if not the one from which many constructivists depart. And Wendt's *Social Theory of International Politics* (1999) explores the ontological assumptions of constructivism and develops its philosophical underpinnings. Finally, the research done by Deutsch and his collaborators (1957), which focused on community, on the development of 'we-feelings', and on the frequency and meaning of symbols in the development of national identities, certainly qualifies as constructivist. A valuable updating and interpretation of Deutsch's work, focusing on security communities and the values that undergird them, is provided by Adler and Barnett (1998).

Constructivism's debts to earlier work and its links to areas of basic research such as social identity theory are not meant as criticism – far from it. It is valuable to have a foundation in basic theory and, without arguing that there is never anything new under the sun, we would be suspicious if constructivism emerged *de novo*. Also, there has been much new work informed by constructivist principles relating to European integration. Most of this work has concentrated in Western Europe, the EU, the Council of Europe and broader social processes such as changing conceptions of citizenship.

Perhaps the leading constructivist scholar of European integration is Jeffrey Checkel (1998, 1999, 2001). Checkel argues that ideas, norms and identities are important but not just as external constraints. Rational choice theory also argues that these phenomena are important but simply incorporates them into the cost (benefit) function of agents. Norms, then, are simply constraints that agents run up against when they make choices. For Checkel, norms can become constitutive of agents, part of who they are, and deeply internalized. When this occurs, the overall interpretation changes from one based on conscious adjustment to changing costs to one based on enactment of values (a scripted model based on logics of appropriateness rather than a utilitarian one).

Beyond these interpretive differences, Checkel looks for testable implications of the constructivist approach. First, the effects of changing costs and benefits at the margins should be less than is generally assumed in utilitarian theories. If norms have independent explanatory weight, they must have some incremental (additional) advantage over changing costs and benefits. Second, compliance with European rules should be less responsive to changing sanctions and benefits of going alone and more to deep institutional factors, such as the conception of a country of itself as a rule-of-law country, one that lives according to rules regardless of whether they agree with them. The UK, for example, has a very good record of implementing EU laws, even when they are vigorously opposed in legislative and judicial decision-making. Institutional capacity, as well as strong normative presumptions in favor of obeying the law, surely works in favor of compliance. Third, constructivism implies endogenous preferences, not just to the economy, but also to political institutions and social interaction that take place in international contexts. Checkel offers numerous hypotheses about preference changes and identities in 'Social Construction and Integration' (1999).

Much other work has been done by scholars, mostly European, relating to the importance of ideas, values and norms, and identities. Amy Verdun's work (1999) on EMU focuses on the Delors Committee as an evolving epistemic community. Jo Shaw (1999) has elaborated a changing conception of 'postnational constitutionalism' in which citizens rights are not fixed, nor limited to the territorial containers of the state, but responsive to transborder movements and demands that are not easily dealt with by the nation-states. Marcussen et al. (1999), Risse (2001) and Risse et al. (1999) have researched the issue of state identities. Not only is there important variation from one state to the next (France, Germany and Great Britain have different European identities), but these identities may change over time. France's puissance, independence and grandeur, and her conception of herself as a middle-sized country with great clout and autonomy, had to undergo considerable change from the 1960s to the 1990s. The authors argue that for European identity to take root, it must have a fertile soil. It must resonate with existing core elements of national identity. The methodology and data sources used match the theoretical interests of the researchers. Discourse analyses among party élites (including the process of argument, justification, persuasion and possibly value change) were relied upon.

Constructivism has made numerous contributions. At the purely descriptive level, constructivists have provided a missing link between objective material factors and outcomes. While much theoretical work remains to be done, there is nevertheless a bridge between ideational, material and institutional realms. Second, work has begun on endogenizing preferences. Third, the often detailed process-tracing of this approach allows us to better understand the 'how' part of the integration process (for example, how EMU got adopted) as well as the 'what' and 'why' dimensions. Fourth, it provides a point of convergence with rational choice analysis. By probing deeper into the content of shared ideas and norms, there is a stronger foundation for focal point analysis which figures prominently in rational choice theory (Garrett and Weingast, 1993).

Constructivist approaches are mostly in the meta-theoretical stage, and have not yet made the transition to shared theoretical principles, recognized puzzles and common research strategies. In a sense there is no common epistemic community for constructivism in the same way that there is for realism and liberal intergovernmentalism. Making this transition is no small matter and will require the advancement of important hypotheses that are both falsifiable and distinctively supportive of constructivist views. Second, and related, variables central to constructivism, such as norms and institutions, will be judged increasingly in terms of their value-added to other explanations, most prominently those that are based on self-interest. While this may be to some extent unfair, in the sense that it privileges rationalist explanations, the tables can be turned. We can (and should) ask how well rationalist explanations perform over and above constructivist explanations. Indeed, when one actually engages in good empirical tests of theories, this is almost always done, since empirical testing requires the evaluation of a variety of specifications, some of which will inevitably privilege one or another viewpoint.

A third challenge concerns the need to better identify exactly what a logic of appropriateness is. It is often posited as a stark alternative to a logic of consequences (based on the calculation of costs and benefits), but this is too simple a dichotomy. Rarely are people acting in one or another capacity, and it must surely be the case that 'appropriate contexts' are not driven purely by norms and institutional factors. While it may be possible to bridge the gap between strategic exchange and socialization (for example, there are strategic repertoires, frames and identities) to maintain its coherence, constructivism must argue that normative frames and skills are not so malleable as to be costlessly downloaded to meet the strategic situation. If 'European', 'Italian', 'Tuscan' and 'Florentine' are simply frames fluidly adjustable to changing circumstance, there is no need to talk about identities at all. Some hard conceptual spadework, informed by downstream theoretical usage, needs to be undertaken if constructivism is to fulfill its promise.

Multi-Level Governance

An increasing number of scholars are shifting the focus from the study of regional integration in favor of considering the EU as a polity or a complex system of multi-level governance. In effect, they are announcing that Lindberg and Scheingold's *Europe's Would-Be Polity* (1970) has arrived as a political entity worthy of consideration in its present dimensions, quite apart from its future evolution. Just as extant nation-states such as the US and Germany are subject to federalizing and decentralizing pressures, so too may the EU change. As the EU makes the transition from a decentralized system of states to a vertically and horizontally integrated system characterized by thick institutions, this shift in focus becomes more understandable.

With this parametric shift also comes a change in the main research problematic from explaining coordination, collaboration and integration to explaining policy-making, implementation, and pressure group activities in much the same way as in domestic politics (Boerzel, 2001; Jachtenfuchs and Kohler-Koch, 1996; Scharpf, 1988, 1994). Numerous scholars have contributed within this framework, including Hix (1998), Hooghe (1995), Marks et al. (1996), Scharpf (1988) and Tarrow (1998). Our comments are most closely addressed to the work of Marks and his collaborators.

The main idea of the multi-level governance model is that neither the EU nor the member states, nor some other political entity, enjoys a monopoly of power and decision-making competence in the EU. The EU along with the states and subnational regions are best seen as part of a complex system of multi-level governance interacting in numerous ways with one another and with private actors. Marks et al. (1996) posit that to understand EU politics, one has to understand these interactions and to take seriously into account levels below and above the state. This is especially true with regard to issues such as regional policies, but it is also the case for regulatory and distributive issue areas. Regional integration is a process that may involve growing centralization of competence 'in Brussels' (an ambiguous phrase in itself), growth in the power of member states (or specific institutional parts such as executives and courts), and expanded influence for subnational actors. Further, in contrast to a state-centric model that sees social influences as funneled through the state, interest groups may outflank the state and go directly to Brussels.

Multi-level governance approaches have expanded our sense of the range of relevant actors. While pointing to different actors is not the same as theorizing about them, it is a prerequisite to it. It is difficult to theorize about multiple levels of decision-making before one admits that multiple levels matter. Second, Marks et al. argue that political arenas and economic actors are interconnected but not necessarily nested (1996: 346). This makes it possible to imagine channels of influence that do not run from subnational units through the state. Finally, the multi-level governance model strongly suggests theories built around multiple levels of decision-making (Scharpf, 1988) and veto point analysis (Heritier, 2001).

The major challenges to multi-level governance theory are two. First, there is a need to come up with a conception of causality that is not dependent on 'where' some activity takes place. Some scholars seem to think that if something happens 'in Brussels' or 'in Munich' it is *ipso facto* proof of the causal importance of these locations and the institutions headquartered there. The geographical site of activity is taken to be direct evidence for causality. Second, there is a need to move from a specification of actors to core research problematics. Will multi-level governance organize its theoretical energies around decision-making, veto analysis, federal models of territorial politics, or some other crucial problematic? An answer to the first question may help to fill in the blanks about the second one.

KEY ISSUES IN THE STUDY OF REGIONAL INTEGRATION

Regionalism and Globalism

From the standpoint of the global economy, regionalism poses an interesting issue. Economically speaking, a world of distinct regions is preferable to a world of commercially separate states, each with its own tariff barriers and restrictions. But it is not necessarily preferable to a globally integrated world of free trade. So distinct groups of countries, organized on a regional basis with zero tariffs, are not as economically efficient as a world of free trade. Given our imperfect world and the low probability of complete global integration, the prudent response might be to take half a loaf. After all, to oppose regional integration on grounds that it falls short of the global optimum is to allow the best to become the enemy of the good.

However, from the standpoint of those outside flourishing regional unions things may look different. Member states of the region may appear to be turning inward, preoccupied with improving conditions inside all the while caring less for those outside. Regional members may increase their own rate of growth, shift the terms of trade in their favor against the interests of non-members, and exploit the differences between external tariffs and zero regional tariffs to shift trade from non-members to members (trade diversion). These events are not just hypothetical. Most of them have already been realized (Petith, 1977).

Ever since the inception of the EEC in 1958, fears of exclusion, discriminatory treatment, and regional insularity have been prevalent. There are two distinct facets to the dark side of regionalism. One concern is that non-membership in regional associations may imply discriminatory economic treatment. Even a relatively moderate design, such as a free trade area, causes shifts in economic incentives between insiders and outsiders. Consequently, trade diversion may occur from lower-cost non-member states to higher-cost member states. The other anxiety is that regionalism will repel more comprehensive, global efforts to cooperate, that is, regionalism versus globalism. This fear is fueled by remembrance of things past, by the connection between regionalism and autarky during the 1930s and between regionalism and the phenomena of import-substitution and collective self-reliance in the 1950s to 1970s, especially among the less developed countries. The modern expression of this concern comes in the form of realist predictions that the collapse of bipolarity and the end of the Cold War will accentuate regional differences, fuel rivalries and stimulate a return to beggar-thy-neighbor policies (Gilpin, 1987: 394–405).

Granting that a degree of trade diversion exists in regional trading arrangements, these regions are not likely to obstruct global trade liberalization and other efforts to cooperate. A strong deterrent is the possibility of inter-bloc rivalry and trade wars, which are likely to be triggered by any attempt by a regional bloc to take advantage of its market power (Krugman, 1991: 16). In addition, the dividing lines drawn between regional blocs are getting fuzzier as many countries have overlapping membership in a number of regional groups (Bhalla and Bhalla, 1997: 20–2). The number of North–South regional integration attempts, infrequently heard of before the mid-1980s, has also increased in recent years. Moreover, inter-regional preferential trading arrangements, with EU as a common node, have proliferated.

What can we say about the relation between regionalism and globalism? There are a number of ways to respond to regional organizations in general and the EU in particular. First of all, both the GATT and the United Nations (UN) have conditionally accepted regional organizations. The UN has rather elaborate rules for governing the relationship between regional and collective security. The GATT/WTO recognizes the legitimacy of regional organizations if such organizations conform to the requirements about average tariffs (they cannot be higher than before the union is formed) and trade-creation versus trade-diversion.

Second, what is the evidence of trade patterns between members and non-members? Various economists have observed that trade is geographically concentrated, and intra-regional trade has increased faster than trade across regions, for most regions (Frankel, 1997: 19–33). This can be observed in Table 25.2. Regional export concentration, as

Table 25.2   *Intra-regional exports as a percentage of all exports in major regional arrangements, 1970–1998*

	1970	1980	1985	1990	1995	1998
European Union	59.5	60.8	59.2	65.9	62.4	55.2
NAFTA	36.0	33.6	43.9	41.4	46.2	51.7
MERCOSUR	9.4	11.6	5.5	8.9	20.3	25.1
ASEAN	22.3	17.2	18.6	18.9	24.3	20.4
APEC	57.9	57.9	67.7	68.5	72.0	69.7

Source: World Bank (2000: 327)

measured by the share of intra-regional exports to all exports, has gone up in major regions, particularly where intra-regional trade barriers are substantially reduced.[7] For example, the figure for NAFTA increased from 41.4 per cent in 1990 to 51.7 per cent in 1998. MERCOSUR's figure is more remarkable, recording a sharp increase from 8.9 per cent in 1990 (it was formed in 1991) to 25.1 per cent in 1998. However, the explanations for the high intra-regional trade concentration ratios differ between those who see geographical proximity as important (Krugman, 1991) and those who argue that discriminatory policies are critical (Bhagwati, 1992).

Determining the impact of regional unions on the rest of the world is difficult because it involves assumptions about different theoretical baselines. One way of approaching the issue would simply be to compare trade patterns between members and non-members before and after formation of regional unions. While this approach has some attractions, the inferences we can draw are likely to be obscured by the presence of dynamic effects of the regional union itself. If the regional union increases growth inside the area (which it is supposed to do) and if external trade is some function of size of the economy (which it almost surely is), then trade between members and non-members should increase in absolute terms, even if the share of trade between members and non-members declines. So the empirical results may depend on which standard is adopted. If we ask 'has the share of trade between the region and outsiders declined?', the answer may well be 'yes'. But if we ask 'has the absolute volume of trade between the region and non-members increased in comparison to our expectation based on the absence of a regional union?', the answer may be 'yes' also. In other words, non-members may do better than they would without regional union, though not as well as they might if they were included as members.

Finally, it is well to ask what the dynamic effects of regionalism are with respect to further globalization. That is, should we expect regional arrangements to freeze the status quo, dividing up the world into a series of privileged clubs providing more or less excludable goods? Or might the opposite be the case, namely, that regionalism becomes the vehicle for further (global) liberalization?

While it is hard to answer this question on theoretical grounds, the Uruguay Round of trade negotiations provides some evidence that the latter pattern is dominating the former. It is well known that the EU, preoccupied with its internal problems and agenda, delayed the beginning and the conclusion of the Uruguay Round. However, as Kahler has argued, regionalism has been used as a bargaining tool as well (1995: 16–17). In particular, Clinton used the APEC (Asia Pacific Economic Cooperation) as a bargaining chip in the final stages of these negotiations, largely as a way of getting some leverage over the EU to reduce agricultural subsidies. Clinton elevated the APEC process just at the time when global negotiations were stalled and suggested that the United States would play the Asian hand if progress were not forthcoming in Europe (Bergsten, 1994). It is hard to tell how general this pattern of regional-global liberalization will be. The results may be very peculiar to the Uruguay Round in which the United States as a powerful country had a material interest in lowering agricultural subsidies in the EU and had an 'Asian hand' to play. It is also possible that preferential trade areas (PTAs), due to their high visibility, can mobilize and unify various protectionist lobbies, which may pose effective challenges to multilateral liberalization. Furthermore, PTAs may divert scarce negotiating resources and attention of individual states away from multilateral trade liberalization.

Political Institutionalization

As Stone Sweet and Sandholtz (1998) have argued, the construction of rules of governance is an elementary component of international transactions. Rules seem to be necessary for exchange to take place, and the existence of externalities may bring a speedy response to those who want to see them controlled. Yet, one of the most glaring empirical differences among East Asia, Western Europe and North America lies in their different degrees of institutionalization.

Western Europe describes a region of dense institutions, with an impressive macro-institutional architecture (the Council of Ministers, Commission, European Court of Justice), elaborate provisions for the making and administration of laws, and the taking of many decisions by qualified majority vote. In terms of comprehensiveness of scope, institutional detail, depth of application, extension of rights to citizens and authoritative backing, the EU far exceeds institutionalization in North America and East Asia.

Why? Economic integration is high in all three areas, so we cannot say that institutionalization necessarily follows from high levels of economic exchange, nor by the externalities created by such exchange. Also, each area has a hegemonic core (Germany or Germany–France in the case of the EU, Japan in the case of East Asia, and the United States in the case of North America). If institutionalization is the result of leadership in the pursuit of public goods, then North America and East Asia should also have high levels of institutionalization.

Working with just three cases, it is difficult to evaluate testable hypotheses. Perhaps the variable institutional patterns have to do with the taming of sovereignty in Western Europe, as well as the waning of nationalism. It is striking to note that Germany, a leader in the process of European integration, thoroughly renounced nationalism after the Second World War and saw European integration as the only viable path toward reincorporation into the international system. This was not the case in North America and East Asia, where the United States and Japan held on to a much more nationalistic conception of their place in the world. In Europe, integration was seen as a solution to the 'German problem' rather than something that aggravated it (though some believed this too). That institutionalization was seen as a way of taming both dominance and hypernationalism certainly worked in favor of institutional as well as economic integration. In fact, economic integration without political integration would have posed problems, for it would have enhanced the position of the German economy without institutional checks on Germany's civilian (market) power (Anderson, 1999; Katzenstein, 1997b).

The analogous situation in East Asia is provided by Japan, the most economically powerful country in the region, and the country that would profit most (in the absolute sense) by economic integration.[8] Yet Japan has had no strong incentive to initiate formal, institutional integration. Germany's position within Europe may be unique and offer little insight into Japan's position within Asia. Germany is the strongest country in Europe, yet allows itself to be bound within institutions that, purely on economic grounds, do not seem to offer net advantages over either the status quo or what it could achieve on a 'go-it-alone' basis (Gruber, 2000). The puzzle as to why Germany accepted EMU (when it was de facto the leader of European monetary policy) is usually resolved by pointing out that Chancellor Kohl wanted to pacify his European neighbors, to soothe their fears that a reunified Germany (a Grossdeutschland) would pose no threat to Europe. A similar downplaying of national sovereignty cannot be expected in East Asia.

Japan's nationalistic disposition, along with the importance attached to national sovereignty among the newly independent East Asian countries, has proven to be a strong impediment to institutional integration. The absence of working regional security arrangements, hot wars waged in Korea and Vietnam and the continuation of the Cold War divide, the fears of domination by Japan and China, and the existence of territorial disputes must have aggravated the concerns about national sovereignty and relative gains from cooperation (Grieco, 1997: 176–8; Krasner, 1995). These realist explanations for the weakness or absence of overarching institutions in East Asia, however, are troubled by the fact that economic integration, in spite of its negative security externalities, has continued to deepen among East Asian countries.

Low levels of institutionalization along with high levels of economic exchange suggest a theoretical foundation for the liberals to claim that East Asian economic cooperation is a 'prisoner's delight', rather than prisoners' dilemma game. In such a situation, actors have no incentive to defect, nor is there a need for binding institutions (Drysdale and Garnaut, 1993: 187–8). This rosy depiction of harmonious economic relations among East Asian countries has to deal with mercantilist economic policies and the visible hand of government in the management of respective economies, as well as the continued existence of political and military conflicts in the region (Choi, 1998: 32–4).

Given the limitations of both realist and liberal explanations in explaining the absence or weakness of institutional integration in East Asia, it may be useful to explore if the question is wrongly posed. Institutional integration in East Asia may be different in form from that which exists in Europe and North America rather than non-existent. Many scholars claim that regional institutions in East Asia are informal, soft (less binding) and open (non-discriminatory), unlike those in Europe and North America. The avoidance of legalization in East Asia (and the Pacific) is largely ascribed to the unique Asian culture based on harmony and consensus, the past experience of colonialism and the fear of superpower domination, or domestic politics and institutions of East Asian countries (Choi, 1998; Kahler, 2000: 559–63; Katzenstein, 1997a).[9] Furthermore, it has been in Japan's interest, considering the widespread fear of Japanese domination, to control East Asia quietly through informal measures; Japan has been quite successful in this regard (Lincoln, 1993; Pyle, 1995).

Another justification for informal institutions comes from the literature on the new institutionalism. Institutions, whose major function is to reduce transaction costs, do not have to be formal to be effective (Keohane, 1989: 4; North, 1990: 36–45). The new institutionalism could argue that East Asia, especially Japan, has maintained an intricate web of intra-regional economic networks. Business networks can reduce the demand for formal/legal protection by internalizing economic relations into various forms of relational contracting, different from arm's length deals in the market, based on long-term commitment and mutual trust (Doner, 1997; Hatch and Yamamura, 1997; Katzenstein, 1997a).

From the perspectives of private businesses, formal regional institutions are a mixed blessing. On the one hand, they can remove barriers to economic exchanges, reduce transaction costs and protect property rights. On the other hand, these institutions can be predatory by formally subjecting the market to the whims of political interests. This is more likely to be the case if member countries have vast economic differences in levels of development, especially between Japan and the rest of the region. Such a fear has been real both to Japanese business leaders, as well as to policy-makers in the government, particularly in its relationship with the ASEAN (Choi, 1998: 270–97). Indeed, Japanese businesses have largely remained silent at both domestic and regional levels over liberalization through formal institutions in East Asia. It is only in recent years that Japanese businesses began to show serious interest in FTAs with selected countries in East Asia as well as the whole region (Keidanren, 2000).

Japanese companies have so far been quite successful in mobilizing private institutional arrangements to cope with risks involved in regional trade and investment. The active support of Japan's economic bureaucracy – by providing supportive laws, investment insurance, market information and tax breaks – was instrumental for the private firms to build production and marketing networks (Hatch and Yamamura, 1996: 115–29). Japan's unique business institutions (for example, practices of relational contracting, *keiretsu*, and the general trading companies) spread throughout East Asia along with the dramatic increase in Japanese FDI from the late 1980s (Aoki, 1995; Doner, 1997; Hatch and Yamamura, 1996).

The rejection of formal, supranational institutions or the utility of informal institutions, however, is not likely to persist in East Asia. Given the closed nature of informal, network relations, the benefits of formal institutions are likely to increase with growing economic interdependence or integration. There is little theoretical reason to assume that culture, history and domestic institutions will continue to resist institutionalization. In fact, East Asian countries have become more receptive to legalistic resolution of trade disputes under the WTO dispute settlement procedures, and ASEAN has developed a more sophisticated institutional structure in recent years (Kahler, 2000: 563–7).

A similar change has occurred in Japan's preference concerning trade disputes with trading partners, especially the United States (Choi, 1998: 167–72). At present, Japan (both government and business) is seriously considering the option to establish a FTA with Singapore, South Korea and other selected countries in the Asia Pacific region.

When compared with East Asia where the demand for political institutions has been either low or informally satisfied, the Americas have achieved higher levels of political institutionalization. For example, NAFTA, living up to its name as a free trade area, has established a sophisticated system of supranational governance for intra-regional trade and investment. The Free Trade Commission is in charge of dismantling trade barriers though it is not seeking explicit harmonization of national standards, and an overarching mechanism for the settlement of intra-regional trade and investment disputes is also put in place. MERCOSUR is much closer in institutional design and intent to the EU, although its level of interdependence is substantially lower than those of NAFTA and East Asia. MERCOSUR implemented common external tariffs (CER) in 1995 and looks ahead to completing a common market with an institutional structure comparable to that of the EU (Pereira, 1999: 14–19). Quite contrary to East Asia, MERCOSUR appears to push economic integration through political institutionalization. The absence of informal institutions could have increased the demand for formal institutions. Considering the insufficiency of conditions favorable to political institutionalization (for example, economic interdependence, dedicated regional leadership, and stable security arrangement), however, it is unlikely that MERCOSUR will establish a workable supranational governance system in the near future.

Regional Institutions and Democracy

Democracy, a complex concept, has both procedural and substantive dimensions. At the procedural level, a democratic system implies participation, elementary rights, institutions to prevent the concentration of power and minimal access to information about how political institutions work (transparency). On the substantive or output side as some put it (Zürn, 2000), democratic policies are those that respond to people's demands, policies that are close to the median voter. There is no necessary reason why these two aspects of democracy go together, indeed an economic institution such as the European Central Bank (ECB) may be quite exclusive in the sense of participation (finance ministers, executives and central bankers) but produce policies that are closer to the median voter than monetary policy made by democratically elected legislatures.

What may seem odd is that the democratic (or non-democratic) nature of regional organizations has not been challenged much earlier. Even for the EU, the most institutionally advanced of the regional organizations, most of the intense dialogue about the democratic deficit has been conducted in the past ten to twelve years, perhaps prodded by the referenda of 1992 and 1993, especially the Danish 'no' to the Treaty on European Union. While the issue of democracy is a lively one in Europe today, it is important to recall that the original construction of the European Economic Community did not facilitate democracy. The European Parliament was not directly elected and in any case did not make laws, the Council of Ministers was composed of national ministers appointed by national executives, and both the Commission and the judges on the ECJ were appointed by national executives. Finally, as Mancini and Keeling (1994: 175) point out, the word 'democracy' did not appear in the preamble and the first part of the Rome Treaty. Instead, the word 'liberty', especially economic liberty, seemed to provide the chief philosophical justification for the EEC.

Two reasons may help us understand this early inattention. First, regional organizations, including the EU in its early stages, are often seen as relatively uncontroversial. The functional approach was to attack the easiest (least controversial) issues first. The first fifteen or so years of European integration focused on achieving a free trade area, customs union and common agricultural policy. Integration in Asia and North America is even more modest in its goals. Without the changes that we have subsequently seen in the development of the EU, it was not clear that this organization was going to alter substantially the way decisions were made with regard to foreign policy, the welfare state and macroeconomic policies. Second, and more important, most of the decisions within international organizations are (or in the case of the EU were) taken by unanimity, thus providing a safeguard to important national interests. Until the mid-1980s, decisions within the EU were subject to a laborious process of universal consent. Efforts to go beyond this by intensifying the use of qualified majority voting in the mid-1960s provoked a major crisis.

As damaging as unanimity was in terms of making decisions difficult, this procedure did have a beneficial effect. It tended to deflect criticism that the EU was an undemocratic body. So long as their own national representatives could hold out in Brussels against unfavorable changes in the status quo, citizens could reason that they had some protection. Perhaps the efficiency of decision-making might suffer, but no important departure from the status quo would take place without the agreement of all.

By the mid-1980s, both of these conditions had changed. The EU, it was clear, was a growing and powerful organization that had increasing competencies in numerous areas, including trade, environment, transportation, social policies such as gender equality, and even monetary policy. While little substantive progress was made in the area of common foreign and security policy, there were even efforts to move ahead in this area. Also, along with the Single European Act of 1987 came an increasing reliance on qualified majority voting as a way of making decisions. In short, as the EU made its 'remarkable transformation from an interstate bargain into a multi-dimensional quasi-federal polity' (Stone Sweet and Sandholtz, 1998: 1), scholars and practitioners were invited to ask 'What about the people?'

The problem of democratic accountability in the EU raises general questions for all international organizations.[10] As they become increasingly important in people's lives, people are bound to ask how they are controlled and to whom they are accountable. Regional organizations affect the distribution of jobs, the transparency with which decisions are made, the distribution of wealth, the environment, national social policies and the relative weight of domestic institutions such as parliaments and executives (Moravcsik, 1994). The focus on the democratization of regionalism is not a 'problem' but rather a sign that regional organizations have moved, at least in some parts of the world, into a new stage of development. These organizations are not simply extensions of their component member states whose national political institutions monitor and control them in the same democratic fashion as issues within the domestic arena. They create new arenas and pose new problems for democratic governance that will challenge the ingenuity of these organizations in the years ahead.

Conclusion

Regionalism is a strong force in the world today. It represents a dynamic compromise between a comprehensive if not homogenous globalization and the more restricted forces of nationalism. If the nation-state is too small to solve the economic problems, and too large to solve (by itself) identity questions, regional integration both expands the economic orbit of the nation-state and adds another potentially important focus of loyalty. Regional movements have proliferated during the past two decades and seem to be more durable than interwar and immediate postwar arrangements. The links between regional organizations and ascendant liberal constituencies seem to account for this durability. Never before have domestic reforms been so closely linked to cooperation to form regional unions.

Since this chapter represents a survey of approaches, it is not our intention to draw conclusions about which approach is the best for explaining integration. Regions and regional integration occur in every area of the world. We do not know if regional integration represents a halfway house on the way to a globalized world or a permanent resting place, but we do know that the regional process is very much alive. We can also say with some confidence that regional organizations, for all their inward orientation in terms of trade shares (see Table 25.2), are very much engaged in more comprehensive global negotiations. Indeed, negotiations within the World Trade Organization (WTO) are often thought of as multilateral negotiations among the EU, the United States (for NAFTA), and Japan and China (representing Asia).

We close by pointing to a tension within the chapter, a tension that we hope has been productive. In deciding how to cast the chapter, we faced an obvious trade-off between being comprehensive (including many regions) and engaging the theoretical debates. Since some of the debates are closely tethered to Europe, including them implied a sacrifice of symmetry with respect to other areas of the world. We decided to include the debates, and it admittedly did mean a disproportionate focus on the European Union. We hope the trade-off was worth it, not only in that as academics we are intrinsically interested in theories and approaches, but also because we believe that increasingly these theories will be useful in understanding regional integration in other areas. As questions relating to deep integration, political institutions, democracy and citizenship rights grow in importance, frameworks tied to the European experience will be more relevant.

Notes

1 There were some instances of unilateral trade preferences by developed countries to underdeveloped countries such as the Lomé Treaty between the EC and ACPs, the US Carribean Basin Initiative, and the Australia–Papua New Guinea Pact.

2 The index of relative acceptance was intended as a measure of transactional integration that took into account (i.e., controlled for) the respective magnitudes of imports and exports of the trading countries. Thus, if country A exports 10 per cent of world exports and country B imports 10 per cent of world imports, the expectation (based on probability) is that B will import 10 per cent of A's exports. In terms of trade partnership and economic integration, this would place A and B at the indifference point, neither particularly close and friendly nor distant and unfriendly. For calculations of the RA index, as well as its mathematical properties, see Savage and Deutsch (1960).

3 Grieco (1997) used these three categories to measure the degree of institutionalization.

4 The original members were Indonesia, Malaysia, the Philippines, Thailand and Singapore. Brunei became a member in 1984. Vietnam, Cambodia, Laos and Myanmar joined in the late 1990s.

5 Moravscik is of course not a functionalist. Our point is not to classify people but to point out the lines of theory and the ways they develop in the literature.

6 This section draws heavily on Caporaso (1998).

7 The EU's figure shows a decline in recent years. It is probably due to the expansion in its membership.

8 This is not an argument about the distribution of gains from trade. It is a statement of what we expect based on total absolute gains across countries based on their respective sizes. Since Japan is the largest country in the area (in the economic sense), we expect Japan to reap the largest absolute gains.

9 The list of domestic factors includes 'rule by law' institutions characterized by state strength and close state–society interaction (Katzenstein); divisions over political regime and the status of domestic legal institutions and a shared history of responding to colonialism (Kahler); and institutional capacity to minimize transaction costs (Choi).

10 A general treatment of problems of democratic accountability is found in James A. Caporaso (2001), 'Challenges of Governance in a Globalized world: Democratic Accountability, Transparency, and Rights in the European Union', paper prepared for a conference on Globalization and Governance, University of California, San Diego, La Jolla, CA, 30–31 March. Also see Joseph S. Nye and John D. Donahue (eds), *Governance in a Globalizing World.* Washington, DC: Brookings Institution (2000).

Bibliography

Abbott, Frederick M. (2000) 'NAFTA and the Legalization of World Politics', *International Organization,* 54 (3): 519–47.

Adler, Emmanuel and Barnett, Michael (eds) (1998) *Security Communities.* Cambridge: Cambridge University Press.

Anderson, Jeffrey (1999) *German Unification and the Union of Europe.* Cambridge, Cambridge University Press.

Aoki, Takeshi (1995) 'Integration in the Asia Pacific Rim: Formation of Networks by Japanese Foreign Direct Investment as the Driving Force to Integrate', in Denis Fred Simon (ed.), *Corporate Strategies in the Pacific Rim: Global and Regional Trend.* London and New York: Routledge. pp. 334–80.

Ash, Timothy Garton (1999) 'The Puzzle of Central Europe', *The New York Review of Books,* 46 (5): 31–4.

Axline, W. Andrew (1977) 'Underdevelopment, Dependence, and Integration: The Politics of Regionalism in the Third World', *International Organization,* 31 (1): 83–105.

Balassa, Bela A. (1961) *The Theory of Economic Integration.* Homewood: Irwin.

Berger, Peter and Luckmann, Thomas (1966) *The Social Construction of Reality.* New York: Doubleday.

Bergsten, C. Fred (1994) 'Sunrise in Seattle', *International Economic Insight*, 5 (1): 18–20.

Bhagwati, Jagdish (1992) 'Regionalism vs. Multilateralism', *World Economy*, 15 (5): 535–56.

Bhalla, A.S. and Bhalla, P. (1997) *Regional Blocs: Building Blocks or Stumbling Blocks?* New York: St Martin's Press.

Boerzel, Tanja A. (2001) 'Europeanization and Territorial Institutional Change: Toward Cooperative Regionalism?', in Maria Green Cowles, James Caporaso and Thomas Risse (eds), *Transforming Europe: Europeanization and Domestic Change*. Ithaca: Cornell University Press. pp. 137–58.

Burley, Anne-Marie and Mattli, Walter (1993) 'Europe before the Court: A Political Theory of Legal Integration', *International Organization*, 47 (1): 41–76.

Cameron, David R. (1998) 'Creating Supranational Authority in Monetary and Exchange Rate Policy: The Sources and Effects of EMU', in Wayne Sandholtz and Alec Stone Sweet (eds), *European Integration and Supranational Governance*. Oxford: Oxford University Press. pp. 188–216.

Caporaso, James A. (1993) 'Global Political Economy', in Ada Finifter (ed.), *Political Science: The State of the Discipline*. Washington, DC: American Political Science Association. pp. 451–81.

Caporaso, James A. (1998) 'Regional Integration Theory: Understanding our Past and Anticipating Our Future', in Wayne Sandholtz and Alec Stone Sweet (eds), *European Integration and Supranational Governance*. Oxford: Oxford University Press. pp. 334–51.

Caporaso, James A. (2000) *The European Union: Dilemmas of Regional Integration*. Boulder: Westview.

Caporaso, James A. (2001) 'Challenges of Governance in a Globalized World: Democratic Accountability, Transparency, and Rights in the European Union', paper prepared for a conference on Globalization and Governance, University of California, San Diego. 30–31 March.

Caporaso, James A. and Keeler, John T.S. (1995) 'The European Union and Regional Integration Theory', in Carolyn Rhodes and Sonia Mazey (eds), *The State of the European Union: Building a European Polity?* Boulder: Lynne Rienner. pp. 29–62.

Checkel, Jeffrey T. (1998) 'The Constructivist Turn in International Relations Theory', *World Politics*, 50 (2): 324–48.

Checkel, Jeffrey T. (1999) 'Social Construction and Integration', *Journal of European Public Policy*, 6 (4): 545–60.

Checkel, Jeffrey T. (2001) 'The Europeanization of Citizenship?' in Maria Green Cowles, James A. Caporaso and Thomas Risse (eds), *Transforming Europe: Europeanization and Domestic Change*. Ithaca: Cornell University Press. pp. 180–97.

Choi, Young Jong (1998) 'Institutionalizing Asia and the Pacific: Interdependence, States, and Institutional Preferences – Japan's Policy in Comparative Perspective', PhD dissertation, University of Washington, Seattle, WA.

Dell, Sidney Samuel (1966) *A Latin American Common Market?* New York: Oxford University Press.

Deutsch, Karl W., Burrell, Sidney A., Kann, Robert A. et al. (1957) *Political Community and the North Atlantic Area: International Organization in the Light of Historical Experience*. Princeton: Princeton University Press.

Doner, Richard F. (1997) 'Japan in East Asia: Institutions and Regional Leadership', in Peter J. Katzenstein and Takashi Shiraishi (eds), *Network Power: Japan and Asia*. Ithaca: Cornell University Press. pp. 197–233.

Drysdale, Peter and Garnaut, Ross (1993) 'The Pacific: An Application of a General Theory of Economic Integration', in C. Fred Bergsten and Marcus Noland (eds), *Pacific Dynamism and the International Economic System*. Washington, DC: Institute for International Economics. pp. 183–224.

Etzioni, Amitai (1965) *Political Unification: A Comparative Study of Leaders and Forces*. New York: Holt, Rinehart and Winston.

Frankel, Jeffrey A. (1997) *Regional Trading Blocs in the World Economic System*. Washington, DC: Institute for International Economics.

Garrett, Geoffrey and Weingast, Barry R. (1993) 'Ideas, Interests, and Institutions: Constructing the European Community's Internal Market', in Judith Goldstein and Robert O. Keohane (eds), *Ideas and Foreign Policy*. Ithaca: Cornell University Press. pp. 173–206.

Gilpin, Robert (1987) *The Political Economy of International Relations*. Princeton: Princeton University Press.

Gowa, Joanne (1989) 'Bipolarity, Multipolarity and Free Trade', *American Political Science Review*, 83 (4): 1245–56.

Grieco, Joseph M. (1993) 'Understanding the Problem of International Cooperation: The Limits of Neoliberal Institutionalism and the Future of Realist Theory', in David A. Baldwin (ed.), *Neorealism and Neoliberalism*. New York: Columbia University Press. pp. 301–38.

Grieco, Joseph M. (1995) 'The Maastricht Treaty, Economic and Monetary Union, and the Neo-realist Research Programme', *Review of International Studies*, 21 (1): 21–40.

Grieco, Joseph M. (1996) 'State Interests and International Rule Trajectories: A Neorealist Interpretation of the Maastricht Treaty and European Economic and Monetary Union', *Security Studies*, 5 (3): 261–306.

Grieco, Joseph M. (1997) 'Systemic Sources of Variation in Regional Institutionalization in West Europe, East Asia, and the Americas', in Edward D. Mansfield and Helen V. Milner (eds), *The Political Economy of Regionalism*. New York: Columbia University Press. pp. 164–87.

Gruber, Lloyd (2000) *Ruling the World: Power Politics and the Rise of Supranational Institutions*. Princeton: Princeton University Press.

Haas, Ernst B. (1968) 'Technocracy, Pluralism, and the New Europe', in Joseph S. Nye Jr (ed.), *International Regionalism: Readings*. Boston, MA: Little, Brown. pp. 149–76.

Haas, Ernst B. and Schmitter, Philippe C. (1964) 'Economics and Differential Patterns of Political Integration: Projections about Unity in Latin America', *International Organization*, 18 (3): 705–37.

Haggard, Stephan (1995) *Developing Nations and the Politics of Global Integration*. Washington, DC: Brookings Institution.

Hatch, Walter and Yamamura, Kozo (1997) *Asia in Japan's Embrace*. Cambridge: Cambridge University Press.

Heritier, Adrienne (2001) 'Differential Europe: National Administrative Responses to Community Policy', in Maria Green Cowles, James A. Caporaso and Thomas Risse (eds), *Transforming Europe: Europeanization and Domestic Change*. Ithaca: Cornell University Press. pp. 44–59.

Hix, Simon (1998) 'The Study of the European Union II: The "New Governance" Agenda and its Rival', *Journal of European Public Policy*, 5 (1): 38–65.

Hooghe, Liesbet (1995) 'Subnational Mobilization in the European Union', *West European Politics*, 18 (1): 175–98.

Jachtenfuchs, Markus and Kohler-Koch, Beate (1996) 'Einleitung: Regieren im dynamischen Mehrebenensystem', in Markus Jachtenfuchs and Beate Kohler-Koch (eds), *Europaische Integration*. Opladen: Leske and Budrich. pp. 15–44.

Jupille, Joseph (2000) 'Procedural Politics: Issues, Interests, and Choice in the European Union', PhD dissertation, University of Washington, Seattle, WA.

Kahler, Miles (1995) *International Institutions and the Political Economy of Integration*. Washington, DC: Brookings Institution.

Kahler, Miles (2000) 'Legalization as Strategy: The Asia–Pacific Case', *International Organization*, 54 (3): 549–71.

Katzenstein, Peter J. (1997a) 'Introduction: Asian Regionalism in Comparative Perspective', in Peter J. Katzenstein and Takashi Shiraishi (eds), *Network Power: Japan and Asia*. Ithaca: Cornell University Press. pp. 1–46

Katzenstein, Peter J. (1997b) 'Unified Germany in an Integrating Europe', in Peter J. Katzenstein (ed.), *Tamed Power: Germany in Europe*. Ithaca: Cornell University Press. pp. 1–48.

Keidanren (Japan Federation of Economic Organization) (2000) 'Urgent Call for Active Promotion of Free Trade Agreements – Toward a New Dimension in Trade Policy', *www.keidanren.or.jp/english/policy/2000/033/proposal.htlm* (1 March 2001)

Keohane, Robert O. (1989) *International Institutions and State Power: Essays in International Relations Theory*. Boulder: Westview.

Krasner, Stephan D. (1995) 'The Parameters of the Global Political Economy', in Denis Fred Simon (ed.), *Corporate Strategies in the Pacific Rim: Global versus Regional Trends*. London: Routledge. pp. 28–54.

Krugman, Paul (1991) 'The Move to Free Trade Zones', in *Policy Implications of Trade and Currency Zones*, proceedings of a symposium sponsored by the Federal Reserve Bank of Kansas City, Jackson Hole, Wyoming. pp. 7–41.

Krugman, Paul (1993) 'Regionalism versus Multilateralism', in Jaime de Melo and Arvind Panagariya (eds), *New Dimensions in Regional Integration*. New York: Cambridge University Press. pp. 58–79.

Kundera, Milan (1984) 'The Tragedy of Central Europe', *The New York Review of Books*, 31 (26 April): 1–4.

Laird, Sam (1997) 'MERCOSUR: Objectives and Achievements', *www.itd.org/forums/merco61.doc* (29 November 2000).

Lincoln, Edward J. (1993) *Japan's New Global Role*. Washington, DC: Brookings Institution.

Lindberg, Leon N. and Scheingold, Stuart A. (1970) *Europe's Would-Be Polity*. Englewood Cliffs: Prentice Hall.

Lipsey, Richard G. (1960) 'The Theory of Customs Union', *Economic Journal*, 70: 496–513.

Ludlow, Peter (1991) 'The European Commission', in Robert O. Keohane and Stanley Hoffmann (eds), *The New European Community: Decisionmaking and Institutional Change*. Boulder: Westview. pp. 85–132.

Mancini, Federico and Veeling, David, T. (1994) 'Democracy and the European Court of Justice', *Moreen Law Review*, 57 (2): 175–90.

Mansfield, Edward D. and Milner, Helen V. (1999) 'The New Wave of Regionalism', *International Organization*, 53 (3): 589–628.

Marcussen, Martin, Risse, Thomas, Englemann-Mastin, Daniela, et al. (1999) 'Constructing Europe: The Evolution of French, British, and German Identities', *Journal of European Public Policy*, 6 (4): 614–33.

Marks, Gary, Hooghe, Liesbet and Blank, Kermit (1996) 'European Integration from the 1980s: State-Centric vs. Multi-Level Governance', *Journal of Common Market Studies*, 34 (3): 341–78.

McNamara, Kathleen R. (1998) *The Currency of Ideas*. Ithaca: Cornell University Press.

Mearsheimer, John (1990) 'Back to the Future: Instability in Europe after the Cold War', *International Security*, 19 (1): 5–56.

Mitrany, David (1968) 'The Prospect of Integration: Federal or Functional?', in Joseph S. Nye (ed.), *International Regionalism: Readings*. Boston: Little, Brown. pp. 43–74.

Moravcsik, Andrew (1993) 'Preferences and Power in the European Community: A Liberal Intergovernmental Approach', *Journal of Common Market Studies*, 31 (4): 473–523.

Moravcsik, Andrew (1994) 'Why the European Community Strengthens the State: Domestic Politics and International Cooperation', Working Paper number 52, Harvard University, Cambridge, MA.

Moravcsik, Andrew (1998) *The Choice for Europe*. Ithaca: Cornell University Press.

North, Douglass (1990) *Institutions, Institutional Change and Economic Performance*. New York: Cambridge University Press.

Nye, Joseph S., Jr (1966) 'East African Economic Integration', in *International Political Communities: An Anthology*. New York: Doubleday. pp. 405–36.

Nye, Joseph S., Jr (1968) 'Comparative Regional Integration: Concepts and Measurement', *International Organization*, 22 (4): 855–80.

Nye, Joseph S., Jr (1970) 'Comparing Common Markets: A Revised Neo-Functionalist Model', *International Organization*, 24 (4): 796–835.

Nye, Joseph S., Jr and Donahue, John D. (eds) (2000) *Governance in a Globalizing World*. Washington, DC: Brookings Institution.

Onuf, Nicholas (1989) *World of Our Making*. Columbia: University of South Carolina Press.

Pereira, Lia Valls (1999) 'Toward the Common Market of the South: Mercosur's Origins, Evolution, and Challenges', in Riordan Roett (ed.), *MERCOSUR*. Boulder: Lynne Rienner. pp. 1–23.

Petith, Howard (1977) 'European Integration and the Terms of Trade', *Economic Journal*, 87 (2): 262–72.

Pierson, Paul (1996) 'The Path to European Integration: A Historical Institutional Analysis', *Comparative Political Studies*, 29 (1): 123–63.

Pyle, Kenneth B. (1995) 'The Context of APEC: US–Japan Relations', *NBR Analysis*, 6 (3): 37–53.

Ravenhill, John (1995) 'Economic Cooperation in Southeast Asia: Changing Incentives', *Asian Survey*, 25 (9): 850–66.

Risse, Thomas (2001) 'A European Identity: Europeanization and the Evolution of Nation-State Identities', in Maria Green Cowles, James A. Caporaso and Thomas Risse (eds), *Transforming Europe: Europeanization and Domestic Change*. Ithaca: Cornell University Press. pp. 198–216.

Risse, Thomas, Engelmann, Daniela, Knopf, Hans-Joachim and Roscher, Klaus (1999) 'To Euro or not to Euro: The EMU and Identity Politics in the European Union', *European Journal of International Relations*, 5 (2): 147–87.

Ruggie, John Gerard (1998) *Constructing the World Polity*. London and New York: Routledge.

Russett, Bruce (1967) *International Regions and the International System: A Study in Political Ecology*. Chicago: Rand–McNally.

Sandholtz, Wayne (1993) 'Choosing Union: Monetary Politics and Maastricht', *International Organization*, 47 (1): 1–39.

Sandholtz, Wayne (1996) 'Membership Matters: Limits to the Functionalist Approach to European Institutions', *Journal of Common Market Studies*, 34 (3): 403–29.

Savage, Richard I. and Deutsch, Karl W. (1960) 'A Statistical Model of the Gross Analysis of Transaction Flows', *Econometrika*, 28 (3): 551–72.

Sbragia, Alberta M. (2001) 'Italy Pays for Europe: Political Leadership, Political Choice, and Institutional Adaptation', in Maria Green Cowles, James A. Caporaso and Thomas Risse (eds), *Transforming Europe: Europeanization and Domestic Change*. Ithaca: Cornell University Press. pp. 79–96.

Scharpf, Fritz W. (1988) 'The Joint Decision Trap: Lessons from German Federalism and European Integration', *Public Administration*, 66 (2): 239–78.

Scharpf, Fritz W. (1994) 'Community and Autonomy: Multi-Level Policy Making in the European Union', *Journal of European Public Policy*, 1 (1): 219–42.

Scharpf, Fritz W. (1999) *Governing in Europe: Effective and Democratic*? Oxford: Oxford University Press.

Schmitter, Philippe C. (1969) 'Three Neofunctionalist Hypotheses about International Integration', *International Organization*, 23 (1): 161–6.

Schmitter, Philippe C. (1970) 'A Revised Theory of Regional Integration', *International Organization*, 24 (4): 836–68.

Shaw, Jo (1999) 'Postnational Constitutionalism in the European Union', *Journal of European Public Policy*, 6 (4): 579–97.

Smith, James McCall (2000) 'The Politics of Dispute Settlement Design: Examining Legalism in Regional Trade Pacts', *International Organization*, 54 (1): 137–80.

Stone Sweet, Alec (1999) 'Judicialization and the Construction of Governance', *Comparative Political Studies*, 32 (2): 147–84.

Stone Sweet, Alec and Caporaso, James A. (1998) 'From Free Trade to Supranational Polity: The European Court and Integration', in Wayne Sandholtz and Alec Stone Sweet (eds), *European Integration and Supranational Governance*. Oxford: Oxford University Press. pp. 92–133.

Stone Sweet, Alec and Sandholtz, Wayne (1998) 'Integration, Supranational Governance, and the Institutionalization of the European Polity', in Wayne Sandholtz and Alec Stone Sweet (eds), *European Integration and Supranational Governance*. Oxford: Oxford University Press. pp. 1–26.

Tarrow, Sidney (1998) 'Building a Composite Polity: Popular Contention in the European Union', Working Papers, Institute for European Studies. Ithaca: Cornell University. pp. 1–34.

Verdun, Amy (1999) 'The Role of the Delors Committee in Creating EMU: An Epistemic Community?', *Journal of European Public Policy*, 6 (2): 308–28.

Wendt, Alexander (1999) *Social Theory of International Politics*. Cambridge: Cambridge University Press.

Wessels, Wolfgang (1991) 'The EC Council: the Community's Decisionmaking Center', in Robert O. Keohane and Stanley Hoffmann (eds), *The New European Community*. Boulder: Westview. pp. 133–54.

Wionczek, Miguel (1970) 'The Rise and Decline of Latin American Economic Integration', *Journal of Common Market Studies*, 9 (1): 49–66.

World Bank (2000) *World Development Indicators*. Washington, DC.

WTO (1999) 'Mapping of Regional Integration', background note by the Secretariat', *www.itd.org/forums/mapping1.pdf* (20 November 2000)

Yoffie, David B. (1983) *Power and Protectionism: Strategies of the Newly Industrializing Countries*. New York: Columbia University Press.

Zürn, Michael (2000) 'Democratic Governance Beyond the Nation-State: The EU and other International Institutions', *European Journal of International Relations*, 6 (2): 183–221.

26

International Environment

RONALD B. MITCHELL

What political, economic and social forces cause the variety of international environmental problems we face? Why do some of these environmental problems become international issues while others do not? What explains why solutions are devised for some of these international problems but not for others? Why do some of the international policies devised mitigate, and sometimes eliminate, the problems they address while others fail miserably? Finally, what determines global society's success at evaluating and improving its attempts to protect the global environment? These questions regarding five stages of the international policy process constitute the primary focus of a growing literature on international environmental politics and policy (IEP).

Scholars working in this sub-field face an uneasy tension between pessimism and optimism: pessimism born from recognizing that structural factors often dictate international environmental outcomes; perhaps unwarranted optimism born from observing that human agency has sometimes protected the natural environment and from believing that humans can make better choices. Thus, issues of structure and agency central to the field of international relations (IR) also frame much IEP research (Dessler, 1989; Wendt, 1987). Fully understanding outcomes, and how they vary over policy stages, requires recognition that structures constrain the choices agents can make but leave room for political skill and energy in determining which of a more or less narrow range of potential outcomes actually occurs (Keohane, 1996: 24; Underdal, 2001: 37). Equally important, human choices, over time, can transform 'normally invariant' structural forces that 'shape how publics and officials ... experience and cope with the diverse challenges posed by environmental issues' (Dessler, 1989: 461; Rosenau, 1993: 262).

Dividing the literature on IEP into 'policy stages' serves more than merely as an organizational tool. The usual distinctions of rationalism and constructivism; realism, institutionalism, and liberalism; or power-based, interest-based and knowledge-based certainly apply to IEP (Hasenclever et al., 1997; Ruggie, 1998). Yet, within IEP, differing theoretical, normative, and methodological perspectives generally coexist in complementary ways that enrich our understanding of global environmental politics. Thus, analyzing the literature along lines of policy process mirrors its tendency to cut across traditional boundaries with mid-range theory that pays careful attention to policy issues. Most importantly, a policy-process approach highlights how structural constraints on choices, on the one hand, and the participation, choices, and influence of state and non-state actors, on the other, vary across policy stages.

A BRIEF HISTORY OF THE FIELD

The nature of international environmental problems makes IEP interdisciplinary, extending from the natural sciences to philosophy and religion. Several textbooks cover the issues broadly (Conca et al., 1996; Hurrell and Kingsbury, 1992; Vig and Axelrod, 1999), while others narrate the history of environmental politics, describe environmental problems, propose policy solutions, and exhort greater efforts to protect the environment (Porter and Brown, 1991; Soroos, 1999; World Resources Institute, 1992–3). The work of international lawyers (Birnie and Boyle, 1992; Cameron et al., 1996; Sands, 1994) and economists (Barrett, 1994; Swanson and Johnston, 1999) complements and informs political science. Yet, to do justice to that sub-set of the literature concerned primarily with causal explanations of IEP, I exclude many of these important literatures from this review.

The study of international environmental issues only gained recognition among international relations scholars in the late 1980s. A few scholars addressed IEP during the 1970s and 1980s (Caldwell, 1984; Falk, 1971; Kay and Jacobson, 1983; M'Gonigle and Zacher, 1979; Ophuls, 1977; Orr and Soroos, 1979; Sprout and Sprout, 1971; Young, 1981). With the exception of a special issue of *International Organization* on 'International Institutions and the Environmental Crisis' in 1972 (coinciding with the UN Conference on the Human Environment), IEP articles in major IR journals were infrequent. This changed rapidly around 1989, in no small part due to Peter Haas's work developing John Ruggie's notion of epistemic communities to explain the Mediterranean Action Plan (Haas, 1989; 1990: 55 n. 22; Ruggie, 1975). Indeed, Haas's work is a rare case in which theories developed within IEP have influenced IR scholarship generally, instead of vice versa (Haas, 1992b).

The end of the Cold War and the 1992 UN Conference on Environment and Development (UNCED) made international environmental issues both politically and intellectually more salient. Two journals dedicated to the issues were launched, *International Environmental Affairs* and the *Journal of Environment and Development*, and IEP articles became more common in mainstream journals and edited volumes devoted to international relations. Sole-authored and edited books dedicated to international environmental issues became increasingly common (Choucri, 1993; Haas et al., 1993; Lipschutz and Conca, 1993; Young, 1994; Young and Osherenko, 1993). A new crop of scholars began publishing doctoral and subsequent research (Bernauer, 1995; Dauvergne, 1997; Keohane and Levy, 1996; Litfin, 1994; Miller, 1995; Mitchell, 1994a; O'Neill, 2000; Princen, 1996; Sprinz and Vaahtoranta, 1994; Wapner, 1996; Young, 1998b). Indeed, recent growth in the amount and diversity of the literature has made it increasingly difficult to track.

As in the early stages of most sub-fields, the generation of theoretical propositions has outpaced their operationalization and testing. New terms and taxonomies overlap with, but seem unaware of, earlier ones. The major debates that structure most sub-fields have yet to emerge, in part because key concepts and theories are not yet refined enough to generate competing predictions. Theories are tested through single cases with insufficient attention to variable definition, case selection and generalizability (Mitchell and Bernauer, 1998). Databases to allow large-*n* studies are only now being developed. But the sub-field is maturing in ways that, if continued, will remedy these shortcomings.

CAUSES OF INTERNATIONAL ENVIRONMENTAL PROBLEMS

Growth in the number and magnitude of harms humans inflict on the natural environment and in our awareness of those harms has produced a plethora of theories on why international environmental problems are both ubiquitous and increasing. Some analysts see the increase in international environmental problems and variation across countries and issues within that trend as functions of the relationship between the supply of environmental amenities and the demands placed on them. Since Malthus, people have recognized that both the carrying capacities of natural systems (the amount and rate at which they can supply human demands) and the magnitude and types of human demands placed on them vary (Malthus and Appleman, 1976). These supply–demand conflicts are exacerbated because capitalist, socialist and communist economies actively create incentives to disregard the environment and passively fail to remedy situations involving Tragedies of the Commons and other externalities, that is, situations involving actions that bestow benefits on those who engage in them but impose larger costs on society as a whole (Hardin, 1968).

Others see sovereignty and international anarchy as making states even more likely than individuals to generate negative externalities by leading them to worry about relative, not absolute, gains and security rather than environmental protection (Conca, 1994; Litfin, 1998). Governance structures are less available, effective and robust at the international, than domestic, level. The security concerns of states and the profit motives of multinational corporations (MNCs) incline both to disregard environmental protection unless pressed by environmental movements and non-governmental organizations (NGOs) (Lipschutz and Conca, 1993; Lipschutz and Mayer, 1996). Scholars developing deep ecology, ecofeminism and other 'radical ecologies' further identify environmental degradation as merely the inherent and predictable result of the increasing domination of modernity and Western normative structures that devalue nature (Devall and Sessions, 1985; Merchant, 1996; Naess, 1973).

If structural forces make environmental degradation likely, they leave room for human actions that avoid it being inevitable. Policies cannot change carrying capacities but can shape demands on natural systems to better reflect them. Intergovernmental regulation or transnational civil society can create constraints and incentives to induce internalization of externalities. Over time, individuals and groups can consciously transform the values of global society to reflect environmental concerns (Stokke, 1998: 140). Research can remedy problems that stem from ignorance of human impacts on the environment and can identify new ways of meeting human needs sustainably. Although theories regarding the sources of international environmental problems are implicit in the theories regarding their resolution outlined below, there is considerable room for political scientists to develop a more complete and integrated theory of the political, social, cultural and economic forces that lead environmental problems to appear in some regions and issue areas but not in others, and to appear with increasing regularity around the globe.

AGENDA-SETTING

Why do only some of the many human impacts on the global environment capture international political and policy attention? Why do some that receive policy attention later 'vanish without a trace' while others are actively addressed? And, what determines how issues are discussed, whether in economic, moral, equity, or other framings?

Structural Forces and Constraints

Political context, material characteristics of the issue and immediate catalysts are three major determinants of the political attention devoted to a problem. Broad contextual factors alter the ease with which environmental issues gain attention. Trends in economic, cultural and informational interdependence, and in views of government's role in economic and social affairs, have made environmental issues politically more important. The end of the Cold War created more diplomatic space for environmental issues. Trade liberalization has created pressures to harmonize environmental standards. Increased awareness of environmental problems has fostered a proliferation of environmental conferences and negotiations (Meyer et al., 1997). The rise of 'post-material values' in civil societies of agenda-setting states has expanded the number, type, geographic scope and time horizon of environmental problems being addressed (Inglehart, 1995).

Contextual factors also influence the discourse of an issue, and the discursive context itself influences how issues play on the policy agenda. A precautionary discourse (that encourages environmental protection despite scientific uncertainty regarding the magnitude and causes of environmental harm from human activities) can move problems onto the agenda and toward policy action more quickly than traditional discourses that require scientific certainty before taking action (Litfin, 1994: 10). Although we have yet to determine why certain framings become dominant, it is clear that different framings can influence whether states view a problem as involving irreconcilable values or a jointly sub-optimal outcome, with the latter view helping states go beyond recognizing the problem to seeking solutions (Young, 1998a: 70).

If contextual forces explain broad patterns in agendas, a problem's material characteristics help explain variation within those patterns. We can expect environmental problems involving transboundary impacts, large and dramatic risks or direct and immediate threats to humans, and clearly understood trends, sources and solutions to appear on the international agenda more often than those lacking such traits. Environmental concern reflects 'objective' impacts on, and 'subjective' valuation of, an environmental amenity as well as the perceptions and incidence of the costs and benefits of mitigating the harm, factors that vary across issues and across and within countries (Jasanoff, 1986).

Paralleling other realms, powerful actors' interests are most likely to gain international attention. Environmental problems, even those with readily available solutions, often remain unaddressed if their costs, however great, are borne by developing countries. Fresh water supply, indoor air pollution and pollution-related illnesses kill millions of people annually in the developing world but remain unaddressed while international policy focuses on ozone depletion and other issues that pose smaller and more distant risks. Environmental problems in developing countries tend to garner attention only when people in agenda-setting states become concerned and, even then, these issues may languish or fail to lead to adequate solutions.

Variation in the level and type of environmental concern around the globe usually demands linkages among interests to get on the agenda (Young, 1998a: 57, 83). Governments, scientists, NGOs and individuals can link local environmental impacts and concerns to broader political agendas (Princen and Finger, 1994). Discursive links can make states more willing to work toward problem resolution, as when developing states attended UNCED because it successfully linked environment and development (World Commission on Environment and Development, 1987). More tactical links also can work, as evident in the financial mechanisms of several recent treaties and the participation of Soviet bloc states in European acid rain negotiations in the 1970s to promote *détente* (Levy, 1993).

One consistent, though undertheorized, finding of much IEP literature is that crises, accidents and other shocks prompt policy action by clearing 'a space for the consideration of new ideas on how to explain and solve problems' (Litfin, 1994: 185). International negotiations promptly followed the Chernobyl nuclear accident, the Sandoz spill in the Rhine, forest die-off in Germany and North Sea algae blooms. Scientific breakthroughs can also put issues on the agenda or increase their urgency

(Keohane, 1996: 27). The press mediates the influence of such events, headlining some issues while relegating others to the back pages. To give but one example, maritime regulation quickly followed pollution incidents near developed states even though much larger disasters off Africa and Latin America had occurred many years before. Yet, catalysts have heavily contingent causal power – they 'are not driving forces like material conditions, interests, or ideas' but move things forward only when deeper forces and conditions align (Haas, 1992b: 14; Young, 1998a: 77). Obviously, more systematic analysis would allow us to take such vague claims and identify more precisely whether catalytic events are necessary for policy action, what types are most influential and what factors and processes condition their influence.

Agents as Policy Entrepreneurs

Astute politicians, of course, do not simply wait for catalytic events to occur (Connolly, 1996: 364). Individuals, NGOs, states and international organizations consciously and strategically expend 'political capital in an effort to persuade others to recognize [certain] issues as priority agenda items' (Young, 1998a: 7; see also Risse, 2001). Scientists and the epistemic communities they compose can raise concern by clarifying environmental impacts and proposing solutions (Haas, 1990: 224). Although the legitimacy accorded to scientific research and discourse allows global environmental assessments to have considerable influence on the environmental agenda, as evident with the reports of the Intergovernmental Panel on Climate Change, many assessments still 'sink without a trace' (Corell, 1999; Shea, 1997). Nor are the biases and parochial interests that we expect from industry and NGO lobbyists always absent from scientific inputs to the policy process (Boehmer-Christiansen and Skea, 1991).

NGOs provide information, conduct research and propose and evaluate policies, transmitting both ideas and political pressure between polities and governments (Princen and Finger, 1994; Raustiala, 1997c). Pressure from American NGOs led the World Bank to add environmental concerns to project approval processes (McCormick, 1999: 65). The International Union for the Conservation of Nature (IUCN), the Worldwide Fund for Nature (WWF) and the World Resources Institute (WRI) self-consciously sought to make biodiversity an international issue, in part by conducting their own scientific research (Raustiala, 1997b). Although NGOs certainly can influence the debate, we still lack models that clarify the conditions and factors that facilitate or impede such influence.

Interest groups in powerful, agenda-setting states can make domestic issues international (DeSombre, 2000; Schreurs and Economy, 1997). Environmental movements in former Soviet bloc states coupled environmental concerns with nationalist movements to link domestically legitimate forms of discourse with transnational environmental concerns (Dawson, 1996). Corporations often support international actions to delay unilateral regulations, replace them with less stringent international ones, and avoid the economic costs of unilateral action (DeSombre, 2000).

In response to such efforts or on their own, states, individual bureaucratic entrepreneurs and international organizations often initiate and maintain pressure for international action. Regimes on Arctic environmental cooperation exhibit such state leadership even without epistemic community or NGO pressure (Young, 1998a: 7, 76). International regimes develop expertise and focus resources on certain issues. The UN Environment Program (UNEP) has promoted several regional seas agreements. Both the Convention on Long-Range Transboundary Air Pollution (LRTAP) and the International Maritime Organization have negotiated agreements on many atmospheric and marine pollutants, respectively, even in the absence of catalyzing events. In a spillover-type process, international cooperation to prevent a particular type of pollution or protect a particular species seems to promote cooperation on other pollutants and species.

States and international institutions generally do not look for problems to resolve but respond to issues put before them by environmental crises or by the activism of scientists, NGOs or individuals. Although some actors wield more influence, many actors have at least some. The international policy agenda is neither a systematic ranking of global environmental risk nor simply a list of problems whose resolution provides large benefits and entails few costs. Costs and benefits matter, but subtle and deeply embedded biases in the problems scientists study influence whether we become aware of or develop solutions to a problem. 'Mundane' problems and 'mundane' solutions receive less attention than issues on the cutting edge of science and technology (Kammen and Dove, 1997). The policy agenda reflects the goals, funding incentives and expertise of all the activists, politicians and bureaucrats involved. What issues ultimately get addressed and how they are prioritized reflect the interests of states but also reflect the pressures of multiple interest groups and the simple influence of catalytic events.

Framing of Issues on the Agenda

Precisely because the question of how to define and address a problem 'is up for grabs' during agenda formation, framing is crucial to what issues get on the agenda and how they progress through the policy process (Young, 1998a: 23, 83). Successful framing makes environmental concerns more salient to those not otherwise interested (Sebenius, 1983; Young, 1998a: 82). Although material factors constrain how a problem can be defined and delimit possible policy solutions, scientists, NGOs and governments can still wield influence within those constraints (Litfin, 1994: 9). Problems can be framed as regional or global, as symmetric Tragedies of the Commons (where all parties are both victims and perpetrators) or asymmetric externalities (where some parties are victims and others are perpetrators), a stand-alone problem or an ecosystemic one, or deserving weak regulation or a complete ban. Which framing is chosen, in turn, influences whether the problem garners attention, how broadly or narrowly the problem is defined, and what responses are considered.

Issue framing involves a dynamic political struggle between 'various networks of power/knowledge' in which policy-makers and stakeholders interpret and frame knowledge 'in light of specific interests, so that information begets counterinformation' (Litfin, 1994: 8 and 13; Stokke, 1998: 135). But, we know very little about 'the process through which a discourse crystallizes around a problem on the international political agenda', or how and when rhetorical power resources can overthrow more material resources to replace dominant discourses with alternative ones (Litfin, 1994: 10; Young, 1998a: 189). Analysis of why issues get onto and become prominent on the international stage and why they are debated and discussed in the terms they are remains in its infancy. Moving forward in this arena will require developing more specific, contingent and testable propositions about why certain environmental problems remain unaddressed and prescriptions about how that might change.

POLICY FORMULATION

Consensus about a problem's existence, causes and importance need not create consensus regarding what, or even whether, action is warranted. The efforts of those most concerned about an issue, whether they be states or non-state actors, often fail to prompt international action. I focus here on factors that facilitate or hinder inter-state regime formation but also note state unilateralism, direct NGO activism and MNC voluntarism as alternatives to inter-state efforts.

Structural Determinants
of Regime Formation

Explaining regime formation has been a major focus of neo-institutionalism, especially its international environmental variant. Most IEP scholars, due

to theoretical predispositions or convinced by environmental evidence, accept the institutionalist claim that inter-state cooperation is difficult but possible and focus on identifying factors that make it more likely. Realists, on the other hand, have largely ignored international environmental cooperation, taking one of three positions: (a) relative gains concerns hinder cooperation as much in environmental affairs as in other realms (Waltz, 1979: 195ff); (b) the 'low politics' of environmental issues are outside the domain of realist claims; or (c) the 'low politics' of environmental issues have so little impact on state survival that states can afford to pursue absolute gains.

Refining more general IR arguments, many IEP scholars have investigated the influence of the structure of interests on regime formation and design. Questioning the common assumption that international environmental problems are all Tragedies of the Commons, scholars have proposed various typologies of interest configurations and conflict types to explain the likelihood of regime formation. Proposals that problems can be identified as ranging from benign to malign (Underdal, 2001; Young, 1999b: 118) have fostered careful empirical research that allows independent categorization of problems in ways that help explain why regimes arise to resolve some problems but not others (Miles and Underdal, 2001; Wettestad, 1999; Young, 1998a).

The malign–benign distinction is too blunt a tool, however, to predict what type of regime will form. That requires using the more specific design implications provided by such distinctions as those among assurance, coordination, collaboration and suasion games; coordination and incongruity problems; symmetric and asymmetric problems; conflicts over values, means, relatively assessed goods, and absolutely assessed goods; and commons problems, shared natural resource problems and transboundary externalities (Barkin and Shambaugh, 1999; Hasenclever et al., 1997; Martin, 1992b; Underdal, 2001). Specific compliance mechanisms should be more common in regimes addressing collaboration games and compelling focal points more common in those addressing coordination games (Zürn, 1998: 629). Symmetric Tragedies of the Commons should lead to reciprocity being used while asymmetric problems (involving perpetrators who are not also victims) should lead to positive incentives being used (Mitchell and Keilbach, 2001). Compromise solutions that set maximum thresholds for harmful activities have become less common as policy-makers realize that only complete bans can adequately address unpredictable and irreversible environmental problems (Princen, 1996: 150–2). Of course, the implications of many other distinctions continue to need development.

At this point, empirical assessment of competing predictions about what kind of regime will form requires carefully identifying what kind of problem states face. That, in turn, requires carefully identifying state preferences independent of their policy positions and identifying the pattern of those preferences across states to identify the structure of the problem being addressed. The benefits and costs of international regulation help predict state positions as leaders or laggards (Levy, 1993; Sprinz and Vaahtoranta, 1994: 78). But preferences for environmental protection also vary based on factors as varied as policy styles, party politics, bureaucratic structures, industrial interests, NGOs and transnational linkages (DeSombre, 2000; O'Neill, 2000; Schreurs and Economy, 1997). These and other factors influence the value individual states place on environmental protection and the constellation of levels of concern which influences the ability to reach agreement and the shape of agreements reached. Categorizing real-world environmental problems as involving a Tragedy of the Commons, an asymmetry of interests, a conflict over a relatively assessed good, or a suasion game involving powerful actors attempting to assert their interests requires careful attention to actor preferences that avoids the tendency toward superficial and aggregate analogizing (Hasenclever et al., 1997; Martin, 1992a; Underdal, 2001). Many environmental problems involve intertwined strategic problems, as with stratospheric ozone loss, which may best be characterized as a Tragedy of the Commons among concerned developed states and an asymmetric externality between these states and less concerned, 'upstream', developing states (Mitchell and Keilbach, 2001).

Preferences also influence the aggressiveness of regime goals. States will find it easier to form a regime if they have low ambitions for it. Regimes initiated with framework conventions, cooperative research programs, or non-binding agreements (Brown Weiss, 1997) may reflect universally low concern, an inability to resolve conflict between concerned and unconcerned states, or high concern but uncertainty about the best way to address the problem. Indeed, the nature of the solution shapes interests as much as the nature of the problem. Regimes with ecologically unambitious goals may nonetheless induce significant resistance if the regime design involves high costs or imposes costs on powerful economic sectors. Thus, the climate convention evoked considerable resistance even though its emission reduction goals fall far short of what climatologists consider necessary to prevent climate change. Regimes that seek broad or deep cooperation, provide little flexibility and involve stringent enforcement will generally be resisted, *ceteris paribus*, but may be adopted if states expect large benefits (Downs et al., 1996). Unfortunately, we know little about how different institutional designs, whether market incentives, financial and technological transfers, or differing legal structures, increase or retard the willingness of states to join.

Regimes may not always reflect self-conscious, voluntary cooperation (Gruber, 2000). Hegemonic states, or groups of states, can impose regimes (Young, 1989: 84–6). Most whaling states accepted the moratorium on commercial whaling only under pressure from the United States. Likewise, regimes addressing industrialized states' concerns are more likely to be negotiated quickly and implemented fully than those addressing developing states' concerns (Haas, 1992a: 221).

Yet, in environmental affairs, structural power provides less explanatory leverage than realists might have us believe (Zürn, 1998: 625). Issue-specific power, in the ability to influence outcomes if no agreement is reached as well as in voting and bargaining power within treaty regimes, gives states considerable power over what gets done, when and how. China and India refused to join the ozone regime until industrialized states codified financial transfers in formal amendments. Although lacking any formal veto, Brazil can effectively prevent progress in protecting tropical rainforests, just as Botswana, Namibia and Zimbabwe can in protecting elephants. At the same time, when the states needed to resolve a problem also share a desire to resolve it, formal regimes may prove unnecessary. Spontaneous patterns of social practice can develop to resolve problems without resort to voting, formal rules and compliance procedures (Young, 1989: 84–6).

Discourses, Framing and Knowledge

Discussing situation structure statically assumes states have 'relatively well-developed conceptions of their own interests' that they bring to, and maintain during, negotiations (Young, 1998a: 97). Yet, preferences will be less clear and stable when issues are complex, knowledge is uncertain, and material interests are 'weakly or ambiguously affected' (Stokke, 1998: 132–3). High levels of uncertainty make interests hard to identify, creating a 'veil of uncertainty' that may facilitate or hinder regime formation (Zürn, 1998: 629–30). Regime bargaining exhibits elements of rationalist, game-theoretic perspectives in which preferences, strategies and possible outcomes are 'identifiable and fixed' and of constructivist perspectives in which these features result from, rather than being inputs to, the negotiation (Zürn, 1998: 627). Words persuade as well as communicate interests, threats and promises. Evaluating rationalist and constructivist claims requires comparing precise, observable, non-trivial and competing predictions to the empirical evidence.

Science has received particular attention as a force promoting environmental cooperation. Scientific identification of the existence of, causes of and solutions to an environmental problem seems at least necessary to regime formation. Yet, even in the

extensively studied case of ozone depletion, debate
continues over whether scientific consensus was a
proximate cause of the Montreal Protocol and even
whether it emerged before 'the real decisions had
been made' (Haas, 1992a: 224). Some argue that
policy-makers delegate power to epistemic communities under conditions of uncertainty, thereby avert-
ing otherwise-debilitating conflicts of interests
(Haas, 1992a: 188, 215). Others are more skeptical,
noting that the values and power embedded in scientific information often rationalize or reinforce rather
than reduce political conflict (Jasanoff, 1990; Litfin,
1994: 186). Scientists certainly do influence international negotiations, not least because scientists'
methods and rules of discursive legitimacy are an
alternative to strictly interest-based bargaining. That
said, those methods and rules do not prevent bias and
partiality in the arguments and facts scientists offer
and even less prevent policy-makers from selectively
using or ignoring science to support interest-based
positions.

Discursive forces also alter perceived interests
and, hence, whether and what type of regimes form.
Framing a problem as 'global' gives 'every participant in the negotiation process real bargaining
leverage' and veto power (Young, 1998a: 14).
Framing the problem as regional may facilitate
evolutionary progress, as evident in UNEP's
regional seas agreements and the European regime
for marine pollution enforcement whose imitation
in other regions has, over time, produced an
increasingly global regime.

Crucial questions now involve not whether interests, power and discourse influence whether and
how regimes emerge, but how to distinguish structural, material and discursive influences and the
conditions of their influence. We need more careful,
rather than more, theorizing to predict when states
bring fixed interests to negotiations and when they
identify their interests through negotiations, when
science is influential and when irrelevant, and
which types of discourses facilitate, instead of hinder, agreement.

Actors and Processes

Within the constraints imposed by interests, power,
discourse and knowledge, actors still can influence
regime formation. Although different scholars have
focused on states, epistemic communities, NGOs,
domestic political constituencies and individual
leaders, the similarities in their lists of how these
different groups influence the negotiation process
suggests a more useful distinction based on the functions they perform (Haas, 1992b: 18; McCormick,
1999; Raustiala, 1997c). Mirroring the literature,
the following discussion highlights the tasks that
state and non-state actors perform that aid international regime formation. Yet, it deserves note that

such actors are not always influential and may
hinder as well as facilitate cooperation.

Clarifying the problem and its causes   Those
who understand environmental trends and their
causes can motivate negotiators by leading them to
revise their estimates of the costs of reaching, or
failing to reach, agreement. If claims by other
governments regarding causes and solutions are
often suspect, policy-makers often seek advice from
epistemic communities and NGOs perceived as
more impartial (Haas, 1992b: 12; Raustiala, 1997c:
727). Indeed, many NGOs, seeking the legitimacy
and influence accorded to scientists, have sought
out resources and expertise to supplement traditional advocacy with impartial information provision. NGOs also provide negotiators with insight
into, and influence on, various constituencies' subjective perceptions of environmental harms
(Princen and Finger, 1994: 217).

Pushing for problem resolution   At local,
national and international levels, NGOs, industry
trade groups and even epistemic communities
lobby, promote media coverage, campaign, protest,
or engage in ecosabotage to raise issue salience. By
providing information on the progress of international negotiations to constituencies, environmental
NGOs and corporations bring pressure to bear on
negotiators to support some agreements and oppose
others (Lipschutz and Conca, 1993; Lipschutz and
Mayer, 1996; Wapner, 1996). Using different
tactics, interest groups press state officials directly
or via public pressure to take action on a given
issue. Scientists, corporate representatives and environmental activists also can 'infiltrate' domestic
and international levels of governance, joining
national delegations and working with intergovernmental organizations (IGOs) (Haas, 1992b: 27;
Raustiala, 1997c: 730). They thereby influence perceptions of the interests in and importance of an
issue area. Individuals, whether representing states
or non-state actors, can become 'determined champions' who promote certain proposals and stage catalytic events to prompt action at crucial junctures
(Haas, 1992a: 222; Young, 1998a: 72, 188; Young
and Osherenko, 1993).

*Designing policies, facilitating agreement and
maintaining momentum*   Regime design is
intimately connected with negotiation progress. The
desire of each state to negotiate, sign and ratify an
agreement is not independent of the terms of that
agreement. Framework-protocol approaches work
precisely because states are willing to accept collective decision-making that they know will lead to
substantive agreement before they are willing to
reach substantive agreement itself. Adding redistributive financial transfers to regulatory agreements may make potential donors more resistant but

will attract potential recipients (Lowi, 1972). Indeed, the redistributive effects of different compliance costs regularly lead states to continue negotiating rather than accept the agreement on the table. When states view transparency as crucial, devising acceptable inspection procedures can slow, and even prevent, agreement. Decision-making rules, proscriptions and prescriptions, implementation provisions, and withdrawal and renegotiation clauses can all become deal-breakers.

This setting rewards those who can design proposals that balance enough competing interests to foster a final agreement. 'Deft diplomacy' is crucial to 'add and subtract issues to facilitate the bargaining process, craft the terms of negotiating texts, and broker the deals needed to achieve consensus' (Young, 1998a: 23; see also Sebenius, 1983). Although material resources are certainly helpful, high-ranking IGO officials, diplomats, bureaucrats, or NGO and corporate representatives often facilitate agreement without such resources (Young, 1998a: 23). States often table proposals themselves but, equally often, non-state actors introduce proposals directly to intergovernmental negotiating bodies or through sympathetic governments. They not only provide local knowledge that contributes to policy design at the international level but also evaluate policy proposals (Haas, 1992b: 15; McCormick, 1999: 67; Princen and Finger, 1994; Raustiala, 1997c: 727).

Particularly when exogenous forces make reaching agreement more difficult or less urgent, maintaining 'political momentum' becomes crucial (Young, 1998a: 87–8). IGOs help by providing a forum for discussion and by proposing regulative and institutional models (List and Rittberger, 1998: 70–1). States have granted NGOs (particularly, the Earth Negotiations Bulletin) access to negotiations because they want detailed and impartial daily reporting and will accept, in exchange, its public dissemination (Raustiala, 1997c: 730). NGOs and issue networks also help mobilize international opinion when agreements near completion or require ratification (Princen and Finger, 1994). Entrepreneurial leaders employ various techniques to ensure progress can be made when political conditions ripen, as evident in UNEP executive director Mostafa Tolba's proposals that fostered the ozone regime negotiations (Keohane, 1996: 26; Young, 1998a: 119).

Unilateral State Action and Non-state Action

While most arms control, trade and human rights regimes target state behavior, most environmental regimes ultimately target private actors. Scholars are increasingly highlighting efforts to protect the international environment without regimes, through state unilateralism, NGO action or changes in MNC policies. States sometimes act to protect the global environment when doing so appears materially irrational. The United States has sanctioned violations of international environmental laws, even when others harmed by those violations fail to do so (DeSombre, 2000). European states often provide bilateral assistance for environmental projects that yield few material benefits (Keohane and Levy, 1996). Such unilateralism does not imply that states act against their material interests, but that domestic environmental interests can align themselves with economic interests in ways that foster international environmental protection without regimes.

Items that fail to get the attention of states need not languish, however. Indeed, if 'states are the problem', circumventing their power may be preferred as quicker, easier and more open to innovation (Deudney, 1990). NGOs and transnational issue networks can engage in 'world civic politics', directly attempting to influence the values and behaviors of individuals and corporations (Lipschutz and Mayer, 1996; Wapner, 1996). NGOs can use rhetorical persuasion, rather than coopting the coercive power of the state, to target places where state control is weak, outcomes are less predetermined, and behavior is more 'amenable to alternative practices' (Wapner, 1996: 156–60).

NGOs regularly operate projects directly with local communities without significant governmental or intergovernmental involvement (McCormick, 1999: 66). NGOs acquire and protect ecosystems directly and through debt-for-nature swaps (Jakobeit, 1996). NGOs prompt consumer boycotts and 'buy green' campaigns that directly shape corporate incentives (Wapner, 1996). Direct NGO pressure, more diffuse pressure from an increasingly 'green' market and the personal values of employees all contribute to domestic corporations, MNCs and trade organizations including environmental concerns in the production calculus (Garcia-Johnson, 2000). The Forest Stewardship Council, International Organization for Standardization (ISO), and other groups that include corporate representatives, NGOs or both, have developed ecolabeling schemes and voluntary codes of conduct that skirt government regulation and provide information directly to consumers (Clapp, 1998). NGOs and industry are rarely averse to, and often are observed, working with governments on programs such as these, but increasingly proceed with them when government cooperation is absent.

POLICY IMPLEMENTATION AND EFFECTIVENESS

Ultimately, the value of formulating new inter-state, state and non-state policies depends on whether they alter human behaviors in ways that improve the environment. Promulgating good policy requires understanding which policies are most likely to be implemented in ways that will produce desired behavioral changes and environmental benefits. Even more than policy formulation, work on policy implementation and effectiveness in international environmental affairs has been dominated by the study of regimes. During the 1990s, individuals and teams representing differing disciplines, countries and theoretical approaches examined numerous cases to produce a remarkably coherent research program. Just English-language edited volumes directly evaluating environmental regime effectiveness identify a plethora of factors and forces considered influential (Andresen and Wettestad, 1995; Brown Weiss and Jacobson, 1998; Cameron et al., 1996; Haas, et al., 1993; Keohane and Levy, 1996; Miles and Underdal, 2001; Underdal and Hanf, 2000; Victor et al., 1998; Young, 1999a; Zürn, 1998: 619 n. 4).

Defining the Dependent Variables

Agreement about what constitutes successful regime formation (states negotiating an agreement) is not matched by agreement about what constitutes policy effectiveness. To determine how much movement toward some goal a policy induced involves three tasks: identifying an appropriate goal, an appropriate metric of movement and an appropriate indicator of the share of that movement to attribute to the policy.

Identifying an appropriate goal for evaluating regime 'effectiveness' proves problematic because regimes can have so many effects, from the direct, immediate and intentional to the indirect, distant and perverse. Scholars have usefully distinguished implementation and compliance (or behavioral change) from environmental (or problem-solving) effectiveness (Brown Weiss and Jacobson, 1998; Peterson, 1998; Underdal, 2001: 4; Victor et al., 1998). We can start with the last of these, asking 'how well did this regime resolve the problem that led to its formation' (Bernauer, 1995: 366; Young, 1999b: 109). Thus, agreed-upon goals in a treaty's preamble or elsewhere become an appropriate metric. However, participants often establish regimes without agreement on objectives or change their objectives over time (Young, 1999b: 109). Indeed, much hard law and most non-binding soft law involves vague or ambiguous language that makes identifying a goal against which to evaluate performance almost impossible.

Equally important, analysts may want to evaluate progress toward goals other than those held by the parties involved (Helm and Sprinz, 1999; Underdal, 2001). Thus, the nominal goal of the whaling convention is 'to provide for the proper conservation of whale stocks and thus make possible the orderly development of the whaling industry', but we may want to know how it has contributed to promoting a norm of a whales' right to life (D'Amato and Chopra, 1991). Indeed, analysts have begun trying to identify 'collective optima', that is, what full environmental protection would have required, as an additional metric of environmental effectiveness (Underdal, 2001).

Second, an interest in environmental improvement quickly shifts when we recognize that achieving that goal requires human behavior change. Equally important, environmental regimes generally target behavioral changes at state and sub-state levels, in a post-negotiation two-level game (Putnam, 1988). Regime effects are evident in implementation – laws, regulations and governmental use of sanctions, rewards and other policies – and in behavior changes by the ultimate targets of the regime. For the latter, legal compliance is a useful, and usually readily available, metric but misses 'overcompliance' and 'good faith non-compliance' that also constitute evidence of regime influence (Mitchell, 1996). For example, the influence of the LRTAP convention was more evident in the otherwise-unlikely 10 per cent reductions in Hungarian sulfur emissions than from reductions by many other countries that far surpassed the 30 per cent requirement (Levy, 1993). The problem, of course, with using behavior is that regimes may induce significant behavioral change that falls far short of the environmental goals established by regime negotiators, let alone scientists or environmental advocates.

Finally, regime efficiency, cost-effectiveness and equity have yet to receive much analytic attention (Bernauer, 1995: 358; Brown Weiss, 1989). Although some scholars have sought to promote one metric or definition of effectiveness as superior to others, progress requires that the research community, even if not individual scholars, adopt an inclusive set of definitions so we can assess how even a single regime varies across various dimensions of effectiveness. The choice of which dimension to evaluate will reflect different analytic goals and normative preferences, making it futile and potentially counterproductive to give one primacy over another. And, in any event, a broad approach will be crucial to evaluating the many regimes with multiple, ambiguous, implicit, or misleading goals and with effects that are less intended and more far-ranging than usually assumed.

Beyond identifying a goal for evaluation, the analyst must identify a criterion of effectiveness. Two basic categories of criteria have been identified: relative improvement and goal achievement (Underdal, 2001: 5). The first compares the observed value of some effectiveness parameter to a no-regime baseline. The second compares that observed value to the desired value of that parameter, as defined by regime negotiators ('goal achievement') or an independent analyst ('collective optimum') (Underdal, 2001: 6). These standards are complementary, with the former 'glass half full' criteria asking how far have we come and the second 'glass half empty' criteria asking how far have we yet to go. Helm and Sprinz have proposed a metric that combines these criteria, involving actual performance relative to a no-regime baseline expressed as a fraction of total possible improvement relative to that same baseline (Helm and Sprinz, 1999). This provides a valuable first step toward transcending claims that a regime 'made a difference' to evaluating how much of a regime's 'potential' was realized and allowing comparison of relative effectiveness across regimes.

All efforts to identify the influence of a regime require comparison of observed outcomes to a carefully hypothesized counterfactual state of affairs in the absence of the regime. Indeed, the literature's focus on behaviors, enforcement, implementation and compliance rather than environmental improvement does not reflect a lack of environmental concern but that our skill in estimating counterfactuals of environmental resource quality (a product of natural variation, human behavior, and myriad other factors) is even more limited than in estimating human behavior (Brown Weiss and Jacobson, 1998; Miles and Underdal, 2001; Victor et al., 1998; Young, 1999a). Behavioral change provides a useful but limited proxy for regime effects: regimes that cause no behavior change are certainly ineffective in behavioral and environmental terms; those that cause some behavior change are behaviorally effective but may nonetheless be environmentally ineffective (Underdal, 2001: 4). Thus, whether by counterfactuals, contrasting cases, or process tracing, the goal is to distinguish regime influences from the myriad other influences on human behavior or the environment.

Several additional aspects of regime effectiveness research deserve comment. Work has only begun to evaluate how success varies over a regime's life cycle (Gehring, 1994). Likewise, research to date has focused on absolute effectiveness, that is, 'do regimes matter?', a question answerable through single case studies. Research on relative effectiveness that compares one regime to another is crucial but must surmount obstacles such as whether the regimes being compared addressed similar problems, were at similar stages in their life cycle and held other determinants of effectiveness constant (Underdal, 2001: 13–14; Young, 1999b: 114). Some, but still not enough, research has begun to move away from 'sterile debates' about whether regimes influence behavior toward policy-relevant identification of the features and conditions that help regimes perform better (see also Bernauer, 1995: 374; Underdal, 2001: 8; Young, 1999b: 116).

Structural Forces and Constraints

Building on Brown Weiss and Jacobson, I categorize regime effectiveness as dependent on characteristics of the issue area, the international setting, the targeted actor and the regime (Brown Weiss and Jacobson, 1998: 535–42). The first three can be considered as structural forces that establish a range of potential influence in which regime design then determines outcomes (Young, 1999a: 124).

Issue area An issue area's structure influences a regime's effectiveness by shaping how willing and able targeted actors, whether states or non-state actors, are to alter their behavior. Regimes must manipulate these 'baseline' incentives and abilities to induce actors otherwise inclined to behave contrary to regime goals to align their behavior with regime goals and rules (Miles and Underdal, 2001). A regime's ability to alter behavior depends on how the incentives and abilities to engage in existing behaviors match those for desired new behaviors (Hasenclever et al., 1997: 62ff.; Martin, 1992b; Underdal, 2001: 1; Victor et al., 1998; Young, 1999b: 117). Situation structure shapes the types of problems a regime will face. Prisoners' dilemma type problems will encourage clandestine cheating while offering rewards to upstream states to induce reduced pollution may prompt public declarations of non-compliance to extract greater rewards. Those who are more ecologically vulnerable will tend to outperform those who are less (Sprinz and Vaahtoranta, 1994). Those for whom change is costly will be more recalcitrant than those for whom it is cheap. Problems whose resolution requires new behaviors will face violations due to incentives and incapacity while regimes that require only restraint will face only those due to incentives.

Material sources of interests are intertwined with how relevant actors define and perceive the environmental problem. Whether poor environmental quality translates into high environmental concern and behavior change depends on where environmental protection fits in a state or non-state actor's value system and on broader domestic and international norms regarding the importance of environmental protection. Certainly, actors will ignore a regime's dictates when they have strong, immediate and clear material interests in doing so. But the values held by individuals, civil society, epistemic communities, NGOs and MNCs wield considerable influence over their own responses and those of the states they compose.

Overlaying power onto the pattern of interests provides additional insight into patterns of regime effectiveness. Powerful states that have independent incentives to meet their commitments often attempt to reassure more cautious states enough to induce them also to cooperate (Chayes and Chayes, 1995). Likewise, powerful states that oppose a regime can induce less adherence by states that might otherwise have changed their behaviors. Other issue-specific factors also influence behavioral incentives, including the number of other actors involved, levels of uncertainty about the science of the problem or its resolution, the inherent transparency of relevant behaviors, the role and position of MNCs and the concentration of the activity being regulated (Brown Weiss and Jacobson, 1998: Figure 15.2, p. 536).

Actor characteristics The responses of states and sub-state actors also vary within and across regimes because of actor-level traits. Variation in beliefs, interests and capacities that are independent of the issue area will produce different levels of commitment to a regime. Countries vary in their levels of domestic environmental concern, government efficiency and effectiveness in responding to those concerns, and political and administrative capacity to implement international commitments (Haas et al., 1993). Brown Weiss and Jacobson attribute variation in compliance levels to national characteristics ranging from previous behavior, history and physical size to number of neighbors, type of economy and institutions, and level of knowledge (Brown Weiss and Jacobson, 1998). Others focus on support from corporate and private actors for regime goals and the means chosen to implement regime rules (Raustiala, 1997a; Underdal, 1998; Underdal and Hanf, 2000; Young, 1998a: 142–54). Such support, in turn, depends on the power and participation of regulated and countervailing groups, economic forces and market conditions, political environmental mobilization and the strength of regulatory and administrative structures (Raustiala and Victor, 1998).

Variation in the capacity to implement regimes also influences their success. Some environmental agreements involve positive commitments requiring large expenditures or developing new technologies while others involve negative commitments requiring only that actors refrain from certain actions. In most regimes, the distribution of burdens is likely to mean at least some actors are financially, technically or administratively incapable of complying. Although claims of incapacity often will mask a lack of incentives to comply, violations often can truly stem from incapacity.

International context A regime's capacity to alter actors' behaviors also depends on the broader international context (Brown Weiss and Jacobson, 1998; Young, 1999b: 123). Regimes have an easier task when their goals align with the current intellectual order and forms of discourse (such as economic integration and political liberalization), the frequency and visibility of major international environmental conferences, the number and strength of environmental NGOs and the attention being given

to environmental issues generally (Brown Weiss and Jacobson, 1998: 536; Victor et al., 1998; Young, 1992). Since these factors enhance or inhibit a regime's ability to influence behavior, they also serve as important alternative explanations of a regime's effectiveness.

Regime Design

Were realist theory always correct, then characteristics of the issue area, actors and international context would determine behavioral outcomes. Institutionalists have shown, however, that regime design and 'problem-solving capacity' also influence outcomes (Mitchell, 1994b; Underdal, 2001: 1). What follows attempts to make sense of the 'plethora of propositions as to which types of institutions are likely to be more effective' (Bernauer, 1995: 374).

The social and political process of defining what problem a regime will address and what strategies and how aggressively to address it determine effectiveness by defining the regime's goal, how hard and costly it will be to achieve, and how much resistance there will be to achieving it. Aggressive goals may motivate significant behavior change by those who try yet fail to meet them, or may be ignored as unachievable. More realistic goals may achieve visible results quickly, but may provide few incentives for actors to do more. At this stage, both theoretical and empirical work on the goals–behavior link is needed.

The means of goal achievement also surely matters. Yet, simple questions of whether binding regulations induce more change than non-binding ones remain open (Brown Weiss, 1997). Clear regulatory rules may seem crucial to behavioral change, but we do not yet know whether such regimes induce more or less behavior change than procedural regimes that facilitate recurring collective choice, programmatic regimes that pool resources toward collective goals, or generative regimes that foster development of new norms and social practices (Young, 1998a: 145; 1999b: 24ff.). The conditions for success of regulatory regimes have been more fully specified, however (if only because their explicitness makes measuring effectiveness easier), providing the foundation for what follows.

Regulatory regimes induce compliance through their primary rule system, compliance information system and non-compliance response system (Mitchell, 1996). Effective regimes design these systems so that they respond to or 'fit' the environmental and behavioral demands of the problem they address. For any given problem, regime designers must choose among behavioral prescriptions and proscriptions. When these primary rules can apply to different actors, deciding which activity to regulate dictates which actors with what interests and capacities must change their behavior, how large and costly those changes will be, and whether other factors will reinforce or undercut compliance incentives. Designing more specific rules clarifies what is expected for those predisposed to comply and removes the opportunity to claim inadvertence or misinterpretation for those predisposed to violate. Even the perception that the rules were generated and implemented in equitable and reasonable ways can influence the willingness to change behavior (Brown Weiss and Jacobson, 1998; Victor et al., 1993: 468–71). Regulating highly visible or transparent activities or those that involve transactions between actors can reassure each actor that others are complying and allow them to protect their interests if they are not.

A regime can further increase transparency through design of the compliance information system. Whether regimes include reciprocity, sanctions, or rewards, altering behavior requires that actors know their behaviors will be noticed. Although most regimes rely on self-reporting, systems that supply incentives and build the capacity to report work better than others that sanction non-reporting or fail to address practical obstacles to reporting (Mitchell, 1998). Intrusive monitoring systems have been authorized in several environmental agreements and rising environmental concern may make them more common. Regimes can also increase transparency by rewarding compliance only if actors also supply reports or allow inspections.

Beyond clear rules, transparency and other such features, a regime's influence depends on how it responds to those who comply and those who do not. The direct tit-for-tat that can discourage violations of economic and arms control agreements proves less useful in environmental realms where regime supporters are unwilling to harm the environment as a retaliatory sanction and, even if they did, would not influence the intended targets unconcerned about the environment. Recognizing this, many scholars and practitioners stress the need for treaties to couple economic sanctions with careful monitoring and verification mechanisms to trigger them (Bernauer, 1995: 363; Downs et al., 1996; Wettestad, 1995). In a seminal piece, Chayes and Chayes (1995) argued that such an enforcement model was less effective than a more 'managerial' approach, employing diplomacy, norms and rewards. Rewards can induce actors, especially unconcerned 'upstream' actors, to alter their behavior (Bernauer, 1995: 371). Theoretical debate and empirical research continues to attempt to determine whether sanctions are always needed or needed only for 'deep' cooperation, and under what conditions, if any, rewards may prove more effective (Downs et al., 1996; Underdal, 2001: 13).

Beyond sanctions and rewards, 'systems of implementation review' and 'sunshine methods' involving reporting, monitoring and review may induce compliance even without explicit and direct responses (Brown Weiss and Jacobson, 1998; Victor et al., 1998). Ecolabeling, certification and prior informed consent rules may induce behavioral changes via marketplace incentives (Krueger, 1999). Norms, argument and persuasion can influence behavior by altering notions of appropriate and inappropriate action (Finnemore, 1996). Thus, the wetland treaty's vague norm to make 'wise use' of wetlands has prompted ongoing discussions about what wise use means, slowly altering traditional perceptions that wetlands are wastelands. The difficulty of demonstrating the influence of norms should not lead us to disregard their potential importance. Crucial questions remain regarding which of various strategies work best in which circumstances, controlling for characteristics of the issue area, international context and actors.

Finally, regime design involves attention to those who support implementation. The material and intellectual power, resources and expertise of the secretariat, other international organizations and supportive NGOs can contribute significantly to implementation (List and Rittberger, 1998: 72; Peterson, 1998; Ringius, 1997; Sandford, 1996). Even MNCs can aid implementation, as when major chemical corporations hastened the phase-out of CFCs because, fearing international regulation, they developed alternatives that were cheaper.

POLICY EVOLUTION AND SOCIAL LEARNING

Evolution and learning constitute something like a fifth policy stage facilitating revision and improvement in the other stages. Policy change may involve simple repetition of the policy process under changed circumstances. New environmental problems may develop and be identified, move onto the international agenda, be addressed through a transnational or international policy process, and be implemented through new mechanisms. When such changes result from changes in exogenous factors, they may deserve our attention but, conceptually, involve simply new instances of these policy processes.

Recent scholarship has begun to investigate the more self-conscious process of how human societies and institutions 'get better' at global environmental management (Social Learning Group, 2001). How do international institutions and processes improve what we know about the environment, human impacts on the environment and our ability to reduce those impacts? These meta-questions are complex and crucial, requiring understanding 'how discoveries, experience, and innovations present in one part of the [global environmental] management system spread to others' (Social Learning Group,

2001: 6). Institutions and society can spiral rather than cycle through policy stages, becoming increasingly proficient at managing human–environment interactions (Haas and Haas, 1995).

Especially in environmental affairs, a crucial but understudied question is how to alter behavior through complex, double-loop learning that alters underlying goals rather than single-loop learning that simply alters preferences across strategies (Parson and Clark, 1995). Regimes and intergovernmental organizations can evolve dynamically, identifying 'new and sharpened rules, stricter standards and improved procedures' (List and Rittberger, 1998: 76; see also Gehring, 1994). Yet questions such as whether framework-protocol approaches work better than alternatives, why some regimes develop progressive regulatory structures and how non-state actors foster social learning remain only vaguely understood.

CONCLUSION

The study of international environmental politics parallels policy efforts to improve global environmental management. Scholars have generated theories and cases demonstrating why global environmental problems are so common; how they get raised to the international agenda; why states form regimes for some but not others; what factors facilitate regime effectiveness; and how evolution and learning occur. Structural forces and agents' choices wield different amounts and types of influence at different policy stages. Non-state actors wield different, and perhaps more, influence earlier in the process. Conscious social engineering appears able to resolve problems of policy formulation and implementation more than agenda-setting.

Given the many important questions still unaddressed in IEP, progress will require new and concerted efforts. Theoretically, we need a framework to make sense, for each stage of the policy process, of which factors are influential under a wide range of circumstances, which are influential only in limited circumstances, and which are simply not influential despite earlier theorizing. Methodologically, we need to supplement the almost-exclusive use of case studies with quantitative methods, formal modeling and simulation. Substantively, we need to examine more than the ozone depletion, climate change and acid rain cases that have been the empirical testbeds for too many theories. Empirically, we need to develop data for qualitative and large-*n* quantitative comparisons across issues (Breitmeier et al., 1996; Haas and Sundgren, 1993). These efforts have begun but opportunities abound for scholars to move the sub-field forward.

If scholars of IEP are to contribute to global environmental management, we must begin developing contingent knowledge that identifies how the choices actors make promote environmental protection, the structural constraints on their ability to do so, and the conditions under which the former can help us overcome the latter.

Notes

This chapter has benefited from the criticism and suggestions of Walter Carlsnaes, Peter Haas, David Patel, M.J. Peterson, Kal Raustiala, Thomas Risse, Beth Simmons, Detlef Sprinz, Paul Steinberg, Paul Wapner, Oran Young and a particularly insightful anonymous reviewer. Generous research support was provided by the University of Oregon's Department of Political Science and Stanford University's Center for Environmental Science and Policy.

Bibliography

Andresen, Steinar and Wettestad, Jørgen (1995) 'International Problem-Solving Effectiveness: The Oslo Project Story So Far', *International Environmental Affairs*, 7 (2): 127–49.

Barkin, J. Samuel and Shambaugh, George (eds) (1999) *Anarchy and the Environment: The International Relations of Common Pool Resources*. Albany: State University of New York Press.

Barrett, Scott (1994) 'Self-enforcing International Environmental Agreements', *Oxford Economic Papers*, 46 (Special Issue): 878–93.

Bernauer, Thomas (1995) 'The Effect of International Environmental Institutions: How We Might Learn More', *International Organization*, 49 (2): 351–77.

Birnie, Patricia W. and Boyle, Alan E. (1992) *International Law and the Environment*. Oxford: Oxford University Press.

Boehmer-Christiansen, Sonja A. and Skea, James (1991) *Acid Politics: Environmental and Energy Policies in Britain and Germany*. London: Belhaven Press.

Breitmeier, Helmut, Levy, Marc A., Young, Oran R. and Zürn, Michael (1996) 'The International Regimes Database as a Tool for the Study of International Cooperation', WP-96-160. Laxenburg, Austria: International Institute for Applied Systems Analysis.

Brown Weiss, Edith (1989) *In Fairness to Future Generations: International Law, Common Patrimony, and Intergenerational Equity*. Dobbs Ferry, NY: Transnational Publishers.

Brown Weiss, Edith (ed.) (1997) *International Compliance with Nonbinding Accords*. Washington, DC: American Society of International Law.

Brown Weiss, Edith and Jacobson, Harold K. (eds) (1998) *Engaging Countries: Strengthening Compliance with International Environmental Accords*. Cambridge, MA: MIT Press.

Caldwell, Lynton Keith (1984) *International Environmental Policy*. Durham, NC: Duke University Press.

Cameron, James, Werksman, Jacob and Roderick, Peter (eds) (1996) *Improving Compliance with International Environmental Law*. London: Earthscan.

Chayes, Abram and Chayes, Antonia Handler (1995) *The New Sovereignty: Compliance with International Regulatory Agreements*. Cambridge, MA: Harvard University Press.

Choucri, Nazli (ed.) (1993) *Global Accord: Environmental Challenges and International Responses*. Cambridge, MA: MIT Press.

Clapp, Jennifer (1998) 'The Privatization of Global Environmental Governance: ISO 14000 and the Developing World', *Global Governance*, 4 (3): 295–316.

Conca, Ken (1994) 'Rethinking the Ecology–Sovereignty Debate', *Millennium*, 23 (3): 1–11.

Conca, Ken, Alberty, Michael and Dabelko, Geoffrey (eds) (1996) *Green Planet Blues*. Boulder: Westview.

Connolly, Barbara (1996) 'Increments for the Earth: The Politics of Environmental Aid', in Robert O. Keohane and Marc A. Levy (eds), *Institutions for Environmental Aid: Pitfalls and Promise*. Cambridge, MA: MIT Press. pp. 327–65.

Corell, Elisabeth (1999) 'The Negotiable Desert: Expert Knowledge in the Negotiations of the Convention to Combat Desertification', PhD dissertation, Linkoping University, Linkoping, Sweden.

D'Amato, Anthony and Chopra, Sudhir K. (1991) 'Whales: Their Emerging Right to Life', *American Journal of International Law*, 85 (1): 21–62.

Dauvergne, Peter (1997) *Shadows in the Forest: Japan and the Politics of Timber in Southeast Asia*. Cambridge, MA: MIT Press.

Dawson, Jane (1996) *Eco-Nationalism*. Durham, NC: Duke University Press.

DeSombre, Elizabeth R. (2000) *Domestic Sources of International Environmental Policy: Industry, Environmentalists, and US Power*. Cambridge, MA: MIT Press.

Dessler, David (1989) 'What's at Stake in the Agent–Structure Debate?', *International Organization*, 43 (3): 441–73.

Deudney, Daniel (1990) 'The Case Against Linking Environmental Degradation and National Security', *Millennium*, 19 (3): 461–76.

Devall, Bill and Sessions, George (1985) *Deep Ecology*. Salt Lake City: Peregrine Smith Books.

Downs, George W., Rocke, David M. and Barsoom, Peter N. (1996) 'Is the Good News about Compliance Good News about Cooperation?', *International Organization*, 50 (3): 379–406.

Falk, Richard (1971) *This Endangered Planet: Prospects and Proposals for Human Survival*. New York: Vintage.

Finnemore, Martha (1996) *National Interests in International Society*. Ithaca: Cornell University Press.

Garcia-Johnson, Ronie (2000) *Exporting Environmentalism: US Multinational Chemical Corporations in Brazil and Mexico*. Cambridge, MA: MIT Press.

Gehring, Thomas (1994) *Dynamic International Regimes: Institutions for International Environmental Governance*. Frankfurt-am-Main: P. Lang.

Gruber, Lloyd (2000) *Ruling the World*. Princeton: Princeton University Press.

Haas, Peter M. (1989) 'Do Regimes Matter? Epistemic Communities and Mediterranean Pollution Control', *International Organization*, 43 (3): 377–403.

Haas, Peter M. (1990) *Saving the Mediterranean: The Politics of International Environmental Cooperation*. New York: Columbia University Press.

Haas, Peter M. (1992a) 'Banning Chlorofluorocarbons', *International Organization*, 46 (1): 187–224.

Haas, Peter M. (1992b) 'Epistemic Communities and International Policy Coordination', *International Organization*, 46 (1): 1–35.

Haas, Peter M. and Haas, Ernst B. (1995) 'Learning to Learn: Improving International Governance', *Global Governance*, 1 (3): 255–85.

Haas, Peter, M. and Sundgren, Jan (1993) 'Evolving International Environmental Law: Changing Practices of National Sovereignty', in Nazli Choucri (ed.), *Global Accord: Environmental Challenges and International Responses*. Cambridge, MA: MIT Press. pp. 401–29.

Haas, Peter M., Keohane, Robert O. and Levy, Marc A. (eds) (1993) *Institutions for the Earth: Sources of Effective International Environmental Protection*. Cambridge, MA: The MIT Press.

Hardin, Garrett (1968) 'The Tragedy of the Commons', *Science*, 162 (3859): 1243–8.

Hasenclever, Andreas, Mayer, Peter and Rittberger, Volker (1997) *Theories of International Regimes*. Cambridge: Cambridge University Press.

Helm, Carsten and Sprinz, Detlef (1999) 'Measuring the Effectiveness of International Environmental Regimes', 52. Potsdam: Potsdam Institute for Climate Impact Research.

Hurrell, Andrew and Kingsbury, Benedict (eds) (1992) *The International Politics of the Environment: Actors, Interests, and Institutions*. Oxford: Oxford University Press.

Inglehart, Ronald (1995) 'Public Support for Environmental Protection: The Impact of Objective Problems and Subjective Values in 43 Societies', *Political Science and Politics*, 27 (1): 57–71.

Jakobeit, Cord (1996) 'Nonstate Actors Leading the Way: Debt-for-Nature Swaps', in Robert O. Keohane and Marc A. Levy (eds), *Institutions for Environmental Aid: Pitfalls and Promise*. Cambridge, MA: MIT Press. pp. 127–66.

Jasanoff, Sheila (1986) *Risk Management and Political Culture: A Comparative Study of Science in the Policy Context*. New York: Russell Sage Foundation.

Jasanoff, Sheila (1990) *The Fifth Branch: Science Advisers as Policymakers*. Cambridge, MA: Harvard University Press.

Kammen, Daniel M. and Dove, Michael R. (1997) 'The Virtues of Mundane Science', *Environment*, 39 (6): 10–9.

Kay, David A. and Jacobson, Harold K. (eds) (1983) *Environmental Protection: The International Dimension*. Totowa: Allanheld, Osmun & Co.

Keohane, Robert O. (1996) 'Analyzing the Effectiveness of International Environmental Institutions', in Robert O. Keohane, and Marc A. Levy (eds),

Institutions for Environmental Aid: Pitfalls and Promise. Cambridge, MA: MIT Press. pp. 3–27.

Keohane, Robert O. and Levy, Marc A. (eds) (1996) *Institutions for Environmental Aid: Pitfalls and Promise.* Cambridge, MA: MIT Press.

Krueger, Jonathan (1999) *International Trade and the Basel Convention.* London: Royal Institute of International Affairs.

Levy, Marc (1993) 'European Acid Rain: The Power of Tote-Board Diplomacy', in Peter Haas, Robert O. Keohane and Marc Levy (eds), *Institutions for the Earth: Sources of Effective International Environmental Protection.* Cambridge, MA: MIT Press. pp. 75–132.

Lipschutz, Ronnie D. and Conca, Ken (eds) (1993) *The State and Social Power in Global Environmental Politics.* New York: Columbia University Press.

Lipschutz, Ronnie D. and Mayer, Judith (1996) *Global Civil Society and Global Environmental Governance: The Politics of Nature From Place to Planet.* Albany: State University of New York.

List, Martin and Rittberger, Volker (1998) 'The Role of Intergovernmental Organizations in the Formation and Evolution of International Environmental Regimes', in Arild Underdal (ed.), *The Politics of International Environmental Management.* Dordrecht: Kluwer Academic. pp. 67–81.

Litfin, Karen T. (1994) *Ozone Discourses: Science and Politics in Global Environmental Cooperation.* New York: Columbia University Press.

Litfin, Karen T. (ed.) (1998) *The Greening of Sovereignty in World Politics.* Cambridge, MA: MIT Press.

Lowi, Theodore J. (1972) 'Four Systems of Policy, Politics, and Choice', *Public Administration Review,* 32 (4): 298–310.

Malthus, T.R. and Appleman, Philip (1976) *An Essay on the Principle of Population: Text, Sources and Background, Criticism.* New York: W.W. Norton.

Martin, Lisa L. (1992a) *Coercive Cooperation: Explaining Multilateral Economic Sanctions.* Princeton: Princeton University Press.

Martin, Lisa L. (1992b) 'Interests, Power, and Multilateralism', *International Organization,* 46 (4): 765–92.

McCormick, John (1999) 'The Role of Environmental NGOs in International Regimes', in Norman J. Vig and Regina S. Axelrod (eds), *The Global Environment: Institutions, Law, and Policy.* Washington, DC: CQ Press. pp. 52–71.

Merchant, Carolyn (1996) *Earthcare: Women and the Environment.* New York: Routledge.

Meyer, John W., Frank, David John, Hironaka, Ann, Schofer, Evan and Tuma, Nancy Brandon (1997) 'The Structuring of a World Environmental Regime, 1870–1990', *International Organization,* 51 (4): 623–9.

M'Gonigle, R. Michael and Zacher, Mark W. (1979) *Pollution, Politics, and International Law: Tankers at Sea.* Berkeley, CA: University of California Press.

Miles, Edward L. and Underdal, Arild (eds) (2001) *Explaining Environmental Regime Effectiveness: Confronting Theory with Evidence.* Cambridge, MA: The MIT Press.

Miller, Marian A.L. (1995) *The Third World in Global Environmental Politics.* Boulder: Lynne Rienner.

Mitchell, Ronald B. (1994a) *Intentional Oil Pollution at Sea: Environmental Policy and Treaty Compliance.* Cambridge, MA: MIT Press.

Mitchell, Ronald B. (1994b) 'Regime Design Matters: Intentional Oil Pollution and Treaty Compliance', *International Organization,* 48 (3): 425–58.

Mitchell, Ronald B. (1996) 'Compliance Theory: An Overview', in James Cameron, Jacob Werksman and Peter Roderick (eds), *Improving Compliance with International Environmental Law.* London: Earthscan. pp. 3–28.

Mitchell, Ronald B. (1998) 'Sources of Transparency: Information Systems in International Regimes', *International Studies Quarterly,* 42 (1): 109–30.

Mitchell, Ronald B. and Bernauer, Thomas (1998) 'Empirical Research on International Environmental Policy: Designing Qualitative Case Studies', *Journal of Environment and Development,* 7 (1): 4–31.

Mitchell, Ronald B. and Keilbach, Patricia M. (2001) 'Situation Structure and Institutional Design: Reciprocity, Coercion, and Exchange', *International Organization,* 55 (4): 893–919.

Naess, Arne (1973) 'The Shallow and the Deep, Long-Range Ecology Movement: A Summary', *Inquiry,* 16 (1): 95–100.

O'Neill, Kate (2000) *Waste Trading Among Rich Nations.* Cambridge, MA: MIT Press.

Ophuls, William (1977) *Ecology and the Politics of Scarcity: Prologue to a Political Theory of the Steady State.* San Francisco: W.H. Freeman.

Orr, David W. and Soroos, Marvin S. (eds) (1979) *The Global Predicament: Ecological Perspectives on World Order.* Chapel Hill: University of North Carolina Press.

Parson, Edward A. and Clark, William C. (1995) 'Sustainable Development as Social Learning: Theoretical Perspectives and Practical Challenges for the Design of a Research Program', in Lance Gunderson, C.S. Holling and Stephen S. Light (eds), *Barriers and Bridges to the Renewal of Ecosystems and Institutions.* New York: Columbia University Press.

Peterson, M.J. (1998) 'International Organizations and the Implementation of Environmental Regimes', in Oran R. Young (ed.), *Global Governance: Drawing Insights from the Environmental Experience.* Cambridge, MA: MIT Press. pp. 115–51.

Porter, Gareth and Brown, Janet Welsh (1991) *Global Environmental Politics.* Boulder: Westview.

Princen, Thomas (1996) 'The Zero Option and Ecological Rationality in International Environmental Politics', *International Environmental Affairs,* 8 (2): 147–76.

Princen, Thomas and Finger, Matthias (1994) *Environmental NGOs in World Politics: Linking the Local and the Global.* New York: Routledge.

Putnam, Robert D. (1988) 'Diplomacy and Domestic Politics: The Logic of Two-Level Games', *International Organization,* 42 (3): 427–60.

Raustiala, Kal (1997a) 'Domestic Institutions and International Regulatory Cooperation: Comparative Responses to the Convention on Biological Diversity', *World Politics*, 49 (4): 482–509.

Raustiala, Kal (1997b) 'The Domestic Politics of Global Biodiversity Protection in the United Kingdom and the United States', in Miranda A. Schreurs and Elizabeth Economy (eds), *The Internationalization of Environmental Protection*. Oxford: Oxford University Press. pp. 42–73.

Raustiala, Kal (1997c) 'States, NGOs, and International Environmental Institutions', *International Studies Quarterly*, 41 (4): 719–40.

Raustiala, Kal and Victor, David G. (1998) 'Conclusions', in David G. Victor, Kal Raustiala and Eugene B. Skolnikoff (eds), *The Implementation and Effectiveness of International Environmental Commitments: Theory and Practice*. Cambridge, MA: MIT Press. pp. 659–707.

Ringius, Lasse (1997) 'Environmental NGOs and Regime Change: The Case of Ocean Dumping of Radioactive Waste', *European Journal of International Relations*, 3 (1): 61–104.

Risse, Thomas (2001) 'Transnational Politics and Non-state Actors', in Walter Carlsnaes, Thomas Risse and Beth Simmons (eds), *Handbook of International Relations*. London: Sage.

Rosenau, James N. (1993) 'Environmental Challenges in a Global Context', in Sheldon Kamieniecki (ed.), *Environmental Politics in the International Arena*. Albany: State University of New York Press. pp. 257–74.

Ruggie, John Gerard (1975) 'International Responses to Technology: Concepts and Trends', *International Organization*, 29 (3): 557–83.

Ruggie, John Gerard (1998) 'What Makes the World Hang Together? Neo-Utilitarianism and the Social Constructivist Challenge', *International Organization*, 52 (4): 855–85.

Sandford, Rosemary (1996) 'International Environmental Treaty Secretariats: A Case of Neglected Potential?', *Environmental Impact Assessment Review*, 16 (1): 3.

Sands, Philippe (ed.) (1994) *Greening International Law*. New York: The New Press.

Schreurs, Miranda A. and Economy, Elizabeth (eds) (1997) *The Internationalization of Environmental Protection*. Oxford: Oxford University Press.

Sebenius, James K. (1983) 'Negotiation Arithmetic: Adding and Subtracting Issues and Parties', *International Organization*, 37 (2): 281–316.

Shea, Eileen (ed.) (1997) *A Critical Evaluation of Global Environmental Assessments: The Climate Experience*. Boulder: Center for the Application of Research on the Environment.

Social Learning Group (eds) (2001) *Learning to Manage Global Environmental Risks: A Comparative History of Social Responses to Climate Change, Ozone Depletion, and Acid Rain*. Cambridge: MIT Press.

Soroos, Marvin S. (1999) 'Global Institutions and the Environment: An Evolutionary Perspective', in Norman J. Vig and Regina S. Axelrod (eds), *The Global Environment: Institutions, Law and Policy*. Washington, DC: CQ Press. pp. 27–51.

Sprinz, Detlef and Vaahtoranta, Tapani (1994) 'The Interest-Based Explanation of International Environmental Policy', *International Organization*, 48 (1): 77–105.

Sprout, Harold Hance and Sprout, Margaret Tuttle (1971) *Toward a Politics of the Planet Earth*. New York: Van Nostrand Reinhold.

Stokke, Olav Schram (1998) 'Understanding the Formation of International Environmental Regimes: The Discursive Challenge', in Arild Underdal (ed.), *The Politics of International Environmental Management*. Dordrecht: Kluwer Academic. pp. 129–48.

Swanson, Timothy M. and Johnston, Sam (1999) *Global Environmental Problems and International Environmental Agreements: The Economics of International Institution Building*. Cheltenham: Edward Elgar.

Underdal, Arild (ed.) (1998) *The Politics of International Environmental Management*. Dordrecht: Kluwer Academic.

Underdal, Arild (2001) 'One Question, Two Answers', in Edward L. Miles and Arild Underdal (eds), *Explaining Environmental Regime Effectiveness: Confronting Theory with Evidence*. Cambridge, MA: MIT Press. pp. 1–47.

Underdal, Arild and Hanf, Kenneth (eds) (2000) *International Environmental Agreements and Domestic Politics: The Case of Acid Rain*. Aldershot: Ashgate.

Victor, David G., Chayes, Abram and Skolnikoff, Eugene B. (1993) 'Pragmatic Approaches to Regime Building for Complex International Problems', in Nazli Choucri (ed.), *Global Accord: Environmental Challenges and International Responses*. Cambridge, MA: MIT Press. pp. 453–74.

Victor, David G., Raustiala, Kal and Skolnikoff, Eugene B. (eds) (1998) *The Implementation and Effectiveness of International Environmental Commitments*. Cambridge, MA: MIT Press.

Vig, Norman J. and Axelrod, Regina S. (eds) (1999) *The Global Environment: Institutions, Law and Policy*. Washington, DC: CQ Press.

Waltz, Kenneth (1979) *Theory of International Politics*. Reading, MA: Addison–Wesley.

Wapner, Paul (1996) *Environmental Activism and World Civic Politics*. Albany: State University of New York Press.

Wendt, Alexander (1987) 'The Agent Structure Problem in International Relations Theory', *International Organization*, 41 (3): 335–70.

Wettestad, Jørgen (1995) 'Science, Politics and Institutional Design: Some Initial Notes on the Long-Range Transboundary Air Pollution Regime', *Journal of Environment and Development*, 4 (2): 165–83.

Wettestad, Jørgen (1999) *Designing Effective Environmental Regimes: The Key Conditions*. Cheltenham: Edward Elgar.

World Commission on Environment and Development (1987) *Our Common Future*. New York: Oxford University Press.

World Resources Institute (1992–3) *World Resources, 1992–93*. New York: Basic Books.

Young, Oran R. (1981) *Natural Resources and the State: The Political Economy of Resource Management*. Berkeley: University of California Press.

Young, Oran R. (1989) *International Cooperation: Building Regimes for Natural Resources and the Environment*. Ithaca: Cornell University Press.

Young, Oran R. (1992) 'The Effectiveness of International Institutions: Hard Cases and Critical Variables', in James N. Rosenau and Ernst-Otto, Czempiel (eds), *Governance Without Government: Change and Order in World Politics*. New York: Cambridge University Press. pp. 160–94.

Young, Oran R. (1994) *International Governance: Protecting the Environment in a Stateless Society*. Ithaca: Cornell University Press.

Young, Oran R. (1998a) *Creating Regimes: Arctic Accords and International Governance*. Ithaca: Cornell University Press.

Young, Oran R. (ed.) (1998b) *Global Governance: Drawing Insights from the Environmental Experience*. Cambridge, MA: MIT Press.

Young, Oran R. (ed.) (1999a) *Effectiveness of International Environmental Regimes: Causal Connections and Behavioral Mechanisms*. Cambridge, MA: MIT Press.

Young, Oran R. (1999b) *Governance in World Affairs*. Ithaca: Cornell University Press.

Young, Oran R. and Osherenko, Gail (eds) (1993) *Polar Politics: Creating International Environmental Regimes*. Ithaca: Cornell University Press.

Zürn, Michael (1998) 'The Rise of International Environmental Politics: A Review of Current Research', *World Politics*, 50 (4): 617–49.

27

International Human Rights

HANS PETER SCHMITZ
AND KATHRYN SIKKINK

WHAT ARE HUMAN RIGHTS?

Human rights are a set of principled ideas about the treatment to which all individuals are entitled by virtue of being human. Over time, these ideas have gained widespread acceptance as international norms defining what was necessary for humans to thrive, both in terms of being protected from abuses and provided with the elements necessary for a life in dignity. Human rights norms create a relationship between individual (and very occasionally collective) right holders and other entities (usually states) that have obligations. The human rights discourse is universal in character and includes claims of equality and non-discrimination. Belief systems in which rights are granted only in exchange for the performance of duties, or where different categories of people have different categories of rights, contradict the basic idea that all people are entitled to equal rights. Human rights are clear examples of what constructivists call 'social constructions' – invented social categories that exist only because people believe and act as if they exist, that nevertheless come to have the capacity to shape the social and political world. The idea of rights has developed a grip on human imaginations that has exerted an increasingly powerful impact on world politics. Brzezinski called human rights 'the single most magnetic political idea of the contemporary time' (cited in Forsythe, 1998: 511).

The idea that the state should respect the human rights of its citizens is an old one, dating back to the struggles for religious freedom and the secular writings of Kant, Locke and Rousseau. The US Bill of Rights and the French Declaration of the Rights of Man and of the Citizen were the most significant early translations of efforts to give the individual special and inalienable protections (Jellinek, [1901] 1979; Weissbrodt and O'Toole, 1988). What has emerged more recently is the idea that not only states, but individuals can be subjects in international law and that human rights should be an integral part of foreign policy and international relations. As recently as 1970, most policy-makers still thought that the promotion of human rights was a moral concern that was not an appropriate part of international politics. But only a brief perusal of any recent daily newspaper shows the extent to which human rights issues are today part of a global discourse. This growing salience of the human rights language in international politics has been accompanied by significant improvements in human rights conditions around the world, but also by a growing awareness of major episodes of gross human rights violations. Indeed, the growing influence of human rights norms in international politics makes us more aware of their violations and the often inadequate responses by governments and international organizations. The success has also led to numerous challenges of the universal and secular character of the rights language and opened important debates about potential conflicts among rights.

Initial work by Donnelly (1989) and Forsythe (1983, 1991) highlighted the increasing relevance of international human rights to political scientists and international relations theorists. Donnelly argued that the concept of a right arose in the West, primarily in response to the rise of the modern state and industrialization, as a social construction that provided the conceptual tools to help protect individuals from the increasingly invasive powers of the state and the market. While the intellectual groundwork of the international human rights discourse was mainly developed in Europe and the United States, their establishment on the international level as well as their justification reflects more culturally diverse sources. Lauren (1998) and Morsink (1999) give extensive evidence on global sources of human rights thinking and activism as well as the crucial role of non-Western participants in the drafting of the 1948 Universal Declaration of Human Rights (UDHR). The values enshrined in the Universal Declaration reflect a secularized 'agreement across cultures' (Glendon, 1998: 1156), which intentionally left questions of deeper justification and priorities among rights open (Ignatieff, 1999). Whatever the disagreements about the definitions and origins of human rights ideas, the passage of the Universal Declaration of Human Rights in 1948, and the subsequent widespread ratification of the two general human rights treaties, the Covenant on Civil and Political Rights, and the Covenant on Economic, Social and Cultural Rights provide international standard definitions and benchmarks for what constitutes international human rights (Newman and Weissbrodt, 1996).

This chapter reviews the progress in establishing international human rights norms and institutions as well as the ability of various international relations theories to account for this development. In the next section we discuss the literature on the causes of human rights violations. We argue that any theory of norm promotion and compliance cannot be complete without an understanding of the potential causes for non-compliance and violation. Then we turn to theories of international relations as potential explanations for change in the international human rights field. We present the basic assumptions of realist, liberal and constructivist theories regarding the role of human rights norms in international relations. In the final section we confront those theories with the existing evidence on the origins, evolution and enforcement of human rights norms.

WHY DO HUMAN RIGHTS VIOLATIONS OCCUR?

Political science did not develop a substantive literature on 'causes of repression' to parallel the 'causes of war' literature until well into the 1980s, although far more people in the world were killed or tortured by their own governments than during international wars and violent conflicts.[1] The emerging literature on the causes of repression is an important line of research, both for its theoretical insights and its potential policy implications, because any effort to limit human rights violations could gain from a credible theory identifying the main causes of repression. Much like human rights research and

promotion in general, this is a project with an intrinsically interdisciplinary perspective. While we cannot expect to arrive at a single, unified theory explaining repression around the globe, research has identified some of the more important factors associated with systematic human rights abuses. The causes of human rights violations identified in the literature can be divided into three broad categories:

1 *Political explanations*: Political explanations focus attention on regime type and real or perceived threats to regimes such as civil and international war, separatist movements and terrorism.

2 *Economic explanations*: Economic explanations highlight such broad factors as levels of economic development, material inequality, or globalization in the areas of trade and finance.

3 *Cultural, ideological and psychological explanations*: Cultural, ideological and psychological explanations focus on deeply ingrained patterns of inter-communal hatred or 'revenge' for past abuses, predispositions to obey orders to commit human rights violations, and particular ideologies associated with human rights violations.

The quantitative research on the causes of repression is still a relatively new field, but it has already produced important empirical findings (Poe, 1997). This literature defines the dependent variable – violations of human rights – quite narrowly, as violations of personal integrity, including extra-judicial killings, torture, disappearances and political imprisonment. To distinguish this narrower variable from the wider range of human rights, we will refer to it as repression. Although a variety of methods have been used to measure repression, the most common and accepted measure has been developed by coding Amnesty International and State Department annual human rights country reports to create a five-point 'Political Terror Scale' (Poe and Tate, 1994; Stohl et al., 1984).

Political Explanations

The quantitative literature draws hypotheses about the causes of human rights violations from a wide range of theories. This literature initially used simple bivariate correlations of data from multiple countries at a single moment in time (Mitchell and McCormick, 1988), but the more recent research is testing theories using multivariate regression models over extended periods of time. Based on this work, the emerging consensus holds that real or imagined threats to a regime are almost always the source of violations. The bulk of the studies indicate that regime type, economic development and the presence of armed conflicts correlate with levels of human rights violations (Henderson, 1991; Poe and Tate, 1994; Poe et al., 1999).

One of the most robust political explanations is that democratic regimes are less likely to engage in repression than non-democratic regimes (Poe and Tate, 1994; Poe et al., 1999). Not only are democracies less likely to carry out repression, they also do a better job in promoting economic and social rights (Heinisch, n.d.). These findings may seem tautological, but they put to rest a lingering debate about the superiority of authoritarian regimes in delivering economic goods. Some qualitative researchers also stress how particular state forms are associated with repression. Stanley (1996), for example, argues that repression in El Salvador was the result of a particular authoritarian state form – a 'protection-racket state' in which the military gained a concession to govern the country in exchange for 'its willingness to use violence against class enemies of the country's relatively small but powerful economic élite'.

Countries engaged in international wars are also more likely to engage in repression than countries not at war (Poe and Tate, 1994; Poe et al., 1999). Leaders that confront other threats to the stability and/or continued existence of their rule by civil war, separatist movements, or insurgent or terrorist groups are also more likely to engage in repression than governments that do not face such a threat (Davenport, 2000; Poe and Tate, 1994; Poe et al., 1999).[2] Further evidence for these findings is contained in recent studies of transitions to democracy. There is 'more murder in the middle' (Fein, 1995) as non-democratic states make the transition to democracy. Ethnic conflict and resulting human rights violations are most likely to occur during the early stages of such a process (Snyder, 2000). Cases of repression within formal democracies can also be explained by threats to their leadership and population. In Israel, the country's supreme court only recently declared the mistreatment of many Palestinian prisoners (Ron, 1997) unconstitutional. In Turkey, the Kurdish minority continues to be a victim of repression because of its desire to gain greater autonomy and possibly political independence. The stronger the real or perceived threats are, the more likely it is that they offset the civilizing impact of democratic rule.

Economic Explanations

There are two distinct debates relating economic conditions and related activities to human rights violations. The first asserts that poor countries are more likely to be repressive than richer countries (Mitchell and McCormick, 1988; Poe and Tate, 1994; Poe et al., 1999). With fewer resources to distribute, domestic conflicts are more likely to lead to real or perceived threats that cause repression. Research further suggests that both absolute poverty and high levels of inequality are positively

associated with repression (Heinisch, n.d.; Henderson, 1991). It is not surprising that human rights are associated with both economic development and democracy, since development and democracy are themselves highly correlated. Recent work has reconfirmed the strong correlation of democracy and wealth, but rejected the causal and normative argument that economic growth always precedes the introduction of political and civil freedoms (Przeworski and Limongi, 1997). A growing number of studies have argued that basic freedoms are a condition for the generation of wealth[3] or that 'basic human rights' should be a concern independent of wealth and democracy (Shue, 1980).

The second debate assumes a diminishing role of the state in affecting domestic human rights conditions. Here, two opposing arguments about free trade and foreign direct investment establish direct links between economic globalization and domestic human rights. Defenders of economic globalization claim that expanding free trade and capitalist investment will lead to improvements in human rights conditions (Meyer, 1996, 1999). An opposite argument holds that involvement with the 'capitalist center', and high levels of direct foreign investment, are positively correlated with human rights violations (Chomsky and Herman, 1979). Smith et al. (1999) find no positive correlation between high levels of direct foreign investment and political and civil rights, although they do report a small negative impact on social and economic rights. Free trade alone is unlikely to improve civil and political rights and its short-term effects on working conditions of the poor around the world are certainly ambiguous. Researchers are only beginning to systematically explore the current era of growing interactions between the globalization of markets and their effects on local (human rights) conditions.

Cultural Ideological and Psychological Explanations

The more qualitative literature on the ideological and psychological explanations for human rights violations points in particular to the role of dehumanizing ideologies (Kuper, 1981) or beliefs that have the effect of 'excluding individuals from the realm of obligation' (Fein, 1993). Kuper argues that ideologies that depict other groups as animals or diseases have the effect of dehumanizing victims and making human rights abuses such as genocide possible. Likewise, ideologies in which the 'ends justify the means' so that some desired endpoint – a pure Aryan race, communist society, or 'Western and Christian civilization' – is seen as so compelling, that repressive means are justified, or seen as necessary for achieving those ends.

Studies of ideologies as diverse as Nazism in Germany, the Khmer Rouge in Cambodia (Quinn, 1989); or the National Security Doctrine in many repressive authoritarian regimes in Latin America, have identified this common ideological element of exclusively focusing on ends (Heinz and Frühling, 1999; Perelli, 1990; Pion-Berlin and Lopez, 1991).

Ideological explanations for human rights violations can either supplement political explanations or offer competing hypotheses. As competing accounts for gross human rights violations they point to deeper layers of group consciousness that might be important to understand decisions for human rights abuses by political leaders. A recent prominent example for this debate is Daniel Goldhagen's argument that the Holocaust was enabled by a particular culture of anti-semitism in the larger German-speaking population, rather than being a 'functionalist' outcome of political or economic choices of the Nazi leadership (Goldhagen, 1996).[4] Lauren (1996) offers an account where an ideological explanation supplements an explanation based on power. He argues that ideologies and power structures interacted to sustain slavery, the slave trade, racial discrimination and apartheid, but changes in power structures later opened space for ideas against racism to bring about change.

There has also been important psychological research on repression which looks at a predisposition to obey authority, even if this involved administering pain to another individual (Millgram, 1965), the societal and psychological origins of genocide and other atrocities, including tendencies towards scapegoating (Gourevitch, 1998; Staub, 1989), and types of training used for soldiers and law-enforcement personnel who engage in human rights violations (Conroy, 2000; Gibson and Haritos-Fatouros, 1986). Psychological explanations of human rights violations often complement rather than compete with political factors of repression. These accounts give an individual level account of why authoritarian leaders can actually use the population to carry out human rights abuses. Such mechanisms can also account for different forms of denial affecting bystanders and even the victims themselves. Furthermore, the mass media has recently come under scrutiny for its responsibility for 'compassion fatigue' (Moeller, 1999) and the growing difficulties of activists to enlist the global public against gross human rights violations (Cohen, 2001).

Linking Domestic and International Factors of Repression

The literature on causes of repression is still far from developing an integrated theory. The quantitative literature on causes of repression suffers from some of the same problems as the quantitative literature on the causes of war and democratic peace. It has discovered strong empirical regularities, but does not yet have a compelling theory to explain these findings. Efforts at such theory-building are under way; one such proposed theory, by Steven Poe, starts with the assumption of a rational decision-maker engaged in choices of how much repression to use. He argues that the decision-maker is influenced by both his or her perceptions of threat to the regime, and his or her perception of the regime strength, which may be diminished or heightened by the other factors considered here, such as economic development (Poe, 1997). Because policy-makers are seen as choosing repression from a 'menu' of possible policy alternatives, decision-making is thus also influenced both by variables that affect the alternatives that appear on the menu, as well as variables that affect the choice among alternatives.

This explanation is consistent with the conclusions of an exhaustive study on the Rwandan genocide of 1994. The author concludes that the genocide was the result of a deliberate choice of a modern élite when faced with threats to their power by the success of their opponents on the battlefield and at the negotiating table. The study concludes that the failure of international actors to raise the perceived costs of genocide permitted domestic actors to carry out their program of mass murder (Des Forges, 1999).

The international relations theorist will note that these theories almost uniformly stress the domestic sources of repression. With the exception of international war and levels of international trade and investment, all the hypothesized causes of repression are domestic factors: democracy, economic development, civil war, state type and perceptions of domestic threat. However, Poe's rational actor theory of repression opens space to consider international elements, and provides one point of possible intersection between the quantitative literature and the more constructivist accounts of ending human rights violations in repressive countries, discussed below. Risse et al. (1999) have argued, for example, that transnational advocacy networks have contributed to decreasing repression in a series of countries through providing information, socialization, and economic and political pressures. Rephrased in the language of the more rationalist and quantitative studies, they argue that international human rights activism has both succeeded in removing certain alternatives from the decision-makers' menu, or increasing the cost of repression on that menu so that it is a less attractive alternative to choose. For example, international and regional norms in favor of democracy have played an important role in virtually removing certain options – like military coups – from the policy menu in certain regions, such as Europe, and increasingly, the Americas. Policy-makers may have chosen repression in the past because it was an effective and relatively cheap policy alternative. However, as a result of increasing international publicity and possible economic and political sanctions the perceived costs of repression have increased. The description and explanation of this process is at the center of the following sections.

HUMAN RIGHTS CHANGE AND THEORIES OF INTERNATIONAL RELATIONS (IR)

Most international human rights treaties agreed upon after 1945 regulate the domestic behavior of governments towards their own citizens. Before the second half of the twentieth century human rights had not been a significant issue in international politics. With the expansion of such regimes within the past fifty years, state actors face growing formal and informal limits to the policy choices they have. Human rights have become part of a norms cascade in the past two decades and have contributed to a significant transformation of the international system. In 1975, only 33 countries had ratified the International Covenant on Civil and Political Rights, equaling 23 per cent of the UN membership at that time (144). By July 2001, 147 states had ratified the treaty (equaling 76 per cent of the total UN membership of 189) and 97 the Optional Protocol accepting supervisory powers of the Human Rights Committee. In addition, 157 states have ratified the Convention against Racial Discrimination, 145 the Covenant on Economic, Social and Cultural Rights, 168 the Women's Rights convention, 125 the Convention against Torture, and 191 the Convention on the Rights of the Child (United Nations High Commissioner for Human Rights, 2001).

Assuming that human rights norms challenge state sovereignty expressed in the norm of non-intervention (Krasner, 1999), this widespread acceptance of international human rights norms is puzzling to the traditional IR scholar. If international human rights rhetoric actually affects domestic practices, then we need to better understand under what conditions international norms matter. In the following sections, we will present the main differences between realist, liberal and constructivist accounts of change in the field of international human rights policy. They give different answers to the following questions:

- Which are the most significant actors in the issue area?
- How and why do human rights norms emerge and become institutionalized?
- Do internationally codified human rights norms make a difference?
- What actions or processes are most likely to lead to norm compliance?

Power Politics, Liberalism and Constructivism

(Neo)Realist thought assumes that international policy outcomes are determined by the distribution of material power capabilities among states. Neo-realists do not recognize norms such as human rights or non-governmental actors as significant and independent forces in international relations. Realists regard principles such as human rights as a potential threat to the overall stability of the international system and advocate state sovereignty as a central organizing principle of international relations. If states make the domestic conduct of other states a regular concern of their actions, this might increase the likelihood of international conflict. More subtly, Krasner showed that state sovereignty consists of a conflicting set of norms where the right to self-help and the norm of non-interference are in a potential conflict (Krasner, 1993). Realists argue that such a conflict is resolved in favor of the materially stronger party involved.

Liberal international relations theory places emphasis on the domestic sources of state preferences as the determinant of outcomes in international politics (Moravcsik, 1997). In this, it differs from neoliberal institutionalism, which shares with neorealism a more state-centric view of the international system. Neoliberal institutionalists emphasize that states have interests in entering international institutional arrangements to prevent sub-optimal outcomes of uncoordinated action. Human rights violations rarely represent a classical dilemma of interdependence, and thus cooperation in the area of human rights is difficult to explain from a neoliberal institutionalist perspective. Hence, a liberal theory with a focus on domestic preferences or an assumption about a community of 'liberal states' seen as a sphere of peace and democracy has been more useful in studying human rights (Slaughter, 1995). Liberal theory argues that behavior within this community is distinctly different from behavior towards non-liberal outsiders.

Constructivist theories[5] highlight the independent role of norms and ideas in affecting international and domestic policy outcomes. Constructivists shift attention from how states pursue their interests to how they define those interests in the first place (Finnemore, 1996a). Norms and principled ideas are assumed to have constitutive effects on the identity formation of actors, rather than simply intervening between interests and behavior. Reflecting a shift towards a sociological perspective, constructivists see agents embedded in a set of norms and rules often described as 'world culture' (Meyer et al., 1997). Constructivists also suggest that long-term systemic change cannot be understood with causal models exclusively focused on immediate consequences of action. Constructivists often take a longer perspective in linking norm-induced change in identities and institutions to changes in behavioral patterns (Iriye, 1997; Mueller, 1995). Wendt's 'Kantian culture' is such an interpretation of the norms cascade, where a 'critical mass of states' (Wendt, 2000) joins other, often non-governmental actors in the process of a profound transformation of the international system.

There are two emerging strands within this constructivist effort for a more sociological understanding of the international system. One set of arguments claims that rules become a part of the identity of actors through an active process of socialization and internalization (Risse et al., 1999). A second version argues that individuals and groups rhetorically adopt such rules not because they inherently believe in them, but because they conform or emulate scripts of legitimate statehood (Meyer et al., 1997). The difference between the two strands has less significance with regard to questions of norm origins and evolution, but leads to fundamentally diverging expectations about the behavioral consequences of rules and norms. The second, weaker constructivist account puts less emphasis on fundamendal identity transformation and traces behavioral changes to more traditional consequentialist calculations.

In the following section, we discuss more explicitly how each type of IR theory explains (1) norm emergence and evolution, as well as (2) norm diffusion and effectiveness/compliance in the area of human rights.

Norm Origins and Evolution

For realists, international norms such as human rights emerge and gain acceptance when they are embraced and promoted by a hegemon or a dominant group of states (Ikenberry and Kupchan, 1990). 'The content of human rights issues that were at the forefront in various historical periods reflected the concerns of those states which possessed a preponderance of economic and military power' (Krasner, 1993: 166). Realists assume that norms are epiphenomenal to the distribution of material and military capabilities in the international system. Prevalent norms change with the rise and fall of powerful states.

Moravcsik's liberal interpretation argues that states accept binding human rights treaties mainly as a means of political survival – that is, newly democratizing states are most likely to ratify legal human rights instruments to protect the still unstable democratic regime against non-democratic opponents (Moravcsik, 2000). The establishment of international human rights institutions is a rational and self-interested move to selectively delegate sovereignty to a supranational body in order to secure the desired domestic outcome of strengthened democratic governance. Hence, the emergence and evolution of human rights institutions is mainly a function of domestic threat perceptions of newly democratic governments, rather than the result of outward-projected activities by the established and most powerful democracies in the international system. When realists emphasize coercion, liberals claim voluntary, self-interested and rational behavior of state actors in accepting long-term limits to state sovereignty.

Constructivism questions a narrow interest-based explanation referring either to a state's position in the international system or domestic preferences. Ruggie argued that knowing the international power structure helps us understand the form of order, but not the content (Ruggie, 1983). We need additional information about prevalent norms and ideas, or what Ruggie calls the structure of social purpose, to know the content and consequences of particular regimes (Schmitz, 1995). For constructivists, norms such as human rights gain strength because of their intrinsic universalistic qualities. These norms give guidance with regard to the fundamental purpose of statehood (Finnemore, 1996b). First, constructivists argue that the normative strength is either directly linked to their Western origins or derives from their potential to resonate with basic ideas of human dignity shared in many cultures around the world (Boli and Thomas, 1999; Keck and Sikkink, 1998; Thomas et al., 1987). Second, certain windows of opportunities such as wars, revolutions and upheavals can lead to shifts of power that accelerate the acceptance and evolution of new ideas and norms (Lauren, 1996). In times of national or global crisis old power structures are cracked open and fundamental questions about the identity and purpose of social systems are more likely to be contested. Morsink (1999) and others have argued that common revulsion toward the Holocaust provided the consensus needed to adopt the Universal Declaration of Human Rights, as the initial step in the global recognition of human rights. The paradoxical strength of the UDHR emanates from its writers' audacity to 'reestablish the idea of human rights at the precise historical moment in which they had been shown to have no moral purchase whatsoever' (Ignatieff, 1999: 4). Third, a number of non-state organizations such as Amnesty International have emerged during the past forty years as principled actors in human rights matters on a global scale (Clark, 2001). Their participation in the evolution of the international human rights regime is still formally limited. However, they have offset these formal limits by acquiring independent authority based on their reliable work and virtual information monopoly.

Norm Diffusion and Effectiveness

For realists the recent spread of human rights norms throughout the international system is caused by a dominance of powerful democracies that force weaker countries to adopt their own domestic standards. In the absence of overriding security or economic motives, realists conclude that any change within the issue area of human rights 'is a function of the extent to which more powerful states in the system are willing to enforce the principles and norms of the regime' (Krasner, 1993: 141). The stronger and the more assertive the democratic camp of states within the international system, the more likely it is that international human rights norms become established. 'Only when powerful states enforce principles and norms were international human rights regimes consequential' (Krasner, 1993: 141). Coercive practices such as sanctions are the preferred means of enforcement.

Liberal theory accepts a limited independent role for international institutions in promoting common norms and cooperation. However, such claims are mainly articulated within the context of a liberal community of states. For outsider states, liberal theory takes a more traditional view of sovereign states negotiating to maximize their self-interests. Liberal theory arrives at this distinction between democratic and non-democratic states based on the emphasis given to the domestic political structure. Domestic structures filter and mediate outside interventions in a two-step process. First, they determine what kinds of *access points* are available to actors seeking to initiate domestic change (issue resonance). Second, these structures consist of potential domestic allies and enemies for outside actors. Domestic structures determine the size and requirements for *winning coalitions* (Risse-Kappen, 1995: 25). A liberal perspective assumes that the success of norms diffusion is mainly determined by the compatibility with pre-existing domestic structures.

For constructivists, the global acceptance of human rights norms since 1948 originates in a two-stage process of a 'norm cascade' (Finnemore and Sikkink, 1998; Sunstein, 1997). Support for a particular norm gathers slowly until it reaches a 'tipping point'.[6] Afterwards, the adoption by other members in the community occurs more rapidly and leads to a cascading effect. This opens questions about the individual state's motivation to rhetorically accept a specific set of norms. Is the norm cascade an inconsequential commitment on the part of state actors to weakly institutionalized human rights norms, or does it actually signal a profound transformation of international and domestic politics? Constructivist scholarship has developed distinct state-centric (Wendt, 1999) and non-statist answers (Keck and Sikkink, 1998; Risse et al., 1999) to this question. Some state-centrists have adopted the language of sociological institutionalism (Thomas et al., 1987) in order to account for the growing international salience of human rights norms, while at the same time denying the transformative effects of this process. Krasner recently argued that state actors engage in 'mimetic imitation' in a superficial way because 'they are unsure about what to do' (Krasner, 1999: 64).

In contrast, non-statist perspectives have adopted a language of a more fundamental normative 'socialization' (Risse et al., 1999) and highlight non-state actors as distinct agents of change. Socialization theorists will accept the possibility of an initial superficial rhetoric of norm adoption, but their ultimate goal is to show that such norms have a profound long-term impact on the identity of state and non-state actors. For sociological institutionalists, sustained 'decoupling' (Boli and Thomas, 1999: 18; Meyer et al., 1997) between norm rhetoric and behavior is the rule, while for socialization theorists the work of non-state human rights actors begins right there. In order to decide which claim is correct, we need to empirically show either an ultimately 'civilizing force of hypocrisy' (Elster, 1998: 12) induced by non-governmental activism or a ubiquitous and sustained hypocrisy with regard to international human rights norms.

In conceptualizing possible agents for change, non-statists have taken two distinct approaches. The first works 'bottom-up' and extends the social movement literature to the transnational realm (Smith et al., 1997). The second, more IR-oriented approach takes internationally codified norms as a starting point and develops a concept of 'transnational advocacy networks' to highlight the emergence of a new category of norm-promoting actors (Keck and Sikkink, 1998). This network concept captures cooperation among NGOs, but also connections to potentially like-minded actors in church or union organizations, foundations, the media, international governmental organizations, or government bureaucracies. These transnational advocacy networks circumvent repressive state authorities and build direct connections between the international and domestic realm.[7] The subsequent support can range from the basic protection of the right to life to the sustainable creation and expansion of domestic space for civil society activism. The emergence of a transnational advocacy network is seen as a necessary, but not a sufficient condition for sustainable domestic norm compliance. While principled pressure 'from above' has often a positive effect on the initial norm adoption and cascade pattern, sustained rule-consistent behavior shifts attention to domestic-level processes of norm education, monitoring and socialization. Human rights norms are only sustainable and of independent value to researchers, if the gap between rhetoric and actual behavior narrows over time. The following table summarizes the realist, liberal and constructivist perspectives on the emergence, evolution, and consequences of international human rights norms.

Table 27.1   *Current perspectives on international human rights norms*

	Origins	Evolution	Paths of compliance	Dominant mode of action
Realist theory (Krasner, 1993)	Hegemonic imposition	Hegemonic domination	Coercive practices	Domination and adaptation
Liberal theory (Moravcsik, 2000)	Voluntary agreement among state leaders	Supra-national institutionalization	Legal process, domestic structure	Self-interested logic of consequentialism
Sociological institutionalism/ state-centric constructivist theory (Krasner, 1999;[10] Meyer et al., 1997)	'Scripts' of world culture	Mimetic imitation	Passive acceptance; 'decoupling' of rhetoric (aimed at outside actors) and action (aimed at domestic actors)	Outward: logic of appropriateness Inward: self-interested logic of consequentialism
Non-statist constructivist theory (Keck and Sikkink 1998; Risse et al., 1999)	Normative mobilization by norm entrepreneurs	'Norm cascade' and transnational socialization	Active acceptance; Socialization by transnational advocacy networks	Logic of appropriateness; moral argumentation

INTERNATIONAL HUMAN RIGHTS INSTITUTIONS AFTER 1945

In this section of the chapter we will evaluate international relations (IR) theories with regard to their ability to account for the origins and evolution of international human rights institutions as well as the variation in observable compliance around the world. We investigate existing regional and global human rights institutions as well as evidence from foreign policy studies and work on the role of transnational advocacy networks.

Our investigation of the international human rights regime as a regulating set of norms begins in the 1940s when these norms became progressively institutionalized on a global and regional level. This applies to human rights concerns in peacetime as well as to situations of armed conflict and war. The international precursors to the human rights issue included the movement for the respect for human rights during armed conflict, the campaign for the abolition of the slave trade and slavery, the work within the League of Nations for the protection of minority rights, the early work on the rights of workers in the International Labor Organization, and the campaign for women's suffrage. But each of these efforts fell short of a full-fledged demand for attention to human rights as a legitimate topic of international action. During the past half century, the Universal Declaration of Human Rights served as a basis for an expanding international human

rights agenda. Moreover, the repeated occurrence of mass atrocities as part of armed conflicts has spurred a growing convergence of international human rights law, humanitarian concerns, and laws of war creating the distinct concept of 'crimes against humanity' (Robertson, 1999).

Although in principle human rights norms are indivisible, in practice the norms included in the Universal Declaration have subsequently enjoyed different levels of attention by the international public and policy-makers. Significant differences also mark the development of regional systems of human rights protection. Europe and the Americas feature today the most advanced human rights institutions, while the African regional human rights body has only weakly developed promotional and monitoring capabilities. Asia and the Arab world are still without significant regional human rights systems.

The Origins of International Human Rights Institutions

The origins of human rights norms and their rhetorical acceptance by state actors have drawn little attention from traditional IR scholarship, because they were either seen as inconsequential or epiphenomenal to the distribution of material power capabilities in the international system. The origins of such norms became only more recently an acceptable research topic, following constructivists' claims that international human rights norms have tangible effects on the interest formation and behavior of state actors. The evidence we can present here is mainly based on case studies and a few more systematic, comparative efforts. These initial results confirm the dominant role of state actors in formally controlling the process of *norm creation* on an international level, but give also ample evidence for the relevance of non-governmental actors in setting the agenda for such processes. Government representatives have drafted human rights treaties, but advocacy networks have often played a pivotal behind-the-scene role in putting human rights norms on the international agenda in the first place and in influencing the result of the subsequent codification efforts (Clark, 2001). Formal exclusion from decision-making organs remains the rule, but non-governmental actors have gained informal influence based on their principled positions and expertise (Korey, 1998).

The Universal Declaration of Human Rights and the Genocide convention were a result of extensive agenda-setting and lobbying efforts by non-governmental groups and activists proposing human rights issues be included in the new United Nations Charter (Burgers, 1992; Glendon, 2001; Ignatieff, 2001; Korey, 1998). From the early 1940s on, the Catholic Church, the American Institute of Law, the American Jewish Committee, but also the International Labor Organization drew up blueprints of such a Bill of Rights (Morsink, 1999: 1–3). Although most governments remained skeptical, the non-governmental mobilization achieved the adoption of a non-binding human rights declaration, a binding convention against genocide as well as a brief reference to the promotion of human rights in Articles 55 and 56 of the UN Charter. Cold War rivalry delayed subsequent efforts to translate the Universal Declaration into binding conventions. These conventions, the Covenant on Civil and Political Rights, and the Covenant for Economic, Social and Cultural Rights, entered into force in 1976. As part of the norm cascade, a growing number of human rights instruments followed, with significant roles played by non-governmental actors (Clark, 2001; van Boven, 1989; Weissbrodt, 1984), including the agreements against racial discrimination (1969), for the protection of women (1981), against torture (1987; Burgers and Danelius, 1988), for the protection of the child (1990; Price Cohen, 1990), and a declaration for the protection of human rights defenders (1999).

On the regional level, Moravcsik's comparative research on the establishment of the strong European human rights system in the early 1950s confirms a liberal explanation that newly democratizing states were most active in building a binding human rights regime. Evidence from the Inter-American case, however, does not clearly confirm this result since established democracies in the Americas have (except for the United States) supported a regional and global human rights system from the start. After the wave of redemocratization in the Americas between 1978 and 1991, the newly democratizing countries also rapidly ratified international and regional human rights treaties. Along the lines of liberal theory suggested by Moravcsik, it is likely that part of the motivation to ratify these treaties was the self-interested desire to lock in their democracies against the danger of being overthrown by their opponents.

There are still questions about the ability of liberal theory to explain the emergence of regional human rights norms. If European leaders were profoundly concerned about the survival of their new regime, why would they expect much help from still to be established international institutions, in particular after the experience with Nazi Germany? Why should a system built on liberal domestic legitimacy and self-determination accept a supranational oversight that in itself lacks the democratic legitimacy of many domestic political institutions? European leaders at that time saw the establishment of regional human rights mechanisms as a parallel process to the (stalled) process of promoting such norms within the United Nations and as a signal for the creation of a liberal community of states right next to the emerging Soviet Bloc. Hence, they were as much intrinsically motivated by the norms themselves as they were convinced that these norms were in their self-interest.

More research is needed to better understand the emergence and establishment of human rights norms on global and regional levels. States still formally control this process, but non-governmental actors have always played a pivotal role in setting the agenda and pushing for the acceptance of specific standards. Further, with the more systematic recognition of social, economic and cultural rights within the global human rights discourse, norm-setting efforts will increasingly target other actors than states. Additional knowledge about the role and motivations of state actors in the process of establishing international human rights norms is necessary. Such knowledge will be part of a larger effort to better understand differences in norm evolution and salience.

The Evolution of International Human Rights Institutions

The evolution of international institutions is treated separately, because it can indicate the extent of autonomy, robustness and authority these entities develop over time.[8] In the area of human rights, evolution is particularly important because the initial recognition of a norm or even binding conventions have often highlighted, rather than immediately narrowed, the gap between rhetoric and practice. Focusing solely on this gap may be misleading because the long-term evolution of human rights norms and institutions has the potential of fundamentally transforming the international system. The idea of human rights puts individuals rather than states and their interests at the center of organizing global cooperation. If the human rights logic becomes more salient, this transformative force deserves heightened attention within international relations theory, no matter how slow this process might be. The question during the past fifty years has not been *if* human rights institutions evolve at all, but *which* human rights norms were strengthened, *how* such a process was set and kept in motion, and what kind of regional differences developed or persisted.

Jack Donnelly concluded in a 1986 article that growth in the international human rights regime was 'easy' in the past, but will be difficult in the future because state actors are unwilling to agree to 'major qualitative increase in the commitment' (Donnelly, 1986: 633). He predicted that human rights institutions would remain declaratory and promotional, rather than move on to develop implementation and enforcement mechanisms. At that time, this position sought to account for the growing international recognition of human rights without challenging the basic premises of the still dominant state-centric realist and (emerging) liberal-institutionalist discourse. Realists do not expect international institutions to develop some form of independent status. If they have influence, it is part of a geopolitical strategy of a hegemon. For liberal theory, international institutionalization is more likely, but will be limited to the self-interest of and voluntary agreement among state leaders and their domestic audience. Constructivist theory highlights the power of human rights norms, institutions and/or non-governmental actors. International human rights institutions are expected to secure increasing autonomy from state actors and develop along their human rights mandate rather than state preferences.

The United Nations human rights system
Since the adoption of the Universal Declaration, human rights institutions in the United Nations system have both increased in numbers and often evolved beyond a declaratory and promotional status. Using Ernst Haas's complex model of change within international organizations (Haas, 1990), the dominant logic for most United Nations human rights instruments has shifted from a logic of 'incremental growth' (adaptation) to a more proactive model of 'managed interdependence' (learning). UN human rights institutions are often mere 'arenas' or 'instruments' (Archer, 1992) of state competition, but states have increasingly changed their own roles from 'shapers' to either 'breakers' or 'takers' (Kent, 1999) of the norms promoted by those mechanisms. The more consistent and robust

UN human rights mechanisms became, the greater were the costs of non-compliance. The increasing visibility of the UN in human rights matters is expressed in a consistent expansion of the treaty-based system as well as an increasing activism of charter-based organs led by the Commission on Human Rights (Alston, 1992a: 1–21). The Universal Declaration has evolved from a non-binding declaration to a generally accepted standard of state behavior (Buergenthal, 1995: 37). In 1966, the two International Covenants turned human rights into binding international law. Additionally, the Covenant on Civil and Political Rights provided for the creation of the Human Rights Committee as a monitoring body of the covenant. In its main function of evaluating state reports, the Committee has slowly increased its independence by drawing systematically on NGO evidence and by issuing 'General Comments' to interpret the meaning of particular articles of the Covenant (Buergenthal, 1995: 45). The Committee has also taken a more proactive role in its investigation of individual complaints brought under the First Optional Protocol. Since 1990, the Committee on Economic, Social and Cultural Rights has also received and reviewed state reports, but no mechanism yet exists for receiving individual complaints under that Covenant. In one of its first decisions, the Committee for the Covenant on Social, Economic and Cultural Rights decided in 1990 that the obligations in the convention are not only long-term goals, but also directly enforceable rights.

In 1984, after a successful mobilization effort by non-governmental actors (Baehr, 1989; Burgers and Danelius, 1988), the UN General Assembly accepted the Convention against Torture and other Cruel, Inhumane or Degrading Treatment or Punishment. Non-governmental groups were able to translate some of their demands into convention articles, including an absolute non-derogation clause (Art. 2), universal jurisdiction, the right to initiate an investigation for the monitoring committee (Art. 20), and an individual complaint procedure (Art. 21). Other UN human rights treaties, often with much weaker monitoring mechanisms, have targeted genocide (1948), racial discrimination (1965), apartheid (1973), the discrimination of women (1979) and the situation of children (1989). The number of state parties for each of these treaties has consistently increased, albeit the period of the respective norm cascades varied significantly. The 1998 Rome compromise on the establishment of a permanent International Criminal Court indicates continued innovation and strengthening within the UN treaty-based system, but also the growing focus on crimes against humanity. The establishment of individual responsibility for such crimes represents a major step towards the direct enforcement of a specific set of international human rights norms. A similar trend prevails within the parallel UN Charter-based system.

Charter-based human rights institutions at the UN have been much more politicized than the treaty-based institutions. States become subject to treaty-based institutions by explicit signature and ratification of human rights treaties. In contrast, simple membership in the UN makes states subject to the charter-based institutions charged with human rights, the 'nerve center' of which is the Commission on Human Rights (CHR). The continuous and often successful efforts of governments to manipulate these institutions for their narrow self-interests has led to unintended consequences whereby those institutions acquired strengthened monitoring capabilities and autonomy. The politicization of many human rights debates at the Commission exemplifies how the use of universal human rights language can strengthen the underlying norms overtime. In the most recent and prominent case, the People's Republic of China avoids condemnation by the CHR for its human rights record year after year, while the political resources it is forced to spend on this effort reflect the growing salience of the issue (Donnelly, 1998: 128). Human rights promotion through the Charter system has evolved considerably, moving from the 1947 assertion that the CHR had 'no power to take any action in regard to any complaints concerning human rights' (ECOSOC Resolution 75, V, 1947) to the current system of working groups and rapporteurs with specific country and thematic mandates (Rodley, 1997; Weissbrodt, 1986) as well as the Security Council's decisions declaring gross human rights violations as threats to international security and peace.

This process of strengthening Charter-based human rights institutions began during the 1960s as a result of the influx of newly independent states from the Southern hemisphere into the United Nations. Their representatives saw the Charter-based system as a potential instrument in their fight against Portugal's colonial policies in Angola and Mozambique, South Africa's *apartheid* regime as well as (since 1968) Israel's occupational policies in the Middle East. In 1967, ECOSOC resolution 1235 effectively ended the 'no power to act' doctrine of the CHR and called for the public investigation of human rights violations. While the new majority of states pushed for an explicit focus on racism and colonialism, the compromise formula kept the mandate open to investigate other situations as well. In 1970, resolution 1503 added a confidential 'petition-information' system to investigate cases 'which appear to reveal a consistent pattern of gross and reliably attested violations of human rights and fundamental freedoms' (Buergenthal, 1995: 87–95). As a consequence of these political victories, the universal claim of human rights was reaffirmed and began slowly to emancipate itself from narrow state interests. Two years after the 1973 coup of General Pinochet, Chile became the precedent for extending the

agenda beyond issues of colonialism and racism (Kamminga, 1992). At the same time, the United Nations still failed to investigate other ongoing human rights crises such as in Argentina, the Central African Republic, Uganda, or Uruguay.

By the late 1970s, the growing success of the non-governmental human rights movement created enough pressure for more innovations, including the 1978 decision of the CHR to publish an annual list of states under the 1503 procedure. One year later, the CHR began to create extra-conventional mechanisms to investigate human rights issues either on a country-specific or a thematic basis. The first such mechanism, investigating the practice of 'disappearances', emerged out of the many NGO–state confrontations at the annual meetings of the CHR (Rodley, 1987: 195). Since then, the CHR has established working groups and named rapporteurs for a total of fifteen country situations – as well as twenty-one thematic human rights mandates. Many of the rapporteurs and working groups have begun to adopt NGO-like strategies in their work, inaugurating a year-round effort of human rights promotion by the United Nations system. They have 'proven to be far more flexible, innovative, and persistent than either their original detractors or proponents would have dared to think' (Alston, 1992b: 175). Moreover, these mechanisms give non-governmental actors additional platforms of mobilization, where they can use their wealth of information to effectively counter the decision-making monopoly of state actors. In 1994, the Charter-based human rights system was further strengthened when the United Nations established the Office of the High Commissioner on Human Rights. The High Commissioner has established on-site presences in twenty-seven countries, sometimes with the agreement of the governments (Newman and Weissbrodt, 1996). The Security Council's decisions to create the *ad hoc* International Tribunals for the former Yugoslavia (1993) and Rwanda (1995) were certainly inadequate and could not detract from the failure of the international community to intervene in time to prevent mass atrocities. However, they also became an important precedent for the pursuit of criminal justice on the international level, later translated into the intergovernmental human rights treaty for the establishment of a permanent International Criminal Court (1998).

The UN human rights system is a reflection of the contested status of human rights around the world. Substantial innovations and strengthening in some areas such as the fight against torture and gross human rights violations have not been the rule for all human rights issues. Some mechanisms such as the women's convention have become strongly contested once the UN put them into place. The clearest consensus of action within the widening human rights catalogue has emerged with regard to crimes against humanity. However, no matter whether states are more likely to follow conventions or whether they contest them, both reactions indicate an evolutionary process whereby the issues gain growing recognition on the international level. The variation in the salience of human rights issues is increasingly a result of an interaction between NGO activism and United Nations human rights mechanisms. A coalition of 'like-minded' states has often led human rights initiatives in the United Nations. However, the United States as a self-professed international leader has not been at the forefront of such activities, as most recently expressed by its stance against the ICC and the landmines convention.

Regional human rights mechanisms Innovation and evolution during the past fifty years have also taken place within regional human rights mechanisms. However, stark differences remain between the more advanced and dynamic systems in Europe and the Americas, and the weakly developed or non-existent mechanisms in Africa, Asia and for the Arab nations. The intergovernmental Council of Europe, the European Convention for the Protection of Human Rights and Fundamental Freedoms (1953) as well as the European Commission and Court of Human Rights have played the leading role in the promotion of human rights within Europe (Harris et al., 1999). A major innovation occurred in 1998 when a new, now full-time Court began to operate. Between 1983 and 1999, the number of new cases before the Court increased from about 500 to over 8,000. In addition to the West European mechanism, the 1975 Helsinki Accord of the Conference on Security and Cooperation in Europe (CSCE) put human rights on the agenda of East–West cooperation. Although this agreement was non-binding and initially frowned upon by many observers, it turned out to play 'an important role in legitimating human rights discourse within Eastern Europe, providing a focus for nongovernmental activities at both the domestic and international levels' (Steiner and Alston, 1996: 578; also: Thomas, 2001). After the end of the Cold War, the norms established by the Council of Europe apply to all aspiring new member states of the Council and the European Union (Schimmelfennig, 2000).

While authoritarian rule alongside a regional human rights mechanism was the exception in Europe (Greece, 1967–1974), it was the rule for an extended period of time in the system established by the Organization of American States (OAS). The 1948 American Declaration of the Rights and Duties of Man was followed in 1959 by the establishment of the Inter-American Commission on Human Rights, and in 1969 by the OAS's own treaty-based system built around the American Convention on Human Rights and the Inter-American Court of Human Rights (including an

individual complaint procedure). The 1970 Protocol of Buenos Aires revised the Charter and strengthened the Commission. Dozens of protocols and conventions followed, indicating another regional norms cascade, which either addressed the initial weaknesses of the OAS system or expanded the mandate and strength of the Court and Commission (Lutz and Sikkink, 2000). In addition to its work on individual cases, the Commission has produced dozens of country reports, some of which have had an important impact on the human rights situation in member countries. After a slow start, the Inter-American Court is increasing its caseload, and its decisions on cases of disappearances in Honduras, and most recently, on torture and execution in Guatemala have established important precedents. Evolution has also taken place in the much weaker mechanisms under the African Charter on Human and People's Rights. In 1998, the Head of States of the Organization of African Unity (OAU) decided to establish an African Human Rights Court to supplement the work of the existing Commission (Mutua, 1999). There are also advanced efforts within the Association of Southeast Asian Nations (ASEAN) to establish a regional human rights mechanism.

The evolution of international human rights institutions has not (yet) featured as a major research question for international relations theorists. Liberal theory tends exclusively to focus on those human rights institutions capable of imposing real sovereignty costs on states. This limits the research to a small handful of human rights treaties that carry real teeth and leaves uninvestigated the great bulk of human rights norm activity that does not involve binding treaties or strong enforcement mechanisms. At the other extreme are constructivists who treat the world polity and its norms as a constant force pulling states towards rhetorical compliance. Both perspectives neglect the political battles around the creation of a global norm catalogue. While realists often dismiss such institutions as inconsequential, they also suggest that hegemonic leaders determine the content and evolution of the dominant norms in international society.

Constructivists hold that non-governmental actors and their principled mobilization play an increasingly important role in determining the social environment of state actors. The evolution of international human rights norms since the late 1940s at the UN and regional levels contains evidence for liberal and constructivist perspectives. States remain formally in control of decision-making procedures, while non-governmental actors acquire increasing authority in shaping the direction of those decisions. All human rights norms originally codified in the Universal Declaration have been subject to some form of progressive 'international legalization' (Abbott et al., 2000) either with regard to the extent of *obligation*, their *precision*, or the use of *delegation* as a means of increasing compliance. At the same time, human rights norms have traveled with different speed from 'soft' to 'hard' along these three dimensions. Future research should move confidently beyond the question of relevance and trace not only the origins, but also the evolution of international human rights institutions within the framework of international relations theories. In the face of serious political challenges, the international human rights regime has passed the test of robustness and successfully defended its basic standards and values as well as authority.

Compliance with International Human Rights Norms

The significance of the origins, acceptance and evolution of norms for international relations scholars hinges on their ability to influence actual behavior beyond mere rhetorical commitment. We can think of compliance with human rights norms as a continuum including (1) the ratification of a human rights treaty, (2) the fulfillment of reporting and other requests by supervisory bodies, (3) the implementation of norms in domestic law, (4) and rule-consistent behavior on the domestic level (Kent, 1999: 236; Risse et al., 1999). Since some of the compliance issues have been discussed above, we will concentrate here on the final stages of the continuum. While compliance understood as rhetorical commitment to international human rights norms has consistently increased since 1948, advancements in more substantive compliance understood as rule-consistent behavior are much less consistent. Camp Keith (1999) recently argued that there is no significant statistical correlation between the increase in ratifications for the International Covenant for Civil and Political Rights and actual human rights behavior measured with the Political Terror Scale (see p. 518). This result supports the claim that international human rights norms are not self-enforcing, but require some form of agency to bring them to the domestic level. Formal acceptance by a state party is often not the end, but the beginning of a prolonged struggle about the implementation of the norms.

Rather than resulting in consistently decreasing human rights violations around the world, the growing rhetorical commitment to human rights often intensifies the frustration among activists about a widening gap between rhetoric and (non-)action. Some of this is a result of vastly increased non-governmental monitoring practices. However, the 1994 genocide in Rwanda and 'ethnic cleansing' in Bosnia and Kosovo in 1994/95 and 1999 are only the most recent instances of continued gross human rights violations committed around the world. Almost thirty years after starting its first global campaign against torture, Amnesty International declared in 2000 that the organization had received credible reports of torture from more than 150 countries since 1997, in about half of these nations torture was widespread.[9] The proliferation of 'truth commissions' around the world (Hayner, 2000) is not only a sign of strengthened human rights norms, but also a reminder of the recurrence of human rights abuses. What are the conditions for successfully enforcing human rights norms? Are the most successful strategies based on sanctions, material incentives, civil society support, transnational mobilization, or combinations of those tactics?

The answers to these questions vary with the particular human rights issue, ranging from the shaming strategies of non-governmental actors to humanitarian interventions by a group or the whole community of states. With a focus on human rights treaties 'with real teeth', liberal theory conceives of compliance mainly as an issue of institutional design and judicial process. For realists, compliance is mainly a question of choosing the appropriate material means of enforcement in a world of state actors. Constructivists fall into two distinct camps with regard to the question of compliance. One side argues that non-compliance and 'decoupling' between norms and behavior is the rule (Krasner, 1999). Other norm-driven arguments maintain that transnational advocacy networks can socialize and 'entrap' (Risse, 2000: 32) state actors using the latter's rhetorical commitment to the norms. In the following sections, we will begin with a discussion of traditional foreign policy instruments and move then to the role of non-governmental actors and transnational advocacy networks.

Human rights in foreign policy   Thirty years ago, human rights were considered a peripheral and even inappropriate topic for foreign policy. Today, many countries have incorporated human rights concerns into their foreign policy agendas. Many questions still remain about to what degree human rights concerns actually influence foreign policy decisions, and whether such human rights policies actually improve domestic conditions in the target country. We will address both questions in turn.

Do human rights considerations affect foreign policy decisions?   A growing number of quantitative and qualitative studies explore how consistently donor nations take human rights into account when allocating military and economic aid. Such studies indicate that human rights have gained increasing salience in foreign policy and aid bureaucracies in many countries of the Northern Hemisphere. In the United States the activism of non-governmental organizations in the early 1970s created a climate of public opinion which encouraged Members of Congress to use the human rights agenda in their challenge of a presidency weakened by Watergate and Vietnam (Forsythe, 2000a: 175; Livezey, 1988; Sikkink, 1993). The creation of a lasting human rights bureaucracy was the result of non-governmental pressure on Congress and began long before the Carter administration took office (Weissbrodt, 1981). The Carter administration policy gave a higher profile and additional rhetorical commitment to the human rights cause.

A series of quantitative studies have focused on the impact of US human rights legislation on changing patterns of military and economic aid (Mitchell and McCormick, 1988; Poe, 1997; Stohl et al., 1984). By comparing levels of aid with human rights practices in a large number of aid recipients, this research explores to what degree US human rights legislation has actually led to a changing pattern of military and economic aid. Although there was very substantial disagreement in the early studies, the most recent work has found that human rights is taken into account in making military and economic aid decisions, but they compete with a range of other policy goals, including the economic need of the target country and strategic and ideological concerns (Apodaca and Stohl, 1999).

Research on foreign policies of the Netherlands, Canada and Norway suggests that states with a reputation for 'human internationalism' often also subordinated human rights concerns to economic and security interests (Matthews and Pratt, 1988). While human rights considerations are neither the only nor the primary factor in determining foreign aid, the literature indicates how human rights as part of 'good governance' have increased in prominence. The application of such standards is very uneven, in particular for the United States as one of the most outspoken and self-professed defenders of democracy. Geostrategic considerations have consistently overridden such concerns in much of the Arab world and for many Asian countries. A recent quantitative study argues that both the European Union and the United States have an increasingly consistent record of punishing human rights violators, albeit with different sanctioning instruments (Hazelzet, 2001).

Apart from the aid decisions of bi- and multilateral donors, the growing salience of human rights norms has led to a 'humanization of humanitarian law' (Meron, 2000) as reflected in the daily decisions of the Rwanda and Yugoslavia tribunals on issues such as command responsibility and the prosecution of sexual crimes. Under the leadership of the US government, the UN Security Council has gradually expanded the scope of Chapter VII of the UN Charter to link the security of peoples within a country to international peace and security. Under this provision domestic human rights violations in the former Yugoslavia, Northern Iraq, or Somalia have become a concern for the world community and makers of foreign policy. Transnational advocacy networks and international media attention to human rights crises around the world have pressured state actors and international organizations to take human rights considerations more seriously. Forsythe concluded that 'the presence or absence, the number and resources, the emphases and orientations of private human rights groups were subjects worthy of analysis in understanding foreign policy and human rights' (Forsythe, 2000b: 5).

Are current foreign policy instruments effective means to improve human rights conditions abroad? Many academics and policy-makers are skeptical when it comes to the use of sanctions as a means to promote human rights (for examples see Drezner, 1999: 10–11). They point out that sanctions are often not taken with an aim to affect change, but to deflect criticism at the home front (Eland, 1995: 29). In such cases of mixed or diffuse motives it is unlikely that policy-makers actually choose appropriate and effective sanctions instruments. During the Kosovo crisis in early 1999, Western leaders jeopardized the success of the military intervention by excluding the possibility of sending in ground troops, which was seen as problematic in the light of the public opinion at home (Garton Ash, 2000). In the target state, domestic élites are the least likely victims of sanctions and many leaders from Cuba to North Korea have been able to strengthen their positions by capitalizing on a 'rally-around-the-flag' effect. Worse still the UN sanctions regime against Iraq during the 1990s has both massively negative consequences for domestic human rights conditions and helped the regime to further demoralize the domestic opposition. Yet in the cases of Rhodesia and South Africa, multilateral and bilateral sanctions had an impact in the long term. A recent study combining qualitative and quantitative analysis argues that US sanctions involving military intervention with an explicit pro-democracy agenda can contribute to enduring democratization in target countries (Peceny, 1999).

Regan (1995) suggests that aid decisions have a small positive effect on changing repression levels. An earlier study by Jan Egeland argued that Norway was more successful in promoting human rights abroad than the United States (Egeland, 1984). Egeland claimed that smaller states develop more coherent and effective human rights policies. However, a closer look at Egeland's measures of effectiveness reveals that consistence and coherence in policy implementation was the main criterion of effectiveness, rather than any actual changes in target country human rights practices. The smaller parliamentary states of Europe that have adopted human rights policies – Norway, Denmark, Sweden and the Netherlands – have indeed had more consistent and unambiguous policies than the United States, but it does not necessarily follow that these policies have been more effective.

Qualitative studies of the effectiveness of US human rights policy reconfirm that the success of outside interventions depends on the concomitant links built between sender and target country. Chances for success increase when Congress and the executive unite in adopting a forceful human rights policy at a time when groups in the target country can use such outside pressures internally (Martin and Sikkink, 1993). Poe also argues that it is necessary to study the strategic interaction between donor and recipient regimes over time in order to better understand the linkage between aid and repression (Poe, 1997). Particularly important is the communication process involved in aid cut-offs, because such measures might weaken the material basis of a regime, but they are also an opportunity for targeted leaders to reinvent themselves as 'victims' of outside intervention (Schmitz, 2001). Moreover, if aid cuts are accompanied by contradictory messages such as concerns about the 'stability' of the country or region, they are likely to be ineffective.

Kaempfer and Lowenberg (1999) have recently used the greater potential for ambiguous communications to argue that multilateral sanctions are less effective than unilateral ones. What is still lacking in many cases of state-led human rights policies are (1) a clear definition of goals, (2) a conscious selection of appropriate means, (3) the consistent application of the measures, including communications with the target government and (4) a long-term follow-up. We argue below that such measures are more likely to be successful if they are part of a larger effort that systematically recognizes and includes the work of transnational advocacy networks. This also requires a broadening of our understanding of sanctions to include both identity-based and material measures (Crawford and Klotz, 1999). We argue below that the combination of norm cascades, non-governmental mobilization, and state foreign policies and multilateral action have proved to be very consequential for human rights violators.

Non-state actors and transnational advocacy networks

Research on the effectiveness of global human rights institutions suggests a complex model of norm diffusion to the national level. This model is not exclusively built on one of the theories of human rights change discussed in this chapter, but includes realist, liberal and constructivist ingredients. Because processes of principled mobilization are seen as the main engine of the process, however, constructivist theorizing and non-governmental networks are at the center of the explanation. These networks emerged during the 1960s and 1970s as a reaction to the failure of the United Nations to respond adequately to systematic human rights violations around the world (Korey, 1998: 139–80). The network members began to lobby international organizations, liberal states and the international public to join their efforts to mobilize against human rights violators. The first result of this research has been that even strong states in the international system are followers, not leaders of such mobilization efforts. Non-governmental mobilization precedes and causes state action on behalf of human rights. Many major human rights victories such as women's suffrage, the global campaign against *apartheid*, or the ban on landmines saw state actors either as increasingly convinced followers or reluctant bystanders (Klotz, 1995; Ramirez et al., 1997).

A second, more preliminary result of non-governmental mobilization traces the direct influence of these principled campaigns on human rights violators. An evaluation of eleven comparative case studies suggests a 'spiral model' of human rights change (Risse et al., 1999). The process starts with (1) a situation of domestic repression, (2) moves to initial non-governmental mobilization and governmental denial, (3) tactical concessions, (4) rhetorical acceptance of human rights norms and ends with (5) rule-consistent behavior. Since countries may spend extended time periods in each of these phases, the question is what kinds of strategies are most likely to move a country towards the next phase of the model. Corresponding to all three major theoretical perspectives, several hypotheses can be generated to account for the timing, including pressure from other states or international organizations, network mobilization strategies, issue characteristics, density or strength of the network (Brysk, 1994; Keck and Sikkink, 1998) and the nature of the domestic structure (Checkel, 1999).

Invariably, principled human rights NGOs set this process in motion by disseminating information provided by domestic victims of systematic human rights abuses. Transnational advocacy networks 'shame' the human rights violator and mobilize further international support from like-minded liberal states and international organizations. In many cases, United Nations human rights mechanisms will start their own investigations and comment on the domestic situation. Repressive governments often deny that human rights abuses occurred and invoke the norm of non-intervention against outside criticism. If a violent or fundamentalist opposition leads the domestic struggle, state leaders have more success in undermining the beginning mobilization by arguing for 'stability' and against further outside action. The most important transition in the spiral model occurs when state leaders move from denial to the stage of tactical concessions. This period has a distinct international and domestic component. On the international level, state representatives will start to accept the human rights norms and admit to the existence of human rights abuses. Domestically, this will open space for civil society actors to reclaim a more independent role in domestic politics. Transnational actors will continue to mobilize and link with those domestic groups and individuals. Research on the spiral model and the rhetorical behavior of state and non-governmental actors provided initial evidence that 'human rights talk' is not cheap. Studies on government responses to human rights criticism (van Ravels-Smulders, 1998) suggest an independent role for processes of moral argumentation and normative socialization (Risse, 2000). Moral argumentation rarely leads to direct behavioral change. Instead, state actors are forced to defend their human rights record in a social environment of world opinion and international institutions. This institutional context does not determine outcomes, but it does create a corridor of narrowing choices for policy-makers.

Ann Kent shows in her study of China's changing attitudes towards UN human rights institutions (1971–1998) that the Chinese government has been socialized within about ten years after Tiananmen into 'an acceptance of basic international human rights procedures' (Kent, 1999: 247), but remains recalcitrant when it comes to the domestic application of those norms. Considering the importance of China in international politics and its prominent role in the debate about 'Asian values', this crucial case study reconfirms the results of the initial research on the effects of norm socialization. However, because of the continuing gap between international rhetoric and domestic action and the expected time lag, there is still not enough evidence to conclude whether this is a case of 'decoupling' or successful norm socialization (see Table 27.1). The successful transition through the phase of tactical concessions ends either with sustainable policy change or the demise of the authoritarian regime altogether. State leaders will now fully accept the human rights norms, ratify international treaties and begin to implement those domestically. This stage of 'de jure compliance' or 'prescriptive status' is not identical with rule-consistent behavior. In most cases, continued network mobilization and a strong domestic support for human rights is necessary to move further along the spiral model and reach full de facto compliance.

Realists and liberals, with their emphasis on material interests, can account for states choosing not to promote human rights issues in other countries. However, when it comes to explaining participation in a process of positive human rights change, constructivist theory carries the main weight. Network strategies of non-governmental actors have been identified as crucial ingredients in many cases of human rights enforcement. Liberal theory's emphasis on domestic structure adds additional insights on the degree of initial resonance of international norms on the domestic level. This perspective can also help to understand why civil societies in some countries are quicker in (re)claiming the political space opened by transnational mobilization. The research on the effectiveness of

international human rights norms is still in its early stages. The spiral model allows us to ask the right questions about crucial periods and actors of human rights change, but it does not necessarily answer those questions.

CONCLUSION

Scholars of international relations have made considerable progress in understanding the international politics of human rights in the past two decades, but many of the most pressing issues still need more systematic scholarly attention. Hence, this chapter has not only focused on presenting the state of the art, but also made a conscious effort to identify important research questions for the future. Constructivist scholarship has transformed our understanding of international human rights and established the subject on the agenda of international relations scholars. The chapter traces how human rights norms have enjoyed consistently growing recognition in international politics since 1945. It also shows how non-governmental actors and advocacy networks shaped this process in crucial ways. Moreover, we argue that the growing rhetorical commitment to human rights norms affects how state actors calculate their self-interests and make decisions. In many cases, proving such an effect is difficult, because a decision *not* to engage in overt repression is hard to identify. Still, many of the global changes described here are still rhetorical and have not yet led to a process of irreversible norm socialization. A globally declining pattern of abuses even of the most basic human rights is still not clearly discernible. The human rights issue deserves attention because it has become a dominant framework for many political struggles within and across national boundaries. Its alternative logic based on individual well-being slowly transforms the state-centric view of international relations with its claim that violations of rights are a shared global concern. Human rights debates have become a dynamic undercurrent influencing and bypassing conventional inter-state politics.

Despite the role of constructivism in establishing human rights as an acceptable research agenda in international relations scholarship, much remains to be done in bringing together separate theoretical debates both within political science and across disciplinary divides. In particular, there are two almost separate debates occurring – one among quantitative scholars on the causes of repression, and the degree to which human rights norms have influenced foreign policy decisions over aid – and a second among more qualitative international relations scholars over liberal, realist and constructivist explanations for the origins, evolution and effectiveness of human rights norms and institutions.

These debates could benefit from engaging more directly with one another, as the possibilities for theoretical advances may lie in synthesizing insights from both literatures. Developing stronger theories of the causes and remedies for repression is not only important for IR theory, but has potentially powerful policy implications. Rather than allow ourselves to be mired down in sterile debates over which IR theory is confirmed by the human rights case, we need to use whatever eclectic theoretical tools are at our disposal that most accurately help us explain the ebbs and flows of repression in the world.

Notes

1 Rudolf Rummel estimates that government mass murder left four times more people dead in the twentieth century than civil and international wars combined (Rummel, 1994).

2 This argument is consistent with Guillermo O'Donnell's (1973) study of bureaucratic authoritarian regimes in Latin America, which also hypothesized that bureaucratic regimes, with their attendant human rights violations, emerged in response to a perceived threat not only to the political system, but to the political-economic order in general.

3 The strong correlation quantitative research has found between democracy and economic well-being has also been confirmed by studies looking at the status of economic and social rights (as measured by a quality of life index that includes infant mortality, life expectancy and literacy). Amartya Sen showed, for example, that famines have not occurred under democracy, apparently because a free press and democratic political institutions draw attention to food shortages before they reach famine levels (Sen, 1994; also Park, 1987; Heinisch, n.d.).

4 Goldhagen (1996) is also a good example for an 'overreaching' ideological explanation that neglects the crucial leadership role necessary to select and privilege certain ideological ideas and make these relevant for action.

5 In accordance with the other contributions in this hand book, we use 'constructivism' as a label for norm-driven, ideational theories.

6 The cascade model is designed to capture an observable pattern of norm adoption. So far, it is still unclear how such a cascade occurs and where crucial events such as the tipping point are to be found. Finnemore and Sikkink (1998) have suggested the entry into force of a treaty as a proxy for the beginning of the cascade.

7 For a description of the 'boomerang effect' see (Chapter 13) Risse in this volume and Keck and Sikkink, 1998: 12–13.

8 For a presentation of such criteria within the 'regime theory' literature, see Levy et al., 1995.

9 See the most recent report by Amnesty International at: http://www.stoptorture.org/

10 Krasner has recently used some ideas of sociological institutionalists to account for an 'organized hypocrisy'

with regard to the application of international norms. His conclusion is that political leaders' main motive is to stay in power, rather than to adhere to international norms. Occasional overlap of this basic self-interest and prescriptions of international norms are an exception to the rule. Krasner claims that constructivists misinterpret such overlaps as instances of norms shaping self-interests of state actors.

Bibliography

Abbott, Kenneth W., Keohane, Robert O., Moravcsik, Andrew, Slaughter, Anne-Marie and Snidal, Duncan (2000) 'The Concept of Legalization', *International Organization*, 54 (3): 401–19.

Alston, Philip (1992a) *The United Nations and Human Rights: A Critical Appraisal*. Oxford: Clarendon Press.

Alston, Philip (1992b) 'The Commission on Human Rights', in Philip Alston (ed.), *The United Nations and Human Rights. A Critical Appraisal*. Oxford: Clarendon Press. pp. 126–210.

Apodaca, Clair and Stohl, Michael (1999) 'United States Human Rights Policy and Foreign Assistance', *International Studies Quarterly*, 43: 185–98.

Archer, Clive (1992) *International Organizations*. London: Routledge.

Baehr, Peter (1989) 'The General Assembly. Negotiating the Convention on Torture', in David P. Forsythe (ed.), *The United Nations in the World Political Economy*. Houndmills: Macmillan.

Boli, John and Thomas, George (1999) 'INGOs and the Organization of World Culture', in John Boli and George Thomas (eds), *Constructing World Culture: International Nongovernmental Organizations since 1875*. Stanford: Stanford University Press. pp. 13–49.

Brysk, Alison (1994) *The Politics of Human Rights in Argentina: Protest, Change, and Democratization*. Stanford: Stanford University Press.

Buergenthal, Thomas (1995) *International Human Rights in a Nutshell*, 2nd edn. St. Paul, MN: West Publishing.

Burgers, J. Herman (1992) 'The Road to San Francisco: The Revival of the Human Rights Idea in the Twentieth Century', *Human Rights Quarterly*, 14 (4): 447–77.

Burgers, J. Herman and Danelius, Hans (1988) *The United Nations Convention against Torture*. Dordrecht: Martinus Nijhoff.

Camp Keith, Linda (1999) 'The United Nations International Covenant on Civil and Political Rights: Does it Make a Difference in Human Rights Behavior?', *Journal of Peace Research*, 36 (1): 95–118.

Checkel, Jeffrey T. (1999) 'Norms, Institutions, and National Identity in Contemporary Europe', *International Studies Quarterly*, 43: 83–114.

Chomsky, Noam and Herman, Edward (1979) *The Political Economy of Human Rights: The Washington Connection and Third World Fascism*. Boston: South End Press.

Clark, Ann Marie (2001) *Diplomacy of Conscience: Amnesty International and Changing Human Rights Norms.* Princeton: Princeton University Press.

Cohen, Stanley (2001) *States of Denial: Knowing About Atrocities and Suffering.* Cambridge: Polity.

Conroy, John (2000) *Unspeakable Acts, Ordinary People: The Dynamics of Torture.* New York: Alfred A. Knopf.

Crawford, Neta C. and Klotz, Audie (eds) (1999) *How Sanctions Work: Lessons from South Africa.* New York: St Martin's Press.

Davenport, Christian (ed.) (2000) *Paths to State Repression. Human Rights Violations and Contentious Politics.* Lanham: Rowman and Littlefield.

Des Forges, Alison (1999) *Leave None to Tell the Story: Genocide in Rwanda.* New York: Human Rights Watch.

Donnelly, Jack (1986) 'International Human Rights: A Regime Analysis', *International Organization*, 40 (3): 599–642.

Donnelly, Jack (1989) *Universal Human Rights in Theory and Practice.* Ithaca: Cornell University Press.

Donnelly, Jack (1998) *International Human Rights.* Boulder: Westview.

Drezner, Daniel W. (1999) *The Sanctions Paradox. Economic Statecraft and International Relations.* Cambridge: Cambridge University Press.

Egeland, Jan (1984) 'Human Rights – Ineffective Big States, Potent Small States', *Journal of Peace Research*, 21 (3): 207–13.

Eland, Ivan (1995) 'Economic Sanctions as Tools of Foreign Policy', in David Cortright and George A. Lopez (eds), *Economic Sanctions: Panacea or Peacebuilding in a Post-Cold War World?* Boulder: Westview. pp. 29–42.

Elster, Jon (1998) 'Introduction', in Jon Elster (ed.), *Deliberative Democracy.* New York: Cambridge University Press. pp. 1–18.

Fein, Helen (1993) *Genocide: A Sociological Perspective.* London: Sage.

Fein, Helen (1995) 'More Murder in the Middle: Life Integrity Violations and Democracy in the World, 1987', *Human Rights Quarterly*, 17 (1): 170–91.

Finnemore, Martha (1996a) *National Interests in International Society.* Ithaca: Cornell University Press.

Finnemore, Martha (1996b) 'Norms, Culture, and World Politics: Insights from Sociology's Institutionalism', *International Organization*, 50 (2): 325–47.

Finnemore, Martha and Sikkink, Kathryn (1998) 'International Norm Dynamics and Political Change', *International Organization*, 52 (4): 887–917.

Forsythe, David P. (1983) *Human Rights and World Politics.* Lincoln: University of Nebraska Press.

Forsythe, David P. (1991) *The Internationalization of Human Rights.* Lexington: Lexington Books.

Forsythe, David P. (1998) 'Human Rights Fifty Years after the Universal Declaration: Reconciling American Political Science and the Study of Human Rights', *PS: Political Science and Politics*, 31 (3): 507–12.

Forsythe, David P. (2000a) *Human Rights in International Relations.* Cambridge: Cambridge University Press.

Forsythe, David P. (2000b) 'Introduction', in David Forsythe (ed.), *Human Rights and Comparative Foreign Policy.* Tokyo: United Nations University Press.

Garton Ash, Timothy (2000) 'Kosovo: Was it Worth it?', *New York Review of Books*, 21 September.

Gibson, Janice T. and Haritos-Fatouros, Mika (1986) 'The Education of a Torturer', *Psychology Today*, 20: 50–8.

Glendon, Mary Ann (1998) 'Knowing the Universal Declaration of Human Rights', *Notre Dame Law Review*, 73 (5): 1153–81.

Glendon, Mary Ann (2001) *A World Made New: Eleanor Roosevelt and the Universal Declaration of Human Rights.* New York: Random House.

Goldhagen, Daniel J. (1996) *Hitler's Willing Executioners: Ordinary Germans and the Holocaust.* New York: Alfred A. Knopf.

Gourevitch, Philip (1998) *We Wish to Inform You that Tomorrow We Will be Killed With Our Families: Stories from Rwanda.* New York: Farrar, Straus and Giroux.

Haas, Ernst B. (1990) *When Knowledge is Power: Three Models of Change in International Organizations.* Berkeley: University of California Press.

Harris, David J., O'Boyle, Michael and Warbrick, C. (1999) *Law of the European Convention on Human Rights*, 2nd edn. London: Butterworths.

Hayner, Priscilla B. (2000) *Unspeakable Truths. Confronting State Terror and Atrocity.* London: Routledge.

Hazelzet, Hadewych (2001) 'Carrots or Sticks? EU and US Sanctions in Reaction to Human Rights Violations', PhD thesis, European University Institute.

Heinisch, Reinhard (n.d.) 'Basic Human Rights: Does Regime Matter?', unpublished paper.

Heinz, Wolfgang S. and Frühling, Hugo (1999) *Determinants of Gross Human Rights Violations by State and State-Sponsored Actors in Brazil, Uruguay, Chile, and Argentina, 1960–1990.* The Hague: Martinus Nijhoff.

Henderson, Conway (1991) 'Conditions Affecting the Use of Political Repression', *Journal of Conflict Resolution*, 35: 120–42.

Ignatieff, Michael (1999) 'Human Rights: The Midlife Crisis', *New York Review of Books*, 20 May.

Ignatieff, Michael (2001) 'The Danger of a World Without Enemies. Lemkin's Word', *The New Republic*, 2 February: 25–8.

Ikenberry, G. John and Kupchan, Charles (1990) 'Socialization and Hegemonic Power', *International Organization*, 44 (3): 283–315.

Iriye, Akira (1997) *Cultural Internationalism and World Order.* Baltimore: Johns Hopkins University Press.

Jellinek, Georg ([1901] 1979) *The Declaration of the Rights of Man and Citizens: A Contribution to Modern Constitutional History* (trans. by Max Farrand). Westport: Hyperion.

Kaempfer, William and Lowenberg, Anton D. (1999) 'Unilateral versus Multilateral International Sanctions: A Public Choice Perspective', *International Studies Quarterly*, 43: 37–58.

Kamminga, Menno T. (1992) *Inter-State Accountability for Violations of Human Rights*. Philadelphia: University of Pennsylvania Press.

Keck, Margaret and Sikkink, Kathryn (1998) *Activists Beyond Borders: Advocacy Networks in International Politics*. Ithaca: Cornell University Press.

Kent, Ann (1999) *China, the United Nations, and Human Rights. The Limits of Compliance*. Philadelphia: University of Pennsylvania Press.

Klotz, Audie (1995) *Norms in International Relations: The Struggle against Apartheid*. Ithaca: Cornell University Press.

Korey, William (1998) *NGOs and the Universal Declaration of Human Rights: A Curious Grapevine*. New York: St Martin's Press.

Krasner, Stephen D. (1993) 'Sovereignty, Regimes, and Human Rights', in Volker Rittberger (ed.), *Regime Theory and International Relations*. Oxford: Clarendon Press. pp. 139–67.

Krasner, Stephen D. (1999) *Sovereignty: Organized Hypocrisy*. Princeton: Princeton University Press.

Kuper, Leo (1981) 'Warrant for Genocide: Ideological Aspects', in *Genocide*. New Haven: Yale University Press. pp. 84–100.

Lauren, Paul Gordon (1996) *Power and Prejudice: The Politics of Racial Discrimination*, 2nd edn. Boulder: Westview.

Lauren, Paul Gordon (1998) *The Evolution of International Human Rights: Visions Seen*. Philadelphia: University of Pennsylvania Press.

Levy, Marc A., Young, Oran R. and Zürn, Michael (1995) 'The Study of International Regimes', *European Journal of International Relations*, 1 (3): 268–312.

Livezey, Lowell W. (1988) *Non-Governmental Organizations and the Idea of Human Rights*. Princeton: Princeton University Press.

Lutz, Ellen and Sikkink, Kathryn (2000) 'International Human Rights Law and Practice in Latin America', *International Organization*, 54 (3): 633–59.

Martin, Lisa L. and Sikkink, Kathryn (1993) 'US Policy and Human Rights in Argentina and Guatemala, 1973–1980', in Peter B. Evans, Harold K. Jacobson and Robert D. Putnam (eds), *Double-Edged Diplomacy: International Bargaining and Domestic Politics*. Berkeley: University of California Press. pp. 330–62.

Matthews, Robert O. and Pratt, Cranford (eds) (1988) *Human Rights in Canadian Foreign Policy*. Montreal: McGill–Queen's University Press.

Meron, Theodor (2000) 'The Humanization of Humanitarian Law', *American Journal of International Law*, 94 (2): 239–78.

Meyer, John W., Boli, John, Thomas, George M. and Ramirez, Francisco O. (1997) 'World Society and the Nation-State', *American Journal of Sociology*, 103 (1): 144–81.

Meyer, William H. (1996) 'Human Rights and MNCs: Theory versus Quantitative Analysis', *Human Rights Quarterly*, 18 (2): 368–97.

Meyer, William H. (1999) 'Confirming, Infirming, and "Falsifying" Theories of Human Rights: Reflections on

Smith, Bolyard, and Ippolito through the Lens of Lakatos', *Human Rights Quarterly*, 21 (1): 220–8.

Millgram, Stanley (1965) 'Some Conditions of Obedience and Disobedience to Authority', *Human Relations*, 18 (1): 57–75.

Mitchell, Neil J. and McCormick, James M. (1988) 'Economic and Political Explanations of Human Rights Violations', *World Politics*, 40 (2): 476–98.

Moeller, Susan D. (1999) *Compassion Fatigue: How the Media Sell Disease, Famine, War, and Death*. London: Routledge.

Moravcsik, Andrew (1997) 'Taking Preferences Seriously: A Liberal Theory of International Politics', *International Organization*, 51 (4): 513–53.

Moravcsik, Andrew (2000) 'The Origins of Human Rights Regimes: Democratic Delegation in Postwar Europe', *International Organization*, 54 (2): 217–52.

Morsink, Johannes (1999) *The Universal Declaration of Human Rights: Origins, Drafting, and Intent*. Philadelphia: University of Pennsylvania Press.

Mueller, John E. (1995) *Quiet Cataclysm: Reflections on the Recent Transformation in World Politics*. New York: Basic Books.

Mutua, Makau (1999) 'The African Human Rights Court. A Two–Legged Stool?', *Human Rights Quarterly*, 21 (2): 342–63.

Newman, Frank and Weissbrodt, David (1996) *International Human Rights: Law, Policy, and Process*, 2nd edn. Cincinnati: Anderson Publishing.

O'Donnell, Guillermo A. (1973) *Modernization and Bureaucratic-Authoritarianism: Studies in South American Politics*. Berkeley: University of California Press.

Park, Han S. (1987) 'Correlates of Human Rights. Global Tendencies', *Human Rights Quarterly*, 9 (2): 405–13.

Peceny, Mark (1999) *Democracy at the Point of Bayonets*. University Park: Pennsylvania State University Press.

Perelli, Carina (1990) 'The Military's Perception of Threat in the Southern Cone of South America', in Louis W. Goodman, Johanna S.R. Mendelson and Juan Rial (eds), *The Military and Democracy:The Future of Civil-Military Relations in Latin America*. Lexington: Lexington Books. pp. 93–105.

Pion-Berlin, David and Lopez, George A. (1991) 'Of Victims and Executioners: Argentine State Terror, 1975–1979', *International Studies Quarterly*, 35 (1): 63–87.

Poe, Steven (1997) 'The Decision to Repress: An Integrative Theoretical Approach to the Research on Human Rights and Repression', unpublished manuscript.

Poe, Steven and Tate, C. Neal (1994) 'Human Rights and Repression to Personal Integrity in the 1980s: A Global Analysis', *American Political Science Review*, 88: 853–72.

Poe, Steven, Tate, C. Neal and Camp Keith, Linda (1999) 'Repression of the Human Right to Personal Integrity Revisited: A Global Crossnational Study Covering the Years 1976–1993', *International Studies Quarterly*, 43: 291–315.

Price Cohen, Cynthia (1990) 'The Role of NGOs in the Drafting of the Convention on the Rights of the Child', *Human Rights Quarterly*, 12 (1): 137–47.

Przeworski, Adam and Limongi, Fernando (1997) 'Modernization: Theories and Facts', *World Politics*, 49 (2): 155–83.

Quinn, Kenneth (1989) 'Explaining the Terror', in Karl Jackson (ed.), *Cambodia 1975–1978: Rendez-vous with Death*. Princeton: Princeton University Press. pp. 215–40.

Ramirez, Francisco, Soysal, Yasemin and Shanahan, Suzanne (1997) 'The Changing Logic of Political Citizenship: Cross-National Acquisition of Women's Suffrage Rights, 1890–1990', *American Sociological Review*, 62: 735–45.

Regan, Patrick A. (1995) 'US Economic Aid and Political Repression: An Empirical Evaluation of US Foreign Policy', *Political Research Quarterly*, 48 (3): 613–29.

Risse, Thomas (2000) 'Let's Argue! Communicative Action in World Politics', *International Organization*, 54 (1): 1–39.

Risse, Thomas, Ropp, Stephen and Sikkink, Kathryn (eds) (1999) *The Power of Human Rights: International Norms and Domestic Change*. Cambridge: Cambridge University Press.

Risse-Kappen, Thomas (1995) 'Bringing Transnational Relations Back In: Introduction', in Thomas Risse-Kappen (ed.), *Bringing Transnational Relations Back In. Non-State Actors, Domestic Structures and International Institutions*. Cambridge: Cambridge University Press. pp. 3–33.

Robertson, Geoffrey (1999) *Crimes Against Humanity. The Struggle for Global Justice*. London: Penguin.

Rodley, Nigel S. (1987) *The Treatment of Prisoners under International Law*. New York: Oxford University Press.

Rodley, Nigel S. (1997) 'The Evolution of United Nations Charter-Based Machinery for the Protection of Human Rights', *European Human Rights Law Review*, 1 (1): 4–10.

Ron, James (1997) 'Varying Methods of State Violence', *International Organization*, 51 (2): 275–300.

Ruggie, John G. (1983) 'International Regimes, Transactions, and Change: Embedded Liberalism in the Postwar Economic Order', *International Organization*, 36 (2): 379–416.

Rummel, Rudolf (1994) 'Power, Genocide, and Mass Murder', *Journal of Peace Research*, 31 (1): 1–10.

Schimmelfennig, Frank (2000) 'International Socialization in the New Europe. Rational Action in an Institutional Environment', *European Journal of International Relations*, 6 (1): 109–39.

Schmitz, Hans Peter (1995) 'Konflikte in die UNESCO. Neorealistische Thesen zum Nord-Süd-Verhältnis', *Zeitschrift für Internationale Beziehungen*, 2 (1): 107–39.

Schmitz, Hans Peter (2001) 'When Networks Blind. Human Rights and Politics in Kenya', in Thomas Callaghy, Ronald Kassimir and Robert Latham (eds), *Authority and Intervention in Africa*. Cambridge: Cambridge University Press. pp. 149–72.

Sen, Amartya (1994) 'An Argument for the Primacy of Political Rights: Freedoms and Needs', *The New Republic*, 10/17 January: 31–8.

Shue, Henry (1980) *Basic Rights. Subsistence, Affluence, and US Foreign Policy*. Princeton: Princeton University Press.

Sikkink, Kathryn (1993) 'The Power of Principled Ideas: Human Rights Policies in the United States and Western Europe', in Judith Goldstein and Robert Keohane (eds), *Ideas and Foreign Policy*. Ithaca: Cornell University Press. pp. 139–70.

Slaughter, Ann-Marie (1995) 'International Law in a World of Liberal States', *The European Journal of International Law*, 6: 139–70.

Smith, Jackie, Chatfield, Charles and Pagnucco, Ron (eds) (1997) *Transnational Social Movements and Global Politics: Solidarity Beyond the State*. Syracuse: Syracuse University Press.

Smith, Jackie, Bolyard, Melissa and Ippolito, Anna (1999) 'Human Rights and the Global Economy', *Human Rights Quarterly*, 21 (1): 207–19.

Snyder, Jack L. (2000) *From Voting to Violence: Democratization and Nationalist Conflict*. New York: W.W. Norton.

Stanley, William (1996) *The Protection Racket State: Elite Politics, Military Extortion, and Civil War in El Salvador*. Philadelphia: Temple University Press.

Staub, Ervin (1989) 'Summary and Conclusions: The Societal and Psychological Origins of Genocide and Other Atrocities', in *The Roots of Evil*. Cambridge: Cambridge University Press. pp. 232–45.

Steiner, Henry J. and Alston, Philip (1996) *International Human Rights in Context: Law, Politics, Morals*. Oxford: Clarendon Press.

Stohl, Michael, Carleton, David and Johnson, Steven E. (1984) 'Human Rights and US Foreign Assistance from Nixon to Carter', *Journal of Peace Research*, 21 (2): 215–26.

Sunstein, Cass (1997) 'Social Norms and Social Roles', in Cass Sunstein (ed.), *Free Markets and Social Justice*. New York: Oxford University Press.

Thomas, Daniel (2001) *The Helsinki Effect: International Norms, Human Rights, and the Demise of Communism*. Princeton: Princeton University Press.

Thomas, George M., Meyer, John W., Ramirez, Francisco O. and Boli, John (eds) (1987) *Institutional Structure: Constituting State, Society and Individual*. Newbury Park: Sage.

United Nations High Commissioner for Human Rights (2001) *Status of Ratifications of the Principal International Human Rights Treaties, as of 16 July 2001*. Geneva: UNHCHR.

van Boven, Theodor C. (1989) 'The Role of Non-Governmental Organizations in International Human Rights Standard-Setting: A Prerequisite of Democracy', *California Western International Law Journal*, 20 (2): 207–25.

van Ravels-Smulders, Chris (1998) 'An Account of China's Response to Allegations of Human Rights Violations', in Mielle Bulterman, Aart Hendriks and

Jacqueline Smith (eds), *To Beahr in Our Minds: Essays on Human Rights from the Heart of the Netherlands*. Utrecht: Netherlands Institute of Human Rights. pp. 289–312.

Weissbrodt, David S. (1981) 'The Influence of Interest Groups on the Development of United States Human Rights Policies', in Natalie Kaufman Hevener (ed.), *The Dynamics of Human Rights in US Foreign Policy*. New Brunswick: Transaction. pp. 229–78.

Weissbrodt, David S. (1984) 'The Contribution of International Non-Governmental Organization to the Protection of Human Rights', in Theodor Meron (ed.), *Human Rights in International Law: Legal and Policy Issues*. Oxford: Clarendon Press.

Weissbrodt, David S. (1986) 'The Three "Theme" Special Rapporteurs of the UN Commission on Human Rights', *American Journal of International Law*, 80 (3): 685–99.

Weissbrodt, David S. and O'Toole, Teresa (1988) 'The Development of International Human Rights Law', in *The Universal Declaration of Human Rights: Human Rights, The United Nations, and Amnesty International*. New York: Amnesty International.

Wendt, Alexander (1999) *Social Theory of International Politics*. Cambridge: Cambridge University Press.

Wendt, Alexander (2000) 'On the Via Media: A Response to Critics', *Review of International Studies*, 26 (1): 165–80.

28

International Law, International Relations and Compliance

KAL RAUSTIALA
AND ANNE-MARIE SLAUGHTER

Commitments are a persistent feature of international affairs. Disagreement over the effect of international commitments and the causes of compliance with them is equally persistent. Yet in the last decade the long-standing divide between those who believed that international rules *per se* shaped state behavior and those who saw such rules as epiphenomenal or insignificant has given way to a more nuanced and complex debate. Regime theory, originally focused on the creation and persistence of regimes, increasingly emphasizes variations in regimes and in their impact on behavior. The legal quality of regime rules is one important source of regime variation. At the same time the proliferation and evolution of international legal agreements, organizations and judicial bodies in the wake of the Cold War has provided the empirical predicate and a policy imperative for heightened attention to the role of international law.

Across many issue-areas, the use of law to structure world politics seems to be increasing. This phenomenon of legalization raises several questions. What factors explain the choice to create and use international law? If law is a tool or method to organize interaction, how does it work? Does the use of international law make a difference to how states or domestic actors behave? These questions are increasingly of interest to IR theorists and policy-makers alike. The core issue is the impact of law and legalization on state behavior, often understood in terms of compliance. While the distinction should not be overstated, legal rules and institutions presume compliance in a way that non-legal rules and institutions do not. Law and compliance are conceptually linked because law explicitly aims to produce compliance with its rules: legal rules set the standard by which

compliance is gauged. Explanations of why and when states comply with international law can help account for the turn to law as a positive phenomenon, but they also provide critical policy guidance for the design of new institutions and agreements.

This chapter surveys the study of compliance in both the international relations (IR) and international law (IL) literature.[1] In many ways, the compliance literature is a microcosm of developments in both fields, and particularly of the rapprochement between them (Abbott, 1989; Koh, 1997; Slaughter Burley, 1993; Slaughter et al., 1998b). For IR scholars interested in reviving the study of international law in their discipline, it was a natural step to focus first on questions of whether, when and how law 'mattered' to state behavior. For international lawyers eager to use IR theory to address a host of theoretical and practical legal problems, the mechanisms of compliance were an equally natural starting point. Indeed, it is a rare conference or collaborative project between scholars from both disciplines in which compliance is not the focus of at least one paper. Future studies on compliance are also likely to prove an important empirical testing ground for the value of theoretically sophisticated interdisciplinary work. Our overview of theories of compliance is thus in many ways a review of the burgeoning body of 'IR–IL' scholarship.

The first part of this chapter defines the concept of compliance, distinguishing it from the related but distinct concepts of implementation and effectiveness. We also focus primarily on compliance with treaties, rather than with the broader categories of rules that international lawyers term 'customary international law'. The second part reviews the major theories advanced by IR and IL scholars through the 1990s, setting forth a chronological account. Part three situates these theories in the context of a typology of six different sets of variables that scholars from both disciplines have identified as influencing the existence and degree of compliance. Part four reviews a range of more recent empirical studies of compliance, as well as the results of cognate analyses of regime design, legalization and the choice of hard law versus soft law. The chapter concludes by identifying a number of open questions.

COMPLIANCE AS A CONCEPTUAL VARIABLE

We define compliance as a state of conformity or identity between an actor's behavior and a specified rule (Fisher, 1981: 20; Mitchell, 1994: 30). Some analysts distinguish 'compliance', in the sense of conformity for instrumental reasons such as avoidance of punishment, from 'obedience', defined as behavior resulting from the internalization of norms (Koh, 1997; Kratochwil, 1989). For present purposes, however, we do not gauge compliance by reference to motivations. Compliance as a concept, in our definition, is agnostic about causality. Compliance is also not uniquely applicable to *legal* rules, though that is our focus here. Nor is the impact of legal rules limited to compliance – as we discuss below, legal rules may change state behavior even when states fail to comply. The important point to underscore is that most theories of compliance with international law are at bottom theories of the behavioral influence of legal rules. Indeed, in practice the line between theories of compliance and theories of the 'effectiveness' or impact of rules can blur. We return to this issue below.

Political scientists have traditionally not distinguished legal from non-legal rules or norms, or have treated the difference as causally insignificant. By contrast, most IL scholarship treats compliance with treaties and compliance with non-legally binding commitments as driven by quite different processes. Law *qua* law, in this view, carries particular obligations and implicates special norms of behavior and decision processes. However, IR scholars are increasingly interested in distinguishing legal from non-legal rules, and IL scholars are increasingly interested in 'soft law' or non-legal rules. Despite this convergence, an interdisciplinary assessment of compliance theory must be sensitive to these disciplinary differences in conceptualizing the dependent variable.

Compliance is distinct from, but closely related to, two concepts that are increasingly important in contemporary regime theory: implementation and effectiveness (Victor et al., 1998). Implementation is the process of putting international commitments into practice: the passage of legislation, creation of institutions (both domestic and international) and enforcement of rules. Implementation is typically a critical step toward compliance, but compliance can occur without implementation; that is, without any effort or action by a government or regulated entity. If an international commitment matches current practice, for instance, implementation is unnecessary and compliance is automatic. Compliance can also occur for reasons entirely exogenous to the agreement: economic collapse in the former Soviet Union, for example, has produced perfect, but coincidental, compliance with many environmental agreements. Or implementation may be thorough but be overwhelmed by exogenous, uncontrollable factors. Thus implementation is conceptually neither a necessary nor a sufficient condition for compliance, but in practice is frequently critical.

Effectiveness is a concept defined in varying ways: for example, as the degree to which a rule induces changes in behavior that further the rule's goals; improves the state of the underlying problem; or achieves its policy objective (Keohane et al., 1993: 7; Young, 1994: 140–62). The connection between compliance and effectiveness is also neither necessary nor sufficient. Rules or regimes can be effective in any of these senses even if compliance is low. And while high levels of compliance can indicate high levels of effectiveness, they can also indicate low, readily met and ineffective standards. Many international agreements reflect a lowest common denominator dynamic that makes compliance easy but results in a negligible influence on behavior. Here is the source of the vexing question of the significance of high observed levels of compliance. From an effectiveness perspective more compliance is better, *ceteris paribus*. But regimes with significant non-compliance can still be effective if they induce changes in behavior. The key point is that the sheer existence (or lack) of compliance may indicate little about international law's impact on behavior; consequently, studies of compliance must be translated into normative prescriptions about institutional design with great care.

THE LITERATURE: GENERAL THEORIES OF COMPLIANCE

A review of the IR and IL literatures on compliance can be organized into many different narratives: the progression of each discipline separately; the conjunction of the two disciplines as captured by cross-cutting analytical categories; the ways in which each discipline responds to the other. We tell the story chronologically, noting important work in each discipline as it arises. The story is a bit longer, but ultimately more interesting and enlightening. At times the two disciplines interact dialectically; at other times they speak past each other. Increasingly, IR and IL scholars are working collaboratively.

We skim the literature through the 1980s, noting only the most visible features of the landscape, but review the 1990s in greater detail. For much of the Cold War, IL scholarship on compliance was part of the larger project of demonstrating that 'international law mattered' (Falk, 1968).[2] The standard move, although it took many different guises, was to deny or downplay the relevance of a layman's domestic vision of law as something to be enforced. Enforcement requires an enforcer, which the international system manifestly does not have. Law, however, can and does perform many functions other than constraint.

The leading legal scholars of the Cold War era, such as McDougal, Chayes, Henkin, Schachter and Falk, all developed accounts of international law in which rules and institutions both reflect and advance state interests. The American Society of International Law sponsored a series of monographs on important international crises in which scholars traced the 'role of international law', not in determining the outcome, but in shaping or facilitating it. Looking back, many contemporary scholars have been inclined to see writers in this period as making a virtue of necessity: the Cold War froze international law in a primarily facilitative mode. In fact, however, much of the scholarship during this period laid the foundation for the compliance theories that have dominated the debate in recent years.

How Nations Behave

Henkin first published his celebrated book, *How Nations Behave*, in the late 1960s. As his title suggests, he ranges well beyond law, embracing politics and policy and explicitly focusing on the impact of law on behavior. He argued that nations behave largely in compliance with international law. Advancing an argument common among IL scholars, Henkin suggested that norms of respect for law shape decisions in myriad ways that often escape attention because they are quiet and routine. This produces selection bias that causes critics to focus on the rare cases of non-compliance rather than the overwhelming cases of compliance – hence his famous aphorism that 'it is probably the case that *almost all nations observe almost all principles of international law and almost all of their obligations almost all of the time*' (Henkin, [1968] 1979: 47; emphasis in original). Yet on the question immediately posed by political scientists – *why* do nations comply? – Henkin is less clear. He invoked legal process arguments to show how the need for plausible justification and argument in international law – its necessary procedural, discursive qualities – bounds

state behavior and systematically encourages states to move closer to the compliance end of the spectrum.[3] But he also claimed that a suite of factors – reputation, reciprocity, norm observation, domestic politics and many others – weighs in favor of compliance in almost every case.

This list of factors influencing compliance is remarkably rich. It is too rich, however, to yield a clear theory of why and when states do and do not comply. Henkin offered instead an argument *of* compliance, coupled to a wide-ranging but largely unweighted analysis of relevant factors. None the less, his work set the standard of the period and remains a touchstone for compliance scholars.

Replacing Law with Regimes

In the 1980s American political scientists rediscovered international law under the banner of regime theory.[4] The famous 'Regimes' volume recapitulates many of the functionalist and constructivist insights advanced by IL scholars in the 1960s and 1970s.[5] On the other hand, to give IR scholarship its due, *After Hegemony* and its progeny formalized and systematized many of the insights generated by the international lawyers. Regime theory was genuinely a theory, or rather a collection of theories. It assumed that compliance with international commitments was possible, even likely. States would only establish regimes when it was in their long-term interest to cooperate. They thus needed mechanisms to prevent short-term defection at the expense of other states. But once assured that other states were cooperating and complying, each should perceive its own interest in following suit.

Regime theory flourished through the 1980s, as scholars demonstrated its applicability to security issues as well as economic problems and expanded the repertoire of causal mechanisms through which regimes facilitate cooperation. The initial focus, however, was more on regime formation than impact. Nevertheless, a divide between rationalist and constructivist approaches to compliance was already emerging, one that would become much more apparent in the focus on regime compliance through the 1990s. Early constructivist scholars emphasized mechanisms that drew on the normative power of rules and the importance of shared knowledge and discourse in shaping identity and interests (Keohane, 1988; Kratochwil, 1989). While constructivists in IR have not generally tackled compliance *per se*, they are starting to (Checkel, 2000; Risse et al., 1999). From a constructivist perspective, compliance is less a matter of rational calculation or imposed constraints than of internalized identities and norms of appropriate behavior. It is a line of theory that is particularly congenial to many IL scholars; we discuss this linkage further below.

Legitimacy Rules

By the end of the 1980s, IL scholars were finally off the defensive of the Cold War years. A decade of obsession with 'regimes', coupled with the fall of the Berlin Wall and the promise of a new era of global cooperation, created an opening for a new scholarly focus on the particular properties of law. Speaking for the international legal profession, Franck proclaimed that 'we are in a post-ontological era' (1992). Freed from the need to demonstrate the existence, much less the relevance, of international law as law, he set forth a bold argument about compliance and legitimacy (Franck, 1990).

Franck's central thesis was that 'in a community organized around rules, compliance is secured – to whatever degree it is – at least in part by the perception of a rule as legitimate by those to whom it is addressed' (1988: 706). Despite this prefatory hedging of dependent and independent variables, he presented the theory as a general theory of compliance in which legitimacy is the crucial causal factor. The legitimacy of rules exerts a 'compliance pull' on governments that explains the high observed levels of compliance of international law. This notion of compliance-pull, rather than compliance itself, is actually the dependent variable of the analysis. Franck defined legitimacy in terms of four elements. Textual determinacy refers to the clarity and transparency of the commitment itself. This is not simplicity *per se*; rather, the rule must be able to clearly 'communicate its intent' in specific situations. Symbolic validation is the communication of authority through ritual or regularized practice. Coherence refers to consistency in application and in context with other rules. Adherence means the degree a rule fits within the normative hierarchy of rules about rule-making, or secondary rules, in Hart's influential schema (Hart, 1994). Together, these four characteristics determine 'right process'. Right process, by creating the perception of legitimacy, in turn determines the compliance pull of a rule. Ultimately, the theory claims a chain (or cycle) of causation between right process and state behavior. Legitimacy determines compliance pull, but compliance pull is also the measure of legitimacy. While influential in IL circles, Franck's theory faced criticism from IR scholars: from a rationalist-instrumentalist perspective, the argument is essentially circular (Keohane, 1997: 493).

What distinguishes the legitimacy theory of compliance is its focus on rule-making processes, and the qualities of rules themselves, rather than on rational, strategic interaction. While Franck did not explicitly engage the then-emerging constructivist literature, his argument is quite consistent with many constructivist assumptions and insights. The theory of state behavior embedded in legitimacy theory is non-instrumental: rather than game theory or bureaucratic politics, Franck invokes theories of legal process and obligation. The recurring image is of international society rather than cooperation under anarchy.

Compliance with International Court Decisions

With the end of the Cold War both international and 'supranational' courts and tribunals proliferated (New York University Journal of International Law and Politics Symposium, 1999).[6] Members of the international community created war crimes tribunals for Rwanda and Yugoslavia, negotiated an international criminal court and added a standing Appellate Body and new dispute settlement rules to the World Trade Organization. Implicit in these moves to create new judicial institutions was a belief that legal decisions are distinctive; that law provides a way to engage complex political issues in a more neutral, less overtly power-laden, and perhaps more predictable manner. Some existing judicial bodies also saw their role and power grow in the 1980s and 1990s. One of the most significant and interesting examples was the European Court of Justice (ECJ). This global turn to judicial bodies spawned a wide-ranging literature, with many implications for compliance theory.

In Europe, 1992 marked the completion of the single market in the European Community; the accompanying hoopla refocused attention on the process and mechanisms of European integration. The ECJ, a key player in this process, was credited by some with having 'constitutionalized' the Treaty of Rome and laid the legal foundation for the single market. Legal scholars and judges such as Stein, Weiler and Mancini offered detailed and powerful accounts of how the ECJ had gradually secured compliance with its judgments and created a far more powerful role for itself than the founders of the Community had ever envisaged (Mancini, 1989; Stein, 1981; Weiler, 1991). Political scientists such as Garrett and Weingast, on the other hand, portrayed the ECJ as the relatively docile creature of state interests (Garrett and Weingast, 1993).

Slaughter[7] and Mattli, a lawyer and a political scientist, drew on the legal literature in developing (or reviving) a neofunctionalist account of compliance with supranational judicial decisions. They argued that the ECJ had adroitly built bridges between supra- and sub-national actors, created spillover of various kinds, and exploited its nominally apolitical character to insulate itself from direct political interference. The result was that European governments could not ignore or reject ECJ decisions without countering their own courts and thus opening themselves to charges of flouting the rule of law domestically (Burley and Mattli, 1993). Garrett countered with further evidence of both rational expectation on the part of state actors and apparent acquiescence on the part of the ECJ; the resulting debate extended for several years (Garrett, 1995; Mattli and Slaughter, 1995; Garrett et al., 1998; Mattli and Slaughter, 1998).

The key issue in this debate was the extent to which the ECJ had engineered greater compliance with its decisions relating to the Treaty of Rome and subsidiary Community legislation than the member states either expected or desired. Proponents of this view emphasized domestic linkages as the key causal mechanism in fostering compliance – links between the ECJ and domestic litigants and courts. Scholars such as Weiler, Stone Sweet and Alter developed distinctive variants of this basic explanation, exploring the motives of domestic courts for engaging in such linkages, cross-national variation, and variation among different types and levels of courts in one country (Slaughter et al., 1998a; Volcansek, 1997; Weiler, 1994).[8]

At the same time, the study of compliance with supranational court decisions has extended well beyond Europe to issue-areas such as human rights, trade and the environment. In 1997 Helfer and Slaughter distilled the experience of the ECJ and the European Court of Human Rights in terms of three sets of factors that appear to have contributed to the effectiveness of those two tribunals (Helfer and Slaughter, 1997). A number of legal scholars have applied the 'checklist' developed in this article to other tribunals, such as the Inter-American Court of Human Rights and the NAFTA Commission on Environmental Cooperation (Knox, 2001). Other more general theories of effective supranational adjudication highlight features of institutional design such as judicial independence, access by private litigants, the degree of 'embeddedness' in domestic and transnational society, and the reliance on progressively linked caselaw (Keohane et al., 2001; Schneider, 1998; Stone Sweet, 1999, 2000).

Among international courts other than the ECJ, arguably the most widely studied and influential is that of the GATT/WTO system. The number of disputes before GATT/WTO panels has increased dramatically since the late 1970s, and the creation of the WTO substantially legalized the GATT dispute process. Two leading trade law figures, Jackson and Hudec, have long debated the impact of legalization on compliance with GATT/WTO decisions, prefiguring the broader studies of legalization now under way among IR scholars. Jackson (and many others) insist that the steady shift to more formal rules and processes in GATT dispute resolution, culminating with the WTO provision that panel decisions be automatically binding, has enhanced compliance with those decisions and hence the effectiveness of not only the dispute resolution process but the trade regime as a whole. Hudec, on the other hand, agrees that legalization of the dispute process altered compliance, but challenges the view that further legalization will have any impact (Hudec, 1999).

Whether the WTO has struck the appropriate balance and achieved 'optimal legalization' is now debated by IR and IL scholars alike (Barfield, 2001; Goldstein and Martin, 2001). Part of that equation is the impact of legalization on compliance. As many have noted, non-compliance with WTO rulings is likely to remain a problem so long as the system permits long delays between bringing suit and a final ruling and so long as the compensation that may be authorized is limited to plaintiff's 'damages' rather than defendant's gains. Why, when and how the WTO – and the GATT before it – produces compliance with rulings remain critical questions that have been taken up by many scholars interested in compliance and the role of law; we discuss some of the current research below.

Many readers are likely to draw an immediate and instinctive distinction between compliance with the decisions of international tribunals, whether courts or arbitral panels, and compliance with more general international rules. Differences certainly exist – tribunal decisions are targeted toward specific parties in a specific dispute; the background conditions that ultimately gave rise to some kind of adjudication may suggest that the parties either are particularly likely or particularly unlikely to comply (they may be exhausted or they may have just begun to fight!); the decisions may or may not have wider precedential value. On the other hand, given that compliance with domestic law is often measured in the first instance by a willingness to comply with the decisions of domestic courts, the two types of compliance are clearly deeply related in many ways. They may both be the product of a deeper variable, such as a more general predisposition to uphold the rule of law, or they may reinforce one another. One of the challenges for future compliance research is to sort out some of these similarities and differences.

Theorizing Across the IR–IL Divide

In 1993 Chayes and Chayes published a general theory of compliance in *International Organization* (Chayes and Chayes, 1993). The theory was 'managerial' in that it rejected sanctions and other 'hard' forms of enforcement in favor of collective management of (non)performance. This approach tied together many themes in the IL literature with insights from IR theory. Managerialism begins with the premise that states have a propensity to comply with their international commitments. This propensity stems from three factors. First, because international legal rules are largely endogenous, an assumption of rational behavior predicts that states have an interest in compliance with rules.[9] Second, compliance is efficient from an internal, decisional perspective. Once a complex bureaucracy is directed to comply, explicit calculation of costs and benefits for every decision is itself costly. The agreement may also create a domestic bureaucracy with a vested interest in compliance. Third, extant norms induce a sense of obligation in states to comply with legal undertakings. This sense of obligation, managerialists argue, is empirically self-evident in state behavior, particularly the 'time and energy … [that states devote] to preparing, negotiating, and monitoring treaty obligations' (Chayes and Chayes, 1993: 186–7). Following Henkin, Chayes and Chayes conceive of compliance as a continuum with the appropriate or tolerable level of compliance set through an interactive, sometimes tacit process. The Anti-Ballistic Missile regime, for example, tolerated several installations by the Soviet Union that skirted, if not crossed, the margin of compliance, yet were not fully challenged by the United States. While instances of non-compliance clearly occur, the key managerial claim is that they are generally inadvertent. They result from state incapacity or serious resource constraints; from interpretively contestable treaty provisions, meaning that the commitment itself is ambiguous; or from unavoidable or unanticipated time lags between commitment and performance. For these reasons the managerial model has been dubbed the 'no-fault' theory of compliance.[10]

Prescriptively, Chayes and Chayes's theory of compliance suggests several ways to improve compliance. For example, ambiguity can be reduced through more specific rules (though specificity may come at the price of increased bargaining costs). Agreements can promote compliance by incorporating a transparent information system, with transparency referring to the adequacy, accuracy and availability of information about policies and actions of other states (Finel and Lord, 1999; Mitchell, 1998). Extensive review of performance can create assurance among the parties. Assistance, either technical or financial, can help put non-compliant states back on track. The overall focus should be non-confrontational, forward-looking and facilitative in nature. As Chayes and Chayes note, many of their prescriptions are already common diplomatic practice.[11] But managerialism provides a synthesizing theory that justifies and draws them together into a coherent whole.

'On Compliance' and later *The New Sovereignty* launched an important and heated debate about the sources and significance of compliance at a time when IR and IL theorists were increasingly talking to one another. In a trenchant critique, Downs, Rocke and Barsoom advanced what is sometimes called the political economy or enforcement theory of compliance. This theory emphasizes the strategic dimensions of cooperation, the central role of enforcement, and the endogenous quality of rules and institutions (Downs, 1998; Downs et al., 1996). Of central importance to the political economy approach is the relationship between enforcement

and the nature of regime commitments – specifically, their 'depth'. As regimes deepen, demanding greater changes from the status quo, the gains from cooperation grow. Yet incentives to behave opportunistically – to violate the agreement – also grow. Deeper agreements as a result require correspondingly harsher punishments to deter non-compliance and sustain cooperation.

Thus enforcement theory suggests that much of the evidence of high compliance with international law is merely indicative of the 'shallowness' of many international agreements and should not be generalized to more demanding cases. As Downs, Rocke and Barsoom put it, the empirical findings of the managerial school 'are interesting and important but … its policy inferences are dangerously contaminated by selection problems' (1996: 379–80). In deeper, more demanding cooperative regimes, the domestic interests affected and the costs and benefits involved are more significant, and, they argue, the deepest regimes have in fact used the most extensive enforcement systems. The precise level of enforcement can be understood based on state incentives. In the GATT, as noted, sanctions for non-compliance correspond to the victim's losses, rather than the defector's gains. If enforcement is the key to compliance, Downs and Rocke argue, this provision 'guarantees that [GATT sanctions] will not function as an effective deterrent' (1995: 134). Yet they argue deductively that these weak sanctions make sense when the power of informational uncertainty about domestic demands for non-compliance (in this context, trade protection) is taken into account. If domestic demands for protection were fully known *ex ante*, they could be incorporated into the agreement itself.[12] Instead, moderate sanctions preserve the overall cooperative system while permitting some politically necessary acts of non-compliance.[13] Thus a domestic attribute – uncertainty about domestic demands for non-compliance – helps determine the level of enforcement and hence the observed levels of compliance. The politically optimal regime, in this case, is one with some non-compliance.[14]

The debate between managerialists and enforcement theorists is important and ongoing. It has deep roots; at its heart it reflects a fundamental division about the nature of law that permeates domestic as well as international jurisprudence. Law can be understood as rules and as process; it can be embraced and enforced; it is both an instrument of its makers and an autonomous entity.

Political scientists all too often assume a relatively flat and formal conception of law, at least when contrasted with the complexity and range of lawyers' understandings of law. At the same time, however, political scientists are often less constrained than lawyers in challenging those understandings and demanding empirical evidence. As the management–enforcement debate demonstrates, the clash of different understandings can yield very different policy implications; it also invites onlookers to determine which empirical situations best fit which model. And it yields a very rich agenda for further research.

Norms and Compliance

In the 1990s the rise of constructivist theory dovetailed with work by legal scholars long interested in the normative basis of compliance (Checkel, 1999). Both strands of research built on or reflected earlier treatments of the role of norms and law, in particular the work of the English School scholars, such as Bull (1977), and early constructivists such as Kratochwil (1989) and Ruggie (1975). Much IL scholarship echoes the flavor and ontology of constructivist theory. Franck's legitimacy theory suggested that state behavior is determined not by rational calculation but by normative processes and specifically legitimacy. Even managerial theory stresses the key role of norms of behavior and the social context within which non-compliance is addressed. In these norm-oriented theories enmeshment in a legitimate, iterated, transnational process of legal production and interpretation cabins state behavior *vis-à-vis* international law.

A more recent exemplar of this approach is Koh's theory of 'obedience' with international law. Obedience is rule-induced behavior caused when a party has 'internalized [a] norm and incorporated it into its own value system' (Koh, 1997, 1998: 628). Thus obedience is compliance motivated not by anticipation of enforcement but via the incorporation of rules and norms into domestic legal systems. Incorporation in turn stems from what he terms 'transnational legal process'. This transnational legal process has three sequential components: interaction, interpretation and internalization. States comply with or obey rules because of variations in this process of internalization. Full internalization produces obedience rather than simply compliance.

Ultimately, Koh's definition of obedience conflates the theory's independent and dependent variables – internalization defines obedience but also explains it – limiting the power of the argument. As a result, rather than explaining why and when states follow international rules, Koh instead describes an empirical pathway to obedience – or, more precisely, a pathway to norm incorporation into domestic law – and details the ways in which transnational actors and practices influence this process.

In some cases internalization involves slow acquiescence to an emerging standard governing a coordination problem, as was the case with US adoption of elements of the Law of the Sea Convention. The most theoretically interesting instances of internalization, however, begin with norm entrepreneurs and issue-networks (Keck and Sikkink, 1998; Nadelmann, 1990). These transnational actors require stages upon which to interact – what Koh terms 'law-declaring fora' – and it is in these courts, legislatures and international organizations that an interpretive community develops. Once such a community construes a norm and finds a state in violation, 'a complex process occurs, whereby international legal norms seep into, are internalized, and become embedded in domestic legal and political processes' (Koh, 1996: 205). This argument closely resembles the 'spiral model' of human rights norms developed by Risse, Ropp and Sikkink (1999).

A core implication of Koh's argument is that compliance is driven by the efficacy of domestic law; what creates compliance with an international rule is its transformation into a domestic rule. While this analysis seemingly puts domestic politics and institutions in a central position, Koh argues that the effectiveness of internalization depends primarily on the characteristics of the rule in question, not on domestic attributes of the state in question. As other commentators have noted, doing so downplays a potentially major explanatory variable (Keohane, 1998). And because he does not look at compliance and non-compliance comparatively, Koh cannot say when non-compliance should occur or what the optimal response should be. Yet his analysis has been influential, perhaps because, with its focus on 'obedience' and internalization, it taps into the widespread belief that compliance with legal rules is qualitatively different than compliance with other sorts of rules or standards and cannot be captured through rational choice or strategic analysis.

Our broadly chronological review of the literature through the 1990s reveals a number of vigorous debates and plenty of propositions for empirical testing. It also reveals growing links between the disciplines. Currently, a small but increasing number of legal scholars are drawing on IR paradigms to refine their analyses (Slaughter, forthcoming); IR theorists are looking to IL scholarship for data, hypotheses and empirical insights. From the perspective of IR theory, it may be tempting to discount many of the arguments and analyses put forward by IL scholars on the grounds that they are insufficiently rigorous or methodologically flawed. Lawyers similarly often dismiss much of the IR literature on the grounds that it is impenetrable and largely irrelevant to the pressing practical problems lawyers observe. But both sides risk losing the forest for the trees.

IL scholars are often more creative and insightful in conceptualizing what they experience both as scholars and as working lawyers. They may not test the theories they generate; the theories themselves may also be insufficiently specified. Nevertheless, they generate new ideas, new hypotheses and sharp analyses of what they observe. IR scholars, on the other hand, often seem more focused on working out models than grappling with pressing policy questions – over the short or long term – confronting states in the international system. Yet their ingrained skepticism, insistence on specifying precise causal relationships, and determination to examine as wide a range of cases as possible to avoid generalizing from a very particular set of particulars, challenge IL scholars in productive ways.

COMPONENTS OF COMPLIANCE

The contemporary study of compliance is becoming more self-consciously theoretical and careful as it becomes more interdisciplinary. Some theories of compliance, particularly but not exclusively those developed by lawyers, mix multiple types of variables. The advantage of these approaches is their potential for multicausal synthesis; the disadvantage is the difficulty of disentangling and weighing the relative importance of different variables. Disaggregating compliance theories into their component parts should help sharpen and refine them for empirical testing, not necessarily to exclude or disprove the impact of particular variables but to understand better how they interrelate (Finnemore and Sikkink, 1998: 909–15; Moravcsik, 1997: 541–7).

To clarify the causal basis of many of the theories we have reviewed, we cluster potential explanatory variables under six broad conceptual categories: problem structure; solution structure; solution process; norms; domestic linkages; and international structure. We describe these categories briefly and illustrate them with examples drawn from the theories reviewed above. Although these categories are not mutually exclusive, they provide a template to help situate and compare different theories. They also provide an overview of the breadth of possible influences on compliance as a whole.

Problem Structure

The category of problem structure encompasses strategic interaction and the nature of the underlying substantive problem. At the most basic level, incentives to comply in coordination games differ from those in collaboration games. Similarly, problems that involve small numbers of states may dampen the public goods nature of enforcement efforts and thus enjoy higher levels of compliance than comparable multilateral agreements. Some relevant behaviors are more transparent than others, allowing them to be more easily monitored. The regulatory scope and complexity of the underlying problem can also influence the capacity to comply and hence the likelihood, *ceteris paribus*, of observed compliance. Compliance with the International Whaling Convention, for example, which requires little action by most states, should be higher than compliance with many narcotics agreements, which require pervasive and costly domestic regulation action.

To illustrate, both managerial and enforcement approaches emphasize variables of problem structure, notwithstanding their many differences. They share a common focus on explicit treaty commitments in regulatory arenas marked by collaboration games, domestic–international interactions and complex social learning. Issues such as trade, arms control and environmental protection are marked by the complex nature of the underlying problems, the regulation of diffuse, private actors, and the intersection of pre-existing domestic regulatory regimes and nascent international regimes (Raustiala, 1997). From an enforcement perspective, the nature of the necessary enforcement institution flows from the nature of the problem: the type and degree of cooperation that must be achieved. Managerialists share this emphasis; they simply disagree on the impact of the problem structure. They reason that failures to comply are not due to the depth and severity of the demands imposed and the resulting domestic opposition, but rather to the capacity to comply and different understandings of what compliance requires. They would thus design very different institutions to address these problems.

Solution Structure

Solution structure, closely related to problem structure, comprises the specific institutional design choices of agreement, such as the nature and content of the primary rules of behavior, the employment of punitive measures, or the use of capacity-building programs. These design elements range widely. For example, conduct rules can be more or less specific. The activity that is chosen as the primary focus of regulation can be more or less transparent and hence more or less monitorable (Mitchell, 1998). The choice of rules can raise the costs of compliance or lower them; for example, the choice of tradable pollution permits in the Kyoto Protocol on climate change may lower aggregate compliance costs compared to discrete, non-transferable pollution targets, thereby promoting compliance.

The debate over compliance with ECJ decisions illustrates the intersection of problem structure and solution structure variables. Garrett and his co-authors argue that states faced the problem of how to deepen integration among themselves – a problem of deep cooperation – and deliberately granted power to the ECJ as a pre-commitment mechanism to help them overcome predictable obstacles to achieving their long-term goals. Given the problem structure, the ECJ was an ideal solution due to the tradition of judicial independence and to the likelihood that national courts would enforce ECJ judgments. Mattli, Slaughter, Alter, Stone Sweet, Weiler and others generally agree on the diagnosis of the problem, but would point out that some states were prepared to commit themselves more whole-heartedly than others and that they all expected the ECJ to function more like an international court, without direct means of enforcing its judgments. These authors argue that compliance with EU rules is much more a function of solution structure, but in ways unanticipated by member states. Creating the ECJ, and specific rules allowing national courts to send cases involving EU law to the ECJ for decision, let the ECJ build an independent power base through links to domestic courts and constituencies. It also served to transform many political disputes into legal disputes, thereby harnessing the symbolic and practical impact of legal discourse.

Solution Process

Solution process encompasses the methods by which the cooperative solution is developed, and the qualities of the processes by which the institution operates. The inclusiveness, fairness and perceived legitimacy of the process of creating collective rules may influence the degree that states or other actors accept and internalize those rules. Theories employing process variables of this type are largely found in the legal literature, but these theories often draw upon a societal conception of international relations well developed by the English School.[15]

IL scholars have long emphasized the ways in which the legal discourse created by a treaty and developed within an international institution establishes a common language and shared assumptions that can gradually contribute toward a common interest in resolving problems of compliance (Chayes and Chayes, 1995). This 'construction' of common interests through repeated interaction is the causal mechanism for how legal process affects state behavior. Koh makes this argument explicitly, drawing on constructivist IR literature and focusing on transnational rather than international legal process. States come to *obey* through changes in their perceived interests over time, changes that occur due to enmeshment in a transnational process of legal production and legal interpretation. Legitimacy theory is similar: many of Franck's key variables relate to the process by which the legal rule is developed, and his overarching claim – that compliance stems from the legitimacy derived from 'right process' – is fundamentally a solution process argument. More recent work in IR theory focused on deliberation and argument also reflects, to the degree it engages with compliance issues, solution process variables.[16]

Norms

Under this broad rubric are variables focused on the strength and quality of international norms. The adoption or inculcation of new norms within states may lead to changes in state interests, identity and behavior. Because norms are collective, the role of socialization looms large in many norm-based accounts and hence there is substantial overlap with the previous category of solution process. Constructivists acknowledge that states may comply with norms instrumentally, 'to demonstrate that they have adapted to the social environment' (Finnemore and Sikkink, 1998: 903). But states also operate in part by figuring out, or being socialized toward, the 'right thing' in a particular or general context. In other words, they may follow a logic of appropriateness rather than one of consequences (Finnemore and Sikkink, 1998: 888; March and Olsen, 1998).[17] Socialization is the causal mechanism or pathway through which norms operate; socialization, in turn, results from long-term participation in a norm-governed process. But some norms apparently have more influence than others; they are more likely to be internalized, more likely to trigger justifications in the event of deviation. Why?

For a norm-based theory the answer must lie in the properties of norms themselves: both in their substantive character and in whether they are legalized or not, and to what degree. Mainstream legal analyses argue that the status of a commitment as law implicates norms of obligation flowing from the special role of law as an ordering principle within societies.[18] Emblematic is the statement in a leading legal treatise that 'the fact that the USA has promised *by treaty* to defend the European members of NATO against … attack means that the USA is more likely to honor its promise than it would have been in the absence of a *legally* binding promise …' (Akehurst, 1993: 5, emphasis in original). Non-compliance with legal norms usually entails particular forms of justification. This justificatory discourse can bound the range of possibilities and alter the costs of non-compliance. One can point to seemingly effective non-binding agreements, such as the Helsinki Final Act, to challenge these claims, but the formal or informal nature of international agreements may have different causes and consequences for compliance.[19]

As discussed above, Franck and Koh take norm-based analysis a step further, suggesting that compliance-inducing properties vary even among legal rules. Thus, Franck argues, drawing on his legitimacy theory, that each legal rule or obligation has 'an inherent pull power that is independent of the circumstances in which it is exerted, and that varies from rule to rule' (1988: 712). Similarly, Koh's transnational legal process theory posits that the effectiveness of internalization depends primarily on the characteristics of the norm or rule at stake.

Domestic Linkages

A growing number of compliance theories emphasize structural links between international institutions and domestic actors.[20] This linkage can operate in at least three distinct ways. Some institutions are designed to be enforced through the provision of access to domestic actors who have an incentive to promote enforcement. Second, the operation of the agreement or regime may itself alter the preferences or power of domestic actors, promoting or inhibiting compliance. Third, some theories look beyond individual domestic actors and link the likelihood of establishing such mechanisms and making them work to the political and legal systems of participating states.

Several of the theories reviewed above rely strongly on domestic linkages, as do analyses of different issues in world politics that do not present themselves as theories of compliance but provide relevant insights. Mattli and Slaughter, following Weiler, emphasize both the ability of the ECJ to develop links with national courts and the European lower courts' willingness to interact with the ECJ. Alter has subsequently challenged the uniformity of this willingness, but relies equally on the importance of domestic actors to overall compliance levels (Alter, 1998, 2001). Many scholars also point to the desire and capacity of individual litigants to seek remedies in supranational tribunals and monitor the results. More generally, Koh's entire theory of transnational legal process depends on the incorporation of international obligations into transnational and from thence domestic legal processes. Closing the loop, Helen Milner's work on protectionism in advanced industrial states suggests that international regimes may create changes in the preferences of domestic actors that lead to greater incentives for compliance (Milner, 1988; Moravcsik, 1997). In short, shifts in the preferences of societal actors, whatever the proximate cause, can in turn shift the compliance preferences of governments.

Yet under what conditions are such linkages to domestic actors, with their associated effects, possible? Here theorists must look to a range of domestic factors: political, legal, economic, social and cultural. Mattli and Slaughter argued that an important factor in explaining relative compliance levels between the ECJ and other supranational tribunals is the ability of the ECJ to hook into domestic rule of law traditions. European governments cannot flout the judgments of domestic courts that incorporate an ECJ ruling without risking the subversion of the entire domestic legal system (Alter, 1998: 134). Such opportunities simply do not arise with supranational tribunals exercising jurisdiction over states without a strong domestic rule of law tradition. Helfer and Slaughter generalize these claims to all supranational tribunals, noting further that at least in the human rights context, states with strong domestic legal systems premised on a commitment to the rule of law generate the types of cases that are well-suited for supranational tribunals (Helfer and Slaughter, 1997: 333–4).

An even further step is to posit a more general relationship between domestic regime type or institutions and propensity to comply. Slaughter, following Keohane and Nye, Henkin, and Doyle, argued that legal relations among liberal states are likely to be different than relations among non-liberal states or between liberal states and non-liberal states (Slaughter, 1995).[21] She defined 'liberal states' as states with some form of representative democracy, a market economy based on private property rights, and constitutional protections of civil and political rights (1995: 509).[22] Raustiala and Victor suggest that, at least in environmental cooperation, liberal states appear more likely than illiberal states to create and participate in the structures for regularized monitoring and implementation review that often enhance compliance (Raustiala and Victor, 1998). Checkel, in his study of compliance with European social and legal norms, argues that 'the structure of domestic institutions seems to be key in explaining variance in the mechanisms through which compliance occurs' (2000: 34). Other research has disaggregated the concept of a 'liberal state', measuring democracy separately from 'rule of law systems', defined 'by the willingness of their citizens to employ peaceful means of dispute resolution and by key institutions, such as a strong court system' (Kahler, 2001: 674; Simmons, 2001). Here the results get more complicated. Brown Weiss and Jacobson conclude: 'democratic governments are more likely to do a better job of implementing and complying with international environmental accords than nondemocratic governments ... This generalization does not always hold, however, and democratization does not necessarily lead automatically or quickly to improved compliance' (1998b: 533). Based on a study of the international monetary regime, Simmons doubts 'that democracy itself is a positive influence on the rule of law in international relations. On the contrary, there is more reason to associate compliance with the extent to which the polity in question respects institutional channels for mediating domestic conflict and protecting property rights than with a participatory or competitive political system' (2000b: 599–600). Busch and Reinhardt similarly cast doubt on the propensity of democracies to comply with GATT rulings, arguing that the data indicate that democracies are in fact less likely to comply (Busch and Reinhardt, 2000).

Yet a further distinction should be drawn between the propensity of liberal states to comply with international rules generally versus the decisions of supranational tribunals. Although the experience of the EU, for which liberal democracy is a prerequisite to admission, appears to offer strong evidence of covariance between compliance with domestic judicial decisions and willingness to comply with supranational decisions, the relationship may in fact be inverse in many cases. Moravcsik, for instance, has demonstrated that at least in the context of human rights regimes, liberal states with strong and stable domestic legal systems may be less likely to enter into regimes with strong enforcement mechanisms likely to change domestic law (Helfer and Slaughter, 1997: 332–3; Moravcsik, 2000: 220). The United States has shown only a limited willingness to abide by rulings of the International Court of Justice; similarly, compliance by liberal and/or democratic states with decisions of the WTO Appellate Body has been mixed. Overall, the relationship between liberal democracy and compliance is more complex and less predictable than often assumed.

International Structure

By generally influencing state behavior, systemic or international structural variables may also alter compliance levels and compliance choices. Highly institutionalized systems may create positive spirals of compliance by embedding states in regularized processes of cooperation that are mutually reinforcing (Ikenberry, 1998/9). Bipolarity may increase compliance with rules within alliances while multipolarity may decrease it by inducing shifting balances and creating credible threats of exit. Hegemonic systems may permit a single state to coerce compliance or use its market power to induce compliance. Chayes and Chayes advance a more unconventional structural variable. In their view, the international system itself has become a 'tightly woven fabric of international agreements, organizations, and institutions that shape [states'] relations with each other and penetrate deeply into their internal economics and politics' (Chayes and Chayes, 1995: 26). This transformation goes beyond interdependence, which highlights mutual dependence and vulnerability but which still assumes a baseline of separation, autonomy and defined boundaries. Chayes and Chayes argue instead that fundamental changes in the structure of the international system – from a largely unregulated place to a landscape criss-crossed by regulatory agreements and institutions – have changed the very meaning of sovereignty. Sovereignty is now best conceptualized not as freedom from interference but as 'status', which in turn depends critically on participation in international regimes (Chayes and Chayes, 1995: 27).[23]

How do these structural transformations affect compliance? This 'connection to the rest of the world and the political ability to be an actor in it are more important than any tangible benefits in explaining compliance with international regulatory agreements' (Chayes and Chayes, 1995: 27). The logic here is a constructivist logic of appropriateness, rejecting cost–benefit calculations in favor of far less tangible benefits, closer to the sense of 'we-feeling' that Karl Deutsch identified as a key dimension of security communities (Adler and Barnett, 1998). Nevertheless, the key variable explaining increased compliance is a structural shift.

This structural explanation is likely to be more powerful when combined with the domestic-level variables discussed above. Some states are more likely to seek status through standing in international institutions than others. Studies of newly democratizing countries in Eastern and Central Europe and their willingness to bear remarkable burdens in the hope of becoming a member of NATO and the EU identify both rational calculations about security and economic benefits and constructivist yearnings for political validation of a particular social and historic identity (Checkel, 2000). These debates will have to be resolved empirically. Overall, however, it seems likely that the desire to participate in international institutions, as well as to enter into specific agreements, will vary along all sorts of historic, political and even ethnic lines.

TESTING OLD THEORIES AND GENERATING NEW ONES

The theories of compliance discussed above have proliferated against a backdrop of the rising salience of compliance issues in contemporary international affairs. Interdependence, particularly thick among the OECD states, has led to a panoply of regimes addressing a wide array of issues raised by the deepening economic and social ties among many states. The complexity of these regimes and the powerful political and economic interests influenced by them have made compliance a central concern. Also noteworthy is the remarkable and largely contemporaneous increase in international judicial bodies. Compliance is consequently rising in importance as a field of inquiry. Yet compliance remains a relatively young field. Many core concepts are debated and empirical testing of compliance theories is limited. The lack of systematic, multi-case comparative studies has restricted the nature of the claims and prescriptions that compliance theorists can offer. Brown Weiss and Jacobson have attempted such a venture, with results that require further testing and that demonstrate the difficulty of the task (Brown Weiss and Jacobson, 1998a). Yet notwithstanding their difficulty, empirical case studies help refine theoretical hypotheses and determine the conditions under which particular claims are valid or invalid.

More is needed. Simmons emphasizes the need for careful validation of claims, the identification of baselines against which to measure compliance, and the importance of finding objective ways to measure intersubjective understandings (Simmons, 2000a). Joerges and Zürn are undertaking a major research initiative comparing levels of compliance at the national, European and international levels (Joerges, 2000; Zürn, 2000). In addition, empirical work is proliferating in various areas that do not necessarily focus on compliance, but nevertheless generate important evidence and insights for compliance debates. This section reviews the current literature in four interrelated categories: the role of enforcement, regime design, legalization, and the choice between 'hard' and 'soft' law. All four categories are cutting edge areas for IR/IL scholarship, increasingly conducted by IR and IL scholars working together. Each contains a number of the components of compliance identified above; scholars working in these areas could usefully examine their results in light of this broader overarching framework. Such an effort would be a valuable step toward more cumulative knowledge.

The Role and Importance of Enforcement

A number of recent studies have produced evidence germane to the managerial–enforcement debate. Consistent with the prescriptions of enforcement theory, the reform of the GATT dispute resolution process as part of the creation of the WTO strengthened the enforcement powers of the WTO and the retaliatory powers of member states in tandem with an increase in depth of cooperation. However, recent work by IR scholars, often using statistical analyses of GATT/WTO disputes, indicates a more mixed story about the influence of GATT enforcement that substantially alters and extends the debate. In terms of compliance with GATT dispute decisions, Busch and Reinhardt, building on Hudec's pioneering work, show that total non-compliance with GATT panel rulings approached 30 per cent, and almost 60 per cent of rulings failed to elicit full compliance (Busch, 2000; Busch and Reinhardt, 2000). This low level of compliance does not, however, indicate that the GATT dispute process was ineffective. Rather, the major effect of the dispute process seemed to *precede* the issuance of a ruling (Busch and Reinhardt, 2000; Reinhardt, 2001). The key variables explaining compliance with panel decisions were economic; for example, the more highly dependent a losing defendant was on the plaintiff's export market, the more likely was compliance. More interestingly, contrary to many intuitions about democracy and law, democracies were comparatively *less* likely to comply with GATT rulings (Busch and Reinhardt, 2000).

Ultimately, Busch and Reinhardt's findings suggest, echoing arguments made by others, that a focus on compliance can obscure other important aspects of the role of legal rules. While the role of enforcement structures in promoting compliance appears more nuanced than previously thought, so is the role of compliance management. Many environmental treaties contain implementation and compliance review institutions that broadly follow managerial precepts (Raustiala, 2001a). These review institutions generally include regularized collection of relevant data – often self-reported by governments, reviews of performance, and processes for the adjustment of regime commitments in light of new information (Victor et al., 1998). By creating an ongoing process of performance review, for example, the institutions of the Montreal Protocol – which include an Implementation Committee, a Non-Compliance Procedure, a Multilateral Fund for developing country parties and various expert 'assessment panels' – manage compliance with the complex regulatory requirements. Human rights accords employ similar review systems: the UN Human Rights Committee considers its function to 'assist State parties in fulfilling their obligations under the [International Covenant on Civil and Political Rights], to make available to them the experience the Committee has acquired in its examination of other reports and to discuss with them various issues relating to the enjoyment of rights enshrined' in the Covenant.[24] These review institutions, with their largely non-confrontational and forward-looking approach, engage in the collective supervision and facilitation of performance that lies at the heart of managerial theory.

Yet empirical research into the Montreal Protocol highlights the ways in which actual regimes often combine enforcement with managerial elements – sometimes in informal ways. The Protocol's Non-Compliance Procedure, in which the Implementation Committee meets with non-compliant parties in closed sessions and recommends a compliance plan, has received extensive attention. In practice, part of the power of the Committee to address non-compliance has stemmed from a decision by the Global Environment Facility (GEF), an organization formally external to the Protocol which funds projects related to ozone depletion. In the first cases of non-compliance, involving several Eastern European states and Russia, the GEF was providing funds for the incremental costs of implementing the Protocol (Victor, 1998). The GEF decided to withhold additional funds for those states until their compliance plans were approved by the Implementation Committee. The GEF played no formal role in the content of the plans, but continued disbursement of funds was in practice predicated on a positive 'report card' from the Committee. As Raustiala and Victor argue, this aid conditionality can be interpreted as supporting either managerial or enforcement theory (Raustiala and Victor, 1998). The existence of assistance tied to a discursive process fits with the cooperative, capacity-building thrust of managerialism, while the link between compliance and funding, which in practice has been critical to the success of the procedure, is consistent with enforcement theory.

Positive Theories of Regime Design

For many political scientists, compliance issues are becoming a sub-set of the larger domain of regime design. As Mitchell frames the issue: 'Why do states design regimes the way they do? ... Why do some regimes appear to rely on tough sanctions, others on financial incentives, and others on what appear to be little more than exhortation?' (1999: 1). Mitchell first analyzed regime design in terms of compliance with the intentional oil pollution regime, which governs routine pollution resulting from tanker operations (1994). Two distinct sub-regimes existed, one based on ship equipment standards and one on discharge standards at sea. Compliance with the ship equipment regime has been far higher than with the discharge standard regime. Mitchell attributed this variation to the structure of the treaty provisions, specifically the way in which the equipment sub-regime ensured that actors who had the incentives to comply with and enforce the treaty had the ability and legal authority to do so (Mitchell, 1994: 327).

More recently, Mitchell has explored the sources of regime transparency, arguing that transparency is influenced both by features of an issue area and by the regime information system (Mitchell, 1998). Specifically, 'effectiveness-oriented systems' impose transparency requirements that are usually easier to satisfy than 'compliance-oriented systems' (Mitchell, 1998: 114–15). In a similar vein, Mitchell and Keilbach analyze state responses to a typology of problems, focusing particularly on situations of asymmetric externalities (Mitchell and Keilbach, 2001). They distinguish between problems involving externalities imposed on strong victims versus weak victims. These different situations lead states to choose among three mechanisms to deter non-compliance: issue-specific reciprocity, coercion (linking non-compliant behavior to sanctions) or exchange (linking compliant behavior to rewards).

This latter research is part of a larger collaborative project on regime design. Directed by Koremenos, Lipson and Snidal, the project advances hypotheses about the relationship between distribution problems and enforcement problems, on the one hand, and regime scope, membership and centralization of enforcement mechanisms, on the other (Mitchell and Keilbach, 2001; Koremenos et al., 2001).[25] This kind of research may play an important role in advancing understanding of compliance and its connection to discrete institutional choices. Analyzing multiple cases and controlling for key variables – whether problem structure, solution structure, or others – allows an assessment of the *relative* effectiveness of different strategies.

Legalization

As political scientists discovered and embraced regime theory in the 1980s and 1990s, many international lawyers questioned the value of lumping 'rules, norms, principles and decision-making procedures' together. Some insisted that '[IR] scholars need to be told that international law is different from the other factors they study' (Byers, 1997: 205; Farer, 1991: 196).[26] A growing number of IR theorists are seeking to understand how *legal* rules affect behavior differently from non-legal rules, or, more broadly, from norms. The phenomenon of international 'legalization', however, has a number of definitions. In one formulation, it refers not only to the obligatory status of a rule as part of the system of international law, but also to the rule's relative precision and the delegation of its interpretation and application to a third-party tribunal (Abbott and Snidal, 2000).[27] For other analysts the question involves the 'judicialization' of international affairs as much as 'legalization'.[28] Definitions aside, the core issue of interest is the significance and impact of law and courts in the international system, as compared to less formal and binding prescriptions and dispute resolution mechanisms.

A recent special issue of *International Organization* devoted to legalization poses two general questions: why do governments choose legalized institutions over other forms of institutions, and what are the consequences of legalization? Kahler distills a number of the 'functionalist' reasons typically advanced to explain the choice of legalized rules and a third-party mechanism to interpret and apply them: 'Government commitments are more credible under precise agreements of high obligation; delegated authority to interpret those commitments may also strengthen compliance. Legalization may be particularly important in providing an institutional solution to commitments fulfilled over an extended period of time' (Abbott and Snidal, 2000; Kahler, 2001: 279). From this perspective, the consequences *are* the cause.

The studies in the IO volume yield some interesting preliminary results relevant to questions of compliance. First is the importance of power asymmetries among states establishing a new regime, with power defined not only in terms of material resources but also in terms of relative access to legal resources (Kahler, 2001: 665–6). Asian governments, for instance, have resisted legalization within APEC largely due to the far greater legal resources available to the United States, which give it a substantial advantage in disputes framed in legal rather than diplomatic terms (Kahler, 2001: 665–6). A second finding supports the importance of domestic and transnational actors in enhancing compliance. Many of the authors in the IO volume detail the role of domestic actors in enhancing compliance with legalized regimes, particularly through the formation of 'compliance constituencies'. These can include lawyers, judges and members of the business community. In addition, national politicians may favor legalized agreements to tie their hands in dealing with domestic interest groups whose demands they seek to resist or to bind their successors to policies they favor (Goldstein, 1996: 556–7; Moravcsik, 1997: 225–9).

More constructivist treatments of legalization emphasize the significance, for bureaucrats, litigants and politicians, of engaging in legal discourse and framing disputes as legal issues. In a separate study of the growing role of courts in France, the EU and the WTO, Stone Sweet develops a theory of judicialized governance that depends on the incentives of individuals to bring disputes before a third-party tribunal, the incentive of judges to maintain and maximize their legitimacy, the resulting creation and expansion of law, and the resulting likelihood that still more disputes will be framed in legal terms and brought before a third-party tribunal (Stone Sweet, 1999, 2000). This argument, like that of many others in the legalization debate, stresses the role of the individuals and groups that are constituencies for compliance.

Yet what exactly motivates the formation of a compliance constituency? Is it the material benefits to be gained by actors whose interests are advanced through a particular international agreement? Or is it, as Stone Sweet and Koh would argue, the *process* of engaging domestic actors in ongoing discursive practices of explanation, justification and persuasion framed by both the existence of legal rules and a tribunal to interpret them? Are these two sets of variables interrelated? How can they best be harnessed as a matter of regime design to enhance compliance?

Another core issue concerns the capacity of legalization to trigger resistance to international regimes and hence diminish compliance. A number of scholars argue that legal constraints may prove undesirably tight. Hudec, and Goldstein and Martin, have made this claim regarding the GATT governments' decision to render panel decisions automatically binding under the WTO agreement (Barfield, 2001; Goldstein and Martin, 2001; Hudec, 1999). Similarly, Alter describes ways in which the progressive construction of the EU legal system has resulted in a greater ability for resistant national courts to block compliance with EU law (Alter, 1998, 2001). Stone Sweet concludes that European constitutional courts enjoy social legitimacy due to their ability to draw 'an ever-widening range of actors, public and private', into normative discourse (Stone Sweet, 2000: 149, 152). But the flipside is that social legitimacy is likely to be limited to those actors with the capacity to participate in legal discourse. Those who lack such capacity, as Kahler points out, are likely to resent and resist the expansion of law. At a time of rumbling opposition to 'globalization' and many of the international legal institutions associated with it, compliance research could usefully incorporate a distributional analysis of precisely who is empowered and disempowered by the growing expansion of law and legal discourse.

Soft Law versus Hard Law

In practice, states legalize agreements or institutions in different ways. IL scholars have long noted the existence of 'soft law': instruments or rules that have some indicia of international law but lack explicit and agreed legal bindingness. Soft law is seemingly proliferating, and scholars have begun to explore the relative advantages and disadvantages of hard and soft law and the ways these advantages may explain the choices of states. Much of the debate over soft law among IL scholars, which is too extensive to chronicle here,[29] either addresses the question whether soft law will ultimately undermine the entire international legal system or tries within a doctrinal framework to determine whether soft law is law at all (Dupuy, 1991; Nanda, 1996; Weil, 1983). From an IR perspective, however, the more interesting question concerns the causality of the observed variation, and its significance for behavioral outcomes of interest, such as compliance.

For example, Abbott and Snidal claim that states often 'deliberately choose softer forms of legalization as superior institutional arrangements' (2000: 423).[30] Echoing a number of IL scholars, they argue that different factors condition states' choice of soft law, including transaction costs, uncertainty, implications for national sovereignty, divergence of preferences and power differentials (Abbott and Snidal, 2000: 423). While soft law is less credible than hard law, it provides needed flexibility under conditions of uncertainty. This argument is rationalist and functional in nature. In contrast, Toope offers a constructivist analysis of soft law, using Kratochwil's conception of law as the result of 'a continuing dialogue between norm and fact, and between means (process) and ends (substance)' (2000: 97; Kratochwil, 1989: 181–211). For Toope, the rhetoric of law shapes politics and leads to the emergence of 'common meanings' (Toope, 2000: 97). From common meanings, common values can coalesce that can in turn underpin 'more far-reaching rules of international law' (Toope, 2000: 98). What does such a conception of law mean for soft law? Soft law creates a crucial framework for conversation, in which states in turn may alter their conception of their interests and even identity. Ultimately agreement on harder rules becomes possible. Understanding this continuum is useful to counter 'the professional instinct of lawyers … to negotiate seemingly "binding" agreements as soon as possible' (Toope, 2000: 98). On the contrary, Toope argues, the 'pre-legal or "contextual" regime may actually be more effective in guiding the relations of international actors' (2000: 98).

While these two analyses of soft law differ dramatically, they share the claim that soft law agreements are not just failed treaties but can be a superior institutional choice. Raustiala and Victor link this argument directly to compliance, suggesting that when uncertainty about implementation costs and outcomes is high – as is often the case with complex environmental treaties – concern with compliance systematically leads states to negotiate lower standards, creating agreements that are readily complied with but largely ineffective as prods to behavioral change (Raustiala and Victor, 1998). In other words, *contra* Abbott and Snidal, they argue that uncertainty does not always lead states to choose soft law. In some cases, states opt for legally binding but substantively weak accords instead. In this context soft law agreements may be normatively preferable, because they avoid the detrimental impact of compliance concerns on the relevant legal standards but energize many of the processes that influence state behavior and effectiveness. This analysis also introduces domestic level variables into the hard–soft question: domestic political preferences and governmental responses, rather than purely functional concerns, often account for the choice of hard or soft law (Raustiala, 2001b).

Other studies have looked explicitly at soft law compliance, with many scholars claiming that compliance is very high (Brown Weiss, 1997; Shelton, 2000). While this observation has been taken to demonstrate the utility of soft law agreements, it raises many of the same methodological and theoretical concerns about compliance analysis that legally binding treaties do. High compliance with soft law, as with hard law, can reflect selection bias and/or indicate a shallow rather than a successful regime. Consequently, Raustiala argues that comprehensive analysis of international agreements – whether hard or soft – should distinguish three separate dimensions: the form of the agreement; the substance of the agreement, understood following Downs et al. (1996) as deep or shallow; and the structure for review of performance, whether judicial dispute tribunal or simple self-reporting (Raustiala, 2001b). States, as the architects of regimes, trade these three dimensions off one another. Since each dimension is an endogenous element of regime design, a failure to control for substance or structure can confound efforts to assess compliance – and similarly can confound efforts to understand the choice between hard and soft law.

CONCLUSION AND OPEN QUESTIONS

Research on compliance with international law is gradually coalescing around several basic approaches at the theoretical level, turning to more systematic empirical research to test hypotheses, and engaging an increasing number of IR and IL scholars, often together. It is also generating questions as fast as it is answering them. We conclude by presenting a few of the more central and interesting open questions.

Reconceptualizing the Means of Production of Compliance

Debates about compliance often revolve around alternative means for the production of compliance. Assistance and deterrence – carrots and sticks – dominate. Relatively less explored have been prevention and *ex ante* controls. Prevention refers to the construction of barriers to non-compliance as a part of a regime's solution structure. For example, to prevent the saving and planting of proprietary, patented bio-engineered seeds, Monsanto initially chose not to rely upon farmers' compliance with intellectual property laws or on enforcement mechanisms within domestic jurisdictions. Instead Monsanto developed what is popularly dubbed 'the terminator gene': a gene that causes the next generation of seed to be sterile (Mann, 1999).[31] Non-compliance with intellectual property law – copying – is effectively prevented. Similarly, Mitchell's study of the oil pollution regime illustrates how tankers built with equipment standards were rendered incapable of illegally discharging oil. While the ship-building process was contingent on the behavior of other actors (such as classification societies) the outcome was the permanent prevention of non-compliance by ship operators.[32]

Prevention thus defined is part of a broader class of *ex ante* strategies. Most compliance strategies are *ex post* strategies, relying on the delivery or threat of a sanction in the event of breach. An *ex ante* process promotes compliance by changing internal decision processes or preventing non-compliance. *Ex ante* control strategies have been explored in domestic politics; they could be usefully extended to studies of international compliance (McCubbins et al., 1989).

Primary Rules and Solution Process versus Secondary Rules and Problem Structure

Our review reveals a clear divide between theories focusing on primary rules (solution structure) and solution process and those that emphasize secondary rules and problem structure. Franck and Koh, for instance, each insist on the quality of primary rules (solution structure) and the solution process as central determinants of compliance variation. Legitimacy, rule-making processes and coherence within the structure of existing rules are central threads in their arguments about compliance. Most IR scholars instead stress solution structure largely in terms of secondary rules – rules about non-compliance and enforcement – and emphasize problem structure, a concept that rarely appears in IL treatments. When the quality of primary rules is identified as causally relevant, as in the oil pollution case, it is the mapping of problem structure onto solution structure that is important: the way in which the shift to equipment standards tapped into existing industry practices and avoided the monitoring problems associated with discharge standards (Mitchell, 1994). Similarly, much of the literature on compliance with the decisions of international tribunals emphasizes solution structure not in terms of the process that produces the rules, but rather the design of a dispute resolution process that creates incentives for litigants and national courts to promote the enforcement of treaty provisions (Keohane et al., 2001). The rules governing dispute resolution fall within the category of secondary rules; their power lies not in their pedigree as legal rules so much as in their responsiveness to a problem structure in which states are disinclined to sue one another and domestic constituencies able to stalemate each other in the domestic political process.

This divide is testable. What is required is a research design and careful selection of case studies to highlight variation in primary rules – such as relatively legitimate rules versus less legitimate rules – versus variation in secondary rules and their relationship to problem structure.

Compliance versus Effectiveness

The distinction between compliance and effectiveness has been central to much recent regime research, in particular for environmental regimes. Most studies of effectiveness employ a behavioral definition, looking not to actual changes in a given problem but rather to behavioral changes that are causally linked to the regime. Some relevant research has, as a result, ignored compliance in favor of a focus on effectiveness. Other research has attempted to understand how compliance and effectiveness interact. For example, in his study of the European acid rain regime, Levy argues that non-compliance can be part of a successful regulatory strategy. The early acid rain treaties were not designed to establish binding rules. Rather they acted as 'a normative register, indicating both what behavior was considered legitimate and which countries had accepted such a standard as a guide to national policy' (Levy, 1993: 77). Failure to comply with these normative benchmarks led to increased domestic and international pressure and to a re-evaluation of interests. Weaker standards might have produced higher compliance, but would not have induced this process of normative benchmarking and persuasion. This argument highlights the complexity of the interaction between compliance and effectiveness.

Much of the contemporary debate over compliance revolves around the causes of compliance and issues of regime design. In the end, however, the study of compliance goes beyond these questions, and implicitly examines the foundations of international institutions and of international order. If compliance with international rules is ephemeral, or results purely from the exercise of power and coercion, the ability of international law and institutions to order world politics is greatly limited. Conversely, if compliance is empirically demonstrable, theoretically understandable and prescriptively manageable, then the case for the role of international law and institutions in achieving global order is strong. IR and IL scholars have a joint agenda in compliance research, an issue that now lies at the heart of international relations theory.

Notes

1 One of the byproducts of the increased focus on compliance has been a proliferation of reviews of the compliance literature: Kingsbury, 1998; Koh, 1997; Scott, 1994; Simmons, 1998.

2 Various intellectual histories of the evolution of international law and international relations from 1945 forward can be found in Kennedy, 1999; Koh, 1997; Slaughter Burley, 1993.

3 Henkin recognized that for certain, 'political' accords, meaning accords relating to core security issues, legal process matters much less. (Henkin, [1968] 1979).

4 This is, of course, an oversimplification. Scholars such as John Ruggie and Oran Young, who were already writing about regimes in the 1970s, had never lost sight of international law (Ruggie, 1975; Young, 1979). And 'English School' scholars such as Hedley Bull had continued to emphasize the study of international law as a pillar of international order (Bull, 1977).

5 See Slaughter Burley, 1993: 220.

6 Supranational refers to tribunals that hear cases from individuals as well as states.

7 Formerly Anne-Marie Burley.

8 The volume *The European Court and National Courts – Doctrine and Jurisprudence* includes country studies by European scholars applying a common template to explore issues of compliance with ECJ decisions, as well as a set of cross-cutting analyses placing these compliance issues in a wider context (Slaughter et al., 1998a).

9 This is, of course, highly dependent on the structure of the strategic environment. The essence of the *n*-person prisoners' dilemma is that actors have an interest in collective rules that diverges from their individual incentives.

10 An early version of Downs et al. (1996) used this phrase in the title.

11 For example, Checkel notes that the Council of Europe is very reluctant to impose sanctions on non-compliant states, and has instead sought to use 'a new, non-public monitoring procedure designed not to sanction, but persuade recalcitrant members to move toward compliance' (2000: 32).

12 Downs and Rocke suggest this explains the exceptional treatment of agriculture, textiles and other sensitive areas (Downs and Rocke, 1995).

13 One might term this 'the Goldilocks theory' of compliance – the sanctions are not too strong or too weak, but rather 'just right' under the circumstances.

14 This echoes the theory of efficient breach; a concept within contract theory that breach is efficient – and therefore should be permitted – if the costs of performance to the breaching party are so large that the breach would in theory permit compensation to the aggrieved party yet still leave the breaching party better off than under an enforced performance rule.

15 See, for example, Bull, 1977.

16 See, for example, Checkel, 2000; Risse, 2000.

17 By contrast, 'rationalists' envision states engaging in careful calculations of costs and benefits, following a logic of consequences (Finnemore and Sikkink, 1998). Norms of conduct may influence actors in both ways, even over time: in her study of contractual norms in the diamond industry, Bernstein quotes a dealer stating that 'when I first entered the business, the conception was that truth and trust were simply *the* way to do business, and nobody decent would consider doing it differently. Although many transactions are still consummated on the basis of trust and truthfulness, this is done because these qualities are viewed as good for business, a way to make a profit' (Bernstein, 1992: 157).

18 'There is an influence for law observance in the very quality of law, in the sense of obligation which it implies' (Henkin, [1968] 1979: 60). Of course, this statement can be seen as merely restating the issue: law is followed because law is obligatory.

19 Analyses of variation in form include Abbott and Snidal, 2000; Hillgenberg, 1999; Lipson, 1991; Raustiala, 2001b.

20 Liberal theories focus on variation in the preferences of individuals and groups in domestic and transnational society as well as variation in their representation by domestic government institutions. Liberal theories of compliance,

like all Liberal theories, are more likely to start from the ground up, emphasizing the conditions necessary for some states to be more likely to comply than others or some institutions to be more embedded than others. Institutionalist theories can point to the importance of embedding international institutions in domestic society without focusing on variation in the relative ease or likelihood of embeddedness.

21 See also Doyle, 1983a. Henkin suggests that this may be so because the liberal democracies of the West, the creators of most extant international law, created it in their own image and interest (1979: 3).

22 See also Keohane and Nye, 1977.

23 Sovereignty as status is old as well as new; see Gong, 1984.

24 Work of the Human Rights Committee Under Article 40 of the Covenant on Civil and Political Rights, UN GAOR, Human Rights Committee, UN Doc A/48/40 (1993).

25 For an explication of the overall design of the project and the hypotheses advanced by the editors and tested by the various authors, see Koremenos et al., 2001.

26 In addition to the various political scientists and international lawyers engaged in the legislation debate, see Arend, 1998.

27 Compare Alec Stone Sweet's definition of legal norms as a 'sub-set of social norms', a sub-set 'distinguished by their higher degree of clarity, formalization, and binding authority' (Stone Sweet, 2000: 11).

28 Stone Sweet is the most prominent scholar studying the 'judicialization' of politics, both within specific countries, across countries and in the international realm (Stone Sweet, 1992, 1999, 2000).

29 See, for example, Cassese and Weiler, 1988; Dupuy, 1991; Schachter, 1977; Shelton, 2000.

30 As Abbott and Snidal acknowledge, they are building here on the pioneering work of Charles Lipson. Lipson's work presaged the current debate by almost a decade (Lipson, 1991).

31 Monsanto has since withdrawn the planned terminator technology.

32 See also Lessig, 1995.

Bibliography

Abbott, Kenneth W. (1989) 'Modern International Relations Theory: A Prospectus for International Lawyers', *Yale Journal of International Law*, 14 (2): 335–411.

Abbott, Kenneth W. and Snidal, Duncan (2000) 'Hard and Soft Law in International Governance', *International Organization*, 54 (3): 421–56.

Abbott, Kenneth W. and Snidal, Duncan (2001) 'Hard and Soft Law in International Governance', in Judith L. Goldstein, Miles Kahler, Robert O. Keohane and Anne-Marie Slaughter (eds), *Legalization and World Politics*. Cambridge, MA: MIT Press. pp. 37–72.

Adler, Emanuel and Barnett, Michael (eds) (1998) *Security Communities*. Cambridge: Cambridge University Press.

Akehurst, Michael (1993) *A Modern Introduction to International Law*, 6th edn. New York: Routledge.

Alter, Karen J. (1998) 'Who are the Masters of the Treaty? European Governments and the European Court of Justice', *International Organization*, 52 (1): 121–47.

Alter, Karen J. (2001) 'The European Union's Legal System and Domestic Policy: Spillover or Backlash?', in Judith L. Goldstein, Miles Kahler, Robert O. Keohane and Anne-Marie Slaughter (eds), *Legalization and World Politics*. Cambridge, MA: MIT Press. pp. 105–34.

Arend, Anthony Clark (1998) 'Do Legal Rules Matter? International Law and International Politics', *Virginia Journal of International Law*, 38 (2): 107–53.

Barfield, Claude (2001) *Free Trade, Sovereignty, Democracy: The Future of the WTO*. Washington DC: AEI Press.

Bernstein, Lisa (1992) 'Opting Out of the Legal System', *Journal of Legal Studies*, 21 (1): 115–57.

Brown Weiss, Edith (ed.) (1997) *International Compliance with Nonbinding Accords*. Washington, DC: American Society of International Law.

Brown Weiss, Edith and Jacobson, Harold K. (1998a) *Engaging Countries: Strengthening Compliance with International Accords*. Cambridge, MA: MIT Press.

Brown Weiss, Edith and Jacobson, Harold K. (1998b) 'Assessing the Record and Designing Strategies to Engage Countries', in Edith Brown Weiss and Harold K. Jacobson, *Engaging Countries: Strengthening Compliance with International Accords*. Cambridge, MA: MIT Press. pp. 511–54.

Bull, Hedley (1977) *The Anarchical Society*. New York: Columbia University Press.

Burley, Anne-Marie and Mattli, Walter (1993) 'Europe Before the Court: A Political Theory of Legal Integration', *International Organization*, 47 (1): 41–76.

Busch, Marc (2000) 'Democracy, Consultation, and the Paneling of Disputes Under GATT', *Journal of Conflict Resolution*, 44 (4): 425–46.

Busch, Marc and Reinhardt, Eric (2000) 'Testing International Trade Law: Empirical Studies of GATT/WTO Dispute Settlement', unpublished manuscript.

Byers, Michael (1997) 'Taking the Law out of International Law: A Critique of the "Iterative Perspective"', *Harvard International Law Journal*, 38 (1): 201–5.

Byers, Michael (ed.) (2000) *The Role of Law in International Politics: Essays in International Relations and International Law*. Oxford: Oxford University Press.

Cassese, Antonio and Weiler, Joseph H.H. (eds) (1988) *Change and Stability in International Law-Making*. New York: De Gruyter.

Chayes, Abram and Chayes, Antonia Handler (1993) 'On Compliance', *International Organization*, 47 (2): 175–205.

Chayes, Abram and Chayes, Antonia Handler (1995) *The New Sovereignty: Compliance with International Regulatory Agreements*. Cambridge, MA: Harvard University Press.

Checkel, Jeffrey T. (1999) 'Why Comply? Constructivism, Social Norms, and the Study of International Institutions', ARENA Working Paper, 99/24.

Checkel, Jeffrey T. (2000) 'Compliance and Domestic Institutions', paper presented at the 2000 Annual Meeting of the American Political Science Association Annual Convention, Washington, DC.

Downs, George W. (1998) 'Enforcement and the Evolution of Cooperation', *Michigan Journal of International Law*, 19 (2): 319–44.

Downs, George W. and Rocke, David M. (1995) *Optimal Imperfection? Domestic Uncertainty and Institutions in International Relations*. Princeton: Princeton University Press.

Downs, George W., Rocke, David and Barsoom, Peter (1996) 'Is the Good News about Compliance Good News about Cooperation', *International Organization*, 50 (3): 379–406.

Doyle, Michael W. (1983a) 'Kant, Liberal Legacies, and Foreign Affairs, Part 1', *Philosophy and Public Affairs*, 12 (4): 205–35.

Doyle, Michael W. (1983b) 'Kant, Liberal Legacies, and Foreign Affairs, Part 2', *Philosophy and Public Affairs*, 12 (4): 323–53.

Dupuy, Pierre-Marie (1991) 'Soft Law and the International Law of the Environment', *Michigan Journal of International Law*, 12 (2): 420–35.

Falk, Richard A. (1968) 'The Relevance of Political Context to the Nature and Functioning of International Law: An Intermediate View', in Karl W. Deutsch and Stanley Hoffmann (eds), *The Relevance of International Law: Essays in Honor of Leo Gross*. Cambridge, MA: Schenkman. pp. 133–52.

Farer, Tom J. (1991) 'An Inquiry into the Legitimacy of Humanitarian Intervention', in Lori Fisler Damrosch and David J. Scheffer (eds), *Law and Force in the New International Order*. Boulder: Westview. pp. 185–201.

Finel, Bernard I. and Lord, Kristen M. (1999) 'The Surprising Logic of Transparency', *International Studies Quarterly*, 43 (2): 315–39.

Finnemore, Martha and Sikkink, Kathryn (1998) 'International Norm Dynamics and Political Change', *International Organization*, 52 (4): 887–917.

Fisher, Roger (1981) *Improving Compliance with International Law*. Charlottesville: University Press of Virginia.

Franck, Thomas M. (1988) 'Legitimacy in the International System', *American Journal of International Law*, 82 (4): 705–59.

Franck, Thomas M. (1990) *The Power of Legitimacy Among Nations*. New York: Oxford University Press.

Franck, Thomas M. (1992) 'Principles of Fairness in International Law', paper presented at the Annual Meeting of American Political Science Association, Chicago.

Garrett, Geoffrey (1995) 'The Politics of Legal Integration in the European Union', *International Organization*, 49 (1): 171–81.

Garrett, Geoffrey and Weingast, Barry R. (1993) 'Ideas, Interests, and Institutions: Constructing the European Community's Internal Market', in Judith Goldstein and Robert O. Keohane (eds), *Ideas in Foreign Policy: Beliefs, Institutions, and Political Change*. Ithaca: Cornell University Press. pp. 173–206.

Garrett, Geoffrey, Kelemen, R. Daniel and Schulz, Heiner (1998) 'The European Court of Justice, National Governments, and Legal Integration in the European Union', *International Organization*, 52 (1): 149–76.

Goldstein, Judith (1996) 'International Law and Domestic Institutions: Reconciling North American "Unfair" Trade Laws', *International Organization*, 50 (4): 541–64.

Goldstein, Judith L. and Martin, Lisa L. (2001) 'Legalization, Trade Liberalization, and Domestic Politics: A Cautionary Note', in Judith L. Goldstein, Miles Kahler, Robert O. Keohane and Anne-Marie Slaughter (eds), *Legalization and World Politics*. Cambridge, MA: MIT Press. pp. 219–48.

Goldstein, Judith L., Kahler, Miles, Keohane, Robert O. and Slaughter, Anne-Marie (eds) (2001) *Legalization and World Politics*. Cambridge, MA: MIT Press.

Gong, Gerrit W. (1984) *The Standard of 'Civilization' in International Society*. Oxford: Clarendon Press.

Hart, H.L.A. (1994) *The Concept of Law*, 2nd edn. Oxford: Clarendon Press.

Hasenclever, Andreas, Mayer, Peter and Rittberger, Volker (1997) *Theories of International Regimes*. Cambridge: Cambridge University Press.

Helfer, Laurence R. and Slaughter, Anne-Marie (1997) 'Toward a Theory of Effective Supranational Adjudication', *Yale Law Journal*, 107 (2): 273–391.

Henkin, Louis ([1968] 1979) *How Nations Behave*, 2nd edn. New York: Columbia University Press.

Hillgenberg, Hartmut (1999) 'A Fresh Look at Soft Law', *European Journal of International Law*, 10 (3): 499–515.

Hudec, Robert E. (1992) 'The Judicialization of GATT Dispute Settlement', in Michael M. Hart and Debra P. Steger (eds), *In Whose Interest? Due Process and Transparency in International Trade*. Ottawa: Center for Trade Policy and Law. pp. 9–43.

Hudec, Robert E. (1999) 'The New WTO Dispute Settlement Procedure: An Overview of the First Three Years', *Minnesota Journal of Global Trade*, 8 (1): 1–53.

Ikenberry, G. John (1998/9) 'Institutions, Strategic Restraint, and the Persistence of the American Postwar Order', *International Security*, 23 (3): 43–78.

Joerges, Christian (2000) 'Compliance Research in Legal Perspective', paper presented at 'Comparing Compliance at the National, European and International Levels', European University Institute, Florence.

Kahler, Miles (2001) 'Conclusion: The Causes and Consequences of Legalization', in Judith L. Goldstein, Miles Kahler, Robert O. Keohane and Anne-Marie Slaughter (eds), *Legalization and World Politics*. Cambridge, MA: MIT Press. pp. 277–99.

Keck, Margaret E. and Sikkink, Kathryn (1998) *Activists Beyond Borders: Advocacy Networks in International Politics*. Ithaca: Cornell University Press.

Kennedy, David (1999) 'The Disciplines of International Law and Policy', *Leiden Journal of International Law*, 12 (1): 9–133.

Keohane, Robert O. (1988) 'International Institutions: Two Approaches', *International Studies Quarterly*, 32: 379–96.

Keohane, Robert O. (1989) *International Institutions and State Power: Essays in International Relations Theory*. Boulder: Westview.

Keohane, Robert O. (1997) 'International Relations and International Law: Two Optics', *Harvard Journal of International Law*, 38 (2): 487–502.

Keohane, Robert O. (1998) 'When Does International Law Come Home?', *Houston Law Review*, 35 (3): 699–713.

Keohane, Robert O. and Nye, Joseph S., Jr (1977) *Power and Interdependence: World Politics in Transition*. Boston: Little, Brown.

Keohane, Robert O., Haas, Peter M. and Levy, Marc A. (1993) 'The Effectiveness of International Environmental Institutions', in Peter M. Haas, Robert O. Keohane and Marc A. Levy (eds), *Institutions for the Earth: Sources of Effective International Environmental Protection*. Cambridge, MA: MIT Press. pp. 3–24.

Keohane, Robert O., Moravcsik, Andrew and Slaughter, Anne-Marie (2001) 'Legalized Dispute Resolution: Interstate and Transnational', in Judith L. Goldstein, Miles Kahler, Robert O. Keohane and Anne-Marie Slaughter (eds), *Legalization and World Politics*. Cambridge, MA: MIT Press. pp. 73–104.

Kingsbury, Benedict (1998) 'The Concept of Compliance as a Function of Competing Conceptions of International Law', *Michigan Journal of International Law*, 19 (2): 345–72.

Knox, John H. (2001) 'A New Approach to Compliance with International Environmental Law: The Submissions Procedure of the NAFTA Environmental Commission', *Ecology Law Quarterly*, 28: 1.

Koh, Harold H. (1996) 'Transnational Legal Process', *Nebraska Law Review*, 75: 181–207.

Koh, Harold H. (1997) 'Why Do Nations Obey International Law?', *Yale Law Journal*, 106: 2598–659.

Koh, Harold H. (1998) 'Bringing International Law Home', *Houston Law Review*, 35 (3): 623–82.

Koremenos, Barbara, Lipson, Charles and Snidal, Duncan (eds) (2001) 'Introduction' *Rational Design: Explaining the Form of International Institutions'*, Special Issue of *International Organization*, 54 (4).

Kratochwil, Friedrich V. (1989) *Rules, Norms, and Decisions on the Conditions of Practical and Legal Reasoning in International Relations and Domestic Affairs*. Cambridge: Cambridge University Press.

Lessig, Lawrence (1995) 'The Regulation of Social Meaning', *University of Chicago Law Review*, 62 (3): 968–73.

Levy, Marc A. (1993) 'European Acid Rain: The Power of Tote-Board Diplomacy', in Peter M. Haas, Robert O. Keohane and Marc A. Levy, *Institutions for the Earth: Sources of Effective International Environmental Protection*. Cambridge, MA: MIT Press. pp. 75–132.

Lipson, Charles (1991) 'Why Are Some Agreements Informal?', *International Organization*, 45 (4): 495–538.

Mancini, G. Frederico (1989) 'The Making of a Constitution for Europe', *Common Market Law Review*, 26: 595–614.

Mann, Charles (1999) 'Biotech Goes Wild', *Technology Review*, July/August: 36–43.

March, James G. and Olsen, Johan P. (1998) 'The Institutional Dynamics of International Political Orders', *International Organization*, 52 (4): 943–69.

Mattli, Walter and Slaughter, Anne-Marie (1995) 'Law and Politics in the European Union: A Reply to Garrett', *International Organization*, 49 (1): 183–90.

Mattli, Walter and Slaughter, Anne-Marie (1998) 'Revisiting the European Court of Justice', *International Organization*, 52 (1): 177–209.

McCubbins, Mathew D., Noll, Roger G. and Weingast, Barry R. (1989) 'Structure and Process, Politics and Policy: Administrative Arrangements and the Political Control of Agencies', *Virginia Law Review*, 75: 431–82.

Milner, Helen (1988) *Resisting Protectionism: Global Industries and the Politics of International Trade*. Princeton: Princeton University Press.

Mitchell, Ronald B. (1994) *Intentional Oil Pollution at Sea: Environmental Policy and Treaty Compliance*. Cambridge, MA: MIT Press.

Mitchell, Ronald B. (1998) 'Sources of Transparency: Information Systems in International Regimes', *International Studies Quarterly*, 42 (1): 109–30.

Mitchell, Ronald B. (1999) 'Situation Structure and Regime Implementation Mechanisms', paper presented at the American Political Science Association Conference, Atlanta, GA.

Mitchell, Ronald B. and Keilbach, Patricia M. (2001) 'Situation Structure and Institutional Design: Reciprocity, Coercion and Exchange', *Rational Design: Explaining the Form of Institutional Organization*. Special Issue of *International Organization*, 55 (4).

Moravcsik, Andrew (1997) 'Taking Preferences Seriously: A Liberal Theory of International Politics', *International Organization*, 51 (4): 513–53.

Moravcsik, Andrew (2000) 'The Origins of Human Rights Regimes: Democratic Delegation in Postwar Europe', *International Organization*, 54 (2): 217–52.

Nadelmann, Ethan A. (1990) 'Global Prohibition Regimes: The Evolution of Norms in International Society', *International Organization*, 44 (4): 479–526.

Nanda, Ved P. (1996) 'Development as an Emerging Human Right under International Law', *Denver Journal of International Law and Policy*, 13 (2–3): 161–79.

New York University Journal of International Law and Politics (1999) 'Symposium: The Proliferation of International Tribunals: Piecing Together the Puzzle', *New York University Journal of International Law and Politics*, 31 (4): 679–933.

Raustiala, Kal (1997) 'Domestic Institutions and International Regulatory Cooperation: Comparative Responses to the Global Biodiversity Regime', *World Politics*, 49 (4): 482–509.

Raustiala, Kal (2000) 'Compliance and Effectiveness in International Regulatory Cooperation', *Case Western Reserve Journal of International Law*, 32: 387–440.

Raustiala, Kal (2001a) *Review Institutions in Ten MEAs*. UN Environment Programme.

Raustiala, Kal (2001b) 'Form and Substance in International Agreements', work in progress.

Raustiala, Kal and Victor, David G. (1998) 'Conclusions', in David G. Victor, Kal Raustiala and Eugene B. Skolnikoff (eds), *The Implementation and Effectiveness of International Environmental Commitments*. Cambridge, MA: MIT Press. pp. 659–707.

Reinhardt, Eric (2001) 'Adjudication without Enforcement in GATT Disputes', *Journal of Conflict Resolution*.

Risse, Thomas (2000) '"Let's Argue!": Communicative Action in World Politics', *International Organization*, 54 (1): 1–39.

Risse, Thomas, Ropp, Stephen C. and Sikkink, Kathryn (1999) *The Power of Human Rights: International Norms and Domestic Change*. Cambridge: Cambridge University Press.

Rittberger, Volker (1993) *Regime Theory and International Relations*. Oxford: Clarendon Press.

Ruggie, John Gerard (1975) 'International Responses to Technology: Concepts and Trends', *International Organization*, 29 (3): 557–84.

Schachter, Oscar (1977) 'The Twilight Existence of Nonbinding International Agreements', *American Journal of International Law*, 71: 296–304.

Schneider, Andrea K. (1998) 'Democracy and Dispute Resolution in the Free Trade Area of the Americas: An Essay in Trade Governance', *University of Pennsylvania Journal of International Economic Law*, 19 (2): 587–638.

Schneider, Andrea Kupfer (1999) 'Getting Along: The Evolution of Dispute Resolution Regimes in International Trade Organizations', *Michigan Journal of International Law*, 20 (4): 697–773.

Scott, Shirley V. (1994) 'International Law as Ideology: Theorizing the Relation between International Law and International Politics', *European Journal of International Law*, 5 (3): 313–25.

Shelton, Dinah (ed.) (2000) *Commitment and Compliance: The Role of Non-Binding Norms in the International Legal System*. Oxford: Oxford University Press.

Simmons, Beth A. (1998) 'Compliance with International Agreements', in Nelson W. Polsby (ed.), *Annual Review of Political Science*, vol. 1. Palo Alto: Annual Reviews. pp. 75–94.

Simmons, Beth A. (2000a) 'Compliance in International Relations', paper presented at the 2000 Annual Meeting of the American Political Science Association, Washington, DC.

Simmons, Beth A. (2000b) 'The Legalization of International Monetary Affairs', *International Organization*, 54 (3): 573–602.

Simmons, Beth A. (2001) 'The Legalization of International Monetary Affairs', in Judith L. Goldstein, Miles Kahler, Robert O. Keohane and Anne-Marie Slaughter (eds), *Legalization and World Politics*. Cambridge, MA: MIT Press. pp. 189–218.

Slaughter, Anne-Marie (1995) 'International Law in a World of Liberal States', *European Journal of International Law*, 6 (4): 503–38.

Slaughter, Anne-Marie (forthcoming) 'International Law and International Relations', *Recueil des Cours*, Hague Academy of International Law.

Slaughter, Anne-Marie, Stone Sweet, Alec and Weiler, Joseph H.H. (eds) (1998a) *The European Court and National Courts – Doctrine and Jurisprudence: Legal Change in Its Social Context*. Oxford: Hart Publishing.

Slaughter, Anne-Marie, Tulumello, Andrew S. and Wood, Stephan (1998b) 'International Law and International Relations Theory: A New Generation of Interdisciplinary Scholarship', *American Journal of International Law*, 92 (3): 367–97.

Slaughter Burley, Anne-Marie (1993) 'International Law and International Relations Theory: A Dual Agenda', *American Journal of International Law*, 87 (2): 205–39.

Stein, Eric (1981) 'Lawyers, Judges, and the Making of a Transnational Constitution', *American Journal of International Law*, 75 (1): 1–27.

Stone Sweet, Alec (1992) *The Birth of Judicial Politics in France: The Constitutional Council in Comparative Perspective*. New York: Oxford University Press.

Stone Sweet, Alec (1999) 'Judicialization and the Construction of Governance', *Comparative Political Studies,* 32 (2): 147–84.

Stone Sweet, Alec (2000) *Governing with Judges: Constitutional Politics in Europe*. Oxford: Oxford University Press.

Toope, Stephen J. (2000) 'Emerging Patterns of Governance and International Law', in Michael Byers (ed.), *The Role of Law in International Politics: Essays in International Relations and International Law*. Oxford: Oxford University Press. pp. 91–108.

Victor, David (1998) 'The Operation and Effectiveness of the Montreal Protocol's Non-Compliance Procedure', in David G. Victor, Kal Raustiala and Eugene B. Skolnikoff (eds), *The Implementation and Effectiveness of International Environmental Commitments*. Cambridge, MA: MIT Press. pp. 137–76.

Victor, David G., Raustiala, Kal and Skolnikoff, Eugene B. (1998) 'Introduction and Overview', in David G. Victor, Kal Raustiala and Eugene B. Skolnikoff (eds), *The Implementation and Effectiveness of International Environmental Commitments*. Cambridge, MA: MIT Press. pp. 1–46.

Volcansek, Mary L. (ed.) (1997) *Law Above Nations: Supranational Courts and the Legalization of Politics*. Gainesville, FL: University Press of Florida.

Weil, Prosper (1983) 'Towards Relative Normativity in International Law?', *American Journal of International Law*, 77 (3): 413–42.

Weiler, J.H.H. (1991) *The Transformation of Europe*. New Haven: Yale Law Journal Co.

Weiler, J.H.H. (1994) 'A Quiet Revolution: The European Court of Justice and Its Interlocutors', *Comparative Political Studies*, 26 (4): 510–34.

Young, Oran R. (1979) *Compliance and Public Authority: A Theory with International Applications*. Baltimore: Johns Hopkins University Press.

Young, Oran R. (1994) *International Governance: Protecting the Environment in a Stateless Society*. Ithaca: Cornell University Press.

Zürn, Michael (2000) 'Law and Compliance at Different Levels', paper presented at 'Comparing Compliance at the National, European and International Levels', European University Institute, Florence.

Index

The following abbreviations have been used in the index:
IR International Relations
NGO non-governmental organization

Abbott, K.W., 551
absolutist state, 158–9
academic field of study, IR as, 5–6, 8, 27
actors (*see also* agency, non-state actors; states, as
    actors; transnational actors): aggregate, 75, 82; consti-
    tution of subjectivity, 65–7; endogenous/exogenous,
    54, 62–7, 84–5; preference formation, 62–5; primacy
    of, 339; and social structures, 335, 344
adjudication, 394, 405n
Adler, E. 99, 104, 131
Africa, states in, 160, 161
African Human Rights Court, 528
agency, 57, 61, 62, 120, 126, 144; constructivism and,
    54, 102, 104–6, 107–8; in environmental politics, 500,
    503, 509–10; and foreign policy analysis, 337–9; and
    interdependence, 240–1
agency-structure problem, 24, 54, 104–6; in foreign
    policy analysis, 343, 344; and security dilemma, 379
agenda setting, 265, 502
Aggarwal, V., 199, 432
aggregation, 82, 85, 223
Alker, H., 99
alliances, 370, 371–2
Allison, G.T., 316–17, 334, 337, 338
Alter, K.J., 551
Amnesty International, 261, 522
analytic narratives, 81–2
anarchy, 9, 12, 309, 353, 486–7, 501; and security
    cooperation, 371, 373, 374, 383
Anderson, B., 131, 301, 410
Anderson, P., 158
Andrews, D., 438, 439
Angell, N., 27, 164, 356
Angell, R., 241
Anti-Ballistic Missile regime, 543
anti-foundationalism, 15–16
APEC (Asia Pacific Economic Cooperation), 481, 484,
    492, 551
arbitration, 394, 405n
ASEAN (Association of Southeast Asian Nations),
    304, 371, 484
attribution theory, 338
authoritarianism, 317, 318, 319; and human rights, 528

authority, 162, 167, 168–9, 171; competing claims,
    169–70, 171; in economic affairs, 433, 442
autonomy, 242–4, 343
Axelrod, R., 124, 126, 218

Baden, S., 279
balance of power, 158, 159, 414; asymmetry in, 396,
    403, 404; theories, 178, 182, 353, 354–5
balances of capabilities, 371, 372, 400–1
Bank for International Settlements, 431
bargaining, 218, 227, 506, 507; in mediation, 392, 395,
    396–7, 397–8, 400, 404–5; and negotiation, 217–19;
    and problem-solving, 218
Barnett, M., 104, 131–2
Barry, B., 140
Barston, R.P., 216
Barth, F., 413
Bates, M., 464, 473, 474
Bates, R., 81
BATNA (Best Alternative to a Negotiated Agreement),
    224
Bauer, R., 310, 451
Becker, G.S., 84
behavioralism, 7, 9, 10, 28–31; in foreign policy, 333;
    and scientism, 11, 13–15
Beitz, C., 139
belief systems, 293, 294, 340, 438
beliefs, 63, 66, 75, 343; desire and, 120, 122
Bercovitch, J., 395, 397, 403
Berger, P., 97, 489
Bernhard, W., 440
Bhaskar, R., 36
bias, 294, 295, 296–7
bipolarity, 336, 361, 455, 458, 487, 548
Blainey, G., 395
Boserup, E., 279
Bosnia, *see* former Yugoslavia
Boucher, D., 7, 138
Boulding, K., 123
boundaries, 161, 172; hard/soft, 164, 165, 166
Braidotti, R., 279–80
Brecher, M., 123, 333
Bretton Woods system, 430–1
Breuilly, J., 131
Brooks, R.A., 315
Brown Weiss, E., 510, 547, 548
Broz, L., 441

Brubaker, R., 410
Bryant, R., 438
Bueno de Mesquita, B., 360
Bukovansky, M., 159
Bull, H., 3–4, 11, 30, 142, 148, 197
Bunce, V., 420
bureaucratic enmeshment, 145–6
bureaucratic politics, 333, 334, 338–9
Burguieres, M., 286
Burton, J., 11, 397–8
Busch, M., 394, 453, 454, 547, 549
Bush, George, 294, 295
Butterfield, H., 8, 28
Buzan, B., 14, 100, 369

Cameron, D., 456, 468
Camp Keith, L., 529
Campbell, D., 34, 37, 40, 99, 381
Canada, 299
capabilities: balance of, 371, 372, 400–1; military, 372;
    ranking, 182–3
capital controls, 438, 440, 441
capital mobility, 437, 438, 439–43
Capital Mobility hypothesis, 439–40, 441
Caporaso, J., 465, 466–7
Caprioli, M., 286
Cardoso, F.H., 452, 465, 466, 467
Carlsnaes, W., 100, 105, 106
Carr, E.H., 144
causation (see also explanations, causal), 37–8, 75–6,
    132, 341, 343; constructivism and, 101, 106–7;
    relation of norms to, 144–5
Cederman, L.E., 126, 159
Cerny, P., 438, 441, 442
Chayes, A. & A.H., 142, 511, 542, 543, 548
Chechnya, 160
Checkel, J., 108, 198, 489, 547
Chemical Weapons Convention, 379, 384
Chin, C., 282
China, People's Republic of, and human rights, 527, 532
choice, psychological explanations, 292, 293–8, 302, 303
civil society, 319; global, 146, 260
civil wars, 321, 351, 395
civilizations, 160; clash of, 148–9, 414
Clapham, C., 149
Clausewitz, C. von, 350
Cobden, R., 182
coercive diplomacy, 213
cognitive consistency, 338
cognitive dissonance, 338
cognitive factors, in explanation of foreign policy
    actions, 333, 334, 337–8, 340
cognitive interest debate, 107
cognitive mapping, 338
cognitive psychology, 110, 124, 125, 302–3; and
    collective choice, 297–8; and individual choice, 293
Cohen, B.C., 332
Cohen, B.J., 429, 435, 443
Cohen, R., 221
Cohn, C., 283

Cold War, 64, 160, 163, 336; and development, 463,
    464; end of, 98, 258, 275, 487; and trade policy, 455
collaboration, 196, 437, 504, 545
collective identity, 245, 298–302
commitments, 224
communication, 213–14, 221, 226–7, 374–5, 382, 398;
    intercultural, 219–20
communicative action, 102, 341
communicative rationality, 102–3, 110
comparative foreign policy analysis, 333, 342
compensation hypothesis, 474
complexity theory, 110–11, 295
compliance, 86, 200, 265, 297; with environmental
    policies, 504, 505, 508, 510–11, 549; in human rights,
    529–32; with international law, 538–53
Comte, A., 29
conflict (see also ethnic conflict), 227; psychological
    explanations, 292–304
conflict resolution, 392–4; mediation and, 394–405;
    psychology and, 301–2
constellations, 382
constitution, 106–7
constitutive theory, 38, 101, 130
constructivism, 16, 95, 98–100, 109–11, 302; added
    value, 101–3; and agency, 54, 102, 104–6, 107–8;
    common ground, 98, 100–1, 107, 111; comparative
    nation-, 417–19; and compliance, 540, 544, 546, 551;
    debates within, 104–9; and democracy, 318–19, 322;
    and epistemology, 56–7, 98, 101; and evidence,
    127–32; and feminism, 276, 339, 340; and human
    rights, 517, 521–2, 523, 524, 526, 528, 529, 532; and
    ideas, 58, 59; and international institutions, 198;
    methodology, 101; modernist linguistic, 98, 101;
    modernist (neoclassical), 34–5, 97–8, 101, 107, 109,
    339, 340; and nationalism, 422; ontology, 53, 57, 100;
    philosophical and sociological foundations, 96–8;
    postmodernist, 339; and power, 185; psychological
    explanations, 303–4; and rationalism, 52–3, 58–68, 74,
    108–9, 432; and rationality, 102–3, 108; and regional
    integration, 489–90; and security cooperation,
    379–82, 385; state centric-, 411, 413; systemic nation-
    419–22; and transnational relations, 258
contextualism, 5, 16, 81, 161
contract zones, 224
Convention on Long-Range Transboundary Air
    Pollution, 503
Conventional Forces in Europe Treaty, 376
conventions, 66–7, 506
convergence-divergence debate, 313–14
convergence hypothesis, 263
Conybeare, J., 455
Cooper, F., 471
Cooper, R., 236, 242, 429
cooperation (see also security cooperation), 128, 195,
    223, 227, 320; among enemies, 372; empirical studies,
    199–200; with environmental policies, 5–4;
    globalization/interdependence and, 241–2;
    monetary, 433–4; rational choice and, 77–9, 83, 85,
    195; role of values, 149–50
coordination, 196, 437, 504, 545

Copenhagen School, 340, 382
Corbridge, S., 472
Correlates of War, 121, 124, 125, 181, 185
Cottam, R., 131
Council of Europe, 528
counterfactual analysis, 200, 337, 341, 509
Covenant on Civil and Political Rights, 518, 526, 549
Covenant on Economic, Social and Cultural Rights, 518, 521, 526
'covering law' model of explanation, 41
Cowles, M., 320
Cox, R.W., 98, 99, 259, 471, 474
Crawford, N., 98
credible commitments, conflicts of, 403–4
crimes against humanity, 527–8
critical realism, 106
critical theory, 31, 33, 97, 107, 127, 141, 276; postmodern, 276, 279–80; and transnational relations, 262, 263
CSCE (Conference on Security and Cooperation in Europe), 220, 528
Cuban missile crisis, 64, 316–17
culture, 148–9, 417, 418, 522; and domestic politics, 318–19; and ethnicity, 414, 415–16; and negotiation, 219–20; and norms, 147–50; in security field, 315–16
curve-fitting, 80, 82
Cyprus, 395–6
Czempiel, E.O., 241, 242

Dahl, R.A., 177, 178, 181, 185
Dalby, S., 384
DAWN (Development Alternatives for Women for a New Era), 279
decision-making, 123–4; collective, 297–8; in foreign policy, 333, 334, 337
defensive realism, 372–3
democracy (see also democratic peace hypothesis), 163, 202, 269, 270, 377, 378–9; effect of globalization, 244–5; and human rights, 519; international institutions and, 316–18; rule of law, 547; trade and, 453–4, 457, 458
democratic deficit, 269–70, 320
democratic peace hypothesis, 123, 161, 358–61, 376–9, 382, 385, 393; democratic norms model, 359; game theory model, 360; institutional constraints model, 359–60; multimethod research, 361
dependency theory, 258, 462, 463, 466–8, 470
dependentistas, 159, 262, 467, 469
Der Derian, J., 99, 214
Derrida, J., 97, 99
desecuritization, 383
desires, 59, 120, 122
Dessler, D., 99, 105
deterrence, 165, 166, 373
deterritorialization of money, 443
Deudney, D., 162
Deutsch, K., 99, 131, 257, 421, 481, 489
development, gender in, 278–80
development economics, 463–4
developmental state, 160, 317, 468–9

development studies, 462, 470–5; intellectual history, 463–70; pragmatic/eclectic, 471–2; post-structural, 472–3; rational-positivist political economy and, 473–5
Dilthey, W., 97
diplomacy, 159, 212–17, 227; definitions, 213–14, 217; development of, 216–17; functions, 215; history, 214–15; and technological change, 217
'disappearances', 527, 528
disarmament, 384–5
discounting, 293
discursive enmeshment, 145
discourse theory, 340–1; and the environment, 502, 503, 505
disintegration, 416
dispositional dimension of foreign policy analysis, 342–3
distributional models, 85, 201
dollar glut/shortage, 430, 431
domestic politics, 110, 309–22; and foreign policy, 334, 342; impact of transnational actors, 266–7; and international institutions, 202–3; and international law, 544, 547–8; and national power, 187–8; trade policy preferences and, 450–3
domestic service, 282
Donnelly, J., 9, 517, 526
Doremus, P.N., 261
Doty, R., 106
Downs, G.W., 78, 86, 195, 200, 374, 543
Drazen, A., 474
Duffield, J.S., 199
Dunant, H., 381
Duvall, R., 99
dynamics, 82–4

EAEC (East Asian Economic Caucus), 481, 484
East Asia, institutional integration, 493–4
Easton, D., 28, 30
economic integration, 493–4
economic interdependence, 238, 257, 258; effects, 242–4; and peace, 356–8, 361, 455, 457
economic security, 369
Edwards, S., 440
efficiency hypothesis, 474
Egeland, J., 530
egocentric bias, 294
Eichengreen, B., 434, 435
Eising, R., 312
Eley, G., 131
Elgstrom, O., 220
Elkins, Z., 322, 474
Elster, J., 81–2, 144
Emerson, R., 131
empire, 159–60
empirical constructivism, 103–4
empirical testing, 73–4, 79–82, 122, 123, 124, 127, 129–30, 548–9
empiricism, 34, 37, 43
endogeneity/exogeneity, 62–7, 76
endogenous macro theory, 311, 322
endogenous preferences, 84–5

enforcement, 86; of environmental policies, 506, 511
enforcement theory of compliance, 543, 545,
    549–50
English School, 5, 15, 100, 110, 544, 546; and
    international institutions, 197–8, 205; and NGOs, 319;
    and norms, 139, 141, 147–8
enlargement, 401, 402
Enlightenment, 27, 63
Enloe, C., 278, 281, 284
environmental crises, 502–3, 505
environmental regimes, *see* international
    environmental regimes
environmental security, 369
environmental treaties, 549
epistemic communities, 99, 101, 112n, 204, 258, 260,
    266–7, 380, 506
epistemological debates, 106–7
epistemology, 35, 39, 42, 335, 336; constructivist,
    56–7, 98, 101; positivist, 26, 30, 43n; postmodern, 35;
    rational positivist, 473; scientific realist, 36
equilibrium, 66, 67, 75, 76, 82, 83, 85; multiple,
    79, 86, 196
Esping-Andersen, G., 314
essentialism, 413; double, 413–16; systemic-nation- ,
    416–19, 420
Esteva, G., 472
ethics of responsibility, 139–40
ethnic activism, 299, 300
ethnic conflict, 352, 409, 414–16, 417
ethnic groups, 411, 413, 414–16
ethnocentrism, 298
Etzioni, A., 481
Europe, states in, 160, 161
European Bank for Reconstruction and
    Development, 168
European Commission, 260, 261
European Convention for the Protection of
    Human Rights, 528
European Court of Human Rights, 169, 528, 542
European Court of Justice, 483, 541, 542,
    545–6, 547
European integration, 482, 483, 487, 489
European Monetary Union (EMU), 435, 487
European Roundtable, 263
European Union, 202, 223–4, 320–1, 483, 490,
    492, 495
Evangelista, M., 266
Evans, P., 159
Evans, T., 197
evidence (*see also* theory) 119
evolution, and state disintegration, 321
evolutionary models, 84
exchange rate regime, 430–1
'expected utility' theory of war, 80, 124
explanation, 32–3, 36, 37, 43, 105, 106, 107; causal, 57,
    58, 62–3, 65–6, 101, 106–7; constitutive, 58, 63, 65–7,
    106–7; 'covering law' model, 41; in foreign policy
    analysis, 335–42
externalities, 240, 487, 501, 504

'faces of power' debate, 179
factor specificity, 311
failed states, 160, 161, 166, 170
Faletto, E., 465, 466, 467
Falk, R., 142
fascist state, 160
Fearon, J., 78, 80, 83, 123, 397, 415, 416, 422
feminist perspectives, 33–4, 276–8; beginnings of,
    275–6; future of, 286–7
Ferejohn, J., 59
Ferguson, Y., 10
Ferry, J., 160
Feyerabend, P., 23, 33, 36, 43n
financial globalization, 165, 170, 262–3; causes, 437–8;
    consequences, 437, 438–43
Finnemore, M., 100, 103, 104, 108–9, 128, 129,
    198, 340, 381
fiscal policy, 441
Fischerkeller, M., 127
Fisher, R., 218
fixed preferences, 80, 84
folk theorem, 78, 79
Follett, M.P., 13
foreign policy, 331–44; human rights in, 529–31
formalization, 73, 74, 77–9, 80
former Yugoslavia, 163, 299, 300, 301, 414, 415,
    420, 527, 529
formula, 225
Forsythe, D.P., 530
Foucault, M., 35, 97, 99
Fox, W.T.R., 14
fractionation, 401, 402
framework conventions, 506
framing, 296; environmental politics, 502,
    503–4, 505–6
Franck, T.M., 541, 544, 546, 553
Frank, A.G., 476n
Franzese, R.J., 314
free trade, 311, 449, 455, 519
free trade areas, 480
Freeden, M., 140
Frey, F., 181, 188
Frieden, J.A., 311, 432, 440
Frost, M., 40, 137
Fukuyama, F., 285
functionalism, 257, 482, 485, 486
fundamental attribution error, 294, 295
fungibility, 180, 187

Gallagher, N., 286
game theory/models, 59, 76, 79, 82–3; collaboration/
    coordination, 504, 545; and ethnic conflict, 415;
    evolutionary, 54, 65, 77; incomplete information, 63;
    and interaction, 126, 188; in negotiation studies,
    218–19, 223, 224, 226, 396; non-cooperative, 56, 63,
    77, 86, 88n, 201; prisoners' dilemma, 64, 77, 78, 196,
    218–19, 220, 374, 400, 509; Rambo, 347; two-level
    games, 110, 226, 309, 321
Garrett, G., 435, 474, 541, 545

GATT (General Agreement on Tariffs and Trade), 393, 394, 450, 455, 458; compliance with, 542, 543, 549; Tokyo Round, 247; Uruguay Round, 247, 449, 492
Gause, G., 132
Geertz, C., 413
Gehring, T., 196
Gellner, E., 131, 411, 417, 418
gender hierarchy, 276, 280, 286
gender ideology, 281
general will, 163
generalization, 76, 80, 101, 129, 130
genocide, 420, 520, 529
George, A., 124
Germain, K., 442
Germany, 314, 315, 341, 354, 381, 493
Gerschenkron, A., 310, 466
Giddens, A., 158
Gill, S., 438
Gilpin, R., 158, 177, 259, 310, 429, 431, 434
Glaser, C., 372
Glennon, M.J., 204
global cooperation, 370–1
global economy, gender in, 280–3
Global Environment Facility, 549
global governance, 104, 244–8, 255, 268–70, 442–3
globalism, 482, 491–2
globalization (see also financial globalization), 84, 161, 170, 171, 235; causes, 239; challenge to IR theory, 244, 248–9; debate on, 258, 262; domestic politics and, 313–14; effects, 242–4; multi-national corporations, 262–3; as societal denationalization, 236–7
goal–seeking, 74–5
Goetz, A., 279
gold exchange standard, 430
Goldhagen, D.J., 520
Goldmann, K., 10
Goldstein, J., 59, 551
Goldstein, M., 311
Goodmann, J.B., 439
Gorbachev, M., 373, 380
Gordon, A., 281
Gourevitch, P., 322, 342, 467, 468
governance (see also global governance): beyond nation-state, 247, 248–9; challenges to, 239–40; effects of globalization, 244–8; levels of, 197, 490–1; system, 434–7
Gowa, J., 432, 455, 487
Grant, R., 277–8, 283
great debates (see also third debate), 4, 10–16, 31, 67–8; rationalism versus constructivism, 54–67
Green, D.P., 474
Grieco, J.M., 78, 122, 373, 436, 487
group decision-making, 297–8
Group of Seven (G7), 431, 439
groupthink, 337
Gruber, L., 195
Gunnell, J., 5, 14, 16, 25–6

Gurr, T., 415, 465
Guzzini, S., 9, 17, 333

Haas, E., 99, 127, 131, 421, 481, 485, 526
Haas, P., 199, 204, 501
Habeeb, M., 220
Habermas, J., 33, 97
Haggard, S., 318, 438, 452, 453, 454, 455
Hadenius, A., 457
Hall, J., 409
Hall, P.A., 314
Halliday, F., 275, 286, 287
Hamada, K., 432
Hamilton, K., 213, 214, 216
Hardin, R., 415, 419
Hathaway, O., 456
Haufler, V., 442
Hechter, M., 150
hegemonic realism, 354–5
hegemonic war, 351, 355
hegemony, 431, 434–5; theory of hegemonic stability, 355, 357, 434–5, 455, 458
Heidegger, M., 97
Held, D., 142, 269
Helfer, L.R., 542, 547
Helleiner, E., 438, 441
Helm, C., 509
Helsinki Final Act, 546
Henkin, L., 540
Henning, C.R., 436
Hermann, R., 127
hermeneutics, 25, 32, 341; objective/subjective, 97, 98
heuristics, 294
Hinsley, F.H., 157, 162
Hintze, O., 421
Hirschman, A.O., 310
Hiscox, M.J., 311
historicity, 102
historiography of IR, 5, 6–16
history: of diplomacy, 214–15; of IR, 4–17, 26–32
Hobbes, T., 26–7
Hobson, J.A., 160
Hocking, B., 216
Hoffman, M., 33
Hoffmann, S., 5, 6, 30
holism, 65–6, 335, 336, 342; methodological, 57–8, 65, 66–7
holistic-interpretative approach, 340
Hollis, M., 32, 143, 146, 335, 337, 341, 342; agent-structure problem, 105, 106; positivism, 36, 37; scientific realism, 35
Holsti, K.J., 14, 245
Hopmann, P.T., 220
Horowitz, D., 409, 416
Houston, A., 395, 397, 403
Hroch, M., 417, 418
Hudec, R.E., 542, 551
human nature, 28, 30

human rights, 150, 163, 169, 261, 265, 266, 549;
    definitions, 517–18
human rights institutions: evolution, 525–9;
    origins, 524–5
human rights norms, 517, 521, 532; compliance
    with, 529–32; creation, 522; diffusion, 522–3, 531;
    evolution, 522, 528; spiral model, 267, 531, 532
human rights violations, 521, 530; cultural/ideological
    explanations, 519–20; economic explanations, 519;
    political explanations, 518–19
human security, 369
humanitarian aid, 530–1
humanitarian law of war, 381
Hume, D., 77
Huntington, S., 148, 201, 315, 414, 465, 468
Husserl, E., 97

idealism, 9–10, 12, 13, 27, 40, 111n; versus realism,
    10–11
idealization, 140
ideas, 102, 127–8; for cooperation, 380; in foreign policy
    explanations, 343–4; and materialism, 39–40, 57,
    58–60
identity, 103–4, 148, 161, 171, 313, 340; collective,
    130–2; and democratic deficit, 320; national, 412,
    417, 419, 423; and preference-shaping, 381;
    reshaping, 301–2, 303
identity conflict, 299–301, 402
identity formation, 299, 412
Iida, K., 436
Ikenberry, J., 433
Ikle, F., 220–1, 223
image theory, 338
imagery, hostile, 124, 294–5, 298, 300, 301, 378–9
impartiality/partiality, in mediation, 396, 398–9
imperial state, 159–60, 166, 167
implementation, 539; of environmental policies,
    507, 508, 511
inclusion/exclusion, 383–4
incommensurability, 31
incongruence, 242, 244
index of relative acceptance, 481
individualism, 335, 336, 342; methodological, 58, 65
indivisibility, mediating conflicts, 401–3
influence, 177
information, incomplete, and mediation, 397–401
information processing, 293–4
informational models, 201
inherent bad faith model, 124
Innenpolitik, 334
institutional constraints model of domestic peace, 359–60
institutional design, 85
institutional effects, measures of, 203–4
institutional form, 196–7
institutionalism (see also neoliberal institutionalism),
    355–6; English School, 197–8; rational functionalist,
    195–7, 202; realist, 194–5; social constructivist,
    197–9; sociological, 523, 524
institutionalization, 309, 310, 492–4

institutions (see also human rights institutions;
    international institutions), 6, 75, 83, 311–12, 319, 473;
    constructivism, 104; informal, 493–4; and norm
    creation, 146, 147; power and, 187; problematizing,
    312–13; regional, 494–5; and regional integration,
    482, 485, 486, 488, 492–3; and trade policy, 449,
    453–5, 458
instrumental agency, 259–60
instrumentalism, 29, 41
integration (see also regional integration), 139, 242, 245
intentional dimension of foreign policy analysis,
    342, 343
intentions, 59, 180–1
interaction, 54, 126–7, 314, 340; domestic/international,
    310, 320–1, 322
Inter-American Commission on Human Rights, 528
Inter-American Court of Human Rights, 542
interdependence, 11–12, 13, 235, 236; agency and,
    240–1; measurement, 237–9; structural effects, 239–40
interest groups, 311, 315, 319, 488; environmental,
    502, 503, 506; trade policy, 450, 453, 457–8
interests, 120, 312–13, 339, 343, 488; as ideas, 102,
    127–8; role of norms, 129
intergovernmentalism, 487–8
internalization, 544
International Court of Justice, 168, 548
International Criminal Court, 247, 526
International Criminal Tribunal for former Yugoslavia,
    527, 541
International Criminal Tribunal for Rwanda, 527, 541
international environmental problems, 501–3, 505
international environmental regimes, 150, 199–200;
    design, 505, 506, 510–11; effectiveness, 507–11;
    formation, 504–7, 508; imposed, 504
international institutions, 192, 194, 201–5, 245, 261, 265;
    democracy and, 245; and development, 466;
    globalization and, 246–8; and human rights, 523,
    524–32; and interdependence, 241, 242, 258, 259;
    membership, 84–5; and trade, 455–6, 458
International Labor Organization, 282
international law, 86, 143–4, 146, 538; compliance with,
    538–53; environment and, 505, 508
International Maritime Organization, 503
International Monetary Fund (IMF), 168, 430, 431,
    436–7, 455, 456, 469
international obligations, 162, 163
international organizations, 13, 103, 192–3, 377, 436;
    and conflict resolution, 393; ideas and, 127–8;
    transnational actors and, 259–60, 264–5
international political economy, 177–8, 310–13, 467–8
international regimes (see also International institutions),
    193–4, 204, 258; empirical studies, 199–200;
    theoretical approaches, 194–9
international relations theory: globalization and, 244,
    248–9; interdisciplinary character, 6, 100; power in,
    182–4
international security, gender in, 283–6
international system, 14, 142
international trade, 150, 448–59, 491–2

International Whaling Convention, 545
interpretativism, 342, 372–3
intervention, 161, 162, 165, 166; external, 163, 164
irredentism, 416–17
Israel (*see also* Middle East), 354, 396, 402
Iversen, T., 314

Jackson, R.H., 144, 149
Jacobeit, C., 204
Jacobson, H.K., 510, 547, 548
James, A., 162
James, S., 456
Japan, 315, 317, 493–4
Jefferson, Thomas, 162
Jervis, R., 124, 224, 373
Joerges, C., 549
Johnston, A.I., 129
judiciary, 202
Jupille, J., 48
justice, 139, 140–1

Kahler. M., 10, 436, 550, 551
Kant, I., 1, 96, 256, 377, 393–4; and conflict
    resolution, 393, 404
Kaplan, A., 28, 29, 178, 184, 185
Kaplan, M., 11, 30
Kaplan, R., 414
Katzenstein, P., 99, 103, 108, 339, 340, 342, 456, 467–8
Kaufman, R., 318, 454
Kaufmann, C.D., 319, 414
Keck, M., 204, 259, 266, 267, 319
Kent, A., 532
Keohane, R., 59, 108, 144, 241, 431, 434, 466, 467;
    and gender in conflict resolution, 286, 287; and
    hegemony, 431, 434; and institutions, 128, 194, 195,
    199; rationalist/reflectivist debate, 38–9, 40, 99–100;
    minor refs., 11, 257
Kielmannsegg, P.G., 245
Kier, E., 317
Kindleberger, C., 310, 429, 433, 434
Kissinger, Henry, 222, 375
Kleiboer, M., 221, 394–5, 396
Klotz, A., 103, 340
Knorr, K., 187
knowledge (*see also* epistemology), 27;
    constructivism and, 95, 96, 101, 102, 107
Koh, H.H., 142, 544, 546, 547, 553
Krasner, S., 108, 194, 195, 243, 261, 436, 523;
    dependency theory, 468; norms, 129, 143, 144, 145;
    sovereignty, 161–2, 248, 521
Kratochwil, F., 34, 35, 99, 100, 143, 144–5, 198
Kriesberg, L., 226
Krueger, A., 452, 469
Kubota, K., 454
Kugler, J., 7
Kuhn, T., 9, 10, 23, 30–2, 33, 97
Kuper, L., 519
Kydd, A., 354, 373
Kyoto Protocol on Climate Change, 545

Laitin, D., 410, 415, 416, 417, 418, 422
Lakatos, I., 9, 23, 31
Lake, D., 188, 196, 321, 435, 456
landmine campaign, 380–1
Lane, R., 28
Langhorne, R., 213, 214, 216
language, 97, 103, 340; culture and, 148;
    in low/high-context cultures, 220;
    and negotiations, 227
Lapid, Y., 12, 33, 99
Larsen, H., 340
Larson, D., 338
Laski, H., 13
Lasswell, H., 14, 28, 178, 184, 185
Latin America, 315, 466
Latour, B., 97
Lauren, P.G., 518, 520
law, hard and soft, 551–2
leadership, 223, 338, 360, 434–5
League of Nations, 13, 165
learning, 110, 311–12, 338, 380
Leblang, D., 440
legal internalization, 146
legalization, 538, 542, 550–1, 553
legitimacy, 162–3, 269; theory of compliance
    541, 544, 546
Legro, J., 198
Lenin, V.I., 160, 257
levels of analysis, 14, 105, 309, 350, 411–12,
    432–3
leverage, 398, 402, 404
Levy, J., 312
Levy, M.A., 199, 200, 553
liberal feminism, 277, 279
liberal states, 140, 158, 547–8
liberal theories of war and peace, 355–61
liberalism (*see also* neoliberalism), 227, 302, 432;
    and compliance, 554n; foreign policy, 339; and human
    rights, 521, 522, 523, 524, 526, 528, 529, 532; and
    security cooperation, 376–9, 385; and transnational
    relations, 256–7, 258
Light, M., 275
Lijphart, A., 9, 10, 13, 31, 312
Lim, L., 281
Linklater, A., 33, 98, 99, 138, 141, 142
Lipson, C., 450
Liska, G., 11
Litfin, K., 98, 266
Little, R., 13, 14, 27
logic of appropriateness, 60, 80, 337, 490;
    norms and, 102, 128, 129, 144
logic of arguing, 341
logic of consequences, 60, 80, 144, 337
logical positivism (*see also* positivism), 8–9, 28–9
Lohmann, S., 454
loss aversion, 296, 299, 338
Luckmann, T., 97, 489
Lumsdaine, D., 198
Lustick, I., 132

MacIntyre, A.J., 312, 318
Mackenzie, W.J.M., 32
Mackinder, H., 160
macro-historical IR theory, 420–2
Magalhaes, J.C. de, 213, 216
Mahan, A.T., 164
managerialism, 181, 185–6; and compliance, 542–3,
    544, 545
manipulation, 224–5
Mann, M., 158
Mansbach, R., 10
Mansfield, E., 453, 454, 455
Marchand, M., 277, 280, 286
markets, states and, 437–43
Marks, G., 490
Martin, L., 199, 437, 551
Marx, K., 24, 159
Marxist-Leninist theories of imperialism, 362n
masculinity, 283, 286, 288n; hegemonic, 283;
    heroic, 283; war and, 284
mass politics, 160
material/ideational split, 39–40, 58–60
materialism, 42, 57, 58–9, 111n
maternal thinking, 285
Mattli, W., 541, 547
Maxfield, S., 438, 439, 440
McGlen, N., 285
McNamara, K., 433
Mearsheimer, J., 194, 195, 336, 487
media, and environmental problems, 503, 506
mediation, 221–2, 392, 393, 394, 395–405
mediators: credibility, 404; neutrality, 398, 399;
    partiality, 398, 399, 403
membership, 128, 298; of international
    institutions, 84–5
Menzel, U., 262
MERCOSUR, 483, 484, 494
Merriam, C., 14
Mesquita, B.B. de, 124
metaphysics, 96, 106
metatheory, 15, 33, 334, 335, 339, 342, 350
methodology, 26, 30, 42, 68; constructivist, 101, 109
Mexico, 166, 472
microeconomic theory, 54, 55–6
Middle East, 104, 132, 294, 296, 300, 301, 402
middle ground, 37, 40
military force, 184, 187, 357
military-industrial complex, 378
military prostitution, 284
Miller, D., 141
Millikan, M., 465, 466
Milliken, J., 340
Milner, H.V., 321–2, 454, 456, 547
Misra, J., 287
missile defence system, 165
Mitchell, C., 226
Mitchell, R.B., 199, 550
Mitrany, D., 131, 257, 482
mobilization, nationalist, 418–19

models (see also game theory/models), 55–6, 76,
    82, 126, 132; mathematical, 77–9; thin and thick, 59
modernization theory, 262, 463, 464–5, 468, 470;
    and transnationalism, 466
monetary cooperation, 434, 435–7
monetary policy, 441
monetary power, 433–4
monetary sovereignty, 430, 439–43
Monnet, Jean, 485
Montevideo Convention on Rights and
    Duties of States, 162
Montreal Protocol on Substances that
    Deplete the Ozone Layer, 549
Moon, K., 284
Moravcsik, A., 65, 320, 339, 486, 488, 522, 548
Morgenthau, H., 9, 13, 129, 158, 165, 215;
    anti-scientism, 27–8; power interests, 120, 121,
    182, 183, 194–5, 333
morphogenesis theory, 112n
Morse, E., 466
Morsink, J., 518, 522
Mostov, J., 165
motivation, 120, 121, 122, 124
Muir, R., 241
Müller, H., 200
multi-ethnic coalitions, 301
multi-ethnic states, 171
multilateralism, 216, 221, 222–3, 227, 241
multilevel governance, 490–1
multimethod research, 361–2
multinational corporations (MNCs), 255, 256, 258,
    261, 262–3; and environmental politics, 501, 503, 507
multipolarity, 336, 361, 455
Mundell-Fleming model, 439, 440, 441
Musil, M., 144
Mutimer, D., 384
mutual recognition, 301
myth making, 300

NAFTA (North American Free Trade Agreement),
    168, 481, 483, 494; Commission on Environment
    Cooperation, 542
Nagel, J., 179, 180
Nardin, T., 139, 142
nation, 159, 320–1; definition of, 410;
    ethnic groups and, 411
nation-state, 159, 160–1, 165, 166, 248, 410, 418–19;
    globalization and, 244, 245, 246
national currencies, 430
national security state, 160, 161, 166
nationalism, 131, 148, 161, 409, 413–14, 417–19, 421,
    422–3; counter-state, 418, 419; definitions of, 411;
    hypernationalism, 414; methodological, 248–9;
    separatist, 411; state–frames, 411; unification,
    411, 418
NATO (North Atlantic Treaty Organization),
    203, 370, 373, 376, 546
naturalism, 23, 24, 37, 41n
naturalization, 57

negotiating style, national, 219
negotiation, 215, 217; asymmetrical, 220–1;
    bargaining and, 217–19; culture and, 219–20;
    dynamics of, 224–7; institutionalized, 223–4;
    multilateral, 221, 222–3; stages of, 225–6
neoclassical economics, 463–4, 469–70
neoclassical realism, 336–7
neofunctionalism, 257, 485–6, 541
neoinstitutionalism (see also neoliberalism,
    and institutionalism), 374–6, 504
neoKantian hermeneutics, 96–7
neoliberalism, 263, 339, 340, 413, 438;
    and institutionalism, 128, 258, 309–10, 320, 337, 521;
    and neorealism, 15; and the state, 158, 161, 166, 302,
    310, 322, 521
neorealism, 12, 15, 146, 195; and anarchy, 9,
    158, 371; and foreign policy, 336–7, 340;
    and offensive/defensive states, 122, 123;
    and power, 182–4, 227; research on war and
    peace, 361–2
networks (see also transnational advocacy networks),
    165, 172
Neufeld, M., 33
Neumann, I., 100
neutrality, 398, 402
Newland, K., 277–8
NGOs (non-government organizations), 146, 170,
    171, 204; advocacy networks, 263–8;
    disarmament-specialized, 380–1; environmental,
    503, 504, 506, 507, 511; and human rights, 523, 526,
    527, 531–2; international, 255, 256, 260–1, 263–8,
    319–20; in security cooperation, 380–1
Nicholson, M., 26, 37
Nicolson, H., 213
nominalism, 41, 111n
non-compliance, 544, 549, 552; prevention of, 552; sanc-
    tions, 543, 554n
non-democratic states, 164
non-government organizations, see NGOs
non-state actors (see also NGOs), 84–5, 108, 147, 204,
    255, 259; competing claims of authority, 169–70;
    and international economy, 465, 466; and international
    finance, 431
norm cascades, 523, 531
norm creation, 265
norm socialization, 532, 546
normative analysis, 85–6, 137–41
norms (see also human rights norms), 60, 61–2, 144–7;
    compliance and, 539, 544–5, 546; conflict and, 128–9;
    constructivism and, 103, 198, 340, 489; and cultural
    diversity, 147–50; definitions of, 143–4;
    environmental, 510, 511; and interests, 129; and
    international regimes, 193–4, 196; normative
    structures, 142–4, 380–1; as preferences, 61, 318–19
North, D.C., 158, 317
North Atlantic Treaty Organization see NATO
Northern Ireland, 396
nuclear deterrence, 165, 166, 216, 373, 380
nuclear non-proliferation, 373, 376, 381

Nuclear Non-Proliferation Treaty, 201, 376, 381
Nye, J., 11, 185, 186, 241, 257, 259, 465, 466,
    467, 481

Oatley, T., 440
obedience, 544
objectivism, 120, 121–3, 127, 342
Odell, J., 220, 432, 433
offensive/defensive states, 122–3
Offer, A., 150
O'Halloran, S., 454
Olson, M., 77–8, 310
O'Neill, B., 77
O'Neill, O., 140
ontology, 26, 42, 67, 335, 336; constructivism and,
    52–3, 100–1, 105; positivism and, 30, 39
Onuf, N., 99, 200, 339, 489
operational codes, 338
operationalism, 29, 42
Organization of African Unity (OAU), 528
Organization of American States (OAS), 528
organizational process, 337
Ottawa Convention, 384–5
Oye, K., 432

Packard, R., 471
Papayoanou, P.A., 315
Pape, R.A., 319
paradigms, 9–10, 31–2, 52
Parpart, J., 277
parsimony, 80, 85
partisanship, and trade policy, 454
partition, 414
Patomaki, H., 35, 100, 106
patriarchy, 277, 281
Pauly, L., 436, 439, 442
Payer, C., 436
Payne, A., 474
peace (see also democratic peace hypothesis)
    257, 351; interdependence and, 241–2, 356–8;
    negative/positive, 393; women and, 283–4, 285–6
peacekeeping, 370
peacemaking, 392–405
Pearson, B., 285
perceptions, 123, 124–5, 127
performativity, 54
Peterson, S., 281, 286
phenomenological strategy, 41, 120, 123–6, 127
philosophy of science, 25–32
philosophy of social science, 32–41
Philpott, D., 142
pluralism, 10, 12, 13, 31, 40, 139, 146
Poe, S., 520, 531
policy convergence, 242–4
political fragmentation, 245–6
political institutionalization, regional integration
    and, 492–4
political prudence, 27
political restructuring, 240–1

political science, 6, 9, 25–6, 27, 28
political theory, 7, 15; normative, 137–41
Pollard, A.F., 182
Popper, K., 23, 35, 97
Posen, B., 317, 414, 415
positivism, 25, 26, 111n; feminism and, 276, 277;
    rationalism and, 39; science as, 28–9, 30, 33,
    35–6, 37, 38, 40
post-colonialism, 279
post-development studies, 472–3
post-liberal feminism, 277
post-material values, 502
postmodern state, 158, 161
postmodernism, 15, 34, 35, 54, 107, 111n, 340;
    in development studies, 471, 472; and security
    cooperation, 382–5
post-national constellation, 247
post-positivism, 12, 15–16, 32, 33, 36, 37, 98–9, 276;
    and norms, 138
post-structuralism, 34, 111n, 340
post-war security arrangements, 370
Potter, P., 13
Poulantzas, N., 159
Powell, R., 78, 83, 122, 188
power (see also balance of power), 103, 120–3,
    168, 186, 220; dimensions of, 178–9; distribution of,
    188; environmental regimes, 505, 506, 509; forms of,
    186–7; measurement, 121, 181–2; monetary, 433–4;
    in negotiations, 220; potential, 179–80; relational, 178,
    183, 184–5, 186, 433, 434; structural, 184–5;
    of transnational actors, 260
power activation, 122–3
power analysis, 179–82
power determinism, 121–2
power transition theory, 83, 355, 400–1, 403–4
pragmatic realism, 98, 107
pragmatism, 97
Prakash, M.S., 472
precautionary principle, 502
preferences (see also state preferences; trade policy
    preferences); 59, 63–5, 310–11, 402, 547; changing,
    84–5; endogenous/exogenous, 63–4, 84–5; fixed, 80,
    84; formation of, 62–5, 312, 488; norms as, 61,
    318–19; problematizing, 312–13
presentism, 5, 8–9
preventive war, 354
Price, R., 107, 128, 129, 340, 384
prisoners' dilemma, 64, 77, 78, 196, 509; in negotiation,
    218–19, 220, 400; in security negotiation, 374
problem representation, 292, 297, 302–3
problem-solving, 401, 402
process tracing, 81
Processes of International Negotiation, 218
property rights, 158, 162
prospect theory, 296, 299, 303, 338, 399, 403
protectionism, 311, 449, 450–1, 452–5, 456, 547
prudence, 27, 150
Prugl, E., 282
Pruitt, D., 226

psychological factors in explaining foreign policy
    actions, 333, 334, 337–8, 340
psychology (see also cognitive psychology;
    social psychology), 79, 124–5
public policy, 332
Puchala, D.J., 30
Putnam, R., 110, 321, 436

qualitative analysis, 361, 512
qualitative testing, 81, 101
quantitative analysis, 361, 512
quantitative testing, 80–1, 101

radical constructivism, 98, 99
radical feminism, 277
rape, in war, 284
Rapoport, A., 218
rational choice, 74–7, 132, 280, 338, 343;
    challenges to, 73–4; and conflict, 298, 302, 303, 392;
    empirical evaluations of arguments, 79–82;
    and ethnicity and nationalism, 414, 415, 422;
    explanations for war, 396–404; feminism and, 283;
    and formalization, 77; and legalization, 85–6;
    and political economy, 463, 473–4; and security
    cooperation, 374–6, 385; substantive challenges for,
    82–6; values, 149–50
rational design, 81
rational functionalism, international institutions
    and, 195–7, 201, 202, 204–5
rational positivist political economy, 473–5
rationalism (see also rational choice), 35, 54–5;
    and constructivism, 52–3, 58–60, 67–8, 74, 108–9,
    432; misunderstandings about, 55–6; norms and,
    61–2, 144–5; and preference formation, 62–5, 312;
    and reflectivism, 37, 38–9; and subjectivity, 65–7
rationality, 56, 102–3, 108–9
Ratzel, F., 164
Raustiala, K., 547, 549–50, 552
Rawls, J., 139, 140
Raymond, G., 394
realism (see also neorealism), 14, 16, 98, 107, 309, 333;
    aggressive/defensive, 336; and collective identities,
    298; and environmentalism, 504, 510; and great
    debates, 10–11, 11–12, 14; and human rights, 521,
    522, 523, 524, 526, 528, 529, 532; and idealism,
    10–11; and institutionalism, 194–5;
    and multi-national corporations, 262; neoclassical,
    336–7; optimistic and pessimistic, 372–4;
    as paradigm, 9; and rational choice, 59, 83, 302;
    and regional integration, 486–7; science and, 26, 27,
    29–30, 35, 334; scientific, 34–5, 43n, 111–12n, 120–7;
    and security cooperation, 371–4, 385
Realpolitik, 334
reasons, 38, 140
reciprocal trade legislation, 311–12
recognition, 157, 162, 164; changing norms of, 169;
    criteria, 162–3, 167
reductionism, 334
reflectivism, 37, 38–9, 100

Regan, P.A., 530
Regan, P.M., 399
regime theory, 197, 538, 540
region, definition of, 481–2
region-state, 166
regional human rights mechanisms, 528–9
regional integration, 131, 166, 491–6; definitions, 481–3;
    and institutionalization, 492–4; theories of, 257,
    485–91
regional trading arrangements, 480
regionalism, 482, 495–6; globalization and, 240, 246,
    491–2
Reinecke, W., 442
Reinhardt, E., 547, 549
Reiter, D., 125, 354
relative gains, 78, 122, 195, 357, 372; asymmetrical,
    371, 375–6
representation, diplomacy as, 213, 215
repression, 518, 519, 520–1
resonance hypothesis, 266–7
Reus-Smit, C., 104, 107, 142
revolutions, American and French, 159, 162, 421
rewards, in environmental regimes, 511
Reynolds, C., 32
Rhodes, C., 160
Rice, C., 341
Richardson, L.F., 77, 317
Riker, W., 125
ripeness, 226
risk, 296, 303
Risse, T., 100, 341, 520
Rittberger, V., 194, 196, 199
Rocke, D., 78, 374
Rodrik, D., 452, 453, 456, 457, 474
Rogoff, K., 436
Rogowski, R., 310–11, 312, 450, 453, 456, 457
role theory, 342
Roman Catholic Church, 261
Rome, Treaty of, 495, 541, 542
Rosati, J.A., 338
Rose, G., 336
Rosenau, J.N., 257, 334, 339
Rosendorff, B., 454
Rostow, W., 464
Rubin, J., 226
Ruddick, S., 285
Ruggie, J., 37, 58, 59, 65, 99, 489; neoclassical
    constructivism, 34–5, 100; on norms, 145, 198, 522
rules (see also legal rules; norms); 193, 194, 198, 434
Rummell, R.J., 393
Russett, B., 481, 482
Rwanda, 300, 420, 520, 527, 529, 530

Saint-Paul, G., 473, 474
Samuelson, P., 77
sanctions, 81, 506–7, 511; human rights and,
    523, 530; for non-compliance, 543; positive, 186
Sandholtz. W., 482, 486, 492
Sarkees, M., 285

Sassen, S., 165
Savage, R., 481
Scharpf, F., 202, 314
Schattschneider, E.E., 310, 450
Schelling, T.C., 69n, 70n, 79, 218, 224
schema, 293; revision of, 295–6
Scheve, K., 451
Schmidt, V., 314
Schmitt, C., 162, 165
Schmitter, P., 481, 485
Schoppa, L., 320
Schultz, K.A., 360
Schumpeter, J.A., 257
Schweller, R., 371, 372
science, 8–9, 10, 23, 97, 98, 158, 505–6; 'behavioral
    revolt', 28–30; philosophy of, 25–32; as positivism,
    28–9, 30, 33, 35–6, 37, 38, 40
scientific realism, 34–5, 43n, 111–12n, 120–7
scientism: formal models, 55; versus traditionalism, 11,
    13–15, 28, 31, 32
Searle, J., 35, 58, 97
secession, 416–17
'second image reversed', 322, 342
second-wave feminism, 277
security, 122, 150, 160, 340, 369; domestic politics of,
    315–16
security communities, 131–2, 382
security cooperation, 370–85
security cultures, 381–2
security dilemma, 127, 128, 354, 371–2, 373,
    379, 383, 415
seigniorage, 440
selection bias, 394, 403, 416
self-determination, 159, 171, 421
Sen, A., 316
sensitivity interdependence, 236
shadow of the future, 78, 223, 375, 437
Shapiro, I., 474
Sharp, P., 213, 215
Shaw, J., 489
Shinn, J., 313
side-payments, 402, 404
signaling, 77, 224, 360, 363n, 397; diplomatic, 218, 227;
    and security cooperation, 372–3
Sikkink, K., 108–9, 204, 259, 266, 267, 319
Simmons, B., 322, 437, 452, 474, 549
Simon, H., 55, 124
simulation, 126
Sinclair, T., 442
Slaughter, A.-M., 142, 451, 541, 547
Smith, A., 77
Smith, J., 519
Smith, R., 201
Smith, S., 15, 32, 34, 335, 337, 341, 342; agent-structure
    problem, 105, 106; incommensurability, 31;
    positivism, 26, 36, 37, 38; scientific realism, 35;
    minor refs., 10, 17
Snidal, D., 78, 455, 551
Snyder, G., 371–2

Snyder, R.C., 341
Sobel, A., 438, 439
social constructivism, 167, 171, 339–40
social facts, 100, 109
social identity theory, 303–4
social-institutional perspective of foreign policy actions,
    339–41, 343
social psychology, 392, 397, 404; and international
    conflict, 297–302, 303
social reality, 96, 98, 102, 107
social sciences, 5, 8, 127, 350; philosophy of, 32–41
social structures, 335, 344
social theory, 96, 106, 335
socialist feminism, 281
socialist state, 160
socialization, 335, 523, 546
sociational analysis, 417–19, 422
societal denationalization, (see also globalization),
    236–7
societal security, 369
soft law, 539, 551–2
Soskice, D., 314
sovereignty, 9, 12–13, 104, 138, 157, 548; challenges to,
    248–9; changing forms, 161–4, 167–8, 170, 171;
    conditioned, 166; external/internal, 165, 168;
    human rights and, 521, 523, 528; popular, 158, 421;
    as social construct, 167
Special Drawing Rights, 430
specific-factors model of trade, 450–1
speech acts, 98, 103, 318
spiral model of human rights norms, 267, 531, 532
Sprinz, D., 509
Sprout, H. and M., 179, 180, 183
Spruyt, H., 62
Stam, A.C., 399
standpoint feminism, 277, 288
Stanley, W., 519
state/s, 108, 121, 157, 412–13, 414, 416–17, 421; as
    actors, 75, 83, 84, 85, 105, 106, 108; authority claims,
    170–1; behavior of, 121–2; birth of, 421; compliance
    with international law, 540; definition of, 410;
    in development theory, 462, 468–70; forms, 158–61,
    170–1; and international finance, 431–4; markets and,
    437–43; and norm creation, 146; offensive/defensive,
    122–3; regional integration, 487, 488; and security,
    369, 381; sovereignty of, 161–4, 521, 523, 528;
    transformation of, 420
state-building, 171, 320–1, 351
statecraft, comparative techniques, 187
state disintegration, 321
state preferences, 110, 264, 339, 374, 486, 488, 505
Stearns, J., 278
Stedman, S., 226
Stein, A., 437
stereotypes, 294–5, 298, 304
Stigler, G.J., 84
Stocking, G., 8
Stone Sweet, A., 147, 482, 486, 492, 551
Strange, S., 168, 216, 429, 430, 431, 433–4, 439, 442
Strauss, L., 30

Streeck, W., 314
Streeton, P., 472
structural effects of interdependence, 239–40
structural dimension of foreign policy analysis, 332,
    336–7, 342–3
structuralism, 34, 334
structuration theory, 112n
structures (see also agency-structure problem),
    34, 142, 380
subjectivity, 57, 65–7
Suganami, H., 37
Suny, R., 131
superstate, 160, 161
supranational courts/tribunals, 541–2, 547
supranationalism, 246–8, 482
Sylvester, C., 33
system constructivism, 310
system governance, 434–7
systems approach, 14, 309–10

Tannenwald, N., 128, 340
target vulnerability, 268
Tellis, A.J., 26, 35
territorial acquisition, 164–5
territorial state, 160, 163
territory, 157; conceptions of, 164–7, 172
Thacker, S., 436
theoretical debates, in constructivism, 107–9
theory, linking to evidence, 119–20, 133, 138, 140–1;
    constructivist theories, 127–32; rationalist theories,
    120–7
'third debate', 11–12, 15–16, 33, 99, 276
Thompson, K., 6
Thomson, J.E., 260
Thucydides, 25, 26, 182, 183, 362n
Tickner, A., 99
Tilly, C., 158
time inconsistency problem, 436
Todaro, M.P., 474
Toope, S.J., 551–2
torture, 526, 528, 529
totalitarian state, 158
Touval, S., 221, 395, 397, 399, 403
trade legislation, reciprocal, 311–12
trade liberalization, 449, 451, 452–3, 453–4,
    456, 457, 458, 491, 502
trade policy, 448, 449–50, 457–9; domestic
    politics and, 450–3; international politics
    and, 453–7
trade policy preferences, 450–3, 458; political
    institutions and, 454–5
trade-promotes-peace hypothesis, 356–8, 361
trading with the enemy, 358
tradition, 7–8
traditionalism, 464; versus scientism, 11, 13–15,
    28, 31, 32
Tragedy of the Commons, 501, 504, 505
transaction costs, 238
transboundary protection of goods and bads, 238–9
transitions to democracy, 359, 519, 522

transnational actors, 258, 259–62, 269–70; impact on world politics, 262–8

transnational advocacy networks, 169–70, 260, 264–8, 269, 530; and human rights, 520, 523, 530, 531–2

transnational legal process (*see also* international law), 544, 546, 547

transnational relations, 255, 256, 465–7, 470; history of, 256–9

transparency, 377, 507, 511, 550

Transparency International, 267–8

truth, 29

truth commissions, 529

Turkey, 519

Udayagiri, M., 280

uncertainty, 505, 510, 552

Underhill, G., 442

understanding, 37, 105, 319, 342; shared, 142

unholy Trinity, 439, 441

unilateralism, 507

United Nations, 264, 491; Conference on Environment and Development, 501, 502; Environment Program, 503, 506; Human Rights Commission, 526, 527, 549; human rights system, 526–8; humanitarian intervention, 168

United Nations Charter, 161, 165

United Nations Security Council, 370, 394, 527, 530

United States of America, 160, 163, 430, 431, 434; aid to developing nations, 463, 530, 531; discipline of IR in, 6, 8, 15; hegemony of, 130, 259, 455

Universal Declaration of Human Rights, 169, 518, 522, 524, 526

universalism, in development studies, 464, 470, 473

Ury, W., 218

USSR, 162–3, 266

value conflict, 149

values, 12, 140, 141; cultural diversity and, 149–50; deduction of, 125, 126; shared, 147–8

Van Apeldoorn, B., 263

Vasquez, J., 9–10, 14, 28

verbal theory, 80

Verdier, D., 312, 454

Verdun, A., 489

Vernon, R., 310

Vertzberger, Y.I., 338

Vico, G., 25

Victor, D.G., 547, 549–50, 552

Vienna Convention on Diplomatic Relations, 216, 217

violence, 298, 299–300, 409, 414, 415

voice opportunity thesis, 487

vulnerability interdependence, 236

Wade, R., 468

Waever, O., 6, 7, 10, 12, 15, 17, 33, 100, 340

Wagner, R., 400

Walker, R.B.J., 99

Wallander, C., 199

Wallerstein, I., 11, 476n

Walt, S., 77, 122, 371

Waltz, K., 7, 14, 30, 104–5, 158, 322; levels of analysis, 432; and materialism, 59; neorealism, 11–12, 182–3, 353; power theory, 122; ranking states, 182–3; theory of war, 353

Walzer, M., 140, 144

war, 350–2, 396, 399; effects on women, 284; hegemonic, 351, 355; liberal theories, 355–61; masculinity and, 284; realist theories, 352–5

Washington Consensus, 317, 469

Watson, A., 160, 197

weapons of mass destruction, 128–9, 340

Webb, M., 439

Weber, M., 32–3, 35, 97, 159, 180, 410

Weber, S., 199

Weiner, M., 420

Weingast, B.R., 317

Weldes, J., 64, 98

welfare state, 160

Wendt, A., 16, 40, 99, 185, 319, 380, 416; agent-structure problem, 104–5, 142, 344; constitutive theory, 101, 106–7; science, 35, 36, 38; state, 108; international politics, 331; minor refs., 34, 339

Westphalian ideal state, 143, 157, 162, 167, 236; transformation of, 246–8

whaling, 505, 508

Whig interpretation of history, 8, 332

Whitworth, S., 276

Wight, C., 35, 106

Wight, M., 7, 159

Williamson, J., 469

Wilson, P., 197

Wilson, Woodrow, 159

Winch, P., 32, 38, 97

Wintrobe, R., 453

Wionczck, M., 481

Wittgenstein, L., 97

Wittman, D., 401

women, 278; effects of war on, 284; in military, 284; and peace, 283–4, 285–6; socioeconomic status, 280–3

Women in Development (WID), 279

Women's Strike for Peace, 285

Woolgar, S., 97

World Bank, 168, 264; Inspection Panel, 169

world security, 369

World Trade Organization, 168, 169, 247, 449, 455, 456, 480, 496; and compliance, 541, 542, 549

World War I, 354

World War II, 11

Wren, A., 314

Wright, Q., 6, 14, 28

Yee, A.S., 416

Young, O.R., 200, 223

Zartman, T.W., 220, 221, 395, 397, 399, 403

Zelikow, P., 341

Zürn, M., 196, 202, 549